ISBN 978-0-365-23699-3
PIBN 10086228

INTRODUCTORY NOTICE.

PHILIP MASSINGER, the author of the nineteen plays contained in this volume, and of eighteen others, which, it is to be feared, are irrecoverably lost, was born in the year 1584; twenty years after Shakspeare and Marlowe, ten after Jonson, eight after Fletcher, and within two of Beaumont and Ford. Contemporary with him also were Greene, Webster, Peele, Chapman, Middleton, Shirley, Kyd, Decker, Marston, Daniel, Fulke Greville, and others of hardly inferior mark, "all of whom spoke nearly the same language and had a set of moral feelings in common." Such was the imperial manner in which Shakspeare and his brother dramatists of the great race took possession of the English stage, and filled

> " The spacious times of great Elizabeth,
> With sounds that echo still."

Never before or since has the earth witnessed such a simultaneous outburst of minds of kindred power. Napoleon and his marshals did not make their appearance in a thicker cluster. When one thinks of the Burghley men, and the Armada men, who were sinking one by one into their graves : of Bacon and Raleigh in the full flush of their genius : of the Hampdens, and Cromwells, and Jeremy Taylors, and Miltons, who about the same time were being rocked in their cradles : lastly of old Queen Bess herself :—when one considers also that the entire population of England in those days was probably not more than that of our present London,—it is impossible not to feel an emotion of pride in belonging to the same "happy breed of men" from which they sprung, and in being born like them in

> " This blessed plot, this earth, this realm, this England."

The same authorities which give 1584 for the year, fix Salisbury for the place, of Massinger's birth. The books of its churches have been searched in vain for any record of his baptism, but as one of the principal of them fell down in 1653, and there is a vacuum in its registers extending over the period in which the name might have appeared, it is probable that the infant son of Arthur Massinger received the name of Philip at the font of St. Edmund's. Hartley Coleridge indulges the pleasing fancy that he must have had for sponsor the greatest Englishman who has ever borne that name, the poet-soldier in whose "sweetly constituted mind no ugly thought or unhandsome meditation could find a harbour; who turned all that he touched into images of honour and virtue;" and who himself derived it from the arch-enemy of his country and his religion. And the circumstance of the sponsorship is in itself not improbable, for was not Sidney's sister Pembroke's wife, and the poet's father was a trusted and honoured "servant" of the Herbert family. Arthur Massinger indeed must have been a man of birth, education, energy, and high principle, for recent research has brought to light a letter from Henry Earl of Pembroke to the great Earl of Burghley, dated 28th March, 1587, recommending him in the strongest manner for the reversion of the office of Examiner in the Court of the Marches towards South Wales; and ten years afterwards, when a matrimonial arrangement of some sort was pending between these two powerful families, it was to Arthur Massinger that the delicate negociation was confided.—[*Notes and Queries*, 1st S. iii. 52.]

In the dedication to *A New Way to Pay Old Debts* the poet states that he " was born a devoted servant to the thrice noble family " of Herbert, and the probability is that he was brought up as a page to the Countess of Pembroke at Wilton. His allusions to the position and minute duties of pages are perpetual. In that particular palace, if anywhere in England, he would learn to admire the combination of rank and power, and stately yet flowing courtesy, which in after life he was so fond of bestowing upon his favourite characters. So successful indeed is he in these delineations that, without the knowledge that such in all likelihood had been his upbringing, a biographer would be led to assume that it was so in order to account for the confident and consummate ease with which he treads the halls, and ascends the staircases, and enters the tents, and sits down at the banquets of his great dukes and emperors, and viceroys and proconsuls. But beyond this general idea which irresistibly forces itself upon us, we know nothing whatever of his early life. Not a single fact, not even a barren date, has come down to us until Friday, the 14th of May, 1602, when " Philip Massinger, a Salisbury man, the son of a gentleman" (Sarisburiensis, generosi filii), was entered at St. Alban's Hall in the University of Oxford. He must then have been about eighteen years old.

After this brief gleam of light, darkness again closes in—darkness that may be felt. Anthony à Wood says that the young student's expenses at the University were defrayed by the Earl of Pembroke, and that " he gave his mind more to poetry and romances for about four years or more, than to logic and philosophy, which he ought to have done, as he was patronized to that end." Langbaine, on the contrary, asserts that during his residence he applied himself closely to his studies; and that his whole support was drawn from his father. Tom Davies, his next biographer, considers that it was very wrong of him to neglect his logic and his philosophy, and thereby provokes the grim merriment of Gifford, who hints that the worthy fellow (whom one forgives for " mouthing a sentence as curs mouth a bone," in consideration of his having introduced Boswell to Johnson), neither possessed himself nor knew the meaning of " these valuable acquisitions." Gifford himself adopts the view of Langbaine, both as regards the studies and the means of living, and, after calling Wood a tasteless drudge, adds that the young man " must have applied himself to study with uncommon energy, for his literary acquisitions at this early period appear to be multifarious and extensive." The representatives of the " tasteless drudge" school might here retort on the logical and caustic critic, and inquire the names of the works in which at this period his literary acquisitions are made manifest.

It is agreed that Massinger left Oxford in 1606 abruptly, and without taking a degree; and, as it appears certain that his father died about the same time, it is reasonable to connect these circumstances together, and thence to conclude that at the age of twenty he found himself cast penniless on the world. The old Earl of Pembroke had died in January, 1601, and had been succeeded by his eldest son, who, according to Wood, was " not only a great favourer of learned and ingenious men, but was himself *endowed to admiration with a poetical geny,*" and " was the very picture and *viva effigies* of nobility." Clarendon, in more weighty language, describes him as " the most universally beloved and esteemed of any man of that age. . . . of a pleasant facetious humour, and a disposition affable and magnificent." On every account, therefore, one would have supposed that a young man of such abilities would as a matter of course have been taken by the hand by a nobleman of such dispositions, who would have felt an additional pride in presenting him to the world as the son of his father's most cherished retainer. But the biographers, who agree in little else, are unanimous in saying that whatever may have been his claims to patronage, no patronage of any kind was afforded to him. To account for this singular neglect, Gifford is reduced to what I cannot but think the still more singular assumption, that Massinger had forfeited the Earl of Pembroke's favour by " having, during his residence at the University, exchanged the religion of his father for one at this time the object of persecution, hatred, and terror,"—in short, he had turned Roman Catholic. It requires a bold man to differ with Gifford on any point connected with Massinger, but is not a change of this sort the precise kind of circumstance the memory of which would have lingered longest among the cloisters of what Bunsen calls the Queen of Cities? Wood was entered at Merton forty-one years after Massinger quitted St. Alban's Hall, and it is not necessary to assume that there were Dr. Rouths in those days in order to feel convinced that he had opportunities of conversing with contemporaries of the poet. A freshman of 1868, of an enquiring turn of mind, would be tolerably certain to learn as much as he cared to hear about any distinguished character who had left the University in 1827. Besides, the fact would have been of particular interest to old Anthony, as he was himself again and again accused of exhibiting in his writings a strong leaning to all who were Papists or papistically inclined. But granting the force of the arguments as to the conversion, was the Earl of Pembroke a man likely to have been influenced as Gifford supposes? It is true that Clarendon says he was "a great lover of his country, and of the religion and justice which he believed could only support it; and his friendships were only with men of these principles;" but it was Puritanism, not Roman Catholicism, that was running in the Chancellor's head when he wrote these lines, and it must have been political rather than moral reasons that swayed the Earl in the choice of his friendships. Clarendon goes on to say that "he was clouded by great infirmities, which he had in too exorbitant proportion: he indulged to himself the pleasures of all kinds, almost in all excesses, and to women he was immoderately given up." For such an one to have been as strait-laced as Gifford's theory seems to require is to anticipate the pious fears of Goldsmith's soldier, in the exquisite dialogue in the *Citizen of the World.*

Gifford seems to think that this estrangement was limited to William, the then head of the house of Herbert, and speaks of Massinger's *anxiously avoiding* all mention of him individually, as contrasted with his *perpetually recurring* to his hereditary obligations to the family generally. But as far as I can discover, his mention of the family at all is limited to three occasions (viz., in the dedications to *The Bondman*, 1624, the *New Way to Pay Old Debts*, 1633, and in a copy of verses 1636), so that the terms "anxious avoidance" and "perpetual recurrence" are at least as strong as the circumstances will justify. In one of these dedications also he expressly states that so late as 1624 he "had not arrived at the happiness to be made known to" Earl Philip, who up to that time, therefore, had neglected him as much as Earl William. Before dropping the subject, it will not be out of place to mention that the elder of these brothers is generally considered to be the mysterious W. H., the "only begetter" of sundry world-renowned sonnets; and that, only a year before the date above given, a certain folio volume had been dedicated to the two earls jointly as "the most noble and incomparable pair of brethren," whose "dignity" the editors "could not but know to be greater than to descend to the reading of these trifles"—the said trifles including, amongst other small matters, *Lear, Hamlet, Macbeth,* and *Othello.*

But to leave this long digression and return to Massinger. He left Oxford in 1606, and appears at once to have enlisted himself amongst "divers whose necessitous fortunes made literature their profession." He thus wrote of himself in the autumn of his days, when we know tolerably well how his time was employed; but of their spring and summer we can hardly say more than that they must have passed away in one long struggle for bare existence. The first distinct record of his independent doings is the performance at Court, in 1621, of his lost comedy of the *Woman's Plot.* But during this interval of fifteen years he must have produced

  1. *The Forced Lady*, tragedy.
  2. *Noble Choice*, comedy.
  3. *The Wandering Lovers*, comedy.
  4. *Philenzo and Hippolita*, tragi-comedy.

5. *Antonio and Vallia,* comedy.
6. *The Tyrant,* tragedy.
7. *Fast and Welcome,* comedy.
8. *The Woman's Plot,* comedy.

It is sad to think that the manuscripts of all these plays were in existence in the middle of the last century, and that not a trace of them now remains. They fell into the hands of one John Warburton, F.R.S. and F.S.A., Somerset Herald, a vulgar, illiterate, sordid, and unprincipled ex-exciseman, whose passion it was to glean up everything either in print or manuscript which bore in any way on a subject which interested him, making the collections over to the care of the domestic who discharged the double duties of cook and librarian, until he could find a person with education enough to write something fit for publication regarding them. In this way he had collected no less than fifty-five genuine unpublished English dramas of the golden period, unfortunately written upon paper suited for culinary purposes, every one of which, except three at the bottom of the pile, was appropriated leaf by leaf by this wretched kitchen wench for coverings for her pastry.*

Besides these "martyrs of pies," as Pope would have called them, the four following surviving plays must be put down to the same period :—

9. *The Old Law,* comedy.
10. *The Virgin Martyr,* tragedy.†
11. *The Unnatural Combat,* tragedy.
12. *The Duke of Milan,* tragedy.

But when, after a careful calculation, it has been considered proved that fifteen pounds is the largest sum that even a writer of established reputation could reckon upon clearing by a single play, it is evident that Massinger must have had other sources of support for fifteen years than these twelve dramas could have afforded him. But it was the frequent fashion of those days, and a "noble practice" it was too, says Charles Lamb, for two or more writers to join in the composition of the same play, and Massinger's powers were such as peculiarly fitted him for the ready execution of this kind of mosaic. Langbaine has preserved some doggrel which describes his Pegasus as an easy hack that would

"Amble o'er
Some three-score miles of fancy in an hour ;'

and "he wrote with that equability of all the passions which made his English style the purest and most free from violent metaphors and harsh constructions of any of the dramatists who were his contemporaries." My present task has led me to peruse his works many times over, and again and again have his extraordinary fluency and facility led me to compare his powers to those of the statesman who could speak a king's speech off-hand.‡ That he lent such assistance to Fletcher, for one, we know from

---

* There must have been something particularly hateful about this Warburton's character. Francis Grose, his brother herald, the "fine fat 'odgel wight" of Burns, and the best-natured of men, quite exults in telling that "he died a beggar ;" another friend seems to derive gratification from relating that he had a great abhorrence to the idea of worms crawling over him, and ordered his corpse to be packed in a particular manner : this packing fermented and burst the coffin during the funeral. But the feeling does not end even in the grave. His only son, we are told, happened to go into France in 1793, and was guillotined at Lyons. And here, in 1868, I plead guilty to feeling a certain sort of satisfaction in penning this note !

† Regarding this fine tragedy a brief note has been discovered in the Office Book of Sir George Buck, Master of the Revels, Oct. 6, 1620. "For new reforming the *Virgin Martyr* for the *Red Bull,* 40s."

‡ Macaulay describes Pitt's oratory as "lofty, sonorous, and commanding." But *he* only knew him at second-hand ; while Cobbett, who must have heard him often, ad-

two altogether independent sources. Sir Aston Cockayne, a true friend, if not a true poet, has mentioned the fact on three separate occasions—the exact number which, according to Gifford, constitutes "perpetual recurrence." In the first, addressing his cousin Charles Cotton, and speaking of Beaumont, he says:—

> " His own renown no such addition needs
> To have a fame sprung from another's deeds ;
> And my good friend, old Philip Massinger,
> With Fletcher writ in some that we see there. "

Again, in his address to Mr. Humphrey Mosley and Mr. Humphrey Robinson, he comes to the same point :

> " For Beaumont of those many writ in few,
> *And Massinger in other few."*

Lastly, in some lines to which I shall again have to refer, he says of the pair Fletcher and Massinger :—

> " Plays they did write together—were great friends."

To all this quasi poetical testimony from his " worthy friend " must now be added the following most prosaic and most melancholy evidence under his own hand. It was discovered by Malone among the archives at Dulwich College, and may be left to tell its own sad and instructive story :—

" To our most loving friend Mr. Phillipp Hinchlow, Esquire, these :—

" Mr. Hinchlow,—You understand our unfortunate extremity, and I do not think you so void of Christianity, but that you would throw so much money into the Thames as we request now of you ; rather than endanger so many innocent lives ; you know there is ten pound more at least to be received of you for the play, we desire you to lend us five pound of that, which shall be allowed to you, without which we cannot be bailed, nor I play any more till this be dispatched. It will lose you twenty pound ere the end of the next week, beside the hindrance of the next new play. Pray, sir, consider our cases with humanity, and now give us cause to acknowledge you our true friend in time of need. We have entreated Mr. Davison to deliver this note, as well to witness your love as our promises, and always acknowledgment to be ever

" Your most thankful and loving friends,
" NAT : FIELD.

" The money shall be abated out of the money remains for the play of Mr. Fletcher and ours. " ROB : DABORNE.

" I have ever found you a true loving friend to me, and in so small a suit, it being honest, I hope you will not fail us. " PHILIP MASSINGER."

It was of course impossible to refuse a request at once so urgent, so reasonable, so modest, and so " honest,"—*i.e.,* honourable ; but still it is satisfactory to be able to transcribe the following endorsement, which I copy literatim in order to show the spelling of the names, which no doubt to a certain extent preserves the pronunciation :—

" Rec. by me Robert Davison of Mr. Hinshloe for the use of Mr. Dauboern, Mr. Feeld, Mr. Messenger the some of v*l.* " ROBERT DAVISON."

This document is without date, but it must be before January 1616, when Henslow died, and therefore, which is worthy of note, during the lifetime of Francis Beaumont, who died on the 6th of March of the same year. The date of the tripartite letter is

---

dresses him in one of his " Rural Rides," " Yes—*you loud snorting bawler."* Is it possible for words to be more graphic ?

conjectured to be some time in either 1613 or 1614, and the research of Mr. Collier has discovered yet another document in the same quarry, which must also be given at length.

"Noverint Universi, &c., 4° die Julii, 1615.

"The condition of this obligation is such, that if the above bounden Robert Daborn and Philip Massinger, or either of them, should pay or cause to be paid unto the above-named Philip Henslowe, his executors, administrators, or assigns, the full and entire sum of three pounds of lawful money of England, at or upon the first day of August next ensuing the date of these presents, at the now dwelling-house of the said Philip Henslowe, situate on the Bankside, without fraud or farther delay, then and from thenceforth this present obligation to be null and void and of no effect, or else to remain and abide in full power, strength, and virtue.

"Rob. Daborne,
"Philip Massinger."

When such uncommon pains are taken about so small a sum as three pounds, it is, I am afraid, evidence that the circumstances of the borrowers were such as to lead the lender to apprehend some difficulty in recovering his advance.

With the exception of the brief note of Sir George Buck regarding the *Virgin Martyr*, the first mention of Massinger's labours in the Office-book of the Master of the Revels, is on the 3rd of December, 1623, when

13. *The Bondman*, tragi-comedy,

was brought upon the boards. Philip Earl of Montgomery was present at the first performance, on which occasion, as Massinger states it, his "lordship's liberal suffrage taught others to allow it for current." When in the following year the play was printed and dedicated to the Earl, it is to be hoped that the "liberal suffrage" assumed a more substantial shape than the forty shillings which was the customary payment for these compliments. Massinger's old comrade Field, as Mr. Collier tells us, when he printed his play *Woman is a Weathercock*, addressed it to "any woman that hath been no weathercock," boastingly asserting that he did so "because forty shillings I care not for." Matters at this time must have been better with him than when he penned that sad tripartite letter.

On April 17, 1624, Massinger produced

14. *The Renegado*, Tragi-comedy;

and on November 3 of the same year—

15. *The Parliament of Love*, Comedy.

They were both acted at the Cockpit, and are entered in Sir Henry Herbert's Office-book.

16. *The Spanish Viceroy*, Comedy,

which was one of the martyrs to Mr. Warburton's pies, is supposed to have been full of allusions to Gondomar, the Spanish Ambassador, and stood no chance of being licensed by the Master of the Revels. The players therefore resolved to act it on their own responsibility, and for this piece of insolence or of independence were required to make a most humble apology to Sir Henry Herbert, and to sign a promise "not to act any play without your hand or substitute's hereafter, nor do anything that may prejudice the authority of your office." I find this circumstance recorded in the Life of John Lowin, and as Mr. Collier makes no allusion to Massinger being the author of the play, and as the date of the apology, December 20th, treads so closely on the date of performance of the *Parliament of Love*, I am led to suspect that Gifford may have admitted *The Spanish Viceroy* into his list on insufficient grounds. Malone, however, mentions that a play of Massinger's called *The Spanish Viceroy ;* or, *the Honour of Women*, was entered at Stationers' Hall for Humphrey Mosely in 1653. If, indeed, Massinger were the author of a play in ridicule of Gondomar and his countrymen, would it not settle the question of his having become a Papist?

On October 11th, 1626, the King's Company performed—

17. *The Roman Actor*, Tragedy.

In dedicating this piece three years afterwards to Sir Philip Knyvett and Sir Thomas Jeay, he says, with manly self-confidence, "if the gravity and height of the subject dis. taste such as are only affected with jigs and ribaldry (as I presume it will), their con. demnation of me and my poem can no way offend me; my reason teaching me such malicious and ignorant detractors deserve rather contempt than satisfaction." He adds, "I ever held this the most perfect work of my Minerva." And surely (*pace* Gifford) the character of Paris is a noble conception, upheld to the end with a grand consistency. In these respects it is only to be surpassed by that of Charalois in the *Fatal Dowry*—a Hamlet whose mind hâs not been sicklied o'er by the pale cast of thought.

Of his next play,

18. *The Judge*,

I find only the fact that it was acted by the King's Company on June 6th, 1627. It has perished, and left no trace behind. It does not appear to be known whether it was a tragedy or a comedy.

19. *The Great Duke of Florence*, Comedy,

was acted at the Phœnix, Drury Lane, on July 5th, 1627, under the name simply of *The Great Duke*.

20. *The Honour of Women*

was acted May 6th, 1628, and is now lost. If this were indeed the same as No. 16, *The Spanish Viceroy*, the perilous stuff must have been purged out of it to adapt it for representation.

21. *The Maid of Honour*, Tragi-Comedy,

was acted at the Phœnix, Drury Lane, but the date of its first appearance is unknown.

22. *The Picture*, Tragi-Comedy,

was first acted June 8th, 1629.

23. *Minerva's Sacrifice*, Tragedy,

perished by the hands of Mr. Warburton's kitchen wench. It was first acted Nov. 3rd, 1629, by the King's Company.

24. *The Emperor of the East*, Tragi-Comedy,

was acted March 11th, 1631, at Blackfriars, and was printed the following year.

We now come to

25. *Believe as You List*, Tragedy,

which was always described as a comedy, and believed to have been one of the many victims of that insatiable *barathrum* of the drama, the oven of the pie-eating Somerset Herald; and that one copy did so perish there can be very little doubt. Colley Cibber, however, had mentioned his having seen a transcript of it, with the stage directions inserted in the margin; and in the year 1844, "concealed in a vast mass of rubbish," this very transcript turned up once more. The lucky discoverer, Mr. Beltz, was fortunately a liberal and enlightened man, and lost no time in making a present of It to the public, through the medium of the long-defunct Percy Society.* It was issued in 1848, under the nominal editorship of Mr. Crofton Croker, but might just as well have had no editor at all. I have not myself seen the manuscript, nor am I aware of the place of its deposit. An attempt was made to correct a few of the grosser errors by a writer in the fourth volume of the "Shakspeare Society's Papers," under the signature of a "Member of both Societies." Of his capabilities for the task I will only give two

---

* The publisher of the present edition has not asked anybody's permission to make this reprint, simply because, when finder, editor, and "Society" had all alike gone to their graves, he was unable even to guess the quarter in which it would have been courteous to make the application

examples, taken for convenience, one from the Prologue, the other from the Epilogue.
The latter, according to Mr. Crofton Croker, opens as follows :—

> " The end of Epilogues is to inquire
> The *conjure* of the play, or to desire
> Pardon for what's amiss."

The word " conjure" in the second line is of course absurd, and the critic proposes to
change it to *fortune,* which is not much better in meaning, and very unlike it in
appearance. The true word, no doubt, is *censure,* which in those days, and much
nearer our own time, was used for *judgment.* Congreve somewhere invites a "*favourable
censure.*" In the Prologue Massinger had begged pardon in case it should be found
that

> "What's Roman here,
> Grecian or Asiatic, *draw too near*
> *A late and sad example.*"

The critic must needs have it that the " late and sad example" could only refer to the
fate of Charles I. ; and as that king was not executed till eighteen years after the date
of the play, he had to post-date the performance, which brought it to a period when
acting was prohibited ! He finds too the closest resemblance between the careers of
Charles and Massinger's Antiochus, while beyond the salmons-in-both style of likeness
there is literally no similarity whatever. On my own first perusal of the play I saw
that no one individual of antiquity could possibly be identified with the hero of
Massinger, and the introduction of a Proconsul of *Lusitania,* and the talk about seeking
aid from the *Batavians* led me to suspect that he drew from a much more modern
source. I then remembered that Mr. Collier in his "Annals of the Stage" (ii. 26) made
mention of "Sir Henry Herbert on the 11th January," 1630-1, refusing to license a
play by Massinger, *the name of which he does not give,* ' because it did contain dangerous
matter, as the deposing of Sebastian, King of Portugal, by Philip II., and there being
a peace sworn 'twixt the Kings of England and Spain.'" I then turned to the
first book of reference at hand, and discovered, as I expected, that the story of *Believe
As You List* was, down to the most minute points, identical with that of the hero of
Portugal. The book from which Massinger must have derived it is, "The True
History of the *Late* and *Lamentable* Adventures of Don Sebastian, King of Portugal,
after his imprisonment in Spain until this present day," London, 1602.* And thus,
what the critic calls "those mysterious words, a late and sad example," were at once
rendered plain, and at the same time a point in Massinger's history cleared up.

Sir Henry Herbert must have made a good thing of his office as Master of the
Revels. In this matter of *Believe As You List,* he seems to have acted on the principle
of the attorney in *Joe Miller,* who made the double charge, " To calling at your house,
6s. 8d. ; to not finding you at home, 6s. 8d." After noting the refusal, he has recorded
in his book, " I had my fee notwithstanding, which belongs to me for reading it
over, and ought to be brought always with a book." In some respects he is
quite Pepys-like in his communicativeness. On the 17th July, 1626, Mr. Hemmings pays him £3 " for a courtesie done him about their Blackfriar's house ;" and on
the 11th April, 1627, the same Mr. Hemmings gives him £5, "to forbid the playing
of Shakspeare's plays to the Red Bull Company." Two years later, some women
actors came over from France, and made their appearance here, which is thus spoken
of by Prynne, in his *Histriomastix.* "Some French women, or monsters, rather, in
Michaelmas term, 1629, attempted to act a French play at the playhouse in Blackfriars,

---

* Of this pamphlet I know no more than the title, which I have taken from Mr. Hazlitt's laborious work, " The Bibliography of Old English Literature."

an impudent, shameful, unwomanish, graceless, if not more than' whorish, attempt." For this *attempt* Sir Henry Herbert says he received £2, which was a high fee, considering that the poor people were "hissed, hooted, and pippin-pelted from the stage." He had another fee "for allowinge of the Frenche at the Red Bull for a day, 22nd Nov., 1629;" and again, "for allowing of a French Companie at the Fortune, to play one afternoone, this 14th day of August, 1629, £1," to which he adds the following characteristic note,—"I should have had another piece, but in respect of their ill-fortune I was content to bestow a piece back !" Well may Gifford call him "a mean and rapacious overseer." These notes are so necessary to a right understanding of the state of the Stage in Massinger's time, that I make no apology for inserting them, except to my old friend Mr. Collier, from whose work they are stolen bodily.

To the refusal to license the *Believe As You List*, on the 11th January, 1631, the poet appears to me to allude in the prologue to the *Emperor of the East*, which was spoken on the 11th March following, when he says—

" He cannot 'scape their censures who delight
To misapply whatever he shall write ;"

and from the desponding tone of the second prologue to the same play, which was composed for an occasion considerably later than the delivery of the first, and subsequent to the *acting* of *Believe As You List*, I cannot help thinking that both these plays were "damned" on their first appearance. In no other way can I account for the opening words of the Prologue to the *Guardian*, which was spoken October 31st, 1633.

" After twice putting forth to sea, his fame
Shipwrecked in either, and his once known name
In two years silence buried."

26. *The Unfortunate Piety*, a Tragedy, was first acted by the King's Company, June 13th, 1631. It is lost.

27. *The Fatal Dowry*, Tragedy, and

28. *A New Way to Pay Old Debts*, Comedy.

29. *The City Madam*, Comedy.

30. *The Guardian*, Comedy, will be spoken of in another place.

31. *Cleander*, Tragedy, was acted May 7th, 1634, by the King's Company, and drew Queen Henrietta Maria to Blackfriars. "A remarkable circumstance," says Gifford, "at that time when our sovereigns were not accustomed to visit the public theatres. It is to be hoped that it was the poet's benefit day. The circumstance is recorded by the Master of the Revels."

32. *A Very Woman*, Tragi-Comedy, will be spoken of in another place.

33. *The Orator*. This play, which is lost, was first acted June 10th, 1635, by the King's Company.

34. *The Bashful Lover*, Tragi-Comedy, will be spoken of in another place.

35. *The King and the Subject*, was first acted June 5th, 1638, by the King's Company, and is now lost. Of this play a remarkable anecdote is related by the Master of the Revels, who would appear to have had doubts about the propriety of licensing it, and referred the manuscript to King Charles for his own decision. The following is the entry in Sir Henry Herbert's book:—"At Greenwich, this 4th of June, 1638, Mr. W. Murray gave me power from the King to allow of *The King and the Subject*, and told me that he would warrant it.'

> " Monies ! we'll raise supplies what way we please
> And force you to subscribe to blanks, in which
> We'll mulct you as we shall think fit. The Cæsars
> In Rome were wise, acknowledging no laws
> But what their swords did ratify ; the wives
> And daughters of the senators bowing to
> Their will, as deities,"* &c.

"This is a piece taken out of Philip Massenger's play called *The King and the Subject*, and entered here for ever to be remembered by my son, and those that cast their eyes on it, in honour of King Charles, my master, who, reading over the play at Newmarket, set his mark upon the place with his own hand, and in these words— *This is too insolent and to be changed.* Note, that the poet makes it the speech of a king, Don Pedro of Spain." Had the *judgment* of King Charles been as sound as his *taste* was excellent, the history of England might have been different from what we find it. He would at any rate have made a very different Master of the Revels from Sir Henry Herbert, as witness the following entry in the latter's book, under date January 1634 :—"The King is pleased to take *faith, death, slight,* for asseverations and no oaths, to which I do humbly submit as my master's judgment ; but under favour conceive them to be oaths, and enter them here to declare my opinion and submission." And this is the man who screwed money from the poor painted women from France, and from the English players and poets who were poorer still.

36. *Alexius,* or the *Chaste Lover,* and

37. *The Fair Anchoress of Pausilippo,*
acted respectively on Sept. 25th, 1639, and Jan. 26th, 1640, both by the King's company, are the two last plays of Massinger which appear in the book of the Master of the Revels, and, although Gifford was not aware of the circumstance, *both were posthumous.* It is impossible now to discover whether they were really his latest compositions, or merely two unacted plays of earlier date found among his papers after his death. If the former, it is hardly possible to overrate the value of what we have lost ; for Massinger's mind was not one of those barren soils which forfeited any of its fertility by thirty years of cropping. His six last plays have all the vigour of his six first, but the judgment which guides his powers is riper and more serene. Strange to say, his *humour* kept growing brighter to the last. The *New Way to Pay Old Debts* and *The City Madam* are among the dozen finest comedies in the English language, and the slave-dealing scene in *A Very Woman* stands altogether by itself for the elastic play of a merry invention.

Of the personal history of Massinger during these last busy years nothing is known beyond what may be gleaned from hints dropped in his dedications, and these, alas, are but too uniformly manly confessions of poverty, and manly thanks for wants relieved. The Earl of Pembroke and Montgomery seems to have made up in these latter years for his own and his brother's early neglect ; and his son-in-law the gallant Earl of Carnarvon likewise befriended him. Without the aid of Sir Francis Foljambe and Sir Thomas Bland, he tells us, " he had hardly subsisted ;" and he "stood much engaged to the noble Society of the Inner Temple for their so frequent bounties." He also derived "extraordinary content" from the "remembrance" of Lord Mohun's love, which was conveyed to him by his lordship's nephew and his own zealous friend Sir Aston Cockayne.

This life of toil and care was suddenly brought to an end about the middle of March 1639—not 1640 as stated by Gifford and all previous biographers. He went to bed

---

* It was probably this passage which led Malone to suppose that this play was identical with *The Tyrant,* one of the "Martyrs of pies." Sir H. Herbert mentions that the title was "changed," but whether *to* or *from The King and the Subject* does not appear.

in good health, says Langbaine, and was found dead in the morning in his own house on the Bankside. He was buried in the church of St. Saviour's, Southwark, and the "monthly accounts" give this record of the circumstance :*—

"1638. March 18th. Philip Massinger, stranger, in the church . . . 2 li."

More than twelve years earlier the following entry is found in the same gloomy record :—

"1625. August 29.· John Fletcher, a poet, in the church."

The charges for Fletcher's grave are entered as 20s., and 2s. for gr: and cl : (the grave digger and the clerk). The charges for Massinger were probably greater, as being a "stranger," or non-parishioner. Sir Aston Cockayne, who evidently was greatly attached to him, wrote the following "Epitaph on Mr. John Fletcher and Mr. Philip Massinger :"—

> "In the same grave Fletcher was buried, here
> Lies the stage poet Philip Massinger :
> Playes they did write together, were great friends :
> And now one grave includes them at their ends :
> So whom on earth nothing did part, beneath
> Here, in their fames, they lie in spight of death."

I am very reluctant to differ from so eminent an authority as my friend Mr. Dyce, who thinks the "same grave" means nothing more than the "same place of interment," but it will be observed that the idea is repeated in the fourth line, in a yet more definite shape, and the whole epitaph, to my thinking, bears unmistakeable marks of being designed by its writer for cutting on the stone which covered their common grave. I also please myself by imagining that the arrangement was made in accordance with an expressed wish of Massinger himself.

The old Priory Church of St. Saviour's was, next to St. Paul's and the Abbey, the noblest church in London, and not being hemmed in as now by warehouses and breweries and railway stations, nor shorn of its fair proportions by fatal decay and more fatal repairs, must have dominated like a cathedral over the brothels and bear gardens that surrounded it. Massinger could not have crossed the ancient bridge or taken boat to the Temple or Queenhithe without having it ever in his view, and considering the circumstances of his life, what is more natural to suppose than that he should often desire to be resting in peace by the side of his illustrious friend and fellow labourer? But it is vain to speculate on a point which can never be decided. In Gifford's time every stone and every fragment of a stone was examined in the hope of finding some indication of the particular spot where these great poets were interred; and had there been anything in the shape of an inscription regarding either, it must have been discovered or have finally perished in the general levelling and destruction of 1832. The monument of that dry old stick Gower was then removed to its present site and "painted and repaired" by the pious care of his namesake, the Duke of Sutherland, but the dust of the authors of *The Faithful Shepherdess* and *The Fatal Dowry* most probably has found its last resting-place under the kitchen floor of some house in Doddington Grove, Kennington, S.W., which is built, we are told, on the "three feet surface of earth" removed from St. Saviour's, Southwark.

Having thus followed Massinger to his grave, and beyond it, I have only to record the subsequent fate of his works. The last play acted during his life, and the two which were produced immediately after his death, have perished, as have also fifteen

---

* This extract was first correctly printed by the 1841 editor of Campbell's "Specimens," who also showed that "stranger" meant nothing more than non-parishioner. But he failed to point out that March 1638 meant March 1639—not March, 1639-40. This was left to Mr. Collier in his "Memoirs of Actors," p. xiii.

others. A much-damaged transcript of *The Parliament of Love* was discovered by Malone, who made it over to Gifford, when he first announced his intention of becoming the poet's editor. In sending it to him Malone said, "the piece is in such a mutilated state, wanting the whole of the first act and part of the second (to say nothing of its other defects from damp and time), that it is feared it can be of little use." Gifford worked diligently and reverently, and in six weeks sent Malone a transcript which "quite astonished" the veteran commentator. The circumstances under which *Believe as You List* was recovered have been already detailed.

Popular as Massinger must have been during the latter part of his life, he was utterly forgotten during the rule of the Puritans, and scarcely remembered for many years after the Restoration. During this period, indeed, the dramatists of the preceding generation seem to have been valued in proportion as indecency predominated in their writings, and Beaumont and Fletcher were greatly more popular than Shakspeare. But the public taste in every way was perverted, and if others had been as honest as Samuel Pepys we should have had many such records as—"To Deptford by water, reading *Othello, Moor of Venice*, which I ever heretofore esteemed a mighty good play, but having so lately read *The Adventures of Five Houres, it seems a mean thing*." Betterton indeed detected the fine opening which *The Bondman* and *The Roman Actor* afforded to his grand powers of declamation, but it is probable that the exhibition was attended with more pleasure to the player than to the public. At length Nicholas Rowe, sixty-four years after Massinger's death, determined upon collecting and publishing his works, but after mature deliberation considered it more judicious to plunder the dead man rather than attempt to revive him. Nothing can show more decisively the oblivion into which Massinger had fallen than that Rowe should think it possible to escape detection in his wholesale *looting*. For a time, too, he was thoroughly successful. His "Gay Lothario" took such a hold in the English mind that he still dwells in the English *tongue*, and nearly eighty years later, when Johnson pronounced this shameless plagiarism to be "one of the most pleasing tragedies on the stage, where it still keeps its turns of appearing, and probably will long keep them, for there is scarcely any work of any poet at once so interesting by the fable, and so delightful by the language," he was evidently not aware that everything in the play really deserving admiration, except the mere harmonious versification, was the work of another man. And yet Johnson was himself a Shakspearian commentator! Of the baseness and shabbiness of Rowe's conduct in the affair it is impossible to speak with patience, and one feels quite grateful to the Earl of Oxford for leading him that famous dance about the Spanish language. Time too has already put the matter square. The once fashionable *Fair Penitent* is read by no one, and will probably never be reprinted, while *The Fatal Dowry* is perused year after year by increasing numbers with increasing admiration.

"Massinger thus robbed and abandoned by Rowe, was after a considerable time taken up by Coxeter," whose gatherings formed the basis of the first collected edition of 1751. This was re-issued in 1761, with new title-pages and introductory matter by Tom Davies and George Colman, and is considered as the second collected edition. The third was brought out in 1779 by a Mr. John Monck Mason, who mentions in his preface that he had never heard of Massinger till two years before he edited him. It is not William Gifford's fault if everybody who now hears of Massinger does not hear also of John Monck Mason. The gentleman's only crime was his being inferior as an editor to the man who came after him; and to that man, as he appears in the Massinger volumes, very few "editors" would not be inferior. Gifford's knowledge of books was very great, although in the particular line of old English literature he may have been excelled by others who have taken up the same work; but in knowledge of mankind, in knowledge of the language and ways of thinking of all the different professions and ranks of life in England, none of them have approached him. He had witnessed, while quite a child, his father sinking into the grave overwhelmed with drink and with debt—itself a terrible training. He had held the plough; he had been not only a "ship-boy on the high and giddy mast," but also in the cabin, where for a whole twelvemonth every menial office fell to his lot. He had been apprenticed to a sordid shoemaker, who debarred him from pen, ink, and paper, till he was reduced " to beat out pieces of leather as smooth as possible, and work his problems upon them with a blunted awl." He had been the object of " A subscription for purchasing the remaining time of William Gifford, and for enabling him to improve himself in writing and English grammar." He had at last received the full benefits of an Oxford education, and had been invited per-manently to reside on terms of affection and esteem with one of the greatest noblemen of England. Few men have ever passed through such a varied career, and a careful student of his notes on Massinger will find that there is hardly a portion of that career which has not been made to throw light on the text of his author. Besides this, he was gifted with an enthusiasm which led him to regard Massinger first, and Ben Jonson afterwards, with the fierce affection which a tigress bears to her cubs. He considered that Coxeter and Monck Mason had not done their duty by Massinger, and there is hardly a page in his four thick volumes in which one or other of these gentlemen was not sneered at, or snarled at, or loaded with gross abuse. Charles Lamb, in some of those charming notes which he appended to his " Specimens of the English Dramatic Poets," had, as I venture to think unjustly, underrated the powers of Massinger, as compared with some of the less known of his contemporaries, and this no doubt was the cause of that unhappy passage in the Quarterly Review, for the writing of which Gifford is said to have sorrowed with the same depth of feeling which actuated Sir William Napier when he wrote his noble letter to the mother of Sir James Outram. The result of these qualities and qualifications was the production of what is said to be the very best edition that has ever appeared of an old English writer. I am told, on competent authority, that the same pains are not by any means visible in his reproduction of Ford and Ben Jonson, while he shows himself, if possible, still more acrimonious and abusive; and his shafts being too often covertly aimed at higher game than those small deer Mason and Coxeter, whom nobody cares to be angry about, the notes are less amusing, and appear to have a great deal more of arrogance and self-assertion.

Of all the critics who have written upon Massinger, Hallam probably was the ablest, and he is certainly the one who has assigned him the highest position. As a tragic writer he appears to him second only to Shakspeare; and, in the higher comedy, he can hardly think him inferior to Jonson. His genius, he says, was not eminently pathetic, nor energetic enough to display the utmost intensity of devotion, but it "abounded in sweetness and dignity," was "apt to delineate the loveliness of virtue, and to delight in its recompense after trial." "His most striking excellence is his conception of character," and in this he inclines to place him above Fletcher, and, if he may venture to say it, above Jonson also. " He is free from the hard outline of the one, and the negligent looseness of the other." He thinks him deficient in variety, and somewhat given to repetition. He shows great mastery in the delineation of vil-lains, but "his own disposition led him more willingly to pictures of moral beauty. A peculiar refinement, a mixture of gentleness and benignity with noble daring belong to some of his favourite characters; to Pisander in The Bondman, to Antonio in A Very Woman, to Charalois in The Fatal Dowry. It may be readily supposed that his female characters are not wanting in these graces. He seems to have more variety in his women than in the other sex, and that they are less mannered than the heroines of Fletcher. A slight degree of error or passion in Sophia, Eudocia, Marcelia, without weakening our sympathy, serves both to prevent the monotony of perpetual rectitude, so often insipid in fiction, and to bring forward the development of the story."

" Next to the grace and dignity of sentiment in Massinger " Hallam praises the same qualities in h's style. "Every modern critic has been struck by the peculiar beauty of his language. In his harmonious swell of numbers, in his pure and genuine idiom, which a text by good fortune and the diligence of its last editor, far less corrupt than that of Fletcher, enables us to enjoy, we find an unceasing charm. The poetical talents of Massinger were very considerable, his taste superior to that of his contemporaries; the colouring of his imagery is rarely overcharged; a certain redundancy as some may account it, gives fulness, or what the painters would call *impasto*, to his style, and if it might not always conduce to effect on the stage, is on the whole suitable to the character of his composition."

To say that a writer is in tragedy second only to Shakspeare, and in the higher comedy not inferior to Jonson, while in conception of character he excels both Ben and Fletcher, is in effect to assign him the highest place among the illustrious brethren of the unapproachable Swan of Avon. Charles Lamb has pronounced a very different verdict, and regarding their merits from his own special and peculiar point of view, no one will be inclined to dispute the opinions he has expressed. His love and reverence for these old writers was so extreme that he dealt with them as a connoisseur of another description deals with his cabinet of costly liqueurs. He treated them like the most precious cordials, pouring them into the smallest glasses, and only allowing them to trickle drop by drop over his palate. In this way, and in this way alone, in my humble opinion, could he have arrived at the conclusion that Massinger was vastly inferior in the higher branches of poetic art, not to Ford and Webster only, but to Decker, Marston, Middleton, Heywood, Tourneur, Rowley, *and others*. But Massinger, above any writer with whom I am acquainted, requires to be judged of in the *full draught*. Not only should no scene or no act be read separately, but for the thorough relish of him too great a pause should not be made between play and play. Hallam, I have no doubt, penned his criticism fresh from a continuous perusal of this nature, and I can easily understand, therefore, how two judges, each in his way so admirably qualified as himself and Lamb, should have arrived at such very opposite conclusions. Am I wrong in thinking that the general opinion of the public sides with the historian of the Middle Ages rather than with the author of the Essays of Elia? Massinger, indeed, never has occupied, and never will occupy, the same space in the public eye, or the same place in the public heart, which has long been filled by Rare Old Ben. He was certainly not his equal in general literary abilities; and in that most popular of all accomplishments, the art of paying exquisite compliments, whether in polished and honeyed stanzas, or in vigorous though rugged couplets, Jonson is altogether without an equal. Massinger could never have written the marvellous "Drink to me only with thine eyes," the "Epitaph on the Countess of Pembroke," the lines on "Lord Bacon's Birthday," or those "To the memory of my beloved Master William Shakspeare." It only remains now to speak of Massinger's art in the construction and conduct of his plots, and on this point a writer may be quoted whose authority on such a question admits of no dispute. "Although Massinger's plays," says Sir Walter Scott, "are altogether irregular, yet he well understood the advantage of a strong and defined interest; and in unravelling the intricacy of his intrigues, he often displays the management of a master. Art, therefore, not perhaps in its technical, but in its most valuable sense, was Massinger's as well as Jonson's, and in point of composition, many passages of his plays are not unworthy of Shakespeare. Were we to distinguish Massinger's peculiar excellence, we should name that first of dramatic attributes, a full conception of character, a strength in bringing out, and consistency in adhering to it. He does not indeed always introduce his personages to the audience in their own proper character; it dawns forth gradually in the progress of the piece, as in the hypocritical Luke or the heroic Marullo. But upon looking back we are always surprised and delighted to trace from the very beginning intimations of what the personage is to prove as the play advances."

The following notes on the various printed Plays would have been inserted in the: Narrative, but for the fear of making it even more confused than it already is.

[THE VIRGIN-MARTYR.] Of this Tragedy, which appears to have been very popular, there are four editions in quarto, 1622, 1631, 1651, and 1661; the last of. which is infinitely the worst. It is not possible to ascertain when it was first produced, but it was certainly amongst the author's earliest efforts. In the composition of it, he was assisted by Decker, a poet of no mean reputation, and the writer of several plays. much esteemed by his contemporaries.—W. G.

Charles Lamb extracts the scene between Angelo and Dorothea (p. 9), and says, " This scene has beauties of so very high an order that, with all my respect for Massinger, I do not think he had poetical enthusiasm capable of furnishing them. His associate Decker, · who wrote *Old Fortunatus*, had poetry enough for any. thing. The very impurities which obtrude themselves among the sweet pieties of this play (like Satan among the Sons of Heaven) have a strength of contrast, a raciness, and a glow in them, which are above Massinger. They set off the religion of the rest, somehow as Caliban serves to show Miranda."

This play was frequently patched and altered. In Sir George Buck's Office-book is the following entry, " 1620, Oct. 6.—For new reforming *The Virgin-Martyr* for the Red Bull, 40s.;" and in Sir Henry Herbert's book, " 1624, July 7.—Received for the adding of a new scene to *The Virgin-Martyr*, 10s."

[THE UNNATURAL COMBAT.] Of this tragedy there is but one edition, which was printed for John Waterson, in 1639. It does not occur in Sir Henry Herbert's Office-book; so that it is probably of a very early date; and indeed Massinger himself calls it an " old tragedy." Like the *Virgin-Martyr*, it has neither Prologue nor Epilogue, for which the author accounts in his Dedication by observing that the play was composed at a time " when such by-ornaments were not advanced above the fabric of the whole work." It is said in the title-page to have been " presented by the King's Majesty's Servants, at the Globe."—W. G.

[THE DUKE OF MILAN.] Of this tragedy there are two editions in quarto; the first, which is very correct, and now very rare, bears date 1623; the other, of little value, 1638. It does not appear in the Office-book of the licenser; from which we may be pretty certain that it was among the author's earliest performances. It is said, in the title-page, to " have been often acted by His Majesty's servants at the Black Friars."—W. G.

[THE BONDMAN.] The *Bondman* was allowed by the Master of the Revels, and. performed at the Cockpit in Drury Lane, on the 3rd December, 1623. It was printed in the following year, and again in 1638. This last edition is full of errors. Mr. W. C. Hazlitt mentions *two* editions of 1638.

[THE RENEGADO.] This tragi-comedy, for so Massinger terms it, appears, from the Office-book of the Master of the Revels, to have been first produced on the stage April 17th, 1624: it was not given to the public till several years after; the entry in the Stationers' Register, bearing date March 6th, 1629–30. It is said in the title-page. to have been " often acted by the Queen's Majesty's servants at the private playhouse in Drury Lane."—W. G.

[THE PARLIAMENT OF LOVE.] A comedy of this name was entered on the books. of the Stationers' Company, June 29th, 1660; and a manuscript play so called, and said to be written by W. Rowley, was in the number of those destroyed by Mr. Warburton's.

servant. I suspect this to be the drama before us. It is, beyond all possibility of doubt, the genuine work of Massinger, and was licensed for the stage by Sir H. Herbert on the 3rd June, 1624. I have elsewhere mentioned my obligations to Mr. Malone for the use of the manuscript. The play was acted at the Cockpit in Drury Lane.—W. G. It was first printed by Gifford in 1805.

[THE ROMAN ACTOR.] This tragedy was licensed by Sir H. Herbert, Oct. 11th, 1626, and given to the press in 1629. This play was successful in the representation, and appears to have been well received by the critics of those times, since it is preceded by commendatory copies of verses from Ford, Harvey, May, Taylor, and others. Taylor, an admirable actor, who played the part of Paris, calls it "the best of many good;" and Massinger himself declares that he "ever held it as the most perfect birth of his Minerva." Too much stress must not be laid upon this expression; it is proper in adverting to it, to consider how few dramatic pieces Massinger had produced when it was used.

This tragedy was revived by Betterton, who took for himself the part of Paris, in which he was highly celebrated. The old title-page says that it had been "divers times acted with good allowance, at the private playhouse in the Black Friars, by the King's Majesty's servants."—W. G.

[THE GREAT DUKE OF FLORENCE.] The "Great Duke" was licensed by Sir H. Herbert for the "Queen's Servants," July 5th, 1627. This, Mr. Malone conjectures with every appearance of probability, to be the "Comical History" before us. This play was not committed to the press till 1636, when it was preceded by two commendatory copies of verses by G. Donne and J. Ford. Though highly, and indeed deservedly popular, it was not reprinted. It was acted "by her Majesty's servants at the Phœnix in Drury Lane," where, the title adds, it was "often presented."—W. G.

[THE MAID OF HONOUR.] This tragi-comedy does not appear, under the present title, in the Office-book of Sir H. Herbert; but a play called *The Honour of Women* was entered there May 6th, 1628, which Mr. Malone conjectures to be the piece before us. He speaks, however, with some hesitation on the subject, as a play of Massinger's, called the *Spanish Viceroy ; or, the Honour of Women*, was entered at Stationers' Hall for Humphrey Moseley in 1653. Mr. Malone says that the *Maid of Honour* was printed in 1631. All the copies which I have seen (for there is but one edition) are dated 1632, which was probably the earliest period of its appearance. This play was always a favourite, and, indeed, with strict justice; for it has a thousand claims to admiration and applause. It was frequently acted, the old title-page tells us, "at the Phœnix in Drury Lane, with good allowance, by the Queen's Majesties Servants."—W. G.

[THE PICTURE.] This tragi-comedy, or as the old 4to calls it, this "true Hungarian History," was licensed by Sir H. Herbert, June 8th, 1629. The play was much approved at its first appearance, when it was acted, as the phrase is, by the whole strength of the house. Massinger himself speaks of it with complacency; and, indeed, its claims to admiration are of no common kind. It was printed in 1630, but seems not to have reached a second edition. It is said, in the title-page, to have been "often presented at the Globe and Black Friar's playhouses by the King's Majesty's servants." An unsuccessful attempt was made to revive this play by the Rev. Henry Bate: *Magnis excidit ausis.* We tolerate no magic now but Shakspeare's, and, without it, the *Picture* can have but little interest.—W.G.

Charles Lamb quotes the first scene of Act I., and adds, "The good sense, rational fondness, and chastised feeling of this dialogue, make it more valuable than many of those scenes in which this writer has attempted a deeper passion and more tragical interest. Massinger had not the higher requisites of his art in anything like the degree in which they were possessed by Ford, Webster, Tourneur, Heywood and others. He never.shakes or disturbs the mind with grief. He is read with composure and placid delight. He wrote with that equability of all the passions, which made his English style the purest and most free from violent metaphors and harsh constructions of any of the dramatists who were his contemporaries."

[THE EMPEROR OF THE EAST.] This tragi-comedy was licensed for the stage,. March 11th, 1631, and printed in the following year. Notwithstanding the excellence of this play it met with some opposition at its first appearance; its distinguished merits, however, procured it a representation at Court, and it finally seems to have grown into very general favour. It was frequently acted, as the title-page tells us, "at the Black Friars and Globe Play-houses, by the King's Majesty's Servants."—W.G.

[THE FATAL DOWRY:] This most excellent tragedy does not appear to have been licensed by Sir H. Herbert, nor is it accompanied by any prologue or epilogue; circumstances from which Mr. Malone concludes that it was produced previous to 1620. However this may be, it was not printed till 1632, before which time the title-page says it "had been often acted at the private house in Blackfriars, by his Majesty's Servants." Massinger was assisted in the writing of it by Nathaniel Field.

From this play Rowe borrowed, or, according to Cicero's distinction, stole, the plan of the *Fair Penitent*, a performance by which he is now chiefly known.—W.G.

Richard Cumberland in an elaborate and masterly criticism has established the immeasurable superiority of the old dramatist over his copyist. I have ventured to insert the songs in their proper places, and in one of them to print a single line as a couplet,. of which no one will dispute the propriety. The songs were retained by Gifford in ignominious banishment, but at p. 377 the dramatic action was injured by their absence.

[A NEW WAY TO PAY OLD DEBTS.] This comedy does not appear in Sir Henry Herbert's book; it must, however, have been produced on the stage before 1633, in which year it had been printed for Henry Scyle. It was extremely well received on its first appearance, and, as the quarto informs us, "often acted at the Phœnix, in Drurie Lane." It has been revived at different periods with considerable success, and still holds a distinguished place on the stage.—W.G.

Hallam says very truly that Sir Giles Overreach is an "original, masterly, and inimitable conception," and sufficient of itself to establish the rank of Massinger in this great province of dramatic art.

[THE CITY MADAM.] This comedy, of which it is not easy to speak in appropriate terms of praise, was licensed by Sir Henry Herbert, May 25th, 1632, and acted by the King's Company. It was received, as the quarto says, with great applause; but was kept in the players' hand till 1659, when it was given to the press by Andrew Pennycuicke, one of the actors. I have seen one copy with the date 1658 on the title. It was probably thrown off in 1658-59.—W. G.

[THE GUARDIAN.] This "Comical History" was licensed by the Master of the Revels, October 31st, 1633, but not printed till 1655, when it was put to the press,. together with the *Bashful Lover*, and the *Very Woman*, by Humphrey Moseley, the general publisher of that age. This popular drama was produced "at the private house in Black-fryers." From a memorandum in the Office-book of Sir Henry Herbert, we learn that shortly after its appearance it was acted before the king. "*The*

Guardian, a play of Mr. Massinger's, was performed at Court on Sunday, the 12th of January, 1633, by the king's players and well likte."—W. G.

[A Very Woman.] This "tragi-comedy," as it is called, was licensed for the stage, June 6th, 1634. From the prologue it appears to be a revision of a former play which had been well received, and which the author modestly insinuates that he was induced to *review* by the command of his patron. If this patron was, as it has been supposed, the Earl of Pembroke, we are indebted to him for one of the most delightful compositions in the English language. The present play was most favourably received; and often acted, the old title-page says, "at the private house in Black Friars, by his late Majesty's Servants, with great applause." Its popularity seems to have tempted the author's good friend, Sir Aston Cockaine, to venture on an imitation of it, which he has executed, not very happily, in his comedy of *The Obstinate Lady.* It was printed with *The Bashful Lover* and *The Guardian* in 1655.—W. G.

[The Bashful Lover.] This tragi-comedy was licensed by the Master of the Revels, May 9th, 1636. It is the latest of Massinger's pieces which are come down to us, though he continued to write for the stage to the period of his death, which happened about four years after the date of the present play. It was extremely well received at its first appearance; it continued to be a favourite, and was "often acted," the old copy says, "by his late Majesty's servants with great applause." It was performed at Blackfriars. This play, together with *The Guardian* and *A Very Woman,* was printed in 8vo by H. Moseley, 1655. I know of no prior edition.—W. G.

[The Old Law.] Of this comedy, which is said to have been written by Massinger, Middleton, and Rowley, in conjunction, there is but one edition, the quarto of 1656, which appears to be a hasty transcript from the prompter's book, made, as I have observed, when the necessities of the actors, now grievously oppressed by the republicans, compelled them for a temporary resource to take advantage of a popular name, and bring forward such pieces as they yet possessed in manuscript. Of Middleton and Rowley I have spoken elsewhere, and need only repeat my persuasion that the share of Massinger in this strange composition is not the most considerable of the three. This drama was very popular. The title of the quarto is "The excellent comedy called *The Old Law,* or *A New Way to Please You.* Acted before the King and Queen at Salisbury House, and at several other places, with great applause."—W. G

Charles Lamb says of it, "There is an exquisiteness of moral sensibility, making one to gush out tears of delight, and a poetical strangeness in all the improbable circumstances of this wild play, which are unlike anything in the dramas which Massinger wrote alone. The pathos is of a subtler edge. Middleton and Rowley, who assisted in this play, had both of them finer geniuses than their associate."

The Virgin-Martyr.

DRAMATIS PERSONÆ.

Dioclesian, } *Emperors of Rome.*
Maximinus, }
King of Pontus.
King of Epire.
King of Macedon.
Sapritius, *Governor of* Cæsarea.
Theophilus, *a zealous persecutor of the Christians*
Sempronius, *captain of* Sapritius' *guards.*
Antoninus, *son to* Sapritius.
Macrinus, *friend to* Antoninus.
Harpax, *an evil spirit, following* Theophilus *in the shape of a secretary.*

Angelo, *a good spirit, serving* Dorothea *in the habit of a page.*
Hircins, *a whoremaster,* } *servants of*
Spungius, *a drunkard,* } Dorothea.
Julianus, } *servants of* Theophilus.
Geta, }
Priest of Jupiter.
British slave.
Artemia, *daughter to* Dioclesian.
Calista, } *daughters to* Theophilus.
Christeta, }
Dorothea, *the Virgin-Martyr.*
Officers and Executioners.

SCENE,—Cæsarea.

ACT I.

SCENE I.—*The Governor's Palace.*

Enter Theophilus *and* Harpax.

Theoph. Come to Cæsarea to-night!
Harp. Most true, sir.
Theoph. The emperor in person!
Harp. Do I live?
Theoph. 'Tis wondrous strange! The marches of great princes,
Like to the motions of prodigious meteors,
Are step by step observ'd; and loud-tongued Fame
The harbinger to prepare their entertainment:
And, were it possible so great an army,
Though cover'd with the night, could be so near,
The governor cannot be so unfriended
Among the many that attend his person,
But, by some secret means, he should have notice
Of Cæsar's purpose;—in this, then, excuse me,
If I appear incredulous.
Harp. At your pleasure.
Theoph. Yet, when I call to mind you never fail'd me
In things more difficult, but have discover'd
Deeds that were done thousand leagues distant from me,
When neither woods, nor caves, nor secret vaults,
No, nor the Power they serve, could keep these Christians

Or from my reach or punishment, but thy magic
Still laid them open; I begin again
To be as confident as heretofore,
It is not possible thy powerful art
Should meet a check, or fail.

Enter the Priest of Jupiter, *bearing an Image, and followed by* Calista *and* Christeta.

Harp. Look on the Vestals,
The holy pledges that the gods have given you,
Your chaste, fair daughters. Wer't not to upbraid
A service to a master not unthankful,
I could say these, in spite of your prevention,
Seduced by an imagined faith, not reason,
(Which is the strength of nature,) quite forsaking
The Gentile gods, had yielded up themselves
To this new-found religion. This I cross'd,
Discover'd their intents, taught you to use,
With gentle words and mild persuasions,
The power and the authority of a father,
Set off with cruel threats; and so reclaim'd them:
And, whereas they with torment should have died,
(Hell's furies to me, had they undergone it!) [*Aside.*
They are now votaries in great Jupiter's temple,
And, by his priest instructed, grown familiar

B

With all the mysteries, nay, the most ab-
struse ones,
Belonging to his deity.
Theoph. 'Twas a benefit,
For which I ever owe you.—Hail, Jove's
flamen!
Have these my daughters reconciled them-
selves,
Abandoning for ever the Christian way,
To your opinion?
Priest. And are constant in it.
They teach their teachers with their depth
of judgment,
And are with arguments able to convert
The enemies to our gods, and answer all
They can object against us.
Theoph. My dear daughters!
Cal. We dare dispute against this new-
sprung sect,
In private or in public.
Harp. My best lady,
Perséver in it.
Chris. And what we maintain,
We will seal with our bloods.
Harp. Brave resolution!
I e'en grow fat to see my labours prosper.
Theoph. I young again. To your devotions.
Harp. Do—
My prayers be present with you.
       [*Exeunt* Priest, Cal. *and* Chris.
Theoph. O my Harpax!
Thou engine of my wishes, thou that steel'st
My bloody resolutions, thou that arm'st
My eyes 'gainst womanish tears and soft
compassion,
Instructing me, without a sigh, to look on
Babes torn by violence from their mothers'
breasts
To feed the fire, and with them make one
flame;
Old men, as beasts, in beasts' skins torn by
dogs;
Virgins and matrons tire the executioners;
Yet I, unsatisfied, think their torments easy—
Harp. And in that, just, not cruel.
Theoph. Were all sceptres
That grace the hands of kings, made into one,
And offer'd me, all crowns laid at my feet,
I would contemn them all,—thus spit at them;
So I to all posterities might be call'd
The strongest champion of the Pagan gods,
And rooter out of Christians.
Harp. Oh, mine own,
Mine own dear lord! to further this great
work,
I ever live thy slave.

Enter Sapritius *and* Sempronius.
Theoph. No more—The governor.

Sap. Keep the ports close, and let the
guards be doubled;
Disarm the Christians; call it death in any
To wear a sword, or in his house to have one.
Semp. I shall be careful, sir.
Sap. 'Twill well become you.
Such as refuse to offer sacrifice
To any of our gods, put to the torture.
Grub up this growing mischief by the roots;
And know, when we are merciful to them,
We to ourselves are cruel.
Semp. You pour oil
On fire that burns already at the height:
I know the emperor's edict, and my charge,
And they shall find no favour.
Theoph. My good lord,
This care is timely for the entertainment
Of our great master, who this night in person
Comes here to thank you.
Sap. Who! the emperor?
Harp. To clear your doubts, he doth re-
turn in triumph,
Kings lackeying by his triumphant chariot;
And in this glorious victory, my lord,
You have an ample share: for know, your son,
The ne'er-enough commended Antoninus,
So well hath flesh'd his maiden sword, and
dyed
His snowy plumes so deep in enemies' blood,
That, besides public grace beyond his hopes,
There are rewards propounded.
Sap. I would know
No mean in thine, could this be true.
Harp. My head
Answer the forfeit.
Sap. Of his victory
There was some rumour: but it was assured,
The army pass'd a full day's journey higher,
Into the country.
Harp. It was so determined;
But, for the further honour of your son,
And to observe the government of the city,
And with what rigour, or remiss indulgence,
The Christians are pursued, he makes his
stay here: [*Trumpets.*
For proof, his trumpets speak his near arrival.
Sap. Haste, good Sempronius, draw up
our guards.
And with all ceremonious pomp receive
The conquering army. Let our garrison speak
Their welcome in loud shouts, the city shew
Her state and wealth.
Semp. I'm gone.
Sap. O, I am ravish'd
With this great honour! cherish, good Theo-
philus,
This knowing scholar. Send [for] your fair
daughters;
I will present them to the emperor,

And in their sweet conversion, as a mirror,
Express your zeal and duty.

Theoph. Fetch them, good Harpax.

[*Exit* Harpax.

Enter Sempronius, *at the head of the guard,
soldiers leading three kings bound;* Antoninus *and* Macrinus *bearing the* Emperor's *eagles;* Dioclesian *with a gilt
laurel on his head, leading in* Artemia: Sapritius *kisses the* Emperor's *hand,
then embraces his* Son; Harpax *brings
in* Calista *and* Christeta. *Loud shouts.*

Diocle. So: at all parts I find Cæsarea
Completely govern'd : the licentious soldier
Confined in modest limits, and the people
Taught to obey, and ·not compell'd with
 rigour :
The ancient Roman discipline revived,
Which raised Rome to her greatness, and
 ·proclaim'd her
The glorious mistress of the conquer'd world ;
But, above all, the service of the gods,
So zealously observed, that, good Sapritius,
In words to thank you for your care and duty,
Were much unworthy Dioclesian's honour,
Or his magnificence to his loyal servants.—
But I shall find a time with noble titles
To recompense your merits.

Sap. Mightiest Cæsar,
Whose power upon this globe of earth is equal
To Jove's in heaven ; whose victorious
 triumphs
On proud rebellious kings that stir against it,
Are perfect figures of his immortal trophies
Won in the Giants' war ; whose conquering
 sword,
Guided by his strong arm, as deadly kills
As did His thunder ! all that I have done,
Or, if my strength were centupled, could do,
Comes short of what my loyalty must challenge,
But, if in anything I have deserved
Great Cæsar's smile, 'tis in my humble care
Still to preserve the honour of those gods,
That make him what he is : my zeal to them
I ever have express'd in my fell hate
Against the Christian sect that, with one blow,
(Ascribing all things to an unknown Power,)
Would strike down all their temples, and
 allows them
Nor sacrifice nor altars.

Diocle. Thou, in this,
Walk'st hand in hand with me : my will and
 power
Shall not alone confirm, but honour all
That are in this most forward.

Sap. Sacred Cæsar,
If your imperial majesty stand pleased

To shower your favours upon such as are
The boldest champions of our religion ;
Look on this reverend man, [*points to Theophilus.*] to whom the power
Of searching out, and punishing such deliuquents,
Was by your choice committed ; and, for
 proof,
He hath deserved the grace imposed upon
 him,
And with a fair and even hand proceeded,
Partial to none, not to himself, or those
Of equal nearness to himself ; behold
This pair of virgins.

Diocle. What are these ?

Sap. His daughters.

Artem. Now by your sacred fortune, they
 are fair ones,
Exceeding fair ones : would 'twere in my
 power
To make them mine !

Theoph. They are the gods', great lady,
They were most happy in your service else !
On these, when they fell from their father's
 faith,
I used a judge's power, entreaties failing
(They being seduced) to win them to adore
The holy Powers we worship ; I put on
The scarlet robe of bold authority,
And, as they had been strangers to my blood,
Presented them in the most horrid form,
All kinds of tortures ; part of which they
 suffer'd
With Roman constancy.

Artem. And could you endure, ·
Being a father, to behold their limbs
Extended on the rack ?

Theoph. I did ; but must
Confess there was a strange contention in me,
Between the impartial office of a judge,
And pity of a father ; to help justice
Religion stept in, under which odds
Compassion fell :—yet still I was a father.
For e'en then, when the flinty hangman's
 whips
Were worn with stripes spent on their tender
 limbs,
I kneel'd, and wept, and begg'd them,
 though they would
Be cruel to themselves, they would take pity
On my grey hairs : now note a sudden change,
Which I with joy remember ; those, whom
 torture,
Nor fear of death could terrify, were o'ercome
By seeing of my sufferings ; and so won,
Returning to the faith that they were born in,
I gave them to the gods. And be assured,
I that used justice with a rigorous hand,
Upon such beauteous virgins, and mine own,

B 2

Will use no favour, where the cause com-
mands me,
To any other ; but, as rocks, be deaf
To all entreaties.
    Diocle. Thou deserv'st thy place ;
Still hold it, and with honour. Things
thus order'd
Touching the gods, 'tis lawful to descend
To human cares, and exercise that power
Heaven has conferr'd upon me ;—which that
you,
Rebels and traitors to the power of Rome,
Should not with all extremities undergo,
What can you urge to qualify your crimes,
Or mitigate my anger !
    K. of Epire. We are now
Slaves to thy power, that yesterday were
kings,
And had command o'er others ; we confess
Our grandsires paid yours tribute, yet left us,
As their forefathers had, desire of freedom.
And, if you Romans hold it glorious honour,
Not only to defend what is your own,
But to enlarge your empire, (though our
fortune
Denies that happiness,) who can accuse
The famish'd mouth, if it attempt to feed?
Or such, whose fetters eat into their free-
doms,
If they desire to shake them off?
    K. of Pontus. We stand
The last examples, to prove how uncertain
All human happiness is ; and are prepared
To endure the worst.
    K. of Macedon. That spoke, which now
is highest
In Fortune's wheel, must, when she turns it
next,
Decline as low as we are. This consider'd,
Taught the Ægyptian Hercules, Sesostris,
That had his chariot drawn by captive kings,
To free them from that slavery ;—but to hope
Such mercy from a Roman, were mere
madness :
We are familiar with what cruelty
Rome, since her infant greatness, ever used
Such as she triumph'd over ; age nor sex
Exempted from her tyranny ; scepter'd
princes
Kept in her common dungeons, and their
children,
In scorn train'd up in base mechanic arts,
For public bondmen. In the catalogue
Of those unfortunate men, we expect to have
Our names remember d.
    Diocle. In all growing empires,
Even cruelty is useful : some must suffer,
And be set up examples to strike terror
In others, though far off : but, when a state

Is raised to her perfection, and her bases
Too firm to shrink, or yield, we may use
mercy,
And do't with safety : but to whom? not
cowards,
Or such whose baseness shames the con-
queror,
And robs him of his victory, as weak Perseus
Did great Æmilius. Know, therefore, kings
Of Epire, Pontus, and of Macedon,
That I with courtesy can use my prisoners,
As well as make them mine by force, pro-
vided
That they are noble enemies : such I found
you,
Before I made you mine ; and, since you
were so,
You have not lost the courages of princes,
Although the fortune. Had you borne your-
selves
Dejectedly, and base, no slavery
Had been too easy for you : but such is
The power of noble valour, that we love it
Even in our enemies, and taken with it,
Desire to make them friends, as I will you.
    K. of Epire. Mock us not, Cæsar.
    Diocle. By the gods, I do not.
Unloose their bonds :—I now as friends
embrace you.
Give them their crowns again.
    K. of Pontus. We are twice o'ercome ;
By courage, and by courtesy.
    K. of Macedon. But this latter,
Shall teach us to live ever faithful vassals
To Dioclesian, and the power of Rome.
    K. of Epire. All kingdoms fall before her !
    K. of Pontus. And all kings
Contend to honour Cæsar !
    Diocle. I believe
Your tongues are the true trumpets of your
hearts,
And in it I most happy. Queen of fate,
Imperious Fortune ! mix some light disaster
With my so many joys, to season them,
And give them sweeter relish : I'm girt round
With true felicity ; faithful subjects here,
Here bold commanders, here with new-made
friends :
But, what's the crown of all, in thee, Artemia,
My only child, whose love to me and duty,
Strive to exceed each other !
    Artem. I make payment
But of a debt, which I stand bound to tender
As a daughter and a subject.
    Diocle. Which requires yet
A retribution from me, Artemia,
Tied by a father's care, how to bestow
A jewel, of all things to me most precious :
Nor will I therefore longer keep thee from

The chief joys of creation, marriage rites ;
Which that thou may'st with greater plea-
sures taste of,
Thou shalt not like with mine eyes, but thine
own.
Among these kings, forgetting they were
captives ;
Or those, remembering not they are my sub-
jects,
Make choice of any : By Jove's dreadful
thunder,
My will shall rank with thine.
   Artem. It is a bounty
The daughters of great princes seldom meet
with ;
For they, to make up breaches in the state,
Or for some other public ends, are forced
To match where they affect not. May my life
Deserve this favour !
   Diocle. Speak ; I long to know
The man thou wilt make happy.
   Artem. If that titles,
Or the adored name of Queen could take me,
Here would I fix mine eyes, and look no
further ;
But these are baits to take a mean-born lady,
Not her, that boldly may call Cæsar father :
In that I can bring honour unto any,
But from no king that lives receive addition :
To raise desert and virtue by my fortune,
Though in a low estate, were greater glory,
Than to mix greatness with a prince that
owes
No worth but that name only.
   Diocle. I commend thee ;
'Tis like myself.
   Artem. If, then, of men beneath me,
My choice is to be made, where shall I seek,
But among those that best deserve from you ?
That have served you most faithfully ; that
in dangers
Have stood next to you ; that have interposed
Their breasts as shields of proof, to dull the
swords
Aim'd at your bosom ; that have spent their
blood
To crown your brows with laurel ?
   Macr. Cytherea,
Great Queen of Love, be now propitious to
me !
   Harp. [*to* Sap.] Now mark what I foretold.
   Anton. Her eye's on me.
Fair Venus' son, draw forth a leaden dart,
And, that she may hate me, transfix her
with it ;
Or, if thou needs wilt use a golden one,
Shoot it in the behalf of any other :
Thou know'st I am thy votary elsewhere.
                          [*Aside.*

   Artem. [*advances to* Anton.) Sir.
   Theoph. How he blushes !
   Sap. Welcome, fool, thy fortune.
Stand like a block when such an angel
courts thee !
   Artem. I am no object to divert your eye
From the beholding.
   Anton. Rather a bright sun,
Too glorious for him to gaze upon,
That took not first flight from the eagle's
aerie.
As I look on the temples, or the gods,
And with that reverence, lady, I behold you,
And shall do ever.
   Artem. And it will become you,
While thus we stand at distance ; but, if love,
Love born out of the assurance of your vir-
tues,
Teach me to stoop so low—
   Anton. O, rather take
A higher flight.
   Artem. Why, fear you to be raised ?
Say I put off the dreadful awe that waits
On majesty, or with you share my beams,
Nay, make you to outshine me ; change the
name
Of Subject into Lord, rob you of service
That's due from you to me, and in me
make it
Duty to honour you, would you refuse me ?
   Anton. Refuse you, madam ! such a worm
as I am,
Refuse what kings upon their knees would
sue for !
Call it, great lady, by another name ;
An humble modesty, that would not match
A molehill with Olympus.
   Artem. He that's famous
For honourable actions in the war,
As you are, Antoninus, a proved soldier,
Is fellow to a king.
   Anton. If you love valour,
As 'tis a kingly virtue, seek it out,
And cherish it in a king ; there it shines
brightest,
And yields the bravest lustre. Look on
Epire,
A prince, in whom it is incorporate ;
And let it not disgrace him that he was
O'ercome by Cæsar ; it was victory,
To stand so long against him : had you
seen him,
How in one bloody scene he did discharge
The parts of a commander and a soldier,
Wise in direction, bold in execution ;
You would have said, Great Cæsar's self ex-
cepted,
The world yields not his equal.
   Artem. Yet I have heard,

Encountering him alone in the head of his
  troop,
You took him prisoner.
    K. of Epire. 'Tis a truth, great princess ;
I'll not detract from valour.
    Anton. 'Twas mere fortune ;
Courage had no hand in it.
    Theoph. Did ever man
Strive so against his own good ?
    Sap. Spiritless villain !
How I am tortured ! By the immortal gods,
I now could kill him.
    Diocle. Hold, Sapritius, hold,
On our displeasure hold !
    Harp. Why, this would make
A father mad ; 'tis not to be endured ;
Your honour's tainted in't.
    Sap. By heaven, it is :
I shall think of it.
    Harp. 'Tis not to be forgotten.
    Artem. Nay, kneel not, sir, I am no
  ravisher,
Nor so far gone in fond affection to you,
But that I can retire, my honour safe :—
Yet say, hereafter, that thou hast neglected
What, but seen in possession of another,
Will make thee mad with envy.
    Anton. In her looks
Revenge is written.
    Mac. As you love your life,
Study to appease her.
    Anton. Gracious madam, hear me.
    Artem. And be again refused ?
    Anton. The tender of
My life, my service, or, since you vouch-
safe it,
My love, my heart, my all : and pardon me,
Pardon, dread princess, that I made some
  scruple
To leave a valley of security,
To mount up to the hill of majesty,
On which, the nearer Jove, the nearer light-
  ning.
What knew I, but your grace made trial
  of me ;
Durst I presume to embrace, where but to
  touch
With an unmanner'd hand, was death?
  the fox,
When he saw first the forest's king, the lion,
Was almost dead with fear ; the second view
Only a little daunted him ; the third,
He durst salute him boldly : pray you, ap-
  ply this ;
And you shall find a little time will teach me
To look with more familiar eyes upon you,
Than duty yet allows me.
    Sap. Well excused.
    Artem. You may redeem all yet.

    Diocle. And, that he may
Have means and opportunity to do so,
Artemia, I leave you my substitute
In fair Cæsarea.
    Sap. And here, as yourself,
We will obey and serve her.
    Diocle. Antoninus,
So you prove hers, I wish no other heir ;
Think on't :—be careful of your charge, Theo-
  philus ;
Sapritius, be you my daughter's guardian.
Your company I wish, confederate princes,
In our Dalmatian wars ; which finished
With victory I hope, and Maximinus,
Our brother and copartner in the empire,
At my request won to confirm as much,
The kingdoms I took from you we'll restore,
And make you greater than you were before.
    [*Exeunt all but* Antoninus *and* Macrinus.
    Anton. Oh, I am lost for ever ! lost,
  Macrinus !
The anchor of the wretched, hope, forsakes
  me,
And with one blast of Fortune all my light
Of happiness is put out.
    Mac. You are like to those
That are ill only, 'cause they are too well ;
That, surfeiting in the excess of blessings,
Call their abundance want. What could you
  wish,
That is not fall'n upon you? honour, greatness,
Respect, wealth, favour, the whole world for
  a dower ;
And with a princess, whose excelling form
Exceeds her fortune.
    Anton. Yet poison still is poison,
Though drunk in gold ; and all these flat-
  tering glories
To me, ready to starve, a painted banquet,
And no essential food. When I am scorch'd
With fire, can flames in any other quench me !
What is her love to me, greatness, or empire,
That am slave to another, who alone
Can give me ease or freedom ?
    Mac. Sir, you point at
Your dotage on the scornful Dorothea :
Is she, though fair, the same day to be
  named
With best Artemia ? In all their courses,
Wise men propose their ends : with sweet
  Artemia,
There comes along pleasure, security,
Usher'd by all that in this life is precious :
With Dorothea (though her birth be noble,
The daughter to a senator of Rome,
By him left rich, yet with a private wealth,
And far inferior to yours) arrives
The emperor's frown, which, like a mortal
  plague,

Speaks death is near ; the princess' heavy
    scorn,
Under which you will shrink ; your father's
    fury,
Which to resist, even, piety forbids :—
And but remember that she stands suspected
A favourer of the Christian sect ; she brings
Not danger, but assured destruction with her.
This truly weigh'd, one smile of great Artemia
Is to be cherish'd, and preferr'd before
All joys in Dorothea : therefore leave her.
    Anton. In what thou think'st thou art
    most wise, thou art
Grossly abused, Macrinus, and most foolish.
For any man to match above his rank,
Is but to sell his liberty. With Artemia
I still must live a servant ; but enjoying
Divinest Dorothea, I shall rule,
Rule as becomes a husband : for the *danger*,
Or call it, if you will, *assured destruction*,
I slight it thus.—If, then, thou art my friend,
As I dare swear thou art, and wilt not take
A governor's place upon thee, be my helper.
    Mac. You know I dare, and will do any-
    thing ;
Put me unto the test.
    Anton. Go then, Macrinus,
To Dorothea ; tell her I have worn,
In all the battles I have fought, her figure,
Her figure in my heart, which, like a deity,
Hath still protected me. Thou canst speak
    well ;
And of thy choicest language spare a little,
To make her understand how much I love her,
And how I languish for her. Bear these jewels,
Sent in the way of sacrifice, not service,
As to my goddess : all lets thrown behind me,
Or fears that may deter me, say, this morning
I mean to visit her by the name of friendship :
—No words to contradict this.
    Mac. I am yours :
And, if my travail this way be ill spent,
Judge not my readier will by the event.
                       [Exeunt.

ACT II.

SCENE I.—*A Room in* Dorothea's *House.*

Enter Spungius, *and* Hircins.

    Spun. Turn Christian ! Would he that
first tempted me to have my shoes walk upon
Christian soles, had turn'd me into a capon ;
for I am sure now, the stones of all my
pleasure, in this fleshly life, are cut off.
    Hir. So then, if any coxcomb has a gal-
loping desire to ride, here's a gelding, if he
can but sit him.
    Spun. I kick, for all that, like a horse ;—
look else.

    Hir. But that is a kickish jade, fellow
Spungius. Have not I as much cause to
complain as thou hast? When I was a pagan,
there was an infidel punk of mine, would have
let me come upon trust for my curvetting :
a pox on your Christian cockatrices ! they
cry, like poulterers' wives :—no money, no
coney.
    Spun. Bacchus, the god of brew'd wine
and sugar, grand patron of rob-pots, upsy-
freesy tipplers, and super-naculum takers ;
this Bacchus, who is head warden of Vintner's-
hall, ale-conner, mayor of all victualling-
houses, the sole liquid benefactor to bawdy-
houses ; lanceprezade to red noses, and invincible adelantado over the armado of
pimpled, deep-scarleted, rubified, and car-
buncled faces——
    Hir. What of all this ?
    Spun. This boon Bacchanalian skinker,
did I make legs to.
    Hir. Scurvy ones, when thou wert drunk.
    Spun. There is no danger of losing a
man's ears by making these indentures ; he
that will not now and then be Calabingo, is
worse than a Calamoothe. When I was a
pagan, and kneeled to this Bacchus, I durst
out-drink a lord ; but your Christian lords
out-bowl me. I was in hope to lead a sober
life, when I was converted ; but, now amongst
the Christians, I can no sooner stagger out
of one alehouse, but I reel into another :
they have whole streets of nothing but drink-
ing-rooms, and drabbing-chambers, jumbled
together.
    Hir. Bawdy Priapus, the first school-
master that taught butchers how to stick
pricks in flesh, and make it swell, thou
know'st, was the only ningle that I cared
for under the moon ; but, since I left him to
follow a scurvy lady, what with her praying
and our fasting, if now I come to a wench,
and offer to use her anything hardly, (telling
her, being a Christian, she must endure,)
she presently handles me as if I were a clove,
and cleaves me with disdain, as if I were a
calf's head.
    Spun. I see no remedy, fellow Hircins,
but that thou and I must be half pagans,
and half Christians ; for we know very fools
that are Christians.
    Hir. Right : the quarters of Christians
are good for nothing but to feed crows.
    Spun. True : Christian brokers, thou
know'st, are made up of the quarters of
Christians ; parboil one of these rogues,
and he is not meat for a dog : no, no, I am
resolved to have an infidel's heart, though in
shew I carry a Christian's face.

Hir. Thy last shall serve my foot: so will I.

Spun. Our whimpering lady and mistress sent me with two great baskets full of beef, mutton, veal, and goose, fellow Hircins——

Hir. And woodcock, fellow Spungius.

Spun. Upon the poor lean ass-fellow, on which I ride, to all the almswomen: what think'st thou I have done with all this good cheer?

Hir. Eat it; or be choked else.

Spun. Would my ass, basket and all, were in thy maw, if I did! No, as I am a demi-pagan, I sold the victuals, and coined the money into pottle pots of wine.

Hir. Therein thou shewed'st thyself a perfect demi-Christian too, to let the poor beg, starve, and hang, or die of the pip. Our puling, snotty-nose lady sent me out likewise with a purse of money, to relieve and release prisoners:—Did I so, think you?

Spun. Would thy ribs were turned into grates of iron then.

Hir. As I am a total pagan, I swore they should be hanged first: for, sirrah Spungius, I lay at my old ward of lechery, and cried, a pox on your two-penny wards! and so I took scurvy common flesh for the money.

Spun. And wisely done; for our lady, sending it to prisoners, had bestowed it out upon lousy knaves: and thou, to save that labour, cast'st it away upon rotten whores.

Hir. All my fear is of that pink-an-eye jack-an-apes boy, her page.

Spun. As I am a pagan from my codpiece downward, that white-faced monkey frights me too. I stole but a dirty pudding, last day, out of an almsbasket, to give my dog when he was hungry, and the peaking chitty-face page hit me in the teeth with it.

Hir. With the dirty pudding! so he did me once with a cow-turd, which in knavery I would have crumb'd into one's porridge, who was half a pagan too. The smug dandiprat smells us out, whatsoever we are doing.

Spun. Does he? let him take heed I prove not his back-friend: I'll make him curse his smelling what I do.

Hir. 'Tis my lady spoils the boy; for he is ever at her tail, and she is never well but in his company.

Enter Angelo *with a book, and a taper lighted; seeing him, they counterfeit devotion.*

Ang. O! now your hearts make ladders of your eyes,
In shew to climb to heaven, when your devotion

Walks upon crutches. Where did you waste your time,
When the religious man was on his knees,
Speaking the heavenly language?

Spun. Why, fellow Angelo, we were speaking in pedlar's French, I hope.

Hir. We have not been idle, take it upon my word.

Ang. Have you the baskets emptied, which your lady
Sent, from her charitable hands, to women
That dwell upon her pity?

Spun. Emptied them! yes; I'd be loth to have my belly so empty: yet, I am sure, I munched not one bit of them neither.

Ang. And went your money to the prisoners?

Hir. Went! no; I carried it, and with these fingers paid it away.

Ang. What way? the devil's way, the way of sin,
The way of hot damnation, way of lust?
And you, to wash away the poor man's bread,
In bowls of drunkenness?

Spun. Drunkenness! yes, yes, I use to be drunk; our next neighbour's man, called Christopher, hath often seen me drunk, hath he not?

Hir. Or me given so to the flesh: my cheeks speak my doings.

Ang. Avaunt, ye thieves, and hollow hypocrites!
Your hearts to me lie open like black books,
And there I read your doings.

Spun. And what do you read in my heart?

Hir. Or in mine? come, amiable Angelo, beat the flint of your brains.

Spun. And let's see what sparks of wit fly out to kindle your cerebrum.

Ang. Your names even brand you; you are Spungius call'd,
And like a spunge, you suck up lickerish wines,
Till your soul reels to hell.

Spung. To hell! can any drunkard's legs carry him so far?

Ang. For blood of grapes you sold the widows' food.
And, starving them, 'tis murder; what's this but hell?——
Hircius your name, and goatish is your nature;
You snatch the meat out of the prisoner's mouth,
To fatten harlots: is not this hell too?
No angel, but the devil, waits on you.

Spun. Shall I cut his throat?

Hir. No; better burn him, for I think he is a witch: but sooth, sooth him.

Spun. Fellow Angelo, true it is, that

falling into the company of wicked he-
Christians, for my part——

Hir. And she ones, for mine,—we have
them swim in shoals hard by——

Spun. We must confess, I took too much
out of the pot; and he of t'other hollow
commodity.

Hir. Yes, indeed, we laid Jill on both of
us; we cozen'd the poor; but 'tis a common
thing: many a one, that counts himself a
better Christian than we two, has done it,
by this light!

Spun. But pray, sweet Angelo, play not
the tell-tale to my lady; and, if you take us
creeping into any of these mouse-holes of
sin any more, let cats flay off our skins.

Hir. And put nothing but the poison'd
tails of rats into those skins.

Ang. Will you dishonour her sweet charity,
Who saved you from the tree of death and
shame?

Hir. Would I were hang'd, rather than
thus be told of my faults!

Spun. She took us, 'tis true, from the
gallows; yet I hope she will not bar yeomen
sprats to have their swing.

Ang. She comes,—beware, and mend.

Hir. Let's break his neck, and bid him
mend.

Enter Dorothea.

Dor. Have you my messages, sent to the
poor,
Deliver'd with good hands, not robbing them
Of any jot was theirs?

Spun. Rob them, lady! I hope neither
my fellow nor I am thieves.

Hir. Delivered with good hands, madam!
else let me never lick my fingers more when
I eat butter'd fish.

Dor. Who cheat the poor, and from them
pluck their alms,
Pilfer from heaven; and there are thunder-
bolts,
From thence to beat them ever. Do not lie;
Were you both faithful, true distributers?

Spun. Lie, madam! what grief is it to
see you turn swaggerer, and give your poor-
minded rascally servants the lie!

Dor. I'm glad you do not; if those
wretched people,
Tell you they pine for want of any thing,
Whisper but to mine ear, and you shall
furnish them.

Hir. Whisper! nay, lady, for my part I'll
cry whoop.

Ang. Play no more, villains, with so good
a lady;
For, if you do——

Spun. Are we Christians?

Hir. The foul fiend snap all pagans for me!

Ang. Away, and, once more, mend.

Spun. 'Takes us for botchers.

Hir. A patch, a patch!

[*Exeunt* Spun. *and* Hir.

Dor. My book and taper.

Ang. Here, most holy mistress.

Dor. Thy voice sends forth such music,
that I never
Was ravish'd with a more celestial sound.
Were every servant in the world like thee,
So full of goodness, angels would come down
To dwell with us: thy name is Angelo,
And like that name thou art; get thee to rest,
Thy youth with too much watching is opprest.

Ang. No, my dear lady, I could weary stars,
And force the wakeful moon to lose her eyes,
By my late watching, but to wait on you.
When at your prayers you kneel before the
altar,
Methinks I'm singing with some quire in
heaven,
So blest I hold me in your company:
Therefore, my most loved mistress, do not bid
Your boy, so serviceable, to get hence;
For then you break his heart.

Dor. Be nigh me still, then:
In golden letters down I'll set that day,
Which gave thee to me. Little did I hope
To meet such worlds of comfort in thyself,
This little, pretty body; when I, coming
Forth of the temple, heard my beggar-boy,
My sweet-faced, godly beggar-boy, crave an
alms,
Which with glad hand I gave, with lucky
hand!—
And, when I took thee home, my most chaste
bosom,
Methought, was fill'd with no hot wanton fire,
But with a holy flame, mounting since higher,
On wings of cherubins, than it did before.

Ang. Proud am I, that my lady's modest eye
So likes so poor a servant.

Dor. I have offer'd
Handfuls of gold but to behold thy parents.
I would leave kingdoms, were I queen of
some,
To dwell with thy good father; for, the son
Bewitching me so deeply with his presence,
He that begot him must do't ten times more.
I pray thee, my sweet boy, shew me thy
parents;
Be not ashamed.

Ang. I am not: I did never
Know who my mother was; but, by yon
palace,
Fill'd with bright heavenly courtiers, I dare
assure you,

And pawn these eyes upon it, and this hand,
My father is in heaven : and, pretty mistress,
If your illustrious hourglass spend his sand,
No worse than yet it does ; upon my life,
You and I both shall meet my father there,
And he shall bid you welcome.
Dor. A blessed day !
We all long to be there, but lose the way.
[*Exeunt.*

SCENE II.—*A S*t*reet, near* Dorothea's
House.

Enter Macrinus, *met by* Theophilus *and*
Harpax.

Theoph. The Sun, god of the day, guide
thee, Macrinus !
Mac. And thee, Theophilus !
Theoph. Glad'st thou in such scorn?
I call my wish back.
Mac. I'm in haste.
Theoph. One word,
Take the least hand of time up :—stay.
Mac. Be brief.
Theoph. As thought : I prithee tell me,
good Macrinus,
How health and our fair princess lay together
This night, for you can tell ; courtiers have
flies,
That buzz all news unto them.
Mac. She slept but ill.
Theoph. Double thy courtesy ; how does
Antoninus?
Mac. Ill, well, straight, crook'd,—I know
not how.
Theoph. Once more ;—
Thy head is full of windmills !—when doth
the princess
Fill a bed full of beauty, and bestow it
On Antoninus, on the wedding-night?
Mac. I know not.
Theoph. No! thou art the manuscript,
Where Antoninus writes down all his secrets :
Honest Macrinus, tell me.
Mac. Fare you well, sir. [*Exit.*
Harp. Honesty is some fiend, and frights
him hence ;
A many courtiers love it not.
Theoph. What piece
Of this state-wheel, which winds up Anto-
ninus,
Is broke, it runs so jarringly? the man
Is from himself divided : O thou, the eye,
By which I wonders see, tell me, my Harpax,
What gad-fly tickles this Macrinus so,
That, flinging up the tail, he breaks thus
from me.
Harp. Oh, sir, his brain-pan is a bed of
snakes,

Whose stings shoot through his eye-balls,
whose poisonous spawn
Ingenders such a fry of speckled villainies,
That, unless charms more strong than ada-
mant
Be used, the Roman angel's wings shall melt,
And Cæsar's diadem be from his head
Spurn'd by base feet ; the laurel which he
wears,
Returning victor, be enforced to kiss
That which it hates, the fire.   And can this
ram,
This Antoninus-Engine, being made ready
To so much mischief, keep a steady motion?—
His eyes and feet, you see, give strange
assaults.
Theoph. I'm turu'd a marble statue at thy
language,
Which printed is in such crabb'd characters,
It puzzles my reading : what, in the name
Of Pluto, now is hatching?
Harp. This Macrinus,
The line is, upon which love-errands run
'Twixt Antoninus and that ghost of women,
The bloodless Dorothea ; who in prayer
And meditation, mocking all your gods,
Drinks up her ruby colour : yet Antoninus
Plays the Endymion to this pale-faced Mcon,
Courts, seeks to catch her eyes—
Theoph. And what of this?
Harp. These are but creeping billows,
Not got to shore yet : but if Dorothea
Fall on his bosom, and be fired with love,
(Your coldest women do so),—had you ink
Brew'd from the infernal Styx, not all that
blackness
Can make a thing so foul, as the dishonours,
Disgraces, buffetings, and most base affronts
Upon the bright Artemia, star o' the court,
Great Cæsar's daughter.
Theoph. I now conster thee.
Harp. Nay, more ; a firmament of clouds,
being fill'd
With Jove's artillery, shot down at once,
To pash your gods in pieces, cannot give,
With all those thunderbolts, so deep a blow
To the religion there, and pagan lore,
As this ; for Dorothea hates your gods,
And, if she once blast Antoninus' soul,
Making it foul like hers, Oh ! the example—
Theoph. Eats through Cæsarea's heart like
liquid poison.
Have I invented tortures to tear Christians,
To see but which, could all that feel hell's
torments
Have leave to stand aloof here on earth's
stage,
They would be mad till they again descended,
Holding the pains most horrid of such souls,

May-games to those of mine ; has this my
    hand
Set down a Christian's execution
In such dire postures, that the very hangman
Fell at my foot dead, hearing but their figures ;
And shall Macrinus and his fellow-masquer
Strangle me in a dance?
   Harp. No :—on ; I hug thee,
For drilling thy quick brains in this rich plot
Of tortures 'gainst these Christians : on ; I
    hug thee !
   Theoph. Both hug and holy me : to this
    Dorothea,
Fly thou and I in thunder.
   Harp. Not for kingdoms
Piled upon kingdoms : there's a villain page
Waits on her, whom I would not for the world
Hold traffic with ; I do so hate his sight,
That, should I look on him, I must sink down.
   Theoph. I will not lose thee then, her to
    confound :
None but this head with glories shall be
   crown'd.
   Harp. Oh! mine own as I would wish
    thee !   [*Exeunt.*

SCENE III.—*A Room in* Dorothea's *House.*

   Enter Dorothea, Macrinus, *and* Angelo.

   Dor. My trusty Angelo, with that curious
    eye
Of thine, which ever waits upon my business,
I prithee watch those my still-negligent
   servants,
That they perform my will, in what's enjoin'd
   them
To the good of others ; else will you find
   them flies,
Not lying still, yet in them no good lies :
Be careful, dear boy.
   Ang. Yes, my sweetest mistress. [*Exit.*
   Dor. Now, sir, you may go on.
   Mac. I then must study
A new arithmetic, to sum up the virtues
Which Antoninus gracefully become.
There is in him so much man, so much
   goodness,
So much of honour, and of all things else,
Which make our being excellent, that from
   his store
He can enough lend others ; yet, much ta'en
   from him,
The want shall be as little, as when seas
Lend from their bounty, to fill up the poorness
Of needy rivers.
   Dor. Sir, he is more indebted
To you for praise, than you to him that
   owes it.
   Mac. If queens, viewing his presents paid
    to the whiteness

Of your chaste hand alone, should be am-
   bitious
But to be parted in their numerous shares :
This he counts nothing : could you see main
   armies
Make battles in the quarrel of his valour,
That 'tis the best, the truest ; this were
   nothing :
The greatness of his state, his father's voice,
And arm, awing Cæsarea, he ne'er boasts of ;
The sunbeams which the emperor throws
   upon him,
Shine there but as in water, and gild him
Not with one spot of pride : no, dearest
   beauty,
All these, heap'd up together in one scale,
Cannot weigh down the love he bears to you,
Being put into the other.
   Dor. Could gold buy you
To speak thus for a friend, you, sir, are
   worthy
Of more than I will number ; and this your
   language
Hath power to win upon another woman,
'Top of whose heart the feathers of this
   world
Are gaily stuck : but all which first you
   named,
And now this last, his love, to me are nothing.
   Mac. You make me a sad messenger ;—
but himself

       Enter Antoninus.

Being come in person, shall, I hope, hear
   from you
Music more pleasing.
   Anton. Has your ear, Macrinus,
Heard none, then?
   Mac. None I like,
   Anton. But can there be
In such a noble casket, wherein lie
Beauty and chastity in their full perfections,
A rocky heart, killing with cruelty
A life that's prostrated beneath your feet?
   Dor. I am guilty of a shame I yet ne'er
   knew,
Thus to hold parley with you ;—pray, sir,
   pardon.   [*Going.*
   Anton. Good sweetness, you now have it,
   and shall go :
Be but so merciful, before your wounding me
With such a mortal weapon as Farewell,
To let me murmur to your virgin ear,
What I was loth to lay on any tongue
But this mine own.
   Dor. If one immodest accent
Fly out, I hate you everlastingly.
   Anton. My true love dares not do it.
   Mac. Hermes inspire thee !

Enter above, Artemia, Sapritius, Theophilus,
Spungius, *and* Hircius.

Spun. So, now, do you see?—Our work
is done ; the fish you angle for is nibbling
at the hook, and therefore untruss the cod-
piece-point of our reward, no matter if the
breeches of conscience fall about our heels.

Theoph. The gold you earn is here ; dam
up your mouths,
And no words of it.

Hir. No ; nor no words from you of too
much damning neither. I know women
sell themselves daily, and are hacknied out
for silver : why may not we, then, betray a
scurvy mistress for gold ?

Spun. She saved us from the gallows, and,
only to keep one proverb from breaking his
neck, we'll hang her.

Theoph. 'Tis well done ; go, go, you're
my fine white boys.

Spun. If your red boys, 'tis well known
more ill-favoured faces than ours are painted.

Sap. Those fellows trouble us.

Theoph. Away, away !

Hir. I to my sweet placket.

Spun. And I to my full pot.
                [*Exeunt Hir. and Spun.*

Anton. Come, let me tune you :—glaze
not thus your eyes
With self-love of a vow'd virginity,
Make every man your glass ; you see our sex
Do never murder propagation ;
We all desire your sweet society,
But if you bar me from it, you do kill me,
And of my blood are guilty.

Artem. O base villain !

Sap. Bridle your rage, sweet princess.

Anton. Could not my fortunes,
Rear'd higher far than yours, be worthy of
you,
Methinks my dear affection makes you mine.

Dor. Sir, for your fortunes, were they
mines of gold,
He that I love is richer ; and for worth,
You are to him lower than any slave,
Is to a monarch.

Sap. So insolent, base Christian !

Dor. Can I, with wearing out my knees
before him,
Get you but be his servant, you shall boast
You're equal to a king.

Sap. Confusion on thee,
For playing thus the lying sorceress !

Anton. Your mocks are great ones ; none
beneath the sun
Will I be servant to.—On my knees I beg it,
Pity me, wondrous maid.

Sap. I curse thy baseness.

Theoph. Listen to more.

Dor. O kneel not, sir, to me.

Anton. This knee is emblem of an hum-
bled heart :
That heart which tortured is with your dis-
dain,
Justly for seorning others, even this heart,
To which for pity such a princess sues,
As in her hand offers me all the world,
Great Cæsar's daughter.

Artem. Slave, thou liest.

Anton. Yet this
Is adamant to her, that melts to you
In drops of blood.

Theoph. A very dog !

Anton. Perhaps
'Tis my religion makes you knit the brow ;
Yet be you mine, and ever be your own :
I ne'er will screw your conscience from that
Power,
On which you Christians lean.

Sap. I can no longer
Fret out my life with weeping at thee, villain.
Sirrah !   [*Aloud.*
Would, when I got thee, the high Thun-
derer's hand
Had struck thee in the womb !

Mac. We are betray'd.

Artem. Is that the idol, traitor, which
thou kneel'st to,
Trampling upon my beauty !

Theoph. Sirrah, bandog !
Wilt thou in pieces tear our Jupiter
For her? our Mars for her? our Sol for her?—
A whore ! a hell-hound ! In this globe of
brains,
Where a whole world of furies for such
tortures
Have fought, as in a chaos, which should
exceed,
These nails shall grubbing hie from skull to
skull,
To find one horrider than all, for you,
You three !

Artem. Threaten not, but strike : quick
vengeance flies
Into my bosom ; caitiff ! here all love dies.
                [*Exeunt above.*

Anton. O ! I am thunderstruck ! We are
both o'erwhelm'd——

Mac. With one high-raging billow.

Dor. You a soldier,
And sink beneath the violence of a woman !

Anton. A woman ! a wrong'd princess.
From such a star,
Blazing with fires of hate, what can be
looked for,
But tragical events? my life is now
The subject of her tyranny.

Dor.   That fear is base,
Of 'death, when that death doth but life
    displace
Out of her house of earth ; you only dread
The stroke, and not what follows when you're
    dead ;
There's the great fear, indeed : come, let
    your eyes
Dwell where mine do, you'll scorn their
    tyrannies.

Re-enter below, Artemia, Sapritius, Theo-
    philus, *a guard ;* Angelo *comes and
    stands close by* Dorothea.

Artem. My father's nerves put vigour in
    mine arm,
And I his strength must use. Because I once
Shed beams of favour on thee; and, with the
    lion,
Play'd with thee gently, when thou struck'st
    my heart,
I'll not insult on a base, humbled prey,
By lingering out thy terrors ; but, with one
    frown,
Kill thee :—hence with them all to execution.
Seize him ; but let even death itself be weary
In torturing her. I'll change those smiles
    to shrieks ;
Give the fool what she's proud of, martyrdom:
In pieces rack that bawd too.
                          [*Points to* Macr.
Sap. Albeit the reverence
I owe our gods and you, are, in my bosom,
Torrents so strong, that pity quite lies
    drown'd
From saving this young man ; yet, when I see
What face death gives him, and that a
    thing within me
Says, 'tis my son, I am forced to be a man,
And grow fond of his life, which thus I beg.
Artem. And I deny.
Anton. Sir, you dishonour me,
To sue for that which I disclaim to have.
I shall more glory in my sufferings gain,
Than you in giving judgment, since I offer
My blood up to your anger ; nor do I kneel
To keep a wretched life of mine from ruin :
Preserve this temple, builded fair as yours is,
And Cæsar never went in greater triumph,
Than I shall to the scaffold.
Artem. Are you so brave, sir?
Set forward to his triumph, and let those two
Go cursing along with him.
Dor. No, but pitying,
For my part, I, that you lose ten times more
By torturing me, than I that dare your
    tortures :
Through all the army of my sins, I have even

Labour'd to break, and cope with death to
    th' face.
The visage of a hangman frights not me ;
The sight of whips, racks, gibbets, axes, fires,
Are scaffoldings by which my soul climbs up
To an eternal habitation.
Theoph. Cæsar's imperial daughter, hear
    me speak.
Let not this Christian thing, in this her
    pageantry
Of proud deriding both our gods and Cæsar,
Build to herself a kingdom in her death,
Going laughing from us : no ; her bitterest
    torment
Shall be, to feel her constancy beaten down ;
The bravery of her resolution lie
Batter'd, by argument, into such pieces,
That she again shall, on her belly, creep
To kiss the pavements of our paynim gods.
Artem. How to be done?
Theoph. I'll send my daughters to her,
And they shall turn her rocky faith to wax ;
Else spit at me, let me be made your slave,
And meet no Roman's but a villain's grave.
Artem. Thy prisoner let her be, then ;
    and, Sapritius,
Your son and that, be yours : death shall be
    sent
To him that suffers them, by voice or letters,
To greet each other. Rifle her estate ;
Christians to beggary brought, grow des-
    perate.
Dor. Still on the bread of poverty let me feed.
Ang. O ! my admired mistress, quench
    not out
The holy fires within you, though temptations
Shower down upon you? Clasp thine armour
    on,
Fight well, and thou shalt see, after these wars,
Thy head wear sunbeams, and thy feet
    touch stars.   [*Exeunt all but* Angelo.

Enter Hircius *and* Spungius.

Hir. How now, Angelo ; how is it, how
    is it?
What thread spins that whore Fortune upon
    her wheel now?
Spun. Com' esta, com esta, poor knave?
*Hir. Comment portez-vous, comment
portez-vous, mon petit garçon ?*
Spun. My pretty wee comrade, my half-
inch of man's flesh, how run the dice of this
cheating world, ha?
Ang. Too well on your sides ; you are hid
    in gold,
O'er head and ears.
Hir. We thank our fates, the sign of the
gingle-boys hangs at the doors of our
pockets.

Spun. Who would think that we, coming
forth of the a—, as it were, or fag-end of
the world, should yet see the golden age,
when so little silver is stirring ?

Hir. Nay, who can say any citizen is an
ass, for loading his own back with money
till his soul cracks again, only to leave his
son like a gilded coxcomb behind him ? Will
not any fool take me for a wise man now,
seeing me draw out of the pit of my treasury
this little god with his belly full of gold ?

Spun. And this, full of the same meat,
out of my ambry ?

Ang. That gold will melt to poison.

Spun. Poison ! would it would ! whole
pints for healths should down my throat.

Hir. Gold, poison ! there is never a she-
thrasher in Cæsarea, that lives on the flail
of money, will call it so.

Ang. Like slaves you sold your souls for
   golden dross,
Bewraying her to death, who stept between
You and the gallows.

Spun. It was an easy matter to save us,
she being so well back'd.

Hir. The gallows and we fell out : so
she did but part us.

Ang. The misery of that mistress is mine
   own ;
She beggar'd, I left wretched.

Hir. I can but let my nose drop in
sorrow, with wet eyes for her.

Spun. The petticoat of her estate is
unlaced, I confess.

Hir. Yes, and the smock of her charity
is now all to pieces.

Ang. For love you bear to her, for some
   good turns
Done you by me, give me one piece of silver.

Hir. How ! a piece of silver ! if thou
wert an angel of gold, I would not put thee
into white money, unless I weighed thee ;
and I weigh thee not a rush.

Spun. A piece of silver ! I never had but
two calves in my life, and those my mother
left me ; I will rather part from the fat of
them, than from a mustard-token's worth
of argent.

Hir. And so, sweet nit, we crawl from thee.

Spun. Adieu, demi-dandiprat, adieu !

Ang. Stay,—one word yet ; you now are
full of gold.

Hir. I would be sorry my dog were so
full of the pox.

Spun. Or any sow of mine of the meazles
   either.

Ang. Go, go ! you're beggars both ; you
are not worth
That leather on your feet.

Hir. Away, away, boy !

Spun. Page, you do nothing but set
patches on the soles of your jests.

Ang. I am glad I tried your love, which,
   see ! I want not,
So long as this is full.

Both. And so long as this, so long as this.

Hir. Spungius, you are a pickpocket.

Spun. Hircins, thou hast nimm'd :—*So
long as !*—not so much money is left as will
buy a louse.

Hir. Thou art a thief, and thou liest in
that gut through which thy wine runs, if
thou deniest it.

Spun. Thou liest deeper than the bottom
of mine enraged pocket, if thou affrontest it.

Ang. No blows, no bitter language ;—
all your gold gone !

Spun. Can the devil creep into one's
breeches ?

Hir. Yes, if his horns once get into the
codpiece.

Ang. Come, sigh not ; I so little am in love
With that whose loss kills you, that, see !
'tis yours,
All yours : divide the heap in equal share,
So you will go along with me to prison,
And in our mistress' sorrows bear a part :
Say, will you ?

Both. Will we !

Spun. If she were going to hanging, no
gallows should part us.

Hir. Let us both be turned into a rope
of onions, if we do not.

Ang. Follow me, then ; repair your bad
   deeds past ;
Happy are men, when their best days are
   last !

Spun. True, master Angelo ; pray, sir,
lead the way.   [*Exit* Angelo.

Hir. Let him lead that way, but follow
thou me this way.

Spun. I live in a gaol !

Hir. Away, and shift for ourselves :—
She'll do well enough there ; for prisoners
are more hungry after mutton, than catch-
poles after prisoners.

Spun. Let her starve then, if a whole gaol
will not fill her belly.   [*Exeunt.*

_____

ACT III.

SCENE I.—*A Room in* Dorothea's *House.*

Enter Sapritius, Theophilus, Priest, Calista,
   and Christeta.

Sap. Sick to the death, I fear.

Theoph. I meet your sorrow,
With my true feeling of it.

Sap. She's a witch,
A sorceress, Theophilus ; my son
Is charm'd by her enchanting eyes ; and, like
An image made of wax, her beams of beauty
Melt him to nothing : all my hopes in him,
And all his gotten honours, find their grave
In his strange dotage on her. ·Would, when first
He saw and loved her, that the earth had open'd,
And swallow'd both alive !
  Theoph. There's hope left yet.
  Sap. Not any : though the princess were appeased,
All title in her love surrender'd up ;
Yet this coy Christian is so transported
With her religion, that unless my son
(But let him perish first !) drink the same potion,
And be of her belief, she'll not vouchsafe
To be his lawful wife.
  Priest. But, once removed
From her opinion, as I rest assured
The reasons of these holy maids will win her,
You'll find her tractable to anything,
For our content or his.
  Theoph. If she refuse it,
The Stygian damps, breeding infectious airs,
The mandrake's shrieks, the basilisk's killing eye,
The dreadful lightning that does crush the bones,
And never singe the skin, shall not appear
Less fatal to her, than my zeal made hot
With love unto my gods. I have deferr'd it,
In hopes to draw back this apostata,
Which will be greater honour than her death,
Unto her father's faith ; and, to that end,
Have brought my daughters hither.
  Cal. And we doubt not
To do what you desire.
  Sap. Let her be sent for.
Prosper in your good work ; and were I not
To attend the princess, I would see and hear
How you succeed.
  Theoph. I am commanded too,
I'll bear you company.
  Sap. Give them your ring,
To lead her as in triumph, if they win her,
Before her highness.   [*Exit.*
  Theoph. Spare no promises,
Persuasions, or threats, I do conjure you :
If you prevail, 'tis the most glorious work
You ever undertook.

        Enter Dorothea *and* Angelo.

  Priest. She comes.
  Theoph. We leave you ;

Be constant, and be careful.
              [*Exeunt* Theoph. *and* Priest.
  Cal. We are sorry
To meet you under guard.
  Dor. But I more grieved
You are at liberty. So well I love you,
That I could wish, for such a cause as mine,.
You were my fellow-prisoners : Prithee, Angelo,
Reach us some chairs.   Please you sit——
  Cal. We thank you :
Our visit is for love, love to your safety.
  Christ. Our conference must be private,.
pray you, therefore,
Command your boy to leave us.
  Dor. You may trust him
With any secret that concerns my life,
Falsehood and he are strangers : had you, ladies,
Been bless'd with such a servant, you had never
Forsook that way, your journey even half ended,
That leads to joys eternal.   In the place
Of loose lascivious mirth, he would have stirr'd you
To holy meditations ; and so far
He is from flattery, that he would have told
you,
Your pride being at the height, how miserable
And wretched things you were, that, for an hour
Of pleasure here, have made a desperate sale
Of all your right in happiness hereafter.
He must not leave me ; without him I fall :
In this life he's my servant, in the other
A wish'd companion.
  Ang. 'Tis not in the devil,
Nor all his wicked arts, to shake such goodness.
  Dor. But you were speaking, lady.
  Cal. As a friend
And lover of your safety, and I pray you
So to receive it ; and, if you remember .
How near in love our parents were, that we,
Even from the cradle, were brought up together,
Our amity increasing with our years,
We cannot stand suspected.
  Dor. To the purpose.
  Cal. We come, then, as good angels, Dorothea,
To make you happy ; and the means so easy,
That, be not you an enemy to yourself,
Already you enjoy it.
  Christ. Look on us,
Ruin'd as you are, once, and brought unto it,
By your persuasion.
  Cal. But what follow'd, lady ?

Leaving those blessings which our gods gave
    freely,
And shower'd upon us with a prodigal hand,
As to be noble born, youth, beauty, wealth,
And the free use of these without control,
Check, curb, or stop, such is our law's in-
    dulgence !
All happiness forsook us ; bonds and fetters,
For amorous twines ; the rack and hang-
    man's whips,
In place of choice delights ; our parents'
    curses
Instead of blessings; scorn, neglect, contempt,
Fell thick upon us.
    Christ. This consider'd wisely,
We made a fair retreat ; and reconciled
To our forsaken gods, we live again
In all prosperity.
    Cal. By our example,
Bequeathing misery to such as love it,
Learn to be happy. The Christian yoke's
    too heavy
For such a dainty neck ; it was framed rather
To be the shrine of Venus, or a pillar,
More precious than crystal, to support
Our Cupid's image : our religion, lady,
Is but a varied pleasure ; yours a toil
Slaves would shrink under.
    Dor. Have you not cloven feet ? are you
    not devils ?
Dare any say so much, or dare I hear it
Without a virtuous and religious anger ?
Now to put on a virgin modesty,
Or maiden silence, when His power is
    question'd
That is omnipotent, were a greater crime,
Than in a bad cause to be impudent.
Your gods ! your temples ! brothel houses
    rather,
Or wicked actions of the worst of men,
Pursued and practised. Your religious rites !
Oh ! call them rather juggling mysteries,
The baits and nets of hell : your souls the prey
For which the devil angles ; your false plea-
    sures
A steep descent, by which you headlong fall
Into eternal torments.
    Cal. Do not tempt
Our powerful gods.
    Dor. Which of your powerful gods ?
Your gold, your silver, brass, or wooden ones,
That can nor do me hurt, nor protect you ?
Most pitied women ! will you sacrifice
To such,—or call them gods or goddesses,
Your parents would disdain to be the same,
Or you yourselves ? O blinded ignorance !
Tell me, Calista, by the truth, I charge you,
Or anything you hold more dear, would you,
To have him deified to posterity,

Desire your father an adulterer,
A ravisher, almost a parricide,
A vile incestuous wretch ?
    Cal. That, piety
And duty answer for me.
    Dor. Or you, Christeta,
To be hereafter register'd a goddess,
Give your chaste body up to the embraces
Of goatish lust? have it writ on your forehead,
" This is the common whore, the prostitute,
The mistress in the art of wantonness,
Knows every trick and labyrinth of desires
That are immodest ?"
    Christ. You judge better of me,
Or my affection is ill placed on you ;
Shall I turn strumpet ?
    Dor. No, I think you would not.
Yet Venus, whom you worship, was a whore ;
Flora, the foundress of the public stews,
And has, for that, her sacrifice ; your great
    god,
Your Jupiter, a loose adulterer,
Incestuous with his sister : read but those
That have canonized them, you'll find them
    worse
Than, in chaste language, I can speak them
    to you.
Are they immortal then, that did partake
Of human weakness, and had ample share
In men's most base affections ; subject to
Unchaste loves, anger, bondage, wounds,
    as men are ?
Here, Jupiter, to serve his lust, turu'd bull,
The shape, indeed, in which he stole Europa ;
Neptune, for gain, builds up the walls of
    Troy,
As a day-labourer ; Apollo keeps
Admetus' sheep for bread ; the Lemnian
    smith
Sweats at the forge for hire ; Prometheus
    here,
With his still-growing liver, feeds the vulture ;
Saturn bound fast in hell with adamant
    chains ;
And thousands more, on whom abused error
Bestows a deity. Will you then, dear sisters,
For I would have you such, pay your devo-
    tions
To things of less power than yourselves ?
    Cal. We worship
Their good deeds in their images.
    Dor. By whom fashion'd ?
By sinful men. I'll tell you a short tale,
Nor can you but confest it is a true one :
A king of Egypt, being to erect
The image of Osiris, whom they honour,
Took from the matrons' necks the richest
    jewels,
And purest gold, as the materials,

To finish up his work ; which perfected,
With all solemnity he set it up,
To be adored, and served himself his idol ;
Desiring it to give him victory
Against his enemies : but, being overthrown,
Enraged against his god, (these are fine gods,
Subject to human fury !) he took down
The senseless thing, and melting it again,
He made a basin, in which eunuchs wash'd
His concubine's feet; and for this sordid use,
Some months it served : his mistress proving
  false,
As most indeed do so, and grace concluded
Between him and the priests, of the same
  bason
He made his god again !—Think, think, of
  this,
And then consider, if all worldly honours,
Or pleasures that do leave sharp stings be-
  hind them,
Have power to win such as have reasonable
  souls,
To put their trust in dross.

Cal. Oh, that I had been born
Without a father !

Christ. Piety to him
Hath ruin'd us for ever.

Dor. Think not so ;
You may repair all yet : the attribute
That speaks his Godhead most, is merciful :
Revenge is proper to the fiends you worship,
Yet cannot strike without his leave.—You
  weep,—
Oh, 'tis a heavenly shower ! celestial balm
To cure your wounded conscience ! let it fall,
Fall thick upon it ; and, when that is spent,
I'll help it with another of my tears :
And may your true repentance prove the child
Of my true sorrow, never mother had
A birth so happy !

Cal. We are caught ourselves,
That came to take you ; and, assured of
  conquest,
We are your captives.

Dor. And in that you triumph :
Your victory had been eternal loss,
And this your loss immortal gain. Fix here,
And you shall feel yourselves inwardly arm'd
'Gainst tortures, death, and hell :—but, take
  heed, sisters,
That, or through weakness, threats, or mild
  persuasions,
Though of a father, you fall not into
A second and a worse apostacy.

Cal. Never, oh never ! steel'd by your
  example,
We dare the worst of tyranny.

Christ. Here's our warrant,
You shall along and witness it.

Dor. Be confirm'd then ;
And rest assured, the more you suffer here,
The more your glory, you to heaven more
  dear.   *[Exeunt.*

SCENE II.—*The* Governor's *Palace.*

Enter Artemia, Sapritius, Theophilus, *and*
Harpax.

Artem. Sapritius, though your son deserve
  no pity,
We grieve his sickness : his contempt of us,
We cast behind us, and look back upon
His service done to Cæsar, that weighs down
Our just displeasure. If his malady
Have growth from his restraint, or that you
  think
His liberty can cure him, let him have it :
Say, we forgive him freely.

Sap. Your grace binds us,
Ever your humblest vassals.

Artem. Use all means,
For his recovery ; though yet I love him,
I will not force affection. If the Christian,
Whose beauty hath out-rivall'd me, be won
To be of our belief, let him enjoy her ;
That all may know, when the cause wills,
  I can
Command my own desires.

Theoph. Be happy then,
My lord Sapritius : I am confident,
Such eloquence and sweet persuasion dwell
Upon my daughters' tongues, that they
  will work her
To anything they please.

Sap. I wish they may !
Yet 'tis no easy task to undertake,
To alter a perverse and obstinate woman.
     [A shout within : loud music.

Artem. What means this shout ?

Sap. 'Tis seconded with music,
Triumphant music.—Ha !

Enter Sempronius.

Semp. My lord, your daughters,
The pillars of our faith, having converted,
For so report gives out, the Christian lady,
The image of great Jupiter borne before them,
Sue for access.

Theoph. My soul divined as much.
Blest be the time when first they saw this light !
Their mother, when she bore them to support
My feeble age, filled not my longing heart
With so much joy, as they in this good work,
Have thrown upon me.

Enter Priest *with the Image of Jupiter, incense and censers ; followed by* Calista *and*
Christeta, *leading* Dorothea.

Welcome, oh, thrice welcome,
Daughters, both of my body and my mind !
                    c

Let me embrace in you my bliss, my comfort ;
And Dorothea, now more welcome too,
Then if you never had fallen off ! I am ravish'd
With the excess of joy : — speak, happy
    daughters,
The blest event.
    Cal. We never gain'd so much
By any undertaking.
    Theoph. O my dear girl,
Our gods reward thee !
    Dor. Nor was ever time,
On my part, better spent.
    Christ. We are all now
Of one opinion.
    Theoph. My best Christeta !
Madam, if ever you did grace to worth,
Vouchsafe your princely hands.
    Artem. Most willingly——
Do you refuse it ?
    Cal. Let us first deserve it.
    Theoph. My own child still ! here set our
    god ; prepare
The incense quickly : Come, fair Dorothea,
I will myself support you ;—now kneel down,
And pay your vows to Jupiter.
    Dor. I shall do it
Better by their example.
    Theoph. They shall guide you,
They are familiar with the sacrifice.
Forward, my twins of comfort, and, to teach
    her,
Make a joint offering.
    Christ. Thus—[*they both spit at the image,*
    Cal. And thus — [*throw it down, and*
    spurn it.
    Harp. Profane,
And impious ! stand you now like a statue ?
Are you the champion of the gods ? where is
Your holy zeal, your anger ?
    Theoph. I am blasted ;
And, as my feet were rooted here, I find
I have no motion ; I would I had no sight
    too !
Or if my eyes can serve to any use,
Give me, thou injured Power ! a sea of tears,
To expiate this madness in my daughters ;
For, being themselves, they would have
    trembled at
So blasphemous a deed in any other :——
For my sake, hold awhile thy dreadful
    thunder,
And give me patience to demand a reason
For this accursed act.
    Dor. 'Twas bravely done.
    Theoph. Peace, damn'd enchantress,
    peace !—I should look on you
With eyes made red with fury, and my hand,
That shakes with rage, should much outstrip
    my tongue,

And seal my vengeance on your hearts ;—
    but nature,
To you that have fallen once, bids me again
To be a father.   Oh ! how durst you tempt
The anger of great Jove ?
    Dor. Alack, poor Jove !
He is no swaggerer ; how smug he stands !
He'll take a kick, or anything.
    Sap. Stop her mouth.
    Dor. It is the patient'st godling ! do not
    fear him ;
He would not hurt the thief that stole away
Two of his golden locks ; indeed he could not :
And still 'tis the same quiet thing.
    Theoph. Blasphemer !
Ingenious cruelty shall punish this :
Thou art past hope : but for you yet, dear
    daughters,
Again bewitch'd, the dew of mild forgiveness
May gently fall, provided you deserve it,
With true contrition : be yourselves again ;
Sue to the offended deity.
    Christ. Not to be
The mistress of the earth.
    Cal. I will not offer
A grain of incense to it, much less kneel,
Nor look on it but with contempt and scorn,
To have a thousand years conferr'd upon me
Of worldly blessings.   We profess ourselves
To be, like Dorothea, Christians ;
And owe her for that happiness.
    Theoph. My ears
Receive, in hearing this, all deadly charms,
Powerful to make man wretched.
    Artem. Are these they
You bragg'd could convert others !
    Sap. That want strength
To stand, themselves !
    Harp. Your honour is engaged,
The credit of your cause depends upon it ;
Something you must do suddenly.
    Theoph. And I will.
    Harp. They merit death ; but, falling by
    your hand,
'Twill be recorded for a just revenge,
And holy fury in you.
    Theoph. Do not blow
The furnace of a wrath thrice hot already ;
Ætna is in my breast, wildfire burns here,
Which only blood must quench.   Incensed
    Power !
Which from my infancy I have adored,
Look down with favourable beams upon
The sacrifice, though not allow'd thy priest,
Which I will offer to thee ; and be pleased,
My fiery zeal inciting me to act,
To call that justice others may style murder.
Come, you accurs'd, thus by the hair I drag
    you

Before this holy altar ; thus look on you,
Less pitiful than tigers to their prey :
And thus, with mine own hand, I take that life
Which I gave to you.   [*Kills them.*
    Dor. O, most cruel butcher !
    Theoph. My anger ends not here : hell's
        dreadful porter,
Receive into thy ever-open gates,
Their damned souls, and let the Furies' whips
On them alone be wasted ; and, when death
Closes these eyes, &twill be Elysium to me
To hear their shrieks and howlings.   Make
    me, Pluto,
Thy instrument to furnish thee with souls
Of that accursed sect; nor let me fall,
Till my fell vengeance hath consumed them
    all.   [*Exit with* Harpax.
    Artem. 'Tis a brave zeal.

Enter Angelo, *smiling.*

    Dor. Oh, call him back again,
Call back your hangman ! here's one pri-
    soner left
To be the subject of his knife.
    Artem. Not so ;
We are not so near reconciled unto thee ;
Thou shalt not perish such an easy way.
Be she your charge, Sapritius, now ; and
Suffer none to come near her, till we have
Found out some torments worthy of her.
    Ang. Courage, mistress ;
These martyrs but prepare your glorious fate;
You shall exceed them, and not imitate.
                              [*Exeunt.*

SCENE III.—*A Room in* Dorothea's *House.*

Enter Spungius *and* Hircius, *ragged, at
opposite doors.*

    Hir. Spungius !
    Spun. My fine rogue, how is it? how
goes this tattered world?
    Hir. Hast any money?
    Spun. Money ! no. The tavern ivy clings
about my money, and kills it.   Hast thou
any money?
    Hir. No. My money is a mad bull ; and
finding any gap opened, away it runs.
    Spun. I see then a tavern and a bawdy-
house have faces much alike ; the one hath
red grates next the door, the other hath
peeping-holes within doors : the tavern hath
evermore a bush, the bawdyhouse sometimes
neither hedge nor bush.   From a tavern a
man comes reeling ; from a bawdyhouse not
able to stand.   In the tavern you are cozen'd
with paltry wine ; in a bawdyhouse by a
painted whore : money may have wine, and
a whore will have money ; but to neither can

you cry, Drawer, you rogue ! or, Keep door,
rotten bawd ! without a silver whistle :—We
are justly plagued, therefore, for running
from our mistress.
    Hir. Thou didst ; I did not : Yet I had
run too, but that one gave me turpentine
pills, and that staid my running.
    Spun. Well ! the thread of my life is
drawn through the needle of necessity,
whose eye, looking upon my lousy breeches,
cries out it cannot mend them ; which so
pricks the linings of my body, (and those
are heart, lights, lungs, guts, and midriff,)
that I beg on my knees, to have Atropos,
the tailor to the Destinies, to take her shears,
and cut my thread in two ; or to heat the
iron goose of mortality, and so press me to
death.
    Hir. Sure thy father was some botcher,
and thy hungry tongue bit off these shreds
of complaints, to patch up the elbows of
thy nitty eloquence.
    Spun. And what was thy father?
    Hir. A low-minded cobler, a cobler
whose zeal set many a woman upright ; the
remembrance of whose awl (I now having
nothing) thrusts such scurvy stitches into my
soul, that the heel of my happiness is gone
awry.
    Spun. Pity that e'er thou trod'st thy shoe
awry.
    Hir. Long I cannot last ; for all sowterly
wax of comfort melting away, and misery
taking the length of my foot, it boots not
me to sue for life, when all my hopes are
seam-rent, and go wet-shod.
    Spun. This shows thou art a cobler's
son, by going through stitch : O Hircins,
would thou and I were so happy to be coblers !
    Hir. So would I ; for both of us being
weary of our lives, should then be sure of
shoemaker's ends.
    Spun. I see the beginning of my end, for
I am almost starved.
    Hir. So am not I ; but I am more than
famished.
    Spun. All the members in my body are
in a rebellion one against another.
    Hir. So are mine, and nothing but a
cook, being a constable, can appease them,
presenting to my nose, instead of his painted
staff, a spit full of roast meat.
    Spun. But in this rebellion, what uproars
do they make ! my belly cries to my mouth,
Why not gape and feed me?
    Hir. And my mouth sets out a throat to
my hand, Why dost thou not lift up meat,
and cram my chops with it ?
    Spun. Then my hand hath a fling at mine

C 2

eyes, because they look not out, and shark for victuals.

Hir. Which mine eyes seeing, full of tears, cry aloud, and curse my feet, for not ambling up and down to feed colon ; sithence if good meat be in any place, 'tis known my feet can smell.

Spun. But then my feet, like lazy rogues, lie still, and had rather do nothing, than run to and fro to purchase anything.

Hir. Why, among so many millions of people, should thou and I only be miserable tatterdemallions, ragamuffins, and lousy desperates?

Spun. Thou art a mere I-am-an-o, I-am-an-as : consider the whole world, and 'tis as we are.

Hir. Lousy, beggarly ! thou whoreson assafœtida !

Spun. Worse ; all tottering, all out of frame, thou fooliamini !

Hir. As how, arsenic? come, make the world smart.

Spun. Old honour goes on crutches, beggary rides caroched ; honest men make feasts, knaves sit at tables, cowards are lapp'd in velvet, soldiers (as we) in rags ; beauty turns whore ; whore, bawd ; and both die of the pox : why then, when all the world stumbles, should thou and I walk upright?

Hir. Stop, look ! who's yonder?

Enter Angelo.

Spun. Fellow Angelo! how does my little man? well?

Ang. Yes ;
And would you did so too! Where are your clothes?

Hir. Clothes ! You see every woman almost go in her loose gown, and why should not we have our clothes loose?

Spun. Would they were loose !

Ang. Why, where are they?

Spun. Where many a velvet cloak, I warrant, at this hour, keeps them company ; they are pawned to a broker.

Ang. Why pawn'd? where's all the gold I left with you?

Hir. The gold ! we put that into a scrivener's hands, and he hath cozen'd us.

Spun. And therefore, I prithee, Angelo, if thou hast another purse, let it be confiscate, and brought to devastation.

Ang. Are you made all of lies? I know which way
Your guilt-wing'd pieces flew. I will no more
Be mock'd by you : be sorry for your riots,

Tame your wild flesh by labour; eat the bread
Got with hard hands ; let sorrow be your whip,
To draw drops of repentance from your heart :
When I read this amendment in your eyes,
You shall not want ; till then, my pity dies.
                                   [*Exit.*

Spun. Is it not a shame, that this senrvy puerilis should give us lessons?

Hir. I have dwelt, thou know'st, a long time in the suburbs of conscience, and they are ever bawdy ; but now my heart shall take a house within the walls of honesty.

Enter Harpax *behind.*

Spun. O you drawers of wine, draw me no more to the bar of beggary ; the sound of S*core a pottle of sack,* is worse than the noise of a scolding oysterwench, or two cats incorporating.

Harp. This must not be—I do not like when conscience
Thaws ;   keep her frozen still.   [*Comes forward.*] How now, my masters !
Dejected? drooping? drown'd in tears? clothes torn?
Lean, and ill colour'd? sighing? where's the whirlwind
Which raises all these mischiefs? I have seen you
Drawn better on't. O ! but a spirit told me
You both would come to this, when in you thrust
Yourselves into the service of that lady,
Who shortly now must die. Where's now her praying?
What good got you by wearing out your feet,
To run on seurvy errands to the poor,
And to bear money to a sort of rogues,
And lousy prisoners?

Hir. Pox on them ! I never prospered since I did it.

Spun. Had I been a pagan still, I should not have spit white for want of drink ; but come to any vintner now, and bid him trust me, because I turned Christian, and he cries, Poh !

Harp. You're rightly served ; before that peevish lady
Had to do with you, women, wine, and money
Flow'd in abundance with you, did it not?

Hir. O, those days ! those days !

Harp. Beat not your breasts, tear not your hair in madness ;
Those days shall come again, be ruled by me;
And better, mark me, better.

Spun. I have seen you, sir, as I take it, an attendant on the lord Theophilus.

Harp. Yes, yes ; in shew his servant : but —hark, hither !—

Take heed nobody listens.

Spun. Not a mouse stirs.

Harp. I am a prince disguised.

Hir. Disguised ! how ? drunk ?

Harp. Yes, my fine boy ! I'll drink too, and be drunk ;

I am a prince, and any man by me,

Let him but keep my rules, shall soon grow rich,

Exceeding rich, most infinitely rich :

He that shall serve me, is not starved from pleasures

As other poor knaves are ; no, take their fill.

Spun. But that, sir, we're so ragged——

Harp. You'll say, you'd serve me ?

Hir. Before any master under the zodiac.

Harp. For clothes no matter ; I've a mind to both.

And one thing I like in you ; now that you see

The bonfire of your lady's state burnt out,

You give it over, do you not ?

Hir. Let her be hang'd !

Spun. And pox'd !

Harp. Why, now you're mine ;

Come, let my bosom touch you.

Spun. We have bugs, sir.

Harp. There's money, fetch your clothes home ; there's for you.

Hir. Avoid, vermin ! give over our mistress ! a man cannot prosper worse, if he serve the devil.

Harp. How ! the devil ? I'll tell you what now of the devil,

He's no such horrid creature ; cloven-footed,

Black, saucer-eyed, his nostrils breathing fire,

As these lying Christians make him.

Both. No !

Harp. He's more loving

To man, than man to man is.

Hir. Is he so ? Would we two might come acquainted with him !

Harp. You shall ; he's a wondrous good fellow, loves a cup of wine, a whore, anything ; if you have money, it's ten to one but I'll bring him to some tavern to you or other.

Spun. I'll bespeak the best room in the house for him.

Harp. Some people he cannot endure.

Hir. We'll give him no such cause.

Harp. He hates a civil lawyer, as a soldier does peace.

Spun. How a commoner ?

Harp. Loves him from the teeth outward.

Spun. Pray, my lord and prince, let me encounter you with one foolish question : does the devil eat any mace in his broth !

Harp. Exceeding much, when his burning fever takes him ; and then he has the knuckles of a bailiff boiled to his breakfast.

Hir. Then, my lord, he loves a catchpole, does he not ?

Harp. As a bearward doth a dog. A catchpole ! he hath sworn, if ever he dies, to make a serjeant his heir, and a yeoman his overseer.

Spun. How if he come to any great man's gate, will the porter let him come in, sir ?

Harp. Oh ! he loves porters of great men's gates, because they are ever so near the wicket.

Hir. Do not they whom he makes much on, for all his stroaking their cheeks, lead hellish lives under him ?

Harp. No, no, no, no ; he will be damn'd before he hurts any man : do but you (when you are thoroughly acquainted with him) ask for anything, see if it does not come.

Spun. Anything !

Harp. Call for a delicate rare whore, she is brought you.

Hir. Oh ! my elbow itches. Will the devil keep the door ?

Harp. Be drunk as a beggar, he helps you home.

Spun. O my fine devil ! some watchman, I warrant ; I wonder who is his constable.

Harp. Will you swear, roar, swagger ? he claps you——

Hir. How——? on the chaps ?

Harp. No, on the shoulder ; and cries, O, my brave boys ! Will any of you kill a man ?

Spun. Yes, yes ; I, I.

Harp. What is his word ? Hang ! hang ! 'tis nothing.—Or stab a woman ?

Hir. Yes, yes ; I, I.

Harp. Here is the worst word he gives you : A pox on't, go on !

Hir. O inveigling rascal !—I am ravish'd.

Harp. Go, get your clothes ; turn up your glass of youth,

And let the sands run merrily : nor do I care

From what a lavish hand your money flies,

So you give none away to beggars——

Hir. Hang them !

Harp. And to the scrubbing poor.

Hir. I'll see them hang'd first.

Harp. One service you must do me.

Both. Anything.

Harp. Your mistress, Dorothea, ere she suffers,

Is to be put to tortures : have you hearts

To tear her into shrieks, to fetch her soul

Up in the pangs of death, yet not to die ?

Hir. Suppose this she, and that I had no
  hands, here's my teeth.
Spun. Suppose this she, and that I had no
  teeth, here's my nails.
Hir. But will not you be there, sir?
Harp. No, not for hills of diamonds ; the
  grand master,
Who schools her in the Christian discipline,
Abhors my company : should I be there,
You'd think all hell broke loose, we should
  so quarrel.
Ply you this business ; he, her flesh who spares,
Is lost, and in my love never more shares.
                                      [*Exit.*
Spun. Here's a master, you rogue !
Hir. Sure he cannot choose but have a
  horrible number of servants. [*Exeunt.*

ACT IV.

SCENE I.—*The* Governor's *Palace.*

Antoninus *on a couch, asleep, with* Doctors
  about him ; Sapritius *and* Macrinus.

Sap. O you, that are half gods, lengthen
  that life
Their duties lend us ; turn o'er all the volumes
Of your mysterious Æsculapian science,
T' increase the number of this young man's
  days :
And, for each minute of his time prolong'd,
Your fee shall be a piece of Roman gold
With Cæsar's stamp, such as he sends his
  captains
When in the wars they earn well : do but
  save him,
And, as he's half myself, be you all mine.
  1 *Doct.* What art can do, we promise ;
  physic's hand
As apt is to destroy as to preserve,
If heaven make not the med'cine : all this
  while,
Our skill hath combat held with his disease ;
But 'tis so arm'd, and a deep melancholy,
To be such in part with death, we are in fear
The grave must mock our labours.
  Mac. I have been
His keeper in this sickness, with such eyes
As I have seen my mother watch o'er me ;
And, from that observation, sure I find
It is a midwife must deliver him.
  Sap. Is he with child ? a midwife !
  Mac. Yes, with child ;
And will, I fear, lose life, if by a woman
He is not brought to bed. Stand by his pillow
Some little while, and, in his broken slumbers,
Him shall you hear cry out on Dorothea ;
And, when his arms fly open to catch her,
Closing together, he falls fast asleep,

Pleased with embracings of her airy form.
Physicians but torment him, his disease
Laughs at their gibberish language ; let him
  hear
The voice of Dorothea, nay, but the name,
He starts up with high colour in his face ;
She, or none, cures him ; and how that can be,
The princess' strict command barring that
  happiness,
To me impossible seems.
  Sap. To me it shall not ;
I'll be no subject to the greatest Cæsar
Was ever crown'd with laurel, rather than
  cease
To be a father.   [*Exit.*
  Mac. Silence, sir, he wakes.
  Anton. Thou kill'st me, Dorothea ; oh,
  Dorothea !
  Mac. She's here :—enjoy her.
  Anton. Where ? Why do you mock me ?
Age on my head hath stuck no white hairs yet,
Yet I'm an old man, a fond doting fool
Upon a woman. I, to buy her beauty,
(In truth I am bewitch'd,) offer my life,
And she, for my acquaintance, hazards hers :
Yet for our equal sufferings, none holds out
A hand of pity.
  1 *Doct.* Let him have some music.
  Anton. Hell on your fidling !
                      [*Starting from his couch.*
  1 *Doct.* Take again your bed, sir ;
Sleep is a sovereign physic.
  Anton. Take an ass's head, sir :
Confusion on your fooleries, your charms !—
Thou stinking clyster-pipe, where's the god
  of rest,
Thy pills and base apothecary drugs
Threaten'd to bring unto me ? Out, you
  impostors !
Quacksalving, cheating mountebanks ! your
  skill
Is to make sound men sick, and sick men kill.
  Mac. Oh, be yourself, dear friend.
  Anton. Myself, Macrinus !
How can I be myself, when I am mangled
Into a thousand pieces ? here moves my head,
But where's my heart ? wherever—that lies
  dead.

Re-enter Sapritius, *dragging in* Dorothea *by
  the hair,* Angelo *following.*

  Sap. Follow me, thou damn'd sorceress !
  Call up thy spirits,
And, if they can, now let them from my hand
Untwine these witching hairs.
  Anton. I am that spirit :
Or, if I be not, were you not my father,
One made of iron should hew that hand in
  pieces,

That so defaces this sweet monument
Of my love's beauty.
Sap. Art thou sick ?
Anton. To death.
Sap. Wouldst thou recover?
Anton. Would I live in bliss !
Sap. And do thine eyes shoot daggers at
that man
That brings thee health?
Anton. It is not in the world.
Sap. It's here.
Anton. To treasure, by enchantment lock'd
In caves as deep as hell, am I as near.
Sap. Break that enchanted cave : enter,
and rifle
The spoils thy lust hunts after ; I descend
To a base office, and become thy pander,
In bringing thee this proud thing : make her
thy whore,
Thy health lies here ; if she deny to give it,
Force it : imagine thou assault'st a town's
Weak wall ; to't, 'tis thine own, but beat this
down.
Come, and, unseen, be witness to this bat-
tery,
How the coy strumpet yields.
1 *Doct.* Shall the boy stay, sir?
Sap. No matter for the boy :—pages are
used
To these odd bawdy shufflings; and, indeed,
are
Those little young snakes in a Fury's head,
Will sting worse than the great ones.——
Let the pimp stay.
[*Exeunt* Sap. Mac. *and* Doet.
Dor. O, guard me, angels !
What tragedy must begin now?
Anton. When a tiger
Leaps into a timorous herd, with ravenous
jaws,
Being hunger-starv'd, what tragedy then
begins?
Dor. Death; I am happy so; you, hitherto,
Have still had goodness sphered within your
eyes,
Let not that orb be broken.
Ang. Fear not, mistress ;
If he dare offer violence, we two
Are strong enough for such a sickly man.
Dor. What is your horrid purpose, sir?
your eye
Bears danger in it.
Anton. I must——
Dor. What?
Sap. [*within.*] Speak it out.
Anton. Climb that sweet virgin tree.
Sap. [*within.*] Plague o' your trees !
Anton. And pluck that fruit which none,
I think, e'er tasted.

Sap. [*within.*] A soldier, and stand fumb-
ling so !
Dor. Oh, kill me, [*kneels.*
And heaven will take it as a sacrifice;
But, if you play the ravisher, there is
A hell to swallow you.
Sap. [*within*] Let her swallow thee !
Anton. Rise :—for the Roman empire,
Dorothea,
I would not wound thine honour. Pleasures
forced,
Are unripe apples ; sour, not worth the
plucking :
Yet, let me tell you, 'tis my father's will,
That I should seize upon you, as my prey ;
Which I abhor, as much as the blackest sin.
The villainy of man did ever act.
[*Sapritius breaks in with* Macrinus.
Dor. Die happy for this language !
Sap. Die a slave,
A blockish idiot !
Mac. Dear sir, vex him not.
Sap. Yes, and vex thee too; both, I think,
are geldings :
Cold, phlegmatic bastard, thou'rt no brat of
mine ;
One spark of me, when I had heat like thine,
By this had made a bonfire : a tempting
whore,
For whom thou'rt mad, thrust e'en into
thine arms,
And stand'st thou puling ! Had a tailor
seen her
At this advantage, he, with his cross capers,
Had ruffled her by this : but thou shalt curse
Thy dalliance, and here, before her eyes,
Tear thy own flesh in pieces, when a slave
In hot lust bathes himself, and gluts those
pleasures
Thy niceness durst not touch. Call out a
slave ;
You, captain of our guard, fetch a slave hither.
Anton. What will you do, dear sir ?
Sap. Teach her a trade, which many a
one would learn
In less than half an hour,—to play the whore.

Enter Soldiers with a Slave.

Mac. A slave is come ; what now ?
Sap. Thou hast bones and flesh
Enough to ply thy labour : from what country
Wert thou ta'en a prisoner, here to be our
slave ?
Slave. From Britain.
Sap. In the west ocean ?
Slave. Yes.
Sap. An island?
Slave. Yes.
Sap. I'm fitted : of all nations

Our Roman swords e'er conquer'd, none
  comes near
The Briton for true whoring. Sirrah fellow,
What wouldst thou do to gain thy liberty?
  Slave. Do! liberty! fight naked with a
    lion,
Venture to pluck a standard from the heart
Of an arm'd legion. Liberty! I'd thus
Bestride a rampire, and defiance spit
I' the face of death, then, when the batter-
  ing-ram
Was fetching his career backward, to pash
Me with his horns in pieces. To shake my
  chains off,
And that I could not do't but by thy death,
Stood'st thou on this dry shore, I on a rock
Ten pyramids high, down would I leap to
  kill thee,
Or die myself: what is for man to do,
I'll venture on, to be no more a slave.
  Sap. Thou shalt, then, be no slave, for I
    will set thee
Upon a piece of work is fit for man;
Brave for a Briton:—drag that thing aside,
And ravish her.
  Slave. And ravish her! is this your manly
    service?
A devil scorns to do it; 'tis for a beast,
A villain, not a man: I am, as yet,
But half a slave; but, when that work is past,
A damned whole one, a black ugly slave,
The slave of all base slaves:—do't thyself,
  Roman,
'Tis drudgery fit for thee.
  Sap. He's bewitched too:
Bind him, and with a bastinado give him,
Upon his naked belly, two hundred blows.
  Slave. Thou art more slave than I.
                 [He is carried in.
  Dor. That power supernal, on whom
    waits my soul,
Is captain o'er my chastity.
  Anton. Good sir, give o'er:
The more you wrong her, yourself's vex'd
  the more.
  Sap. Plagues light on her and thee!—
    thus down I throw
Thy harlot, thus by the hair nail her to earth.
Call in ten slaves, let every one discover
What lust desires, and surfeit here his fill.
Call in ten slaves.

     Enter Slaves.

  Mac. They are come, sir, at your call.
  Sap. Oh, oh!   *[Falls down.*

    Enter Theophilus.

  Theoph. Where is the governor?
  Anton. There's my wretched father.

  Theoph. My lord Sapritius — he's not
    dead!—my lord!
That witch there—
  Anton. 'Tis no Roman gods can strike
These fearful terrors. O, thou happy maid,
Forgive this wicked purpose of my father.
  Dor. I do.
  Theoph. Gone, gone; he's pepper'd. It
    is thou
Hast done this act infernal.
  Dor. Heaven pardon you!
And if my wrongs from thence pull ven-
  geance down,
(I can no miracles work,) yet, from my soul,
Pray to those Powers I serve, he may recover.
  Theoph. He stirs—help, raise him up,—
    my lord!
  Sap. Where am I?
  Theoph. One cheek is blasted.
  Sap. Blasted! where's the lamia
That tears my entrails? I'm bewitch'd;
  seize on her.
  Dor. I'm here; do what you please.
  Theoph. Spurn her to the bar.
  Dor. Come, boy, being there, more near
  to heaven we are.
  Sap. Kick harder; go out, witch!
                    [Exeunt.
  Anton. O bloody hangmen! Thine own
  gods give thee breath!
Each of thy tortures is my several death.
                       [Exit.

    SCENE II.—*A Public Square.*

  Enter Harpax, Hircius, *and* Spungius.

  Harp. Do you like my service now? say,
  am not I
A master worth attendance?
  Spun. Attendance! I had rather lick
clean the soles of your dirty boots, than
wear the richest suit of any infected lord,
whose rotten life hangs between the two
poles.
  Hir. A lord's suit! I would not give up
the cloak of your service, to meet the splay-
foot estate of any left-eyed knight above
the antipodes; because they are unlucky to
meet.
  Harp. This day I'll try your loves to me;
  'tis only
But well to use the agility of your arms.
  Spun. Or legs, I'm lusty at them.
  Hir. Or any other member that has no legs.
  Spun. Thou'lt run into some hole.
  Hir. If I meet one that's more than my
match, and that I cannot stand in their
hands, I must and will creep on my knees.
  Harp. Hear me, my little team of villains,
  hear me;

I cannot teach you fencing with these cudgels,
Yet you must use them ; lay them on but
　　soundly ;
That's all.

Hir. Nay, if we come to mauling once,
　　pah !

Spun. But what walnut-tree is it we must
beat ?

Harp. Your mistress.

Hir. How ! my mistress ? I begin to have
a Christian heart made of sweet butter. I
melt ; I cannot strike a woman.

Spun. Nor I, unless she scratch ; bum
my mistress !

Harp. You're coxcombs, silly animals.

Hir. What's that ?

Harp. Drones, asses, blinded moles, that
　　dare not thrust
Your arms out to catch fortune ; say, you
　　fall off,
It must be done. You are converted rascals,
And, that once spread abroad, why every
　　slave
Will kick you, call you motley Christians,
And half-faced Christians.

Spun. The guts of my conscience begin
to be of whitleather.

Hir. I doubt me, I shall have no sweet
butter in me.

Harp. Deny this, and each pagan whom
　　you meet,
Shall forked fingers thrust into your eyes——

Hir. If we be cuckolds.

Harp. Do this, and every god the Gentiles
　　bow to,
Shall add a fathom to your line of years.

Spun. A hundred fathom, I desire no more.

Hir. I desire but one inch longer.

Harp. The senators will, as you pass along,
Clap you upon your shoulders with this hand,
And with this give you gold : when you are
　　dead,
Happy that man shall be, can get a nail,
The paring,—nay, the dirt under the nail,
Of any of you both, to say, this dirt
Belonged to Spungius or Hircius.

Spun. They shall not want dirt under my
nails, I will keep them long of purpose, for
now my fingers itch to be at her.

Hir. The first thing I do, I'll take her
over the lips.

Spun. And I the hips,—we may strike
anywhere ?

Harp. Yes, anywhere.

Hir. Then I know where I'll hit her.

Harp. Prosper, and be mine own ; stand
by, I must not
To see this done, great business calls me
　　hence :

He's made can make her curse his violence.
　　　　　　　　　　　　　　　[*Exit.*

Spun. Fear it not, sir ; her ribs shall be
　　basted.

Hir. I'll come upon her with rounce,
robble-hobble, and thwick-thwack-thirley
bouncing.

Enter Dorothea, *led prisoner ;* Sapritius,
Theophilus, Angelo, *and a* Hangman,
who sets up a pillar ; Sapritius *and* Theophilus *sit ;* Angelo *stands by* Dorothea.
A guard attending.

Sap. According to our Roman customs,
　　bind
That Christian to a pillar.

Theoph. Infernal Furies,
Could they into my hand thrust all their
　　whips
To tear thy flesh, thy soul, 'tis not a torture
Fit to the vengeance I should heap on thee,
For wrongs done me ; me ! for flagitious facts,
By thee done to our gods ; yet, so it stand,
To great Cæsarea's governor's high pleasure,
Bow but thy knee to Jupiter, and offer
Any slight sacrifice ; or do but swear
By Cæsar's fortune, and——be free.

Sap. Thou shalt.

Dor. Not for all Cæsar's fortune, were it
　　chain'd
To more worlds than are kingdoms in the
　　world,
And all those worlds drawn after him. I defy
Your hangmen ; you now shew me whither
　　to fly.

Sap. Are her tormentors ready ?

Ang. Shrink not, dear mistress.

Spun and Hir. My lord, we are ready
for the business.

Dor. You two ! whom I like foster'd
　　children fed,
And lengthen'd out your starved life with
　　bread.
You be my hangmen ! whom, when up the
　　ladder
Death haled you to be strangled, I fetch'd
　　down,
Clothed you, and warm'd you, you two my
　　tormentors !

Both. Yes, we.

Dor. Divine Powers pardon you !

Sap. Strike.
　　　[*They strike at her !* Angelo *kneeling
　　　holds her fast.*

Theoph. Beat out her brains.

Dor. Receive me, you bright angels !

Sap. Faster, slaves.

Spun. Faster ! I am out of breath, I am

sure; if I were to beat a buck, I can strike no harder.

Hir. O mine arms! I cannot lift them to my head.

Dor. Joy above joys! are my tormentors weary
In torturing me, and, in my sufferings,
I fainting in no limb! tyrants, strike home,
And feast your fury full.

Theoph. These dogs are curs,
[*Comes from his seat.*
Which snarl, yet bite not. See, my lord, her face
Has more bewitching beauty than before:
Proud whore, it smiles! cannot an eye start out,
With these?

Hir. No, sir; nor the bridge of her nose fall; 'tis full of iron work.

Sap. Let's view the cudgels, are they not counterfeit?

Ang. There fix thine eye still;—thy glorious crown must come
Not from soft pleasure, but by martyrdom.
There fix thine eye still;—when we next do
· meet,
Not thorns, but roses, shall bear up thy feet:
There fix thine eye still. [*Exit.*

Dor. Ever, ever, ever! ·

Enter Harpax, *sneaking.*

Theoph. We're mock'd; these bats have power to fell down giants,
Yet her skin is not scarr'd.

Sap. What rogues are these?

Theoph. Cannot these force a shriek?
[*Beats* Spungius.

Spun. Oh! a woman has one of my ribs, and now five more are broken.

Theoph. Cannot this make her roar?
[*Beats* Hircins; *he roars.*

Sap. Who hired these slaves? what are they?

Spun. We serve that noble gentleman, there; he enticed us to this dry beating; oh! for one half pot.

Harp. My servants! two base rogues, and sometime servants
To her, and for that cause forbear to hurt her.

Sap. Unbind her; hang up these.

Theoph. Hang the two hounds on the next tree.

Hir. Hang us! master Harpax, what a devil, shall we be thus used?

Harp. What bandogs but you two would worry a woman?
Your mistress? I but clapt you, you flew on.
Say I should get your lives, each rascal beggar

Would, when he met you, cry out, Hell-hounds! traitors!
Spit at you, fling dirt at you; and no woman
Ever endure your sight: 'tis your best course
Now, had you secret knives, to stab yourselves;—
But, since you have not, go and be hang'd.

Hir. I thank you.

Harp. 'Tis your best course.

Theoph. Why stay they trifling here?
To the gallows drag them by the heels;—away!

Spun. By the heels! no, sir, we have legs to do us that service.

Hir. Ay, ay, if no woman can endure my sight, away with me.

Harp. Dispatch them.

Spun. The devil dispatch thee!
[*Exeunt Guard with* Spungius *and* Hircins.

Sap. Death this day rides in triumph, Theophilus.
See this witch made away too.

Theoph. My soul thirsts for it;
Come, I myself the hangman's part could play.

Dor. O haste me to my coronation day!

SCENE III.—*The Place of Execution. A scaffold, block, &c.*

Enter Antoninus, *supported by* Macrinus, *and* Servants.

Anton. Is this the place, where virtue is . to suffer,
And heavenly beauty, leaving this base earth,
To make a glad return from whence it came?
Is it, Macrinus?

Mac. By this preparation,
You well may rest assured that Dorothea
This hour is to die here.

Anton. Then with her dies
The abstract of all sweetness that's in woman!
Set me down, friend, that, ere the iron hand
Of death close up mine eyes, I once more may
Take my last leave both of this light and her:
For, she being gone, the glorious sun himself
To me's Cimmerian darkness.

Mac. Strange affection!
Cupid once more hath changed his shafts with Death,
And kills instead of giving life.

Anton. Nay, weep not;
Though tears of friendship be a sovereign balm,
On me they're cast away. It is decreed
That I must die with her; our clue of life
Was spun together.

Mac. Yet, sir, 'tis my wonder,
That you, who, hearing only what she suffers,
Partake of all her tortures, yet will be,
To add to our calamity, an eyewitness

Of her last tragic scene, which must pierce
   deeper,
And make the wound more desperate.

  Anton. Oh, Macrinus!
'Twould linger out my torments else, not
   kill me,
Which is the end I aim at : being to die too,
What instrument more glorious can I wish for,
Than what is made sharp by my constant love
And true affection? It may be, the duty
And loyal service, with which I pursued her,
And seal'd it with my death, will be re-
   member'd
Among her blessed actions ; and what honour
Can I desire beyond it?

Enter a Guard bringing in Dorothea, *a
Headsman before her : followed by* Theophilus, Sapritius, *and* Harpax.

   See, she comes ;
How sweet her innocence appears ! more like
To heaven itself, than any sacrifice
That can be offer'd to it. By my hopes
Of joys hereafter, the sight makes me doubtful
In my belief ; nor can I think our gods
Are good, or to be served, that take delight
In offerings of this kind : that, to maintain
Their power, deface the masterpiece of
   nature,
Which they themselves come short of. She
   ascends,
And every step raises her nearer heaven.
What god soe'er thou art, that must enjoy her,
Receive in her a boundless happiness !

  Sap. You are to blame
To let him come abroad.

  Mac. It was his will ;
And we were left to serve him, not command
   him.

  Anton. Good sir, be not offended ; nor
   deny
My last of pleasures in this happy object,
That I shall e'er be blest with.

  Theoph. Now, proud contemner
Of us, and of our gods, tremble to think,
It is not in the Power thou serv'st to save
   thee.
Not all the riches of the sea, increased
By violent shipwrecks, nor the unsearch'd
   mines,
(Mammon's unknown exchequer,) shall re-
   deem thee :
And, therefore, having first with horror
   weigh'd
What 'tis to die, and to die young ; to part
   with
All pleasures and delights ; lastly, to go
Where all antipathies to comfort dwell,
Furies behind, about thee, and before thee ;

And, to add to affliction, the remembrance
Of the Elysian joys thou might'st have tasted,
Hadst thou not turn'd apostata to those gods
That so reward their servants ; let despair
Prevent the hangman's sword, and on this
   scaffold
Make thy first entrance into hell.

  Anton. She smiles,
Unmoved, by Mars ! as if she were assured
Death, looking on her constancy, would
   forget
The use of his inevitable hand.

  Theoph. Derided too ! dispatch, I say.

  Dor. Thou fool !
That gloriest in having power to ravish
A trifle from me I am weary of,
What is this life to me? not worth a thought ;
Or, if it be esteem'd, 'tis that I lose it
To win a better : even thy malice serves
To me but as a ladder to mount up
To such a height of happiness, where I shall
Look down with scorn on thee, and on the
   world ;
Where, circled with true pleasures, placed
   above
The reach of death or time, 'twill be my glory
To think at what an easy price I bought it.
There's a perpetual spring, perpetual youth:
No joint-benumbing cold, or scorching heat,
Famine, nor age, have any being there.
Forget, for shame, your Tempe ; bury in
Oblivion your feign'd Hesperian orchards :—
The golden fruit, kept by the watchful
   dragon,
Which did require a Hercules to get it,
Compared with what grows in all plenty
   there,
Deserves not to be named. The Power I
   serve,
Laughs at your happy Araby, or the
Elysian shades ; for he hath made his bowers
Better in deed, than you can fancy yours.

  Anton. O, take me thither with you !

  Dor. Trace my steps,
And be assured you shall.

  Sap. With my own hands
I'll rather stop that little breath is left thee,
And rob thy killing fever.

  Theoph. By no means ;
Let him go with her : do, seduced young
   man,
And wait upon thy saint in death ; do, do :
And, when you come to that imagined place
That place of all delights—pray you, ob-
   serve me,
And meet those cursed things I once called
   Daughters,
Whom I have sent as harbingers before you ;
If there be any truth in your religion,

In thankfulness to me, that with care hasten
Your journey thither, pray you send me some
Small pittance of that curious fruit you boast
of.

Anton. Grant that I may go with her, and
I will.

Sap. Wilt thou in thy last minute damn
thyself?

Theoph. The gates to hell are open.

Dor. Know, thou tyrant,
Thou agent for the devil, thy great master,
Though thou art most unworthy to taste
of it,
I can, and will.

Enter Angelo, *in the Angel's habit.*

Harp. Oh! mountains fall upon me,
Or hide me in the bottom of the deep,
Where light may never find me!

Theoph. What's the matter?

Sap. This is prodigious, and confirms her
witchcraft.

Theoph. Harpax, my Harpax, speak!

Harp. I dare not stay:
Should I but hear her once more, I were lost.
Some whirlwind snatch me from this cursed
place,
To which compared, (and with what now I
suffer,)
Hell's torments are sweet slumbers! [*Exit.*

Sap. Follow him.

Theoph. He is distracted, and I must not
lose him.
Thy charms upon my servant, cursed witch,
Give thee a short reprieve. Let her not die,
Till my return. [*Exeunt* Sap. *and* Theoph.

Anton. She minds him not: what object
Is her eye fix'd on?

Mac. I see nothing.

Anton. Mark her.

Dor. Thou glorious minister of the Power
I serve!
(For thou art more than mortal,) is't for me,
Poor sinner, thou art pleased awhile to leave
Thy heavenly habitation, and vouchsafest,
Though glorified, to take my servant's
habit?—
For, put off thy divinity, so look'd
My lovely Angelo.

Ang. Know, I am the same;
And still the servant to your piety.
Your zealous prayers, and pious deeds first
won me
(But 'twas by His command to whom you
sent them)
To guide your steps. I tried your charity,
When in a beggar's shape you took me up,
And clothed my naked limbs, and after fed,

As you believed, my famish'd mouth. Learn
all,
By your example, to look on the poor
With gentle eyes! for in such habits, often,
Angels desire an alms. I never left you,
Nor will I now; for I am sent to carry
Your pure and innocent soul to joys eternal,
Your martyrdom once suffer'd; and before it,
Ask any thing from me, and rest assured,
You shall obtain it.

Dor. I am largely paid
For all my torments. Since I find such grace,
Grant that the love of this young man to me,
In which he languisheth to death, may be
Changed to the love of heaven.

Ang. I will perform it;
And in that instant when the sword sets free
Your happy soul, his shall have liberty.
Is there aught else?

Dor. For proof that I forgive
My persecutor, who in scorn desired
To taste of that most sacred fruit I go to;
After my death, as sent from me, be pleased
To give him of it.

Ang. Willingly, dear mistress.

Mac. I am amazed.

Anton. I feel a holy fire,
That yields a comfortable heat within me;
I am quite alter'd from the thing I was.
See! I can stand, and go alone; thus kneel
To heavenly Dorothea, touch her hand
With a religious kiss. [*Kneels.*

Re-enter Sapritius *and* Theophilus.

Sap. He is well now,
But will not be drawn back.

Theoph. It matters not,
We can discharge this work without his help.
But see your son.

Sap. Villain!

Anton. Sir, I beseech you,
Being so near our ends, divorce us not.

Theoph. I'll quickly make a separation of
them:
Hast thou aught else to say?

Dor. Nothing, but to blame
Thy tardiness in sending me to rest;
My peace is made with heaven, to which
my soul
Begins to take her flight: strike, O! strike
quickly;
And, though you are unmoved to see my
death,
Hereafter, when my story shall be read,
As they were present now, the hearers shall
Say this of Dorothea, with wet eyes,
"She lived a virgin, and a virgin dies"
[*Her head is struck off.*

Anton. 'O' take my soul along, to wait on
    thine !
Mac. Your son sinks too.
                       [*Antoninus falls.*
Sap. Already dead !
Theoph. Die all
That are, or favour this accursed sect :
I triumph in their ends, and will raise up
A hill of their dead carcasses, to o'erlook
The Pyrenean hills, but I'll root out
These superstitious fools, and leave the world
No name of Christian.
        [*Loud music: Exit* Angelo, *having
          first laid his hand upon the
          mouths of* Anton. *and* Dor.
Sap. Ha ! heavenly music !
Mac. 'Tis in the air.
Theoph. Illusions of the devil,
Wrought by some witch of her religion,
That fain would make her death a miracle ;
It frights not me.   Because he is your son,
Let him have burial ; but let her body
Be east forth with contempt in some high-
    way,
And be to vultures and to dogs a prey.
                            [*Exeunt.*

ACT V.

SCENE I.—Theophilus *discovered sitting
in his* Study: *books about him.*

Theoph. Is 't holiday, O Cæsar, that thy
    servant,
Thy provost, to see execution done
On these base Christians in Cæsarea,
Should now want work? Sleep these ido-
    laters,
That none are stirring?—As a curious painter,
When he has made some honourable piece,
Stands off, and with a searching eye ex-
    amines
Each colour, how 'tis sweeten'd ; and then
    hugs
Himself for his rare workmanship—so here,
Will I my drolleries, and bloody landscapes,
Long past wrapt up, unfold, to make me
    merry
With shadows, now I want the substances.
My muster-book of hell-hounds.   Were
    the Christians,
Whose names stand here, alive and arm'd,
    not Rome
Could move upon her hinges.   What I've
    done,
Or shall hereafter, is not out of hate
To poor tormented wretches ; no, I'm carried
With violence of zeal, and streams of service
I owe our Roman gods.   *Great Britain,—*
    what ?   [*reads.*

*A thousand wives, with brats sucking their
    breasts,*
*Had hot irons pinch them off, and thrown
    to swine ;*
*And then their fleshy back-parts, hew'd with
    hatchets,*
*Were minced and baked in pies, to feed
    starv'd Christians.*
Ha ! ha !
Again, again,—*East Angies,*—oh, *East
    Angies :*
Bandogs, kept three days hungry, worried
A thousand British rascals, stied up fat
Of purpose, stripped naked, and disarm'd.
I could outstare a year of suns and moons,
To sit at these sweet bull-baitings, so I
Could thereby but one Christian win to fall
In adoration to my Jupiter.—*Twelve hun-
    dred*
Eyes bored with augers out—Oh ! *eleven
    thousand*
*Torn by wild beasts : two hundred ramm'd
    in the earth*
*To the armpits, and full platters round
    about them,*
But far enough for reaching : Eat, dogs,
    ha ! ha ! ha !   [*He rises..*
Tush, all these tortures are but fillipings,
Fleabitings ; I, before the Destinies

Enter Angelo *with a basket filled with fruit
    and flowers.*

My bottom did wind up, would flesh myself
Once more upon some one remarkable
Above all these.   This Christian slut was
    well,
A pretty one ; but let such horror follow
The next I feed with torments, that when
    Rome
Shall hear it, her foundation at the sound
May feel an earthquake.   How now?
                            [*Music.*
Ang. Are you amazed, sir?
So great a Roman spirit—and doth it
    tremble !
Theoph. How cam'st thou in? to whom
    thy business?
Ang. To you :
I had a mistress, late sent hence by you
Upon a bloody errand ; you entreated,
That, when she came into that blessed garden
Whither she knew she went, and where,
    now happy,
She feeds upon all joy, she would send to you
Some of that garden fruit and flowers ;
    which here
To have her promise saved, are brought by
    me.
Theoph. Cannot I see this garden ?

Ang. Yes, if the master
Will give you entrance.   [*He vanishes.*
  Theoph. 'Tis a tempting fruit,
And the most bright-cheek'd child I ever
  view'd ;
Sweet smelling, goodly fruit.   What flowers
  are these ?
In Dioclesian's gardens, the most beauteous,
Compared with these, are weeds : is it not
  February,
The second day she died ? frost, ice, and
  snow,
Hang on the beard of winter : where's the sun
That gilds this summer ? pretty, sweet boy,
  say,
In what country shall a man find this gar-
  den ?—
My delicate boy,—gone ! vanish'd ! within
  there,
Julianus ! Geta !—

Enter Julianus *and* Geta.

Both. My lord.
  Theoph. Are my gates shut ?
  Geta. And guarded.
  Theoph. Saw you not
A boy ?
  Jul. Where ?
  Theoph. Here he enter'd ; a young lad ;
A thousand blessings danced upon his eyes :
A smoothfaced glorious thing, that brought
  this basket.
  Geta. No, sir !
  Theoph. Away—but be in reach, if my voice
  calls you.   [*Exeunt* Jul. *and* Geta.
No !—vanish'd, and not seen !—be thou a
  spirit, sent from that witch to mock me,
  I am sure
This is essential, and, howe'er it grows,
Will taste it.   [*Eats of the fruit.*
  Harp. [*within.*] Ha, ha, ha, ha !
  Theoph. So good ! I'll have some more,
  sure.
  Harp. Ha, ha, ha, ha ! great liquorish fool !
  Theoph. What art thou ?
  Harp. A fisherman.
  Theoph. What dost thou catch ?
  Harp. Souls, souls ; a fish call'd souls.
  Theoph. Geta !

Re-enter Geta.

Geta. My lord.
  Harp. [*within.*] Ha, ha, ha, ha !
  Theoph. What insolent slave is this, dares
  laugh at me ?
Or what is 't the dog grins at so ?
  Geta. I neither know, my lord, at what,
  nor whom ; for there is none without, but

my fellow Julianus, and he is making a gar-
  land for Jupiter.
  Theoph. Jupiter ! all within me is not well ;
And yet not sick.
  Harp. [*within.*] Ha, ha, ha, ha !
  Theoph. What's thy name, slave ?
  Harp. [*at one end of the room.*] Go look.
  Geta. 'Tis Harpax' voice.
  Theoph. Harpax ! go, drag the caitiff to
  my foot,
That I may stamp upon him.
  Harp. [*at the other end.*] Fool, thou liest !
  Geta. He's yonder, now, my lord.
  Theoph. Watch thou that end,
Whilst I make good this.
  Harp. [*in the middle.*] Ha, ha, ha, ha ha !
  Theoph. He is at barley-break, and the
  last couple
Are now in hell. [*Exit* Geta.] All this ground,
  methinks, is bloody,
And paved with thousands of those Chris-
  tians' eyes
Whom I have tortured ; and they stare upon
  me.
What was this apparition ? sure it had
A shape angelical.   Mine eyes, though
  dazzled,
And daunted at first sight, tell me, it wore
A pair of glorious wings ; yes, they were wings ;
And hence he flew :——'tis vanish'd ! Jupiter,
For all my sacrifices done to him,
Never once gave me smile.—How can stone
  smile ?
Or wooden image laugh ? [*music.*] Ha ! I
  remember,
Such music gave a welcome to mine ear,
When the fair youth came to me :—'tis in
  the air,
Or from some better place ; a Power divine,
Through my dark ignorance, on my soul
  does shine,
And makes me see a conscience all stain'd o'er,
Nay, drown'd and damn'd for ever in Chris-
  tian gore.
  Harp. [*within.*] Ha, ha, ha !
  Theoph. Again !—What dainty relish on
  my tongue
This fruit hath left ! some angel hath me fed ;
If so toothfull, I will be banqueted.
                              [*Eats again.*

Enter Harpax *in a fearful shape, fire flash-
  ing out of the Study.*

Harp. Hold !
  Theoph. Not for Cæsar.
  Harp. But for me thou shalt.
  Theoph. Thou art no twin to him that last
  was here.

Ye Powers, whom my soul bids me reverence,
  guard me!
What art thou?   *&*
  Harp. I am thy master.
  Theoph. Mine!
  Harp. And thou my everlasting slave:
    that Harpax,
Who hand in hand hath led thee to thy hell,
Am I.
  Theoph. Avaunt!
  Harp. I will not; cast thou down
That basket with the things in 't, and fetch up
What thou hast swallow'd and then take a
  drink,
Which I shall give thee, and I'm gone.
  Theoph. My fruit!
Does this offend thee! see!   *[Eats again.*
  Harp. Spit it to the earth,
And tread upon it, or I'll piecemeal tear thee.
  Theoph. Art thou with this affrighted?
  see, here's more.
    [Pulls out a handful of flowers.
  Harp. Fling them away. I'll take thee
  . else, and hang thee
In a contorted chain of icicles,
In the frigid zone: down with them!
  Theoph. At the bottom
One thing I found not yet. See!
    [Holds up a cross of flowers.
  Harp. Oh! I am tortured.
  Theoph. Can this do 't? hence, thou fiend
  infernal, hence!
  Harp. Clasp Jupiter's image, and away
  with that.
  Theoph. At thee I'll fling that Jupiter; for
  methinks,
I serve a better master: he now checks me
For murdering my two daughters, put on by
  thee,—
By thy damned rhetoric did I hunt the life
Of Dorothea, the holy virgin-martyr.
She is not angry with the axe, nor me,
But sends these presents to me; and I'll
  travel
O'er worlds to find, and from her white
  hand
Beg a forgiveness.
  Harp. No; I'll bind thee here.
  Theoph. I serve a strength above thine;
  this small weapon,
Methinks, is armour hard enough.
  Harp. Keep from me.
      [Sinks a little.
  Theoph. Art posting to thy centre? down,
  hell-hound! down!
Me thou hast lost. That arm, which hurls
  thee hence, ·   *[Harpax disappears.*
Save me, and set me up, the strong defence,
In the fair Christian's quarrel!

Enter Angelo.
  Ang. Fix thy foot there,
Nor be thou shaken with a Cæsar's voice,
Though thousand deaths were in it; and I
  then
Will bring thee to a river, that shall wash
Thy bloody hands clean and more white than
  snow;
And to that garden where these blest things
  grow,
And to that martyr'd virgin, who hath sent
That heavenly token to thee: spread this
  brave wing,
And serve, than Cæsar, a far greater king.
                    [Exit.
  Theoph. It is, it is, some angel. Vanish'd
  again!
Oh, come back, ravishing boy! bright mes-
  senger,
Thou hast, by these mine eyes fix'd on thy
  beauty,
Illumined all my soul. Now look I back
On my black tyrannies, which, as they did
Outdare the bloodiest, thou, blest spirit, that
  lead'st me,
Teach me what I must to do, and, to do well,
That my last act the best may parallel. *[Exit.*

SCENE II.—Dioclesian's *Palace.*

Enter Dioclesian, Maximinus, *the Kings of*
. Epire, Pontus, *and* Macedon, *meeting*
  Artemia; *Attendants.*
  Artem. Glory and conquest still attend
  upon
Triumphant Cæsar!
  Diocle. Let thy wish, fair daughter,
Be equally divided; and hereafter
Learn thou to know and reverence Maxi-
  minus,
Whose power, with mine united, makes one
  Cæsar.
  Max. But that I fear, 'twould be held
  flattery,
The bonds consider'd in which we stand tied,
As love and empire, I should say, till now
I ne'er had seen a lady I thought worthy
To be my mistress.
  Artem. Sir, you shew yourself
Both courtier and soldier; but take heed,
Take heed, my lord, though my dull-pointed
  beauty,
Stain'd by a harsh refusal in my servant,
Cannot dart forth such beams as may inflame
  you,
You may encounter such a powerful one,
That with a pleasing heat will thaw your heart,
Though bound in ribs of ice. Love still is
  Love ·

His bow and arrows are the same : Great
   Julius,
That to his successors left the name of Cæsar,
Whom war could never tame, that with dry
   eyes
Beheld the large plains of Pharsalia cover'd
With the dead carcasses of senators,
And citizens of Rome, when the world knew
No other lord but him, struck deep in years
   too,
(And men gray-bair'd forget the lusts of
   youth,)
After all this, meeting fair Cleopatra,
A suppliant too, the magic of her eye,
Even in his pride of conquest, took him
   captive :
Nor are you more secure.

   Max. Were you deform'd,
(But, by the gods, you are most excellent,)
Your gravity and discretion would o'ercome
   me ;
And I should be more proud in being prisoner
To your fair virtues, than of all the honours,
Wealth, title, empire, that my sword hath
   purchased.

   Diocle. This meets my wishes. Welcome
it, Artemia,
With outstretch'd arms, and study to forget
That Antoninus ever was : thy fate
Reserved thee for this better choice ; em-
   brace it.

   Max. This happy match brings new
   nerves to give strength
To our continued league.

   Diocle. Hymen himself
Will bless this marriage, which we'll solemnize
In the presence of these kings.

   K. of Pontus. Who rest most happy,
To be eyewitnesses of a match that brings
Peace to the empire.

   Diocle. We much thank your loves :
But where's Sapritius, our governor,
And our most zealous provost, good Theo-
   philus !
If ever prince were blest in a true servant,
Or could the gods be debtors to a man,
Both they and we stand far engaged to cherish
His piety and service.

   Artem. Sir, the governor
Brooks sadly his son's loss, although he turu'd
Apostata in death ; but bold Theophilus,
Who for the same cause, in my presence,
   seal'd
His holy anger on his daughters' hearts ;
Having with tortures first tried to convert her,
Dragg'd the bewitching Christian to the
   scaffold,
And saw her lose her head.

   Diocle. He is all worthy :

And from his own mouth I would gladly hear
The manner how she suffer'd.

   Artem. 'Twill be deliver'd
With such contempt and scorn, (I know his
   nature,)
That rather 'twill beget your highness'
   laughter,
Than the least pity.

   Diocle. To. that end I would hear it.

Enter Theophilus, Sapritius, *and* Macrinus.

   Artem. He comes : with him the governor.

   Diocle. O, Sapritius,
I am to chide you for your tenderness ;
But yet, remembering that you are a father,
I will forget it. Good Theophilus, .
I'll speak with you anon.—Nearer, your ear.
                [*To* Sapritius.

   Theoph. [*Aside to* Macrinus.] ·By An-
toninus' soul, I do conjure you,
And though not for religion, for bis friendship,
Without demanding what's the cause that
   moves me,
Receive my signet :—By the power of this,
Go to my prisons, and release all Christians,
That are in fetters there by my command.

   Mac. But what shall follow ?

   Theoph. Haste then to the port ;
You there shall find two tall ships ready rigg'd,
In which embark the poor distressed souls,
And bear them from the reach of tyranny.
Enquire not whither you are bound : the
   Deity
That they adore will give you prosperous
   winds,
And make your voyage such, and largely
   pay for
Your hazard, and your travail. Leave me
   here ;
There is a scene that I must act alone :
Haste, good Macrinus ; and the great God
   guide you !

   Mac. I'll undertake it ; there's something
   prompts me to it ;
'Tis to save innocent blood, a saint-like act :
And to be merciful has never been
By moral men themselves esteem'd a sin.
                [*Exit.*

   Diocle. You know your charge ?

   Sap. And will with care observe it.

   Diocle. For I profess he is not Cæsar's
   friend,
That sheds a tear for any torture that
A Christian suffers. Welcome, my best
   servant,
My careful, zealous provost ! thou hast toil'd
To satisfy my will, though in extremes :
I love thee for 't ; thou art firm rock, no
   changeling.

Prithee deliver, and for my sake do it,
Without excess of bitterness, or scoffs,
Before my brother and these kings, how took
The Christian her death?
   Theoph. And such a presence,
Though every private head in this large
   room
Were circled round with an imperial crown,
Her story will deserve, it is so full
Of excellence and wonder.
   Diocle. Ha! how is this?
   Theoph. O! mark it, therefore, and with
   that attention,
As you would hear an embassy from heaven
By a wing'd legate; for the truth deliver'd,
Both how, and what, this blessed virgin
   suffer'd,
And Dorothea but hereafter named,
You will rise up with reverence, and no more,
As things unworthy of your thoughts, re-
   member
What the canonized Spartan ladies were,
Which lying Greece so boasts of. Your
   own matrons,
Your Roman dames, whose figures you yet
   keep
As holy relics, in her history
Will find a second urn: Gracchus' Cornelia,
Paulina, that in death desired to follow
Her husband Seneca, nor Brutus' Portia,
That swallow'd burning coals to overtake
   him,
Though all their several worths were given
   to one,
With this is to be mention'd.
   Max. Is he mad?
   Diocle. Why, they did die, Theophilus,
   and boldly;
This did no more.
   Theoph. They, out of desperation,
Or for vain glory of an after-name,
Parted with life: this had not mutinous sons,
As the rash Gracchi were; nor was this saint
A doating mother, as Cornelia was.
This lost no husband, in whose overthrow
Her wealth and honour sunk; no fear of
   want
Did make her being tedious; but, aiming
At an immortal crown, and in His cause
Who only can bestow it; who sent down
Legions of ministering angels to bear up
Her spotless soul to heaven, who entertain'd it
With choice celestial music, equal to
The motion of the spheres; she, uncompell'd,
Changed this life for a better. My lord
   Sapritius,
You w   present at her death; did you e'er
   hear
Such ravishing sounds?

   Sap. Yet you said then 'twas witchcraft,
And devilish illusions.
   Theoph. I then heard it
With sinful ears, and belch'd out blasphe-
   mous words
Against his Deity, which then I knew not,
Nor did believe in him.
   Diocle. Why, dost thou now?
Or dar'st thou, in our hearing——
   Theoph. Were my voice
As loud as is His thunder, to be heard
Through all the world, all potentates on
   earth
Ready to burst with rage, should they but
   hear it;
Though hell, to aid their malice, lent her
   furies,
Yet I would speak, and speak again, and
   boldly,
I am a Christian, and the Powers you wor-
   ship,
But dreams of fools and madmen.
   Max. Lay hands on him.
   Diocle. Thou twice a child! for doating
   age so makes thee,
Thou couldst not else, thy pilgrimage of life
Being almost past through, in this last mo-
   ment
Destroy whate'er thou hast done good or
   great.
Thy youth did promise much; and, grown a
   man,
Thou mad'st it good, and, with increase of
   years,
Thy actions still better'd: as the sun,
Thou did'st rise gloriously, kept'st a constant
   course
In all thy journey; and now, in the evening,
When thou should'st pass with honour to thy
   rest,
Wilt thou fall like a meteor?
   Sap. Yet confess
That thou art mad, and that thy tongue and
   heart
Had no agreement.
   Max. Do; no way is left, else,
To save thy life, Theophilus.
   Diocle. But, refuse it,
Destruction as horrid, and as sudden,
Shall fall upon thee, as if hell stood open,
And thou wert sinking thither.
   Theoph. Hear me, yet;
Hear, for my service past.
   Artem. What will he say?
   Theoph. As ever I deserved your favour,
   hear me,
And grant one boon; 'tis not for life I sue
   for;
Nor is it fit that I, that ne'er knew pity

                  D

To any Christian, being one myself,
Should look for any : no, I rather beg
The utmost of your cruelty.   I stand
Accomptable for thousand Christians' deaths ;
And, were it possible that I could die
A day for every one, then live again
To be again tormented, 'twere to me
An easy penance, and I should pass through
A gentle cleansing fire ; but, that denied me,
It being beyond the strength of feeble nature,
My suit is, you would have no pity on me.
In mine own house there are a thousand
  engines
Of studied cruelty, which I did prepare
For miserable Christians ; let me feel,
As the Sicilian did his brazen bull,
The horrid'st you can find ; and I will say,
In death, that you are merciful.
  Diocle. Despair not ;
In this thou shalt prevail.   Go fetch them
  hither :   [*Exit some of the Guard.*
Death shall put on a thousand shapes at once,
And so appear before thee ; racks, and
  whips !——
Thy flesh, with burning pincers torn, shall
  feed
The fire that heats them ; and what's want-
  ing to
The torture of thy body, I'll supply
In punishing thy mind.   Fetch all the
  Christians
That are in hold ; and here, before his face,
Cut them in pieces.
  Theoph. 'Tis not in thy power :
It was the first good deed I ever did.
They are removed out of thy reach ; howe'er,
I was determined for my sins to die,
I first took order for their liberty ;
And still I dare thy worst.

Re-enter Guard *with racks and other instru-*
ments of torture.

  Diocle. Bind him, I say ;
Make every artery and sinew crack :
The slave that makes him give the loudest
  shriek,
Shall have ten thousand drachmas : wretch !
I'll force thee
To curse the Power thou worship'st.
  Theoph. Never, never :
No breath of mine shall e'er be spent on Him,
    [*They torment him.*
But what shall speak His majesty or mercy.
I'm honour'd in my sufferings.   Weak tor-
  mentors,
More tortures, more :—alas ! you are un-
  skilful—
For heaven's sake more ; my breast is yet
  untorn :

Here purchase the reward that was pro-
  pounded.
The irons cool,—here are arms yet, and
  thighs ;
Spare no part of me.
  Max. He endures beyond
The sufferance of a man.
  Sap. No sigh nor groan,
To witness he hath feeling.
  Diocle. Harder, villains !
    Enter Harpax.
  Harp. Unless that he blaspheme, he's lost
  for ever.
If torments ever could bring forth despair,
Let these compel him to it :—Oh me !
My ancient enemies again !   [*Falls down.*

Enter Dorothea *in a white robe, a crown*
  upon her head, led in by Angelo; Antoninus, Calista, *and* Christeta *following,*
  all in white, but less glorious ; Angelo
  holds out a crown to Theophilus.

    Theoph. Most glorious vision !—
Did e'er so hard a bed yield man a dream
So heavenly as this ?· I am confirm'd,
Confirm'd, you blessed spirits, and make
  haste
To take that crown of immortality
You offer to me.   Death ! till this blest
  minute,
I never thought thee slow-paced ; nor would I
Hasten thee now, for any pain I suffer,
But that thou keep'st me from a glorious
  wreath,
Which through this stormy way I would
  creep to,
And, humbly kneeling, with humility wear it.
Oh ! now I feel thee :—blessed spirits ! I
  come ;
And, witness for me all these wounds and
  scars,
I die a soldier in the Christian wars.   [*Dies.*
  Sap. I have seen thousands tortured, but
  ne'er yet.
A constancy like this.
  Harp. I am twice damn'd.
  Ang. Haste to thy place appointed, cursed
  fiend !
  [Harpax *sinks with thunder and lightning.*
In spite of hell, this soldier's not thy prey ;
'Tis I have won, thou that hast lost the day.
    [*Exit with Dor. &c.*
  Diocle. I think the centre of the earth be
  crack'd—
Yet I stand still unmoved, and will go on :
The persecution that is here begun,
Through all the world with violence shall
  run.   [*Flourish.   Exeunt.*

The Unnatural Combat.

DRAMATIS PERSONÆ.

Beaufort *senior, governor of* Marseilles.
Beaufort *junior, his son.*
Malefort *senior, admiral of* Marseilles.
Malefort *junior, his son.*
Chamont, ⎫
Montaigne, ⎬ *assistants to the governor.*
Lanour, ⎭
Montreville, *a pretended friend to* Malefort *senior.*
Belgarde, *a poor captain.*

Three *Sea Captains, of the navy of* Malefort *junior.*
A Steward.
An Usher.
A Page.
Theocrine, *daughter to* Malefort *senior.*
Two Waiting-women.
Two Courtezans.
A Bawd.
Servants and Soldiers.

SCENE,—Marseilles.

ACT I.

SCENE I.—*A Hall in the Court of Justice.*

Enter Montreville, Theocrine, Usher, Page, *and* Waiting-women.

Montr. Now to be modest, madam, when you are
A suitor for your father, would appear
Coarser than boldness ; you awhile must part with
Soft silence, and the blushings of a virgin :
Though I must grant, did not this cause command it,
They are rich jewels you have ever worn
To all men's admiration. In this age,
If, by our own forced importunity,
Or others purchased intercession, or
Corrupting bribes, we can make our approaches
To justice, guarded from us by stern power,
We bless the means and industry.
Ush. Here's music
In this bag shall wake her, though she had drunk opium,
Or eaten mandrakes. Let commanders talk
Of cannons to make breaches, give but fire
To this petard, it shall blow open, madam,
The iron doors of a judge, and make you entrance ;
When they (let them do what they can) with all
Their mines, their culverins, and basiliscos,
Shall cool their feet without ; this being the picklock
That never fails.
Montr. 'Tis true, gold can do much,
But beauty more. Were I the governor,
Though the admiral, your father, stood convicted
Of what he's only doubted, half a dozen
Of sweet close kisses from these cherry lips,
With some short active conference in private,
Should sign his general pardon.
Theoc. These light words, sir,
Do ill become the weight of my sad fortune ;
And I much wonder, you, that do profess
Yourself to be my father's bosom friend,
Can raise mirth from his misery.
Montr. You mistake me ;
I share in his calamity, and only
Deliver my thoughts freely, what I should do
For such a rare petitioner : and if
You'll follow the directions I prescribe,
With my best judgment I'll mark out the way
For his enlargement.
Theoc. With all real joy
I shall put what you counsel into act,
Provided it be honest.
Montr. Honesty
In a fair she client (trust to my experience)
Seldom or never prospers ; the world's wicked.
We are men, not saints, sweet lady ; you must practise
The manners of the time, if you intend
To have favour from it : do not deceive yourself,
By building too much on the false foundations
Of chastity and virtue. Bid your waiters
Stand further off, and I'll come nearer to you.
1 *Wom.* Some wicked counsel, on my life.
2 *Wom.* Ne'er doubt it,
If it proceed from him.

D 2

Page. I wonder that
My lord so much affects him.
   Ush. Thou'rt a child,
And dost not understand on what strong basis
This friendship's raised between this Montre-
   ville
And our lord, Monsieur Malefort ; but I'll
   teach thee :
From thy years they have been joint pur-
   chasers
In fire and water works, and truck'd together.
   Page. In fire and water works !
   Ush. Commodities, boy, '
Which you may know hereafter.
   Page. And deal in them,
When the trade has given you over, as ap-
   pears by
The increase of your high forehead.
   Ush. Here's a crack !
I think they suck this knowledge in their
   milk.
   Page. I had an ignorant nurse else. I
   have tied, sir,
My lady's garter, and can guess——
   Ush. Peace, infant ;
Tales out of school ! take heed, you will be
   breech'd else.
   1 *Wom.* My lady's colour changes.
   2 *Wom.* She falls off too.
   Theoc. You are a naughty man, indeed you
   are ;
And I will sooner perish with my father,
Than at this price redeem him.
   Montr. Take your own way,
Your modest, legal way : 'tis not your veil,
Nor mourning habit, nor these creatures
   taught
To howl, and cry, when you begin to
   whimper ;
Nor following my lord's coach in the dirt,
Nor that which you rely upon, a bribe,
Will do it, when there's something he likes
   better.
These courses in an old crone of threescore,
That had seven years together tired the court
With tedious petitions, and clamours,
For the recovery of a straggling husband,
To pay, forsooth, the duties of one to her ;—
But for a lady of your tempting beauties,
Your youth, and ravishing features, to hope
   only
In such a suit as this is, to gain favour,
Without exchange of courtesy—you con-
   ceive me—

   Enter Beaufort *junior, and* Belgarde.

Were madness at the height.   Here's brave
   young Beaufort,
The meteor of Marseillés, one that holds

The governor his father's will and power
In more awe than his own !   Come, come,
   advance,
Present your bag, cramm'd with crowns of
   the sun ;
Do you think he cares for money ? he loves
   pleasure.
Burn your petition, burn it ; he doats on
   you,
Upon my knowledge : to his cabinet, do,
And he will point you out a certain course,
Be the cause right or wrong, to have your
   father
Released with much facility.   [*Exit.*
   Theoc. Do you hear ?
Take a pander with you.
   Beauf. jun. I tell thee there is neither
Employment yet, nor money.
   Belg. I have commanded,
And spent my own means in my country's
   service,
In hope to raise a fortune.
   Beauf. jun. Many have hoped so ;
But hopes prove seldom certainties with
   soldiers.
   Belg. If no preferment, let me but re-
   ceive
My pay that is behind, to set me up
A tavern, or a vaulting-house ; while men
   love
Or drunkenness, or lechery, they'll ne'er fail
   me :
Shall I have that ?
   Beauf. jun. As our prizes are brought in ;
Till then you must be patient.
   Belg. In the mean time,
How shall I do for clothes ?
   Beauf. jun. As most captains do :
Philosopher-like, carry all you have about
   you.
   Belg. But how shall I do, to satisfy colon,
   monsieur ?
There lies the doubt.
   Beauf. jun. That's easily decided ;
My father's table's free for any man
That hath borne arms.
   Belg. And there's good store of meat ?
   Beauf. jun. Never fear that.
   Belg. I'll seek no other ordinary then,
But be his daily guest without invitement ;
And if my stomach hold, I'll feed so heartily,
As he shall pay me suddenly, to be quit of
   me.
   Beauf. jun. 'Tis she.
   Belg. And further——
   Beauf. jun. Away, you are troublesome ;
Designs of more weight——
   Belg. Ha ! fair Theocrine.
Nay, if a velvet petticoat move in the front,

Buff jerkins must to the rear; I know my
    manners :
This is, indeed, great business, mine a gew-
    gaw.
I may dance attendance, this must be dis-
    patch'd,
And suddenly, or all will go to wreck ;
Charge her home in the flank, my lord : nay,
    I am gone, sir.   [*Exit.*
Beauf. jun. [*raising* Theoc. *from her
    knees.*] Nay, pray you, madam, rise,
    or I'll kneel with you.
Page. I would bring you on your knees,
    were I a woman.
Beauf. jun. What is it can deserve so
    poor a name,
As a suit to me ? This more than mortal
    form
Was fashion'd to command, and not entreat :
Your will but known is served.
    Theoc. Great sir, my father,
My brave, deserving father ;—but that sor-
    row
Forbids the use of speech——
    Beauf. jun. I understand you,
Without the aids of those interpreters
That fall from your fair eyes : I know you
    labour
The liberty of your father ; at the least,
An equal hearing to acquit himself :
And, 'tis not to endear my service to you,
Though I must add, and pray you with pa-
    tience hear it,
'Tis hard to be effected, in respect
The state's incensed against him : all pre-
    suming,
The world of outrages his impious son,
Turu'd worse than pirate in his cruelties,
Express'd to this poor country, could not be
With such ease put in execution, if
Your father, of late our great admiral,
Held not or correspondence, or connived
At his proceedings.
    Theoc. And must he then suffer,
His cause unheard ?
    Beauf. jun. As yet it is resolved so,
In their determination. But suppose
(For I would nourish hope, not kill it, in you)
I should divert the torrent of their purpose,
And render them, that are implacable,
Impartial judges, and not sway'd with
    spleen ;
Will you, I dare not say in recompense,
For that includes a debt you cannot owe me,
But in your liberal bounty, in my suit
To you, be gracious?
    Theoc. You entreat of me, sir,
What I should offer to you, with confession
That you much undervalue your own worth,

Should you receive me, since there come with
    you
Not lustful fires, but fair and lawful flames.
But I must be excused, 'tis now no time
For me to think of Hymeneal joys.
Can he (and pray you, sir, consider it)
That gave me life, and faculties to love,
Be, as he's now, ready to be devour'd
By ravenous wolves, and at that instant, I
But entertain a thought of those delights,
In which, perhaps, my ardour meets with
    yours !
Duty and piety forbid it, sir.
    Beauf. jun. But this effected, and your
    father free,
What is your answer ?
    Theoc. Every minute to me
Will be a tedious age, till our embraces
Are warrantable to the world.
    Beauf. jun. I urge no more ;
Confirm it with a kiss.
    Theoc. [*Kissing him.*] I doubly seal it.
    Ush. This would do better abed, the busi-
    ness ended :—
They are the loving'st couple !

    Enter Beaufort *senior,* Montaigne,
        Chamont, *and* Lanour.

    Beauf. jun. Here comes my father,
With the Council of War : deliver your pe-
    tition,
And leave the rest to me.
        [Theoc. *offers a paper.*
    Beauf. sen. I am sorry, lady,
Your father's guilt compels your innocence
To ask what I in justice must deny.
    Beauf. jun. For my sake, sir, pray you
receive and read it.
    Beauf. sen. Thou foolish boy ! I can deny
thee nothing.
        [*Takes the paper from* Theoc.
    Beauf. jun. Thus far we are happy,
madam : quit the place ;
You shall hear how we succeed.
    Theoc. Goodness reward you !
        [*Exeunt* Theocrine, Usher, Page,
        and Women.
    Mont. It is apparent ; and we stay too long
To censure Malefort as he deserves.
        [*They take their seats.*
    Cham. There is no colour of reason that
makes for him :
Had he discharged the trust committed to
    him,
With that experience and fidelity
He practised heretofore, it could not be
Our navy should be block'd up, and, in our
    sight,

Our goods made prize, our sailors sold for
    slaves,
By his prodigious issue.
    Lan. I much grieve,
After so many brave and high achievements,
He should in one ill forfeit all the good
He ever did his country.
    Beauf. sen. Well, 'tis granted.
    Beauf. jun. I humbly thank you, sir.
    Beauf. sen. He shall have hearing,
His irons too struck off; bring him before us,
But seek no further favour.
    Beauf. jun. Sir, I dare not.   [*Exit.*
    Beauf. sen. Monsieur Chamont, Mon-
taigne, Lanour, assistants,
By a commission from the most Christian
    king,
In punishing or freeing Malefort,
Our late great admiral : though I know you
    need not
Instructions from me, how to dispose of
Yourselves in this man's trial, that exacts
Your clearest judgments, give me leave, with
    favour,
To offer my opinion.   We are to hear him,
A little looking back on his fair actions,
Loyal, and true demeanour ; not as now
By the general voice already he's condemn'd.
But if we find, as most believe, he hath held
Intelligence with his accursed son,
Fallen off from all allegiance, and turn'd
(But for what cause we know not) the most
    bloody
And fatal enemy this country ever
Repented to have brought forth ; all com-
    passion
[Of his years pass'd over, all consideration]
Of what he was, or may be, if now pardon'd ;
We sit engaged to censure him with all
Extremity and rigour.
    Cham. Your lordship shews us
A path which we will tread in.
    Lan. He that leaves
To follow, as you lead, will lose himself.
    Mont. I'll not be singular.

Re-enter Beaufort *junior, with* Montreville,
Malefort *senior,* Belgarde, *and Officers.*

    Beauf. sen. He comes, but with
A strange distracted look.
    Malef. sen. Live I once more
To see these hands and arms free ! these,
    that often,
In the most dreadful horror of a fight,
Have been as seamarks to teach such as were
Seconds in my attempts, to steer between
The rocks of too much daring, and pale fear,
To reach the port of victory ! when my sword,
Advanced thus, to my enemies appear'd

A hairy comet, threatening death and ruin
To such as durst behold it ! These the legs,
That, when our ships were grappled, carried
    me
With such swift motion from deck to deck,
As they that saw it, with amazement cried,
He does not run, but flies !
    Mont. He still retains
The greatness of his spirit.
    Malef. sen. Now crampt with irons,
Hunger, and cold, they hardly do support
  . me—
But I forget myself.   O, my good lords,
That sit there as my judges, to determine
The life, and death of Malefort, where are now
Those shouts, those cheerful looks, those loud
    applauses,
With which, when I return'd loaden with spoil,
You entertain'd your admiral ? all's forgotten :
And I stand here to give account of that
Of which I am as free and innocent
As he that never saw the eyes of him,
For whom I stand suspected.
    Beauf. sen. Monsieur Malefort,
Let not your passion so far transport you,
As to believe from any private malice,
Or envy to your person, you are question'd :
Nor do the suppositions want weight,
That do invite us to a strong assurance,
Your son——
    Malef. sen. My shame !
    Beauf. sen. Pray you, hear with patience,
    —never
Without assistance or sure aids from you,
Could, with the pirates of Argiers and Tunis,
Even those that you had almost twice de-
    feated,
Acquire such credit, as with them to be
Made absolute commander ; (pray you ob-
    serve me ;)
If there had not some contract pass'd
    between you,
That, when occasion serv'd, you would join
    with them,
To the ruin of Marseilles ?
    Mont. More, what urged
Your son to turn apostata ?
    Cham. Had he from
The state, or governor, the least neglect,
Which envy could interpret for a wrong ?
    Lan. Or, if you slept not in your charge,
    how could
So many ships as do infest our coast,
And have in our own harbour shut our navy,
Come in unfought with ?
    Beauf. jun. They put him hardly to it.
    Malef. sen. My lords, with as much
    brevity as I can,
I'll answer each particular objection

With which you charge me. The main
ground, on which
You raise the building of your accusation,
Hath reference to my son: should I now
curse him,
Or wish, in the agony of my troubled soul,
Lightning had found him in his mother's
womb,
You'll say 'tis from the purpose; and I,
therefore,
Betake him to the devil, and so leave him!
Did never loyal father but myself
Beget a treacherous issue? was 't in me,
With as much ease to fashion up his mind,
As, in his generation, to form,
The organs to his body? Must it follow,
Because that he is impious, I am false :——
I would not boast my actions, yet 'tis lawful
To upbraid my benefits to unthankful men.
Who sunk the Turkish gallies in the streights,
But Malefort? Who rescued the French
merchants,
When they were boarded, and stow'd under
hatches
By the pirates of Argiers, when every minute
They did expect to be chain'd to the oar,
But your now doubted admiral? then you
fill'd
The air with shouts of joy, and did proclaim,
When hope had left them, and grim-look'd
despair
Hover'd with sail-stretch'd wings over their
heads,
To me, as to the Neptune of the sea,
They owed the restitution of their goods,
Their lives, their liberties. O, can it then
Be probable, my lords, that he that never
Became the master of a pirate's ship,
But at the mainyard hung the captain up,
And caused the rest to be thrown over-
board;
Should, after all these proofs of deadly hate,
So oft express'd against them, entertain
A thought of quarter with them; but much
less
(To the perpetual ruin of my glories)
To join with them to lift a wicked arm
Against my mother-country, this Marseilles,
Which, with my prodigal expense of blood,
I have so oft protected!
   Beauf. sen. What you have done
Is granted and applauded; but yet know
This glorious relation of your actions
Must not so blind our judgments, as to suffer
This most unnatural crime you stand accused
of,
To pass unquestion'd.
   Cham. No; you must produce
Reasons of more validity and weight,

To plead in your defence, or we shall hardly
Conclude you innocent.
   Mont. The large volume of
Your former worthy deeds, with your ex-
perience,
Both what and when to do, but makes
against you.
   Lan. For had your care and courage been
the same
As heretofore, the dangers we are plunged in
Had been with ease prevented.
   Malef. sen. What have I
Omitted, in the power of flesh and blood,
Even in the birth to strangle the designs of
This hell-bred wolf, my son? alas! my lords,
I am no god, nor like him could foresee
His cruel thoughts, and cursed purposes :
Nor would the sun at my command forbear
To make his progress to the other world,
Affording to us one continued light.
Nor could my breath disperse those foggy
mists,
Cover'd with which, and darkness of the night,
Their navy undiscern'd, without resistance,
Beset our harbour! make not that my fault,
Which you in justice must ascribe to fortune—
But if that nor my former acts, nor what
I have deliver'd, can prevail with you,
To make good my integrity and truth;
Rip up this bosom, and pluck out the heart
That hath been ever loyal.
                              [*A trumpet within.*
   Beauf. sen. How! a trumpet?
Enquire the cause.   [*Exit* Montreville.
   Malef. sen. Thou searcher of men's
hearts,
And sure defender of the innocent,
(My other crying sins—awhile not look'd on)
If I in this am guilty, strike me dead,
Or by some unexpected means confirm,
I am accused unjustly!   [*Aside.*

Re-enter Montreville *with a* Sea Captain.

   Beauf. sen. Speak, the motives
That bring thee hither?
   Capt. From our admiral thus:
He does salute you fairly, and desires
It may be understood no public hate
Hath brought him to Marseilles; nor seeks he
The ruin of his country, but aims only
To wreak a private wrong : and if from you
He may have leave and liberty to decide it
In single combat, he'll give up good pledges,
If he fall in the trial of his right,
We shall weigh anchor, and no more molest
This town with hostile arms.
   Beauf. sen. Speak to the man,
If in this presence he appear to you,
To whom you bring this challenge.

Capt. 'Tis to you.
Beauf. sen. His father!
Montr. Can it be?
Beauf. jun. Strange and prodigious!
Malef. sen. Thou seest I stand unmoved:
    were thy voice thunder,
It should not shake me; say, what would
    the viper?
Capt. The reverence a father's name may
    challenge,
And duty of a son no more remember'd,
He does defy thee to the death.
    Malef. sen. Go on.
    Capt. And with his sword will prove it on
    thy head,
Thou art a murderer, an atheist;
And that all attributes of men turn'd furies,
Cannot express thee: this he will make
    good,
If thou dar'st give him meeting.
    Malef. sen. Dare I live!
Dare I, when mountains of my sins o'er-
    whelm me,
At my last gasp ask for mercy! How I bless
Thy coming, captain; never man to me
Arrived so opportunely; and thy message,
However it may seem to threaten death,
Does yield to me a second life in curing
My wounded honour. Stand I yet suspected
As a confederate with this enemy,
Whom of all men, against all ties of nature,
He marks out for destruction! you are just,
Immortal Powers, and in this merciful;
And it takes from my sorrow, and my shame
For being the father to so bad a son,
In that you are pleased to offer up the
    monster
To my correction. Blush and repent,
As you are bound, my honourable lords,
Your ill opinions of me. Not great Brutus,
The father of the Roman liberty,
With more assured constancy beheld
His traitor sons, for labouring to call home
The banish'd Tarquins, scourged with rods
    to death,
Than I will shew, when I take back the life
This prodigy of mankind received from me.
    Beauf. sen. We are sorry, monsieur Male-
    fort, for our error,
And are much taken with your resolution;
But the disparity of years and strength,
Between you and your son, duly consider'd,
We would not so expose you.
    Malef. sen. Then you kill me, .
Under pretence to save me, O my lords,
As you love honour, and a wrong'd man's
    fame,
Deny me not this fair and noble means
To make me right again to all the world.

Should any other but myself be chosen
To punish this apostata with death,
You rob a wretched father of a justice
That to all after times will be recorded.
I wish his strength were centuple, his skill
    equal
To my experience, that in his fall
He may not shame my victory! I feel
The powers and spirits of twenty strong men
    in me.
Were he with wild fire circled, I undaunted
Would make way to him.—As you do affect,
    sir,
My daughter Theocrine; as you are
My true and ancient friend; as thou art
    valiant;
And as all love a soldier, second me
    [*They all sue to the* Governor.
In this my just petition. In your looks
I see a grant, my lord.
    Beauf. sen. You shall o'erbear me;
And since you are so confident in your cause,
Prepare you for the combat.
    Malef. sen. With more joy
Than yet I ever tasted: by the next sun,
The disobedient rebel shall hear from me,
And so return in safety. [*To the* Captain.]
    My good lords,
To all my service.—I will die, or purchase
Rest to Marseilles; nor can I make doubt,
But his impiety is a potent charm,
To edge my sword, and add strength to my
    arm.   [*Exeunt.*

ACT II.

SCENE I.—*An open Space without the
    City.*

Enter three Sea Captains.

    2 *Capt.* He did accept the challenge, then!
    1 *Capt.* Nay more,
Was overjoy'd in't; and, as it had been
A fair invitement to a solemn feast,
And not a combat to conclude with death,
He cheerfully embraced it.
    3 *Capt.* Are the articles
Sign'd to on both parts?
    1 *Capt.* At the father's suit,
With much unwillingness the governor
Consented to them.
    2 *Capt.* You are inward with
Our admiral; could you yet never learn
What the nature of the quarrel is, that
    renders
The son more than incensed, implacable,
Against the father?
    1 *Capt.* Never; yet I have,
As far as manners would give warrant to it,

With my best curiousness of care observed
him.
I have sat with him in his cabin a day together,
Yet not a syllable exchanged between us.
Sigh he did often, as if inward grief
And melancholy at that instant would
Choke up his vital spirits, and now and then
A tear or two, as in derision of
The toughness of his rugged temper, would
Fall on his hollow cheeks, which but once
felt,
A sudden flash of fury did dry up ;
And laying then his hand upon his sword,
He would murmur, but yet so as I oft heard
him,
We shall meet, cruel father, yes, we shall ;
When I'll exact, for every womanish drop
Of sorrow from these eyes, a strict accompt
Of much more from thy heart.
  2 *Capt.* 'Tis wondrous strange.
  3 *Capt.* And past my apprehension.
  1 *Capt.* Yet what makes
The miracle greater, when from the maintop
A sail's descried, all thoughts that do concern
Himself laid by, no lion, pinch'd with
hunger,
Rouses himself more fiercely from his den,
Than he comes on the deck ; and there how
wisely
He gives directions, and how stout he is
In his executions, we, to admiration,
Have been eyewitnesses : yet he never minds
The booty when 'tis made ours ; but as if
The danger, in the purchase of the prey,
Delighted him much more than the reward,
His will made known, he does retire himself
To his private contemplation, no joy
Express'd by him for victory.

Enter Malefort *junior.*

  2 *Capt.* Here he comes,
But with more cheerful looks than ever yet
I saw him wear.
  Malef. jun. It was long since resolved on,
Nor must I stagger now in't. May the cause,
That forces me to this unnatural act
Be buried in everlasting silence,
And I find rest in death, or my revenge !
To either I stand equal. Pray you, gentle-
men,
Be charitable in your censures of me,
And do not entertain a false belief
That I am mad, for undertaking that
Which must be, when effected, still repented.
It adds to my calamity, that I have
Discourse and reason, and but too well
know
I can nor live, nor end a wretched life,

But both ways I am impious. Do not, there-
fore,
Ascribe the perturbation of my soul
To a servile fear of death : I oft have view'd
All kinds of his inevitable darts,
Nor a they terrible. Were I condemn'd to
leap
From the cloud-cover'd brows of a steep rock,
Into the deep ; or, Curtius like, to fill up,
For my country's safety, and an after-name,
A bottomless abyss, or charge through fire,
It could not so much shake me, as th' en-
counter
Of this day's single enemy.
  1 *Capt.* If you please, sir,
You may shun it, or defer it.
  Malef. jun. Not for the world :
Yet two things I entreat you ; the first is,
You'll not enquire the difference between
Myself and him, which as a father once
I honour'd, now my deadliest enemy ;
The last is, if I fall, to bear my body
Far from this place, and where you please
inter it.—
I should say more, but by his sudden coming
I am cut off.

Enter Beaufort *junior and* Montreville,
leading in Malefort *senior ;* Belgarde
following, with others.

  Beauf. jun. Let me, sir, have the honour
To be your second.
  Montr. With your pardon, sir,
I must put in for that, since our tried friend-
ship
Hath lasted from our infancy.
  Belg. I have served
Under your command, and you have seen
me fight,
And handsomely, though I say it ; and if now,
At this downright game, I may but hold
your cards,
I'll not pull down the side.
  Malef. sen. I rest much bound
To your so noble offers, and I hope
Shall find your pardon, though I now refuse
them ;
For which I'll yield strong reasons, but as
briefly
As the time will give me leave. For me to
borrow
(That am supposed the weaker) any aid
From the assistance of my second's sword,
Might write me down in the black list of those
That have nor fire nor spirit of their own ;
But dare, and do, as they derive their courage
From his example, on whose help and valour
They wholly do depend. Let this suffice,
In my excuse, for that. Now, if you please,

On both parts, to retire to yonder mount,
Where you, as in a Roman theatre,
May see the bloody difference determined,
Your favours meet my wishes.
　Malef. jun. 'Tis approved of
By me ; and I command you [*To his* Cap-
　tains.] lead the way,
And leave me to my fortune.
　Beauf. jun. I would gladly
Be a spectator (since I am denied
To be an actor) of each blow and thrust,
And punctually observe them.
　Malef. jun. You shall have
All you desire ; for in a word or two
I must make bold to entertain the time,
If he give suffrage to it.
　Malef. sen. Yes, I will ;
I'll hear thee, and then kill thee : nay, farewell.
　Malef. jun. Embrace with love on both
　sides,
Leave deadly hate and fury.
　Malef. sen. From this place
You ne'er shall see both living.
　Belg. What's past help, is
Beyond prevention.
　　[*They embrace on both sides, and take
　　leave severally of the father and
　　son.*
. *Malef. sen.* Now we are alone, sir ;
And thou hast liberty to unload the burthen
Which thou groan'st under. Speak thy griefs.
　Malef. jun. I shall, sir ;
But in a perplex'd form and method, which
You only can interpret : Would you had not
A guilty knowledge in your bosom, of
The language which you force me to deliver,
So I were nothing ! As you are my father,
I bend my knee, and, uncompell'd, profess
My life, and all that's mine, to be your gift ;
And that in a son's duty I stand bound
To lay this head beneath your feet, and run
All desperate hazards for your ease and safety :
But this confest on my part, I rise up,
And not as with a father, (all respect,
Love, fear, and reverence cast off,) but as
A wicked man, I thus expostulate with you.
Why have you done that which I dare not
　speak,
And in the action changed the humble shape
Of my obedience, to rebellious rage,
And insolent pride ? and with shut eyes con-
　strain'd me
To run my bark of honour on a shelf
I must not see, nor, if I saw it, shun it ?
In my wrongs nature suffers, and looks
　backward,
And mankind trembles to see me pursue
What beasts would fly from. For when I
　· advance

This sword, as I must do, against your head,
Piety will weep, and filial duty mourn,
To see their altars which you built up in me,
In a moment razed and ruin'd. That you could
(From my grieved soul I wish it) but produce,
To qualify, not excuse, your deed of horror,
One seeming reason, that I might fix here,
And move no further !
　Malef. sen. Have I so far lost
A father's power, that I must give account
Of my actions to my son ? or must I plead
As a fearful prisoner at the bar, while he
That owes his being to me sits a judge
To censure that, which only by myself
Ought to be question'd ? mountains sooner fall
Beneath their valleys, and the lofty pine
Pay homage to the bramble, or what else is
Preposterous in nature, ere my tongue
In one short syllable yield satisfaction
To any doubt of thine ; nay, though it were
A certainty disdaining argument !
Since, though my deeds wore hell's black
　livery,
To thee they should appear triumphal robes,
Set off with glorious honour, thou being bound
To see with my eyes, and to hold that reason,
That takes or birth or fashion from my will.
　Malef. jun. This sword divides that slavish
　knot.
　Malef. sen. It cannot :
It cannot, wretch ; and if thou but remember
From whom thou hadst this spirit, thou dar'st
　not hope it.
Who train'd thee up in arms but I ? Who
　taught thee
Men were men only when they durst look down
With scorn on death and danger, and
　contemn'd
All opposition, till plumed Victory
Had made her constant stand upon their
　helmets ?
Under my shield thou hast fought as securely
As the young eaglet, cover'd with the wings
Of her fierce dam, learns how and where to
　prey.
All that is manly in thee, I call mine ;
But what is weak and womanish, thine own.
And what I gave, since thou art proud, un-
　grateful,
Presuming to contend with him, to whom
Submission is due, I will take from thee.
Look, therefore, for extremities, and expect
　not
I will correct thee as a son, but kill thee
As a serpent swollen with poison ; who sur-
　viving
A little longer, with infectious breath,
Would render all things near him, like itself,
Contagious. Nay, now my anger's up,

Ten thousand virgins kneeling at my feet,
And with one general cry howling for mercy,
Shall not redeem thee.

Malef. jun. Thou incensed Power,
Awhile forbear thy thunder! let me have
No aid in my revenge, if from the grave
My mother——

Malef. sen. Thou shalt never name her
    more.   [*They fight.*

Beaufort *junior*, Montreville, Belgarde, *and
    the three* Sea Captains, *appear on the*
Mount.

Beauf. jun. They are at it.

2 *Capt.* That thrust was put strongly home.

Montr. But with more strength avoided.

Belg. Well come in ;
He has drawn blood of him yet : well done,
    old cock.

1 *Capt.* That was a strange miss.

Beauf. jun. That a certain hit.
                    [*Young Malefort is slain.*

Belg. He's fallen, the day is ours !

2 *Capt.* The admiral's slain.

Montr. The father is victorious !

Belg. Let us haste
To gratulate his conquest.

1 *Capt.* We to mourn
The fortune of the son.

Beauf. jun. With utmost speed
Acquaint the governor with the good success,
That he may entertain, to his full merit,
The father of his country's peace and safety.
                              [*They retire.*

Malef. sen. Were a new life hid in each
    mangled limb,
I would search, and find it : and howe'er to
    some
I may seem cruel thus to tyrannize
Upon this senseless flesh, I glory in it.—
That I have power to be unnatural,
Is my security ; die all my fears,
And waking jealousies, which have so long
Been my tormentors ! there's now no sus-
    picion :
A fact, which I alone am conscious of,
Can never be discover'd, or the cause
That call'd this duel on, I being above
All perturbations ; nor is it in
The power of fate, again to make me
    wretched.

Re-enter Beaufort *junior*, Montreville, Bel-
    garde, *and the three* Sea Captains.

Beauf. jun. All honour to the conqueror !
    who dares tax
My friend of treachery now ?

Belg. I am very glad, sir,
You have sped so well : but I must tell you
    thus much,

To put you in mind that a low ebb must
    follow
Your high-swoll'n tide of happiness, you
    have purchased
This honour at a high price.

Malef. 'Tis, Belgarde,
Above all estimation, and a little
To be exalted with it cannot savour
Of arrogance. That to this arm and sword
Marseillés owes-the freedom of her fears,
Or that my loyalty, not long since eclipsed,
Shines now more bright than ever, are not
    things
To be lamented : though, indeed, they may
Appear too dearly bought, my falling glories
Being made up again, and cémented
With a son's blood. 'Tis true, he was my son,
While he was worthy ; but when he shook off
His duty to me, (which my fond indulgence,
Upon submission, might perhaps have par-
    don'd,)
And grew his country's enemy, I look'd on
    him
As a stranger to my family, and a traitor
Justly proscribed, and he to be rewarded
That could bring in his head. . I know in this
That I am censured rugged, and austere,
That will vouchsafe not one sad sigh or tear
Upon his slaughter'd body : but I rest . .
Well satisfied in myself, being assured that
Extraordinary virtues, when they soar
Too high a pitch for common sights to judge·
    of,
Losing their proper splendour, are condemn'd
For most remarkable vices.

Beauf. jun. 'Tis too true, sir,
In the opinion of the multitude ;
But for myself, that would be held your·
    friend,
And hope to know you by a nearer name,
They are as they deserve, received.

Malef. My daughter
Shall thank you for the favour.

Beauf. jun. I can wish
No happiness beyond it.

1 *Capt.* Shall we have leave
To bear the corpse of our dead admiral,
As he enjoin'd us, from this coast ?

Malef. Provided
The articles agreed on be observed,
And you depart hence with it, making oath
Never hereafter, but as friends, to touch
Upon this shore.

1 *Capt.* We'll faithfully perform it.

Malef. Then as you please dispose of it :
    'tis an object
That I could wish removed. His sins die
    with him !
So far he has my charity.

1 *Capt.* He shall have
A soldier's funeral.
[*The* Captains *bear the body off, with
sad music.*
Malef. Farewell!
Beauf. jun. These rites
Paid to the dead, the conqueror that survives
Must reap the harvest of his bloody labour.
Sound all loud instruments of joy and
triumph,
And with all circumstance and ceremony,
Wait on the patron of our liberty,
Which he at all parts merits.
Malef. I am honour'd
Beyond my hopes.
Beauf. jun. 'Tis short of your deserts.
Lead on : oh, sir, you must ; you are too
modest. [*Exeunt with loud music.*

SCENE II.—*A Room in* Malefort's *House.*

Enter Theocrine, Page, *and* Waiting-
women.

Theoc. Talk not of comfort ; I am both
ways wretched,
And so distracted with my doubts and fears,
I know not where to fix my hopes. My loss
Is certain in a father, or a brother,
Or both ; such is the cruelty of my fate,
And not to be avoided.
1 *Wom.* You must bear it
With patience, madam.
2 *Wom.* And what's not in you
To be prevented, should not cause a sorrow
Which cannot help it.
Page. Fear not my brave lord,
Your noble father ; fighting is to him
Familiar as eating. He can teach
Our modern duellists how to cleave a button,
And in a new way, never yet found out
By old Caranza.
1 *Wom.* May he be victorious,
And punish disobedience in his son !
Whose death, in reason, should at no part
move you,
He being but half your brother, and the
nearness
Which that might challenge from you, for-
feited
By his impious purpose to kill him, from
whom
He received life. [*A shout within.*
2 *Wom.* A general shout——
1 *Wom.* Of joy.
Page. Look up, dear lady ; sad news
never came
Usher'd with loud applause.
Theoc. I stand prepared
To endure the shock of it.

Enter Usher.

Ush. I am out of breath
With running to deliver first——
Theoc. What?
Ush. We are all made.
My lord has won the day ; your brother's
slain ;
The pirates gone : and by the governor,
And states, and all the men of war, he is
Brought home in triumph :—nay, no musing,
pay me
For my good news hereafter.
Theoc. Heaven is just !
Ush. Give thanks at leisure ; make all
haste to meet him.
I could wish I were a horse, that I might
bear you
To him upon my back.
Page. Thou art an ass,
And this is a sweet burthen.
Ush. Peace, you crack-rope ! [*Exeunt.*

SCENE III.—*A Street.*

Loud music. Enter Montreville, Belgarde,
Beaufort *senior,* Beaufort *junior ;* Malefort, *followed by* Montaigne, Chamont,
and Lanour.

Beauf. sen. All honours we can give you,
and rewards,
Though all that's rich or precious in Mar-
seilles
Were laid down at your feet, can hold no
weight
With your deservings : let me glory in
Your action, as if it were mine own ;
And have the honour, with the arms of love,
To embrace the great performer of a deed
Transcending all this country e'er could
boast of.
Mont. Imagine, noble sir, in what we may
Express our thankfulness, and rest assured
It shall be freely granted.
Cham. He's an enemy
To goodness and to virtue, that dares think
There's anything within our power to give,
Which you in justice may not boldly chal-
lenge.
Lan. And as your own ; for we will ever be
At your devotion.
Malef. Much honour'd sir,
And you, my noble lords, I can say only,
The greatness of your favours overwhelms
me,
And like too large a sail, for the small bark
Of my poor merits, sinks me. That I stand
Upright in your opinions, is an honour
Exceeding my deserts, I having done
Nothing but what in duty I stood bound to :

And to expect a recompense were base,
Good deeds being ever in themselves re-
warded.
Yet since your liberal bounties tell me that
I may, with your allowance, be a suitor,
To you, my lord, I am an humble one,
And must ask that, which known, I fear you
   will
Censure me over bold.
   Beauf. sen. It must be something
Of a strange nature, if it find from me
Denial or delay.
   Malef. Thus then, my lord,
Since you encourage me : you are happy in
A worthy son, and all the comfort that
Fortune has left me, is one daughter ; now,
If it may not appear too much presumption,
To seek to match my lowness with your
   height,
I should desire (and if I may obtain it,
I write *nil ultra* to my largest hopes)
She may in your opinion be thought worthy
To be received into your family,
And married to your son : their years are
   equal,
And their desires, I think, too ; she is not
Ignoble, nor my state contemptible,
And if you think me worthy your alliance,
'Tis all I do aspire to.
   Beauf. jun. You demand
That which with all the service of my life
I should have labour'd to obtain from you.
O sir, why are you slow to meet so fair
And noble an offer? can France show a virgin
That may be parallel'd with her ? is she not
The phœnix of the time, the fairest star
In the bright sphere of women?
   Beauf. sen. Be not rapt so :
Though I dislike not what is motion'd, yet
In what so near concerns me, it is fit
I should proceed with judgment.

    Enter Usher, Theocrine, Page, *and*
     Waiting-women.

   Beauf. jun. Here she comes :
Look on her with impartial eyes, and then
Let envy, if it can, name one graced feature
In which she is defective.
   Malef. Welcome, girl!
My joy, my comfort, my delight, my all,
Why dost thou come to greet my victory
In such a sable habit? This shew'd well
When thy father was a prisoner, and sus-
   pected ;
But now his faith and loyalty are admired,
Rather than doubted, in your outward gar-
   ments
You are to express the joy you feel within:

Nor should you with more curiousness and
   care
Pace to the temple to be made a bride,
Than now, when all men's eyes are fixt upon
   you,
You should appear to entertain the honour
From me descending to you, and in which
You have an equal share.
   Theoc. Heaven has my thanks,
With all humility paid for your fair fortune,
And so far duty binds me ; yet a little
To mourn a brother's loss, however wicked,
The tenderness familiar to our sex
May, if you please, excuse.
   Malef. Thou art deceived.
He, living, was a blemish to thy beauties,
But in his death gives ornament and lustre
To thy perfections, but that they are
So exquisitely rare, that they admit not
The least addition. Ha ! here's yet a print
Of a sad tear on thy cheek; how it takes
   from
Our present happiness ! with a father's lips,
A loving father's lips, I'll kiss it off,
The cause no more remember'd.
   Theoc. You forget, sir,
The presence we are in.
   Malef. 'Tis well consider'd ;
And yet, who is the owner of a treasure
Above all value, but, without offence,
May glory in the glad possession of it ?
Nor let it in your excellence beget wonder,
Or any here, that looking on the daughter,
I feast myself in the imagination
Of those sweet pleasures, and allowed de-
   lights,
I tasted from the mother, who still lives
In this her perfect model ; for she had
Such smooth and high-arch'd brows, such
   sparkling eyes,
Whose every glance stored Cupid's emptied
   quiver,
Such ruby lips,—and such a lovely bloom,
Disdaining all adulterate aids of art,
Kept a perpetual spring upon her face,
As Death himself lamented, being forced
To blast it with his paleness : and if now,
Her brightness dimm'd with sorrow, take
   and please you,
Think, think, young lord, when she appears
   herself,
This veil removed, in her own natural pure-
   ness,
How far she will transport you.
   Beauf. jun. Did she need it,
The praise which you (and well deserved)
   give to her,
Must of necessity raise new desires
In one indebted more to years ; to me

Your words are but as oil pour'd on a fire,
That flames already at the height.
  Malef. No more ;
I do believe you, and let me from you
Find so much credit ; when I make her yours,
I·do possess you of a gift, which I
With much unwillingness part from.   My
    good lords,
Forbear your further trouble ; give me leave,
For on the sudden I am indisposed,
To retire to my own house, and rest : to-
    morrow,
As you command me, I will be your guest,
And having deck'd my daughter like herself,
You shall have further conference.
  Beauf. sen. You are master
·Of your own will ; but fail not, I'll expect
    you.
  Malef. Nay, I will be excused ; I must
    part with you.
            [*To young* Beaufort *and the rest.*
My dearest Theocrine, give me thy hand,
I will support thee.
  Theoc. You gripe it too hard, sir.
  Malef. Indeed I do, but have no further
    end in it
But love and tenderness, such as I may
    challenge,
And you must grant.   Thou art a sweet
    one ; yes,
And to be cherish'd.
  Theoc. May I still deserve it !
            [*Exeunt several ways.*

ACT III.

SCENE I.—*A Banqueting-room in*
        Beaufort's *House.*

Enter Beaufort *senior, and* Steward.

  Beauf. sen. Have you been careful ?
  Stew. With my best endeavours.
Let them bring stomachs, there's no want
    of meat, sir.
Portly and curious viands are prepared,
To please all kinds of appetites.
  Beauf. sen. 'Tis well.
I love a table furnish'd with full plenty,
And store of friends to eat it : but with this
    caution,
I would not have my house a common inn,
For some men that come rather to devour
    me,
Than to present their service.   At this time,
    too,
It being a serious and solemn meeting,
I must not have my board pester'd with
    shadows,

That, under other men's protection, break in
Without invitement.
  Stew. With your favour, then,
You must double your guard, my lord, for
    on my knowledge,
There are some so sharp set, not to be kept
    out
By a file of musketeers : and 'tis less danger,
I'll undertake, to stand at push of pike,
With an enemy in a breach, that under-
    mined too,
And the cannon playing on it, than to stop
One harpy, your perpetual guest, from en-
    trance,
When the dresser, the cook's drum, thun-
    ders, Come on,
The service will be lost else !
  Beauf. sen. What is he ?
  Stew. As tall a trencherman, that is most
    certain,
As e'er demolish'd pye-fortification
As soon as batter'd ; and if the rim of his
    belly
Were not made up of a much tougher stuff
Than his buff jerkin, there were no defence
Against the charge of his guts : you needs
    must know him,
He's eminent for his eating.
  Beauf. sen. O, Belgarde !
  Stew. The same ; one of the admiral's
    cast captains,
Who swear, there being no war, nor hope
    of any,
The only drilling is to eat devoutly,
And to be ever drinking—that's allow'd of,
But they know not where to get it, there's
    the spite on't.
  Beauf. sen. The more their misery ; yet,
    if you can,
For this day put him off.
  Stew. It is beyond
The invention of man.
  Beauf. sen. No :—say this only,
            [*Whispers to him.*
And as from me ; you apprehend me ?
  Stew. Yes, sir.
  Beauf. sen. But it must be done gravely.
  Stew. Never doubt me, sir.
  Beauf. sen. We'll dine in the great room,
    but let the music
And banquet be prepared here.   [*Exit.*
  Stew. This will make him
Lose his dinner at the least, and that will
    vex him.
As for the sweetmeats, when they are trod
    under foot,
Let him take his share with the pages and
    the lackies,
Or scramble in the rushes.

Enter Belgarde.

Belg. 'Tis near twelve ;
I keep a watch within me never misses.—
Save thee, master steward !
Stew. You are most welcome, sir.
Belg. Has thy lord slept well to-night?
I come to enquire.
I had a foolish dream, that, against my will,
Carried me from my lodging, to learn only
How he's disposed.
Stew. He's in most perfect health, sir.
Belg. Let me but see him feed heartily at
dinner,
And I'll believe so too ; for from that ever
I make a certain judgment.
Stew. It holds surely
In your own constitution.
Belg. And in all men's,
'Tis the best symptom ; let us lose no time,
Delay is dangerous.
Stew. Troth, sir, if I might,
Without offence, deliver what my lord has
Committed to my trust, I shall receive it
As a special favour.
Belg. We'll see it, and discourse,
As the proverb says, for health sake, after
dinner,
Or rather after supper ; willingly then
I'll walk a mile to hear thee.
Stew. Nay, good sir,
I will be brief and pithy.
Belg. Prithee be so.
Stew. He bid me say, of all his guests,
that he
Stands most affected to you, for the freedom
And plainness of your manners. He ne'er
observed you
To twirl a dish about, you did not like of,
All being pleasing to you ; or to take
A say of venison, or stale fowl, by your
nose,
Which is a solecism at another's table ;
But by strong eating of them, did confirm
They never were delicious to your palate,
But when they were mortified, as the Hugonot
says,
And so your part grows greater ; nor do you
Find fault with the sauce, keen hunger being
the best,
Which ever, to your much praise, you bring
with you ;
Nor will you with impertinent relations,
Which is a master-piece when meat's before
you,
Forget your teeth, to use your nimble tongue,
But do the feat you come for.
Belg. Be advised,
And end your jeering ; for, if you proceed,

You'll feel, as I can eat I can be angry ;
And beating may ensue.
Stew. I'll take your counsel,
And roundly come to the point : my lord
much wonders,
That you, that are a courtier as a soldier,
In all things else, and every day can vary
Your actions and discourse, continue constant
To this one suit.
Belg. To one ! 'tis well I have one,
Unpawn'd, in these days ; every cast com-
mander
Is not blest with the fortune, I assure you.
But why this question? does this offend him?
Stew. Not much ; but he believes it is the
reason
You ne'er presume to sit above the salt ;
And therefore, this day, our great admiral,
With other states, being invited guests,
He does entreat you to appear among them,
In some fresh habit.
Belg. This staff shall not serve
To beat the dog off ; these are soldier's gar-
ments,
And so by consequence grow contemptible.
Stew. It has stung him.   [*Aside.*
Belg. I would I were acquainted with the
players,
In charity they might furnish me : but
there is
No faith in brokers ; and for believing tailors,
They are only to be read of, but not seen ;
And sure they are confined to their own hells,
And there they live invisible. Well, I must not
Be fubb'd off thus : pray you, report my service
To the lord governor ; I will obey him :
And though my wardrobe's poor, rather
than lose
His company at this feast, I will put on
The richest suit I have, and fill the chair
That makes me worthy of.   [*Exit.*
Stew. We are shut of him,
He will be seen no more here : how my
fellows
Will bless me for his absence ! he had
starved them,
Had he staid a little longer. Would he
could,
For his own sake, shift a shirt ! and that's
the utmost
Of his ambition : adieu, good captain.
                                    [*Exit.*

SCENE II.—*The same.*

Enter Beaufort *senior, and* Beaufort *junior.*

Beauf. sen. 'Tis a strange fondness.
Beauf. jun. 'Tis beyond example.
His resolution to part with his estate,
To make her dower the weightier, is nothing ;

But to observe how curious he is
In his own person, to add ornament
To his daughter's ravishing features, is the
wonder.
I sent a page of mine in the way of courtship
This morning to her, to present my service,
From whom I understand all. There he
found him
Solicitous in what shape she should appear ;
This gown was rich, but the fashion stale ;
the other
Was quaint, and neat, but the stuff not rich
enough :
Then does he curse the tailor, and in rage
Falls on her shoemaker, for wanting art
To express in every circumstance the form
Of her most delicate foot ; then sits in council
With much deliberation, to find out
What tire would best adorn her ; and one
chosen,
Varying in his opinion, he tears off,
And stamps it under foot ; then tries a second,
A third, and fourth, and satisfied at length,
With much ado, in that, he grows again
Perplex'd and troubled where to place her
jewels,
To be most mark'd, and whether she should
wear
This diamond on her forehead, or between
Her milkwhite paps, disputing on it both
ways.
Then taking in his hand a rope of pearl,
(The best of France,) he seriously considers,
Whether he should dispose it on her arm,
Or on her neck ; with twenty other trifles,
Too tedious to deliver.
   Beauf. sen. I have known him
From his first youth, but never yet observed,
In all the passages of his life and fortunes,
Virtues so mixed with vices : valiant the
world speaks him,
But with that, bloody ; liberal in his gifts too,
But to maintain his prodigal expense,
A fierce extortioner ; an impotent lover
Of women for a flash, but, his fires quench'd,
Hating as deadly : the truth is, I am not
Ambitious of this match ; nor will I cross you
In your affections.
   Beauf. jun. I have ever found you
(And 'tis my happiness) a loving father.
                      [Loud music.
And careful of my good :—by the loud music,
As you gave order, for his entertainment,
He's come into the house. Two long hours
sinee,
The colonels, commissioners, and captains,
To pay him all the rites his worth can
challenge,
Went to wait on him hither.

Enter Malefort, Montaigne, Chamont, Lanour, Montreville, Theocrine, Usher,
Page, *and* Waiting-women.

   Beauf. sen. You are most welcome,
And what I speak to you, does from my heart
Disperse itself to all.
   Malef. You meet, my lord,
Your trouble.
   Beauf. sen. Rather, sir, increase of honour,
When you are pleased to grace my house.
   Beauf. jun. The favour
Is doubled on my part, most worthy sir,
Since your fair daughter, my incomparable
mistress,
Deigns us her presence.
   Malef. View her well, brave Beaufort,
But yet at distance ; you hereafter may
Make your approaches nearer, when the
priest
Hath made it lawful : and were not she mine,
I durst aloud proclaim it, Hymen never
Put on his saffron-colour'd robe, to change
A barren virgin name, with more good omens
Than at her nuptials. Look on her again,
Then tell me if she now appear the same,
That she was yesterday.
   Beauf. sen. Being herself,
She cannot but be excellent ; these rich
And curious dressings, which in others might
Cover deformities, from her take lustre,
Nor can add to her.
   Malef. You conceive her right,
And in your admiration of her sweetness,
You only can deserve her. Blush not, girl,
Thou art above his praise, or mine ; nor can
Obsequious Flattery, though she should use
Her thousand oil'd tongues to advance thy
worth,
Give aught, (for that's impossible,) but take
from
Thy more than human graces ; and even then,
When she hath spent herself with her best
strength,
The wrong she has done thee shall be so
apparent,
That, losing her own servile shape and name,
She will be thought Detraction : but I
Forget myself ; and something whispers to me,
I have said too much.
   Mont. I know not what to think on't,
But there's some mystery in it, which I fear
Will be too soon discover'd.
   Malef. I much wrong
Your patience, noble sir, by too much hug-
ging
My proper issue, and, like the foolish crow,
Believe my black brood swans.
   Beauf. sen. There needs not, sir,

The least excuse for this ; nay, I must have
Your arm, you being the master of the feast,
And this the mistress.
Theoc. I am any thing
That you shall please to make me.
Beauf. jun. Nay, 'tis yours,
Without more compliment.
Mont. Your will's a law, sir.
    [*Loud music. Exeunt* Beaufort *se-
    nior,* Malefort, Theocrine, Beau-
    fort *junior,* Montaigne, Cha-
    mont, Lanour, Montreville.
Ush. Would I had been born a lord !
1 *Wom.* Or I a lady !
Page. It may be you were both begot in
court,
Though bred up in the city; for your
mothers,
As I have heard, loved the lobby; and
there, nightly,
Are seen strange apparitions : and who
knows
But that some noble faun, heated with wine,
And cloy'd with partridge, had a kind of
longing
To trade in sprats? this needs no exposi-
tion :—
But can you yield a reason for your wishes ?
Ush. Why, had I been born a lord, I had
been no servant.
1 *Wom.* And whereas now necessity
makes us waiters,
We had been attended on.
2 *Wom.* And might have slept then
As long as we pleased, and fed when we
had stomachs,
And worn new clothes, nor lived as now, in
hope
Of a cast gown, or petticoat.
Page. You are fools,
And ignorant of your happiness. Ere I was
Sworn to the pantofle, I have heard my tutor
Prove it by logic, that a servant's life
Was better than his masters ; and by that
I learn'd from him, if that my memory fail
not,
I'll make it good.
Ush. Proceed, my little wit
In decimo sexto.
Page. Thus then : From the king
To the beggar, by gradation, all are ser-
vants ;
And you must grant, the slavery is less
To study to please one, than many.
Ush. True.
Page. Well then ; and first to you, sir :
you complain
You serve one lord, but your lord serves a
thousand,

Besides his passions, that are his worst
masters ;
You must humour him, and he is bound to
sooth
Every grim sir above him : if he frown,
For the least neglect you fear to lose your
place ;
But if, and with all slavish observation,
From the minion's self, to the groom of his
close-stool,
He hourly seeks not favour, he is sure
To be eased of his office, though perhaps he
bought it.
Nay, more ; that high disposer of all such
That are subordinate to him, serves and fears
The fury of the many-headed monster,
The giddy multitude : and as a horse
Is still a horse, for all his golden trappings,
So your men of purchased titles, at their
best, are
But serving-men in rich liveries.
Ush. Most rare infant !
Where learnd'st thou this morality ?
Page. Why, thou dull pate,
As I told thee, of my tutor.
2 *Wom.* Now for us, boy.
Page. I am cut off :—the governor.

Enter Beaufort *senior and* Beaufort *junior ;*
Servants *setting forth a banquet.*

Beauf. sen. Quick, quick, sirs.
See all things perfect.
Serv. Let the blame be ours else.
Beauf. sen. And, as I said, when we are
at the banquet,
And high in our cups, for 'tis no feast with-
out it,
Especially among soldiers ; Theocrine
Being retired, as that's no place for her,
Take you occasion to rise from the table,
And lose no opportunity.
Beauf. jun. 'Tis my purpose ;
And if I can win her to give her heart,
I have a holy man in readiness
To join our hands ; for the admiral, her
father,
Repents him of his grant to me, and seems
So far transported with a strange opinion
Of her fair features, that, should we defer it,
I think, ere long, he will believe, and
strongly,
The dauphin is not worthy of her : I
Am much amazed with't.
Beauf. sen. Nay, dispatch there, fellows.
    [*Exeunt* Beaufort *senior and* Beau-
    fort *junior.*
Serv. We are ready, when you please.
Sweet forms, your pardon !
It has been such a busy time, I could not

E

Tender that ceremonious respect
Which you deserve; but now, the great
  work ended,
I will attend the less, and with all care
Observe and serve you.
  Page. This is a penn'd speech,
And serves as a perpetual preface to
A dinner made of fragments.
  Ush. We wait on you.   [*Exeunt.*

SCENE III.—*The same. A Banquet set
        forth.*

Loud music. Enter Beaufort *senior*, Malefort, Montaigne, Chamont, Lanour, Beaufort *junior*, Montreville, *and* Servants.

  Beauf. sen. You are not merry, sir.
  Malef. Yes, my good lord,
You have given us ample means to drown
  all cares :—
And yet I nourish strange thoughts, which
  I would
Most willingly destroy.   [*Aside.*
  Beauf. sen. Pray you, take your place.
  Beauf. jun. And drink a health ; and let
  it be, if you please,
To the worthiest of women.—Now observe
  him.
  Malef. Give me the bowl ; since you do
  me the honour,
I will begin it.
  Cham. May we know her name, sir?
  Malef. You shall ; I will not choose a
  foreign queen's,
Nor yet our own, for that would relish of
Tame flattery ; nor do their height of title,
Or absolute power, confirm their worth and
  goodness,
These being heaven's gifts, and frequently
  conferr'd
On such as are beneath them ; nor will I
Name the king's mistress, howsoever she
In his esteem may carry it : but if I,
As wine gives liberty, may use my freedom,
Not sway'd this way or that, with confidence,
(And I will make it good on any equal,)
If it must be to her whose outward form
Is better'd by the beauty of her mind,
She lives not that with justice can pretend
An interest to this so sacred health,
But my fair daughter. He that only doubts it,
I do pronounce a villain : this to her, then.
                          [*Drinks.*
  Mont. What may we think of this ?
  Beauf. sen. It matters not.
  Lan. For my part, I will sooth him, rather
  than
Draw on a quarrel.
  Cham. It is the safest course ;
And one I mean to follow.

  Beauf. jun. It has gone round, sir.
                          [*Exit.*
  Malef. Now you have done her right ; if
  there be any
Worthy to second this, propose it boldly,
I am your pledge.
  Beauf. sen. Let's pause here, if you please,
And entertain the time with something else.
Music there ! in some lofty strain ; the song
  too
That I gave order for ; the new one, call'd
The Soldier's Delight.
                      [*Music and a Song.*

Enter Belgarde *in armour, a case of
        carbines by his side.*

  Belg. Who stops me now?
Or who dares only say that I appear not
In the most rich and glorious habit that
Renders a man complete? What court so
  set off
With state and ceremonious pomp, but, thus
Accoutred, I may enter? Or what feast,
Though all the elements at once were
  ransack'd
To store it with variety transcending
The curiousness and cost on Trajan's birth-
  day ;
(Where princes only, and confederate kings,
Did sit as guests, served and attended on
By the senators of Rome,) at which a soldier,
In this his natural and proper shape,
Might not, and boldly, fill a seat, and by
His presence make the great solemnity
More honour'd and remarkable?
  Beauf. sen. 'Tis acknowledged ;
And this a grace done to me unexpected.
  Mont. But why in armour ?
  Malef. What's the mystery?
Pray you, reveal that.
  Belg. Soldiers out of action,
That very rare * * * * *
* * * * * but, like unbidden guests,
Bring their stools with them, for their own
  defence,
At court should feed in guantlets ; they may
  have
Their fingers cut else : there your carpet
  knights,
That never charged beyond a mistress' lips,
Are still most keen, and valiant. But to you,
Whom it does most concern, my lord, I will
Address my speech, and, with a soldier's
  freedom,
In my reproof, return the bitter scoff
You threw upon my poverty : you contemn'd
My coarser outside, and from that concluded
(As by your groom you made me under-
  stand)

I was unworthy to sit at your table,
Among these tissues and embroideries,
Unless I changed my habit : I have done it,
And shew myself in that which I have worn
In the heat and fervour of a bloody fight ;
And then it was in fashion, not as now,
Ridiculous and despised. This hath past
    through
A wood of pikes, and everyone aim'd at it,
Yet scorn'd to take impression from their
    fury :
With this, as still you see it, fresh and new,
I've charged through fire that would have
    singed your sables,
Black fox, and ermines, and changed the
    proud colour
Of scarlet, though of the right Tyrian die.—
But now, as if the trappings made the man,
Such only are admired that come adorn'd
With what's no part of them. This is mine
    own,
My richest suit, a suit I must not part from,
But not regarded now : and yet remember,
'Tis we that bring you in the means of feasts,
Banquets, and revels, which, when you
    possess,
With barbarous ingratitude you deny us
To be made sharers in the harvest, which
Our sweat and industry reap'd, and sow'd
    for you.
The silks you wear, we with our blood spin
    for you ;
This massy plate, that with the ponderous
    weight
Does make your cupboards crack, we (un-
    affrighted
With tempests, or the long and tedious way,
Or dreadful monsters of the deep, that wait
With open jaws still ready to devour us,)
Fetch from the other world. Let it not then,
In after ages, to your shame be spoken,
That you, with no relenting eyes, look on
Our wants that feed your plenty : or con-
    sume,
In prodigal and wanton gifts on drones,
The kingdom's treasure, yet detain from us
The debt that with the hazard of our lives,
We have made you stand engaged for ; or
    force us,
Against all civil government, in armour
To require that, which with all willingness
Should be tendered ere demanded.
    Beauf. sen. I commend
This wholesome sharpness in you, and
    prefer it
Before obsequious tameness ; it shews lovely :
Nor shall the rain of your good counsel
    fall
Upon the barren sands, but spring up fruit,

Such as you long have wish'd for. And the
    rest
Of your profession, like you, discontented
For want of means, shall, in their present
    payment,
Be bound to praise your boldness : and
    hereafter
I will take order you shall have no cause,
For want of change, to put your armour on,
But in the face of an enemy ; not as now,
Among your friends. To that which is due
    to you,
To furnish you like yourself, of mine own
    bounty
I'll add five hundred crowns.
    Cham. I, to my power,
Will follow the example.
    Mont. Take this, captain,
'Tis all my present store ; but when you
    please,
Command me further.
    Lan. I could wish it more.
    Belg. This is the luckiest jest ever came
    from me.
Let a soldier use no other scribe to draw
The form of his petition. This will speed,
When your thrice-humble supplications,
With prayers for increase of health and
    honours
To their grave lordships, shall, as soon as
    read,
Be pocketed up, the cause no more re-
    member'd :
When this dumb rhetoric [*Aside.*]—Well, I,
    have a life,
Which I, in thankfulness for your great
    favours,
My noble lords, when you please to com-
    mand it,
Must never think mine own.—Broker, be
    happy,
These golden birds fly to thee.   [*Exit.*
    Beauf. sen. You are dull, sir,
And seem not to be taken with the passage
You saw presented.
    Malef. Passage ! I observed none,
My thoughts were elsewhere busied. Ha !
    she is
In danger to be lost, to be lost for ever,.
If speedily I come not to her rescue,
For so my genius tells me.
    Montr. What chimeras
Work on your fantasy ?
    Malef. Fantasies ! they are truths.
Where is my Theocrine ? you have plotted
To rob me of my daughter ; bring me to her,
Or I'll call down the saints to witness for me,
You are inhospitable.
    Beauf. sen. You amaze me.

Your daughter's safe, and now exchanging
      courtship
With my son, her servant. Why do you hear
      this
With such distracted looks, since to that end
You brought her hither?
  Malef. 'Tis confess'd I did ;
But now, pray you, pardon me ; and, if you
      please,
Ere she delivers up her virgin fort,
I would observe what is the art he uses
In planting his artillery against it :
She is my only care, nor must she yield,
But upon noble terms.
  Beauf. sen. 'Tis so determined.
  Malef. Yet I am jealous.
  Mont. Overmuch, I fear.
What passions are these?   [*Aside.*
  Beauf. sen. Come, I will bring you
Where you, with these, if they so please,
      may see
The love-scene acted.
  Montr. There is something more
Than fatherly love in this.   [*Aside.*
  Mont. We wait upon you.   [*Exeunt.*

SCENE IV.—*Another Room in* Beaufort's
            House.

Enter Beaufort *junior, and* Theocrine.

  Beauf. jun. Since then you meet my flames
      with equal ardour,
As you profess, it is your bounty, mistress,
Nor must I call it debt ; yet 'tis your glory,
That your excess supplies my want, and
      makes me
Strong in my weakness, which could never be,
But in your good opinion.
  Theoc. You teach me, sir,
What I should say ; since from your sun of
      favour,
I, like dim Phœbe, in herself obscure,
Borrow that light I have.
  Beauf. jun. Which you return
With large increase, since that you will o'er-
      come,
And I dare not contend, were you but pleased
To make what's yet divided one.
  Theoc. I have
Already in my wishes ; modesty
Forbids me to speak more.
  Beauf. jun. But what assurance,
But still without offence, may I demand,
That may secure me that your heart and
      tongue
Join to make harmony?
  Theoc. Choose any,
Suiting your love, distinguished from lust,
To ask, and mine to grant.

Enter at a distance Beaufort *senior*, Male-
      fort, Montreville, *and the rest.*

  Beauf. sen. Yonder they are.
  Malef. At distance too ! 'tis yet well.
  Beauf. jun. I may take then
This hand, and with a thousand burning
      kisses,
Swear 'tis the anchor to my hopes?
  Theoc. You may, sir.
  Malef. Somewhat too much.
  Beauf. jun. And this done, view myself
In these true mirrors?
  Theoc. Ever true to you, sir :
And may they lose the ability of sight,
When they seek other object !
  Malef. This is more
Than I can give consent to.
  Beauf. jun. And a kiss
Thus printed on your lips, will not distaste you?
  Malef. Her lips !
  Montr. Why, where should he kiss? are
      you distracted?
  Beauf. jun. Then, when this holy man
      hath made it lawful——
              [*Brings in a* Priest.
  Malef. A priest so ready too ! I must
      break in.
  Beauf. jun. And what's spoke here is re-
      gister'd above ;
I must engross those favours to myself
Which are not to be named.
  Theoc. All I can give,
But what they are I know not.
  Beauf. jun. I'll instruct you.
  Malef. O how my blood boils !
  Montr. Pray you, contain yourself ;
Methinks his courtship's modest.
  Beauf. jun. Then being mine,
And wholly mine, the river of your love
To kinsmen and allies, nay, to your father,
(Howe'er out of his tenderness he admires
      you,)
Must in the ocean of your affection
To me, be swallow'd up, and want a name,
Compared with what you owe me.
  Theoc. 'Tis most fit, sir.
The stronger bond that binds me to you, must
Dissolve the weaker.
  Malef. I am ruin'd, if
I come not fairly off.
  Beauf. sen. There's nothing wanting
But your consent.
  Malef. Some strange invention aid me !
This ! yes, it must be so.   [*Aside.*
  Montr. Why do you stagger,
When what you seem'd so much to wish, is
      offer'd,
Both parties being agreed too?

Beauf. sen. I'll not court
A grant from you, nor do I wrong your
   daughter,
Though I say my son deserves her.
   Malef. 'Tis far from
My humble thoughts to undervalue him
I cannot prize too high : for howsoever
From my own fond indulgence I have sung
Her praises with too prodigal a tongue,
That tenderness laid by, I stand confirm'd,
All that I fancied excellent in her,
Balanced with what is really his own,
Holds weight in no proportion.
   Montr. New turnings !
   Beauf. sen. Whither tends this?
   Malef. Had you observed, my lord,
With what a sweet gradation he woo'd,
As I did punctually, you cannot blame her,
Though she did listen with a greedy ear
To his fair modest offers : but so great
A good as then flow'd to her, should have been
With more deliberation entertain'd,
And not with such haste swallow'd ; she shall
   first
Consider seriously what the blessing is,
And in what ample manner to give thanks
   for't,
And then receive it. And though I shall think
Short minutes years, till it be pérfected,
I will defer that which I most desire ;
And so must she, till longing expectation,
That heightens pleasure, makes her truly
   know
Her happiness, and with what outstretch'd
   arms
She must embrace it.
   Beauf. jun. This is curiousness
Beyond example.
   Malef. Let it then begin
From me : in what's mine own I'll use my will,
And yield no further reason. I lay claim to
The liberty of a subject. [*Rushes forward
   and seizes* Theoc.]—Fall not off,
But be obedient, or by the hair
I'll drag thee home. Censure me as you please,
I'll take my own way.—O, the inward fires
That, wanting vent, consume me !
       [*Exit with* Theocrine.
   Montr. 'Tis most certain
He's mad, or worse.
   Beauf. sen. How worse?
   Montr. Nay, there I leave you ;
My thoughts are free.
   Beauf. jun. This I foresaw.
   Beauf. sen. Take comfort,
He shall walk in clouds, but I'll discover him :
And he shall find and feel, if he excuse not,
And with strong reasons, this gross injury,
I can make use of my authority. [*Exeunt.*

ACT IV.

SCENE I.—*A Room in* Malefort's *House.*

Enter Malefort.

What flames are these my wild desires fan
   in me?
The torch that feeds them was not lighted at
Thy altars, Cupid : vindicate thyself,
And do not own it ; and confirm it rather,
That this infernal brand, that turns me
   cinders,
Was by the snake-hair'd sisters thrown into
My guilty bosom. O that I was ever
Accurs'd in having issue ! my son's blood,
(That like the poison'd shirt of Hercules
Grows to each part about me,) which my hate
Forced from him with much willingness, may
   admit
Some weak defence ; but my most impious love
To my fair daughter Theocrine, none ;
Since my affection (rather wicked lust)
That does pursue her, is a greater crime
Than any detestation, with which
I should afflict her innocence. With what
   cunning
I have betray'd myself, and did not feel
The scorching heat that now with fury rages !
Why was I tender of her? cover'd with
That fond disguise, this mischief stole upon
   me.
I thought it no offence to kiss her often,
Or twine mine arms about her softer neck,
And by false shadows of a father's kindness
I long deceived myself : but now the effect
Is too apparent. How I strove to be
In her opinion held the worthiest man
In courtship, form, and feature ! envying him
That was preferr'd before me ; and yet then
My wishes to myself were not discover'd.
But still my fires increased, and with delight
I would call her mistress, willingly forgetting
The name of daughter, choosing rather she
Should style me servant, than, with reverence,
   father :
Yet, waking, I ne'er cherish'd obscene hopes,
But in my troubled slumbers often thought
She was too near to me, and then sleeping
   blush'd
At my imagination ; which pass'd,
(My eyes being open not condemning it,)
I was ravish'd with the pleasure of the dream.
Yet, spite of these temptations, I have reason
That pleads against them, and commands
   me to
Extinguish these abominable fires
And I will do it ; I will send her back
To him that loves her lawfully. Within
   there !

Enter Theocrine.

Theoc. Sir, did you call?
Malef. I look no sooner on her,
But all my boasted power of reason leaves me,
And passion again usurps her empire.—
Does none else wait me?
Theoc. I am wretched, sir,
Should any owe more duty.
Malef. This is worse
Than disobedience ; leave me.
Theoc. On my knees, sir,
As I have ever squared my will by yours,
And liked and loath'd with your eyes, I be-
seech you
To teach me what the nature of my fault is,
That hath incens'd you ; sure 'tis one of
weakness
And not of malice, which your gentler temper,
On my submission, I hope, will pardon :
Which granted by your piety, if that I,
Out of the least neglect of mine hereafter,
Make you remember it, may I sink ever
Under your dread command, sir.
Malef. O my stars !
Who can but doat on this humility,
That sweetens——Lovely in her tears !——
The fetters
That seem'd to lessen in their weight but now,
By this grow heavier on me.   [*Aside.*
Theoc. Dear sir—
Malef. Peace !
I must not hear thee.
Theoc. Nor look on me?
Malef. No,
Thy looks and words are charms.
Theoc. May they have power then
To calm the tempest of your wrath ! Alas,
sir,
Did I but know in what I give offence,
In my repentance I would show my sorrow
For what is past, and, in my care hereafter,
Kill the occasion, or cease to be :
Since life, without your favour, is to me
A load I would cast off.
Malef. O that my heart
Were rent in sunder, that I might expire,
The cause in my death buried ! yet I know
not——
With such prevailing oratory 'tis begg'd
from me,
That to deny thee would convince me to
Have suck'd the milk of tigers ; rise, and I,
But in a perplex'd and mysterious method,
Will make relation : That which all the world
Admires and cries up in thee for perfections,
Are to unhappy me foul blemishes,
And mulcts in nature.   If thou hadst been
born

Deform'd and crooked in the features of
Thy body, as the manners of thy mind ;
Moor-lipp'd, flat-nosed, dim-eyed, and
beetle-brow'd,
With a dwarf's stature to a giant's waist ;
Sour-breath'd, with claws for fingers on thy
hands,
Splay-footed, gouty-legg'd, and over all
A loathsome leprosy had spread itself,
And made thee shunn'd of human fellow-
ships ;
I had been blest.
Theoc. Why, would you wish a monster
(For such a one, or worse, you have de-
scribed)
To call you father?
Malef. Rather than as now,
(Though I had drown'd thee for it in the sea,)
Appearing, as thou dost, a new Pandora,
With Juno's fair cow-eyes, Minerva's brow,
Aurora's blushing cheeks, Hebe's fresh
youth,
Venus' soft paps, with Thetis' silver feet.
Theoc. Sir, you have liked and loved
them, and oft forced,
With your hyperboles of praise pour'd on
them,
My modesty to a defensive red,
Strew'd o'er that paleness, which you then
were pleased
To style the purest white.
Malef. And in that cup
I drank the poison I now feel dispersed
Through every vein and artery.   Wherefore
art thou
So cruel to me?   This thy outward shape
Brought a fierce war against me, not to be
By flesh and blood resisted : but to leave me
No hope of freedom, from the magazine
Of thy mind's forces, treacherously thou
drew'st up
Auxiliary helps to strengthen that
Which was already in itself too potent.
Thy beauty gave the first charge, but thy duty,
Seconded with thy care and watchful studies
To please, and serve my will, in all that might
Raise up content in me, like thunder brake
through
All opposition ; and, my ranks of reason
Disbanded, my victorious passions fell
To bloody execution, and compell'd me
With willing hands to tie on my own chains,
And, with a kind of flattering joy, to glory
In my captivity.
Theoc. In this you speak, sir,
Am ignorance itself.
Malef. And so continue ;
For knowledge of the arms thou bear'st
against me,

Would make thee curse thyself, but yield no
    aids
For thee to help me : and 'twere cruelty
In me to wound that spotless innocence,
Howe'er it make me guilty. In a word,
Thy plurisy of goodness is thy ill ;
Thy virtues vices, and thy humble lowness
Far worse than stubborn sullenness and pride ;
Thy looks, that ravish all beholders else,
As killing as the basilisk's, thy tears,
Express'd in sorrow for the much I suffer,
A glorious insultation, and no sign
Of pity in thee ; and to hear thee speak
In thy defence, though but in silent action,
Would make the hurt, already deeply fester'd,
Incurable : and therefore, as thou wouldst not
By thy presence raise fresh furies to torment
    me,
I do conjure thee by a father's power,
(And 'tis my curse I dare not think it lawful
To sue unto thee in a nearer name,)
Without reply to leave me.
    Theoc. My obedience
Never learn'd yet to question your commands,
But willingly to serve them ; yet I must,
Since that your will forbids the knowledge of
My fault, lament my fortune. [*Exit.*
    Malef. O that I
Have reason to discern the better way,
And yet pursue the worse ! When I look
    on her,
I burn with heat, and in her absence freeze
With the cold blasts of jealousy, that another
Should e'er taste those delights that are
    denied me ;
And which of these afflictions brings less
    torture,
I hardly can distinguish : Is there then
No mean? no ; so my understanding tells me,
And that by my cross fates it is determined
That I am both ways wretched.

    Enter Usher *and* Montreville.

    Ush. Yonder he walks, sir,
In much vexation : he hath sent my lady,
His daughter, weeping in ; but what the
    cause is,
Rests yet in supposition.
    Montr. I guess at it,
But must be further satisfied ; I will sift him
In private, therefore quit the room.
    Ush. I am gone, sir. [*Exit.*
    Malef. Ha ! who disturbs me? Montre-
    ville ! your pardon.
    Montr. Would you could grant one to
    yourself ! I speak it
With the assurance of a friend, and yet,
Before it be too late, make reparation
Of the gross wrong your indiscretion offer'd

To the governor and his son ; nay, to yourself ;
For there begins my sorrow.
    Malef. Would I had
No greater cause to mourn, than their dis-
    pleasure !
For I dare justify——
    Montr. We must not do
All that we dare. We're private, friend. I
    observed
Your alterations with a stricter eye,
Perhaps, than others ; and, to lose no time
In repetition, your strange demeanour
To your sweet daughter.
    Malef. Would you could find out
Some other theme to treat of !
    Montr. None but this ;
And this I'll dwell on ; how ridiculous,
And subject to construction——
    Malef. No more !
    Montr. You made yourself, amazes me,
    and if
The frequent trials interchanged between us
Of love and friendship, be to their desert
Esteem'd by you, as they hold weight with me,
No inward trouble should be of a shape
So horrid to yourself, but that to me
You stand bound to discover it, and unlock
Your secret'st thoughts ; though the most
    innocent were
Loud crying sins.
    Malef. And so, perhaps, they are :
And therefore be not curious to learn that
Which, known, must make you hate me.
    Montr. Think not so.
I am yours in right and wrong ; nor shall you
    find
A verbal friendship in me, but an active ;
And here I vow, I shall no sooner know
What the disease is, but, if you give leave,
I will apply a remedy.   Is it madness ?
I am familiarly acquainted with
A deep-read man, that can with charms and
    herbs
Restore you to your reason : or, suppose
You are bewitch'd,—he with more potent
    spells
And magical rites shall cure you.   Is't
    heaven's anger?
With penitence and sacrifice appease it.——
Beyond this, there is nothing that I can
Imagine dreadful : in your fame and fortunes
You are secure ; your impious son removed
    too,
That render'd you suspected to the state ;
And your fair daughter——
    Malef. Oh ! press me no further.
    Montr. Are you wrung there !   Why,
    what of her? hath she
Made shipwreck of her honour, or conspired

Against your life? or scal'd a contract with
The devil of hell, for the recovery of
Her young Inamorato?
  Malef. None of these;
And yet, what must increase the wonder
    in you,
Being innocent in herself, she hath wounded
    me;
But where, enquire not. Yet, I know not how
I am persuaded, from my confidence
Of your vow'd love to me, to trust you with
My dearest secret; pray you chide me for it,
But with a kind of pity, not insulting
On my calamity.
  Montr. Forward.
  Malef. This same daughter——
  Montr. What is her fault?
  Malef. She is too fair to me.
  Montr. Ha! how is this?
  Malef. And I have looked upon her
More than a father should, and languish to
Enjoy her as a husband.
  Montr. Heaven forbid it!
  Malef. And this is all the comfort you
    can give me!
Where are your promised aids, your charms,
    your herbs,
Your deep-read scholar's spells and magic
    rites?
Can all these disenchant me? No, I must be
My own physician, and upon myself
Practise a desperate cure.
  Montr. Do not contemn me:
Enjoin me what you please, with any hazard
I'll undertake it. What means have you
    practised
To quench this hellish fire?
  Malef. All I could think on,
But to no purpose; and yet sometimes
    absence
Does yield a kind of intermission to
The fury of the fit.
  ·Montr. See her no more, then.
  Malef. 'Tis my last refuge; and 'twas my
    intent,
And still 'tis, to desire your help.
  Montr. Command it.
  Malef. Thus then: you have a fort, of
    which you are
The a s   lord, whither, I pray you, bear
    her olute
And that the sight of her may not again
Nourish those flames, which I feel something
  · lessen'd,
By all the ties of friendship I conjure you,
And by a solemn oath you must confirm it,
That though my now calm'd passions should
    rage higher
Than ever heretofore, and so compel me

Once more to wish to see her; though I use
Persuasions mix'd with threatenings, (nay,
    add to it,
That I, this failing, should with hands held
    up thus,
Kneel at your feet, and bathe them with my
    tears,)
Prayers or curses, vows or imprecations,
Only to look upon her, though at distance,
You still must be obdurate.
  Montr. If it be
Your pleasure, sir, that I shall be unmoved,
I will endeavour.
  Malef. You must swear to be
Inexorable, as you would prevent
The greatest mischief to your friend, that fate
Could throw upon him.
  Montr. Well, I will obey you.
But how the governor will be answer'd yet,
And 'tis material, is not consider'd.
  Malef. Leave that to me. I'll presently
    give order
How you shall surprise her; be not frighted
    with
Her exclamations.
  Montr. Be you constant to
Your resolution, I will not fail
In what concerns my part.
  Malef. Be ever bless'd for't! [*Exeunt.*

SCENE II.—*A Street.*

Enter Beaufort *junior,* Chamont, *and*
Lanour.

  Cham. Not to be spoke with, say you?
  Beauf. jun. No.
  Lan. Nor you
Admitted to have conference with her?
  Beauf. jun. Neither.
His doors are fast lock'd up, and solitude
Dwells round about them, no access allow'd
To friend or enemy; but——
  Cham. Nay, be not moved, sir;
Let his passion work, and, like a hot-rein'd
    horse,
'Twill quickly tire itself.
  Beauf. jun. Or in his death,
Which, for her sake, till now I have forborn,
I will revenge the injury he hath done to
My true and lawful love.
  Lan. How does your father,
The governor, relish it?
  Beauf. jun. Troth, he never had
Affection to the match; yet in his pity
To me, he's gone in person to his house,
Nor will he be denied; and if he find not
Strong and fair reasons, Malefort will hear
    from him
In a kind he does not look for.

Cham. In the mean time,
Pray you put on cheerful looks.

Enter Montaigne.

Beauf. jun. Mine suit my fortune.
Lan. O, here's Montaigne.
Mont. I never could have met you
More opportunely. I'll not stale the jest
By my relation ; but if you will look on
The malecontent·Belgarde, newly rigg'd up,
With the train that follows him, 'twill be an
· object
Worthy of your noting.
Beauf. jun. Look you the comedy
Make good the prologue, or the scorn will
dwell
Upon yourself.
Mont. I'll hazard that ; observe now.

*Belgarde comes out of his house in a gallant
habit ; stays at the door with his sword
drawn.*

Several voices within. Nay, captain! glo-
rions captain !
Belg. Fall back, rascals !
Do you make an owl of me ? this day I will
Receive no more petitions.—
Here are bills of all occasions, and all sizes!
If this be the pleasure of a rich suit, would
I were
Again in my buff jerkin, or my armour !
Then I walk'd securely by my creditors' noses,
Not a dog mark'd me ; every officer shunn'd
me,
And not one lousy prison would receive me :
But now, as the ballad says, *I am turn'd
gallant,*
There does not live that thing I owe a sous to,
But does torment me. A faithful cobler told
me,
With his awl in his hand, I was behindhand
with him
For setting me upright, and bade me look
to myself.
A sempstress too, that traded but in socks,
Swore she would set a serjeant on my back
For a borrow'd shirt : my pay, and the
benevolence
The governor and the states bestow'd upon
me,
The city cormorants, my money-mongers,
Have swallow'd down already ; they were
sums,
I grant,—but that I should be such a fool,
Against my oath, being a cashier'd captain,
To pay debts, though grown up to one and
twenty,
Deserves more reprehension, in my judg-
ment,

Than a shopkeeper, or a lawyer that lends
money,
In a long dead vacation.
Mont. How do you like
His meditation?
Cham. Peace ! let him proceed.
Belg. I cannot now go on the score for
shame,
And where I shall begin to pawn—ay, marry,
That is consider'd timely ! I paid for
This train of yours, dame Estridge, fourteen
crowns,
And yet it is so light, 'twill hardly pass ·
For a tavern reckoning, unless it be,
To save the charge of painting, nail'd on a
post,
For the sign of the feathers. · Pox upon the
fashion,
That a captain cannot think himself a captain,.
If he wear not this, like a fore-horse ! yet it
is not
Staple commodity : these are perfumed too
O' the Roman wash, and yet a stale red
herring
Would fill the belly better, and hurt the head
less :
And this is Venice gold ; would I had it again
In French crowns in my pocket? O you com-
manders,
That, like me, have no dead pays, nor can
cozen
The commissary at a muster, let me stand
For an example to you ! as you would
Enjoy your privileges, *videlicet,.*
To pay your debts, and take your letchery
gratis ;
To have your issue warm'd by others fires ;
To be often drunk, and swear, yet pay no·
forfeit
To the poor, but when you share with one
another ;
With all your other choice immunities :
Only of this I seriously advise you,
Let courtiers trip like courtiers, and your.
lords
Of dirt and dunghills mete their woods and
acres,
In velvets, satins, tissues ; but keep you
Constant to cloth and shamois.
Mont. Have you heard
Of such a penitent homily ?
Belg. I am studying now
Where I shall hide myself till the rumour of
My wealth and bravery vanish : let me see,
There is a kind of vaulting-house not far
off,
Where I used to spend my afternoons, among
Suburb she-gamesters ; and yet, now I think
on't,

I have crack'd a ring or two there, which
 they made
Others to solder : No——

Enter a Bawd, *and two* Courtezans, *with
  two Children.*

1 *Court.* O ! have we spied you !
Bawd. Upon him without ceremony !
 now's the time,
While he's in the paying vein.
2 *Court.* Save you, brave captain !
Beauf. jun. 'Slight, how he stares ! they
 are worse than she-wolves to him.
Belg. Shame me not in the streets ; I was
 coming to you.
1 *Court.* O, sir, you may in public pay
 for the fiddling
You had in private.
 2 *Court.* We hear you are full of crowns,
 sir.
1 *Court.* And therefore, knowing you are
 open-handed,
Before all be destroy'd, I'll put you in mind,
 sir,
Of your young heir here.
 2 *Court.* Here's a second, sir,
That looks for a child's portion.
Bawd. There are reckonings
For muscadine and eggs too, must be
 thought on.
1 *Court.* We have not been hasty, sir.
Bawd. But staid your leisure :
But now you are ripe, and loaden with
 fruit——
 2 *Court.* 'Tis fit you should be pull'd ;
 here's a boy, sir,
Pray you, kiss him ; 'tis your own, sir.
 1 *Court.* Nay, buss this first,
It hath just your eyes ; and such a pro-
 mising nose,
That, if the sign deceive me not, in time
'Twill prove a notable striker, like his father.
Belg. And yet you laid it to another.
1 *Court.* True,
While you were poor ; and it was policy ;
But she that has variety of fathers,
And makes not choice of him that can
 maintain it,
Ne'er studied Aristotle.
Lan. A smart quean !
Belg. Why, braches, will you worry me ?
2 *Court.* No, but ease you
Of your golden burthen ; the heavy carriage
 may
Bring you to a sweating sickness.
Belg. Very likely ;
I foam all o'er already.
 1 *Court.* Will you come off, sir ?

Belg. Would I had ne'er come on ! Hear
 me with patience,
Or I will anger you. Go to, you know me ;
And do not vex me further : by my sins,
And your diseases, which are certain truths,
Whate'er you think, I am not master, at
This instant, of a livre.
 2 *Court.* What, and in
Such a glorious suit !
Belg. The liker, wretched things,
To have no money.
Bawd. You may pawn your clothes, sir.
1 *Court.* Will you see your issue starve ?
2 *Court.* Or the mothers beg ?
Belg. Why, you unconscionable strumpets,
 would you have me,
Transform my hat to double clouts and
 biggins ?
My corslet to a cradle ? or my belt
To swaddlebands ? or turn my cloak to
 blankets ?
Or to sell my sword and spurs, for soap and
 candles ?
Have you no mercy ? what a chargeable devil
We carry in our breeches !
Beauf. jun. Now 'tis time
To fetch him off. [*They come forward.*

Enter Beaufort *senior.*

Mont. Your father does it for us.
Bawd. The governor !
Beauf. sen. What are these ?
1 *Court.* An it like your lordship,
Very poor spinsters.
Bawd. I am his nurse and laundress.
Belg. You have nurs'd and launder'd me,
 hell take you for it !
Vanish !
 Cham. Do, do, and talk with him hereafter.
1 *Court.* 'Tis our best course.
2 *Court.* We'll find a time to fit him.
   [*Exeunt* Bawd *and* Courtezans.
Beauf. sen. Why in this heat, Belgarde ?
Belg. You are the cause of 't.
Beauf. sen. Who, I ?
Belg. Yes, your pied livery and your gold
Draw these vexations on me ; pray you strip
 me,
And let me be as I was : I will not lose
The pleasures and the freedom which I had
In my certain poverty, for all the wealth
Fair France is proud of.
Beauf. sen. We at better leisure
Will learn the cause of this.
Beauf. jun. What answer, sir,
From the admiral ?
Beauf. sen. None ; his daughter is removed
To the fort of Montreville, and he himself
In person fled, but where, is not discover'd :

I could tell you wonders, but the time denies
me
Fit liberty. In a word, let it suffice
The power of our great master is contemn'd,
The sacred laws of God and man profaned ;
And if I sit down with this injury,
I am unworthy of my place, and thou
Of my acknowledgment : draw up all the
troops ;
As I go, I will instruct you to what purpose.
Such as have power to punish, and yet spare,
From fear or from connivance, others ill,
Though not in act, assist them in their will.
[*Exeunt.*

——

ACT V.

SCENE I.—*A Street near* Malefort's *House.*
Enter Montreville *and* Servants, *with* Theocrine, Page, *and* Waiting-women.

Montr. Bind them, and gag their mouths
sure ; I alone
Will be your convoy.
  1 *Wom.* Madam !
  2 *Wom.* Dearest lady !
  Page. Let me fight for my mistress.
  Serv. 'Tis in vain,
Little cockerel of the kind.
  Montr. Away with them,
And do as I command you.
[*Exeunt* Servants *with* Page *and*
Waiting-women.
  Theoc. Montreville,
You are my father's friend ; nay more, a
soldier,
And if a right one, as I hope to find you,
Though in a lawful war you had surprised
A city, that bow'd humbly to your pleasure,
In honour you stand bound to guard a virgin
From violence ; but in a free estate,
Of which you are a limb, to do a wrong
Which noble enemies never consent to,
Is such an insolence——
  Montr. How her heart beats !
Much like a partridge in a sparhawk's foot,
That with a panting silence does lament
The fate she cannot fly from !—Sweet, take
comfort,
You are safe, and nothing is intended to you,
But love and service.
  Theoc. They came never clothed
In force and outrage. Upon what assurance
(Remembering only that my father lives,
Who will not tamely suffer the disgrace,)
Have you presumed to hurry me from his
house,
And, as I were not worth the waiting on,
To snatch me from the duty and attendance
Of my poor servants ?

  Montr. Let not that afflict you,
You shall not want observance ; I will be
Your page, your woman, parasite, or fool,
Or any other property, provided
You answer my affection.
  Theoc. In what kind ?
  Montr. As you had done young Beaufort's.
  Theoc. How !
  Montr. So, lady ;
Or, if the name of wife appear a yoke
Too heavy for your tender neck, so I
Enjoy you as a private friend or mistress,
'Twill be sufficient.
  Theoc. Blessed angels guard me !
What frontless impudence is this? what devil
Hath, to thy certain ruin, tempted thee
To offer me this motion ? by my hopes
Of after joys, submission nor repentance
Shall expiate this foul intent.
  Montr. Intent !
'Tis more, I'll make it act.
  Theoc. Ribald, thou darest not :
And if (and with a fever to thy soul)
Thou but consider that I have a father,
And such a father, as, when this arrives at
His knowledge, as it shall, the terror of
His vengeance, which as sure as fate must
follow,
Will make thee curse the hour in which lust
taught thee
To nourish these bad hopes ;—and 'tis my
wonder
Thou darest forget how tender he is of me,
And that each shadow of wrong done to me,
Will raise in him a tempest not to be
But with thy heart-blood calm'd : this, when
I see him——
  Montr. As thou shalt never.
  Theoc. Wilt thou murder me ?
  Montr. No, no, 'tis otherwise determined,
fool.
The master which in passion kills his slave
That may be useful to him, does himself
The injury : know, thou most wretched
creature,
That father thou presumest upon, that father,
That, when I sought thee in a noble way,
Denied thee to me, fancying in his hope
A higher match, from his excess of dotage,
Hath in his bowels kindled such a flame
Of impious and most unnatural lust,
That now he fears his furious desires
May force him to do that, he shakes to
think on.
  Theoc. O me, most wretched !
  Montr. Never hope again
To blast him with those eyes : their golden
beams
Are unto him arrows of death and hell,

But unto me divine artil'ery.
And therefore, since what I so long in vain
Pursued, is offer'd to me, and by him
Given up to my possession ; do not flatter
Thyself with an imaginary hope,
But that I'll take occasion by the forelock,
And make use of my fortune.   As we walk,
I'll tell thee more.
    Theoc. I will not stir.
    Montr. I'll force thee.
    Theoc. Help, help !
    Montr. In vain.
    Theoc. In me my brother's blood
Is punish'd at the height.
    Montr. The coach there !
    Theoc. Dear sir——
    Montr. Tears, curses, prayers, are alike
to me ;
I can, and must enjoy my present pleasure,
And shall take time to mourn for it at leisure.
                [He bears her off.
   SCENE II.—*A Space before the Fort.*
        Enter Malefort.

I have play'd the fool, the gross fool, to believe
The bosom of a friend will hold a secret,
Mine own could not contain ; and my industry
In taking liberty from my innocent daughter,
Out of false hopes of freedom to myself,
Is, in the little help it yields me, punish'd.
She's absent, but I have her figure here ;
And every grace and rarity about her,
Are by the pencil of my memory,
In living colours painted on my heart.
My fires too, a short interim closed up,
Break out with greater fury.   Why was I,
Since 'twas my fate, and not to be declined,
In this so tender-conscienced ?   Say I had
Enjoy'd what I desired, what had it been
But incest ? and there's something here that
    tells me
I stand accountable for greater sins
I never check'd at.   Neither had the crime
Wanted a precedent : I have read in story,
Those first great heroes, that, for their brave
    deeds,
Were in the world's first infancy styled gods,
Freely enjoy'd what I denied myself.
Old Saturn, in the golden age, embraced
His sister Ops, and, in the same degree,
The Thunderer Juno, Neptune Thetis, and,
By their example, after the first deluge,
Deucalion Pyrrha.   Universal nature,
As every day 'tis evident, allows it
To creatures of all kinds : the gallant horse
Covers the mare to which he was the sire ;
The bird with fertile seed gives new increase
To her that hatch'd him : why should envious
    man then

Brand that close act, which adds proximity
To what's most near him, with the abhorred
    title
Of incest ? or our later laws forbid,
What by the first was granted ?   Let old men,
That are not capable of these delights,
And solemn superstitious fools, prescribe
Rules to themselves ; I will not curb my
    freedom,
But cons'antly go on, with this assurance,
I but walk in a path which greater men
Have trod before me.   Ha ! this is the fort :
Open the gate !   Within, there !
       Enter two Soldiers.
    1 *Sold.* With your pardon
We must forbid your entrance.
    Malef. Do you know me?
    2 *Sold.* Perfectly, my lord.
    Malef. I am [your] captain's friend.
    1 *Sold.* It may be so ; but till we know his
    pleasure,
You must excuse us.
    2 *Sold.* We'll acquaint him with
Your waiting here.
    Malef. Waiting, slave ! he was ever
By me commanded.
    1 *Sold.* As we are by him.
    Malef. So punctual ! pray you then, in
    my name entreat
His presence.
    2 *Sold.* That we shall do. [*Exeunt* Sold.
    Malef. I must use
Some strange persuasions to work him to
Deliver him, and to forget the vows,
And horrid oaths, I, in my madness, made him
Take to the contrary : and may I get her
Once more in my possession, I will bear her
Into some close cave or desert, where we'll end
Our lusts and lives together.
  Enter Montreville *and* Soldiers, *upon the*
           Walls.
    Montr. Fail not, on
The forfeit of your lives, to execute
What I command.   [*Exeunt* Soldiers.
    Malef. Montreville ! how is't friend?
    Montr. I am glad to see you wear such
    cheerful looks ;
The world's well alter'd.
    Malef. Yes, I thank my stars :
But methinks thou art troubled.
    Montr. Some light cross,
But of no moment.
    Malef. So I hope : beware
Of sad and impious thoughts ; you know
    how far
They wrought on me.
    Montr. No such come near me, sir.

I have, like you, no daughter, and much
  wish
You never had been curs'd with one.
  Malef. Who, I?
Thou art deceived, I am most happy in her.
  Montr. I am glad to hear it.
  Malef. My incestuous fires
To'ards her are quite burnt out; I love her
  now
As a father, and no further.
  Montr. Fix there then
Your constant peace, and do not try a second
Temptation from her.
  Malef. Yes, friend, though she were
By millions of degrees more excellent
In her perfections; nay, though she could
  borrow
A form angelical to take my frailty,
It would not do: and therefore, Montre-
  ville,
My chief delight next her, I come to tell
  thee,
The governor and I are reconciled,
And I confirm'd, and with all possible speed,
To make large satisfaction to young Beau-
  fort,
And her, whom I have so much wrong'd;
  and for
Thy trouble in her custody, of which
I'll now discharge thee, there is nothing in
My nerves or fortunes, but shall ever be
At thy devotion.
  Montr. You promise fairly,
Nor doubt I the performance; yet I would
  not
Hereafter be reported to have been
The principal occasion of your falling
Into a relapse: or but suppose, out of
The easiness of my nature, and assurance
You are firm and can hold out, I could con-
  sent;
You needs must know there are so many lets
That make against it, that it is my wonder
You offer me the motion; having bound me,
With oaths and imprecations, on no terms,
Reasons, or arguments, you could propose,
I ever should admit you to her sight,
Much less restore her to you.
  Malef. Are we soldiers,
And stand on oaths!
  Montr. It is beyond my knowledge
In what we are more worthy, than in keeping
Our words, much more our vows.
  Malef. Heaven pardon all!
How many thousands, in our heat of wine,
Quarrels, and play, and in our younger days,
In private I may say, between ourselves,
In points of love, have we to answer for,
Should we be scrupulous that way?

  M ntr. You say well:
And very aptly call to memory
Two oaths, against all ties and rites of
  friendship,
Broken by you to me.
  Malef. No more of that.
  Montr. Yes, 'tis material, and to the pur-
  pose:
The first (and think upon't) was, when I
  brought you
As a visitant to my mistress then, (the mother
Of this same daughter,) whom, with dread-
  ful words,
Too hideous to remember, you swore deeply
For my sake never to attempt; yet then,
Then, when you had a sweet wife of your own,
I know not with what arts, philtres, and
  charms
(Unless in wealth and fame you were above
  me)
You won her from me; and, her grant ob-
  tain'd,
A marriage with the second waited on
The burial of the first, that to the world
Brought your dead son: this I sat tamely
  down by,
Wanting, indeed, occasion and power
To be at the height revenged.
  Malef. Yet this you seem'd
Freely to pardon.
  Montr. As perhaps I did.
Your daughter Theocrine growing ripe,
(Her mother too deceased,) and fit for mar-
  riage,
I was a suitor for her, had your word,
Upon your honour, and our friendship made
Authentical, and ratified with an oath,
She should be mine: but vows with you
  being like
To your religion, a nose of wax
To be turn'd every way, that very day
The governor's son but making his approaches
Of courtship to her, the wind of your ambition
For her advancement, scatter'd the thin sand
In which you wrote your full consent to me,
And drew you to his party. What hath pass'd
  since,
You bear a register in your own bosom,
That can at large inform you.
  Malef. Montreville,
I do confess all that you charge me with
To be strong truth, and that I bring a cause
Most miserably guilty, and acknowledge
That though your goodness made me mine
  own judge,
I should not shew the least compassion
Or mercy to myself. O, let not yet
My foulness taint your pureness, or my false-
  hood

Divert the torrent of your loyal faith !
My ills, if not return'd by you, will add
Lustre to your much good ; and to o'ercome
With noble sufferance, will express your
    strength,
And triumph o'er my weakness. If you
    please too,
My black deeds being only known to you,
And, in surrendering up my daughter, buried,
You not alone make me your slave, (for I
At no part do deserve the name of friend,)
But in your own breast raise a monument
Of pity to a wretch, on whom with justice
You may express all cruelty.
    Montr. You much move me.
    Malef. O that I could but hope it ! To
    revenge
An injury, is proper to the wishes
Of feeble women, that want strength to act it :
But to have power to punish, and yet pardon,
Peculiar to princes. See ! these knees,
                                    [*Kneels.*
That have been ever stiff to bend to heaven,
To you are supple. Is there aught beyond
    this
That may speak my submission? or can pride
(Though I well know it is a stranger to you)
Desire a feast of more humility,
To kill her growing appetite ?
    Montr. I required not
To be sought to this poor way ; yet 'tis so far
A kind of satisfaction, that I will
Dispense a little with those serious oaths
You made me take : your daughter shall
    come to you,
I will not say, as you deliver'd her,
But, as she is, you may dispose of her
As you shall think most requisite.   [*Exit.*
    Malef. His last words
Are riddles to me. Here the lion's force
Would have proved useless, and, against
    my nature,
Compell'd me from the crocodile to borrow
Her counterfeit tears : there's now no turn-
    ing backward.
May I but quench these fires that rage with-
    in me,
And fall what can fall, I am arm'd to bear it !

Enter Soldiers *below, thrusting forth* Theocrine ; *her garments loose, her hair dishe-
velled.*

    2 *Sold.* You must be packing.
    Theoc. Hath he robb'd me of
Mine honour, and denies me now a room
To hide my shame !
    2 *Sold.* My lord the admiral
Attends your ladyship.

    1 *Sold.* Close the port, and leave them.
                            [*Exeunt* Soldiers.
    Malef. Ha ! who is this? how alter'd !
    how deform'd !
It cannot be : and yet this creature has
A kind of a resemblance to my daughter,
My Theocrine ! but as different
From that she was, as bodies dead are, in
Their best perfections, from what they were
When they had life and motion.
    Theoc. 'Tis most true, sir ;
I am dead indeed to all but misery.
O come not near me sir, I am infectious :
To look on me at distance, is as dangerous
As, from a pinnacle's cloud-kissing spire,
With giddy eyes to view the deep descent ;
But to acknowledge me, a certain ruin.
O, sir !
    Malef. Speak, Theocrine, force me not
To further question ; my fears already
Have choked my vital spirits.
    Theoc. Pray you turn away
Your face and hear me, and with my last
    breath
Give me leave to accuse you: What offence,
From my first infancy, did I commit,
That for a punishment you should give up
My virgin chastity to the treacherous guard
Of goatish Montreville ?
    Malef. What hath he done ?
    Theoc. Abused me, sir, by violence ; and
    this told,
I cannot live to speak more : may the cause
In you find pardon, but the speeding curse
Of a ravish'd maid fall heavy, heavy on
    him !—
Beaufort, my lawful love, farewell for ever.
                                    [*Dies.*
    Malef. Take not thy flight so soon, im-
    maculate spirit !
'Tis fled already.—How the innocent,
As in a gentle slumber, pass away !
But to cut off the knotty thread of life
In guilty men, must force stern Atropos
To use her sharp knife often. I would help
The edge of hers with the sharp point of mine,
But that I dare not die, till I have rent
This dog's heart piecemeal. O, that I had
    wings
To scale these walls, or that my hands were
    cannons,
To bore their flinty sides, that I might bring
The villain in the reach of my good sword !
The Turkish empire offer'd for his ransom,
Should not redeem his life. O that my voice
Were loud as thunder, and with horrid sounds
Might force a dreadful passage to his ears,
And through them reach his soul ! Libidinous
    monster !

Foul ravisher ! as thou durst do a deed
Which forced the sun to hide his glorious face
Behind a sable mask of clouds, appear,
And as a man defend it ; or, like me,
Shew some compunction for it.

Enter Montreville *on the Walls, above.*

Montr. Ha, ha, ha !
Malef. Is this an object to raise mirth ?
Montr. Yes, yes.
Malef. My daughter's dead.
Montr. Thou hadst best follow her ;
Or, if thou art the thing thou art reported,
Thou shouldst have led the way.   Do tear
      thy hair,
Like a village nurse, and mourn, while I
      laugh at thee.
Be but a just examiner of thyself,
And in an equal balance poise the nothing,
Or little mischief I have done, compared
With the pond'rous weight of thine : and
      how canst thou
Accuse or argue with me ? mine was a rape,
And she being in a kind contracted to me,
The fact may challenge some qualification :
But thy intent made nature's self run back-
      ward,
And done, had caused an earthquake.

Enter Soldiers *above.*

1 *Sold.* Captain !
Montr. Ha !
2 *Sold.* Our outworks are surprised, the
      sentinel slain,
The corps de guard defeated too.
Montr. By whom ?
1 *Sold.* The sudden storm and darkness
      of the night
Forbids the knowledge ; make up speedily,
Or all is lost.   [*Exeunt.*
Montr. In the devil's name, whence comes
this ?   [*Exit.*
[*A storm ; with thunder and lightning.*
Malef. Do, do rage on ! rend open, Æolus,
Thy brazen prison, and let loose at once
Thy stormy issue ! Blustering Boreas,
Aided with all the gales the pilot numbers
Upon his compass, cannot raise a tempest
Through the vast region of the air, like that
I feel within me : for I am possess'd
With whirlwinds, and each guilty thought
      to me is
A dreadful hurricano.   Though this centre
Labour to bring forth earthquakes, and hell
      open
Her wide-stretch'd jaws, and let out all her
      furies,
They cannot add an atom to the mountain
Of fears and terrors that each minute threaten
To fall on my accursed head.—

Enter the Ghost of young Malefort, *naked
from the waist, full of wounds, leading in
the Shadow of a Lady, her face leprous.*

              Ha ! is't fancy ?
Or hath hell heard me, and makes proof if I
Dare stand the trial ?   Yes, I do ; and now
I view these apparitions, I feel
I once did know the substances.   For what
come you ?
Are your aerial forms deprived of language,
And so denied to tell me, that by signs
      [*The* Ghosts *use various gestures.*
You bid me ask here of myself ?   'Tis so ;
And there is something here makes answer
      for you.
You come to lance my sear'd-up conscience ;
      yes,
And to instruct me, that those thunderbolts,
That hurl'd me headlong from the height of
      glory,
Wealth, honours, worldly happiness, were
      forged
Upon the anvil of my impious wrongs,
And cruelty to you !   I do confess it ;
And that my lust compelling me to make
      way
For a second wife, I poison'd thee ; and that
The cause (which to the world is undis-
      cover'd)
That forced thee to shake off thy filial duty
To me, thy father, had its spring and source
From thy impatience, to know thy mother,
That with all duty and obedience served me,
(For now with horror I acknowledge it,)
Removed unjustly : yet, thou being my son,
Wert not a competent judge mark'd out by
      heaven
For her revenger, which thy falling by
My weaker hand confirm'd.—[*Answered still
by signs.*]—'Tis granted by thee.
Can any penance expiate my guilt,
Or can repentance save me ?—
              [*The* Ghosts *disappear.*
              They are vanish'd !
What's left to do then ?   I'll accuse my fate,
That did not fashion me for nobler uses :
For if those stars, cross to me in my birth,
Had not denied their prosperous influence
      to it,
With peace of conscience, like to innocent
      men,
I might have ceased to be, and not as now,
To curse my cause of being——
      [*He is kill'd with a flash of lightning.*

Enter Belgarde, *with* Soldiers.

Belg. Here's a night
To season my silks !   Buff-jerkin, now I miss
      thee :

Thou hast endured many foul nights, but
  never
One like to this.   How fine my feather looks
  now !
Just like a capon's tail stol'n out of the pen,
And hid in the sink ; and yet 't had been
  dishonour
To have charged without it.—Wilt thou
  never cease ?
Is the petard, as I gave directions, fasten'd
On the portcullis ?
    1 *Sold.* It hath been attempted
By divers, but in vain.
    Belg. These are your gallants,
That at a feast take the first place, poor I
Hardly allow'd to follow ; marry, in
These foolish businesses they are content
That I shall have precedence ; I much thank
Their manners, or their fear.   Second me,
  soldiers ;
They have had no time to undermine, or if
They have, it is but blowing up, and fetching
A caper or two in the air ; and I will do it,
Rather than blow my nails here.
    2 *Sold.* O brave captain !   [*Exeunt.*

*An Alarum ; noise and cries within.   After
  a flourish, enter* Beaufort *senior,* Beaufort
  junior, Montaigne, Chamont, Lanour,
  Belgarde, *and* Soldiers, *with* Montreville
  prisoner.

    Montr. Racks cannot force more from me
  than I have

Already told you : I expect no favour ;
I have cast up my accompt.
    Beauf. sen. Take you the charge
Of the fort, Belgarde ; your dangers have
  deserved it.
    Belg. I thank your excellence : this will
  keep me safe yet
From being pull'd by the sleeve, and bid
  remember
The thing I wot of.
    Beauf. jun. All that have eyes to weep,
Spare one tear with me.   Theocrine's
  dead.
    Mont. Her father too lies breathless here,
  I think
Struck dead with thunder.
    Cham. 'Tis apparent : how
His carcass smells !
    Lan. His face is alter'd to
Another colour.
    Beauf. jun. But here's one retains
Her native innocence, that never yet
Call'd down heaven's anger.
    Beauf. sen. 'Tis in vain to mourn
For what's past help.—We will refer, bad
  man,
Your sentence to the king.   May we make
  use of
This great example, and learn from it,
  that
There cannot be a want of power above,
To punish murder, and unlawful love !
                                [*Exeunt.*

The Duke of Milan.

***

DRAMATIS PERSONÆ.

Ludovico Sforza, *supposed duke of* Milan.
Francisco, *his especial favourite.*
Tiberio, } *lords of his council.*
Stephano, }
Graccho, *a creature of* Mariana.
Julio, } *courtiers.*
Giovanni, }
Charles, *the Emperor.*
Pescara, *an imperialist, but a friend to* Sforza.
Hernando, }
Medina, } *captains to the Emperor.*
Alphonso, }

Three Gentlemen.
Fiddlers.
An Officer.
Two Doctors.   Two Couriers.
Marcelia, *the dutchess, wife to* Sforza.
Isabella, *mother to* Sforza.
Mariana, *wife to* Francisco, *and sister to* Sforza.
Eugenia, *sister to* Francisco.
A Gentlewoman.
Guards, Servants, Attendants.

SCENE,—*for the first and second acts, in* Milan ; *during part of the third, in the* Imperial Camp *near* Pavia ; *the rest of the play, in* Milan, *and its neighbourhood.*

ACT I.

SCENE I.—Milan.   *An outer Room in the Castle.*

Enter Graccho, Julio, *and* Giovanni, *with Flaggons.*

Grac. Take every man his flaggon : give the oath
To all you meet ; I am this day the state-drunkard,
I am sure against my will ; and if you find
A man at ten that's sober, he's a traitor,
And, in my name, arrest him.
   Jul. Very good, sir :
But, say he be a sexton?
   Grac. If the bells
Ring out of tune, as if the street were burning,
And he cry, '*Tis rare music !* bid him sleep :
'Tis a sign he has ta'en his liquor ; and if you meet
An officer preaching of sobriety,
Unless he read it in Geneva print,
Lay him by the heels.
   Jul. But think you 'tis a fault
To be found sober?
   Grac. It is capital treason :
Or, if you mitigate it, let such pay
Forty crowns to the poor : but give a pension
To all the magistrates you find singing catches,
Or their wives dancing ; for the courtiers reeling,

And the duke himself, I dare not say dis-temper'd,
But kind, and in his tottering chair carousing,
They do the country service. If you meet
One that eats bread, a child of ignorance,
And bred up in the darkness of no drinking,
Against his will you may initiate him
In the true posture ; though he die in the taking
His drench, it skills not : what's a private man,
For the public honour !   We've nought else to think on.
And so, dear friends, copartners in my travails,
Drink hard ; and let the health run through the city,
Until it reel again, and with me cry,
Long live the dutchess !

Enter Tiberio *and* Stephano.

   Jul. Here are two lords ;—what think you?
Shall we give the oath to them ?
   Grac. Fie ! no : I know them,
You need not swear them ; your lord, by his patent,
Stands bound to take his rouse.   Long live the dutchess !
   [*Exeunt* Grac. Jul. *and* Gio.
   Steph. The cause of this? but yesterday the court
Wore the sad livery of distrust and fear ;
No smile, not in a buffoon to be seen,
Or common jester : the Great Duke himself

F

Had sorrow in his face ! which, waited on
By his mother, sister, and his fairest dutchess,
Dispersed a silent mourning through all
    Milan ;
As if some great blow had been given the
    state,
Or were at least expected.
    Tib. Stephano,
I know as you are noble, you are honest,
And capable of secrets of more weight
Than now I shall deliver.   If that Sforza,
The present duke, (though his whole life
    hath been
But one continued pilgrimage through
  . dangers,
Affrights, and horrors, which his fortune,
    guided   .
By his strong judgment, still hath overcome,)
Appears now shaken, it deserves no wonder :
All that his youth hath labour'd for, the
    harvest
Sown by his industry ready to be reap'd too,
Being now at stake ; and all his hopes con-
    firm'd,
Or lost for ever.
    Steph. I know no such hazard :
His guards are strong and sure, his coffers
    full ;
The people well affected ; and so wisely
His provident care hath wrought, that
    though war rages
In most parts of our western world, there is
No enemy near us.
    Tib. Dangers, that we see
To threaten ruin, are with ease prevented ;
But those strike deadly, that come unex-
    pected :
The lightning is far off, yet, soon as seen,
We may behold the terrible effects
That it produceth.   But I'll help your know-
    ledge,
And make his cause of fear familiar to you.
The wars so long continued between
The emperor Charles, and Francis the
    French king, ·
Have interess'd, in either's cause, the most
Of the Italian princes ; among which, Sforza,
As one of greatest power, was sought by
    both ;
But with assurance, having one his friend,
The other lived his enemy.
    Steph. 'Tis true :
And 'twas a doubtful choice.
    Tib. But he, well knowing,
And hating too, it seems, the Spanish pride,
Lent his assistance to the king of France :
Which hath so far incensed the emperor,
That all his hopes and honours are embark'd
With his great patron's fortune.

    Steph. Which stands fair,
For aught I yet can hear.
    Tib. But should it change,
The duke's undone.   They have drawn to
    the field
Two royal armies, full of fiery youth ;
Of equal spirit to dare, and power to do :
So near intrench'd, that 'tis beyond all hope
Of human counsel they can e'er be severed,
Until it be determined by the sword,
Who hath the better cause : for the success,
Concludes the victor innocent, and the van-
    quish'd
Most miserably guilty.   How uncertain
The fortune of the war is, children know ;
And, it being in suspense, on whose fair tent
Wing'd Victory will make her glorious stand,
You cannot blame the duke, though he
    appear
Perplex'd and troubled.
    Steph. But why, then,
In such a time, when every knee should bend
For the success and safety of his person,
Are these loud triumphs? in my weak opinion,
They are unseasonable.
    Tib. I judge so too ;
But only in the cause to be excused.
It is the dutchess' birthday, once a year
Solemnized with all pomp and ceremony ;
In which the duke is not his own, but hers :
Nay, every day, indeed, he is her creature,
For never man so doated ;—but to tell
The tenth part of his fondness to a stranger
Would argue me of fiction.
    Steph. She's, indeed,
A lady of most exquisite form.
    Tib. She knows it,
And how to prize it.
    Steph. I ne'er heard her tainted
In any point of honour.
    Tib. On my life,
She's constant to his bed, and well deserves
His largest favours.   But, when beauty is
Stamp'd on great women, great in birth and
    fortune,
And blown by flatterers greater than it is
'Tis seldom unaccompanied with pride ;
Nor is she that way free : presuming on
The duke's affection, and her own desert,
She bears herself with such a majesty,
Looking with scorn on all as things beneath
    her,
That Sforza's mother, that would lose no
    part
Of what was once her own, nor his fair sister,
A lady too acquainted with her worth,
Will brook it well ; and howsoe'er their hate
Is smother'd for a time, 'tis more than fear'd
It will at length break out.

Steph. He in whose power it is,
Turn all to the best!
Tib. Come, let us to the court;
We there shall see all bravery and cost,
That art can boast of.
Steph. I'll bear you company.
[*Exeunt.*

SCENE II.—*Another Room in the same.*

Enter Francisco, Isabella, *and* Mariana.

Mari. I will not go; I scorn to be a spot
In her proud train.
Isab. Shall I, that am his mother,
Be so indulgent, as to wait on her
That owes me duty?
Fran. 'Tis done to the duke,
And not to her: and, my sweet wife, re-
member,
And, madam, if you please, receive my
counsel,
As Sforza is your son, you may command
him;
And, as a sister, you may challenge from
him
A brother's love and favour: but, this
granted,
Consider he's the prince, and you his sub-
jects,
And not to question or contend with her
Whom he is pleased to honour. Private
men
Prefer their wives; and shall he, being a
prince,
And blest with one that is the paradise
Of sweetness and of beauty, to whose charge
The stock of women's goodness is given up,
Not use her like herself?
Isab. You are ever forward
To sing her praises.
Mari. Others are as fair;
I am sure, as noble.
Fran. I detract from none,
In giving her what's due. Were she deform'd,
Yet being the dutchess, I stand bound to
serve her;
But, as she is, to admire her. Never wife
Met with a purer heat her husband's fervour;
A happy pair, one in the other blest!
She confident in herself he's wholly hers,
And cannot seek for change; and he secure,
That 'tis not in the power of man to tempt her.
And therefore to contest with her, that is
The stronger and the better part of him,
Is more than folly: you know him of a nature
Not to be played with; and, should you forget
To obey him as your prince, he'll not re-
member
The duty that he owes you.

Isab. 'Tis but truth:
Come, clear our brows, and let us to the
banquet;
But not to serve his idol.
Mari. I shall do
What may become the sister of a prince;
But will not stoop beneath it.
Fran. Yet, be wise;
Soar not too high, to fall; but stoop to rise.
[*Exeunt.*

SCENE III.—*A State Room in the same.*

Enter three Gentlemen, *setting forth a
banquet.*

1 *Gent.* Quick, quick, for love's sake! let
the court put on
Her choicest outside: cost and bravery
Be only thought of.
2 *Gent.* All that may be had
To please the eye, the ear, taste, touch, or
smell,
Are carefully provided.
3 *Gent.* There's a masque:
Have you heard what's the invention?
1 *Gent.* No matter:
It is intended for the dutchess' honour;
And if it give her glorious attributes,
As the most fair, most virtuous, and the rest,
'Twill please the duke [*Loud music*]. They
come.
3 *Gent.* All is in order.

Flourish. Enter Tiberio, Stephano, Francisco, Sforza, Marcelia, Isabella, Mariana,
and Attendants.

Sfor. You are the mistress of the feast—
sit here,
O my soul's comfort! and when Sforza bows
Thus low to do you honour, let none think
The meanest service they can pay my love,
But as a fair addition to those titles
They stand possest of. Let me glory in
My happiness, and mighty kings look pale
With envy, while I triumph in mine own.
O mother, look on her! sister, admire her!
And, since this present age yields not a
woman
Worthy to be her second, borrow of
Times past, and let imagination help,
Of those canonized ladies Sparta boasts of,
And, in her greatness, Rome was proud to
owe,
To fashion one; yet still you must confess,
The phœnix of perfection ne'er was seen,
But in my fair Marcelia.
Fran. She's, indeed,
The wonder of all times.
Tib. Your excellence,

Though I confess, you give her but her own,
Forces her modesty to the defence
Of a sweet blush.
   Sfor. It need not, my Marcelia;
When most I strive to praise thee, I appear
A poor detractor : for thou art, indeed,
So absolute in body and in mind,
That, but to speak the least part to the height,
Would ask an angel's tongue, and yet then end
In silent admiration !
   Isab. You still court her,
As if she were a mistress, not your wife.
   Sfor. A mistress, mother ! she is more to me,
And every day deserves more to be sued to.
Such as are cloy'd with those they have embraced,
May think their wooing done : no night to me
But is a bridal one, where Hymen lights
His torches fresh and new ; and those delights,
Which are not to be clothed in airy sounds,
Enjoy'd, beget desires as full of heat,
And jovial fervour, as when first I tasted
Her virgin fruit.—Blest night ! and be it number'd
Amongst those happy ones, in which a blessing
Was, by the full consent of all the stars,
Conferr'd upon mankind.
   Marc. My worthiest lord !
The only object I behold with pleasure,—
My pride, my glory, in a word, my all !
Bear witness, heaven, that I esteem myself
In nothing worthy of the meanest praise
You can bestow, unless it be in this,
That in my heart I love and honour you.
And, but that it would smell of arrogance,
To speak my strong desire and zeal to serve you,
I then could say, these eyes yet never saw
The rising sun, but that my vows and prayers
Were sent to heaven for the prosperity
And safety of my lord : nor have I ever
Had other study, but how to appear
Worthy your favour ; and that my embraces
Might yield a fruitful harvest of content
For all your noble travail, in the purchase
Of her that's still your servant : By these lips,
Which, pardon me, that I presume to kiss——
   Sfor. O swear, for ever swear !
   Marc. I ne'er will seek
Delight but in your pleasure : and desire,
When you are sated with all earthly glories,

And age and honours make you fit for heaven,
That one grave may receive us.
   Sfor. 'Tis believed,
Believed, my blest one.
   Mari. How she winds herself
Into his soul !
   Sfor. Sit all.—Let others feed
On those gross cates, while Sforza banquets with
Immortal viands ta'en in at his eyes.
I could live ever thus.—[Command the eunuch
To sing the ditty that I last composed,

        Enter a Courier.

In praise of my Marcelia.——From whence ?
   Cour. From Pavia, my dread lord.
   Sfor. Speak, is all lost ?
   Cour. [*Delivers a letter.*] The letter will inform you.   [*Exit.*
   Fran. How his hand shakes,
As he receives it !
   Mari. This is some allay
To his hot passion.
   Sfor. Though it bring death, I'll read it :

May it please your excellence to under-
stand, that the very hour I wrote this, I
heard a bold defiance delivered by a herald
from the emperor, which was cheerfully re-
ceived by the king of France. The battailes
being ready to join, and the vanguard com-
mitted to my charge, enforces me to end
abruptly.
     Your Highness's humble servant.
                GASPERO.

Ready to join !—By this, then, I am nothing,
Or my estate secure.   [*Aside.*
   Marc. My lord.
   Sfor. To doubt,
Is worse than to have lost ; and to despair,
Is but to antedate those miseries
That must fall on us ; all my hopes depending
Upon this battle's fortune. In my soul,
Methinks, there should be that imperious power,
By supernatural, not usual means,
T' inform me what I am. The cause consider'd,
Why should I fear ? The French are bold and strong,
Their numbers full, and in their councils wise ;
But then, the haughty Spaniard is all fire,
Hot in his executions ; fortunate
In his attempts ; married to victory :—
Ay, there it is that shakes me.   [*Aside.*
   Fran. Excellent lady,
This day was dedicated to your honour ;

One gale of your sweet breath will easily
Disperse these clouds; and, but yourself, there's none
That dare speak to him.
Marc. I will run the hazard.—
My lord!
    Sfor. Ha!—pardon me, Marcelia, I am troubled;
And stand uncertain, whether I am master
Of aught that's worth the owning.
    Marc. I am yours, sir;
And I have heard you swear, I being safe,
There was no loss could move you. This day, sir,
Is by your gift made mine. Can you revoke
A grant made to Marcelia? your Marcelia?—
For whose love, nay, whose honour, gentle sir,
All deep designs, and state-affairs deferr'd,
Be, as you purposed, merry.
    Sfor. Out of my sight!
      [*Throws away the letter.*
And all thoughts that may strangle mirth forsake me.
Fall what can fall, I dare the worst of fate:
Though the foundation of the earth should shrink,
The glorious eye of heaven lose his splendour,
Supported thus, I'll stand upon the ruins,
And seek for new life here. Why are you sad?
No other sports! by heaven, he's not my friend,
That wears one furrow in his face. I was told
There was a masque.
    Fran. They wait your highness' pleasure,
And when you please to have it.
    Sfor. Bid them enter:
Come, make me happy once again. I am rapt—
'Tis not to-day, to-morrow, or the next,
But all my days, and years, shall be employ'd
To do thee honour.
    Marc. And my life to serve you.
      [*A horn without.*
    Sfor. Another post! Go hang him, hang him, I say;
I will not interrupt my present pleasures,
Although his message should import my head:
Hang him, I say.
    Marc. Nay, good sir, I am pleased
To grant a little intermission to you;
Who knows but he brings news we wish to hear,
To heighten our delights.
    Sfor. As wise as fair!

Enter another Courier.

From Gaspero?
    Cour. That was, my lord.
    Sfor. How! dead?
    Cour. [*Delivers a letter.*] With the delivery of this, and prayers,
To guard your excellency from certain dangers,
He ceased to be a man.   [*Exit.*
    Sfor. All that my fears
Could fashion to me, or my enemies wish,
Is fallen upon me.—Silence that harsh music;
'Tis now unseasonable: a tolling bell,
As a sad harbinger to tell me, that
This pamper'd lump of flesh must feast the worms,
Is fitter for me:—I am sick.
    Marc. My lord!
    Sfor. Sick to the death, Marcelia. Remove
These signs of mirth; they were ominous, and but usher'd
Sorrow and ruin.
    Marc. Bless us, heaven!
    Isab. My son.
    Marc. What sudden change is this?
    Sfor. All leave the room;
I'll bear alone the burden of my grief,
And must admit no partner. I am yet
Your prince, where's your obedience?—Stay, Marcelia;
I cannot be so greedy of a sorrow,
In which you must not share.
    [*Exeunt* Tiberio, Stephano, Francisco, Isabella, Mariana, *and* Attendants.
    Marc. And cheerfully
I will sustain my part. Why look you pale?
Where is that wonted constancy and courage,
That dared the worst of fortune? where is Sforza,
To whom all dangers that fright common men,
Appear'd but panic terrors? why do you eye me
With such fix'd looks? Love, counsel, duty, service,
May flow from me, not danger.
    Sfor. O, Marcelia!
It is for thee I fear; for thee, thy Sforza
Shakes like a coward: for myself, unmoved,
I could have heard my troops were cut in pieces,
My general slain, and he, on whom my hopes
Of rule, of state, of life, had their dependence,
The king of France, my greatest friend, made prisoner
To so proud enemies.

Marc. Then you have just cause
To shew you are a man.
    Sfor. All this were nothing,
Though I add to it, that I am assured,
For giving aid to this unfortunate king,
The emperor, incens'd, lays his command
On his victorious army, flesh'd with spoil,
And bold of conquest, to march up against
    me,
And seize on my estates : suppose that done
    too,
The city ta'en, the kennels running blood,
The ransack'd temples falling on their saints :
My mother, in my sight, toss'd on their pikes,
And sister ravish'd ; and myself bound fast
In chains, to grace their triumph ; or what
    else
An enemy's insolence could load me with,
I would be Sforza still.   But, when I think
That my Marcelia, to whom all these
Are but as atoms to the greatest hill,
Must suffer in my cause, and for me suffer !
All earthly torments, nay, even those the
    damn'd
Howl for in hell, are gentle strokes, .com-
    pared
To what I feel, Marcelia.
    'Marc. Good sir, have patience :
I can as well partake your adverse fortune,
As I thus long have had an ample share
In your prosperity.   'Tis not in the power
Of fate to alter me ; for while I am,
In spite of it, I'm yours.
    Sfor. But should that will
To be so [be] forced, Marcelia ; and I live
To see those eyes I prize above my own,
Dart favours, though compell'd, upon an-
    other ;
Or those sweet lips, yielding immortal nectar,
Be gently touch'd by any but myself ;
Think, think, Marcelia, what a cursed thing
I were, beyond expression !
    Marc. Do not feed
Those jealous thoughts ; the only blessing
    that
Heaven hath bestow'd on us, more than on
    beasts,
Is, that 'tis in our pleasure when to die.
Besides, were I now in another's power,
There are so many ways to let out life,
I would not live, for one short minute, his ;
I was born only yours, and I will die so.
    Sfor. Angels reward the goodness of this
    woman !

            Enter Francisco.

All I can pay is nothing.—Why, uncall'd
    for ?

    Fran. It is of weight, sir, that makes me
        thus press
Upon your privacies. Your constant friend,
The marquis of Pescara, tired with haste,
Hath business that concerns your life and
    fortunes,
And with speed, to impart.
    Sfor. Wait on him hither.
                    [*Exit* Francisco.
And, dearest, to thy closet. Let thy prayers
Assist my councils.
    Marc. To spare imprecations
Against myself, without you I am nothing.
                            [*Exit.*
    Sfor. The marquis of Pescara ! a great
    soldier ;
And, though he serv'd upon the adverse
    party,
Ever my constant friend.

        Re-enter Francisco *with* Pescara.

    Fran. Yonder he walks,
Full of sad thoughts.
    Pesc. Blame him not, good Francisco,
He hath much cause to grieve ; would I
    might end so,
And not add this,—to fear !
    Sfor. My dear Pescara ;
A miracle in these times ! a friend, and
    happy,
Cleaves to a falling fortune !
    Pesc. If it were
As well in my weak power, in act, to raise it,
As 'tis to bear a part of sorrow with you,
You then should have just cause to say,
    Pescara
Look'd not upon your state, but on your
    virtues,
When he made suit to be writ in the list
Of those you favour'd.——But my haste for-
    bids
All compliment ; thus, then, sir, to the pur-
    pose :
The cause that, unattended, brought me
    hither,
Was not to tell you of your loss, or danger;
For fame hath many wings to bring ill
    tidings,
And I presume you've heard it ; but to give
    you
Such friendly counsel, as, perhaps, may make
Your sad disaster less.
    Sfor. You are all goodness ;
And I give up myself to be disposed of,
As in your wisdom you think fit.
    Pesc. Thus, then, sir :
To hope you can hold out against the em-
    peror,
Were flattery in yourself, to your undoing :

Therefore, the safest course that you can
  take,
Is, to give up yourself to his discretion,
Before you be compell'd ; for, rest assured,
A voluntary yielding may find grace,
And will admit defence, at least, excuse :
But, should you linger doubtful, till his
  powers
Have seized your person and estates perforce,
You must expect extremes.
    Sfor. I understand you ;
And I will put your counsel into act,
And speedily. I only will take order
For some domestical affairs, that do
Concern me nearly, and with the next sun
Ride with you : in the mean time, my best
  friend,
Pray take your rest.
    Pesc. Indeed, I have travell'd hard ;
And will embrace your counsel.   [*Exit.*
    Sfor. With all care,
Attend my noble friend. Stay you, Francisco.
You see how things stand with me ?
    Fran. To my grief :
And if the loss of my poor life could be
A sacrifice to restore them as they were,
I willingly would lay it down.
    Sfor. I think so ;
For I have ever found you true and thank-
  ful,
Which makes me love the building I have
  raised
In your advancement; and repent no grace
I have conferr'd upon you. And, believe me,
Though now I should repeat my favours to
  you,
The titles I have given you, and the means
Suitable to your honours ; that I thought you
Worthy my sister and my family,
And in my dukedom made you next myself;
It is not to upbraid you ; but to tell you
I find you are worthy of them, in your love
And service to me.
    Fran. Sir, I am your creature ;
And any shape, that you would have me
  wear,
I gladly will put on.
    Sfor. Thus, then, Francisco :
I now am to deliver to your trust
A weighty secret ; of so strange a nature,
And 'twill, I know, appear so monstrous to
  you,
That you will tremble in the execution,
As much as I am tortured to command it :
For 'tis a deed so horrid, that, but to hear it,
Would strike into a ruffian flesh'd in mur-
  ders,
Or an obdurate hangman, soft compassion ;
And yet, Francisco, of all men the dearest,

And from me most deserving, such my state
And strange condition is, that thou alone
Must know the fatal service, and perform it.
    Fran. These preparations, sir, to work a
  stranger,
Or to one unacquainted with your bounties,
Might appear useful ; but to me they are
Needless impertinencies : for I dare do
Whate'er you dare command.
    Sfor. But you must swear it ;
And put into the oath all joys or torments
That fright the wicked, or confirm the good ;
Not to conceal it only, that is nothing,
But, whensoe'er my will shall speak, Strike
  now !
To fall upou't like thunder.
    Fran. Minister
The oath in any way or form you please,
I stand resolved to take it.
    Sfor. Thou must do, then,
What no malevolent star will dare to look
  on,
It is so wicked : for which men will curse
  thee
For being the instrument ; and the blest
  angels
Forsake me at my need, for being the au-
  thor :
For 'tis a deed of night, of night, Francisco !
In which the memory of all good actions
We can pretend to, shall be buried quick :
Or, if we be remember'd, it shall be
To fright posterity by our example,
That have outgone all precedents of villains
That were before us ; and such as succeed,
Though taught in hell's black school, shall
  ne'er come near us.—
Art thou not shaken yet?
    Fran. I grant you move me :
But to a man confirm'd——
    Sfor. I'll try your temper :
What think you of my wife ?
    Fran. As a thing sacred ;
To whose fair name and memory I pay
  gladly
These signs of duty.
    Sfor. Is she not the abstract
Of all that's rare, or to be wish'd in woman ?
    Fran. It were a kind of blasphemy to
  dispute it :
But to the purpose, sir.
    Sfor. Add too, her goodness,
Her tenderness of me, her care to please me,
Her unsuspected chastity, ne'er equall'd ;
Her innocence, her honour :—O, I am lost
In the ocean of her virtues and her graces,
When I think of them !
    Fran. Now I find the end
Of all your conjurations; there's some service

To be done for this sweet lady. If she have
enemies,
That she would have removed——
Sfor. Alas! Francisco,
Her greatest enemy is her greatest lover ;
Yet, in that hatred, her idolater.
One smile of hers would make a savage
tame ;
One accent of that tongue would calm the
seas,
Though all the winds at once strove there
for empire.
Yet I, for whom she thinks all this too little,
Should I miscarry in this present journey,
From whence it is all number to a cipher,
I ne'er return with honour, by thy hand
Must have her murder'd.
Fran. Murder'd !—She that loves so,
And so deserves to be beloved again !
And I, who sometimes you were pleased to
favour,
Pick'd out the instrument !
Sfor. Do not fly off :
What is decreed can never be recall'd ;
'Tis more than love to her, that marks her
out
A wish'd companion to me in both fortunes :
And strong assurance of thy zealous faith,
That gives up to thy trust a secret, that
Racks should not have forced from me. O,
Francisco !
There is no heaven without her ; nor a hell,
Where she resides. I ask from her but justice,
And what I would have paid to her, had
sickness,
Or any other accident, divorced
Her purer soul from her unspotted body.
The slavish Indian princes, when they die,
Are cheerfully attended to the fire,
By the wife and slave that, living, they loved
best,
To do them service in another world :
Nor will I be less honour'd, that love more.
And therefore trifle not, but, in thy looks,
Express a ready purpose to perform
What I command ; or, by Marcelia's soul,
This is thy latest minute.
Fran. 'Tis not fear
Of death, but love to you, makes me em-
brace it ;
But for mine own security, when 'tis done,
What warrant have I? If you please to sign
one,
I shall, though with unwillingness and horror,
Perform your dreadful charge.
Sfor. I will, Francisco :
But still remember, that a prince's secrets
Are balm conceal'd ; but poison, if dis-
cover'd.

I may come back ; then this is but a trial
To purchase thee, if it were possible,
A nearer place in my affection :—but
I know thee honest.
Fran. 'Tis a character
I will not part with.
Sfor. I may live to reward it. [*Exeunt.*

———

. ACT II.

SCENE I.—*The same. An open space
before the Castle.*

Enter Tiberio *and* Stephano.

Steph. How ! left the court?
Tib. Without guard or retinue
Fitting a prince.
Steph. No enemy near, to force him
To leave his own strengths, yet deliver up
Himself, as 'twere, in bonds, to the discretion
Of him that hates him ! 'tis beyond example.
You never heard the motives that induced
him
To this strange course?
Tib. No, those are cabinet councils,
And not to be communicated, but
To such as are his own, and sure. Alas !
We fill up empty places, and in public
Are taught to give our suffrages to that
Which was before determined ; and are
safe so.
Signior Francisco (upon whom alone
His absolute power is, with all strength, con-
ferr'd,
During his absence) can with ease resolve
you :
To me they are riddles.
Steph. Well, he shall not be
My Œdipus ; I'll rather dwell in darkness.
But, my good lord Tiberio, this Francisco
Is, on the sudden, strangely raised.
Tib. O sir,
He took the thriving course ; he had a sister,
A fair one too, with whom, as it is rumour'd,
The duke was too familiar ; but she, cast off,
(What promises soever past between them,)
Upon the sight of this, forsook the court,
And since was never seen. To smother this,
As honours never fail to purchase silence,
Francisco first was graced, and, step by step,
Is raised up to this height.
Steph. But how is
His absence born?
Tib. Sadly, it seems, by the dutchess ;
For since he left the court,
For the most part she hath kept her private
chamber,
No visitants admitted. In the church.
She hath been seen to pay her pure devotions,

Season'd with tears ; and sure her sorrow's
    true,
Or deeply counterfeited ; pomp, and state,
And bravery cast off : and she, that lately
Rivall'd Poppæa in her varied shapes,
Or the Egyptian queen, now, widow-like,
In sable colours, as her husband's dangers
Strangled in her the use of any pleasure,
Mourns for his absence.
    Steph. It becomes her virtue,
And does confirm what was reported of her.
    Tib. You take it right ; but, on the other
    side.
The darling of his mother, Mariana,
As there were an antipathy between
Her and the dutchess' passions ; and as
She'd no dependence on her brother's for-
    tune,
She ne'er appear'd so full of mirth.
    Steph. 'Tis strange.

Enter Graccho *with* Fiddlers.

But see ! her favourite, and accompanied,
To your report.
    Grac. You shall scrape, and I will sing
A scurvy ditty to a scurvy tune,
Repine who dares.
    1 *Fid.* But if we should offend,
The dutchess having silenced us ; and these
    lords
Stand by to hear us.—
    Grac. They in name are lords
But I am one in power : and, for the dutchess,
But yesterday we were merry for her pleasure,
We now 'll be for my lady's.
    Tib. Signior Graccho.
    Grac. A poor man, sir, a servant to the
    princess ;
But you, great lords and counsellors of state,
Whom I stand bound to reverence.
    Tib. Come ; we know
You are a man in grace.
    Grac. Fie ! no : I grant,
I bear my fortunes patiently ; serve the
    princess,
And have access at all times to her closet,
Such is my impudence ! when your grave
    lordships
Are masters of the modesty to attend
Three hours, nay sometimes four ; and then
    bid wait
Upon her the next morning.
    Steph. He derides us.
    Tib. Pray you, what news is stirring?
    you know all.
    Grac. Who, I ? alas ! I've no intelligence
At home nor abroad ; I only sometimes guess
The change of the times : I should ask of
    your lordships,

Who are to keep their honours, who to lose
    them ;
Who the dutchess smiled on last, or on
    whom frown'd,
You only can resolve me ; we poor waiters
Deal, as you see, in mirth, and foolish fiddles :
It is our element ; and—could you tell me
What point of state 'tis that I am commanded
To muster up this music, on mine honesty,
You should much befriend me.
    Steph. Sirrah, you grow saucy.
    Tib. And would be laid by the heels.
    Grac. Not by your lordships,
Without a special warrant ; look to your
    own stakes ;
Were I committed, here come those would
    bail me :
Perhaps, we might change places too.

Enter Isabella, *and* Mariana ; Graccho
    whispers the latter.

    Tib. The princess !
We must be patient.
    Steph. There is no contending.
    Tib. See, the informing rogue !
    Steph. That we should stoop
To such a mushroom !
    Mari. Thou dost mistake ; they durst not
Use the least word of scorn, although pro-
    voked,
To anything of mine.—Go, get you home,
And to your servants, friends, and flatterers,
    number
How many descents you're noble :—look to
    your wives too ;
The smooth-chinned courtiers are abroad.
    Tib. No way to be a freeman !
        [*Exeunt* Tiberio *and* Stephano.
    Grac. Your Excellence hath the best gift
    to dispatch
These arras pictures of nobility,
I ever read of.
    Mari. I can speak sometimes.
    Grac. And cover so your bitter pills with
    sweetness
Of princely language to forbid reply,
They are greedily swallow'd.
    Isab. But the purpose, daughter,
That brings us hither? Is it to bestow
A visit on this woman, that, because
She only would be thought truly to grieve
The absence and the dangers of my son,
Proclaims a general sadness ?
    Mari. If to vex her
May be interpreted to do her honour,
She shall have many of them. I'll make use
Of my short reign : my lord now governs all ;
And she shall know that her idolater,

My brother, being not by now to protect her,
I am her equal.

Grac. Of a little thing,
It is so full of gall! A devil of this size,
Should they run for a wager to be spiteful,
Gets not a horse-head of her.   [*Aside.*

Mari. On her birthday,
We were forced to be merry, and now she's
   musty,
We must be sad, on pain of her displeasure :
We will, we will! this is her private chamber,
Where, like an hypocrite, not a true turtle,
She seems to mourn her absent mate ; her
   servants
Attending her like mutes : but I'll speak to
   her,
And in a high key too.—Play anything
That's light and loud enough but to torment
   her,
And we will have rare sport.
             [*Music and a song.*

Marcelia *appears at a window above, in
   black.*

Isab. She frowns as if
Her looks could fright us.

Mari. May it please your greatness,
We heard that your late physic hath not
   work'd ;
And that breeds melancholy, as your doctor
   tells us :
To purge which, we, that are born your
   highness' vassals,
And are to play the fool to do you service,
Present you with a fit of mirth. What think
   you
Of a new antic?

Isab. 'Twould shew rare in ladies. .

Mari. Being intended for so sweet a
   creature,
Were she but pleased to grace it.

Isab. Fie ! she will,
Be it ne'er so mean ; she's made of courtesy.

Mari. The mistress of all hearts. One
   smile, I pray you,
On your poor servants, or a fiddler's fee ;
Coming from those fair hands, though but a
   ducat,
We will enshrine it as a holy relic.

Isab. 'Tis wormwood, and it works.

Marc. If I lay by
My fears and griefs, in which you should be
   sharers,
If doting age could let you but remember,
You have a son ; or frontless impudence,
You are a sister ; and, in making answer
To what was most unfit for you to speak,
Or me to hear, borrow of my just anger——

Isab. A set speech, on my life.

Mari. Penn'd by her chaplain.

Marc. Yes, it can speak, without instruction speak,
And tell your want of manners, that you are
   rude,
And saucily rude, too.

Grac. Now the game begins.

Marc. You durst not, else, on any hire or
   hope,
Remembering what I am, and whose I am,
Put on the desperate boldness, to disturb
The least of my retirements.

Mari. Note her, now.

Marc. For both shall understand, though
   the one presume
Upon the privilege due to a mother,
The duke stands now on his own legs, and
   needs
No nurse to lead him.

Isab. How, a nurse !

Marc. A dry one,
And useless too :—but I am merciful,
And dotage signs your pardon.

Isab. I defy thee ;
Thee, and thy pardons, proud one !

Marc. For you, puppet——

Mari. What of me, pine-tree?

Marc. Little you are, I grant,
And have as little worth, but much less wit ;
You durst not else, the duke being wholly
   mine,
His power and honour mine, and the alle-
   giance,
You owe him as a subject, due to me——

Mari. To you ?

Marc. To me : and therefore, as a vassal,
From this hour learn to serve me, or you'll
   feel
I must make use of my authority,
And, as a princess, punish it.

Isab. A princess ! .

Mari. I had rather be a slave unto a
   Moor,
Than know thee for my equal.

Isab. Scornful thing !
Proud of a white face.

Mari. Let her but remember
The issue in her leg.

Isab. The charge she puts
The state to, for perfumes.

Mari. And howsoe'er
She seems, when she's made up, as she's
   herself,
She stinks above the ground. O that I
   could reach you !
The little one you scorn so, with her nails
Would tear your painted face, and scratch
   those eyes out.

Do but come down.

Marc. Were there no other way,
But leaping on thy neck, to break my own,
Rather than be outbraved thus.

                    [*She retires.*
  Grac. Forty ducats
Upon the little hen ; she's of the kind,
And will not leave the pit.   [*Aside.*
  Mari. That it were lawful
To meet her with a poniard and a pistol !
But these weak hands shall shew my spleen—

      Re-enter Marcelia *below.*

  Marc. Where are you,
You modicum, you dwarf !
  Mari. Here, giantess, here.

Enter Francisco, Tiberio, Stephano, *and*
          Guards.

  Fran. A tumult in the court !
  Mari. Let her come on.
  Fran. What wind hath raised this tempest ?
ever them, I command you. What's the
    cause ?
speak, Mariana.
  Mari. I am out of breath ;
But we shall meet, we shall.—And do you
  hear, sir !
Or right me on this monster, ((she's three feet
Too high for a woman,)) or ne'er look to have
A quiet hour with me.
  Isab. If my son were here,
And would endure this, may a mother's curse
Pursue and overtake him !
  Fran. O forbear :
n me he's present, both in power and will ;
And, madam, I much grieve that, in his absence,
There should arise the least distaste to move
  you ;
It being his principal, nay, only charge,
To have you in his absence, served and
  honour'd,
As when himself perform'd the willing office.
  Mari. This is fine, i' faith.
  Grac. I would I were well off !
  Fran. And therefore, I beseech you,
  madam, frown not,
Till most unwittingly he hath deserved it,
On your poor servant ; to your excellence
I ever was and will be such ; and lay
The duke's authority, trusted to me,
With willingness at your feet.
  Mari. O base !
  Isab. We are like
To have an equal judge !
  Fran. But, should I find
That you are touch'd in any point of honour,

Or that the least neglect is fall'n upon you,
I then stand up a prince.
  1 *Fid.* Without reward,
Pray you dismiss us.
  Grac. Would I were five leagues hence !
  Fran. I will be partial
To none, not to myself ;
Be you but pleased to shew me my offence,
Or if you hold me in your good opinion,
Name those that have offended you.
  Isab. I am one,
And I will justify it.
  Mari. Thou art a base fellow,
To take her part.
  Fran. Remember, she's the dutchess.
  Marc. But used with more contempt, than
  if I were
A peasant's daughter ; baited, and hooted at,
Like to a common strumpet ; with loud
  noises
Forced from my prayers ; and my private
  chamber,
Which with all willingness, I would make
  my prison
During the absence of my lord, denied me :
But if he e'er return——
  Fran. Were you an actor
In this lewd comedy?
  Mari. Ay, marry was I ;
And will be one again.
  Isab. I'll join with her,
Though you repine at it.
  Fran. Think not, then, I speak,
For I stand bound to honour, and to serve
  you ;
But that the duke, that lives in this great
  lady,
For the contempt of him in her, commands
  you
To be close prisoners.
  Isab. *Mari.* Prisoners !
  Fran. Bear them hence ;
This is your charge, my lord Tiberio,
And, Stephano, this is yours.
  Marc. I am not cruel,
But pleased they may have liberty.
  Isab. Pleased, with a mischief !
  Mari. I'll rather live in any loathsome
  dungeon,
Than in a paradise at her entreaty :
And, for you, upstart——
  Steph. There is no contending.
  Tib. What shall become of these ?
  Fran. See them well whipp'd,
As you will answer it.
  Tib. Now, signior Graccho,
What think you of your greatness ?
  Grac. I preach patience,
And must endure my fortune.

1 *Fid.* I was never yet
At such a hunt's-up, nor was so rewarded.
[*Exeunt all but Francisco and Marcelia.*
Fran. Let them first know themselves,
and how you are
To be served and honour'd ; which, when
they confess,
You may again receive them to your favour :
And then it will shew nobly.
Marc. With my thanks
The duke shall pay you his, if he return
To bless us with his presence.
Fran. There is nothing
That can be added to your fair acceptance ;
That is the prize, indeed; all else are blanks,
And of no value. As, in virtuous actions,
The undertaker finds a full reward,
Although conferr'd upon unthankful men ;
So, any service done to so much sweetness,
However dangerous, and subject to
An ill construction) in your favour finds
A wish'd, and glorious end.
Marc. From you, I take this
As loyal duty ; but, in any other,
It would appear gross flattery.
Fran. Flattery, madam !
You are so rare and excellent in all things,
And raised so high upon a rock of goodness,
As that vice cannot reach you ; who but
looks on
This temple, built by nature to perfection,
But may bow to it ; and out of that zeal,
Not only learn to adore it, but to love it ?
Marc. Whither will this fellow ? [*Aside.*
Fran. Pardon, therefore, madam,
If an excess in me of humble duty,
Teach me to hope, and though it be not in
The power of man to merit such a blessing,
My piety, for it is more than love,
May find reward.
Marc. You have it in my thanks ;
And, on my hand, I am pleased that you
shall take
A full possession of it : but, take heed
That you fix here, and feed no hope beyond
it ;
If you do, it will prove fatal.
Fran. Be it death,
And death with torments tyrants ne'er
found out,
Yet I must say, I love you.
Marc. As a subject ;
And 'twill become you.
Fran. Farewell, circumstance !
And since you are not pleased to understand
me,
But by a plain and usual form of speech ;
All superstitious reverence laid by,
I love you as a man, and, as a man,

I would enjoy you. Why do you start, a
fly me ?
I am no monster, and you but a woman,
A woman made to yield, and by example
Told it is lawful : favours of this nature
Are, in our age, no miracles in the greates
And, therefore, lady——
Marc. Keep off !—O you Powers !
Libidinous beast ! and, add to that, u
thankful !
A crime, which creatures wanting reas
fly from.
Are all the princely bounties, favour
honours,
Which, with some prejudice to his ov
wisdom,
Thy lord and raiser hath conferr'd up
thee,
In three days' absence buried ? Hath l
made thee,
A thing obscure, almost without a name,
The envy of great fortunes ? Have I grac
thee,
Beyond thy rank, and entertain'd thee, as
A friend, and not a servant ? and is this,
This impudent attempt to taint mi
honour,
The fair return of both our ventured favour
Fran. Hear my excuse.
Marc. The devil may plead mercy,
And, with as much assurance, as thou yiel
one.
Burns lust so hot in thee ? or is thy pride
Grown up to such a height, that, but
princess,
No woman can content thee ; and, add to it
His wife and princess, to whom thou art tie
In all the bonds of duty ? Read my life,
And find one act of mine so loosely carried,
That could invite a most self-loving fool,
Set off with all that fortune could throw on
him,
To the least hope to find way to my favour;
And what's the worst mine enemies could
wish me,
I'll be thy strumpet.
Fran. 'Tis acknowledged, madam,
That your whole course of life hath been a
pattern
For chaste and virtuous women. In your
beauty,
Which I first saw, and loved, as a fair
crystal,
I read your heavenly mind, clear and un-
tainted ;
And while the duke did prize you to your
value,
Could it have been in man to pay that duty,
I well might envy him, but durst not hope

To stop you in your full career of goodness:
But now I find that he's fall'n from his for-
    tune,
And, howsoever he would appear doting,
Grown cold in his affection; I presume,
From his most barbarous neglect of you,
To offer my true service. Nor stand I
    bound,
To look back on the courtesies of him,
That, of all living men, is most unthankful.
  Marc. Unheard-of impudence !
  Fran. You'll say I am modest,
When I have told the story. Can he tax
    me;
That have received some worldly trifles
    from him,
For being ungrateful ; when he, that first
    tasted,
And hath so long enjoy'd, your sweet em-
    braces,
In which all blessings that our frail condition
Is capable of, are wholly comprehended,
As cloy'd with happiness, contemns the
    giver
Of his felicity ; and, as he reach'd not
The masterpiece of mischief which he aims
    at,
Unless he pay those favours he stands bound
    to,
With fell and deadly hate !—You think he
    loves you
With unexampled fervour; nay, dotes on
    you,
As there were something in you more than
    woman :
When, on my knowledge, he long since
    hath wish'd
You were among the dead ;—and I, you
    scorn so,
Perhaps, am your preserver.
  Marc. Bless me, good angels,
Or I am blasted ! Lies so false and wicked,
And fashion'd to so damnable a purpose,
Cannot be spoken by a human tongue.
My husband hate me ! give thyself the lie,
False and accurs'd ! Thy soul, if thou hast
    any,
Can witness, never lady stood so bound
To the unfeign'd affection of her lord,
As I do to my Sforza. If thou wouldst work
Upon my weak credulity, tell me, rather,
That the earth moves; the sun and stars
    stand still ;
The ocean keeps nor floods nor ebbs ; or
    that
There's peace between the lion and the
    lamb ;
Or that the ravenous eagle and the dove
Keep in one aerie, and bring up their young;

Or anything that is averse to nature :
And I will sooner credit it, than that
My lord can think of me, but as a jewel,
He loves more than himself, and all the
    world.
  Fran. O innocence abused ! simplicity
    cozen'd !
It were a sin, for which we have no name,
To keep you longer in this wilful error.
Read his affection here ;—[*Gives her a paper.*]
    —and then observe
How dear he holds you ! 'Tis his character,
Which cunning yet could never counterfeit.
  Marc. 'Tis his hand, I'm resolv'd of it.
    I'll try
What the inscription is.
  Fran. Pray you, do so.

  Marc. [reads.] *You know my pleasure,
and the hour of Marcelia's death, which fail
not to execute, as you will answer the contrary, not with your head alone, but with
the ruin of your whole family. And this,
written with mine own hand, and signed
with my privy signet, shall be your sufficient
warrant.*

                        LODOVICO SFORZA.

I do obey it ! every word's a poniard,
And reaches to my heart.   [*Swoons.*
  Fran. What have I done?
Madam ! for heaven's sake, madam !—O my
    fate !
I'll bend her body : this is yet some pleasure :
I'll kiss her into a new life.   Dear lady !—
She stirs. For the duke's sake, for Sforza's
    sake——
  Marc. Sforza's ! stand off ; though dead,
    I will be his,
And even my ashes shall abhor the touch
Of any other.—O unkind, and cruel !
Learn, women, learn to trust in one another ;
There is no faith in man : Sforza is false,
False to Marcelia !
  Fran. But I am true,
And live to make you happy. All the pomp,
State, and observance you had, being his,
Compared to what you shall enjoy, when
    mine,
Shall be no more remember'd. Lose his
    memory,
And look with cheerful beams on your new
    creature ;
And know, what he hath plotted for your
    good,
Fate cannot alter. If the emperor
Take not his life, at his return he dies.
And by my hand : my wife, that is his heir,
Shall quickly follow :—then we reign alone !

For with this arm I'll swim through seas of
    blood,
Or make a bridge, arch'd with the bones of
    men,
But I will grasp my aims in you, my dearest,
Dearest, and best of women !
    Marc. Thou art a villain !
All attributes of arch-villains made into one,
Cannot express thee. I prefer the hate
Of Sforza, though it mark me for the grave,
Before thy base affection.   I am yet
Pure and unspotted in my true love to him ;
Nor shall it be corrupted, though he's
    tainted :
Nor will I part with innocence, because
He is found guilty.   For thyself, thou art
A thing, that, equal with the devil himself,
I do detest and scorn.
    Fran. Thou, then, art nothing :
Thy life is in my power, disdainful woman !
Think on't, and tremble.
    Marc. No, though thou wert now
To play thy hangman's part.—Thou well
    may'st be
My executioner, and art only fit
For such employment ; but ne'er hope to have
The least grace from me.   I will never see
    thee,
But as the shame of men ; so, with my curses
Of horror to thy conscience in this life,
And pains in hell hereafter, I spit at thee ;
And, making haste to make my peace with
    heaven,
Expect thee as my hangman.   [*Exit.*
    Fran. I am lost
In the discovery of this fatal secret.
Curs'd hope, that flatter'd me, that wrongs
    could make her
A stranger to her goodness ! all my plots
Turn back upon myself ; but I am in,
And must go on : and, since I have put off
From the shore of innocence, guilt be now
    my pilot !
Revenge first wrought me ; murder's his
    twin brother :
One deadly sin, then, help to cure another !
                                [*Exit.*

                ———

            ACT III.

SCENE I.—*The* Imperial Camp, *before*
            Pavia.

Enter Medina, Hernando, *and* Alphonso.

    Med. The spoil, the spoil ! 'tis that the
        soldier fights for.
Our victory, as yet, affords us nothing
But wounds and empty honour.   We have
    pass'd

The hazard of a dreadful day, and forced
A passage with our swords through all the
    dangers
That, page-like, wait on the success of war ;
And now expect reward.
    Hern. Hell put in
The enemy's mind to be desperate, and hold
    out !
Yieldings and compositions will undo us ;
And what is that way given, for the most part,
Comes to the emperor's coffers to defray
The charge of the great action, as 'tis ru-
    mour'd :
When, usually, some thing in grace, that
    ne'er heard
The cannon's roaring tongue, but at a tri-
    umph,
Puts in, and for his intercession shares
All that we fought for ; the poor soldier left
To starve, or fill up hospitals.
    Alph. But, when
We enter towns by force, and carve our-
    selves,
Pleasure with pillage, and the richest wines
Open our shrunk-up veins, and pour into
    them
New blood and fervour——
    Med. I long to be at it ;
To see these chuffs, that every day may
    spend
A soldier's entertainment for a year,
Yet make a third meal of a bunch of raisins ;
These sponges, that suck up a kingdom's
    fat,
Battening like scarabs in the dung of
    peace,
To be squeezed out by the rough hand of
    war ;
And all that their whole lives have heap'd
    together,
By cozenage, perjury, or sordid thrift,
With one gripe to be ravish'd.
    Hern. I would be tousing
Their fair madonas, that in little dogs,
Monkeys, and paraquittos, consume thou-
    sands ;
Yet, for the advancement of a noble action,
Repine to part with a poor piece of eight :
War's plagues upon them !   I have seen
    them stop
Their scornful noses first, then seem to
    swoon,
At sight of a buff jerkin, if it were not
Perfumed, and hid with gold : yet these
    nice wantons,
Spurr'd on by lust, cover'd in some disguise,
To meet some rough court-stallion, and be
    leap'd,
Durst enter into any common brothel,

Though all varieties of stink contend there ;
Yet praise the entertainment.
  Med. I may live
To see the tatter'd'st rascals of my troop
Drag them out of their closets, with a vengeance !
When neither threat'ning, flattering, kneeling, howling,
Can ransome one poor jewel, or redeem
Themselves, from their blunt wooing.·
  Hern. My main hope is,
To begin the sport at Milan : there's enough,
And of all kinds of pleasure we can wish for,
To satisfy the most covetous.
  Alph. Every day
We look for a remove.
  Med. For Lodowick Sforza,
The duke of Milan, I, on mine own knowledge,
Can say thus much : he is too much a soldier,
Too confident of his own worth, too rich too,
And understands too well the emperor hates him,
To hope for composition.
  Alph. On my life,
We need not fear his coming in.
  Hern. On mine,
I do not wish it : I had rather that,
To shew his valour, he'd put us to the trouble
To fetch him in by the ears.
  Med. The emperor !

Flourish. Enter Charles, Pescara, *and Attendants.*

  Charl. You make me wonder :—nay, it is no counsel,
You may partake it, gentlemen : who'd have thought,
That he, that scorn'd our proffer'd amity
When he was sued to, should, ere he be summon'd,
(Whether persuaded to it by base fear,
Or flatter'd by false hope, which, 'tis uncertain,)
First kneel for mercy?
  Med. When your majesty
Shall please to instruct us who it is, we may
Admire it with you.
  Charl. Who, but the duke of Milan,
The right hand of the French ! of all that stand
In our displeasure, whom necessity
Compels to seek our favour, I would have sworn
Sforza had been the last.
  Hern. And should be writ so,
In the list of those you pardon. Would his city

Had rather held us out a siege, like Troy,
Than, by a feign'd submission, he should cheat you
Of a just revenge ; or us, of those fair glories
We have sweat blood to purchase !
  Med. With your honour
You cannot hear him.
  Alph. The sack alone of Milan
Will pay the army.
  Charl. I am not so weak,
To be wrought on, as you fear ! nor ignorant
That money is the sinew of the war ;
And on what terms soever he seek peace,
'Tis in our power to grant it, or deny it :
Yet, for our glory, and to shew him that
We've brought him on his knees, it is resolved
To hear him as a supplicant. Bring him in ;
But let him see the effects of our just anger,
In the guard that you make for him.
                     [Exit Pescara.
  Hern. I am now
Familiar with the issue ; all plagues on it !
He will appear in some dejected habit,
His countenance suitable, and, for his order,
A rope about his neck : then kneel and tell
Old stories, what a worthy thing it is
To have the power, and not to use it ; then
add to that
A tale of king Tigranes, and great Pompey,
Who said, forsooth, and wisely ! 'twas more honour
To make a king than kill one ; which, applied
To the emperor, and himself, a pardon's granted
To him an enemy ; and we, his servants,
Condemn'd to beggary.   *[Aside to Med.*
  Med. Yonder he comes ;
But not as you expected.

Re-enter Pescara *with* Sforza, *strongly guarded.*

  Alph. He looks as if
He would outface his dangers.
  Hern. I am cozen'd :
A suitor, in the devil's name !
  Med. Hear him speak.
  Sfor. I come not, emperor, to invade thy mercy,
By fawning on thy fortune ; nor bring with me
Excuses, or denials. I profess,
And with a good man's confidence, even this instant
That I am in thy power, I was thine enemy ;
Thy deadly and vow'd enemy : one that wish'd
Confusion to thy person and estates ;
And with my utmost powers, and deepest counsels,

Had they been truly follow'd, further'd it.
Nor will I now, although my neck were under
The hangman's axe, with one poor syllable
Confess, but that I honour'd the French king,
More than thyself, and all men.

   Med.   By Saint Jacques,
This is no flattery.

   Hern. There is fire and spirit in't ;
But not long-lived, I hope.

   Sfor.   Now give me leave,
My hate against thyself, and love to him
Freely acknowledged, to give up the reasons
That make me so affected : In my wants
I ever found him faithful ; had supplies
Of men and monies from him ; and my
    hopes,
Quite sunk, were, by his grace, buoy'd up
    again ;
He was, indeed, to me, as my good angel
To guard me from all dangers. I dare speak,
Nay, must and will, his praise now, in as
    high
And loud a key, as when he was thy equal.—
The benefits he sow'd in me, met not
Unthankful ground, but yielded him his own
With fair increase, and I still glory in it.
And, though my fortunes, poor, compared
    to his,
And Milan, weigh'd with France, appear as
    nothing,
Are in thy fury burnt, let it be mention'd,
They served but as small tapers to attend
The solemn flame at this great funeral ;
And with them I will gladly waste myself,
Rather than undergo the imputation
Of being base, or unthankful.

   Alph. Nobly spoken !

   Hern. I do begin, I know not why, to
    hate him
Less than I did.

   Sfor. If that, then, to be grateful
For courtesies received, or not to leave
A friend in his necessities, be a crime
Amongst you Spaniards, which other nations
That, like you, aim'd at empire, loved, and
    cherish'd
Where'er they found it, Sforza brings his head
To pay the forfeit. Nor come I as a slave,
Pinion'd and fetter'd, in a squalid weed,
Falling before thy feet, kneeling and howling,
For a forestall'd remission : that were poor,
And would but shame thy victory; for con-
    quest
Over base foes, is a captivity,
And not a triumph. I ne'er feared to die,
More than I wish'd to live. When I had
    reach'd
My ends in being a duke, I wore these robes,
This crown upon my head, and to my side

This sword was girt ; and witness truth,
    that, now
'Tis in another's power, when I shall part
With them and life together, I'm the same :
My veins then did not swell with pride ;
    nor now
Shrink they for fear. Know, sir, that Sforza
    stands
Prepared for either fortune.

   Hern.   As I live,
I do begin strangely to love this fellow ;
And could part with three quarters of my
    share in
The promised spoil, to save him.

   Sfor.   But, if example
Of my fidelity to the French, whose honours,
Titles, and glories, are now mix'd with yours,
As brooks, devour'd by rivers, lose their
    names,
Has power to invite you to make him a
    friend,
That hath given evident proof he knows to
    love,
And to be thankful : this my crown, now
    yours,
You may restore me, and in me instruct
These brave commanders, should your for-
    tune change,
Which now I wish not, what they may
    expect
From noble enemies, for being faithful.
The charges of the war I will defray,
And, what you may, not without hazard,
    force,
Bring freely to you : I'll prevent the cries
Of murder'd infants, and of ravish'd maids,
Which in a city sack'd, call on heaven's
    justice,
And stop the course of glorious victories :
And, when I know the captains and the
    soldiers,
That have in the late battle done best service,
And are to be rewarded, I myself,
According to their quality and merits,
Will see them largely recompensed.—I have
    said,
And now expect my sentence.

   Alph. By this light,
'Tis a brave gentleman.

   Med. How like a block
The emperor sits !

   Hern. He hath deliver'd reasons,
Especially in his purpose to enrich
Such as fought bravely, (I myself am one,
I care not who knows it,) as I wonder that
He can be so stupid. Now he begins to stir :
Mercy, an't be thy will !

   Charl. Thou hast so far
Outgone my expectation, noble Sforza,

For such I hold thee ;—and true constancy,
Raised on a brave foundation, bears such
   palm
And privilege with it, that where we be-
   hold it,
Though in an enemy, it does command us
To love and honour it. By my future hopes,
I am glad for thy sake, that in seeking favour,
Thou did'st not borrow of vice her indirect,
Crooked, and abject means, and for mine
   own,
That, since my purposes must now be
   changed
Touching thy life and fortunes, the world
   cannot
Tax me of levity in my settled counsels ;
I being neither wrought by tempting bribes,
Nor servile flattery ; but forced into it
By a fair war of virtue.
  Hern. This sounds well.
  Charl. All former passages of hate be
   buried :
For thus with open arms I meet thy love,
And as a friend embrace it ; and so far
I am from robbing thee of the least honour,
That with my hands, to make it sit the faster,
I set thy crown once more upon thy head ;
And do not only style thee, Duke of Milan,
But vow to keep thee so. Yet, not to take
From others to give only to myself,
I will not hinder your magnificence
To my commanders, neither will I urge it ;
But in that, as in all things else, I leave you
To be your own disposer.
      [*Flourish. Exit with Attendants.*
  Sfor. May I live
To seal my loyalty, though with loss of life,
In some brave service worthy Cæsar's favour,
And I shall die most happy ! Gentlemen,
Receive me to your loves ; and, if henceforth
There can arise a difference between us,
It shall be in a noble emulation
Who hath the fairest sword, or dare go
   farthest,
To fight for Charles the emperor.
  Hern. We embrace you,
As one well read in all the points of honour :
And there we are your scholars.
  Sfor. True ; but such
As far outstrip the master. We'll contend
In love hereafter : in the meantime, pray you,
Let me discharge my debt, and, as an earnest
Of what's to come, divide this cabinet :
In the small body of it there are jewels
Will yield a hundred thousand pistolets,
Which honour me to receive.
  Med. You bind us to you.
  Sfor. And when great Charles commands
   me to his presence,

If you will please to excuse my abrupt de-
   parture,
Designs that most concern me, next this
   mercy,
Calling me home, I shall hereafter meet you,
And gratify the favour.
  Hern. In this, and all things,
We are your servants.
  Sfor. A name I ever owe you.
      [*Exeunt* Medina, Hernando, *and*
           . Alphonso.
  Pesc. So, sir ; this tempest is well over-
   blown,
And all things fall out to our wishes : but,
In my opinion, this quick return,
Before you've made a party in the court
Among the great ones, (for these needy
   captains
Have little power in peace,) may beget
   danger,
At least suspicion.
  Sfor. Where true honour lives,
Doubt hath no being : I desire no pawn
Beyond an emperor's word, for my assurance.
Besides, Pescara, to thyself, of all men,
I will confess my weakness :—though my
   state
And crown's restored me, though I am in
   grace,
And that a little stay might be a step
To greater honours, I must hence. Alas !
I live not here ; my wife, my wife, Pescara,
Being absent, I am dead. Prithee, excuse,
And do not chide, for friendship's sake, my
   fondness,
But ride along with me ; I'll give you reasons,
And strong ones, to plead for me.
  Pesc. Use your own pleasure ;
I'll bear you company,
  Sfor. Farewell, grief ! I am stored with
Two blessings most desired in human life,
A constant friend, an unsuspected wife.
                   [*Exeunt.*

SCENE II.—Milan. *A Room in the Castle.*
   Enter an Officer *with* Graccho.

  Offic. What I did, I had warrant for ; you
   have tasted
My office gently, and for those soft strokes,
Flea-bitings to the jerks I could have lent
   you,
There does belong a feeing.
  Grac. Must I pay
For being tormented, and dishonour'd ?
  Offic. Fie ! no,
Your honour's not impair'd in't. What's the
   letting out
Of a little corrupt blood, and the next way
   too?

                               G

There is no surgeon like me, to take off
A courtier's itch that's·rampant at great
   ladies,
Or turns knave for preferment, or grows
   proud
Of his rich cloaks and suits, though got by
   brokage,
And so forgets his betters.
  Grac. Very good, sir :
But am I the first man of quality
That e'er came under your fingers?
  Offic. Not by a thousand ;
And they have said I have a lucky hand too :
Both men and women of all sorts have bow'd
Under this sceptre. I have had a fellow
That could endite, forsooth, and make fine
   metres
To tinkle in the ears of ignorant madams,
That, for defaming of great men, was sent
   me
Threadbare and lousy, and in three days
   after,
Discharged by another that set him on. I
   have seen him
Cap à pié gallant, and his stripes wash'd off
With oil of angels.
  Grac. 'Twas a sovereign cure.·
  Offic. There was a sectary too, that would
   not be
Conformable to the orders of the church,
Nor yield to any argument of reason,
But still rail at authority, brought to me,
When I had worm'd his tongue, and truss'd
   his haunches,
Grew a fine pulpit man, and was beneficed :
Had he not cause to thank me?
  Grac. There was physic
Was to the purpose.
  Offic. Now, for women, sir,
For your more consolation, I could tell you
Twenty fine stories, but I'll end in one,
And 'tis the last that's memorable.
  Grac. Prithee, do ;
For I grow weary of thee.
  Offic. There was lately
A fine she-waiter in the court, that doted
Extremely of a gentleman, that had
His main dependence on a signior's favour
I will not name, but could not compass him
On any terms. This wanton, at dead mid-
   night,
Was found at the exercise behind the arras,
With the 'foresaid signior : he got clear off,
But she was seized on, and, to save his
   honour,
Endured the lash ; and, though I made her
   often
Cúrvet and caper, she would never tell
Who play'd at pushpin with her.

  Grac. But what follow'd?
Prithee be brief.
  Offic. Why this, sir : She deliver'd,
Had store of crowns assign'd her by her
   patron,
Who forced the gentleman, to save her credit,
To marry her, and say he was the party
Found in Lob's pound : so she, that, before,
   gladly
Would have been his whore, reigns o'er him
   as his wife ;
Nor dares he grumble at it. Speak but
   truth, then,
Is not my office lucky?
  Grac. Go, there's for thee ;
But what will be my fortune?
  Offic. If you thrive not
After that soft correction, come again.
  Grac. I thank you, knave.
  Offic. And then, knave, I will fit you.
                         [Exit.
  Grac. Whipt like a rogue ! no lighter
   punishment serve
To balance with a little mirth ! 'Tis well ;
My credit sunk for ever, I am now
Fit company only for pages and for footboys,
That have perused the porter's lodge.

     Enter Julio *and* Giovanni.

  Giov. See, Julio,
Yonder the proud slave is. How he looks
   now,
After his castigation !
  Jul. As he came
From a close fight at sea under the hatches,
With a she-Dunkirk, that was shot before
Between wind and water ; and he hath
   sprung a leak too,
Or I am cozen'd.
  Giov. Let's be merry with him.
  Grac. How they stare at me ! am I turn'd
   to an owl?—
The wonder, gentlemen?
  Jul. I read, this morning,
Strange stories of the passive fortitude
Of men in former ages, which I thought
Impossible, and not to be believed :
But now I look on you, my wonder ceases.
  Grac. The reason, sir?
  Jul. Why, sir, you have been whipt,
Whipt, signior Graccho ; and the whip, I
   take it,
Is to a gentleman, the greatest trial
That may be of his patience.
  Grac. Sir, I'll call you
To a strict account for this.
  Giov. I'll not deal with you,
Unless I have a beadle for my second :
And then I'll answer you.

Jul. Farewell, poor Graccho.
            [*Exeunt* Julio *and* Giovanni.
Grac. Better and better still. If ever
    wrongs
Could teach a wretch to find the way to
    vengeance,

        Enter Francisco *and a* Servant.

Hell now inspire me! How, the lord pro-
    tector!
My judge; I thank him! Whither thus in
    private?
I will not see him.   [*Stands aside.*
Fran. If I am sought for,
Say I am indisposed, and will not hear
Or suits, or suitors.
    Serv. But, sir, if the princess
Enquire, what shall I answer?
    Fran. Say, I am rid
Abroad to take the air; but by no means
Let her know I'm in court.
    Serv. So I shall tell her.   [*Exit.*
Fran. Within there, ladies!

        Enter a Gentlewoman.

Gentlew. My good lord, your pleasure?
Fran. Prithee, let me beg thy favour for
    access
To the dutchess.
    Gentlew. In good sooth, my lord, I dare
    not;
She's very private.
    Fran. Come, there's gold to buy thee
A new gown, and a rich one.
    Gentlew. I once swore
If e'er I lost my maidenhead, it should be
With a great lord, as you are; and, I know
    not how,
I feel a yielding inclination in me,
If you have appetite.
    Fran. Pox on thy maidenhead!
Where is thy lady?
    Gentlew. If you venture on her,
She's walking in the gallery; perhaps,
You will find her less tractable.
    Fran. Bring me to her.
    Gentlew. I fear you'll have cold entertain-
    ment, when
You are at your journey's end; and 'twere
    discretion
To take a snatch by the way.
    Fran. Prithee, leave fooling:
My page waits in the lobby; give him sweet-
    meats;
He is train'd up for his master's ease,
And he will cool thee.
            [*Exeunt* Fran. *and* Gentlew.
Grac. A brave discovery beyond my hope,
A plot even offer'd to my hand to work on!

If I am dull now, may I live and die
The scorn of worms and slaves!—Let me
    consider:
My lady and her mother first committed,
In the favour of the dutchess; and I whipt!
That, with an iron pen, is writ in brass
On my tough heart, now grown a harder
    metal.—
And all his bribed approaches to the dutchess
To be conceal'd! good, good. This to my lady
Deliver'd, as I'll order it, runs her mad.—
But this may prove but courtship! let it be,
I care not, so it feed her jealousy.   [*Exit.*

SCENE III.—*Another Room in the same.*

    Enter Marcelia *and* Francisco.

Marc. Believe thy tears or oaths! can it
    be hoped,
After a practice so abhorr'd and horrid,
Repentance e'er can find thee?
    Fran. Dearest lady,
Great in your fortune, greater in your good-
    ness,
Make a superlative of excellence,
In being greatest in your saving mercy.
I do confess, humbly confess my fault,
To be beyond all pity; my attempt
So barbarously rude, that it would turn
A saint-like patience into savage fury.
But you, that are all innocence and virtue,
No spleen or anger in you of a woman,
But when a holy zeal to piety fires you,
May, if you please, impute the fault to love,
Or call it beastly lust, for 'tis no better:
A sin, a monstrous sin! yet with it many
That did prove good men after, have been
    tempted;
And, though I'm crooked now, 'tis in your
    power
To make me straight again.
    Marc. Is't possible
This can be cunning!   [*Aside.*
    Fran. But, if no submission,
Nor prayers can appease you, that you may
    know
'Tis not the fear of death that makes me sue
    thus,
But a loath'd detestation of my madness,
Which makes me wish to live to have your
    pardon;
I will not wait the sentence of the duke,
Since his return is doubtful, but I myself
Will do a fearful justice on myself,
No witness by but you, there being no more
When I offended. Yet, before I do it,
For I perceive in you no signs of mercy,
I will disclose a secret, which dying with me,
May prove your ruin.

                                    G 2

Marc. Speak it ; it will take from
The burthen of thy conscience.
 Fran. Thus, then, madam ; .
The warrant by my lord sign'd for your
 death,
Was but conditional ; but you must swear
By your unspotted truth, not to reveal it,
Or I end here abruptly.
 Marc. By my hopes
Of joys hereafter. On.
 Fran. Nor was it hate
That forced him to it, but excess of love.
And, if I ne'er return, (so said great Sforza,)
No living man deserving to enjoy
My best Marcelia, with the first news
That I am dead, (for no man after me
Must e'er enjoy her,) fail not to kill her——
But till certain proof
Assure thee I am lost, (these were his words,)
Observe and honour her, as if the soul
Of woman's goodness only dwelt in hers.
This trust I have abused, and basely
 wrong'd ;
And, if the excelling pity of your mind
Cannot forgive it, as I dare not hope it,
Rather than look on my offended lord,
I stand resolved to punish it.
       [*Draws his sword.*
 Marc. Hold ! 'tis forgiven,
And by me freely pardon'd. In thy fair life
Hereafter, study to deserve this bounty,
Which thy true penitence, such I believe it,
Against my resolution hath forced from me.—
But that my lord, my Sforza, should esteem
My life fit only as a page, to wait on
The various course of his uncertain fortunes ;
Or cherish in himself that sensual hope,
In death to know me as a wife, afflicts me ;
Nor does his envy less deserve mine anger,
Which though, such is my love, I would not
 nourish,
Will slack the ardour that I had to see him
Return in safety.
 Fran. But if your entertainment
Should give the least ground to his jealousy,
To raise up an opinion I am false,
You then destroy your mercy. . Therefore,
 madam,
(Though I shall ever look on you as on
My life's preserver, and the miracle
Of human pity,) would you but vouchsafe,
In company, to do me those fair graces,
And favours, which your innocence and
 honour
May safely warrant, it would to the duke,
I being to your best self alone known guilty,
Make me appear most innocent.
 Marc. Have your wishes ;
And something I may do to try his temper,

At least, to make him know a constant wife
Is not so slaved to her husband's doting
 humours,
But that she may deserve to live a widow,
Her fate appointing it.
 Fran. It is enough ;
Nay, all I could desire, and will make way
To my revenge, which shall disperse itself
On him, on her, and all.
  [*Aside and exit.—Shout and flourish.*
 Marc. What shout is that?

   Enter Tiberio *and* Stephano.

 Tib. All happiness to the dutchess, that
 may flow
From the duke's new and wish'd return !
 Marc. He's welcome.
 Steph. How coldly she receives it !
 Tib. Observe the encounter.

 Flourish. *Enter* Sforza, Pescara, Isabella,
  Mariana, Graccho, *and Attendants.*
 Mari. What you have told me, Graccho,
 is believed,
And I'll find time to stir in't.
 Grac. As you see cause ;
I will not do ill offices.
 Sfor. I have stood
Silent thus long, Marcelia, expecting
When, with more than a greedy haste, thou
 wouldst
Have flown into my arms, and on my lips
Have printed a deep welcome. My desires
To glass myself in these fair eyes, have
 borne me
With more than human speed : nor durst I
 stay
In any temple, or to any saint
To pay my vows and thanks for my return,
Till I had seen thee.
 Marc. Sir, I am most happy
To look upon you safe, and would express
My love and duty in a modest fashion,
Such as might suit with the behaviour
Of one that knows herself a wife, and how
To temper her desires, not like a wanton
Fired with hot appetite; nor can it wrong me
To love discreetly.
 Sfor. How ! why, can there be
A mean in your affections to Sforza?
Or any act, though ne'er so loose, that may
Invite or heighten appetite, appear
Immodest or uncomely? Do not move me ;
My passions to you are in extremes,
And know no bounds :—come ; kiss me.
 Marc. I obey you.
 Sfor. By all the joys of love, she does
 salute me
As if I were her grandfather ! What witch,

With cursed spells, · hath quench'd the amorous heat
That lived upon these lips? Tell me, Marcelia,
And truly tell me, is't a fault of mine ·
That hath begot this coldness? or neglect
Of others, in my absence?·
  Marc. Neither, sir :
I stand indebted to your substitute,
Noble and good Francisco, for his care·
And fair observance of me : there was nothing
With which you, being present, could supply me,
That I dare say I wanted.
  Sfor. How!
  Marc. The pleasures
That sacred Hymen warrants us, excepted,
Of which, in troth, you are too great a doter ;
And·there is more of beast in it than man.
Let us love temperately ; things violent last not,
And too much dotage rather argues folly
Than true affection.
  Grac. Observe but this,
And how she praised my lord's care and observance ;
And then judge, madam, if my intelligence
Have any ground of truth.
  Mari. No more ; I mark it.
  Steph. How the duke stands!
  Tib. As he were rooted there,
And had no motion.
  Pesc. My lord, from whence
Grows this amazement?
  Sfor. It is more, dear my friend ;
For I am doubtful whether I've a being,
But certain that my life's a burden to me.
Take me back, good Pescara, shew me to Cæsar
In all his rage and fury ; I disclaim
His mercy : to live now, which is his gift,
Is worse than death, and with all studied torments.
Marcelia is unkind, nay, worse, grown cold
In her affection ; my excess of fervour,
Which yet was never equall'd, grown distasteful.
— But have thy wishes, woman ; thou shalt know
That I can be myself, and thus shake off
The fetters of fond dotage. From my sight,
Without reply ; for I am apt to do
Something I may repent.—[*Exit Marc.*—
  Oh ! who would place
His happiness in most accursed woman,
In whom obsequiousness engenders pride ;
And harshness deadly hatred ! From this hour

I'll labour to forget there are such creatures ;
True friends be now my mistresses. Clear your brows,
And, though my heart-strings crack for't I will be
To all a free example of delight.
We will have sports of all kinds, and pro-pound
Rewards to such as can produce us new ;
Unsatisfied, though we surfeit in their store ;
And never think of curs'd Marcelia more.·
  [*Exeunt.*

ACT IV.

SCENE I.—*The same. A Room in the Castle.*

Enter Francisco *and* Graccho.

  Fran. And is it possible thou shouldst forget
A wrong of such a nature, and then study
My safety and content?
  Grac. Sir, but allow me
Only to have read the elements of courtship,
Not the abstruse and hidden arts to thrive there ;
And you may please to grant me so much knowledge,
That injuries from one in grace, like you,
Are noble favours. Is it not grown common, ·
In every sect, for those that want, to suffer
From such as have to give? Your captain cast,
If poor, though not thought daring, but approved so,
To raise a coward into name, that's rich,
Suffers disgraces publicly ; but receives ·
Rewards for them in private.
  Fran. Well observed.
Put on ; we'll be familiar, and discourse
A little of this argument. That day, ·
In which it was first rumour'd, then confirm'd,
Great Sforza thought me worthy of his favour,
I found myself to be another thing ;
Not what I was before. I passed then
For a pretty fellow, and of pretty parts too,
And was perhaps received so ; but, once raised,
The liberal courtiers made me master of
Those virtues which I ne'er knew in myself:
If I pretended to a jest, 'twas made one
By their interpretation ; if I offer'd
To reason of philosophy, though absurdly,
They had helps to save me, and without a blush

Would swear that I, by nature, had more
    knowledge,
Than others could acquire by any labour :
Nay, all I did, indeed, which in another
Was not remarkable, in me shew'd rarely.
    Grac. But then they tasted of your bounty.
    Fran. True :
They gave me those good parts I was not
    born to,
And, by my intercession, they got that
Which, had I cross'd them, they durst not
    have hoped for.
    Grac. All this is oracle : and shall I, then,
For a foolish whipping, leave to honour
    him,
That holds the wheel of fortune ? no ; that
    savours
Too much of the ancient freedom. Since
    great men
Receive disgraces and give thanks, poor
    knaves
Must have nor spleen, nor anger. Though
    I love
My limbs as well as any man, if you had
    now
A humour to kick me lame into an office,
Where I might sit in state and undo others,
Stood I not bound to kiss the foot that
    did it ?
Though it seem strange, there have been
    such things seen
In the memory of man.
    Fran. But to the purpose,
And then, that service done, make thine
    own fortunes.
My wife, thou say'st, is jealous I am too
Familiar with the dutchess.
    Grac. And incensed
For her commitment in her brother's ab-
    sence ;
And by her mother's anger is spurr'd on
To make discovery of it. This her purpose
Was trusted to my charge, which I declined
As much as in me lay ; but, finding her
Determinately bent to undertake it,
Though breaking my faith to her may de-
    stroy
My credit with your lordship, I yet thought,
Though at my peril, I stood bound to re-
    veal it.
    Fran. I thank thy care, and will deserve
    this secret,
In making thee acquainted with a greater,
And of more moment. Come into my
    bosom,
And take it from me : Canst thou think,
    dull Graccho,
My power and honours were conferr'd upon
    me,

And, add to them, this form, to have my
    pleasures
Confined and limited ? I delight in change,
And sweet variety ; that's my heaven on
    earth,
For which I love life only. I confess,
My wife pleased me a day, the dutchess,
    two,
(And yet I must not say I have enjoy'd her,)
But now I care for neither : therefore,
    Graccho,
So far I am from stopping Mariana
In making her complaint, that I desire thee
To urge her to it.
    Grac. That may prove your ruin ;
The duke already being, as 'tis reported,
Doubtful she hath play'd false.
    Fran. There thou art cozen'd ;
His dotage, like an ague, keeps his course,
And now 'tis strongly on him. But I lose
    time,
And therefore know, whether thou wilt or
    no,
Thou art to be my instrument ; and, in spite
Of the old saw, that says, It is not safe
On any terms to trust a man that's wrong'd,
I dare thee to be false.
    Grac. This is a language,
My lord, I understand not.
    Fran. You thought, sirrah,
To put a trick on me for the relation
Of what I knew before, and, having won
Some weighty secret from me, in revenge
To play the traitor. Know, thou wretched
    thing,
By my command thou wert whipt ; and
    every day
I'll have thee freshly tortured, if thou miss
In the least charge that I impose upon thee.
Though what I speak, for the most part, is
    true :
Nay, grant thou hadst a thousand witnesses
To be deposed they heard it, 'tis in me
With one word, such is Sforza's confidence
Of my fidelity not to be shaken,
To make all void, and ruin my accusers.
Therefore look to't ; bring my wife hotly on
To accuse me to the duke—I have an end
    in't,
Or think what 'tis makes man most mise-
    rable,
And that shall fall upon thee. Thou wert
    a fool
To hope, by being acquainted with my
    courses,
To curb and awe me ; or that I should live
Thy slave, as thou didst saucily divine :
For prying in my counsels, still live mine.
                        [Exit.

Grac. I am caught on both sides.   This
'tis for a puisne
In policy's Protean school, to try conclusions
With one that hath commenced, and gone
   out doctor.
If I discover what but now he bragg'd of,
I shall not be believed : if I fall off
From him, his threats and actions go to-
   gether,
And there's no hope of safety.   Till I get
A plummet that may sound his deepest
   counsels,
I must obey and serve him : Want of skill
Now makes me play the rogue against my
   will.   [*Exit.*

SCENE II.—*Another Room in the same.*

Enter Marcelia, Tiberio, Stephano, *and*
   Gentlewoman.

Marc. Command me from his sight, and
   with such scorn
As he would rate his slave !
Tib. 'Twas in his fury.
Steph. And he repents it, madam.
Marc. Was I born
To observe his humours ! or, because he
   dotes,
Must I run mad ?
Tib. If that your Excellence
Would please but to receive a feeling know-
   ledge
Of what he suffers, and how deep the least
Unkindness wounds from you, you would
   excuse
His hasty language.
Steph. He hath paid the forfeit
Of his offence, I'm sure, with such a sorrow,
As, if it had been greater, would deserve
A full remission.
Marc. Why, perhaps, he hath it ;
And I stand more afflicted for his absence,
Than he can be for mine :—so, pray you,
   tell him.
But, till I have digested some sad thoughts,
And reconciled passions that are at war
Within myself, I purpose to be private :
And have you care, unless it be Francisco,
That no man be admitted.
                                [*Exit Gentlewoman.*
Tib. How ! Francisco ?
Steph. He, that at every stage keeps
   livery mistresses ;
The stallion of the state !
Tib. They are things above us,
And so no way concern us.
Steph. If I were
The duke, (I freely must confess my weak-
   ness,)

Enter Francisco.

I should wear yellow breeches.   Here he
   comes.
Tib. Nay, spare your labour, lady, we
   know our duty,
And quit the room.
Steph. Is this her privacy !
Though with the hazard of a check, perhaps,
This may go to the duke.
                             [*Exeunt* Tiberio *and* Stephano.
Marc. Your face is full
Of fears and doubts : the reason ?
Fran. O, best madam,
They are not counterfeit.   I, your poor
   convert,
That only wish to live in sad repentance,
To mourn my desperate attempt of you,
That have no ends nor aims, but that your
   goodness
Might be a witness of my penitence,
Which seen, would teach you how to love
   your mercy,
Am robb'd of that last hope.   The duke,
   the duke,
I more than fear, hath found that I am guilty.
Marc. By my unspotted honour, not from
   me ;
Nor have I with him changed one syllable,
Since his return, but what you heard.
Fran. Yet malice
Is eagle eyed, and would see that which is
   not ;
And jealousy's too apt to build upon
Unsure foundations.
Marc. Jealousy !
Fran. [*Aside.*] It takes.
Marc. Who dares but only think I can
   be tainted ?
But for him, though almost on certain proof,
To give it hearing, not belief, deserves
My hate for ever.
Fran. Whether grounded on
Your noble, yet chaste favours shewn unto
   me ;
Or her imprisonment, for her contempt
To you, by my command, my frantic wife
Hath put it in his head.
Marc. Have I then lived
So long, now to be doubted ? Are my favours
The themes of her discourse ? or what I do,
That never trod in a suspected path,
Subject to base construction ? Be un-
   daunted ;
For now, as of a creature that is mine,
I rise up your protectress : all the grace
I hitherto have done you, was bestow'd
With a shut hand ; it shall be now more free,
Open, and liberal.   But let it not,

Though counterfeited to the life, teach you
To nourish saucy hopes.
Fran. May I be blasted,
When I prove such a monster!
Marc. I will stand then
Between you and all danger. He shall know,
Suspicion overturns what confidence builds;
And he that dares but doubt when there's no
    ground,
Is neither to himself nor others sound.
                      [*Exit.*
Fran. So, let it work! Her goodness,
    that denied
My service, branded with the name of lust,
Shall now destroy itself; and she shall find,
When he's a suitor, that brings cunning
    arm'd
With power, to be his advocates, the denial
Is a disease as killing as the plague,
And chastity a clue that leads to death.
Hold but thy nature, duke, and be but rash
And violent enough, and then at leisure
Repent; I care not.
And let my plots produce this long'd-for birth,
In my revenge I have my heaven on earth.
                      [*Exit.*

SCENE III.—*Another Room in the same.*

Enter Sforza, Pescara, *and three* Gentlemen.

Pesc. You promised to be merry.
  1 *Gent.* There are pleasures,
And of all kinds, to entertain the time.
  2 *Gent.* Your excellence vouchsafing to
  make choice
Of that which best affects you.
  Sfor. Hold your prating.
Learn manners too; you are rude.
  3 *Gent.* I have my answer,
Before I ask the question.   [*Aside.*
  Pesc. I must borrow
The privilege of a friend, and will; or else
I am like these, a servant, or, what's worse,
A parasite to the sorrow Sforza worships
In spite of reason.
  Sfor. Pray you, use your freedom;
And so far, if you please, allow me mine,
To hear you only; not to be compell'd
To take your moral potions. I am a man,
And if though philosophy, your mistress, rage
  or't,
Now I have cause to grieve I must be sad;
And I dare shew it.
  Pesc. Would it were bestow'd
Upon a worthier subject!
  Sfor. Take heed, friend.
You rub a sore, whose pain will make me
  mad;
And I shall then forget myself and you.
Lance it no further.

Pesc. Have you stood the shock
Of thousand enemies, and outfaced the
  anger
Of a great emperor, that vow'd your ruin,
Though by a desperate, a glorious way,
That had no precedent? are you return'd
  with honour,
Loved by your subjects? does your fortune
  court you,
Or rather say, your courage does command
  it?
Have you given proof, to this hour of your
  life,
Prosperity, that searches the best temper,
Could never puff you up, nor adverse fate
Deject your valour? Shall, I say, these
  virtues,
So many and so various trials of
Your constant mind, be buried in the frown
(To please you, I will say so) of a fair
  woman?
—Yet I have seen her equals.
  Sfor. Good Pescara,
This language in another were profane;
In you it is unmannerly.—Her equal!
I tell you as a friend, and tell you plainly,
(To all men else my sword should make
  reply,)
Her goodness does disdain comparison,
And, but herself, admits no parallel.
But you will say she's cross; 'tis fit she
  should be,
When I am foolish; for she's wise, Pescara,
And knows how far she may dispose her
  bounties,
Her honour safe; or, if she were averse,
'Twas a prevention of a greater sin
Ready to fall upon me; for she's not igno-
  rant,
But truly understands how much I love her,
And that her rare parts do deserve all honour.
Her excellence increasing with her years
  too,
I might have fallen into idolatry,
And, from the admiration of her worth,
Been taught to think there is no Power
  above her;
And yet I do believe, had angels sexes,
The most would be such women, and as-
  sume
No other shape, when they were to appear
In their full glory.
  Pesc. Well, sir, I'll not cross you,
Nor labour to diminish your esteem,
Hereafter, of her. Since your happiness,
As you will have it, has alone dependence
Upon her favour, from my soul I wish you
A fair atonement.
  Sfor. Time, and my submission,

Enter Tiberio *and* Stephano.

May work her to it.—O ! you are well re-
    turn'd ;
Say, am I blest? hath she vouchsafed to
    hear you?
Is there hope left that she may be appeased ?
Let her propound, and gladly I'll subscribe
To her conditions.
    Tib. She, sir, yet is froward,
And desires respite, and some privacy.
    Steph. She was harsh at first ; but, ere we
    parted, seem'd not
Implacable.
    Sfor. There's comfort yet : I'll ply her
Each hour with new ambassadors of more
    honours,
Titles, and eminence : my second self,
Francisco, shall solicit her.
    Steph. That a wise man,
And what is more, a prince that may com-
    mand,
Should sue thus poorly, and treat with his
    wife,
As she were a victorious enemy,
At whose proud feet, himself, his state, and
    country,
Basely begg'd mercy !
    Sfor. What is that you mutter?
I'll have thy thoughts.
    Steph. You shall. You are too fond,
And feed a pride that's swollen too big
    already,
And surfeits with observance.
    Sfor. O my patience !
My vassal speak thus?
    Steph. Let my head answer it,
If I offend. She, that you think a saint,
I fear, may play the devil.
    Pesc. Well said, old fellow.   [*Aside.*
    Steph. And he that hath so long engross'd
    your favours,
Though to be named with reverence, lord
    Francisco,
Who, as you purpose, shall solicit for you,
I think's too near her.
    [Sforza *lays his hand on his sword.*
    Pesc. Hold, sir ! this is madness.
    Sieph. It may be they confer of joining
    lordships ;
I'm sure he's private with her.
    Sfor. Let me go,
I scorn to touch him ; he deserves my pity,
And not my anger. Dotard ! and to be one
Is thy protection, else thou durst not think
That love to my Marcelia hath left room
In my full heart for any jealous thought :—
That idle passion dwell with thick-skinn'd
    tradesmen,   /

The undeserving lord, or the unable !
Lock up thy own wife, fool, that must take
    physic
From her young doctor, physic upon her
    back,
Because thou hast the palsy in that part—
That makes her active. I could smile to
    think
What wretched things they are that dare be
    jealous :
Were I match'd to another Messaline,
While I found merit in myself to please her,
I should believe her chaste, and would not
    seek
To find out my own torment ; but, alas !
Enjoying one that, but to me, 's a Dian,
I am too secure.
    Tib. This is a confidence
Beyond example.

Enter Graccho, Isabella, *and* Mariana.

    Grac. There he is— now speak,
Or be for ever silent.
    Sfor. If you come
To bring me comfort, say that you have made
My peace with my Marcelia.
    Isab. I had rather
Wait on you to your funeral.
    Sfor. You are my mother ;
Or, by her life, you were dead else.
    Mari. Would you were,
To your dishonour ! and, since dotage makes
    you
Wilfully blind, borrow of me my eyes,
Or some part of my spirit. Are you all flesh ?
A lump of patience only? no fire in you?
But do your pleasure :—here your mother
    was
Committed by your servant, (for I scorn
To call him husband,) and myself, your sister,
If that you dare remember such a name,
Mew'd up, to make the way open and free
For the adultress, I am unwilling
To say, a part of Sforza.
    Sfor. Take her head off !
She hath blasphemed, and by our law must
    die.
    Isab. Blasphemed ! for calling of a whore,
    a whore ?
    Sfor. O hell, what do I suffer !
    Mari. Or is it treason
For me, that am a subject, to endeavour
To save the honour of the duke, and that
He should not be a wittol on record ?
For by posterity 'twill be believed,
As certainly as now it can be proved,
Francisco, the great minion, that sways all,
To meet the chaste embraces of the dutchess,
Hath leap'd into her bed.

Sfor. Some proof, vile creature !
Or thou hast spoke thy last.
   Mari. The public fame,
Their hourly private meetings ; and, e'en
   now,
When, under a pretence of grief or anger,
You are denied the joys due to a husband,
And made a stranger to her, at all times
The door stands open to him. To a Dutch-
   man
This were enough, but to a right Italian
A hundred thousand witnesses.
   Isab. Would you have us
To be her bawds?
   Sfor. O the malice
And envy of base women, that, with horror,
Knowing their own defects and inward guilt,
Dare lie, and swear, and damn, for what's
   most false,
To cast aspersions upon one untainted !
Ye are in your natures devils, and your ends,
Knowing your reputation sunk for ever,
And not to be recover'd, to have all
Wear your black livery. Wretches ! you
   have raised
A monumental trophy to her pureness,
In this your studied purpose to deprave her :
And all the shot made by your foul detrae-
   tion,
Falling upon her sure-arm'd innocence,
Returns upon yourselves ; and, if my love
Could suffer an addition, I'm so far
From giving credit to you, this would teach
   me
More to admire and serve her. You are not
   worthy
To fall as sacrifices to appease her ;
And therefore live till your own envy burst
   you.
   Isab. All is in vain ; he is not to be moved.
   Mari. She has bewitch'd him.
   Pesc. 'Tis so past belief,
To me it shews a fable.

   Enter Francisco, *speaking to a* Servant
      within.

   Fran. On thy life,
Provide my horses, and without the port
With care attend me.
   Serv. [*within.*] I shall, my lord.
   Grac. He's come.
What gimcrack have we next?
   Fran. Great sir.
   Sfor. Francisco,
Though all the joys in women are fled from
   me,
In thee I do embrace the full delight
That I can hope from man.
   Fran. I would impart,

Please you to lend your ear, a weighty secret,
I am in labour to deliver to you.
   Sfor. All leave the room.
      [*Exeunt* Isab. Mari. *and* Graccho.
Excuse me, good Pescara,
Ere long I will wait on you.
   Pesc. You speak, sir,
The language I should use.   [*Exit.*
   Sfor. Be within call,
Perhaps we may have use of you.
   Tib. We shall, sir.
      [*Exeunt* Tib. *and* Steph.
   Sfor. Say on, my comfort.
   Fran. Comfort ! no, your torment,
For so my fate appoints me. I could curse
The hour that gave me being.
   Sfor. What new monsters
Of misery stand ready to devour me ?
Let them at once dispatch me.
   Fran. Draw your sword then,
And, as you wish your own peace, quickly
   kill me ;
Consider not, but do it.
   Sfor. Art thou mad?
   Fran. Or, if to take my life be too much
   mercy,
As death, indeed, concludes all human sor-
   rows,
Cut off my nose and ears ; pull out an eye,
The other only left to lend me light
To see my own deformities. Why was I
   born
Without some mulct imposed on me by
   nature?
Would from my youth a loathsome leprosy
Had run upon this face, or that my breath
Had been infectious, and so made me
   shunn'd
Of all societies ! Curs'd be he that taught
   me
Discourse or manners, or lent any grace
That makes the owner pleasing in the eye
Of wanton women ! Since those parts, which
   others
Value as blessings, are to me afflictions,
Such my condition is.
   Sfor. I am on the rack :
Dissolve this doubtful riddle.
   Fran. That I alone,
Of all mankind, that stand most bound to
   love you,
And study your content, should be ap-
   pointed,
Not by my will, but forced by cruel fate,
To be your greatest enemy !—not to hold
   you
In this amazement longer, in a word,
Your dutchess loves me.
   Sfor. Loves thee !

Fran. Is mad for me,·
Pursues me hourly.
Sfor. Oh !
Fran. And from hence grew
Her late neglect of you.
Sfor. O women ! women !
Fran. I labour'd to divert her by per-
  suasion,
Then urged your much love to her, and the
  danger ;
Denied her, and with scorn.
Sfor. 'Twas like thyself.
Fran. But when I saw her smile, then
  heard her say,
Your love and extreme dotage, as a cloak,
Should cover our embraces, and your power
Fright others from suspicion ; and all fa-
  vours
That should preserve her in her innocence,
By lust inverted to be used as bawds ;
I could not but in duty (though I know
That the relation kills in you all hope
Of peace hereafter, and in me 'twill shew
Both base and poor to rise up her accuser)
Freely discover it.
Sfor. Eternal plagues
Pursue and overtake her ! for her sake,
To all posterity may he prove a cuckold,
And, like to me, a thing so miserable
As words may not express him, that gives
  trust
To all-deceiving women ! Or, since it is
The will of heaven, to preserve mankind,
That we must know and couple with these
  serpents,
No wise man ever, taught by my example,
Hereafter use his wife with more respect ·
Than he would do his horse that does him
  service ;
Base woman being in her creation made
A slave to man. But, like a village nurse,
Stand I now cursing and considering, when
The tamest fool would do !—Within there !
  Stephano,
Tiberio, and the rest !——I will be sudden,
And she shall know and feel, love in ex-
  tremes
Abused, knows no degree in hate.

        Enter Tiberio *and* Stephano.

Tib. My lord.
Sfor. Go to the chamber of that wicked
  woman—
Steph. What wicked woman, sir ?
Sfor. The devil, my wife.
Force a rude entry, and, if she refuse
To follow you, drag her hither by the hair,
And know no pity ; any gentle usage
To her will call on cruelty from me,

To such as shew it.—Stand you staring ? Go,
And put my will in act.
Steph. There's no disputing.
Tib. But 'tis a tempest, on the sudden
  raised,
Who durst have dream'd of ?
        [*Exeunt* Tiberio *and* Stephano.
Sfor. Nay, since she dares damnation,
I'll be a fury to her.
Fran. Yet, great sir,
Exceed not in your fury ; she's yet guilty
Only in her intent.
Sfor. Intent, Francisco !
It does include all fact ; and I might sooner
Be won to pardon treason to my crown,
Or one that kill'd my father.
Fran. You are wise,
And know what's best to do :—yet, if you
  please,
To prove her temper to the height, say only
That I am dead, and then observe how far
She'll be transported. I'll remove a little,
But be within your call.—Now to the up-
  shot !
Howe'er, I'll shift for one.
        [*Aside and exit.*

    Re-enter Tiberio, Stephano, *and* Guard
        with Marcelia.

Marc. Where is this monster,
This walking tree of jealousy, this dreamer,
This horned beast that would be ? Oh ! are
  you here, sir ?
Is it by your commandment or allowance,
I am thus basely used ? Which of my virtues,
My labours, services, and cares to please
  you,
For, to a man suspicious and unthankful,
Without a blush I may be mine own trumpet,
Invites this barbarous course ? dare you look
  on me
Without a seal of shame ?
Sfor. Impudence,
How ugly thou appear'st now ! Thy intent
To be a whore, leaves thee not blood enough
To make an honest blush : what had the
  act done ?
Marc. Return'd thee the dishonour thou
  deserv'st ;
Though willingly I had given up myself
To every common letcher.
Sfor. Your chief minion,
Your chosen favourite, your woo'd Francisco,
Has dearly paid for't ; for, wretch ! know,
  he's dead,
And by my hand.
Marc. The bloodier villain thou !
But 'tis not to be wonder'd at, thy love

Does know no other object :—thou hast
  kill'd then,
A man I do profess I loved ; a man
For whom a thousand queens might well be
  rivals.
But he, I speak it to thy teeth, that dares be
A jealous fool, dares be a murderer,
And knows no end in mischief.
  Sfor. I begin now
In this my justice.   [*Stabs her.*
  Marc. Oh ! I have fool'd myself
Into my grave, and only grieve for that
Which, when you know you've slain an
  innocent,
You needs must suffer.
  Sfor. An innocent ! Let one
Call in Francisco ;—for he lives, vile creature,
       [*Exit* Stephano.
To justify thy falsehood, and how often,
With whorish flatteries, thou hast tempted
  him ;
I being only fit to live a stale,
A bawd and property to your wantonness.

    Re-enter Stephano.

  Steph. Signior Francisco, sir, but even now
Took horse without the ports.
  Marc. We are both abused,
And both by him undone. Stay, death, a
  little,
Till I have clear'd me to my lord, and then
I willingly obey thee.—O, my Sforza !
Francisco was not tempted, but the tempter ;
And, as he thought to win me, shew'd the
  warrant
That you sign'd for my death.
  Sfor. Then I believe thee ;
Believe thee innocent too.
  Marc. But, being contemn'd,
Upon his knees with tears he did beseech me,
Not to reveal it ; I, soft-hearted fool,
Judging his penitence true, was won unto it :
Indeed, the unkindness to be sentenced by
  you,
Before that I was guilty in a thought,
Made me put on a seeming anger towards you,
And now—behold the issue ! As I do,
May heaven forgive you !   [*Dies.*
  Tib. Her sweet soul has left
Her beauteous prison.
  Steph. Look to the duke ; he stands
As if he wanted motion.
  Tib. Grief hath stopp'd
The organ of his speech.
  Steph. Take up this body,
And call for his physicians.
  Sfor. O, my heart-strings !   [*Exeunt.*

    ACT V.

SCENE I.—*The* Milanese.   *A Room in*
    Eugenia's *House.*

Enter Francisco, *and* Eugenia *in male attire.*

  Fran. Why, could'st thou think, Eugenia,
  that rewards,
Graces, or favours, though strew'd thick
  upon me,
Could ever bribe me to forget mine honour ?
Or that I tamely would sit down, before
I had dried these eyes still wet with showers
  of tears,
By the fire of my revenge ? look up, my
  dearest !
For that proud fair, that, thief-like, stepp'd
  between
Thy promis'd hopes, and robb'd thee of a
  fortune
Almost in thy possession, hath found,
With horrid proof, his love, she thought her
  glory,
And an assurance of all happiness,
But hastened her sad ruin.
  Eug. Do not flatter
A grief that is beneath it ; for, however
The credulous duke to me proved false and
  cruel,
It is impossible he could be wrought
To look on her, but with the eyes of dotage,
And so to serve her.
  Fran. Such, indeed, I grant,
The stream of his affection was, and ran
A constant course, till I, with cunning
  malice—
And yet I wrong my act, for it was justice,
Made it turn backwards ; and hate, in ex-
  tremes,
(Love banish'd from his heart,) to fill the
  room :
In a word, know the fair Marcelia's dead.
  Eug. Dead !
  Fran. And by Sforza's hand. Does it not
  move you?
How coldly you receive it ! I expected
The mere relation of so great a blessing,
Borne proudly on the wings of sweet revenge,
Would have call'd on a sacrifice of thanks,
And joy not to be bounded or conceal'd.
You entertain it with a look, as if
You wish'd it were undone.
  Eug. Indeed I do :
For, if my sorrows could receive addition,
Her sad fate would increase, not lessen them.
She never injured me, but entertain'd
A fortune humbly offer'd to her hand,
Which a wise lady gladly would have kneel'd
  for.

Unless you would impute it as a crime,
She was more fair than.I, and had discretion
Not to deliver up her virgin fort,
Though strait besieged with flatteries, vows,
    and tears,
Until the church had made it safe and lawful.
And had I been the mistress of her judgment
And constant temper, skilful in the know-
    ledge
Of man's malicious falsehood, I had never,
Upon his hell-deep oaths to marry me,
Given up my fair name, and my maiden
    honour,
To his foul lust; nor lived now, being
    branded
In the forehead for his whore, the scorn and
    shame
Of all good women.
   Fran. Have you then no gall,
Anger, or spleen, familiar to your sex?
Or is it possible, that you could see
Another to possess what was your due,
And not grow pale with envy?
   Eug. Yes, of him
That did deceive me.: There's no passion,
    that
A maid so injured ever could partake of,
But I have dearly suffer'd. These three years,
In my desire and labour of revenge,
Trusted to you, I have endured the throes
Of teeming women; and will hazard all
Fate can inflict on me, but I will reach
Thy heart, false Sforza! You have trifled
    with me,
And not proceeded with that fiery zeal,
I look'd for from a brother of your spirit.
Sorrow forsake me, and all signs of grief
Farewell for ever! Vengeance, arm'd with
    fury,
Possess me wholly now!
   Fran. The reason, sister,
Of this strange metamorphosis?
   Eug. Ask thy fears:
Thy base, unmanly fears, thy poor delays,
Thy dull forgetfulness equal with death;
My wrong, else, and the scandal which can
    never
Be wash'd off from our house, but in his
    blood,
Would have stirr'd up a coward to a deed
In which, though he had fallen, the brave
    intent
Had crown'd itself with a fair monument
Of noble resolution. In this shape
I hope to get access; and, then, with shame,
Hearing my sudden execution, judge
What honour thou hast lost, in being
    transcended
By a weak woman.

   Fran. Still mine own, and dearer!
And yet in this you but pour oil on fire,
And offer your assistance where it needs not,
And, that you may perceive I lay not fallow,
But had your wrongs stamp'd deeply on my
    heart
By the iron pen of vengeance, I attempted,
By whoring her, to cuckold him: that failing,
I did begin his tragedy in her death,
To which it served as prologue, and will
    make
A memorable story of your fortunes
In my assured revenge: Only, best sister,
Let us not lose ourselves in the performance,
By your rash undertaking: we will be
As sudden as you could wish.
   Eug. Upon those terms
I yield myself and cause to be disposed of
As you think fit.

       Enter a Servant.

   Fran. Thy purpose?.
   Serv. There's one Graccho,
That follow'd you, it seems, upon the track,
Since you left Milan, that's importunate
To have access, and will not be denied:
His haste, he says, concerns you.
   Fran. Bring him to me.   [*Exit* Servant.
Though he hath laid an ambush for my life,
Or apprehension, yet I will prevent him,
And work mine own ends out.

       Enter Graccho.

   Grac. Now for my whipping!
And if I now outstrip him not, and catch
    him,
And by a new and strange way too, hereafter
I'll swear there are worms in my brains.
                    [*Aside.*
   Fran. Now, my good Graccho!
We meet as 'twere by miracle.
   Grac. Love, and duty,
And vigilance in me for my lord's safety,
First taught me to imagine you were here,
And then to follow you. All's come forth,
    my lord,
That you could wish conceal'd. The
    dutchess' wound,
In the duke's rage put home, yet gave her
    leave
To acquaint him with your practices, which
    your flight
Did easily confirm.
   Fran. This I expected;
But sure you come provided of good counsel,
To help in my extremes.
   Grac. I would not hurt you.
   Fran. How! hurt me? such another
    word's thy death;

Why, dar'st thou think it can fall in thy will,
To outlive what I determine?
  Grac. How he awes me !   [*Aside.*
— *Fran.* Be brief; what brought thee hither?
  Grac. Care to inform you
You are a condemn'd man, pursued and
    sought for,
And your head rated at ten thousand ducats
To him that brings it.
  Fran. Very good.
  Grac. All passages
Are intercepted, and choice troops of horse
Scour o'er the neighbour plains; your picture
    sent
To every state confederate with Milan :
That, though I grieve to speak it, in my
    judgment,
So thick your dangers meet, and run upon
    you,
It is impossible you should escape
Their curious search.
  Eug. Why, let us then turn Romans,
And, falling by our own hands, mock their
    threats,
And dreadful preparations.
  Fran. 'Twould show nobly ;
But that the honour of our full revenge
Were lost in the rash action. No, Eugenia,
Graccho is wise, my friend too, not my
    servant,
And I dare trust him with my latest secret.
We would, and thou must help us to perform
    it,
First kill the duke—then, fall what can upon
    us !
For injuries are writ in brass, kind Graccho,
And not to be forgotten.
  Grac. He instructs me
What I should do.   [*Aside.*
  Fran. What's that?
  Grac. I labour with
A strong desire to assist you with my service ;
And now I am deliver'd of 't.
  Fran. I told you.—
Speak, my oraculous Graccho.
  Grac. I have heard, sir,
Of men in debt that, lay'd for by their cre-
    ditors,
In all such places where it could be thought
They would take shelter, chose, for sanc-
    tuary,
Their lodgings underneath their creditors'
    noses,
Or near that prison to which they were de-
    sign'd,
If apprehended ; confident that there
They never should be sought for.
  Eug. 'Tis a strange one !
  Fran. But what infer you from it?

  Grac. This, my lord ;
That, since all ways of your escape are
    stopp'd,
In Milan only, or, what's more, in the court,
Whither it is presumed you dare not come,
Conceal'd in some disguise, you may live safe.
  Fran. And not to be discover'd ?
  Grac. But by myself.
  Fran. By thee ! Alas ! I know thee honest,
    Graccho,.
And I will put thy counsel into act,
And suddenly. Yet, not to be ungrateful
For all thy loving travail to preserve me,
What bloody end soe'er my stars appoint,
Thou shalt be safe, good Graccho.—Who's
    within there?
  Grac. In the devil's name, what means he !

          Enter Servants.

  Fran. Take my friend
Into your custody, and bind him fast :
I would not part with him.
  Grac. My good lord.
  Fran. Dispatch :
'Tis for your good, to keep you honest,
    Graccho !
I would not have ten thousand ducats tempt
    you,
Being of a soft and wax-like disposition,
To play the traitor ; nor a foolish itch
To be revenged for your late excellent whip-
    ping,
Give you the opportunity to offer
My head for satisfaction. Why, thou fool !
I can look through and through thee ; thy
    intents
Appear to me as written in thy forehead,
In plain and easy characters : and but that
I scorn a slave's base blood should rust that
    sword
That from a prince expects a scarlet dye,
Thou now wert dead ; but live, only to pray
For good success to crown my undertakings ;
And then, at my return, perhaps, I'll free
    thee,
To make me further sport. Away with him !
I will not hear a syllable.
          [*Exeunt* Servants *with* Graccho.
                    We must trust
Ourselves, Eugenia ; and though we make
    use of
The counsel of our servants, that oil spent,
Like snuffs that do offend, we tread them
    out.—
But now to our last scene, which we'll so
    carry,
That few shall understand how 'twas begun,
Till all, with half an eye, may see 'tis done.
          [*Exeunt.*

SCENE II.—Milan. *A Room in the Castle.*

Enter Pescara, Tiberio, *and* Stephano.

Pesc. The like was never read of.

Steph. In my judgment,
To all that shall but hear it, 'twill appear
A most impossible fable.

Tib. For Francisco,
My wonder is the less, because there are
Too many precedents of unthankful men
Raised up to greatness, which have after
    studied
The ruin of their makers.

Steph. But that melancholy,
Though ending in distraction, should work
So far upon a man, as to compel him
To court a thing that has nor sense nor being,
Is unto me a miracle.

Pesc. 'Troth, I'll tell you,
And briefly as I can, by what degrees
He fell into this madness. When, by the care
Of his physicians, he was brought to life,
As he had only pass'd a fearful dream,
And had not acted what I grieve to think on,
He call'd for fair Marcelia, and being told
That she was dead, he broke forth in ex-
    tremes,
(I would not say blasphemed,) and cried
    that heaven,
For all the offences that mankind could do,
Would never be so cruel as to rob it
Of so much sweetness, and of so much
    goodness ;
That not alone was sacred in herself,
But did preserve all others innocent,
That had but converse with her. Then it
    came
Into his fancy that she was accused
By his mother and his sister ; thrice he curs'd
    them,
And thrice his desperate hand was on his
    sword
T'have kill'd them both ; but he restrain'd,
    and they
Shunning his fury, spite of all prevention
He would have turned his rage upon himself ;
When wisely his physicians, looking on
The dutchess' wound, to stay his ready hand,
Cried out, it was not mortal.

Tib. 'Twas well thought on.

Pes. He easily believing what he wish'd,
More than a perpetuity of pleasure
In any object else ; flatter'd by hope,
Forgetting his own greatness, he fell prostrate
At the doctors' feet, implored their aid, and
    swore,
Provided they recover'd her, he would live
A private man, and they should share his
    dukedom.

They seem'd to promise fair, and every hour
Vary their judgments, as they find his fit
To suffer intermission or extremes :
For his behaviour since——

Sfor. [*within.*] As you have pity
Support her gently.

Pes. Now, be your own witnesses ;
I am prevented.

Enter Sforza, Isabella, Mariana, Doctors,
    and Servants *with the body of* Marcelia.

Sfor. Carefully, I beseech you,
The gentlest touch torments her ; and then
    think
What I shall suffer. O you earthly gods,
You second natures, that from your great
    master,
Who join'd the limbs of torn Hippolitus,
And drew upon himself the Thunderer's envy,
Are taught those hidden secrets that restore
To life death-wounded men ! you have a
    patient,
On whom to express the excellence of art,
Will bind even heaven your debtor, though
    it pleases
To make your hands the organs of a work
The saints will smile to look on, and good
    angels
Clap their celestial wings to give it plaudits,
How pale and wan she looks ! O pardon me,
That I presume (dyed o'er with bloody guilt,
Which makes me, I confess, far, far un-
    worthy)
To touch this snow-white hand. How cold
    it is !
This once was Cupid's fire-brand, and still
'Tis so to me. How slow her pulses beat too !
Yet in this temper, she is all perfection,
And mistress of a heat so full of sweetness,
The blood of virgins, in their pride of youth,
Are balls of snow or ice compared unto her.

Mari. Is not this strange ?

Isab. Oh ! cross him not, dear daughter ;
Our conscience tells us we have been abused,
Wrought to accuse the innocent, and with
    him
Are guilty of a fact——

Enter a Servant, *and whispers* Pescara.

Mari. 'Tis now past help.

Pesc. With me ? What is he ?

Serv. He has a strange aspect ;
A Jew by birth, and a physician
By his profession, as he says, who, hearing
Of the duke's frenzy, on the forfeit of
His life will undertake to render him
Perfect in every part :—provided that
Your lordship's favour gain him free access,

And your power with the duke a safe pro-
tection,
Till the great work be ended.
    Pesc. Bring me to him ;
As I find cause, I'll do.
                    [*Exeunt* Pesc. *and* Serv.
    Sfor. How sound she sleeps !
Heaven keep her from a lethargy !——How
    long
(But answer me with comfort, I beseech you)
Does your sure judgment tell you that these
    lids,
That cover richer jewels than themselves,
Like envious night, will bar these glorious
    suns
From shining on me ?
    1 *Doct.* We have given her, sir,
A sleepy potion, that will hold her long,
That she may be less sensible of the torment
The searching of her wound will put her to.
    2 *Doct.* She now feels little ; but, if we
        should wake her,
To hear her speak would fright both us and
    you,
And therefore dare not hasten it.
    Sfor. I am patient.
You see I do not rage, but wait your pleasure.
What do you think she dreams of now ? for
    sure,
Although her body's organs are bound fast,
Her fancy cannot slumber.
    1 *Doct.* That, sir, looks on
Your sorrow for your late rash act, with pity
Of what you suffer for it, and prepares
To meet the free confession of your guilt
With a glad pardon.
    Sfor. She was ever kind ;
And her displeasure, though call'd on, short-
    lived
Upon the least submission. O you Powers,
That can convey our thoughts to one another
Without the aid of eyes or ears, assist me !
Let her behold me in a pleasing dream
                            [*Kneels.*
Thus, on my knees before her ; (yet that duty
In me is not sufficient ;) let her see me
Compel my mother, from whom I took life,
And this my sister, partner of my being,
To bow thus low unto her ; let her hear us
In my acknowledgment freely confess
That we in a degree as high are guilty
As she is innocent. Bite your tongues, vile
    creatures,
And let your inward horror fright your souls,
For having belied that pureness, to come
    near which,
All women that posterity can bring forth
Must be, though striving to be good, poor
    rivals.

And for that dog Francisco, that seduced me,
In wounding her, to rase a temple built
To chastity and sweetness, let her know
I'll follow him to hell, but I will find him,
And there live a fourth fury to torment him.
Then, for this curs'd hand and arm that
    guided
The wicked steel, I'll have them, joint by
    joint,
With burning irons sear'd off, which I will
    eat,
I being a vulture fit to taste such carrion ;
Lastly——
    1 *Doct.* You are too loud, sir ; you disturb
Her sweet repose.
    Sfor. I am hush'd. Yet give us leave,
Thus prostrate at her feet, our eyes bent
    downwards,
Unworthy, and ashamed, to look upon her,
To expect her gracious sentence.
    2 *Doct.* He's past hope.
    1 *Doct.* The body too will putrify, and then
We can no longer cover the imposture.
    Tib. Which, in his death, will quickly be
        discover'd.
I can but weep his fortune.
    Steph. Yet be careful
You lose no minute to preserve him ; time
May lessen his distraction.

Re-enter Pescara, *with* Francisco, *as a Jew
    doctor, and* Eugenia *disguised as before.*

    Fran. I am no god, sir,
To give a new life to her ; yet I'll hazard
My head, I'll work the senseless trunk
    t'appear
To him as it had got a second being,
Or that the soul, that's fled from't, were call'd
    back
To govern it again. I will preserve it
In the first sweetness, and by a strange
    vapour,
Which I'll infuse into her mouth, create
A seeming breath ; I'll make her veins run
    high too,
As if they had true motion.
    Pesc. Do but this,
Till we use means to win upon his passions
T'endure to hear she's dead with some small
    patience,
And make thy own reward.
    Fran. The art I use
Admits no looker on : I only ask
The fourth part of an hour, to perfect that
I boldly undertake.
    Pesc. I will procure it.
    2 *Doct.* What stranger's this ?
    Pesc. Sooth me in all I say ;
There's a main end in it.

Fran. Beware !

Eug. I am warn'd.

Pesc. Look up, sir, cheerfully ; comfort in me
Flows strongly to you.

Sfor. From whence came that sound ?
Was it from my Marcelia ? If it were,

                        [Rises.
I rise, and joy will give me wings to meet it.

Pesc. Nor shall your expectation be deferr'd
But a few minutes. Your physicians are
Mere voice, and no performance ; I have found
A man that can do wonders. Do not hinder
The dutchess' wish'd recovery, to enquire
Or what he is, or to give thanks, but leave him
To work this miracle.

Sfor. Sure, 'tis my good angel.
I do obey in all things : be it death
For any to disturb him, or come near,
Till he be pleased to call us. O, be prosperons,
And make a duke thy bondman !

    [Exeunt all but Francisco *and* Eugenia.

Fran. 'Tis my purpose ;
If that to fall a long-wish'd sacrifice
To my revenge can be a benefit.
I'll first make fast the doors ;—so !

Eug. You amaze me :
What follows now ?

Fran. A full conclusion.
Of all thy wishes. Look on this, Eugenia,
Even such a thing, the proudest fair on earth
(For whose delight the elements are ransack'd,
And art with nature studied to preserve her,)
Must be, when she is summon'd to appear
In the court of Death. But I lose time.

Eug. What mean you ?

Fran. Disturb me not.—Your ladyship looks pale ;
But I, your doctor, have a ceruse for you.—
See, my Eugenia, how many faces,
That are adorned in court, borrow these helps,

                     [Paints the cheeks.
And pass for excellence, when the better part
Of them are like to this.—Your mouth smells sour too,
But here is that shall take away the scent ;
A precious antidote old ladies use,
When they would kiss, knowing their gums are rotten.   *[Paints the lips.*
These hands, too, that disdained to take a touch
From any lip, whose owner writ not lord,
Are now but as the coarsest earth ; but I
Am at the charge, my bill not to be paid too,

To give them seeming beauty.

                   [Paints the hands.
So ! 'tis done.
How do you like my workmanship ?

Eug. I tremble :
And thus to tyrannize upon the dead,
Is most inhuman.

Fran. Come we for revenge,
And can we think on pity ! Now to the upshot,
And, as it proves, applaud it.—My lord the duke !
Enter with joy, and see the sudden change
Your servant's hand hath wrought.

    Re-enter Sforza *and the rest.*

Sfor. I live again
In my full confidence that Marcelia may
Pronounce my pardon. Can she speak yet ?

Fran. No :
You must not look for all your joys at once ;
That will ask longer time.

Pesc. 'Tis wondrous strange !

Sfor. By all the dues of love I have had from her,
This hand seems as it was when first I kiss'd it.
These lips invite too : I could ever feed
Upon these roses, they still keep their colour
And native sweetness : only the nectar's wanting.
That, like the morning dew in flowery May,
Preserved them in their beauty.

    Enter Graccho *hastily.*

Grac. Treason, treason !

Tib. Call up the guard.

Fran. Graccho ! then we are lost.
                     [Aside.

    Enter Guard.

Grac. I am got off, sir Jew ; a bribe hath done it,
For all your serious charge ; there's no disguise
Can keep you from my knowledge.

Sfor. Speak.

Grac. I am out of breath,
But this is——

Fran. Spare thy labour, fool,—Francisco.

All. Monster of men !

Fran. Give me all attributes
Of all you can imagine, yet I glory
To be the thing I was born. I AM Francisco ;
Francisco, that was raised by you, and made
The minion of the time ; the same Francisco,
That would have whored this trunk, when it had life ;
And, after, breathed a jealousy upon thee,

H

As killing as those damps that belch out
　　plagues
When the foundation of the earth is shaken :
I made thee do a deed heaven will not pardon,
Which was—to kill an innocent.
　　Sfor. Call forth the tortures
For all that flesh can feel.
　　Fran. I dare the worst.
Only, to yield some reason to the world
Why I pursued this course, look on this face,
Made old by thy base falsehood : 'tis Eugenia.
　　Sfor. Eugenia !
　　Fran. Does it start you, sir ? my sister,
Seduced and fool'd by thee : but thou must
　　pay
The forfeit of thy falsehood.　Does it not
　　work yet !—
Whate'er becomes of me, which I esteem not,
THOU art mark'd for the grave : I've given
　　thee poison
In this cup, now observe me, which, thy lust
Carousing deeply of, made thee forget
Thy vow'd faith to Eugenia.
　　Pesc. O damn'd villain !
　　Isab. How do you, sir ?
　　Sfor. Like one
That learns to know in death what punish-
　　ment
Waits on the breach of faith.　Oh ! now I
　　feel
An Ætna in my entrails.—I have lived
A prince, and my last breath shall be com-
　　mand.
—I burn, I burn ! yet ere life be consumed,

Let me pronounce upon this wretch all
　　torture
That witty cruelty can invent.
　　Pesc. Away with him !
　　Tib. In all things we will serve you.
　　Fran. Farewell, sister !
Now I have kept my word, torments I scorn :
I leave the world with glory.　They are
　　men,
And leave behind them name and memory,
That, wrong'd, do right themselves before
　　they die.
　　　　　　[*Exeunt* Guard *with* Francisco.
　　Steph. A desperate wretch !
　　Sfor. I come : Death ! I obey thee.
Yet I will not die raging ; for, alas !
My whole life was a frenzy. Good Eugenia,
In death forgive me.—As you love me, bear
　　her
To some religious house, there let her spend
The remnant of her life : when I am ashes,
Perhaps she'll be appeased, and spare a
　　prayer
For my poor soul.　Bury me with Marcelia,
And let our epitaph be——　　　[*Dies.*
　　Tib. His speech is stopp'd.
　　Steph. Already dead !
　　Pesc. It is in vain to labour
To call him back.　We'll give him funeral,
And then determine of the state affairs :
And learn, from this example, There's no
　　trust
In a foundation that is built on lust.　　.
　　　　　　　　　　　　　　　　[*Exeunt.*

The Bondman.

DRAMATIS PERSONÆ.

Timoleon, *the general, of* Corinth.
Archidamus, *prætor of* Syracusa.
Diphilus, *a senator of* Syracusa.
Cleon, *a fat impotent lord.*
Marullo, *the* Bondman (*i.e.* Pisander, *a gentleman of* Thebes ; *disguised as a slave.*)
Poliphron, *friend to Marullo ; also disguised as a slave.*
Leosthenes, *a gentleman of* Syracusa, *enamoured of* Cleora.
Asotus, *a foolish lover, and the son of* Cleon.

Timagoras, *the son of* Archidamus.
Gracculo, } *slaves.*
Cimbrio, }
A Gaoler.
Cleora, *daughter of* Archidamus.
Corisca, *a proud wanton lady, wife to* Cleon.
Olympia, *a rich widow.*
Timandra, *slave to* Cleora (*i.e.* Statilia, *sister to* Pisander.)
Zanthia, *slave to* Corisca.
Other Slaves, Soldiers, Officers, Senators.

SCENE,—Syracuse, *and the adjacent country.*

ACT I.

SCENE I.—*The Camp of* Timoleon, *near* Syracuse.

Enter Timagoras *and* Leosthenes.

Timag. Why should you droop, Leosthenes, or despair
My sister's favour ? What, before, you purchased
By courtship and fair language, in these wars,
(For from her soul you know she loves a soldier)
You may deserve by action.
    Leost. Good Timagoras,
When I have said my friend, think all is spoken
That may assure me yours ; and pray you believe,
The dreadful voice of war that shakes the city,
The thundering threats of Carthage, nor their army
Raised to make good those threats, affright not me.—
If fair Cleora were confirm'd his prize,
That has the strongest arm and sharpest
    sword,
I'd court Bellona in her horrid trim,
As if she were a mistress ; and bless fortune,
That offers my young valour to the proof,
How much I dare do for your sister's love.
But, when that I consider how averse
Your noble father, great Archidamus,
Is, and hath ever been, to my desires,
Reason may warrant me to doubt and fear,
What seeds soever I sow in these wars

Of noble courage, his determinate will
May blast, and give my harvest to another,
That never toil'd for it.
    Timag. Prithee, do not nourish
These jealous thoughts ; I am thine, (and
    pardon me,
Though I repeat it,) thy Timagoras,
That, for thy sake, when the bold Theban
    sued,
Far-famed Pisander, for my sister's love,
Sent him disgraced and discontented home.
I wrought my father then ; and I, that
    stopp'd not
In the career of my affection to thee,
When that renowned worthy, that, brought
    with him
High birth, wealth, courage, as fee'd advocates
To mediate for him ; never will consent
A fool, that only has the shape of man,
Asotus, though he be rich Cleon's heir,
Shall bear her from thee.
    Leost. In that trust I love.
    Timag. Which never shall deceive you.

Enter Marullo.

Mar. Sir, the general,
Timoleon, by his trumpets hath given
    warning
For a remove.
    Timag. 'Tis well ; provide my horse.
    Mar. I shall, sir.   [*Exit.*
    Leost. This slave has a strange aspect.
    Timag. Fit for his fortune ; 'tis a strong-limb'd knave :
My father bought him for my sister's litter.

H 2

O pride of women ! Coaches are too com-
   mon—
They surfeit in the happiness of peace,
And ladies think they keep not state enough,
If, for their pomp and ease, they are not born
In triumph on men's shoulders.
   Leost. Who commands
The Carthaginian fleet !
   Timag. Gisco's their admiral,
And 'tis our happiness ; a raw young fellow,
One never train'd in arms, but rather
   fashion'd
To tilt with ladies' lips, than crack a lance ;
Ravish a feather from a mistress' fan,
And wear it as a favour. A steel helmet,
Made horrid with a glorious plume, will crack
His woman's neck.
   Leost. No more of him.—The motives,
That Corinth gives us aid?
   Timag. The common danger ;
For Sicily being afire, she is not safe :
It being apparent that ambitious Carthage,
That, to enlarge her empire, strives to fasten
An unjust gripe on us that live free lords
Of Syracusa, will not end, till Greece
Acknowledge her their sovereign.
   Leost. I am satisfied.
What think you of our general?
   Timag. He's a man   [*Trumpets within.*
Of strange and reserved parts ; but a great
   soldier.
His trumpets call us, I'll forbear his cha-
   racter :
To morrow, in the senate-house, at large
He will express himself.
   Leost. I'll follow you.   [*Exeunt.*

SCENE II.—Syracuse. *A Room in* Cleon's
     House.

   Enter Cleon, Corisca, *and* Gracculo.

   Coris. Nay, good chuck.
   Cleon. I've said it ; stay at home :
I cannot brook your gadding ; you're a fair
   one,
Beauty invites temptations, and short heels
Are soon tripp'd up.
   Coris. Deny me ! by my honour,
You take no pity on me. I shall swoon
As soon as you are absent ; ask my man else,
You know he dares not tell a lie.
   Grac. Indeed,
You are no sooner out of sight, but she
Does feel strange qualms ; then sends for her
   young doctor,
Who ministers physic to her on her back,
Her ladyship lying as she were entranced :
(I've peep'd in at the keyhole, and observed
   them :)
And sure his potions never fail to work,

For she's so pleasant in the taking them,
She tickles again.
   Coris. And all's to make you merry,
When you come home.
   Cleon. You flatter me ; I am old,
And wisdom cries, Beware ! .
   Coris. Old ! duck. To me
You are a young Adonis.
   Grac. Well said, Venus !
I am sure she Vulcans him.   [*Aside.*
   Coris. I will not change thee
For twenty boisterous young things without
   beards.
These bristles give the gentlest titillations,
And such a sweet dew flows on them, it cures
My lips without pomatum. Here's a round
   belly !
'Tis a down pillow to my back ; I sleep
So quietly by it : and this tunable nose,
Faith, when you hear it not, affords such
   music,
That I curse all night-fiddlers.
   Grac. This is gross.
Not finds she flouts him !   [*Aside.*
   Coris. As I live, I am jealous.
   Cleon. Jealous of me, wife?
   Coris. Yes ; and I have reason ;
Knowing how lusty and active a man you
   are.
   Cleon. Hum, hum !
   Grac. This is no cunning quean ! 'slight,
   she will make him
To think that, like a stag, he has cast his
   horns,
And is grown young again.   [*Aside.*
   Coris. You have forgot
What you did in your sleep, and, when you
   waked,
Call'd for a caudle.
   Grac. It was in his sleep ;
For, waking, I durst trust my mother with
   him.   [*Aside.*
   Coris. I long to see the man of war :
   Cleora,
Archidamus' daughter, goes, and rich
   Olympia :
I will not miss the show.
   Cleon. There's no contending :
For this time I am pleased, but I'll no more
on't.   [*Exeunt*

SCENE III.—*The Same. The Senate-house.*

   Enter Archidamus, Cleon, Diphilus, Olympia, Corisca, Cleora, *and* Zanthia.

   Archid. So careless we have been, my
   noble lords,
In the disposing of our own affairs,
And ignorant in the art of government,
That now we need a stranger to instruct us.

Yet we are happy that our neighbour Corinth,
Pitying the unjust gripe Carthage would lay
On Syracusa, hath vouchsafed to lend us
Her man of men, Timoleon, to defend
Our country and our liberties.
   Diph. 'Tis a favour
We are unworthy of, and we may blush
Necessity compels us to receive it.
   Archid. O shame! that we, that are a
    populous nation,
Engaged to liberal nature, for all blessings
An island can bring forth; we, that have
   limbs,
And able bodies; shipping, arms, and
   treasure,
The sinews of the war, now we are call'd
To stand upon our guard, cannot produce
One fit to be our general.
   Cleon. I am old and fat;
I could say something, else.
   Archid. We must obey
The time and our occasions; ruinous build-
   ings,
Whose bases and foundations are infirm,
Must use supporters: we are circled round
With danger; o'er our heads, with sail-
   stretch'd wings,
Destruction hovers, and a cloud of mischief
Ready to break upon us; no hope left us
That may divert it, but our sleeping virtue,
Roused up by brave Timoleon.
   Cleon. When arrives he?
   Diph. He is expected every hour.
   Archid. The braveries
Of Syracusa, among whom my son,
Timagoras, Leosthenes, and Asotus,
Your hopeful heir, lord Cleon, two days
   since
Rode forth to meet him, and attend him to
The city; every minute we expect
To be bless'd with his presence.
   [*Shouts within; then a flourish of*
    trumpets.
   Cleon. What shout's this?
   Diph. 'Tis seconded with loud music.
   Archid. Which confirms
His wish'd-for entrance. Let us entertain
   him
With all respect, solemnity, and pomp,
A man may merit, that comes to redeem us
From slavery and oppression.
   Cleon. I'll lock up
My doors, and guard my gold: these lads
   of Corinth
Have nimble fingers, and I fear them more,
Being within our walls, than those of
   Carthage;
They are far off.
   Archid. And, ladies, be it your care

To welcome him and his followers with all
   duty:
For rest resolved, their hands and swords
   must keep you
In that full height of happiness you live;
A dreadful change else follows.
   [*Exeunt* Archidamus, Cleon, *and*
    Diphilus.
   Olymp. We are instructed.
   Coris. I'll kiss him for the honour of my
    country,
With any she in Corinth.
   Olymp. Were he a courtier,
I've sweetmeat in my closet shall content
   him,
Be his palate ne'er so curious.
   Coris. And, if need be,
I have a couch and a banqueting-house in
   my orchard,
Where many a man of honour has not scorn'd
To spend an afternoon.
   Olymp. These men of war,
As I have heard, know not to court a lady.
They cannot praise our dressings, kiss our
   hands,
Usher us to our litters, tell love-stories,
Commend our feet and legs, and so search
   upwards;
A sweet becoming boldness! they are rough,
Boisterous, and saucy, and at the first sight
Ruffle and touze us, and, as they find their
   stomachs,
Fall roundly to it.
   Coris. 'Troth, I like them the better:
I can't endure to have a perfumed sir
Stand cringing in the hams, licking his lips
Like a spaniel over a furmenty-pot, and yet
Has not the boldness to come on, or offer
What they know we expect.
   Olymp. We may commend
A gentleman's modesty, manners, and fine
   language,
His singing, dancing, riding of great horses,
The wearing of his clothes, his fair com-
   plexion;
Take presents from him, and extol his
   bounty:
Yet, though he observe, and waste his estate
   upon us,
If he be staunch, and bid not for the stock
That we were born to traffic with; the truth
   is,
We care not for his company.
   Coris. Musing, Cleora?
   Olymp. She's studying how to entertain
   these strangers,
And to engross them to herself.
   Cleo. No, surely;
I will not cheapen any of their wares,

Till you have made your market; you will
  buy,
I know, at any rate.
  Coris. She has given it you.
  Olymp. No more; they come: the first
    kiss for this jewel.

Flourish of trumpets. Enter Timagoras,
  Leosthenes, Asotus, Timoleon *in black,
  led in by* Archidamus, Diphilus, *and*
  Cleon; *followed by* Marullo, Gracculo,
  Cimbrio, *and other* Slaves.

  Archid. It is your seat: which, with a
    general suffrage,
            [*Offering* Timoleon *the state.*
As to the supreme magistrate, Sicily tenders,
And prays Timoleon to accept.
  Timol. Such honours
To one ambitious of rule or titles,
Whose heaven on earth is placed in his
  command,
And absolute power o'er others, would with
  joy,
And veins swollen high with pride, be en-
  tertain'd.
They take not me; for I have ever loved
An equal freedom, and proclaim'd all such
As would usurp on others' liberties,
Rebels to nature, to whose bounteous bless-
  ings
All men lay claim as true legitimate sons:
But such as have made forfeit of themselves
By vicious courses, and their birthright lost,
'Tis not injustice they are mark'd for slaves,
To serve the virtuous. For myself, I know
Honours and great employments are great
  burthens,
And must require an Atlas to support them.
He that would govern others, first should be
The master of himself, richly endued
With depth of understanding, height of
  courage,
And those remarkable graces which I dare
  not
Ascribe unto myself.
  Archid. Sir, empty men
Are trumpets of their own deserts; but you,
That are not in opinion, but in proof,
Really good, and full of glorious parts,
Leave the report of what you are to fame;
Which, from the ready tongues of all good
  men,
Aloud proclaims you.
  Diph. Besides, you stand bound,
Having so large a field to exercise
Your active virtues offer'd you, to impart
Your strength to such as need it.
  Timol. 'Tis confess'd:
And, since you'll have it so, such as I am,

For you, and for the liberty of Greece,
I am most ready to lay down my life:
But yet consider, men of Syracusa,
Before that you deliver up the power,
Which yet is yours, to me,—to whom 'tis
  given;
To an impartial man, with whom nor
  threats,
Nor prayers, shall prevail; for I must steer
An even course.
  Archid. Which is desired of all.
  Timol. Timophanes, my brother, for
    whose death
I am tainted in the world, and foully
  tainted;
In whose remembrance I have ever worn,
In peace and war, this livery of sorrow,
Can witness for me how much I detest
Tyrannous usurpation. With grief,
I must remember it; for, when no persuasion
Could win him to desist from his bad
  practice,
To change the aristocracy of Corinth
Into an absolute monarchy, I chose rather
To prove a pious and obedient son
To my country, my best mother, than to lend
Assistance to Timophanes, though my
  brother,
That, like a tyrant, strove to set his foot
Upon the city's freedom.
  Timag. 'Twas a deed
Deserving rather trophies than reproof.
  Leost. And will be still remember'd to
    your honour,
If you forsake not us.
  Diph. If you free Sicily
From barbarous Carthage' yoke, it will be
  said,
In him you slew a tyrant.
  Archid. But, giving way
To her invasion, not vouchsafing us
That fly to your protection, aid and comfort,
'Twill be believed, that, for your private ends,
You kill'd a brother.
  Timol. As I then proceed,
To all posterity may that act be crown'd
With a deserved applause, or branded with
The mark of infamy!—Stay yet; ere I take
This seat of justice, or engage myself
To fight for you abroad, or to reform
Your state at home, swear all upon my sword,
And call the gods of Sicily to witness
The oath you take, that whatsoe'er I shall
Propound for safety of your commonwealth,
Not circumscribed or bound in, shall by
  you
Be willingly obey'd.
  Archid. Diph. Cleon. So may we prosper,
As we obey in all things!

Timag. Leost. Asot. And observe
All your commands as oracles !
  Timol. Do not repent it. [*Takes the state.*
  Olymp. He ask'd not our consent.
  Coris. He's a clown, I warrant him.
  Olymp. I offer'd myself twice, and yet the churl
Would not salute me.
  Coris. Let him kiss his drum !
I'll save my lips, I rest on it.
  Olymp. He thinks women
No part of the republic.
  Coris. He shall find
We are a commonwealth.
  Cleo. The less your honour.
  Timol. First, then, a word or two, but without bitterness,
(And yet mistake me not, I am no flatterer,)
Concerning your ill government of the state ;
In which the greatest, noblest, and most rich,
Stand, in the first file, guilty.
  Cleon. Ha ! how's this?
  Timol. You have not, as good patriots should do, studied
The public good, but your particular ends ;
Factious among yourselves, preferring such
To offices and honours, as ne'er read
The elements of saving policy ;
But deeply skill'd in all the principles
That usher to destruction.
  Leost. Sharp !
  Timag. The better.
  Timol. Your senate-house, which used not to admit
A man, however popular, to stand
At the helm of government, whose youth was not
Made glorious by action ; whose experience,
Crown'd with gray hairs, gave warrant to his counsels,
Heard and received with reverence, is now fill'd
With green heads, that determine of the state
Over their cups, or when their sated lusts
Afford them leisure ; or supplied by those
Who, rising from base arts and sordid thrift,
Are eminent for their wealth, not for their wisdom :
Which is the reason that to hold a place
In council, which was once esteem'd an honour,
And a reward for virtue, hath quite lost
Lustre and reputation, and is made
A mercenary purchase.
  Timag. He speaks home.
  Leost. And to the purpose.
  Timol. From whence it proceeds,
That the treasure of the city is engross'd
By a few private men, the public cofiers

Hollow with want ; and they, that will not spare
One talent for the common good, to feed
The pride and bravery of their wives, consume,
In plate, in jewels, and superfluous slaves,
What would maintain an army.
  Coris. Have at us !
  Olymp. We thought we were forgot.
  Cleo. But it appears,
You will be treated of.
  Timol. Yet, in this plenty,
And fat of peace, your young men ne'e were train'd
In martial discipline ; and your ships unrigg'd,
Rot in the harbour : no defence prepared,
But thought unuseful ; as if that the gods,
Indulgent to your sloth, had granted you
A perpetuity of pride and pleasure,
No change fear'd or expected. Now you find
That Carthage, looking on your stupid sleeps,
And dull security, was invited to
Invade your territories.
  Archid. You have made us see, sir,
To our shame, the country's sickness : now, from you,
As from a careful and a wise physician,
We do expect the cure.
  Timol. Old fester'd sores
Must be lanced to the quick, and cauterized ;
Which born with patience, after I'll apply
Soft unguents. For the maintenance of the war,
It is decreed all monies in the hand
Of private men, shall instantly be brought
To the public treasury.
  Timag. This bites sore.
  Cleon. The cure
Is worse than the disease ; I'll never yield to't :
What could the enemy, though victorious,
Inflict more on us ? All that my youth hath toil'd for,
Purchas'd with industry, and preserved with care,
Forced from me in a moment !
  Diph. This rough course
Will never be allow'd of.
  Timol. O blind men !
If you refuse the first means that is offer'd
To give you health, no hope's left to recover
Your desperate sickness. Do you prize your muck
Above your liberties ; and rather choose
To be made bondmen, than to part with that
To which already you are slaves ? Or can it
Be probable in your flattering apprehensions,

You can capitulate with the conquerors,
And keep that yours which they come to
  possess,
And, while you kneel in vain, will ravish
  from you?
—But take your own ways ; brood upon
  your gold.
Sacrifice to your idol, and preserve
The prey entire, and merit the report
Of careful stewards : yield a just account
To your proud masters, who, with whips of
  iron,
Will force you to give up what you conceal,
Or tear it from your throats : adorn your
  walls
With Persian hangings wrought of gold and
  pearl ;
Cover the floors, on which they are to tread,
With costly Median silks ? perfume the
  rooms
With cassia and amber, where they are
To feast and revel ; while, like servile
  grooms,
You wait upon their trenchers : feed their
  eyes
With massy plate, until your cupboards crack
With the weight that they sustain ; set forth
  your wives
And daughters in as many varied shapes
As there are nations, to provoke their lusts,
And let them be embraced before your eyes,
The object may content you ! and, to perfect
Their entertainment, offer up your sons,
And able men, for slaves; while you, that
  are
Unfit for labour, are spurn'd out to starve,
Unpitied, in some desert, no friend by,
Whose sorrow may spare one compassionate
  tear,
In the remembrance of what once you were.
  Leost. The blood turns.
  Timag. Observe how old Cleon shakes,
As if in picture he had shown him what
He was to suffer.
  Coris. I am sick ; the man
Speaks poniards and diseases.
  Olymp. O my doctor !
I never shall recover.
  Cleo. [*coming forward.*] If a virgin,
Whose speech was ever yet usher'd with fear ;
One knowing modesty and humble silence
To be the choicest ornaments of our sex,
In the presence of so many reverend men
Struck dumb with terror and astonishment,
Presume to clothe her thought in vocal
  sounds,
Let her find pardon. First to you, great sir,
A bashful maid's thanks, and her zealous
  prayers

Wing'd with pure innocence, bearing them
  to heaven,
For all prosperity that the gods can give
To one whose piety must exact their care,
Thus low I offer.
  Timol. 'Tis a happy omen.
Rise, blest one, and speak boldly. On my
  virtue,
I am thy warrant, from so clear a spring
Sweet rivers ever flow.
  Cleo. Then, thus to you,
My noble father, and these lords, to whom
I next owe duty : no respect forgotten
To you, my brother, and these bold young
  men,
(Such I would have them,) that are, or
  should be,
The city's sword and target of defence.
To all of you I speak ; and, if a blush
Steal on my cheeks, it is shown to reprove
Your paleness, willingly I would not say,
Your cowardice or fear : Think you all
  treasure
Hid in the bowels of the earth, or ship-
  wreck'd
In Neptune's wat'ry kingdom, can hold
  weight,
When liberty and honour fill one scale,
Triumphant Justice sitting on the beam ?
Or dare you but imagine that your gold is
Too dear a salary for such as hazard
Their blood and lives in your defence ? For
  me,
An ignorant girl, bear witness, heaven ! so far
I prize a soldier, that, to give him pay,
With such devotion as our flamens offer
Their sacrifices at the holy altar,
I do lay down these jewels, will make sale
Of my superfluous wardrobe, to supply
The meanest of their wants.
  [*Lays down her jewels, &c.; the rest
    follow her example.*
  Timol. Brave masculine spirit !
  Diph. We are shown, to our shame, what
  we in honour
Should have taught others.
  Archid. Such a fair example
Must needs be follow'd.
  Timag. Ever my dear sister,
But now our family's glory !
  Leost. Were she deform'd,
The virtues of her mind would force a stoic
To sue to be her servant.
  Cleon. I must yield ;
And, though my heart-blood part with it, I
  will
Deliver in my wealth.
  Asot. I would say something ;
But, the truth is, I know not what.

Timol. We have money ;
And men must now be thought on.
  Archid. We can press
Of labourers in the country, men inured
To cold and heat, ten thousand.
  Diph. Or, if need be,
Enrol our slaves, lusty and able varlets,
And fit for service.
  Cleon. They shall go for me ;
I will not pay and fight too.
  Cleo. How ! your slaves?
O stain of honour !——Once more, sir, your
    pardon ;
And, to their shames, let me deliver what
I know in justice you may speak.
  Timol. Most gladly :
I could not wish my thoughts a better organ
Than your tongue, to express them.
  Cleo. Are you men !
(For age may qualify, though not excuse,
The backwardness of these,) able young
    men !
Yet, now your country's liberty's at the
    stake,
Honour and glorious triumph made the
    garland
For such as dare deserve them ; a rich feast
Prepared by Victory, of immortal viands,
Not for base men, but such as with their
    swords
Dare force admittance, and will be her
    guests :
And can you coldly suffer such rewards
To be proposed to labourers and slaves ?
While you, that are born noble, to whom
    these,
Valued at their best rate, are next to horses,
Or other beasts of carriage, cry aim !
Like idle lookers on, till their proud worth
Make them become your masters !
  Timol. By my hopes,
There's fire and spirit enough in this to
    make
Thersites valiant.
  Cleo. No ; far, far be it from you :
Let these of meaner quality contend
Who can endure most labour ; plough the
    earth,
And think they are rewarded when their
    sweat
Brings home a fruitful harvest to their lords ;
Let them prove good artificers, and serve
    you
For use and ornament, but not presume
To touch at what is noble. If you think
    them
Unworthy to taste of those cates you feed on,
Or wear such costly garments, will you grant
    them

The privilege and prerogative of great
    minds,
Which you were born to? Honour won in
    war,
And to be styled preservers of their country,
Are titles fit for free and generous spirits,
And not for bondmen: had I been born a
    man,
And such ne'er-dying glories made the prize
To bold heroic courage, by Diana,
I would not to my brother, nay, my father,
Be bribed to part with the least piece of
    honour
I should gain in this action !
  Timol. She's inspired,
Or in her speaks the genius of your country,
To fire your blood in her defence : I am
    rapt
With the imagination. Noble maid,
Timoleon is your soldier, and will sweat
Drops of his best blood, but he will bring
    home
Triumphant conquest to you. Let me wear
Your colours, lady ; and though youthful
    heats,
That look no further than your outward
    form,
Are long since buried in me ; while I live,
I am a constant lover of your mind,
That does transcend all precedents.
  Cleo. 'Tis an honour,   [*Gives her scarf.*
And so I do receive it.
  Coris. Plague upon it !
She has got the start of us : I could even
    burst
With envy at her fortune.
  Olymp. A raw young thing !
We have too much tongue sometimes, our
    husbands say,—
And she outstrip us !
  Leost. I am for the journey.
  Timag. May all diseases sloth and letchery
    bring,
Fall upon him that stays at home !
  Archid. Though old,
I will be there in person.
  Diph. So will I :
Methinks I am not what I was ; her words
Have made me younger, by a score of years,
Than I was when I came hither.
  Cleon. I am still
Old Cleon, fat and unwieldy ; I shall never
Make a good soldier, and therefore desire
To be excused at home.
  Asot. 'Tis my suit too :
I am a gristle, and these spider fingers
Will never hold a sword. Let us alone
To rule the slaves at home : I can so yerk
    them—

But in my conscience I shall never prove
Good justice in the war.
  Timol. Have your desires ;
You would be burthens to us, no way
    aids.—
Lead, fairest, to the temple ; first we'll pay
A sacrifice to the gods for good success :
For all great actions the wish'd course do
    run,
That are, with their allowance, well begun.
    [*Exeunt all but* Mar. Grac. *and* Cimb.
  Mar. Stay, Cimbrio and Gracculo.
  Cimb. The business ?
  Mar. Meet me to-morrow night near to
    the grove,
Neighbouring the east part of the city.
  Grac. Well.
  Mar. And bring the rest of our condition
    with you :
I've something to impart may break our
    fetters,
If you dare second me.
  Cimb. We'll not fail.
  Grac. A cart-rope
Shall not bind me at home.
  Mar. Think on't, and prosper. [*Exeunt.*

ACT II.

SCENE I.—*The Same. A Room in*
    Archidamus's *House.*

Enter Archidamus, Timagoras, Leosthenes,
    with gorgets ; and Marullo.

  Archid. So, so, 'tis well : how do I look ?
  Mar. Most sprightfully.
  Archid. I shrink not in the shoulders ;
    though I'm old
I'm tough, steel to the back ; I have not
    wasted
My stock of strength in feather-beds : here's
    an arm too ;
There's stuff in't, and I hope will use a sword
As well as any beardless boy of you all.
  Timag. I'm glad to see you, sir, so well
    prepared
To endure the travail of the war.
  Archid. Go to, sirrah !
I shall endure, when some of you keep your
    cabins,
For all your flaunting feathers ; nay, Leos-
    thenes,
You are welcome too, all friends and fellows
    now.
  Leost. Your servant, sir.
  Archid. Pish ! leave these compliments,
They stink in a soldier's mouth ; I could be
    merry,
For, now my gown's off, farewell gravity !

And must be hold to put a question to you,
Without offence, I hope.
  Leost. Sir, what you please.
  Archid. And you will answer truly ?
  Timag. On our words, sir.
  Archid. Go to, then : I presume you will
    confess
That you are two notorious whoremasters—
Nay, spare your blushing, I've been wild
    myself,
A smack or so for physic does no harm ;
Nay, it is physic, if used moderately ;
But to lie at rack and manger——
  Leost. Say we grant this,
For if we should deny't, you will not believe
    us,
What will you infer upon it ?
  Archid. What you'll groan for,
I fear, when you come to the test. Old
    stories tell us,
There's a month call'd October, which
    brings in
Cold weather ; there are trenches too, 'tis
    rumour'd,
In which to stand all night to the knees in
    water,
In gallants.breeds the toothach ; there's a
    sport too,
Named *lying perdue,* do you mark me ? 'tis
    a game
Which you must learn to play at : now in
    these seasons,
And choice variety of exercises,
(Nay, I come to you,) and fasts, not for de-
    votion,
Your rambling hunt-smock feels strange al-
    terations ;
And, in a frosty morning, looks as if
He could with ease creep in a pottle-pot,
Instead of his mistress' placket. Then he
    curses
The time he spent in midnight visitations ;
And finds what he superfluously parted with,
To be reported good at length, and well
    breath'd,
If but retrieved into his back again,
Would keep him warmer than a scarlet
    waistcoat,

    Enter Diphilus *and* Cleora.

Or an armour lined with fur —O welcome !
    welcome !
You have cut off my discourse ; but I will
    pérfect
My lecture in the camp.
  Diph. Come, we are stay'd for ;
The general's afire for a remove,
And longs to be in action.
  Archid. 'Tis my wish too.

We must part—nay, no tears, my best Cleora;
I shall melt too, and that were ominous.
Millions of blessings on thee! All that's mine
I give up to thy charge; and, sirrah, look
                    [*To* Marullo.
You with that care and reverence observe her,
Which you would pay to me.—A kiss; farewell, girl!
  Diph. Peace wait upon you, fair one!
    [*Exeunt* Archidamus, Diphilus, *and*
       Marullo. .
  Timag. 'Twere impertinence
To wish you to be careful of your honour,
That ever keep in pay a guard about you
Of faithful virtues: farewell!—Friend, I leave you
To wipe our kisses off; I know that lovers
Part with more circumstance and ceremony:
Which I give way to.   [*Exit.*
  Leost. 'Tis a noble favour,
For which I ever owe you. We are alone;
But how I should begin, or in what language
Speak the unwilling word of parting from you,
I am yet to learn.
  Cleo. And still continue ignorant:
For I must be most cruel to myself,
If I should teach you.
  Leost. Yet it must be spoken,
Or you will chide my slackness. You have fired me
With the heat of noble action to deserve you;
And the least spark of honour that took life
From your sweet breath, still fanu'd by it and cherish'd,
Must mount up in a glorious flame, or I
Am much unworthy.
  Cleo. May it not burn here,
And, as a seamark, serve to guide true lovers,
Toss'd on the ocean of luxurious wishes,
Safe from the rocks of lust into the harbour
Of pure affection? rising up an example
Which aftertimes shall witness, to our glory,
First took from us beginning.
  Leost. 'Tis a happiness
My duty to my country, and mine honour
Cannot consent to; besides, add to these,
It was your pleasure, fortified by persuasion,
And strength of reason, for the general good,
That I should go.
  Cleo. Alas! I then was witty
To plead against myself; and mine eye, fix'd
Upon the hill of honour, ne'er descended
To look into the vale of certain dangers,
Through which you were to cut your passage to it.
  Leost. I'll stay at home, then.
  Cleo. No, that must not be;

For so, to serve my own ends, and to gain
A petty wreath myself, I rob you of
A certain triumph, which must fall upon you,
Or Virtue's turu'd a handmaid to blind Fortune.
How is my soul divided! to confirm you
In the opinion of the world, most worthy
To be beloved, (with me you're at the height,
And can advance no further,) I must send you
To court the goddess of stern war, who, if
She see you with my eyes, will ne'er return you,
But grow enamour'd of you.
  Leost. Sweet, take comfort!
And what I offer you, you must vouchsafe me
Or I am wretched. All the dangers that
I can encounter in the war, are trifles;
My enemies abroad to be contemn'd:
The dreadful foes, that have the power to hurt me,
I leave at home with you.
  Cleo. With me!
  Leost. Nay, in you,
In every part about you, they are arm'd
To fight against me.
  Cleo. Where?
  Leost. There's no perfection
That you are mistress of, but musters up
A legion against me, and all sworn
To my destruction.
  Cleo. This is strange!
  Leost. But true, sweet;
Excess of love can work such miracles!
Upon this ivory forehead are intrench'd
Ten thousand rivals, and these suns command
Supplies from all the world, on pain to forfeit
Their comfortable beams; these ruby lips,
A rich exchequer to assure their pay:
This hand, Sibylla's golden bough to guard them
Through hell, and horror, to the Elysian springs:
Which who'll not venture for? and, should I name
Such as the virtues of your mind invite,
Their numbers would be infinite.
  Cleo. Can you think
I may be tempted?
  Leost. You were never proved.
For me, I have conversed with you no further
Than would become a brother. I ne'er tuned
Loose notes to your chaste ears; or brought rich presents
For my artillery, to batter down
The fortress of your honour; nor endeavour'd
To make your blood run high at solemn feasts,

With viands that provoke ; the speeding
   philtres :
I work'd no bawds to tempt you ; never
   practised
The cunning and corrupting arts they study,
That wander in the wild maze of desire ;
Honest simplicity and truth were all
The agents I employ'd ; and when I came
To see you, it was with that reverence
As I beheld the altars of the gods : .
And Love, that came along with me, was
   taught
To leave his arrows and his torch behind,
Quench'd in my fear to give offence.
   Cleo. And 'twas
That modesty that took me, and preserves
   me,
Like a fresh rose, in mine own natural
   sweetness ;
Which, sullied with the touch of impure
   hands,
Loses both scent and beauty.
   Leost. But, Cleora,
When I am absent, as I must go from you,
(Such is the cruelty of my fate,) and leave
   you,
Unguarded, to the violent assaults
Of loose temptations ; when the memory
Of my so many years of love and service
Is lost in other objects ; when you are
   courted
By such as keep a catalogue of their con-
   quests,
Won upon credulous virgins ; when nor
   father
Is here to owe you, brother to advise you,
Nor your poor servant by, to keep such off,
By lust instructed how to undermine,
And blow your chastity up ; when your weak
   senses,
At once assaulted, shall conspire against you,
And play the traitors to your soul, your
   virtue ;
How can you stand ? 'Faith, though you
   fall, and I
The judge, before whom you then stood
   accused,
I should acquit you.
   Cleo. Will you then confirm
That love and jealousy, though of different
   natures,
Must of necessity be twins ; the younger
Created only to defeat the elder,
And spoil him of his birthright ? 'tis not well.
But being to part, I will not chide, I will not ;
Nor with one syllable or tear, express
How deeply I am wounded with the arrows
Of your distrust : but when that you shall
   hear,

At your return, how I have born myself,
And what an austere penance I take on me,
To satisfy your doubts ; when, like a Vestal,
I shew you, to your shame, the fire still
   burning,
Committed to my charge by true affection,
The people joining with you in the wonder ;
When, by the glorious splendour of my suf-
   ferings,
The prying eyes of jealousy are struck blind,
The monster too that feeds on fears, e'en
   starv'd
For want of seeming matter to accuse me ;
Expect, Leosthenes, a sharp reproof
From my just anger.
   Leost. What will you do?
   Cleo. Obey me,
Or from this minute you are a stranger to
   me ;
And do't without reply. All-seeing sun,
Thou witness of my innocence, thus I close
Mine eyes against thy comfortable light,
Till the return of this distrustful man !
Now bind them sure ;—nay, do't :
          [*He binds her eyes with her scarf.*
          If, uncompell'd,
I loose this knot, until the hands that made it
Be pleased to untie it, may consuming
   plagues
Fall heavy on me! pray you guide me to
   your lips.
This kiss, when you come back, shall be a
   virgin
To bid you welcome ; nay, I have not done
   yet :
I will continue dumb, and, you once gone,
No accent shall come from me. Now to my
   chamber,
My tomb, if you miscarry : there I'll spend
My hours in silent mourning, and thus much
Shall be reported of me to my glory,
And you confess it, whether I live or die,
My chastity triumphs o'er your jealousy.
          [*Exeunt.*

SCENE II.—*The same. A Room in*
      Cleon's *House.*

   Enter Asotus, *driving in* Gracculo.

   Asot. You slave ! you dog ! down, cur.
   Grac. Hold, good young master,
For pity's sake !
   Asot. Now am I in my kingdom :—
Who says I am not valiant ? I begin
To frown again : quake, villain !
   Grac. So I do, sir !
Your looks are agues to me.
   Asot. Are they so, sir !
'Slight, if I had them at this bay that flout me,

And say I look like a sheep and an ass, I'd
  make them
Feel that I am a lion.
  Grac. Do not roar, sir,
As you are a valiant beast : but do you know
Why you use me thus ?
  Asot. I'll beat thee a little more,
Then study for a reason. O ! I have it :
One brake a jest on me, and then I swore,
(Because I durst not strike him,) when I
  came home,
That I would break thy head.
  Grac. Plague on his mirth !
I'm sure I mourn for't.
  Asot. Remember, too, I charge you,
To teach my horse good manners yet ; this
  morning,
As I rode to take the air, the untutor'd jade
Threw me, and kicked me.
  Grac. I thank him for't.   *[Aside.*
  Asot. What's that ?
  Grac. I say, sir, I will teach him to hold
  his heels,
If you will rule your fingers.
  Asot. I'll think upon't.
  Grac. I am bruised to jelly : better be a
  dog,
Than slave to a fool or coward.   *[Aside.*
  Asot. Here's my mother,

Enter Corisca *and* Zanthia.

She is chastising too: how brave we live,
That have our slaves to beat, to keep us in
  breath
When we want exercise !
  Coris. Careless harlotry, *[Striking her.*
Look to't ; if a curl fall, or wind or sun
Take my complexion off, I will not leave
One hair upon thine head.
  Grac. Here's a second show
Of the family of pride !   *[Aside.*
  Coris. Fie on these wars !
I'm starv'd for want of action ; not a
  gamester left
To keep a woman play. If this world last
A little longer with us, ladies must study
Some new-found mystery to cool one another,
We shall burn to cinders else. I have heard
  there have been
Such arts in a long vacation ; would they
  were
Reveal'd to me ! they have made my doctor,
  too,
Physician to the army : he was used
To serve the turn at a pinch ; but I am now
Quite unprovided.
  Asot. My mother-in-law is, sure,
At her devotion.
  Coris. There are none but our slaves left,

Nor are they to be trusted. Some great
  women,
Which I could name, in a dearth of visitants,
Rather than be idle, have been glad to play
At small game ; but I am so queasy-
  stomach'd,
And from my youth have been so used to
  dainties,
I cannot taste such gross meat. Some that
  are hungry
Draw on their shoemakers, and take a fall
From such as mend mats in their galleries ;
Or when a tailor settles a petticoat on,
Take measure of his bodkin ; fie upon't !
'Tis base ; for my part, I could rather lie with
A gallant's breeches, and conceive upon
  them,
Than stoop so low.
  Asot. Fair madam, and my mother.
  Coris. Leave the last out, it smells rank
  of the country,
And shews coarse breeding ; your true
  courtier knows not
His niece, or sister, from another woman,
If she be apt and cunning.—I could tempt
  now
This fool, but he will be so long a working !
Then he's my husband's son :—the fitter to
Supply his wants ; I have the way already,
I'll try if it will take.—When were you with
Your mistress, fair Cleora ?
  Asot. Two days sithence ;
But she's so coy, forsooth, that ere I can
Speak a penn'd speech I have bought and
  studied for her,
Her woman calls her away.
  Coris. Here's a dull thing !
But better taught, I hope.—Send off your
  man.
  Asot. Sirrah, begone.
  Grac. This is the first good turn
She ever did me.   *[Aside and exit.*
  Coris. We'll have a scene of mirth ;
I must not have you shamed for want of
  practice.
I stand here for Cleora, and, do you hear,
  minion,
That you may tell her what her woman
  should do,
Repeat the lesson over that I taught you,
When my young lord came to visit me : if
  you miss
In a syllable or posture——
  Zant. I am perfect.
  Asot. Would I were so ! I fear I shall
  be out.
  Coris. If you are, I'll help you in. Thus
  I walk musing :
You are to enter, and, as you pass by,

Salute my woman ;—be but bold enough,
You'll speed, I warrant you.   Begin.
Asot. Have at it——
Save thee, sweetheart ! a kiss.
  Zant. Venus forbid, sir,
I should presume to taste your honour's lips
Before my lady.
  Coris. This is well on both parts.
  Asot. How does thy lady ?
  Zant. Happy in your lordship,
As oft as she thinks on you.
  Coris. Very good ;
This wench will learn in time.
  Asot. Does she think of me?
  Zant. O, sir ! and speaks the best of you ;
admires
Your wit, your clothes, discourse ; and
swears, but that
You are not forward enough for a lord, you
were
The most complete and absolute man,—I'll
show
Your lordship a secret.
  Asot. Not of thine own?
  Zant. O ! no, sir,
'Tis of my lady : but, upon your honour,
You must conceal it.
  Asot. By all means.
  Zant. Sometimes
I lie with my lady, as the last night I did ;
She could not say her prayers for thinking
of you :
Nay, she talk'd of you in her sleep, and
sigh'd out,
O sweet Asotus, sure thou art so backward,
That I must ravish thee! and in that fer-
vour
She took me in her arms, threw me upon
her,
Kiss'd me, and hugg'd me, and then waked,
and wept,
Because 'twas but a dream.
  Coris. This will bring him on,
Or he's a block.—A good girl !
  Asot. I am mad,
Till I am at it.
  Zant. Be not put off, sir,
With, *Away, I dare not ;—fie, you are im-*
modest ;—
My brother's up ;—My father will hear.—
Shoot home, sir,
You cannot miss the mark.
  Asot. There's for thy counsel.
This is the fairest interlude—if it prove
earnest,
I shall wish I were a player.
  Coris. Now my turn comes.—
I am exceeding sick, pray you send my
page

For young Asotus, I cannot live without
him ;
Pray him to visit me ; yet, when he's present,
I must be strange to him.
  Asot. Not so, you are caught :
Lo, whom you wish ; behold Asotus here !
  Coris. You wait well, minion ; shortly I
shall not speak
My thoughts in my private chamber, but
they must
Lie open to discovery.
  Asot. 'Slid, she's angry.
  Zant. No, no, sir, she but seems so.   To
her again.
  Asot. Lady, I would descend to kiss your
hand,
But that 'tis gloved, and civet makes me
sick ;
And to presume to taste your lip's not safe,
Your woman by.
  Coris. I hope she's no observer
Of whom I grace. [*Zanthia looks on a book.*
  Asot. She's at her book, O rare !
                      [*Kisses her.*
  Coris. A kiss for entertainment is suffi-
cient ;
Too much of one dish cloys me.
  Asot. I would serve in
The second course ; but still I fear your
woman.
  Coris. You are very cautelous.
              [*Zanthia seems to sleep.*
  Asot. 'Slight, she's asleep !
'Tis pity these instructions are not printed ;
They would sell well to chambermaids. 'Tis
no time now
To play with my good fortune, and your
favour ;
Yet to be taken, as they say :—a scout,
To give the signal when the enemy comes,
               [*Exeunt* Zanthia.
Were now worth gold.—She's gone to watch.
A waiter so train'd up were worth a million
To a wanton city madam.
  Coris. You are grown conceited.
  Asot. You teach me.   Lady, now your
cabinet—
  Coris. You speak as it were yours.
  Asot. When we are there,
I'll shew you my best evidence. [*Seizing her.*
  Coris. Hold ! you forget,
I only play Cleora's part.
  Asot. No matter,
Now we've begun, let's end the act.
  Coris. Forbear, sir ;
Your father's wife !——
  Asot. Why, being his heir, I am bound,
Since he can make no satisfaction to you,
To see his debts paid.

Re-enter Zanthia *running.*

Zant. Madam, my lord!
Coris. Fall off:
I must trifle with the time too, hell confound it!
Asot. Plague on his toothless chaps! he cannot do't
Himself, yet hinders such as have good stomachs.

Enter Cleon.

Cleon. Where are you, wife? I fain would go abroad,
But cannot find my slaves that bear my litter;
I am tired. Your shoulder, son;—nay, sweet, thy hand, too:
A turn or two in the garden, and then to supper,
And so to bed.
Asot. Never to rise, I hope, more. [*Aside.*
                                        [*Exeunt.*

SCENE III.—*A Grove near the Walls of* Syracuse.

Enter Marullo *and* Poliphron. *A Table set out with Wine, &c.*

Mar. 'Twill take, I warrant thee.
Poliph. You may do your pleasure;
But, in my judgment, better to make use of
The present opportunity.
Mar. No more.
Poliph. I am silenced.
Mar. More wine; prithee drink hard, friend,
And when we're hot, whatever I propound,

Enter Cimbrio, Gracculo, *and other Slaves.*

Second with vehemence.—Men of your words, all welcome!
Slaves use no ceremony; sit down, here's a health.
Poliph. Let it run round, fill every man his glass.
Grac. We look for no waiters;—this is wine!
Mar. The better,
Strong, lusty wine: drink deep, this juice will make us
As free as our lords.   [*Drinks.*
Grac. But if they find we taste it,
We are all damn'd to the quarry during life,
Without hope of redemption.
Mar. Pish! for that
We'll talk anon: another rouse! we lose time;   [*Drinks.*
When our low blood's wound up a little higher,

I'll offer my design; nay, we are cold yet;
These glasses contain nothing;—do me right,   [*Takes the bottle.*
As e'er you hope for liberty. 'Tis done bravely;
How do you feel yourselves now?
Cimb. I begin
To have strange conundrums in my head.
Grac. And I
To loath base water: I would be hang'd in peace now,
For one month of such holidays.
Mar. An age, boys,
And yet defy the whip; if you are men,
Or dare believe you have souls.
Cimb. We are no brokers.
Grac. Nor whores, whose marks are out of their mouths, they have none;
They hardly can get salt enough to keep them
From stinking above ground.
Mar. Our lords are no gods——
Grac. They are devils to us, I am sure.
Mar. But subject to
Cold, hunger, and diseases.
Grac. In abundance.
Your lord that feels no ach in his chine at twenty,
Forfeits his privilege; how should their surgeons build else,
Or ride on their footcloths?
Mar. Equal Nature fashion'd us
All in one mould. The bear serves not the bear,
Nor the wolf the wolf; 'twas odds of strength in tyrants,
That pluck'd the first link from the golden chain
With which that THING OF THINGS bound in the world.
Why then, since we are taught, by their examples,
To love our liberty, if not command,
Should the strong serve the weak, the fair, deform'd ones?
Or such as know the cause of things, pay tribute
To ignorant fools? All's but the outward gloss,
And politic form, that does distinguish us.—
Cimbrio, thou art a strong man; if, in place
Of carrying burthens, thou hadst been train'd up
In martial discipline, thou might'st have proved
A general, fit to lead and fight for Sicily,
As fortunate as Timoleon.
Cimb. A little fighting
Will serve a general's turn.

Mar. Thou, Gracculo,
Hast fluency of language, quick conceit ;
And, I think, cover'd with a senator's robe,
Formally set on the bench, thou wouldst appear
As brave a senator.
  Grac. Would I had lands,
Or money to buy a place ! and if I did not
Sleep on the bench with the drowsiest of them, play with my chain,
Look on my watch, when my guts chimed twelve, and wear
A state beard, with my barber's help, rank with them
In their most choice peculiar gifts ; degrade me,
And put me to drink water again, which, now
I have tasted wine, were poison !
  Mar. 'Tis spoke nobly,
And like a gownman : none of these, I think too,
But would prove good burghers.
  Grac. Hum ! the fools are modest ;
I know their insides : here's an ill-faced fellow,
(But that will not be seen in a dark shop,)
If he did not in a month learn to outswear,
In the selling of his wares, the cunning'st tradesman
In Syracuse, I have no skill. Here's another,
Observe but what a cozening look he has !—
Hold up thy head, man ; if, for drawing gallants
Into mortgages for commodities, cheating heirs
With your new counterfeit gold thread, and gumm'd velvets,
He does not transcend all that went before him,
Call in his patent : pass the rest ; they'll all make
Sufficient beccos, and, with their brow-antlers,
Bear up the cap of maintenance.
  Mar. Is't not pity, then,
Men of such eminent virtues should be slaves ?
  Cimb. Our fortune.
  Mar. 'Tis your folly ; daring men
Command and make their fates. Say, at this instant,
I mark'd you out a way to liberty ;
Possess'd you of those blessings; our proud lords
So long have surfeited in ; and, what is sweetest,
Arm you with power, by strong hand to revenge

Your stripes, your unregarded toil, the pride
The insolence of such as tread upon
Your patient sufferings ; fill your famish'd mouths
With the fat and plenty of the land ; redeem you
From the dark vale of servitude, and seat you
Upon a hill of happiness ; what would you do
To purchase this, and more ?
  Grac. Do ! any thing :
To burn a church or two, and dance by the light on't,
Were but a May-game.
  Poliph. I have a father living ;
But, if the cutting of his throat could work this,
He should excuse me.
  Cimb. 'Slight ! I would cut mine own,
Rather than miss it ; so I might but have
A taste on't, ere I die.
  Mar. Be resolute men ;
You shall run no such hazard, nor groan under
The burthen of such crying sins.
  Cimb. The means ?
  Grac. I feel a woman's longing.
  Poliph. Do not torment us
With expectation.
  Mar. Thus, then : Our proud masters,
And all the able freemen of the city,
Are gone unto the wars——
  Poliph. Observe but that.
  Mar. Old men, and such as can make no resistance,
Are only left at home——
  Grac. And the proud young fool,
My master—if this take, I'll hamper him.
  Mar. Their arsenal, their treasure 's in our power,
If we have hearts to seize them. If our lords fall
In the present action, the whole country's ours ;
Say they return victorious, we have means
To keep the town against them ; at the worst,
To make our own conditions. Now, if you dare
Fall on their daughters and their wives, break up
Their iron chests, banquet on their rich beds,
And carve yourselves of all delights and pleasures
You have been barr'd from, with one voice cry with me,
Liberty ! liberty !
  All. Liberty ! liberty !
  Mar. Go then, and take possession : use all freedom ;

But shed no blood. [*Exeunt* Slaves.]—So,
this is well begun ;
But not to be commended, till't be done.
[*Exit.*

ACT III.

SCENE I.—*The same. A Gallery in*
Archidamus's *House.*

Enter Marullo *and* Timandra.

Mar. Why, think you that I plot against
myself ?
Fear nothing, you are safe : these thick-
skinn'd slaves,
I use as instruments to serve my ends,
Pierce not my deep designs ; nor shall they
dare
To lift an arm against you.
Timand. With your will.
But turbulent spirits, raised beyond them-
selves
With ease, are not so soon laid ; they oft
prove
Dangerous to him that call'd them up.
Mar. 'Tis true,
In what is rashly undertook. Long since
I have considered seriously their natures,
Proceeded with mature advice, and know
I hold their will and faculties in more awe
Than I can do my own. Now, for their
license,
And riot in the city, I can make
A just defence and use : it may appear too
A politic prevention of such ills
As might, with greater violence and danger,
Hereafter be attempted ; though some smart
for 't,
It matters not :—however, I'm resolved ;
And sleep you with security. Holds Cleora
Constant to her rash vow ?
Timand. Beyond belief ;
To me, that see her hourly, it seems a fable.
By signs I guess at her commands, and serve
them
With silence ; such her pleasure is, made
known
By holding her fair hand thus. She eats little,
Sleeps less, as I imagine ; once a day
I lead her to this gallery, where she walks
Some half a dozen turns, and, having offer'd
To her absent saint a sacrifice of sighs,
She points back to her prison.
· *Mar.* Guide her hither,
And make her understand the slaves' revolt ;
And, with your utmost eloquence, enlarge
Their insolence, and rapes done in the city.
Forget not too, I am their chief, and tell her
You strongly think my extreme dotage on her,

As I'm Marullo, caused this sudden uproar,
To make way to enjoy her.
Timand. Punctually
I will discharge my part.   [*Exit.*

Enter Poliphron.

Poliph. O, sir, I sought you :
You've missed the best sport ! Hell, I think's
broke loose ;
There's such variety of all disorders,
As leaping, shouting, drinking, · dancing,
whoring,
Among the slaves ; answer'd with crying,
howling,
By the citizens and their wives ; such a con-
fusion,
In a word, not to tire you, as I think,
The like was never read of.
Mar. I share in
The pleasure, though I'm absent. This is
some
Revenge for my disgrace.
Poliph. But, sir, I fear,
If your authority restrain them not,
They'll fire the city, or kill one another,
They are so apt to outrage ; neither know I
Whether you wish it, and came therefore to
Acquaint you with so much.
Mar. I will among them ;
But must not long be absent.
Poliph. At your pleasure.   [*Exeunt.*

SCENE II.—*The same. A Room in the
same.*

Shouts within. Enter Cleora *and* Timandra.

Timand. They are at our gates : my heart !
affrights and horrors
Increase each minute. No way left to save
us,
No flattering hope to comfort us, or means,
But miracle, to redeem us from base lust
And lawless rapine ! Are there gods, yet
suffer
Such innocent sweetness to be made the spoil
Of brutish appetite ? or since they decree
To ruin nature's masterpiece, of which
They have not left one pattern, must they
choose,
To set their tyranny off, slaves to pollute
The spring of chastity, and poison it
With their most loath'd embraces ? and, of
those,
He that should offer up his life to guard it,
Marullo, curs'd Marullo, your own bond-
man,
Purchased to serve you, and fed by your
favours ?—
Nay, start not : it is he : he, the grand
captain

I

Of these libidinous beasts, that have not left
One cruel act undone, that barbarous con-
   quest
Yet ever practised in a captive city,
He, doating on your beauty, and to have
   fellows
In his foul sin, hath raised these mutinous
   slaves,
Who have begun the game by violent rapes
Upon the wives and daughters of their
   lords:
And he, to quench the fire of his base lust,
By force, comes to enjoy you—do not wring
Your innocent hands, 'tis bootless ; use the
   means
That may preserve you. 'Tis no crime to
   break
A vow when you are forced to it ; shew your
   face,
And with the majesty of commanding
   beauty,
Strike dead his loose affections : if that fail,
Give liberty to your tongue, and use en-
   treaties ;
There cannot be a breast of flesh and blood,
Or heart so made of flint, but must receive
Impression .from your words ; or eyes so
   stern,
But, from the clear reflection of your tears,
Must melt, and bear them company. Will
   you not
Do these good offices to yourself? poor I,
   then,
Can only weep your fortune : here he comes.

Enter Marullo, *speaking at the door.*

Mar. He that advances
A foot beyond this, comes upon my sword :
You have had your ways, disturb not mine.
Timand. Speak gently,
Her fears may kill her else.
Mar. Now Love inspire me !
Still shall this canopy of envious night
Obscure my suns of comfort? and those
   dainties
Of purest white and red, which I take in at
My greedy eyes, denied my famish'd
   senses ?—
The organs of your hearing yet are open ;
And you infringe no vow, though you vouch-
   : safe
To give them warrant to convey unto
Your understanding parts the story of
A tortured and despairing lover, whom
Not fortune but affection marks your slave :—
Shake not, best lady ! for believ't, you are
As far from danger as I am from force :
All violence I shall offer, tends no further

Than to relate my sufferings, which I dare
   not
Presume to do, till, by some gracious sign,
You shew you are pleased to hear me.
Timand. If you are,
Hold forth your right hand.
   [Cleora *holds forth her right hand.*
Mar. So, 'tis done ; and I
With my glad lips seal humbly on your foot,
My soul's thanks for the favour : I forbear
To tell you who I am, what wealth, what
   honours
I made exchange of, to become your ser-
   vant :
And, though I knew worthy Leosthenes
(For sure he must be worthy, for whose love
You have endured so much) to be my rival ;
When rage and jealousy counsell'd me to
   kill him,
Which then I could have done with much
   more ease,
Than now, in fear to grieve you, I dare
   speak it,
Love, seconded with duty, boldly told me
The man I hated, fair Cleora favour'd :
And that was his protection. [Cleora *bows.*
Timand. See, she bows
Her head in sign of thankfulness.
Mar. He removed by
The occasion of the war, (my fires increasing
By being closed and stopp'd up,) frantic
   affection
Prompted me to do something in his absence,
That might deliver you into my power,
Which you see is effected : and, even now,
When my rebellious passions chide my dul-
   ness,
And tell me how much I abuse my fortunes,
Now it is in my power to bear you hence,
   [Cleora *starts.*
Or take my wishes here, (nay, fear not,
   madam,)
True love's a servant, brutish lust a tyrant,)
I dare not touch those viands that ne'er
   taste well,
But when they're freely offer'd : only thus
   much,
Be pleased I may speak in my own dear
   cause,
And think it worthy your consideration,
(I have loved truly, cannot say deserved,
Since duty must not take the name of merit,)
That I so far prize your content, before
All blessings that my hope can fashion to me,
That willingly I entertain despair,
And, for your sake, embrace it : for I know,
This opportunity lost, by no endeavour
The like can be recover'd. To conclude,
Forget not, that I lose myself to save you :

For what can I expect but death and torture,
The war being ended? and, what is a task
Would trouble Hercules to undertake,
I do deny you to myself, to give you,
A pure unspotted present, to my rival.
I have said: If it distaste not, best of virgins,
Reward my temperance with some lawful
favour,
Though you contemn my person.
   [Cleora *kneels, then pulls off her glove,
   and offers her hand to* Marullo.
Timand. See, she kneels;
And seems to call upon the gods to pay
The debt she owes your virtue: to perform
which,
As a sure pledge of friendship, she vouch-
safes you
Her fair right hand.
Mar. I am paid for all my sufferings.
Now, when you please, pass to your pri-
vate chamber:
My love and duty, faithful guards, shall
keep you
From all disturbance; and when you are
sated
With thinking of Leosthenes, as a fee
Due to my service, spare one sigh for me.
   [*Exeunt.* Cleora *makes a low courtesy
   as she goes off.*

SCENE III.—*The same. A Room in*
Cleon's *House.*

Enter Gracculo, *leading* Asotus *in an ape's
habit, with a chain about his neck;* Zanthia *in* Corisca's *clothes, she bearing up
her train.*

Grac. Come on, sir.
Asot. Oh!
Grac. Do you grumble? you were ever
A brainless ass; but if this hold, I'll teach
you
To come aloft and do tricks like an ape.
Your morning's lesson: if you miss——
Asot. O no, sir.
Grac. What for the Carthaginians?
   [Asotus *makes moppes.*] A good beast.
What for ourself, your lord? [*Dances.*]
Exceeding well.
There's your reward. [*Gives him an apple.*]
—Not kiss your paw! So, so, so.
Zant. Was ever lady, the first day of her
bonour,
So waited on by a wrinkled crone? She
looks now,
Without her painting, curling, and perfumes,
Like the last day of January; and stinks
worse
Than a hot brache in the dogdays. Further
off!

So—stand there like an image; if you stir,
Till, with a quarter of a look, I call you,
You know what follows.
Coris. O, what am I fallen to!
But 'tis a punishment for my lust and
pride,
Justly return'd upon me.
Grac. How dost thou like
Thy ladyship, Zanthia?
Zant. Very well; and bear it
With as much state as your lordship.
Grac. Give me thy hand:
Let us, like conquering Romans, walk in
triumph,
Our captives following; then mount our
tribunals,
And make the slaves our footstools.
Zant. Fine, by Jove!
Are your hands clean, minion?
Coris. Yes, forsooth.
Zant. Fall off then.
So! now come on; and having made your
three duties——
Down, I say—are you stiff in the hams?—
now kneel,
And tie our shoe: now kiss it, and be happy.
Grac. This is state, indeed!
Zant. It is such as she taught me;
A tickling itch of greatness, your proud ladies
Expect from their poor waiters: we have
changed parts;
She does what she forced me to do in her
reign,
And I must practise it in mine.
Grac. 'Tis justice:
O! here come more.

Enter Cimbrio, Cleon, Poliphron, *and*
Olympia.

Cimb. Discover to a drachma,
Or I will famish thee.
Cleon. O! I am pined already.
Cimb. Hunger shall force thee to cut off
the brawns
From thy arms and thighs, then broil them
on the coals
For carbonadoes.
Poliph. Spare the old jade, he's founder'd,
Grac. Cut his throat then,
And hang him out for a scarecrow.
Poliph. You have all your wishes
In your revenge, and I have mine. You see
I use no tyranny: when I was her slave,
She kept me as a sinner, to lie at her back
In frosty nights, and fed me high with dainties,
Which still she had in her belly again ere
morning;
And in requital of those courtesies,

I 2

Having made one another free, we are mar-
ried :
And, if you wish us joy, join with us in
A dance at our wedding.
    Grac. Agreed ; for I have thought of
A most triumphant one, which shall express
We are lords, and these our slaves.
    Poliph. But we shall want
A woman.
    Grac. No, here's Jane-of-apes shall serve;
Carry your body swimming.—Where's the
music ?
    Poliph. I have placed it in yon window.
    Grac. Begin then sprightly.
            [*Music, and then a dance.*

      Enter Marullo *behind.*

    Poliph. Well done on all sides ! I have
    prepared a banquet ;
Let's drink and cool us.
    Grac. A good motion.
    Cimb. Wait here ;
You have been tired with feasting, learn to
    fast now.
    Grac. I'll have an apple for jack, and may
    be some scraps
May fall to your share.
        [*Exeunt* Grac. Zant. Cimb. Poliph.
           and Olymp.
    Coris. Whom can we accuse
But ourselves, for what we suffer? Thou art
    just,
Thou all-creating Power ! and misery
Instructs me now, that yesterday acknow-
    ledged
No deity beyond my lust and pride,
There is a heaven above us, that looks down
With the eyes of justice, upon such as number
Those blessings freely given, in the accompt
Of their poor merits : else it could not be,
Now miserable I, to please whose palate
The elements were ransack'd, yet complain'd
Of nature, as not liberal enough
In her provision of rarities
To sooth my taste, and pamper my proud flesh,
Should wish in vain for bread.
    Cleon. Yes, I do wish too,
For what I fed my dog's with.
    Coris. I, that forgot
I was made of flesh and blood, and thought
    the silk
Spun by the diligent worm out of their
    entrails,
Too coarse to clothe me, and the softest
    down
Too hard to sleep on ; that disdain'd to look
On virtue being in rags, that stopp'd my nose
At those that did not use adulterate arts

To better nature ; that from those that served
    me
Expected adoration, am made justly
The scorn of my own bondwoman.
    Asot. I am punish'd,
For seeking to cuckold mine own natural
    father :
Had I been gelded then, or used myself
Like a man, I had not been transform'd, and
    forced
To play an overgrown ape.
    Cleon. I know I cannot
Last long, that's all my comfort. Come, I
    forgive both :
'Tis in vain to be angry ; let us, therefore,
Lament together like friends.
    Mar. What a true mirror
Were this sad spectacle for secure greatness !
Here they, that never see themselves, but in
The glass of servile flattery, might behold
The weak foundation upon which they build
Their trust in human frailty. Happy are
    those,
That knowing, in their births, they are sub-
    ject to
Uncertain change, are still prepared, and
    arm'd
For either fortune : a rare principle,
And with much labour, learn'd in wisdom's
    school !
For, as these bondmen, by their actions, shew
That their prosperity, like too large a sail
For their small bark of judgment, sinks them
    with
A fore-right gale of liberty, ere they reach
The port they long to touch at : so these
    wretches,
Swollen with the false opinion of their worth,
And proud of blessings left them, not ac-
    quired ;
That did believe they could with giant arms
Fathom the earth, and were above their fates,
Those borrow'd helps, that did support them,
    vanish'd,
Fall of themselves, and by unmanly suffering,
Betray their proper weakness, and make
    known
Their boasted greatness was lent, not their
    own.
    Cleon. O for some meat ! they sit long.
    Coris. We forgot,
When we drew out intemperate feasts till
    midnight ;
Their hunger was not thought on, nor their
    watchings ;
Nor did we hold ourselves served to the
    height,
But when we did exact and force their duties
Beyond their strength and power.

Asot. We pay for 't now :
I now could be content to have my head
Broke with a rib of beef, or, for a coffin,
Be buried in the dripping-pan.

Re-enter Poliphron, Cimbrio, Gracculo,
Zanthia, *and* Olympia, *drunk and quarrelling.*

Cimb. Do not hold me :
Not kiss the bride !
Poliph. No, sir.
Cimb. She's common good,
And so we'll use her.
Grac. We'll have nothing private.
Mar. [*coming forward.*] Hold !
Zant. Here's Marullo.
Olymp. He's your chief.
Cimb. We are equals ;
I will know no obedience.
Grac. Nor superior——
Nay, if you are lion drunk, I will make one ;
For lightly ever he that parts the fray,
Goes away with the blows.
Mar. Art thou mad too?
No more, as you respect me.
Poliph. I obey, sir.
Mar. Quarrel among yourselves !
Cimb. Yes, in our wine, sir,
And for our wenches.
Grac. How could we be lords else ?
Mar. Take heed ; I've news will cool this
heat, and make you
Remember what you were.
Cimb. How !
Mar. Send off these,
And then I'll tell you.
          [*Zanthia beats* Corisca.
Olymp. This is tyranny,
Now she offends not.
Zant. 'Tis for exercise,
And to help digestion. What is she good
for else ?
To me, it was her language.
Mar. Lead her off.
And take heed, madam minx, the wheel
may turn.
Go to your meat, and rest ; and from this
hour
Remember, he that is a lord to-day,
May be a slave to-morrow.
Cleon. Good morality !
          [*Exeunt* Cleon, Asot. Zant. Olymp.
          and Coris.
Cimb. But what would you impart ?
Mar. What must invite you
To stand upon your guard, and leave your
feasting ;
Or but imagine what it is to be.

Most miserable, and rest assured you are so.
Our masters are victorious.
All. How !
Mar. Within
A day's march of the city, flesh'd with spoil,
And proud of conquest ; the armado sunk,
The Carthaginian admiral, hand to hand,
Slain by Leosthenes.
Cimb. I feel the whip
Upon my back already.
Grac. Every man
Seek a convenient tree, and hang himself.
Poliph. Better die once, than live an age
to suffer
New tortures every hour.
Cimb. Say, we submit,
And yield us to their mercy ?——
Mar. Can you flatter
Yourselves with such false hopes? Or dare
you think
That your imperious lords, that never fail'd
To punish with severity petty slips
In your neglect of labour, may be won
To pardon those licentious outrages
Which noble enemies forbear to practise
Upon the conquer'd? What have you
omitted,
That may call on their just revenge with
horror,
And studied cruelty? we have gone too far
To think now of retiring ; in our courage,
And daring, lies our safety : if you are not
Slaves in your abject minds, as in your
fortunes,
Since to die is the worst, better expose
Our naked breasts to their keen swords,
and sell
Our lives with the most advantage, than to
trust
In a forestall'd remission, or yield up
Our bodies to the furnace of their fury,
Thrice heated with revenge.
Grac. You led us on.
Cimb. And 'tis but justice you should
bring us off.
Grac. And we expect it.
Mar. Hear then, and obey me ;
And I will either save you, or fall with you.
Man the walls strongly, and make good the
ports ;
Boldly deny their entrance, and rip up
Your grievances, and what compell'd you to
This desperate course : if they disdain to hear
Of composition, we have in our powers
Their aged fathers, children, and their wives,
Who, to preserve themselves, must willingly
Make intercession for us. 'Tis not time
now
To talk, but do : a glorious end, or freedom,

Is now proposed us; stand resolved for either,
And, like good fellows, live or die together.
[*Exeunt.*

SCENE IV.—*The Country near* Syracuse.
The Camp of Timoleon.

Enter Leosthenes *and* Timagoras.

Timag. I am so far from envy, I am proud
You have outstripp'd me in the race of
  honour.
O 'twas a glorious day, and bravely won!
Your bold performance gave such lustre to
Timoleon's wise directions, as the army
Rests doubtful, to whom they stand most
  engaged
For their so great success.
  Leost. The gods first honour'd,
The glory be the general's; 'tis far from me
To be his rival.
  Timag. You abuse your fortune,
To entertain her choice and gracious favours
With a contracted brow; plumed Victory
Is truly painted with a cheerful look,
Equally distant from proud insolence,
And base dejection.
  Leost. O, Timagoras,
You only are acquainted with the cause
That loads my sad heart with a hill of lead;
Whose ponderous weight, neither my new-
  got honour,
Assisted by the general applause
The soldier crowns it with, nor all war's
  glories,
Can lessen or remove: and, would you please,
With fit consideration, to remember
How much I wrong'd Cleora's innocence
With my rash doubts; and what a grievous
  penance
She did impose upon her tender sweetness,
To pluck away the vulture, jealousy,
That fed upon my liver; you cannot blame
  me,
But call it a fit justice on myself,
Though I resolve to be a stranger to
The thought of mirth or pleasure.
  Timag. You have redeem'd
The forfeit of your fault with such a ransom
Of honourable action, as my sister
Must of necessity confess her sufferings,
Weigh'd down by your fair merits; and,
  when she views you,
Like a triumphant conqueror, carried
  through
The streets of Syracusa, the glad people
Pressing to meet you, and the senators
Contending who shall heap most honours on
  you;
The oxen, **crown'd** with garlands, led before
  you,

Appointed for the sacrifice; and the altars
Smoaking with thankful incense to the gods:
The soldiers chanting loud hymns to your
  praise,
The windows fill'd with matrons and with
  virgins,
Throwing upon your head, as you pass by,
The choicest flowers, and silently invoking
The queen of love, with their particular vows,
To be thought worthy of you; can Cleora
(Though, in the glass of self-love, she behold
Her best deserts) but with all joy acknow-
  ledge,
What she endured was but a noble trial
You made of her affection? and her anger,
Rising from your too amorous cares, soon
  drench'd
In Lethe, and forgotten.
  Leost. If those glories
You so set forth were mine, they might plead
  for me;
But I can lay no claim to the least honour
Which you, with foul injustice, ravish from
  her.
Her beauty in me wrought a miracle,
Taught me to aim at things beyond my
  power,
Which her perfections purchased, and gave
  to me
From her free bounties; she inspired me with
That valour which I dare not call mine own;
And, from the fair reflexion of her mind,
My soul received the sparkling beams of
  courage.
She, from the magazine of her proper good-
  ness,
Stock'd me with virtuous purposes; sent me
  forth
To trade for honour; and, she being the
  owner
Of the bark of my adventures, I must yield
  her
A just account of all, as fits a factor.
And, howsoever others think me happy,
And cry aloud, I have made a prosperous
  voyage;
One frown of her dislike at my return,
Which, as a punishment for my fault, I
  look for,
Strikes dead all comfort.
  Timag. Tush! these fears are needless;
She cannot, must not, shall not, be so cruel.
A free confession of a fault wins pardon,
But, being seconded by desert, commands it.
The general is your own, and, sure, my
  father
Repents his harshness; for myself, I am
Ever your creature.—One day shall be happy
In your triumph, and your marriage.

Leost. May it prove so,
With her consent and pardon.
Timag. Ever touching
On that harsh string ! She is your own,
   and you
Without disturbance seize on what's your
   due.   *[Exeunt.*

ACT IV.

SCENE I.—Syracuse. *A Room in*
   Archidamus's *House.*

Enter Marullo *and* Timandra.

Mar. She has her health, then?
Timand. Yes, sir ; and as often
As I speak of you, lends attentive ear
To all that I deliver ; nor seems tired,
Though I dwell long on the relation of
Your sufferings for her, heaping praise on
   praise
On your unequall'd temperance, and com-
   mand
You hold o'er your affections.
Mar. To my wish :   .
Have you acquainted her with the defeature
Of the Carthaginians, and with what ho-
   nours
Leosthenes comes crown'd home with?
Timand. With all care.
Mar. And how does she receive it? .
Timand. As I guess,
With a seeming kind of joy ; but yet ap-
   pears not
Transported, or proud of his happy fortune.
But when I tell her of the certain ruin
You must encounter with at their arrival
In Syracusa, and that death, with torments,
Must fall upon you, which you yet repent not,
Esteeming it a glorious martyrdom,
And a reward of pure unspotted love,
Preserved in the white robe of innocence,
Though she were in your power ; and, still
   spurr'd on
By insolent lust, you rather chose to suffer
The fruit untasted, for whose glad possession
You have call'd on the fury of your lord,
Than that she should be grieved, or tainted
   in
Her reputation——
Mar. Doth it work compunction?
Pities she my misfortune?
Timand. She express'd
All signs of sorrow which, her vow observed,
Could witness a grieved heart. At the first
   hearing,
She fell upon her face, rent her fair hair,
Her hands held up to heaven, and vented
   sighs,

In which she silently seemed to complain
Of heaven's injustice.
Mar. 'Tis enough : wait carefully,
And, on all watched occasions, continue
Speech and discourse of me : 'tis time must
   work her.
Timand. I'll not be wanting, but still
strive to serve you.   *[Exit.*

Enter Poliphron.

Mar. Now, Poliphron, the news?
Poliph. The conquering army   .
Is within ken.
Mar. How brook the slaves the object?
Poliph. Cheerfully yet ; they do refuse no
   labour,   .
And seem to scoff at danger ; 'tis your
   presence
That must confirm them : with a full consent
You are chosen to relate the tyranny
Of our proud masters ; and what you sub-
   scribe to,
They gladly will allow of, or hold out
To the last man.   .
Mar. I'll instantly among them.
If we prove constant to ourselves, good
   fortune
Will not, I hope, forsake us.
Poliph. 'Tis our best refuge.   *[Exeunt.*

SCENE II.—*Before the Walls of* Syracuse.

Enter Timoleon, Archidamus, Diphilus,
   Leosthenes, Timagoras, *and* Soldiers.

Timol. Thus far we are return'd victorious ;
   crown'd
With wreaths triumphant, (famine, blood,
   and death,   .
Banish'd your peaceful confines,) and bring
   home
Security and peace. . 'Tis therefore fit   `
That such as boldly stood the shock of war,
And with the dear expense of sweat and
   blood
Have purchased honour, should with plea-
   sure reap
The harvest of their toil : and we stand
   bound,
Out of the first file of the best deservers,
(Though all must be considered to their
   merits,)
To think of you, Leosthenes, that stand,
And worthily, most dear in our esteem,
For your heroic valour.
Archid. When I look on
The labour of so many men and ages,
This well-built city, not long since design'd
To spoil and rapine, by the favour of
The gods, and you, their ministers, pre-
   served,

I cannot, in my height of joy, but offer
These tears for a glad sacrifice.
   Diph. Sleep the citizens?
Or are they overwhelm'd with the excess
Of comfort that flows to them?
   Leost. We receive
A silent entertainment.
   Timag. I long since
Expected that the virgins and the matrons,
The old men striving with their age, the
   priests,
Carrying the images of their gods before
   them,
Should have met us with procession.— Ha !
   the gates
Are shut against us !
   Archid. And, upon the walls,
Arm'd men seem to defy us !

Enter above, on the Walls, Marullo, Poliphron, Cimbrio, Gracculo, *and other*
   Slaves.

   Diph. I should know
These faces : they are our slaves.
   Timag. The mystery, rascals !
Open the ports, and play not with an anger
That will consume you.
   Timol. This is above wonder.
   Archid. Our bondmen stand against us !
   Grac. Some such things
We were in man's remembrance. The
   slaves are turn'd
Lords of the town, or so—nay, be not angry :
Perhaps, upon good terms, giving security
You will be quiet men, we may allow you
Some lodgings in our garrets or outhouses :
Your great looks cannot carry it.
   Cimb. The truth is,
We've been bold with your wives, toy'd with
   your daughters——
   Leost. O my prophetic soul !
   Grac. Rifled your chests,
Been busy with your wardrobes.
   Timag. Can we endure this?
   Leost. O my Cleora !
   Grac. A caudle for the gentleman ;
He'll die o' the pip else.
   Timag. Scorn'd too ! are you turn'd
   stone?
Hold parley with our bondmen ! force our
   entrance,
Then, villains, expect——
   Timol. Hold ! You wear men's shapes,
And if, like men, you have reason, shew a
   cause
That leads you to this desperate course,
   which must end
In your destruction.

   Grac. That, as please the Fates ;
But we vouchsafe——Speak, captain.
   Timag. Hell and furies !
   Archid. Bay'd by our own curs !
   Cimb. Take heed you be not worried.
   Poliph. We are sharp set.
   Cimb. And sudden.
   Mar. Briefly thus, then,
Since I must speak for all—Your tyranny
Drew us from our obedience.   Happy those
   times
When lords were styled fathers of families,
And not imperious masters ! when they
   number'd
Their servants almost equal with their sons,
Or one degree beneath them ! when their
   labours
Were cherish'd and rewarded, and a period
Set to their sufferings ; when they did not
   press
Their duties or their wills, beyond the power
And strength of their performance ! all
   things order'd
With such decorum, as wise lawmakers,
From each well-govern'd private house de-
   rived
The perfect model of a commonwealth.
Humanity then lodged in the hearts of men,
And thankful masters carefully provided
For creatures wanting reason.   The noble
   horse,
That, in his fiery youth, from his wide nostrils
Neigh'd courage to his rider, and brake
   through
Groves of opposed pikes, bearing his lord
Safe to triumphant victory ; old or wounded,
Was set at liberty, and freed from service.
The Athenian mules, that from the quarry
   drew
Marble, hew'd for the temples of the gods,
The great work ended, were dismiss'd, and fed
At the public cost ; nay, faithful dogs have
   found
Their sepulchres ; but man, to man more
   cruel,
Appoints no end] to the sufferings of his
   slave ;
Since pride stepp'd in and riot, and o'erturn'd
This goodly frame of concord, teaching
   masters
To glory in the abuse of such as are
Brought under their command ; who, grown
   unuseful,
Are less esteem'd than beasts.—This you
   have practised,
Practised on us with rigour ; this hath forced
   us
To shake our heavy yokes off ; and, if redress
Of these just grievances be not granted us,

We'll right ourselves, and by strong hand
defend
What we are now possess'd of.
  Grac. And not leave
One house unfired.
  Cimb. Or throat uncut of those
We have in our power.
  Poliph. Nor will we fall alone ;
You shall buy us dearly.
  Timag. O the gods !
Unheard-of insolence !
  Timol. What are your demands?
  Mar. A general pardon first, for all
offences
Committed in your absence. Liberty
To all such as desire to make return
Into their countries ; and, to those that stay,
A competence of land freely allotted
To each man's proper use, no lord acknow-
ledged :
Lastly, with your consent, to choose them
wives
Out of your families.
  Timag. Let the city sink first.
  Leost. And ruin seize on all, ere we sub-
scribe
To such conditions.
  Archid. Carthage, though victorious.
Could not have forced more from us.
  Leost. Scale the walls ;
Capitulate after.
  Timol. He that wins the top first,
Shall wear a mural wreath.   [*Exeunt.*
  Mar. Each to his place.
                [*Flourish and alarms.*
Or death or victory! Charge them home,
and fear not.
                [*Exeunt* Marullo *and* Slaves.

  Re-enter Timoleon, Archidamus, *and*
                Senators.

  Timol. We wrong ourselves, and we are
justly punish'd,
To deal with bondmen, as if we encounter'd
An equal enemy.
  Archid. They fight like devils ;
And run upon our swords, as if their breasts
Were proof beyond their armour.

  Re-enter Leosthenes *and* Timagoras.

  Timag. Make a firm stand.
The slaves, not satisfied they have beat us off,
Prepare to sally forth.
  Timol. They are wild beasts,
And to be tamed by policy. Each man take
A tough whip in his hand, such as you used
To punish them with, as masters : in your
looks
Carry severity and awe ; 'twill fright them

More than your weapons. Savage lions fly
from
The sight of fire ; and these, that have forgot
That duty you ne'er taught them with your
swords,
When, unexpected, they behold those terrors
Advanced aloft, that they were made to
shake at,
'Twill force them to remember what they are,
And stoop to due obedience.
  Archid. Here they come.

  Enter, from the City, Cimbrio, Gracculo,
                and other Slaves.

  Cimb. Leave not a man alive ; a wound's
but a flea-biting,
To what we suffer'd, being slaves.
  Grac. O, my heart !
Cimbrio, what do we see? the whip ! our
masters !
  Timag. Dare you rebel, slaves !
      [*The* Senators *shake their whips, the*
                Slaves *throw away their weapons,
                and run off.*
  Cimb. Mercy ! mercy ! where
Shall we hide us from their fury ?
  Grac. Fly, they follow.
O, we shall be tormented !
  Timol. Enter with them,
But yet forbear to kill them : still remember
They are part of your wealth ; and being
disarm'd,
There is no danger.
  Archid. Let us first deliver
Such as they have in fetters, and at leisure
Determine of their punishment.
  Leost. Friend, to you
I leave the disposition of what's mine :
I cannot think I am safe without your sister,
She is only worth my thought ; and, till I see
What she has suffer'd, I am on the rack,
And Furies my tormentors.   [*Exeunt.*

SCENE III.—Syracuse. *A Room in*
                Archidamus's *House.*

  Enter Marullo *and* Timandra.

  Mar. I know I am pursued ; nor would
I fly
Although the ports were open, and a convoy
Ready to bring me off: the baseness of
These villains, from the pride of all my hopes,
Hath thrown me to the bottomless abyss
Of horror and despair : had they stood firm,
I could have bought Cleora's free consent
With the safety of her father's life, and
brother's ;
And forced Leosthenes to quit his claim,
And kneel a suitor for me.
  Timand. You must not think

What might have been, but what must now
  be practised,
And suddenly resolve.

Mar. All my poor fortunes
Are at the stake, and I must run the hazard.
Unseen, convey me to Cleora's chamber ;
For in her sight, if it were possible,
I would be apprehended : do not enquire
The reason why, but help me.
                [Knocking within.
Timand. Make haste,—one knocks.
                   [Exit Marullo.
Jove turn all to the best !

     Enter Leosthenes.

              You are welcome, sir.
Leost. Thou giv'st it in a heavy tone.
Timand. Alas ! sir,
We have so long fed on the bread of sorrow,
Drinking the bitter water of afflictions,
Made loathsome too by our continued fears,
Comfort's a stranger to us.
  Leost. Fears ! your sufferings :——
For which I am so overgone with grief,
I dare not ask, without compassionate tears,
The villain's name that robbed thee of thy
  honour :
For being train'd up in chastity's cold school,
And taught by such a mistress as Cleora,
'Twere impious in me to think Timandra
Fell with her own consent.
  Timand. How mean you, fell, sir ?
I understand you not.
  Leost. I would thou did'st not,
Or that I could not read upon thy face,
In blushing characters, the story of
Libidinous rape : confess it, for you stand not
Accountable for a sin, against whose strength
Your o'ermatched innocence could make no
  resistance ;
Under which odds, I know, Cleora fell too,
Heaven's help in vain invoked ; the amazed
  sun
Hiding his face behind a mask of clouds,
Nor daring to look on it ! In her sufferings
All sorrow's comprehended : what Timandra,
Or the city, has endured, her loss consider'd,
Deserves not to be named.
  Timand. Pray you, do not bring, sir,
In the chimeras of your jealous fears,
New monsters to affright us.
  Leost. O, Timandra,
That I had faith enough but to believe thee !
I should receive it with a joy beyond
Assurance of Elysian shades hereafter,
Or all the blessings, in this life, a mother
Could wish her children crown'd with—but
  I must not
Credit impossibilities ; yet I strive

To find out that whose knowledge is a curse,
And ignorance a blessing. Come, discover
What kind of look he had that forced thy
  lady,
(Thy ravisher I will enquire at leisure,)
That when, hereafter, I behold a stranger,
But near to him in aspéct, I may conclude,
Though men and angels should proclaim him
  honest,
He is a hell bred villain.
  Timand. You are unworthy
To know she is preserved, preserved un-
  tainted :
Sorrow, but ill bestow'd, hath only made
A rape upon her comforts in your absence.
Come forth, dear madam. [*Leads in* Cleora.
  Leost. Ha !   [*Kneels.*
  Timand. Nay, she deserves
The bending of your heart ; that, to content
  you,
Has kept a vow, the breach of which a Vestal,
Though the infringing it had call'd upon her
A living funeral, must of force have shrunk at.
No danger could compel her to dispense
  with
Her cruel penance, though hot lust came
  arm'd
To seize upon her ; when one look or accent
Might have redeem'd her.
  Leost. Might ! O do not shew me
A beam of comfort, and straight take it
  from me.
The means by which she was freed ? speak,
  O speak quickly ;
Each minute of delay's an age of torment ;
O speak, Timandra.
  Timand. Free her from her oath ;
Herself can best deliver it.
  Leost. O blest office ! [*Unbinds her eyes.*
Never did galley-slave shake off his chains,
Or look'd on his redemption from the oar,
With such true feeling of delight, as now
I find myself possess'd of.—Now I behold
True light indeed ; for, since these fairest
  stars,
Cover'd with clouds of your determinate will,
Denied their influence to my optic sense,
The splendour of the sun appear'd to me
But as some little glimpse of his bright beams
Convey'd into a dungeon, to remember
The dark inhabitants there, how much they
  wanted.
Open these long shut lips, and strike mine
  ears
With music more harmonious than the spheres
Yield in their heavenly motions : and if ever
A true submission for a crime acknowledged,
May find a gracious hearing, teach your
  tongue,

In the first sweet articulate sounds it utters,
To sign my wish'd-for pardon.
Cleo. I forgive you.
Leost. How greedily I receive this ! Stay,
  best lady,
And let me by degrees ascend the height
Of human happiness ! all at once deliver'd,
The torrent of my joys will overwhelm me:—
So! now a little more ; and pray excuse me,
If, like a wanton epicure, I desire
The pleasant taste these cates of comfort
  yield me,
Should not too soon be swallow'd. Have
  you not,
By your unspotted truth I do conjure you
To answer truly, suffer'd in your honour,
By force, I mean, for in your will I free you,
Since I left Syracusa?
Cleo. I restore
This kiss, so help me goodness ! which I
  borrow'd,
When I last saw you.
Leost. Miracle of virtue !
One pause more, I beseech you: I am like
A man whose vital spirits consumed and
  · wasted
With a long and tedious fever, unto whom
Too much of a strong cordial, at once taken,
Brings death, and not restores him. Yet I
  cannot
Fix here; but must enquire the man to whom
I stand indebted for a benefit,
Which to requite at full, though in this hand
I grasp all sceptres the world's empire bows to,
Would leave me a poor bankrupt. Name
  him, lady;
If of a mean estate, I'll gladly part with
My utmost fortunes to him ; but if noble,
In thankful duty study how to serve him ;
Or if of higher rank, erect him altars,
And as a god adore him.
Cleo. If that goodness,
And noble temperance, the queen of virtues,
Bridling rebellious passions, to whose sway,
Such as have conquer'd nations have lived
  slaves,
Did ever wing great minds to fly to heaven,
He, that preserved mine honour, may hope
  boldly
To fill a seat among the gods, and shake off
Our frail corruption.
Leost. Forward.
Cleo. Or if ever
The Powers above did mask in human shapes,
To teach mortality, not by cold precepts
Forgot as soon as told, but by examples,
To imitate their pureness, and draw near
To their celestial natures, I believe
He's more than man.

Leost. You do describe a wonder.
Cleo. Which will encrease, when you shall
  understand
He was a lover.
Leost. Not yours, lady?
Cleo. Yes ;
Loved me, Leosthenes ; nay, more, so doted,
(If e'er affections scorning gross desires
May without wrong be styled so,) that he
  durst not,   .
With an immodest syllable or look,
In fear it might take from me, whom he made
The object of his better part, discover
I was the saint he sued to.
Leost. A rare temper !
Cleo. I cannot speak it to the worth : all
  praise
I can bestow upon it will appear
Envious detraction. Not to rack you further,
Yet make the miracle full, though, of all
  men,
He hated you, Leosthenes, as his rival,
So high yet he prized my content, that,
  knowing
You were a man I favour'd, he disdain'd not,
Against himself, to serve you.
Leost. You conceal still
The owner of these excellencies.
Cleo. 'Tis Marullo,
My father's bondman.
Leost. Ha, ha, ha !
Cleo. Why do you laugh?
Leost. To hear the labouring mountain of
  your praise
Deliver'd of a mouse.
Cleo. The man deserves not
This scorn, I can assure you.
Leost. Do you call
What was his duty, merit?
Cleo. Yes, and place it
As high in my esteem, as all the honours
Descended from your ancestors, or the glory,
Which you may call your own, got in this
  action,
In which, I must confess, you have done
  nobly ;
And I could add, as I desired, but that
I fear 'twould make you proud.
Leost. Why, lady, can you
Be won to give allowance, that your slave
Should dare to love you ?
Cleo. The immortal gods
Accept the meanest altars, that are raised
By pure devotions ; and sometimes prefer
An ounce of frankincense, honey or milk,
Before whole hecatombs, or Sabæan gums,
Offer'd in ostentation.—Are you sick
Of your old disease? I'll fit you. [*Aside.*
Leost. You seem moved.

Cleo. Zealous, I grant, in the defence of
     virtue.
Why, good Leosthenes, though I endured
A penance for your sake, above example ;
I have not so far sold myself, I take it,
To be at your devotion, but I may
Cherish desert in others, where I find it.
How would you tyrannize, if you stood
     possess'd of
That which is only yours in expectation,
That now prescribe such hard conditions to
     me?
Leost. One kiss, and I am silenced.
Cleo. I vouchsafe it ;
Yet, I must tell you 'tis a favour that
Marullo, when I was his, not mine own,
Durst not presume to ask : no ; when the city
Bow'd humbly to licentious rapes and lust,
And when I was, of men and gods forsaken,
Deliver'd to his power, he did not press me
To grace him with one look or syllable,
Or urged the dispensation of an oath
Made for your satisfaction :—the poor
     wretch,
Having related only his own sufferings,
And kiss'd my hand, which I could not
     deny him,
Defending me from others, never since
Solicited my favours.
Leost. Pray you, end   :
The story does not please me.
Cleo. Well, take heed
Of doubts and fears ;—for know, Leosthenes,
A greater injury cannot be offer'd
To innocent chastity, than unjust suspicion.
I love Marullo's fair mind, not his person ;
Let that secure you.   And I here command
     you,
If I have any power in you, to stand
Between him and all punishment, and
     oppose
His temperance to his folly ; if you fail——
No more ; I will not threaten.   [*Exit.*
Leost. What a bridge
Of glass I walk upon, over a river
Of certain ruin, mine own weighty fears
Cracking what should support me! and
     those helps,
Which confidence lends to others, are from
     me
Ravish'd by doubts, and wilful jealousy.
                              [*Exit.*

SCENE IV.—*Another Room in the same.*

Enter Timagoras, Cleon, Asotus, Corisca,
     and Olympia.

Cleon. But are you sure we are safe ?
Timag. You need not fear ;

They are all under guard, their fangs pared
     off :
The wounds their insolence gave you, to be
     cured
With the balm of your revenge.
Asot. And shall I be
The thing I was born, my lord ?
Timag. The same wise thing.
'Slight, what a beast they have made thee !·
     Africk never
Produced the like.
Asot. I think so :—nor the land
Where apes and monkeys grow, like crabs
     and walnuts,
On the same tree.   Not all the catalogue
Of conjurers or wise women bound together
Could have so soon transform'd me, as my
     rascal
Did with his whip ; for not in outside only,
But in my own belief, I thought myself
As perfect a baboon——
Timag. An ass thou wert ever.
Asot. And would have given one leg,
     with all my heart,
For good security to have been a man
After three lives, or one and twenty years,
Though I had died on crutches.
Cleon. Never varlets
So triumph'd o'er an old fat man : I was
     famish'd.
Timag. Indeed you are fallen away.
Asot. Three years of feeding
On cullises and jelly, though his cooks
Lard all he eats with marrow, or his doctors
Pour in his mouth restoratives as he sleeps,
Will not recover him.
Timag. But your ladyship looks
Sad on the matter, as if you had miss'd
Your ten-crown amber possets, good to
     smooth
The cutis, as you call it, and prepare you
Active, and high, for an afternoon's en-
     counter
With a rough gamester, on your couch.
     Fie on't !
You are grown thrifty, smell like other
     women ;
The college of physicians have not sat,
As they were used, in counsel, how to fill
The crannies in your cheeks, or raise a
     rampire
With mummy, ceruses, or infants' fat,
To keep off age and time.
Coris. Pray you, forbear ;
I am an alter'd woman.
Timag. So it seems ;
A part of your honour's ruff stands out of
     rank too.
Coris. No matter, I have other thoughts.

Timag. O strange !
Not ten days since it would have vex'd you more
Than the loss of your good name : pity, this cure
For your proud itch came no sooner !
Marry, Olympia
Seems to bear up still.
Olymp. I complain not, sir ;
I have borne my fortune patiently.
Timag. Thou wert ever
An excellent bearer ; so is all your tribe,
If you may choose your carriage.

Enter Leosthenes *and* Diphilus *with a Guard.*

How now, friend !
Looks our Cleora lovely ?
Leost. In my thoughts, sir.
Timag. But why this guard ?
Diph. It is Timoleon's pleasure :
The slaves have been examin'd, and confess
Their riot took beginning from your house ;
And the first mover of them to rebellion,
Your slave Marullo.
[*Exeunt* Diph. *and* Guard.
Leost. Ha ! I more than fear.
Timag. They may search boldly.

Enter Timandra, *speaking to the* Guard *within.*

Timand. You are unmanner'd grooms,
To pry into my lady's private lodgings ;
There's no Marullos there.

Re-enter Diphilus, *and* Guard *with Marullo.*

Timag. Now I suspect too.
Where found you him ?
Diph. Close hid in your sister's chamber.
Timag. Is that the villain's sanctuary ?
Leost. This confirms
All she deliver'd, false.
Timag. But that I scorn
To rust my good sword in thy slavish blood,
Thou now wert dead.
Mar. He's more a slave than fortune
Or misery can make me, that insults
Upon unweapon'd innocence.
Timag. Prate you, dog !
Mar. Curs snap at lions in the toil, whose looks
Frighted them, being free.
Timag. As a wild beast,
Drive him before you.
Mar. O divine Cleora !
Leost. Dar'st thou presume to name her ?
Mar. Yes, and love her ;
And may say, have deserved her.

Timag. Stop his mouth,
Load him with irons too.
[*Exit* Guard *with* Marullo.
Cleon. I am deadly sick
To look on him.
Asot. If he get loose, I know it,
I caper like an ape again : I feel
The whip already.
Timand. This goes to my lady. [*Exit.*
Timag. Come, cheer you, sir ; we'll urge his punishment
To the full satisfaction of your anger.
Leost. He is not worth my thoughts. No corner left
In all the spacious rooms of my vex'd heart,
But is fill'd with Cleora : and the rape
She has done upon her honour, with my wrong,
The heavy burthen of my sorrow's song.
[*Exeunt.*

ACT V.

SCENE I.—*The same. A Room in Archidamus's House.*

Enter Archidamus *and* Cleora.

Archid. Thou art thine own disposer.
Were his honours
And glories centupled, as I must confess,
Leosthenes is most worthy, yet I will not,
However I may counsel, force affection.
Cleo. It needs not, sir ; I prize him to his worth,
Nay, love him truly ; yet would not live slaved
To his jealous humours : since, by the hopes of heaven,
As I am free from violence, in a thought
I am not guilty.
Archid. 'Tis believed, Cleora ;
And much the rather, our great gods be praised for't !
In that I find, beyond my hopes, no sign
Of riot in my house, but all things order'd,
As if I had been present.
Cleo. May that move you
To pity poor Marullo !
Archid. 'Tis my purpose
To do him all the good I can, Cleora ;
But this offence, being against the state,
Must have a public trial. In the mean time,
Be careful of yourself, and stand engaged
No further to Leosthenes, than you may
Come off with honour ; for, being once his wife,
You are no more your own, nor mine, but must
Resolve to serve, and suffer his commands,

And not dispute them :—ere it be too late,
Consider it duly. I must to the senate.
                                        [*Exit.*
Cleo. I am much distracted : in Leos-
thenes,
I can find nothing justly to accuse,
But his excess of love, which I have
studied
To cure with more than common means ;
yet still
It grows upon him. And, if I may call
My sufferings merit, I stand bound to think
on
Marullo's dangers—though I save his life,
His love is unrewarded :—I confess,
Both have deserved me ; yet, of force, must
be
Unjust to one ; such is my destiny.—

            Enter Timandra.

How now ! whence flow these tears ?
  Timand. I have met, madam,
An object of such cruelty, as would force
A savage to compassion.
  Cleo. Speak, what is it ?
  Timand. Men pity beasts of rapine, if
o'ermatch'd,
Though baited for their pleasure ; but these
monsters,
Upon a man that can make no resistance,
Are senseless in their tyranny. Let it be
granted,
Marullo is a slave, he's still a man ;
A capital offender, yet in justice
Not to be tortured, till the judge pronounce
His punishment.
  Cleo. Where is he ?
  Timand. Dragg'd to prison
With more than barbarous violence ; spurn'd
and spit on
By the insulting officers, his hands
Pinion'd behind his back ; loaden with
fetters :
Yet, with a saint-like patience, he still offers
His face to their rude buffets.
  Cleo. O my grieved soul !—
By whose command ?
  Timand. It seems, my lord your brother's,
For he's a looker-on : and it takes from
Honour'd Leosthenes, to suffer it,
For his respect to you, whose name in vain
The grieved wretch loudly calls on.
  Cleo. By Diana,
'Tis base in both ; and to their teeth I'll
tell them
That I am wrong'd in't.   [*Going forth.*
  Timand. What will you do?
  Cleo. In person
Visit and comfort him.

  Timand. That will bring fuel
To the jealous fires which burn too hot
already
In lord Leosthenes.
  Cleo. Let them consume him !
I am mistress of myself. Where cruelty
reigns,
There dwells nor love, nor honour. [*Exit.*
  Timand. So ! it works.
Though hitherto I have run a desperate
course
To serve my brother's purposes, now 'tis fit

      Enter Leosthenes *and* Timagoras.

I study mine own ends. They come :—assist
me
In these my undertakings, Love's great
patron,
As my intents are honest !
  Leost. 'Tis my fault :
Distrust of others springs, Timagoras,
From diffidence in ourselves : but I will strive,
With the assurance of my worth and merits,
To kill this monster, jealousy.
  Timag. 'Tis a guest,
In wisdom, never to be entertain'd
On trivial probabilities ; but, when
He does appear in pregnant proofs, not
fashion'd
By idle doubts and fears, to be received :
They make their own horns that are too
secure,
As well as such as give them growth and being
From mere imagination.   Though I prize
Cleora's honour equal with mine own,
And know what large additions of power
This match brings to our family, I prefer
Our friendship, and your peace of mind so far
Above my own respects, or hers, that if
She hold not her true value in the test,
'Tis far from my ambition, for her cure
That you should wound yourself.
  Timand. This argues for me.   [*Aside.*
  Timag. Why she should be so passionate
for a bondman,
Falls not in compass of my understanding,
But for some nearer interest : or he raise
This mutiny, if he loved her, as, you say,
She does confess he did, but to enjoy,
By fair or foul play, what he ventured for,
To me's a riddle.
  Leost. Pray you, no more ; already
I have answered that objection, in my strong
Assurance of her virtue.
  Timag. 'Tis unfit then,
That I should press it further.
  Timand. Now I must
Make in, or all is lost.
              [*Rushes forward distractedly.*

Timag. What would Timandra?
Leost. How wild she looks! How is it
 with thy lady?
Timag. Collect thyself, and speak.
Timand. As you are noble,
Have pity, or love piety.—Oh!
Leost. Take breath.
Timag. Out with it boldly.
Timand. O, the best of ladies,
I fear, is gone for ever.
Leost. Who, Cleora?
Timag. Deliver, how? 'Sdeath, be a man,
 sir!—Speak.
Timand. Take it then in as many sighs
 as words,
My lady——
Timag. What of her?
Timand. No sooner heard
Marullo was imprison'd, but she fell
Into a deadly swoon.
Timag. But she recover'd:
Say so, or he will sink too; hold, sir; fie!
This is unmanly.
Timand. Brought again to life,
But with much labour, she awhile stood
 silent,
Yet in that interim vented sighs, as if
They labour'd, from the prison of her flesh,
To give her grieved soul freedom. On the
 sudden,
Transported on the wings of rage and sorrow,
She flew out of the house, and, unattended,
Entered the common prison.
Leost. This confirms
What but before I fear'd.
Timand There you may find her;
And, if you love her as a sister——
Timag. Damn her!
Timand. Or you respect her safety as a
 lover,
Procure Marullo's liberty.
Timag. Impudence
Beyond expression!
Leost. Shall I be a bawd
To her lust, and my dishonour?
. *Timand.* She'll run mad, else,
Or do some violent act upon herself:
My lord, her father, sensible of her sufferings,
Labours to gain his freedom.
Leost. O, the devil!
Has she bewitch'd him too?
Timag. I'll hear no more.
Come, sir, we'll follow her; and if no per-
 suasion
Can make her take again her natural form,
Which by lust's powerful spell she has cast off,
This sword shall disenchant her.
Leost. O my heart-strings!
 [*Exeunt* Leosthenes *and* Timagoras.

Timand. I knew 'twould take. Pardon
 me, fair Cleora,
Though I appear a traitress; which thou
 wilt do,
In pity of my woes, when I make known
My lawful claim, and only seek mine own.
 [*Exit.*

SCENE II.—*A Prison.* Marullo *discovered
 in chains.*

 Enter Cleora *and* Gaoler.

Cleo. There's for your privacy. Stay, un-
 bind his hands.
Gaol. I dare not, madam.
Cleo. I will buy thy danger:
Take more gold;—do not trouble me with
 thanks,
I do suppose it done. [*Exit* Gaoler.
Mar. My better angel
Assumes this shape to comfort me, and
 wisely;
Since, from the choice of all celestial figures,
He could not take a visible form so full
Of glorious sweetness. [*Kneels.*
Cleo. Rise. I am flesh and blood,
And do partake thy tortures.
Mar. Can it be,
That charity should persuade you to descend
So far from your own height, as to vouchsafe
To look upon my sufferings? How I bless
My fetters now, and stand engaged to fortune
For my captivity—no, my freedom, rather!
For who dare think that place a prison, which
You sanctify with your presence? or believe,
Sorrow has power to use her sting on him,
That is in your compassion arm'd, and made
Impregnable, though tyranny raise at once
All engines to assault him?
Cleo. Indeed virtue,
With which you have made evident proofs
 that you
Are strongly fortified, cannot fall, though
 shaken
With the shock of fierce temptations; but
 still triumphs
In spite of opposition. For myself,
I may endeavour to confirm your goodness,
(A sure retreat, which never will deceive you,)
And with unfeigned tears express my sorrow
For what I cannot help.
Mar. Do you weep for me!
O, save that precious balm for nobler uses:
I am unworthy of the smallest drop,
Which, in your prodigality of pity,
You throw away on me. Ten of these pearls
Were a large ransom to redeem a kingdom
From a consuming plague, or stop heaven's
 vengeance,

Call'd down by crying sins, though, at that
    instant,
In dreadful flashes falling on the roofs
Of bold blasphemers. I am justly punish'd
For my intent of violence to such pureness ;
And all the torments flesh is sensible of,
A soft and gentle penance.
    Cleo. Which is ended
In this your free confession.

Enter Leosthenes *and* Timagoras *behind.*

    Leost. What an object
Have I encountered !
    Timag. I am blasted too :
Yet hear a litle further.
    Mar. Could I expire now,
These white and innocent hands closing my
    eyes thus,
'Twere not to die, but in a heavenly dream
To be transported, without the help of
    Charon,
To the Elysian shades. You make me bold ;
And, but to wish such happiness, I fear,
May give offence.
    Cleo. No ; for believ't, Marullo,
You've won so much upon me, that I know
    not
That happiness in my gift, but you may
    challenge.
    Leost. Are you yet satisfied ?
    Cleo. Nor can you wish
But what my vows will second, though it were
Your freedom first, and then in me full power
To make a second tender of myself,
And you receive the present. By this kiss,
From me a virgin bounty, I will practise
All arts for your deliverance ; and that pur-
    chased,
In what concerns your further aims, I
    speak it,
Do not despair, but hope——
    [Timagoras *and* Leosthenes *come forward.*
    Timag. To have the hangman,
When he is married to the cross, in scorn
To say *Gods give you joy !*
    Leost. But look on me,
And be not too indulgent to your folly ;
And then, but that grief stops my speech,
    imagine
What language I should use.
    Cleo. Against thyself :
Thy malice cannot reach me.
    Timag. How ?
    Cleo. No, brother,
Though you join in the dialogue to accuse
    me :
What I have done, I'll justify ; and these
    favours,

Which, you presume, will taint me in my
    honour, .
Though jealousy use all her eyes to spy out
One stain in my behaviour, or envy.
As many tongues to wound it, shall appear
My best perfections. For, to the world,
I can in my defence allege such reasons,
As my accusers shall stand dumb to hear
    them ; .
When in his fetters this man's worth and
    virtues,
But truly told, shall shame your boasted
    glories,
Which fortune claims a share in.
    Timag. The base villain
Shall never live to hear it.
                  [*Draws his sword.*
    Cleo. Murder ! help !
Through me, you shall pass to him.

Enter Archidamus, Diphilus, *and* Officers.

    Archid. What's the matter ?
On whom is your sword drawn ? are you a
    judge ?
Or else ambitious of the hangman's office,
Before it be design'd you?—You are bold, too;
Unhand my daughter.
    Leost. She's my valour's prize.
    Archid. With her consent, not otherwise.
    You may urge
Your title in the court ; if it prove good,
Possess her freely.—Guard him safely off too.
    Timag. You'll hear me, sir ?
    Archid. If you have aught to say,
Deliver it in public ; all shall find
A just judge of Timoleon.
    Diph. You must
Of force now use your patience.
    [*Exeunt all but* Timagoras *and* Leosthenes.
    Timag. Vengeance rather !
Whirlwinds of rage possess me : you are
    wrong'd
Beyond a Stoic sufferance ; yet you stand
As you were rooted.
    Leost. I feel something here,
That boldly tells me, all the love and service
I pay Cleora is another's due,
And therefore cannot prosper.
    Timag. Melancholy ;
Which now you must not yield to.
    Leost. 'Tis apparent :
In fact your sister's innocent, however
Changed by her violent will.
    Timag. If you believe so,
Follow the chase still ; and in open court
Plead your own interest : we shall find the
    judge
Our friend, I fear not.

Leost. Something I shall say,
But what——
Timag. Collect yourself as we walk thither.
[*Exeunt.*

SCENE III.—*The Court of Justice.*

Enter Timoleon, Archidamus, Cleora, *and*
Officers.

Timol. 'Tis wonderous strange! nor can
it fall within
The reach of my belief, a slave should be
The owner of a temperance which this age
Can hardly parallel in freeborn lords,
Or kings proud of their purple.
Archid. 'Tis most true;
And, though at first it did appear a fable,
All circumstances meet to give it credit;
Which works so on me, that I am compell'd
To be a suitor, not to be denied,
He may have equal hearing.
Cleo. Sir, you graced me
With the title of your mistress; but my fortune
Is so far distant from command, that I
Lay by the power you gave me, and plead
humbly
For the preserver of my fame and honour.
And pray you, sir, in charity believe,
That, since I had ability of speech,
My tongue has been so much inured to
truth,
I know not how to lie.
Timol. I'll rather doubt
The oracles of the gods, than question what
Your innocence delivers; and, as far
As justice and mine honour can give way,
He shall have favour. Bring him in unbound:
[*Exeunt* Officers.
And though Leosthenes may challenge from
me,
For his late worthy service, credit to
All things he can allege in his own cause,
Marullo, so, I think, you call his name,
Shall find I do reserve one ear for him,

Enter Cleon, Asotus, Diphilus, Olympia,
and Corisca.

To let in mercy. Sit, and take your places;
The right of this fair virgin first determined,
Your bondmen shall be censured.
Cleon. With all rigour,
We do expect.
Coris. Temper'd, I say, with mercy.

Enter at one door Leosthenes *and* Timagoras;
at the other, Officers *with* Marullo, *and*
Timandra.

Timol. Your hand, Leosthenes: I cannot
doubt,
You, that have been victorious in the war,

Should, in a combat fought with words,
come off
But with assured triumph.
Leost. My deserts, sir,
If, without arrogance, I may style them such,
Arm me from doubt and fear.
Timol. 'Tis nobly spoken.
Nor be thou daunted (howsoe'er thy fortune
Has mark'd thee out a slave) to speak thy
merits:
For virtue, though in rags, may challenge
more
Than vice, set off with all the trim of greatness.
Mar. I had rather fall under so just a
judge,
Than be acquitted by a man corrupt,
And partial in his censure.
Archid. Note his language;
It relishes of better breeding than
His present state dares promise.
Timol. I observe it.
Place the fair lady in the midst, that both,
Looking with covetous eyes upon the prize
They are to plead for, may, from the fair
object,
Teach Hermes eloquence.
Leost. Am I fallen so low?
My birth, my honour, and, what's dearest
to me,
My love, and, witness of my love, my service,
So undervalued, that I must contend
With one, where my excess of glory must
Make his o'erthrow a conquest? Shall my
fulness
Supply defects in such a thing, that never
Knew anything but want and emptiness,
Give him a name, and keep it such, from
this
Unequal competition? If my pride,
Or any bold assurance of my worth,
Has pluck'd this mountain of disgrace
upon me,
I am justly punish'd, and submit; but if
I have been modest, and esteem'd myself
More injured in the tribute of the praise,
Which no desert of mine, prized by self-love,
Ever exacted, may this cause and minute
For ever be forgotten! I dwell long
Upon mine anger, and now turn to you,
Ungrateful fair one; and, since you are such,
'Tis lawful for me to proclaim myself,
And what I have deserved.
Cleo. Neglect and scorn
From me, for this proud vaunt.
Leost. You nourish, lady,
Your own dishonour in this harsh reply,
And almost prove what some hold of your
sex,
You are all made up of passion: for, if reason

K

Or judgment could find entertainment with
 you,
Or that you would distinguish of the objects
You look on, in a true glass, not seduced
By the false light of your too violent will,
I should not need to plead for that which
 you,
With joy, should offer.   Is my high birth a
 blemish?
Or does my wealth, which all the vain ex-
 pense
Of women cannot waste, breed loathing in
 you?
The honours I can call mine own, thought
 scandals?
Am I deform'd, or, for my father's sins,
Mulcted by nature? If you interpret these
As crimes, 'tis fit I should yield up myself
Most miserably guilty.   But, perhaps,
(Which yet I would not credit,) you have
 seen
This gallant pitch the bar, or bear a burthen
Would crack the shoulders of a weaker
 bondman :
Or any other boisterous exercise,
Assuring a strong back to satisfy
Your loose desires, insatiate as the grave.
 Cleo. You are foul-mouth'd.
 Archid. Ill-manner'd too.
 Leost. I speak
In the way of supposition, and entreat you,
With all the fervour of a constant lover,
That you would free yourself from these
 aspersions,
Or any imputation black-tongued slander
Could throw on your unspotted virgin white-
 ness :
To which there is no easier way, than by
Vouchsafing him your favour ; him, to whom,
Next to the general, and the gods and
 fautors,
The country owes her safety.
 Timag. Are you stupid?
'Slight, leap into his arms, and there ask
 pardon—
Oh ! you expect your slave's reply ; no doubt
We shall have a fine oration : I will teach
My spaniel to howl in sweeter language,
And keep a better method.
 Archid. You forget
The dignity of the place.
 Diph. Silence !
 Timol. [*to* Marullo.] Speak boldly.
 Mar. 'Tis your authority gives me a
 tongue,
I should be dumb else ; and I am secure,
I cannot clothe my thoughts, and just
 defence,
In such an abject phrase, but 'twill appear

Equal, if not above my low condition.
I need no bombast language stolen from
 such
As make nobility from prodigious terms
The hearers understand not ; I bring with me
No wealth to boast of, neither can I number
Uncertain fortune's favours with my merits ;
I dare not force affection, or presume
To censure her discretion, that looks on me
As a weak man, and not her fancy's idol.
How I have loved, and how much I have
 suffer'd,
And with what pleasure undergone the
 burthen
Of my ambitious hopes, (in aiming at
The glad possession of a happiness,
The abstract of all goodness in mankind
Can at no part deserve,) with my confession
Of mine own wants, is all that can plead for
 me.
But if that pure desires, not blended with
Foul thoughts, that, like a river, keeps his
 course,
Retaining still the clearness of the spring
From whence it took beginning, may be
 thought
Worthy acceptance ; then I dare rise up,
And tell this gay man to his teeth, I never
Durst doubt her constancy, that, like a rock,
Beats off temptations, as that mocks the
 fury
Of the proud waves ; nor, from my jealous
 fears,
Question that goodness to which, as an altar
Of all perfection, he that truly loved
Should rather bring a sacrifice of service,
Than raze it with the engines of suspicion :
Of which, when he can wash an Æthiop
 white,
Leosthenes may hope to free himself ;
But, till then, never.
 Timag. Bold, presumptuous villain !
 Mar. I will go further, and make good
 upon him,   .
I' the pride of all his honours, birth, and
 fortunes,
He's more unworthy than myself.
 Leost. Thou liest.
 Timag. Confute him with a whip, and,
 the doubt decided,
Punish him with a halter.
 Mar. O the gods !
My ribs, though made of brass, cannot
 contain
My heart, swollen big with rage. The lie !—
 a whip !
Let fury then disperse these clouds, in which
I long have march'd disguised ; [*Throws off
 his disguise.*] that, when they know

Whom they have injured, they may faint with
   horror
Of my revenge, which, wretched men!
   expect,
As sure as fate, to suffer.
   Leost. Ha! Pisander!
   Timag. 'Tis the bold Theban!
   A sot. There's no hope for me then:
I thought I should have put in for a share,
And borne Cleora from them both; but now,
This stranger looks so terrible, that I dare
   not
So much as look on her.
   Pisan. Now as myself,
Thy equal at thy best, Leosthenes.
For you, Timagoras, praise heaven you were
   born
Cleora's brother, 'tis your safest armour.
But I lose time,—The base lie cast upon me,
I thus return: Thou art a perjured man,
False, and perfidious, and hast made a tender
Of love and service to this lady, when
Thy soul, if thou hast any, can bear witness,
That thou wert not thine own: for proof of
   this,
Look better on this virgin, and consider,
This Persian shape laid by, and she appear-
   ing
In a Greekish dress, such as when first you
   saw her,
If she resemble not Pisander's sister,
One call'd Statilia?
   Leost. 'Tis the same! My guilt
So chokes my spirits, I cannot deny
My falsehood, nor excuse it.
   Pisan. This is she,
To whom thou wert contracted: this the
   lady,
That, when thou wert my prisoner, fairly
   taken
In the Spartan war, that, begg'd thy liberty,
And with it gave herself to thee, ungrate-
   ful!
   Statil. No more, sir, I entreat you: I
   perceive
True sorrow in his looks, and a consent
To make me reparation in mine honour;
And then I am most happy.
   Pisan. The wrong done her,
Drew me from Thebes, with a full intent to
   kill thee:
But this fair object met me in my fury,
And quite disarm'd me. Being denied to
   have her,
By you, my lord Archidamus, and not able
To live far from her; love, the mistress of
All quaint devices, prompted me to treat
With a friend of mine, who, as a pirate,
   sold me

For a slave to you, my lord, and gave my
   sister,
As a present, to Cleora.
   Timol. Strange meanders!
   Pisan. There how I bare myself, needs no
   relation:
But, if so far descending from the height
Of my then flourishing fortunes, to the
   lowest
Condition of a man, to have means only
To feed my eye with the sight of what I
   honour'd;
The dangers too I underwent, the suffer-
   ings;
The clearness of my interest, may deserve
A noble recompense in your lawful favour;
Now 'tis apparent that Leosthenes
Can claim no interest in you, you may
   please
To think upon my service.
   Cleo. Sir, my want
Of power to satisfy so great a debt,
Makes me accuse my fortune; but if that,
Out of the bounty of your mind, you think
A free surrender of myself full payment,
I gladly tender it.
   Archid. With my consent too,
All injuries forgotten.
   Timag. I will study,
In my future service, to deserve your favour,
And good opinion.
   Leost. Thus I gladly fee
This advocate to plead for me.
              [*Kissing* Statilia.
   Pisan. You will find me
An easy judge. When I have yielded
   reasons
Of your bondmen's falling off from their
   obedience,
Then after, as you please, determine of me.
I found their natures apt to mutiny
From your too cruel usage, and made trial
How far they might be wrought on; to in-
   struct you
To look with more prevention and care
To what they may hereafter undertake
Upon the like occasions. The hurt's little
They have committed; nor was ever cure,
But with some pain, effected. I confess,
In hope to force a grant of fair Cleora,
I urged them to defend the town against
   you;
Nor had the terror of your whips, but that
I was preparing for defence elsewhere,
So soon got entrance: In this I am guilty;
Now, as you please, your censure.
   Timol. Bring them in;
And, though you've given me power, I do
   entreat

Such as have undergone their insolence,
It may not be offensive, though I study
Pity, more than revenge.
  Coris. 'Twill best become you.
  Cleon. I must consent.
  Asot. For me, I'll find a time
To be revenged hereafter.

Enter Gracculo, Cimbrio, Poliphron, Zanthia, *and the other* Slaves, *with halters
about their necks.*

  Grac. Give me leave ;
I'll speak for all.
  Timol. What canst thou say, to hinder
The course of justice?
  Grac. Nothing.—You may see
We are prepared for hanging, and confess
We have deserved it : our most humble
    suit is,
We may not twice be executed.
  Timol. Twice !
How meanest thou?
  Grac. At the gallows first, and after in a
 · ballad
Sung to some villainous tune.   There are
    ten-groat rhymers
About the town, grown fat on these occa-
    sions.
Let but a chapel fall, or a street be fired,
A foolish lover hang himself for pure love,

Or any such like accident, and, before
They are cold in their graves, some damn'd
    ditty's made,
Which makes their ghosts walk.—Let the
    state take order
For the redress of this abuse, recording
'Twas done by my advice, and, for my part,
I'll cut as clean a caper from the ladder,
As ever merry Greek did.
  Timol. Yet I think
You would shew more activity to delight
Your master for a pardon.
  Grac. O ! I would dance,
As I were all air and fire.   [*Capers.*
  Timol. And ever be
Obedient and humble?
  Grac. As his spaniel,
Though he kick'd me for exercise ; and the
    like
I promise for all the rest.
  Timol. Rise then, you have it.
  All the Slaves. Timoleon ! Timoleon !
  Timol. Cease these clamours.
And now, the war being ended to our wishes,
And such as went the pilgrimage of love,
Happy in full fruition of their hopes,
'Tis lawful, thanks paid to the Powers
    divine,
To drown our cares in honest mirth and
    wine.   [*Exeunt.*

The Renegado.

DRAMATIS PERSONÆ.	ACTORS' NAMES.
Asambeg, *viceroy of* Tunis	John Blanye.
Mustapha, *basha of* Aleppo	John Sumner.
Vitelli, *a Venetian gentleman, disguised as a merchant*	Mich. Bowyer.
Francisco, *a Jesuit*	Wm. Reignalds.
Antonio Grimaldi, the RENEGADO	Wm. Allen.
Carazie, *an eunuch*	Wm. Robins.
Gazet, *servant to* Vitelli	Ed. Shakerley.
Aga.	
Capiaga.	
Janizaries.	
Master.	
Boatswain.	
Sailors.	
A Gaoler. Turks.	
Donusa, *niece to* Amurath	Ed. Rogers.
Paulina, *sister to* Vitelli	Theo. Bourne.
Manto, *servant to* Donusa,	

SCENE,—Tunis.

ACT I.

SCENE I.—*A Street near the* Bazaar.

Enter Vitelli *and* Gazet.

Vitel. You have hired a shop, then?

Gaz. Yes, sir ; and our wares,
Though brittle as a maidenhead at sixteen,
Are safe unladen ; not a crystal crack'd,
Or China dish needs soldering ; our choice
        pictures,
As they came from the workman, without
        blemish :
And I have studied speeches for each piece,
And, in a thrifty tone, to sell them off,
Will swear by Mahomet and Termagant,
That this is mistress to the great duke of
        Florence,
That, niece to old king Pepin, and a third,
An Austrian princess by her Roman nose,
Howe'er my conscience tells me they are
        figures
Of bawds and common courtezans in Venice.

Vitel. You make no scruple of an oath,
        then?

Gaz. Fie, sir !
'Tis out of my indentures ; I am bound there,
To swear for my master's profit, as securely
As your intelligencer must for his prince,
That sends him forth an honourable spy,
To serve his purposes. And, if it be lawful
In a Christian shopkeeper to cheat his father,
I cannot find but to abuse a Turk
In the sale of our commodities, must be
        thought
A meritorious work.

Vitel. I wonder, sirrah,
What's your religion?

Gaz. Troth, to answer truly,
I would not be of one that should command
        me
To feed upon poor John, when I see pheasants
And partridges on the table : nor do I like
The other, that allows us to eat flesh
In Lent, though it be rotten, rather than be
Thought superstitious ; as your zealous
        cobler,
And learned botcher, preach at Amsterdam,
Over a hotchpotch. I would not be confined
In my belief : when all your sects and sectaries
Are grown of one opinion, if I like it,
I will profess myself,—in the mean time,
Live I in England, Spain, France, Rome,
        Geneva,
I'm of that country's faith.

Vitel. And what in Tunis?
Will you turn Turk here?

Gaz. No : so I should lose
A collop of that part my Doll enjoin'd me
To bring home as she left it : 'tis her venture,
Nor dare I barter that commodity,
Without her special warrant.

Vitel. You are a knave, sir :

Leaving your roguery, think upon my business,
It is no time to fool now.
Remember where you are too : though this
  mart time
We are allow'd free trading, and with safety,
Temper your tongue, and meddle not with
  the Turks,
Their manners, nor religion.
  Gaz. Take you heed, sir,
What colours you wear.   Not two hours
  since, there landed
An English pirate's whore, with a green
  apron,
And, as she walked the streets, one of their
  muftis,
We call them priests at Venice, with a razor
Cuts it off, petticoat, smock and all, and
  leaves her
As naked as my nail ; the young fry wondering
What strange beast it should be.   I scaped
  a scouring——
My mistress's busk point, of that forbidden
  colour,
Then tied my codpiece ; had I been dis-
  cover'd,
I had been capon'd.
  Vitel. And had been well served.
Haste to the shop, and set my wares in order,
I will not long be absent.
  Gaz. Though I strive, sir,
To put off melancholy, to which you are ever
Too much inclined, it shall not hinder me,
With my best care to serve you.   [*Exit.*

  Enter Francisco.

  Vitel. I believe thee.—
O welcome, sir ! stay of my steps in this life,
And guide to all my blessed hopes hereafter.
What comforts, sir ? Have your endeavours
  prosper'd ?
Have we tired Fortune's malice with our
  sufferings ?
Is she at length, after so many frowns,
Pleased to vouchsafe one cheerful look upon
  us ?
  Fran. You give too much to fortune and
  your passions,
O'er which a wise man, if religious, triumphs.
That name fools worship ; and those tyrants,
  which
We arm against our better part, our reason,
May add, but never take from our afflictions.
  Vitel. Sir, as I am a sinful man, I cannot
But like one suffer.
  Fran. I exact not from you
A fortitude insensible of calamity,
To which the saints themselves have how'd
  and shown

They are made of flesh and blood ; all that
  I challenge,
Is manly patience.   Will you, that were
  train'd up
In a religious school, where divine maxims
Scorning comparison with moral precepts,
Were daily taught you, bear your con-
  stancy's trial,
Not like Vitelli, but a village nurse,
With curses in your mouth, tears in your
  eyes?—
How poorly it shows in you.
  Vitel. I am school'd, sir,
And will hereafter, to my utmost strength,
Study to be myself.
  Fran. So shall you find me
Most ready to assist you ; neither have I
Slept in your great occasions : since I left you,
I have been at the viceroy's court, and press'd,
As far as they allow, a Christian entrance ;
And something I have learn'd, that may
  concern
The purpose of this journey.
  Vitel. Dear sir, what is it ?
  Fran. By the command of Asambeg, the
  viceroy,
The city swells with barbarous pomp and
  pride,
For the entertainment of stout Mustapha,
The basha of Aleppo, who in person
Comes to receive the niece of Amurath,
The fair Donusa, for his bride.
  Vitel. I find not
How this may profit us.
  Fran. Pray you, give me leave.
Among the rest that wait upon the viceroy,
Such as have, under him, command in Tunis,
Who, as you've often heard, are all false
  pirates,
I saw the shame of Venice, and the scorn
Of all good men, the perjured RENEGADO,
Antonio Grimaldi.
  Vitel. Ha ! his name
Is poison to me.
  Fran. Yet again?
  Vitel. I have done, sir.
  Fran. This debauch'd villain, whom we
  ever thought
(After his impious scorn done, in St. Mark's,
To me, as I stood at the holy altar)
The thief that ravish'd your fair sister from
  you,
The virtuous Paulina, not long since,
As I am truly given to understand,
Sold to the viceroy a fair Christian virgin
On whom, maugre his fierce and cruel nature,
Asambeg dotes extremely.
  Vitel. 'Tis my sister :
It must be she, my better angel tells me

'Tis poor Paulina. Farewell all disguises !
I'll show, in my revenge, that I am noble.
 Fran. You are not mad?
 Vitel. No, sir ; my virtuous anger
Makes every vein an artery; I feel in me
The strength of twenty men ; and, being
  arm'd
With my good cause, to wreak wrong'd
  innocence,
I dare alone run to the viceroy's court,
And with this poniard, before his face,
Dig out Grimaldi's heart.
 Fran. Is this religious?
 Vitel. Would you have me tame now?
  Can I know my sister
Mew'd up in his seraglio, and in danger
Not alone to lose her honour, but her soul ;
The hell-bred villain by too, that has sold
  both
To black destruction, and not haste to send
  him
To the devil, his tutor? To be patient now,
Were, in another name, to play the pander
To the viceroy's loose embraces, and cry aim !
While he, by force or flattery, compels her
To yield her fair name up to his foul lust,
And, after, turn apostata to the faith
That she was bred in.
 Fran. Do but give me hearing,
And you shall soon grant how ridiculous
This childish fury is. A wise man never
Attempts impossibilities ; 'tis as easy
For any single arm to quell an army,
As to effect your wishes. We come hither
To learn Paulina's fate, and to redeem her :
Leave your revenge to heaven. I oft have
  told you
Of a relic that I gave her, which has power,
If we may credit holy men's traditions,
To keep the owner free from violence :
This on her breast she wears, and does pre-
  serve
The virtue of it, by her daily prayers.
So, if she fall not by her own consent,
Which it were sin to think, I fear no force.
Be, therefore, patient ; keep this borrow'd
  shape,
Till time and opportunity present us
With some fit means to see her ; which per-
  form'd,
I'll join with you in any desperate course
For her delivery.
 Vitel. You have charm'd me, sir,
And I obey in all things : pray you, pardon
The weakness of my passion.
 Fran. And excuse it.
Be cheerful, man ; for know that good intents
Are, in the end, crown'd with as fair events.
 [*Exeunt.*

SCENE II.—*A Room in* Donusa's *Palace.*

Enter Donusa, Manto, *and* Carazie.

 Don. Have you seen the Christian captive,
The great basha is so enamour'd of?
 Mant. Yes, and it please your excellency,
I took a full view of her, when she was
Presented to him.
 Don. And is she such a wonder,
As 'tis reported?
 Mant. She was drown'd in tears then,
Which took much from her beauty ; yet, in
  spite
Of sorrow, she appear'd the mistress of
Most rare perfections ; and, though low of
  stature,
Her well-proportion'd limbs invite affection ;
And, when she speaks, each syllable is music
That does enchant the hearers : but your
  highness,
That are not to be parallel'd, I yet never
Beheld her equal.
 Don. Come, you flatter me ;
But I forgive it. We, that are born great,
Seldom distaste our servants, though they
  give us
More than we can pretend to. I have heard
That Christian ladies live with much more
  freedom
Than such as are born here. Our jealous
  Turks,
Never permit their fair wives to be seen,
But at the public bagnios, or the mosques,
And, even then, veil'd and guarded. Thou,
  Carazie,
Wert born in England ; what's the custom
  there,
Among your women? Come, be free and
  merry :
I am no severe mistress ; nor hast thou met with
A heavy bondage.
 Car. Heavy ! I was made lighter
By two stone weight; at least, to be fit to
  serve you.
But to your question, madam ; women in
  England,
For the most part, live like queens. Your
  country ladies
Have liberty to hawk, to hunt, to feast,
To give free entertainment to all comers,
To talk, to kiss ; there's no such thing known
  there
As an Italian girdle. Your city dame,
Without leave, wears the breeches, has her
  husband
At as much command as her 'prentice ; and,
  if need be,
Can make him cuckold by her father's copy.
 Don. But your court lady?

Car. She, I assure you, madam,
Knows nothing but her will; must be allow'd
Her footmen, her caroch, her ushers, pages,
Her doctor, chaplains; and, as I have heard,
They're grown of late so learn'd, that they
    maintain
A strange position, which their lords, with all
Their wit, cannot confute.
 Don. What's that, I prithee?
 Car. Marry, that it is not only fit, but
    lawful,
Your madam there, her much rest and high
    feeding
Duly consider'd, should, to ease her husband,
Be allow'd a private friend: they have drawn
    a bill
To this good purpose, and, the next assem-
    bly,
Doubt not to pass it.
 Don. We enjoy no more,
That are o' the Othoman race, though our
    religion
Allows all pleasure. I am dull: some music.
Take my chapines off. So, a lusty strain.
   [*A galliard. Knocking within.*
Who knocks there?
  [*Manto goes to the door, and returns.*
 Mant. 'Tis the basha of Aleppo,
Who humbly makes request he may present
His service to you.
 Don. Reach a chair. We must
Receive him like ourself, and not depart with
One piece of ceremony, state, and greatness,
That may beget respect and reverence
In one that's born our vassal. Now admit
 him.

Enter Mustapha; *he puts off his yellow
   pantofles.*

 Musta. The place is sacred; and I am to
    enter
The room where she abides, with such de-
    votion
As pilgrims pay at Mecca, when they visit
The tomb of our great prophet. [*Kneels.*
 Don. Rise; the sign
   [Carazie *takes up the pantofles.*
That we vouchsafe your presence.
 Musta. May those Powers
That raised the Othoman empire, and still
    guard it,
Reward your highness for this gracious favour
You throw upon your servant! It hath
    pleased
The most invincible, mightiest Amurath,
(To speak his other titles would take from
    him
That in himself does comprehend all great-
    ness,)

To make me the unworthy instrument
Of his command. Receive, divinest lady,
    [*Delivers a letter.*
This letter, sign'd by his victorious hand,
And made authentic by the imperial seal.
There, when you find me mention'd, far be
    it from you
To think it my ambition to presume
At such a happiness, which his powerful will,
From his great mind's magnificence, not my
    merit,
Hath shower'd upon me. But, if your consent
Join with his good opinion and allowance,
To perfect what his favours have begun,
I shall, in my obsequiousness and duty,
Endeavour to prevent all just complaints,
Which want of will to serve you may call on me.
 Don. His sacred majesty writes here, that
    your valour
Against the Persian hath so won upon him,
That there's no grace or honour in his gift,
Of which he can imagine you unworthy;
And, what's the greatest you can hope, or
    aim at,
It is his pleasure you should be received
Into his royal family—provided,
For so far I am unconfined, that I
Affect and like your person. I expect not
The ceremony which he uses in
Bestowing of his daughters and his nieces:
As that he should present you for my slave,
To love you, if you pleased me; or deliver
A poniard, on my least dislike, to kill you.
Such tyranny and pride agree not with
My softer disposition. Let it suffice,
For my first answer, that thus far I grace
    you: [*Gives him her hand to kiss.*
Hereafter, some time spent to make enquiry
Of the good parts and faculties of your mind,
You shall hear further from me.
 Musta. Though all torments
Really suffer'd, or in hell imagined
By curious fiction, in one hour's delay
Are wholly comprehended; I confess
That I stand bound in duty, not to check at
Whatever you command, or please to impose,
For trial of my patience.
 Don. Let us find
Some other subject; too much of one theme
    cloys me:
Is 't a full mart?
 Musta. A confluence of all nations
Are met together: there's variety, too,
Of all that merchants traffic for.
 Don. I know not—
I feel a virgin's longing to descend
So far from my own greatness, as to be,
Though not a buyer, yet a looker on
Their strange commodities.

Musta. If without a train
You dare be seen abroad, I'll dismiss mine,
And wait upon you as a common man,
And satisfy your wishes.
  Don. I embrace it.
Provide my veil ; and, at the postern gate,
Convey us out unseen. I trouble you.
  Musta. It is my happiness you deign to
    command me.   [*Exeunt.*

SCENE III.—*The* Bazar.

Gazet *in his Shop;* Francisco *and* Vitelli
    walking before it.

  Gaz. What do you lack? Your choice
China dishes, your pure Venetian crystal of
all sorts, of all neat and new fashions, from
the mirror of the madam, to the private
utensil of her chambermaid ; and curious
pictures of the rarest beauties of Europe :
What do you lack, gentlemen?
  Fran. Take heed, I say ; howe'er it may
    appear
Impertinent, I must express my love,
My advice, and counsel. You are young,
    Vitelli,
And may be tempted ; and these Turkish
    dames,
(Like English mastiffs, that increase their
    fierceness
By being chain'd up,) from the restraint of
    freedom,
If lust once fire their blood from a fair object,
Will run a course the fiends themselves would
    shake at,
To enjoy their wanton ends.
  Vitel. Sir, you mistake me :
I am too full of woe, to entertain
One thought of pleasure, though all Europe's
    queens
Kneel'd at my feet, and courted me ; much
    less
To mix with such, whose difference of faith
Must, of necessity, (or I must grant
Myself neglectful of all you have taught me,)
Strangle such base desires.
  Fran. Be constant in
That resolution ; I'll abroad again,
And learn, as far as it is possible,
What may concern Paulina. Some two hours
Shall bring me back.   [*Exit.*
  Vitel. All blessings wait upon you !
  Gaz. Cold doings, sir ? a mart do you call
this ? 'slight !
A pudding-wife, or a witch with a thrum cap,
That sells ale underground to such as come
To know their fortunes in a dead vacation,
Have, ten to one, more stirring.
  Vitel. We must be patient.

  Gaz. Your seller by retail ought to be
    angry,
But when he's fingering money.

Enter Grimaldi, Master, Boatswain, Sailors,
    and Turks.

  Vitel. Here are company——
Defend me, my good angel, [*seeing* Gri-
    maldi.] I behold
A basilisk !
  Gaz. What do you lack? what do you lack?
pure China dishes, clear crystal glasses, a
dumb mistress to make love to? What do
you lack, gentlemen?
  Grim. Thy mother for a bawd ; or, if thou
    hast
A handsome one, thy sister for a whore ;
Without these, do not tell me of your trash,
Or I shall spoil your market.
  Vitel. —Old Grimaldi !
  Grim. 'Zounds, wherefore do we put to
    sea, or stand
The raging winds, aloft, or p—— upon
The foamy waves, when they rage most ;
    deride
The thunder of the enemy's shot, board boldly
A merchant's ship for prize, though we behold
The desperate gunner ready to give fire,
And blow the deck up? wherefore shake we off
Those scrupulous rags of charity and con-
    science,
Invented only to keep churchmen warm,
Or feed the hungry mouths of famish'd
    beggars ;
But, when we touch the shore, to wallow in
All sensual pleasures?
  Mast. Ay, but, noble captain,
To spare a little for an after-clap,
Were not improvidence.
  Grim. Hang consideration !
When this is spent, is not our ship the same,
Our courage too the same, to fetch in more?
The earth, where it is fertilest, returns not
More than three harvests, while the glorious
    sun
Posts through the zodiac, and makes up the
    year :
But the sea, which is our mother, (that em-
    braces
Both the rich Indies in her outstretch'd
    arms,)
Yields every day a crop, if we dare reap it.
No, no, my mates, let tradesmen think of
    thrift,
And usurers hoard up ; let our expense
Be, as our comings in are, without bounds.
We are the Neptunes of the ocean,
And such as traffic shall pay sacrifice
Of their best lading ; I will have this canvass

Your boy wears, lined with tissue, and the
    cates
You taste, serv'd up in gold :—Though we
    carouse
The tears of orphans in our Greekish wines,
The sighs of undone widows paying for
The music bought to cheer us, ravish'd virgins
To slavery sold, for coin to feed our riots,
We will have no compunction.
    Gaz. Do you hear, sir?
We have paid for our ground.
    Grim. Hum!
    Gaz. And hum, too!
For all your big words, get you further off,
And hinder not the prospect of our shop,
Or——
    Grim. What will you do?
    Gaz. Nothing, sir—but pray
Your worship to give me handsel.
    Grim. [*Seizing him.*] By the ears,
Thus, sir, by the ears.
    Mast. Hold, hold!
    Vitel. You'll still be prating.
    Grim. Come, let's be drunk ; then each
    man to his whore.
'Slight, how do you look? you had best go
    find a corner
To pray in, and repent : do, do, and cry ;
It will shew fine in pirates.   [*Exit.*
    Mast. We must follow,
Or he will spend our shares.
    Boatsw. I fought for mine.
    Mast. Nor am I so precise but I can drab
    too :
We will not sit out for our parts.
    Boatsw. Agreed.
        [*Exeunt* Mast. Boatsw. Sailors.
    Gaz. The devil gnaw off his fingers ! If
    he were
In London, among the clubs, up went his
    heels,
For striking of a prentice.—What do you lack?
What do you lack, gentlemen?
    1 *Turk.* I wonder how the viceroy can
    endure
The insolence of this fellow.
    2 *Turk.* He receives profit
From the prizes he brings in ; and that excuses
Whatever he commits. Ha ! what are these?

Enter Mustapha *with* Donusa *veiled.*

    1 *Turk.* They seem of rank and quality :
    observe them.
    Gaz. What do you lack? see what you
    please to buy ;
Wares of all sorts, most honourable madona.
    Vitel. Peace, sirrah, make no noise ;
    these are not people
To be jested with.

    Don. Is this the Christians' custom,
In the venting their commodities?
    Musta. Yes, best madam.
But you may please to keep your way, here's
    nothing
But toys and trifles, not worth your observing.
    Don. Yes, for variety's sake : pray you,
    shew us, friend,
The chiefest of your wares.
    Vitel. Your ladyship's servant ;
And if, in worth, or title you are more,
My ignorance plead my pardon !
    Don. He speaks well.
    Vitel. Take down the looking-glass. Here
    is a mirror
Steel'd so exactly, neither taking from
Nor flattering the object it returns
To the beholder, that Narcissus might
(And never grow enamour'd of himself)
View his fair feature in't.
    Don. Poetical, too!
    Vitel. Here China dishes to serve in a
    banquet,
Though the voluptuous Persian sat a guest.
Here crystal glasses, such as Ganymede
Did fill with nectar to the Thunderer,
When he drank to Alcides, and received him
In the fellowship of the gods ; true to the
    owners :
Corinthian plate, studded with diamonds,
Conceal'd oft deadly poison ; this pure metal
So innocent is, and faithful to the mistress
Or master that possesses it, that, rather
Than hold one drop that's venomous, of itself
It flies in pieces, and deludes the traitor.
    Don. How movingly could this fellow
    treat upon
A worthy subject, that finds such discourse
To grace a trifle !
    Vitel. Here's a picture, madam ;
The master-piece of Michael Angelo,
Our great Italian workman ; here's another,
So perfect at all parts, that had Pygmalion
Seen this, his prayers had been made to
    Venus
To have given it life, and his carved ivory
    image
By poets ne'er remember'd. They are, in-
    deed,
The rarest beauties of the Christian world,
And no where to be equall'd.
    Don. You are partial
In the cause of those you favour ; I believe
I instantly could show you one, to theirs
Not much inferior.
    Vitel. With your pardon, madam,
I am incredulous.
    Don. Can you match me this ?
        [*Lifts her veil hastily.*

Vitel. What wonder look I on! I'll search
above,
And suddenly attend you.   [*Exit.*
Don. Are you amazed I
I'll bring you to yourself.
                    [*Throws down the glasses.*
Musta. Ha! what's the matter?
Gaz. My master's ware!—We are undone!
—O strange!
A lady to turn roarer, and break glasses!
'Tis time to shut up shop then.
Musta. You seem moved:
If any language of these Christian dogs
Have called your anger on, in a frown shew it,
And they are dead already.
Don. The offence
Looks not so far. The foolish, paltry fellow,
Shew'd me some trifles, and demanded of me,
For what I valued at so many aspers,
A thousand ducats. I confess he moved me;
Yet I should wrong myself, should such a
beggar
Receive least loss from me.
Musta. Is it no more?
Don. No, I assure you. Bid him bring
his bill
To-morrow to the palace, and enquire
For one Donusa; that word gives him passage
Through all the guard: say, there he shall
receive
Full satisfaction. Now, when you please.
Musta. I wait you.
              [*Exeunt* Musta. *and* Don.
1 *Turk.* We must not know them.—Let's
shift off, and vanish. [*Exeunt* Turks.
Gaz. The swine's-pox overtake you! there's
a curse
For a Turk, that eats no hog's flesh.

Re-enter Vitelli.

Vitel. Is she gone?
Gaz. Yes: you may see her handywork.
Vitel. No matter.
Said she aught else?
Gaz. That you should wait upon her,
And there receive court payment; and, to
pass
The guards, she bids you only say you come
To one Donusa.
Vitel. How! Remove the wares;
Do it without reply. The sultan's niece!
I have heard among the Turks, for any lady
To shew her face bare, argues love, or speaks
Her deadly hatred. What should I fear? my
fortune
Is sunk so low, there cannot fall upon me
Aught worth my shunning. I will run the
hazard:

She may be a means to free distress'd
Paulina—
Or, if offended, at the worst, to die
Is a full period to calamity.   [*Exeunt.*

ACT II.

SCENE I.—*A Room in* Donusa's *Palace.*

Enter Carazie *and* Manto.

Car. In the name of wonder, Manto, what
hath my lady
Done with herself, since yesterday?
Mant. I know not.
Malicious men report we are all guided
In our affections by a wandering planet:
But such a sudden change in such a person,
May stand for an example, to confirm
Their false assertion.
Car. She's now pettish, froward;
Music, discourse, observance, tedious to her.
Mant. She slept not the last night; and
yet prevented
The rising sun, in being up before him:
Call'd for a costly bath, then will'd the rooms
Should be perfumed; ransack'd her cabinets
For her choice and richest jewels, and
appears now
Like Cynthia in full glory, waited on
By the fairest of the stars.
Car. Can you guess the reason,
Why the aga of the janizaries, and he
That guards the entrance of the inmost port,
Were call'd before her?
Mant. They are both her creatures,
And by her grace preferred: but I am
ignorant
To what purpose they were sent for.

Enter Donusa.

Car. Here she comes,
Full of sad thoughts: we must stand further
off.
What a frown was that!
Mant. Forbear.
Car. I pity her.
Don. What magic hath transform'd me
from myself?
Where is my virgin pride? how have I lost
My boasted freedom? what new fire burns up
My scorched entrails; what unknown desires
Invade, and take possession of my soul,
All virtuous objects vanish'd? I, that have
stood
The shock of fierce temptations, stopp'd
mine ears
Against all Syren notes lust ever sung,
To draw my bark of chastity (that with
wonder

Hath kept a constant and an honour'd
    course)
Into the gulf of a deserved ill-fame,
Now fall unpitied ; and, in a moment,
With mine own hands, dig up a grave to
    bury
The monumental heap of all my years,
Employ'd in noble actions. O my fate !
—But there is no resisting. I obey thee,
Imperious god of love, and willingly
Put mine own fetters on, to grace thy
    triumph :
'Twere therefore more than cruelty in thee,
To use me like a tyrant. What poor means
Must I make use of now ! and flatter such,
To whom, till I betray'd my liberty,
One gracious look of mine would have
    erected
An altar to my service ! How now,
    Manto !—
My ever careful woman ; and Carazie,
Thou hast been faithful too.
    Car. I dare not call
My life mine own, since it is yours, but
    gladly
Will part with it, whene'er you shall com-
    mand me ;
And think I fall a martyr, so my death
May give life to your pleasures.
    Mant. But vouchsafe
To let me understand what you desire
Should be effected ; I will undertake it,
And curse myself for cowardice, if I paused
To ask the reason why.
    Don. I am comforted
In the tender of your service, but shall be
Confirm'd in my full joys, in the perfor-
    mance.
Yet, trust me, I will not impose upon
But what you stand engaged for to a mis-
    tress,
Such as I have been to you. All I ask,
Is faith and secrecy.
    Car. Say but you doubt me,
And, to secure you, I'll cut out my tongue ;
I am libb'd in the breech already.
    Mant. Do not hinder
Yourself, by these delays.
    Don. Thus then I whisper
Mine own shame to you.—O that I should
    blush
To speak what I so much desire to do !
And, further—[*Whispers, and uses vehement
    action.*
    Mant. Is this all?
    Don. Think it not base ;
Although I know the office undergoes
A coarse construction.
    Car. Coarse ! 'tis but procuring ;

A smock employment, which has made more
    knights,
In a country I could name, than twenty
    years
Of service in the field.
    Don. You have my ends.
    Mant. Which say you have arrived at :
    be not wanting
To yourself, and fear not us.
    Car. I know my burthen ;
I'll bear it with delight.
    Mant. Talk not, but do.
                    [*Exeunt* Car. *and* Mant.
    Don. O love, what poor shifts thou dost
    force us to !   [*Exit.*

SCENE II.—*A Court in the same.*

Enter Aga, Capiaga, *and* Janizaries.

    Aga. She was ever our good mistress, and
    our maker,
And should we check at a little hazard for
    her,
We were unthankful.
    Cap. I dare pawn my head,
'Tis some disguised minion of the court,
Sent from great Amurath, to learn from her
The viceroy's actions.
    Aga. That concerns not us ;
His fall may be our rise : whate'er he be,
He passes through my guards.
    Cap. And mine—provided
He give the word.

                Enter Vitelli.

Vitel. To faint now, being thus far,
Would argue me of cowardice.
    Aga. Stand : the word ;
Or, being a Christian, to press thus far,
Forfeits thy life.
    Vitel. Donusa.
    Aga. Pass in peace.
                [*Exeunt* Aga *and* Janizaries.
Vitel. What a privilege her name bears !
'Tis wondrous strange ! If the great officer,
The guardian of the inner port, deny not—
    Cap. Thy warrant : Speak, or thou art
    dead.
    Vitel. Donusa.
    Cap. That protects thee ;
Without fear enter. So :—discharge the
    watch. [*Exeunt* Vitelli *and* Capiaga.

SCENE III.—*An outer Room in the same.*

Enter Carazie *and* Manto.

    Car. Though he hath past the aga and
    chief porter,
This cannot be the man.
    Mant. By her description,
I am sure it is.

Car. O women, women,
What are you? A great lady dote upon
A haberdasher of small wares!
Mant. Pish! thou hast none.
: *Car.* No; if I had, I might have served
the turn:
This 'tis to want munition, when a man
Should make a breach, and enter.

Enter Vitelli.

Mant. Sir, you are welcome:
Think what 'tis to be happy, and possess it.
Car. Perfume the rooms there, and make
way. Let music
With choice notes entertain the man the
princess
Now purposes to honour.
Vitel. I am ravish'd. [*Exeunt.*

SCENE IV.—*A Room of State in the same.
A table set forth, with jewels and bags of
money upon it.*
Loud music. Enter Donusa, (*followed by*
Carazie,) *and takes her seat.*

Don. Sing o'er the ditty that I last com-
posed
Upon my love-sick passion: suit your voice
To the music that's placed yonder, we shall
hear you
With more delight and pleasure.
Car. I obey you. [*Song.*

During the song, enter Manto *and* Vitelli.

Vitel. Is not this Tempe, or the blessed
shades,
Where innocent spirits reside? or do I dream,
And this a heavenly vision? Howsoever,
It is a sight too glorious to behold,
For such a wretch as I am.
Car. He is daunted.
Mant. Speak to him, madam; cheer him
up, or you
Destroy what you have built.
Car. Would I were furnish'd
With his artillery, and if I stood
Gaping as he does, hang me. [*Aside.*
[*Exeunt* Carazie *and* Manto.
Vitel. That I might
Ever dream thus! [*Kneels.*
Don. Banish amazement:
You wake; your debtor tells you so, your
debtor.
And, to assure you that I am a substance,
And no aerial figure, thus I raise you.
Why do you shake? my soft touch brings
no ague;
No biting frost is in this palm; nor are
My looks like to the Gorgon's head, that
turn

Men into statues; rather they have power,
Or I have been abused, where they bestow
Their influence, (let me prove it truth in you,)
To give to dead men motion.
Vitel. Can this be?
May I believe my senses? Dare I think
I have a memory, or that you are
That excellent creature that of late disdain'd
not .
To look on my poor trifles?
Don. I am she.
Vitel. The owner of that blessed name,
Donusa,
Which, like a potent charm, although pro-
nounced
By my profane, but much unworthier,
tongue,
Hath brought me safe to this forbidden
place,
Where Christian ne'er yet trod?
Don. I am the same.
Vitel. And to what end, great lady—pardon
me,
That I presume to ask, did your command
Command me hither? Or what am I, to
whom
You should vouchsafe your favours; nay,
your angers?
If any wild or uncollected speech,
Offensively deliver'd, or my doubt
Of your unknown perfections, have displeased
you,
You wrong your indignation to pronounce,
Yourself, my sentence: to have seen you only,
And to have touch'd that fortune-making
hand,
Will with delight weigh down all tortures,
that
A flinty hangman's rage could execute,
Or rigid tyranny command with pleasure.
Don. How the abundance of good flowing
to thee,
Is wronged in this simplicity! and these
bounties,
Which all our Eastern kings have kneeled
in vain for,
Do, by thy ignorance, or wilful fear,
Meet with a false construction! Christian,
know,
(For till thou art mine by a nearer name,
That title, though abhorr'd here, takes not
from
Thy entertainment) that 'tis not the fashion
Among the greatest and the fairest dames
This Turkish empire gladly owes and bows to,
To punish where there's no offence, or nourish
Displeasures against those, without whose
mercy
They part with all felicity. Prithee, be wise,

And gently understand me; do not force her,
That ne'er knew aught but to command, nor
e'er read
The elements of affection, but from such
As gladly sued to her, in the infancy
Of her new-born desires, to be at once
Importunate and immodest.
Vitel. Did I know,
Great lady, your commands; or, to what
purpose
This personated passion tends, (since 'twere
A crime in me deserving death, to think
It is your own,) I should, to make you sport,
Take any shape you please t'impose upon me;
And with joy strive to serve you.
Don. Sport! thou art cruel,
If that thou canst interpret my descent
From my high birth and greatness, but to be
A part, in which I truly act myself:
And I must hold thee for a dull spectator,
If it stir not affection, and invite
Compassion for my sufferings. Be thou
taught
By my example, to make satisfaction
For wrongs unjustly offer'd. Willingly
I do confess my fault; I injured thee.
In some poor petty trifles; thus I pay for
The trespass I did to thee. Here—receive
These bags, stuff'd full of our imperial coin;
Or, if this payment be too light, take here
These gems, for which the slavish Indian
dives
To the bottom of the main: or, if thou scorn
These as base dross, which take but common
minds,
But fancy any honour in my gift,
Which is unbounded as the sultan's power,
And be possest of it.
Vitel. I am overwhelm'd
With the weight of happiness you throw
upon me:
Nor can it fall in my imagination,
What wrong you e'er have done me; and
much less
How, like a royal merchant, to return
Your great magnificence.
Don. They are degrees,
Not ends, of my intended favours to thee.
These seeds of bounty I yet scatter on
A glebe I have not tried:—but, be thou
thankful;
The harvest is to come.
Vitel. What can be added
To that which I already have received,
I cannot comprehend.
Don. The tender of
Myself. Why dost thou start? and in that
gift,
Full restitution of that virgin freedom

Which thou hast robb'd me of. Yet, I
profess,
I so far prize the lovely thief that stole it,
That, were it possible thou couldst restore
What thou unwittingly hast ravish'd from me,
I should refuse the present.
Vitel. How I shake
In my constant resolution! and my flesh,
Rebellious to my better part, now tells me,
As if it were a strong defence of frailty,
A hermit in a desert, trench'd with prayers,
Could not resist this battery.
Don. Thou an Italian,
Nay more, I know't, a natural Venetian,
Such as are courtiers born to please fair
ladies,
Yet come thus slowly on!
Vitel. Excuse me, madam:
What imputation soe'er the world
Is pleased to lay upon us, in myself
I am so innocent, that I know not what 'tis
That I should offer.
Don. By instinct I'll teach thee,
And with such ease as love makes me to
ask it.
When a young lady wrings you by the hand,
thus,
Or with an amorous touch presses your foot,
Looks babies in your eyes, plays with your
locks,
Do not you find, without a tutor's help,
What 'tis she looks for?
Vitel. I am grown already
Skilful in the mystery.
Don. Or, if thus she kiss you,
Then tastes your lips again——[*Kisses him.*
Vitel. That latter blow
Has beat all chaste thoughts from me.
Don. Say, she points to
Some private room the sunbeams never
enter,
Provoking dishes passing by, to heighten
Declined appetite, active music ushering
Your fainting steps, the waiters too, as born
dumb,
Not daring to look on you.
[*Exit, inviting him to follow.*
Vitel. Though the devil
Stood by, and roar'd, I follow: Now I find
That virtue's but a word, and no sure guard,
If set upon by beauty and reward. [*Exit.*

SCENE V.—*A Hall in* Asambeg's *Palace.*

Enter Aga, Capiaga, Grimaldi, Master,
Boatswain, *and* Sailors.

Aga. The devil's in him, I think.
Grim. Let him be damn'd too.
I'll look on him, though he stared as wild as
hell;

Nay, I'll go near to tell him to his teeth,
If he mends not suddenly, and proves more
    thankful,
We do him too much service.   Were't not
    for shame now,
I could turn honest, and forswear my trade;
Which, next to being truss'd up at the
    mainyard
By some low country butterbox, I hate
As deadly as I do fasting, or long grace
When meat cools on the table.
    Cap. But take heed ;
You know his violent nature.
    Grim. Let his whores
And catamites know't !   I understand my-
    self,
And how unmanly 'tis to sit at home,
And rail at us, that run abroad all hazards,
If every week we bring not home new pillage,
For the fatting his seraglio.

Enter Asambeg, Mustapha, *and* Attendants.

    Aga. Here he comes.
    Cap. How terrible he looks !
    Grim. To such as fear him.
The viceroy, Asambeg ! were he the sultan's
    self
He'll let us know a reason for his fury ;
Or we must take leave, without his allowance,
To be merry with our ignorance.
    Asam. Mahomet's hell
Light on you all !   You crouch and cringe
    now :—Where
Was the terror of my just frowns, when you
    suffer'd
Those thieves of Malta, almost in our harbour,
To board a ship, and bear her safely off,
While you stood idle lookers on?
    Aga. The odds
In the men and shipping, and the suddenness
Of their departure, yielding us no leisure
To send forth others to relieve our own,
Deterr'd us, mighty sir.
    Asam. Deterr'd you, cowards !
How durst you only entertain the knowledge
Of what fear was, but in the not performance
Of our command?   In me great Amurath
    spake ;
My voice did echo to your ears his thunder,
And will'd you, like so many sea-born tritons,
Arm'd only with the trumpets of your courage,
To swim up to her, and, like remoras
Hanging upon her keel, to stay her flight,
Till rescue, sent from us, had fetch'd you off.
You think you're safe now.   Who durst but
    dispute it,
Or make it questionable, if, this moment,
I charged you, from yon hanging cliff, that
    glasses

His rugged forehead in the neighbouring lake,
To throw yourselves down headlong? or, like
    faggots,
To fill the ditches of defended forts,
While on your backs we march'd up to the
    breach?
    Grim. What would not I.
    Asam. Ha !
    Grim. Yet I dare as much
As any of the sultan's boldest sons,
Whose heaven and hell hang on his frown
    or smile,
His warlike janizaries.
    Asam. Add one syllable more,
Thou dost pronounce upon thyself a sentence
That, earthquake-like, will swallow thee.
    Grim. Let it open,
I'll stand the hazard : those contemned
    thieves,
Your fellow-pirates, sir, the bold Maltese,
Whom with your looks you think to quell, at
    Rhodes
Laugh'd at great Solyman's anger : and, if
    treason
Had not delivered them into his power,
He had grown old in glory as in years,
At that so fatal siege ; or risen with shame,
His hopes and threats deluded.
    Asam. Our great prophet !
How have I lost my anger and my power !
    Grim. Find it, and use it on thy flatterers,
And not upon thy friends, that dare speak
    truth.
These knights of Malta, but a handful to
Your armies, that drink rivers up, have stood
Your fury at the height, and with their
    crosses
Struck pale your horned moons ; these men
    of Malta,
Since I took pay from you, I've met and
    fought with
Upon advantage too ; yet, to speak truth,
By the soul of honour, I have ever found them
As provident to direct, and bold to do,
As any train'd up in your discipline,
Ravish'd from other nations.
    Musta. I perceive
The lightning in his fiery looks ; the cloud
Is broke already.   [*Aside.*
    Grim. Think not, therefore, sir,
That you alone are giants, and such pigmies
You war upon.
    Asam. Villain ! I'll make thee know
Thou hast blasphemed the Othoman power,
    and safer,
At noonday, might'st have given fire to St.
    Mark's,
Your proud Venetian temple.—Seize upon
    him :

I am not so near reconciled to him,
To bid him die ; that were a benefit
The dog's unworthy of. To our use con-
fiscate
All that he stands possess'd of; let him taste
The misery of want, and his vain riots,
Like to so many walking ghosts, affright
him,
Where'er he sets his desperate foot. Who is't
That does command you?
    Grim. Is this the reward
For all my service, and the rape I made
On fair Paulina?
    Asam. Drag him hence :—he dies,
That dallies but a minute.
    [*Grimaldi is dragg'd off, his head covered.*
    Boatsw. What's become of
Our shares now, master?
    Mast. Would he had been born dumb !
The beggar's cure, patience, is all that's
left us.
    [*Exeunt* Master, Boatswain, *and* Sailors.
    Musta. 'Twas but intemperance of speech,
excuse him ;
Let me prevail so far. Fame gives him out
For a deserving fellow.
    Asam. At Aleppo,
I durst not press you so far; give me leave
To use my own will, and command in Tunis ;
And, if you please, my privacy.
    Musta. I will see you,
When this high wind's blown o'er.   [*Exit.*
    Asam. So shall you find me
Ready to do you service. Rage, now leave me ;
Stern looks, and all the ceremonious forms
Attending on dread majesty, fly from
Transformed Asambeg. Why should I hug
                    [*Pulls out a key.*
So near my heart, what leads me to my prison ;
Where she that is inthrall'd, commands her
keeper,.
And robs me of the fierceness I was born
with?
Stout men quake at my frowns, and, in return,
I tremble at her softness. Base Grimaldi
But only named Paulina, and the charm
Had almost choak'd my fury, ere I could
Pronounce his sentence. Would, when first
I saw her,
Mine eyes had met with lightning, and, in
place
Of hearing her enchanting tongue, the shrieks
Of mandrakes had made music to my slum-
bers !
For now I only walk a loving dream,
And, but to my dishonour, never wake ;
And yet am blind, but when I see the object,
And madly dote on it. Appear, bright spark
    [*Opens a door; Paulina comes forth.*

Of all perfection ! any simile
Borrow'd from diamonds, or the fairest stars,
To help me to express how dear I prize
Thy unmatch'd graces, will rise up, and
chide me
For poor detraction.
    Paul. I despise thy flatteries :
Thus spit at them, and scorn them ; and
being arm'd
In the assurance of my innocent virtue,
I stamp upon all doubts, all fears, all tortures
Thy barbarous cruelty, or, what's worse, thy
dotage,
The worthy parent of thy jealousy,
Can shower upon me.
    Asam. If these bitter taunts
Ravish me from myself, and make me think
My greedy ears receive angelical sounds ;
How would this tongue, tuned to a loving note,
Invade, and take possession of my soul,
Which then I durst not call mine own !
    Paul. Thou art false,
Falser than thy religion. Do but think me
Something above a beast, nay more, a
monster
Would fright the sun to look on, and then
tell me,
If this base usage can invite affection?
If to be mewed up, and excluded from
Human society ; the use of pleasures ;
The necessary, not superfluous duties
Of servants, to discharge those offices
I blush to name——
    Asam. Of servants ! Can you think
That I, that dare not trust the eye of heaven
To look upon your beauties ; that deny
Myself the happiness to touch your pureness,
Will e'er consent an eunuch, or bought
    handmaid,
Shall once approach you?—There is some-
thing in you
That can work miracles, or I am cozen'd ;
Dispose and alter sexes, to my wrong,
In spite of nature. I will be your nurse,
Your woman, your physician, and your fool ;
Till, with your free consent, which I have
vow'd
Never to force, you grace me with a name
That shall supply all these.
    Paul. What is it?
    Asam. Your husband.
    Paul. My hangman, when thou pleasest.
    Asam. Thus I guard me
Against your further angers.
                    [*Leads her to the door.*
    Paul. Which shall reach thee,
Though I were in the centre.
    [*Asambeg closes the door upon her, and
    locks it.*

Asam. Such a spirit,
In such a small proportion, I ne'er read of,
Which time must alter. Ravish her I dare not;
The magic that she wears about her neck,
I think, defends her :—this devotion paid
To this sweet saint, mistress of my sour pain,
'Tis fit I take mine own rough shape again.
                                        [*Exit.*

SCENE VI.—*A Street near* Donusa's
           Palace.

Enter Francisco *and* Gazet.

Fran. I think he's lost.
Gaz. 'Tis ten to one of that ;
I ne'er knew citizen turn courtier yet,
But he lost his credit though he saved himself.
Why, look you, sir, there are so many lobbies,
Out-offices, and dispartations here,
Behind these Turkish hangings, that a
   Christian
Hardly gets off but circumcised.

Enter Vitelli, *richly habited,* Carazie, *and*
       Manto.

Fran. I am troubled,
Troubled exceedingly. Ha! what are these?
Gaz. One, by his rich suit, should be some
   French ambassador :
For his train, I think they are Turks.
Fran. Peace! be not seen.
Car. You are now past all the guards,
   and, undiscover'd,
You may return.
Vitel. There's for your pains ; forget not
My humblest service to the best of ladies.
Mant. Deserve her favour, sir, by making
   haste
For a second entertainment.
               [*Exeunt* Carazie *and* Manto.
Vitel. Do not doubt me ;
I shall not live till then.
Gaz. The train is vanish'd :
They have done him some good office, he's
   so free
And liberal of his gold.—Ha! do I dream,
Or is this mine own natural master?
Fran. 'Tis he :
But strangely metamorphosed.—You have
   made, sir,
A prosperous voyage ; heaven grant it be
   honest,
I shall rejoice then, too.
Gaz. You make him blush,
To talk of honesty :—you were but now
In the giving vein, and may think of Gazet,
Your worship's prentice.
Vitel. There's gold : be thou free too,
And master of my shop, and all the wares
We brought from Venice.

Gaz. Rivo ! then.
Vitel. Dear sir,
This place affords not privacy for discourse ;
But I can tell you wonders : my rich habit
Deserves least admiration ; there is nothing
That can fall in the compass of your wishes,
Though it were to redeem a thousand slaves
From the Turkish gallies, or, at home, to
   erect
Some pious work, to shame all hospitals,
But I am master of the means.
Fran. 'Tis strange.
Vitel. As I walk, I'll tell you more.
Gaz. Pray you, a word, sir ; ·
And then I will put on : I have one boon
   more.
Vitel. What is't? speak freely.
Gaz. Thus then : As I am master
Of your shop and wares, pray you help me
   to some trucking
With your last she-customer ; though she
   crack my best piece,
I will endure it with patience.
Vitel. Leave your prating.
Gaz. I may : you have been doing ; we
   will do too.
Fran. I am amazed, yet will not blame
   nor chide you,
Till you inform me further : yet must say,
They steer not the right course, nor traffic
   well,
That seek a passage to reach heaven through
   hell.   [*Exeunt.*

ACT III.

SCENE I.—*A Room in* Donusa's *Palace.*

Enter Donusa *and* Manto.

Don. When said he he would come again ?
Mant. He swore,
Short minutes should be tedious ages to
   him,
Until the tender of his second service ;
So much he seemed transported with the
   first.
Don. I'm sure I was. I charge thee, Manto,
   tell me,
By all my favours, and my bounties, truly,
Whether thou art a virgin, or, like me,
Hast forfeited that name ?
Mant. A virgin, madam,
At my years ! being a waiting-woman, and
   in court too !
That were miraculous. I so long since lost
That barren burthen, I almost forget
That ever I was one.
Don. And could thy friends

L

Read in thy face, thy maidenhead gone, that
　　thou
Had'st parted with it?
　Mant. No, indeed: I past
For current many years after, till, by fortune,
Long and continued practice in the sport
Blew up my deck; a husband then was found
　　out
By my indulgent father, and to the world
All was made whole again.. What need you
　　fear, then,
That, at your pleasure, may repair your
　　honour,
Durst any envious or malicious tongue
Presume to taint it?

　　　　　Enter Carazie.

Don. How now?
Car. Madam, the basha
Humbly desires access.
Don. If it had been
My neat Italian, thou hadst met my wishes.
Tell him we would be private.
　Car. So I did,
But he is much importunate.
Mant. Best despatch him:
His lingering here else will deter the other
From making his approach.
Don. His entertainment
Shall not invite a second visit. Go;
Say we are pleased.

　　　　　Enter Mustapha.

Musta. All happiness——
Don. Be sudden.
'Twas saucy rudeness in you, sir, to press
On my retirements; but ridiculous folly
To waste the time, that might be better spent,
In complimentary wishes.　　　*
　Car. There's a cooling
For his hot encounter!　　.　　[*Aside.*
Don. Come you here to stare?
If you have lost your tongue, and use of
　　speech,
Resign your government; there's a mute's
　　place void
In my uncle's court, I hear; and you may
　　work me,
To write for your preferment.
Musta. This is strange!
I know not, madam, what neglect of mine ·
Has call'd this scorn upon me.
　Don. To the purpose——
My will's a reason, and we stand not bound
To yield account to you.
Musta. Not of your angers:
But with erected ears I should hear from you
The story of your good opinion of me,
Confirm'd by love and favours.

Don. How deserved?
I have considered you from head to foot,
And can find nothing in that wainscot face,
That can teach me to dote; nor am I taken
With your grim aspéct, or tadpole-like
　　complexion.
Those scars you glory in, I fear to look on;
And had much rather·hear a merry tale,
Than all your battles won with blood and
　　sweat,
Though you belch forth the stink too in the
　　service,
And swear by your mustachios all is true.
You are yet too rough for me: purge and
　　take physic.
Purchase perfumers, get me some French
　　tailor
To new-create you; the first shape you were
　　made with
Is quite worn out: let your barber wash
　　your face too,
You look yet like a bugbear to fright children;
Till when I take my leave.—Wait me, Carazie.
　　　　　[*Exeunt* Donusa *and* Carazie.
Musta. Stay you, my lady's cabinet-key.
　　　　　　　　　[*Seizes* Manto.
Mant. How's this, sir?
Musta. Stay, and stand quietly, or you
　　shall fall else,
Not to firk your belly up, flounder-like, but
　　never
To rise again. Offer but to unlock
These doors that stop your fugitive tongue,
　　(observe me,)
And, by my fury, I'll fix there this bolt
　　　　　　　　[*Draws his scimitar.*
To bar thy speech for ever. So! be safe now;
And but resolve me, not of what I doubt,
But bring assurance to a thing believed,
Thou makest thyself a fortune; not depending
On the uncertain favours of a mistress,
But art thyself one. I'll not so far question
My judgment and observance, as to ask
Why I am slighted and contemn'd; but in
Whose favour it is done? I, that have read
The copious volume of all women's falsehood,
Commented on by the heart-breaking groans
Of abused lovers; all the doubts wash'd off
With fruitless tears, the spider's cobweb veil
Of arguments alleged in their defence,
Blown off with sighs of desperate men, and
　　they
Appearing in their full deformity;
Know that some other hath displanted me,
With her dishonour. Has she given it up?
Confirm it in two syllables.
　Mant. She has.
·*Musta.* I cherish thy confession thus, and
　　thus;　　　　　　[*Gives her jewels.*

Be mine. Again I court thee thus, and thus :
Now prove but constant to my ends.
  Mant. By all——
  Musta. Enough ; I dare not doubt thee.
—O land crocodiles,
Made of Egyptian slime, accursed women !
But 'tis no time to rail—come, my best
  Manto.   *[Exeunt.*

SCENE II.—*A Street.*

Enter Vitelli *and* Francisco.

  Vitel. Sir, as you are my confessor, you
stand bound
Not to reveal whatever I discover
In that religious way ; nor dare I doubt you.
Let it suffice you have made me see my follies,
And wrought, perhaps, compunction ; for I
  would not
Appear an hypocrite. But, when you impose
A penance on me beyond flesh and blood
To undergo, you must instruct me how
To put off the condition of a man ;
Or, if not pardon, at the least, excuse
My disobedience. Yet, despair not, sir ;
For, though I take mine own way, I shall do
Something that may hereafter, to my glory,
Speak me your scholar.
  Fran. I enjoin you not
To go, but send.
  Vitel. That were a petty trial ;
Not worth one, so long taught, and exercised,
Under so grave a master. Reverend Fran-
  cisco,
My friend, my father, in that word, my all !
Rest confident you shall hear something of
  me,   .
That will redeem me in your good opinion ;
Or judge me lost for ever. Send Gazet
(She shall give order that he may have en-
  trance)
To acquaint you with my fortunes.   *[Exit.*
  Fran. Go, and prosper.
Holy saints guide and strengthen thee !
  however,
As thy endeavours are, so may they find
Gracious acceptance.

Enter Gazet, *and* Grimaldi *in rags.*

  Gaz. Now, you do not roar, sir ;
You speak not tempests, nor take ear-rent
  from
A poor shop-keeper. Do you remember
  that, sir?
I wear your marks here still.
  Fran. Can this be possible?
All wonders are not ceased, then.
  Grim. Do, abuse me,
Spit on me, spurn me, pull me by the nose,

Thrust out these fiery eyes, that yesterday
Would have look'd thee dead.
  Gaz. O save me, sir !
  Grim. Fear nothing.
I am tame and quiet ; there's no wrong can
  force me
To remember what I was. I have forgot
I e'er had ireful fierceness, a steel'd heart,
Insensible of compassion to others ;
Nor is it fit that I should think myself
Worth mine own pity. Oh !
  Fran. Grows this dejection
From his disgrace, do you say?
  Gaz. Why, he's cashier'd, sir ;
His ships, his goods, his livery-punks, con-
  fiscate :
And there is such a punishment laid upon
  him !—
The miserable rogue must steal no more,
Nor drink, nor drab.
  Fran. Does that torment him ?
  Gaz. O, sir,
Should the state take order to bar men of
  acres
From these two laudable recreations,
Drinking and whoring, how should panders
  purchase,
Or thrifty whores build hospitals ? 'Slid ! if I,
That, since I am made free, may write myself
A city gallant, should forfeit two such charters,
I should be stoned to death, and ne'er be
  pitied
By the liveries of those companies.
  Fran. You'll be whipt, sir,
If you bridle not your tongue. Haste to the
  palace,
Your master looks for you.
  Gaz. My quondam master.
Rich sons forget they ever had poor fathers ;
In servants 'tis more pardonable : as a com-
  panion,
Or so, I may consent : but, is there hope,
  sir,
He has got me a good chapwoman? pray
  you, write
A word or two in my behalf.
  Fran. Out, rascal !
  Gaz. I feel some insurrections.
  Fran. Hence !
  Gaz. I vanish.   *[Exit.*
  Grim. Why should I study a defence or
  comfort,
In whom black guilt and misery, if balanced,
I know not which would turn the scale?
  look upward
I dare not ; for, should it but be believed
That I, died deep in hell's most horrid colours,
Should dare to hope for mercy, it would leave
No check or feeling in men innocent,
                      L 2

To catch at sins the devil ne'er taught man-
kind yet.
No! I must downward, downward; though
repentance
Could borrow all the glorious wings of grace,
My mountainous weight of sins would
crack their pinions,
And sink them to hell with me.
Fran. Dreadful! Hear me,
Thou miserable man.
Grim. Good sir, deny not
But that there is no punishment beyond
Damnation.

Enter Master *and* Boatswain.

Master. Yonder he is; I pity him.
Boatsw. Take comfort, captain; we live
still to serve you.
Grim. Serve me! I am a devil already:
leave me—
Stand further off, you are blasted else! I
have heard
Schoolmen affirm man's body is composed
Of the four elements; and, as in league to-
gether
They nourish life, so each of them affords
Liberty to the soul, when it grows weary
Of this fleshy prison. Which shall I make
choice of?
The fire? no; I shall feel that hereafter;
The earth will not receive me. Should
some whirlwind
Snatch me into the air, and I hang there,
Perpetual plagues would dwell upon the earth;
And those superior bodies, that pour down
Their cheerful influence, deny to pass it,
Through those vast regions I have infected.
The sea? ay, that is justice: there I ploúgh'd
up
Mischief as deep as hell: there, there, I'll hide
This cursed lump of clay. May it turn rocks,
Where plummet's weight could never reach
· the sands,
And grind the ribs of all such barks as press
The ocean's breast in my unlawful course!
I haste then to thee; let thy ravenous womb,
Whom all things else deny, be now my tomb!
[*Exit.*
· *Master.* Follow him, and restrain him.
[*Exit Boatswain.*
Fran. Let this stand
For an example to you. I'll provide
A lodging for him, and provide such cures
To his wounded conscience, as heaven hath
lent me.
He's now my second care; and my profession
Binds me to teach the desperate to repent,
As far as to confirm the innocent. [*Exeunt.*

SCENE III.—*A Room in* Asambeg's *Palace.*
Enter Asambeg, Mustapha, Aga, *and*
Capiaga.

Asam. Your pleasure?
Musta. 'Twill exact your private ear;
And, when you have received it, you will
think
Too many know it.
Asam. Leave the room; but be
Within our call.—
[*Exeunt* Aga, *and* Capiaga.
Now, sir, what burning secret
(With which, it seems, you are turn'd cinders)
bring you,
To quench in my advice or power?
Musta. The fire
Will rather reach you.
Asam. Me!
Musta. And consume both;
For 'tis impossible to be put out,
But with the blood of those that kindle it:
And yet one vial of it is so precious,
In being borrow'd from the Othoman spring,
That better 'tis, I think, both we should
perish,
Than prove the desperate means that must
restrain it
From spreading further.
Asam. To the point, and quickly:
These winding circumstances in relations,
Seldom environ truth.
Musta. Truth, Asambeg!
Asam. Truth, Mustapha. I said it, and
add more,
You touch upon a string that, to my ear,
Does sound Donusa.
Musta. You then understand
Who 'tis I aim at.
Asam. Take heed, Mustapha;
Remember what she is, and whose we are:
'Tis her neglect, perhaps, that you complain
of;
And, should you practise to revenge her
scorn,
With any plot to taint her in her honour,——
Musta. Hear me.
Asam. I will be heard first,—there's no
tongue
A subject owes, that shall out-thunder mine.
Musta. Well, take your way.
Asam. I then again repeat it;
If Mustapha dares with malicious breath,
On jealous suppositions, presume
To blast the blossom of Donusa's fame,
Because he is denied a happiness
Which men of equal, nay, of more desert,
Have sued in vain for——
Musta. More!

Asam. More. 'Twas I spake it.
The basha of Natolia and myself
Were rivals for her ; either of us brought
More victories, more trophies, to plead for us
To our great master, than you dare lay claim
   to ;
Yet still, by his allowance, she was left
To her election : each of us owed nature
As much for outward form and inward worth,
To make way for us to her grace and favour,
As you brought with you. We were heard,
   repulsed ;
Yet thought it no dishonour to sit down
With the disgrace, if not to force affection
May merit such a name.
   Musta. Have you done yet ?
   Asam. Be, therefore, more than sure the
   ground on which
You raise your accusation, may admit
No undermining of defence in her :
For if, with pregnant and apparent proofs,
Such as may force a judge, more than inclined,
Or partial in her cause, to swear her guilty,
You win not me to set off your belief ;
Neither our ancient friendship, nor the rites
Of sacred hospitality, to which
I would not offer violence, shall protect you :
—Now, when you please.
   Musta. I will not dwell upon
Much circumstance ; yet cannot but profess,
With the assurance of a loyalty
Equal to yours, the reverence I owe
The sultan, and all such his blood makes
   sacred ;
That there is not a vein of mine, which yet is
Unemptied in his service, but this moment
Should freely open, so it might wash off
The stains of her dishonour. Could you
   think,
Or, though you saw it, credit your own eyes,
That she, the wonder and amazement of
Her sex, the pride and glory of the empire,
That hath disdain'd you, slighted me, and
   boasted
A frozen coldness, which no appetite
Or height of blood could thaw ; should now
   so far
Be hurried with the violence of her lust,
As, in it burying her high birth, and fame,
Basely descend to fill a Christian's arms ;
And to him yield her virgin honour up,
Nay, sue to him to take it ?
   Asam. A Christian !
   Musta. Temper
Your admiration :—and what Christian,
   think you ?
No prince disguised, no man of mark, nor
   honour ;
No daring undertaker in our service,

But one, whose lips her foot should scorn
   to touch ;
A poor mechanic pedlar.
   Asam. He !
   Musta. Nay, more ;
Whom do you think she made her scout,
   nay bawd,
To find him out, but me ? What place
   make choice of
To wallow in her foul and loathsome
   pleasures,
But in the palace ? Who the instruments
Of close conveyance, but the captain of
Your guard, the aga, and that man of trust,
The warden of the inmost port ?—I'll prove
   this :
And, though I fail to shew her in the act,
Glued like a neighing gennet to her stallion,
Your incredulity shall be convinced
With proofs I blush to think on.
   Asam. Never yet
This flesh felt such a fever. By the life
And fortune of great Amurath, should our
   prophet
(Whose name I bow to) in a vision speak
   this,
'Twould make me doubtful of my faith !—
   Lead on ;
And, when my eyes and ears are, like yours,
   guilty,
My rage shall then appear ; for I will do
Something—but what, I am not yet de-
   termin'd.   [*Exeunt.*

SCENE IV.—*An outer room in* Donusa's
      Palace.

Enter Carazie, Manto, *and* Gazet *gaily
    dressed.*

   Car. They are private to their wishes ?
   Mant. Doubt it not.
   Gaz. A pretty structure this ! a court do
you call it ?
Vaulted and arch'd ! O, here has been old
   jumbling
Behind this arras.
   Car. Prithee let's have some sport
With this fresh codshead.
   Mant. I am out of tune,
But do as you please.—My conscience !—
   tush ! the hope
Of liberty throws that burthen off ; I must
Go watch, and make discovery.
              [*Aside, and exit.*
   Car. He is musing,
And will talk to himself ; he cannot hold :
The poor fool's ravish'd.
   Gaz. I am in my master's clothes,
They fit me to a hair too ; let but any

Indifferent gamester measure us inch by
    inch,
Or weigh us by the standard, I may pass:
I have been proved and proved again true
    metal.
  Car. How he surveys himself!
  Gaz. I have heard, that some
Have fooled themselves at court into good
    fortunes,
That never hoped to thrive by wit in the
    city,
Or honesty in the country. If I do not
Make the best laugh at me, I'll weep for
    myself,
If they give me hearing: 'tis resolved—I'll
    try
What may be done. By your favour, sir,
    I pray you,
Were you born a courtier?
  Car. No, sir; why do you ask?
  Gaz. Because I thought that none could
    be preferred,
But such as were begot there.
  Car. O, sir! many;
And, howsoe'er you are a citizen born,
Yet if your mother were a handsome woman,
And ever long'd to see a masque at court,
It is an even lay, but that you had
A courtier to your father; and I think so,
You bear yourself so sprightly.
  Gaz. It may be;
But pray you, sir, had I such an itch upon
    me
To change my copy, is there hope a place
May be had here for money?
  Car. Not without it,
That I dare warrant you.
  Gaz. I have a pretty stock,
And would not have my good parts undis-
    cover'd:
What places of credit are there?
  Car. There's your beglerbeg.
  Gaz. By no means that; it comes too near
    the beggar,
And most prove so, that come there.
  Car. Or your sanzacke.
  Gaz. Sauce-jack! fie, none of that.
  Car. Your chiaus.
  Gaz. Nor that.
  Car. Chief gardener.
  Gaz. Out upon't!
'Twill put me in mind my mother was an
    herb-woman.
What is your place, I pray you?
  Car. Sir, an eunuch.
  Gaz. An eunuch! very fine, i'faith; an
    eunuch!
And what are your employments?
  Car. Neat and easy:

In the day, I wait on my lady when she eats,
Carry her pantofles, bear up her train;
Sing her asleep at night, and, when she
    pleases,
I am her bedfellow.
  Gaz. How! her bedfellow?
And lie with her?
  Car. Yes, and lie with her.
  Gaz. O rare!
I'll be an eunuch, though I sell my shop for't,
And all my wares.
  Car. It is but parting with
A precious stone or two: I know the price on't.
  Gaz. I'll part with all my stones; and
    when I am
An eunuch, I'll so toss and touse the
    ladies——
Pray you help me to a chapman.
  Car. The court surgeon
Shall do you that favour.
  Gaz. I am made! an eunuch!

    Enter Manto.

  Mant. Carazie, quit the room.
  Car. Come, sir; we'll treat of
Your business further.
  Gaz. Excellent! an eunuch! [*Exeunt.*

SCENE V.—*An inner Room in the same.*

    Enter Donusa *and* Vitelli.

  Vitel. Leave me, or I am lost again: no
    prayers,
No penitence, can redeem me.
  Don. Am I grown
Old or deform'd since yesterday?
  Vitel. You are still,
(Although the sating of your lust hath sullied
The immaculate whiteness of your virgin
    beauties,)
Too fair for me to look on: and, though
    pureness,
The sword with which you ever fought and
    conquer'd,
Is ravish'd from you by unchaste desires,
You are too strong for flesh and blood to
    treat with,
Though iron grates were interpos'd between
    us,
To warrant me from treason.
  Don. Whom do you fear?
  Vitel. That human frailty I took from my
    mother,
That, as my youth increased, grew stronger
    on me;
That still pursues me, and, though once
    recover'd,
In scorn of reason, and, what's more, religion,
Again seeks to betray me.
  Don. If you mean, sir,

To my embraces, you turn rebel to
The laws of nature, the great queen and
	mother
Of all productions, and deny allegiance,
Where you stand bound to pay it.
	Vitel. I will stop
Mine ears against these charms, which, if
	Ulysses
Could live again, and hear this second Syren,
Though bound with cables to his mast, his
	ship too
Fasten'd with all her anchors, this enchant-
	ment
Would force him, in despite of all resistance,
To leap into the sea, and follow her ;
Although destruction, with outstretch'd arms,
Stood ready to receive him.
	Don. Gentle sir,
Though you deny to hear me, yet vouchsafe
To look upon me: though I use no language,
The grief for this unkind repulse will print
Such a dumb eloquence upon my face,
As will not only plead but prevail for me.
	Vitel. I am a coward. I will see and
	hear you,
The trial, else, is nothing; nor the conquest,
My temperance shall crown me with here-
	after,
Worthy to be remember'd. Up, my virtue !
And holy thoughts and resolutions arm me
Against this fierce temptation ! give me voice
Tuned to a zealous anger, to express
At what an over-value I have purchased
The wanton treasure of your virgin bounties;
That, in their false fruition, heap upon me
Despair and horror.—That I could with
	that ease
Redeem my forfeit innocence, or cast up
The poison I received into my entrails,
From the alluring cup of your enticements,
As now I do deliver back the price
	[*Returns the jewels.*
And salary of your lust ! or thus unclothe me
Of sin's gay trappings, the proud livery
	[*Throws off his cloak and doublet.*
Of wicked pleasure, which but worn and
	heated
With the fire of entertainment and consent,
Like to Alcides' fatal shirt, tears off
Our flesh and reputation both together,
Leaving our ulcerous follies bare and open
To all malicious censure !
	Don. You must grant,
If you hold that a loss to you, mine equals,
If not transcends it. If you then first tasted
That poison, as you call it, I brought with
	me
A palate unacquainted with the relish
Of those delights, which most, as I have heard,

Greedily swallow ; and then the offence,
If my opinion may be believed,
Is not so great : howe'er, the wrong no more,
Than if Hippolitus and the virgin huntress
Should meet and kiss together.
	Vitel. What defences
Can lust raise to maintain a precipice

	Enter Asambeg *and* Mustapha, *above.*

To the abyss of looseness !—but affords not
The least stair, or the fastening of one foot,
To reascend that glorious height we fell from.
	Musta. By Mahomet, she courts him !
		[*Donusa kneels.*
	Asam. Nay, kneels to him !
Observe, the scornful villain turns away too,
As glorying in his conquest.
	Don. Are you marble ?
If Christians have mothers, sure they share in
The tigress' fierceness ; for, if you were
	owner
Of human pity, you could not endure
A princess to kneel to you, or look on
These falling tears which hardest rocks
	would soften,
And yet remain unmoved. Did you but
	give me
A taste of happiness in your embraces,
That the remembrance of the sweetness of it
Might leave perpetual bitterness behind it ?
Or shew'd me what it was to be a wife,
To live a widow ever ?
	Asam. She has confest it !——
Seize on him, villains.

	Enter Capiaga *and* Aga, *with* Janizaries.

		O the Furies !
	[*Exeunt* Asambeg *and* Mustapha *above.*
	Don. How !
Are we betray'd ?
	Vitel. The better ; I expected
A Turkish faith.
	Don. Who am I, that you dare this ?
'Tis I that do command you to forbear
A touch of violence.
	Aga. We, already, madam,
Have satisfied your pleasure further than
We know to answer it.
	Cap. Would we were well off !
We stand too far engaged, I fear.
	Don. For us ?
We'll bring you safe off : who dares contra-
	dict
What is our pleasure ?

	Re-enter Asambeg *and* Mustapha, *below.*

	Asam. Spurn the dog to prison.
I'll answer you anon.
	Vitel. What punishment

Soe'er I undergo, I am still a Christian.
          [Exit Guard *with* Vitelli.
  Don. What bold presumption's this?
    Under what law
Am I to fall, that set my foot upon
Your statutes and decrees?
  Musta. The crime committed,
Our Alcoran calls death.
  Don. Tush! who is here,
That is not Amurath's slave, and so, unfit
To sit a judge upon his blood?
  Asam. You have lost,
And shamed the privilege of it; robb'd me
    too
Of my soul, my understanding, to behold
Your base unworthy fall from your high
    virtue.
  Don. I do appeal to Amurath.
  Asam. We will offer
No violence to your person, till we know
His sacred pleasure; till when, under guard
You shall continue here.
  Don. Shall!
  Asam. I have said it.
  Don. We shall remember this.
  Asam. It ill becomes.
Such as are guilty, to deliver threats
Against the innocent.
          [*The* Guard *leads off* Donusa.
I could tear this flesh now,
But 'tis in vain; nor must I talk, but do.
Provide a well-mann'd galley for Constanti-
    nople:
Such sad news never came to our great master.
As he directs, we must proceed, and know
No will but his, to whom what's ours we owe.
                    [Exeunt.

ACT IV.

SCENE I.—*A Room in* Grimaldi's *House.*

Enter Master *and* Boatswain.

  Mast. He does begin to eat?
  Boatsw. A little, master;
But our best hope for his recovery is, that
His raving leaves him; and those dreadful
    words,
Damnation and despair, with which he ever
Ended all his discourses, are forgotten.
  Mast. This stranger is a most religious
    man sure;
And I am doubtful, whether his charity
In the relieving of our wants, or care
To cure the wounded conscience of Grimaldi,
Deserves more admiration.
  Boatsw. Can you guess
What the reason should be, that we never
    mention

The church, or the high altar, but his
    melancholy
Grows and increases on him?
  Mast. I have heard him,
When he gloried to profess himself an atheist,
Talk often, and with much delight and
    boasting,
Of a rude prank he did ere he turn'd pirate;
The memory of which, as it appears,
Lies heavy on him,
  Boatsw. Pray you, let me understand it.
  Mast. Upon a solemn day, when the
    whole city
Join'd in devotion, and with barefoot steps
Passed to St. Mark's, the duke, and the
    whole signiory,
Helping to perfect the religious pomp
With which they were received; when all
    men else
Were full of tears, and groan'd beneath the
    weight
Of past offences, of whose heavy burthen
They came to be absolved and freed; our
    captain,
Whether in scorn of those so pious rites
He had no feeling of, or else drawn to it
Out of a wanton, irreligious madness,
(I know not which,) ran to the holy man,
As he was doing of the work of grace,
And snatching from his hands the sanctified
    means,
Dash'd it upon the pavement.
  Boatsw. How escaped he,
It being a deed deserving death with torture?
  Mast. The general amazement of the people
Gave him leave to quit the temple, and a
    gondola,
Prepared, it seems, before, brought him
    aboard;
Since which he ne'er saw Venice. The re-
    membrance
Of this, it seems, torments him; aggravated
With a strong belief he cannot receive pardon
For this foul fact, but from his hands,
    against whom
It was committed.
  Boatsw. And what course intends
His heavenly physician, reverend Francisco,
To beat down this opinion?
  Mast. He promised
To use some holy and religious fineness,
To this good end; and, in the meantime,
    charged me
To keep him dark, and to admit no visitants;
But on no terms to cross him. Here he comes.

Enter Grimaldi, *with a book.*

  Grim. For theft, he that restores treble
    the value,

Makes satisfaction ; and, for want of means
To do so, as a slave must serve it out,
Till he hath made full payment. There's
    hope left here.
Oh ! with what willingness would I give up
My liberty to those that I have pillaged ;
And wish the numbers of my years, though
    wasted
In the most sordid slavery, might equal
The rapines I have made ; till, with one voice,
My patient sufferings might exact, from my
Most cruel creditors, a full remission,
An eye's loss with an eye, limb's with a limb :
A sad account !—yet, to find peace within
    here,
Though all such as I have maim'd and dis-
    member'd
In drunken quarrels, or o'ercome with rage,
When they were given up to my power, stood
    here now,
And cried for restitution ; to appease them,
I would do a bloody justice on myself :
Pull out these eyes, that guided me to ravish
Their sight from others ; lop these legs, that
    bore me
To barbarous violence ; with this hand cut off
This instrument of wrong, till nought were
    left me
But this poor bleeding limbless trunk, which
    gladly
I would divide among them.—Ha ! what
    think I

Enter Francisco *in a cope, like a Bishop.*

Of petty forfeitures ! In this reverend habit,
'All that I am turn'd into eyes, I look on
A deed of mine so fiend-like, that repentance,
Though with my tears I taught the sea new
    tides,
Can never wash off : all my thefts, my rapes,
Are venial trespasses, compared to what
I offer'd to that shape, and in a place too,
Where I stood bound to kneel to 't. [*Kneels.*
    Fran. 'Tis forgiven :
I with his tongue, whom, in these sacred
    vestments,
With impure hands thou didst offend, pro-
    nounce it.
I bring peace to thee ; see that thou deserve it
In thy fair life hereafter.
    Grim. Can it be !
Dare I believe this vision, or hope
A pardon e'er may find me ?
    Fran. Purchase it
By zealous undertakings, and no more
'Twill be remembered.
    Grim. What celestial balm   [*Rises.*
I feel now pour'd into my wounded con-
    science !

What penance is there I'll not undergo,
Though ne'er so sharp and rugged, with
    more pleasure
Than flesh and blood e'er tasted ! show me
    true Sorrow,
Arm'd with an iron whip, and I will meet
The stripes she brings along with her, as if
They were the gentle touches of a hand
That comes to cure me. Can good deeds
    redeem me ?
I will rise up a wonder to the world,
When I have given strong proofs how I am
    alter'd.
I, that have sold such as profess'd the faith
That I was born in, to captivity,
Will make their number equal, that I shall
Deliver from the oar ; and win as many
By the clearness of my actions, to look on
Their misbelief, and loath it. I will be
A convoy for all merchants ; and thought
    worthy
To be reported to the world, hereafter,
The child of your devotion ; nurs'd up,
And made strong by your charity, to break
    through
All dangers hell can bring forth to oppose me.
Nor am I, though my fortunes were thought
    desperate,
Now you have reconciled me to myself,
So void of worldly means, but, in despite
Of the proud viceroy's wrongs, I can do
    something
To witness of my change : when you please,
    try me,
And I will perfect what you shall enjoin me,
Or fall a joyful martyr.
    Fran. You will reap
The comfort of it ; live yet undiscover'd,
And with your holy meditations strengthen
Your Christian resolution : ere long,
You shall hear further from me.   [*Exit.*
    Grim. I'll attend
All your commands with patience ;—come,
    my mates,
I hitherto have lived an ill example,
And, as your captain, led you on to mischief ;
But now will truly labour, that good men
May say hereafter of me, to my glory,
(Let but my power and means hand with my
    will,)
His good endeavours did weigh down his ill.
    [*Exeunt.*

Re-enter Francisco, *in his usual habit.*

    Fran. This penitence is not counterfeit :
    howsoever,
Good actions are in themselves rewarded.
My travail's to meet with a double crown.

If that Vitelli come off safe, and prove
Himself the master of his wild affections——

Enter Gazet.

O, I shall have intelligence; how now,
      Gazet,
Why these sad looks and tears?
    Gaz. Tears, sir! I have lost
My worthy master.   Your rich heir seems
      to mourn for
A miserable father, your young widow,
Following a bedrid husband to his grave,
Would have her neighbours think she cries
      and roars,
That she must part with such a goodman
      Do-nothing;
When 'tis, because he stays so long above
      ground,
And hinders a rich suitor.—All's come out,
      sir.
We are smok'd for being coney-catchers:
      my master
Is put in prison; his she-customer
Is under guard too; these are things to weep
      for:—
But mine own loss consider'd, and what a
      fortune
I have had, as they say, snatch'd out of my
      chops,
Would make a man run mad.
    Fran. I scarce have leisure,
I am so wholly taken up with sorrow
For my loved pupil, to enquire thy fate;
Yet I will hear it.
    Gaz. Why, sir, I had bought a place,
A place of credit too, an I had gone through
      with it;
I should have been made an eunuch: there
      was honour
For a late poor prentice! when, upon the
      sudden,
There was such a hurly-burly in the court,
That I was glad to run away, and carry
The price of my office with me.
    Fran. Is that all?
You have made a saving voyage: we must
      think now,
Though not to free, to comfort sad Vitelli;
My grieved soul suffers for him.
    Gaz. I am sad too;
But had I been an eunuch——
    Fran. Think not on it.   [*Exeunt.*

SCENE II.—*A Hall in* Asambeg's *Palace.*

Enter Asambeg; *he unlocks a door, and*
      Paulina *comes forth.*

    Asam. Be your own guard: obsequious-
      ness and service
Shall win you to be mine.   Of all restraint

For ever take your leave, no threats shall
      awe you,
No jealous doubts of mine disturb your
      freedom,
No fee'd spies wait upon your steps: your
      virtue,
And due consideration in yourself
Of what is noble, are the faithful helps
I leave you, as supporters, to defend you
From falling basely.
    Paul. This is wondrous strange:
Whence flows this alteration?
    Asam. From true judgment;
And strong assurance, neither grates of iron,
Hemm'd in with walls of brass, strict guards,
      high birth,
The forfeiture of honour, nor the fear
Of infamy or punishment, can stay
A woman slaved to appetite, from being
False, and unworthy.
    Paul. You are grown satirical
Against our sex. Why, sir, I durst produce
Myself in our defence, and from you chal-
      lenge
A testimony that's not to be denied,
All fall not under this unequal censure.
I, that have stood your flatteries, your
      threats,
Borne up against your fierce temptations;
      scorn'd
The cruel means you practised to supplant
      me,
Having no arms to help me to hold out,
But love of piety, and constant goodness;
If you are unconfirm'd, dare again boldly,
Enter into the lists, and combat with
All opposites man's malice can bring forth
To shake me in my chastity, built upon
The rock of my religion.
    Asam. I do wish
I could believe you; but, when I shall shew
      you
A most incredible example of
Your frailty, in a princess, sued and
      sought to
By men of worth, of rank, of eminence;
      courted
By happiness itself, and her cold temper
Approved by many years; yet she to fall,
Fall from herself, her glories, nay, her safety,
Into a gulf of shame and black despair;
I think you'll doubt yourself, or, in beholding
Her punishment, for ever be deterr'd
From yielding basely.
    Paul. I would see this wonder;
'Tis, sir, my first petition.
    Asam. And thus granted:
Above, you shall observe all.
                              [*Exit* Paulina.

Enter Mustapha.

Musta. Sir, I sought you,
And must relate a wonder. Since I studied,
And knew what man was, I was never witness
Of such invincible fortitude as this Christian
Shews in his sufferings : all the torments that
We could present him with, to fright his constancy,
Confirm'd, not shook it ; and those heavy chains,
That eat into his flesh, appear'd to him
Like bracelets made of some loved mistress' hairs,
We kiss in the remembrance of her favours.
I am strangely taken with it, and have lost
Much of my fury.
Asam. Had he suffer'd poorly,
It had call'd on my contempt ; but manly patience,
And all-commanding virtue, wins upon
An enemy. I shall think upon him.—Ha !

Enter Aga, *with a black box.*

So soon return'd ! This speed pleads in excuse
Of your late fault, which I no more remember.
What's the grand signior's pleasure ?
Aga. 'Tis enclosed here.
The box too that contains it may inform you
How he stands affected : I am trusted with
Nothing but this, On forfeit of your head,
She must have a speedy trial.
Asam. Bring her in
In black, as to her funeral : [*Exit* Aga.] 'tis the colour
Her fault wills her to wear, and which, in justice,
I dare not pity. Sit, and take your place :
However in her life she has degenerated,
May she die nobly, and in that confirm
Her greatness and high blood !

Solemn music. Re-enter the Aga, *with the*
Capiaga *leading in* Donusa *in black, her*
train borne up by Carazie *and* Manto. *A*
Guard attending. Paulina *enters above.*

Musta. I now could melt—
But soft compassion leave me.
Mant. I am affrighted
With this dismal preparation. Should the enjoying
Of loose desires find ever such conclusions,
All women would be Vestals.
Don. That you clothe me
In this sad livery of death, assures me
Your sentence is gone out before, and I
Too late am call'd for, in my guilty cause
To use qualification or excuse——

Yet must I not part so with mine own strengths,
But borrow, from my modesty, boldness, to
Enquire by whose authority you sit
My judges, and whose warrant digs my grave
In the frowns you dart against my life ?
Asam. See here,
This fatal sign and warrant ! This, brought to
A general, fighting in the head of his
Victorious troops, ravishes from his hand
His even then conquering sword ; this,
shewn unto
The sultan's brothers, or his sons, delivers
His deadly anger ; and, all hopes laid by,
Commands them to prepare themselves for heaven ;
Which would stand with the quiet of your soul,
To think upon, and imitate.
Don. Give me leave
A little to complain ; first, of the hard
Condition of my fortune, which may move you,
Though not to rise up intercessors for me,
Yet, in remembrance of my former life,
(This being the first spot tainting mine honour,)
To be the means to bring me to his presence :
And then I doubt not, but I could allege
Such reasons in mine own defence, or plead
So humbly, (my tears helping,) that it should
Awake his sleeping pity.
Asam. 'Tis in vain.
If you have aught to say, you shall have hearing ;
And, in me, think him present.
Don. I would thus then
First kneel, and kiss his feet ; and after, tell him
How long I had been his darling ; what delight
My infant years afforded him ; how dear
He prized his sister in both bloods, my mother :
That she, like him, had frailty, that to me
Descends as an inheritance ; then conjure him,
By her blest ashes, and his father's soul,
The sword that rides upon his thigh, his right hand
Holding the sceptre and the Othoman fortune,
To have compassion on me.
Asam. But suppose
(As I am sure) he would be deaf, what then
Could you infer ?
Don. I, then, would thus rise up,
And to his teeth tell him he was a tyrant,
A most voluptuous and insatiable epicure
In his own pleasures ; which he hugs so dearly,

As proper and peculiar to himself,
That he denies a moderate lawful use
Of all delight to others. And to thee,
Unequal judge, I speak as much, and
    charge thee,
But with impartial eyes to look into
Thyself, and then consider with what justice
Thou canst pronounce my sentence. Un-
    kind nature,
To make weak women servants, proud men
    masters !
Indulgent Mahomet, do thy bloody laws
Call my embraces with a Christian death,
Having my heat and May of youth, to plead
In my excuse? and yet want power to punish
These that, with scorn, break through thy
    cobweb edicts,
And laugh at thy decrees? To tame their
    lusts
There's no religious bit : let her be fair,
And pleasing to the eye, though Persian,
    Moor,
Idolatress, Turk, or Christian, you are privi-
    leged,
And freely may enjoy her. At this instant,
I know, unjust man, thou hast in thy power
A lovely Christian virgin ; thy offence
Equal, if not transcending mine : why, then,
(We being both guilty,) dost thou not descend
From that usurp'd tribunal, and with me
Walk hand in hand to death?
    Asam. She raves ; and we
Lose time to hear her : Read the law.
    Don. Do, do ;
I stand resolved to suffer.   ·
    Aga. [reads.] *If any virgin, of what
degree, or quality soever, born a natural
Turk, shall be convicted of corporal loose-
ness, and incontinence with any Christian,
she is, by the decree of our great prophet,
Mahomet, to lose her head.*
    Asam. Mark that, then tax our justice !
    *Aga. Ever provided, That if she, the said
offender, by any reasons, arguments, or persuasion, can win and prevail with the said
Christian offending with her, to alter his
religion, and marry her, that then the winning of a soul to the Mahometan sect, shall
acquit her from all shame, disgrace, and
punishment whatsoever.*
    Don. I lay hold on that clause, and chal-
    lenge from you
The privilege of the law.
    Musta. What will you do?
    Don. Grant me access and means, I'll
    undertake
To turn this Christian Turk, and marry him :
This trial you cannot deny.
    Musta. O base !

Can fear to die make you descend so low
From your high birth, and brand the Otho-
    man line
With such a mark of infamy?
    Asam. This is worse
Than the parting with your honour. Better
    suffer
Ten thousand deaths, and without hope to
    ·   have
A place in our great prophet's paradise,
Than have an act to aftertimes remember'd,
So foul as this is.
    Musta. Cheer your spirits, madam ;
To die is nothing, 'tis but parting with
A mountain of vexations.
    Asam. Think of your honour :
In dying nobly, you make satisfaction
For your offence, and you shall live a story
Of bold heroic courage.
    Don. You shall not fool me
Out of my life : I claim the law, and sue for
A speedy trial ; if I fail, you may
Determine of me as you please.
    Asam. Base woman !
But use thy ways, and see thou prosper in
    them ;
For, if thou fall again into my power,
Thou shalt in vain, after a thousand tortures,
Cry out for death, that death which now
    thou fliest from.
Unloose the prisoner's chains. Go, lead
    her on,
To try the magic of her tongue. I follow :
                    [*Exeunt all but* Asambeg.
I'm on the rack—descend, my best Paulina.
                    [*Exit with* Paulina.

SCENE III.—*A Room in the Prison.*

Enter Francisco *and* Gaoler.

    Fran. I come not empty-handed ; I will
    purchase
Your favour at what rate you please. There's
    gold.
    Gaol. 'Tis the best oratory. I will hazard
A check for your content.—Below, there !
    Vitel. [*below.*] Welcome !
Art thou the happy messenger, that brings
    me
News of my death?
    Gaol. Your hand.   [*Plucks up* Vitelli.
    Fran. Now, if you please,
A little privacy.
    Gaol. You have bought it, sir ;
Enjoy it freely.   [*Exit.*
    Fran. O, my dearest pupil !
Witness these tears of joy, I never saw you,
Till now, look lovely ; nor durst I ever glory
In the mind of any man I had built up

With the hands of virtuous and religious
precepts,
Till this glad minute. Now you have made
good
My expectation of you. By my order,
All Roman Cæsars, that led kings in chains,
Fast bound to their triumphant chariots, if
Compared with that true glory and full lustre
You now appear in; all their boasted
honours,
Purchased with blood and wrong, would
lose their names,
And be no more remember'd !
  Vitel. This applause,
Confirm'd in your allowance, joys me more
Than if a thousand full-cramm'd theatres
Should clap their eager hands, to witness that
The scene I act did please, and they ad-
mire it.
But these are, father, but beginnings, not
The ends, of my high aims. I grant, to
have master'd
The rebel appetite cf flesh and blood,
Was far above my strength ; and still owe
for it
To that great Power that lent it : but, when I
Shall make't apparent the grim looks of Death
Affright me not, and that I can put off
The fond desire of life, (that, like a garment,
Covers and clothes our frailty,) hastening to
My martyrdom, as to a heavenly banquet,
To which I was a choice invited guest ;   .
Then you may boldly say, you did not plough,
Or trust the barren and ungrateful sands
With the fruitful grain of your religious
counsels.
  Fran. You do instruct your teacher. Let
the sun
Of your clear life, that lends to good men
light,
But set as gloriously as it did rise,
(Though sometimes clouded,) you may write
nil ultra
To human wishes.
  Vitel. I have almost gain'd
The end o' the race, and will not faint or
tire now.

Re-enter Gaoler *with* Aga.

  Aga. Sir, by your leave,—nay, stay not,
[*to the* Gaoler, *who goes out.*] I bring
comfort.
The viceroy, taken with the constant bearing
Of your afflictions ; and presuming too
You will not change your temper, does
command
Your irons should be ta'en off. [*They take
off his irons.*] Now arm yourself
With your old resolution ; suddenly

You shall be visited. You must leave the
room too,
And do it without reply.
  Fran. There's no contending :
Be still thyself, my son.
                    [*Exeunt* Aga *and* Francisco.
  Vitel. 'Tis not in man

Enter Donusa, *followed at a distance by*
Asambeg, Mustapha, *and* Paulina.

To change or alter me.
  Paul. Whom do I look on ?
My brother? 'tis he !—but no more, my
tongue ;
Thou wilt betray all.   [*Aside.*
  Asam. Let us hear this temptress :
The fellow looks as he would stop his ears
Against her powerful spells.
  Paul. He is undone else.   [*Aside.*
  Vitel. I'll stand the encounter—charge
me home.
  Don. I come, sir,   [*Bows herself.*
A beggar to you, and doubt not to find
A good man's charity, which if you deny,
You are cruel to yourself; a crime a wise man
(And such I hold you) would not willingly
Be guilty of : nor let it find less welcome,
Though I, a creature you contemn, now
shew you
The way to certain happiness ; nor think it
Imaginary or fantastical,
And so not worth the acquiring, in respect
The passage to it is nor rough nor thorny ;
No steep hills in the way which you must
climb up,
No monsters to be conquer'd, no enchant-
ments
To be dissolved by counter charms, before
You take possession of it.
  Vitel. What strong poison
Is wrapp'd up in these sugar'd pills ?
  Don. My suit is,
That you would quit your shoulders of a
burthen,
Under whose ponderous weight you wilfully
Have too long groan'd, to cast those fetters
off,
With which, with your own hands, you
chain your freedom :
Forsake a severe, nay, imperious mistress,
Whose service does exact perpetual cares,
Watchings, and troubles ; and give enter-
tainment
To one that courts you, whose least favours
are
Variety, and choice of all delights
Mankind is capable of.
  Vitel. You speak in riddles.

What burthen, or what mistress, or what
fetters,
Are those you point at?
　Don. Those which your religion,
The mistress you too long have served, com-
pels you
To bear with slave-like patience.
　Vitel. Ha!
　Paul. How bravely
That virtuous anger shews?
　Don. Be wise, and weigh
The prosperous success of things; if bless-
ings
Are donatives from heaven, (which, you
must grant,
Were blasphemy to question,) and that
They are call'd down and pour'd on such as
are
Most gracious with the great Disposer of
them,
Look on our flourishing empire, if the
splendor,
The majesty, and glory of it dim not
Your feeble sight; and then turn back, and
see
The narrow bounds of yours, yet that poor
remnant
Rent in as many factions and opinions
As you have petty kingdoms;—and then, if
You are not obstinate against truth and
reason,
You must confess the Deity you worship
Wants care or power to help you.
　Paul. Hold out now,
And then thou art victorious.　　　[*Aside.*
　Asam. How he eyes her!
　Musta. As if he would look through her.
　Asam. His eyes flame too,
As threatening violence.
　Vitel. But that I know
The devil, thy tutor, fills each part about thee,
And that I cannot play the exorcist
To dispossess thee, unless I should tear
Thy body limb by limb, and throw it to
The Furies, that expect it; I would now
Pluck out that wicked tongue, that hath
blasphemed
The great Omnipotency, at whose nod
The fabric of the world shakes.　Dare you
bring
Your juggling prophet in comparison with
That most inscrutable and infinite Essence,
That made this All, and comprehends his
work!—
The place is too profane to mention him .
Whose only name is sacred.　O Donusa!
How much, in my compassion, I suffer,
That thou, on whom this most excelling
form,

And faculties of discourse, beyond a woman,
Were by his liberal gift conferr'd, shouldst
still
Remain in ignorance of him that gave it!
I will not foul my mouth to speak the sorceries
Of your seducer, his base birth, his whore-
doms,
His strange impostures; nor deliver how
He taught a pigeon to feed in his ear,
Then made his credulous followers believe
It was an angel, that instructed him
In the framing of his Alcoran—pray you,
mark me.
　Asam. These words are death, were he in
nought else guilty.
　Vitel. Your intent to win me .
To be of your belief, proceeded from
Your fear to die.　Can there be strength in
that
Religion, that suffers us to tremble
At that which every day, nay hour, we
haste to?　　　　　　　　.
　Don. This is unanswerable, and there's .
something tells me
I err in my opinion.
　Vitel. Cherish it,
It is a heavenly prompter; entertain
This holy motion, and wear on your forehead
The sacred badge he arms his servants with;
You shall, like me, with scorn look down
upon
All engines tyranny can advance to batter
Your constant resolution.　Then you shall
Look truly fair, when your mind's pureness
answers
Your outward beauties.
　Don. I came here to take you,
But I perceive a yielding in myself
To be your prisoner.
　Vitel. 'Tis an overthrow,
That will outshine all victories.　O Donusa,
Die in my faith, like me; and 'tis a marriage
At which celestial angels shall be waiters,
And such as have been sainted welcome us :
Are you confirm'd?
　Don. I would be; but the means
That may assure me?
　Vitel. Heaven is merciful,
And will not suffer you to want a man
To do that sacred office, build upon it.　.
　Don. Then thus I spit at Mahomet.
　Asam. [*coming forward.*] Stop her mouth:
In death to turn apostata!　I'll not hear
One syllable from any.—Wretched creature!
With the next rising sun prepare to die.—
Yet, Christian, in reward of thy brave courage,
Be thy faith right or wrong, receive this
favour;
In person I'll attend thee to thy death :

And boldly challenge all that I can give,
But what's not in my grant, which is—to
    live.   [*Exeunt.*

ACT V.

SCENE I.—*A Room in the Prison.*

Enter Vitelli *and* Francisco.

Fran. You are wondrous brave and jo-
    cund.

Vitel. Welcome, father.
Should I spare cost, or not wear cheerful
    looks
Upon my wedding day, it were ominous,
And shew'd 'I did repent it ; which I dare
    not,
It being a marriage, howsoever sad
In the first ceremonies that confirm it,
That will for ever arm me against fears,
Repentance, doubts, or jealousies, and bring
Perpetual comforts, peace of mind, and quiet
To the glad couple.

Fran. I well understand you ;
And my full joy to see you so resolved
Weak words cannot express. What is the
    hour
Design'd for this solemnity?

Vitel. The sixth :
Something before the setting of the sun,
We take our last leave of his fading light,
And with our scul's eyes seek for beams
    eternal.
Yet there's one scruple with which I am much
Perplex'd and troubled, which I know you can
Resolve me of.

Fran. What is't?

Vitel. This, sir ; my bride,
Whom I first courted, and then won, not with
Loose lays, poor flatteries, apish compliments,
But sacred and religious zeal, yet wants
The holy badge that should proclaim her fit
For these celestial nuptials : willing she is,
I know, to wear it, as the choicest jewel,
On her fair forehead ; but to you, that well
Could do that work of grace, I know the
    viceroy
Will never grant access. Now, in a case
Of this necessity, I would gladly learn,
Whether, in me, a layman, without orders,
It may not be religious and lawful,
As we go to our deaths, to do that office?

Fran. A question in itself with much
    ease answer'd :
Midwives, upon necessity, perform it ;
And knights that, in the Holy Land, fought
    tor
The freedom of Jerusalem, when full

Of sweat and enemies' blood, have made
    their helmets
The fount, out of which, with their holy hands
They drew that heavenly liquor ; 'twas ap-
    proved then
By the holy church, nor must I think it now,.
In you, a work less pious.

Vitel. You confirm me ;
I will find a way to do it. In the mean time,
Your holy vows assist me !

Fran. They shall ever
Be present with you.

Vitel. You shall see me act
This last scene to the life.

Fran. And though now fall,
Rise a bless'd martyr.

Vitel. That's my end, my all.   [*Exeunt.*

SCENE II.—*A* S*treet.*

Enter Grimaldi, Master, Boatswain, *and*
    Sailors.

Boatsw. Sir, if you slip this opportunity,
Never expect the like.

Mast. With as much ease now
We may steal the ship out of the harbour,
    captain,
As ever gallants, in a wanton bravery,
Have set upon a drunken constable,
And bore him from a sleepy rug-gown'd
    watch :
Be therefore wise.

Grim. I must be honest too.
And you shall wear that shape, you shall
    observe me,
If that you purpose to continue mine.
Think you ingratitude can be the parent
To our unfeign'd repentance? Do I owe
A peace within here, kingdoms could not.
    purchase,
To my religious creditor, to leave him
Open to danger, the great benefit
Never remember'd ! no ; though in her
    bottom
We could stow up the tribute of the Turk ;
Nay, grant the passage safe too ; I will never
Consent to weigh an anchor up, till he,
That only must, commands it.

Boatsw. This religion
Will keep us slaves and beggars.

Mast. The fiend prompts me
To change my copy : plague upon't ! we
    are seamen ;
What have we to do with't, but for a snatch
    or so,
At the end of a long Lent?

Enter Francisco.

Boatsw. Mum : see who is here.

Grim. My father !

Fran. My good convert. I am full
Of serious business which denies me leave
To hold long conference with you : only
 thus much
Briefly receive ; a day or two, at the most,
Shall make me fit to take my leave of Tunis,
Or give me lost for ever.
 Grim. Days nor years,
Provided that my stay may do you service,
But to me shall be minutes.
 Fran. I much thank you :
In this small scroll you may in private read
What my intents are ; and, as they grow ripe,
I will instruct you further : in the mean time
Borrow your late distracted looks and gesture ;
The more dejected you appear, the less
The viceroy must suspect you.
 ` *Grim.* I am nothing,·
But what you please to have me be.
 Fran. Farewell, sir.
Be cheerful, master, something we will do,
That shall reward itself in the performance ;
And that's true prize indeed.
 Mast. I am obedient.
 Boatsw. And I : there's no contending.
   [*Exeunt* Grim. Mast. Boatsw. *and*
    Sailors.
 Fran. Peace to you all !
Prosper, thou Great Existence, my en-
 deavours,
As they religiously are undertaken,
And distant equally from servile gain,

 Enter Paulina, Carazie, *and* Manto.

Or glorious ostentation !—I am heard,
In this blest opportunity, which in vain
I long have waited for. I must show myself.
O, she has found me ! now if she prove right,
All hope will not forsake us.
 Paul. Further off ;
And in that distance know your duties too.
You were bestow'd on me as slaves to serve me,
And not as spies to pry into my actions,
And after, to betray me. You shall find
If any look of mine be unobserved,
I am not ignorant of a mistress' power,
And from whom I receive it.
 Car. Note this, Manto,
The pride and scorn with which she enter-
 tains us,
Now we are made hers by the viceroy's gift !
Our sweet condition'd princess, fair Donusa,
Rest in her death wait on her ? never used us
With such contempt. I would he had sent me
To the gallies, or the gallows, when he
 gave me
To this proud little devil.
 Mant. I expect
All tyrannous usage, but I must be patient ;

And though, ten times a day, she tears these
 locks,
Or makes this face her footstool, 'tis but
 justice.
 Paul. 'Tis a true story of my fortunes,
 father.
My chastity preserved by miracle,
Or your devotions for me ; and, believe it,
What outward pride soe'er I counterfeit,
Or state, to these appointed to attend me,
I am not in my disposition alter'd,
But still your humble daughter, and share
 with you
In my poor brother's sufferings :—all hell's
 torments
Revenge it on accurs'd Grimaldi's soul,
That, in his rape of me, gave a beginning
To all the miseries that since have follow'd !
 Fran. Be charitable, and forgive him,
 gentle daughter.
He's a changed man, and may redeem his
 fault
In his fair life hereafter. You must bear too
Your forced captivity, for 'tis no better,
Though you wear golden fetters, and of him,
Whom death affrights not, learn to hold
 out nobly.
 Paul. You are still the same good coun-
 sellor.
 Fran. And who knows,
(Since what above is purposed, is inscru-
 table,)
But that the viceroys's extreme dotage on you
May be the parent of a happier birth
Than yet our hopes dare fashion. Longer
 conference
May prove unsafe for you and me ; however
(Perhaps for trial) he allows you freedom.—
     [*Delivers a paper.*
From this learn therefore what you must
 attempt,
Though with the hazard of yourself : heaven
 guard you,
And give Vitelli patience ! then I doubt not
But he will have a glorious day, since some
Hold truly,—such as suffer, overcome.
       [*Exeunt.*

SCENE III.—*A Hall in* Asambeg's *Palace.*

 Enter Asambeg, Mustapha, Aga, *and*
   Capiaga.

 Asam. What we commanded, see per-
 form'd ; and fail not
In all things to be punctual.
 Aga. We shall, sir.
    [*Exeunt* Aga *and* Capiaga.
 Musta. 'Tis strange, that you should use
 such circumstance
To a delinquent of so mean condition.

Asam. Had he appeared in a more sordid
  shape
Than disguised greatness ever deign'd to
  mask in,
The gallant bearing of his present fortune
Aloud proclaims him noble.
  Musta. If you doubt him
To be a man built up for great employments,
And, as a cunning spy, sent to explore
The city's strength or weakness, you by
  torture
May force him to discover it.
  Asam. That were base ;
Nor dare I do such injury to virtue
And bold assured courage ; neither can I
Be won to think, but if I should attempt it,
I shoot against the moon.   He that hath
  stood
The roughest battery, that captivity
Could ever bring to shake a constant temper ;
Despised the fawnings of a future greatness,
By beauty, in her full perfection, tender'd ;
That hears of death as of a quiet slumber,
And from the surplusage of his own firmness,
Can spare enough of fortitude, to assure
A feeble woman ; will not, Mustapha,
Be alter'd in his soul for any torments
We can afflict his body with.
  Musta. Do your pleasure :
I only offer'd you a friend's advice,
But without gall or envy to the man
That is to suffer. But what do you determine
Of poor Grimaldi? the disgrace call'd on him,
I hear, has run him mad.
  Asam. There weigh the difference
In the true temper of their minds. The one,
A pirate, sold to mischiefs, rapes, and all
That make a slave relentless and obdurate,
Yet, of himself wanting the inward strengths
That should defend him, sinks beneath
  compassion
Or pity of a man : whereas this merchant,
Acquainted only with a civil life ;
Arm'd in himself, intrench'd and fortified
With his own virtue, valuing life and death
At the same price, poorly does not invite
A favour, but commands us to do him right ;
Which unto him, and her we both once
  honour'd
As a just debt, I gladly pay ;—they enter.
Now sit we equal hearers.

*A dreadful music. Enter at one door, the
Aga, Janizaries, Vitelli, Francisco, and
Gazet ; at the other, Donusa, (her train
borne up), Paulina, Carazie, and Manto.*

  Musta. I shall hear
And see, sir, without passion ; my wrongs
  arm me.

  Vitel. A joyful preparation ! To whose
  bounty
Owe we our thanks for gracing thus our
  hymen ?
The notes, though dreadful to the ear, sound
  here
As our epithalamium were sung
By a celestial choir, and a full chorus .,
Assured us future happiness.   These that
  lead me
Gaze not with wanton eyes upon my bride,
Nor for their service are repaid by me
With jealousies or fears ; nor do they envy
My passage to those pleasures from which
  death
Cannot deter me.   Great sir, pardon me :.
Imagination of the joys I haste to.
Made me forget my duty ; but the form
And ceremony past, I will attend you,
And with our constant resolution feast you ;
Not with coarse cates, forgot as soon as
  tasted,
But such as shall, while you have memory,
Be pleasing to the palate.
  Fran. Be not lost
In what you purpose.   [*Exit.*
  Gaz. Call you this a marriage !
It differs little from hanging ; I cry at it.
  Vitel. See, where my bride appears ! in
  what full lustre !
As if the virgins that bear up her train
Had long contended to receive an honour
Above their births, in doing her this service.
Nor comes she fearful to meet those delights,
Which, once past o'er, immortal pleasures
  follow.
I need not, therefore, comfort or encourage
Her forward steps ; and I should offer wrong
To her mind's fortitude, should I but ask
How she can brook the rough high-going
  sea,
Over whose foamy back our ship, well rigg'd
With hope and strong assurance, must
  transport us.
Nor will I tell her, when we reach the haven,
Which tempests shall not hinder, what loud
  welcome
Shall entertain us ; nor commend the place,
To tell whose least perfection would strike
  dumb
The eloquence of all boasted in story,
Though join'd together.
  Don. 'Tis enough, my dearest,
I dare not doubt you ; as your humble
  shadow,
Lead where you please, I follow.
  Vitel. One suit, sir,
And willingly I cease to be a beggar ;
And that you may with more security hear it,

                                          M

Know, 'tis not life I'll ask, nor to defer .
Our deaths, but a few minutes.
   Asam. Speak ; 'tis granted.
   Vitel. We being now to take our latest
     leave,
And grown of one belief, I do desire
I may have your allowance to perform it,
But in the fashion which we Christians use
Upon the like occasions.
   Asam. 'Tis allow'd of.
   Vitel. My service : haste, Gazet, to the
     next spring,
And bring me of it.
   Gaz. Would I could as well
Fetch you a pardon ; I would not run but fly,
And be here in a moment.   [*Exit.*
   Musta. What's the mystery
Of this ? discover it.
   Vitel. Great sir, I'll tell you.
Each country hath its own peculiar rites :
Some, when they are to die, drink store of
    wine,
Which, pour'd in liberally, does oft beget
A bastard valour, with which arm'd, they bear
The not-to-be declined charge of death
With less fear and astonishment : others take
Drugs to procure a heavy sleep, that so
They may insensibly receive the means
That casts them in an everlasting slumber ;
Others——

     Re-enter Gazet, *with water.*

       O welcome !
   Asam. Now the use of yours ?
   Vitel. The clearness of this is a perfect sign
Of innocence : and as this washes off
Stains and pollutions from the things we
    wear ;
Thrown thus upon the forehead, it hath
    power
To purge those spots that cleave upon the
    mind,   [*Sprinkles it on her face.*
If thankfully received.
   Asam. 'Tis a strange custom.
   Vitel. How do you entertain it, my
    Donusa?
Feel you no alteration, no new motives,
No unexpected aids, that may confirm you
In that to which you were inclined before ?
   Don. I am another woman ;—till this
    minute
I never lived, nor durst think how to die.
How long have I been blind ! yet on the
    sudden,
By this blest means, I feel the films of error
Ta'en from my soul's eyes. O divine phy-
    sician !
That hast bestow'd a sight on me, which
    Death,

Though ready to embrace me in his arms,
Cannot take from me : let me kiss the hand
That did this miracle, and seal my thanks
Upon those lips from whence these sweet
    words vanish'd,
That freed me from the cruellest of prisons,
Blind ignorance and misbelief. False pro-
    phet !
Impostor Mahomet !——
   Asam. I'll hear no more,
You do abuse my favours ; sever them :
Wretch, if thou hadst another life to lose,
This blasphemy deserved it ;—instantly
Carry them to their deaths.
   Vitel. We part now, blest one,
To meet hereafter in a kingdom, where
Hell's malice shall not reach us.
   Paul. Ha ! ha ! ha !
   Asam. What means my mistress ?
   Paul. Who can hold her spleen,
When such ridiculous follies are presented,
The scene, too, made religion ? O, my lord,
How from one cause two contrary effects
Spring up upon the sudden !
   Asam. This is strange.
   Paul. That which hath fool'd her in her
    death, wins me,
That hitherto have barr'd myself from
    pleasure,
To live in all delight.
   Asam. There's music in this.
   Paul. I now will run as fiercely to your
    arms
As ever longing woman did, borne high
On the swift wings of appetite.
   Vitel. O devil !
   Paul. Nay, more ; for there shall be no
    odds betwixt us,
I will turn Turk.
   Gaz. Most of your tribe do so,
When they begin in whore.   [*Aside.*
   Asam. You are serious, lady?
   Paul. Serious !—but satisfy me in a suit
That to the world may witness that I have
Some power upon you, and to-morrow
    challenge
Whatever's in my gift ; for I will be
At your dispose.
   Gaz. That's ever the subscription
To a damn'd whore's false epistle. [*Aside.*
   Asam. Ask this hand,
Or, if thou wilt, the heads of these. I am
    rapt
Beyond myself with joy. Speak, speak,
    what is it ?
   Paul. But twelve short hours' reprieve
for this base couple.
   Asam. The reason, since you hate them ?
   Paul. That I may

Have time to triumph o'er this wretched
  woman.
I'll be myself her guardian; I will feast,
Adorned in her choice and richest jewels :
Commit him to what guards you please.
  Grant this,
I am no more mine own, but yours.
  Asam. Enjoy it ;
Repine at it who dares : bear him safe off
To the black tower, but give him all things
  useful :
The contrary was not in your request ?
  Paul. I do contemn him.
  Don. Peace in death denied me !
  Paul. Thou shalt not go in liberty to thy
  grave ;
For one night a sultana is my slave.
  Musta. A terrible little tyranness !
  Asam. No more ;
Her will shall be a law. Till now ne'er happy !
                          [*Exeunt.*

SCENE IV.—*A Street.*

Enter Francisco, Grimaldi, Master, Boatswain, *and* Sailors.

  Grim. Sir, all things are in readiness ;
  the Turks,
That seized upon my ship, stow'd under
  hatches ;
My men resolved and cheerful. Use but
  means
To get out of the ports, we will be ready
To bring you aboard, and then (heaven be
  but pleased)
This, for the viceroy's fleet !
  Fran. Discharge your parts ;
In mine I'll not be wanting: Fear not,
  master ;
Something will come along to fraught your
  bark,
That you will have just cause to say you
  never
Made such a voyage.
  Must. We will stand the hazard.
  Fran. What's the best hour ?
  Boatsw. After the second watch.
  Fran. Enough ; each to his charge.
  Grim. We will be careful.   [*Exeunt.*

SCENE V.—*A Room in* Asambeg's *Palace.*

Enter Paulina, Donusa, Carazie, *and*
          Manto.

  Paul. Sit, madam, it is fit that I attend
  you ;
And pardon, I beseech you, my rude
  language,
To which the sooner you will be invited,
When you shall understand, no way was
  left me

To free you from a present execution,
But by my personating that which never
My nature was acquainted with.
  Don. I believe you.
  Paul. You will, when you shall under-
  stand I may
Receive the honour to be known unto you
By a nearer name :—and, not to rack you
  further,
The man you please to favour is my brother ;
No merchant, madam, but a gentleman
Of the best rank in Venice.
  Don. I rejoice in't ;
But what's this to his freedom ? for myself,
Were he well off, I were secure.
  Paul. I have
A present means, not plotted by myself,
But a religious man, my confessor,
That may preserve all, if we had a servant
Whose faith we might rely on.
  Don. She, that's now
Your slave, was once mine ; had I twenty
  lives,
I durst commit them to her trust.
  Mant. O madam !
I have been false,—forgive me : I'll re-
  deem it
By anything, however desperate,
You please to impose upon me.
  Paul. Troth, these tears,
I think, cannot be counterfeit ; I believe
  her,
And, if you please, will try her.
  Don. At your peril ;
There is no further danger can look towards
  me.
  Paul. This only then—canst thou use
  means to carry
This bake-meat to Vitelli ?
  Mant. With much ease ;
I am familiar with the guard ; beside,
It being known it was I that betray'd him,
My entrance hardly will of them be ques-
  tion'd.
  Paul. About it then.   Say, that 'twas
  sent to him
From his Donusa ; bid him search the midst
  of it,
He there shall find a cordial.
  Mant. What I do
Shall speak my care and faith.   [*Exit.*
  Don. Good fortune with thee !
  Paul. You cannot eat ?
  Don. The time we thus abuse
We might employ much better.
  Paul. I am glad
To hear this from you. As for you, Carazie,
If our intents do prosper, make choice,
  whether

                                    M 2

You'll steal away with your two mistresses,
Or take your fortune.
    Car. I'll be gelded twice first ;
Hang him that stays behind.
    Paul. I wait you, madam.
Were but my brother off, by the command
Of the doting viceroy there's no guard dare
        stay me ;
And I will safely bring you to the place,
Where we must expect him.
    Don. Heaven be gracious to us ! [*Exeunt.*

SCENE VI.—*A Room in the Black Tower.*
Enter Vitelli, Aga, *and* Guard, *at the door.*

    Vitel. Paulina to fall off thus ! 'tis to me
More terrible than death, and, like an earth-
        quake,
Totters this walking building, such I am ;
And in my sudden ruin would prevent,
By choaking up at once my vital spirits,
This pompous preparation for my death.
But I am lost ; that good man, good Fran-
    cisco,
Deliver'd me a paper, which till now
I wanted leisure to peruse. [*Reads the paper.*
    Aga. This Christian
Fears not, it seems, the near approaching sun,
Whose second rise he never must salute.

    Enter Manto *with the baked-meat.*

    1 *Guard.* Who's that ?
    2 *Guard.* Stand.
    Aga. Manto !
    Mant. Here's the viceroy's ring,
Gives warrant to my entrance ; yet you may
Partake of anything I shall deliver.
'Tis but a present to a dying man,
Sent from the princess that must suffer with
    him.
    Aga. Use your own freedom.
    Mant. I would not disturb
This his last contemplation.
    Vitel. O, 'tis well !
He has restored all, and I at peace again
With my Paulina.
    Mant. Sir, the sad Donusa,
Grieved for your sufferings, more than for
    her own,
Knowing the long and tedious pilgrimage
You are to take, presents you with this
    cordial,
Which privately she wishes you should taste
    of ;
And search the middle part, where you
    shall find
Something that hath the operation to
Make death look lovely.
    Vitel. I will not dispute
What she commands, but serve it.   [*Exit.*

    Aga. Prithee, Manto,
How hath the unfortunate princess spent
    this night,
Under her proud new mistress?
    Mant. With such patience
As it o'ercomes the other's insolence,
Nay, triumphs o'er her pride. My much
    haste now
Commands me hence ; but, the sad tragedy
    past,
I'll give you satisfaction to the full
Of all hath pass'd, and a true character
Of the proud Christian's nature.   [*Exit.*
    Aga. Break the watch up ;
What should we fear i' the midst of our own
    strengths ?
'Tis but the basha's jealousy.   Farewell,
    soldiers !   [*Exeunt.*

SCENE VII.—*An upper Room in the same.*
    Enter Vitelli *with the baked-meat.*

    Vitel. There's something more in this
    than means to cloy
A hungry appetite, which I must discover.
She will'd me search the midst : thus, thus
    I pierce it.
—Ha ! what is this? a scroll bound up in
    packthread !
What may the mystery be ?   [*Reads.*
    *Son, let down this packthread at the west
window of the castle.   By it you shall draw
up a ladder of ropes, by which you may
descend : your dearest Donusa with the rest
of your friends below attend you.   Heaven
prosper you !*
O best of men ! he that gives up himself
To a true religious friend, leans not upon
A false deceiving reed, but boldly builds
Upon a rock ; which now with joy I find
In reverend Francisco, whose good vows,
Labours, and watchings, in my hoped-for
    freedom,
Appear a pious miracle.   I come,
I come with confidence ; though the descent
Were steep as hell, I know I cannot slide,
Being call'd down by such a faithful guide.
    [*Exit.*

SCENE VIII.—*A Room in* Asambeg's
    Palace.
Enter Asambeg, Mustapha, *and* Janizaries.

    Asam. Excuse me, Mustapha, though
    this night to me
Appear as tedious as that treble one
Was to the world, when Jove on fair Alcmena
Begot Alcides. Were you to encounter
Those ravishing pleasures, which the slow-
    paced hours

(To me they are such) bar me from, you would,
With your continued wishes, strive to imp
New feathers to the broken wings of time,
And chide the amorous sun, for too long dalliance
In Thetis' watery bosom.
Musta. You are too violent
In your desires, of which you are yet uncertain ;
Having no more assurance to enjoy them,
Than a weak woman's promise, on which wise men
Faintly rely.
Asam. Tush ! she is made of truth ;
And what she says she will do, holds as firm
As laws in brass, that know no change :
[*A chamber shot off.*
What's this?
Some new prize brought in, sure—

Enter Aga *hastily.*

Why are thy looks
So ghastly? Villain, speak !
Aga. Great sir, hear me,
Then after, kill me :—we are all betray'd.
The false Grimaldi, sunk in your disgrace,
With his confederates, has seized his ship,
And those that guarded it stowed under hatches.
With him the condemn'd princess, and the merchant,
That, with a ladder made of ropes, descended
From the black tower, in which he was enclosed,
And your fair mistress——
Asam. Ha!
Aga. With all their train,
And choicest jewels, are gone safe aboard :
Their sails spread forth, and with a fore-right gale
Leaving our coast, in scorn of all pursuit,
As a farewell, they shew'd a broadside to us.
Musta. Now note your confidence !
Asam. No more.
O my credulity ! I am too full
Of grief and rage to speak. Dull, heavy fool !
Worthy of all the tortures that the frown
Of thy incensed master can throw on thee,
Without one man's compassion ! I will hide
This head among the desarts, or some cave
Fill'd with my shame and me ; where I alone
May die without a partner in my moan.
[*Exeunt.*

The Parliament of Love.

ACT I.

SCENE IV.—*A Room in* Bellisant's *House.*

Enter Chamont *and* Bellisant.

Cham. . . . .
. . . .
I did discharge the trust imposed upon me,
Being your guardian.
Bell. 'Tis with truth acknowledged.
Cham. The love I then bore to you, and desire
To do you all good offices of a friend,
Continues with me, nay, increases, lady ;
And, out of this assurance, I presume,
What, from a true heart, I shall now deliver,
Will meet a gentle censure.
Bell. When you speak,
Whate'er the subject be, I gladly hear.
Cham. To tell you of the greatness of your state,
And from what noble stock you are derived,
Were but impertinence, and a common theme,
Since you well know both. What I am to speak of,
Touches you nearer ; therefore, give me leave
To say, that, howsoever your great bounties,
Continual feasting, princely entertainments,
May gain you the opinion of some few
Of a brave generous spirit, (the best harvest
That you can hope for from such costly seed,)
You cannot yet, amongst the multitude,

(Since, next unto the princes of the blood,
The eyes of all are fix'd on you,) but give
Some wounds, which will not close without a scar,
To your fair reputation, and good name ;
In suffering such a crew of riotous gallants,
Not of the best repute, to be so frequent
Both in your house and presence : this, 'tis rumour'd,
Little agrees with the curiousness of honour,
Or modesty of a maid.
Bell. Not to dwell long
Upon my answer, I must thank your goodness,
And provident care, that have instructed me
What my revenues are, by which I measure
How far I may expend ; and yet I find not
That I begin to waste ; nor would I add
To what I now possess. I am myself ;
And for my fame, since I am innocent here,
This, for the world's opinion !
Cham. Take heed, madam.
That [world's] opinion, which you slight, confirms
This lady for immodest, and proclaims
Another for a modest ; whereas the first
Ne'er knew what loose thoughts were, and the praised second
Had never a cold dream.
Bell. I dare not argue :
But what means to prevent this ?
Cham. Noble marriage.
Bell. Pardon me, sir ; and do not think I scorn

Your grave advice, which I have ever fol-
lowed,
Though not pleased in it.——
Would you have me match with wealth? I
need it not:
Or hunt for honour, and increase of titles?
In truth, I rest ambitious of no greater
Than what my father left. Or do you judge
My blood to run so high, that 'tis not in
Physic to cool me? I yet feel no such heat:
But when, against my will, it grows upon me,
I'll think upon your counsel.
Cham. If you resolve, then,
To live a virgin, you have   .   .
To which you may retire, and ha-   .   .
To   .   .   .   .   .   .
In   .   .   .   .   .   .
And live cont-   .   .   .   .
Bell. What proof
Should I give of my continence, if I lived
Not seen, nor seeing any? Spartan Helen,
Corinthian Lais, or Rome's Messaline,
So mew'd up, might have died as they were
born,
By lust untempted : no, it is the glory
Of chastity to be tempted, tempted home too,
The honour else is nothing! I would be
The first example to convince, for liars,
Those poets, that with sharp and bitter
rhymes
Proclaim aloud, that chastity has no being,
But in a cottage : and so confident
I am in this to conquer, that I will
Expose myself to all assaults ; see masques,
And hear bewitching sonnets ; change dis-
course
With one that, for experience, could teach
Ovid
To write, a better way, his *Art of Love:*
Feed high, and take and give free entertain-
ment,
Lend Cupid eyes, and new artillery,
Deny his mother for a deity ;
Yet every burning shot he made at me,
Meeting with my chaste thoughts, should
lose their ardour ;
Which when I have o'ercome, malicious
men
Must, to their shame, confess it's possible,
For a young lady, (some say fair,) at court,
To keep her virgin honour.
Cham. May you prosper
In this great undertaking! I'll not use
A syllable to divert you : but must be
A suitor in another kind.
Bell. Whate'er it be,
'Tis granted.
Cham. It is only to accept
A present from me.

Bell. Call you this a suit?
Cham. Come in, Calista.

Enter Beaupré, *disguised as a Moorish*
Slave.

                    This is one I would
Bestow upon you.
Bell. 'Tis the handsomest,
I e'er saw of her country ; she hath neither
Thick lips, nor rough curl'd hair.
Cham. Her manners, lady,
Upon my honour, better her good shape :
She speaks our language too, for being sur-
prised
In Barbary, she was bestow'd upon
A pirate of Marseilles, with whose wife
She lived five years, and learn'd it ; there I
bought her,
As pitying her hard usage ; if you please
To make her yours, you may.
Bell. With many thanks.
Come hither, pretty one ; fear not, you shall
find me
A gentle mistress.
Beau. With my care and service,
I'll study to preserve you such.
Bell. Well answered.
Come, follow me ; we'll instantly to court,
And take my guests along.
Chamb. They wait you, madam.
                              [*Exeunt.*

SCENE V.—*A State-room in the Palace.*

Flourish. Enter Charles, Orleans, Nemours,
Philamour, *and* Lafort.

Char. What solitude does dwell about our
court!
Why this dull entertainment? Have I
march'd
Victorious through Italy, enter'd Rome,
Like a triumphant conqueror, set my foot
Upon the neck of Florence, tamed the pride
Of the Venetians, scourged those petty
tyrants,
That   .   .   den of the world, to be
.   .   home, nay, my house neglected!
   (*New Speaker.*)   .   .   the courtiers
   would appear
   .   .   .   therefore they presumed

   (*New Speaker.*)   .   .   the ladies, sir,
.   .   .   that glad time
.   .   .   .   the choice.

Enter Bellisant, Leonora, Lamira, Cla-
rinda, Chamont, Montrose, Cleremond,
Clarindore, Perigot, Novall, *and other*
Courtiers.

Phil. Here they come.

Ladies. All happiness to your majesty!
Courtiers. And victory sit ever on your sword!
Char. Our thanks to all.
But wherefore come you in divided troops,
As if the mistresses would not accept
Their servants' guardship, or the servants, slighted,
Refuse to offer it? You all wear sad looks:
On Perigot appears not that blunt mirth
Which his face used to promise; on Montrose
There hangs a heavy dulness; Cleremond
Droops e'en to death, and Clarindore hath lost
Much of his sharpness; nay, these ladies too,
Whose sparkling eyes did use to fire the court
With various inventions of delight,
Part with their splendour. What's the cause? from whence
Proceeds this alteration?
Peri. I am troubled
With the toothache, or with love, I know not whether;
There is a worm in both. [*Aside.*
Clarin. It is their pride.
Bell. Or your unworthiness.
Cler. The honour that
The French dames held for courtesy, above
All ladies of the earth, dwells not in these,
That glory in their cruelty.
Leon. The desert
The chevaliers of France were truly lords of,
And which your grandsires really did possess,
At no part you inherit.
Bell. Ere they durst
Presume to offer service to a lady,
In person they perform'd some gallant acts:
The fame of which prepared them gracious hearing,
Ere they made their approaches: what coy she, then,
Though great in birth, not to be parallel'd
For nature's liberal bounties, both set off
With fortune's trappings, wealth; but, with delight,
Gladly acknowledged such a man her servant,
To whose heroic courage, and deep wisdom,
The flourishing commonwealth, and thankful king,
Confess'd themselves for debtors? Whereas, now,
If you have travelled Italy, and brought home
Some remnants of the language, and can set
Your faces in some strange and ne'er-seen posture,
Dance a lavolta, and be rude and saucy;

Protest, and swear, and damn, (for these are acts
That most think grace them,) and then view yourselves
In the deceiving mirror of self-love,
You do conclude there hardly is a woman
That can be worthy of you.
Mont. We would grant
We are not equal to our ancestors
In noble undertakings, if we thought,
In us a free confession would persuade you,
Not to deny your own most wilful errors:
And where you tax us for unservice, lady,
I never knew a soldier yet, that could
Arrive into your favour: we may suffer
The winter's frost, and scorching summer's heat,
When the hot lion's breath singeth the fields,
To seek out victory; yet, at our return,
Though honour'd in our manly wounds, well taken,
You say they do deform us, and the loss
Of much blood that way, renders us unfit
To please you in your chambers.
Clarin. I must speak
A little in the general cause: Your beauties
Are charms that do enchant so . . .
. . . .
Knowing that we are fastened in your toils;
In which to struggle, or strive to break out,
Increases the captivity. Never Circe,
Sated with such she purposed to transform,
Or cunning Siren, for whose fatal music
Nought but the hearer's death could satisfy,
Knew less of pity. Nay, I dare go further,
And justify your majesty hath lost
More resolute and brave courageous spirits
In this same dull and languishing fight of love,
Than e'er your wars took from you.
Char. No reply:——
This is a cause we will determine of,
And speedily redress: Tamed Italy,
With fear, confesses me a warlike king,
And France shall boast I am a prince of love.
Shall we, that keep perpetual parliaments
For petty suits, or the least injury
Offer'd the goods or bodies of our subjects,
Not study a cure for the sickness of the mind,
Whose venomous contagion hath infected
Our bravest servants, and the choicest beauties
Our court is proud of? These are wounds require
A kingly surgeon, and the honour worthy
By us to be accepted.
Phil. It would add
To the rest of your great actions.

Laf. But the means
Most difficult, I fear.
    Cham. You shall do more, sir,
If you perform this, than I e'er could read
The sons of Saturn, that by lot divided
The government of the air, the sea, and hell,
Had spirit to undertake.
    Char. Why, this more fires me;
And now partake of my design. With speed
Erect a place of justice near the court,
Which we'll have styled, the PARLIAMENT
OF LOVE:
Here such whose humble service is not con-
    sider'd
By their proud mistresses, freely may com-
    plain;
And shall have hearing and redress.
    Nov. O rare!
    Peri. I like this well.
    Char. And ladies that are wrong'd
By such as do profess themselves their ser-
    vants,
May cite them hither, and their cause de-
    liver'd
Or by their own tongues, or fee'd advocates,
Find sudden satisfaction.
    Nov. What a rascal
Was I to leave the law! I might have had
Clients and clients. Ne'er was such a time
For any smooth-chinn'd advocate.
    Peri. They will get the start
Of the ladies' spruce physicians, starve their
    chaplains,
Though never so well timber'd.
    Char. 'Tis our will,
Nor shall it be disputed. Of this court,
Or rather, sanctuary of pure lovers,
My lord of Orleans, and Nemours, assisted
By the messieurs Philamour and Lafort, are
    judges.
You have worn Venus's colours from your
    youth,
And cannot, therefore, but be sensible
Of all her mysteries: what you shall deter-
    mine,
In the way of penance, punishment, or
    reward,
Shall . the trial; a month we grant you
. . . amours, which expired,
. make your complaints, and be assured
. . impartial hearing; this determined,
. . . rest of our affairs. [*Exeunt.*

        ACT II.

SCENE I.—*A Room in* Clarindore's *House.*
Enter Clarindore, Montrose, Perigot, *and*
    Novall.
    Peri. I do not relish

The last part of the king's speech, though I
    was
Much taken with the first.
    Nov. Your reason, tutor?
    Peri. Why, look you, pupil; the decree,
    that women
Should not neglect the service of their
    lovers,
But pay them from the exchequer they were
    born with,
Was good and laudable; they being created
To be both tractable and tactable,
When they are useful: but to have it order'd,
All women that have stumbled in the dark,
Or given, by owl-light, favours, should com-
    plain,
Is most intolerable: I myself shall have,
Of such as trade in the streets, and scaped
    my pockets,
Of progress laundresses, and marketwomen,
When the king's pleasure's known, a thou-
    sand bills
Preferr'd against me.
    Clarin. This is out of season:
Nothing to madam Bellisant, that, in public,
Hath so inveigh'd against us.
    Nov. She's a Fury,
I dare no more attempt her.
    Peri. I'll not venture
To change six words with her for half her
    state,
Or stay, till she be trimm'd, from wine and
    women,
For any new monopoly.
    Mont. I will study
How to forget her, shun the tempting poison
Her looks, and magic of discourse, still offer,
And be myself again: since there's no hope,
'Twere madness to pursue her.
    Peri. There are madams
Better brought up, 'tis thought, and wives
    that dare not
Complain in parliament; there's safe trading,
    pupil:
And, when she finds she is of all forsaken,
Let my lady Pride repent in vain, and mump,
And envy others' markets.
    Clarin. May I ne'er prosper
But you are three of the most fainting spirits,
That ever I conversed with! You do well
To talk of progress laundresses, punks, and
    beggars;
The wife of some rich tradesman with three
    teeth,
And twice so many hairs:—truck with old
    ladies,
That nature hath given o'er, that owe their
    doctors
For an artificial life, that are so frozen,

That a sound plague cannot thaw them ;
   but despair,
I give you over : never hope to take
A velvet petticoat up, or to commit
With an Italian cutwork smock, when torn
   too.
Mont. And what hopes nourish you?
Clarin. Troth, mine are modest.
I am only confident to win the lady
You dare not look on, and now, in the height
Of her contempt and scorn, to humble her,
And teach her at what game her mother
   play'd,
When she was got ; and, cloy'd with those
   poor toys,
As I find her obedient and pleasing,
I may perhaps descend to marry her :
Then, with a kind of state, I take my chair,
Command a sudden muster of my servants,
And, after two or three majestic hums,
It being known all is mine, peruse my
   writings,
Let out this manor, at an easy rate,
To such a friend, lend this ten thousand
   crowns,
For the redemption of his mortgaged land,
Give to each by-blow I know mine, a farm,
Erect   .   .   . this in conse- .   .
.   .   .   .
That pleased me in my youth, but now
   grown stale.
These things first ordered by me, and con-
   firm'd
By Bellisant, my wife, I care not much
If, out of her own lands, I do assign her
Some pretty jointure.
Peri. Talk'st thou in thy sleep?
Nov. Or art thou mad?
Clarin. A little elevated
With the assurance of my future fortune :
Why do you stare and grin? I know this
   must be,
And I will lay three thousand crowns, within
A month I will effect this.
Mont. How !
Clarin. Give proof
I have enjoy'd fair Bellisant, evident proof
I have pluck'd her virgin rose, so long pre-
   served,
Not, like a play-trick, with a chain or ring
Stolen by corruption, but, against her will,
Make her confess so much.
Mont. Impossible.
Clarin. Then the disgrace be mine, the
   profit yours.
If that you think her chastity a rock
Not to be moved or shaken, or hold me
A flatterer of myself, or overweener,
Let me pay for my foolery.

Peri. I'll engage
Myself for a thousand.
Nov. I'll not out for a second.
Mont. I would gladly lose a third part for
   assurance
No virgin can stand constant long.
Clarin. Leave that
To the trial : let us to a notary,
Draw the conditions, see the crowns de-
   posited,
And then I will not cry, St. Dennis for me !
But—Love, blind archer, aid me !
Peri. Look you thrive ;
I would not be so jeer'd and hooted at,
As you will be else.
Clarin. I will run the hazard. [*Exeunt.*

SCENE II.—*A Room in* Leonora's *House.*

Enter Leonora *and a* Servant.

Serv. He will not be denied.
Leon. Slave, beat him back.
I feed such whelps !——
Serv. Madam, I rattled him,
Rattled him home.
Leon. Rattle him hence, you rascal,
Or never see me more.

Enter Cleremond.

Serv. He comes : a sword !
What would you have me do? Shall I cry
   murder,
Or raise the constable ?
Leon. Hence, you shaking coward !
Serv. I am glad I am so got off : here's
   a round sum [*Looking at his money.*
For a few bitter words ! Be not shook off,
   sir ;
I'll see none shall disturb you. [*Exit.*
Cler. You might spare
These frowns, good lady, on me ; they are
   useless,
I am shot through and through with your
   disdain,
And on my heart the darts of scorn so thick,
That there's no vacant place left to receive
Another wound : their multitude is grown
My best defence, and do confirm me that
You cannot hurt me further.
Leon. Wert thou not
Made up of impudence, and slaved to folly,
Did any drop of noble blood remain
In thy lustful veins, hadst thou or touch, or
   relish,
Of modesty, civility, or manners,
Or but in thy deformed outside only
Thou didst retain the essence of a man,
.   .   .   . so many   .   .   .
.   .   .   .

And loathing to thy person, thou wouldst not
Force from a blushing woman that rude language,
Thy baseness first made me acquainted with.
Cler. Now saint-like patience guard me!
Leon. I have heard
Of mountebanks, that to vent their drugs and oils,
Have so enured themselves to poison, that
They could digest a venom'd toad, or spider,
Better than wholesome viands : in the list
Of such I hold thee ; for that bitterness
Of speech, reproof, and scorn, by her de-livered
Whom thou professest to adore, and shake at,
Which would deter all mankind but thyself,
Do nourish in thee saucy hopes, with pleasure.
Cler. Hear but my just defence.
Leon. Yet, since thou art
So spaniel-like affected, and thy dotage
Increases from abuse and injury,
That way I'll once more feast thee. Of all men
I ever saw yet, in my settled judgment,
Spite of thy barber, tailor, and perfumer,
And thine adulterate and borrow'd helps,
Thou art the ugliest creature ; and when trimm'd up
To the height, as thou imagin'st, in mine eyes,
A leper with a clap-dish, (to give notice
He is infectious,) in respect of thee,
Appears a young Adonis.
Cler. You look on me
In a false glass, madam.
Leon. Then thy dunghill mind,
Suitable to the outside, never yet
Produced one gentle thought, knowing her want
Of faculties to put it into act.
Thy courtship, as absurd as any zany's,
After a practised manner ; thy discourse,
Though full of bombast phrase, never brought matter
Worthy the laughing at, much less the hearing.—
But I grow weary ; for, indeed, to speak thee,
Thy ills I mean, and speak them to the full,
Would tire a thousand women's voluble tongues,
And twice so many lawyers'—for a farewell,
I'll sooner clasp an incubus, or hug
A fork'd-tongued adder, than meet thy em-braces, .
Which, as the devil, I fly from.
Cler. Now you have spent
The utmost of your spleen, I would not say

Your malice, set off to the height with fiction,
Allow me leave, (a poor request, which judges
Seldom deny unto a man condemn d,)
A little to complain : for, being censured,
Or to extenuate, or excuse my guilt,
Were but to wash an Ethiop. How oft,.
with tears,
When the inhuman porter has forbid
My entrance by your most severe commands,
Have these eyes wash'd your threshold !
Did there ever
Come novelty to Paris, rich or rare,
Which but as soon as known was not pre--sented,
Howe'er with frowns refused ? Have I not brought
The braveries of France before your window,.
To fight at barriers, or to break a lance,
Or, in their full career, to take the ring,
To do you honour ? and then, being refused
To speak my grief, my arms, my impresses,
The colours that I wore, in a dumb sorrow
Express'd how much I suffer'd in the rigour
Of your displeasure.
Leon. Two months hence I'll have
The . . . . .
Cler. Stay, best madam,
I am growing to a period.
Leon. Pray you do;
I here shall take a nap else, 'tis so pleasing.
Cler. Then only this : the voice you now contemn,
You once did swear was musical ; you have met too
These lips in a soft encounter, and have·brought
An equal ardour with you : never lived
A happier pair of lovers. I confess,
After you promised marriage, nothing want-ing
But a few days expired, to make me happy,
My violent impatience of delay
Made me presume, and with some amorous·force,
To ask a full fruition of those pleasures
Which sacred Hymen to the world makes·lawful,
Before his torch was lighted ; in this only,
You justly can accuse me.
Leon. Dar'st thou think
That this offence can ever find a pardon,
Unworthy as thou art !
Cler. But you most cruel,
That, in your studied purpose of revenge,
Cast both divine and human laws behind you,.
And only see their rigour, not their mercy.
Offences of foul shape, by holy writ
Are warranted remission, provided
That the delinquent undergo the penance

Imposed upon him by his confessor :
But you, that should be mine, and only can
Or punish or absolve me, are so far
From doing me right, that you disdain to
    hear me.
    Leon. Now I may catch him in my long-
    wish'd toils ;
My hate help me to work it ! [*Aside.*]—To
    what purpose,
Poor and pale spirited man, should I expect
From thee the satisfaction of a wrong, ·
Compared to which, the murder of a brother
Were but a gentle injury ?
    Cler. Witness, heaven,
All blessings hoped by good men, and all
    tortures
The wicked shake at, no saint left unsworn
    by,
That, uncompell'd, I here give up myself
Wholly to your devotion : if I fail
To do whatever you please to command,
To expiate my trespass to your honour,
So that, the task perform'd, you likewise
    swear,
First to forgive, and after marry me, ·
May I endure more sharp and lingering
    torments
Than ever tyrants found out ! may my friends
With scorn, not pity, look upon my suffer-
    ings,
And at my last gasp, in the place of hope,
Sorrow, despair, possess me !
    Leon. You are caught,
Most miserable fool, but fit to be so ;—
And 'tis but justice that thou art delivered
Into her power that's sensible of a wrong,
And glories to revenge it.   Let me study
What dreadful punishment, worthy my fury,
I shall inflict upon thee ; all the malice
Of injured women help me ! Death ? that's
    nothing,
'Tis, to a conscious wretch, a benefit,
And not a penance ; else, on the next tree,
For sport's sake I would make thee hang
    thyself.
    Cler. What have I done?
    Leon. What cannot be recall'd.
To row for seven years in the Turkish gallies?
A flea-biting !   To be sold to a brothel,
Or a common bagnio? that's a trifle too !
. . . Furies, .   .   .
The lashes of their whips pierce through the
    mind.
I'll imitate them :—I have it too.
    Cler. Remember
You are a woman.
    Leon. I have heard thee boast,
That of all blessings in the earth next me,
The number of thy trusty, faithful friends,

Made up thy happiness : out of these, I
    charge thee,
And by thine own repeated oaths conjure thee,
To kill the best deserver.   Do not start ;
I'll have no other penance. Then to practise,
To find some means he that deserves thee
    best,
By undertaking something others fly from :
This done, I am thine.
    Cler. But hear me.
    Leon. Not a syllable :
And till then, never see me.   [*Exit.*
    Cler. I am lost,
Foolishly lost and sunk by mine own base-
    ness :
I'll say only,
With a heart-breaking patience, yet not rave,
Better the devil's than a woman's slave.
    [*Exit.*

SCENE III.—*A Room in* Bellisant's
    House.

Enter Clarindore *and* Beaupré.

    Clarin. Nay, prithee, good Calista—
    Beau. As I live, sir,
She is determined to be private, and charged
    me,
Till of herself she broke up her retirement,
Not to admit a visitant.
    Clarin. Thou art a fool,
And I must have thee learn to know thy
    strength ;
There never was a sure path to the mistress,
But by her minister's help, which I will pay
    for :   [*Gives her his purse.*
But yet this is but trash ; hark in thine ear—
By love ! I like thy person, and will make
Full payment that way ; be thou wise.
    Beau. Like me, sir !
One of my dark complexion !
    Clarin. I am serious :
The curtains drawn, and envious light shut
    out,
The soft touch heightens appetite, and takes
    more
Than colour, Venus' dressing, in the day time,
But never thought on in her midnight revels.
Come, I must have thee mine.
    Beau. But how to serve you ?
    Clarin. Be speaking still my praises to thy
    lady,
How much I love and languish for her
    bounties :
You may remember too, how many madams
Are rivals for me, and, in way of caution,
Say you have heard, when I was wild, how
    dreadful
My name was to a profess'd courtezan,
Still asking more than she could give—

Enter Bellisant.

Beau. My lady !

Bell. Be within call :—

[*Aside, to the* Servants *within.*
How now, Clarindore,
Courting my servant ! Nay, 'tis not my envy—
You now express yourself a complete lover,
That, for variety's sake, if she be woman,
Can change discourse with any.

Clarin. All are foils
I practise on, but when you make me happy
In doing me that honour : I desired
To hear her speak in the Morisco tongue ;
Troth, 'tis a pretty language.

Bell. Yes, to dance to :—
Look now those sweetmeats. [*Exit* Beaupré.

Clarin. How ! by heaven, she aims
To speak with me in private ! [*Aside.*

Bell. Come, sit down ;
Let's have some merry conference.

Clarin. In which . . . .
It . . . .
That my whole life employ'd to do you
service,
At no part can deserve.

Bell. If you esteem it
At such a rate, do not abuse my bounty,
Or comment on the granted privacy, further
Than what the text may warrant ; so you shall
Destroy what I have built.

Clarin. I like not this. [*Aside.*

Bell. This new-erected Parliament of
Love,
It seems, has frighted hence my visitants :
How spend Montrose and Perigot their hours ?
Novall and Cleremond vanish'd in a moment ;
I like your constancy yet.

Clarin. That's good again ;
She hath restored all : [*Aside.*]—Pity them,
good madam ;
The splendour of your house and entertain-
ment,
Enrich'd with all perfections by yourself,
Is too, too glorious for their dim eyes :
You are above their element ; modest fools,
That only dare admire ! and bar them from
Comparing of these eyes to the fairest flowers,
Giving you Juno's majesty, Pallas' wit,
Diana's hand, and Thetis' pretty foot ;
Or, when you dance, to swear that Venus leads
The Loves and Graces from the Idalian green,
And such hyperboles stolen out of playbooks,
They would stand all day mute, and, as you
were
Some curious picture only to be look'd on,
Presume no further.

Bell. Pray you, keep your distance,
And grow not rude.

Clarin. Rude, lady ! manly boldness
Cannot deserve that name ; I have studied
you,
And love hath made an easy gloss upon
The most abstruse and hidden mysteries
Which you may keep conceal'd. You well
may praise
A bashful suitor, that is ravish'd with
A feather of your fan, or if he gain
A riband from your shoe, cries out, *Nil'
ultra !*

Bell. And what would satisfy you ?

Clarin. Not such poor trifles,
I can assure you, lady. Do not I see
You are gamesome, young, and active ? that
you love
A man that, of himself, comes boldly on,
That will not put your modesty to trouble,
To teach him how to feed, when meat's
before him !
That knows that you are flesh and blood, a
creature,
And born with such affections, that, like me,
Now I have opportunity, and your favour,
Will not abuse my fortune ? Should I stand
now
Licking my fingers, cry Ah me ! then kneel,
And swear you were a goddess, kiss the
skirts
Of your proud garments, when I were gone,
I am sure
I should be kindly laugh'd at for a coxcomb ;.
The story made the subject of your mirth,
At your next meeting, when you sit in
council,
Among the beauties.

Bell. Is this possible ?
All due respect forgotten !

Clarin. Hang respect !
Are we not alone ? See, I dare touch this
hand,
And without adoration unglove it.
A spring of youth is in this palm ; here
Cupid,
The moisture turu'd to diamonds, heads his
arrows :
The far-famed English Bath, or German
Spa,
One drop of this will purchase. Shall this
nectar
Run useless, then, to waste ? or . . .
these lips,
That open like the morn, breathing perfumes
On such as dare approach them, be un-
touch'd ?
They must,—nay, 'tis in vain to make resis-
tance,—
Be often kiss'd and tasted : You seem angry
At . . . I have displeased you.

Bell. [*to the* Servants *within.*]   .   .   .
And come prepared, as if some Africk monster,
By force, had broke into my house.

    Enter Servants *with drawn swords.*

  Clarin. How's this?
  Bell. Circle him round with death, and if
he stir,
Or but presume to speak, till I allow it,
His body be the navel to the wheel,
In which your rapiers, like so many spokes,
Shall meet and fix themselves.
  Clarin. Were I off with life,
This for my wager!   [*Aside.*
  Bell. Villain, shake and tremble
At my just anger! Which, of all my actions,
Confined in virtuous limits, hath given life
And birth to this presumption? Hast thou
ever
Observed in me a wanton look or gesture,
Not suiting with a virgin? Have I been
Prodigal in my favours, like so many spokes,
To nourish such attempts? swear, and swear
truly,
What in thy soul thou think'st of me.
  Clarin. As of one
Made up of chastity; and only tried,
Which I repent, what this might work upon
you.
  Bell. The intent deserves not death; but,
sirrah, know
'Tis in my power to look thee dead.
  Clarin. 'Tis granted.
  Bell. I am not so cruel; yet, for this
insolence,
Forbear my house for ever: if you are hot,
You, ruffian-like, may force a parting kiss,
As from a common gamester.
  Clarin. I am cool:—
She's a virago.   [*Aside.*
  Bell. Or you may go boast,
How bravely you came on, to your com-
panions;
I will not bribe your silence: no reply.—
Now thrust him headlong out of doors, and
see
He never more pass my threshold.   [*Exit.*
  Clarin. This comes of
My daring: all hell's plagues light on the
proverb
That says, *Faint heart*——but it is stale.
  Serv. Pray you walk, sir,
We must shew you the way else.
  Clarin. Be not too officious.
I am no bar for you to try your strength on.—
Sit quietly by this disgrace I cannot:
Some other course I must be forced to take,
Not for my wager now, but honour's sake.
           [*Exeunt.*

ACT III.

SCENE I.—*A Room in* Chamont's *House.*

Enter Chamont, Perigot, Novall, Dinant,
Lamira, *and* Clarinda.

  Peri. 'Twas prince-like entertainment.
  Cham. You o'erprize it.
  Din. Your cheerful looks made every dish
a feast,
And 'tis that crowns a welcome.
  Lam. For my part,
I hold society and honest mirth
The greatest blessing of a civil life.
  Cla. Without good company, indeed, all
dainties
Lose their true relish, and, like painted
grapes,
Are only seen, not tasted.·
  Nov. By this light,
She speaks well, too! I'll have a fling at
her:
She is no fit electuary for a doctor:
A coarser julap may well cool his worship;
This cordial is for gallants.   [*Aside.*
  Cham. Let me see,
The night grows old: pray you often be my
guests.
Such as dare come unto a   .   .   .
table,
Although not crack'd with curious delicates,
Have liberty to command it as their own:
I may do the like with you, when you are
married.
  Peri. Yes, 'tis likely,
When there's no forage to be had abroad,
Nor credulous husbands left to father chil-
dren
Of bachelors' begetting; when court wives
Are won to grant variety is not pleasing,
And that a friend at a pinch is useless to
them,
I   .   .   .   .   .   but till then
.   .   .   .
  Cham. You have a merry time of't;—
But we forget ourselves;—Gallants, good
night.
Good master doctor, when your leisure
serves,
Visit my house; when we least need their
art,
Physicians look most lovely.
  Din. All that's in me,
Is at your lordship's service. Monsieur
Perigot,
Monsieur Novall, in what I may be useful,
Pray you command me.
  Nov. We'll wait on you home.
  Din. By no means, sir; good night.
     [*Exeunt all but* Novall *and* Perigot.

Nov. The knave is jealous.

Peri. 'Tis a disease few doctors cure themselves of.

Nov. I would he were my patient !

Peri. Do but practise
To get his wife's consent, the way is easy.

Nov. You may conclude so; for myself,
I grant
I never was so taken with a woman,
Nor ever had less hope.

Peri. Be not dejected ;
Follow but my directions, she's your own :
I'll set thee in a course that shall not fail.—
I like thy choice ; but more of that here-
after :
Adultery is a safe and secret sin ;
The purchase of a maidenhead seldom quits
The danger and the labour : build on this,
He that puts home shall find all women
coming,
The frozen Bellisant ever excepted.
Could you believe the fair wife of Chamont,
A lady never tainted in her honour,
Should, at the first assault, (for till this night
I never courted her,) yield up the fort
That she hath kept so long ?

Nov. 'Tis wondrous strange.
What winning language used you?

Peri. Thou art a child ;
'Tis action, not fine speeches, take a woman.
Pleasure's their heaven ; and he that gives
assurance
That he hath strength to tame their hot
desires,
Is the prevailing orator : she but saw me
Jump over six join'd stools, and after cut
Some forty capers ; tricks that never miss,
In a magnificent masque, to draw the eyes
Of all the beauties in the court upon me,
But straight she wrung my hand, trod on
my toe,
And said my mistress could not but be happy
In such an able servant. I replied
Bluntly, I was ambitious to be hers ;
And she, nor coy, nor shy, straight enter-
tain'd me :
I begg'd a private meeting, it was granted,
The time and place appointed.

Nov. But remember,
Chamont is your friend.

Peri. Now out upon thee, puisne !
As if a man so far e'er loved that title,
But 'twas much more delight and tickling to
him,
To hug himself, and say, This is my cuckold !

Nov. But did he not observe thee ?

Peri. Though he did,
As I am doubtful, I will not desist ;
The danger will endear the sport.

Enter Clarindore.

Nov. Forbear ;
Here's Clarindore.

Peri. We will be merry with him ;
I have heard his entertainment.   Join but
with me,
And we will jeer this self-opinion'd fool
Almost to madness.

Nov. He's already grown
Exceeding melancholy, and some say
That's the first step to frenzy.

Peri. I'll upon him.—
Save you, good monsieur ! no reply ? grown
proud
Of your success? it is not well   .   .

Clar. 'Tis come out ; these goslings
Have heard of my   .   .   .

Nov. We gratulate,
Though we pay for't, your happy entrance to
The certain favours, nay, the sure possession,
Of madam Bellisant.

Clarin. The young whelp too !—
'Tis well, exceeding well.

Peri. 'Tis so, with you, sir ;
But bear it modestly, faith it will become you:
And being arrived at such a lordly revenue,
As this your happy match instates you with,
Two thousand crowns from me, and from
Novall,
Though we almost confess the wager lost,
Will be a small addition.

Nov. You mistake him ;
Nor do I fear, out of his noble nature,
But that he may be won to license us
To draw our venture.

Clarin. Spend your frothy wits,
Do, do ; you snarl, but hurt not.

Nov. O, give leave
To losers for to speak.

Peri. 'Tis a strange fate
Some men are born to, and a happy star
That reigned at your nativity ! it could not
be else,
A lady of a constancy like a rock,
Not to be moved, and held impregnable,
Should yield at the first assault !

Nov. 'Tis the reward
Of a brave daring spirit.

Peri. Tush ! we are dull ;
Abuse our opportunities.

Clarin. Have you done yet ?

Peri. When he had privacy of discourse,
he knew
How to use that advantage ; did he stand
Fawning, and crouching? no; he ran up
boldly,
Told her what she was born to, ruffled her,
Kiss'd her, and toused her :—all the passages

Are at court already; and, 'tis said, a patent
Is granted him, if any maid be chaste,
For him to humble her, and a new name
  given him,
The scornful-virgin tamer.
   Clarin. I may tame
Your buffoon tongues, if you proceed.
   Nov. No anger.
I have heard that Bellisant was so taken with
Your manly courage, that she straight pre-
  pared you
A sumptuous banquet.
   Peri. Yet his enemies
Report it was a blanket.
   Nov. Malice! malice!
She was shewing him her chamber too, and
  call'd for
Perfumes, and cambric sheets.
   Peri. When, see the luck on't!
Against her will, her most unmannerly
  grooms,
For so 'tis rumour'd, took him by the
  shoulders,
And thrust him out of doors.
   Nov. Faith, sir, resolve us;
How was it? we would gladly know the truth,
To stop the mouth of calumny.
   Clarin. Troth, sir, I'll tell you .·
One took me by the nose thus,—and a second
Made bold with me thus—but one word
  more, you shall
Feel new expressions—and so, my gentle
  boobies,
Farewell, and be hang'd.   [*Exit.*
   Nov. We have nettled him.
   Peri. Had we stung him to death, it were
  but justice,
An overweening braggard!
   Nov. This is nothing
To the doctor's wife.
   Peri. Come, we'll consult of it,
And suddenly.   ·
   Nov. I feel a woman's longing
Till I am at it.
   Peri. Never fear; she's thine own, boy.
            [*Exeunt.*

     SCENE II.—*A Street.*

     Enter Cleremond.

   Cler. What have my sins been, heaven?
  yet thy great pleasure
Must not be argued. Was wretch ever bound
On such a black adventure, in which only
To wish to prosper is a greater curse
·Than to .   .   .   . me
Of reason, understanding, and true judgment.
'Twere a degree of comfort to myse'f
I were stark mad; or, like a beast of prey,
Prick'd on by griping hunger, all my thoughts

And faculties were wholly taken up
To cloy my appetite, and could look no
  further:
But I rise up a new example of
Calamity, transcending all before me;
And I should gild my misery with false com-
  forts,
If I compared it with an Indian slave's,
That, with incessant labour to search out
Some unknown mine, dives almost to the
  centre;
And, if then found, not thank'd of his proud
  master.   .
But this, if put into an equal scale
With my unparalleled fortune, will weigh
  nothing;
For from a cabinet of the choicest jewels
That mankind e'er was rich in, whose least
  gem
All treasure of the earth, or what is hid
In Neptune's watery bosom, cannot pur-
  chase,
I must seek out the richest, fairest, purest,
And when by proof 'tis known it holds the
  value,
As soon as found destroy it. O most cruel!
And yet, when I consider of the many
That have professed themselves my friends,
  and vow'd
Their lives were not their own, when my en-
  gagements
Should summon them to be at my devotion,
Not one endures the test; I almost grow
Of the world's received opinion, that holds
Friendship but a mere name, that binds no
  further
Than to the altar—to retire with safety.
Here comes Montrose.

    Enter Montrose *and* Beaupré.

       What sudden joy transports him?
I never saw man rapt so.
   Mon. Purse and all,
And 'tis too little, though it were cramm'd full
With crowns of the sun. O blessed, blessed
  paper!
But made so by the touch of her fair hand.
What shall I answer? Say, I am her creature.
Or, if thou canst find out a word, that may
Express subjection in an humbler style,
Use it, I prithee; add too, her commands
Shall be with as much willingness perform'd,
As I in this fold, this, receive her favours.
   Beau. I shall return so much.
   Mont. And that two hours
Shall bring me to attend her.
   Beau. With all care
And circumstance of service from yourself,
I will deliver it.

Mont. I am still your debtor.

[*Exit* Beaupré.

Cler. I read the cause now clearly ; I'll slip by :
For though, even at this instant, he should prove
Himself, which others' falsehood makes me doubt,
That constant and best friend I go in quest of,
It were inhuman in their birth to strangle
His promising hopes of comfort.

Mont. Cleremond
Pass by me as a stranger ! at a time too
When I am filled with such excess of joy,
So swollen and surfeited with true delight,
That had I not found out a friend, to whom
I might impart them, and so give them vent,
In their abundance they would force a passage,
And let out life together ! Prithee, bear,
For friendship's sake, a part of that sweet burthen
Which I shrink under ; and when thou hast read
Fair Bellisant subscribed, so near my name too,
Observe but that,—thou must, with me, confess,
There cannot be room in one lover's heart
Capacious enough to entertain
Such multitudes of pleasures.

Cler. I joy with you,
Let that suffice, and envy not your blessings;
May they increase ! Farewell, friend.

Mont. How ! no more ?
By the snow white hand that writ these characters,
It is a breach to courtesy and manners,
So coldly to take notice of his good,
Whom you call friend ! See further : here she writes
That she is truly sensible of my sufferings,
And not alone vouchsafes to call me servant,
But to employ me in a cause that much
Concerns her in her honour ; there's a favour !
Are you yet stupid?—and that, two hours hence,
She does expect me in the private walks
Neighbouring the Louvre : cannot all this move you ?
I could be angry. A tenth of these bounties
But promised to you from Leonora,
To witness my affection to my friend,
In his behalf had taught me to forget,
All mine own miseries.

Cler. Do not misinterpret
This coldness in me ; for alas ! Montrose,
I am a thing so made up of affliction,
So every way contemn'd, that I conclude

My sorrows are infectious ; and my company,
Like such as have foul ulcers running on them,
To be with care avoided. May your happiness,
In the favour of the matchless Bellisant,
Hourly increase ! and—my best wishes guard you !
'Tis all that I can give.

Mont. You must not leave me.

Cler. Indeed I must and will ; mine own engagements
Call me away.

Mont. What are they ? I presume
There cannot be a secret of that weight,
You dare not trust me with ; and should you doubt me,
I justly might complain that my affection
Is placed unfortunately.

Cler. I know you are honest ;
And this is such a business, and requires
Such sudden execution, that it cannot
Fall in the compass of your will, or power,
To do me a friend's office. In a word,
On terms that near concern me in mine honour,
I am to fight the quarrel, mortal too,
The time some two hours hence, the place
ten miles
Distant from Paris ; and when you shall know
I yet am unprovided of a second,
You will excuse my sudden parting from you.
Farewell, Montrose !

Mont. Not so ; I am the man
Will run the danger with you ; and must tell you,
That, while I live, it was a wrong to seek
Another's arm to second you. Lead the way ;
My horse stands ready.

Cler. I confess 'tis noble,
For you to offer this, but it were base
In me to accept it.

Mont. Do not scorn me, friend.

Cler. No ; but admire and honour you ;
and from that
Serious consideration, must refuse
The tender of your aid. France knows you valiant,
And that you might, in single opposition,
Fight for a crown ; but millions of reasons
Forbid me your assistance. You forget
Your own designs ; being, the very minute
I am to encounter with mine enemy,
To meet your mistress, such a mistress too,
Whose favour you so many years have sought :
And will you then, when she vouchsafes access,
Nay more, invites you, check at her fair offer?
Or shall it be repeated, to my shame,
For my own ends I robb'd you of a fortune
Princes might envy? Can you even hope

N

She ever will receive you to her presence,
If you neglect her now?—Be wise, dear friend,
And, in your prodigality of goodness,
Do not undo yourself. Live long and happy,
And leave me to my dangers.

Mont. Cleremond,
I have with patience heard you, and con-
    sider'd
The strength of your best arguments;
    weigh'd the dangers
I run in mine own fortunes : but again,
When I oppose the sacred name of friend
Against those joys I have so long pursued,
Neither the beauty of fair Bellisant,
Her wealth, her virtues, can prevail so far,
In such a desperate case as this, to leave
    you.——
To have it to posterity recorded,
At such a time as this I proved true gold,
And current in my friendship, shall be to me
A thousand mistresses, and such embraces
As leave no sting ·behind them ; therefore,
    on :
I am resolved, unless you beat me off,
I will not leave you.

Cler. Oh ! here is a jewel
Fit for the cabinet of the greatest monarch !
But I of all men miserable——

Mont. Come, be cheerful ;
Good fortune will attend us.

Cler. That, to me,
To have the greatest blessing, a true friend,
Should be the greatest curse!—Be yet advised.

Mont. It is in vain.

Cler. That e'er I should have cause
To wish you had loved less !

Mont. The hour draws on :
We'll talk more as we ride.

Cler. Of men most wretched !   [*Exeunt.*

SCENE III.—*A Room in* Bellisant's *House.*

Enter Bellisant *and* Beaupré.

Bell. Nay, pray you, dry your eyes, or
    your sad story,
Whose every accent still, methinks, I hear,
'Twas with such passion, and such grief de-
    liver'd,
Will make mine bear yours company. All
    my fear is,
The rigorous repulse this worst of men,
False, perjured Clarindore—I am sick to
    name him—
Received at his last visit, will deter him
From coming again.

Beau. No ; he's resolved to venture ;
And has bribed me, with hazard of your anger,
To get him access, but in another shape :
The time prefix'd draws near too.

Bell. 'Tis the better.   [*Knocking within.*
One knocks.

Beau. I am sure 'tis he.·

Bell. Convey him in ;
But do it with a face of fear :
                        [*Exit* Beaupré.
                        I cannot
Resolve yet with what looks to entertain him.
You Powers that favour innocence, and
    revenge
Wrongs done by such as scornfully deride
Your awful names, inspire me !
                        [*Walks aside.*

Re-enter Beaupré *with* Clarindore *disguised.*

Beau. Sir, I hazard
My service, in this action.

Clarin. Thou shalt live
To be the mistress of thyself and others,
If that my projects hit : all's at the stake now;
And as the die falls, I am made most happy,
Or past expression wretched.

Bell. Ha ! who's that?
What bold intruder usher you?   This rude-
    ness !—
From whence? what would he ?

Beau. He brings letters, madam,
As he says, from lord Chamont.

Clarin. How her frowns fright me !

Bell. From lord Chamont ?   Are they of
    such import,
That you, before my pleasure be enquired,
Dare bring the bearer to my private chamber ?
No more of this : your packet, sir ?

Clarin. The letters
Deliver'd to my trust and faith are writ
In such mysterious and dark characters,
As will require the judgment of your soul,
More than your eye, to read and understand
    them.

Bell. What riddle's this? [*Discovering*
Clarin.]—Ha ! am I then contemn'd ?
Dare you do this, presuming on my soft
And gentle nature ?—Fear not, I must shew
A seeming anger. [*Aside to* Beaupré.]—
    What new boist'rous courtship,
After your late loose language, and forced
    kiss,
Come you to practise?   I know none be-·
    yond it.
If you imagine that you may commit
A rape in mine own house, and that my
    servants
Will stand tame lookers on——

Clarin. If I bring with me
One thought, but of submission and sorrow,
Or nourish any hope, but that your goodness
May please to sign my pardon, may I perish
In your displeasure ! which, to me, is more

Than fear of hell hereafter. I confess,
The violence I offered to your sweetness,
In my presumption, with lips impure,
To force a touch from yours, a greater crime
Than if I should have mix'd lascivious flames
With those chaste fires that burn at Dian's
 altar.
That 'twas a plot of treason to your virtues,
To think you could be tempted, or believe
You were not fashion'd in a better mould,
And made of purer clay, than other women.
Since you are, then, the phœnix of your time,
And e'en now, while you bless the earth,
 partake
Of their angelical essence, imitate
Heaven's aptness to forgive, when mercy's
 sued for,
And once more take me to ycur grace and
 favour.
Bell. What charms are these ! What an
 enchanting tongue !
What pity 'tis, one that can speak so well,
Should, in his actions, be so ill !
Beau. Take heed,
Lose not yourself.
Bell. So well, sir, you have pleaded,
And like an advocate, in your own cause,
That, though your guilt were greater, I ac-
 quit you,
The fault no more remember'd ; and for proof,
My heart partakes in my tongue, thus seal
 your pardon ; [*Kisses him.*
And with this willing favour (which forced
 from me,
Cail'd on my anger) make atonement with
 you.
Clarin. If I dream now, O, may I never
 wake,
But slumber thus ten ages !
Bell. Till this minute,
You ne'er to me look'd lovely.
Clarin. How !
Bell. Nor have I
E'er seen a man, in my opinion, worthy
The bounty I vouchsafe you ; therefore fix
 here,
And make me understand that you can bear
Your fortune modestly.
Clarin. I find her coming :
This kiss was but the prologue to the play,
And not to seek the rest, were cowardice.
Help me, dissimulation ! [*Aside.*]—Pardon,
 madam,
Though now, when I should put on cheerful
 looks,
In being blest with what I durst not hope for,
I change the comic scene, and do present
 you
With a most tragic spectacle.

Bell. Heaven avert
This prodigy ! What mean you ?
Clarin. To confirm,
In death, how truly I have loved. I grant
Your favours done me, yield this benefit,
As to make way for me to pass in peace
To my long rest ; what I have tasted from you,
Informs me only of the much I want :
For in your pardon, and the kiss vouchsafed
 me,
You did but point me out a fore-right way
To lead to certain happiness, and then will'd
 me
To move no further. Pray you, excuse me,
 therefore,
Though I desire to end a lingering torment.
And, if you please, with your fair hand, to
 make me
A sacrifice to your chastity, I will meet
The instrument you make choice of, with
 more fervour
Than ever Cæsar did, to hug the mistress,
He doated on, plumed Victory : but if that
You do abhor the office, as too full
Of cruelty, and horror, yet give leave,
That, in your presence, I myself may be
Both priest and offering. [*Draws his sword.*
Bell. Hold, hold, frantic man !
The shrine of love shall not be bathed in blood.
Women, though fair, were made to bring
 forth men,
And not destroy them ; therefore, hold, I say !
I had a mother, and she look'd upon me
As on a true epitome of her youth :
Nor can I think I am forbid the comfort
To bring forth little models of myself,
If heaven be pleased (my nuptial joys per-
 form'd)
To make me fruitful.
Clarin. Such celestial music
Ne'er blest these ears. O ! you have argued
 better
For me, than I could for myself.
Bell. For you !
What, did I give you hope to be my husband ?
Clarin. Fallen off again ! [*Aside.*
Bell. Yet since you have given sure proof
Of love and constancy, I'll unmask those
 thoughts,
That long have been conceal'd ; I am yours,
 but how ?
In an honourable way.
Clarin. I were more than base,
Should I desire you otherwise.
Bell. True affection
Needs not a contract : and it were to doubt me,
To engage me further ; yet, my vow expired,
Which is, to live a virgin for a year,
Challenge my promise.

Clarin. For a year! O, madam!
Play not the tyranness; do not give me hopes,
And in a moment change them to despair.
A year! alas, this body, that's all fire,
If you refuse to quench it with your favour,
Will in three days be cinders; and your mercy
Will come too late then. Dearest lady,
marriage
Is but a ceremony; and a hurtful vow
Is in the breach of it better commended,
Than in the keeping. O l I burn, I burn;
And if you take not pity, I must fly
To my last refuge. [*Offers to stab himself.*
Bell. Hold! Say I could yield
This night, to satisfy you to the full,
And you should swear, until the wedding day,
To keep the favours I now grant conceal'd;
You would be talking.
Clarin. May my tongue rot out, then!
Bell. Or boast to your companions of
your conquest,
And of my easiness.
Clarin. I'll endure the rack first.
Bell. And, having what you long for, cast
me off,
As you did madam Beaupré.
Clarin. May the earth
First gape, and swallow me!
Bell. I'll press you no further.
Go in, your chamber's ready: if you have
A bedfellow, so: but silence I enjoin you,
And liberty to leave you when I please:
I blush, if you reply.
Clarin. Till now ne'er happy! [*Exit.*
Beau. What means your ladyship?
Bell. Do not ask, but do
As I direct you: though as yet we tread
A rough and thorny way, faint not; the ends
I hope to reach shall make a large amends.
[*Exeunt.*

ACT IV.

SCENE I.—*A Room in* Dinaut's *House.*

Enter Novall *and* Dinant.

Din. You are welcome first, sir; and that
spoke, receive
A faithful promise, all that art, or long
Experience, hath taught me, shall enlarge
Themselves for your recovery.
Nov. Sir, I thank you,
As far as a weak, sick, and unable man
Has power to express; but what wants in
my tongue,
My hand (for yet my fingers feel no gout)
Shall speak in this dumb language.
[*Gives him his purse.*
Din. You are too magnificent.

Nov. Fie! no, sir; health is, sure, a
precious jewel,
We cannot buy it too dear.
Din. Take comfort, sir;
I find not, by your urine, nor your pulse,
Or any outward symptom, that you are
In any certain danger.
Nov. Oh! the more my fear:
Infirmities that are known are   .   .   .
cured,
But when the causes of them are conceal'd,
As these of mine are, doctor, they prove
mortal:
Howe'er, I'll not forget you while I live,
Do but your parts.
Din. Sir, they are at your service.
I'll give you some preparatives, to instruct me
Of your inward temper; then, as I find
cause,
Some gentle purge.
Nov. Yes, I must purge; I die else:
But where, dear doctor, you shall not find
out.
This is a happy entrance, may it end well!
I'll mount your nightcap, Doddipol. [*Aside.*
Din. In what part,
(We are sworn to secrecy, and you must be
free,)
Do you find your greatest agony?
Nov. Oh! I have
Strange motions on the sudden; villainous
tumours,
That rise, then fall, then rise again; oh,
doctor!
Not to be shewn or named.
Din. Then, in my judgment,
You had best leave Paris: choose some
fresher air;
That does help much in physic.
Nov. By no means.
Here, in your house, or no where, you must
cure me:
The eye of the master fats the horse; and
when
His doctor's by, the patient may drink wine
In a fit of a burning fever: for your presence
Works more than what you minister. Take
physic,
Attended on by ignorant grooms, mere
strangers
To your directions, I must hazard life,
And you your reputation! whereas, sir,
I hold your house a college of your art,
And every boy you keep, by you instructed,
A pretty piece of a Galenist: then the
females,
From your most fair wife to your kitchen
drudge,
Are so familiar with your learned courses,

That, to an herb, they know to make thin
  broth ?
Or, when occasion serves, to cheer the heart,
And such ingredient I shall have most need of,
How many cocks o' the game make a strong
  cullis,
Or pheasant's eggs a caudle.
  Din. I am glad
To hear you argue with such strength.

  Enter Clarinda, *and whispers* Dinant.

  Nov. A flash, sir :
But now I feel my fit again.—She is
Made up of all perfection ; any danger
That leads to the enjoying so much sweetness
Is pleasure at the height : I am ravish'd with
The mere imagination.   O happiness !—
                                [Aside.
  Din. How's this ! One from the duke
  Nemours ?
  Cla. Yes, sir.
  Din. 'Tis rank :
The sight of my wife hath forced him to
  forget
To counterfeit : [*Aside.*]—I now guess at
  your sickness,
And if I fit you not——
  Cla. The gentleman stays you.
  Din. I come to him presently ; in the
  meantime, wife,
Be careful of this monsieur ; nay, no coyness,
You may salute him boldly ; his pale lips
Enchant not in the touch.
  Nov. Hers do, I'm sure.
  Din. Kiss him again.
  Cla. Sir, this is more than modest.
  Din. Modest ! why, fool, desire is dead
  in him :
Call it a charitable, pious work,
If it refresh his spirits.
  Nov. Yes, indeed, sir.
I find great ease in it.
  Din. Mark that ! and would you
Deny a sick man comfort ? meat's against
  .   .   .   physic, must be granted too,
  .   .   .   wife   .   .   you shall,
In person, wait on him ; nay, hang not off,
I say you shall : this night, with your own
  hands,
I'll have you air his bed, and when he eats
Of what you have prepared, you shall sit by
  him,
And, with some merry chat, help to repair
Decayed appetite ; watch by him when he
  slumbers ;
Nay, play his page's part : more, I durst
  trust you,
Were this our wedding day, you yet a virgin,
To be his bedfellow ; for well I know

Old Priam's impotence, or Nestor's hernia is
Herculean activeness, if but compared
To his debility : put him to his oath,
He'll swear he can do nothing.
  Nov. Do ! O no, sir ;
I am past the thought of it.
  Din. But how do you like
The method I prescribe ?
  Nov. Beyond expression :
Upon the mere report I do conceive
Hope of recovery.
  Cla. Are you mad ?
  Din. Peace, fool.
This night you shall take a cordial to
  strengthen
Your feeble limbs :—'twill cost ten crowns a
  draught.
  Nov. No matter, sir.
  Din. To-morrow you shall walk
To see my garden ; then my wife shall show
  you
The choice rooms of my house ; when you'
  are weary,
Cast yourself on her couch.
  Nov. Oh, divine doctor !
What man in health would not be sick, on
  purpose
To be your patient ?
  Din. Come, sir, to your chamber ;
And now I understand where your disease
  lies,
(Nay, lead him by the hand,) doubt not I'll
  cure you.   [*Exeunt.*

SCENE II.—*An open part of the Country
            near Paris.*

  Enter Cleremond *and* Montrose.

  Cler. This is the place.
  Mont. An even piece of ground,
Without advantage ; but be jocund, friend :
The honour to have entered first the field,
However we come off, is ours.
  Cler. I need not,
So well I am acquainted with your valour,
To dare, in a good cause, as much as man,
Lend you encouragement ; and should I add,
Your power to do, which Fortune, howe'er
  blind,
Hath ever seconded, I cannot doubt
But victory still sits upon your sword,
And must not now forsake you.
  Mont. You shall see me
Come boldly up ; nor will I shame your'
  cause,
By parting with an inch of ground not
  bought
With blood on my part.
  Cler. 'Tis not to be question'd :

That which I would entreat, (and pray you
   grant it,)
Is, that you would forget your usual softness,
Your foe being at your mercy; it hath been
A custom in you, which I dare not praise,
Having disarm'd your enemy of his sword,
To tempt your fate, by yielding it again;
Then run a second hazard.
   Mont. When we encounter
A noble foe, we cannot be too noble.
   Cler. That I confess; but he that's now
   to oppose you,
I know for an archvillain; one that hath lost
All feeling of humanity, one that hates
Goodness in others, 'cause he's ill himself;
A most ungrateful wretch, (the name's too
   gentle,
All attributes of wickedness cannot reach
   him,)
Of whom to have deserved, beyond example,
Or precedent of friendship, is a wrong
Which only death can satisfy.
   Mont. You describe
A monster to me.
   Cler. True, Montrose, he is so.
Afric, though fertile of strange prodigies,
Never produced his equal! be wise, therefore,
And if he fall into your hands, dispatch him:
Pity to him is cruelty. The sad father,
That sees his son stung by a snake to death,
May, with more justice, stay his vengeful
   hand,
And let the worm escape, than you vouch-
   safe him
A minute to repent: for 'tis a slave
So sold to hell and mischief; that a traitor
To his most lawful prince, a church-robber,
A parricide, who, when his garners are
Cramm'd with the purest grain, suffers his
   parents,
Being old, and weak, to starve for want of
   bread;
Compared to him, are innocent.
   Mont. I ne'er heard
Of such a cursed nature; if long-lived,
He would infect mankind: rest you assured,
He finds from me small courtesy.
   Cler. And expect
As little from him: blood is that he thirsts
   for,
Not honourable wounds.
   Mont. I would I had him
Within my sword's length!
   Cler. Have thy wish: Thou hast!
      [*Cleremond draws his sword.*
Nay, draw thy sword, and suddenly; I am
That monster, temple-robber, parricide,
Ingrateful wretch; friend-hater, or what else
Makes up the perfect figure of the devil,

Should he appear like man. Banish amaze-
   ment,
And call thy ablest spirits up to guard thee
From him that's turn'd a Fury. I am made
Her minister, whose cruelty but named,
Would with more horror strike the pale-
   cheek'd stars,
Than all those dreadful words which con-
   jurors use,
To fright their damn'd familiars. Look not
   on me
As I am Cleremond; I have parted with
The essence that was his, and entertain'd
The soul of some fierce tigress, or a wolf's
New-hang'd for human slaughter, and 'tis fit:
I could not else be an apt instrument
To bloody Leonora.
   Mont. To my knowledge
I never wrong'd her.
   Cler. Yes, in being a friend
To me she hated, my best friend; her malice
Would look no lower:—and for being such,
By her commands, Montrose, I am to kill
   thee.
Oh, that thou hadst, like others, been all
   words,
And no performance! or that thou hadst
   made
Some little stop in thy career of kindness!
Why would'st thou, to confirm the name of
   friend,
Despise the favours of fair Bellisant,
And all those certain joys that waited for
   thee?
Snatch at this fatal offer of a second,
Which others fled from?—'Tis in vain to
   mourn now,
When there's no help; and therefore, good
   Montrose,
Rouse thy most manly parts, and think thou
   stand'st now
A champion for more than king or country;
Since, in thy fall, goodness itself must suffer.
Remember too, the baseness of the wrong
   . . . . friendship; let it edge thy sword,
And kill compassion in thee; and forget not
I will take all advantages: and so,
Without reply have at thee!
      [*They fight.* Cleremond *falls.*
   Mont. See, how weak
An ill cause is! you are already fallen:
What can you look for now?
   Cler. Fool, use thy fortune:
And so he counsels thee, that, if we had
Changed places, instantly would have cut
   thy throat,
Or digg'd thy heart out.
   Mont. In requital of
That savage purpose, I must pity you;

Witness these tears, not tears of joy for con-
quest,
But of true sorrow for your misery.
Live, O live, Cleremond, 'and, like a man,
Make use of reason, as an exorcist
To cast this devil out, that does abuse you ;
This fiend of false affection.
  Cler. Will you not kill me ?
You are then more tyrannous than Leonora.
An easy thrust will do it : you had ever
A charitable hand ; do not deny me,
For our old friendship's sake : no ! will 't
  not be ?
There are a thousand doors to let out life ;
You keep not guard of all : and I shall find,
By falling headlong from some rocky cliff,
Poison, or fire, that long rest which your
  sword
Discourteously denies me.   [*Exit.*
  Mont. I will follow ;
And something I must fancy, to dissuade
  him
From doing sudden violence on himself :
That's now my only aim ; and that to me,
Succeding well, is a true victory. [*Exit.*

SCENE III.—Paris. *An outer Room in*
    Chamont's *House.*

Enter Chamont *disguised, and* Dinant.

  Din. Your lady tempted too !
  Cham. And tempted home ;
Summon'd to parley, the fort almost yielded,
Had not I stepp'd in 'to remove the siege :
But I have countermined his works, and if
You second me, will blow the letcher up,
And laugh to see him caper.
  Din. Anything :
Command me as your servant, to join with
  you ;
All ways are honest we take, to revenge us
On these lascivious monkies of the court,
That make it their profession to dishonour
Grave citizens' wives ; nay, those of higher
  rank,
As 'tis, in yours, apparent. My young
  rambler,
That thought to cheat me with a feign'd
  disease,
I have in the toil already ; I have given him,
Under pretence to make him high and active,
A cooler :—I dare warrant it will yield
Rare sport to see it work ; I would your lord-
  ship
Could be a spectator.
  Cham. It is that I aim at :
And might I but persuade you to dispense
A little with your candour, and consent
To make your house the stage, on which
  we'll act

A comic scene ; in the pride of all their hopes,
We'll show these shallow fools sunk-eyed
  despair,
And triumph in their punishment.
  Din. My house,
Or whatsoever else is mine, shall serve
As properties to grace it.
  Cham. In this shape, then,
Leave me to work the rest.
  Din. Doubt not, my lord,
You shall find all things ready.   [*Exit.*

Enter Perigot.

  Cham. This sorts well
With my other purposes. Perigot ! to my
  wish.
Aid me, invention !
  Peri. Is the quean fallen off ?
I hear not from her ?—'tis the hour and place
That she appointed.
What have we here ? This fellow has a
  pimp's face,
And looks as if he were her call, her fetch——
With me ?
  Cham. Sir, from the party,
The lady you should truck with, the lord's
  wife
Your worship is to dub, or to make free
Of the company of the horners.
  Peri. Fair Lamira ?
  Cham. The same, sir.
  Peri. And how, my honest squire o'
  dames ? I see
Thou art of her privy council.
  Cham. Her grant holds, sir.
  Peri. O rare ! But when ?
  Cham. Marry, instantly.
  Peri. But where ?
  Cham. She hath outgone the cunning of
  a woman,
In ordering it both privately and securely :
You know Dinant, the doctor ?
  Peri. Good.
  Cham. His house
And him she has made at her devotion, sir.
Nay, wonder not ; most of these empirics
Thrive better by connivance in such cases,
Than their lame practice ; framing some dis-
  temper,
The fool, her lord——
  Peri. Lords may be what they please ;
I question not their patent.
  Cham. Hath consented,
That this night, privately, she shall take a
  clyster ;
Which he believes the doctor ministers,
And never thinks of you.
  Peri. A good wench still.
  Cham. And there, without suspicion——

Peri. Excellent !
I make this lord my cuckold?
Cham. True ; and write
The reverend drudging doctor, my copartner,
And fellow bawd : next year we will have
   him warden
Of our society.
Peri. There ! there ! I shall burst,
I am so swollen with pleasure ; no more
   talking,
Dear keeper of the vaulting door ; lead on.
Cham. Charge you as boldly.
Peri. Do not fear ; I have
A staff to taint, and bravely.
Cham. Save the splinters,
If it break in the encounter.
Peri. Witty rascal !   ·   [*Exeunt.*

SCENE IV.—*A room in* Bellisant's *House.*

Enter Clarindore, Bellisant, *and* Beaupré.

Clarin. Boast of your favours, madam !
Bell. Pardon, sir,
My fears, since it is grown a general custom,
In our hot youth, to keep a catalogue
Of conquests this way got ; nor do they think
Their victory complete, unless they publish,
To their disgrace, that are made captives to
   them,
How far they have prevail'd.
Clarin. I would have such rascals
First gelded, and then hang'd.
Bell. Remember too, sir,
To what extremities your love had brought
   you ;
And, since I saved your life, I may, with
   justice,
By silence charge you to preserve mine
   honour ;
Which, howsoever to my conscious self
I am tainted, foully tainted, to the world
I am free from all suspicion.
Clarin. Can you think
I'll do myself that wrong? although I had
A lawyer's mercenary tongue, still moving,
. . le this precious carcanet, these jewels,
. . of your magnificence, would keep me
A Pythagorean, and ever silent.
No, rest secure, sweet lady ; and excuse
My sudden and abrupt departure from you :
And if the fault makes forfeit of your grace,
A quick return shall ransome and redeem it.
Bell. Be mindful of your oaths.
          [*Walks aside with* Beaupré.
Clarin. I am got off,
And leave the memory of them behind me.
Now, if I can find out my scoffing gulls,
Novall and Perigot, besides my wager,
Which is already sure, I shall return

Their bitter jests, and wound them with my
   tongue,
Much deeper than my sword. Oh ! but the
   oaths
I have made to the contrary, and her credit,
Of which I should be tender :—tush ! both
   hold
With me an equal value. The wise say,
That the whole fabric of a woman's lighter
Than wind or feathers : what is then her
   fame?
A kind of nothing ;—not to be preserved
With the loss of so much money : 'tis sound
   doctrine
And I will follow it.   [*Exit.*
Bell. Prithee, be not doubtful ;
Let the wild colt run his course.
Beau. I must confess
I cannot sound the depth of what you pur-
   pose,
But I much fear——
Bell. That he will blab ; I know it,
And that a secret scalds him : that he suffers
Till he hath vented what I seem to wish
He should conceal ;—but let him, I am
   arm'd for't.   [*Exeunt.*

SCENE V.—*A Room in* Dinaut's *House.*

Enter Chamont, Diuant, Lamira, Clarinda,
         and Servants.

Cham. For Perigot, he's in the toil ne'er
   doubt it.
O, had you seen how his veins swell'd with
   lust,
When I brought him to the chamber ! how
   he gloried,
And stretch'd his limbs, preparing them for
   action ;
And, taking me to be a pander, told me
'Twas more delight to have a lord his cuckold,
Than to enjoy my lady !—there I left him
In contemplation, greedily expecting
Lamira's presence ; but, instead of her,
I have prepared him other visitants.——
You know what you have to do?
   1 *Serv.* Fear not, my lord,
He shall curvet, I warrant him, in a blanket.
   2 *Serv.* We'll discipline him with dog-
   whips, and take off
His rampant edge.
Cham. His life ; save that—remember,
You cannot be too cruel.
Din. For his pupil,
My wife's Inamorato, if cold weeds,
Removed but one degree from deadly poison,
Have not forgot their certain operation,
You shall see his courage cool'd ; and in
   that temper,

Till he have howl'd himself into my pardon,
I vow to keep him.
Nov. [*within.*] Ho, doctor! master doctor!
Din. The game's afoot; we will let slip: conceal
Yourselves a little. [*Exeunt all but* Dinant.

Enter Novall.

Nov. Oh! a thousand agues
Play at barley-break in my bones; my blood's
a pool
On the sudden frozen, and the isicles
Cut every vein: 'tis here, there, everywhere;
Oh dear, dear, master doctor!
Din. I must seem
Not to understand him; 'twill increase his
torture.— [*Aside.*
How do you, sir? has the potion wrought?
do you feel
An alteration? have your swellings left you?
Is your blood still rebellious?
Nov. Oh, good doctor,
I am a ghost! I have nor flesh, nor blood,
Nor heat, nor warmth, about me.
Din. Do not dissemble;
I know you are high and jovial.
Nov. Jovial! doctor;
No, I am all amort, as if I had lain
Three days in my grave already.
Din. I will raise you:
For, look you, sir, you are a liberal patient,
Nor must I, while you can be such, part with
you;
'Tis against the laws of our college. Pray
you, mark me;
I have with curiosity consider'd
Your constitution to be hot and moist,
And that at your nativity Jupiter
And Venus were in conjunction, whence it
follows,
By necessary consequence, you must be
A most insatiate letcher.
Nov. Oh! I have been,
I have been, I confess: but now I cannot
Think of a woman.
Din. For your health you must, sir,
Both think, and see, and touch; you're but
a dead man else.
Nov. That way, I am already.
Din. You must take,
And suddenly ('tis a conceal'd receipt),
A buxom, juicy wench.
Nov. Oh! 'twill not down, sir;
I have no swallow for't.
Din. Now, since I would
Have the disease as private as the cure,
(For 'tis a secret,) I have wrought my wife
To be both physic and physician,
To give you ease :—will you walk to her?

Nov. Oh! doctor,
I cannot stand; in every sense about me
I have the palsy, but my tongue.
Din. Nay then,
You are obstinate, and refuse my gentle offer;
Or else 'tis foolish modesty :—Come hither;
Come, my Clarinda,

Re-enter Clarinda.

'tis not common courtesy;
Comfort the gentleman.
Nov. This is ten times worse.
Cham. [*within.*] He does torment him
rarely.
Din. She is not coy, sir.
What think you, is not this a pretty foot,
And a clean instep? I will leave the calf
For you to find and judge of: here's a hand
too;
Try it, the palm is moist; the youthful blood
Runs strong in every azure vein: the face too
Ne'er knew the help of art; and, all together,
May serve the turn, after a long sea-voyage,
For the captain's self.
Nov. I am a swabber, doctor,
A bloodless swabber; have not strength
enough
To cleanse her poop.
Din. Fie! you shame yourself,
And the profession of your rutting gallants,
That hold their doctors' wives as free for
them,
As some of us do our apothecaries'!
Nov. Good sir, no more.
Din. Take her aside; cornute me;
I give you leave: what should a quacksalve,
A fellow that does deal with drugs, as I do,
That has not means to give her choice of
gowns,
Jewels, and rich embroidered petticoats,
Do with so fair a bedfellow? she being
fashion'd
To purge a rich heir's reins, to be the
mistress
Of a court gallant? Did you not tell her so?
Nov. I have betray'd myself! I did, I did.
Din. And that rich merchants, advocates,
and doctors,
Howe'er deserving from the commonwealth,
On forfeit of the city's charter, were
Predestined cuckolds?
Nov. Oh, some pity, doctor!
I was an heretic, but now converted.
Some little, little respite!
Din. No, you town-bull;
. . venge all good men's wrongs,
And now will play the tyrant. To dissect
thee,
Eat thy flesh off with burning corrosives,

Or write with aquafortis in thy forehead,
Thy last intent to wrong my bed, were justice;
And to do less were foolish pity in me :
I speak it, ribald !
Nov. Perigot ! Perigot !
Woe to thy cursed counsel.

Re-enter Chamont *and* Lamira.

Cham. Perigot !
Did he advise you to this course?
Nov. He did.
Cham. And he has his reward for't.
Peri. [*within.*] Will you murder me !
Serv. [*within.*] Once more, aloft with him.
Peri. [*within.*] Murder! murder! murder!

Re-enter Servants, *with* Perigot *in a blanket.*

Cham. What conceal'd bake-meats have
    you there? a present?
Is it goat's flesh? It smells rank.
    1 *Serv.* We have had
Sweet work of it, my lord.
    2 *Serv.* I warrant you 'tis tender,
It wants no cooking ; yet, if you think fit,
We'll bruise it again.
    Peri. As you are Christians, spare me !
I am jelly within already, and without
Embroider'd all o'er with statute lace.
What would you more ?
    Nov. My tutor in the gin, too !
This is some comfort : he is as good as
    drench'd ;
And now we'll both be chaste.
    Cham. What, is't a cat
You have encounter'd, monsieur, you are
    scratch'd so?
My lady, sure, forgot to pare her nails,
Before your soft embraces.
    Din. He has ta'en great pains :
What a sweat he's in !
    Cham. O ! he's a master-dancer,
Knows how to caper into a lady's favour :
One lofty trick more, dear monsieur.
    Nov. That I had
But strength enough to laugh at him !
    blanketted like a dog,
And like a cut-purse whipt ! I am sure that
    now,
He cannot jeer me.
    Peri. May not a man have leave
To hang himself !
    Cham. No ; that were too much mercy.
Live to be wretched ; live to be the talk
Of the conduit, and the bakehouse. I will
    have thee
Pictured as thou art now, and thy whole story
Sung to some villainous tune in a lewd ballad;
And make thee so notorious to the world,

That boys in the streets shall hoot at thee :
    come, Lamira,
And triumph o'er him.—Dost thou see this
    lady,
My wife, whose honour foolishly thou
    thought'st
To undermine, and make a servant to
Thy brutish lusts, laughing at thy affliction?
And, as a sign she scorns thee, set her foot
Upon thy head? Do so :—'Sdeath ! but
    resist,
Once more you caper.
    Peri. I am at the stake,
And must endure it.
    Cham. Spurn him, too.
    Lam. Troth, sir,
I do him too much grace.
    Cham. Now, as a schoolboy
Does kiss the rod that gave him chastisement,
To prove thou art a slave, meet, with thy lips,
This instrument that corrects thee.
    Peri. Have you done yet?
    Din. How like a pair of crest-fallen jades
    they look now !
    Cla. They are not worth our scorn.
    Peri. O pupil, pupil !
    Nov. Tutor, I am drench'd : let us con-
    dole together.
    Cham. And where's the tickling itch now,
    my dear monsieur,
To say, *This lord's my cuckold !*—I am tired:
That we had fresh dogs to hunt them !

Enter Clarindore.

Clarin. . . . . . . *
.   .   I am acquainted with the story ;
The doctor's man has told me all.
    Din. Upon them.
    Peri. Clarindore ! worst of all :—for him
    to know this,
Is a second blanketting to me.
    Nov. I again
Am drench'd to look on him.
    Clarin. How is't ? nay, bear up ;
You that commend adultery, I am glad
To see it thrive so well. Fie, Perigot !
Dejected?   Haply thou wouldst have us
    think,
This is the first time that thou didst curvet,
And come aloft in a blanket. By St. Dennis !
Here are shrewd scratches too ; but nothing to
A man of resolution, whose shoulders
Are of themselves armour of proof, against
A bastinado, and will tire ten beadles.
    Peri. Mock on ; know no mercy.
    Clarin. Thrifty young men !
What a charge is saved in wenching ! and
    'tis timely——

A certain wager of three thousand crowns
Is lost, and must be paid, my pair of puppies:
The coy dame, Bellisant, hath stoop'd ! bear
    witness
This chain and jewels you have seen her wear.
The fellow, that her grooms kick'd down
    the stairs,
Hath crept into her bed ; and, to assure you
There's no deceit, she shall confess so much,
I have enjoy'd her.
  Cham. Are you serious?
  Clarin. Yes, and glory in it.
  Cham. Nay then, give over fooling.——
Thou liest, and art a villain, a base villain,
To slander her.
  Clarin. You are a lord, and that
Bids me forbear you ; but I will make good
Whatever I have said.
  Cham. I'll not lose time
To change words with thee. The king hath
    ordain'd
A Parliament of Love to right her wrongs,
To which I summon thee.   [*Exit.*
  Clarin. Your worst : I care not.—Fare-
well, babions !   [*Exit.*
  Din. Here was a sudden change !
Nay, you must quit my house : shog on,
    kind patient,
And, as you like my physic, when you are
Rampant again, you know I have that can
    cool you.
Nay, monsieur Perigot, help your pupil off
    too,
Your counsel brought him on. Ha ! no reply?
Are you struck dumb? If you are wrong'd,
    complain.
  Peri. We shall find friends to right us.
  Din. And I justice,
The cause being heard ; I ask no more.
Hence ! vanish !   [*Exeunt.*

ACT V.

SCENE I.—*A Court of Justice.*

Enter Chamont, Philamour, *and* Lafort.

  Phil. Montrose slain ! and by Cleremond !
  Cham. 'Tis too true.
  Laf. But wondrous strange, that any dif-
ference,
Especially of such a deadly nature,
Should e'er divide so eminent a friendship.
  Phil. The miracle is greater, that a lady,
His most devoted mistress, Leonora,
Against the usual softness of her sex,
Should with such violence and heat pursue
Her amorous servant ; since I'm inform'd
That he was apprehended by her practice,

And, when he comes to trial for his life,
She'll rise up his accuser.
  Cham. So 'tis rumour'd :
And that's the motive that young Cleremond
Makes it his humble suit, to have his cause
Decided in the Parliament of Love ;
For he pretends the bloody quarrel grew
From grounds that claim a reference to that
    place :
Nor fears he, if you grant him equal hearing,
But, with unanswerable proof, to render
The cruel Leonora tainted with
A guilt beyond his.
  Laf. The king is acquainted
Already with the accident ; besides,
He hath vouchsafed to read divers petitions
Preferr'd on several causes ; one against
Monsieur Dinant, his doctor, by Novall ;
A second, in which madam Bellisant
Complains 'gainst Clarindore ; there is a
    bill too,
Brought in by Perigot, against your lordship ;
All which, in person, he resolves to hear,
Then, as a judge, to censure.
    [*A flourish within.*
  Phil. See the form !
Choice musick ushers him.
  Cham. Let us meet the troop,
And mix with them.
  Phil. 'Twill poize your expectation.
    [*Exeunt.*

Loud Music. Enter Charles *followed by*
Orleans, Nemours, Chamont, Lafort, *and*
Philamour. *A Priest with the image of*
Cupid : *then enter* Cleremond, Clarin-
dore, Perigot, Novall, Bellisant, Leonora,
Beaupré, Lamira, Clarinda, *and* Officers.
Montrose *is brought forward on a bier,*
and placed before the bar.

  Char. Let it not seem a wonder, nor beget
An ill opinion in this fair assembly,
That here I place this statue ; 'tis not done,
Upon the forfeit of our grace, that you
Should, with a superstitious reverence,
Fall down and worship it : nor can it be
Presumed, we hope, young Charles, that
    justly holds
The honour'd title of *most Christian King*,
Would ever nourish such idolatrous thoughts.
'Tis rather to instruct deceived mankind,
How much pure Love, that has his birth in
    heaven,
And scorns to be received a guest, but in
A noble heart prepared to entertain him,
Is, by the gross misprision of weak men,
Abused and injured. That celestial fire,
Which hieroglyphically is described
In this his bow, his quiver, and his torch,

First warm'd their bloods, and after gave a
   name
To the old heroic spirits : such as Orpheus,
That drew men, differing little then from
   beasts,
To civil government ; or famed Alcides,
The tyrant-queller, that refused the plain
And easy path leading to vicious pleasures,
And ending in a precipice deep as hell,
To scale the ragged cliff, on whose firm top
Virtue and Honour, crown'd with wreaths
   of stars,
Did sit triumphant. But it will be answer'd,
(The world decaying in her strength,) that
   now
We are not equal to those ancient times,
And therefore 'twere impertinent and tedious
To cite more precedents of that reverend age,
But rather to endeavour, as we purpose,
To give encouragement, by reward, to such
As with their best nerves imitate that old
   goodness ;
And, with severe correction, to reform
The modern vices.— Begin ; read the bills.
   Peri. Let mine be first, my lord ; 'twas
   first preferr'd.
   Bell. But till my cause be heard, our
   whole sex suffers——
   Off. Back ! keep back, there !
   Nov. Prithee, gentle officer,
Handle me gingerly, or I fall to pieces,
Before I can plead mine.
   Peri. I am bruised   .   .
   Omnes. Justice ! justice !
   Char. Forbear these clamours, you shall
   all be heard :
And, to confirm I am no partial judge,
By lottery decide it ; here's no favour.——
Whcse bill is first, Lafort ?
        [*The names are drawn.*
   Laf. 'Tis Cleremond's.
   Char. The second ?
   Laf. Perigot's ; the third Novall's.
   Nov. Our cases are both lamentable, tutor.
   Peri. And I am glad they shall be heard
   together ;
We cannot stand asunder.
   Char. What's the last ?
   Laf. The injured lady Bellisant's.
   Char. To the first, then ;
And so proceed in order.
   Phil. Stand to the bar.
        [*Cler.* comes forward.
   Leon. Speak, Cleremond, thy grief, as I
   will mine.
   Peri. A confident little pleader ! were I in
   case,
I would give her a double fee.
   Nov. So would I, tutor.

   Off. Silence ! silence !
   Cler. Should I rise up to plead my inno-
   cence,
Though, with the favour of the court, I stood
Acquitted to the world, yea, though the
   wounds
Of my dead friend, (which, like so many
   mouths
With bloody tongues, cry out aloud against
   me,)
By your authority, were closed ; yet here,
A not to be corrupted judge, my conscience,
Would not alone condemn me, but inflict
Such lingering tortures on me, as the hang-
   man,
Though witty in his malice, could not equal.
I therefore do confess a guilty cause,
Touching the fact, and, uncompell'd, ac-
   knowledge
Myself the instrument of a crime the sun,
Hiding his face in a thick mask of clouds,
As frighted with the horror, durst not look on.
But if your laws with greater rigour punish
Such as invent a mischief, than the organs
By whom 'tis put in act, (they truly being
The first great wheels by which the lesser
   move,)
Then stand forth, Leonora ; and I'll prove
The white robe of my innocence tainted with
But one black spot of guilt, and even that one
By thy hand cast on me ; but thine, dyed o'er,
Ten times in grain, in hell's most ugly colours.
   Leon. The fellow is distracted : see how
   he raves !
Now as I live, if detestation of
His baseness would but give me leave, I should
Begin to pity him.
   Cler. Frontless impudence,
And not to be replied be ! Sir, to you,
And these subordinate ministers of yourself,
I turn my speech : to her I do repent
I e'er vouchsafed a syllable. My birth
Was noble as 'tis ancient, nor let it relish
Of arrogance, to say my father's care,
With curiousness and cost, did train me up
In all those liberal qualities that commend
A gentleman : and when the tender down
Upon my chin told me I was a man,
I came to court ; there youth, ease, and ex-
   ample,
First made me feel the pleasing pangs of love :
And there I saw this woman ; saw, and loved
   her
With more than common ardour : for that
   deity,
(Such our affection makes him,) whose dread
   power
.   .   .   .   .   .
.   .   . the choicest arrow, headed with

Not loose but loyal flames, which aim'd at
   me,
Who came with greedy haste to meet the
   shaft,
.   . ing,' that my captive heart was made
.   .   .   . Love's divine artillery,
.   .   . preserved . . no relation.
But the shot made at her was not, like mine,
Of gold, nor of pale lead that breeds disdain ;
Cupid himself disclaims it : I think rather,
As by the sequel 'twill appear, some Fury
From burning Acheron snatch'd a sulphur
   brand,
That smoak'd with hate, the parent of red
   murder,
And threw it in her bosom. Pardon me,
Though I dwell long upon the cause that did
Produce such dire effects ; and, to omit, *
For your much patience' sake, the cunning
   trap   .
In which she caught me, and, with horrid
   oaths,
Embark'd me in a sea of human blood,
I come to the last scene——
   Leon. 'Tis time ; for this
Grows stale and tedious.
   Cler. When, I say, she had,
To satisfy her fell rage, as a penance,
Forced me to this black deed, her vow, too,
   given,
That I should marry her, and she conceal
   me ;
When to her view I brought the slaughter'd
   body
Of my dear friend, and labour'd with my
   tears
To stir compunction in her, aided too
By the sad object, which might witness for
   me,
At what an over-rate I had made purchase
Of her long-wish'd embraces ; then, great
   sir,—
But that I had a mother, and there may be
Some two or three of her .   .   sex
   less faulty,
I should affirm she was the perfect image
Of the devil, her tutor, that had left hell empty,
To dwell in wicked woman.
   Leon. Do ; rail on.
   Cler. For not alone she gloried in my
   sufferings,
Forswore what she had vow'd, refused to
   touch me,
Much less to comfort me, or give me harbour ;
But, instantly, ere I could recollect
My scatter'd sense, betray'd me to your
   justice,
Which I submit to ; hoping, in your wisdom,
That as, in me, you lop a limb of murder,

You will, in her, grub up the root. I have
   said, sir.
   Leon. Much, I confess, but much to little
   purpose.
And though, with your rhetorical flourishes,
You strive to gild a rotten cause, the touch
Of reason, fortified by truth, delivered
From my unletter'd tongue, shall shew it
   dust ;
And so to be contemn'd : You have trimm'd up
All your deservings, should I grant them
   such,
With more care than a maiden of threescore
Does hide her wrinkles, which, if she en-
   counter
The rain, the wind, or sun, the paint wash'd off,
Are to dim eyes discover'd. I forbear
The application, and in a plain style
Come roundly to the matter. 'Tis confess'd,
This pretty, handsome, gentleman, (for
   thieves
Led to the gallows are held proper men,
And so I now will call him,) would needs
   make me
The mistress of his thoughts ; nor did I
   scorn,
For truth is truth, to grace him as a servant.
Nay, he took pretty ways to win me too,
For a court novice ; every year I was
His Valentine, and, in an anagram,
My name worn in his hat ; he made me
   banquets,
As if he thought that ladies, like to flies,
Were to be caught with sweetmeats ; quar-
   rell'd with
My tailor, if my gown were not the first
Of that edition ; beat my shoemaker,
If the least wrinkle on my foot appear'd,
As wronging the proportion ; and, in time,
Grew bolder, usher'd me to masques, and .
Or else paid him that wrote them ; .   .
With such a deal of p   .   .   .
And of good rank, are taken with such
   gambols :
In a word, I was so ; and a solemn contract
Did pass betwixt us ; and the day appointed,
That should make our embraces warrantable,
And lawful to the world : all things so car-
   ried,
As he meant nought but honourable love.
   Char. A pretty method.
   Phil. Quaintly, too, deliver'd.
   Leon. But, when he thought me sure, he
   then gave proof
That foul lust lurk'd in the fair shape of love ;
For, valuing neither laws divine, nor human,
His credit, nor my fame, with violence born
On black-sail'd wings of loose and base de-
   sires,

As if his natural parts had quite forsook him,
And that the pleasures of the marriage bed
Were to be reaped with no more ceremony
Than brute beasts couple,—I yet blush to
    speak it,
He tempted me to yield my honour up
To his libidinous' twines ; and, like an
    atheist,
Scoff'd at the form and orders of the church ;
Nor ended so, but, being by me reproved,
He offered violence ; but was prevented.
   Char. Note, a sudden change.
   Laf. 'Twas foul in Cleremond.
   Leon. I, burning then with a most vir-
    tuous anger,
Razed from my heart the memory of his
    name,
Reviled, and spit at him ; and knew 'twas
    justice
That I should take those deities he scorn'd,
Hymen and Cupid, into my protection,
And be the instrument of their revenge :
And so I cast him off, scorn'd his submission,
His poor and childish whinings, will'd my
    servants
To shut my gates against him : but, when
    neither
Disdain, hate, or contempt, could free me
    from
His loathsome importunities, (and fired too,
To wreak mine injured honour,) I took
    gladly
Advantage of his execrable oaths
To undergo what penance I enjoin'd him ;
Then, to the terror of all future ribalds,
That make no difference between love and
    lust,
Imposed this task upon him. I have said,
    too :
Now, when you please, a censure.
   Char. She has put
The judges to their whisper.
   Nov. What do you think of these pro-
    ceedings, tutor ?
   Peri. The truth is,
I like not the severity of the court ;
Would I were quit, and in an hospital,
I could let fall my suit !
   Nov. 'Tis still your counsel.
   Char. We are resolved, and with an
    equal hand
Will hold the scale of justice ; pity shall not
Rob us of strength and will to draw her sword,
Nor passion transport us : let a priest
And headsman be in readiness ;—do you
    start,
To hear them named ? Some little pause
    we grant you,
To take examination of yourselves,

What either of you have deserved, and why
These instruments of our power are now
    thought useful :
You shall hear more, anon.——
   Cler. I like not this.   [*Aside.*
   Leon. A dreadful preparation ! I confess
It shakes my confidence.   [*Aside.*
   Clarin. I presumed this court
Had been in sport erected ; but now find,
With sorrow to the strongest hopes I built on,
That 'tis not safe to be the subject of
The   .   . of kings.
   (*New Speaker.*) To the second cause.
   Laf.   .   .   Perigot's.
   Nov. Nay, take me along too ;
And, since that our complaints differ not
    much,
Dispatch us both together. I accuse
This devilish doctor.
   Peri. I, this wicked lord.
   Nov. 'Tis known I was an able, lusty man,
Fit to get soldiers to serve my king
And country in the wars ; and howsoever
'Tis said I am not valiant of myself,
I was a striker, one that could strike home
    too ;
And never did beget a girl, though drunk.
To make this good, I could produce brave
    boys,
That others father, twigs of mine own graft-
    ing,
That loved a drum at four, and ere full ten,
Fought battles for the parish they were born
    in ;
And such by-blows, old stories say, still
    proved
Fortunate captains : now, whereas, in justice,
I should have had a pension from the state
For my good service, this ingrateful doctor,
Having no child, and never like to have one,
Because, in pity of his barrenness,
I plotted how to help him to an heir,
Has, with a drench, so far disabled me,
That the great Turk may trust me with his
    virgins,
And never use a surgeon. Now consider,
If this be not hard measure, and a wrong to
Little Dan Cupid, if he be the god
Of coupling, as 'tis said ; and will undo,
If you give way to this, all younger brothers
That carry their revenue in their breeches.—
Have I not nick'd it, tutor ? [*Aside to* Peri.
   Peri. To a hair, boy :
Our bills shall pass, ne'er fear it. [*Aside.*]—
   For my case,
It is the same, sir ; my intent as noble
As was my pupil's.
   Cham. Plead it not again, then :
It takes much from the dignity of the court

But to give audience to such things as these,
That do, in their defence, condemn them-
selves,
And need not an accuser. To be short, sir,
And in a language as far from obsceneness,
As the foul cause will give me leave, be
pleased
To know thus much : This hungry pair of
flesh-flies,
And most inseparable pair of coxcombs,
Though born of divers mothers, twins in
baseness,
Were frequent at my table, had free welcome
And entertainment fit for better men ;
In the return of which, this thankful monsieur
Tempted my wife, seduced her, at the least
To him it did appear so ; which discover'd,
And with what treacheries he did abuse
My bounties, treading underneath his feet
All due respect of hospitable rights,
Or the honour of my family; though the
intent
Deserved a stab, and at the holy altar,
I borrow'd so much of your power to right
me,
As to make him caper.
   Din. For this gallant, sir,
I do confess I cool'd him, spoil'd his ram-
bling ;
Would all such as delight in it, were served so !
And since you are acquainted with the
motives
That did induce me to it, I forbear
A needless repetition.
   Cham. 'Tis not worth it.
The criminal judge is fitter to take . .
Of pleas of this base nature. Be . .
An injured lady, for whose wrong . .
I see the statue of the god of love
Drop down tears of compassion, his sad
mother,
And fair cheek'd Graces, that attend on her,
Weeping for company, as if that all
The ornaments upon the Paphian shrine
Were, with one gripe, by sacrilegious hands,
Torn from the holy altar : 'tis a cause, sir,
That justly may exact your best attention ;
Which if you truly understand and censure,
You not alone shall right the present times,
But bind posterity to be your debtor.
Stand forth, dear madam :—
      [Bellisant *comes forward.*
      Look upon this face,
Examine every feature and proportion,
And you with me must grant, this rare piece
finish'd,
Nature, despairing e'er to make the like,
Brake suddenly the mould in which 'twas
fashion'd.

Yet, to increase your pity, and call on
Your justice with severity, this fair outside
Was but the cover of a fairer mind.
Think, then, what punishment he must
deserve,
And justly suffer, that could arm his heart
With such impenetrable flinty hardness,
To injure so much sweetness.
   Clarin. I must stand
The fury of this tempest, which already
Sings in my ears.
   Bell. Great sir, the too much praise
This lord, my guardian once, has shower'd
upon me,
Could not but spring up blushes in my cheeks,
If grief had left me blood enough to speak
My humble modesty : and so far I am
From being litigious, that though I were
robb'd
Of my whole estate, provided my fair name
Had been unwounded, I had now been silent,
But since the wrongs I undergo, if smother'd,
Would injure our whole sex, I must lay by
My native bashfulness, and put on boldness,
Fit to encounter with the impudence
Of this bad man, that from his birth hath been
So far from nourishing an honest thought,
That the abuse of virgins was his study,
And daily practice. His forsaking of
His wife, distressed Beaupré ; his lewd wager
With these, companions like himself, to
abuse me ;
His desperate resolution, in my presence,
To be his own assassin ; to prevent which,
Foolish compassion forced me to surrender
The life of life, my honour, I pass over :
I'll only touch his foul ingratitude,
To scourge which monster, if your laws
provide not
A punishment with rigour, they are useless.
Or if the sword, the gallows, or the wheel,
Be due to such as spoil us of our goods ;
Perillus' brazen bull, the English rack,
The German pincers, or the Scotch oil'd-
boots,
Though join'd together, yet come short of
torture,
To their full merit, those accursed wretches,
That steal our reputations, and good names,
As this base villain has done mine :—
      Forgive me,
If rage provoke me to uncivil language ;
The cause requires it. Was it not enough
That, to preserve thy life, I lost my honour,
  .   in recompense of such a gift
  .   . publish it, to my disgrace ?
  .   . whose means, unfortunate I,
Whom, but of late, the city, nay, all France,
Durst bring in opposition for chaste life,

With any woman in the Christian world,
Am now become a by-word, and a scorn,
In mine own cóuntry.
   Char. As I live, she moves me.
Is this true, Clarindore?
   Nov. Oh! 'tis very true, sir ;
He bragg'd of it to me.
   Peri. And me.
Nay, since we must be censured, we'll give
   evidence ;
'Tis comfort to have fellows in affliction :
You shall not 'scape, fine monsieur.
   Clarin. Peace, you dog-bolts !—
Sir, I address myself to you, and hope
You have preserved one ear for my defence,
The other freely given to my accuser :
This lady, that complains of injury,
If she have any, was herself the cause
That brought it to her; for being young,
   and rich,
And fair too, as you see, and from that proud,
She boasted of her strength, as if it were not
In the power of love to undermine the fort
On which her chastity was strongly raised :
I, that was bred a courtier, and served
Almost my whole life under Cupid's ensigns,
Could not, in justice, but interpret this
As an affront to the great god of love,
And all his followers, if she were not brought
To due obedience : these strong reasons, sir,
Made me to undertake her. How I woo'd,
Or what I swore, it skills not ; (since 'tis said,
And truly, Jupiter and Venus smile
At lovers' perjuries ;) to be brief, she yielded,
And I enjoy'd her : if this be a crime,
And all such as offend this pleasant way
Are to be punish'd, I am sure you would
   have
Few followers in the court : you are young
   yourself, sir,
And what would you in such a cause ?——
   Laf. Forbear.
   Phil. You are rude and insolent.
   Clarin. Good words, gentle judges.
I have no oil'd tongue ; and I hope my
   bluntness
Will not offend.
   Char. But did you boast your conquest
Got on this lady?
   Clarin. After victory ;
A little glory in a soldier's mouth
Is not uncomely ; love being a kind of war
   too :
And what I did achieve, was full of labour
As his that wins strong towns, and merits
   triumphs.
I thought it could not but take from my
   hoûour,
(Besides the wager of three thousand crowns

Made sure by her confession of my service,)
If it had been conceal'd.
   Char. Who would have thought
That such an impudence could e'er have
   harbour
In the heart of any gentleman?   In this,
Thou dost degrade thyself of all the honours
Thy ancestors left thee, and, in thy base
   nature,
'Tis too apparent that thou art a peasant.
Boast of a lady's favours ! this confirms
Thou art the captain of that .   .   .
That glory in their sins, and .   .   .
With name of courtship ; such as dare bely
Great women's bounties, and repuls'd and
   scorn'd, .
Commit adultery with their good names,
And never touch their persons.   I am sorry,
For your sake, madam, that I cannot make
Such reparation for you in your <u>honour</u>
As I desire ; for, if I should compel him
To marry you, it were to him a blessing,
To you a punishment ; he being so unworthy :
I therefore do resign my place to you ;
Be your own judge ; whate'er you shall de-
   termine,
By my crown, I'll see perform'd.
   Clarin. I am in a fine case,
To stand at a woman's mercy.   [*Aside.*
   Bell. Then thus, sir :
I am not bloody, nor bent to revenge ;
And study his amendment, not his ruin :
Yet, since you have given up your power to
   me,
For punishment, I do enjoin him to
Marry this Moor.
   Clarin. A devil ! hang me rather.
   Char. It is not to be alter'd.
   Clarin. This is cruelty
Beyond expression, .   . I have a wife.
   Cham. Ay, too good for thee.   View her
   well,
And then, this varnish from her face wash'd
   off,
Thou shalt find Beaupré.
   Clarin. Beaupré !
   Bell. Yes, his wife, sir,
But long by him with violence cast off :
And in this shape she serv'd me ; all my
   studies
Aiming to make a fair atonement for her,
To which your majesty may now constrain
   him.
   Clarin. It needs not ; I receive her, and
   ask pardon
Of her and you.
   Bell. On both our parts 'tis granted.
This was your bedfellow, and fill'd your
   arms,

When you thought you embraced me ; I am
    yet
A virgin ; nor had ever given consent,
In my chaste house, to such a wanton passage,
But that I knew that her desires were lawful.—
But now no more of personated passion :
This is the man I loved, [*pointing to the
    bier*,] that I loved truly,
However I dissembled ; and, with him,
Dies all affection in me. So, great sir,
Resume your seat.
    Char. An unexpected issue,
Which I rejoice in. Would 'twere in our
    power
To give a period to the rest, like this,
And spare our heavy censure ! but the death
Of good Montrose forbids it. Cleremond,
Thou instantly shall marry Leonora ;
Which done, as suddenly thy head cut off,
And corpse interr'd, upon thy grave I'll build
A room of eight feet square, in which this
    lady,
For punishment of her cruelty, shall die
An anchoress.
    Leon. I do repent, and rather
Will marry him, and forgive him.
    Clarin. Bind her to
Her word, great sir ; Montrose lives ; this a
    plot
To catch this obstinate lady.
    Leon. I am glad
To be so cheated.
    Mont. [*rises from the bier*]. .   . Lady,
.   .   . deceived ; do not repent
Your good opinion of me when thought dead.
Nor let not my neglect to wait upon you,
Considering what a business of import
Diverted me, be thought unpardonable.

Bell. For my part 'tis forgiven ; and thus
    I seal   .   .   .   .   .   .
Char. Nor are we averse ·
To your desires ; may you live long, and
    happy :
Nov. Mercy to us, great sir.
Peri. We will become
Chaste and reform'd men.
    Cham. and Din. We both are suitors,
On this submission, for your pardon, sir.
    Cham. Which we in part will grant : but,
    to deter
Others, by their example, from pursuing
Unlawful lusts, that think adultery
A sport to be oft practised ; fix on them
Two satyrs' heads ; and so, in capital letters
Their foul intents writ on their breasts, we'll
    have them
Led thrice through Paris ; then, at the court
    gate,
To stand three hours, where Clarindore shall
    make
His recantation for the injury
Done to the lady Bellisant ; and read
A sharp invective, ending with a curse
Against all such as boast of ladies' favours :
Which done, both truly penitent, my doctor
Shall use his best art to restore your strength,
And render Perigot a perfect man.——
So break we up LOVE'S PARLIAMENT,
    which, we hope,
*Being for mirth intended, shall not meet
    with
An ill construction; and if then, fair ladies,
You please to approve it, we hope you'll
    invite
Your friends to see it ften, with delight.*
[*Exeunt.*

The Roman Actor.

DRAMATIS PERSONÆ.	ACTORS' NAMES.
Domitianus Cæsar	J. Lowin.
Paris, the ROMAN ACTOR	J. Taylor.
Ælius Lamia, ⎫	T. Pollard.
Junius Rusticus, ⎬ *senators*	Rob. Benfield,
Palphurius Sura, ⎭	W. Patricke.
Fulcinius,	
Parthenius, Cæsar's *freedman*	R. Sharpe.
Aretinus, Cæsar's *spy*	E. Swanstone.
Stephanos, Domitilla's *freedman.*	
Æsopus, ⎱ *players*	R. Robinson.
Latinus, ⎰	C. Greville.
Philargus, *a rich miser; father to* Parthenius . . .	A. Smith.
Ascletario, *an astrologer.*	
Sejeius, ⎱ *conspirators*	G. Vernon.
Entellus, ⎰	J. Horne.
Domitia, *wife of* Ælius Lamia	J. Tompson.
Domitilla, *cousin-german to* Cæsar	T. Hunnieman.
Julia, *daughter of* Titus	W. Trigge.
Cænis, Vespasian's *concubine*	A. Gough.
A Lady.	

Tribunes, Lictors, Centurions, Soldiers, Hangmen, Servants, Captives.

SCENE,—Rome.

ACT I.

SCENE I.—*The Theatre.* *Enter* Paris, Latinus, *and* Æsopus.

Æsop. What do we act to-day?

Lat. Agave's frenzy,
With Pentheus' bloody end.

Par. It skills not what ;
The times are dull, and all that we receive
Will hardly satisfy the day's expense.
The Greeks, to whom we owe the first invention
Both of the buskin'd scene, and humble sock,
That reign in every noble family,
Declaim against us ; and our theatre,
Great Pompey's work, that hath given full delight
Both to the eye and ear of fifty thousand
Spectators in one day, as if it were
Some unknown desart, or great Rome unpeopled,
Is quite forsaken.

Lat. Pleasures of worse natures
Are gladly entertain'd; and they that shun us,
Practise, in private, sports the stews would blush at.
A litter borne by eight Liburnian slaves,

To buy diseases from a glorious strumpet,
The most censorious of our Roman gentry,
Nay, of the garded robe, the senators,
Esteem an easy purchase.

Par. Yet grudge us,
That with delight join profit, and endeavour
To build their minds up fair, and on the stage
Decipher to the life what honours wait
On good and glorious actions, and the shame
That treads upon the heels of vice, the salary
Of six *sestertii.*

Æsop. For the profit, Paris,
And mercenary gain, they are things beneath us ;
Since, while you hold your grace and power with Cæsar,
We, from your bounty, find a large supply,
Nor can one thought of want ever approach us.

Par. Our aim is glory, and to leave our names
To aftertime.

Lat. And, would they give us leave,
There ends all our ambition.

Æsop. We have enemies,
And great ones too, I fear. 'Tis given out lately,

The consul Aretinus, Cæsar's spy,
Said at his table, ere a month expired,
For being gall'd in our last comedy,
He'd silence us for ever.

Par. I expect
No favour from him ; my strong Aventine is,
That great Domitian, whom we oft have
cheer'd
In his most sullen moods, will once return,
Who can repair, with ease, the consul's ruins.

Lat. 'Tis frequent in the city, he hath
subdued
The Catti and the Daci, and, ere long,
The second time will enter Rome in triumph.

Enter two Lictors.

Par. Jove hasten it? With us?—I now
believe
The consul's threats, Æsopus.

1 Lict. You are summon'd
To appear to-day in senate.

2 Lict. And there to answer
What shall be urged against you.

Par. We obey you.
Nay, droop not, fellows ; innocence should
be bold.
We, that have personated in the scene
The ancient heroes, and the falls of princes,
With loud applause ; being to act ourselves,
Must do it with undoubted confidence.
Whate'er our sentence be, think 'tis in sport :
And, though condemn'd, let's hear it without
sorrow,
As if we were to live again to-morrow.

1 Lict. 'Tis spoken like yourself.

Enter Ælius Lamia, Junius Rusticus, *and*
Palphurius Sura.

Lam. Whither goes Paris?

1 Lict. He's cited to the senate.

Lat. I am glad the state is
So free from matters of more weight and
trouble,
That it has vacant time to look on us.

Par. That reverend place, in which the
affairs of kings
And provinces were determined, to descend
To the censure of a bitter word, or jest,
Dropp'd from a poet's pen ! Peace to your
lordships !
We are glad that you are safe.
[*Exeunt* Lictors, Paris, Latinus, *and*
Æsopus.

Lam. What times are these !
To what 's Rome fallen ! may we, being
alone,
Speak our thoughts freely of the prince and
state,
And not fear the informer?

Rust. Noble Lamia,
So dangerous the age is, and such bad acts
Are practised every where, we hardly sleep,
Nay, cannot dream with safety. All our
actions
Are call'd in question ; to be nobly born
Is now a crime ; and to deserve too well,
Held capital treason. Sons accuse their
fathers,
Fathers their sons ; and, but to win a smile
From one in grace at court, our chastest
matrons
Make shipwreck of their honours. To be
virtuous
Is to be guilty. They are only safe
That know to sooth the prince's appetite,
And serve his lusts.

Sura. 'Tis true ; and 'tis my wonder,
That two sons of so different a nature
Should spring from good Vespasian. We
had a Titus,
Styl'd, justly, "the Delight of all Man-
kind,"
Who did esteem that day lost in his life
In which some one or other tasted not
Of his magnificent bounties. One that had
A ready tear, when he was forced to sign
The death of an offender : and so far
From pride, that he disdain'd not the con-
verse
Even of the poorest Roman.

Lam. Yet his brother,
Domitian, that now sways the power of things,
Is so inclined to blood, that no day passes
In which some are not fasten'd to the hook,
Or thrown down from the Gemonies. His
freed men
Scorn the nobility, and he himself,
As if he were not made of flesh and blood,
Forgets he is a man.

Rust. In his young years,
He shew'd what he would be when grown
to ripeness :
His greatest pleasure was, being a child,
With a sharp-pointed bodkin to kill flies,
Whose rooms now men supply. For his
escape
In the Vitellian war, he raised a temple
To Jupiter, and proudly placed his figure
In the bosom of the god : and, in his edicts,
He does not blush, or start, to style himself
(As if the name of emperor were base)
Great Lord and God Domitian.

Sura. I have letters
He's on his way to Rome, and purposes
To enter with all glory. The flattering senate
Decrees him divine honours ; and to cross it,
Were death with studied torments : — for
my part,

O 2

I will obey the time ; it is in vain
To strive against the torrent.
   Rust. Let's to the curia,
And, though unwillingly, give our suffrages,
Before we are compell'd.
   Lam. And since we cannot
With safety use the active, let's make use of
The passive fortitude, with this assurance,
That the state, sick in him, the gods to friend,
Though at the worst, will now begin to mend.
                       [Exeunt.

SCENE II.—*A Room in* Lamia's *House.*
   Enter Domitia *and* Parthenius.

   Dom. To me this reverence !
   Parth. I pay it, lady,
As a debt due to her that's Cæsar's mistress:
For understand with joy, he that commands
All that the sun gives warmth to, is your
   servant ;
Be not amazed, but fit you to your fortunes.
Think upon state and greatness, and the
   honours
That wait upon Augusta, for that name
Ere long, comes to you :—still you doubt
   your vassal—   *[Presents a letter.*
But, when you've read this letter, writ and
   sign'd
With his imperial hand, you will be freed
From fear and jealousy; and, I beseech you,
When all the beauties of the earth bow to
   you,
And senators shall take it for an honour,
As I do now, to kiss these happy feet ;
                      [Kneels.
When every smile you give is a preferment,
And you dispose of provinces to your crea-
   tures,
Think on Parthenius.
   Dom. Rise. I am transported,
And hardly dare believe what is assured here.
The means, my good Parthenius, that
   wrought Cæsar,
Our god on earth, to cast an eye of favour
Upon his humble handmaid?
   Parth. What, but your beauty ?
When nature framed you for her masterpiece,
As the pure abstract of all rare in woman,
She had no other ends but to design you
To the most eminent place. I will not say
(For it would smell of arrogance, to insinuate
The service I have done you) with what zeal
I oft have made relation of your virtues,
Or how I've sung your goodness, or how
   Cæsar
Was fired with the relation of your story :
I am rewarded in the act, and happy
In that my project prosper'd.
   Dom. You are modest :

And were it in my power, I would be thankful.
If that, when I was mistress of myself,
And in my way of youth, pure and untainted,
The emperor had vouchsafed to seek my
   favours,
I had with joy given up my virgin fort,
At the first summons, to his soft embraces ;
But I am now another's, not mine own.
You know I have a husband :—for my
   honour,
I would not be his strumpet ; and how law
Can be dispensed with to become his wife,
To me's a riddle.
   Parth. I can soon resolve it :
When power puts in his plea the laws are
   silenced.
The world confesses one Rome, and one
   Cæsar,
And as his rule is infinite, his pleasures
Are unconfined ; this syllable, his *will,*
Stands for a thousand reasons.
   Dom. But with safety,
Suppose I should consent, how can I do it ?
My husband is a senator, and of a temper
Not to be jested with.

   Enter Lamia.

   Parth. As if he durst
Be Cæsar's rival !—here he comes ; with ease
I will remove this scruple.
   Lam. How ! so private !
My own house made a brothel ! *[Aside.]*—
   Sir, how durst you,
Though guarded with your power in court,
   and greatness,
Hold conference with my wife? As for you,
   minion,
I shall hereafter treat——
   Parth. You are rude and saucy,
Nor know to whom you speak.
   Lam. This is fine, i'faith !
Is she not my wife ?
   Parth. Your wife ! But touch her, that
   respect forgotten
That's due to her whom mightiest Cæsar
   favours,
And think what 'tis to die. Not to lose time,
She's Cæsar's choice : it is sufficient honour
You were his taster in this heavenly nectar ;
But now must quit the office.
   Lam. This is rare !
Cannot a man be master of his wife
Because she's young and fair, without a
   patent ?
I in my own house am an emperor,
And will defend what's mine. Where are
   my knaves ?
If such an insolence escape unpunish'd——

Parth. In yourself, Lamia—Cæsar hath
  forgot
To use his power, and I, his instrument,
In whom, though absent, his authority
  speaks,
Have lost my faculties !   [*Stamps.*

Enter a Centurion *with* Soldiers.

Lam. The guard ! why, am I
Design'd for death?
Dom. As you desire my favour
Take not so rough a course.
Parth. All your desires
Are absolute commands : Yet give me leave
To put the will of Cæsar into act.
Here's a bill of divorce between your lordship
And this great lady : if you refuse to sign it,
And so as if you did it uncompell'd,
Won to 't by reasons that concern yourself,
Her honour too untainted, here are clerks,
Shall in your best blood write it new, till
  torture
Compel you to perform it.
Lam. Is this legal?
Parth. Monarchs that dare not do unlaw-
  ful things,
Yet bear them out, are constables, not kings.
Will you dispute?
Lam. I know not what to urge
Against myself, but too much dotage on her,
Love, and observance.
Parth. Set it under your hand,
That you are impotent, and cannot pay
The duties of a husband ; or, that you are
  mad ;
Rather than want just cause, we'll make
  you so.
Dispatch, you know the danger else ;—de-
  liver it,
Nay, on your knee.—Madam, you now are
  free,
And mistress of yourself.
Lam. Can you, Domitia,
Consent to this?
Dom. 'Twould argue a base mind
To live a servant, when I may command.
I now am Cæsar's : and yet, in respect
I once was yours, when you come to the
  palace,
Provided you deserve it in your service,
You shall find me your good mistress. Wait
  me, Parthenius ;
And now farewell, poor Lamia !
              [*Exeunt all but* Lamia.
Lam. To the gods
I bend my knees, (for tyranny hath banish'd
Justice from men,) and as they would deserve
Their altars, and our vows, humbly invoke
  them,

That this my ravish'd wife may prove as fatal
To proud Domitian, and her embraces
Afford him, in the end, as little joy
As wanton Helen brought to him of Troy !
              [*Exit.*

SCENE III.—*The Curia or Senate-house.*

Enter Lictors, Aretinus, Fulcinius, Rusticus,
  Sura, Paris, Latinus, *and* Æsopus.

Aret. Fathers conscript, may this our
  meeting be
Happy to Cæsar and the commonwealth !
Lict. Silence !
Aret. The purpose of this frequent senate
Is, first, to give thanks to the gods of Rome,
That, for the propagation of the empire,
Vouchsafe us one to govern it, like themselves.
In height of courage, depth of understanding,
And all those virtues, and remarkable graces,
Which make a prince most eminent, our
  Domitian
Transcends the ancient Romans : I can never
Bring his praise to a period. What good man,
That is a friend to truth, dares make it
  doubtful,
That he hath Fabius' staidness, and the
  courage
Of bold Marcellus, to whom Hannibal gave
The style of Target, and the Sword of Rome?
But he has more, and every touch more
  Roman ;
As Pompey's dignity, Augustus' state,
Antony's bounty, and great Julius' fortune,
With Cato's resolution. I am lost
In the ocean of his virtues : in a word,
All excellencies of good men meet in him,
But no part of their vices.
Rust. This is no flattery !
Sura. Take heed, you'll be observed.
Aret. 'Tis then most fit
That we, (as to the father of our country,
Like thankful sons, stand bound to pay true
  service
For all those blessings that he showers upon
  us,)
Should not connive, and see his government
Depraved and scandalized by meaner men,
That to his favour and indulgence owe
Themselves and being.
Par. Now he points at us.
Aret. Cite Paris, the tragedian.
Par. Here.
Aret. Stand forth.
In thee, as being the chief of thy profession,
I do accuse the quality of treason,
As libellers against the state and Cæsar.
Par. Mere accusations are not proofs, my
  lord ;
In what are we delinquents ?

Aret. You are they
That search into the secrets of the time,
And, under feign'd names, on the stage,
     present
Actions not to be touch'd at ; and traduce
Persons of rank and quality of both sexes,
And, with satirical, and bitter jests,
Make even the senators ridiculous
To the plebeians.
     Par. If I free not myself,
And, in myself, the rest of my profession,
From these false imputations, and prove
That they make that a libel which the poet
Writ for a comedy, so acted too ;
It is but justice that we undergo
The heaviest censure.
     Aret. Are you on the stage,
You talk so boldly?
     Par. The whole world being one,
This place is not exempted ; and I am
So confident in the justice of our cause,
That I could wish Cæsar, in whose great
     name
All kings are comprehended, sat as judge,
To hear our plea, and then determine of us.—
If, to express a man sold to his lusts,
Wasting the treasure of his time and fortunes
In wanton dalliance, and to what sad end
A wretch that's so given over does arrive at ;
Deterring careless youth, by his example,
From such licentious courses ; laying open
The snares of bawds, and the consuming arts
Of prodigal strumpets, can deserve reproof ;
Why are not all your golden principles,
Writ down by grave philosophers to instruct
     us
To choose fair virtue for our guide, not
     pleasure,
Condemn'd unto the fire ?
     Sura. There's spirit in this.
     Par. Or if desire of honour was the base
On which the building of the Roman empire
Was raised up to this height ; if, to inflame
The noble youth with an ambitious heat
T' endure the frosts of danger, nay, of death,
To be thought worthy the triumphal wreath
By glorious undertakings, may deserve
Reward, or favour from the commonwealth ;
Actors may put in for as large a share
As all the sects of the philosophers :
They with cold precepts (perhaps seldom
     read)
Deliver, what an honourable thing
The active virtue is : but does that fire
The blood, or swell the veins with emulation,
To be both good and great, equal to that
Which is presented on our theatres ?
Let a good actor, in a lofty scene,
Show great Alcides honour'd in the sweat

Of his twelve labours ; or a bold Camillus,
Forbidding Rome to be redeem'd with gold
From the insulting Gauls ; or Scipio,
After his victories, imposing tribute
On conquer'd Carthage : if done to the life,
As if they saw their dangers, and their glories,
And did partake with them in their rewards,
All that have any spark of Roman in them,
The slothful arts laid by, contend to be
Like those they see presented.
     Rust. He has put
The consuls to their whisper.
     Par. But, 'tis urged
That we corrupt youth, and traduce superiors,
When do we bring a vice upon the stage,
That does go off unpunish'd ? Do we teach,
By the success of wicked undertakings,
Others to tread in their forbidden steps?
We shew no arts of Lydian panderism,
Corinthian poisons, Persian flatteries,
But mulcted so in the conclusion, that
Even those spectators that were so inclined,
Go home changed men. And, for traducing
     such
That are above us, publishing to the world
Their secret crimes, we are as innocent
As such as are born dumb. When we present
An heir, that does conspire against the life
Of his dear parent, numbering every hour
He lives, as tedious to him ; if there be,
Among the auditors, one whose conscience
     tells him
He is of the same mould,—WE CANNOT
     HELP IT.
Or, bringing on the stage a loose adulteress,
That does maintain the riotous expense
Of him that feeds her greedy lust, yet suffers
The lawful pledges of a former bed
To starve the while for hunger ; if a matron,
However great in fortune, birth, or titles,
Guilty of such a foul unnatural sin,
Cry out, 'Tis writ for me,—WE CANNOT
     HELP IT.
Or, when a covetous man's express'd, whose
     wealth
Arithmetic cannot number, and whose lord-
     ships
A falcon in one day cannot fly over ;
Yet he so sordid in his mind, so griping,
As not to afford himself the necessaries
To maintain life ; if a patrician,
(Though honour'd with a consulship,) find
     himself
Touch'd to the quick in this,—WE CANNOT
     HELP IT.
Or, when we shew a judge that is corrupt,
And will give up his sentence, as he favours
The person, not the cause ; saving the guilty,
If of his faction, and as oft condemning

The innocent, out of particular spleen ;
If any in this reverend assembly,
Nay, even yourself, my lord, that are the
 ' image
Of absent Cæsar, feel something in your
 bosom
That puts you in remembrance of things
 past,
Or things intended,—'TIS NOT IN US TO
 HELP IT.
I have said, my lord : and now, as you find
 cause,
Or censure us, or free us with applause.
Lat. Well pleaded, on my life ! I never
 saw him
Act an orator's part before.
Æsop. We might have given
Ten double fees to Regulus, and yet
Our cause deliver'd worse. [*A shout within.*

Enter Parthenius.

Aret. What shout is that ?
Parth. Cæsar, our lord, married to con-
quest, is
Return'd in triumph.
Ful. Let's all haste to meet him.
Aret. Break up the court ; we will reserve
 to him
The censure of this cause.
All. Long life to Cæsar ! [*Exeunt.*

SCENE IV.—*The Approach to the Capitol.*

Enter Julia, Cænis, Domitilla, *and* Domitia.

Cænis. Stand back—the place is mine.
Jul. Yours ! Am I not
Great Titus' daughter, and Domitian's niece?
Dares any claim precedence ?
Cænis. I was more : .
The mistress of your father, and, in his
 right,
Claim duty from you.
Jul. I confess, you were useful
To please his appetite.
Dom. To end the controversy,
For I'll have no contending, I'll be bold
To lead the way myself.
Domitil. You, minion !
Dom. Yes ;
And all, ere long, shall kneel to catch my
 favours.
Jul. Whence springs this flood of great-
ness ?
Dom. You shall know
Too soon, for your vexation, and perhaps
Repent too late, and pine with envy, when
You see whom Cæsar favours.
Jul. Observe the sequel.

Enter Captains *with laurels*, Domitian *in*
 his triumphant chariot, Parthenius, Paris,
 Latinus, *and* Æsopus, *met by* Aretinus.
 Sura, Lamia, Rusticus, Fulcinins, Soldiers,
 and Captives.

Cæs. As we now touch the height of human
 glory,
Riding in triumph to the capitol,
Let these, whom this victorious arm hath.
 made
The scorn of fortune, and the slaves of Rome,
Taste the extremes of misery. Bear them off
To the common prisons, and there let them.
 prove
How sharp our axes are.
 [*Exeunt* Soldiers *with* Captives.
Rust. A bloody entrance ! [*Aside.*
Cæs. To tell you you are happy in your
 prince,
Were to distrust your love, or my desert ;
And either were distasteful : .or to boast
How much, not by my deputies, but myself,
I have enlarged the empire ; or what horrors.
The soldier, in our conduct, hath broke
 through,
Would better suit the mouth of Plautus'
 braggart,
Than the adored monarch of the world.
 Sura. This is no boast ! [*Aside.*
Cæs. When I but name the Daci,
And gray-eyed Germans, whom I have sub-
 dued,
The ghost of Julius will look pale with envy,
And great Vespasian's and Titus' triumph,
(Truth must take place of father and of
 brother,)
Will be no more remember'd. I am above
All honours you can give me : and the style
Of Lord and God, which thankful subjects.
 give me,
Not my ambition, is deserved.
 Aret. At all parts
Celestial sacrifice is fit for Cæsar,
In our acknowledgment.
 Cæs. Thanks, Aretinus ;
Still hold our favour. Now, the god of war,
And famine, blood, and death, Bellona's
 pages,
Banish'd from Rome to Thrace, in our good.
 fortune,
With justice he may taste the fruits of peace,
Whose sword hath plough'd the ground, and
 reap'd the harvest
Of your prosperity. Nor can I think
That there is one among you so ungrateful,
Or such an enemy to thriving virtue,
That can esteem the jewel he holds dearest,
Too good for Cæsar's use.

Sura. All we possess—
Lam. Our liberties—
Ful. Our children—
Par. Wealth—
Aret. And throats,
Fall willingly beneath his feet.
Rust. Base flattery !
What Roman can endure this?   [*Aside.*
Cæs. This calls on
My love to all, which spreads itself among
you.
The beauties of the time! [*seeing the ladies.*]
Receive the honour
To kiss the hand which, rear'd up thus,
holds thunder ;
To you 'tis an assurance of a calm.
Julia, my niece, and Cænis, the delight
Of old Vespasian ; Domitilla, too,
A princess of our blood.
Rust. 'Tis strange his pride
Affords no greater courtesy to ladies
Of such high birth and rank.
Sura. Your wife's forgotten.
Lam. No, she will be remember'd, fear it
not ;
She will be graced and greased.
Cæs. But, when I look on
Divine Domitia, methinks we should meet
(The lesser gods applauding the encounter)
As Jupiter, the Giants lying dead
On the Phlegræan plain, embraced his Juno.
Lamia, it is your honour that she's mine.
Lam. You are too great to be gainsaid.
Cæs. Let all
That fear our frown, or do affect our favour,
Without examining the reason why,
Salute her (by this kiss I make it good)
With the title of Augusta.
Dom. Still your servant.
All. Long live Augusta, great Domitian's
empress !
Cæs. Paris, my hand.
Par. [*kissing it.*] The gods still honour
Cæsar !
Cæs. The wars are ended, and, our arms
laid by,
We are for soft delights. Command the poets
To use their choicest and most rare invention,
To entertain the time ; nor be you careful
To give it action : we'll provide the people
Pleasures of all kinds.—My Domitia, think
not
I flatter, though thus fond.—On to the capitol:
'Tis death to him that wears a sullen brow.
This 'tis to be a monarch, when alone
He can command all, but is awed by none.
                                  [*Exeunt.*

ACT II.

SCENE I.—*A State Room in the Palace.*

Enter Philargus *in rags, and* Parthenius.

Phil. My son to tutor me ! Know your
obedience,
And question not my will.
Parth. Sir, were I one,
Whom want compell'd to wish a full pos-
session
Of what is yours : or had I ever number'd
Your years, or thought you lived too long,
with reason
You then might nourish ill opinions of me :
Or did the suit that I prefer to you
Concern myself, and aim'd not at your good,
You might deny, and I sit down with patience,
And after never press you.
Phil. In the name of Pluto,
What wouldst thou have me do?
Parth. Right to yourself ;
Or suffer me to do it. Can you imagine
This nasty hat, this tatter'd cloak, rent shoe
This sordid linen, can become the master
Of your fair fortunes? whose superfluous
means,
Though I were burthensome, could clothe
you in
The costliest Persian silks, studded with
jewels,
The spoils of provinces, and every day
Fresh change of Tyrian purple.
Phil. Out upon thee !
My monies in my coffers melt to hear thee.
Purple ! hence, prodigal ! Shall I make my
mercer,
Or tailor heir, or see my jeweller purchase ?
No, I hate pride.
Parth. Yet decency would do well.
Though, for your outside, you will not be
alter'd,
Let me prevail so far yet, as to win you
Not to deny your belly nourishment ;
Neither to think you've feasted, when 'tis
cramm'd
With mouldy barley-bread, onions, and leeks,
And the drink of bondmen, water.
Phil. Wouldst thou have me
Be an Apicius, or a Lucullus,
And riot out my state in curious sauces ?
Wise nature with a little is contented ;
And, following her, my guide, I cannot err.
Parth. But you destroy her in your want
of care
(I blush to see, and speak it) to maintain her
In perfect health and vigour ; when you suffer,
Frighted with the charge of physic, rheums,
catarrhs,

The scurf, ach in your bones, to grow upon
    you,
And hasten on your fate with too much
    sparing :
When a cheap purge, a vomit, and good diet,
May lengthen it.   Give me but leave to send
The emperor's doctor to you.
    Phil. I'll be borne first,
Half rotten, to the fire that must consume me!
His pills, his cordials, his electuaries,
His syrups, julaps, bezoar stone, nor his
Imagined unicorn's horn, comes in my belly ;
My mouth shall be a draught first, 'tis re-
    solved.
No ; I'll not lessen my dear golden heap,
Which, every hour increasing, does renew
My youth and vigor ; but, if lessen'd, then,
Then my poor heart-strings crack.   Let me
    enjoy it,
And brood o'er't, while I live, it being my life,
My soul, my all : but when I turn to dust,
And part from what is more esteem'd, by me,
Than all the gods Rome's thousand altars
    smoke to,
Inherit thou my adoration of it,
And, like me, serve my idol.   [*Exit.*
    Parth. What a strange torture
Is avarice to itself ! what man, that looks on
Such a penurious spectacle, but must
Know what the fable meant of Tantalus,
Or the ass whose back is crack'd with curious
    viands,
Yet feeds on thistles. Some course I must take,
To make my father know what cruelty
He uses on himself.

Enter Paris.

    Par. Sir, with your pardon,
I make bold to enquire the emperor's pleasure ;
For, being by him commanded to attend,
Your favour may instruct us what's his will
Shall be this night presented.
    Parth. My loved Paris,
Without my intercession, you well know,
You may make your own approaches, since
    his ear
To you is ever open.
    Par. I acknowledge
His clemency to my weakness, and, if ever
I do abuse it, lightning strike me dead !
The grace he pleases to confer upon me,
(Without boast I may say so much,) was never
Employ'd to wrong the innocent, or to incense
His fury.
    Parth. 'Tis confess'd : many men owe you
For provinces they ne'er hoped for ; and
    their lives,
Forfeited to his anger :—you being absent,
I could say more.

    Par. You still are my good patron ;
And, lay it in my fortune to deserve it,
You should perceive the poorest of your clients
To his best abilities thankful.
    Parth. I believe so.
Met you my father ?
    Par. Yes, sir, with much grief,
To see him as he is.   Can nothing work him
To be himself ?
    Parth. O, Paris, 'tis a weight
Sits heavy here ; and could this right hand's
    loss
Remove it, it should off : but he is deaf
To all persuasion.
    Par. Sir, with your pardon,
I'll offer my advice : I once observed,
In a tragedy of ours, in which a murder
Was acted to the life, a guilty hearer,
Forced by the terror of a wounded conscience,
To make discovery of that which torture
Could not wring from him. Nor can it appear
Like an impossibility, but that
Your father, looking on a covetous man
Presented on the stage, as in a mirror,
May see his own deformity, and loath it.
Now, could you but persuade the emperor
To see a comedy we have, that's styled
The Cure of Avarice, and to command
Your father to be a spectator of it,
He shall be so anatomized in the scene,
And see himself so personated, the baseness
Of a self-torturing miserable wretch
Truly described, that I much hope the object
Will work compunction in him.
    Parth. There's your fee ;
I ne'er bought better counsel.   Be you in
    readiness,
I will effect the rest.
    Par. Sir, when you please ;
We'll be prepar'd to enter.—Sir, the emperor.
                                    [*Exit.*

Enter Cæsar, Aretinus, *and* Guard.

    Cæs. Repine at us !
    Aret. 'Tis more, or my informers,
That keep strict watch upon him, are deceived
In their intelligence : there is a list
Of malcontents, as Junius Rusticus,
Palphurius Sura, and this Ælius Lamia,
That murmur at your triumphs, as mere
    pageants ;
And, at their midnight meetings, tax your
    justice,
(For so I style what they call tyranny,)
For Pætus Thrasea's death, as if in him
Virtue herself were murdered : nor forget
    they
Agricola, who, for his service done
In the reducing Britain to obedience,

They dare affirm to be removed with poison
And he compell'd to write you a coheir
With his daughter, that his testament might
    stand,
Which, else, you had made void. Then
    your much love
To Julia your niece, censured as incest,
And done in scorn of Titus, your dead
    brother :
But the divorce Lamia was forced to sign
To her you honour with Augusta's title,
Being only named, they do conclude there was
A Lucrece once, a Collatine, and a Brutus ;
But nothing Roman left now but, in you,
The lust of Tarquin.
    Cæs. Yes, his fire, and scorn
Of such as think that our unlimited power
Can be confined. Dares Lamia pretend
An interest to that which I call mine ;
Or but remember she was ever his,
That's now in our possession? Fetch him
    hither.   [*Exit* Guard.
I'll give him cause to wish he rather had
Forgot his own name, than e'er mention'd
    hers.
Shall we be circumscribed? Let such as
    cannot
By force make good their actions, though
    wicked,
Conceal, excuse, or qualify their crimes !
What our desires grant leave and privilege to,
Though contradicting all divine decrees,
Or laws confirm'd by Romulus and Numa,
Shall be held sacred.
    Aret. You should, else, take from
The dignity of Cæsar.
    Cæs. Am I master
Of two and thirty legions, that awe
All nations of the triúmphed world,
Yet tremble at our frown, to yield account
Of what's our pleasure, to a private man !
Rome perish first, and Atlas's shoulders
    shrink,
Heaven's fabric fall, (the sun, the moon,
    the stars
Losing their light and comfortable heat,)
Ere I confess that any fault of mine
May be disputed !
    Aret. So you preserve your power,
As you should, equal and omnipotent here,
With Jupiter's above.
    [*Parthenius kneeling, whispers* Cæsar.
    Cæs. Thy suit is granted,
Whate'er it be, Parthenius, for thy service
Done to Augusta.——Only so ? a trifle :
Command him hither. If the comedy fail
To cure him, I will minister something to him
That shall instruct him to forget his gold,
And think upon himself.

    Parth. May it succeed well,
Since my intents are pious !   [*Exit.*
    Cæs. We are resolved
What course to take; and, therefore,
    Aretinus,
Enquire no further. Go you to my empress,
And say I do entreat (for she rules him
Whom all men else obey) she would
    vouchsafe
The music of her voice at yonder window,
When I advance my hand, thus. I will·
    blend   [*Exit* Aretinus..
My cruelty with some scorn, or else 'tis lost.
Revenge, when it is unexpected, falling
With greater violence ; and hate clothed in
    smiles,
Strikes, and with horror, dead the wretch
    that comes not
Prepared to meet it.—

    Re-enter Guard *with* Lamia.

    Our good Lamia, welcome.
So much we owe you for a benefit,
With willingness on your part conferr'd
    upon us,
That 'tis our study, we that would not live
Engaged to any for a courtesy,
How to return it.
    Lam. 'Tis beneath your fate
To be obliged, that in your own hand grasp
The means to be magnificent.
    Cæs. Well put off ;
But yet it must not do : the empire, Lamia,
Divided equally, can hold no weight,
If balanced with your gift in fair Domitia——
You, that could part with all delights at
    once,
The magazine of rich pleasures being con-
    tain'd
In her perfections,—uncompell'd, deliver'd
As a present fit for Cæsar. In your eyes,
With tears of joy, not sorrow, 'tis confirm'd
You glory in your act.
    Lam. Derided too !
Sir, this is more——
    Cæs. More than I can requite ;
It is acknowledged, Lamia. There's no drop
Of melting nectar I taste from her lip,
But yields a touch of immortality
To the blest receiver ; every grace and
    feature,
Prized to the worth, bought at an easy rate,
If purchased for a consulship. Her dis-
    course
So ravishing, and her action so attractive,
That I would part with all my other senses,
Provided I might ever see and hear her.
The pleasures of her bed I dare not trust

The winds or air with ; for that would draw
   down,
In envy of my happiness, a war
From all the gods upon me.
  Lam. Your compassion
To me, in your forbearing to insult
On my calamity, which you make your sport,
Would more appease those gods you have
   provoked,
Than all the blasphemous comparisons
You sing unto her praise.

       Domitia appears at the window.

  Cæs. I sing her praise !
'Tis far from my ambition to hope it ;
It being a debt she only can lay down,
And no tongue else discharge.
      [*He raises his hand. Music above.*
        Hark ! I think, prompted
With my consent that you once more should
   hear her,
She does begin. An universal silence
Dwell on this place ! 'Tis death, with linger-
   ing torments,
To all that dare disturb her.—

       A SONG *by* Domitia.

       —Who can hear this,
And fall not down and worship ? In my fancy,
Apollo being judge, on Latmos' hill
Fair-bair'd Calliope, on her ivory lute,
(But something short of this,) sung Ceres'
   praises,
And grisly Pluto's rape on Proserpine.
The motions of the spheres are out of time,
Her musical notes but heard. Say, Lamia,
   say,
Is not her voice angelical ?
  Lam. To your ear :
But I, alas ! am silent.
  Cæs. Be so ever,
That without admiration canst hear her !
Malice to my felicity strikes thee dumb,
And, in thy hope, or wish, to repossess
What I love more than empire, I pronounce
  t ee
Guilty of treason.—Off with his head ! do
  you stare ?
By her that is my patroness, Minerva,
Whose statue I adore of all the gods,
If he but live to make reply, thy life
Shall answer it !
    [*The* Guard *leads off* Lamia,
      stopping his mouth.
    My fears of him are freed now ;
And he that lived to upbraid me with my
   wrong,
For an offence he never could imagine,

In wantonness removed.—Descend, my
   dearest ;
Plurality of husbands shall no more
Breed doubts or jealousies in you : [*Exit*
   Dom. *above.*] 'tis dispatch'd,
And with as little trouble here, as if
I had kill'd a fly.

Enter Domitia, *ushered in by* Aretinus, *her
  train borne up by* Julia, Cænis, *and* Domitilla.

       Now you appear, and in
That glory you deserve ! and these, that stoop
To do you service, in the act much honour'd !
Julia, forget that Titus was thy father ;
Cænis, and Domitilla, ne'er remember
Sabinus or Vespasian. To be slaves
To her is more true liberty, than to live
Parthian or Asian queens. As lesser stars,
That wait on Phœbe in her full of brightness,
Compared to her, you are. Thus, thus I
   seat you
By Cæsar's side, commanding these, that
   once
Were the adored glories of the time,
To witness to the world they are your vassals,
At your feet to attend you.
  Dom. 'Tis your pleasure,
And not my pride. And yet, when I consider
That I am yours, all duties they can pay
I do receive as circumstances due
To her you please to honour.

    Re-enter Parthenius *with* Philargus.

  Parth. Cæsar's will
Commands you hither, nor must you gain-
   say it.
  Phil. Lose time to see an interlude ! must
  I pay too,
For my vexation ?
  Parth. Not in the court :
It is the emperor's charge.
  Phil. I shall endure
My torment then the better
  Cæs. Can it be
This sordid thing, Parthenius, is thy father ?
No actor can express him : I had held
The fiction for impossible in the scene,
Had I not seen the substance.—Sirrah, sit
   still,
And give attention ; if you but nod,
You sleep for ever.—Let them spare the
   prologue,
And all the ceremonies proper to ourself,
And come to the last act—there, where the
   cure
By the doctor is made perfect. The swift
   minutes
Seem years to me, Domitia, that divorce thee

From my embraces : my desires increasing
As they are satisfied, all pleasures else
Are tedious as dull sorrows. Kiss me again :
If I now wanted heat of youth, these fires,
In Priam's veins, would thaw his frozen blood,
Enabling him to get a second Hector
For the defence of Troy.
Dom. You are wanton !
Pray you, forbear. Let me see the play.
Cæs. Begin there.

Enter Paris, *like a doctor of physic, and*
Æsopus : Latinus *is brought forth asleep
in a chair, a key in his mouth.*

*Æsop. O master doctor, he is past recovery ;
A lethargy hath seized him ; and, however
His sleep resemble death, his watchful care
To guard that treasure he dares make no
use of,
Works strongly in his soul.*
    *Par. What's that he holds
So fast between his teeth ?*
    *Æsop. The key that opens
His iron chests, cramm'd with accursed gold,
Rusty with long imprisonment. There's no
duty
In me, his son, nor confidence in friends,
That can persuade him to deliver up
That to the trust of any.*
    Phil. He is the wiser :
'We were fashion'd in one mould.
    *Æsop. He eats with it ;
And when devotion calls him to the temple
Of Mammon, whom, of all the gods, he
kneels to,
THAT held thus still, his orisons are paid :
Nor will he, though the wealth of Rome
were pawn'd
For the restoring of 't, for one short hour
Be won to part with it.*
    Phil. Still, still myself !
And if like me he love his gold, no pawn
Is good security.
    *Par. I'll try if I can force it——
It will not be. His avaricious mind,
Like men in rivers drown'd, make him
gripe fast,
To his last gasp, what he in life held dearest;
And, if that it were possible in nature,
Would carry it with him to the other world.*
    Phil. As I would do to hell, rather than
leave it.
    Æsop. Is he not dead ?
    *Par. Long since to all good actions,
Or to himself, or others, for which wise men
Desire to live. You may with safety pinch
him,
Or under his nails stick needles, yet he stirs
not ;*

*Anxious fear to lose what his soul doats on,
Renders his flesh insensible. We must use
Some means to rouse the sleeping faculties
Of his mind ; there lies the lethargy. Take
a trumpet,
And blow it into his ears ; 'tis to no purpose;
The roaring noise of thunder cannot wake
him :—
And yet despair not; I have one trick left yet.*
    Æsop. What is it ?
    *Par. I will cause a fearful dream
To steal into his fancy, and disturb it
With the horror it brings with it, and so free
His body's organs.*
    Dom. 'Tis a cunning fellow ;
If he were indeed a doctor, as the play says,
He should be sworn my servant ; govern
my slumbers,
And minister to me waking.
    Par. If this fail,   [*A chest brought in.*
*I'll give him o'er. So ; with all violence
Rend ope this iron chest, for here his life lies
Bound up in fetters, and in the defence
Of what he values higher, 'twill return,
And fill each vein and artery.—Louder yet !
—'Tis open, and already he begins
To stir ; mark with what trouble.*
                [*Latinus stretches himself.*
    Phil. As you are Cæsar,
Defend this honest, thrifty man ! they are
thieves,
And come to rob him.
    *Parth. Peace ! the emperor frowns.
    *Par. So ; now pour out the bags upon the
table ;
Remove his jewels, and his bonds.—Again,
Ring a second golden peal. His eyes are open;
He stares as he had seen Medusa's head,
And were turn'd marble.—Once more.*
    *Lat. Murder ! murder !
They come to murder me. My son in the
plot ?
Thou worse than parricide ! if it be death
To strike thy father's body, can all tortures
The Furies in hell practise, be sufficient
For thee, that dost assassinate my soul ?—
My gold ! my bonds ! my jewels ! dost thou
envy
My glad possession of them for a day ;
Extinguishing the taper of my life
Consumed unto the snuff ;*
    *Par. Seem not to mind him.
    *Lat. Have I, to leave thee rich, denied
myself
The joys of human being ; scraped and
hoarded
A mass of treasure, which had Solon seen,
The Lydian Crœsus had appeared to him
Poor as the beggar Irus ? And yet I,*

Solicitous to increase it, when my entrails
Were clemm'd with keeping a perpetual fast,
Was deaf to their loud windy cries, as fearing,
Should I disburse one penny to their use,
My heir might curse me. And, to save
    expense
In outward ornaments, I did expose
My naked body to the winter's cold,
And summer's scorching heat : nay, when
    diseases
Grew thick upon me, and a little cost
Had purchased my recovery, I chose rather
To have my ashes closed up in my urn,
By hasting on my fate, than to diminish
The gold my prodigal son, while I am living,
Carelessly scatters.
    Æsop. Would you'd dispatch and die
    once !
Your ghost should feel in hell, THAT *is my*
    slave
Which was your master.
    Phil. Out upon thee, varlet !
    Par. And what then follows all your carke
    and caring,
And self-affliction ? When your starved
  trunk is
Turn'd to forgotten dust, this hopeful youth
Urines upon your monument, ne'er remem-
    bering
How much for him you suffer'd ; and then
    tells,
To the companions of his lusts and riots,
The hell you did endure on earth, to leave
    him
Large means to be an epicure, and to feast
His senses all at once, a happiness
You never granted to yourself. Your gold,
    then,
Got with vexation, and preserved with
    trouble,
Maintains the public stews, panders, and
    ruffians,
That quaff damnations to your memory,
For living so long here.
    Lat. It will be so ; I see it—
O, that I could redeem the time that's past !
I would live and die like myself ; and make
    true use
Of what my industry purchased.
    Par. Covetous men,
Having one foot in the grave, lament so ever :
But grant that I by art could yet recover
Your desperate sickness, lengthen out your
    life
A dozen of years ; as I restore your body
To perfect health, will you with care en-
    deavour
To rectify your mind ?
    Lat. I should so live then,

As neither my heir should have just cause to·
    think
I lived too long, for being close-handed to him,.
Or cruel to myself.
    Par. Have your desires.
Phœbus assisting me, I will repair
The ruin'd building of your health ; and'
    think not
You have a son that hates you ; the truth is,
This means, with his consent, I practised on·
    you
To this good end : it being a device,
In you to shew the Cure of Avarice.
    [*Exeunt* Paris, Latinus, *and* Æsopus.
    Phil. An old fool, to be gull'd thus ! had.
    he died
As I resolve to do, not to be alter'd,
It had gone off twanging.
    Cæs. How approve you, sweetest,
Of the matter and the actors?
    Dom. For the subject,
I like it not ; it was filch'd out of Horace.
—Nay, I have read the poets :—but the fellow
That play'd the doctor, did it well, by Venus ꞉꞉
He had a tuneable tongue, and neat de-
    livery :
And yet, in my opinion, he would perform
A lover's part much better. Prithee, Cæsar,
For I grow weary, let us see, to-morrow,
Iphis and Anaxarete.
    Cæs. Any thing
For thy delight, Domitia ; to your rest,
Till I can disquiet you : wait upon her..
There is a business that I must dispatch,
And I will straight be with you. [*Exeunt.·*
    Aret. Dom. Julia, Cænis, *and* Domitil.
    Parth. Now, my dread sir,
Endeavour to prevail.
    Cæs. One way or other
We'll cure him, never doubt it. Now,.
    Philargus,
Thou wretched thing, hast thou seen thy·
    sordid baseness,
And but observed what a contemptible
    creature
A covetous miser is ? Dost thou in thyself
Feel true compunction, with a resolution
To be a new man?
    Phil. This crazed body's Cæsar's ;
But for my mind——
    Cæs. Trifle not with my anger.
Canst thou make good use of what was now
    presented ;
And imitate, in thy sudden change of life,
The miserable rich man, that express'd
What thou art to the life?
    Phil. Pray you, give me leave
To die as I have lived. I must not part with
My gold ; it is my life : I am past cure.

And all those glorious constellations
That do adorn the firmament, appointed,
Like grooms, with their bright influence to
    attend
The actions of kings and emperors,
They being the greater wheels that move
    the less.
Bring forth those condemn'd wretches ;—
    [*Exit* Parthenius.]—let me see
One man so lost, as but to pity them,
And though there lay a million of souls
Imprison'd in his flesh, my hangmen's hooks
Should rend it off, and give them liberty.
Cæsar hath said it.

Re-enter Parthenius, *with* Aretinus, *and*
    Guard ; Executioners *dragging in* Junius
    Rusticus *and* Palphurius Sura, *bound back
    to back.*

    Aret. 'Tis great Cæsar's pleasure,
That with fix'd eyes you carefully observe
The people's looks.   Charge upon any man
That with a sigh or murmur does express
A seeming sorrow for these traitors' deaths.
You know his will, perform it.
    Cæs. A good bloodhound,
And fit for my employments.
    Sura. Give us leave
To die, fell tyrant.
    Rust. For, beyond our bodies,
Thou hast no power.
    Cæs. Yes ; I'll afflict your souls,
And force them groaning to the Stygian lake,
Prepared for such to howl in, that blaspheme
The power of princes, that are gods on earth.
Tremble to think how terrible the dream is
After this sleep of death.
    Rust. To guilty men
It may bring terror : not to us, that know
What 'tis to die, well taught by his example
For whom we suffer. In my thought I see
The substance of that pure untainted soul
Of Thrasea, our master, made a star,
That with melodious harmony invites us
(Leaving this dunghill Rome, made hell by
    thee)
To trace his heavenly steps, and fill a sphere
Above yon crystal canopy.
    Cæs. Do invoke him
With all the aids his sanctity of life
Have won on the rewarders of his virtue ;
They shall not save you.—Dogs, do you grin?
    torment them.
    [*The* Executioners *torment them, they
        still smiling.*
So, take a leaf of Seneca now, and prove
If it can render you insensible
Of that which but begins here. Now an oil,
Drawn from the Stoic's frozen principles,

Predominant over fire, were useful for you.
Again, again. You trifle. Not a groan !——
Is my rage lost ? What cursed charms defend
    them !
Search deeper, villains. Who looks pale, or
    thinks
That I am cruel ?
    Aret. Over-merciful :
'Tis all your weakness, sir.
    Parth. I dare not shew
A sign of sorrow ; yet my sinews shrink,
The spectacle is so horrid.   [*Aside.*
    Cæs. I was never
O'ercome till now. For my sake roar a little,
And shew you are corporeal, and not turn'd
Aerial spirits.—Will it not do ? By Pallas,
It is unkindly done to mock his fury
Whom the world styles Omnipotent ! I am
    tortured
In their want of feeling torments.   Marius'
    story,
That does report him to have sat unmoved,
When cunning surgeons ripp'd his arteries
And veins, to cure his gout, compared to this,
Deserves not to be named.   Are they not
    dead ?
If so, we wash an Æthiop.
    Sura. No ; we live.
    Rust. Live to deride thee, our calm pa-
    tience treading
Upon the neck of tyranny.   That securely,
As 'twere a gentle slumber, we endure
Thy hangman's studied tortures, is a debt
We owe to grave philosophy, that instructs us.
The flesh is but the clothing of the soul,
Which growing out of fashion, though it be
Cast off, or rent, or torn, like ours, 'tis then,
Being itself divine, in her best lustre.
But unto such as thou, that have no hopes
Beyond the present, every little scar,
The want of rest, excess of heat or cold,
That does inform them only they are mortal,
Pierce through and through them.
    Cæs. We will hear no more.
    Rust. This only, and I give thee warning
        of it :
Though it is in thy will to grind this earth
As small as atoms, they thrown in the sea
    too,
They shall seem re-collected to thy sense :—
And, when the sandy building of thy greatness
Shall with its own weight totter, look to see
    me
As I was yesterday, in my perfect shape ;
For I'll appear in horror.
    Cæs. By my shaking
I am the guilty man, and not the judge,
Drag from my sight these cursed ominous
    wizards,

That, as they are now, like to double-faced
    Janus,
Which way soe'er I look, are Furies to me.
Away with them! first shew them death,
    . then leave
No memory of their ashes.   I'll mock Fate.
                · [*Exeunt* Executioners *with*
                            Rusticus *and* Sura.
Shall words fright him victorious armies
    circle?
No, no ; the fever does begin to leave me ;

Enter Domitia, Julia, *and* Cænis; Stephanos
        following.

Or, were it deadly, from this living fountain
I could renew the vigour of my youth,
And be a second Virbius.   O my glory !
My life ! command ! my all !
    Dom. As you to me are.
                · [*Embracing and kissing.*
I heard you were sad : I have prepared you
    sport
Will banish melancholy.   Sirrah, Cæsar,
(I hug myself for't,) I have been instructing
The players how to act ; and to cut off
All tedious impertinence, have contracted
The tragedy into one continued scene.
I have the art of't, and am taken more
With my ability that way, than all knowledge
I have but of thy love.
    Cæs. Thou art still thyself,
The sweetest, wittiest,——
    Dom. When we are abed
I'll thank your good opinion.   Thou shalt see
Such an Iphis of thy Paris !—and, to humble
The pride of Domitilla, that neglects me,
(Howe'er she is your cousin,) I have forced
    her
To play the part of Anaxarete——
You are not offended with it?
    Cæs. Any thing
That does content thee yields delight to me :
My faculties and powers are thine.
    Dom. I thank you :
Prithee let's take our places.   Bid them enter
Without more circumstance.

After a short flourish, enter Paris as Iphis.

                How do you like
That shape? methinks it is most suitable
To the aspéct of a despairing lover
The seeming late-fallen, counterfeited tears
That hang upon his cheeks, was my device.
    Cæs. And all was excellent.
    Dom. Now hear him speak.
    Iphis. *That she is fair, (and that an
        epithet*
Too foul to express her,) or descended nobly,
Or rich, or fortunate, are certain truths

In which poor Iphis glories.   But that these
Perfections, in no other virgin found,
Abused, should nourish cruelty and pride
In the divinest Anaxarete,
Is, to my love-sick, languishing soul, a riddle;
And with more difficulty to be dissolv'd,
Than that the monster Sphinx, from the
    steep rock,
Offer'd to Œdipus.   Imperious Love, .
As at thy everflaming altars Iphis,
Thy never-tired votary, hath presented,
With scalding tears, whole hecatombs of
    sighs,
Preferring thy power, and thy Paphian
    mother's,
Before the Thunderer's, Neptune's, or Pluto's
(That, after Saturn, did divide the world,
And had the sway of things, yet were com-
    pell'd
By thy inevitable shafts to yield,
And fight under thy ensigns) be auspicious
To this last trial of my sacrifice
Of love and service !
    Dom. Does he not act it rarely ?
Observe with what a feeling he delivers
His orisons to Cupid ; I am rapt with't.
    Iphis. *And from thy never-emptied quiver*
        take
A golden arrow, to transfix her heart,
And force her love like me ; or cure my wound
With a leaden one, that may beget in me
Hate and forgetfulness of what's now my
    idol——
But I call back my prayer ; I have blas-
    phemed
In my rash wish : 'tis I that am unworthy ;
But she all merit, and may in justice chal-
    lenge,
From the assurance of her excellencies,
Not love but adoration.   Yet, bear witness,
All-knowing Powers! I bring along with me,
As faithful advocates to make intercession,
A loyal heart with pure and holy flames,
With the foul fires of lust never polluted.
And, as I touch her threshold, which with
    tears,
My limbs benumb'd with cold, I oft have
    wash'd,
With my glad lips I kiss this earth, grown
    proud
With frequent favours from her delicate feet.
    Dom. By Cæsar's life he weeps ! and I
    forbear
Hardly to keep him company.
    Iphis. *Blest ground, thy pardon,*
If I profane it with forbidden steps.
I must presume to knock—and yet attempt it
With such a trembling reverence, as if
My hands [were now] held up for expiation
                                        P

To the incensed gods to spare a kingdom.
Within there, ho! something divine come
    forth
To a distressed mortal.

     Enter Latinus *as a* Porter.

Port. *Ha! Who knocks there?*
Dom. What a churlish look this knave has!
Port. *Is't you, sirrah?*
Are you come to pule and whine? Avaunt,
    and quickly;
Dog-whips shall drive you hence, else.
Dom. Churlish devil!
But that I should disturb the scene, as I live
I would tear his eyes out.
Cæs. 'Tis in jest, Domitia.
Dom. I do not like such jesting: if he
    were not
A flinty-hearted slave, he could not use
One of his form so harshly.   How the toad
    swells
At the other's sweet humility!
Cæs. 'Tis his part:
Let them proceed.
Dom. A rogue's part will ne'er leave him.
Iphis. *As you have, gentle sir, the happi-*
    ness
(*When you please*) *to behold the figure of*
The masterpiece of nature, limn'd to the life,
In more than human Anaxarete,
Scorn not your servant, that with suppliant
    hands
Takes hold upon your knees, conjuring
    you,
As you are a man, and did not suck the milk
Of wolves, and tigers, or a mother of
A tougher temper, use some means these eyes,
Before they are wept out, may see your lady.
Will you be gracious, sir?
  Port. *Though I lose my place for't,*
I can hold out no longer.
Dom. Now he melts,
There is some little hope he may die honest.
Port. *Madam!*

     Enter Domitilla *as* Anaxarete.

Anax. *Who calls? What object have we*
    here?
Dom. Your cousin keeps her proud state
    still; I think
I have fitted her for a part.
Anax. *Did I not charge thee*
I ne'er might see this thing more?
Iphis. *I am, indeed,*
What thing you please; a worm that you
    may tread on:
Lower I cannot fall to show my duty,
Till your disdain hath digg'd a grave to
    cover

This body with forgotten dust; and, when
I know your sentence, cruellest of women!
I'll, by a willing death, remove the object
That is an eyesore to you.
  Anax. *Wretch, thou dar'st not:*
That were the last and greatest service to me
Thy doting love could boast of. What dull
    fool
But thou could nourish any flattering hope,
One of my height in youth, in birth and for-
    tune,
Could e'er descend to look upon thy lowness,
Much less consent to make my lord of one
I'd not accept, though offer'd for my slave?
My thoughts stoop not so low.
Dom. There's her true nature:
No personated scorn.
  Anax. *I wrong my worth,*
Or to exchange a syllable or look
With one so far beneath me.
Iphis. *Yet take heed,*
Take heed of pride, and curiously consider,
How brittle the foundation is, on which
You labour to advance it. Niobe,
Proud of her numerous issue, durst contemn
Latona's double burthen; but what follow'd?
She was left a childless mother, and mourn'd
    to marble.
The beauty you o'erprize so, time or sickness
Can change to loath'd deformity; your wealth
The prey of thieves; queen Hecuba, Troy
    fired,
Ulysses' bondwoman: but the love I bring
    you
Nor time, nor sickness, violent thieves, nor
    fate,
Can ravish from you.
  Dom. Could the oracle
Give better counsel!
  Iphis. *Say, will you relent yet,*
Revoking your decree that I should die?
Or, shall I do what you command? resolve;
I am impatient of delay.
  Anax. *Dispatch then:*
I shall look on your tragedy unmoved,
Peradventure laugh at it; for it will prove
A comedy to me.
  Dom. O devil! devil!
Iphis. *Then thus I take my last leave.*
All the curses
Of lovers fall upon you; and, hereafter,
When any man, like me contemn'd, shall
    study,
In the anguish of his soul, to give a name
To a scornful, cruel mistress, let him only
Say, This most bloody woman is to me,
As Anaxarete was to wretched Iphis!——
Now feast your tyrannous mind, and glory
    in

*The ruins you have made: for Hymen's
    bands,
That should have made us one, this fatal
    halter
For ever shall divorce us: at your gate,
As a trophy of your pride and my affliction,
I'll presently hang myself.*
    Dom. Not for the world —
                                    [*Starts from her seat.*
Restrain him, as you love your lives !
    Cæs. Why are you
Transported thus, Domitia ? 'tis a play ;
Or, grant it serious, it at no part merits
This passion in you.
    Par. I ne'er purposed, madam,
To do the deed, in earnest ; though I bow
To your care and tenderness of me.
    Dom. Let me, sir,
Entreat your pardon ; what I saw presented,
Carried me beyond myself.
    Cæs. To your place again,
And see what follows.
    Dom. No, I am familiar
With the conclusion ; besides, upon the
    sudden
I feel myself much indisposed.
    Cæs. To bed then ;
I'll be thy doctor.
    Aret. There is something more
In this than passion,—which I must find out,
Or my intelligence freezes.
    Dom. Come to me, Paris,
To-morrow, for your reward.
    [*Exeunt all but* Domitilla *and* Stephanos.
    Steph. Patroness, hear me ;
Will you not call for your share ? Sit down
    with this,
And, the next action, like a Gaditane
    strumpet,
I shall look to see you tumble !
    Domitil. Prithee be patient.
I, that have suffer'd greater wrongs, bear
    this ;
And that, till my revenge, my comfort is.
                                    [*Exeunt.*

───────

ACT IV.

SCENE I.—*A Room in the Palace.*

Enter Parthenius, Julia, Domitilla, *and*
        Cænis.

    Parth. Why, 'tis impossible.—Paris !
    Jul. You observed not,
As it appears, the violence of her passion,
When personating Iphis, he pretended,
For your contempt, fair Anaxarete,
To hang himself.
    Parth. Yes, yes, I noted that ;

But never could imagine it could work her
To such a strange intemperance of affection,
As to doat on him.
    Domitil. By my hopes, I think not -
That she respects, though all here saw, and
    mark'd it ;
Presuming she can mould the emperor's will,
Into what form she likes, though we, and all
The informers of the world, conspired to,
    cross it.
    Cæn. Then with what eagerness, this
    morning, urging
The want of health and rest, she did entreat
Cæsar to leave her !
    Domitil. Who no sooner absent,
But she calls, *Dwarf!* (so in her scorn she
    styles me,)
*Put on my pantofles; fetch pen and paper,
I am to write:*—and with distracted looks,
In her smock, impatient of so short delay
As but to have a mantle thrown upon her,
She seal'd—I know not what, but 'twas in-
    dorsed,
To my loved Paris.
    Jul. Add to this, I heard her
Say, when a page received it, *Let him wait me,
And carefully, in the walk call'd our Retreat,
Where Cæsar, in his fear to give offence,
Unsent for, never enters.*
    Parth. This being certain,
(For these are more than jealous supposi-
    tions,)
Why do not you, that are so near in blood,
Discover it ?
    Domitil. Alas ! you know we dare not.
'Twill be received for a malicious practice,
To free us from that slavery which her pride
Imposes on us. But, if you would please
To break the ice, on pain to be sunk ever,
We would aver it.
    Parth. I would second you,
But that I am commanded with all speed
To fetch in Ascletario the Chaldæan ;
Who, in his absence, is condemn'd of treason,
For calculating the nativity
Of Cæsar, with all confidence foretelling,
In every circumstance, when he shall die
A violent death. Yet, if you could approve
Of my directions, I would have you speak
As much to Aretinus, as you have
To me deliver'd : he in his own nature
Being a spy, on weaker grounds, no doubt,
Will undertake it ; not for goodness' sake,
(With which he never yet held correspon-
    dence,)
But to endear his vigilant observings
Of what concerns the emperor, and a little
To triumph in the ruins of this Paris,
That cross'd him in the senate-house.—

                                    P 2

Enter Aretinus.

Here he comes,
His nose held up; he hath something in the
    wind,
Or I much err, already.   My designs
Command me hence, great ladies; but I leave
My wishes with you.   [*Exit.*
·*Aret.* Have I caught your Greatness
In the trap, my proud Augusta!
    Domitil. What is't raps him?
    Aret. And my fine Roman Actor! Is't
    even so?
No coarser dish to take your wanton palate,
Save that which, but the emperor, none
    durst taste of!
'Tis very well.   I needs must glory in
This rare discovery: but the rewards
Of my intelligence bid me think, even now,
By an edict from Cæsar, I have power
To tread upon the neck of slavish Rome,
Disposing offices and provinces
To my kinsmen, friends, and clients.
    Domitil. This is more
Than usual with him.
    Jul. Aretinus!
    Aret. How!
No more respect and reverence tender'd to
    me,
But *Aretinus!* 'Tis confess'd that title,
When you were princesses, and commanded
    all,
Had been a favour; but being, as you are,
Vassals to a proud woman, the worst bondage,
You stand obliged with as much adoration
To entertain him, that comes arm'd with
    strength
To break your fetters, as tann'd galley-slaves
Pay such as do redeem them from the oar.
I come not to entrap you; but aloud
Pronounce that you are manumized: and
    to make
Your liberty sweeter, you shall see her fall,
This empress,—this Domitia,—what you
    will,—
That triumph'd in your miseries.
    Domitil. Were you serious,
To prove your accusation I could lend
Some help.
    Cæn. And I.
    Jul. And I.
    Aret. No atom to me.—
My eyes and ears are every where; I know all,
To the line and action in the play that took
    her:
Her quick dissimulation to excuse
Her being transported, with her morning
    passion.
.I bribed the boy that did·convey the letter,

And, having perused it, made it up again:
Your griefs and angers are to me familiar.
—That Paris is brought to her, and how far
He shall be tempted.
    Domitil. This is above wonder.
    Aret. My gold can work much stranger
    miracles,
Than to corrupt poor waiters.   Here, join
    with me—   [*Takes out a petition.*
'Tis a complaint to Cæsar.   This is that
Shall ruin her, and raise you.   Have you
    set your hands
To the accusation?
    Jul. And will justify
What we've subscribed to.
    Cæn. And with vehemence.
    Domitil. I will deliver it.
    Aret. Leave the rest to me then.

Enter Cæsar, *with his* Guard.

    Cæs. Let our lieutenants bring us victory,
While we enjoy the fruits of peace at home:
And being secured from our intestine foes,
(Far worse than foreign enemies,) doubts
    and fears,
Though all the sky were hung with blazing
    meteors,
Which fond astrologers give out to be
Assured presages of the change of empires,
And deaths of monarchs, we, undaunted yet,
Guarded with our own thunder, bid defiance
To them and fate; we being too strongly
    arm'd
For them to wound us.
    Aret. Cæsar!
    Jul. As thou art
More than a man——
    Cæn. Let not thy passions be
Rebellious to thy reason—
    Domitil. But receive
        [*Delivers the petition.*
This trial of your constancy, as unmoved
As you go to or from the capitol,
Thanks given to Jove for triumphs.
    Cæs. Ha!
    Domitil. Vouchsafe
A while to stay the lightning of your eyes,
Poor mortals dare not look on.
    Aret. There's no vein
Of yours that rises with high rage, but is
An earthquake to us.
    Domitil. And, if not kept closed ·
With more than·human patience, in a
    . moment
Will swallow us to the centre.
    Cæn. Not that we
Repine to serve her, are we her accusers.
    Jul. But that she's fallen·so low. ·

Aret. Which on sure proofs
We can make good.
Domitil. And shew she is unworthy
Of the least spark of that diviner fire
You have conferr'd upon her.
Cæs. I stand doubtful,
And unresolved what to determine of you.
In this malicious violence you have offer'd
To the altar of her truth and pureness to me,
You have but fruitlessly labour'd to sully
A white robe of perfection, black-mouth'd
envy
Could belch no spot on.—But I will put off
The deity you labour to take from me,
And argue out of probabilities with you,
As if I were a man. Can I believe
That she, that borrows all her light from me,
And knows to use it, would betray her
darkness
To your intelligence; and make that ap-
parent,
Which, by her perturbations in a play,
Was yesterday but doubted, and find none
But you, that are her slaves, and therefore
hate her,
Whose aids she might employ to make way
for her?
Or Aretinus, whom long since she knew
To be the cabinet counsellor, nay, the key
Of Cæsar's secrets? Could her beauty raise
her
To this unequall'd height, to make her fall
The more remarkable? or must my desires
To her, and wrongs to Lamia, be revenged
By her, and on herself, that drew on both?
Or she leave our imperial bed to court
A public actor?
Aret. Who dares contradict
These more than human reasons, that have
power
To clothe base guilt in the most glorious
shape
Of innocence?
Domitil. Too well she knew the strength
And eloquence of her patron to defend her,
And thereupon presuming, fell securely;
Not fearing an accuser, nor the truth
Produced against her, which your love and
favour
Will ne'er discern from falsehood.
Cæs. I'll not hear
A syllable more that may invite a change
In my opinion of her. You have raised
A fiercer war within me by this fable,
Though with your lives you vow to make it
story,
Than if, and at one instant, all my legions
Revolted from me, and came arm'd against
me.

Here in this paper are the swords pre-
destined
For my destruction; here the fatal stars
That threaten more than ruin; this the
Death's head
That does assure me, if she can prove false,
That I am mortal, which a sudden fever
Would prompt me to believe, and faintly
yield to.
But now in my full confidence what she
suffers,
In that, from any witness but myself,
I nourish a suspicion she's untrue,
My toughness returns to me. Lead on,
monsters,
And, by the forfeit of your lives, confirm
She is all excellence, as you all baseness;
Or let mankind, for her fall, boldly swear
There are no chaste wives now, nor ever
were. [*Exeunt.*

SCENE II.—*A private Walk in the
Gardens of the Palace.*

Enter Domitia, Paris, *and* Servants.

Dom. Say we command, that none pre-
sume to dare,
On forfeit of our favour, that is life,
Out of a saucy curiousness, to stand
Within the distance of their eyes or ears,
Till we please to be waited on.
[*Exeunt* Servants.
And, sirrah,
Howe'er you are excepted, let it not
Beget in you an arrogant opinion
'Tis done to grace you.
Par. With my humblest service
I but obey your summons, and should blush
else,
To be so near you.
Dom. 'Twould become you rather
To fear the greatness of the grace vouch-
safed you
May overwhelm you; and 'twill do no less,
If, when you are rewarded, in your cups
You boast this privacy.
Par. That were, mightiest empress,
To play with lightning.
Dom. You conceive it right.
The means to kill or save is not alone
In Cæsar circumscribed; for, if incensed,
We have our thunder too, that strikes as
deadly.
Par. 'Twould ill become the lowness of
my fortune,
To question what you can do, but with all
Humility to attend what is your will,
And then to serve it.
Dom. And would not a secret,

Suppose we should commit it to your trust,
Scald you to keep it?

Par. Though it raged within me
Till I turn'd cinders, it should ne'er have vent.
To be an age a dying, and with torture,
Only to be thought worthy of your counsel,
Or actuate what you command to me,
A wretched obscure thing, not worth your knowledge,
Were a perpetual happiness.

Dom. We could wish
That we could credit thee, and cannot find
In reason, but that thou, whom oft I have seen
To personate a gentleman, noble, wise,
Faithful, and gainsome, and what virtues else
The poet pleases to adorn you with ;
But that (as vessels still partake the odour
Of the sweet precious liquors they contain'd)
Thou must be really, in some degree,
The thing thou dost present.—Nay, do not tremble ;
We seriously believe it, and presume
Our Paris is the volume in which all
Those excellent gifts the stage hath seen him graced with,
Are curiously bound up.

Par. The argument
Is the same, great Augusta, that I, acting
A fool, a coward, a traitor, or cold cynic,
Or any other weak and vicious person,
Of force I must be such. O, gracious madam,
How glorious soever, or deform'd,
I do appear in the scene, my part being ended,
And all my borrow'd ornaments put off,
I am no more, nor less, than what I was
Before I enter'd.

Dom. Come, you would put on
A wilful ignorance, and not understand
What 'tis we point at. Must we in plain language,
Against the decent modesty of our sex,
Say that we love thee, love thee to enjoy thee ;
Or that in our desires thou art preferr'd,
And Cæsar but thy second? Thou in justice,
If from the height of majesty we can
Look down upon thy lowness, and embrace it,
Art bound with fervor to look up to me.

Par. O, madam ! hear me with a patient ear,
And be but pleased to understand the reasons
That do deter me from a happiness
Kings would be rivals for. Can I, that owe
My life, and all that's mine, to Cæsar's bounties,
Beyond my hopes or merits, shower'd upon me,
Make payment for them with ingratitude,

Falsehood, and treason ! Though you have a shape
Might tempt Hippolitus, and larger power
To help or hurt than wanton Phædra had,
Let loyalty and duty plead my pardon,
Though I refuse to satisfy.

Dom. You are coy,
Expecting I should court you. Let mean ladies
Use prayers and entreaties to their creatures
To rise up instruments to serve their pleasures ;
But for Augusta so to lose herself,
That holds command o'er Cæsar and the world,
Were poverty of spirit. Thou must—thou shalt :
The violence of my passion knows no mean,
And in my punishments, and my rewards,
I'll use no moderation. Take this only,
As a caution from me ; threadbare chastity
Is poor in the advancement of her servants,
But wantonness magnificent ; and 'tis frequent
To have the salary of vice weigh down
The pay of virtue. So, without more trifling,
Thy sudden answer.

Par. In what a strait am I brought in !
Alas ! I know that the denial's death ;
Nor can my grant, discover'd, threaten more.
Yet, to die innocent, and have the glory
For all posterity to report, that I
Refused an empress, to preserve my faith
To my great master ; in true judgment, must
Show fairer, than to buy a guilty life
With wealth and honour. 'Tis the base I build on :
I dare not, must not, will not.

Dom. How ! contemn'd?
Since hopes, nor fears, in the extremes, prevail not,
I must use a mean. [*Aside.*]—Think who 'tis sues to thee.
Deny not that yet, which a brother may
Grant to a sister : as a testimony

Enter Cæsar, Aretinus, Julia, Domitilla,
Cænis, *and a* Guard *behind.*

I am not scorn'd, kiss me ;—kiss me again :
Kiss closer. Thou art now my Trojan Paris,
And I thy Helen.

Par. Since it is your will.

Cæs. And I am Menelaus : but I shall be
Something I know not yet.

Dom. Why lose we time
And opportunity? These are but salads
To sharpen appetite : let us to the feast,
[*Courting* Paris *wantonly.*

Where I shall wish that thou wert Jupiter,
And I Alcmena; and that I had power
To lengthen out one short night into three,
And so beget a Hercules.
 Cæs. [*Comes forward.*] While Amphitrio
Stands by, and draws the curtains.
  Par. Oh!——   [*Falls on his face.*
  Dom. Betray'd!
  Cæs. No; taken in a net of Vulcan's
filing,
Where, in myself, the theatre of the gods
Are sad spectators, not one of them daring
To witness, with a smile, he does desire
To be so shamed for all the pleasure that
You've sold your being for! What shall I
name thee?
Ingrateful, treacherous, insatiate, all
Invectives which, in bitterness of spirit,
Wrong'd men have breathed out against
wicked women,
Cannot express thee! Have I raised thee
from
Thy low condition to the height of greatness,
Command, and majesty, in one base act
To render me, that was, before I hugg'd
thee,
An adder, in my bosom, more than man,
A thing beneath a beast! Did I force these
Of mine own blood, as handmaids to kneel to
Thy pomp and pride, having myself no
thought
But how with benefits to bind thee mine;
And am I thus rewarded! Not a knee,
Nor tear, nor sign of sorrow for thy fault?
Break, stubborn silence: what canst thou
allege
To stay my vengeance?
  Dom. This. Thy lust compell'd me
To be a strumpet, and mine hath return'd it
In my intent and will, though not in act,
To cuckold thee.
  Cæs. O, impudence! take her hence,
And let her make her entrance into hell,
By leaving life with all the tortures that
Flesh can be sensible of. Yet stay. What
power
Her beauty still holds o'er my soul, that
wrongs
Of this unpardonable nature cannot teach me
To right myself, and hate her!—Kill her.—
Hold!
O that my dotage should increase from that
Which should breed detestation. By
Minerva,
If I look on her longer, I shall melt,
And sue to her, my injuries forgot,
Again to be received into her favour;
Could honour yield to it! Carry her to her
 chamber;

Be that her prison, till in cooler blood
I shall determine of her.
    [*Exit* Guard *with* Domitia.
 Aret. Now step I in,
While he's in this calm mood, for my re-
ward.—
Sir, if my service hath deserved——
  Cæs. Yes, yes:
And I'll reward thee. Thou hast robb'd
me of
All rest and peace, and been the principal
means
To make me know that, of which if again
I could be ignorant of, I would purchase it

    Re-enter Guard.

With the loss of empire: Strangle him;
 take these hence too,
And lodge them in the dungeon. Could
your reason,
Dull wretches, flatter you with hope to think
That this discovery, that hath shower'd
 upon me
Perpetual vexation, should not fall
Heavy on you? Away with them!—stop
their mouths;
I will hear no reply.
  [*Exit* Guard *with* Aretinus, Julia,
   Cænis, *and* Domitilla.
   —O, Paris, Paris!
How shall I argue with thee? how begin
To make thee understand, before I kill thee,
With what grief and unwillingness 'tis forced
 from me?
Yet, in respect I have favour'd thee, I'll hear
What thou canst speak to qualify or excuse
Thy readiness to serve this woman's lust;
And wish thou couldst give me such satis-
faction,
As I might bury the remembrance of it.
Look up: we stand attentive.
  Par. O, dread Cæsar!
To hope for life, or plead in the defence
Of my ingratitude, were again to wrong you.
I know I have deserved death; and my
suit is,
That you would hasten it: yet, that your
highness,
When I am dead, (as sure I will not live,)
May pardon me, I'll only urge my frailty,
Her will, and the temptation of that beauty
Which you could not resist. How could
poor I, then,
Fly that which follow'd me, and Cæsar sued
for?
This is all. And now your sentence.
  Cæs. Which I know not
How to pronounce. O that thy fault had been
But such as I might pardon! if thou hadst

In wantonness, like Nero, fired proud Rome,
Betray'd an army, butcher'd the whole senate,
Committed sacrilege, or any crime
The justice of our Roman laws calls death,
I had prevented any intercession,
And freely sign'd thy pardon.
  Par. But for this,
Alas! you cannot, nay, you must not, sir;
Nor let it to posterity be recorded,
That Cæsar, unrevenged, suffer'd a wrong,
Which, if a private man should sit down
    with it,
Cowards would baffle him.
  Cæs. With such true feeling
Thou arguest against thyself, that it
Works more upon me, than if my Minerva,
The grand protectress of my life and empire,
On forfeit of her favour, cried aloud,
Cæsar, show mercy! and, I know not how,
I am inclined to it. Rise. I'll promise
    nothing;
Yet clear thy cloudy fears, and cherish hopes.
What we must do, we shall do: we remember
A tragedy we oft have seen with pleasure,
Call'd *the False Servant.*
  Par. Such a one we have, sir.
  Cæs. In which a great lord takes to his
    protection
A man forlorn, giving him ample power
To order and dispose of his estate
In's absence, he pretending then a journey:
But yet within this restraint that, you no terms,
(This lord suspecting his wife's constancy,
She having play'd false to a former husband,)
The servant, though solicited, should con-
    sent,
Though she commanded him to quench her
    flames.
  Par. That was, indeed, the argument.
  Cæs. And what
Didst thou play in it!
  Par. The *False Servant*, sir.
  Cæs. Thou didst, indeed. Do the players
    wait without?
  Par. They do, sir, and prepared to act
    the story
Your majesty mention'd.
  Cæs. Call them in. Who presents
The injured lord!

  Enter Æsopus, Latinus, *and a* Lady.

  Æsop. 'Tis my part, sir.
  Cæs. Thou didst not
Do it to the life; we can perform it better.
Off with my robe and wreath: since Nero
    scorn'd not
The public theatre, we in private may
Disport ourselves. This cloak and hat,
    without

Wearing a beard, or other property,
Will fit the person.
  Æsop. Only, sir, a foil,
The point and edge rebated, when you act,
To do the murder. If you please to use this,
And lay aside your own sword.
  Cæs. By no means.
In jest nor earnest this parts never from me,
We'll have but one short scene—That, where
    the lady
In an imperious way commands the servant
To be unthankful to his patron: when
My cue's to enter, prompt me:—Nay, begin,
And do it sprightly: though but a new actor,
When I come to execution, you shall find
No cause to laugh at me.
  Lat. In the name of wonder,
What's Cæsar's purpose!
  Æsop. There is no contending.
  Cæs. Why, when?
  Par. I am arm'd:
And, stood grim Death now in my view,
    and his
Inevitable dart aim'd at my breast,
His cold embraces should not bring an ague
To any of my faculties, till his pleasures
Were served and satisfied; which done,
    Nestor's years
To me would be unwelcome.   [*Aside.*
  Lady. *Must we entreat,*
That were born to command? or court a
    servant,
That owes his food and clothing to our bounty,
For that, which thou ambitiously shouldst
    kneel for?
Urge not in thy excuse, the favours of
Thy absent lord, or that thou stand'st engaged
For thy life to his charity; nor thy fears
Of what may follow, it being in my power
To mould him any way.
  Par. *As you may me,*
In what his reputation is not wounded,
Nor I, his creature, in my thankfulness suffer.
I know you're young and fair; be virtuous too,
And loyal to his bed, that hath advanced you
To the height of happiness.
  Lady. *Can my love-sick heart*
Be cured with counsel? or durst reason ever
Offer to put in an exploded plea
In the court of Venus? My desires admit not
The least delay; and therefore instantly
Give me to understand what I must trust to:
For, if I am refused, and not enjoy
Those ravishing pleasures from thee, I run
    mad for,
I'll swear unto my lord, at his return,
(Making what I deliver good with tears,)
That brutishly thou wouldst have forced
    from me

What I make suit for. And then but imagine
What 'tis to die, with these words, slave and
   traitor,
With burning corsives writ upon thy fore-
   head,
And live prepared for't.
   Par. *This he will believe*
Upon her information, 'tis apparent;
And then I'm nothing: and of two extremes,
Wisdom says, choose the less. [Aside.]—
   Rather than fall
Under your indignation, I will yield:
This kiss, and this, confirms it.
   Æsop. Now, sir, now.
   Cæs. I must take them at it?
   Æsop. Yes, sir; be but perfect.
   Cæs. O villain! thankless villain!—I
      should talk now;
But I've forgot my part. But I can do:
Thus, thus, and thus!'   [*Stabs* Paris.
   Par. Oh! I am slain in earnest.
   Cæs. 'Tis true; and 'twas my purpose,
      my good Paris:
And yet, before life leave thee, let the honour
I've done thee in thy death bring comfort to
   thee.
If it had been within the power of Cæsar,
His dignity preserved, he had pardon'd thee:
But cruelty of honour did deny it.
Yet, to confirm I loved thee, 'twas my study,
To make thy end more glorious, to dis-
   tinguish
My Paris from all others; and in that
Have shewn my pity.   Nor would I let
   thee fall
By a centurion's sword, or have thy limbs
Rent piecemeal by the hangman's hook,
   however
Thy crime deserved it: but, as thou didst
   live
Rome's bravest actor, 'twas my plot that
   thou
Shouldst die in action, and to crown it, die,
With an applause enduring to all times,
By our imperial hand.—His soul is freed
From the prison of his flesh; let it mount
   upward!
And for this trunk, when that the funeral pile
Hath made it ashes, we'll see it enclosed
In a golden urn; poets adorn his hearse
With their most ravishing sorrows, and the
   stage
For ever mourn him, and all such as were
His glad spectators, weep his sudden death,
The cause forgotten in his epitaph.
   [*Sad music; the* Players *bear off* Paris'
      body, Cæsar *and the rest following.*

ACT V.

SCENE I.—*A Room in the Palace, with*
   an image of Minerva.

Enter Parthenius, Stephanos, *and* Guard.

   Parth. Keep a strong guard upon him,.
      and admit not
Access to any, to exchange a word
Or syllable with him, till the emperor pleases.
To call him to his presence.—[*Exit* Guard.]
   —The relation
That you have made me, Stephanos, of
   these late
Strange passions in Cæsar, much amaze me.
The informer Aretinus put to death
For yielding him a true discovery
Of the empress' wantonness; poor Paris
   kill'd first,
And now lamented; and the princesses
Confined to several islands; yet Augusta,
The machine on which all this mischief
   moved,
Received again to grace!
   Steph. Nay, courted to it:
Such is the impotence of his affection!
Yet, to conceal his weakness, he gives out
The people made suit for her, whom they
   hate more
Than civil war or famine.   But take heed,
My lord, that, nor in your consent nor wishes,
You lend or furtherance or favour to
The plot contrived against her: should she
   prove it,
Nay, doubt it only, you are a lost man,
Her power o'er doating Cæsar being now
Greater than ever.
   Parth. 'Tis a truth I shake at;
And, when there's opportunity——
   Steph. Say but, Do,
I am yours, and sure.
   Parth. I'll stand one trial more,
And then you shall hear from me.
   Steph. Now observe
The fondness of this tyrant, and her pride.
      [*They stand aside.*

Enter Cæsar *and* Domitia.

   Cæs. Nay, all's forgotten.
   Dom. It may be, on your part.
   Cæs. Forgiven too, Domitia:—'tis a
      favour
That you should welcome with more cheer-
   ful looks.
Can Cæsar pardon what you durst not hope
   for,
That did the injury, and yet must sue
To her, whose guilt is wash'd off by his
   mercy,
Only to entertain it?

Dom. I ask'd none ;
And I should be more wretched to receive
Remission for what I hold no crime,
But by a bare acknowledgment, than if,
By slighting and contemning it, as now,
I dared thy utmost fury.   Though thy flatterers
Persuade thee, that thy murders, lusts, and rapes,
Are virtues in thee ; and what pleases Cæsar,
Though never so unjust, is right and lawful ;
Or work in thee a false belief that thou
Art more than mortal ; yet I to thy teeth,
When circled with thy guards, thy rods, thy axes,
And all the ensigns of thy boasted power,
Will say, Domitian, nay, add to it Cæsar,
Is a weak, feeble man, a bondman to
His violent passions, and in that my slave ;
Nay, more my slave than my affections made me
To my loved Paris.
    Cæs. Can I live and hear this ?
Or hear, and not revenge it ? Come, you know
The strength that you hold on me, do not use it
With too much cruelty ; for though 'tis granted
That Lydian Omphale had less command
O'er Hercules, than you usurp o'er me,
Reason may teach me to shake off the yoke
Of my fond dotage.
    Dom. Never ; do not hope it :
It cannot be.   Thou being my beauty's captive,
And not to be redeem'd, my empire's larger
Than thine, Domitian, which I'll exercise
With rigour on thee, for my Paris' death.
And, when I've forced those eyes, now red with fury,
To drop down tears, in vain spent to appease me,
I know thy fervour such to my embraces,
Which shall be, though still kneel'd for, still denied thee,
That thou with languishment shalt wish my actor
Did live again, so thou mightst be his second
To feed upon those delicates, when he's sated.
    Cæs. O my Minerva.
    Dom. There she is, [*Points to the statue.*] invoke her :
She cannot arm thee with ability
To draw thy sword on me, my power being greater :
Or only say to thy centurions,

Dare none of you do what I shake to think on,
And, in this woman's death, remove the Furies
That every hour afflict me?—Lamia's wrongs,
When thy lust forced me from him, are, in me,
At the height revenged ; nor would I outlive Paris,
But that thy love, increasing with my hate,
May add unto thy torments ; so, with all
Contempt I can, I leave thee.   ˙ [*Exit.*
    Cæs. I am lost ;
Nor am I Cæsar. When I first betray'd
The freedom of my faculties and will
To this imperious siren, I laid down
The empire of the world, and of myself,
At her proud feet.   Sleep all my ireful powers?
Or is the magic of my dotage such,
That I must still make suit to hear those charms
That do increase my thraldom ! Wake, my anger !
For shame, break through this lethargy, and appear
With usual terror, and enable me,
Since I wear not a sword to pierce her heart,
Nor have a tongue to say this, *Let her die,*
Though 'tis done with a fever-shaken hand,
                [*Pulls out a table-book.*
To sign her death.   Assist me, great Minerva,
And vindicate thy votary ! [*writes*] So ; she's now
Among the list of those I have proscribed,
And are, to free me of my doubts and fears,
To die to-morrow.
    Steph. That same fatal book
Was never drawn yet, but some men of rank
Were mark'd out for destruction.   [*Exit.*
    Parth. I begin
To doubt myself.
    Cæs. Who waits there ?
    Parth. [*coming forward.*] Cæsar.
    Cæs. So !
These, that command arm'd troops, quake at my frowns,
And yet a woman slights them. Where's the wizard
We charged you to fetch in ?
    Parth. Ready to suffer
What death you please to appoint him.
    Cæs. Bring him in.
We'll question him ourself.

Enter Tribunes, *and* Guard *with*
Ascletario.

        Now, you, that hold

Intelligence with the stars, and dare prefix
The day and hour in which we are to part
With life and empire, punctually foretelling
The means and manner of our violent end ;
As you would purchase credit to your art,
Resolve me, since you are assured of us,
What fate attends yourself?

Ascle. I have had long since
A certain knowledge, and as sure as thou
Shalt die to-morrow, being the fourteenth of
The kalends of October, the hour five ;
Spite of prevention, this carcass shall be
Torn and devoured by dogs ;—and let that
stand
For a firm prediction.

Cæs. May our body, wretch,
Find never nobler sepulchre, if this
Fall ever on thee ! Are we the great disposer
Of life and death, yet cannot mock the stars
In such a trifle ? Hence with the impostor ;
And having cut his throat, erect a pile,
Guarded with soldiers, till his cursed trunk
Be turu'd to ashes : upon forfeit of
Your life, and theirs, perform it.

Ascle. 'Tis in vain ;
When what I have foretold is made apparent,
Tremble to think what follows.

Cæs. Drag him hence,
[*The* Tribunes *and* Guard *bear off* Ascletario.
And do as I command you. I was never
Fuller of confidence ; for, having got
The victory of my passions, in my freedom
From proud Domitia, (who shall cease to live,
Since she disdains to love,) I rest unmoved :
And, in defiance of prodigious meteors,
Chaldeans' vain predictions, jealous fears
Of my near friends and freedmen, certain hate
Of kindred and alliance, or all terrors
The soldiers' doubted faith, or people's rage
Can bring to shake my constancy, I am
arm'd.
That scrupulous thing styled conscience is
sear'd up,
And I insensible of all my actions,
For which, by moral and religious fools,
I stand condemn'd, as they had never been.
And, since I have subdued triumphant love,
I will not deify pale captive fear,
Nor in a thought receive it : for, till thou,
Wisest Minerva, that from my first youth
Hast been my sole protectress, dost forsake
me,
Not Junius Rusticus' threaten'd apparition,
Nor what this soothsayer but even now fore-
told,
Being things impossible to human reason,
Shall in a dream disturb me. Bring my
couch, there :
A sudden but a secure drowsiness

Invites me to repose myself. [*A couch
brought in.*] Let music,
With some choice ditty, second it :—[*Exit
Parthenius.*]—The mean time,
Rest there, dear book, which open'd, when
I wake,
[*Lays the book under his pillow.*
Shall make some sleep for ever.
[*Music and a song.* Cæsar *sleeps.*

Re-enter Parthenius *and* Domitia.

Dom. Write my name
In his bloody scroll, Parthenius ! the fear's
idle :
He durst not, could not.

Parth. I can assure nothing ;
But I observed, when you departed from him,
After some little passion, but much fury,
He drew it out : whose death he sign'd, I
know not ;
But in his looks appear'd a resolution
Of what before he stagger'd at. What he hath
Determined of is uncertain, but too soon
Will fall on you, or me, or both, or any,
His pleasure known to the tribunes and cen-
turions,
Who never use to enquire his will, but serve it.
Now, if, out of the confidence of your power,
The bloody catalogue being still about him,
As he sleeps you dare peruse it, or remove it,
You may instruct yourself, or what to suffer,
Or how to cross it.

Dom. I would not be caught
With too much confidence. By your leave,
sir. Ha !
No matter !—you lie uneasy, sir,
Let me mend your pillow.
[*Takes away the book.*
Parth. Have you it?
Dom. 'Tis here.
Cæs. Oh !
Parth. You have waked him : softly,
gracious madam,
While we are unknown ; and then consult
at leisure. [*Exeunt.*

Dreadful music. The Apparitions of Junius
Rusticus *and* Palphurius Sura *rise, with
bloody swords in their hands ; they wave
them over the head of* Cæsar, *who seems
troubled in his sleep, and as if praying to
the image of Minerva, which they scornfully seize, and then disappear with it.*

Cæs. [*starting.*] Defend me, goddess, or
this horrid dream
Will force me to distraction ! whither have
These furies borne thee? Let me rise and
follow.
I am bathed o'er with the cold sweat of death,

And am deprived of organs to pursue
These sacrilegious spirits. Am I at once
Robb'd of my hopes and being? No, I live—
                    [*Rises distractedly.*
Yes, live, and have discourse, to know myself
Of gods and men forsaken. What accuser
Within me cries aloud, I have deserved it,
In being just to neither? Who dares speak
      this?
Am I not Cæsar?—How! again repeat it?
Presumptuous traitor, thou shalt die!—
      What traitor?
He that hath been a traitor to himself,
And stands convicted here. Yet who can sit
A competent judge o'er Cæsar? Cæsar. Yes,
Cæsar by Cæsar's sentenced, and must suffer;
Minerva cannot save him. Ha! where is she?
Where is my goddess? vanish'd! I am lost
      then.
No; 'twas no dream, but a most real truth,
That Junius Rusticus and Palphurius Sura,
Although their ashes were cast in the sea,
Were by their innocence made up again,
And in corporeal forms but now appear'd,
Waving their bloody swords above my head,
As at their deaths they threaten'd. And
      methought,
Minerva, ravish'd hence, whisper'd that she
Was, for my blasphemies, disarm'd by Jove,
And could no more protect me. Yes, 'twas so,
                    [*Thunder and lightning.*
His thunder does confirm it, against which,
Howe'er it spare the laurel, this proud wreath

          Enter three Tribunes.

Is no assurance. Ha! come you resolved
To be my executioners?
      1 *Trib.* Allegiance
And faith forbid that we should lift an arm
Against your sacred head.
      2 *Trib.* We rather sue
For mercy.
      3 *Trib.* And acknowledge that in justice
Our lives are forfeited for not performing
What Cæsar charged us.
      1 *Trib.* Nor did we transgress it
In our want of will or care; for, being but
      men,
It could not be in us to make resistance,
The gods fighting against us.
      Cæs. Speak, in what
Did they express their anger? we will hear it,
But dare not say, undaunted.
      1 *Trib.* In brief thus, sir :
The sentence given by your imperial tongue,
For the astrologer Ascletario's death,
With speed was put in execution.
      Cæs. Well.

      1 *Trib.* For, his throat cut, his legs bound,
      and his arms
Pinion'd behind his back, the breathless trunk
Was with all scorn dragg'd to the field of
      Mars,
And there, a pile being raised of old dry wood,
Smear'd ,o'er with oil and brimstone, or what
      else
Could help to feed or to increase the fire,
The carcass was thrown on it ; but no sooner
The stuff, that was most apt, began to flame,
But suddenly, to the amazement of
The fearless soldier, a sudden flash
Of lightning, breaking through the scatter'd
      clouds,
With such a horrid violence forced its passage,
And, as disdaining all heat but itself,
In a moment quench'd the artificial fire :
And before we could kindle it again,
A clap of thunder follow'd with such noise,
As if then Jove, incensed against mankind,
Had in his secret purposes determined
An universal ruin to the world.
This horror past, not at Deucalion's flood
Such a stormy shower of rain (and yet that
      word is
Too narrow to express it) was e'er seen :
Imagine rather, sir, that with less fury
The waves rush down the cataracts of Nile ;
Or that the sea, spouted into the air
By the angry Orc, endangering tall ships
But sailing near it, so falls down again.——
Yet here the wonder ends not, but begins :
For, as in vain we labour'd to consume
The wizard's body, all the dogs of Rome,
Howling and yelling like to famish'd wolves,
Brake in upon us; and though thousands were
Kill'd in th' attempt, some did ascend the pile,
And with their eager fangs seized on the
      carcass.
      Cæs. But have they torn it?
      1 *Trib.* Torn it, and devour'd it.
      Cæs. I then am a dead man, since all
      predictions
Assure me I am lost. O, my loved soldiers,
Your emperor must leave you! yet, however
I cannot grant myself a short reprieve,
I freely pardon you. The fatal hour
Steals fast upon me : I must die this morning
By five, my soldiers ; that's the latest hour
You e'er must see me living.
      1 *Trib.* Jove avert it !
In our swords lies your fate, and we will
      guard it.
      Cæs. O no, it cannot be ; it is decreed
Above, and by no strength here to be alter'd..
Let proud mortality but look on Cæsar,
Compass'd of late with armies, in his eyes
Carrying both life and death, and in his arms

Fathoming the earth ; that would be styled
  a God,
And is, for that presumption, cast beneath
The low condition of a common man,
Sinking with mine own weight.
  1 *Trib*. Do not forsake
Yourself, we'll never leave you.
  2 *Trib*. We'll draw up
More cohorts of your guard, if you doubt
  treason.
  Cæs. They cannot save me. The offended
  gods,
That now sit judges on me, from their envy
Of my power and greatness here, conspire
  against me.
  1 *Trib*. Endeavour to appease them.
  Cæs. 'Twill be fruitless :
I am past hope of remission. Yet, could I
Decline this dreadful hour of five, these
  terrors,
That drive me to despair, would soon fly
  from me :
And could you but till then assure me——
  1 *Trib*. Yes, sir ; .
Or we'll fall with you, and make Rome the urn
In which we'll mix our ashes.
  Cæs. 'Tis said nobly :
I am something comforted : howe'er, to die
Is the full period of calamity.   [*Exeunt*.

SCENE II.—*Another Room in the Palace*.

Enter Parthenius, Domitia, Julia, Cænis,
  Domitilla, Stephanos, Sejeius, *and* En-
  tellus.

  Parth. You see we are all condemn'd ;
  there's no evasion ;
We must do, or suffer.
  Steph. But it must be sudden ;
The least delay is mortal. .
  Dom. Would I were
A man, to give it action !
  Domitil. Could I make my approaches,
  though my stature
Does promise little, I have a spirit as daring
As hers that can reach higher.
  Steph. I will take
That burthen from you, madam. All the
  art is,
To draw him from the tribunes that attend
  him ;
For, could you bring him but within my
  sword's reach,
The world should owe her freedom from a
  tyrant
To Stephanos.
  Sej. You shall not share alone
The glory of a deed that will endure
To all posterity.

  Ent. I will put in
For a part, myself.
  Parth. Be resolv'd, and stand close.
I have conceived a way, and with the hazard
Of my life I'll practise it, to fetch him hither.
But then no trifling.
  Steph. We'll dispatch him, fear not :
A dead dog never bites.
  Parth. Thus then at all.
    [*Exit ; the rest conceal themselves*.

Enter Cæsar *and the* Tribunes.

  Cæs. How slow-paced are these minutes !
  in extremes,
How miserable is the least delay !
Could I imp feathers to the wings of time,
Or with as little ease command the sun
To scourge his coursers up heaven's eastern
  hill,
Making the hour to tremble at, past re-
  calling,
As I can move this dial's tongue to six ;
My veins and arteries, emptied with fear,
Would fill and swell again. How do I look ?
Do you yet see Death about me ?
  1 *Trib*. Think not of him ;
There is no danger : all these prodigies
That do affright you, rise from natural causes ;
And though you do ascribe them to yourself,
Had you ne'er been, had happened.
  Cæs. 'Tis well said,
Exceeding well, brave soldier. Can it be,
That I, that feel myself in health and
  strength,
Should still believe I am so near my end,
And have my guards about me ? perish all
Predictions ! I grow constant they are false,
And built upon uncertainties.
  1 *Trib*. This is right ;
Now Cæsar's heard like Cæsar.
  Cæs. We will to
The camp, and having there confirm'd the
  soldier
With a large donative, and increase of pay,
Some shall——I say no more.

Re-enter Parthenius.

  Parth. All happiness,
Security, long life, attend upon
The monarch of the world !
  Cæs. Thy looks are cheerful.
  Parth. And my relation full of joy and
  wonder.
Why is the care of your imperial body,
My lord, neglected, the fear'd hour being
  past,
In which your life was threaten'd ?
  Cæs. Is't past five ?

Parth. Past six, upon my knowledge; and, in justice,
Your clock-master should die, that hath deferr'd
Your peace so long. There is a post new lighted,
That brings assured intelligence, that your legions
In Syria have won a glorious day,
And much enlarged your empire. I have kept him
Conceal'd, that you might first partake the pleasure
In private, and the senate from yourself
Be taught to understand how much they owe
To you and to your fortune.

Cæs. Hence, pale fear, then!
Lead me, Parthenius.

1 Trib. Shall we wait you?

Cæs. No.
After losses guards are useful. Know your distance.
            [*Exeunt* Cæsar *and* Parthenius.

2 Trib. How strangely hopes delude men! as I live,
The hour is not yet come.

1 Trib. Howe'er, we are
To pay our duties, and observe the sequel.
            [*Exeunt* Tribunes. Domitia *and the rest come forward.*

Dom. I hear him coming. Be constant.

Re-enter Cæsar *and* Parthenius.

Cæs. Where, Parthenius,
Is this glad messenger?

Steph. Make the door fast.—Here;
A messenger of horror.

Cæs. How! betray'd?

Dom. No; taken, tyrant.

Cæs. My Domitia
In the conspiracy!

Parth. Behold this book.

Cæs. Nay, then I am lost. Yet, though
    I am unarm'd,
I'll not fall poorly. [*Overthrows* Stephanos.

Steph. Help me.

Ent. Thus, and thus!   } *They stab*
Sej. Are you so long a falling? }   *him.*

Cæs. 'Tis done basely. [*Falls, and dies.*

Parth. This for my father's death.

Dom. This for my Paris.

Jul. This for thy incest.

Domitil. This for thy abuse
Of Domitilla.   [*They severally stab him.*

Tribunes. [*within.*] Force the doors!

Enter Tribunes.
                                    O Mars!
What have you done?

Parth. What Rome shall give us thanks for.

Steph. Dispatch'd a monster.

1 Trib. Yet he was our prince,
However wicked; and, in you, this murder,—
Which whosoe'er succeeds him will revenge:
Nor will we, that serv'd under his command,
Consent that such a monster as thyself,
(For in thy wickedness Augusta's title
Hath quite forsook thee,) thou, that wert the ground
Of all these mischiefs, shall go hence unpunish'd.
Lay hands on her, and drag her to her sentence.—
We will refer the hearing to the senate,
Who may at their best leisure censure you.
Take up his body: he in death hath paid
For all his cruelties. Here's the difference;
Good kings are mourn'd for after life; but ill,
And such as govern'd only by their will,
And not their reason, unlamented fall;
No good man's tear shed at their funeral.
            [*Exeunt; the* Tribunes *bearing the body of*
                        Cæsar.

The Great Duke of Florence.

DRAMATIS PERSONÆ.

Cozimo, *duke of* Florence.
Giovanni, *nephew to the duke.*
Sanazarro, *the duke's favourite.*
Carolo Charomonte, Giovanni's *tutor.*
Contarino, *secretary to the duke.*
Alphonso, ⎱
Hippolito, ⎰ *counsellors of state.*
Hieronimo, ⎰
Calandrino, *a merry fellow, servant to Gio-vanni.*

Bernardo, ⎱
Caponi, ⎰ *servants to* Charomonte.
Petruchio, ⎰
A Gentleman.
Fiorinda, *duchess of* Urbin.
Lidia, *daughter to* Charomonte.
Calaminta, *servant to* Fiorinda.
Petronella, *a foolish servant to* Lidia.
Attendants, Servants, &c.

SCENE,—*Partly in* Florence, *and partly at the residence of* Charomonte *in the country.*

ACT I.

SCENE I.—*The Country. A Room in* Charomonte's House.

Enter Charomonte *and* Contarino.

Char. You bring your welcome with you.
Cont. Sir, I find it
In every circumstance.
Char. Again most welcome.
Yet, give me leave to wish (and pray you, excuse me,
For I must use the freedom I was born with)
The great duke's pleasure had commanded you
To my poor house upon some other service;
Not this you are design'd to : but his will
Must be obey'd, howe'er it ravish from me
The happy conversation of one
As dear to me as the old Romans held
Their household Lars, whom they believed had power
To bless and guard their families.
Cont. 'Tis received so
On my part, signior ; nor can the duke
But promise to himself as much as may
Be hoped for from a nephew. And 'twere weakness
In any man to doubt, that Giovanni,
Train'd up by your experience and care
In all those arts peculiar and proper
To future greatness, of necessity
Must in his actions, being grown a man,
Make good the princely education
Which he derived from you.
Char. I have discharged,
To the utmost of my power, the trust the duke

Committed to me, and with joy perceive
The seed of my endeavours was not sown
Upon the barren sands, but fruitful glebe,
Which yields a large increase : my noble charge,
By his sharp wit, and pregnant apprehension,
Instructing those that teach him ; making use,
Not in a vulgar and pedantic form,
Of what's read to him, but 'tis straight digested,
And truly made his own. His grave discourse,
In one no more indebted unto years,
Amazes such as hear him : horsemanship,
And skill to use his weapon, are by practice
Familiar to him : as for knowledge in
Music, he needs it not, it being born with him ;
All that he speaks being with such grace deliver'd,
That it makes perfect harmony.
Cont. You describe
A wonder to me.
Char. Sir, he is no less ;
And that there may be nothing wanting that
May render him complete, the sweetness of
His disposition so wins on all
Appointed to attend him, that they are
Rivals, even in the coarsest office, who
Shall get precedency to do him service ;
Which they esteem a greater happiness,
Than if they had been fashion'd and built up
To hold command o'er others.
Cont. And what place
Does he now bless with his presence?
Char. He is now

Running at the ring, at which he's excellent.
He does allot for every exercise
A several hour; for sloth, the nurse of vices,
And rust of action, is a stranger to him.
But I fear I am tedious, let us pass,
If you please, to some other subject, though
    I cannot
Deliver him as he deserves.
    Cont. You have given him
A noble character.
    Char. And how, I pray you,
(For we, that never look beyond our villas,
Must be inquisitive,) are state affairs
Carried in court?
    Cont. There's little alteration :
Some rise, and others fall, as it stands with
The pleasure of the duke, their great dis-
    poser.
    Char. Does Lodovico Sanazarro hold
Weight, and grace with him?
    Cont. Every day new honours
Are shower'd upon him, and without the
    envy
Of such as are good men ; since all confess
The service done our master in his wars
'Gainst Pisa and Sienna may with justice
Claim what's conferr'd upon him.
    Char. 'Tis said nobly ;
For princes never more make known their
    wisdom,
Than when they cherish goodness where
    they find it :
They being men, and not gods, Contarino,
They can give wealth and titles, but no
    virtues ;
That is without their power. When they
    advance,
Not out of judgment, but deceiving fancy,
An undeserving man, howe'er set off
With all the trim of greatness, state, and
    power,
And of a creature even grown terrible
To him from whom he took his giant form,
This thing is still a comet, no true star ;
And when the bounties feeding his false fire
Begin to fail, will of itself go out,
And what was dreadful, proves ridiculous.
But in our Sanazarro 'tis not so,
He being pure and tried man; and any stamp
Of grace, to make him current to the world,
The duke is pleased to give him, will add
    honour
To the great bestower; for he, though
    allow'd
Companion to his master, still preserves
His majesty in full lustre.
    Cont. He, indeed,
At no part does take from it, but becomes
A partner of his cares, and eases him,

With willing shoulders, of a burthen which
He should alone sustain.
    Char. Is he yet married?
    Cont. No, signior, still a bachelor;
    howe'er
It is apparent that the choicest virgin
For beauty, bravery, and wealth, in Florence,
Would, with her parents' glad consent, be
    won,
Were his affection and intent but known,
To be at his devotion.
    Char. So I think too.
But break we off—here comes my princely
    charge.

Enter Giovanni *and* Calandrino.

Make your approaches boldly ; you will find
A courteous entertainment.   [*Cont. kneels.*
    Giov. Pray you, forbear
My hand, good signior ; 'tis a ceremony
Not due to me. 'Tis fit we should embrace
With mutual arms.
    Cont. It is a favour, sir,
I grieve to be denied.
    Giov. You shall o'ercome :
But 'tis your pleasure, not my pride, that
    grants it.
Nay, pray you, guardian, and good sir,
    put on :
How ill it shews to have that reverend head
Uncover'd to a boy !
    Char. Your excellence
Must give me liberty to observe the distance
And duty that I owe you.
    Giov. Owe me duty !
I do profess (and when I do deny it,
Good fortune leave me !) you have been to me
A second father, and may justly challenge,
For training up my youth in arts and arms,
As much respect and service, as was due
To him that gave me life. And did you
    know, sir,
Or will believe from me, how many sleeps
Good Charomonte hath broken, in his care
To build me up a man, you must confess
Chiron, the tutor to the great Achilles,
Compared with him, deserves not to be named.
And if my gracious uncle, the great duke,
Still holds me worthy his consideration;
Or finds in me aught worthy to be loved,
That little rivulet flow'd from this spring ;
And so from me report him.
    Cont. Fame already
Hath fill'd his highness' ears with the true
    story
Of what you are, and how much better'd by
    him.
And 'tis his purpose to reward the travail
Of this grave sir, with a magnificent hand.

For, though his tenderness hardly could con-
sent
To have you one hour absent from his sight,
For full three years he did deny himself
The pleasure he took in you, that you, here,
From this great master, might arrive unto
The theory of those high mysteries
Which you, by action, must make plain in
court.
'Tis, therefore, his request, (and that, from
him,
Your excellence must grant a strict command,)
That instantly (it being not five hours riding)
You should take horse and visit him. These
his letters
Will yield you further reasons.
[*Delivers a packet.*
    Cal. To the court !
Farewell the flower, then, of the country's
garland.
This is our sun, and when he's set, we must not
Expect or spring or summer, but resolve
For a perpetual winter.
    Char. Pray you, observe
            [Giovanni *reading the letters.*
The frequent changes in his face.
    Cont. As if
His much unwillingness to leave your house
Contended with his duty.
    Char. Now he appears
Collected and resolved.
    Giov. It is the duke !
The duke, upon whose favour all my hopes
And fortunes do depend. Nor must I check
At his commands for any private motives
That do invite my stay here, though they are
Almost not to be master'd. My obedience,
In my departing suddenly, shall confirm
I am his highness' creature ; yet, I hope
A little stay to take a solemn farewell
Of all those ravishing pleasures I have tasted
In this my sweet retirement, from my
guardian,
And his incomparable daughter, cannot meet
An ill construction.
    Cont. I will answer that :
Use your own will.
    Giov. I would speak to you, sir,
In such a phrase as might express the thanks
My heart would gladly pay ; but——
    Char. I conceive you :
And something I would say ; but I must not
do it
In that dumb rhetoric which you make
use of ;
For I do wish you all——I know not how,
My toughness melts, and, spite of my dis-
cretion,
I must turn woman. [*Embraces* Giovanni.

    Cont. What a sympathy
There is between them !
    Cal. Were I on the rack,
I could not shed a tear. But I am mad,
And, ten to one, shall hang myself for sorrow,
Before I shift my shirt. But hear you, sir,
(I'll separate you,) when you are gone, what
will
Become of me ?
    Giov. Why, thou shalt to court with me.
            [*Takes* Char. *aside.*
    Cal. To see you worried ?
    Cont. Worried, Calandrine !
    Cal. Yes, sir : for, bring this sweet face
to the court,
There will be such a longing 'mong the
madams,
Who shall engross it first, nay, fight and
scratch for't,
That, if they be not stopp'd, for entertainment
They'll kiss his lips off. Nay, if you'll scape so,
And not be tempted to a further danger,
These succubæ are so sharp set, that you must
Give out you are an eunuch.
    Cont. Have a better
Opinion of court-ladies, and take care
Of your own stake.
    Cal. For my stake, 'tis past caring.
I would not have a bird of unclean feathers
Handsel his lime twig,—and so much for him :
There's something else that troubles me.
    Cont. What's that ?
    Cal. Why, how to behave myself in court,
and tightly.
I have been told the very place transforms
men,
And that not one of a thousand, that before
Lived honestly in the country on plain salads,
But bring him thither, mark me that, and
feed him
But a month or two with custards and court
cake-bread,
And he turns knave immediately.—I'd be
honest ;
But I must follow the fashion, or die a beggar.
    Giov. And, if I ever reach my hopes,
believe it,
We will share fortunes.
    Char. This acknowledgement

            Enter Lidia.

Binds me your debtor ever.—Here comes one
In whose sad looks you easily may read
What her heart suffers, in that she is forced
To take her last leave of you.
    Cont. As I live,
A beauty without parallel !
    Lid. Must you go, then,
So suddenly ?

Q

Giov. There's no evasion, Lidia,
To gain the least delay, though I would buy it
At any rate. Greatness, with private men
Esteem'd a blessing, is to me a curse ;
And we, whom, for our high births, they
conclude
The only freemen, are the only slaves.
Happy the golden mean ! had I been born
In a poor sordid cottage, not nurs'd up
With expectation to command a court,
I might, like such of your condition, sweetest,
Have ta'en a safe and middle course, and
not,
As I am now, against my choice, compell'd
Or to lie grovelling on the earth, or raised
So high upon the pinnacles of state,
That I must either keep my height with
danger,
Or fall with certain ruin.
Lid. Your own goodness
Will be your faithful guard.
Giov. O, Lidia !——
Cont. So passionate ! [*Aside.*
Giov. For, had I been your equal,
I might have seen and liked with mine own
eyes,
And not, as now, with others; I might still,
And without observation, or envy,
As I have done, continued my delights
With you, that are alone, in my esteem,
The abstract of society : we might walk
In solitary groves, or in choice gardens ;
From the variety of curious flowers
Contemplate nature's workmanship, and
wonders :
And then, for change, near to the murmur of
Some bubbling fountain, I might hear you
sing,
And, from the well-tuned accents of your
tongue,
In my imagination conceive
With what melodious harmony a quire
Of angels sing above their Maker's praises.
And then with chaste discourse, as we re-
turu'd,
Imp feathers to the broken wings of time :—
And all this I must part from.
Cont. You forget
The haste imposed upon us.
Giov. One word more,
And then I come. And after this, when, with
Continued innocence of love and service,
I had grown ripe for Hymeneal joys,
Embracing you, but with a lawful flame,
I might have been your husband.
Lid. Sir, I was,
And ever am, your servant ; but it was,
And 'tis, far from me in a thought to cherish
Such saucy hopes. If I had been the heir

Of all the globes and sceptres mankind
bows to,
At my best you had deserved me ; as I am,
Howe'er unworthy, in my virgin zeal
I wish you, as a partner of your bed,
A princess equal to you : such a one
That may make it the study of her life,
With all the obedience of a wife, to please
you.
May you have happy issue, and I live
To be their humblest handmaid !
Giov. I am dumb,
And can make no reply.
Cont. Your excellence
Will be benighted.
Giov. This kiss, bathed in tears,
May learn you what I should say.
Lid. Give me leave
To wait on you to your horse.
Char. And me to bring you
To the one half of your journey.
Giov. Your love puts
Your age to too much trouble.
Char. I grow young,
When most I serve you.
Cont. Sir, the duke shall thank you.
[*Exeunt.*

SCENE II.—Florence. *A Room in the Palace.*

Enter Alphonso, Hippolito, *and* Hieronimo.

Alph. His highness cannot take it ill.
Hip. However,
We with our duties shall express our care
For the safety of his dukedom.
Hier. And our loves

Enter Cozimo.

To his person.—-Here he comes : present it
boldly.
[*They kneel,* Alphonso *tenders a paper.*
Coz. What needs this form ? We are not
grown so proud
As to disdain familiar conference
With such as are to counsel and direct us.
This kind of adoration showed not well
In the old Roman emperors, who, forgetting
That they were flesh and blood, would be
styled gods :
In us to suffer it, were worse. Pray you,
rise. [*Reads.*
Still the old suit ! With too much curious-
ness
You have too often search'd this wound,
which yields
Security and rest, not trouble to me.
For here you grieve, that my firm resolution
Continues me a widower; and that
My want of issue to succeed me in

My government, when I am dead, may
breed
Distraction in the state, and make the name
And family of the Medici, now admired,
Contemptible.
Hip. And with strong reasons, sir.
Alph. For, were you old, and past hope
to beget
The model of yourself, we should be silent.
· *Hier.* But, being in your height and pride
of years,
As you are now, great sir, and having, too,
In your possession the daughter of
The deceased duke of Urbin, and his heir,
Whose guardian you are made ; were you
but pleased
To think her worthy of you, besides chil-
dren,
The dukedom she brings with her for a
dower
Will yield a large increase of·strength and
power
To those fair territories which already
Acknowledge you their absolute lord.
Coz. You press us
With solid arguments, we grant ; and, though
We stand not bound to yield account to any
Why we do this or that, (the full consent
Of our subjects being included in our will,)
We, out of our free bounties, will deliver
The motives that divert us. You well know
That, three years since, to our much grief,
we lost
Our dutchess ; such a dutchess, that the
world,
In her whole course of life, yields not a lady
That can with imitation deserve
To be her second : in her grave we buried
All thoughts of woman : let this satisfy
For any second marriage. Now, whereas
You name the heir of Urbin, as a princess
Of great revenues, 'tis confess'd she is so :
But for some causes private to ourself,
We have disposed her otherwise. Yet despair
· not ;
For you, ere long, with joy shall understand
That in our princely care we have provided
One worthy to succeed us.

Enter Sanazarro.

Hip. We submit,
And hold the counsels of great Cozimo
Oraculous.
Coz. My Sanazarro !—Nay,
Forbear all ceremony. You look sprightly,
friend,
And promise in your clear aspect some novel
That may delight us.
Sanaz. O sir, I would not be

The harbinger of aught that might distaste
you :
And therefore know (for 'twere a sin to torture
Your highness' expectation) your vice-ad-
miral,
By my directions, hath surprised the gallies
Appointed to transport the Asian tribute
Of the great Turk ; a richer prize was never
Brought into Florence.
Coz. Still my nightingale,
That with sweet accents dost assure me that
My spring of happiness comes fast upon me !
Embrace me boldly. I pronounce that wretch
An enemy to brave and thriving action,
That dares believe but in a thought, we are
Too prodigal in our favours to this man,
Whose merits, though with him we should
divide
Our dukedom, still continue us his debtor.
Hip. 'Tis far from me.
Alph. We all applaud it.
Coz. Nay, blush not, Sanazarro, we are
proud
Of what we build up in thee ; nor can our
Election be disparaged, since we have not
Received into our bosom and our grace
A glorious lazy drone, grown fat with feeding
On others' toil, but an industrious bee,
That crops the sweet flowers of our enemies,
And every happy evening returns
Loaden with wax and honey to our hive.
Sanaz. My best endeavours never can
discharge
The service I should pay.
Coz. Thou art too modest ;
But we will study how to give, and when,

Enter Giovanni *and* Contarino.

Before it be demanded.——Giovanni !
My nephew ! let me eye thee better, boy.
In thee, methinks, my sister lives again ;
For her love I will be a father to thee,
For thou art my adopted son.
Giov. Your servant,
And humblest subject.
Coz. Thy hard travel, nephew,
Requires soft rest, and therefore we forbear,
For the present, an account how thou hast
spent
Thy absent hours. See, signiors, see, our care,
Without a second bed, provides you of
A hopeful prince. Carry him to his lodgings,
And, for his further honour, Sanazarro,
With the rest, do you attend him.
Giov. All true pleasures
Circle your highness !
Sanaz. As the rising sun,
We do receive you.
Giov. May this never set,

O 2

But shine upon you ever !
[*Exeunt* Giovanni, Sanazarro, Hieronimo,
    Alphonso, *and* Hippolito.
   Coz. Contarino !
   Cont. My gracious lord.
   Coz. What entertainment found you
From Carolo de Charomonte ?
   Cont. Free,
And bountiful.   He's ever like himself,
Noble and hospitable.
   Coz. But did my nephew
Depart thence willingly ?
   Cont. He obey'd your summons
As did become him.   Yet it was apparent,
But that he durst not cross your will, he would
Have sojourn'd longer there, he ever finding
Variety of sweetest entertainment.
But there was something else ; nor can I blame
His youth, though with some trouble he
    took leave
Of such a sweet companion.
   Coz. Who was it ?
   Cont. The daughter, sir, of signior Carolo,
Fair Lidia, a virgin, at all parts,
But in her birth and fortunes, equal to him.
The rarest beauties Italy can make boast of,
Are but mere shadows to her, she the sub-
    stance
Of all perfection.   And what increases
The wonder, sir, her body's matchless form
Is better'd by the pureness of her soul.
Such sweet discourse, such ravishing be-
    haviour,
Such charming language, such enchanting
    manners,
With a simplicity that shames all courtship,
Flow hourly from her, that I do believe
Had Circe or Calypso her sweet graces,
Wandering Ulysses never had remember'd
Penelope, or Ithaca.
   Coz. Be not rapt so.
   Cont. Your Excellence would be so, had
    you seen her.
   Coz. Take up, take up.—But did your
    observation
Note any passage of affection
Between her and my nephew ?
   Cont. How it should
Be otherwise between them, is beyond
My best imagination.   Cupid's arrows
Were useless there ; for, of necessity,
Their years and dispositions do accord so,
They must wound one another.
   Coz. Umph ! Thou art
My secretary, Contarino, and more skill'd
In politic designs of state, than in
Thy judgment of a beauty ; give me leave,
In this, to doubt it.—Here. Go to my cabinet,
You shall find there letters newly received,

Touching the state of Urbin.
Pray you, with care peruse them : leave the
    search
Of this to us.
   Cont. I do obey in all things.   [*Exit.*
   Coz. Lidia ! a diamond so long conceal'd,
And never worn in court ! of such sweet
    feature !
And he on whom I fix my dukedom's hopes
Made captive to it ! Umph ! 'tis somewhat
    strange.
Our eyes are everywhere, and we will make
A strict inquiry.—Sanazarro !

       Re-enter Sanazarro.

   Sanaz. Sir.
   Coz. Is my nephew at his rest ?
   Sanaz. I saw him in bed, sir.
   Coz. 'Tis well ; and does the princess
    Fiorinda,
Nay, do not blush, she is rich Urbin's heir,
Continue constant in her favours to you ?
   Sanaz. Dread sir, she may dispense them
    as she pleases ;
But I look up to her as on a princess
I dare not be ambitious of, and hope
Her prodigal graces shall not render me
Offender to your highness.
   Coz. Not a scruple.
He whom I favour, as I do my friend,
May take all lawful graces that become him :
But touching this hereafter.   I have now
(And though perhaps it may appear a trifle)
Serious employment for thee.
   Sanaz. I stand ready
For any act you please.
   Coz. I know it, friend.
Have you ne'er heard of Lidia, the daughter
Of Carolo Charomonte ?
   Sanaz. Him I know, sir,
For a noble gentleman, and my worthy friend ;
But never heard of her.
   Coz. She is deliver'd,
And feelingly to us by Contarino,
For a masterpiece in nature.   I would have
    you
Ride suddenly thither to behold this wonder,
But not as sent by us ; that's our first caution :
The second is, and carefully observe it,
That, though you are a bachelor, and en-
    dow'd with
All those perfections that may take a virgin,
On forfeit of our favour do not tempt her :
It may be her fair graces do concern us.
Pretend what business you think fit, to gain
Access unto her father's house, and, there,
Make full discovery of her, and return me
A true relation :—I have some ends in it,
With which we will acquaint you. .

Sanaz. This is, sir,
An easy task.
 Coz. Yet one that must exact
Your secrecy and diligence. Let not
Your stay be long.
 Sanaz. It shall not, sir.
 Coz. Farewell,
And be, as you would keep our favour,
 careful.   [*Exeunt.*

———

ACT II.

SCENE I.—*The same. A Room in*
Fiorinda's *House.*

Enter Fiorinda *and* Calaminta.

Fior. How does this dressing shew?
Calam. 'Tis of itself
Curious and rare; but, borrowing ornament,
As it does from your grace, that deigns
 to wear it,
Incomparable.
 Fior. Thou flatter'st me.
 Calam. I cannot,
Your excellence is above it.
 Fior. Were we less perfect,
Yet, being as we are, an absolute princess,
We of necessity must be chaste, wise, fair,
By our prerogative!—yet all these fail
To move where I would have them. How
 received
Count Sanazarro the rich scarf I sent him
For his last visit?
 Calam. With much reverence,
I dare not say affection. He express'd
More ceremony in his humble thanks,
Than feeling of the favour; and appear'd
Wilfully ignorant, in my opinion,
Of what it did invite him to.
 Fior. No matter;
He's blind with too much light. Have you
 not heard
Of any private mistress he's engaged to?
 Calam. Not any; and this does amaze
 me, madam,
That he, a soldier, one that drinks rich wines,
Feeds high, and promises as much as Venus
Could wish to find from Mars, should in his
 manners
Be so averse to women.
 Fior. Troth, I know not;
He's man enough, and, if he has a haunt,
He preys, far off, like a subtle fox.
 Calam. And that way
I do suspect him: for I learnt last night,
When the great duke went to rest, attended
 by
One private follower, he took horse; but
 whither

He's rid, or to what end, I cannot guess at,
But I will find it out.
 Fior. Do, faithful servant;

Enter Calandrino.

We would not be abused.—Who have we
 here?
 Calam. How the fool stares!
 Fior. And looks as if he were
Conning his neck-verse.
 Cal. If I now prove perfect
In my A B C of courtship, Calandrino
Is made for ever. I am sent—let me see,
On a *How d'ye*, as they call't.
 Calam. What wouldst thou say?
 Cal. Let me see my notes. These are
 her lodgings; well.
 Calam. Art thou an ass?
 Cal. Peace! thou art a court wagtail,
    [*Looking on his instructions.*
To interrupt me.
 Fior. He has given it you.
 Cal. *And then say to the illustrious Fi-o-*
 rin-da—
I have it. Which is she?
 Calam. Why this; fop-doodle.
 Cal. Leave chattering, bull-finch; you
 would put me out,
But 'twill not do.—*Then, after you have made*
Your three obeisances to her, kneel and kiss
The skirt of her gown.—I am glad it is no
 worse.
 Calam. And why so, sir?
 Cal. Because I was afraid
That, after the Italian garb, I should
Have kiss'd her backward.
 Calam. This is sport unlooked for.
 Cal. Are you the princess?
 Fior. Yes, sir.
 Cal. Then stand fair,
For I am choleric; and do not nip
A hopeful blossom. Out again:—*Three low*
 Obeisances.—
 Fior. I am ready.
 Cal. I come on, then.
 Calam. With much formality.
 Cal. Umph! One, two, three.
    [*Makes antic curtesies.*
Thus far I am right. Now for the last.
 [*Kisses the skirt of her gown.*]—O, rare!
She is perfumed all over! Sure great women,
Instead of little dogs, are privileged
To carry musk-cats.
 Fior. Now the ceremony
Is pass'd, what is the substance?
 Cal. I'll peruse
My instructions, and then tell you.—*Her*
 skirt kiss'd,
Inform her highness that your lord——

Calam. Who's that?
Cal. Prince Giovanni, who entreats your
  grace,
That he, with your good favour, may have
  leave
To present his service to you. I think I
  have nick'd it
For a courtier of the first form.
Fior. To my wonder.

Enter Giovanni *and a* Gentleman.

Return unto the prince—but he prevents
My answer. Calaminta, take him off;
And, for the neat delivery of his message,
Give him ten ducats: such rare parts as yours
Are to be cherish'd.
Cal. We will share: I know
It is the custom of the court, when ten
Are promised, five is fair. Fie! fie! the
  princess
Shall never know it, so you dispatch me
  quickly, •
And bid me not come to-morrow.
Calam. Very good, sir.
  [*Exeunt* Calandrino *and* Calaminta.
Giov. Pray you, friend,
Inform the duke I am putting into act
What he commanded.
Gent. I am proud to be employ'd, sir.
  [*Exit.*
Giov. Madam, that, without warrant, I
  presume
To trench upon your privacies, may argue
Rudeness of manners; but the free access
Your princely courtesy vouchsafes to all
That come to pay their services, gives me hope
To find a gracious pardon.
Fior. If you please, not
To make that an offence in your construction,
Which I receive as a large favour from you,
There needs not this apology.
Giov. You continue,
As you were ever, the greatest mistress of
Fair entertainment.
Fior. You are, sir, the master;
And in the country have learnt to outdo
All that in court is practised. But why
  should we
Talk at such distance? You are welcome, sir.
We have been more familiar, and since
You will impose the province (you should
  govern)
Of boldness on me, give me leave to say
You are too punctual. Sit, sir, and discourse
As we were used.
Giov. Your excellence knows so well
How to command, that I can never err
When I obey you.
Fior. Nay, no more of this.

You shall o'ercome; no more, I pray you,
  sir.—
And what delights, pray you be liberal
In your relation, hath the country life
Afforded you?
Giov. All pleasures, gracious madam,
But the happiness to converse with your
  sweet virtues.
I had a grave instructor, and my hours
Design'd to serious studies yielded me
Pleasure with profit in the knowledge of
What before I was ignorant in; the signior,
Carolo de Charomonte, being skilful
To guide me through the labyrinth of wild
  passions,
That labour'd to imprison my free soul
A slave to vicious sloth.
Fior. You speak him well.
Giov. But short of his deserts. Then for
  the time
Of recreation, I was allow'd
(Against the form follow'd by jealous parents
In Italy) full liberty to partake
His daughter's sweet society. She's a virgin
Happy in all endowments which a poet
Could fancy in his mistress; being herself
A school of goodness, where chaste maids
  may learn,
Without the aid of foreign principles,
By the example of her life and pureness,
To be as she is, excellent. I but give you
A brief epitome of her virtues, which,
Dilated on at large, and to their merit,
Would make an ample story.
Fior. Your whole age,
So spent with such a father, and a daughter,
Could not be tedious to you.
Giov. True, great princess:
And now, since you have pleased to grant
  the hearing
Of my time's expense in the country, give
  me leave
To entreat the favour to be made acquainted
What service, or what objects in the court,
Have, in your excellency's acceptance, proved
Most gracious to you.
Fior. I'll meet your demand,
And make a plain discovery. The duke's
  care
For my estate and person holds the first
And choicest place: then, the respect the
  courtiers
Pay gladly to me, not to be contemn'd.
But that which raised in me the most delight,
(For I am a friend to valour) was to hear
The noble actions truly reported
Of the brave count Sanazarro. I profess
When it hath been, and fervently, deliver'd,
How boldly, in the horror of a fight,

Cover'd with fire and smoke, and, as if
nature
Had lent him wings, like lightning he hath
fallen
Upon the Turkish gallies, I have heard it
With a kind of pleasure, which hath whis-
per'd to me,
This worthy must be cherish'd.
 Giov. 'Twas a bounty
You never can repent.
 Fior. I glory in it.
And when he did return, (but still with con-
quest,)
His armour off, not young Antinous
Appear'd more courtly ; all the graces that
Render a man's society dear to ladies,
Like pages waiting on him ; and it does
Work strangely on me.
 Giov. To divert your thoughts,
Though they are fix'd upon a noble subject,
I am a suitor to you.
 Fior. You will ask,
I do presume, what I may grant, and then
It must not be denied.
 Giov. It is a favour
For which I hope your excellence will thank
me.
 Fior. Nay, without circumstance.
 Giov. That you would please
To take occasion to move the duke,
That you, with his allowance, may com-
mand
This matchless virgin, Lidia, (of whom
I cannot speak too much,) to wait upon you.
She's such a one, upon the forfeit of
Your good opinion of me, that will not
Be a blemish to your train.
 Fior. 'Tis rank ! he loves her :
But I will fit him with a suit. [*Aside.*]—I
pause not,
As if it bred or doubt or scruple in me
To do what you desire, for I'll effect it,
And make use of a fair and fit occasion ;
Yet, in return, I ask a boon of you,
And hope to find you, in your grant to me,
As I have been to you.
 Giov. Command me, madam.
 Fior. 'Tis near allied to yours. That
you would be
A suitor to the duke, not to expose,
After so many trials of his faith,
The noble Sanazarro to all dangers,
As if he were a wall to stand the fury
Of a perpetual battery : but now
To grant him, after his long labours, rest
And liberty to live in court ; his arms
And his victorious sword and shield hung up
For monuments.
 Giov. Umph !—I'll embrace, fair princess,

Enter Cozimo.

The soonest opportunity. The duke !
 Coz. Nay, blush not ; we smile on your
privacy,
And come not to disturb you. You are
equals,
And, without prejudice to either's honours,
May make a mutual change of love and
courtship,
Till you are made one, and with holy rites,
And we give suffrage to it.
 Giov. You are gracious.
 Coz. To ourself in this : but now break
off ; too much
Taken at once of the most curious viands,
Dulls the sharp edge of appetite. We are
now
For other sports, in which our pleasure is
That you shall keep us company.
 Fior. We attend you. [*Exeunt.*

SCENE II.—*The Country. A Hall in*
Charomonte's *House.*

Enter Bernardo, Caponi, *and* Petruchio.

 Bern. Is my lord stirring ?
 Cap. No ; he's fast.
 Pet. Let us take, then,
Our morning draught. Such as eat store of
beef,
Mutton, and capons, may preserve their
healths
With that thin composition call'd small beer,
As, 'tis said, they do in England. But Italians,
That think when they have supp'd upon an
olive,
A root, or bunch of raisins, 'tis a feast,
Must kill those crudities rising from cold herbs,
With hot and lusty wines.
 Cap. A happiness
Those tramontanes ne'er tasted.
 Bern. Have they not
Store of wine there ?
 Cap. Yes, and drink more in two hours
Than the Dutchmen or the Dane in four and
twenty.
 Pet. But what is't ? French trash, made
of rotten grapes,
And dregs and lees of Spain, with Welsh
metheglin,
A drench to kill a horse ! But this pure nectar,
Being proper to our climate, is too fine
To brook the roughness of the sea ; the spirit
Of this begets in us quick apprehensions,
And active executions ; whereas their
Gross feeding makes their understanding
like it :
They can fight, and that's their all.
       [*They drink.*

Enter Sanazarro *and* Servant.

Sanaz. Security
Dwells about this house, I think ; the gate's
wide open,
And not a servant stirring.   See the horses
Set up, and clothed.
    Serv. I shall, sir.   [*Exit.*
    Sanaz. I'll make bold
To press a little further.
    Bern. Who is this,
Count Sanazarro ?
    Pet. Yes, I know him.   Quickly
Remove the flaggon.
    Sanaz. A good day to you, friends.
Nay, do not conceal your physic ; I approve it,
And, if you please, will be a patient with you.
    Pet. My noble lord.   [*Drinks.*
    Sanaz. A health to yours. [*Drinks.*] Well
        done !
I see you love yourselves, and I commend you ;
'Tis the best wisdom.
    Pet. May it please your honour
To walk a turn in the gallery, I'll acquaint
My lord with your being here.   [*Exit.*
    Sanaz. Tell him I come
For a visit only.   'Tis a handsome pile this.
                                                  [*Exit.*
    Cap. Why here is a brave fellow, and a
        right one ;
Nor wealth nor greatness makes him proud.
    Bern. There are
Too few of them ; for most of our new
        courtiers,
(Whose fathers were familiar with the prices
Of oil and corn, with when and where to
        vent them,
And left their heirs rich, from their know-
        ledge that way,)
Like gourds shot up in a night, disdain to
    · speak
But to cloth of tissue.

Enter Charomonte *in a nightgown,*
Petruchio *following.*

    Char. Stand you prating, knaves,
When such a guest is under my roof ! See all
The rooms perfumed.   This is the man that
        carries   ·
The sway and swing of the court ; and I
        had rather
Preserve him mine with honest offices,
        than——
But I'll make no comparisons. Bid my
        daughter
Trim herself up to the height ; I know this
        courtier
Must have a smack at her ; and, perhaps,
        by his place,

Expects to wriggle further ; if he does,
I shall deceive his hopes ; for I'll not taint
My honour for the dukedom.   Which way
        went he ?
    Cap. To the round gallery.
    Char. I will entertain him
As fits his worth and quality, but no further.
                                                  [*Exeunt.*

SCENE III.—*A Gallery in the same.*

Enter Sanazarro.

    Sanaz. I cannot apprehend, yet I have
        argued ·
All ways I can imagine, for what reasons
The great duke does employ me hither ; and,
What does increase the miracle, I must
        render
A strict and true account, at my return,
Of Lidia, this lord's daughter, and describe
In what she's excellent, and where defective.
'Tis a hard task : he that will undergo
To make a judgment of a woman's beauty,
And see through all her plasterings and
        paintings,
Had need of Lynceus' eyes, and with more
        ease
May look, like him, through nine mud walls,
        than make
A true discovery of her.   But the intents
And secrets of my prince's heart must be
Served, and not search'd into.

Enter Charomonte.

    Char. Most noble sir,
Excuse my age, subject to ease and sloth,
That with no greater speed I have presented
My service with your welcome.
    Sanaz. 'Tis more fit
That I should ask your pardon, for dis-
        turbing
Your rest at this unseasonable hour.
But my occasions carry me so near
Your hospitable house, my stay being short
        too,
Your goodness, and the name of friend,
        which you
Are pleased to grace me with, gave me
        assurance
A visit would not offend.
    Char. Offend, my lord !
I feel myself much younger for the favour.
How is it with our gracious master ?
    Sanaz. He, sir,
Holds still his wonted greatness, and con-
        fesses
Himself your debtor, for your love and care
To the prince Giovanni ; and had sent
Particular thanks by me, had his grace known

The quick dispatch of what I was design'd to
Would have licensed me to see you.
 Char. I am rich
In his acknowledgment.
 Sanaz. Sir, I have heard
Your happiness in a daughter.
 Char. Sits the wind there ? [*Aside.*
 Sanaz. Fame gives her out for a rare
 masterpiece.
 Char. 'Tis a plain village girl, sir, but
 obedient ;
That's her best beauty, sir.
 Sanaz. Let my desire
To see her, find a fair construction from you :
I bring no loose thought with me.
 Char. You are that way,
My lord, free from suspicion. Her own
 manners,
Without an imposition from me,
I hope, will prompt her to it.

  Enter Lidia *and* Petronella.

    As she is,
She comes to make a tender of that service
Which she stands bound to pay.
 Sanaz. With your fair leave,
I make bold to salute you.
 Lid. Sir, you have it.
 Petron. I am her gentlewoman, will he
 not kiss me too ? .
This is coarse, i'faith. [*Aside.*
 Char. How he falls off !
 Lid. My lord, though silence best becomes
 a maid,
And to be curious to know but what
Concerns myself, and with becoming dis-
 tance,
May argue me of boldness, I must borrow
So much of modesty, as to inquire
Prince Giovanni's health.
 Sanaz. He cannot want
What you are pleased to wish him.
 Lid. Would 'twere so !
And then there is no blessing that can make
A hopeful and a noble prince complete,
But should fall on him. O ! he was our
 north star,
The light and pleasure of our eyes.
 Sanaz. Where am I?
I feel myself another thing ! Can charms
Be writ on such pure rubies? her lips melt
As soon as touch'd ! Not those smooth
 gales that glide
O'er happy Araby, or rich Sabæa,
Creating in their passage gums and spices,
Can serve for a weak simile to express
The sweetness of her breath. Such a brave
 stature

Homer bestow'd on Pallas, every limb
Proportion'd to it !
 Char. This is strange.—My lord !
 Sanaz. I crave your pardon, and yours,
 matchless maid,
For such I must report you.
 Petron. There's no notice
Taken all this while of me. [*Aside.*
 Sanaz. And I must add,
If your discourse and reason parallel
The rareness of your more than human form,
You are a wonder.
 Char. Pray you, my lord, make trial :
She can speak, I can assure you ; and that
 my presence
May not take from her freedom, I will leave
 you :
For know, my lord, my confidence dares trust
 her
Where, and with whom, she pleases.——
 If he be
Taken the right way with her, I cannot fancy
A better match ; and, for false play, I know
The tricks, and can discern them.—Petro-
 nella !
 Petron. Yes, my good lord.
 Char. I have employment for you.
  [*Exeunt* Charomonte *and* Petronella.
 Lid. What's your will, sir?
 Sanaz. Madam, you are so large a theme
 to treat of,
And every grace about you offers to me
Such copiousness of language, that I stand
Doubtful which first to touch at. If I err,
As in my choice I may, let me entreat you,
Before I do offend, to sign my pardon :
Let this, the emblem of your innocence,
Give me assurance.
 Lid. My hand join'd to yours,
Without this superstition, confirms it.
Nor need I fear you will dwell long upon me,
The barrenness of the subject yielding nothing
That rhetoric, with all her tropes and figures,
Can amplify. Yet since you are resolved
To prove yourself a courtier in my praise,
As I'm a woman (and you men affirm
Our sex loves to be flatter'd) I'll endure it.

  Enter Charomonte *above.*

Now, when you please, begin.
 Sanaz. [*turning from her.*] Such Læda's
 paps were,—
(Down pillows styled by Jove,) and their
 pure whiteness
Shames the swan's down, or snow. No heat
 of lust
Swells up her azure veins ; and yet I feel
That this chaste ice but touch'd fans fire in
 me.

Lid. You need not, noble sir, be thus
  transported,
Or trouble your invention to express
Your thought of me : the plainest phrase
  and language
That you can use, will be too high a strain
For such an humble theme.
  Sanaz. If the great duke
Made this his end to try my constant temper,
Though I am vanquish'd, 'tis his fault, not
  mine :
For I am flesh and blood, and have affections
Like other men. Who can behold the
  temples,
Or holy altars, but the objects work
Devotion in him ? And I may as well
Walk over burning iron with bare feet,
And be unscorch'd, as look upon this beauty
Without desire, and that desire pursued too,
Till it be quench'd with the enjoying those
Delights, which to achieve, danger is nothing,
And loyalty but a word.
  Lid. I ne'er was proud ;
Nor can find I am guilty of a thought
Deserving this neglect and strangeness from
  you :
Nor am I amorous.
  Sanaz. Suppose his greatness
Loves her himself, why makes he choice of me
To be his agent ? It is tyranny
To call one pinch'd with hunger to a feast,
And at that instant cruelly deny him
To taste of what he sees. Allegiance
Tempted too far is like the trial of
A good sword on an anvil ; as that often
Flies in pieces without service to the owner,
So trust enforced too far proves treachery,
And is too late repented.
  Lid. Pray you, sir,
Or license me to leave you, or deliver
The reasons which invite you to command
My tedious waiting on you.
  Char. As I live,
I know not what to think on't. Is't his pride,
Or his simplicity ?
  Sanaz. Whither have my thoughts
Carried me from myself ? In this my dulness,
I've lost an opportunity——
  ·   [*Turns to her ; she falls off.*
  Lid. 'Tis true,
I was not bred in court, nor live a star there ;
Nor shine in rich embroideries and pearl,
As they, that are the mistresses of great
  fortunes,
Are every day adorn'd with——
  Sanaz. Will you vouchsafe
Your ear, sweet lady ?
  Lid. Yet I may be bold,
For my integrity and fame, to rank

With such as are more glorious. Though I
  never
Did injury, yet I am sensible
When I'm contemn'd and scorn'd.
  Sanaz. Will you please to bear me ?
  Lid. O the difference of natures ! Giovanni,
A prince in expectation, when he lived here,
Stole courtesy from heaven, and would not to·
The meanest servant in my father's house
Have kept such distance.
  Sanaz. Pray you, do not think me
Unworthy of your ear ; it was your beauty
That turn'd me statue. I can speak, fair lady.
  Lid. And I can hear. The harshness of
  your courtship
Cannot corrupt my courtesy.
  Sanaz. Will you hear me,
If I speak of love ?
  Lid. Provided you be modest ;
I were uncivil, else.
  Char. They are come to parley :
I must observe this nearer.   [*He retires.*
  Sanaz. You are a rare one,
And such (but that my haste commands me·
  hence)
I could converse with ever. Will you grace me·
With leave to visit you again ?
  Lid. So you,
At your return to court, do me the favour
To make a tender of my humble service
To the prince Giovanni.
  Sanaz. Ever touching
Upon that string ! [*Aside.*] And will you.
  give me hope
Of future happiness ?
  Lid. That, as I shall find you :
The fort that's yielded at the first assault
Is hardly worth the taking.

      Re-enter Charomonte *below.*   .

  Char. O, they are at it.
  Sanaz. She is a magazine of all perfection,
And 'tis death to part from her, yet I must—
A parting kiss, fair maid.
  Lid. That custom grants you.
  Char. A homely breakfast does. attend.
  your lordship,
Such as the place affords.
  Sanaz. No ; I have feasted
Already here ; my thanks, and so I leave you :
I will see you again.—Till this unhappy hour·
I was never lost, and what to do, or say,
I have not yet determined.
                          [*Aside and exit.*
  Char. Gone so abruptly !
  'Tis very strange.
  Lid. Under your favour, sir,
His coming hither was to little purpose,
For anything I heard from him.

Char. Take heed, Lidia !
I do advise you with a father's love,
And tenderness of your honour ; as I would not
Have you coarse and harsh in giving enter-
tainment,
So by no means to be credulous : for great
men,
Till they have gain'd their ends, are giants in
Their promises, but, those obtain'd, weak
pigmies
In their performance. And it is a maxim
Allow'd among them, so they may deceive,
They may swear any thing ; for the queen of
love,
As they hold constantly, does never punish,
But smile, at lovers' perjuries.—Yet be wise
too,
And when you are sued to in a noble way,
Be neither nice nor scrupulous.
Lid. All you speak, sir,
I hear as oracles ; nor will digress
From your directions.
Char. So shall you keep
Your fame untainted.
Lid. As I would my life, sir. [*Exeunt.*

ACT III.

SCENE I.—Florence. *An Anteroom
in the Palace.*

Enter Sanazarro *and* Servant.

Sanaz. Leave the horses with my grooms ;
but be you careful,
With your best diligence and speed, to find
out
The prince, and humbly, in my name, entreat
I may exchange some private conference with
him
Before the great duke know of my arrival.
Serv. I haste, my lord.
Sanaz. Here I'll attend his coming :
And see you keep yourself, as much as may be,
Conceal'd from all men else.
Serv. To serve your lordship,
I wish I were invisible. [*Exit.*
Sanaz. I am driven
Into a desperate strait, and cannot steer
A middle course ; and of the two extremes
Which I must make election of, I know not
Which is more full of horror. Never servant
Stood more engaged to a magnificent master,
Than I to Cozimo : and all those honours
And glories by his grace conferr'd upon me,
Or by my prosperous services deserved,
If now I should deceive his trust, and make
A shipwreck of my loyalty, are ruin'd.
And, on the other side, if I discover
Lidia's divine perfections, all my hopes

In her are sunk, never to be buoy'd up :
For 'tis impossible, but, as soon as seen,
She must with adoration be sued to.
A hermit at his beads but looking on her,
Or the cold cynic, whom Corinthian Laïs
(Not moved with her lust's blandishments)
call'd a stone,
At this object would take fire. Nor is the
duke
Such an Hippolytus, but that this Phædra,
But seen, must force him to forsake the
groves,
And Dian's huntmanship, proud to serve
under
Venus' soft ensigns. No, there is no way
For me to hope fruition of my ends,
But to conceal her beauties ;—and how that
May be effected, is as hard a task
As with a veil to cover the sun's beams,
Or comfortable light. Three years the prince
Lived in her company, and Contarino,
The secretary, hath possess'd the duke
What a rare piece she is : - but he's my
creature,
And may with ease be frighted to deny
What he hath said ! and, if my long ex-
perience,
With some strong reasons I have thought
upon,
Cannot o'er-reach a youth, my practice
yields me
But little profit.

Enter Giovanni *with the* Servant.

Giov. You are well return'd, sir.
Sanaz. Leave us.—[*Exit* Servant.] When
that your grace shall know the motives
That forced me to invite you to this trouble,
You will excuse my manners.
Giov. Sir, there needs not
This circumstance between us. You are ever
My noble friend.
Sanaz. You shall have further cause
To assure you of my faith and zeal to serve
you.
And, when I have committed to your trust
(Presuming still on your retentive silence)
A secret of no less importance than
My honour, nay, my head, it will confirm
What value you hold with me.
Giov. Pray you, believe, sir,
What you deliver to me shall be lock'd up
In a strong cabinet, of which you yourself
Shall keep the key : for here I pawn my
honour,
Which is the best security I can give yet,
It shall not be discover'd.
Sanaz. This assurance
Is more than I with modesty could demand

From such a paymaster; but I must be
sudden :
And therefore, to the purpose. Can your
Excellence,
In your imagination, conceive
On what design, or whither, the duke's will
Commanded me hence last night?
   Giov. No, I assure you ;
And it had been a rudeness to enquire
Of that I was not call'd to.
   Sanaz. Grant me hearing,
And I will truly make you understand
It only did concern you.
   Giov. Me, my lord !
   Sanaz. You, in your present state, and
future fortunes ;
For both lie at the stake.
   Giov. You much amaze me.
Pray you, resolve this riddle.
   Sanaz. You know the duke,
If he die issueless, as yet he is,
Determines you his heir.
   Giov. It hath pleased his highness
Oft to profess so much.
   Sanaz. But say, he should
Be won to prove a second wife, on whom
He may beget a son, how, in a moment,
With all those glorious expectations, which
Render you reverenced and remarkable,
Be in a moment blasted, howe'er you are
His much-lov'd sister's son !
   Giov. I must bear it
With patience, and in me it is a duty
That I was born with ; and 'twere much
unfit
For the receiver of a benefit
To offer, for his own ends, to prescribe
Laws to the giver's pleasure.
   Sanaz. Sweetly answer'd,
And like your noble self. This your rare
temper
So wins upon me, that I would not live
(If that by honest arts I can prevent it)
To see your hopes made frustrate. And but
think
How you shall be transform'd from what
you are,
Should this (as heaven avert it !) ever happen.
It must disturb your peace : for whereas now,
Being, as you are, received for the heir ap-
parent,
You are no sooner seen, but wonder'd at ;
The signiors making it a business to
Enquire how you have slept ; and, as you
walk
The streets of Florence, the glad multitude
In throngs press but to see you ; and, with
joy,
The father, pointing with his finger, tells

His son, This is the prince, the hopeful
prince,
That must hereafter rule, and you obey
him.—
Great ladies beg your picture, and make love
To that, despairing to enjoy the substance.—
And, but the last night, when 'twas only
rumour'd
That you were come to court, as if you had
By sea past hither from another world,
What general shouts and acclamations fol-
low'd !
The bells rang loud, the bonfires blazed,
and such
As loved not wine, carousing to your health,
Were drunk, and blush'd not at it. And is
this .
A happiness to part with ?
   Giov. I allow these
As flourishes of fortune, with which princes
Are often sooth'd ; but never yet esteem'd
them
For real blessings.
   Sanaz. Yet all these were paid
To what you may be, not to what you are ;
For if the Great Duke but shew to his ser-
vants
A son of his own, you shall, like one ob-
scure,
Pass unregarded.
   Giov. I confess, command
Is not to be contemn'd, and if my fate
Appoint me to it, as I may, I'll bear it
With willing shoulders. But, my lord, as yet,
You've told me of a danger coming towards
me,
But have not named it.
   Sanaz. That is soon deliver'd.
Great Cozimo, your uncle, as I more
Than guess, for 'tis no frivolous circumstance
That does persuade my judgment to believe it,
Purposes to be married.
   Giov. Married, sir !
With whom, and on what terms ? pray you,
instruct me.
   Sanaz. With the fair Lidia.
   Giov. Lidia !
   Sanaz. The daughter
Of signior Charomonte.
   Giov. Pardon me
Though I appear incredulous ; for, on
My knowledge, he ne'er saw her.
   Sanaz. That is granted :
But Contarino hath so sung her praises,
And given her out for such a masterpiece,
That he's transported with it, sir :—and love
Steals sometimes through the ear into the
heart,
As well as by the eye. The duke no sooner

Heard her described, but I was sent in post
To see her, and return my judgment of her.
Giov. And what's your censure?
Sanaz. 'Tis a pretty creature.
Giov. She's very fair.
Sanaz. Yes, yes, I have seen worse faces.
Giov. Her limbs are neatly form'd.
Sanaz. She hath a waist
Indeed sized to love's wish.
Giov. A delicate hand too.
Sanaz. Then for a leg and foot—
Giov. And there I leave you,
For I presumed no further.
Sanaz. As she is, sir,
I know she wants no gracious part that may
Allure the duke ; and, if he only see her,
She is his own ; he will not be denied,
And then you are lost ; yet, if you'll second me,
(As you have reason, for it most concerns you,)
I can prevent all yet.
Giov. I would you could,
A noble way.
Sanaz. I will cry down her beauties ;
Especially the beauties of her mind,
As much as Contarino hath advanced them ;
And this, I hope, will breed forgetfulness,
And kill affection in him : but you must join
With me in my report, if you be question'd.
Giov. I never told a lie yet ; and I hold it
In some degree blasphémous to disparise
What's worthy admiration : yet, for once,
I will disprase a little, and not vary
From your relation.
Sanaz. Be constant in it.

Enter Alphonso.

Alph. My lord, the duke hath seen your
man, and wonders

Enter Cozimo, Hippolito, Contarino, *and*
Attendants.

You come not to him. See, if his desire
To have conference with you hath not
  brought him hither
In his own person !
Coz. They are comely coursers,
And promise swiftness.
Cont. They are, of my knowledge,
Of the best race in Naples.
Coz. You are, nephew,
As I hear, an excellent horseman, and we
  like it :
'Tis a fair grace in a prince. Pray you, make
  trial
Of their strength and speed ; and, if you
  think them fit
For your employment, with a liberal hand
Reward the gentleman that did present them
From the viceroy of Naples.

Giov. I will use
My best endeavour, sir.
Coz. Wait on my nephew.
        [*Exeunt* Giovanni, Alphonso,
              Hippolito, *and* Attendants.
Nay, stay you, Contarino :—be within call ;
It may be we shall use you.
              [*Exit* Contarino.
You have rode hard, sir,
And we thank you for it : every minute seems
Irksome, and tedious to us, till you have
Made your discovery. Say, friend, have you
  seen
This phœnix of our age ?
Sanaz. I have seen a maid, sir ;
But, if that I have judgment, no such wonder
As she was deliver'd to you.
Coz. This is strange.
Sanaz. But certain truth. It may be, she
was look'd on
With admiration in the country, sir ;
But, if compared with many in your court,
She would appear but ordinary.
Coz. Contarino
Reports her otherwise.
Sanaz. Such as ne'er saw swans,
May think crows beautiful.
Coz. How is her behaviour ?
Sanaz. 'Tis like the place she lives in.
Coz. How her wit,
Discourse, and entertainment ?
Sanaz. Very coarse ;
I would not willingly say poor, and rude :
But, had she all the beauties of fair-women,
The dullness of her soul would fright me
  from her.
Coz. You are curious, sir. I know not
  what to think on't. —   [*Aside.*
Contarino !

Re-enter Contarino.

Cont. Sir.
Coz. Where was thy judgment, man,
To extol a virgin Sanazarro tells me
Is nearer to deformity ?
Sanaz. I saw her,
And curiously perused her ; and I wonder
That she, that did appear to me, that know
What beauty is, not worthy the observing,
Should so transport you.
Cont. Troth, my lord, I thought then——
Coz. Thought ! Didst thou not affirm it ?
Cont. I confess, sir,
I did believe so then ; but now, I hear
My lord's opinion to the contrary,
I am of another faith : for 'tis not fit
That I should contradict him. I am dim, sir ;
But he's sharp-sighted.
Sanaz. This is to my wish.   [*Aside.*

Coz. We know not what to think of this;
yet would not

Re-enter Giovanni, Hippolito, *and*
Alphonso.

Determine rashly of it. [*Aside*]—How do you
like
My nephew's horsemanship?
  Hip. In my judgment, sir,
It is exact and rare.
  Alph. And, to my fancy,
He did present great Alexander mounted
On his Bucephalus.
  Coz. You are right courtiers,
And know it is your duty to cry up
All actions of a prince.
  Sanaz. Do not betray
Yourself, you're safe ; I have done my part.
                [*Aside to* Giovanni.
  Giov. I thank you ;
Nor will I fail.
  Coz. What's your opinion, nephew,
Of the horses?
  Giov. Two of them are, in my judgment,
The best I ever back'd ; I mean the roan, sir,
And the brown bay : but for the chesnut-
colour'd,
Though he be full of metal, hot, and fiery,
He treads weak in his pasterns.
  Coz. So : come nearer ;
This exercise hath put you into a sweat ;
Take this and dry it : and now I command you
To tell me truly what's your censure of
Charomonte's daughter, Lidia.
  Giov. I am, sir,
A novice in my judgment of a lady ;
But such as 'tis, your grace shall have it freely.
I would not speak ill of her, and am sorry,
If I keep myself a friend to truth, I cannot
Report her as I would, so much I owe
Her reverend father ; but I'll give you, sir,
As near as I can, her character in little.
She's of a goodly stature, and her limbs
Not disproportion'd ; for her face, it is
Far from deformity ; yet they flatter her,
That style it excellent : her manners are
Simple and innocent ; but her discourse
And wit deserve my pity, more than praise :
At the best, my lord, she is a handsome
    picture,
And, that said, all is spoken.
  Coz. I believe you :
I ne'er yet found you false.
  Giov. Nor ever shall, sir.—
Forgive me, matchless Lidia! too much love,
And jealous fear to lose thee, do compel me,
Against my will, my reason, and my know-
    ledge,
To be a poor detractor of that beauty,

Which fluent Ovid, if he lived again,
Would want words to express.   [*Aside.*
  Coz. Pray you, make choice of
The richest of our furniture for these horses,
                [*To* Sanazarro.
And take my nephew with you ; we in this
Will follow his directions.
  Giov. Could I find now
The princess Fiorinda, and persuade her
To be silent in the suit that I moved to her,
All were secure.
  Sanaz. In that, my lord, I'll aid you.
  Coz. We will be private ; leave us.
              [*Exeunt all but* Cozimo.
              All my studies
And serious meditations aim no further
Than this young man's good. He was my
    sister's son,
And she was such a sister, when she lived,
I could not prize too much ; nor can I better
Make known how dear I hold her memory,
Than in my cherishing the only issue
Which she hath left behind her. Who's that?

         Enter Fiorinda.
  Fior. Sir.
  Coz. My fair charge ! you are welcome to
    us.
  Fior. I have found it, sir.
  Coz. All things go well in Urbin.
  Fior. Your gracious care to me, an orphan,
    frees me
From all suspicion that my jealous fears
Can drive into my fancy.
  Coz. The next summer,
In our own person, we will bring you thither,
And seat you in your own.
  Fior. When you think fit, sir.
But in the meantime, with your highness'
    pardon,
I am a suitor to you.
  Coz. Name it, madam,
With confidence to obtain it.
  Fior. That you would please
To lay a strict command on Charomonte,
To bring his daughter Lidia to the court :
And pray you, think, sir, that 'tis not my
    purpose
To employ her as a servant, but to use her
As a most wish'd companion.
  Coz. Ha ! your reason?
  Fior. The hopeful prince, your nephew,
    sir, hath given her
To me for such an abstract of perfection
In all that can be wish'd for in a virgin,
As beauty, music, ravishing discourse,
Quickness of apprehension, with choice
    manners
And learning too, not usual with women,

That I am much ambitious (though I shall
Appear but as a foil to set her off)
To be by her instructed, and supplied
In what I am defective.

Coz. Did my nephew
Seriously deliver this?

Fior. I assure your grace,
With zeal and vehemency; and, even when,
With his best words, he strived to set her
    forth,
(Though the rare subject made him eloquent,)
He would complain, all he could say came
    short
Of her deservings.

Coz. Pray you have patience.
                    [Walks aside.
This was strangely carried.—Ha! are we
    trifled with?
Dare they do this? Is Cozimo's fury, that
Of late was terrible, grown contemptible?
Well; we will clear our brows, and under-
    mine
Their secret works, though they have digg'd
    like moles,
And crush them with the tempest of my wrath
When I appear most calm. He is unfit
To command others, that knows not to use it,
And with all rigour: yet my stern looks
    shall not
Discover my intents: for I will strike
When I begin to frown.——You are the
    mistress
Of that you did demand.

Fior. I thank your highness;
But speed in the performance of the grant
Doubles the favour, sir.

Coz. You shall possess it
Sooner than you expect:——
Only be pleased to be ready when my secre-
    tary
Waits on you to take the fresh air. My
    nephew,
And my bosom friend, so to cheat me! 'tis
    not fair.   *[Aside.*

Re-enter Giovanni *and* Sanazarro.

Sanaz. Where should this princess be?
    nor in her lodgings,
Nor in the private walks, her own retreat,
Which she so much frequented!

Giov. By my life,
She's with the duke! and I much more than
    fear
Her forwardness to prefer my suit hath
    ruin'd
What with such care we built up.

Coz. Have you furnish'd
Those coursers, as we will'd you?

Sanaz. There's no sign
Of anger in his looks.

Giov. They are complete, sir.

Coz. 'Tis well: to your rest. Soft sleeps
    wait on you, madam.
To morrow, with the rising of the sun,
Be ready to ride with us.—They with more
    safety
Had trod on fork-tongued adders, than pro-
    voked me.   *[Aside and exit.*

Fior. I come not to be thank'd, sir, for
    the speedy
Performance of my promise touching Lidia:
It is effected.

Sanaz. We are undone.   *[Aside.*

Fior. The duke
No sooner heard me with my best of lan-
    guage
Describe her excellencies, as you taught me,
But he confirm'd it.—You look sad, as if
You wish'd it were undone.

Giov. No, gracious madam,
I am your servant for't.

Fior. Be you as careful
For what I moved to you.—Count Sanazarro,
Now I perceive you honour me, in vouch-
    safing
To wear so slight a favour.

Sanaz. 'Tis a grace
I am unworthy of.

Fior. You merit more,
In prizing so a trifle. Take this diamond;
I'll second what I have begun; for know,
Your valour hath so won upon me, that
'Tis not to be resisted: I have said, sir,
And leave you to interpret it.   *[Exit.*

Sanaz. This to me
Is wormwood. 'Tis apparent we are taken
In our own noose. What's to be done?

Giov. I know not.
And 'tis a punishment justly fallen upon me,
For leaving truth, a constant mistress, that
Ever protects her servants, to become
A slave to lies and falsehood. What excuse
Can be made to the duke, what mercy hope
    for,
Our packing being laid open?

Sanaz. 'Tis not to
Be question'd but his purposed journey is
To see fair Lidia.

Giov. And to divert him
Impossible.

Sanaz. There's now no looking backward.

Giov. And which way to go on with safety,
    not
To be imagined.

Sanaz. Give me leave: I have
An embryon in my brain, which, I despair
    not,

May be brought to form and fashion, pro-
vided
You will be open-breasted.
   Giov. 'Tis no time now,
Our dangers being equal, to conceal
A thought from you.
   Sanaz. What power hold you o'er Lidia?
Do you think that, with some hazard of her
life,
She would prevent your ruin?
   Giov. I presume so:
If, in the undertaking it, she stray not
From what becomes her innocence; and to
that
'Tis far from me to press her: I myself
Will rather suffer.
   Sanaz. 'Tis enough; this night
Write to her by your servant Calandrino,
As I shall give directions; my man

Enter Calandrino, *fantastically dressed.*

Shall bear him company. See, sir, to my wish
He does appear; but much transform'd
from what
He was when he came hither.
   Cal. I confess
I am not very wise, and yet I find
A fool, so he be parcel knave, in court
May flourish and grow rich.
   Giov. Calandrino.
   Cal. Peace!
I am in contemplation.
   Giov. Do not you know me?
   Cal. I tell thee, no; on forfeit of my place,
I must not know myself, much less my father,
But by petition; that petition lined too
With golden birds, that sing to the tune of
profit,
Or I am deaf.
   Giov. But you've your sense of feeling.
                   [*Offering to strike him.*
   Sanaz. Nay, pray you, forbear.
   Cal. I have all that's requisite
To the making up of a signior: my spruce
ruff,
My hooded cloak, long stocking, and paned
hose,
My case of toothpicks, and my silver fork,
To convey an olive neatly to my mouth;—
And, what is all in all, my pockets ring
A golden peal. O that the peasants in the
country,
My quondam fellows, but saw me as I am,
How they would admire and worship me!
   Giov. As they shall;
For instantly you must thither.
   Cal. *My grand signior,*
Vouchsafe a beso la manos, and a cringe
Of the last edition.

   Giov. You must ride post with letters
This night to Lidia.
   Cal. An it please your grace,
Shall I use my coach, or footcloth mule?
   Sanaz. You widgeon,
You are to make all speed; think not of
pomp.
   Giov. Follow for your instructions, sirrah.
   Cal. I have
One suit to you, my good lord.
   Sanaz. What is't?
   Cal. That you would give me
A subtle court-charm, to defend me from
The infectious air of the country.
   Giov. What's the reason?
   Cal. Why, as this court-air taught me
knavish wit,
By which I am grown rich, if that again
Should turn me fool and honest, vain hopes
farewell!
For I must die a beggar.
   Sanaz. Go to, sirrah.
You'll be whipt for this.
   Giov. Leave fooling, and attend us.
                    [*Exeunt.*

ACT IV.

   SCENE I.—The Country. *A Hall in*
Charomonte's *House.*

   Enter Charomonte, *and* Lidia.

   Char. Daughter, I have observed, since
the prince left us,
(Whose absence I mourn with you,) and the
visit
Count Sanazarro gave us, you have nourish'd
Sad and retired thoughts, and parted with
That freedom and alacrity of spirit
With which you used to cheer me.
   Lid. For the count, sir,
All thought of him does with his person die;
But I confess ingenuously, I cannot
So soon forget the choice and chaste delights,
The courteous conversation of the prince,
And without stain, I hope, afforded me
When he made this house a court.
   Char. It is in us
To keep it so without him. Want we know
not,
And all we can complain of, heaven be
praised for't,
Is too much plenty; and we will make use of

   Enter Caponi, Bernardo, Petruchio, *and*
other Servants.

All lawful pleasures. How now, fellows!
when
Shall we have this lusty dance?

Cap. In the afternoon, sir.
'Tis a device, I wis, of my own making,
And such a one as shall make your signior-
    ship know
I have not been your butler for nothing, but
Have crotchets in my head. We'll trip it
    tightly,
And make my sad young mistress merry
    again,
Or I'll forswear the cellar.
    Bern. If we had
Our fellow Calandrino here, to dance
His part, we were perfect.
    Pet. O ! he was a rare fellow ;
But I fear the court hath spoil'd him.
    Cap. When I was young,
I could have cut a caper on a pinnacle :
But now I'm old and wise.—Keep your
    figure fair,
And follow but the sample I shall set you,
The duke himself will send for us, and laugh
    at us ;
And that were credit.

Enter Calandrino.

    Lid. Who have we here ?
    Cal. I find
What was brawn in the country, in the court
    grows tender.
The bots on these jolting jades ! I am bruised
    to jelly.
A coach for my money ! and that the courte-
    zans know well ;
Their riding so makes them last three years
    longer
Than such as are hacknied.
    Char. Calandrino ! 'tis he.
    Cal. Now to my postures.—Let my hand
    have the honour
To convey a kiss from my lips to the cover of
    Your foot, dear signior.
    Char. Fie ! you stoop too low, sir.
    Cal. The hem of your vestment, lady :
    your glove is for princes ;
Nay, I have coun'd my distances.
    Lid. 'Tis most courtly.
    Cap. Fellow Calandrino !
    Cal. Signior de Caponi,
Grand boteler of the mansion.
    Bern. How is't, man?
        [*Claps him on the shoulder.*
    Cal. Be not so rustic in your salutations,
Signior Bernardo, master of the accounts.
Signior Petruchio, may you long continue
Your function in the chamber !
    Cap. When shall we learn
Such gambols in our villa?
    Lid. Sure he's mad.

Char. 'Tis not unlike, for most of such
    mushrooms are so.
What news at court ?
    Cal. Basta! they are mysteries,
And not to be reveal'd. With your favour,
    signior ;
I am, in private, to confer awhile
With this signora : but I'll pawn my honour,
That neither my terse language, nor my habit,
Howe'er it may convince, nor my new shrugs,
Shall render her enamour'd.
    Char. Take your pleasure ;
A little of these apish tricks may pass,
Too much is tedious.   [*Exit.*
    Cal. The prince, in this paper,
Presents his service. Nay, it is not courtly
To see the seal broke open ; so I leave you.—
Signiors of the villa, I'll descend to be
Familiar with you.
    Cap. Have you forgot to dance ?
    Cal. No, I am better'd.
    Pet. Will you join with us?
    Cal. As I like the project.
Let me warm my brains first with the richest
    grape,
And then I'm for you.
    Cap. We will want no wine.
                [*Exeunt all but Lidia.*
    Lid. That this comes only from the best
        of princes,
With a kind of adoration does command me
To entertain it ; and the sweet contents
                [*Kissing the letter.*
That are inscribed here by his hand must be
Much more than musical to me. All the service
Of my life at no part can deserve this favour.
O what a virgin longing I feel on me
To unrip the seal, and read it ! yet, to break
What he hath fastened, rashly, may appear
A saucy rudeness in me.—I must do it,
(Nor can I else learn his commands, or serve
    them,)
But with such reverence, as I would open
Some holy writ, whose grave instructions
    beat down
Rebellious sins, and teach my better part
How to mount upward.—So, [*opens the
    letter*] 'tis done, and I
With eagle's eyes will curiously peruse it.
                [*Reads.*
Chaste Lidia, the favours are so great
On me by you conferr'd, that to entreat
The least addition to them, in true sense
May argue me of blushless impudence.
But, such are my extremes, if you deny
A further grace, I must unpitied die.
Haste cuts off circumstance. As you're ad-
    mired
For beauty, the report of it hath fired

R

The duke my uncle, and, I fear, you'll
prove,
Not with a sacred, but unlawful love.
If he see you as you are, my hoped for light
Is changed into an everlasting night ;
How to prevent it, if your goodness find,
You save two lives, and me you ever bind,
The honourer of your virtues,
                                GIOVANNI.

Were I more deaf than adders, these sweet
   charms
Would through my ears find passage to my
   soul,
And soon enchant it. To save such a prince,
Who would not perish ? virtue in him must
   suffer,
And piety be forgotten. The duke's lust,
Though it raged more than Tarquin's, shall
   not reach me.
All quaint inventions of chaste virgins aid me !
My prayers are heard ; I have't. The duke
   ne'er saw me—
Or, if that fail, I am again provided—
But for the servants !—They will take what
   form
I please to put upon them. Giovanni,
Be safe ; thy servant Lidia assures it.
Let mountains of afflictions fall on me,
Their weight is easy, so I set thee free.
                                [*Exit.*

SCENE II.—*Another Room in the same.*

   Enter Cozimo, Giovanni, Sanazarro,
      Charomonte, *and* Attendants.

Sanaz. Are you not tired with travel, sir?
Coz. No, no ;
I am fresh and lusty.
Char. This day shall be ever
A holiday to me, that brings my prince
Under my humble roof.   [*Weeps.*
Giov. See, sir, my good tutor
Sheds tears for joy.
Coz. Dry them up, Charomonte ;
And all forbear the room, while we exchange
Some private words together.
Giov. O, my lord,
How grossly have we overshot ourselves !
Sanaz. In what, sir?
Giov. In forgetting to acquaint
My guardian with our purpose : all that Lidia
Can do avails us nothing, if the duke
Find out the truth from him.
Sanaz. 'Tis now past help,
And we must stand the hazard :—hope the
   best, sir.
            [*Exeunt* Giovanni, Sanazarro, *and*
               Attendants.
Char. My loyalty doubted, sir !

Coz. 'Tis more. Thou hast
Abused our trust, and in a high degree
Committed treason.
Char. Treason ! 'Tis a word
My innocence understands not. Were my
   breast
Transparent, and my thoughts to be dis-
   cern'd,
Not one spot shall be found to taint the
   candour
Of my allegiance : and I must be bold
To tell you, sir, (for he that knows no guilt
Can know no fear,) 'tis tyranny to o'ercharge
An honest man ; and such, till now, I've
   lived,
And such, my lord, I'll die.
Coz. Sir, do not flatter
Yourself with hope, these great and glo-
   rions words,
Which every guilty wretch, as well as you,
That's arm'd with impudence, can with ease
   deliver,
And with as full a mouth, can work on us :
Nor shall gay flourishes of language clear
What is in fact apparent.
Char. Fact ! what fact?
You, that know only what it is, instruct me,
For I am ignorant.
Coz. This, then, sir : We gave up,
On our assurance of your faith and care,
Our nephew Giovanni, nay, our heir
In expectation, to be train'd up by you
As did become a prince.
Char. And I discharg'd it :
Is this the treason?
Coz. Take us with you, sir.
And, in respect we knew his youth was prone
To women, and that, living in our court,
He might make some unworthy choice,
   before
His weaker judgment was confirm'd, we did
Remove him from it ; constantly presuming,
You, with your best endeavours, rather would
Have quench'd those heats in him, than
   light a torch,
As you have done, to his looseness.
Char. I ! my travail
Is ill-requited, sir ; for, by my soul,
I was so curious that way, that I granted
Access to none could tempt him ; nor did
   ever
One syllable, or obscene accent, touch
His ear, that might corrupt him.
Coz. No ! Why, then,
With your allowance, did you give free way
To all familiar privacy between
My nephew and your daughter ? Or why
   did you
(Had you no other ends in't but our service)

Read to them, and together, as they had
been
Scholars of one form, grammar, rhetoric,
Philosophy, story, and interpret to them
The close temptations of lascivious poets?
Or wherefore, for we still had spies upon you,
Was she still present, when, by your advice,
He was taught the use of his weapon, horse-
manship,
Wrestling, nay, swimming, but to fan in her
A hot desire of him? and then, forsooth,
His exercises ended, cover'd with
A fair pretence of recreation for him,
(When Lidia was instructed in those graces
That add to beauty,) he, brought to admire
her,
Must hear her sing, while to her voice her
hand
Made ravishing music; and, this applauded,
dance
A light lavolta with her.
   Char. Have you ended
All you can charge me with?
   Coz. Nor stopt you there,
But they must unattended walk into
The silent groves, and hear the amorous
birds
Warbling their wanton notes; here, a sure
shade
Of barren sicamores, which the all-seeing sun
Could not pierce through; near that, an
arbour hung
With spreading eglantine; there, a bubbling
spring
Watering a bank of hyacinths and lilies;
With all allurements that could move to lust.
And could this, Charomonte, (should I grant
They had been equals both in birth and
fortune,)
Become your gravity? nay, 'tis clear as air,
That your ambitious hopes to match your
daughter
Into our family, gave connivance to it:
And this, though not in act, in the intent
I call high treason.
   Char. Hear my just defence, sir;
And, though you are my prince, it will not
   take from
Your greatness, to acknowledge with a blush,
In this my accusation you have been
More sway'd by spleen, and jealous suppo-
sitions,
Than certain grounds of reason. You had
a father,
(Blest be his memory!) that made frequent
proofs
Of my loyalty and faith, and, would I boast
The dangers I have broke through in his
service,

I could say more. Nay, you yourself, dread
sir,
Whenever I was put unto the test,
Found me true gold, and not adulterate
metal;
And am I doubted now?
   Coz. This is from the purpose.
   Char. I will come to it, sir: Your grace
well knew,
Before the prince's happy presence made
My poor house rich, the chiefest blessing
which
I gloried in, though now it prove a curse,
Was an only daughter. Nor did you com-
mand me,
As a security to your future fears,
To cast her off: which had you done,
howe'er
She was the light of my eyes, and comfort of
My feeble age, so far I prized my duty
Above affection, she now had been
A stranger to my care. But she is fair!
Is that her fault, or mine? Did ever father
Hold beauty in his issue for a blemish?
Her education and her manners tempt too!
If these offend, they are easily removed:
You may, if you think fit, before my face,
In recompense of all my watchings for you,
With burning corrosives transform her to
An ugly leper; and, this done, to taint
Her sweetness, prostitute her to a brothel.
This I will rather suffer, sir, and more,
Than live suspected by you.
   Coz. Let not passion
Carry you beyond your reason.
   Char. I am calm, sir;
Yet you must give me leave to grieve I find
My actions misinterpreted. Alas! sir,
Was Lidia's desire to serve the prince
Call'd an offence? or did she practise to
Seduce his youth, because with her best zeal
And fervour she endeavoured to attend him?
'Tis a hard construction. Though she be
my daughter,
I may thus far speak her: from her infancy
She was ever civil, her behaviour nearer
Simplicity than craft; and malice dares not
Affirm, in one loose gesture, or light language,
She gave a sign she was in thought unchaste.
I'll fetch her to you, sir; and but look on her,
With equal eyes, you must in justice grant,
That your suspicion wrongs her.
   Coz. It may be;
But I must have stronger assurance of it
Than passionate words: and, not to trifle
time,
As we came unexpected to your house,
We will prevent all means that may pre-
pare her

R 2

How to answer that, with which we come to
  charge her.
And howsoever it may be received
As a foul breach to hospitable rites,
On thy allegiance and boasted faith,
Nay, forfeit of thy head, we do confine thee
Close prisoner to thy chamber, till all doubts
Are clear'd, that do concern us.
  Char. I obey, sir,
And wish your grace had followed my hearse
To my sepulchre, my loyalty unsuspected,
Rather than now—but I am silent, sir,
And let that speak my duty.   [*Exit.*
  Coz. If this man
Be false, disguised treachery ne'er put on
A shape so near to truth. Within, there!

Re-enter Giovanni *and* Sanazarro, *ushering
  in* Petronella. Calandrino *and others
  setting forth a banquet.*

  Sanaz. Sir.
  Coz. Bring Lidia forth.
  Giov. She comes, sir, of herself,
To present her service to you.
  Coz. Ha! this personage
Cannot invite affection.
  Sanaz. See you keep state.
  Petron. I warrant you.
  Coz. The manners of her mind
Must be transcendent, if they can defend
Her rougher outside. May we with your
  liking
Salute you, lady?
  Petron. Let me wipe my mouth, sir,
With my cambric handkerchief, and then
  have at you.
  Coz. Can this be possible?
  Sanaz. Yes, sir; you will find her
Such as I gave her to you.
  Petron. Will your dukeship
Sit down and eat some sugar-plums? Here's
  a castle
Of march-pane too; and this quince-mar-
  malade was
Of my own making; all summ'd up together,
Did cost the setting on: and here is wine too,
As good as e'er was tapp'd. I'll be your
  taster,
For I know the fashion. [*Drinks all off.*—
  Now you must do me right, sir;
You shall nor will not choose.
  Giov. She's very simple.
  Coz. Simple! 'tis worse. Do you drink
  thus often, lady?
  Petron. Still when I am thirsty, and eat
  when I am hungry:
Such junkets come not every day. Once
  more to you,
With a heart and a half, i'faith.

  Coz. Pray you, pause a little;
If I hold your cards, I shall pull down the
  side;
I am not good at the game,
  Petron. Then I'll drink for you.
  Coz. Nay, pray you stay: I'll find you out
  a pledge
That shall supply my place; what think you of
This complete signior? You are a Juno,
And in such state must feast this Jupiter:
What think you of him?
  Petron. I desire no better.
  Coz. And you will undertake this service
  for me?
You are good at the sport.
  Cal. Who, I? a piddler, sir.
  Coz. Nay, you shall sit enthroned, and
  drink
As you were a duke.
  Cal. If your grace will have me,
I'll eat and drink like an emperor.
  Coz. Take your place then:
    [Calandrino *takes the* Duke's *chair.*
We are amazed.
  Giov. This is gross: nor can the imposture
But be discover'd.
  Sanaz. The duke is too sharp-sighted,
To be deluded thus.
  Cal. Nay, pray you eat fair,
Or divide, and I will choose. Cannot you use
Your fork, as I do? Gape, and I will feed
  you.   [*Feeds her.*
Gape wider yet; this is court-like.
  Petron. To choke daws with:——
I like it not.
  Cal. But you like this?
  Petron. Let it come, boy. [*They drink.*
  Coz. What a sight is this! We could be
  angry with you.
How much you did belie her when you told us
She was only simple! this is barbarous rude-
  ness,
Beyond belief.
  Giov. I would not speak her, sir,
Worse than she was.
  Sanaz. And I, my lord, chose rather
To deliver her better parted than she is,
Than to take from her.

Enter Caponi, *with his fellow Servants for
  the dance.*

  Cap. Ere I'll lose my dance,
I'll speak to the purpose. I am, sir, no
  prologue;
But in plain terms must tell you, we are
  provided
Of a lusty hornpipe.
  Coz. Prithee, let us have it,
For we grow dull.

Cap. But to make up the medley,
For it is of several colours, we must borrow
Your grace's ghost here.
Cal. Pray you, sir, depose me ;
It will not do else. I am, sir, the engine
    [*Rises, and resigns his chair.*
By which it moves.
Petron. I will dance with my duke too;
I will not out.
Coz. Begin then.—[*They dance.*]—There's
 more in this,
Than yet I have discover'd. Some Œdipus
Resolve this riddle.
Petron. Did I not foot it roundly. [*Falls.*
Coz. As I live, stark drunk ! away with her.
 We'll reward you,
    [*Exeunt* Servants *with* Petronella.
When you have cool'd yourselves in the cellar.
Cap. Heaven preserve you !
Coz. We pity Charomonte's wretched
 fortune
In a daughter, nay, a monster. Good old
 man !—
The place grows tedious ; our remove shall be
With speed : we'll only, in a word or two,
Take leave, and comfort him.
Sanaz. 'Twill rather, sir,
Increase your sorrow, that you know his
 shame ;
Your grace may do it by letter.
Coz. Who sign'd you
A patent to direct us ? Wait our coming
In the garden.
Giov. All will out.
Sanaz. I more than fear it.
    [*Exeunt* Giovanni *and* Sanazarro.
Coz. These are strange chimeras to us :
 what to judge of't,
Is past our apprehension. One command
Charomonte to attend us.
    [*Exit an* Attendant.
      Can it be
That Contarino could be so besotted,
As to admire this prodigy ! or her father
To doat upon it ! Or does she personate,
For some ends unknown to us, this rude be-
 haviour,
Which, in the scene presented, would appear
Ridiculous and impossible !—O, you are
 welcome.

    Enter Charomonte.

We now acknowledge the much wrong we
 did you
In our unjust suspicion. We have seen
The wonder, sir, your daughter.
Char. And have found her
Such as I did report her. What she wanted

In courtship, was, I hope, supplied in civil
And modest entertainment.
Coz. Pray you, tell us,
And truly, we command you—Did you never
Observe she was given to drink ?
Char. To drink, sir !
Coz. Yes, nay more, to be drunk ?
Char. I had rather see her buried.
Coz. Dare you trust your own eyes, if you
 find her now
More than distemper'd ?
Char. I will pull them out, sir,
If your grace can make this good. And if
 'you please
To grant me liberty, as she is I'll fetch her,
And in a moment.
Coz. Look you do, and fail not,
On the peril of your head.
Char. Drunk !—She disdains it. [*Exit.*
Coz. Such contrarieties were never read of.
Charomonte is no fool ; nor can I think
His confidence built on sand. We are abused,
'Tis too apparent.

   Re-enter Charomonte *with* Lidia.

Lid. I am indisposed, sir :
And that life you once tender'd, much en-
 danger'd
In forcing me from my chamber.
Char. Here she is, sir :
Suddenly sick, I grant ; but, sure, not drunk ;
Speak to my lord the duke.
Lid. All is discover'd. [*Kneels.*
Coz. Is this your only daughter ?
Char. And my heir, sir ;
Nor keep I any woman in my house
(Unless for sordid offices) but one
I do maintain, trimm'd up in her cast habits,
To make her sport : and she, indeed, loves
 wine,
And will take too much of it ; and, perhaps,
 for mirth,
She was presented to you.
Coz. It shall yield
No sport to the contrivers. 'Tis too plain now.
Her presence does confirm what Contarino
Deliver'd of her ; nor can sickness dim
The splendour of her beauties : being her-
 self, then,
She must exceed his praise.
Lid. Will your grace hear me ?
I'm faint, and can say little.
Coz. Here are accents
Whose every syllable is musical !
Pray you, let me raise you, and awhile rest
 here.
False Sanazarro, treacherous Giovanni !
But stand we talking !——
Char. Here's a storm soon raised.

Coz. As thou art our subject, Charomonte,
   swear
To act what we command.
   Char. That is an oath
I long since took.
   Coz. Then, by that oath we charge thee,
Without excuse, denial, or delay,
To apprehend, and suddenly, Sanazarro,
And our ingrateful nephew. We have
   said it.
Do it without reply, or we pronounce thee,
Like them, a traitor to us. See them guarded
In several lodgings, and forbid access
To all, but when we warrant. Is our will
Heard sooner than obey'd?
   Char. These are strange turns ;
But I must not dispute them.   [*Exit.*
   Coz. Be severe in't.—
O my abused lenity ! from what height
Is my power fall'n !
   Lid. O me most miserable !
That, being innocent, makes others guilty.
Most gracious prince——
   Coz. Pray you rise, and then speak to me.
   Lid. My knees shall first be rooted in this
   earth,
And, Myrrha-like, I'll grow up to a tree,
Dropping perpetual tears of sorrow, which
Harden'd by the rough wind, and turu'd to
   amber,
Unfortunate virgins like myself shall wear ;
Before I'll make petition to your greatness,
But with such reverence, my hands held up
   thus,
As I would do to heaven. You princes are
As gods on earth to us, and to be sued to
With such humility, as his deputies
May challenge from their vassals.
   Coz. Here's that form
Of language I expected ; pray you, speak :
What is your suit?
   Lid. That you would look upon me
As an humble thing, that millions of degrees
Is placed beneath you : for what am I, dread
   sir,
Or what can fall in the whole course of my
   life,
That may be worth your care, much less
   your trouble?
As the lowly shrub is to the lofty cedar,
Or a molehill to Olympus, if compared,
I am to you, sir. Or, suppose the prince,
(Which cannot find belief in me,) forgetting
The greatness of his birth and hopes, hath
   thrown
An eye of favour on me, in me punish,
That am the cause, the rashness of his youth.
Shall the queen of the inhabitants of the air,
The eagle, that bears thunder on her wings,

In her angry mood destroy her hopeful young,
For suffering a wren to perch too near them?
Such is our disproportion.
   Coz. With what fervour
She pleads against herself !
   Lid. For me, poor maid,
I know the prince to be so far above me,
That my wishes cannot reach him. Yet I am
So much his creature, that, to fix him in
Your wonted grace and favour, I'll abjure
His sight for ever, and betake myself
To a religious life, (where in my prayers
I may remember him,) and ne'er see man
   more,
But my ghostly father. Will you trust me,
   sir?
In truth I'll keep my word ; or, if this fail,
A little more of fear what may befall him
Will stop my breath for ever.
   Coz. Had you thus argued   [*Raises her.*
As you were yourself, and brought as advo-
   cates
Your health and beauty, to make way for you,
No crime of his could put on such a shape
But I should look with the eyes of mercy on it.
What would I give to see this diamond
In her perfect lustre, as she was before
The clouds of sickness dimm'd it ! Yet,
   take comfort ;
And, as you would obtain remission for
His treachery to me, cheer your drooping
   spirits,
And call the blood again into your cheeks,
And then plead for him ; and in such a habit
As in your highest hopes you would put on,
If we were to receive you for our bride.
   Lid. I'll do my best, sir.
   Coz. And that best will be
A crown of all felicity to me.   [*Exeunt.*

ACT V.

SCENE I.—*The same. An upper Chamber
   in* Charomonte's *House.*

· *Enter* Sanazarro.

   Sanaz. 'Tis proved in me : the curse of
   human frailty,
Adding to our afflictions, makes us know
What's good ; and yet our violent passions
   force us
To follow what is ill. Reason assured me
It was not safe to shave a lion's skin ;
And that to trifle with a sovereign was
To play with lightning : yet imperious beauty,
Treading upon the neck of understanding,
Compell'd me to put off my natural shape
Of loyal duty, to disguise myself
In the adulterate and cobweb-mask

Of disobedient treachery.. Where is now
My borrow'd greatness, or the promised lives
Of following courtiers echoing my will?
In a moment vanish'd ! Power that stands
    not on
Its proper base, which is peculiar only
To absolute princes, falls or rises with
Their frown or favour. The great duke,
    my master,
(Who almost changed me to his other self,)
No sooner takes his beams of comfort from
    me,
But I, as one unknown, or unregarded,
Unpitied suffer. Who makes intercession
To his mercy for me, now? who does re-
    member
The service I have done him? not a man :
And such as spake no language but my lord
The favourite of Tuscany's grand duke,
Deride my madness.—Ha ! what noise of
    horses?
        [*He looks out at the back window.*
A goodly troop ! This back part of my prison
Allows me liberty to see and know them.
Contarino ! yes, 'tis he, and Lodovico :
And the dutchess Fiorinda, Urbin's heir,
A princess I have slighted : yet I wear
Her favours ; and, to teach me what I am,
She who.n I scorn'd can only mediate for me.
This way she makes, yet speak to her I dare
    not :
And how to make suit to her is a task
Of as much difficulty.—Yes, thou blessed
    pledge   [*Takes off the ring.*
Of her affection, aid me ! This supplies
The want of pen and ink ; and this, of paper.
                [*Takes a pane of glass.*
It must be so ; and I in my petition
Concise and pithy.

SCENE II.—*The Court before* Charomonte's *House.*

Enter Contarino *leading in* Fiorinda, Al-
phouso, Hippolito, Hieronimo, *and* Calaminta.

Fior. 'Tis a goodly pile, this.
Hier. But better by the owner.
Alph. But most rich
In the great states it covers.
Fior. The duke's pleasure
Commands us hither.
Cont. Which was laid on us
To attend you to it,
Hip. Signior Charomonte,
To see your excellence his guest, will think
Himself most happy.
Fior.. Tie my shoe.—[*The pane falls
down.*]—What's that ?

A pane thrown from the window, no wind
    stirring !
Calam. And at your feet too fall'n :—
    there's something writ on't.
Cont. Some courtier, belike, would have
    it known
He wore a diamond.
Calam. Ha ! it is directed
To the princess Fiorinda.
Fior. We will read it.   [*Reads.*
*He, whom you pleased to favour, is cast down
Past hope of rising, by the great duke's frown,
If, by your gracious means, he cannot have
A pardon ;—and that got, he lives your slave.
        Of men the most distressed,
                        SANAZARRO.*
Of me the most beloved ; and I will save thee,
Or perish with thee. Sure, thy fault must be
Of some prodigious shape, if that my prayers
And humble intercession to the duke

Enter Cozimo *and* Charomonte.

Prevail not with him. Here he comes ; delay
Shall not make less my benefit.
Coz. What we purpose
Shall know no change, and therefore move
    me not :
We were made as properties, and what we
    shall
Determine of them cannot be call'd rigour,
But noble justice. When they proved disloyal,
They were cruel to themselves. The prince
    that pardons
The first affront offer'd to majesty,
Invites a second, rendering that power
Subjects should tremble at, contemptible.
Ingratitude is a monster, Carolo,
To be strangled in the birth, not to be
    cherish'd.
Madam, you're happily met with.
Fior. Sir, I am
An humble suitor to you; and the rather
Am confident of a grant, in that your grace,
When I made choice to be at your devotion,
Vow'd to deny me nothing.
Coz. To this minute
We have confirm'd it. What's your boon?
Fior. It is, sir,
That you, in being gracious to your servant,
The ne'er sufficiently praised Sanazarro,
That now under your heavy displeasure
    suffers,   ·
Would be good unto yourself. His services,
So many, and so great, (your storm of fury
Calm'd by your better judgment,) must in-
    form you
Some little slip, for sure it is no more,
From his loyal duty, with your justice cannot

Make foul his fair deservings. Great sir, therefore,
Look backward on his former worth, and turning
Your eye from his offence, what 'tis I know not,
And, I am confident, you will receive him
Once more into your favour.
  Coz. You say well,
You are ignorant in the nature of his fault ;
Which when you understand, as we'll instruct you,
Your pity will appear a charity,
It being conferr'd on an unthankful man,
To be repented. He's a traitor, madam,
To you, to us, to gratitude ; and in that
All crimes are comprehended.
  Fior. If his offence
Aim'd at me only, whatsoe'er it is,
'Tis freely pardon'd.
  Coz. This compassion in you
Must make the colour of his guilt more ugly.
The honours we have hourly heap'd upon him,
The titles, the rewards, to the envy of
The old nobility, as the common people,
We now forbear to touch at, and will only
Insist on his gross wrongs to you. You were pleased,
Forgetting both yourself and proper greatness,
To favour him, nay, to court him to embrace
A happiness, which, on his knees, with joy
He should have sued for. Who repined not at
The grace you did him? yet, in recompense
Of your large bounties, the disloyal wretch
Makes you a stale ; and, what he might be by you
Scorn'd and derided, gives himself up wholly
To the service of another. If you can
Bear this with patience, we must say you have not
The bitterness of spleen, or ireful passions
Familiar to women. Pause upon it,
And when you seriously have weigh'd his carriage,
Move us again, if your reason will allow it,
His treachery known : and then, if you continne
An advocate for him, we, perhaps, because
We would deny you nothing, may awake
Our sleeping mercy. Carolo !
  Char. My lord.   [*They talk aside.*
  Fior. To endure a rival that were equal to me,
Cannot but speak my poverty of spirit ;
But an inferior, more : yet true love must not
Know or degrees, or distances. Lidia may be
As far above me in her form, as she

Is in her birth beneath me ; and what I
In Sanazarro liked, he loves in her.
But, if I free him now, the benefit
Being done so timely, and confirming too
My strength and power, my soul's best faculties being
Bent wholly to preserve him, must supply me
With all I am defective in, and bind him
My creature ever. It must needs be so,
Nor will I give it o'er thus.
  Coz. Does our nephew
Bear his restraint so constantly, as you
Deliver it to us ?
  Char. In my judgment, sir,
He suffers more for his offence to you,
Than in his fear of what can follow it.
For he is so collected, and prepared
To welcome that you shall determine of him,
As if his doubts and fears were equal to him.
And sure he's not acquainted with much guilt,
That more laments the telling one untruth,
Under your pardon still, for 'twas a fault, sir,
Than others, that pretend to conscience, do
Their crying secret sins.
  Coz. No more ; this gloss
Defends not the corruption of the text :
Urge it no more.
    [Charomonte *and the others talk aside.*
  Fior. I once more must make bold, sir,
To trench upon your patience. I have
Consider'd my wrongs duly : yet that cannot
Divert my intercession for a man
Your grace, like me, once favour'd. I am still
A suppliant to you, that you would vouchsafe
The hearing his defence, and that I may,
With your allowance, see and comfort him.
Then, having heard all that he can allege
In his excuse, for being false to you,
Censure him as you please.
  Coz. You will o'ercome :
There's no contending with you. Pray you, enjoy
What you desire, and tell him, he shall have
A speedy trial ; in which, we'll forbear
To sit a judge, because our purpose is
To rise up his accuser.
  Fior. All increase
Of happiness wait on Cozimo !
    [*Exeunt* Fiorinda *and* Calaminta.
  Alph. Was it no more ?
  Char. My honour's pawn'd for it.
  Cont. I'll second you.
  Hip. Since it is for the service and the safety
Of the hopeful prince, fall what can fall,
I'll run
The desperate hazard.

Hier. He's no friend to virtue
That does decline it.
[*They all come forward and kneel.*
Coz. Ha! what sue you for?
Shall we be ever troubled? Do not tempt
That anger may consume you.
Char. Let it, sir:
The loss is less, though innocents we perish,
Than that your sister's son should fall, un-
heard,
Under your fury. Shall we fear to entreat
That grace for him, that are your faithful
servants,
Which you vouchsafe the count, like us a
subject?
Coz. Did not we vow, till sickness had
forsook
Thy daughter Lidia, and she appear'd
In her perfect health and beauty to plead for
him,
We were deaf to all persuasion?
Char. And that hope, sir,
Hath wrought a miracle. She is recover'd,
And, if you please to warrant her, will bring
The penitent prince before you.
Coz. To enjoy
Such happiness, what would we not dis-
pense with?
Alph. Hip. Hier. We all kneel for the
prince.
Cont. Nor can it stand
With your mercy, that are gracious to
strangers,
To be cruel to your own.
Coz. But art thou certain
I shall behold her at the best?
Char. If ever
She was handsome, as it fits not me to say so,
She is now much better'd.
Coz. Rise; thou art but dead
If this prove otherwise. Lidia, appear
And feast an appetite almost pined to death
With longing expectation to behold
Thy excellencies: thou, as beauty's queen,
Shalt censure the detractors. Let my nephew
Be led in triumph under her command;
We'll have it so; and Sanazarro tremble
To think whom he hath slander'd. We'll
retire
Ourselves a little, and prepare to meet
A blessing, which imagination tells us
We are not worthy of: and then come
forth,
But with such reverence, as it I were
Myself the priest, the sacrifice my heart,
To offer at the altar of that goodness
That must or kill or save me. [*Exit.*
Char. Are not these
Strange gambols in the duke!

Alph. Great princes have,
Like meaner men, their weakness.
Hip. And may use it
Without control or check.
Cont. 'Tis fit they should:
Their privilege were less else, than their
subjects'.
Hier. Let them have their humours; there's
no crossing them. [*Exeunt.*

SCENE III.—*A State-room in the same.*

Enter Fiorinda, Sanazarro, *and* Calaminta.

Sanaz. And can it be, your bounties
should fall down
In showers on my ingratitude, or the wrongs
Your greatness should revenge, teach you to·
pity?
What retribution can I make, what service
Pay to your goodness, that, in some pro-
portion,
May to the world express I would be thankful?·
Since my engagements are so great, that all
My best endeavours to appear your creature
Can but proclaim my wants, and what I owe
To your magnificence.
Fior. All debts are discharged
In this acknowledgment: yet, since you
please
I shall impose some terms of satisfaction
For that which you profess yourself obliged
for,
They shall be gentle ones, and such as will not,
I hope, afflict you.
Sanaz. Make me understand,
Great princess, what they are, and my
obedience
Shall, with all cheerful willingness, subscribe·
To what you shall command.
Fior. I will bind you to
Make good your promise. First, I then·
enjoin you
To love a lady, that, a noble way,
Truly affects you; and that you would take·
To your protection and care the dukedom
Of Urbin, which no more is mine, but yours.
And that, when you have full possession of
My person as my fortune, you would use me,
Not as a princess, but instruct me in
The duties of an humble wife, for such,
The privilege of my birth no more re-
member'd,
I will be to you. This consented to,
All injuries forgotten, on your lips
I thus sign your *quietus.*
Sanaz. I am wretched,
In having but one life to be employ'd
As you please to dispose it. And, believe it,
If it be not already forfeited
To the fury of my prince, as 'tis your gift,

With all the faculties of my soul I'll study,
In what I may to serve you.
   Fior. I am happy

    Enter Giovanni, *and* Lidia.

In this assurance. What sweet lady's this?
   Sanaz. 'Tis Lidia, madam, she——
   Fior. I understand you.
Nay, blush not; by my life, she is a rare one!
And, if I were your judge, I would not
   blame you
To like and love her. But, sir, you are
   mine now;   ·
And I presume so on your constancy,
That I dare not be jealous.
   Sanaz. All thoughts of her
Are in your goodness buried.
   Lid. Pray you, sir,
Be comforted; your innocence should not
   know
What 'tis to fear; and if that you but look on
The guards that you have in yourself, you
   cannot.
The duke's your uncle, sir, and, though a
   little
Incensed against you, when he sees your
   sorrow,
He must be reconciled. What rugged Tartar,
Or cannibal, though bath'd in human gore,
But, looking on your sweetness, would forget
His cruel nature, and let fall his weapon,
Though then aim'd at your throat?
   Giov. O Lidia,
Of maids the honour, and your sex's glory!
It is not fear to die, but to lose you,
That brings this fever on me. I will now
Discover to you, that which, till this minute,
I durst not trust the air with. Ere you knew
What power the magic of your beauty had,
I was enchanted by it, liked, and loved it,
My fondness still increasing with my years;
And, flatter'd by false hopes, I did attend
Some blessed opportunity to move
The duke with his consent to make you mine:
But now, such is my star-cross'd destiny,
When he beholds you as you are, he cannot
Deny himself the happiness to enjoy you.
And I as well in reason may entreat him
To give away his crown, as to part from
A jewel of more value, such you are.
Yet, howsoever, when you are his dutchess,
And I am turn'd into forgotten dust,
Pray you, love my memory:—I should say
   more,
But I'm cut off.

   Enter Cozimo, Charomonte, Contarino,
   Hieronimo, Hippolito, *and* Alphonso.

   Sanaz. The duke! That countenance,
   once,

When it was clothed in smiles, shew'd like
   an angel's,
But, now 'tis folded up in clouds of fury,
'Tis terrible to look on.
   Lid. Sir.
   Coz. A while
Silence your musical tongue, and let me feast
My eyes with the most ravishing object that
They ever gazed on. There's no miniature
In her fair face, but is a copious theme
Which would, discours'd at large of, make
   a volume.
What clear arch'd brows! what sparkling
   eyes! the lilies
Contending with the roses in her cheeks,
Who shall most set them off. What ruby
   lips!—
Or unto what can I compare her neck,
But to a rock of crystal! every limb
Proportion'd to love's wish, and in their
   neatness
Add lustre to the riches of her habit,
Not borrow from it.
   Lid. You are pleased to shew, sir,
The fluency of your language, in advancing
A subject much unworthy.
   Coz. How! unworthy?
By all the vows which lovers offer at
The Cyprian goddess' altars, eloquence
Itself presuming, as you are, to speak you,
Would be struck dumb!—And what have
   you deserved then,
       [Giovanni *and* Sanazarro *kneel.*
(Wretches, you kneel too late,) that have
   endeavour'd
To spout the poison of your black detraction
On this immaculate whiteness? was it malice
To her perfections? or——
   Fior. Your highness promised
A gracious hearing to the count.
   Lid. And prince too;
Do not make void so just a grant.
   Coz. We will not:
Yet, since their accusation must be urged,
And strongly, ere their weak defence have
   hearing,
We seat you here, as judges, to determine
Of your gross wrongs and ours.
       [*Seats the* Ladies *in the chairs of state.*
And now, remembering
Whose deputies you are, be neither sway'd
Or with particular spleen, or foolish pity,
For neither can become you.
   Char. There's some hope yet,
Since they have such gentle judges.
   Coz. Rise, and stand forth, then,
And hear, with horror to your guilty souls,
What we will prove against you. Could this
   princess,

Thou enemy to thyself, [*To* Sanazarro.]
    stoop her high flight
Of towering greatness to invite thy lowness
To look up to it, and with nimble wings
Of gratitude couldst thou forbear to meet it ?
Were her favours boundless in a noble way,
And warranted by our allowance, yet,
In thy acceptation, there appear'd no sign
Of a modest thankfulness ?
  Fior. Pray you forbear
To press that further ; 'tis a fault we have
Already heard, and pardon'd.
  Coz. We will then
Pass over it, and briefly touch at that
Which does concern ourself, in which both
    being
Equal offenders, what we shall speak points
Indifferently at either. How we raised thee,
Forgetful Sanazarro ! of our grace,
To a full possession of power and honours,
It being too well known, we'll not remember.
And what thou wert, rash youth, in expecta-
    tion,   [*To* Giovanni.
And from which headlong thou hast thrown
    thyself,
Not Florence, but all Tuscany can witness,
With admiration. To assure thy hopes,
We did keep constant to a widowed bed,
And did deny ourself those lawful pleasures
Our absolute power and height of blood
    allow'd us ;
Made both, the keys that open'd our heart's
    secrets,
And what you spake, believed as oracles :
But you, in recompense of this, to him
That gave you all, to whom you owed your
    being,
With treacherous lies endeavour'd to con-
    ceal
This jewel from our knowledge, which ourself
Could only lay just claim to.
  Giov. 'Tis most true, sir.
  Sanaz. We both confess a guilty cause.
  Coz. Look on her.
Is this a beauty fit to be embraced
By any subject's arms ? can any tire
Become that forehead, but a diadem ?
Or, should we grant your being false to us
Could be excused, your treachery to her,
In seeking to deprive her of that greatness
(Her matchless form consider'd) she was
    born to,
Must ne'er find pardon. We have spoken,
    ladies,
Like a rough orator, that brings more truth
Than rhetoric to make good his accusation ;
And now expect your sentence.
     [*The* Ladies *descend from the state.*
  Lid. In your birth, sir,

You were mark'd out the judge of life and
    death,
And we, that are your subjects, to attend,
With trembling fear, your doom.
  Fior. We do resign
This chair, as only proper to yourself.
  Giov. And, since in justice we are lost,
    we fly
Unto your saving mercy.   [*All kneeling.*
  Sanaz. Which sets off
A prince, much more than rigour.
  Char. And becomes him,
When 'tis express'd to such as fell by weak-
    ness,
That being a twin-born brother to affection,
Better than wreaths of conquest.
  Hier. Hip. Cont. Alph. We all speak
Their language, mighty sir.
  Coz. You know our temper,
And therefore with more boldness venture
    on it :
And, would not our consent to your demands
Deprive us of a happiness hereafter
Ever to be despair'd of, we, perhaps,
Might hearken nearer to you ; and could
    wish
With some qualification, or excuse,
You might make less the mountains of your
    crimes,
And so invite our clemency to feast with
    you.
But you, that knew with what impatiency
Of grief we parted from the fair Clarinda,
Our dutchess, (let her memory still be
    sacred !)
And with what imprecations on ourself
We vowed, not hoping e'er to see her equal,
Ne'er to make trial of a second choice,
If nature framed not one that did excel her,
As this maid's beauty prompts us that she
    does : —
And yet, with oaths then mix'd with tears,
    upon
Her monument we swore our eye should
    never
Again be tempted ;—'tis true, and those vows
Are register'd above, something here tells
    me.—
Carolo, thou heardst us swear.
  Char. And swear so deeply,
That if all women's beauties were in this,
(As she's not to be named with the dead
    dutchess,)
Nay, all their virtues bound up in one story,
(Of which mine is scarce an epitome,)
If you should take her as a wife, the weight
Of your perjuries would sink you. If I durst,
I had told you this before.
  Coz. 'Tis strong truth, Carolo :

And yet, what was necessity in us,
Cannot free them from treason.

Char. There's your error ;
The prince, in care to have you keep your
    vows
Made unto heaven, vouchsafed to love my
    daughter.

Lid. He told me so, indeed, sir.

Fior. And the count
Averr'd as much to me.

Coz. You all conspire,
To force our mercy from us.

Char. Which given up,
To aftertimes preserves you unsworn :
An honour which will live upon your tomb,
When your greatness is forgotten.

Coz. Though we know
All this is practice, and that both are false :
Such reverence we will pay to dead Clarinda,
And to our serious oaths, that we are
    pleased
With our own hand to blind our eyes, and
    not
Know what we understand. Here, Giovanni,
We pardon thee ; and take from us, in this,
More than our dukedom : love her. As I
    part
With her, all thoughts of women fly fast
    from us !
Sanazarro, we forgive you : in your service
To this princess, merit it. Yet let not
. others
That are in trust and grace, as you have been,
By the example of our lenity,
Presume upon their sovereign's clemency.

Enter Calandrino *and* Petronella.

All. Long live great Cozimo !

Cal. Sure the duke is
In the giving vein, they are so loud. Come
    on, spouse ;
We have heard all, and we will have our
    boon too.

Coz. What is it ?

Cal. That your grace, in remembrance of
My share in a dance, and that I play'd your
    part,
When you should have drunk hard, would
    get this signior's grant
To give this damsel to me in the church,
For we are contracted. In it you shall do
Your dukedom pleasure.

Coz. How ?

Cal. Why the whole race
Of such as can act naturally fools' parts,
Are quite worn out ; and they that do survive,
Do only zany us : and we will bring you,
If we die not without issue, of both sexes
Such chopping mirth-makers, as shall pre-
    serve
Perpetual cause of sport, both to your grace
And your posterity ; that sad melancholy
Shall ne'er approach you.

Coz. We are pleased in it,.
And will pay her portion.—[*Comes forward.*

          May the passage prove,
Of what's presented, worthy of your love,
And favour, as was aim'd ; and we have all
That can in compass of our wishes fall.
                    [*Exeunt.*

The Maid of Honour.

DRAMATIS PERSONÆ.

Roberto, *king of* Sicily.
Ferdinand, *duke of* Urbin.
Bertoldo, *the king's natural brother, a knight of* Malta.
Gonzaga, *a knight of* Malta, *general to the dutchess of* Sienna.
Astutio, *a counsellor of state.*
Fulgentio, *the minion of* Roberto.
Adorni, *a follower of* Camiola's *father.*
Signior Sylli, *a foolish self-lover.*
Antonio, }
Gasparo, } *two rich heirs city-bred.*
Pierio, *a colonel to* Gonzaga.

Roderigo, }
Jacomo, } *captains to* Gonzaga.
Druso, }
Livio, } *captains to duke* Ferdinand.
Father Paulo, *a priest,* Camiola's *confessor.*
Ambassador from the duke of Urbin.
A Bishop.
A Page.
Aurelia, *dutchess of* Sienna.
Camiola, *the* MAID OF HONOUR.
Clarinda, *her woman.*
Scout, Soldiers, Gaoler, Attendants, Servants, &c.

SCENE,—Partly in Sicily, and partly in the Siennese.

ACT I.

SCENE I.—Palermo. *A State-room in the Palace.*

Enter Astutio *and* Adorni.

Ador. Good day to your lordship.
Ast. Thanks, Adorni.
Ador. May I presume to ask if the ambassador
Employ'd by Ferdinand, the Duke of Urbin,
Hath audience this morning?

Enter Fulgentio.

Ast. 'Tis uncertain;
For, though a counsellor of state, I am not
Of the cabinet council: but there's one, if he please,
That may resolve you.
Ador. I will move him.—Sir!
Ful. If you've a suit, shew water, I am blind else.
Ador. A suit; yet of a nature not to prove
The quarry that you hawk for; if your words
Are not like Indian wares, and every scruple
To be weigh'd and rated, one poor syllable,
Vouchsafed in answer of a fair demand,
Cannot deserve a fee.
Ful. It seems you are ignorant,
I neither speak nor hold my peace for nothing;
And yet, for once, I care not if I answer
One single question, gratis.
Ador. I much thank you.
Hath the ambassador audience, sir, to-day?
Ful. Yes.

Ador. At what hour?
Ful. I promised not so much.
A syllable you begg'd, my charity gave it;
Move me no further. [*Exit.*
Ast. This you wonder at:
With me, 'tis usual.
Ador. Pray you, sir, what is he?
Ast. A gentleman, yet no lord. He hath some drops
Of the king's blood running in his veins, derived
Some ten degrees off. His revenue lies
In a narrow compass, the king's ear; and yields him
Every hour a fruitful harvest. Men may talk
Of three crops in a year in the Fortunate Islands,
Or profit made by wool; but, while there are suitors,
His sheepshearing, nay, shaving to the quick,
Is in every quarter of the moon, and constant.
In the time of trussing a point, he can undo,
Or make a man: his play or recreation,
Is to raise this up, or pull down that; and, though
He never yet took orders, makes more bishops
In Sicily, than the pope himself.

Enter Bertoldo, Gasparo, Antonio, *and a Servant.*

Ador. Most strange!
Ast. The presence fills. He in the Malta habit
Is the natural brother of the king—a by-blow.

Ador. I understand you.

Gasp. Morrow to my uncle.

Ant. And my late guardian :—but at length
I have
The reins in my own hands.

Ast. Pray you, use them well,
Or you'll too late repent it.

Bert. With this jewel
Presented to Camiola, prepare
This night, a visit for me. [*Exit* Servant.] I
shall have
Your company, gallants, I perceive, if that
The king will hear of war.

Ant. Sir, I have horses
Of the best breed in Naples, fitter far
To break a rank than crack a lance ; and are,
In their career, of such incredible swiftness,
They outstrip swallows.

Bert. And such may be useful
To run away with, should we be defeated :
You are well provided, signior.

Ant. Sir, excuse me ;
All of their race, by instinct, know a coward,
And scorn the burthen : they come on, like
lightning ;
Founder'd in a retreat.

Bert. By no means back them ;
Unless you know your courage sympathize
With the daring of your horse.

Ant. My lord, this is bitter.

Gasp. I will raise me a company of foot ;
And, when at push of pike I am to enter
A breach, to shew my valour, I have bought
me
An armour cannon proof.

Bert. You will not leap, then,
O'er an outwork in your shirt ?

Gasp. I do not like
Activity that way.

Bert. You had rather stand
A mark to try their muskets on?

Gasp. If I do
No good, I'll do no hurt.

Bert. 'Tis in you, signior,
A Christian resolution, and becomes you !
But I will not discourage you.

Ant. You are, sir,
A knight of Malta, and, as I have heard,
Have serv'd against the Turk.

Bert. 'Tis true.

Ant. Pray you, shew us
The difference between the city valour,
And service in the field.

Bert. 'Tis somewhat more
Than roaring in a tavern or a brothel,
Or to steal a constable from a sleeping watch,
Then burn their halberds ; or, safe guarded
by
Your tenants' sons, to carry away a May-pole
From a neighbour village. You will not find
there,
Your masters of dependencies, to take up
A drunken brawl, or, to get you the names
Of valiant chevaliers, fellows that will be,
For a cloak with thrice-dyed velvet, and a
cast suit
Kick'd down the stairs. A knave with half
a breech there,
And no shirt, (being a thing superfluous
And worn out of his memory,) if you bear not
Yourselves both in, and upright, with a
provant sword
Will slash your scarlets and your plush a
new way ;
Or, with the hilts, thunder about your ears
Such music as will make your worships dance
To the doleful tune of *Lachrymæ.*

Gasp. I must tell you
In private, as you are my princely friend,
I do not like such fiddlers.

Bert. No ! they are useful
For your imitation ; I remember you,
When you came first to the court, and
talk'd of nothing
But your rents and your entradas, ever
chiming
The golden bells in your pockets ; you be-
lieved
The taking of the wall as a tribute due to
Your gaudy clothes ; and could not walk at
midnight
Without a causeless quarrel, as if men
Of coarser outsides were in duty bound
To suffer your affronts : but, when you had
been
Cudgell'd well twice or thrice, and from the
doctrine
Made profitable uses, you concluded
The sovereign means to teach irregular heirs
Civility, with conformity of manners,
Were two or three sound beatings.

Ant. I confess
They did much good upon me.

Gasp. And on me :
The principles that they read were sound.

Bert. You'll find
The like instructions in the camp.

Ast. The king !

A flourish. Enter Roberto, Fulgentio,
Ambassadors, *and* Attendants.

Rob. [*ascends the throne.*] We sit prepared
to hear.

Amb. Your majesty
Hath been long since familiar, I doubt not,
With the desperate fortunes of my lord ; and
pity

Of the much that your confederate hath
  suffer'd,
You being his last refuge, may persuade you
Not alone to compassionate, but to lend
Your royal 'aids to stay him in his fall
To certain ruin. He, too late, is conscious
That his ambition to encroach upon
His neighbour's territories, with the danger
  of
His liberty, nay, his life, hath brought in
  question
His own inheritance : but youth, and heat
Of blood, in your interpretation, may
Both plead and mediate for him. I must
  grant it
An error in him, being denied the favours
Of the fair princess of Sienna, (though
He sought her in a noble way,) to endeavour
To force affection, by surprisal of
Her principal seat, Sienna.
  Rob. Which now proves
The seat of his captivity, not triumph :
Heaven is still just.
  Amb. And yet that justice is
To be with mercy temper'd, which heaven's
  deputies
Stand bound to minister. The injured
  dutchess,
By reason taught, as nature could not, with
The reparation of her wrongs, but aim at
A brave revenge ; and my lord feels, too late,
That innocence will find friends. The great
  Gonzaga,
The honour of his order, (I must praise
Virtue, though in an enemy,) he whose fights
And conquests hold one number, rallying up
Her scatter'd troops, before we could get
  time
To victual or to man the conquer'd city,
Sat down before it ; and, presuming that
'Tis not to be relieved, admits no parley,
Our flags of truce hung on tin vain : nor will he
Lend an ear to composition, but exacts,
With the rendering up the town, the goods
  and lives
Of all within the walls, and of all sexes,
To be at his discretion.
  Rob. Since injustice
In your duke meets this correction, can you
  press us,
With any seeming argument of reason,
In foolish pity to decline his dangers,
To draw them on ourself? Shall we not be
Waru'd by his harms? The league pro-
  claim'd between us,
Bound neither of us further than to aid
Each other, if by foreign force invaded ;
And so far in my honour I was tied.
But since, without our counsel, or allowance,

He hath ta'en arms ; with his good leave, he
  must
Excuse us as if we steer not on a rock
We see and may avoid. Let other monarchs
Contend to be made glorious by proud war,
And, with the blood of their poor subjects,
  purchase
Increase of empire, and augment their cares.
In keeping that which was by wrongs ex-
  torted,
Gilding unjust invasions with the trim
Of glorious conquests ; we, that would be
  known
The father of our people, in our study
And vigilance for their safety, must not change
Their ploughshares into swords, and force
  them from
The secure shade of their own vines, to be
Scorch'd with the flames of war : or, for our
  sport,
Expose their lives to ruin.
  Amb. Will you, then,
In his extremity, forsake your friend ?
  Rob. No ; but preserve ourself.
  Bert. Cannot the beams
Of honour thaw your icy fears?
  Rob. Who's that ?
  Bert. A kind of brother, sir, howe'er your
  subject ;
Your father's son, and one who blushes that
You are not heir to his brave spirit and
  vigour,
As to his kingdom.
  Rob. How's this !
  Bert. Sir, to be
His living chronicle, and to speak his praise,
Cannot deserve your anger.
  Rob. Where's your warrant
For this presumption ?
  Bert. Here, sir, in my heart :
Let sycophants, that feed upon your favours,
Style coldness in you caution, and prefer
Your ease before your honour ; and conclude,
To eat and sleep supinely is the end
Of human blessings : I must tell you, sir,
Virtue, if not in action, is a vice ;
And, when we move not forward, we go
  backward :
Nor is this peace, the nurse of drones and
  cowards,
Our health, but a disease.
  Gasp. Well urged, my lord.
  Ant. Perfect what is so well begun.
  Amb. And bind
My lord your servant.
  Rob. Hair-brain'd fool ! what reason
Canst thou infer to make this good ?
  Bert. A thousand,
Not to be contradicted. But consider

Where your command lies : 'tis not, sir, in
    France,
Spain, Germany, Portugal, but in Sicily ;
An island, sir. Here are no mines of gold
Or silver to enrich you ; no worm spins
Silk in her womb, to make distinction
Between you and a peasant in your habits ;
No fish lives near our shores, whose blood
    can dye
Scarlet or purple ; all that we possess,
With beasts we have in common : nature did
Design us to be warriors, and to break
    through
Our ring, the sea, by which we are environ'd ;
And we by force must fetch in what is
    wanting,
Or precious to us. Add to this, we are
A populous nation, and increase so fast,
That, if we by our providence are not sent
Abroad in colonies, or fall by the sword,
Not Sicily, though now it were more fruitful
Than when 'twas styled the Granary of great
    Rome,
Can yield our numerous fry bread : we must
    starve,
Or eat up one another.
    Ador. The king hears
With much attention.
    Ast. And seems moved with what
Bertoldo hath delivered.
    Bert. May you live long, sir,
The king of peace, so you deny not us
The glory of the war ; let not our nerves
Shrink up with sloth, nor, for want of em-
    ployment,
Make younger brothers thieves : it is their
    swords, sir,
Must sow and reap their harvest. If examples
May move you more than arguments, look
    on England,
The empress of the European isles,
And unto whom alone ours yields precedence :
When did she flourish so, as when she was
The mistress of the ocean, her navies
Putting a girdle round about the world?
When the Iberian quaked, her worthies
    named ;
And the fair flower-de-luce grew pale, set by
The red rose and the white ! Let not our
    armour
Hung up, or our unrigg'd armada, make us
Ridiculous to the late poor snakes our
    neighbours,
Warm'd in our bosoms, and to whom again
We may be terrible ; while we spend our
    hours
Without variety, confined to drink,
Dice, cards, or whores. Rouse us, sir, from
    the sleep

Of idleness, and redeem our mortgaged
    honours.
Your birth, and justly, claims my father's
    kingdom ;
But his heroic mind descends to me :
I will confirm so much.
    Ador. In his looks he seems
To break ope Janus' temple.
    Ast. How these younglings
Take fire from him !
    Ador. It works an alteration
Upon the king.
    Ant. I can forbear no longer :
War, war, my sovereign !
    Ful. The king appears
Resolv'd, and does prepare to speak.
    Rob. Think not
Our counsel's built upon so weak a base,
As to be overturn'd, or shaken, with
Tempestuous winds of words. As I, my lord,
Before resolv'd you, I will not engage
My person in this quarrel ; neither press
My subjects to maintain it : yet, to shew
My rule is gentle, and that I have feeling
O' your master's sufferings, since these
    gallants, weary
Of the happiness of peace, desire to taste
The bitter sweets of war, we do consent
That, as adventurers and volunteers,
No way compell'd by us, they may make trial
Of their boasted valours.
    Bert. We desire no more.
    Rob. 'Tis well ; and, but my grant in this,
    expect not
Assistance from me. Govern, as you please,
The province you make choice of ; for, I vow
By all things sacred, if that thou miscarry
In this rash undertaking, I will hear it
No otherwise than as a sad disaster,
Fallen on a stranger : nor will I esteem
That man my subject, who, in thy extremes,
In purse or person aids thee. Take your
    fortune :
You know me ; I have said it. So, my lord,
You have my absolute answer.
    Amb. My prince pays,
In me, his duty.
    Rob. Follow me, Fulgentio,
And you, Astutio.
        [*Flourish. Exeunt* Roberto, Fulgen-
        tio, Astutio, *and* Attendants.
    Gasp. What a frown he threw,
At his departure, on you !
    Bert. Let him keep
His smiles for his state catamite, I care not.
    Ant. Shall we aboard to-night ?
    Amb. Your speed, my lord,
Doubles the benefit.
    Bert. I have a business

Requires dispatch ; some two hours hence
I'll meet you.   [*Exeunt.*
     SCENE II.—*The same.   A Room in*
               Camiola's *House.*
Enter Signior Sylli, *walking fantastically,*
     followed by Camiola *and* Clarinda.
Cam. Nay, signior, this is too much
     ceremony,
In my own house.
     Syl. What's gracious abroad,
Must be in private practised.
     Clar. For your mirth's sake
Let him alone ; he has been all this morning
In practise with a peruked gentleman-usher,
To teach him his true amble, and his postures,
               [Sylli *walking by, and practising.*
When he walks before a lady.
     Syl. You may, madam,
Perhaps, believe that I in this use art,
To make you dote upon me, by exposing
My more than most rare features to your view :
But I, as I have ever done, deal simply ;
A mark of sweet simplicity, ever noted
In the family of the Syllis.   Therefore, lady,
Look not with too much contemplation on
     me ;
If you do, you are in the suds.
     Cam. You are no barber ?
     Syl. Fie, no ! not I ; but my good parts
     have drawn
More loving hearts out of fair ladies' bellies,
Than the whole trade have done teeth.
     Cam. Is't possible ?
     Syl. Yes, and they live too : marry, much
     condoling
The scorn of their Narcissus, as they call me,
Because I love myself——
     Cam. Without a rival.
What philters or love-powders do you use,
To force affection ? I see nothing in
Your person but I dare look on, yet keep
My own poor heart still.
     Syl. You are warn'd—be arm'd ;
And do not lose the hope of such a husband,
In being too soon enamour'd.
     Clar. Hold in your head,
Or you must have a martingal.
     Syl. I have sworn
Never to take a wife, but such a one,
O may your ladyship prove so strong ! as can
Hold out a month against me.
     Cam. Never fear it ;
Though your best taking part, your wealth,
     were trebled,
I would not woo you. But since in your pity
You please to give me caution, tell me what
Temptations I must fly from.
     Syl. The first is,

That you never hear me sing, for I'm a Syren :
If you observe, when I warble, the dogs howl,
As ravish'd with my ditties ; and you will
Run mad to hear me.
     Cam. I will stop my ears,
And keep my little wits.
     Syl. Next, when I dance,
And come aloft thus, [*capers.*] cast not a
     sheep's eye
Upon the quivering of my calf.
     Cam. Proceed, sir.
     Syl. But on no terms, for 'tis a main point,
     dream not
O' th' strength of my back, though it will
     bear a burthen
With any porter.
     Cam. I mean not to ride you.
     Syl. Nor I your little ladyship, till you have
Perform'd the covenants.   Be not taken with
My pretty spider-fingers, nor my eyes,
That twinkle on both sides.
     Cam. Was there ever such
A piece of motley heard of ! [*A knocking
     within.*] Who's that ? [*Exit* Clarinda.]
     You may spare
The catalogue of my dangers.
     Syl. No, good madam ;
I have not told you half.
     Cam. Enough, good signior ;
If I eat more of such sweetmeats, I shall
     surfeit.—

               Re-enter Clarinda.

Who is 't ?
     Clar. The brother of the king.
     Syl. Nay, start not.
The brother of the king ! is he no more ?
Were it the king himself, I'd give him leave
To speak his mind to you, for I am not
     jealous ;
And, to assure your ladyship of so much,
I'll usher him in, and, that done—hide my-
     self.   [*Aside, and exit.*
     Cam. Camiola, if ever, now be constant :
This is, indeed, a suitor, whose sweet presence,
Courtship, and loving language, would have
     stagger'd
The chaste Penelope ; and, to increase
The wonder, did not modesty forbid it,
I should ask that from him he sues to me for :
And yet my reason, like a tyrant, tells me
I must nor give nor take it.

               Re-enter Sylli *with* Bertoldo.

     Syl. I must tell you,
You lose your labour. 'Tis enough to prove it,
Signior Sylli came before you ; and you know,
First come first serv'd : yet you shall have my
     countenance
                                             S

To parley with her, and I'll take special care
That none shall interrupt you.
Bert. You are courteous.
Syl. Come, wench, wilt thou hear wisdom?
Clar. Yes, from you, sir.
                   [*They walk aside.*
Bert. If forcing this sweet favour from your
    lips,   .   [*Kisses her.*
Fair madam, argue me of too much boldness,
When you are pleased to understand I take
A parting kiss, if not excuse, at least
'Twill qualify the offence.
   Cam. A parting kiss, sir!
What nation, envious of the happiness
Which Sicily enjoys in your sweet presence,
Can buy you from her? or what climate yield
Pleasures transcending those which you enjoy
   here,
Being both beloved and honour'd; the north-
   star
And guider of all hearts; and, to sum up
Your full accompt of happiness in a word,
The brother of the king?
   Bert. Do you, alone,
And with an unexampled cruelty,
Enforce my absence, and deprive me of
Those blessings which you, with a polish'd
   phrase,
Seem to insinuate that I do possess,
And yet tax me as being guilty of
My wilful exile? What are titles to me,
Or popular suffrage, or my nearness to
The king in blood, or fruitful Sicily,
Though it confess'd no sovereign but myself,
When you, that are the essence of my being,
The anchor of my hopes, the real substance
Of my felicity, in your disdain,
Turn all to fading and deceiving shadows?
   Cam. You tax me without cause.
   Bert. You must confess it.
But answer love with love, and seal the con-
   tract
In the uniting of our souls, how gladly
(Though now I were in action, and assured,
Following my fortune, that plumed Victory
Would make her glorious stand upon my
   tent)
Would I put off my armour, in my heat
Of conquest, and, like Antony, pursue
My Cleopatra! Will you yet look on me,
With an eye of favour?
   Cam. Truth bear witness for me,
That, in the judgment of my soul, you are
A man so absolute, and circular,
In all those wish'd-for rarities that may
   take
A virgin captive, that, though at this instant
All scepter'd monarchs of our western world
Were rivals with you, and Camiola worthy

Of such a competition, you alone
Should wear the garland.
   Bert. If so, what diverts
Your favour from me?
   Cam. No mulct in yourself,
Or in your person, mind, or fortune.
   Bert. What then?
   Cam. The consciousness of mine own
      wants: alas! sir,
We are not parallels; but, like lines divided,
Can ne'er meet in one centre. Your birth, sir,
Without addition, were an ample dowry
For one of fairer fortunes; and this shape,
Were you ignoble, far above all value:
To this so clear a mind, so furnish'd with
Harmonious faculties moulded from heaven,
That though you were Thersites in your
   features,
Of no descent, and Irus in your fortunes,
Ulysses-like, you'd force all eyes and ears
To love, but seen; and, when heard, won-
   der at
Your matchless story: but all these bound up
Together in one volume!—give me leave,
With admiration to look upon them;
But not presume, in my own flattering hopes,
I may or can enjoy them.
   Bert. How you ruin
What you would seem to build up! I know no
Disparity between us; you're an heir,
Sprung from a noble family; fair, rich, young,
And every way my equal.
   Cam. Sir, excuse me;
One aerie with proportion ne'er discloses
The eagle and the wren:—tissue and frieze
In the same garment, monstrous! But
   suppose
That what's in you excessive were diminish'd,
And my desert supplied; the stronger bar,
Religion, stops our entrance: you are, sir,
A knight of Malta, by your order bound
To a single life; you cannot marry me;
And, I assure myself, you are too noble
To seek me, though my frailty should consent,
In a base path.
   Bert. A dispensation, lady,
Will easily absolve me.
   Cam. O take heed, sir!
When what is vow'd to heaven is dispens'd
   with,
To serve our ends on earth, a curse must
   follow,
And not a blessing.
   Bert. Is there no hope left me?
   Cam. Nor to myself, but is a neighbour to
Impossibility. True love should walk
On equal feet; in us it does not, sir:
But rest assured, excepting this, I shall be
Devoted to your service.

Bert. And this is your
Determinate sentence?
Cam. Not to be revoked.
Bert. Farewell then, fairest cruel! all
　　thoughts in me
Of women perish. Let the glorious light
Of noble war extinguish Love's dim taper,
That only lends me light to see my folly :
Honour, be thou my ever-living mistress,
And fond affection, as thy bond-slave, serve
　　thee!　　　　　　　　　　　[*Exit.*
Cam. How soon my sun is set, he being
　　absent,
Never to rise again! What a fierce battle
Is fought between my passions!—methinks
We should have kiss'd at parting.
Syl. I perceive
He has his answer : now must I step in
To comfort her. [*comes forward.*] You have
　　found, I hope, sweet lady,
Some difference between a youth of my pitch,
And this bugbear Bertoldo : men are men,
The king's brother is no more ; good parts
　　will do it,
When titles fail. Despair not ; I may be
In time entreated.
Cam. Be so now, to leave me.—
Lights for my chamber. O my heart!
　　　[*Exeunt* Camiola *and* Clarinda.
Syl. She now,
I know, is going to bed, to ruminate
Which way to glut herself upon my person :
But, for my oath's sake, I will keep her
　　hungry ;
And, to grow full myself, I'll straight—to
　　supper.　　　　　　　　　　[*Exit.*

ACT II.

SCENE I.—*The same. A Room in the
　　Palace.*

Enter Roberto, Fulgentio, *and* Astutio.

Rob. Embark'd to-night, do you say?
Ful. I saw him aboard, sir.
Rob. And without taking of his leave?
Ast. 'Twas strange!
Rob. Are we grown so contemptible?
Ful. 'Tis far
From me, sir, to add fuel to your anger,
That, in your ill opinion of him, burns
Too hot already ; else, I should affirm,
It was a gross neglect.
Rob. A wilful scorn
Of duty and allegiance ; you give it
Too fair a name : but we shall think on't.
　　Can you
Guess what the numbers were, that follow'd
　　him
In his desperate action?

Ful. More than you think, sir.
All ill-affected spirits in Palermo,
Or to your government or person, with
The turbulent swordmen, such whose po-
　　verty forced them
To wish a change, are gone along with him;
Creatures devoted to his undertakings,
In right or wrong : and, to express their zeal
And readiness to serve him, ere they went,
Profanely took the sacrament on their knees,
To live and die with him.
Rob. O most impious!
Their loyalty to us forgot?
Ful. I fear so.
Ast. Unthankful as they are!
Ful. Yet this deserves not
One troubled thought in you, sir ; with your
　　pardon,
I hold that their remove from hence makes
　　more
For your security than danger.
Rob. True ;
And, as I'll fashion it, they shall feel it too.
Astutio, you shall presently be dispatch'd
With letters, writ and sign'd with our own
　　hand,
To the dutchess of Sienna, in excuse
Of these forces sent against her. If you spare
An oath, to give it credit, that we never
Consented to it, swearing for the king,
Though false, it is no perjury.
Ast. I know it.
They are not fit to be state agents, sir,
That without scruple of their conscience,
　　cannot
Be prodigal in such trifles.
Ful. Right, Astutio.
Rob. You must, beside, from us take
　　some instructions,
To be imparted, as you judge them useful,
To the general Gonzaga. Instantly
Prepare you for your journey.
Ast. With the wings
Of loyalty and duty.　　　　　　[*Exit.*
Ful. I am bold
To put your majesty in mind——
Rob. Of my promise,
And aids, to further you in your amorous
　　project
To the fair and rich Camiola? there's my ring ;
Whatever you shall say that I entreat,
Or can command by power, I will make good.
Ful. Ever your majesty's creature.
Rob. Venus prove
Propitious to you!　　　　　　[*Exit.*
Ful. All sorts to my wishes :
Bertoldo was my hindrance ; he removed,
I now will court her in the conqueror's style ;
" Come, see, and overcome."—Boy!
　　　　　　　　　　　　　　S 2

Enter Page.

Page. Sir ; your pleasure ?
Ful. Haste to Camiola ; bid her prepare
An entertainment suitable to a fortune
She could not hope for. Tell her, I vouchsafe
To honour her with a visit.
Page. 'Tis a favour
Will make her proud.
Ful. I know it.
Page. I am gone, sir. [*Exit.*
Ful. Entreaties fit not me ; a man in grace
May challenge awe and privilege, by his
place. [*Exit.*

SCENE II.—*The same. A Room in*
Camiola's *House.*

Enter Adorni, Sylli, *and* Clarinda.

Ador. So melancholy, say you !
Clar. Never given
To such retirement.
Ador. Can you guess the cause ?
Clar. If it hath not its birth and being
from
The brave Bertoldo's absence, I confess
'Tis past my apprehension.
Syl. You are wide,
The whole field wide. I, in my understanding,
Pity your ignorance ; yet, if you will
Swear to conceal it, I will let you know
Where her shoe wrings her.
Clar. I vow, signior,
By my virginity.
Syl. A perilous oath,
In a waiting-woman of fifteen ! and is, indeed,
A kind of nothing.
Ador. I'll take one of something,
If you please to minister it.
Syl. Nay, you shall not swear :
I had rather take your word ; for, should
you vow,
D—n me, I'll do this !—you are sure to
break.
Ador. I thank you, signior ; but resolve us.
Syl. Know, then,
Here walks the cause. She dares not look
upon me ;
My beauties are so terrible and enchanting,
She cannot endure my sight.
Ador. There I believe you.
Syl. But the time will come, be comforted,
when I will
Put off this vizor of unkindness to her,
And shew an amorous and yielding face :
And, until then, though Hercules himself
Desire to see her, he had better eat
His club, than pass her threshold ; for I
will be
Her Cerberus, to guard her.

Ador. A good dog !
Clar. Worth twenty porters.

Enter Page.

Page. Keep you open house here ?
No groom to attend a gentleman ! O, I
spy one.
Syl. He means not me, I am sure.
Page. You, sirrah sheep's-head,
With a face cut on a cat-stick, do you hear ?
You, yeoman fewterer, conduct me to
The lady of the mansion, or my poniard
Shall disembogue thy soul.
Syl. O terrible ! *disembogue!*
I talk'd of Hercules, and here is one
Bound up in *decimo sexto.*
Page. Answer, wretch.
Syl. Pray you, little gentleman, be not so
furious :
The lady keeps her chamber.
Page. And we present,
Sent in an embassy to her ! but here is
Her gentlewoman. Sirrah ! hold my cloak,
While I take a leap at her lips : do it, and
neatly ;
Or, having first tripp'd up thy heels, I'll
make
Thy back my footstool. [*Kisses* Clarinda.
Syl. Tamberlane in little !
Am I turn'd Turk ! What an office am I
put to !
Clar. My lady, gentle youth, is indis-
posed.
Page. Though she were dead and buried,
only tell her,
The great man in the court, the brave Ful-
gentio,
Descends to visit her, and it will raise her
Out of the grave for joy.

Enter Fulgentio.

Syl. Here comes another !
The devil, I fear, in his holiday clothes.
Page. So soon !
My part is at an end then. Cover my
shoulders ;
When I grow great, thou shalt serve me.
Ful. Are you, sirrah,
An implement of the house ? [*To* Sylli.
Syl. Sure he will make
A jointstool of me !
Ful. Or, if you belong [*To* Ador.
To the lady of the place, command her
hither.
Ador. I do not wear her livery, yet ac-
knowledge
A duty to her ; and as little bound
To serve your peremptory will, as she is

To obey your summons. 'Twill become
you, sir,
To wait her leisure ; then, her pleasure
known,
You may present your duty.
Ful. Duty ! Slave,
I'll teach you manners.
Ador. I'm past learning ; make not
A tumult in the house.
Ful. Shall I be braved thus?
[*They draw.*
Syl. O, I am dead ! and now I swoon.
[*Falls on his face.*
Clar. Help ! murder !
Page. Recover, sirrah ; the lady's here.

Enter Camiola.

Syl. Nay, then
I am alive again, and I'll be valiant.
[*Rises.*
Cam. What insolence is this? Adorni,
hold,
Hold, I command you.
Ful. Saucy groom !
Cam. Not so, sir ;
However, in his life, he had dependence
Upon my father, he's a gentleman,
As well born as yourself. Put on your hat.
Ful. In my presence, without leave !
Syl. He has mine, madam.
Cam. And I must tell you, sir, and in plain
language,
Howe'er your glittering outside promise
gentry,
The rudeness of your carriage and behaviour
Speaks you a coarser thing.
Syl. She means a clown, sir ;
I am her interpreter, for want of a better.
Cam. I am a queen in mine own house ;
nor must you
Expect an empire here.
Syl. Sure, I must love her
Before the day, the pretty soul's so valiant.
Cam. What are you? and what would
you with me?
Ful. Proud one,
When you know what I am, and what I
came for,
And may, on your submission, proceed to,
You, in your reason, must repent the coarse-
ness
Of my entertainment.
Cam. Why, fine man? what are you?
Ful. A kinsman of the king's.
Cam. I cry you mercy,
For his sake, not your own. But grant you
are so,
'Tis not impossible but a king may have

A fool to his kinsman,—no way meaning
you, sir.
Ful. You have heard of Fulgentio?
Cam. Long since, sir ;
A suit-broker in court. He has the worst
Report among good men I ever heard of,
For bribery and extortion : in their prayers,
Widows and orphans curse him for a canker
And caterpillar in the state. I hope, sir,
You are not the man ; much less employ'd
by him,
As a smock-agent to me.
Ful. I reply not
As you deserve, being assured you know me ;
Pretending ignorance of my person, only
To give me a taste of your wit : 'tis well, and
courtly ;
I like a sharp wit well.
Syl. I cannot endure it ;
Nor any of the Syllis.
Ful. More ; I know too,
This harsh induction must serve as a foil
To the well-tuned observance and respect
You will hereafter pay me, being made
Familiar with my credit with the king,
And that (contain your joy) I deign to love
you.
Cam. Love me ! I am not rapt with it.
Ful. Hear't again ;
I love you honestly : now you admire me.
Cam. I do, indeed ; it being a word so
seldom
Heard from a courtier's mouth. But, pray
you, deal plainly,
Since you find me simple ; what might be
the motives
Inducing you to leave the freedom of
A bachelor's life, on your soft neck to wear
The stubborn yoke of marriage ; and, of all
The beauties in Palermo, to choose me,
Poor me? that is the main point you must
treat of.
Ful. Why, I will tell you. Of a little thing
You are a pretty peat, indifferent fair too;
And, like a new-rigg'd ship, both tight and
yare,
Well truss'd to bear : virgins of giant size
Are sluggards at the sport ; but, for my
pleasure,
Give me a neat well-timber'd gamester like
you ;
Such need no spurs,—the quickness of your
eye
Assures an active spirit.
Cam. You are pleasant, sir ;
Yet I presume that there was one thing in me,
Unmention'd yet, that took you more than all
Those parts you have remember'd.
Ful. What?

Cam. My wealth, sir.

Ful. You are in the right ; without that, beauty is
A flower worn in the morning, at night trod on :
But beauty, youth, and fortune meeting in you,
I will vouchsafe to marry you.

Cam. You speak well ;
And, in return, excuse me, sir, if I
Deliver reasons why, upon no terms,
I'll marry you : I fable not.

Syl. I am glad
To hear this ; I began to have an ague.

Ful. Come, your wise reasons.

Cam. Such as they are, pray you take them :
First, I am doubtful whether you are a man,
Since, for your shape, trimm'd up in a lady's dressing,
You might pass for a woman ; now I love
To deal on certainties : and, for the fairness
Of your complexion, which you think will take me,
The colour, I must tell you, in a man,
Is weak and faint, and never will hold out,
If put to labour : give me the lovely brown,
A thick curl'd hair of the same dye, broad shoulders,
A brawny arm full of veins, a leg without
An artificial calf ;—I suspect yours ;
But let that pass.

Syl. She means me all this while,
For I have every one of those good parts ;
O Sylli ! fortunate Sylli !

Cam. You are moved, sir.

Ful. Fie ! no ; go on.

Cam. Then, as you are a courtier,
A graced one too, I fear you have been too forward ;
And so much for your person. Rich you are,
Devilish rich, as 'tis reported, and sure have
The aids of Satan's little fiends to get it ;
And what is got upon his back, must be
Spent, you know where ;—the proverb's stale—One word more,
And I have done.

Ful. I'll ease you of the trouble,
Coy and disdainful !

Cam. Save me, or else he'll beat me.

Ful. No, your own folly shall ; and, since you put me
To my last charm, look upon this, and tremble.   [*Shews the king's ring.*

Cam. At the sight of a fair ring ! the king's, I take it ?
I have seen him wear the like : if he hath sent it,
As a favour, to me——

Ful. Yes, 'tis very likely,
His dying mother's gift, prized at his crown !
By this he does command you to be mine ;
By his gift you are so :—you may yet redeem all.

Cam. You are in a wrong account still.
Though the king may
Dispose of my life and goods, my mind's mine own,
And never shall be yours. The king, heaven bless him !
Is good and gracious, and, being in himself
Abstemious from base and goatish looseness,
Will not compel, against their wills, chaste maidens
To dance in his minion's circles. I believe,
Forgetting it when he wash'd his hands, you stole it,
With an intent to awe me. But you are cozen'd ;
I am still myself, and will be.

Ful. A proud haggard,
And not to be reclaim'd ! which of your grooms,
Your coachman, fool, or footman, ministers
Night-physic to you?

Cam. You are foul-mouth'd.

Ful. Much fairer
Than thy black soul ; and so I will proclaim thee.

Cam. Were I a man, thou durst not speak this.

Ful. Heaven
So prosper me, as I resolve to do it
To all men, and in every place : scorn'd by
A tit of ten-pence !
        [*Exeunt* Fulgentio *and* Page.

Syl. Now I begin to be valiant :
Nay, I will draw my sword. O for a brother !
Do a friend's part ; pray you, carry him the length of 't.
I give him three years and a day to match my Toledo,
And then we'll fight like dragons.

Ador. Pray, have patience.

Cam. I may live to have vengeance : my Bertoldo
Would not have heard this.

Ador. Madam——

Cam. Pray you, spare
Your language. Prithee fool, and make me merry.   [*To* Sylli.

Syl. That is my office ever.

Ador. I must do,
Not talk ; this glorious gallant shall hear from me.   [*Exeunt.*

SCENE III.—*The* Siennese. *A Camp before the Walls of* Sienna.

Chambers shot off: a flourish as to an Assault: after which, enter Gonzaga, Pierio, Roderigo, Jacomo, *and* Soldiers.

Gonz. Is the breach made assaultable?

Pier. Yes, and the moat
Fill'd up; the cannoneer hath done his parts;
We may enter six abreast.

Rod. There's not a man
Dares shew himself upon the wall.

Jac. Defeat not
The soldiers' hoped-for spoil.

Pier. If you, sir,
Delay the assault, and the city be given up
To your discretion, you in honour cannot
Use the extremity of war,—but, in
Compassion to them, you to us prove cruel.

Jac. And an enemy to yourself.

Rod. A hindrance to
The brave revenge you have vow'd.

Gonz. Temper your heat,
And lose not, by too sudden rashness, that
Which, be but patient, will be offer'd to you.
Security ushers ruin; proud contempt
Of an enemy three parts vanquish'd, with desire
And greediness of spoil, have often wrested
A certain victory from the conqueror's gripe.
Discretion is the tutor of the war,
Valour the pupil; and, when we command
With lenity, and our direction's follow'd
With cheerfulness, a prosperous end must crown
Our works well undertaken.

Rod. Ours are finish'd——

Pier. If we make use of fortune.

Gonz. Her false smiles
Deprive you of your judgments. The condition
Of our affairs exacts a double care,
And, like bifronted Janus, we must look
Backward, as forward: though a flattering calm
Bids us urge on, a sudden tempest raised,
Not feared, much less expected, in our rear,
May foully fall upon us, and distract us
To our confusion.—

Enter a Scout, *hastily.*

Our scout! what brings
Thy ghastly looks, and sudden speed?

Scout. The assurance
Of a new enemy.

Gonz. This I foresaw and fear'd.
What are they, know'st thou?

Scout. They are, by their colours,
Sicilians, bravely mounted, and the brightness
Of their rich armours doubly gilded with
Reflection of the sun.

Gonz. From Sicily?—— ¶
The king in league! no war proclaim'd!
'tis foul:
But this must be prevented, not disputed.
Ha, how is this? your estridge plumes, that but
Even now, like quills of porcupines, seem'd to threaten
The stars, drop at the rumour of a shower,
And, like to captive colours, sweep the earth!
Bear up; but in great dangers, greater minds
Are never proud. Shall a few loose troops, untrain'd
But in a customary ostentation,
Presented as a sacrifice to your valours,
Cause a dejection in you?

Pier. No dejection.

Rod. However startled, where you lead we'll follow.

Gonz. 'Tis bravely said. We will not stay their charge,
But meet them man to man, and horse horse.
Pierio, in our absence hold our place,
And with our foot men, and those sickly troops,
Prevent a sally: I in mine own person,
With part of the cavalry, will bid
These hunters welcome to a bloody breakfast:—
But I lose time.

Pier. I'll to my charge.   [*Exit,*

Gonz. And we
To ours: I'll bring you on.

Jac. If we come off,
It's not amiss; if not, my state is settled.
                    [*Exeunt. Alarum within.*

SCENE IV.—*The Same.   The Citadel of* Sienna.

Enter Ferdinand, Druso, *and* Livio, *on the Walls.*

Fer. No aids from Sicily! Hath hope forsook us;
And that vain comfort to affliction, pity,
By our vow'd friend denied us? we can nor live
Nor die with honour: like beasts in a toil,
We wait the leisure of the bloody hunter,
Who is not so far reconciled unto us,
As in one death to give a period
To our calamities; but in delaying,
The fate we cannot fly from, starv'd with wants,
We die this night, to live again to-morrow,
And suffer greater torments.

Dru. There is not
Three days provision for every soldier,
At an ounce of bread a day, left in the city.
   Liv. To die the beggar's death, with
      hunger made
Anatomies while we live, cannot but crack
Our heart-strings with vexation.
   Fer. Would they would break,
Break altogether ! How willingly, like Cato,
Could I tear out my bowels, rather than
Look on the conqueror's insulting face ;
But that religion, and the horrid dream
To be suffer'd in the other world, denies it !

Enter a Soldier.

What news with thee?
   Sold. From the turret of the fort,
By the rising clouds of dust, through which,
      like lightning,
The splendour of bright arms sometimes
      brake through,
I did descry some forces making towards us ;
And, from the camp, as emulous of their glory,
The general, (for I know him by his horse,)
And bravely seconded, encounter'd them.
Their greetings were too rough for friends ;
      their swords,
And not their tongues, exchanging cour-
      tesies.
By this the main battalias are join'd ;
And, if you please to be spectators of
The horrid issue, I will bring you where,
As in a theatre, you may see their fates
In purple gore presented.
   Fer. Heaven, if yet
Thou art appeased for my wrong done to
      Aurelia,
Take pity of my miseries ! Lead the way,
      friend.   [*Exeunt.*

SCENE V.—*The same. A Plain near the
      Camp.*

*A long Charge : after which, a Flourish for
   victory ; then enter* Gonzaga, Jacomo, *and*
   Roderigo *wounded ;* Bertoldo, Gasparo,
   and Antonio *Prisoners. Officers and
   Soldiers.*

Gonz. We have them yet, though they
      cost us dear.   This was
Charged home, and bravely follow'd.   Be
   to yourselves
               [*To* Jacomo *and* Roderigo.
True mirrors to each other's worth ; and,
   looking
With noble emulation on his wounds,
                     [*Points to* Bert.
The glorious livery of triumphant war,
Imagine these with equal grace appear

Upon yourselves.   The bloody sweat you
      have suffer'd
In this laborious, nay, toilsome harvest,
Yields a rich crop of conquest ; and the spoil,
Most precious balsam to a soldier's hurts,
Will ease and cure them.   Let me look upon
            [Gasparo *and* Antonio *are brought
                           forward.*
The prisoners' faces.   Oh, how much trans-
      form'd
From what they were !   O Mars ! were these
      toys fashion'd
To undergo the burthen of thy service ?
The weight of their defensive armour bruised
Their weak effeminate limbs, and would
      have forced them,
In a hot day, without a blow to yield.
   Ant. This insultation shews not manly in
      you.
   Gonz. To men I had forborne it ; you
      are women,
Or, at the best, loose carpet-knights.   What
      fury
Seduced you to exchange your ease in court,
For labour in the field ? perhaps, you thought
To charge, through dust and blood, an
      armed foe,
Was but like graceful running at the ring
For a wanton mistress' glove ; and the en-
      counter,
A soft impression on her lips :—but you .
Are gaudy butterflies, and I wrong myself
In parling with you.
   Gasp. Væ victis ! now we prove it.
   Rod. But here's one fashion'd in another
      mould,
And made of tougher metal.
   Gonz. True ;   I owe him
For this wound bravely given.
   Bert. O that mountains
Were heap'd upon me, that I might expire,
A wretch no more remember'd !   [*Aside.*
   Gonz. Look up, sir ;
To be o'ercome deserves no shame.   If you
Had fallen ingloriously, or could accuse
Your want of courage in resistance, 'twere
To be lamented : but, since you perform'd
As much as could be hoped for from a man,
(Fortune his enemy,) you wrong yourself
In this dejection.   I am honour'd in
My victory over you ; but to have these
My prisoners, is, in my true judgment, rather
Captivity than a triumph : you shall find
Fair quarter from me, and your many
      wounds,
Which I hope are not mortal, with such care
Look'd to and cured, as if your nearest friend
Attended on you.
   Bert. When you know me better,

You will make void this promise : can you
   call me
Into your memory?
  Gonz. The brave Bertoldo !
A brother of our order ! By St. John,
Our holy patron, I am more amazed,
Nay, thunderstruck with thy apostacy,
And precipice from the most solemn vows
Made unto heaven, when this, the glorious
   badge
Of our Redeemer, was conferr'd upon thee
By the great master, than if I had seen
A reprobate Jew, an atheist, Turk, or Tartar,
Baptized in our religion !
  Bert. This I look'd for ;
And am resolv'd to suffer.
  Gonz. Fellow-soldiers,
Behold this man, and, taught by his example,
Know that 'tis safer far to play with light-
   ning,
Than trifle in things sacred. In my rage
                     [*Weeps.*
I shed these at the funeral of his virtue,
Faith, and religion :—why, I will tell you ;
He was a gentleman so train'd up and
   fashion'd
For noble uses, and his youth did promise
Such certainties, more than hopes, of great
   achievements,
As—if the Christian world had stood opposed
Against the Othoman race, to try the fortune
Of one encounter,—this Bertoldo had been,
For his knowledge to direct, and matchless
   courage
To execute, without a rival, by
The votes of good men, chosen general ;
As the prime soldier, and most deserving
Of all that wear the cross : which now, in
   justice,
I thus tear from him.
  Bert. Let me die with it
Upon my breast.
  Gonz. No ; by this thou wert sworn,
On all occasions, as a knight, to guard
Weak ladies from oppression, and never
To draw thy sword against them ; whereas
   thou,
In hope of gain or glory, when a princess,
And such a princess as Aurelia is,
Was dispossess'd by violence, of what was
Her true inheritance ; against thine oath
Hast, to thy uttermost, labour'd to uphold
Her falling enemy. But thou shalt pay
A heavy forfeiture, and learn too late,
Valour employ'd in an ill quarrel, turns
To cowardice, and Virtue then puts on
Foul Vice's visor. This is that which cancels
All friendship's bands between us.—Bear
   them off ;

I will hear no reply : and let the ransome
Of these, for they are yours, be highly rated.
In this I do but right, and let it be
Styled justice, and not wilful cruelty.
                   [*Exeunt.*

ACT III.

SCENE I.—*The same. A Camp before the
         Walls of Sienna.*

Enter Gonzaga, Astutio, Roderigo, *and*
         Jacomo.

  Gonz. What I have done, sir, by the law
   of arms
I can and will make good.
  Ast. I have no commission
To expostulate the act. These letters speak
The king my master's love to you, and his
Vow'd service to the dutchess, on whose
   person
I am to give attendance.
  Gonz. At this instant,
She's at Fienza : you may spare the trouble
Of riding thither : I have advertised her
Of our success, and on what humble terms
Sienna stands : though presently I can
Possess it, I defer it, that she may
Enter her own, and, as she please, dispose of
The prisoners and the spoil.
  Ast. I thank you, sir.
In the mean time, if I may have your license,
I have a nephew, and one once my ward,
For whose liberties and ransomes I would
   gladly
Make composition.
  Gonz. They are, as I take it,
Call'd Gasparo and Antonio.
  Ast. The same, sir.
  Gonz. For them, you must treat with
   these : but, for Bertoldo,
He is mine own ; if the king will ransom him,
He pays down fifty thousand crowns ; if not,
He lives and dies my slave.
  Ast. Pray you, a word : [*Aside to* Gonz.
The king will rather thank you to detain him,
Than give one crown to free him.
  Gonz. At his pleasure.
I'll send the prisoners under guard : my
   business
Calls me another way.   [*Exit.*
  Ast. My service waits you.
Now, gentlemen, do not deal like merchants
   with me,
But noble captains ; you know, in great
   minds,
Posse et nolle, nobile.
  Rod. Pray you, speak
Our language.

Jac. I find not, in my commission,
An officer's bound to speak or understand
More than his mother-tongue.
    Rod. If be speak that
After midnight, 'tis remarkable.
    Ast. In plain terms, then,
Antonio is your prisoner ; Gasparo, yours.
    Jac. You are in the right.
    Ast. At what sum do you rate
Their several ransomes ?
    Rod. I must make my market
As the commodity cost me.
    Ast. As it cost you !
You did not buy your captainship? your
    desert,
I hope, advanced you.
    Rod. How ! It well appears
You are no soldier.   Desert in these days !
Desert may make a serjeant to a colonel,
And it may hinder him from rising higher ;
But, if it ever get a company,
A company, pray you mark me, without
    money,
Or private service done for the general's
    mistress,
With a commendatory epistle from her,
I will turn lanceprezado.
    Jac. Pray you observe, sir :
I serv'd two prenticeships, just fourteen years,
Trailing the puissant pike, and half so long
Had the right-hand file ; and I fought well,
    'twas said, too :
But I might have serv'd, and fought, and
    serv'd till doomsday,
And ne'er have carried a flag, but for the
    legacy
A bucksome widow of threescore bequeath'd
    me ;
And that too, my back knows, I labour'd
    hard for,
But was better paid.
    Ast. You are merry with yourselves :
But this is from the purpose.
    Rod. To the point then.
Prisoners are not ta'en every day ; and, when
We have them, we must make the best use
    of them.
Our pay is little to the port we should bear,
And that so long a coming, that 'tis spent
Before we have it, and hardly wipes off
    scores
At the tavern and the ordinary.
    Jac. You may add, too,
Our sport ta'en up on trust.
    Rod. Peace, thou smock vermin !
Discover commanders' secrets !—In a word,
    sir,
We have inquired, and found our prisoners
    rich :

Two thousand crowns apiece our companies
    cost us ;
And so much each of us will have, and that
In present pay.
    Jac. It is too little : yet,
Since you have said the word, I am content ;
But will not go a gazet less.
    Ast. Since you are not
To be brought lower, there is no evading ;
I'll be your paymaster.
    Rod. We desire no better.
    Ast. But not a word of what's agreed be-
    tween us,
Till I have school'd my gallants.
    Jac. I am dumb, sir.

Enter a Guard *with* Bertoldo, Antonio, *and*
    Gasparo, *in irons.*

    Bert. And where removed now ? hath the
    tyrant found out
Worse usage for us ?
    Ant. Worse it cannot be.
My greyhound has fresh straw, and scraps,
    in his kennel ;
But we have neither.
    Gasp. Did I ever think
To wear such garters on silk stockings ? or
That my too curious appetite, that turn'd
At the sight of godwits, pheasant, partridge,
    quails,
Larks, woodcocks, calver'd salmon, as
    coarse diet,
Would leap at a mouldy crust ?
    Ant. And go without it,
So oft as I do ?   Oh ! how have I jeer'd
The city entertainment !   A huge shoulder
Of glorious fat ram-mutton, seconded
With a pair of tame cats or conies, a crab-
    tart,
With a worthy loin of veal, and valiant capon,
Mortified to grow tender !—these I scorn'd,
From their plentiful horn of abundance,
    . though invited :
But now I could carry my own stool to a
    tripe,
And call their chitterlings charity, and bless
    the founder.
    Bert. O that I were no further sensible
Of my miseries than you are ! you, like
    beasts,
Feel only stings of hunger, and complain not
But when you're empty : but your narrow
    souls
(If you have any) cannot comprehend
How insupportable the torments are,
Which a free and noble soul, made captive,
    suffers.
Most miserable men !—and what am I,
    then,

That envy you? Fetters, though made of
　gold,
Express base thraldom : and all delicates
Prepared by Median cooks for epicures,
When not our own, are bitter ; quilts fill'd
　high
With gossamere and roses, cannot yield
The body soft repose, the mind kept waking
With anguish and affliction.
　　Ast. My good lord——
　　Bert. This is no time nor place for flat-
tery, sir :
Pray you, style me as I am, a wretch for-
saken
Of the world, as myself.
　　Ast. I would it were
In me to help you.
　　Bert. If that you want power, sir,
Lip-comfort cannot cure me. Pray you,
　leave me
To mine own private thoughts. [*Walks by.*
　　Ast. [*Comes forward.*] My valiant ne-
phew!
And my more than warlike ward! I am
・　glad to see you,
After your glorious conquests. Are these
　chains,
Rewards for your good service? if they are
You should wear them on your necks, since
　they are massy,
Like aldermen of the war.
　　Ant. You jeer us too!
　　Gasp. Good uncle, name not, as you are
　a man of honour,
・That fatal word of war; the very sound of it
Is more dreadful than a cannon.
　　Ant. But redeem us
From this captivity, and I'll vow hereafter
Never to wear a sword, or cut my meat
With a knife that has an edge or point ; I'll
　starve first.
　　Gasp. I will cry broom, or cat's-meat, in
　Palermo ;
Turn porter, carry burthens, anything,
Rather than live a soldier.
　　Ast. This should have
Been thought upon before. At what price,
　think you,
Your two wise heads are rated ?
　　Ant. A calf's head is
More worth than mine; I'm sure it has more
　brains in't,
Or I had ne'er come here.
　　Rod. And I will eat it
With bacon, if I have not speedy ransome.
　　Ant. And a little garlick too, for your
　own sake, sir :
'Twill boil in your stomach else.
　　Gasp. Beware of mine,

Or the horns may choak you ; I am married,
　sir.
　　Ant. You shall have my row of houses
　near the palace.
　　Gasp. And my villa ; all——
　　Ant. All that we have.
　　Ast. Well, have more wit hereafter ; for
　this time,
You are ransomed.
　　Jac. Off with their irons.
　　Rod. Do, do :
If you are ours again, you know your price.
　　Ant. Pray you dispatch us : I shall ne'er
　believe
I am a free man, till I set my foot
In Sicily again, and drink Palermo,
And in Palermo too.
　　Ast. The wind sits fair,
You shall aboard to-night : with the rising sun
You may touch upon the coast. But take
　your leaves
Of the late general first.
　　Gasp. I will be brief.
　　Ant. And I. My lord, heaven keep you!
　　Gasp. Yours, to use
In the way of peace ; but as your soldiers,
　never.
　　Ant. A pox of war ! no more of war.
　　　　[*Exeunt* Rod. Jac. Ant. *and* Gasp.
　　Bert. Have you
Authority to loose their bonds, yet leave
The brother of your king, whose worth dis-
dains
Comparison with such as these, in irons?
If ransome may redeem them, I have lands,
A patrimony of mine own, assign'd me
By my deceased sire, to satisfy
Whate'er can be demanded for my freedom.
　　Ast. I wish you had, sir ; but the king,
　who yields
No reason for his will, in his displeasure
Hath seized on all you had ; nor will Gonzaga,
Whose prisoner now you are, accept of less
Than fifty thousand crowns.
　　Bert. I find it now,
That misery never comes alone. But, grant
The king is yet inexorable, time
May work him to a feeling of my sufferings.
I have friends that swore their lives and for-
tunes were
At my devotion, and, among the rest,
Yourself, my lord, when forfeited to the law
For a foul murder, and in cold blood done,
I made your life my gift, and reconciled you
To this incensed king, and got your pardon.
—Beware ingratitude. I know you are rich,
And may pay down the sum.
　　Ast. I might, my lord ;
But pardon me.

Bert. And will Astutio prove, then,
To please a passionate man, (the king's no more,)
False to his maker, and his reason, which
Commands more than I ask? O summer-friendship,
Whose flattering leaves, that shadow'd us in our
Prosperity, with the least gust drop off
In the autumn of adversity! How like
A prison is to a grave! when dead, we are
With solemn pomp brought thither, and our heirs,
Masking their joy in false, dissembled tears,
Weep o'er the herse; but earth no sooner covers
The earth brought thither, but they turn away,
With inward smiles, the dead no more remember'd:
So, enter'd in a prison——
Ast. My occasions
Command me hence, my lord.
Bert. Pray you, leave me, do;
And tell the cruel king, that I will wear
These fetters till my flesh and they are one
Incorporated substance. [*Exit* Astutio.] In myself,
As in a glass, I'll look on human frailty,
And curse the height of royal blood: since I,
In being born near to Jove, am near his thunder.
Cedars once shaken with a storm, their own
Weight grubs their roots out.—Lead me where you please;
I am his, not fortune's martyr, and will die
The great example of his cruelty.
[*Exit guarded.*

SCENE II.—Palermo. *A Grove near the Palace.*

Enter Adorni.

Ador. He undergoes my challenge, and contemns it,
And threatens me with the late edict made
'Gainst duellists,—the altar cowards fly to.
But I, that am engaged, and nourish in me
A higher aim than fair Camiola dreams of,
Must not sit down thus. In the court I dare not
Attempt him; and in public, he's so guarded,
With a herd of parasites, clients, fools, and suitors,
That a musket cannot reach him:—my designs
Admit of no delay. This is her birthday,
Which, with a fit and due solemnity,
Camiola celebrates: and on it, all such
As love or serve her usually present

A tributary duty. I'll have something
To give, if my intelligence prove true,
Shall find acceptance. I am told, near this grove
Fulgentio, every morning, makes his markets
With his petitioners; I may present him
With a sharp petition!——Ha! 'tis he: my fate
Be ever bless'd for't!

Enter Fulgentio *and* Page.

Ful. Command such as wait me
Not to presume, at the least for half an hour,
To press on my retirements.
Page. I will say, sir,
You are at your prayers.
Ful. That will not find belief;
Courtiers have something else to do:—be gone, sir. [*Exit* Page.
Challenged! 'tis well; and by a groom! still better.
Was this shape made to fight? I have a tongue yet,
Howe'er no sword, to kill him; and what way,
This morning I'll resolve of. [*Exit.*
Ador. I shall cross
Your resolution, or suffer for you.
[*Exit following him.*

SCENE III.—*The same. A Room in Camiola's House.*

Enter Camiola, *followed by* Servants *with Presents;* Sylli, *and* Clarinda.

Syl. What are all these?
Clar. Servants with several presents,
And rich ones too.
1 *Serv.* With her best wishes, madam,
Of many such days to you, the lady Petula
Presents you with this fan.
2 *Serv.* This diamond,
From your aunt Honoria.
3 *Serv.* This piece of plate
From your uncle, old Vicentio, with your arms
Graven upon it.
Cam. Good friends, they are too
Munificent in their love and favour to me.
Out of my cabinet return such jewels
As this directs you:—[*To* Clarinda.]—for your pains; and yours;
Nor must you be forgotten.
[*Gives them money.*
Honour me
With the drinking of a health.
1 *Serv.* Gold, on my life!
2 *Serv.* She scorns to give base silver.
3 *Serv.* Would she had been
Born every month in the year!
1 *Serv.* Month! every day.

2 Serv. Shew such another maid.

3 Serv. All happiness wait you!

Clar. I'll see your will done.

[*Exeunt* Sylli, Clarinda, *and* Servants.

Enter Adorni *wounded.*

Cam. How, Adorni wounded!

Ador. A scratch got in your service, else not worth
Your observation : I bring not, madam,
In honour of your birthday, antique plate,
Or pearl, for which, the savage Indian dives
Into the bottom of the sea ; nor diamonds
Hewn from steep rocks with danger. Such as give
To those that have, what they themselves want, aim at
A glad return with profit : yet, despise not
My offering at the altar of your favour ;
Nor let the lowness of the giver lessen
The height of what's presented ; since it is
A precious jewel, almost forfeited,
And dimm'd with clouds of infamy, redeem'd,
And, in its natural splendour, with addition
Restored to the true owner.

Cam. How is this?

Ador. Not to hold you in suspense, I bring you, madam,
Your wounded reputation cured, the sting
Of virulent malice, festering your fair name,
Pluck'd out and trod on. That proud man, that was
Denied the honour of your bed, yet durst,
With his untrue reports, strumpet your fame,
Compell'd by me, hath given himself the lie,
And in his own blood wrote it :—you may read
Fulgentio subscribed. [*Offering a paper.*

Cam. I am amazed!

Ador. It does deserve it, madam. Common service
Is fit for hinds, and the reward proportion'd
To their conditions : therefore, look not on me
As a follower of your father's fortunes, or
One that subsists on yours :—you frown! my service
Merits not this aspect.

Cam. Which of my favours,
I might say bounties, hath begot and nourish'd
This more than rude presumption? Since you had
An itch to try your desperate valour, wherefore
Went you not to the war? Couldst thou suppose
My innocence could ever fall so low
As to have need of thy rash sword to guard it
Against malicious slander? O how much

Those ladies are deceived and cheated, when
The clearness and integrity of their actions
Do not defend themselves, and stand secure
On their own bases ! Such as in a colour
Of seeming service give protection to them,
Betray their own strengths. Malice scorn'd, puts out
Itself ; but argued, gives a kind of credit
To a false accusation. In this, your
Most memorable service, you believed
You did me right ; but you have wrong'd me more
In your defence of my undoubted honour,
Than false Fulgentio could.

Ador. I am sorry what was
So well intended is so ill received ;

Re-enter Clarinda.

Yet, under your correction, you wish'd
Bertoldo had been present.

Cam. True, I did :
But he and you, sir, are not parallels,
Nor must you think yourself so.

Ador. I am what
You'll please to have me.

Cam. If Bertoldo had
Punish'd Fulgentio's insolence, it had shewn
His love to her whom, in his judgment, he
Vouchsafed to make his wife ; a height, I hope,
Which you dare not aspire to. The same actions
Suit not all men alike ; but I perceive
Repentance in your looks. For this time, leave me ;
I may forgive, perhaps forget, your folly :
Conceal yourself till this storm be blown over.
You will be sought for ; yet, if my estate
[*Gives him her hand to kiss.*
Can hinder it, shall not suffer in my service.

Ador. This is something yet, though I miss'd the mark I shot at.
[*Aside, and exit.*

Cam. This gentleman is of a noble temper ;
And I too harsh, perhaps, in my reproof :
Was I not, Clarinda?

Clar. I am not to censure
Your actions, madam ; but there are a thousand
Ladies, and of good fame, in such a cause
Would be proud of such a servant.

Cam. It may be ;

Enter a Servant.

Let me offend in this kind. Why, uncall'd for ?

Serv. The signiors, madam, Gasparo and Antonio,

Selected friends of the renown'd Bertoldo,
Put ashore this morning.
 Cam. Without him?
 Serv. I think so.
 Cam. Never think more then.
 Serv. They have been at court,
Kiss'd the king's hand; and, their first duties
 done
To him, appear ambitious to tender
To you their second service.
 Cam. Wait them hither. [*Exit* Servant.
Fear, do not rack me! Reason, now, if ever,
Haste with thy aids, and tell me, such a
 wonder
As my Bertoldo, is, with such care fashion'd,
Must not, nay, cannot, in heaven's providence

Enter Antonio *and* Gasparo.

So soon miscarry!—pray you, forbear; ere
 you take
The privilege, as strangers, to salute me,
(Excuse my manners,) make me first under-
 stand
How it is with Bertoldo.
 Gasp. The relation
Will not, I fear, deserve your thanks.
 Ant. I wish
Some other should inform you.
 Cam. Is he dead?
You see, though with some fear, I dare
 enquire it.
 Gasp. Dead! Would that were the worst;
 a debt were paid then,
Kings in their birth owe nature.
 Cam. Is there aught
More terrible than death?
 Ant. Yes, to a spirit
Like his; cruel imprisonment, and that
Without the hope of freedom.
 Cam. You abuse me:
The royal king cannot, in love to virtue,
(Though all springs of affection were dried
 up,)
But pay his ransome.
 Gasp. When you know what 'tis,
You will think otherwise: no less will do it
Than fifty thousand crowns.
 Cam. A petty sum,
The price weigh'd with the purchase: fifty
 thousand!
To the king 'tis nothing. He that can spare
 more
To his minion for a masque, cannot but
 ransome
Such a brother at a million. You wrong
The king's magnificence.
 Ant. In your opinion;
But 'tis most certain: he does not alone

In himself refuse to pay it, but forbids
All other men.
 Cam. Are you sure of this?
 Gasp. You may read
The edict to that purpose, publish'd by him;
That will resolve you.
 Cam. Possible! pray you, stand off.
If I do not mutter treason to myself,
My heart will break; and yet I will not
 curse him;
He is my king. The news you have de-
 liver'd
Makes me weary of your company; we'll
 salute
When we meet next. I'll bring you to the
 door.
Nay, pray you, no more compliments.
 Gasp. One thing more,
And that's substantial: let your Adorni
Look to himself.
 Ant. The king is much incensed
Against him for Fulgentio.
 Cam. As I am,
For your slowness to depart.
 Both. Farewell, sweet lady.
   [*Exeunt* Gasparo *and* Antonio.
 Cam. O more than impious times! when
 not alone
Subordinate ministers of justice are
Corrupted and seduced, but kings themselves,
The greater wheels by which the lesser move,
Are broken, or disjointed! could it be, else,
A king, to sooth his politic ends, should so
 far
Forsake his honour, as at once to break
The adamant chains of nature and religion,
To bind up atheism, as a defence
To his dark counsels? Will it ever be,
That to deserve too much is dangerous,
And virtue, when too eminent, a crime?,
Must she serve fortune still, or, when
 stripp'd of
Her gay and glorious favours, lose the
 beauties
Of her own natural shape? O, my Bertoldo,
Thou only sun in honour's sphere, how soon
Art thou eclipsed and darken'd! not the
 nearness
Of blood prevailing on the king; nor all
The benefits to the general good dispens'd,
Gaining a retribution! But that
To owe a courtesy to a simple virgin
Would take from the deserving, I find in me
Some sparks of fire, which, fann'd with
 honour's breath,
Might rise into a flame, and in men darken
Their usurp'd splendour. Ha! my aim is
 high,
And, for the honour of my sex, to fall so,

Can never prove inglorious.—'Tis resolv'd :
Call in Adorni.
  Clar. I am happy in
Such an employment, madam.   [*Exit.*
  Cam. He's a man,
I know, that at a reverent distance loves me ;
And such are ever faithful. What a sea
Of melting ice I walk on! what strange
    censures
Am I to undergo! but good intents
Deride all future rumours.

    Re-enter Clarinda *with* Adorni.

  Ador. I obey
Your summons, madam.
  Cam. Leave the place, Clarinda ;
One woman, in a secret of such weight,
Wise men may think too much : [*Exit*
    Clarinda.] nearer, Adorni.
I warrant it with a smile.
  Ador. I cannot ask
Safer protection ; what's your will?
  Cam. To doubt
Your ready desire to serve me, or prepare you
With the repetition of former merits,
Would, in my diffidence, wrong you : but I
    will,
And without circumstance, in the trust that I
Impose upon you, free you from suspicion.
  Ador. I foster none of you.
  Cam. I know you do not.
You are, Adorni, by the love you owe me——
  Ador. The surest conjuration.
  Cam. Take me with you,——
Love born of duty ; but advance no further.
You are, sir, as I said, to do me service,
To undertake a task, in which your faith,
Judgment, discretion—in a word, your all
That's good, must be engaged ; nor must
    you study,
In the execution, but what may make
For the ends I aim at.
  Ador. They admit no rivals.
  Cam. You answer well. You have heard
    of Bertoldo's
Captivity, and the king's neglect ; the great-
    ness
Of his ransom ; fifty thousand crowns,
    Adorni;
Two parts of my estate !
  Ador. To what tends this?   [*Aside.*
  Cam. Yet I so love the gentleman, for to
    you
I will confess my weakness, that I purpose
Now, when he is forsaken by the king,
And his own hopes, to ransom him, and
    receive him
Into my bosom, as my lawful husband——
Why change you colour?

  Ador. 'Tis in wonder of
Your virtue, madam.
  Cam. You must, therefore, to
Sienna for me, and pay to Gonzaga
This ransome for his liberty; you shall
Have bills of exchange along with you.
    Let him swear
A solemn contract to me ; for you must be
My principal witness, if he should—but why
Do I entertain these jealousies? You will
    do this ?
  Ador. Faithfully, madam—but not live
    long after.   [*Aside.*
  Cam. One thing I had forgot : besides
    his freedom,
He may want accommodations ; furnish him
According to his birth : and from Camiola
Deliver this kiss, printed on your lips,
    [*Kisses him.*
Seal'd on his hand. You shall not see my
    blushes :
I'll instantly dispatch you.   [*Exit.*
  Ador. I am half
Hang'd out o' the way already.—Was there
    ever
Poor lover so employ'd against himself,
To make way for his rival? I must do it.
Nay, more, I will. If loyalty can find
Recompense beyond hope or imagination,
Let it fall on me in the other world,
As a reward, for in this I dare not hope it.
    [*Exit.*

ACT IV.

SCENE I.—*The* Siennese. *A Camp before
    the Walls of* Sienna

  Enter Gonzaga, Pierio, Roderigo, *and*
    Jacomo.

  Gonz. You have seized upon the citadel,
    and disarm'd
All that could make resistance ?
  Pier. Hunger had
Done that, before we came ; nor was the
    soldier
Compell'd to seek for prey; the famish'd
    wretches,
In hope of mercy, as a sacrifice offer'd
All that was worth the taking.
  Gonz. You proclaim'd,
On pain of death, no violence should be
    offer'd
To any woman?
  Rod. But it needed not ;
For famine had so humbled them, and ta'en off
The care of their sex's honour, that there
    was not
So coy a beauty in the town, but would,

For half a mouldy biscuit, sell herself
To a poor bisognion, and without shrieking.
Gonz. Where is the duke of Urbin?
Jac. Under guard,
As you directed.
Gonz. See the soldiers set
In rank and file, and, as the dutchess passes,
Bid them vail their ensigns ; and charge
them on their lives,
Not to cry *Whores!*
Jac. The devil cannot fright them
From their military license. Though they
know
They are her subjects, and will part with
being,
To do her service; yet, since she's a woman,
They will touch at her breech with their
tongues ; and that is all
That they can hope for.
[*A shout, and a general cry within,*
Whores ! whores !
Gonz. O the devil ! they are at it.
Hell stop their brawling throats. Again !
make up,
And cudgel them into jelly.
Rod. To no purpose,
Though their mothers were there, they
would have the same name for them.
[*Exeunt.*

SCENE II.—*The same. · Another Part of
the Camp.*

Loud music. Enter Roderigo, Jacomo,
Pierio, Gonzaga, *and* Aurelia *under a
Canopy.* Astutio *presents her with letters.*

Gonz. I do beseech your highness not to
ascribe,
To the want of discipline, the barbarous
rudeness
Of the soldier, in his profanation of
Your sacred name and virtues.
Aurel. No, lord general ;
I've heard my father say oft, 'twas a custom
Usual in the camp ; nor are they to be
punish'd
For words, that have, in fact, deserved so
well :
Let the one excuse the other.
All. Excellent princess !
Aurel. But for these aids from Sicily sent
against us,
To blast our spring of conquest in the bud ;
I cannot find, my lord ambassador,
How we should entertain't but as a wrong,
With purpose to detain us from our own,
Howe'er the king endeavours, in his letters,
To mitigate the affront.
Ast. Your grace hereafter
May hear from me such strong assurances

Of his unlimited desires to serve you,
As will, I hope, drown in forgetfulness
The memory of what's past.
Aurel. We shall take time
To search the depth of 't further, and pro-
ceed
As our council shall direct us.
Gonz. We present you
With the keys of the city ; all lets are remov'd,
Your way is smooth and easy ; at your feet
Your proudest enemy falls.
Aurel. We thank your valours :
A victory without blood is twice achieved,
And the disposure of it, to us tender'd,
The greatest honour. Worthy captains,
thanks !
My love extends itself to all.
Gonz. Make way there.
[*A* Guard *drawn up;* Aurelia *passes.
through them. Loud music.*
[*Exeunt.*

SCENE III.—Sienna. *A Room in the
Prison.*

Bertoldo *is discovered in fetters, reading.*

Bert. "Tis here determined, (great ex-
amples, arm'd
With arguments, produced to make it good,)
That neither tyrants, nor the wrested laws,
The people's frantic rage, sad exile, want,
Nor that which I endure, captivity,
Can do a wise man any injury.
Thus Seneca, when he wrote, thought.—But
then
Felicity courted him ; his wealth exceeding
A private man's ; happy in the embraces
Of his chaste wife Paulina ; his house full
Of children, clients, servants, flattering
friends,
Soothing his lip-positions ; and created
Prince of the senate, by the general voice,
At his new pupil's suffrage : then, no doubt,
He held, and did believe, this. But no sooner
The prince's frowns and jealousies had thrown
him
Out of security's lap, and a centurion
Had offer'd him what choice of death he
pleased,
But told him, die he must ; when straight the
armour
Of his so boasted fortitude fell off,
[*Throws away the book.*
Complaining of his frailty. Can it then
Be censured womanish weakness in me, if,
Thus clogg'd with irons, and the period
To close up all calamities denied me,
Which was presented Seneca, I wish
I ne'er had being ; at least, never knew

What happiness was ; or argue with heaven's
   justice,
Tearing my locks, and, in defiance, throwing
Dust in the air ? or, falling on the ground,
   thus
With my nails and teeth to dig a grave, or
   rend
The bowels of the earth, my step-mother,
And not a natural parent ? or thus practise
To die, and, as I were insensible,
Believe I had no motion? [*Falls on his face.*

   Enter Gonzaga, Adorni, *and* Gaoler.

  Gonz. There he is :
I'll not enquire by whom his ransome's paid,
I am satisfied that I have it ; nor allege
One reason to excuse his cruel usage,
As you may interpret it ; let it suffice
It was my will to have it so. He is yours now,
Dispose of him as you please.   [*Exit.*
  Ador. Howe'er I hate him,
As one preferr'd before me, being a man,
He does deserve my pity. Sir !—he sleeps :—
Or is he dead? would he were a saint in
   heaven !
'Tis all the hurt I wish him. But, I was not
Born to such happiness [*Aside.*] *Kneels by
   him.*]——no, he breathes—come near,
And, if 't be possible, without his feeling,
Take off his irons.—[*His irons taken off.*]—
So ; now leave us private.
               [*Exit Gaoler.*
He does begin to stir ; and, as transported
With a joyful dream, how he stares ! and
   feels his legs,
As yet uncertain whether it can be
True or fantastical.
  Bert. [*rising.*] Ministers of mercy,
Mock not calamity. · Ha ! 'tis no vision !
Or, if it be, the happiest that ever
Appear'd to sinful flesh ! Who's here? his face
Speaks him Adorni ;—but some glorious
   angel,
Concealing its divinity in his shape,
Hath done this miracle, it being not an act
For wolfish man.   Resolve me, if thou
   look'st for
Bent knees in adoration?
  Ador. O forbear, sir !
I am Adorni, and the instrument
Of your deliverance ; but the benefit
You owe another.
  Bert. If he has a name,
As soon as spoken, 'tis writ on my heart
I am his bondman.
  Ador. To the shame of men,
This great act is a woman's.
  Bert. The whole sex
For her sake must be deified. How I wander

In my imagination, yet cannot
Guess who this phœnix should be !
  Ador. 'Tis Camiola.
  Bert. Pray you, speak 't again ; there's music
   in her name.
Once more, I pray you, sir.
  Ador. Camiola,
The MAID OF HONOUR. —
  Bert. Curs'd atheist that I was,
Only to doubt it could be any other ;
Since she alone, in the abstract of herself,
That small but ravishing substance, com-
   prehends
Whatever is, or can be wish'd, in the
Idea of a woman ! O what service,
Or sacrifice of duty, can I pay her,
If not to live and die her charity's slave,
Which is resolved already !
  Ador. She expects not
Such a dominion o'er you : yet, ere I
Deliver her demands, give me your hand :
On this, as she enjoin'd me, with my lips
I print her love and service, by me sent you.
  Bert. I am o'erwhelmed with wonder !
  Ador. You must now,
Which is the sum of all that she desires,
By a solemn contract bind yourself, when she
Requires it, as a debt due for your freedom,
To marry her.
  Bert. This does engage me further ;
A payment ! an increase of obligation.
To marry her !—'twas my *nil ultra* ever :
The end of my ambition. O that now
The holy man, she present, were prepared
To join our hands, but with that speed my
   heart
Wishes mine eyes might see her !
  Ador. You must swear this.
  Bert. Swear it ! Collect all oaths and im-
   precations,
Whose least breach is damnation, and those
Minister'd to me in a form more dreadful ;
Set heaven and hell before me, I will take
   them :
False to Camiola ! never.—Shall I now
Begin my vows to you?
  Ador. I am no churchman ;
Such a one must file it on record : you are
   free ;
And, that you may appear like to yourself,
(For so she wish'd,) here's gold, with which
   you may
Redeem your trunks and servants, and
   whatever
Of late you lost. I have found out the captain
Whose spoil they were ; his name is Roderigo.
  Bert. I know him.
  Ador. I have done my parts.
  Bert. So much, sir,

                            T

As I am ever yours for't. Now, methinks,
I walk in air ! Divine Camiola——
But words cannot express thee : I'll build to
   thee
An altar in my soul, on which I'll offer
A still-increasing sacrifice of duty.   [*Exit.*
  Ador. What will .become of me. now is
   apparent.
Whether a poniard or a halter be
The nearest way to hell, (for I must thither,
After I've kill'd myself,) is somewhat doubtful.
This Roman resolution of self-murder,
Will not hold water at the high tribunal,
When it comes to be argued ; my good Genius
Prompts me to this consideration. He.
That kills himself to avoid misery, fears it,
And, at the best, shews but a bastard valour.
This life's a fort committed to my trust,
Which I must not yield up till it be forced :
Nor will I. He's not valiant that dares die,
But he that boldly bears calamity.   [*Exit.*

  SCENE IV.—*The same. A State-room
      in the Palace.*

  A Flourish. Enter Pierio, Roderigo,
Jacomo, Gonzaga, Aurelia, Ferdinand,
Astutio, *and* Attendants.

  Aurel. A seat here for the duke. It is
   our glory
To overcome with courtesies, not rigour ;
The lordly Roman, who held it the height
Of human happiness to have kings and queens
To wait by his triumphant chariot-wheels,
·In his insulting pride, deprived himself
Of drawing near the nature of the gods,
Best known for such, in being merciful.
Yet, give me leave, but still with gentle
   language,
And with the freedom of a friend, to tell you,
To seek by force, what courtship could not
   win,
Was harsh, and never taught in Love's mild
   school.
Wise poets feign that Venus' coach is drawn
By doves and sparrows, not by bears and
   tigers.
I spare the application.
  Fer. In my fortune,
Heaven's justice hath confirm'd it ; yet,
   great lady,
Since my offence grew from excess of love,
And not to be resisted, having paid, too,
With loss of liberty, the forfeiture
Of my presumption, in your clemency
It may find pardon.
  Aurel. You shall have just cause
To say it hath. The charge of the long siege
Defray'd, and the loss my subjects have sus-
   tain'd

Made good, since so far I must deal with
   caution,
You have your liberty.
  Fer. I could not hope for
Gentler conditions.
  Aurel. My lord Gonzaga,
Since my coming to Sienna, I've heard much
   of
Your prisoner, brave Bertoldo.
  Gonz. Such an one,
Madam, I had.
  Ast. And have still, sir, I hope.
  Gonz. Your hopes deceive you. He is
  ransomed, madam.
  Ast. By whom, I pray you, sir ?
  Gonz. You had best enquire
Of your intelligencer : I am no informer.
  Ast. I like not this.   [*Aside.*
  Aurel. He is, as 'tis reported,
A goodly gentleman, and of noble parts ;
A brother of your order.
  Gonz. He was, madam,
Till he, against his oath, wrong'd you, a
   princess,
Which his religion bound him from.
  Aurel. Great minds,
For trial of their valours, oft maintain
Quarrels that are unjust, yet without malice :
And such a fair construction I make of him :
I would see that brave enemy.
  Gonz. My duty
Commands me to seek for him.
  Aurel. Pray you do ;
And bring him to our presence.
          [*Exit* Gonzaga.
  Ast. I must blast
His entertainment. [*Aside.*] May it please
   your excellency,
He is a man debauch'd, and, for his riots,
Cast off by the king my master ; and that, I
   hope, is
A crime sufficient.
  Fer. To you, his subjects,
That like as your king likes.
  Aurel. But not to us ;
We must weigh with our own scale.

  Re-enter Gonzaga, *with* Bertoldo, *richly
    habited, and* Adorni.

            This is he, sure.
How soon mine eye had found him ! what a
   port
He bears ! how well his bravery becomes
   him !
A prisoner ! nay, a princely suitor, rather !
But I'm too sudden.   [*Aside.*
  Gonz. Madam, 'twas his suit,
Unsent for, to present his service to you,
Ere his departure.

Aurel. With what majesty
He bears himself!   [*Aside.*
Ast. The devil, I think, supplies him.
Ransomed, and thus rich too!
Aurel. You ill deserve
    [Bertoldo *kneeling, kisses her hand.*
The favour of our hand——we are not well,
Give us more air.   [*Descends suddenly.*
Gonz. What sudden qualm is this?
Aurel. — That lifted yours against me.
Bert. Thus, once more,
I sue for pardon.   ·
Aurel. Sure his lips are poison'd,
And through these veins force passage to
    my heart,
Which is already seized on.   [*Aside.*
Bert. I wait, madam,
To know what your commands are ; my de-
    signs
Exact me in another place.
Aurel. Before
You have our license to depart ! If manners,
Civility of manners, cannot teach you
To attend our leisure, I must tell you, sir,
That you are still our prisoner ; nor had you
Commission to free him.
Gonz. How's this, madam?
Aurel. You were my substitute, and
    wanted power,
Without my warrant, to dispose of him :
I will pay back his ransom ten times over,
Rather than quit my interest.
Bert. This is
Against the law of arms.
Aurel. But not of love.   [*Aside.*
Why, hath your entertainment, sir, been
    such,
In your restraint, that, with the wings of fear,
You would fly from it ?
Bert. I know no man, madam,
Enamour'd of his fetters, or delighting
In cold or hunger, or that would in reason
Prefer straw in a dungeon, before
A down-bed in a palace.
Aurel. How !—Come nearer :
Was his usage such?
Gonz. Yes ; and it had been worse,
Had I forseen this.
Aurel. O thou mis-shaped monster !
In thee it is confirm'd, that such as have
No share in nature's bounties, know no pity
To such as have them. Look on him with
    my eyes,
And answer, then, whether this were a man
Whose cheeks of lovely fulness should be
    made
A prey to meagre famine? or these eyes,
Whose every glance store Cupid's emptied
    quiver,

To be dimm'd with tedious watching? or
    these lips,
These ruddy lips, of whose fresh colour
    cherries
And roses were but copies, should grow pale
For want of nectar? or these legs, that bear
A burthen of more worth than is supported
By Atlas' wearied shoulders, should be
    cramp'd
With the weight of iron ?   O, I could dwell
    ever
On this description !
Bert. Is this in derision,
Or pity of me ?
Aurel. In your charity
Believe me innocent. Now you are my
    prisoner,
You shall have fairer quarter? you will shame
The place where you have been, should you
    now leave it,
Before you are recover'd. I'll conduct you
To more convenient lodgings, and it shall be
My care to cherish you. Repine who dare ;
It is our will. You'll follow me?
Bert. To the centre,
Such a Sybilla guiding me.
    [*Exeunt* Aurelia, Bertoldo, *and*
    Attendants.
Gonz. Who speaks first ?
Fer. We stand as we had seen Medusa's
    head.
Pier. I know not what to think, I am so
    amazed.
Rod. Amazed ! I am thunderstruck.
Jac. We are enchanted,
And this is some illusion.
Ador. Heaven forbid !
In dark despair it shews a beam of hope :
Contain thy joy, Adorni.   [*Aside.*
Ast. Such a princess,
And of so long-experienced reserv'dness,
Break forth, and on the sudden, into flashes
Of more than doubted looseness !
Gonz. They come again,
Smiling, as I live ! his arm circling her waist.
I shall run mad :—Some fury hath possess'd
    her.
If I speak, I may be blasted. Ha ! I'll
    mumble
A prayer or two, and cross myself, and then,
Though the devil fart fire, have at him.

Re-enter Bertoldo, *and* Aurelia.

Aurel. Let not, sir,
The violence of my passion nourish in you
An ill opinion ; or, grant my carriage
Out of the road and garb of private women,
'Tis still done with decorum. As I am
    T 2.

A princess, what I do is above censure,
And to be imitated.
   Bert. Gracious madam,
Vouchsafe a little pause ; for I am so rapt
Beyond myself, that, till I have collected
My scatter'd faculties, I cannot tender
My resolution.
   Aurel. Consider of it,
I will not be long from you.
             [*Bertoldo walks by musing.*
   Gonz. Pray I cannot,
This cursed object strangles my devotion :
I must speak, or I burst.—Pray you, fair lady,
If you can, in courtesy direct me to
The chaste Aurelia.
   Aurel. Are you blind ? who are we ?
   Gonz. Another kind of thing. Her blood
    was govern'd
By her discretion, and not ruled her reason :
The reverence and majesty of Jnno
Shined in her looks, and, coming to the camp,
Appear'd a second Pallas. I can see
No such divinities in you : if I,
Without offence, may speak my thoughts,
    you are,
As 'twere, a wanton Helen.
   Aurel. Good ! ere long
You shall know me better.
   Gonz. Why, if you are Aurelia,
How shall I dispose of the soldier ?
   Ast. May it please you
To hasten my dispatch ?
   Aurel. Prefer your suits
Unto Bertoldo ; we will give him hearing,
And you'll find him your best advocate.
                   [*Exit.*
   Ast. This is rare !
   Gonz. What are we come to ?
   Rod. Grown up in a moment
A favourite !
   Ferd. He does take state already.
   Bert. No, no ; it cannot be :—yet, but
    Camiola,
There is no step between me and a crown.
Then my ingratitude ! a sin in which
All sins are comprehended ! Aid me, Virtue,
Or I am lost.
   Gonz. May it please your excellence——
Second me, sir.
   Bert. Then my so horrid oaths,
And hell-deep imprecations made against it !
   Ast. The king, your brother, will thank
    you for the advancement
Of his affairs.
   Bert. And yet who can hold out
Against such batteries as her power and
    greatness
Raise up against my weak defences !
   Gonz. Sir,

          Re-enter Aurelia.

Do you dream waking ? 'Slight, she's here
   again !
Walks she on woollen feet !
   Aurel. You dwell too long
In your deliberation, and come
With a cripple's pace to that which you
   should fly to.
   Bert. It is confess'd : yet why should I,
From you, that hazard all to my poor nothing,
By false play send you off a loser from me ?
I am already too, too much engaged
To the king my brother's anger ; and who
   knows
But that his doubts and politic fears, should
   you
Make me his equal, may draw war upon
Your territories? Were that breach made up,
I should with joy embrace what now I fear
To touch but with due reverence.
   Aurel. That hinderance
Is easily removed. I owe the king
For a royal visit, which I straight will pay
   him ;
And having first reconciled you to his favour,
A dispensation shall meet with us.
   Bert. I am wholly yours.
   Aurel. On this book seal it.
   Gonz. What, hand and lip too ! then the
    bargain's sure.——
You have no employment for me ?
   Aurel. Yes, Gonzaga ;
Provide a royal ship.
   Gonz. A ship ! St. John,
Whither are we bound now ?
   Aurel. You shall know hereafter.
My lord, your pardon, for my too much
   trenching
Upon your patience.
   Ador. Camiola !   [*Aside to* Bertolda.
   Aurel. How do you ?
   Bert. Indisposed ; but I attend you.
           [*Exeunt all but* Adorni.
   Ador. The heavy curse that waits on per-
    jury,
And foul ingratitude, pursue thee ever !
Yet why from me this ? in his breach of
   faith
My loyalty finds reward : what poisons him,
Proves mithridate to me. I have perform'd
All she commanded, punctually ; and now,
In the clear mirror of my truth, she may
Behold his falsehood. O that I had wings
To bear me to Palermo ! This once known,
Must change her love into a just disdain,
And work her to compassion of my pain.
                   [*Exit.*

SCENE V.—Palermo. *A Room in Ca-miola's House.*

Enter Sylli, Camiola, *and* Clarinda, *at several doors.*

Syl. Undone! undone!—poor I, that whilome was
The top and ridge of my house, am, on the sudden,
Turu'd to the pitifullest animal
O' the lineage of the Syllis!
Cam. What's the matter?
Syl. The king—break, girdle, break!
Cam. Why, what of him?
Syl. Hearing how far you doated on my person,
Growing envious of my happiness, and knowing
His brother, nor his favourite, Fulgentio,
Could get a sheep's eye from you, I being present,
Is come himself a suitor, with the awl
Of his authority to bore my nose,
And take you from me—Oh, oh, oh!
Cam. Do not roar so:
The king!
Syl. The king. Yet loving Sylli is not
So sorry for his own, as your misfortune;
If the king should carry you, or you bear him,
What a loser should you be! He can but make you
A queen, and what a simple thing is that,
To the being my lawful spouse! the world can never
Afford you such a husband.
Cam. I believe you.
But how are you sure the king is so inclined?
Did not you dream this?
Syl. With these eyes I saw him
Dismiss his train, and lighting from his coach,
Whispering Fulgentio in the ear.
Cam. If so,
I guess the business.
Syl. It can be no other,
But to give me the bob, that being a matter
Of main importance. Yonder they are; I dare not

Enter Roberto, *and* Fulgentio.

Be seen, I am so desperate: if you forsake me,
Send me word, that I may provide a willow garland,
To wear when I drown myself. O Sylli, Sylli!
[*Exit crying.*
Ful. It will be worth your pains, sir, to observe
The constancy and bravery of her spirit.

Though great men tremble at your frowns,
I dare
Hazard my head, your majesty, set off
With terror, cannot fright her.
Rob. May she answer
My expectation! [*Aside.*
Ful. There she is.
Cam. My knees thus
Bent to the earth, while my vows are sent upward
For the safety of my sovereign, pay the duty
Due for so great an honour, in this favour
Done to your humblest handmaid.
Rob. You mistake me;
I come not, lady, that you may report
The king, to do you honour, made your house
(He being there) his court; but to correct
Your stubborn disobedience. ' A pardon
For that, could you obtain it, were well purchased
With this humility.
Cam. A pardon, sir!
Till I am conscious of an offence,
I will not wrong my innocence to beg one.
What is my crime, sir?
Rob. Look on him I favour,
By you scorn'd and neglected.
Cam. Is that all, sir?
Rob. No, minion; though that were too much. How can you
Answer the setting on your desperate bravo
To murder him?
Cam. With your leave, I must not kneel, sir,
While I reply to this: but thus rise up
In my defence, and tell you, as a man,
(Since, when you are unjust, the deity,
Which you may challenge as a king, parts from you,)
'Twas never read in holy writ, or moral,
That subjects on their loyalty, were obliged
To love their sovereign's vices; your grace, sir,
To such an undeserver is no virtue.
Ful. What think you now, sir?
Cam. Say, you should love wine,
You being the king, and, 'cause I am your subject,
Must I be ever drunk? Tyrants, not kings,
By violence, from humble vassals force
The liberty of their souls. I could not love him;
And to compel affection, as I take it,
Is not found in your prerogative.
Rob. Excellent virgin!
How I admire her confidence! [*Aside.*
Cam. He complains
Oi wrong done him: but, be no more a king,
Unless you do me right. Burn your decrees,

And of your laws and statutes make a fire
To thaw the frozen numbness of delinquents,
If he escape unpunish'd. Do your edicts
Call it death in any man that breaks into
Another's house, to rob him, though of trifles;
And shall Fulgentio, your Fulgentio, live,
Who hath committed more than sacrilege,
In the pollution of my clear fame,
By his malicious slanders?
  Rob. Have you done this?
Answer truly, on your life.
  Ful. In the heat of blood,
Some such thing I reported.
  Rob. Out of my sight!
For I vow, if by true penitence thou win not
This injured virgin to sue out thy pardon,
Thy grave is digg'd already.
  Ful. By my own folly
I have made a fair hand of 't.
             [*Aside, and exit.*
  Rob. You shall know, lady,
While I wear a crown, justice shall use her
    sword
To cut offenders off, though nearest to us.
  Cam. Ay, now you shew whose deputy
    you are :
If now I bathe your feet with tears, it cannot
Be censured superstition.
  Rob. You must rise ;
Rise in our favour and protection ever.
               [*Kisses her.*
  Cam. Happy are subjects, when the prince
    is still
Guided by justice, not his passionate will.
                [*Exeunt.*

————

ACT V.

SCENE I.—*The same. A Room in*
Camiola's House.

Enter Camiola *and* Sylli.

  Cam. You see how tender I am of the
    quiet
And peace of your affection, and what great
    ones
I put off in your favour.
  Syl. You do wisely,
Exceeding wisely ; and when I have said,
I thank you for't, be happy.
  Cam. And good reason,
In having such a blessing.
  Syl. When you have it ;
But the bait is not yet ready. Stay the time,
While I triumph by myself. King, by your
    leave,
I have wiped your royal nose without a
    napkin ;

You may cry, *Willow, willow!* for your
    brother,
I'll only say, *Go by!* for my fine favourite,
He may graze where he please ; his lips may
    water
Like a puppy's o'er a furmenty pot, while Sylli,
Out of his two-leaved cherry-stone dish,
    drinks nectar !
I cannot hold out any longer ; heaven for-
    give me !
'Tis not the first oath I have broke ; I must
    take
A little for a preparative.
    [*Offers to kiss and embrace her.*
  Cam. By no means.
If you forswear yourself, we shall not prosper :
I'll rather lose my longing.
  Syl. Pretty soul !
How careful it is of me ! let me buss yet
Thy little dainty foot for't : that, I'm sure, is
Out of my oath.
  Cam. Why, if thou canst dispense with't
So far, I'll not be scrupulous ; such a favour
My amorous shoe-maker steals.
  Syl. O most rare leather !
           [*Kisses her shoe often.*
I do begin at the lowest, but in time
I may grow higher.
  Cam. Fie ! you dwell too long there :
Rise, prithee rise.
  Syl. O, I am up already.

    Enter Clarinda, *hastily.*

  Cam. How I abuse my hours !—What
    news with thee, now ?
  Clar. Off with that gown, 'tis mine ; mine
    by your promise :
Signior Adorni is return'd ! now upon en-
    trance !
Off with it, off with it, madam !
  Cam. Be not so hasty :
When I go to bed, 'tis thine.
  Syl. You have my grant too ;
But, do you hear, lady, though I give way
    to this,
You must hereafter ask my leave, before
You part with things of moment.
  Cam. Very good ;
When I'm yours I'll be govern'd.
  Syl. Sweet obedience !

    Enter Adorni.

  Cam. You are well return'd.
  Ador. I wish that the success
Of my service had deserved it.
  Cam. Lives Bertoldo ?
  Ador. Yes, and return'd with safety.
  Cam. 'Tis not then
In the power of fate to add to, or take from

My perfect happiness ; and yet—he should
Have made me his first visit.
   Ador. So I think too ;
But he——
   Syl. Durst not appear, I being present ;
That's his excuse, I warrant you.
   Cam. Speak, where is he?
With whom ? who hath deserved more from
   him ?. or
Can be of equal merit ? I in this
Do not except the king.
   Ador. He's at the palace,
With the dutchess of Sienna. One coach
   brought them hither,
Without a third : he's very gracious with her ;
You may conceive the rest.
   Cam. My jealous fears
Make me to apprehend.
   Ador. Pray you dismiss
Signior Wisdom, and I'll make relation to you
Of the particulars.
   Cam. Servant, I would have you
To haste unto the court.
   Syl. I will outrun
A footman for your pleasure.
   Cam. There observe
The dutchess' train, and entertainment.
   Syl. Fear not ;
I will discover all that is of weight,
To the liveries of her pages and her footmen.
This is fit employment for me.   [*Exit.*
   Cam. Gracious with
The dutchess ! sure, you said so ?
   Ador. I will use
All possible brevity to inform you, madam,
Of what was trusted to me, and discharged
With faith and loyal duty.
   Cam. I believe it ;
You ransomed him, and supplied his wants—
   imagine
That is already spoken ; and what vows
Of service he made to me, is apparent ;
His joy of me, and wonder too, perspicuous ;
Does not your story end so?
   Ador. Would the end
Had answered the beginning?—In a word,
Ingratitude and perjury at the height
Cannot express him.
   Cam. Take heed.
   Ador. Truth is arm'd,
And can defend itself. It must out, madam :
I saw (the presence full) the amorous dutchess
Kiss and embrace him ; on his part ac-
   cepted
With equal ardour ; and their willing hands
No sooner join'd, but a remove was publish'd,
And put in execution.
   Cam. The proofs are
Too pregnant. O Bertoldo !

   Ador. He's not worth
Your sorrow, madam.
   Cam. Tell me, when you saw this,
Did not you grieve, as I do now to hear it ?
   Ador. His precipice from goodness raising
   mine,
And serving as a foil to set my faith off,
I had little reason.
   Cam. In this you confess
The devilish malice of your disposition.
As you were a man, you stood bound to
   lament it ;
And not, in flattery of your false hopes,
To glory in it. When good men pursue
The path mark'd out by virtue, the blest saints
With joy look on it, and seraphic angels
Clap their celestial wings in heavenly plau-
   dits,
To see a scene of grace so well presented,
The fiends, and men made up of envy,
   mourning.
Whereas now, on the contrary, as far
As their divinity can partake of passion,
With me they weep, beholding a fair temple,
Built in Bertoldo's loyalty, turu'd to ashes
By the flames of his inconstancy, the damn'd
Rejoicing in the object.—'Tis not well
In you, Adorni.
   Ador. What a temper dwells
In this rare virgin ! [*Aside.*] Can you pity
   him,
That hath shewn none to you?
   Cam. I must not be
Cruel by his example. You, perhaps,
Expect now I should seek recovery
Of what I have lost, by tears, and with bent
   knees
Beg his compassion. No ; my towering
   virtue,
From the assurance of my merit, scorns
To stoop so low. I'll take a nobler course,
And, confident in the justice of my cause,
The king his brother, and new mistress,
   judges,
Ravish him from her arms. You have the
   contract,
In which he swore to marry me?
   Ador. 'Tis here, madam.
   Cam. He shall be, then, against his will,
   my husband ;
And when I have him, I'll so use him !—
   Doubt not,
But that, your honesty being unquestion'd,
This writing, with your testimony, clears all.
   Ador. And buries me in the dark mists of
   error.
   Cam. I'll presently to court ; pray you,
   give order
For my caroch.

Ador. A cart for me were fitter,
To hurry me to the gallows.
                              [*Aside, and exit.*
Cam. O false men!
Inconstant! perjured! My good angel help
    me,
In these my extremities!

            Re-enter Sylli.

Syl. If you e'er will see brave sight,
Lose it not now. Bertoldo and the dutchess
Are presently to be married: there's such
    pomp,
And preparation!
Cam. If I marry, 'tis
This day, or never.
Syl. Why, with all my heart;
Though I break this, I'll keep the next oath
    I make,
And then it is quit.
Cam. Follow me to my cabinet;
You know my confessor, father Paulo?
Syl. Yes: shall he
Do the feat for us?
Cam. I will give in writing
Directions to him, and attire myself
Like a virgin bride; and something I will do,
That shall deserve men's praise, and wonder
    too.
Syl. And I, to make all know I am not
    shallow,
Will have my points of cochineal and yellow.
                              [*Exeunt.*

SCENE II.—*The Same. A State-room in
        the Palace.*

Loud music. Enter Roberto, Bertoldo,
    Aurelia, Ferdinand, Astutio, Gonzaga,
    Roderigo, Jacomo, Pierio, *a Bishop, and
    Attendants.*

Rob. Had our division been greater,
    madam,
Your clemency, the wrong being done to you,
In pardon of it, like the rod of concord,
Must make a perfect union.—Once more,
With a brotherly affection, we receive you
Into our favour: let it be your study
Hereafter to deserve this blessing, far
Beyond your merit.
Bert. As the princess' grace
To me is without limit, my endeavours,
With all obsequiousness to serve her plea-
    sures,
Shall know no bounds: nor will I, being
    made
Her husband, e'er forget the duty that
I owe her as a servant.
Aurel. I expect not
But fair equality, since I well know,

If that superiority be due,
'Tis not to me. When you are made my
    consort,
All the prerogatives of my high birth can-
    cell'd,
I'll practice the obedience of a wife,
And freely pay it. Queens themselves, if they
Make choice of their inferiors, only aiming
To feed their sensual appetites, and to reign
Over their husbands, in some kind commit
Authorized whoredom; nor will I be guilty,
In my intent of such a crime.
Gonz. This done,
As it is promised, madam, may well stand for
A precedent to great women: but, when once
The griping hunger of desire is cloy'd,
And the poor fool advanced, brought on his
    knees,
Most of your eagle breed, I'll not say all,
Ever excepting you, challenge again
What, in hot blood, they parted from.
Aurel. You are ever
An enemy of our sex; but you, I hope, sir,
Have better thoughts.
Bert. I dare not entertain
An ill one of your goodness.
Rob. To my power
I will enable him, to prevent all danger
Envy can raise against your choice. One
    word more
Touching the articles.

Enter Fulgentio, Camiola, Sylli, *and* Adorni.

Ful. In you alone
Lie all my hopes; you can or kill or save me;
But pity in you will become you better
(Though I confess in justice 'tis denied me)
Than too much rigour.
Cam. I will make your peace
As far as it lies in me; but must first
Labour to right myself.
Aurel. Or add or alter
What you think fit; in him I have my all:
Heaven make me thankful for him!
Rob. On to the temple.
Cam. Stay, royal sir; and as you are a
    king,
Erect one here, in doing justice to
An injured maid.
Aurel. How's this?
Bert. O, I am blasted!
Rob. I have given some proof, sweet lady,
    of my promptness
To do you right, you need not, therefore,
    doubt me;
And rest assured, that, this great work dis-
    patch'd,
You shall have audience, and satisfaction
To all you can demand.

Cam. To do me justice
Exacts your present care, and can admit
Of no delay. If, ere my cause be heard,
In favour of your brother you go on, sir,
Your sceptre cannot right me. He's the man,
The guilty man, whom I accuse ; and you
Stand bound in duty, as you are supreme,
To be impartial. Since you are a judge,
As a delinquent look on him, and not
As on a brother : Justice painted blind,
Infers her ministers are obliged to hear
The cause, and truth, the judge, determine
of it :
And not sway'd or by favour or affection,
By a false gloss, or wrested comment, alter
The true intent and letter of the law.
Rob. Nor will I, madam.
Aurel. You seem troubled, sir.
Gonz. His colour changes too.
Cam. The alteration
Grows from his guilt. The goodness of my
cause
Begets such confidence in me, that I bring
No hired tongue to plead for me, that with
gay
Rhetorical flourishes may palliate
That which, stripp'd naked, will appear de-
form'd.
I stand here mine own advocate ; and my
truth,
Deliver'd in the plainest language, will
Make good itself ; nor will I, if the king
Give suffrage to it, but admit of you,
My greatest enemy, and this stranger prince,
To sit assistants with him.
Aurel. I ne'er wrong'd you.
Cam. In your knowledge of the injury, I
believe it ;
Nor will you, in your justice, when you are
Acquainted with my interest in this man,
Which I lay claim to.
Rob. Let us take our seats.
What is your title to him ?
Cam. By this contract,
Seal'd solemnly before a reverend man,
[*Presents a paper to the king.*
I challenge him for my husband.
Syl. Ha ! was I
Sent for the friar for this ? O Sylli ! Sylli !
Some cordial, or I faint.
Rob. This writing is
Authentical.
Aurel. But, done in heat of blood,
Charm'd by her flatteries, as no doubt, he was,
To be dispens'd with.
Fer. Add this, if you please,
The distance and disparity between
Their births and fortunes.
Cam. What can Innocence hope for,

When such as sit her judges are corrupted !
Disparity of birth or fortune, urge you ?
Or Syren charms ? or, at his best, in me
Wants to deserve him ? Call some few days
back,
And, as he was, consider him, and you
Must grant him my inferior. Imagine
You saw him now in fetters, with his honour,
His liberty lost ; with her black wings Despair
Circling his miseries, and this Gonzaga
Trampling on his afflictions ; the great sum
Proposed for his redemption ; the king
Forbidding payment of it ; his near kinsmen,
With his protesting followers and friends,
Falling off from him ; by the whole world
forsaken ;
Dead to all hope, and buried in the grave
Of his calamities ; and then weigh duly
What she deserv'd, whose merits now are
doubted,
That, as his better angel, in her bounties
Appear'd unto him, his great ransom paid,
His wants, and with a prodigal hand, sup-
plied ;
Whether, then, being my manumised slave,
He owed not himself to me ?
Aurel. Is this true ?
Rob. In his silence 'tis acknowledged.
Gonz. If you want
A witness to this purpose, I'll depose it.
Cam. If I have dwelt too long on my
deservings
To this unthankful man, pray you pardon me ;
The cause required it. And though now I add
A little, in my painting to the life
His barbarous ingratitude, to deter
Others from imitation, let it meet with
A fair interpretation. This serpent,
Frozen to numbness, was no sooner warm'd
In the bosom of my pity and compassion,
But, in return, he ruin'd his preserver,
The prints the irons had made in his flesh
Still ulcerous ; but all that I had done,
My benefits, in sand or water written,
As they had never been, no more re-
member'd !
And on what ground, but his ambitious hopes
To gain this dutchess' favour ?
Aurel. Yes ; the object,
Look on it better, lady, may excuse
The change of his affection.
Cam. The object !
In what ? forgive me, modesty, if I say
You look upon your form in the false glass
Of flattery and self-love, and that deceives you.
That you were a dutchess, as I take it, was not
Character'd on your face ; and, that not seen,
For other feature, make all these, that are
Experienced in women, judges of them,

And, if they are not parasites, they must
　　grant,
For beauty without art, though you storm
　　at it,
I may take the right-hand file.
　　Gonz. Well said, i' faith !
I see fair women on no terms will yield
Priority in beauty.
　　Cam. Down, proud heart !
Why do I rise up in defence of that,
Which, in my cherishing of it, hath undone
　　me!　　　．
No, madam, I recant,—you are all beauty,
Goodness, and virtue; and poor I not worthy
As a foil to set you off: enjoy your conquest ;
But do not tyrannize. Yet, as I am,
In my lowness, from your height you may
　　look on me,
And, in your suffrage to me, make him know
That, though to all men else I did appear
The shame and scorn of women, he stands
　　bound
To hold me as the masterpiece.
　　Rob. By my life,
You have shewn yourself of such an abject
　　temper,
So poor and low-condition'd, as I grieve for
Your nearness to me.
　　Fer. I am changed in my
Opinion of you, lady ; and profess
The virtues of your mind an ample fortune
For an absolute monarch.
　　Gonz. Since you are resolved
To damn yourself, in your forsaking of
Your noble order for a woman, do it
For this. You may search through the
　　world, and meet not
With such another phœnix.
　　Aurel. On the sudden
I feel all fires of love quench'd in the water
Of my compassion.—Make your peace ; you
　　have
My free consent ; for here I do disclaim
All interest in you : and, to further your
Desires, fair maid, composed of worth and
　　honour,　　　﹏
The dispensation procured by me,
Freeing Bertoldo from his vow, makes way
To your embraces.
　　Bert. Oh, how have I stray'd,
And wilfully, out of the noble track
Mark'd me by virtue ! till now, I was never
Truly a prisoner. To excuse my late
Captivity, I might allege the malice
Of fortune ; you, that conquer'd me, con-
　　fessing
Courage in my defence was no way wanting.
But now I have surrender'd up my strengths
Into the power of Vice, and on my forehead

Branded, with mine own hand, in capital
　　letters,
DISLOYAL, and INGRATEFUL. Though
　　barr'd from
Human society, and hiss'd into
Some desart ne'er yet haunted with the curses
Of men and women, sitting as a judge
Upon my guilty self, I must confess
It justly falls upon me ; and one tear,
Shed in compassion of my sufferings, more
Than I can hope for.
　　Cam. This compunction
For the wrong that you have done me,
　　though you should
Fix here, and your true sorrow move no
　　further,
Will, in respect I loved once, make these eyes
Two springs of sorrow for you.
　　Bert. In your pity
My cruelty shews more monstrous : yet I
　　am not,
Though most ingrateful, grown to such a
　　height
Of impudence, as, in my wishes only,
To ask your pardon. If, as now I fall
Prostrate before your feet, you will vouchsafe
To act your own revenge, treading upon me
As a viper eating through the bowels of
Your benefits, to whom, with liberty,
I owe my being, 'twill take from the burthen
That now is insupportable.
　　Cam. Pray you, rise ;　　⟩
As I wish peace and quiet to my soul,
I do forgive you heartily : yet, excuse me,
Though I deny myself a blessing that,
By the favour of the dutchess, seconded
With your submission, is offer'd to me ;
Let not the reason I allege for't grieve you,
You have been false once.—I have done :
　　and if,
When I am married, as this day I will be,
As a perfect sign of your atonement with me,
You wish me joy, I will receive it for
Full satisfaction of all obligations
In which you stand bound to me.
　　Bert. I will do it,
And, what's more, in despite of sorrow, live
To see myself undone, beyond all hope
To be made up again.
　　Syl. My blood begins　.
To come to my heart again.
　　Cam. Pray you, signior Sylli,
Call in the holy friar : he's prepared
For finishing the work.
　　Syl. I knew I was
The man : heaven make me thankful !
　　Rob. Who is this?
　　Ast. His father was the banker of Pa-
　　lermo,

And this the heir of his great wealth ; his
wisdom
Was not hereditary.
   Syl. Though you know me not,
Your majesty owes me a round sum ; I have
A seal or two to witness ; yet, if you please
To wear my colours, and dance at my
wedding,
I'll never sue you.
   Rob. And I'll grant your suit.
   Syl. Gracious madonna, noble general,
Brave captains, and my quondam rivals, wear
them,   [*Gives them favours.*
Since I am confident you dare not harbour
A thought but that way current.   [*Exit.*
   Aurel. For my part
I cannot guess the issue.

Re-enter Sylli *with* Father Paulo.

   Syl. Do your duty ;
And with all speed you can, you may dis-
patch us.
   Paul. Thus, as a principal ornament to
the church,
I seize her.
   All. How !
   Rob. So young, and so religious !
   Paul. She has forsook the world.
   Syl. And Sylli too !
I shall run mad.
   Rob. Hence with the fool !—[Sylli *is thrust
off.*]—Proceed, sir.
   Paul. *Look on this* MAID OF HONOUR, *now
Truly honour'd in her vow
She pays to heaven: vain delight
By day, or pleasure of the night
She no more thinks of. This fair hair
(Favours for great kings to wear)
Must now be shorn ; her rich array
Changed into a homely gray :
The dainties with which she was fed,
And her proud flesh pampered,
Must not be tasted ; from the spring,
For wine, cold water we will bring:
And with fasting mortify
The feasts of sensuality.
Her jewels, beads; and she must look
Not in a glass, but holy book,
To teach her the ne'er-erring way
To immortality. O may
She, as she purposes to be
A child new-born to piety,
Persever in it, and good men,
With saints and angels, say, Amen !*

   Cam. This is the marriage ! this the port
to which
My vows must steer me ! Fill my spreading
sails
With the pure wind of your devotions for me,
That I may touch the secure haven, where
Eternal happiness keeps her residence,
Temptations to frailty never entering !
I am dead to the world, and thus dispose
Of what I leave behind me ; and, dividing
My state into three parts, I thus bequeath it :
The first to the fair nunnery, to which
I dedicate the last and better part
Of my frail life ; a second portion
To pious uses ; and the third to thee,
Adorni, for thy true and faithful service.
And, ere I take my last farewell, with hope
To find a grant, my suit to you is, that
You would, for my sake, pardon this young
man,
And to his merits love him, and no further.
   Rob. I thus confirm it.
       [*Gives his hand to* Fulgentio.
   Cam. And, as e'er you hope,
           [*To* Bertoldo.
Like me, to be made happy, I conjure you
To reassume your order ; and in fighting
Bravely against the enemies of our faith,
Redeem your mortgaged honour.
   Gonz. I restore this :
      [*Gives him the white cross.*
Once more brothers in arms.
   Bert. I'll live and die so.
   Cam. To you my pious wishes ! And, to end
All differences, great sir, I beseech you
To be an arbitrator, and compound
The quarrel long continuing between
The duke and dutchess.
   Rob. I will take it into
My special care.
   Cam. I am then at rest. Now, father,
Conduct me where you please.
       [*Exeunt* Paulo *and* Camiola.
   Rob. She well deserves
Her name, THE MAID OF HONOUR ! May
she stand,
To all posterity, a fair example
For noble maids to imitate ! Since to live
In wealth and pleasure's common, but to
part with
Such poison'd baits is rare ; there being
nothing
Upon this stage of life to be commended,
Though well begun, till it be fully ended.
       [*Flourish. Exeunt.*

The Picture.

ACT I.

SCENE I.—*The Frontiers of* Bohemia.

Enter Mathias, Sophia, Corisca, Hilario,
with other Servants.

Math. Since we must part, Sophia, to
    pass further
Is not alone impertinent, but dangerous.
We are not distant from the Turkish camp
Above five leagues, and who knows but
    some party
Of his Timariots, that scour the country,
May fall upon us?—be now, as thy name,
Truly interpreted, hath ever spoke thee,
Wise, and discreet; and to thy understanding
Marry thy constant patience.
    Soph. You put me, sir,
To the utmost trial of it.
    Math. Nay, no melting;
Since the necessity that now separates us,
We have long since disputed, and the reasons
Forcing me to it, too oft wash'd in tears.
I grant that you, in birth, were far above me,
And great men, my superiors, rivals for you;
But mutual consent of heart, as hands,
Join'd by true love, hath made us one, and
    equal:
Nor is it in me mere desire of fame,
Or to be cried up by the public voice,
For a brave soldier, that puts on my armour:
Such airy tumours take not me. You know
How narrow our demeans are, and what's
    more,
Having as yet no charge of children on us,
We hardly can subsist.
    Soph. In you alone, sir,
I have all abundance.
    Math. For my mind's content,
In your own language I could answer you.
You have been an obedient wife, a right one;
And to my power, though short of your
    desert,
I have been ever an indulgent husband.
We have long enjoy'd the sweets of love,
    and though
Not to satiety, or loathing, yet
We must not live such dotards on our
    pleasures,
As still to hug them, to the certain loss
Of profit and preferment. Competent means
Maintains a quiet bed; want breeds dis-
    sention,
Even in good women.
    Soph. Have you found in me, sir,
Any distaste, or sign of discontent,
For want of what's superfluous?
    Math. No, Sophia;
Nor shalt thou ever have cause to repent

Thy constant course in goodness, if heaven
bless
My honest undertakings. 'Tis for thee
That I turn soldier, and put forth, dearest,
Upon this sea of action, as a factor,
To trade for rich materials to adorn
Thy noble parts, and shew them in full lustre.
I blush that other ladies, less in beauty
And outward form, but in the harmony
Of the soul's ravishing music, the same age
Not to be named with thee, should so out-
shine thee
In jewels, and variety of wardrobes ;
While you, to whose sweet innocence both
Indies
Compared are of no value, wanting these,
Pass unregarded.

   Soph. If I am so rich, or—
In your opinion, why should you borrow
Additions for me ?

   Math. Why ! I should be censured
Of ignorance, possessing such a jewel
Above all price, if I forbear to give it
The best of ornaments : therefore, Sophia,
In few words know my pleasure, and obey
me,
As you have ever done. To your discretion
I leave the government of my family,
And our poor fortunes ; and from these com-
mand
Obedience to you, as to myself :
To the utmost of what's mine, live plenti-
fully ;
And, ere the remnant of our store be spent,
With my good sword I hope I shall reap for
you
A harvest in such full abundance, as
Shall make a merry winter.

   Soph. Since you are not
To be diverted, sir, from what you purpose,
All arguments to stay you here are useless :
Go when you please, sir. Eyes, I charge
you waste not
One drop of sorrow ; look you hoard all up
Till in my widow'd bed I call upon you,
But then be sure you fail not. You blest
angels,
Guardians of human life, I at this instant
Forbear t'invoke you : at our parting, 'twere
To personate devotion. My soul ·
Shall go along with you, and, when you are
Circled with death and horror, seek and
find you ;
And then I will not leave a saint unsued to
For your protection. To tell you what
I will do in your absence, would shew
poorly ;
My actions shall speak for me : 'twere to
doubt you,

To beg I may hear from you ; where you are
You cannot live obscure, nor shall one post,
By night or day, pass unexamined by me.—
If I dwell long upon your lips, consider,
               [*Kisses him.*
After this feast, the griping fast that follows,
And it will be excusable ; pray turn from me.
All that I can, is spoken.   [*Exit.*

   Math. Follow your mistress.
Forbear your wishes for me ; let me find them,
At my return, in your prompt will to serve
her.

   Hil. For my part, sir, I will grow lean
with study ·
To make her merry.

   Coris. Though you are my lord,
Yet being her gentlewoman, by my place
I may take my leave ; your hand, or, if you
please
To have me fight so high, I'll not be coy,
But stand a-tip-toe for't.

   Math. O, farewell, girl !   [*Kisses her.*

   Hil. A kiss well begg'd, Corisca.

   Coris. 'Twas my fee ;
Love, how he melts ! I cannot blame my
lady's
Unwillingness to part with such marmalade
lips.   ·
There will be scrambling for them in the
camp ;
And were it not for my honesty, I could
wish now
I were his leaguer laundress ; I would find
Soap of mine own, enough to wash his linen,
Or I would strain hard for't.

   Hil. How the mammet twitters !
Come, come ; my lady stays for us.

   Coris. Would I had been
Her ladyship the last night !

   Hil. No more of that, wench.
   [*Exeunt* Hilario, Corisca, *and the rest.*

   Math. I am strangely troubled, yet why I
should nourish
A fury here, and with imagined food,
Having no real grounds on which to raise
A building of suspicion she was ever
Or can be false hereafter. I in this
But foolishly enquire the knowledge of
A future sorrow, which, if I find out,
My present ignorance were a cheap purchase,
Though with my loss of being. I have al-
ready
Dealt with a friend of mine, a general
scholar,
One deeply read in nature's hidden secrets,
And, though with much unwillingness, have
won him
To do as much as art can, to resolve me
My fate that follows—To my wish, he's come.

Enter Baptista.

Julio Baptista, now I may affirm
Your promise and performance walk
together ;
And therefore, without circumstance, to the
point :
Instruct me what I am.
  Bapt. I could wish you had
Made trial of my love some other way.
  Math. Nay, this is from the purpose.
  Bapt. If you can
Proportion your desire to any mean,
I do pronounce you happy ; I have found
By certain rules of art, your matchless wife
Is to this present hour from all pollution
Free, and untainted.
  Math. Good.
  Bapt. In reason, therefore,
You should fix here, and make no further
search
Of what may fall hereafter.
  Math. O, Baptista,
'Tis not in me to master so my passions ;
I must know further, or you have made good
But half your promise.   While my love stood
by,
Holding her upright, and my presence was
A watch upon her, her desires being met
too
With equal ardour from me, what one proof
Could she give of her constancy, being un-
tempted ?
But when I am absent, and my coming back
Uncertain, and those wanton heats in women,
Not to be quench'd by lawful means, and she
The absolute disposer of herself,
Without control or curb ; nay, more, invited
By opportunity, and all strong temptations,
If then she hold out—
  Bapt. As, no doubt, she will.
  Math. Those doubts must be made cer-
tainties, Baptista,
By your assurance ; or your boasted art
Deserves no admiration.   How you trifle,
And play with my affliction ! I am on
The rack, till you confirm me.
  Bapt. Sure, Mathias,
I am no god, nor can I dive into
Her hidden thoughts, or know what her
intents are ;
That is denied to art, and kept conceal'd
E'en from the devils themselves : they can
but guess,
Out of long observation, what is likely ;
But positively to fortel that shall be,
You may conclude impossible.   All I can,
I will do for you ; when you are distant from
her

A thousand leagues, as if you then were with
her,
You shall know truly when she is solicited,
And how far wrought on.
  Math. I desire no more.
  Bapt. Take then this little model of Sophia,
With more than human skill limn'd to the
life ;   [*Gives him a picture.*
Each line and lineament of it, in the drawing,
So punctually observed, that, had it motion,
In so much 'twere herself.
  Math. It is, indeed,
An admirable piece ! but if it have not
Some hidden virtue that I cannot guess at,
In what can it advantage me ?
  Bapt. I'll instruct you :
Carry it still about you, and as oft
As you desire to know how she's affected,
With curious eyes peruse it : while it keeps
The figure it now has, entire and perfect,
She is not only innocent in fact,
But unattempted ; but if once it vary
From the true form, and what's now white
and red
Incline to yellow, rest most confident
She's with all violence courted, but uncon-
quer'd ;
But if it turn all black, 'tis an assurance
The fort, by composition or surprise,
Is forced, or with her free consent sur-
render'd.
  Math. How much you have engaged me
for this favour,
The service of my whole life shall make good.
  Bapt. We will not part so, I'll along with
you,
And it is needful : with the rising sun,
The armies meet ; yet, ere the fight begin,
In spite of opposition, I will place you
In the head of the Hungarian general's troop,
And near his person.
  Math. As my better angel,
You shall direct and guide me.
  Bapt. As we ride
I'll tell you more.
  Math. In all things I'll obey you.
                   [*Exeunt.*

  SCENE II.—Hungary. *Alba Regalis.*
    A State-room in the Palace.

    Enter Ubaldo *and* Ricardo.

  Ric. When came the post?
  Ubald. The last night.
  Ric. From the camp?
  Ubald. Yes, as 'tis said, and the letter
writ and sign'd
By the general, Ferdinand.
  Ric. Nay, then, sans question,
It is of moment.

Ubald. It concerns the lives
Of two great armies.
  Ric. Was it cheerfully
Received by the king?
  Ubald. Yes ; for being assured
The armies were in view of one another,
Having proclaim'd a public fast and prayer
For the good success, [he] dispatch'd a gen-
    tleman
Of his privy chamber to the general
With absolute authority from him,
To try the fortune of a day.
  Ric. No doubt then
The general will come on, and fight it
    bravely.
Heaven prosper him! This military art,
I grant to be the noblest of professions ;
And yet, I thank my stars for't, I was never
Inclined to learn it : since this bubble honour
(Which is, indeed, the nothing soldiers fight
    for,)
With the loss of limbs or life, is, in my
    judgment,
Too dear a purchase.
  Ubald. Give me our court warfare :
The danger is not great in the encounter
Of a fair mistress.
  Ric. Fair and sound together
Do very well, Ubaldo ; but such are,
With difficulty, to be found out ; and when
    they know
Their value, prized too high. By thy own
    report,
Thou wast at twelve a gamester, and since
    that,
Studied all kinds of females, from the night-
    trader
I' the street, with certain danger to thy pocket,
To the great lady in her cabinet ;
That spent upon thee more in cullises,
To strengthen thy weak back, than would
    maintain
Twelve Flanders mares, and as many
    running horses :
Besides apothecaries and surgeons' bills,
Paid upon all occasions, and those frequent.
  Ubald. You talk, Ricardo, as if yet you
    were
A novice in those mysteries.
  Ric. By no means ;
My doctor can assure the contrary :
I lose no time. I have felt the pain and
    pleasure,
As he that is a gamester, and plays often,
Must sometimes be a loser.
  Ubald. Wherefore, then,
Do you envy me?
  Ric. It grows not from my want,
Nor thy abundance ; but being, as I am,

The likelier man, and of much more ex-
    perience,
My good parts are my curses : there's no
    beauty,
But yields ere it be summon'd ; and, as
    nature
Had sign'd me the monopoly of maidenheads,
There's none can buy till I have made my
    market.
Satiety cloys me ; as I live, I would part
    with
Half my estate, nay, travel o'er the world,
To find that only phœnix in my search,
That could hold out against me.
  Ubald. Be not rapt so ;
You may spare that labour. As she is a
    woman,
What think you of the queen?
  Ric. I dare not aim at
The petticoat royal, that is still excepted :
Yet, were she not my king's, being the ab-
    stract,
Of all that's rare, or to be wish'd in woman,.
To write her in my catalogue, having en-
    joy'd her,
I would venture my neck to a halter—but
    we talk of
Impossibilities : as she hath a beauty
Would make old Nestor young ; such
    majesty
Draws forth a sword of terror to defend it,
As would fright Paris, though the queen of
    love
Vow'd her best furtherance to him.
  Ubald. Have you observed
The gravity of her language, mix'd with
    sweetness?
  Ric. Then, at what distance she reserves
    herself,
When the king himself makes his approaches
    to her—
  Ubald. As she were still a virgin, and his
    life
But one continued wooing.
  Ric. She well knows
Her worth, and values it.
  Ubald. And so far the king is
Indulgent to her humours, that he forbears
The duty of a husband, but when she calls
    for't.
  Ric. All his imaginations and thoughts
Are buried in her ; the loud noise of war
Cannot awake him.
  Ubald. At this very instant,
When both his life and crown are at the
    stake,
He only studies her content, and when
She's pleased to show herself, music and.
    masques

Are with all care and cost provided for
  her.
Ric. This night she promised to appear.
Ubald. You may
Believe it by the diligence of the king,
As if he were her harbinger.

Enter Ladislaus, Eubulus, *and* Attendants
            with perfumes.

Ladis. These rooms
Are not perfumed, as we directed,
  Eubu. Not, sir!
I know not what you would have ; I am
  sure the smoak
Cost treble the price of the whole week's
  provision
Spent in your majesty's kitchens.
  Ladis. How I scorn
Thy gross comparison ! When my Honoria,
The amazement of the present time, and envy
Of all succeeding ages, does descend
To sanctify a place, and in her presence
Makes it a temple to me, can I be
Too curious, much less prodigal to receive
  her ?
But that the splendour of her beams of beauty
Hath struck thee blind—
  Eubu. As dotage hath done you.
  Ladis. Dotage ? O blasphemy ! is it in me
To serve her to her merit ? Is she not
The daughter of a king?
  Eubu. And you the son
Of ours, I take it ; by what privilege else,
Do you reign over us? for my part, I know not
Where the disparity lies.
  Ladis. Her birth, old man,
Old in the kingdom's service, which protects
  thee,
Is the least grace in her : and though her
  beauties
Might make the Thunderer a rival for her,
They are but superficial ornaments,
And faintly speak her : from her heavenly
  mind,
Were all antiquity and fiction lost,
Our modern poets could not, in their fancy,
But fashion a Minerva far transcending
The imagined one whom Homer only dreamt
  of.
But then add this, she's mine, mine, Eubŭlus !
And though she knows one glance from her
  fair eyes
Must make all gazers her idolaters,
She is so sparing of their influence
That, to shun superstition in others,
She shoots her powerful beams only at me.
And can I, then, whom she desires to hold
Her kingly captive above all the world,
Whose nations and empires, if she pleased,

She might command as slaves, but gladly pay
The humble tribute of my love and service,
Nay, if I said of adoration, to her,
I did not err ?
  Eubu. Well, since you hug your fetters,
In Love's name wear them ! You are a king,
  and that
Concludes you wise : your will a powerful
  reason,
Which we, that are foolish subjects, must
  not argue.
And what in a mean man I should call folly,
Is in your majesty remarkable wisdom :
But for me, I subscribe.
  Ladis. Do, and look up,
Upon this wonder.

Loud music. Enter Honoria *in state, under
    a Canopy; her train borne up by* Sylvia
    and Acanthe.

  Ric. Wonder ! It is more, sir.
  Ubald. A rapture, an astonishment.
  Ric. What think you, sir?
  Eubu. As the king thinks ; that is the
    surest guard
We courtiers ever lie at.—Was prince ever
So drown'd in dotage? Without spectacles
I can see a handsome woman, and she is so :
But yet to admiration look not on her.
Heaven, how he fawns ! and, as it were his
  duty,
With what assured gravity she receives it !
Her hand again ! O she at length vouchsafes
Her lip, and as he had sucked nectar from it,
How he's exalted ! Women in their natures
Affect command ; but this humility
In a husband and a king, marks her the way
To absolute tyranny.
        [*The king seats her on his throne.*
            So ! Juno's placed
In Jove's tribunal : and, like Mercury,
(Forgetting his own greatness,) he attends
For her employments. She prepares to
  speak ;
What oracles shall we hear now?   [*Aside.*
  Hon. That you please, sir,
With such assurances of love and favour,
To grace your handmaid, but in being
  yours, sir,
A matchless queen, and one that knows
  herself so,
Binds me in retribution to deserve
The grace conferr'd upon me.
  Ladis. You transcend
In all things excellent : and it is my glory,
Your worth weigh'd truly, to depose myself
From absolute command, surrendering up
My will and faculties to your disposure :
And here I vow, not for a day or year,

But my whole life, which I wish long, to serve you,
That whatsoever I, in justice, may
Exact from these my subjects, you from me
May boldly challenge : and when you require it,
In sign of my subjection, as your vassal,
Thus I will pay my homage.
Hon. O forbear, sir !
Let 'not my lips envy my robe ; on them
Frint your allegiance often : I desire
No other fealty.
Ladis. Gracious sovereign !
Boundless in bounty !
Eubu. Is not here fine fooling !
He's questionless, bewitch'd. Would I were gelt,
So that would disenchant him ! though I forfeit
My life for't, I must speak.—By your good leave, sir— [*Passing before the king.*
I have no suit to you, nor can you grant one,
Having no power: you are like me, a subject,
Her more than serene majesty being present.
And I must tell you, 'tis ill manners in you,
Having deposed yourself, to keep your hat on,
And not stand bare, as we do, being no king,
But a fellow-subject with us. Gentlemen-ushers,
It does belong to your place, see it reform'd ;
He has given away his crown, and cannot challenge
The privilege of his bonnet.
Ladis. Do not tempt me.
Eubu. Tempt you ! in what? in following your example ?
If you are angry, question me hereafter,
As Ladislaus should do Eubulus,
On equal terms. You were of late my sovereign,
But weary of it, I now bend my knee
To her divinity, and desire a boon
From her more than magnificence.
Hon. Take it freely.
Nay, be not moved ; for our mirth's sake let us hear him.
Eubu. 'Tis but to ask a question : Have you ne'er read
The story of Semiramis and Ninus?
Hon. Not as I remember.
Eubu. I will then instruct you,
And 'tis to the purpose: This Ninus was a king,
And such an impotent loving king as this was,
But now he's none ; this Ninus (pray you observe me)
Doted on this Semiramis, a smith's wife ;
(I must confess, there the comparison holds not,

You are a king's daughter, yet, under your correction,
Like her, a woman ;) this Assyrian monarch,
Of whom this is a pattern, to express
His love and service, seated her, as you are,
In his regal throne, and bound by oath his nobles,
Forgetting all allegiance to himself,
One day to be her subjects, and to put
In execution whatever she
Pleased to impose upon them :—pray you command him
To minister the like to us, and then
You shall hear what follow'd.
Ladis. Well, sir, to your story.
Eubu. You have no warrant, stand by ; let me know
Your pleasure, goddess.
Hon. Let this nod assure you.
Eubu. Goddess-like, indeed ! as I live, a pretty idol !
She knowing her power, wisely made use of it ;
And fearing his inconstancy, and repentance
Of what he had granted, (as, in reason, madam,
You may do his,) that he might never have
Power to recall his grant, or question her
For her short government, instantly gave order
To have his head struck off.
Ladis. Is't possible ?
Eubu. The story says so, and commends her wisdom
For making use of her authority.
And it is worth your imitation, madam :
He loves subjection, and you are no queen,
Unless you make him feel the weight of it.
You are more than all the world to him,
and that
He may be so to you, and not seek change,
When his delights are sated, mew him up
In some close prison, (if you let him live,
Which is no policy,) and there diet him
As you think fit, to feed your appetite ;
Since there ends his ambition.
Ubald. Devilish counsel !
Ric. The king's amazed.
Ubald. The queen appears, too, full
Of deep imaginations ; Eubulus
Hath put both to it.
Ric. Now she seems resolved :
I long to know the issue.
 [*Honoria descends from the throne.*
Hon. Give me leave,
Dear sir, to reprehend you for appearing
Perplex'd with what this old man, out of envy
Of your unequal graces shower'd upon me,
Hath, in his fabulous story, saucily
Applied to me.   Sir, that you only nourish
U

One doubt Honoria dares abuse the power
With which she is invested by your favour ;
Or that she ever can make use of it
To the injury of you, the great bestower,
Takes from your judgment. It was your
  delight
To seek to me with more obsequiousness
Than I desired : and stood it with my duty
Not to receive what you were pleased to
  offer?
I do but act the part you put upon me,
And though you make me personate a queen,
And you my subject, when the play, your
  pleasure,
Is at a period, I am what I was
Before I enter'd, still your humble wife,
And you my royal sovereign.
  Ric. Admirable !
  Hon. I have heard of captains taken more
  with dangers
Than the rewards ; and if, in your approaches
To those delights which are your own, and
  freely,
To heighten your desire, you make the pas-
  sage
Narrow and difficult, shall I prescribe you,
Or blame your fondness? or can that swell
  me
Beyond my just proportion ?
  Ubald. Above wonder !
  Ladis. Heaven make me thankful for such
  goodness !
  Hon. Now, sir,
The state I took to satisfy your pleasure,
I change to this humility ; and the oath
You made to me of homage, I thus cancel,
And seat you in your own.
          [*Leads the king to the throne.*
  Ladis. I am transported
Beyond myself.
  Hon. And now, to your wise lordship :
Am I proved a Semiramis? or hath
My Ninus, as maliciously you made him,
Cause to repent the excess of favour to me,
Which you call dotage?
  Ladis. Answer, wretch !
  Eubu. I dare, sir,
And say, however the event may plead
In your defence, you had a guilty cause ;
Nor was it wisdom in you, I repeat it,
To teach a lady, humble in herself,
With the ridiculous dotage of a lover,
To be ambitious.
  Hon. Eubulus, I am so ;
'Tis rooted in me ; you mistake my temper.
I do profess myself to be the most
Ambitious of my sex, but not to hold
Command over my lord ; such a proud torrent
Would sink me in my wishes : not that I

Am ignorant how much I can deserve,
And may with justice challenge.
  Eubu. This I look'd for ;
After this seeming humble ebb, I knew
A gushing tide would follow.   [*Aside.*
  Hon. By my birth,
And liberal gifts of nature, as of fortune,
From you, as things beneath me, I expect
What's due to majesty, in which I am
A sharer with your sovereign.
  Eubu. Good again !
  Hon. And as I am most eminent in place,
In all my actions I would appear so.
  Ladis. You need not fear a rival.
  Hon. I hope not ;
And till I find one, I disdain to know
What envy is.
  Ladis. You are above it, madam.
  Hon. For beauty without art, discourse,
  and free
From affectation, with what graces else
Can in the wife and daughter of a king
Be wish'd, I dare prefer myself, as——
  Eubu. I
Blush for you, lady.   Trumpet your own
  praises !
This spoken by the people had been heard
With honour to you. Does the court afford
No oil-tongued parasite, that you are forced
To be your own gross flatterer ?
  Ladis. Be dumb,
Thou spirit of contradiction !
  Hon. The wolf ,
But barks against the moon, and I contemn it.
The mask you promised.
          [*A horn sounded within.*
  Ladis. Let them enter.

            Enter a Courier.

                  How !
  Eubu. Here's one, I fear, unlook'd for.
  Ladis. From the camp?
  Cour. The general, victorious in your
  fortune,
Kisses your hand in this, sir.
                  [*Delivers a letter.*
  Ladis. That great Power,
Who at his pleasure does dispose of battles,
Be ever praised for't ! Read, sweet, and
  partake it :
The Turk is vanquish'd, and with little loss
Upon our part, in which our joy is doubled.
  Eubu. But let it not exalt you ; bear it, sir,
With moderation, and pay what you owe
  for't.
  Ladis. I understand thee, Eubulus.   I'll
  not now
Enquire particulars.—[*Exit* Courier.]—Our
  delights deferr'd,

With reverence to the temples ; there we'll
    tender
Our souls' devotions to his dread might,
Who edged our swords, and taught us how
    to fight.   [*Exeunt.*

ACT II.

SCENE I.—Bohemia. *A Hall in* Mathias'
    House.

Enter Hilario *and* Corisca.

Hil. You like my speech ?
Coris. Yes, if you give it action
In the delivery.
Hil. If 1 I pity you.
I have play'd the fool before ; this is not the
    first time,
Nor shall be, I hope, the last.
Coris. Nay, I think so too.
Hil. And if I put her not out of her
    dumps with laughter,
I'll make her howl for anger.
Coris. Not too much
Of that, good fellow Hilario : our sad lady
Hath drank too often of that bitter cup ;
A pleasant one must restore her. With what
    patience
Would she endure to hear of the death of
    my lord ;
That, merely out of doubt he may miscarry,
Afflicts herself thus ?
Hil. Umph ! 'tis a question
A widow only can resolve. There be some
That in their husband's sicknesses have wept
Their pottle of tears a day ; but being once
    certain
At midnight he was dead, have in the morning
Dried up their handkerchiefs, and thought no
    more on't.
Coris. Tush, she is none of that race ; if
    her sorrow
Be not true and perfect, I, against my sex,
Will take my oath woman ne'er wept in
    earnest.
She has made herself a prisoner to her
    chamber,
Dark as a dungeon, in which no beam
Of comfort enters. She admits no visits ;
Eats little, and her nightly music is
Of sighs and groans, tuned to such harmony
Of feeling grief, that I, against my nature,
Am made one of the consort. This hour only
She takes the air, a custom every day
She solemnly observes, with greedy hopes,
From some that pass by, to receive assurance
Of the success and safety of her lord.
Now, if that your device will take——
Hil. Ne'er fear it :

I am provided cap-à-pié, and have
My properties in readiness.
Soph. [*within.*] Bring my veil, there.
Coris. Begone, I hear her coming.
Hil. If I do not
Appear, and, what's more, appear perfect,
    hiss me.   [*Exit.*

Enter Sophia.

Soph. I was flatter'd once, I was a star,
    but now
Turn'd a prodigious meteor, and, like one,
Hang in the air between my hopes and fears ;
And every hour, the little stuff burnt out
That yields a waning light to dying comfort,
I do expect my fall, and certain ruin.
In wretched things more wretched is delay ;
And Hope, a parasite to me, being un-
    mask'd,
Appears more horrid than Despair, and my
Distraction worse than madness. Even my
    prayers,
When with most zeal sent upward, are pull'd
    down
With strong imaginary doubts and fears,
And in their sudden precipice o'erwhelm me.
Dreams and fantastic visions walk the round
About my widow'd bed, and every slumber's
Broken with loud alarms : can these be then
But sad presages, girl ?
Coris. You make them so,
And antedate a loss shall ne'er fall on you.
Such pure affection, such mutual love,
A bed, and undefiled on either part,
A house without contention, in two bodies
One will and soul, like to the rod of concord,
Kissing each other, cannot be short-lived,
Or end in barrenness.—If all these, dear
    madam,
(Sweet in your sadness,) should produce no
    fruit,
Or leave the age no models of yourselves,
To witness to posterity what you were ;
Succeeding times, frighted with the example,
But hearing of your story, would instruct
Their faires issue to meet sensually,
Like other creatures, and forbear to raise
True Love, or Hymen, altars.
Soph. O Corisca,
I know thy reasons are like to thy wishes ;
And they are built upon a weak foundation,
To raise me comfort. Ten long days are past,
Ten long days, my Corisca, since my lord
Embark'd himself upon a sea of danger,
In his dear care of me. And if his life
Had not been shipwreck'd on the rock of
    war,
His tenderness of me (knowing how much
I languish for his absence) had provided

Some trusty friend, from whom I might
  receive
Assurance of his safety.
  Coris. Ill news, madam,
Are swallow-wing'd, but what's good walks
  on crutches :
With patience expect it, and, ere long,
No doubt you shall hear from him.
               [A horn without.
  Soph. Ha ! What's that?
  Coris. The fool has got a sowgelder's
  horn. *[Aside.]* A post,
As I take it, madam.
  Soph. It makes this way still ;
Nearer and nearer.
  Coris. From the camp, I hope.

Enter one disguised as a Courier, *with a
  horn ; followed by* Hilario, *in antic
  armour, with long white hair and beard.*

  Soph. The messenger appears, and in
  strange armour.
Heaven ! if it be thy will——
  Hil. It is no boot
To strive ; our horses tired, let's walk on
  foot :
And that the castle, which is very near us,
To give us entertainment, may soon hear us,
Blow lustily, my lad, and drawing nigh-a,
Ask for a lady which is cleped Sophia.
  Coris. He names you, madam.
  Hil. For to her I bring,
Thus clad in arms, news of a pretty thing,
By name Mathias.   *[Exit* Courier.
  Soph. From my lord? O sir,
I am Sophia, that Mathias' wife.
So may Mars favour you in all your battles,
As you with speed unload me of the burthen
I labour under, till I am confirm'd
Both where and how you left him !
  Hil. If thou art,
As I believe, the pigsney of his heart,
Know he's in health, and what's more, full
  of glee ;
And so much I was will'd to say to thee.
  Soph. Have you no letters from him ?
  Hil. No more words.
In the camp we use no pens, but write with
  swords :
Yet, as I am enjoin'd, by word of mouth
I will proclaim his deeds from north to south;
But tremble not, while I relate the wonder,
Though my eyes like lightning shine, and my
  voice thunder.
  Soph. This is some counterfeit braggart.
  Coris. Hear him, madam.
  Hil. The rear march'd first, which fol-
  low'd by the van,
And wing'd with the battalia, no man

Durst stay to shift a shirt, or louse himself ;
Yet, ere the armies join'd, that hopeful elf,
Thy dear, thy dainty duckling, bold Mathias,
Advanced, and stared like Hercules or
  Golias.
A hundred thousand Turks, it is no vaunt,
Assail'd him ; every one a Termagaunt :
But what did he, then ! with his keen-edge
  spear
He cut and carbonaded them : here and
  there
Lay legs and arms ; and, as 'tis said trulee
Of Bevis, some he quarter'd all in three.
  Soph. This is ridiculous.
  Hil. I must take breath ;
Then, like a nightingale, I'll sing his death.
  Soph. His death !
  Hil. I am out.   *[Aside to* Coris.
  Coris. Recover, dunder-head.
  Hil. How he escaped, I should have
  sung, not died ;
For, though a knight, when I said so, I lied.
Weary he was, and scarce could stand up-
  right,
And looking round for some courageous
  knight
To rescue him, as one perplex'd in woe,
He call'd to me, Help, help, Hilario !
My valiant servant, help !
  Coris. He has spoil'd all.
  Soph. Are you the man of arms, then ?
  I'll make bold
To take off your martial beard, you had
  fool's hair
Enough without it. Slave ! how durst thou
  make
Thy sport of what concerns me more than
  life,
In such an antic fashion? Am I grown
Contemptible to those I feed? you, minion,
Had a hand in it too, as it appears ;
Your petticoat serves for bases to this
  warrior.
  Coris. We did it for your mirth.
  Hil. For myself, I hope,
I have spoke like a soldier.
  Soph. Hence, you rascal !
I never but with reverence name my lord,
And can I hear it by thy tongue profaned,
And not correct thy folly? but you are
Transform'd, and turu'd knight-errant ;
  take your course,
And wander where you please; for here I vow
By my lord's life, (an oath I will not break,)
Till his return, or certainty of his safety,
My doors are shut against thee.   *[Exit.*
  Coris. You have made
A fine piece of work on't ! How do you like
  the quality ?

You had a foolish itch to be an actor,
And may stroll where you please.
   Hil. Will you buy my share?
   Coris. No, certainly; I fear I have already
Too much of mine own: I'll only, as a
   damsel,
(As the books say,) thus far help to disarm
   you;
And so, dear Don Quixote, taking my leave,
I leave you to your fortune.   [*Exit.*
   Hil. Have I sweat
My brains out for this quaint and rare in-
   vention,
And am I thus rewarded? I could turn
Tragedian, and roar now, but that I fear
'Twould get me too great a stomach, having
   no meat
To pacify colon: What will become of me?
I cannot beg in armour, and steal I dare not:
My end must be to stand in a corn field,
And fright away the crows, for bread and
   cheese;
Or find some hollow tree in the highway,
And there, until my lord return, sell switches:
No more Hilario, but Dolorio now,
I'll weep my eyes out, and be blind of purpose
To move compassion; and so I vanish.
   [*Exit.*

SCENE II.—*Alba Regalis. An ante-room
   in the Palace.*

Enter Eubulus, Ubaldo, Ricardo, *and
   others.*

   Eubu. Are the gentlemen sent before, as
it was order'd
By the king's direction, to entertain
The general?
   Ric. Long since; they by this have met
   him,
And given him the bienvenu.
   Eubu. I hope I need not
Instruct you in your parts.
   Ubald. How! us, my lord!
Fear not; we know our distances and degrees
To the very inch where we are to salute him.
   Ric. The state were miserable, if the
   court had none
Of her own breed, familiar with all garbs
Gracious in England, Italy, Spain, or France;
With form and punctuality to receive
Stranger ambassadors: for the general,
He's a mere native, and it matters not
Which way we do accost him.
   Ubald. 'Tis great pity
That such as sit at the helm provide no
   better
For the training up of the gentry. In my
   judgment
An academy erected, with large pensions

To such as in a table could set down
The congees, cringes, postures, methods,
   phrase,
Proper to every nation——
   Ric. O, it were
An admirable piece of work!
   Ubald. And yet rich fools
Throw away their charity on hospitals
For beggars and lame soldiers, and ne'er
   study
The due regard to compliment and courtship,
Matters of more import; and are indeed
The glories of a monarchy!
   Eubu. These, no doubt,
Are state points, gallants, I confess; but, sure,
Our court needs no aids this way, since it is
A school of nothing else. There are some
   of you
Whom I forbear to name, whose coining
   heads
Are the mints of all new fashions, that have
   done
More hurt to the kingdom by superfluous
   bravery,
Which the foolish gentry imitate, than a war,
Or a long famine; all the treasure, by
This foul excess, is got into the merchant,
Embroiderer, silkman, jeweller, tailor's hand,
And the third part of the land too, the
   nobility
Engrossing titles only.
   Ric. My lord, you are bitter.
   [*A trumpet.*

Enter a Servant.

   Serv. The general is alighted, and now
enter'd.
   Ric. Were he ten generals, I am prepared,
And know what I will do.
   Eubu. Pray you what, Ricardo?
   Ric. I'll fight at compliment with him.
   Ubald. I'll charge home too.
   Eubu. And that's a desperate service; if
you come off well.

Enter Ferdinand, Mathias, Baptista, *and*
   Captains.

   Ferd. Captain, command the officers to
keep
The soldier, as he march'd, in rank and file,
Till they hear further from me.
   [*Exeunt* Captains.
   Eubu. Here's one speaks
In another key; this is no canting language
Taught in your academy.
   Ferd. Nay, I will present you
To the king myself.
   Math. A grace beyond my merit.

Ferd. You undervalue what I cannot set
Too high a price on.
Eubu. With a friend's true heart,
I gratulate your return.
Ferd. Next to the favour
Of the great king, I am happy in your
    friendship.
Ubald. By courtship, coarse on both sides!
Ferd. Pray you, receive
This stranger to your knowledge ; on my
    credit,
At all parts he deserves it.
Eubu. Your report
Is a strong assurance to me.—Sir, most
    welcome.
Math. This said by you, the reverence of
    your age
Commands me to believe it.
Ric. This was pretty ;
But second me now.——I cannot stoop too
    low
To do your excellence that due observance
Your fortune claims.
Eubu. He ne'er thinks on his virtue !
Ric. For being, as you are, the soul of
    soldiers,
And bulwark of Bellona——
Ubald. The protection
Both of the court and king——
Ric. And the sole minion
Of mighty Mars—
Ubald. One that with justice may
Increase the number of the worthies——
Eubu. Heyday !
Ric. It being impossible in my arms to
    circle
Such giant worth——
Ubald. At distance we presume
To kiss your honour'd gauntlet.
Eubu. What reply now
Can he make to this foppery ?
Ferd. You have said,
Gallants, so much, and hitherto done so little,
That, till I learn to speak, and you to do,
I must take time to thank you.
Eubu. As I live,
Answer'd as I could wish. How the fops
    gape now !
Ric. This was harsh and scurvy.
Ubald. We will be revenged
When he comes to court the ladies, and
    laugh at him.
Eubu. Nay, do your offices gentlemen,
    and conduct
The general to the presence.
Ric. Keep your order.
Ubald. Make way for the general.
                    [*Exeunt all but* Eubulus.
Eubu. What wise man,

That, with judicious eyes, looks on a soldier,
But must confess that fortune's swing is more
O'er that profession, than all kinds else
Of life pursued by man ? They, in a state,
Are but as surgeons to wounded men,
E'en desperate in their hopes : While pain
    and anguish
Make them blaspheme, and call in vain for
    death,
Their wives and children kiss the surgeon's
    knees,
Promise him mountains, if his saving hand
Restore the tortured wretch to former
    strength :
But when grim death, by Æsculapius' art,
Is frighted from the house, and health appears
In sanguine colours on the sick man's face,
All is forgot ; and, asking his reward,
He's paid with curses, often receives wounds
From him whose wounds he cured: so
    soldiers,
Though of more worth and use, meet the
    same fate,
As it is too apparent. I have observ'd,
When horrid Mars, the touch of whose rough
    hand
With palsies shakes a kingdom, hath put on
His dreadful helmet, and with terror fills
The place where he, like an unwelcome guest,
Resolves to revel, how the lords of her, like
The tradesman, merchant, and litigious
    pleader,
And such like scarabs bred in the dung of
    peace,
In hope of their protection, humbly offer
Their daughters to their beds, heirs to their
    service,
And wash with tears their sweat, their dust,
    their scars :
But when those clouds of war, that menaced
A bloody deluge to the affrighted state,
Are, by their breath, dispersed, and over-
    blown,
And famine, blood, and death, Bellona's
    pages,
Whipt from the quiet continent to Thrace ;
Soldiers, that, like the foolish hedge-sparrow,
To their own ruin, hatch this cuckoo, peace,
Are straight thought burthensome ; since
    want of means,
Growing from want of action, breeds con-
    tempt :
And that, the worst of ills, falls to their lot,
Their service, with the danger, soon forgot.

Enter a Servant.

Serv. The queen, my lord, hath made
    choice of this room,
To see the masque.

Eubu. I'll be a looker on :
My dancing days are past.

Loud music. Enter Ubaldo, Ricardo, Ladislaus, Ferdinand, Honoria, Mathias, Syl-
via, Acanthe, Baptista, Captains, *and
others. As they pass, a Song in praise of
war.*

Ladis. This courtesy
To a stranger, my Honoria, keeps fair rank
With all your rarities. After your travail,
Look on our court delights ; but first, from
   your
Relation, with erected ears, I'll hear
The music of your war, which must be sweet,
Ending in victory.

Ferd. Not to trouble
Your majesties with description of a battle
Too full of horror for the place, and to
Avoid particulars, which should I deliver,
I must trench longer on your patience, than
My manners will give way to ;—in a word, sir,
It was well fought on both sides, and almost
With equal fortune, it continuing doubtful
Upon whose tents plumed Victory would take
Her glorious stand. Impatient of delay,
With the flower of our prime gentlemen, I
   charged
Their main battalia, and with their assistance
Brake in ; but, when I was almost assured
That they were routed, by a stratagem
Of the subtile Turk, who opened his gross
   body,
And rallied up his troops on either side,
I found myself so far engaged, for I
Must not conceal my errors, that I knew not
Which way with honour to come off.

Eubu. I like
A general that tells his faults, and is not
Ambitious to engross unto himself
All honour, as some have, in which, with
   justice,
They could not claim a share.

Ferd. Being thus hemm'd in,
Their scimitars raged among us ; and, my
   horse
Kill'd under me, I every minute looked for
An honourable end, and that was all
My hope could fashion to me : circled thus
With death and horror, as one sent from
   heaven,
This man of men, with some choice horse,
   that follow'd
His brave example, did pursue the track
His sword cut for them, and, but that I see
   him
Already blush to hear what he, being present,
I know would wish unspoken, I should say,
   sir,

By what he did, we boldly may believe
All that is writ of Hector.

Math. General,
Pray spare these strange hyperboles.

Eubu. Do not blush
To hear a truth ; here are a pair of monsieurs,
Had they been in your place, would have run
   away,
And ne'er changed countenance.

Ubald. We have your good word still.

Eubu. And shall, while you deserve it.

Ladis. Silence ; on.

Ferd. He, as I said, like dreadful lightning
   thrown
From Jupiter's shield, dispersed the armed
   gire
With which I was environed ; horse and man
Shrunk under his strong arm : more, with
   his looks
Frighted, the valiant fled, with which en-
   couraged,
My soldiers, (like young eaglets preying under
The wings of their fierce dam,) as if from him
They took both spirit and fire, bravely came
   on.
By him I was remounted, and inspired
With treble courage ; and such as fled before
Boldly made head again ; and, to confirm
   them,
It suddenly was apparent, that the fortune
Of the day was ours ; each soldier and com-
   mander
Perform'd his part ; but this was the great
   wheel
By which the lesser moved : and all rewards.
And signs of honour, as the civic garland,
The mural wreath, the enemy's prime horse,
With the general's sword, and armour, (the
   old honours
With which the Romans crown'd their several
   leaders,)
To him alone are proper.

Ladis. And they shall
Deservedly fall on him. Sit ; 'tis our pleasure.

Ferd. Which I must serve, not argue.

Hon. You are a stranger,
But, in your service for the king, a native.
And, though a free queen, I am bound in duty
To cherish virtue wheresoe'er I find it :
This place is yours.

Math. It were presumption in me
To sit so near you.

Hon. Not, having our warrant.
   [*Music within.*

Ladis. Let the masquers enter : by the
   preparation,
'Tis a French brawl, an apish imitation
Of what you really perform in battle :

And Pallas, bound up in a little volume,
Apollo, with his lute, attending on her,
Serve for the induction.

Enter Masquers, *&c.:* Pallas, *accompanied
by* Apollo *on the lute.*

*Though we contemplate to express
    The glory of your happiness,
That, by your powerful arm, have been
    So true a victor, that no sin
Could ever taint you with a blame
    To lessen your deserved fame.*

*Or, though we contend to set
    Your worth in the full height, or get
Celestial singers crown'd with bays,
    With flourishes to dress your praise :
You know your conquest ; but your story
    Lives in your triumphant glory.*
                              [*A Dance.*

Ladis. Our thanks to all.
To the banquet that's prepared to entertain
    them :
            [*Exeunt* Masquers, Apollo, *and* Pallas.
What would my best Honoria?
Hon. May it please
My king, that I, who, by his suffrage, ever
Have had power to command, may now
    entreat
An honour from him.
Ladis. Why should you desire
What is your own? whate'er it be, you are
The mistress of it.
Hon. I am happy in
Your grant : my suit, sir, is, that your com-
    manders,
Especially this stranger, may, as I,
In my discretion, shall think good, receive
What's due to their deserts.
Ladis. What you determine
Shall know no alteration.
Eubu. The soldier
Is like to have good usage, when he depends
Upon her pleasure ! Are all the men so bad,
That, to give satisfaction, we must have
A woman treasurer ? Heaven help all !
Hon. With you, sir,   [*To* Mathias.
I will begin, and, as in my esteem
You are most eminent, expect to have
What's fit for me to give, and you to take.
The favour in the quick dispatch being
    double,
Go fetch my casket, and with speed.
                              [*Exit* Acanthe.
Eubu. The kingdom
Is very bare of money, when rewards
Issue from the queen's jewel-house. Give
    him gold
And store, no question the gentleman wants it.

Good madam, what shall he do with a hoop
    ring,
And a spark of diamond in it? though you
    take it,

        Re-enter Acanthe *with a Casket.*

For the greater honour, from your majesty's
    finger,
'Twill not increase the value.   He must
    purchase
Rich suits, the gay caparison of courtship,
Revel and feast, which, the war ended, is
A soldier's glory ; and 'tis fit that way
Your bounty should provide for him.
Hon. You are rude,
And by your narrow thoughts proportion
    mine.
What I will do now shall be worth the envy
Of Cleopatra.   Open it ; see here
              [Honoria *descends from the state.*
The lapidary's idol !   Gold is trash,
And a poor salary fit for grooms ; wear these,
As studded stars in your armour, and make
    the sun
Look dim with jealousy of a greater light
Than his beams gild the day with : when it is
Exposed to view, call it Honoria's gift,
The queen Honoria's gift, that loves a soldier ;
And, to give ornament and lustre to him,
Parts freely with her own !   Yet, not to take
From the magnificence of the king, I will
Dispense his bounty too, but as a page
To wait on mine ; for other tosses, take
A hundred thousand crowns :—your hand,
    dear sir——— [*Takes off the king's signet.*
And this shall be thy warrant.
Eubu. I perceive
I was cheated in this woman : now she is
In the giving vein to soldiers, let her be proud,
And the king dote, so she go on, I care not.
Hon. This done, our pleasure is, that all
    arrearages
Be paid unto the captains, and their troops ;
With a large donative, to increase their zeal
For the service of the kingdom.
Eubu. Better still :
Let men of arms be used thus, if they do not
Charge desperately upon the cannon's mouth,
Though the devil roar'd, and fight like
    dragons, hang me !
Now they may drink sack : but small beer,
    with a passport
To beg with as they travel, and no money,
Turns their red blood to buttermilk.
Hon. Are you pleased, sir,
With what I have done ?
Ladis. Yes, and thus confirm it,
With this addition of mine own : You have,
    sir,

From our loved queen received some recompense
For your life hazarded in the late action ;
And, that we may follow her great example
In cherishing valour, without limit ask
What you from us can wish.
  Math. If it be true,
Dread sir, as 'tis affirm'd, that every soil,
Where he is well, is to a valiant man
His natural country, reason may assure me
I should fix here, where blessings beyond
   hope,
From you, the spring, like rivers, flow unto
  me.
If wealth were my ambition, by the queen
I am made rich already, to the amazement
Of all that see, or shall hereafter read
The story of her bounty ; if to spend
The remnant of my life in deeds of arms,
No region is more fertile of good knights,
From whom my knowledge that way may be
  better'd,
Than this your warlike Hungary ; if favour,
Or grace in court could take me, by your
  grant,
Far, far, beyond my merit, I may make
In yours a free election ; but, alas ! sir,
I am not mine own, but by my destiny
(Which I cannot resist) forced to prefer
My country's smoke, before the glorious fire
With which your bounties warm me. All I
  ask, sir,
Though I cannot be ignorant it must relish
Of foul ingratitude, is your gracious license
For my departure.
  Ladis. Whither ?
  Math. To my own home, sir,
My own poor home ; which will, at my return,
Grow rich by your magnificence. I am here
But a body without a soul ; and, till I find it
In the embraces of my constant wife,
And, to set off that constancy, in her beauty
And matchless excellences, without a rival,
I am but half myself.
  Hon. And is she then
So chaste and fair as you infer ?
  Math. O, madam,
Though it must argue weakness in a rich man,
To shew his gold before an armed thief,
And I, in praising of my wife, but feed
The fire of lust in others to attempt her ;
Such is my full-sail'd confidence in her virtue,
Though in my absence she were now besieged
By a strong army of lascivious wooers,
And every one more expert in his art,
Than those that tempted chaste Penelope ;
Though they raised batteries by prodigal
  gifts,

By amorous letters, vows made for her service,
With all the engines wanton appetite
Could mount to shake the fortress of her
  honour,
Here, here is my assurance she holds out,
And is impregnable.   [*Kisses the picture.*
  Hon. What's that ?
  Math. Her fair figure.
  Ladis. As I live, an excellent face !
  Hon. You have seen a better.
  Ladis. I ever except yours :—nay, frown
  not, sweetest,
The Cyprian queen, compared to you, in my
Opinion, is a negro. As you order'd,
I'll see the soldiers paid ; and, in my absence,
Pray you use your powerful arguments, to
  stay
This gentleman in our service.
  Hon. I will do
My parts.
  Ladis. On to the camp.
    [*Exeunt* Ladislaus, Ferdinand, Eubulus, Baptista, *and* Officers.
  Hon. I am full of thoughts,
And something there is here I must give
  form to,
Though yet an embryon : [*Aside.*] You,
  signiors,
Have no business with the soldier, as I
  take it,
You are for other warfare; quit the place,
But be within call.
  Ric. Employment, on my life, boy !
  Ubald. If it lie in our road, we are made
  for ever.
    [*Exeunt* Ubaldo *and* Ricardo.
  Hon. You may perceive the king is no
  way tainted
With the disease of jealousy, since he leaves
  me
Thus private with you.
  Math. It were in him, madam,
A sin unpardonable to distrust such pureness,
Though I were an Adonis.
  Hon. I presume
He neither does nor dares : and yet the story
Delivered of you by the general,
With your heroic courage, which sinks deeply
Into a knowing woman's heart, besides
Your promising presence, might beget some
  scruple
In a meaner man; but more of this hereafter.
I'll take another theme now, and conjure you
By the honours you have won, and by the
  love
Sacred to your dear wife, to answer truly
To what I shall demand.

Math. You need not use
Charms to this purpose, madam.
Hon. Tell me, then,
Being yourself assured 'tis not in man
To sully with one spot th' immaculate white-
ness
Of your wife's honour, if you have not, since
The Gordian of your love was tied by mar-
riage,
Play'd false with her?
Math. By the hopes of mercy, never.
Hon. It may be, not frequenting the con-
verse
Of handsome ladies, you were never tempted,
And so your faith's untried yet.
Math. Surely, madam,
I am no woman-hater ; I have been
Received to the society of the best
And fairest of our climate, and have met with
No common entertainment, yet ne'er felt
The least heat that way.
Hon. Strange ! and do you think still,
The earth can show no beauty that can drench
In Lethe all remembrance of the favour
You now bear to your own ?
Math. Nature must find out
Some other mould to fashion a new creature
Fairer than her Pandora, ere I prove
Guilty, or in my wishes or my thoughts,
To my Sophia.
Hon. Sir, consider better ;
Not one in our whole sex ?
Math. I am constant to
My resolution.
Hon. But dare you stand
The opposition, and bind yourself
By oath for the performance ?
Math. My faith else
Had but a weak foundation.
Hon. I take hold
Upon your promise, and enjoin your stay
For one month here.
Math. I am caught !   [*Aside.*
Hon. And if I do not
Produce a lady, in that time, that shall
Make you confess your error, I submit
Myself to any penalty you shall please
To impose upon me : in the mean space,
write
To your chaste wife, acquaint her with your
fortune :
The jewels that were mine you may send
to her,
For better confirmation. I'll provide you
Of trusty messengers : but how far distant
is she ?
Math. A day's hard riding.
Hon. There is no retiring ;
I'll bind you to your word.

Math. Well, since there is
No way to shun it, I will stand the hazard,
And instantly make ready my dispatch :
Till then, I'll leave your majesty.   [*Exit.*
Hon. How I burst
With envy, that there lives, besides myself,
One fair and loyal woman ! 'twas the end
Of my ambition to be recorded
The only wonder of the age, and shall I
Give way to a competitor ? Nay more,
To add to my affliction, the assurances
That I placed in my beauty have deceived me :
I thought one amorous glance of mine could
bring
All hearts to my subjection ; but this stranger,
Unmoved as rocks, contemns me. But I.
cannot
Sit down so with mine honour : I will gain
A double victory, by working him
To my desire, and taint her in her honour,
Or lose myself : I have read that sometime
poison
Is useful.—To supplant her, I'll employ,
With any cost, Ubaldo and Ricardo,
Two noted courtiers, of approved cunning
In all the windings of lust's labyrinth ;
And in corrupting him, I will outgo
Nero's Poppæa : if he shut his ears
Against my Syren notes, I'll boldly swear,
Ulysses lives again ; or that I have found
A frozen cynic, cold in spite of all
Allurements ; one whom beauty cannot move,
Nor softest blandishments entice to love.
[*Exit.*

———

ACT III.

SCENE I.—Bohemia. *A Space near the
Entrance of* Mathias' *House.*

Enter Hilario, *with a pitcher of water,
and a wallet.*

Hil. Thin, thin provision ! I am dieted
Like one set to watch hawks ; and, to keep
me waking,
My croaking guts make a perpetual larum.
Here I stand centinel ; and, though I fright
Beggars from my lady's gate, in hope to have
A greater share, I find my commons mend
not.
I look'd this morning in my glass, the river,
And there appear'd a fish call'd a poor John,
Cut with a lenten face, in my own likeness ;
And it seem'd to speak, and say, *Good
morrow, cousin !*
No man comes this way but has a fling at me :
A surgeon passing by, ask'd at what rate
I would sell myself ; I answered, For what
use ?

To make, said he, a living anatomy,
And set thee up in our hall, for thou art
    transparent
Without dissection ; and, indeed, he had
    reason :
For I am scour'd with this poor purge to
    nothing.
They say that hunger dwells in the camp ;
    but till
My lord returns, or certain tidings of him,
He will not part with me :—but sorrow's dry,
And I must drink howsoever.

    Enter Ubaldo, Ricardo, *and a* Guide.

    Guide. That's her castle,
Upon my certain knowledge.
    Ubald. Our horses held out
To my desire. I am afire to be at it.
    Ric. Take the jades for thy reward ;
    before I part hence,
I hope to be better carried. Give me the
    cabinet :
So ; leave us now.
    Guide. Good fortune to you, gallants !
                      [*Exit.*
    Ubald. Being joint agents, in a design of
    trust too,
For the service of the queen, and our own
    pleasure,
Let us proceed with judgment.
    Ric. If I take not
This fort at the first assault, make me an
    eunuch ;
So I may have precedence,
    Ubald. On no terms.
We are both to play one prize ; he that
    works best
In the searching of this mine, shall carry it,
Without contention.
    Ric. Make you your approaches
As I directed.
    Ubald. I need no instruction ;
I work not on your anvil. I'll give fire
With mine own linstock ; if the powder be
    dank,
The devil rend the touch-hole ! Who have
    we here ?
What skeleton's this ?
    Ric. A ghost ! or the image of famine !
Where dost thou dwell ?
    Hil. Dwell, sir ! my dwelling is
In the highway : that goodly house was once
My habitation, but I am banish'd,
And cannot be call'd home till news arrive
Of the good knight Mathias.
    Ric. If that will
Restore thee, thou art safe.
    Ubald. We come from him,
With presents to his lady.

    Hil. But are you sure
He is in health ?
    Ric. Never so well : conduct us
To the lady.
    Hil. Though a poor snake, I will leap
Out of my skin for joy. Break, pitcher,
    break !
And wallet, late my cupboard, I bequeath thee
To the next beggar ; thou, red herring, swim
To the Red Sea again : methinks I am already
Knuckle deep in the fleshpots ; and, though
    waking, dream
Of wine and plenty !
    Ric. What's the mystery
Of this strange passion ?
    Hil. My belly, gentlemen,
Will not give me leave to tell you ; when I
    have brought you
To my lady's presence, I am disenchanted :
There you shall know all. Follow ; if I
    outstrip you,
Know I run for my belly.
    Ubald. A mad fellow.   [*Exeunt.*

SCENE II.—*A Room in* Mathias' *House.*

    Enter Sophia *and* Corisca.

    Soph. Do not again delude me.
    Coris. If I do,
Send me a grazing with my fellow, Hilario.
I stood as you commanded, in the turret,
Observing all that pass'd by ; and even now,
I did discern a pair of cavaliers,
For such their outside spoke them, with
    their guide,
Dismounting from their horses ; they said
    something
To our hungry centinel, that made him caper
And frisk in the air for joy : and, to confirm
    this,
See, madam, they're in view.

    Enter Hilario, Ubaldo, *and* Ricardo.

    Hil. News from my lord !
Tidings of joy ! these are no counterfeits,
But knights indeed. Dear madam, sign my
    pardon,
That I may feed again, and pick up my
    crumbs ;
I have had a long fast of it.
    Soph. Eat, I forgive thee.
    Hil. O comfortable words ! *Eat, I forgive*
    thee !
And if in this I do not soon obey you,
And ram in to the purpose, billet me again
In the highway. Butler and cook, be ready,.
For I enter like a tyrant.   [*Exit.*
    Ubald. Since mine eyes
Were never happy in so sweet an object,

Without inquiry, I presume you are
The lady of the house, and so salute you.
  Ric. This letter, with these jewels, from
your lord,
Warrant my boldness, madam.
            [*Delivers a letter and a casket.*
  Ubald. In being a servant
To such rare beauty, you must needs deserve
This courtesy from a stranger.
              [*Salutes* Corisca.
  Ric. You are still
Beforehand with me. Pretty one, I descend
To take the height of your lip ; and, if I miss
In the altitude, hereafter, if you please,
I will make use of my Jacob's staff.
              [*Salutes* Corisca.
  Coris. These gentlemen
Have certainly had good breeding, as it ap-
pears
By their neat kissing, they hit me so pat on
the lips,
At the first sight.
      [*In the interim,* Sophia *reads the letter,*
        and opens the casket.
  Soph. Heaven, in thy mercy, make me
Thy thankful handmaid for this boundless
blessing,
In thy goodness shower'd upon me !
  Ubald. I do not like
This simple devotion in her ; it is seldom
Practised among my mistresses.
  Ric. Or mine.
Would they kneel to I know not who, for
the possession
Of such inestimable wealth, before
They thank'd the bringers of it? the poor
lady
Does want instruction, but I'll be her tutor,
And read her another lesson.
  Soph. If I have
Shewn want of manners, gentlemen, in my
slowness
To pay the thanks I owe you for your travail,
To do my lord and me, howe'er unworthy
Of such a benefit, this noble favour,
Impute it, in your clemency, to the excess
Of joy that overwhelm'd me.
  Ric. She speaks well.
  Ubald. Polite and courtly.
  Soph. And howe'er it may
Increase the offence, to trouble you with more
Demands touching my lord, before I have
Invited you to taste such as the coarseness
Of my poor house can offer ; pray you connive
On my weak tenderness, though I entreat
To learn from you something he hath, it
may be,
In his letter left unmention'd.
  Ric. I can only

Give you assurance that he is in health,
Graced by the king and queen.
  Ubald. And in the court
With admiration look'd on.
  Ric. You must therefore
Put off these widow's garments, and appear
Like to yourself.
  Ubald. And entertain all pleasures
Your fortune marks out for you.
  Ric. There are other
Particular privacies, which on occasion
I will deliver to you.
  Soph. You oblige me
To your service ever.
  Ric. Good ! *your service ;* mark that.
  Soph. In the mean time, by your good
acceptance make
My rustic entertainment relish of
The curiousness of the court.
  Ubald. Your looks, sweet madam,
Cannot but make each dish a feast.
  Soph. It shall be
Such, in the freedom of my will to please you.
I'll shew you the way : this is too great an
honour,
From such brave guests, to me so mean an
hostess.   [*Exeunt.*

SCENE III.—*Alba Regalis. An Outer-
room in the Palace.*

Enter Acanthe, *and four or five* Servants
with visors.

  Acan. You know your charge ; give it
action, and expect
Rewards beyond your hopes.
  1 *Serv.* If we but eye them,
They are ours, I warrant you.
  2 *Serv.* May we not ask why
We are put upon this?
  Acan. Let that stop your mouth ;
            [*Gives them money.*
And learn more manners, groom. 'Tis upon
the hour
In which they use to walk here : when you
have them
In your power, with violence carry them to
the place
Where I appointed ; there I will expect you :
Be bold and careful.   [*Exit.*

    Enter Mathias *and* Baptista.

  1 *Serv.* These are they.
  2 *Serv.* Are you sure?
  1 *Serv.* Am I sure I am myself?
  2 *Serv.* Seize on him strongly ; if he have
but means
To draw his sword, 'tis ten to one we smart
for't :
Take all advantages.

Math. I cannot guess
What her intents are ; but her carriage was
As I but now related.
Bapt. Your assurance
In the constancy of your lady is the armour
That must defend you. Where's the picture ?
Math. Here,
And no way alter'd.
Bapt. If she be not perfect,
There is no truth in art.
Math. By this, I hope,
She hath received my letters.
Bapt. Without question :
These courtiers are rank riders, when they are
To visit a handsome lady.
Math. Lend me your ear.
One piece of her entertainment will require
Your dearest privacy.
1 *Serv.* Now they stand fair ;
Upon them. [*They rush forward.*
Math. Villains !
1 *Serv.* Stop their mouths. We come not
To try your valours : kill him, if he offer
To ope his mouth. We have you : 'tis in
vain
To make resistance. Mount them, and away.
[*Exeunt with* Mathias *and* Baptista.

SCENE IV.—*A Gallery in the same.*

Enter Servants with lights, Ladislaus, Ferdinand, *and* Eubulus.

Ladis. 'Tis late. Go to your rest ; but
do not envy
The happiness I draw near to.
Eubu. If you enjoy it
The moderate way, the sport yields, I confess,
A pretty titillation ; but too much of't
Will bring you on your knees. In my
younger days
I was myself a gamester ; and I found
By sad experience, there is no such soaker
As a young spongy wife ; she keeps a thousand
Horse-leeches in her box, and the thieves
will suck out
Both blood and marrow ! I feel a kind of
cramp
In my joints, when I think on't : but it may
be queens,
And such a queen as yours is has the art——
Ferd. You take leave
To talk, my lord.
Ladis. He may, since he can do nothing.
Eubu. If you spend this way too much of
your royal stock,·
Ere long we may be puefellows.
Ladis. The door shut !
Knock gently ; harder. So, here comes her
woman.
Take off my gown.

Enter Acanthe.

Acan. My lord, the queen by me
This night desires your pardon.
Ladis. How, Acanthe !
I come by her appointment ; 'twas her grant ;·
The motion was her own.
Acan. It may be, sir ;
But by her doctors she is since advised,
For her health's sake, to forbear,
Eubu. I do not like
This physical letchery, the old downright
way
Is worth a thousand on't.
Ladis. Prithee, Acanthe,
Mediate for me. [*Offering her a ring.*
Eubu. O the fiends of hell !
Would any man bribe his servant, to make
way
To his own wife ? if this be the court state,·
Shame fall on such as use it !
Acan. By this jewel,
This night I dare not move her, but to·
morrow
I will watch all occasions.
Ladis. Take this,
To be mindful of me.
Eubu. 'Slight, I thought a king
Might have ta'en up any woman at the·
king's price ;
And must he buy his own, at a dearer rate
Than a stranger in a brothel ?
Ladis. What is that
You mutter, sir ?
Eubu. No treason to your honour :
I'll speak it out, though it anger you ; if you·
pay for
Your lawful pleasure in some kind, great sir,
What do you make the queen ? cannot you·
clicket
Without a fee, or when she has a suit
For you to grant ? [Ladis. *draws his sword.·*
Ferd. O hold, sir !
Ladis. Off with his head !
Eubu. Do, when you please ; you but blow·
out a taper
That would light your understanding, and,
in care of 't,
Is burnt down to the socket. Be as you are, sir,
An absolute monarch : it did shew more king-
like
In those libidinous Cæsars, that compell'd
Matrons and virgins of all ranks to bow
Unto their ravenous lusts ; and did admit
Of more excuse than I can urge for you,
That slave yourself to the imperious humour
Of a proud beauty.
Ladis. Out of my sight !
Eubu. I will, sir,

Give way to your furious passion ; but when
    reason
Hath got the better of it, I much hope
The counsel that offends now will deserve
Your royal thanks.   Tranquillity of mind
Stay with you, sir !——I do begin to doubt
There's something more in the queen's
    strangeness than
Is yet disclosed ; and I will find it out,
Or lose myself in the search.
                              [*Aside, and exit.*
    Ferd. Sure he is honest,
And from your infancy hath truly served
    you :
Let that plead for him ; and impute this
    harshness
To the frowardness of his age.
    Ladis. I am much troubled,
And do begin to stagger.   Ferdinand, good
    night !
To-morrow visit us.   Back to our own
    lodgings.   [*Exeunt.*

SCENE V.—*Another Room in the same.*

Enter Acanthe *and the visored* Servants, *with*
    Mathias *and* Baptista *blindfolded.*

    Acan. You have done bravely.   Lock this
    in that room,
There let him ruminate ; I'll anon unhood
    him :   [*They carry off* Baptista.
The other must stay here.   As soon as I
Have quit the place, give him the liberty
And use of his eyes ; that done, disperse
    yourselves
As privately as you can : but, on your lives,
No word of what hath pass'd.   [*Exit.*
    1 *Serv.* If I do, sell
My tongue to a tripe-wife.   Come, unbind
    his arms :
You are now at your own disposure ; and
    however
We used you roughly, I hope you will find
    here
Such entertainment as will give you cause
To thank us for the service : and so I leave
    you.   [*Exeunt* Servants.
    Math. If I am in a prison, 'tis a neat one.
What Œdipus can resolve this riddle ? Ha !
I never gave just cause to any man
Basely to plot against my life :—But what is
Become of my true friend ? for him I suffer
More than myself.
    Acan. [*within.*] Remove that idle fear ;
He's safe as you are.
    Math. Whosoe'er thou art,
For him I thank thee.   I cannot imagine
Where I should be : though I have read the
    tales

Of errant-knighthood, stuff'd with the rela-
    tions
Of magical enchantments ; yet I am not
So sottishly credulous to believe the devil
Hath that way power. [*Music above.*] Ha !
    music ?

The blushing rose, and purple flower,
    Let grow too long, are soonest blasted ;
Dainty fruits, though sweet, will sour,
    And rot in ripeness, left untasted.
Yet here is one more sweet than these :
The more you taste the more she'll please.

Beauty that's enclosed with ice,
    Is a shadow chaste as rare ;
Then how much those sweets entice,
    That have issue full as fair !
Earth cannot yield, from all her powers,
One equal for dame Venus' bowers.

A song too ! certainly, be it he or she
That owes this voice, it hath not been ac-
    quainted
With much affliction.   Whosoe'er you are
That do inhabit here, if you have bodies,
And are not mere aërial forms, appear,

        Enter Honoria *masked.*

And make me know your end with me.
    Most strange !
What have I conjured up ? sure, if this be
A spirit, it is no damn'd one.   What a
    shape's here !
Then, with what majesty it moves ! If Juno
Were now to keep her state among the gods,
And Hercules to be made again her guest,
She could not put on a more glorious habit,
Though her handmaid, Iris, lent her various
    colours,
Or old Oceanus ravish'd from the deep
All jewels shipwreck'd in it.   As you have
Thus far made known yourself, if that your
    face
Have not too much divinity about it
For mortal eyes to gaze on, perfect what
You have begun, with wonder and amaze-
    ment
To my astonish'd senses.
                        [Honoria *unmasks.*
How ! the queen !   [*Kneels.*
    Hon. Rise, sir, and hear my reasons, in
    defence
Of the rape (for so you may conceive) which I,
By my instruments, made upon you.   You,
    perhaps,
May think what you have suffer'd for my
    lust
Is a common practice with me ; but I call
Those ever-shining lamps, and their great
    Maker,

As witnesses of my innocence : I ne'er look'd on
A man but your best self, on whom I ever
(Except the king) vouchsafed an eye of favour.

Math. The king, indeed, and only such a king,
Deserves your rarities, madam ; and, but he,
'Twere giant-like ambition in any,
In his wishes only, to presume to taste
The nectar of your kisses ; or to feed
His appetite with that ambrosia, due
And proper to a prince ; and, what binds more,
A lawful husband. For myself, great queen,
I am a thing obscure, disfurnish'd of
All merit, that can raise me higher than,
In my most humble thankfulness for your bounty,
To hazard my life for you ; and, that way,
I am most ambitious.

Hon. I desire no more
Than what you promise. If you dare expose
Your life, as you profess, to do me service,
How can it be better employ'd than in
Preserving mine ? which only you can do,
And must do, with the danger of your own,
A desperate danger too ! If private men
Can brook no rivals in what they affect,
But to the death pursue such as invade
What law makes their inheritance ; the king,
To whom you know I am dearer than his crown,
His health, his eyes, his after hopes, with all
His present blessings, must fall on that man,
Like dreadful lightning, that is won by prayers,
Threats, or rewards, to stain his bed, or make
His hoped-for issue doubtful !

Math. If you aim
At what I more than fear you do, the reasons
Which you deliver, should, in judgment, rather
Deter me, than invite a grant, with my
Assured ruin.

Hon. True ; if that you were
Of a cold temper, one whom doubt, or fear,
In the most horrid forms they could put on,
Might teach to be ingrateful. Your denial
To me, that have deserved so much, is more,
If it can have addition.

Math. I know not
What your commands are.

Hon. Have you fought so well
Among arm'd men, yet cannot guess what lists
You are to enter, when you are in private
With a willing lady : one, that, to enjoy
Your company this night, denied the king

Access to what's his own ? If you will press me
To speak in plainer language——

Math. Pray you, forbear ;
I would I did not understand too much !
Already, by your words, I am instructed
To credit that, which, not confirm'd by you,
Had bred suspicion in me of untruth,
Though an angel had affirm'd it. But suppose
That, cloy'd with happiness, which is ever built
On virtuous chastity, in the wantonness
Of appetite, you desire to make trial
Of the false delights proposed by vicious lust ;
Among ten thousand, every way more able
And apter to be wrought on, such as owe you
Obedience, being your subjects, why should you
Make choice of me, a stranger ?

Hon. Though yet reason
Was ne'er admitted in the court of love,
I'll yield you one unanswerable. As I urged,
In our last private conference, you have
A pretty promising presence ; but there are
Many, in limbs and feature, who may take,
That way, the right-hand file of you : besides,
Your May of youth is past, and the blood spent
By wounds, though bravely taken, renders you
Disabled for love's service : and that valour
Set off with better fortune, which, it may be,
Swells you above your bounds, is not the hook
That hath caught me, good sir. I need no champion,
With his sword, to guard my honour or my beauty ;
In both I can defend myself, and live
My own protection.

Math. If these advocates,
The best that can plead for me, have no power,
What can you find in me else, that may tempt you,
With irrecoverable loss unto yourself,
To be a gainer from me ?

Hon. You have, sir,
A jewel of such matchless worth and lustre,
As does disdain comparison, and darkens
All that is rare in other men ; and that,
I must or win or lessen.

Math. You heap more
Amazement on me : What am I possess'd of
That you can covet ? make me understand it,
If it have a name.

Hon. Yes, an imagined one ;
But is, in substance, nothing ; being a garment

Worn out of fashion, and long since given o'er
By the court and country : 'tis your loyalty
And constancy to your wife ; 'tis that I dote
    on,
And does deserve my envy ; and that jewel,
Or by fair play or foul, I must win from you.
    Math. These are mere contraries. If you
    love me, madam,
For my constancy, why seek you to destroy
    it ?
In my keeping it preserve me worth your
    favour.
Or, if it be a jewel of that value,
As you with labour'd rhetoric would per-
    suade me,
What can you stake against it ?
    Hon. A queen's fame,
And equal honour.
    Math. So, whoever wins,
Both shall be losers.
    Hon. That is that I aim at :
Yet on the die I lay my youth, my beauty,
This moist palm, this soft lip, and those
    delights
Darkness should only judge of. [*Kisses
    him.*] Do you find them
Infectious in the trial, that you start,
As frighted with their touch ?
    Math. Is it in man
To resist such strong temptations?
    Hon. He begins
To waver.   [*Aside.*
    Math. Madam, as you are gracious,
Grant this short night's deliberation to me ;
And, with the rising sun, from me you shall
Receive full satisfaction.
    Hon. Though extremes
Hate all delay, I will deny you nothing.
This key will bring you to your friend ; you
    are safe both ;
And all things useful that could be prepared
For one I love and honour, wait upon you.
Take counsel of your pillow, such a fortune
As with affection's swiftest wings flies to you,
Will not be often tender'd.   [*Exit.*
    Math. How my blood
Rebels ! I now could call her back—and yet
There's something stays me : if the king
    had tender'd
Such favours to my wife, 'tis to be doubted
They had not been refused : but, being a
    man,
I should not yield first, or prove an example,
For her defence, of frailty. By this, sans
    question,
She's tempted too ; and here I may examine.
                [*Looks on the picture.*
How she holds out. She's still the same,
    the same

Pure crystal rock of chastity.   Perish all
Allurements that may alter me ! The snow
Of her sweet coldness hath extinguish'd quite
The fire that but even now began to flame :
And I by her confirm'd,—rewards nor titles,
Nor certain death from the refused queen,
Shall shake my faith ; since I resolve to be
Loyal to her, as she is true to me.   [*Exit.*

SCENE VI.—Bohemia.   *A Gallery in*
        Mathias' *House.*

        Enter Ubaldo *and* Ricardo.

    Ubald. What we spake on the voley be-
        gins to work ;
We have laid a good foundation.
    Ric. Build it up,
Or else 'tis nothing : you have by lot the
    honour
Of the first assault ; but, as it is condition'd,
Observe the time proportion'd : I'll not part
    with
My share in the achievement ; when I
    whistle,
Or hem, fall off.

        Enter Sophia.

    Ubald. She comes.   Stand by, I'll watch
My opportunity.   [*They walk aside.*
    Soph. I find myself
Strangely distracted with the various stories,
Now well, now ill, then doubtfully, by my
    guests
Deliver'd of my lord : and, like poor beggars
That in their dreams find treasure, by re-
    flection
Of a wounded fancy, make it questionable
Whether they sleep or not ; yet, tickled with
Such a fantastic hope of happiness,
Wish they may never wake.   In some such
    measure,
Incredulous of what I see and touch,
As 'twere a fading apparition, I
Am still perplex'd, and troubled ; and when
    most
Confirm'd 'tis true, a curious jealousy
To be assured, by what means, and from
    whom,
Such a mass of wealth was first deserv'd,
    then gotten,
Cunningly steals into me. I have practised,
For my certain resolution, with these courtiers,
Promising private conference to either,
And, at this hour :—if in search of the truth,
I hear, or say, more than becomes my virtue,
Forgive me, my Mathias.
    Ubald. Now I make in.—
                    [*Comes forward.*
Madam, as you commanded, I attend
Your pleasure.

Soph. I must thank you for the favour.

Ubald. I am no ghostly father; yet, if you have
Some scruples touching your lord, you would be resolved of,
I am prepared.

Soph. But will you take your oath,
To answer truly?

Ubald. On the hem of your smock, if you please :
A vow I dare not break, it being a book
I would gladly swear on.

Soph. To spare, sir, that trouble,
I'll take your word, which, in a gentleman,
Should be of equal value. Is my lord, then,
In such grace with the queen?

Ubald. You should best know, .
By what you have found from him, whether he can
Deserve a grace or no.

Soph. What grace do you mean?

Ubald. That special grace, if you will have it, he
Labour'd so hard for between a pair of sheets,
Upon your wedding night, when your lady-ship
Lost—you know what.

Soph. Fie! be more modest,
Or I must leave you.

Ubald. I would tell a truth
As cleanly as I could, and yet the subject
Makes me run out a little.

Soph. You would put, now,
A foolish jealousy in my head, my lord
Hath gotten a new mistress.

Ubald. One! a hundred ;
But under seal I speak it : I presume
Upon your silence, it being for your profit.
They talk of Hercules' fifty in a night,
'Twas well ; but yet to yours he was a piddler :
Such a soldier and a courtier never came
To Alba Regalis ; the ladies run mad for him,
And there is such contention among them,
Who shall engross him wholly, that the like
Was never heard of.

Soph. Are they handsome women?

Ubald. Fie! no ; coarse mammets : and what's worse, they are old too,
Some fifty, some threescore, and they pay dear for't,
Believing that he carries a powder in his breeches
Will make them young again ; and these suck shrewdly.

Ric. [*whistles.*] Sir, I must fetch you off.
[*Aside.*

Ubald. I could tell you wonders
Of the cures he has done, but a business of import
Calls me away ; but, that dispatch'd, I will
Be with you presently. [*Walks aside.*

Soph. There is something more,
In this, than bare suspicion.

Ric. [*comes forward.*] Save you, lady ;
Now you look like yourself ! I have not look'd on
A lady more complete, yet have seen a madam
Wear a garment of this fashion, of the same stuff too,
One just of your dimensions :—Sat the wind there, boy !

Soph. What lady, sir?

Ric. Nay, nothing ; and methinks
I should know this ruby : very good ! 'tis the same.
This chain of orient pearl, and this diamond too,
Have been worn before ; but much good may they do you !
Strength to the gentleman's back ! he toil'd hard for them,
Before he got them.

Soph. Why, how were they gotten?

Ric. Not in the field with his sword, upon my life ;
He may thank his close stiletto.—[Ubaldo *hems.*]—Plague upon it !
Run the minutes so fast? [*Aside.*]—Pray you, excuse my manners ;
I left a letter in my chamber window,
Which I would not have seen on any terms ;
fie on it,
Forgetful as I am ! but I'll straight attend you. [*Walks aside.*

Soph. This is strange. His letters said these jewels were
Presented him by the queen, as a reward
For his good service, and the trunks of clothes,
That followed them this last night, with haste made up
By his direction.

Ubald. [*comes forward.*] I was telling you
Of wonders, madam.

Soph. If you are so skilful,
Without premeditation answer me ;
Know you this gown, and these rich jewels?

Ubald. Heaven,
How things will come out ! But that I should offend you,
And wrong my more than noble friend, your husband,
(For we are sworn brothers,) in the discovery
Of his nearest secrets, I could——

x

Soph. By the hope of favour
That you have from me, out with it.
  Ubald. 'Tis a potent spell
I cannot resist: Why, I will tell you, madam,
And to how many several women you are
Beholding for your bravery. This was
The wedding gown of Paulina, a rich
  strumpet,
Worn but a day, when she married old Gon-
  zaga,
And left off trading.
  Soph. O my heart!
  Ubald. This chain
Of pearl, was a great widow's, that invited
Your lord to a masque, and the weather
  proving foul,
He lodged in her house all night, and merry
  they were;
But how he came by it, I know not.
  Soph. Perjured man!
  Ubald. This ring was Julietta's, a fine piece,
But very good at the sport: this diamond
Was madam Acanthe's, given him for a song
Prick'd in a private arbour, as she said,
When the queen ask'd for't; and she heard
  him sing too,
And danced to his hornpipe, or there are
  liars abroad.
There are other toys about you, the same
  way purchased;
But, parallel'd with these, not worth the re-
  lation.
You are happy in a husband, never man
Made better use of his strength: would you
  have him waste
His body away for nothing? if he holds out,
There's not an embroider'd petticoat in the
  court,
But shall be at your service.
  Soph. I commend him,
It is a thriving trade; but pray you leave me
A little to myself.
  Ubald. You may command
Your servant, madam.—[*Walks aside.*]—
  She's stung unto the quick, lad.
  Ric. I did my part: if this potion work
  not, hang me!
Let her sleep as well as she can to-night, to-
  morrow
We'll mount new batteries.
  Ubald. And till then leave her.
  [*Exeunt* Ubaldo *and* Ricardo.
  Soph. You Powers, that take into your
  care the guard
Of innocence, aid me! for I am a creature
So forfeited to despair, hope cannot fancy
A ransom to redeem me. I begin
To waver in my faith, and make it doubtful,
Whether the saints, that were canonized for

Their holiness of life, sinn'd not in secret;
Since my Mathias is fallen from his virtue,
In such an open fashion. Could it be, else,
That such a husband, so devoted to me,
So vow'd to temperance, for lascivious hire
Should prostitute himself to common harlots!
Old and deform'd too! Was't for this he
  left me,
And on a feign'd pretence, for want of means
To give me ornament?—or to bring home
Diseases to me? Suppose these are false,
And lustful goats; if he were true and right,
Why stays he so long from me, being made
  rich,
And that the only reason why he left me?
No, he is lost; and shall I wear the spoils
And salaries of lust! they cleave unto me,
Like Nessus' poison'd shirt: no, in my rage,
I'll tear them off, and from my body wash
The venom with my tears. Have I no spleen,
Nor anger of a woman? shall he build
Upon my ruins, and I, unrevenged,
Deplore his falsehood? no; with the same
  trash
For which he had dishonour'd me, I'll pur-
  chase
A just revenge: I am not yet so much
In debt to years, nor so mis-shaped, that all
Should fly from my embraces: Chastity,
Thou only art a name, and I renounce thee!
I am now a servant to voluptuousness.
Wantons of all degrees and fashions,
  welcome!
You shall be entertain'd; and, if I stray,
Let him condemn himself, that led the way.
                              [*Exit.*

————

ACT IV.

SCENE I.—*Alba Regalis. A Room in
                    the Palace.*

Enter Mathias *and* Baptista.

  Bapt. We are in a desperate strait; there's
  no evasion,
Nor hope left to come off, but by your yield-
  ing
To the necessity; you must feign a grant
To her violent passion, or——
  Math. What, my Baptista?
  Bapt. We are but dead else.
  Math. Were the sword now heaved up,
And my neck upon the block, I would not buy
An hour's reprieve with the loss of faith and
  virtue,
To be made immortal here. Art thou a
  scholar,
Nay, almost without parallel, and yet fear
To die, which is inevitable! You may urge

The many years that, by the course of nature,
We may travel in this tedious pilgrimage,
And hold it as a blessing ; as it is,
When innocence is our guide : yet know,
    Baptista,
Our virtues are preferr'd before our years,
By the great Judge : to die untainted in
Our fame and reputation is the greatest ;
And to lose that, can we desire to live ?
Or shall I, for a momentary pleasure,
Which soon comes to a period, to all times
Have breach of faith and perjury remember'd
In a still-living epitaph ? no, Baptista,
Since my Sophia will go to her grave
Unspotted in her faith, I'll follow her
With equal loyalty :—[*Takes out the picture.*]
    But look on this,
Your own great work, your masterpiece, and
    then,
She being still the same, teach me to
    alter !——
Ha ! sure I do not sleep ! or, if I dream,
This is a terrible vision ! I will clear
My eyesight ; perhaps melancholy makes me
See that which is not.
    Bapt. It is too apparent.
I grieve to look upon't : besides the yellow,
That does assure she's tempted, there are
    lines
Of a dark colour, that disperse themselves
O'er every miniature of her face, and those
Confirm——
    Math. She is turn'd whore !
    Bapt. I must not say so.
Yet, as a friend to truth, if you will have me
Interpret it,—in her consent and wishes
She's false, but not in fact yet.
    Math. Fact, Baptista !
Make not yourself a pander to her looseness,
In labouring to palliate what a visor
Of impudence cannot cover. Did e'er woman,
In her will, decline from chastity, but found
    means,
To give her hot lust fuel ? It is more
Impossible in nature for gross bodies,
Descending of themselves, to hang in the air ;
Or with my single arm to underprop
A falling tower ; nay, in its violent course
To stop the lightning, than to stay a woman
Hurried by two furies, lust and falsehood,
In her full career to wickedness !
    Bapt. Pray you, temper
The violence of your passion.
    Math. In extremes
Of this condition, can it be in man
To use a moderation ? I am thrown,
From a steep rock, headlong into a gulph
Of misery, and find myself past hope,
In the same moment that I apprehend

That I am falling : and this, the figure of
My idol, few hours since, while she continued
In her perfection, that was late a mirror,
In which I saw miraculous shapes of duty,
Staid manners, with all excellency a husband
Could wish in a chaste wife, is on the sudden
Turn'd to a magicall glass, and does present
Nothing but horns and horror.
    Bapt. You may yet,
And 'tis the best foundation, build up comfort
On your own goodness.
    Math. No, that hath undone me ;
For now I hold my temperance a sin
Worse than excess, and what was vice, a
    virtue.
Have I refused a queen, and such a queen,
Whose ravishing beauties at the first sight
    had tempted
A hermit from his beads, and changed his
    prayers
To amorous sonnets, to preserve my faith
Inviolate to thee, with the hazard of
My death with torture, since she could inflict
No less for my contempt ; and have I met
Such a return from thee ! I will not curse thee,
Nor, for thy falsehood, rail against the sex ;
'Tis poor, and common : I'll only with wise
    men,
Whisper unto myself, howe'er they seem,
Nor present, nor past times, nor the age to
    come,
Hath heretofore, can now, or ever shall,
Produce one constant woman.
    Bapt. This is more
Than the satirists wrote against them.
    Math. There's no language
That can express the poison of these aspics,
These weeping crocodiles, and all too little
That hath been said against them. But I'll
    mould
My thoughts into another form ; and, if
She can outlive the report of what I have done,
This hand, when next she comes within my
    reach,
Shall be her executioner.

        Enter Honoria *and* Acanthe.

    Bapt. The queen, sir.
    Hon. Wait our command at distance :——
        [*Exit* Acanthe.]—Sir, you too have
Free liberty to depart.
    Bapt. I know my manners,
And thank you for the favour.   [*Exit.*
    Hon. Have you taken
Good rest in your new lodgings ? I expect
    now
Your resolute answer : but advise maturely
Before I hear it.
    Math. Let my actions, madam,

X 2

For no words can dilate my joy, in all
You can command, with cheerfulness to
serve you,
Assure your highness ; and, in sign of my
Submission, and contrition for my error,
My lips, that but the last night shunn'd the
touch
Of yours as poison, taught humility now,
Thus on your foot, and that too great an
honour
For such an undeserver, seal my duty.
A cloudy mist of ignorance, equal to
Cimmerian darkness, would not let me see,
then,
What now, with adoration and wonder,
With reverence I look up to : but those fogs
Dispersed and scatter'd by the powerful
beams
With which yourself, the sun of all perfection,
Vouchsafe to cure my blindness ; like a
suppliant,
As low as I can kneel, I humbly beg
What you once pleased to tender.
  Hon. This is more
Than I could hope ! [*Aside.*]—What find
you so attractive
Upon my face, in so short time to make
This sudden metamorphosis ? pray you,
rise ;
I, for your late neglect, thus sign your par-
don.   [*Kisses him.*
Ay, now you kiss like a lover, and not as
brothers
Coldly salute their sisters.
  Math. I am turn'd
All spirit and fire.
  Hon. Yet, to give some allay
To this hot fervour, 'twere good to remem-
ber
The king, whose eyes and ears are every-
where ;
With the danger too that follows, this dis-
cover'd.
  Math. Danger ! a bugbear, madam ; let
[me] ride once
Like Phaeton in the chariot of your favour,
And I contemn Jove's thunder ; though the
king,
In our embraces stood a looker on,
His hangman, and with studied cruelty,
ready
To drag me from your arms, it should not
fright me
From the enjoying that a single life is
Too poor a price for. O, that now all vigour
Of my youth were re-collected for an hour,
That my desire might meet with yours, and
raw
The envy of all men, in the encounter,

Upon my head ! I should—but we lose
time—
Be gracious, mighty queen.
  Hon. Pause yet a little :
The bounties of the king, and, what weighs
more,
Your boasted constancy to your matchless
wife,
Should not so soon be shaken.
  Math. The whole fabric,
When I but look on you, is in a moment
O'erturn'd and ruin'd ; and, as rivers lose
Their names when they are swallow'd by
the ocean,
In you alone all faculties of my soul
Are wholly taken up ; my wife and king,
At the best, as things forgotten.
  Hon. Can this be ?
I have gain'd my end now.   [*Aside.*
  Math. Wherefore stay you, madam ?
  Hon. In my consideration what a nothing
Man's constancy is.
  Math. Your beauties make it so
In me, sweet lady.
  Hon. And it is my glory :
I could be coy now, as you were, but I
Am of a gentler temper ; howsoever,
And in a just return of what I have suffer'd
In your disdain, with the same measure
grant me
Equal deliberation : I ere long
Will visit you again ; and when I next
Appear, as conquer'd by it, slave-like wait
On my triumphant beauty.   [*Exit.*
  Math. What a change
Is here beyond my fear ! but by thy false-
hood,
Sophia, not her beauty, is't denied me
To sin but in my wishes ? what a frown,
In scorn, at her departure, she threw on me !
I am both ways lost ; storms of contempt
and scorn
Are ready to break on me, and all hope
Of shelter doubtful : I can neither be
Disloyal, nor yet honest ; I stand guilty
On either part ; at the worst, Death will end
all ;
And he must be my judge to right my wrong,
Since I have loved too much, and lived too
long.   [*Exit.*
SCENE II.—Bohemia. *A Room in* Ma-
thias' *House.*

  Enter Sophia, *with a book and a paper.*

  Soph. Nor custom, nor example, nor vast
numbers
Of such as do offend, make less the sin.
For each particular crime a strict account
Will be exacted ; and that comfort which

The damn'd pretend, fellows in misery,
Takes nothing from their torments: every
     one,
Must suffer, in himself, the measure of
His wickedness.   If so, as I must grant,
It being unrefutable in reason,
Howe'er my lord offend, it is no warrant
For me to walk in his forbidden paths:
What penance then can expiate my guilt,
For my consent (transported then with
     passion)
To wantonness? the wounds I give my fame,
Cannot recover his; and, though I have fed
These courtiers with promises and hopes,
I am yet in fact untainted ; and I trust,
My sorrow for it, with my purity,
And love to goodness for itself, made
     powerful,
Though all they have alleged prove true or
     false,
Will be such exorcisms as shall command
This Fury, jealousy, from me? What I have
Determined touching them, I am resolved
To put in execution.   Within, there ! .

Enter Hilario, Corisca, *with other* Servants.

Where are my noble guests?
   Hil. The elder, madam,
Is drinking by himself to your ladyship's
     health,
In muskadine and eggs ; and, for a rasher
To draw his liquor down, he hath got a pie
Of marrowbones, potatoes, and eringos,
With many such ingredients ; and, 'tis said,
He hath sent his man in post to the next
     town,
For a pound of ambergris, and half a peck
Of fishes call'd cantharides.
   Coris. The younger
Prunes up himself, as if this night he were
To act a bridegroom's part ; but to what
     purpose,
I am ignorance itself.
   Soph. Continue so.
          [*Gives the servants the paper.*
Let those lodgings be prepared as this di-
     rects you :
And fail not in a circumstance, as you
Respect my favour.
   1 *Serv.* We have our instructions.
   2 *Serv.* And punctually will follow them.
                    [*Exeunt* Servants.

Enter Ubaldo.

   Hil. Here comes, madam,
The lord Ubaldo.
   Ubald. Pretty one, there's gold
To buy thee a new gown ; [*To* Coris.] and
     there's for thee ;

Grow fat, and fit for service. [*To* Hil.] I
     am now,
As I should be, at the height, and able to
Beget a giant.   O my better angel !
In this you shew your wisdom, when you pay
The letcher in his own coin ; shall you sit
     puling,
Like a Patient Grizzle, and be laughed at? no :
This is a fair revenge.   Shall we to't?
   Soph. To what, sir?
   Ubald. The sport you promised.
   Soph. Could it be done with safety.
   Ubald. I warrant you ; I am sound as a
     bell, a tough
Old blade, and steel to the back, as you
     shall find me
In the trial on your anvil.
   Soph. So ; but how, sir,
Shall I satisfy your friend, to whom, by
     promise,
I am equally engaged?
   Ubald. I must confess,
The more the merrier ; but, of all men living,
Take heed of him : you may safer run upon
The mouth of a cannon when it is unlading,
And come off colder.
   Soph. How ! is he not wholesome?
   Ubald. Wholesome ! I'll tell you, for your
     good : he is
A spittle of diseases, and, indeed,
More loathsome and infectious; the tub is
His weekly bath : he hath not drank this
     seven years,
Before he came to your house, but composi-
     tions
Of sassafras and guaicum ; and dry mutton
His daily portion : name what scratch soever
Can be got by women, and the surgeons
     will resolve you,
At this time, or at that, Ricardo had it.
   Soph. Bless me from him !
   Ubald. 'Tis a good prayer, lady.
It being a degree unto the pox,
Only to mention him : if my tongue burn
     not, hang me,
When I but name Ricardo.
   Soph. Sir, this caution
Must be rewarded.
   Ubald. I hope I have marr'd his market.
                    [*Aside.*
——But when?
   Soph. Why, presently ; follow my woman,
She knows where to conduct you, and will
     serve
To-night for a page.   Let the waistcoat I
     appointed,
With the cambric shirt perfumed, and the
     rich cap,
Be brought into his chamber.

Ubald. Excellent lady !
And a caudle too in the morning.
Coris. I will fit you.
　　　　　[*Exeunt* Ubaldo *and* Corisca.

　　　　　Enter Ricardo.

Soph. So hot on the scent ! Here comes
the other beagle.
Ric. Take purse and all.　　[*To* Hilario.
Hil. If this company would come often,
I should make a pretty term on't.
Soph. For your sake
I have put him off ; he only begg'd a kiss,
I gave it, and so parted.
Ric. I hope better :——
He did not touch your lips ?
Soph. Yes, I assure you.
There was no danger in it ?
Ric. No ! eat presently
These lozenges of forty crowns an ounce,
Or you are undone.
Soph. What is the virtue of them ?
Ric. They are preservatives against stink-
ing breath,
Rising from rotten lungs.
Soph. If so, your carriage
Of such dear antidotes, in my opinion,
May render yours suspected.
Ric. Fie ! no ; I use them
When I talk with him, I should be poison'd
else,
But I'll be free with you : he was once a
creature,
It may be, of God's making, but long since
He is turn'd to a druggist's shop ; the spring
and fall
Hold all the year with him : that he lives,
he owes
To art, not nature ; she has given him o'er.
He moves, like the fairy king, on screws and
wheels,
Made by his doctor's recipes, and yet still
They are out of joint, and every day repairing.
He has a regiment of whores he keeps,
At his own charge, in a lazar-house ; but the
best is,
There's not a nose among them.　　He's
acquainted
With the green water, and the spitting pill's
Familiar to him : in a frosty morning,
You may thrust him in a pottle-pot ; his bones
Rattle in his skin, like beans tossed in a
bladder.
If he but hear a coach, the fomentation,
The friction with fumigation, cannot save
him
From the chine-evil.　In a word, he is
Not one disease, but all ; yet, being my
·　friend,

I will forbear his character, for I would not,
Wrong him in your opinion.
Soph. The best is,
The virtues you bestow on him, to me
Are mysteries I know not ; but, however,
I am at your service.　Sirrah, let it be your
care
To unclothe the gentleman, and with speed ;
delay
Takes from delight.
Ric. Good ! there's my hat, sword, cloak :
A vengeance on these buttons ! off with my
doublet,
I dare shew my skin ; in the touch you will
like it better.
Prithee cut my codpiece-points, and, for this
service,
When I leave them off, they are thine.
Hil. I'll take your word, sir.
Ric. Dear lady, stay not long.
Soph. I may come too soon, sir.
Ric. No, no ; I am ready now.
Hil. This is the way, sir.
　　　　　[*Exeunt* Hilario *and* Ricardo.
Soph. I was much to blame to credit their
reports
Touching my lord, that so traduce each other,
And with such virulent malice ; though I
presume
They are bad enough ; but I have studied
for them
A way for their recovery.
　　　[*A noise of clapping a door ;* Ubaldo
　　　　　appears above in his shirt.
Ubald. What dost thou mean, wench ?
Why dost thou shut the door upon me ? Ha !
My clothes are ta'en away too ! shall I starve
here ?
Is this my lodging ?　I am sure the lady
talk'd of
A rich cap, a perfum'd shirt, and a waistcoat ;
But here is nothing but a little fresh straw,
A petticoat for a coverlet, and that torn too,
And an old woman's biggin, for a night-cap.

　　　　　Re-enter Corisca *below.*

'Slight, 'tis a prison, or a pigsty.　Ha !
The windows grated with iron ! I cannot
force them,
And if I leap down here, I break my neck :
I am betray'd.　Rogues ! Villains ! let me out ;
I am a lord, and that's no common title,
And shall I be used thus ?
Soph. Let him rave, he's fast ;
I'll parley with him at leisure.

　　　Ricardo *entering with a great noise above,*
　　　　　　as fallen.

Ric. Zounds ! have you trapdoors ?

Soph. The other bird's i'the cage too, let
  him flutter.
Ric. Whither am I fallen? into hell!
Ubald. Who makes that noise, there?
Help me, if thou art a friend.
  Ric. A friend! I am where
I cannot help myself; let me see thy face.
Ubald. How, Ricardo! Prithee, throw me
Thy cloak, if thou canst, to cover me; I am
  almost
Frozen to death.
  Ric. My cloak! I have no breeches;
I am in my shirt, as thou art; and here's
  nothing
For myself but a clown's cast suit.
  Ubald. We are both undone.
Prithee, roar a little—Madam!

Re-enter Hilario *below, in* Ricardo's *clothes.*

  Ric. Lady of the house!
  Ubald. Grooms of the chamber!
  Ric. Gentlewomen! Milkmaids!
  Ubald. Shall we be murder'd?
  Soph. No, but soundly punish'd,
To your deserts.
  Ric. You are not in earnest, madam?
  Soph. Judge as you find, and feel it; and
  now hear
What I irrevocably purpose to you.
Being received as guests into my house,
And with all it afforded entertain'd,
You have forgot all hospitable duties;
And, with the defamation of my lord,
Wrought on my woman weakness, in revenge
Of his injuries, as you fashion'd them to me,
To yield my honour to your lawless lust.
  Hil. Mark that, poor fellows!
  Soph. And so far you have
Transgress'd against the dignity of men,
Who should, bound to it by virtue, still defend
Chaste ladies' honours, that it was your trade
To make them infamous: but you are caught
In your own toils, like lustful beasts, and
  therefore
Hope not to find the usage of men from me:
Such mercy you have forfeited, and shall
  suffer
Like the most slavish women.
  Ubald. How will you use us?
  Soph. Ease, and excess in feeding, made
  you wanton.
A plurisy of ill blood you must let out,
By labour, and spare diet that way got too,
Or perish for hunger. Reach him up that
  distaff
With the flax upon it; though no Omphale,
Nor you a second Hercules, as I take it,
As you spin well at my command, and please
  me,

Your wages, in the coarsest bread and water,
Shall be proportionable.
  Ubald. I will starve first.
  Soph. That's as you please.
  Ric. What will become of me now?
  Soph. You shall have gentler work; I have
  oft observed
You were proud to shew the fineness of your
  hands,
And softness of your fingers; you should
  reel well
What he spins, if you give your mind to it, as
  I'll force you.
Deliver him his materials. Now you know
Your penance, fall to work; hunger will teach
  you:
And so, as slaves to your lust, not me, I leave
  you.   [*Exeunt* Sophia *and* Corisca.
  Ubald. I shall spin a fine thread out now!
  Ric. I cannot look
On these devices, but they put me in mind
Of rope-makers.
  Hil. Fellow, think of thy task.
Forget such vanities; my livery there,
Will serve thee to work in.
  Ric. Let me have my clothes yet;
I was bountiful to thee.
  Hil. They are past your wearing,
And mine by promise, as all these can witness.
You have no holidays coming, nor will I work
While these, and this lasts; and so, when you
  please,
You may shut up your shop windows.
                    [*Exit.*
  Ubald. I am faint,
And must lie down.
  Ric. I am hungry too, and cold.
O cursed women!
  Ubald. This comes of our whoring.
But let us rest as well as we can to-night,
But not o'ersleep ourselves, lest we fast to-
  morrow.   [*They withdraw.*

SCENE III.—*Alba Regalis. A Room in
the Palace.*

Enter Ladislaus, Honoria, Eubulus, Ferdinand, Acanthe, *and* Attendants.

  Hon. Now you know all, sir, with the
  motives why
I forced him to my lodging.
  Ladis. I desire
No more such trials, lady.
  Hon. I presume, sir,
You do not doubt my chastity.
  Ladis. I would not;
But these are strange inducements.
  Eubu. By no means, sir.
Why, though he were with violence seized
  upon,

And still detain'd, the man, sir, being no
    soldier,
Nor used to charge his pike when the breach
    is open,
There was no danger in't! You must con-
    ceive, sir,
Being religious, she chose him for a chaplain,
To read old homilies to her in the dark;
She's bound to it by her canons.
    Ladis. Still tormented   ·
With thy impertinence!
    Hon. By yourself, dear sir,
I was ambitious only to o'erthrow
His boasted constancy in his consent;
But for fact, I contemn him : I was never
Unchaste in thought; I laboured to give
    proof
What power dwells in this beauty you ad-
    mire so;
And when you see how soon it has trans-
    form'd him,
And with what superstition he adores it,
Determine as you please.
    Ladis. I will look on
This pageant; but——
    Hon. When you have seen and heard, sir,
The passages which I myself discover'd,
And could have kept conceal'd, had I meant
    basely,
Judge as you please.
    Ladis. Well, I'll observe the issue.
    Eubu. How had you ta'en this, general, in
    your wife?
    Ferd. As a strange curiosity; but queens
Are privileged above subjects, and 'tis fit, sir.
                                    [*Exeunt.*

SCENE IV.—*Another Room in the same.*

    Enter Mathias *and* Baptista.

    Bapt. You are much alter'd, sir, since the
    last night,
When the queen left you, and look cheerfully,
Your dulness quite blown over.
    Math. I have seen a vision
This morning, makes it good; and never was
In such security as at this instant,
Fall what can fall : and when the queen
    appears,
Whose shortest absence now is tedious to me,
Observe the encounter.

    Enter Honoria.   Ladislaus, Eubulus, Fer-
    dinand, *and* Acanthe, *with others, ap-
    pear above.*

    Bapt. She already is
Enter'd the lists.
    Math. And I prepared to meet her.
    Bapt. I know my duty.   [*Going.*

    Hon. Not so, you may stay now,
As a witness of our contract.
    Bapt. I obey
In all things, madam.
    Hon. Where's that reverence,
Or rather superstitious adoration,
Which, captive-like, to my triumphant beauty
You paid last night?   No humble knee, nor
    sign
Of vassal duty! sure this is the foot,
To whose proud cover, and then happy in it,
Your lips were glued; and that the neck
    then offer'd,
To witness your subjection, to be trod on;
Your certain loss of life in the king's anger
Was then too mean a price to buy my favour;
And that false glow-worm fire of constancy
To your wife, extinguish'd by a greater light
Shot from our eyes;—and that, it may be,
    (being
Too glorious to be look'd on,) hath deprived
    you
Of speech and motion : but I will take off
A little from the splendour, and descend
From my own height, and in your lowness
    hear you
Plead as a suppliant.
    Math. I do remember
I once saw such a woman.
    Hon. How!
    Math. And then
She did appear a most magnificent queen,
And, what's more, virtuous, though some-
    what darken'd
With pride, and self-opinion.
    Eubu. Call you this courtship?
    Math. And she was happy in a royal
    husband,
Whom envy could not tax, unless it were
For his too much indulgence to her humours.
    Eubu. Pray you, sir, observe that touch,
    'tis to the purpose;
I like the play the better for't.
    Math. And she lived
Worthy her birth and fortune; you retain
    yet
Some part of her angelical form; but when
Envy to the beauty of another woman,
Inferior to hers, one that she never
Had seen, but in her picture, had dispersed
Infection through her veins, and loyalty,
Which a great queen, as she was, should
    have nourish'd,
Grew odious to her——
    Hon. I am thunderstruck.
    Math. And lust, in all the bravery it could
    borrow
From majesty, howe'er disguised, had ta'en
Sure footing in the kingdom of her heart,

The throne of chastity once, how, in a moment,
All that was gracious, great, and glorious in her,
And won upon all hearts, like seeming shadows
Wanting true substance, vanish'd!
Hon. How his reasons
Work on my soul!
Math. Retire into yourself;
Your own strengths, madam, strongly mann'd with virtue,
And be but as you were, and there's no office
So base, beneath the slavery that men
Impose on beasts, but I will gladly bow to.
But as you play and juggle with a stranger,
Varying your shapes like Thetis, though the beauties
Of all that are by poets' raptures sainted
Were now in you united, you should pass
Pitied by me, perhaps, but not regarded.
Eubu. If this take not, I am cheated.
Math. To slip once,
Is incident, and excused by human frailty;
But to fall ever, damnable. We were both
Guilty, I grant, in tendering our affection;
But, as I hope you will do, I repented.
When we are grown up to ripeness, our life is
Like to this [magick] picture. While we run
A constant race in goodness, it retains
The just proportion; but the journey being
Tedious, and sweet temptation in the way,
That may in some degree divert us from
The road that we put forth in, ere we end
Our pilgrimage, it may, like this, turn yellow,
Or be with blackness clouded: but when we
Find we have gone astray, and labour to
Return unto our never-failing guide,
Virtue, contrition, with unfeigned tears,
The spots of vice wash'd off, will soon restore it
To the first pureness.
Hon. I am disenchanted:
Mercy, O mercy, heavens!   [*Kneels.*
Ladis. I am ravish'd
With what I have seen and heard.
Ferd. Let us descend,
And hear the rest below.
Eubu. This hath fallen out
Beyond my expectation.   [*They retire.*
Hon. How have I wander'd
Out of the track of piety! and misled
By overweening pride, and flattery
Of fawning sycophants, (the bane of greatness,)
Could never meet till now a passenger,
That in his charity would set me right,
Or stay me in my precipice to ruin.
How ill have I return'd your goodness to me!

The horror, in my thought oft, turns me marble:
But if it may be yet prevented——

Re-enter Ladislaus, Eubulus, Ferdinand, Acanthe, *and others, below.*

         O sir,
What can I do to shew my sorrow, or
With what brow ask your pardon?
Ladis. Pray you, rise.   .
Hon. Never, till you forgive me, and receive
Unto your love and favour a changed woman:
My state and pride turn'd to humility, henceforth
Shall wait on your commands, and my obedience
Steer'd only by your will.
Ladis. And that will prove
A second and a better marriage to me.
All is forgotten.
Hon. Sir, I must not rise yet,
Till, with a free confession of a crime
Unknown to you yet, and a following suit,
Which thus I beg, be granted,
Ladis. I melt with you:
'Tis pardon'd, and confirm'd thus.
                [*Raises her.*
Hon. Know then, sir,
In malice to this good knight's wife, I practised
Ubaldo and Ricardo to corrupt her.
Bapt. Thence grew the change of the picture.   [*Aside.*
Hon. And how far
They have prevail'd, I am ignorant: now, if you, sir,
For the honour of this good man, may be entreated
To travel thither, it being but a day's journey,
To fetch them off——
Ladis. We will put on to-night.
Bapt. I, if you please, your harbinger.
Ladis. I thank you.
Let me embrace you in my arms; your service
Done on the Turk, compared with this, weighs nothing.
Math. I am still your humble creature.
Ladis. My true friend.
Ferd. And so you are bound to hold him.
Eubu. Such a plant
Imported to your kingdom, and here grafted,
Would yield more fruit than all the idle weeds
That suck up your rain of favour.
Ladis. In my will
I'll not be wanting. Prepare for our journey.

In act be my Honoria now, not name,
And to all aftertimes preserve thy fame.
　　　　　　　　　　　　　　[*Exeunt.*

————

ACT V.

SCENE I.—Bohemia. *A Hall in* Mathias'
House.

Enter Sophia, Corisca, *and* Hilario.

Soph. Are they then so humble?
Hil. Hunger and hard labour
Have tamed them, madam ; at the first they
　bellow'd
Like stags ta'en in a toil, and would not work
For sullenness ; but when they found, with-
　out it,
There was no eating, and that, to starve to
　death,
Was much against their stomach ; by de-
　grees,
Against their wills, they fell to it.
Coris. And now feed on
The little pittance you allow, with gladness.
Hil. I do remember that they stopp'd their
　noses
At the sight of beef and mutton, as coarse
　feeding
For their fine palates ; but now, their work
　being ended,
They leap at a barley crust, and hold cheese-
　parings,
With a spoonful of pall'd wine pour'd in
　their water,
For festival-exceedings.
Coris. When I examine
My spinster's work, he trembles like a
　prentice,
And takes a box on the ear, when I spy faults
And botches in his labour, as a favour
From a curst mistress.
Hil. The other, too, reels well
For his time ; and if your ladyship would
　please
To see them for your sport, since they want
　airing,
It would do well, in my judgment ; you
　shall hear
Such a hungry dialogue from them !
Soph. But suppose,
When they are out of prison, they should
　grow
Rebellious ?
Hil. Never fear't ; I'll undertake
To lead them out by the nose with a coarse
　thread
Of the one's spinning, and make the other
　reel after,

And without grumbling ; and when you are
　weary of
Their company, as easily return them.
Coris. Dear madam, it will help to drive
　away
Your melancholy.
Soph. Well, on this assurance,
I am content ; bring them hither.
Hil. I will do it
In stately equipage. 　　　　　　[*Exit.*
Soph. They have confess'd, then,
They were set on by the queen, to taint me in
My loyalty to my lord ?
Coris. 'Twas the main cause,
That brought them hither.
Soph. I am glad I know it ;
And as I have begun, before I end
I'll at the height revenge it ; let us step
　aside,
They come : the object's so ridiculous,
In spite of my sad thoughts, I cannot but
　lend
A forced smile to grace it.

Re-enter Hilario, *with* Ubaldo *spinning,
　and* Ricardo *reeling.*

Hil. Come away :
Work as you go, and lose no time, 'tis
　precious ;
You'll find it in your commons.
Ric. Commons, call you it !
The word is proper ; I have grazed so long
Upon your commons, I am almost starv'd
　here.
Hil. Work harder, and they shall be
　better'd.
Ubald. Better'd !
Worser they cannot be : would I might lie
Like a dog under her table, and serve for a
　footstool,
So I might have my belly full of that
Her Iceland cur refuses !
Hil. How do you like
Your airing? is it not a favour?
Ric. Yes ;
Just such a one as you use to a brace of
　greyhounds,
When they are led out of their kennels to
　scumber ;
But our case is ten times harder, we have
　nothing
In our bellies to be vented : if you will be
An honest yeoman-fewterer, feed us first,
And walk us after.
Hil. Yeoman-fewterer !
Such another word to your governor, and
　you go
Supperless to bed for't.
Ubald. Nay, even as you please ;

The comfortable names of breakfasts, din-
ners,
Collations, supper, beverage, are words
Worn out of our remembrance.
  Ric. O· for the steam
Of meat in a cook's shop !
  Ubald. I am so dry
I have not spittle enough to wet my fingers
When, I draw my flax from my distaff.·
  Ric. Nor I strength .
To raise my hand to the top of my reeler. Oh!
I have the cramp all over me.
  Hil. What do you think
Were best to apply to it? A cramp-stone,
as I take it,
Were very useful.
  Ric. Oh ! no more of stones,
We have been used too long like hawks
already.
  Ubald. We are not so high in our flesh
now to need casting,
We will come to an empty fist.
  Hil. Nay, that you shall not.
So ho, birds !—[*Holds up a piece of bread.*]—
How the eyasses scratch and scramble !
Take heed of a surfeit, do not cast your
gorges ;
This is more than I have commission for ;
be thankful.
  Soph. Were all that study the abuse of
women,
Used thus, the city would not swarm with
cuckolds,
Nor so many tradesmen break.
  Coris. Pray you, appear now,
And mark the alteration.
        [Sophia *comes forward.*
  Hil. To your work,
My lady is in presence ; shew your duties :
Exceeding well.
  Soph. How do your scholars profit?
  Hil. Hold up your heads demurely.
Prettily,
For young beginners.
  Coris. And will do well in time,
If they be kept in awe.
  Ric. In awe ! I am sure
I quake like an aspen leaf.
  Ubald. No mercy, lady?
  Ric. Nor intermission ?
  Soph. Let me see your work :
Fie upon't, what a thread's here ! a poor
cobler's wife
Would make a finer to sew a clown's rent
startup ;
And here you reel as you were drunk.
  Ric. I am sure
It is not with wine. .
  Soph. O take heed of wine ;

Cold water is far better for your healths,
Of which I am very tender : you had foul
bodies,
And must continue in this physical diet,
Till the cause of your disease be ta'en away,
For fear of a relapse ; and that is dangerous :
Yet I hope already that you are in some
Degree recover'd, and that way to resolve me,
Answer me truly ; nay, what I propound
Concerns both ; nearer : what would you
now give,
If your means were in your hands, to lie all
night
With a fresh and handsome lady?
  Ubald. How ! a lady?
O, I am past it ; hunger with her razor
Hath made me an eunuch.
  Ric. For a mess of porridge,
Well sopp'd with a bunch of radish and a
carrot,
I would sell my barony ; but for women, oh !
No more of women ; not a doit for a doxy,
After this hungry voyage.
  Soph. These are truly
Good symptoms ; let them not venture too
much in the air,
Till they are weaker.
  Ric. This is tyranny.
  Ubald. Scorn upon scorn.
  Soph. You were so
In your malicious intents to me,

       Enter a Servant.

And therefore 'tis but justice——What's the
business ?
  Serv. My lord's great friend, signior
Baptista, madam,
Is newly lighted from his horse, with certain
Assurance of my lord's arrival.
  Soph. How ?
And stand I trifling here ? Hence with the
mongrels
To their several kennels ; there let them howl
in private ;
I'll be no further troubled.
      [*Exeunt* Sophia *and* Servant.
  Ubald. O that ever
I saw this fury !
  Ric. Or look'd on a woman
But as a prodigy in nature !
  Hil. Silence ;
No more of this.
  Coris. Methinks you have no cause
To repent your being here.
  Hil. Have you not learnt,
When your states are spent, your several
trades to live by,
And never charge the hospital ?
  Coris. Work but tightly,

And we will not use a dish-clout in the house,
But of your spinning.
Ubald. O, I would this hemp
Were turn'd to a halter!
Hil. Will you march?
Ric. A soft one,
Good general, I beseech you.
Ubald. I can hardly
Draw my legs after me.
Hil. For a crutch, you may use
Your distaff; a good wit makes use of all
   things. [*Exeunt.*

SCENE II.—*A Room in the same.*

Enter Sophia *and* Baptista.

Soph. Was he jealous of me?
Bapt. There's no perfect love
Without some touch of't, madam.
Soph. And my picture,
Made by your devilish art, a spy upon
My actions! I ne'er sat to be drawn,
Nor had you, sir, commission for't.
Bapt. Excuse me;
At his earnest suit I did it.
Soph. Very good :—
Was I grown so cheap in his opinion of me?
Bapt. The prosperous events that crown
   his fortunes,
May qualify the offence.
Soph. Good, the events!—
The sanctuary fools and madmen fly to,
When their rash and desperate undertakings
   thrive well :
But good and wise men are directed by
Grave counsels, and with such deliberation
Proceed in their affairs, that chance has
   nothing
To do with them : howsoe'er, take the pains,
   sir,
To meet the honour (in the king and queen's
Approaches to my house) that breaks upon
   me;
I will expect them with my best of care.
Bapt. To entertain such royal guests——
Soph. I know it; Leave that to me, sir. [*Exit* Baptista.
What should move the queen,
So given to ease and pleasure, as fame speaks
   her,
To such a journey! or work on my lord,
To doubt my loyalty, nay, more, to take,
For the resolution of his fears, a course
That is by holy writ denied a Christian?
'Twas impious in him, and perhaps the wel-
   come
He hopes in my embraces, may deceive
               [*Trumpets sounded.*
His expectation. The trumpets speak
The king's arrival: help, a woman's wit now,

To make him know his fault, and my just
   anger! [*Exit.*

SCENE III.—*A Hall in the Same.*

A Flourish. Enter Ladislaus, Ferdinand,
   Eubulus, Mathias, Baptista, Honoria, *and*
   Acanthe, *with* Attendants.

Eubu. Your majesty must be weary.
Hon. No, my lord,
A willing mind makes a hard journey easy.
Math. Not Jove, attended on by Hermes,
   was
More welcome to the cottage of Philemon,
And his poor Baucis, than your gracious self,
Your matchless queen, and all your royal
   train,
Are to your servant and his wife.
Ladis. Where is she?
Hon. I long to see her as my now-loved
   rival.
Eubu. And I to have a smack at her; 'tis
   a cordial
To an old man, better than sack and a toast
Before he goes to supper.
Math. Ha! is my house turn'd
To a wilderness? nor wife nor servants ready,
With all rites due to majesty, to receive
Such unexpected blessings! You assured me
Of better preparation; hath not
The excess of joy transported her beyond
Her understanding?
Bapt. I now parted from her,
And gave her your directions.
Math. How shall I beg
Your majesties' patience! sure my family's
   drunk,
Or by some witch, in envy of my glory,
A dead sleep thrown upon them.

Enter Hilario *and* Servants.

Serv. Sir.
Math. But that
The sacred presence of the king forbids it,
My sword should make a massacre among
   you.
Where is your mistress?
Hil. First, you are welcome home, sir:
Then know, she says she's sick, sir.—There's
   no notice
Taken of my bravery! [*Aside.*
Math. Sick at such a time!
It cannot be : though she were on her death-
   bed,
And her spirit e'en now departed, here stand
   they
Could call it back again, and in this honour,
Give her a second being. Bring me to her;
I know not what to urge, or how to redeem

This mortgage of her manners.
    [*Exeunt* Mathias, Hilario, *and*
    Servants.
Eubu. There's no climate
On the world, I think, where one jade's
    trick or other
Reigns not in women.
    Ferd. You were ever bitter
Against the sex.
    Ladis. This is very strange.
    Hon. Mean women
Have their faults, as well as queens.
    Ladis. O, she appears now.

    Re-enter Mathias *with* Sophia ; Hilario
    following.

    Math. The injury that you conceive I
    have done you
Dispute hereafter, and in your perverseness
Wrong not yourself and me.
    Soph. I am past my childhood,
And need no tutor.
    Math. This is the great king,
To whom I am engaged till death for all
I stand possess'd of.
    Soph. My humble roof is proud, sir,
To be the canopy of so much greatness
Set off with goodness.
    Ladis. My own praises flying
In such pure air as your sweet breath, fair
    lady,
Cannot but please me.
    Math. This is the queen of queens,
In her magnificence to me.
    Soph. In my duty
I kiss her highness' robe.
    Hon. You stoop too low
To her whose lips would meet with yours.
        [*Kisses her.*
    Soph. Howe'er
It may appear preposterous in women,
So to encounter, 'tis your pleasure, madam,
And not my proud ambition.—Do you hear,
    sir?
Without a magical picture, in the touch
I find your print of close and wanton kisses
On the queen's lips.   [*Aside to* Mathias.
    Math. Upon your life be silent :—
And now salute these lords.
    Soph. Since you will have me,
You shall see I am experienced at the game,
And can play it tightly.—You are a brave
    man, sir,   [*To* Ferdinand.
And do deserve a free and hearty welcome :
Be this the prologue to it.   [*Kisses him.*
    Eubu. An old man's turn
Is ever last in kissing. I have lips too,
However cold ones, madam.

    Soph. I will warm them
With the fire of mine.   [*Kisses him.*
    Eubu. And so she has ! I thank you,
I shall sleep the better all night for't.
    Math. You express
The boldness of a wanton courtezan,
And not a matron's modesty ; take up,
Or you are disgraced for ever.
        [*Aside to* Soph.
    Soph. How? with kissing
Feelingly, as you taught me? would you
    have me
Turn my cheek to them, as proud ladies use
To their inferiors, as if they intended
Some business should be whisper'd in their
    ear,
And not a salutation? what I do,
I will do freely ; now I am in the humour,
I'll fly at all : are there any more?
    Math. Forbear,
Or you will raise my anger to a height
That will descend in fury.
    Soph. Why? you know
How to resolve yourself what my intents are,
By the help of Mephostophilus, and your
    picture :
Pray you, look upon't again. I humbly
    thank
The queen's great care of me while you
    were absent.
She knew how tedious 'twas for a young
    wife,
And being for that time a kind of widow,
To pass away her melancholy hours
Without good company, and in charity,
    therefore,
Provided for me : out of her own store,
She cull'd the lords Ubaldo and Ricardo,
Two principal courtiers for ladies' service,
To do me all good offices ; and as such
Employ'd by her, I hope I have received
And entertain'd them ; nor shall they depart,
Without the effect arising from the cause
That brought them hither.
    Math. Thou dost belie thyself :
I know that in my absence thou wert honest,
However now turn'd monster.
    Soph. The truth is,
We did not deal, like you, in speculations
On cheating pictures ; we knew shadows were
No substances, and actual performance
The best assurance. I will bring them
    hither,
To make good in this presence so much for
    me.
Some minutes space I beg your majesties'
    pardon.—
You are moved now :—champ upon this bit
    a little,

Anon you shall have another. Wait me,
 Hilario. [*Exeunt* Sophia *and* Hilario.
Ladis. How now? turn'd statue, sir !
Math. Fly, and fly quickly,
From this cursed habitation, or this Gorgon
Will make you all as I am. In her tongue
Millions of adders hiss, and every hair
Upon her wicked head a snake more dreadful,
Than that Tisiphone threw on Athamas,
Which in his madness forced him to dis-
 member
His proper issue. O that ever I
Reposed my trust in magick, or believed
Impossibilities ! or that charms had power
To sink and search into the bottomless hell
Of a false woman's heart !
Eubu. These are the fruits
Of marriage ! an old bachelor as I am,
And, what's more, will continue so, is not
 troubled
With these fine vagaries.
Ferd. Till you are resolv'd, sir,
Forsake not hope.
Bap. Upon my life, this is
Dissimulation.
Ladis. And it suits not with
Your fortitude and wisdom, to be thus
Transported with your passion.
Hon. You were once
Deceived in me, sir, as I was in you ;
Yet the deceit pleased both.
Math. She hath confess'd all ;
What further proof should I ask?
Hon. Yet remember
The distance that is interposed between
A woman's tongue and her heart ; and you
 must grant,
You build upon no certainties.

Re-enter Sophia, Corisca, *and* Hilario, *with*
 Ubaldo *and* Ricardo *in rags, and spinning
 and reeling, as before.*

Eubu. What have we here?
Soph. You must come on, and shew your-
 selves.
Ubald. The king !
Ric. And queen too ! would I were as far
 under the earth
As I am above it !
Ubald. Some poet will,
From this relation, or in verse or prose,
Or both together blended, render us
Ridiculous to all ages.
Ladis. I remember
This face, when it was in a better plight :
Are not you Ricardo ?
Hon. And this thing, I take it,
Was once Ubaldo.

Ubald. I am now I know not what.
Ric. We thank your majesty for employ-
 ing us
To this subtle Circe.
Eubu. How, my lord ! turn'd spinster !
Do you work by the day, or the great?
Ferd. Is your theorbo
Turn'd to a distaff, signior? and your voice,.
With which you chanted, *Room for a lusty
 gallant !*
Tuned to the note of *Lachrymæ* ?
Eubu. Prithee tell me,
For I know thou'rt free, how oft, and to the
 purpose,
You've been merry with this lady.
Ric. Never, never.
Ladis. Howsoever, you should say so for
 your credit,
Being the only court-bull.
Ubald. O, that ever
I saw this kicking heifer !
Soph. You see, madam,
How I have cured your servants, and what
 favours,
They, with their rampant valour, have won
 from me.
You may, as they are physic'd, I presume,
Trust a fair virgin with them ; they have
 learn'd
Their several trades to live by, and paid
 nothing
But cold and hunger for them ; and may now
Set up for themselves, for here I give them
 over.
And now to you, sir ; why do you not again.
Peruse your picture, and take the advice
Of your learned consort? these are the men,
 or none,
That make you, as the Italian says, a *becco..*
Math. I know not which way to entreat
 your pardon,
Nor am I worthy of it. My Sophia,
My best Sophia, here before the king,
The queen, these lords, and all the lookers on;.
I do renounce my error, and embrace you,
As the great example to all aftertimes,
For such as would die chaste and noble wives,
With reverence to imitate.
Soph. Not so, sir ;
I yet hold off. However I have purged
My doubted innocence, the foul aspersions,
In your unmanly doubts, cast on my honour,.
Cannot so soon be wash'd off.
Eubu. Shall we have
More jiggobobs yet !
Soph. When you went to the wars,
I set no spy upon you, to observe
Which way you wander'd, though our sex by
 nature

Is subject to suspicions and fears ;
My confidence in your loyalty freed me from
    them.
But, to deal, as you did, against your re-
    ligion,
With this enchanter, to survey my actions,
Was more than woman's weakness; therefore
    know,
And 'tis my boon unto the king, I do
Desire a separation from your bed ;
For I will spend the remnant of my life
In prayer and meditation.
    Math. O take pity
Upon my weak condition, or I am
More wretched in your innocence, than if
I had found you guilty.   Have you shewn a
    jewel
Out of the cabinet of your rich mind,
To lock it up again ?—She turns away.
Will none speak for me ? shame and sin have
    robb'd me
Of the use of my tongue.
    Ladis. Since you have conquer'd, madam,
You wrong the glory of your victory,
If you use it not with mercy.   •
    Ferd. Any penance
You please to impose upon him, I dare
    . warrant
He will gladly suffer.
    Eubu. Have I lived to see
But one good woman, and shall we for a
    trifle,
Have her turn nun ? I will first pull down the
    cloister.
To the old sport again, with a good luck to
    you !
'Tis not alone enough that you are good,
We must have some of the breed of you : will
    you destroy
The kind and race of goodness ? I am con-
    verted,
And ask your pardon, madam, for my ill
    opinion

Against the sex ; and shew me but two such
    more,
I'll marry yet, and love them.
    Hon. She that yet
Ne'er knew what 'twas to bend but to the·
    king,
Thus begs remission for him.
    Soph. O, dear madam,
Wrong not your greatness so.   ·
    Omnes. We are all suitors.
    Ubald. I do deserve to be heard among
    the rest.
    Ric. And we have suffer'd for it.
    Soph. I perceive
There's no resistance : but, suppose I pardon
What's past, who can secure me he'll be free
From jealousy hereafter ?
    Math. I will be
My own security ; go, ride, where you please ;
Feast, revel, banquet, and make choice with
    whom,
I'll set no watch upon you ; and, for proof·
    of it,
This cursed picture I surrender up
To a consuming fire.
    Bapt. As I abjure
The practice of my art.
    Soph. Upon these terms
I am reconciled ; and, for these that have·
    paid
The price of their folly, I desire your mercy.
    Ladis. At your request they have it.
    Ubald. Hang all trades now !
    Ric. I will find a new one, and that is, to·
    live honest.
    Hil. These are my fees.
    Ubald. Pray you, take them, with a mis-·
    chief !
    Ladis. So, all ends in peace now.
And, to all married men, be this a caution,
Which they should duly tender as their life,.
Neither to dote too much, nor doubt a wife.·
                              [*Exeunt.*

To be marked in your fair censures.   More than this
I am forbid to promise, and it is
With the most till you confirm it : since we know
Whate'er the shaft be, archer, or the bow
From which 'tis sent, it cannot hit the white,
Unless your approbation guide it right.

PROLOGUE
AT COURT.

As ever, sir, you lent a gracious ear
To oppress'd innocence, now vouchsafe to hear
A short petition.   At your feet, in me,
The poet kneels, and to your majesty
Appeals for justice.   What we now present,
When first conceived, in his vote and intent,
Was sacred to your pleasure ; in each part,
With his best of fancy, judgment, language, art,
Fashion'd and form'd so, as might well, and may
Deserve a welcome, and no vulgar way.
He durst not, sir, at such a solemn feast,
Lard his grave matter with one scurrilous jest;
But labour'd that no passage might appear,
But what the queen without a blush might hear:
And yet this poor work suffered by the rage
And envy of some Catos of the stage:
Yet still he hopes this Play, which then was seen
With sore eyes, and condemn'd out of their spleen,
May be by you, the supreme judge, set free,
And raised above the reach of calumny.

DRAMATIS PERSONÆ.

Theodosius *the younger, the emperor.*
Paulinus, *a kinsman to the emperor.*
Philanax, *captain of the guard.*
Timantus, ⎱ *eunuchs of the emperor's cham-*
Chrysapius, ⎰ *ber.*
Gratianus, ⎰
Cleon, *a traveller, friend to* Paulinus.
Patriarch.
Informer.
Projector.
Master of the Habits and Manners.
Minion of the Suburbs.

Countryman.
Surgeon.
Empiric.
Pulcheria, *the protectress, sister to the em-*
peror.
Athenais, *a strange virgin, afterwards em-*
press, and named Eudocia.
Arcadia, ⎱ *the young sisters of the emperor.*
Flaccilla, ⎰
Officers, Suitors, Attendants, Guards,
Huntsman, Executioners, Servants, &c.

SCENE,—Constantinople.

CT I.

SCENE I.—*A Room in the Palace.*

Enter Paulinus *and* Cleon.

Paul. In your six years' travel, friend, no
doubt, you have met with
Many and rare adventures, and observed
The wonders of each climate, varying in
The manners and the men ; and so return,
For the future service of your prince and
country,
In your understanding better'd.
Cle. Sir, I have made of it
The best use in my power, and hope my
gleanings
After the full crop others reap'd before me,
Shall not, when I am call'd on, altogether
Appear unprofitable : yet I left
The miracle of miracles in our age
At home behind me ; every where abroad,
Fame, with a true though prodigal voice,
deliver'd
Such wonders of Pulcheria, the princess,
To the amazement, nay, astonishment rather,
Of such as heard it, that I found not one,
In all the states and kingdoms that I pass'd
through,
Worthy to be her second.
Paul. She, indeed, is
A perfect phœnix, and disdains a rival.
Her infant years, as you know, promised
much,
But, grown to ripeness, she transcends, and
makes
Credulity her debtor. I will tell you,
In my blunt way, to entertain the time,
Until you have the happiness to see her,
How in your absence she hath borne herself,
And with all possible brevity ; though the
subject
Is such a spacious field, as would require

An abstract of the purest eloquence
(Derived from the most famous orators
The nurse of learning, Athens, shew'd the
world)
In that man, that should undertake to be
Her true historian.
Cle. In this you shall do me
A special favour.
Paul. Since Arcadius' death,
Our late great master, the protection of
The prince, his son, the second Theodosius,
By a general vote and suffrage of the people,
Was to her charge assign'd, with the dis-
posure
Of his so many kingdoms. For his person,
She hath so train'd him up in all those arts
That are both great and good, and to be
wish'd
In an imperial monarch, that the mother
Of the Gracchi, grave Cornelia, Rome still
boasts of,
The wise Pulcheria but named, must be
No more remember'd. She, by her example,
Hath made the court a kind of academy,
In which true honour is both learn'd and
practised :
Her private lodgings a chaste nunnery,
In which her sisters, as probationers, hear
From her, their sovereign abbess, all the
precepts
Read in the school of virtue.
Cle. You amaze me.
Paul. I shall, ere I conclude ; for here the
wonder
Begins, not ends. Her soul is so immense,
And her strong faculties so apprehensive,
To search into the depth of deep designs,
And of all natures, that the burthen, which
To many men were insupportable,
To her is but a gentle exercise,
Made, by the frequent use, familiar to her.

Y

Cle. With your good favour, let me interrupt you.
Being, as she is, in every part so perfect,
Methinks that all kings of our eastern world
Should become rivals for her.
    Paul. So they have ;
But to no purpose. She, that knows her strength
To rule and govern monarchs, scorns to wear
On her free neck the servile yoke of marriage ;
And for one loose desire, envy itself
Dares not presume to taint her. Venus' son
Is blind indeed when he but gazes on her ;
Her chastity being a rock of diamonds,
With which encounter'd, his shafts fly in splinters ;
His flaming torches in the living spring
Of her perfections quench'd : and, to crown all,
She's so impartial when she sits upon
The high tribunal, neither sway'd with pity,
Nor awed by fear, beyond her equal scale,
That 'tis not superstition to believe
Astrea once more lives upon the earth,
Pulcheria's breast her temple.
    Cle. You have given her
An admirable character.
    Paul. She deserves it :
And, such is the commanding power of virtue,
That from her vicious enemies it compels
Pæans of praise, as a due tribute to her.
                [*Loud music.*
  Cle. What means this solemn music?
    Paul. Sir, it ushers
The emperor's morning meditation,
In which Pulcheria is more than assistant.
'Tis worth your observation, and you may
Collect from her expense of time this day,
How her hours, for many years, have been disposed of.
    Cle. I am all eyes and ears.

Enter, after a strain of solemn music,
Philanax, Timantus, Patriarch, Theo-
dosius, Pulcheria, Flaccilla, and Arcadia;
followed by Chrysapius and Gratianus ;
Servants, and Officers.

    Pul. Your patience, sir.
Let those corrupted ministers of the court,
Which you complain of, our devotions ended,
Be cited to appear : for the ambassadors
Who are importunate to have audience,
From me you may assure them, that to-morrow
They shall in public kiss the emperor's robe,
And we in private, with our soonest leisure,

Will give them hearing. Have you especial care too,
That free access be granted unto all
Petitioners. The morning wears.—Pray you, on, sir ;
Time lost is ne'er recover'd.
      [*Exeunt all but* Paulinus *and* Cleon.
  Paul. Did you note
The majesty she appears in?
    Cle. Yes, my good lord ;
I was ravish'd with it.
    Paul. And then, with what speed
She orders her dispatches, not one daring
To interpose ; the emperor himself,
Without reply, putting in act whatever
She pleased to impose upon him.
    Cle. Yet there were some,
That in their sullen looks, rather confess'd
A forced constraint to serve her, than a will
To be at her devotion ; what are they?
    Paul. Eunuchs of the emperor's chamber, that repine
The globe and awful sceptre should give place
Unto the distaff ; for, as such, they whisper
A woman's government, but dare not yet
Express themselves.
    Cle. From whence are the ambassadors
To whom she promised audience?
    Paul. They are
Employ'd by divers princes, who desire
Alliance with our emperor, whose years now,
As you see, write him man. One would advance
A daughter to the honour of his bed ;
A second, his fair sister : to instruct you
In the particulars would ask longer time
Than my own designs give way to. I have letters
From special friends of mine, that to my care
Commend a stranger virgin, whom this morning
I purpose to present before the princess :
If you please, you may accompany me.
    Cle. I'll wait on you.   [*Exeunt.*

SCENE II.—*Another Room in the same.*
Enter the Informer, *with* Officers *bringing*
in the Projector, *the* Minion of the Suburbs,
and the Master of the Habit and Manners.

    Infor. Why should you droop, or hang your working heads?
No danger is meant to you ; pray bear up :
For aught I know, you are cited to receive
Preferment due to your merits.
    Proj. Very likely :
In all the projects I have read and practised,
I never found one man compell'd to come,
Before the seat of justice, under guard,
To receive honour.

Infor. No! it may be, you are
The first example. Men of qualities,
As I have deliver'd you to the protectress,
Who knows how to advance them, cannot
    conceive
A fitter place to have their virtues publish'd,
Than in open court. Could you hope that
    the princess,
Knowing your precious merits, will reward
    them
In a private corner? No; you know not yet
How you may be exalted.
    Min. To the gallows.
    Infor. Fie!
Nor yet depress'd tò the galleys; in your
    names
You carry no such crimes: your specious titles
Cannot but take her:—President of the Pro-
    jectors!
What a noise it makes! The Master of the
    Habit!
How proud would some one country be that
    I know,
To be your first pupil! Minion of the
    Suburbs,
And now and then admitted to the court,
And honour'd with the style of Squire of
    Dames!
What hurt is in it! One thing I must tell you,
As I am the state-scout, you may think me
    an informer.
    Mast. They are synonyma.
    Infor. Conceal nothing from her
Of your good parts, 'twill be the better for you;
Or if you should, it matters not; she can
    conjure,
And I am her ubiquitary spirit,
Bound to obey her:—you have my instruc-
    tions;
Stand by, here's better company.

Enter Paulinus, Cleon, *and* Athenais, *with
a petition.*

    Athen. Can I hope, sir,
Oppressed innocence shall find protection
And justice among strangers, when my
    brothers,
Brothers of one womb, by one sire begotten,
Trample on my afflictions?
    Paul. Forget them,
Remembering those may help you.
    Athen. They have robb'd me
Of all means to prefer my just complaint,
With any promising hope to gain a hearing,
Much less redress: petitions not sweetened
With gold, are but unsavory, oft refused;
Or, if received, are pocketed, not read.
A suitor's swelling tears, by the glowing beams

Of choleric authority are dried up
Before they fall, or, if seen, never pitied.
What will become of a forsaken maid!
My flattering hopes are too weak to encounter
With my strong enemy, despair, and 'tis
In vain to oppose her.
    Cle. Cheer her up; she faints, sir.
    Paul. This argues weakness; though
    your brothers were
Cruel beyond expression, and the judges
That sentenced you, corrupt, you shall find
    here
One of your own fair sex to do you right;
Whose beams of justice, like the sun, extend
Their light and heat to strangers, and are not
Municipal or confined.
    Athen. Pray you, do not feed me
With airy hopes: unless you can assure me
The great Pulcheria will descend to hear
My miserable story, it were better
I died without the trouble.
    Paul. She is bound to it
By the surest chain, her natural inclination
To help the afflicted; nor shall long delays,
More terrible to miserable suitors
Than quick denials, grieve you. Dry your
    fair eyes.
This room will instantly be sanctified
With her bless'd presence; to her ready hand
Present your grievances, and rest assured
You shall depart contented.
    Athen. You breathe in me
A second life.
    Infor. Will your lordship please to hear
Your servant a few words?
    Paul. Away, you rascal!
Did I ever keep such servants?
    Infor. If your honesty
Would give you leave, it would be for your
    profit.
    Paul. To make use of an informer! tell
    me, in what
Can you advantage me?
    Infor. In the first tender
Of a fresh suit never begg'd yet.
    Paul. What's your suit, sir?
    Infor. 'Tis feasible:—here are three ar-
    rant knaves
Discovered by my art.
    Paul. And thou the archknave:
The great devour the less.
    Infor. And with good reason;
I must eat one a month, I cannot live else.
    Paul. A notable cannibal! but should I
    hear thee,
In what do your knaves concern me?
    Infor. In the begging
Of their estates.
    Paul. Before they are condemn'd·

Infor. Yes, or arraign'd : your lordship
  may speak too late else.
They are your own, and I will be content
With the fifth part of a share.
  Paul. Hence, rogue !
  Infor. Such rogues
In this kind will be heard and cherish'd too.
Fool that I was, to offer such a bargain
To a spiced-conscience chapman !—but I
  care not ;
What he disdains to taste, others will swal-
  low.

Loud Music. Enter Theodosius, Pulcheria,
  Arcadia, Flaccilla, Patriarch, Philanax,
  Timantus, Chrysapius, Gratianus, *and*
  Attendants.

  Cle. They are return'd from the temple.
  Paul. See, she appears ;
What think you now ?
  Athen. A cunning painter thus,
Her veil ta'en off, and awful sword and
  balance
Laid by, would picture Justice.
  Pul. When you please,
You may intend those royal exercises
Suiting your birth and greatness : I will bear
The burthen of your cares, and, having
  purged
The body of your empire of ill humours,
Upon my knees surrender it.
  Chry. Will you ever
Be awed thus like a boy ?
  Grat. And kiss the rod
Of a proud mistress ?
  Tim. Be what you were born, sir.
  Phil. Obedience and majesty never lodged
In the same inn.
  Theod. No more ; he never learn'd
The right way to command, that stopp'd his
  ears
To wise directions.
  Pul. Read o'er the papers
I left upon my cabinet, two hours hence
I will examine you.
  Flac. We spend our time well !
Nothing but praying and poring on a book.
It ill agrees with my constitution, sister.
  Arcad. Would I had been born some
  masquing-lady's woman,
Only to see strange sights, rather than live
  thus !
  Flac. We are gone, forsooth ; there is no
  remedy, sister.
            [*Exeunt* Arcadia *and* Flaccilla.
  Grat. What hath his eye found out ?
  Tim. 'Tis fix'd upon
That stranger lady.

  Chry. I am glad yet, that
He dares look on a woman.
    [*All this time the* Informer *is kneeling
       to* Pulcheria, *and delivering papers.*
  Theo. Philanax,
What is that comely stranger ?
  Phil. A petitioner.
  Chry. Will you hear her case, and dis-
  patch her in your chamber ?
I'll undertake to bring her.
  Theo. Bring me to
Some place where I may look on her de-
  meanor :
'Tis a lovely creature !
  Chry. There's some hope in this yet.
    [*Flourish. Exeunt* Theodosius, Pa-
      triarch, Philanax, Timantus, Chrysa-
      pius, *and* Gratianus.
  Pul. No ; you have done your parts.
  Paul. Now opportunity courts you,
Prefer your suit.
  Athen. [*Kneeling.*] As low as misery
Can fall, for proof of my humility,
A poor distressed virgin bows her head,
And lays hold on your goodness, the last altar
Calamity can fly to for protection.
Great minds erect their never-falling trophies
On the firm base of mercy ; but to triumph
Over a suppliant, by proud fortune captived,
Argues a bastard conquest :—'tis to you
I speak, to you, the fair and just Pulcheria,
The wonder of the age, your sex's honour ;
And as such, deign to hear me. As you have
A soul moulded from heaven, and do desire
To have it made a star there, make the means
Of your ascent to that celestial height
Virtue, wing'd with brave action : they draw
  near
The nature and the essence of the gods,
Who imitate their goodness.
  Pul. If you were
A subject of the empire, which your habit
In every part denies——
  Athen. O, fly not to
Such an evasion ! whate'er I am,
Being a woman, in humanity
You are bound to right me. Though the
  difference
Of my religion may seem to exclude me
From your defence, which you would have
  confined ;
The moral virtue, which is general,
Must know no limits. By these blessed feet,
That pace the paths of equity, and tread boldly
On the stiff neck of tyrannous oppression,
By these tears by which I bathe them, I
  conjure you
With pity to look on me !
  Pul. Pray you, rise ;

And, as you rise, receive this comfort from
me.

Beauty, set off with such sweet language,
never

Can want an advocate; and you must bring
More than a guilty cause if you prevail not.
Some business, long since thought upon,
dispatch'd,
You shall have hearing, and, as far as justice
Will warrant me, my best aids.

  Athen. I do desire
No stronger guard; my equity needs no
favour.   [*Walks aside.*

  Pul. Are these the men?

  Proj. We were, an't like your highness,
The men, the men of eminence and mark,
And may continue so, if it please your grace.

  Mast. This speech was well projected.

  Pul. Does your conscience,
I will begin with you, whisper unto you
What here you stand accused of? Are you
named
The President of Projectors?

  Infor. Justify it, man,
And tell her in what thou'rt useful.

  Proj. That is apparent;
And if you please, ask some about the court,
And they will tell you, to my rare inventions
They owe their bravery, perhaps means to
purchase,
And cannot live without me. I, alas!
Lend out my labouring brains to use, and
sometimes
For a drachma in the pound,—the more the
pity
I am all patience, and endure the curses
Of many, for the profit of one patron.

  Pul. I do conceive the rest. What is the
second?

  Infor. The Minion of the Suburbs.

  Pul. What hath he
To do in Constantinople?

  Min. I steal in now and then,
As I am thought useful; marry, there I am
call'd
The Squire of Dames, or Servant of the Sex,
And by the allowance of some sportful ladies,
Honour'd with that title.

  Pul. Spare your character,
You are here decipher'd: stand by with your
compeer.
What is the third? a creature I ne'er heard of:
The Master of the Manners and the Habit!
You have a double office.

  Mast. In my actions
I make both good; for by my theorems
Which your polite and terser gallants practise,
I re-refine the court, and civilize
Their barbarous natures. I have in a table,

With curious punctuality set down,
To a hair's breadth, how low a new-stamp'd
courtier
May vail to a country gentleman, and by
Gradation, to his merchant, mercer, draper,
His linen-man, and tailor.

  Pul. Pray you, discover,
This hidden mystery.

  Mast. If the foresaid courtier
(As it may chance sometimes) find not his
name
Writ in the citizens' books, with a state hum
He may salute them after three days wait-
ing;
But, if he owe them money, that he may
Preserve his credit, let him in policy never
Appoint a day of payment, so they may
hope still:
But, if he be to take up more, his page
May attend them at the gate, and usher them
Into his cellar, and when they are warm'd
with wine,
Conduct them to his bedchamber; and
though then
He be under his barber's hands, as soon as
seen,
He must start up to embrace them, vail
thus low;
Nay, though he call them cousins, 'tis the
better,
His dignity no way wrong'd in't.

  Paul. Here's a fine knave!

  Pul. Does this rule hold without exception, sirrah,
For courtiers in general?

  Mast. No, dear madam,
For one of the last edition; and for him
I have composed a dictionary, in which
He is instructed, how, when, and to whom,
To be proud or humble; at what times of
the year
He may do a good deed for itself, and that is
Writ in dominical letters; all days else
Are his own, and of those days the several
   hours
Mark'd out, and to what use.

  Pul. Shew us your method;
I am strangely taken with it.

  Mast. 'Twill deserve
A pension, I hope. First, a strong cullis
In his bed, to heighten appetite; shuttle-
cock,
To keep him in breath when he rises;
tennis courts
Are chargeable, and the riding of great
horses
Too boisterous for my young courtier: let
the old ones
I think not of, use it; next, his meditation

How to court his mistress, and that he may
  seem witty,
Let him be furnish'd with confederate jests
Between him and his friend, that, on occa-
  sion,
They may vent them mutually: what his
  pace and garb
Must be in the presence, then the length of
  his sword,
The fashion of the hilt—what the blade is
It matters not, 'twere barbarism to use it.
Unless to shew his strength upon an andiron;
So, the sooner broke the better.
    Pul. How I abuse
This precious time! Projector, I treat first
Of you and your disciples; you roar out,
All is the king's, his will above his laws;
And that fit tributes are too gentle yokes
For his poor subjects: whispering in his ear,
If he would have their fear, no man should
  dare
To bring a salad from his country garden,
Without the paying gabel; kill a hen,
Without excise: and that if he desire
To have his children or his servants wear
Their heads upon their shoulders, you affirm
In policy 'tis fit the owner should
Pay for them by the poll; or, if the prince
  want
A present sum, he may command a city
Impossibilities, and for non-performance,
Compel it to submit to any fine
His officers shall impose. Is this the way
To make our emperor happy? can the groans
Of his subjects yield him music? must his
  thresholds
Be wash'd with widows and wrong'd orphans'
  tears,
Or his power grow contemptible?
    Proj. I begin
To feel myself a rogue again.
    Pul. But you are
The squire of dames, devoted to the service
Of gamesome ladies, the hidden mystery
Discover'd, their close bawd, thy slavish
  breath
Fanning the fires of lust; the go-between
This female and that wanton sir; your art
Can blind a jealous husband, and, disguised
Like a milliner or shoemaker, convey
A letter in a pantofle or glove,
Without suspicion, nay, at his table,
In a case of picktooths; you instruct them
  how
To parley with their eyes, and make the
  temple
A mart of looseness:—to discover all
Your subtile brokages, were to teach in
  public

Those private practices which are, in justice,
Severely to be punish'd.
    Min. I am cast:
A jury of my patronesses cannot quit me.
    Pul. You are master of the manners and
  the habit;
Rather the scorn of such as would live men,
And not, like apes, with servile imitation
Study prodigious fashions. You keep
Intelligence abroad, that may instruct
Our giddy youth at home what new-found
  fashion
Is now in use, swearing he's most complete
That first turns monster. Know, villains,
  I can thrust
This arm into your hearts, strip off the flesh
That covers your deformities, and shew you
In your own nakedness. Now, though the
  law
Call not your follies death, you are for ever
Banish'd my brother's court.—Away with
  them;
I will hear no reply.
    [*Exeunt* Informer, *and* Officers *with the*
    Projector, Minion of the Suburbs, *and*
    Master of the Habit and Manners.
    Athenais *comes forward.*

Enter above, Theodosius, Philanax, Timantus, Chrysapius, *and* Gratianus.

    Paul. What think you now?
    Cle. That I am in a dream; or that I see
A second Pallas.
    Pul. These removed, to you
I clear my brow. Speak without fear, sweet
  maid,
Since, with a mild aspect, and ready ear,
I sit prepared to hear you.
    Athen. Know, great princess,
My father, though a pagan, was admired
For his deep search into those hidden studies,
Whose knowledge is denied to common men:
The motion, with the divers operations
Of the superior bodies, by his long
And careful observation were made
Familiar to him; all the secret virtues
Of plants and simples, and in what degree
They were useful to mankind, he could dis-
  course of:
In a word, conceive him as a prophet honour'd
In his own country. But being born a man,
It lay not in him to defer the hour
Of his approaching death, though long fore-
  told:
In this so fatal hour he call'd before him
His two sons and myself, the dearest pledges
Lent him by nature, and with his right hand
Blessing our several heads, he thus began.
    Chry. Mark his attention.

Phil. Give me leave to mark too.

*Athen. If I could leave my understanding
    to you
It were superfluous to make division
Of whatsoever else I can bequeath you:
But, to avoid contention I allot
An equal portion of my possessions
To you, my sons; but unto thee, my daughter,
My joy, my darling,* (pardon me, though I
Repeat his words,) *if my prophetic soul,
Ready to take her flight, can truly guess at
Thy future fate, I leave the strange as-
    surance
Of the greatness thou art born to, unto which
Thy brothers shall be proud to pay their
    service:—*

Paul. And all men else, that honour
    beauty.

Theo. Umph !

*Athen. Yet to prepare thee for that certain
    fortune,
And that I may from present wants defend
    thee,
I leave ten thousand crowns:*—which said,
    being call'd
To the fellowship of our deities, he expired,
And with him all remembrance of the charge
Concerning me, left by him to my brothers.

Pul. Did they detain your legacy?

Athen. And still do.
His ashes were scarce quiet in his urn,
When, in derision of my future greatness,
They thrust me out of doors, denying me
One short night's harbour.

Pul. Weep not.

Athen. I desire,
By your persuasion, or commanding power,
The restitution of mine own ; or that,
To keep my frailty from temptation,
In your compassion of me, you would please,
I, as an handmaid, may be entertain'd
To do the meanest offices to all such
As are honour'd in your service.

Pul. Thou art welcome.
What is thy name?

Athen. The forlorn Athenais.

Pul. The sweetness of thy innocence
    strangely takes me.
        [*Takes her up and kisses her.*
Forget thy brothers wrongs ; for I will be
In my care a mother, in my love a sister to
    thee ;
And, were it possible thou couldst be won
To be of our belief——

Paul. May it please your excellence,
That is an easy task ; I, though no scholar,
Dare undertake it ; clear truth cannot want
Rhetorical persuasions.

Pul. 'Tis a work,

My lord, will well become you.—Break up
    the court :
May your endeavours prosper !

Paul. Come, my fair one ;
I hope, my convert.

Athen. Never : I will die
As I was born,

Paul. Better you ne'er had been. [*Exeunt.*

Phil. What does your majesty think of?
——the maid's gone.

Theo. She's wondrous fair, and in her
    speech appear'd
Pieces of scholarship.

Chry. Make use of her learning
And beauty together ; on my life she will be
    proud
To be so converted.

Theo. From foul lust heaven guard me !
                [*Exeunt.*

───

ACT II.

SCENE I.—*A Room in the Palace.*

Enter Philanax, Timantus, Chrysapius,
    and Gratianus.

Phil. We only talk, when we should do.

Tim. I'll second you ;
Begin, and when you please.

Grat. Be constant in it.

Chry. That resolution which grows cold
    to-day,
Will freeze to-morrow.

Grat. 'Slight ! I think she'll keep him
Her ward for ever, to herself engrossing
The disposition of all the favours
And bounties of the empire.

Chry. We, that by
The nearness of our service to his person,
Should raise this man, or pull down that,
    without
Her license hardly dare prefer a suit,
Or if we do, 'tis cross'd.

Phil. You are troubled for
Your proper ends ; my aims are high and
    honest,
The wrong that's done to majesty I repine at :
I love the emperor, and 'tis my ambition
To have him know himself, and to that
    purpose
I'll run the hazard of a check.

Grat. And I
The loss of my place.

Tim. I will not come behind,
Fall what can fall.

Chry. Let us put on sad aspects,
To draw him on ; charge home, we'll fetch
    you off,
Or lie dead by you.

Enter Theodosius.

Theo. How's this? clouds in the chamber,
And the air clear abroad!
Phil. When you, our sun,
Obscure your glorious beams, poor we that
  borrow
Our little light from you, cannot but suffer
A general eclipse.
Tim. Great sir, 'tis true;
For, till you please to know and be yourself,
And freely dare dispose of what's your own,
Without a warrant, we are falling meteors,
And not fix'd stars.
Chry. The pale-faced moon, that should
Govern the night, usurps the rule of day,
And still is at the full in spite of nature,
And will not know a change.
Theo. Speak you in riddles?
I am no Œdipus, but your emperor,
And as such would be instructed.
Phil. Your command
Shall be obey'd: till now, I never heard you
Speak like yourself; and may that Power, by
  which
You are so, strike me dead, if what I shall
Deliver as a faithful subject to you,
Hath root or growth from malice, or base
  envy
Of your sister's greatness! I could honour
  in her
A power subordinate to yours; but not,
As 'tis, predominant.
Tim. Is it fit that she,
In her birth your vassal, should command
  the knees
Of such as should not bow but to yourself?
Grat. She with security walks upon the
  heads   *
Of the nobility; the multitude,
As to a deity, offering sacrifice   .
For her grace and favour.
Chry. Her proud feet even wearied
With the kisses of petitioners.
Grat. While you,
To whom alone such reverence is proper,
Pass unregarded by.
Tim. You have not yet,
Been master of one hour of your whole life.
Chry. Your will and faculties kept in more
  awe
Than she can do her own.
Phil. And as a bondman,
(O let my zeal find grace, and pardon from
  you,
That I descend so low,) you are design'd
To this or that employment, suiting well
A private man, I grant, but not a prince.
To be a perfect horseman, or to know

The words of the chase, or a fair man of
  arms,
Or to be able to pierce to the depth,
Or write a comment on the obscurest poets,
I grant are ornaments; but your main scope
Should be to govern men, to guard your
  own,
If not enlarge your empire.
Chry. You are built up
By the curious hand of nature, to revive
The memory of Alexander, or by
A prosperous success in your brave actions,
To rival Cæsar.
Tim. Rouse yourself, and let not
Your pleasures be a copy of her will.
Phil. Your pupilage is past, and manly
  actions
Are now expected from you.
Grat. Do not lose
Your subjects' hearts.
Tim. What is't to have the means
To be magnificent, and not exercise
The boundless virtue?
Grat. You confine yourself
To that which strict philosophy allows of,
As if you were a private man.
Tim. No pomp
Or glorious shows of royalty rendering it
Both loved and terrible.
Grat. 'Slight! you live, as it
Begets some doubt, whether you have, or not,
The abilities of a man.
Chry. The firmament
Hath not more stars than there are several
  beauties
Ambitious, at the height, to impart their
  dear
And sweetest favours to you.
Grat. Yet you have not
Made choice of one, of all the sex, to serve
  you,
In a physical way of courtship.
Theo. But that I would not
Begin the expression of my being a man,
In blood, or stain the first white robe I wear
Of absolute power, with a servile imitation
Of any tyrannous habit, my just anger
Prompts me to make you, in your sufferings,
  feel,
And not in words to instruct you, that the
  license
Of the loose and saucy language you now
  practised
Hath forfeited your heads.
Grat. How's this!
Phil. I know not
What the play may prove, but I assure you
  that
I do not like the prologue.

Theo. O the miserable
Condition of a prince; who, though he vary
More shapes than Proteus, in his mind and
    manners
He cannot win an universal suffrage
From the many-headed monster, multitude!
Like Æsop's foolish frogs, they trample on
    him
As a senseless block, if his government be
    easy;
And, if he prove a stork, they croak and rail
Against him as a tyrant.—I will put off
That majesty, of which you think I have
Nor use nor feeling; and in arguing with you,
Convince you with strong proofs of common
    reason,
And not with absolute power, against which,
    wretches,
You are not to dispute. Dare you, that are
My creatures, by my prodigal favours
    fashion'd,
Presuming on the nearness of your service,
Set off with my familiar acceptance,
Condemn my obsequiousness to the wise
    directions
Of an incomparable sister, whom all parts
Of our world, that are made happy in the
    knowledge
Of her perfections, with wonder gaze on?
And yet you, that were only born to eat
The blessings of our mother earth, that are
Distant but one degree from beasts, (since
    slaves
Can claim no larger privilege,) that know
No further than your sensual appetites,
Or wanton lusts, have taught you, undertake
To give your sovereign laws to follow that
Your ignorance marks out to him!
                    [*Walks by.*
  Grat. How were we
Abused in our opinion of his temper!
  Phil. We had forgot 'tis found in holy
    writ,
That kings' hearts are inscrutable.
  Tim. I ne'er read it;
My study lies not that way.
  Phil. By his looks,
The tempest still increases.
  Theo. Am I grown
So stupid, in your judgments, that you dare,
With such security, offer violence
To sacred majesty? will you not know
The lion is a lion, though he shew not
His rending paws, or fill the affrighted air
With the thunder of his roarings?——You
    bless'd saints,
How am I trenched on! Is that temperance
So famous in your cited Alexander,
Or Roman Scipio, a crime in me?

Cannot I be an emperor, unless
Your wives and daughters bow to my proud
    lusts?
And, 'cause I ravish not their fairest build-
 . ings
And fruitful vineyards, or what is dearest,
From such as are my vassals, must you con-
    clude
I do not know the awful power and strength
Of my prerogative? Am I close-handed,
Because I scatter not among you that
I must not call mine own? know you, court-
    leeches,
A prince is never so magnificent
As when he's sparing to enrich a few
With the injuries of many. Could your
    hopes
So grossly flatter you, as to believe
I was born and train'd up as an emperor,
    only
In my indulgence to give sanctuary,
In their unjust proceedings, to the rapine
And avarice of my grooms?
  Phil. In the true mirror
Of your perfections, at length we see
Our own deformities.
  Tim. And not once daring
To look upon that majesty we now slight-
    ed——
  Chry. With our faces thus glued to the
    earth, we beg
Your gracious pardon.
  Grat. Offering our necks
To be trod on, as a punishment for our late
Presumption, and a willing testimony
Of our subjection.
  Theo. Deserve our mercy
In your better life hereafter; you shall find,
Though, in my father's life, I held it mad-
    ness
To usurp his power, and in my youth dis-
    dain'd not
To learn from the instructions of my sister,
I'll make it good to all the world I am
An emperor; and even this instant grasp
The sceptre, my rich stock of majesty
Entire, no scruple wasted.
  Phil. If these tears
I drop proceed not from my joy to hear
    this,
May my eyeballs follow them!
  Tim. I will shew myself,
By your sudden metamorphosis, transform'd
From what I was.
  Grat. And ne'er presume to ask
What fits not you to give.
  Theo. Move in that sphere,
And my light with full beams shall shine
    upon you.

Forbear this slavish courtship, 'tis to me
In a kind idolatrous.
  Phil. Your gracious sister.

    Enter Pulcheria *and* Servant.   •

  Pul. Has he converted her?
  Serv. And, as such, will
Present her, when you please.
  Pul. I am glad of it.
Command my dresser to adorn her with
The robes that I gave order for.
  Serv. I shall.
  Pul. And let those precious jewels I took
last
Out of my cabinet, if't be possible,
Give lustre to her beauties ; and, that done,
Command her to be near us.
  Serv. 'Tis a province
I willingly embrace.   [*Exit.*
  Pul. O my dear sir,
You have forgot your morning task, and
therefore,
With a mother's love, I come to reprehend
you ;
But it shall be gently.
  Theo. 'Twill become you, though
You said, with reverend duty. Know, here-
after,
If my mother lived in you, howe'er her son,
Like you she were my subject.
  Pul. How !
  Theo. Put off
Amazement ; you will find it. Yet I'll hear
you
At distance, as a sister, but no longer
As a governess, I assure you.
  Grat. This is put home.
  Tim. Beyond our hopes.
  Phil. She stands as if his words
Had powerful magic in them.
  Theo. Will you have me
Your pupil ever ? the down on my chin
Confirms I am a man, a man of men,
The emperor, that knows his strength.
  Pul. Heaven grant
You know it not too soon !
  Theo. Let it suffice
My wardship's out. If your design con-
cerns us
As a man, and not a boy, with our allowance
You may deliver it.
  Pul. A strange alteration !
But I will not contend. Be as you wish, sir,
Your own disposer ; uncompell'd I cancel
All bonds of my authority.   [*Kneels.*
  Theo. You in this
Pay your due homage, which perform'd, I
thus

Embrace you as a sister ; [*Raises her.*] no
way doubting
Your vigilance for my safety as my honour ;
And what you now come to impart, I rest
Most confident, points at one of them.
  Pul. At both ;
And not alone the present, but the future
Tranquillity of your mind ; since in the
choice
Of her you are to heat with holy fires,
And make the consort of your royal bed,
The certain means of glorious succession,
With the true happiness of our human being,
Are wholly comprehended.
  Theo. How ! a wife?
Shall I become a votary to Hymen,
Before my youth hath sacrificed to Venus?
'Tis something with the soonest :—yet, to
shew,
In things indifferent, I am not averse
To your wise counsels, let me first survey
Those beauties, that, in being a prince, I
know
Are rivals for me. You will not confine me
To your election ; I must see, dear sister,
With mine own eyes.
  Pul. 'Tis fit, sir. Yet, in this,
You may please to consider, absolute princes
Have, or should have, in policy, less free will
Than such as are their vassals : for, you
must,
As you are an emperor, in this high business
Weigh with due providence, with whom
alliance
May be most useful for the preservation
Or increase of your empire.
  Theo. I approve not
Such compositions for our moral ends,
In what is in itself divine, nay, more,
Decreed in heaven. Yet, if our neighbour
princes,
Ambitious of such nearness, shall present
Their dearest pledges to me, (ever reserving
The caution of mine own content,) I will not
Contemn their courteous offers.
  Pul. Bring in the pictures.
      [*Two pictures brought in.*
  Theo. Must I then judge the substances
by the shadows?
The painters are most envious, if they want
Good colours for preferment : virtuous ladies
Love this way to be flattered, and accuse
The workman of detraction, if he add not
Some grace they cannot truly call their own.
Is't not so, Gratianus? you may challenge
Some interest in the science.
  Grat. A pretender
To the art, I truly honour, and subscribe
To your majesty's opinion.

Theo. Let me see—— [*Reads.*
Cleanthe, daughter to the king of Epire,
Ætatis suæ, the fourteenth : ripe enough,
And forward too, I assure you. Let me
examine
The symmetries. If statuaries could
By the foot of Hercules set down punctually
His whole dimensions, and the countenance
be
The index of the mind, this may instruct me,
With the aids of that I've read touching this
subject,
What she is inward. The colour of her hair,
If it be, as this does promise, pale and faint,
And not a glistering white ; her brow, so so ;
The circles of her sight, too much con-
tracted ;—
Juno's fair cow-eyes by old Homer are
Commended to their merit : here's a sharp
frost,
In the tip of her nose, which, by the length,
assures me
Of storms at midnight, if I fail to pay her
The tribute she expects. I like her not :
What is the other ?
Chry. How hath he commenced
Doctor in this so sweet and secret art,
Without our knowledge ?
Tim. Some of his forward pages
Have robbed us of the honour.
Phil. No such matter ;
He has the theory only, not the practic.
Theo. [*reads.*] *Amasia, sister to the duke*
of Athens ;
Her age eighteen, descended lineally
From Theseus, as by her pedigree
Will be made apparent. Of his lusty kin-
dred,
And lose so much time ! 'tis strange !—as I
live, she hath
A philosophical aspéct ; there is
More wit than beauty in her face ; and when
I court her, it must be in tropes, and figures,
Or she will cry, Absurd ! she will have
her elenchs
To cut off any fallacy I can hope
To put upon her, and expect I should
Ever conclude in syllogisms, and those true
ones
In parte et toto : or she'll tire me with
Her tedious elocutions in the praise of
The increase of generation, for which
Alone, the sport, in her morality,
Is good and lawful, and to be often practised
For fear of missing. Fie on't ! let the race
Of Theseus be match'd with Aristotle's :
I'll none of her.
Pul. You are curious in your choice, sir,
And hard to please ; yet, if that your consent

May give authority to it, I'll present you
With one, that, if her birth and fortunes.
answer
The rarities of her body and her mind,
Detraction durst not tax her.
Theo. Let me see her,
Though wanting those additions, which we
can
Supply from our own store : it is in us
To make men rich and noble ; but to give
Legitimate shapes and virtues does belong
To the great Creator of them, to whose
boúnties
Alone 'tis proper, and in this disdains
An emperor for his rival.
Pul. I applaud
This fit acknowledgment ; since princes then
Grow less than common men, when they
contend
With him, by whom they are so.

Enter Paulinus, Cleon, *and* Athenais,
richly habited.

Theo. I confess it.
Pul. Not to hold you in suspense, behold
the virgin,
Rich in her natural beauties, no way bor-
rowing
The adulterate aids of art. Peruse her
better ;
She's worth your serious view.
Phil. I am amazed too :
I never saw her equal.
Grat. How his eye
Is fix'd upon her !
Tim. And, as she were a fort
He'd suddenly surprise, he measures her
From the bases to the battlements.
Chry. Ha ! now I view her better,
I know her ; 'tis the maid that not long since
Was a petitioner ; her bravery
So alters her, I had forgot her face.
Phil. So has the emperor.
Paul. She holds out yet,
And yields not to the assault.
Cle. She's strongly guarded
In her virgin blushes.
Paul. When you know, fair creature,
It is the emperor that honours you
With such a strict survey of your sweet parts,
In thankfulness you cannot but return
Due reverence for the favour.
Athen. I was lost
In my astonishment at the glorious object,
And yet rest doubtful whether he expects,
Being more than man, my adoration,
Since sure there is divinity about him :
Or will rest satisfied, if my humble knees
In duty thus bow to him.

Theo. Ha! it speaks.
Pul. She is no statue, sir.
Theo. Suppose her one,
And that she had nor organs, voice, nor heat,
Most willingly I would resign my empire,
So it might be to aftertimes recorded
That I was her Pygmalion ; though, like
  him,
I doted on my workmanship, without hope
  too
Of having Cytherea so propitious
To my vows or sacrifice, in her compassion
To give it life or motion.
Pul. Pray you, be not rapt so,
Nor borrow from imaginary fiction
Impossible aids : she's flesh and blood, I
  assure you ;
And if you please to honour her in the trial,
And be your own security, as you'll find
I fable not, she comes in a noble way
To be at your devotion.
Chry. 'Tis the maid
I offer'd to your highness ; her changed
  shape
Conceal'd her from you.
Theo. At the first I knew her,
And a second firebrand Cupid brings, to
  kindle
My flames almost put out : I am too cold,
And play with opportunity.—May I taste
  then
The nectar of her lip ?—[*Kisses her.*]—I do
  not give it
The praise it merits : antiquity is too poor
To help me with a simile to express her :
Let me drink often from this living spring,
To nourish new invention.
Pul. Do not surfeit
In over-greedily devouring that
Which may without satiety feast you often.
From the moderation in receiving them,
The choicest viands do continue pleasing
To the most curious palates. If you think her
Worth your embraces, and the sovereign title
Of the Grecian Empress——
Theo. If! how much you sin,
Only to doubt it ; the possession of her
Makes all that was before most precious to
  me,
Common and cheap : in this you've shewn
  yourself
A provident protectress. I already
Grow weary of the absolute command
Of my so numerous subjects, and desire
No sovereignty but here, and write down
  gladly
A period to my wishes.
Pul. Yet, before
It be too late, consider her condition ;

Her father was a pagan, she herself
A new-converted Christian.
Theo. Let me know
The man to whose religious means I owe
So great a debt.
Paul. You are advanced too high, sir,
To acknowledge a beholdingness ; 'tis dis-
  charged,
And I beyond my hopes rewarded, if
My service please your majesty.
Theo. Take this pledge
Of our assured love.   Are there none here
Have suits to prefer ! on such a day as this
My bounty's without limit.   O my dear-
  est !——
I will not hear thee speak ; whatever in
Thy thoughts is apprehended, I grant freely :
Thou wouldst plead thy unworthiness.   By
  thyself,
The magazine of felicity, in thy lowness
Our eastern queens, at their full height, bow
  to thee,
And are, in their best trim, thy foils and
  shadows !
Excuse the violence of my love, which cannot
Admit the least delay.   Command the pa-
  triarch
With speed to do his holy office for us,
That, when we are made one——
Pul. You must forbear, sir ;
She is not yet baptized.
Theo. In the same hour
In which she is confirmed in our faith,
We mutually will give away each other,
And both be gainers ; we'll hear no reply
That may divert us. On.
Pul. You may hereafter
Please to remember to whose furtherance
You owe this height of happiness.
Athen. As I was
Your creature when I first petition'd you,
I will continue so, and you shall find me,
Though an empress, still your servant.
          [*All go off, but* Philanax, Gratianus,
                    and Timantus.
Grat. Here's a marriage
Made up o' the sudden !
Phil. I repine not at
The fair maid's fortune, though I fear the
  princess
Had some peculiar end in't.
Tim. Who's so simple
Only to doubt it ?
Grat. It is too apparent ;
She hath preferr'd a creature of her own,
By whose means she may still keep to her-
  self
The government of the empire.
Tim. Whereas, if

The emperor had espoused some neighbour
   queen,
Pulcheria, with all her wisdom, could not
Keep her pre-eminence.
  Phil. Be it as it will,
'Tis not now to be alter'd. Heaven, I say,
Turn all to the best!
  Grat. Are we come to praying again?
  Phil. Leave thy profaneness.
  Grat. Would it would leave me !
I am sure I thrive not by it.
  Tim. Come to the temple.
  Grat. Even where you will—I know not
  what to think on't.   [*Exeunt.*

ACT III.

SCENE I.—*A Room in the Palace.*

Enter Paulinus *and* Philanax.

  Paul. Nor this, nor the age before us,
  ever look'd on
The like solemnity.
  Phil. A sudden fever
Kept me at home. Pray you, my lord,
  acquaint me
With the particulars.
  Paul. You may presume
No pomp nor ceremony could be wanting,
Where there was privilege to command, and
  means
To cherish rare inventions.
  Phil. I believe it ;
But the sum of all in brief.
  Paul. Pray you, so take it :
Fair Athenais, not long since a suitor,
And almost in her hopes forsaken, first
Was christen'd and the emperor's mother's
  name,
Eudocia, as he will'd, imposed upon her :
Pulcheria, the ever-matchless princess,
Assisted by her reverend aunt Maria,
Her godmothers.
  Phil. And who the masculine witness?
  Paul. At the new empress' suit, I had the
  honour ;
For which I must ever serve her.
  Phil. 'Twas a grace
With justice you may boast of.
  Paul. The marriage follow'd ;
And, as 'tis said, the emperor made bold
To turn the day to night ; for to bed they
  went
As soon as they had dined, and there are
  wagers
Laid by some merry lords, he hath already
Begot a boy upon her.
  Phil. That is yet
To be determined of ; but I am certain

A prince, so soon in his disposition alter'd,
Was never heard nor read of.
  Paul. But of late,
Frugal and sparing, now nor bounds nor
  limits
To his magnificent bounties. He affirm'd
Having received more blessings by his
  empress
Than he could hope, in thankfulness to
  heaven
He cannot be too prodigal to others.
Whatever's offer'd to his royal hand,
He signs without perusing it.
  Phil. I am here
Enjoin'd to free all such as lie for debt,
The creditors to be paid out of his coffers.
  Paul. And I all malefactors that are not
Convicted or for treason or foul murder :
Such only are excepted.
  Phil. 'Tis a rare clemency !
  Paul. Which we must not dispute, but put
  in practice.   [*Exeunt.*

SCENE II.—*Another Room in the same.*

Loud Music ; Shouts within : Heaven preserve the Emperor ! Heaven bless the
  Empress ! *Then enter in state, the* Patriarch, Chrysapius, Paulinus, Theodosius,
  Eudocia, Pulcheria ; Arcadia *and* Flaccilla, *bearing up* Eudocia's *train ; followed
  by* Philanax, Gratianus, *and* Timantus.
  Several Suitors *present petitions to the*
  Emperor, *which he seals.*

  Pul. Sir, by your own rules of philosophy,
You know things violent last not. Royal
  bounties
Are great and gracious, while they are dis-
  pensed
With moderation ; but, when their excess
In giving giant-bulks to others, takes from
The prince's just proportion, they lose
The name of virtues, and, their natures
  changed,
Grow the most dangerous vices.
  Theo. In this, sister,
Your wisdom is not circular ; they that sow
In narrow bounds, cannot expect in reason
A crop beyond their ventures : what I do
Disperse, I lend, and will with usury
Return unto my heap. I only then
Am rich and happy (though my coffers sound
With emptiness) when my glad subjects feel
Their plenty and felicity is my gift ;
And they will find, when they with cheer-
  fulness
Supply not my defects, I being the stomach
To the politic body of the state, the limbs
Grow suddenly faint and feeble : I could
  urge

Proofs of more fineness in their shape and
　　language,
But none of greater strength.—Dissuade me
　　not ;
What we will, we will do ; yet, to assure you
Your care does not offend us, for an hour
Be happy in the converse of my best
And dearest comfort.　May you please to
　　license
My privacy some few minutes ?
　　Eud.　License, sir !
I have no will but is derived from yours,
And that still waits upon you ; nor can I
Be left with such security with any
As with the gracious princess, who receives
Addition, though she be all excellence,
In being styled your sister.　　·
　　Theo.　O' sweet creature !
Let me be censured fond, and too indulgent,
Nay, though they say uxorious, I care not—
Her love and sweet humility exact
A tribute far above my power to pay
Her matchless goodness.　Forward.
　　　[*Flourish. Exeunt all but* Pulcheria,
　　　　Eudocia, Arcadia, *and* Flaccilla.
　　Pul. Now you find
Your dying father's prophecy, that foretold
Your present greatness, to the full accom-
　　plish'd,
For the poor aids and furtherance I lent you,
I willingly forget.
　　Eud. Even that binds me
To a more strict remembrance of the favour ;
Nor shall you, from my foul ingratitude,
In any circumstance, ever find cause
To upbraid me with your benefit.
　　Pul. I believe so.
Pray you, give us leave :—[Arcadia *and*
　　Flaccilla *walk aside.*]—What now I
　　must deliver
Under the deepest seal of secrecy,
Though it be for your good, will give assu-
　　rance
Of what is look'd for, if you not alone
Hear, but obey my counsels.
　　Eud. They must be
Of a strange nature, if with zealous speed
I put them not in practice.
　　Pul. 'Twere impertinence
To dwell on circumstances, since the wound
Requires a sudden cure ; especially
Since you, that are the happy instrument
Elected to it, though young, in your judg-
　　ment
Write far above your years, and may instruct
Such as are more experienced.
　　Eud. Good madam,
In this I must oppose you ; I am well
Acquainted with my weakness, and it will not

Become your wisdom, by which I am raised
To this titulary height, that should correct
The pride and overweening of my fortune,
To play the parasite to it, in ascribing
That merit to me, unto which I can
Pretend no interest : pray you, excuse
My bold simplicity, and to my weight
Design me where you please, and you shall
　　find,
In my obedience, I am still your creature.
　　Pul. 'Tis nobly answer'd, and I glory in ·
The building I have raised : go on, sweet
　　lady,
In this your virtuous progress : but to the
　　point.
You know, nor do I envy it, you have
Acquired that power which, not long since,
　　was mine,
In governing the emperor, and must use
The strength you hold in the heart of his
　　affections,
For his private, as the public preservation,
To which there is no greater enemy
Than his exorbitant prodigality,
Howe'er his sycophants and flatterers call it
Royal magnificence ; and though you may
Urge what's done for your honour must
　　not be
Curb'd or controll'd by you, you cannot in
Your wisdom but conceive, if that the torrent
Of his violent bounties be not stopp'd or
　　lessen'd,
It will prove most pernicious.　Therefore,
　　madam,
Since 'tis your duty, as you are his wife,
To give him saving counsels, and in being
Almost his idol, may command him to
Take any shape you please, with a powerful
　　hand
To stop him in his precipice to ruin——
　　Eud. Avert it, heaven !
　　Pul. Heaven is most gracious to you,
In choosing you to be the instrument
Of such a pious work.　You see he signs
What suit soever is preferr'd, not once
Enquiring what it is, yielding himself
A prey to all ; I would, therefore, have you,
　　lady,
As I know you will, to advise him, or com-
　　mand him,
As he would reap the plenty of your favours,
To use more moderation in his bounties ;
And that, before he gives, he would consider
The what, to whom, and wherefore.
　　Eud. Do you think
Such arrogance, or ursurpation rather,
Of what is proper and peculiar
To every private husband, and much
　　more

To him, an emperor, can rank with the
   obedience
And duty of a wife? Are we appointed
In our creation (let me reason with you)
To rule, cr to obey? or, 'cause he loves me
With a kind impotence, must I tyrannize
Over his weakness, or abuse the strength
With which he arms me, to his wrong? or,
   like
A prostituted creature, merchandize
Our mutual delight for hire, or to
Serve mine own sordid ends? In vulgar
   nuptials
Priority is exploded, though there be
A difference in the parties; and shall I,
His vassal, from obscurity raised by him
To this so eminent light, presume t' appoint
   him
To do, or not·to do, this, or that? When
   wives
Are well accommodated by their husbands,
With all things both for use and ornament,
Let them fix there, and never dare to
   question
Their wills or actions; for myself, I vow,
Though now my lord would rashly give away
His sceptre and imperial diadem,
Or if there could be anything more precious,
I would not cross it :—but I know this is
But a trial of my temper, and as such
I do receive it; or, if 't be otherwise,
You are so subtle in your arguments,
I dare not stay to hear them.
               [Offers to retire.

Pul. Is it even so?
I have power o'er these yet, and command
   their stay,
To harken nearer to me.

Arcad. We are charged
By the emperor, our brother, to attend
The empress' service.

Flac. You are too mortified, sister,
(With reverence I speak it,) for young ladies,
To keep you company. I am so tired
With your tedious exhortations, doctrines,
   uses,
Of your religious morality,
That, for my health's sake, I must take the
   freedom
To enjoy a little of those pretty pleasures
That I was born to.

Arcad. When I come to your years,
I'll do as you do; but, till then, with your
   pardon,
I'll lose no more time. I have not learn'd to
   dance yet,
Nor sing, but holy hymns, and those to vile
   tunes too;
Nor to discourse, but of schoolmen's opinions.

How shall I answer my suitors, since, I hope,
Ere long I shall have many, without practice
To write, and speak, something that's not
   derived
From the fathers of philosophy?

Flac. We shall shame
Our breeding, sister, if we should go on thus.

Arcad. 'Tis for your credit that we study
How to converse with men; women with
   women
Yields but a barren argument.

Flac. She frowns——
But you'll protect us, madam?·

Eud. Yes, and love
Your sweet simplicity.

Arcad. All young girls are so,
Till they know the way of it.

Flac. But, when we are enter'd,
We shall on a good round pace.

Eud. I'll leave you, madam.

Arcad. And we our duties with you.
   [Exeunt Eudocia, Arcadia, *and* Flaccilla.

Pul. On all hands
Thus slighted! no way left? Am I grown
   stupid
In my invention? can I make no use
Of the emperor's bounties?—Now 'tis
   thought: within, there!

       Enter an Attendant.

Att. Madam.

Pul. It shall be so :—nearer; your ear.
—Draw a petition to this end.
              [Whispers him.

Att. Besides
The danger to prefer it, I believe
'Twill ne'er be granted.

Pul. How's this! are you grown,
From a servant, my director? let me hear
No more of this. Dispatch; *[Exit* Atten-
   dant.] I'll master him
At his own weapon.

  Enter Theodosius, Paulinus, Philanax,
     Timantus, *and* Gratianus.

Theo. Let me understand it,
If yet there be aught wanting that may
   perfect
A general happiness.

Paul. The people's joys
In seas of acclamations flow in,
To wait on yours.

Phil. Their love, with bounty levied,
Is a sure guard: obedience forced from fear,
Paper fortification, which, in danger,
Will yield to the impression of a reed,
Or of itself fall off.

Theo. True, Philanax;

And by that certain compass we resolve
To steer our bark of government.

Re-enter Attendant *with the petition, which
he secretly delivers to* Pulcheria.

Pul. 'Tis well.   [*Kneels.*
Theo. My dearest and my all-deserving
    sister
As a petitioner kneel ! It must not be.
Pray you, rise ; although your suit were half
    my empire,
'Tis freely granted.
Pul. Your alacrity
To give hath made a beggar ; yet, before
My suit is by your sacred hand and seal
Confirm'd, 'tis necessary you peruse
The sum of my request.
                    [*Presents the petition.*
Theo. We will not wrong
Your judgment in conceiving what 'tis fit
For you to ask, and us to grant, so much,
As to proceed with caution ; give me my
    signet :
With confidence I sign it, and here vow
By my father's soul, but with your free consent,
It is irrevocable.
Tim. What if she now,
Calling to memory how often we
Have crossed her government, in revenge
    hath made
Petition for our heads ?
Grat. They must even off then ;
No ransome can redeem us.
Theo. Let those jewels
So highly rated by the Persian merchants,
Be bought, and as a sacrifice from us,
Presented to Eudocia, she being only
Worthy to wear them.   I am angry with
The unresistible necessity
Of my occasions and important cares,
That so long keep me from her.
        [*Exeunt* Theodosius, Paulinus, Phi-
        lanax, Timantus, *and* Gratianus.
Pul. Go to the empress,
And tell her, on the sudden I am sick,
And do desire the comfort of a visit,
If she please to vouchsafe it.   From me use
Your humblest language—[*Exit* Attendant.]
    but, when once I have her
In my possession, I will rise and speak
In a higher strain : say it raise storms, no
    matter ;
Fools judge by the event, my ends are
    honest.   [*Exit.*

SCENE III.—*Another Room in the same.*

Enter Theodosius, Timantus, *and* Philanax.

Theo. What is become of her? Can she,
    that carries

Such glorious excellence of light about her,
Be any where conceal'd ?
Phil. We have sought her lodgings,
And all we can learn from the servants, is,
She, by your majesty's sisters waited on,
The attendance of her other officers,
By her express command, denied——
Theo. Forbear
Impertinent circumstances,—whither went
    she ? speak.
Phil. As they guess, to the laurel grove.
Theo. So slightly guarded !
What an earthquake I feel in me ! and, but
    that   .
Religion assures the contrary,
The poets' dreams of lustful fauns and satyrs
Would make me fear I know not what.

Enter Paulinus.

Paul. I have found her,
An it please your majesty.
Theo. Yes, it doth please me :
But why return'd without her ?
Paul. As she made
Her speediest approaches to your presence,
A servant of the princess's, Pulcheria,
Encounter'd her : what 'twas he whisper'd
    to her
I am ignorant ; but hearing it, she started,
And will'd me to excuse her absence from you
The third part of an hour.
Theo. In this she takes
So much of my life from me : yet, I'll bear it
With what patience I may, since 'tis her
    pleasure.
Go back, my good Paulinus, and entreat her
Not to exceed a minute.
Tim. Here's strange fondness ! [*Exeunt.*

SCENE IV.—*Another Room in the same.*

Enter Pulcheria *and* Servants.

Pul. You are certain she will come ?
1 *Serv.* She is already
Enter'd your outward lodgings.
Pul. No train with her ?
1 *Serv.* Your excellence' sisters only.
Pul. 'Tis the better.
See the doors strongly guarded, and deny
Access to all, but with our special license :
Why dost thou stay ? shew your obedience,
Your wisdom now is useless.
                    [*Exeunt* Servants.

Enter Eudocia, Arcadia, *and* Flaccilla.

Flac. She is sick, sure,
Or, in fit reverence to your majesty,
She had waited you at the door.
Arcad. 'Twould hardly be
                    [Pulcheria *walking by.*

Excused, in civil manners, to her equal:
But with more difficulty to you, that are
So far above her.
   Eud. Not in her opinion;
She hath been too long accustom'd to command,
To acknowledge a superior.
   Arcad. There she walks.
   Flac. If she be not sick of the sullens, I
. see not
The least infirmity in her.
   Eud. This is strange!
. *Arcad.* Open your eyes; the empress.
. *Pul.* Reach that chair:
Now, sitting thus at distance, I'll vouchsafe
To look upon her.
   Arcad. How, sistér! pray you, awake;
Are you in your wits?
   Flac. Grant, heaven, your too much
learning
Does not conclude in madness!
   Eud. You entreated
A visit from me.
   Pul. True, my servant used
Such language; but now, as a mistress, I
Command your service.
   Eud. Service!
   Arcad. She's stark mad, sure.
   Pul. You'll find I can dispose of what's
mine own,
Without a guardian.
. *Eud.* Follow me.—I will see you
When your frantic fit is o'er.—I do begin
To be of your belief.
   Pul. It will deceive you.
Thou shalt not stir from hence:—thus, as
mine own,
I seize upon thee.
   Flac. Help, help! violence
Offer'd to the empress' person!
   Pul. 'Tis in vain:
She was an empress once, but, by my gift;
Which being abused, I do recall my grant.
You are read in story; call to your remembrance
What the great Hector's mother, Hecuba,
Was to Ulysses, Ilium sack'd.
   Eud. A slave.
   Pul. To me thou art so.
   Eud. Wonder and amazement
Quite overwhelm me: how am I transform'd?
How have I lost my liberty?
           [*Knocking within.*
   Pul. Thou shalt know
Too soon, no doubt.

     Enter a Servant.

    Who's that, that with such rudeness
Beats at the door?

   Serv. The prince Paulinus, madam;
Sent from the emperor, to attend upon
The gracious empress.
   Arcad. And who is your slave now?
   Flac. Sister, repent in time, and beg a
pardon
For your presumption.
   Pul. From me return this answer to Paulinus,
She shall not come; she's mine; the emperor
hath
No interest in her.   [*Exit* Servant.
   Eud. Whatsoe'er I am,
You take not from your power o'er me, to
yield
A reason for this usage.
   Pul. Though my will is
Sufficient, to add to thy affliction,
Know, wretched thing, 'tis not thy fate, but
folly,
Hath made thee what thou art: 'tis some
delight
To urge my merits to one so ungrateful;
Therefore with horror hear it. When thou
wert
Thrust, as a stranger, from thy father's
house,
Exposed to all calamities that want
Could throw upon thee, thine own brothers'
scorn,
And in thy hopes, as by the world, forsaken,
My pity the last altar that was left thee, .
I heard thy syren charms, with feeling heard
them, .
And my compassion made mine eyes vie
tears
With thine, dissembling crocodile! and
when queens
Were emulous for thy imperial bed,
The garments of thy sorrows cast aside,
I put thee in a shape as would have forced
Envy from Cleopatra, had she seen thee.
Then, when I knew my brother's blood was
warm'd
With youthful fires, I brought thee to his
presence;
And how my deep designs, for thy good
plotted,
Succeeded to my wishes, is apparent,
And needs no repetition.
   Eud. I am conscious
Of your so many and unequall'd favours;
But find not how I may accuse myself
For any facts committed, that, with justice,
Can raise your anger to this height against
me.
   Pul. Pride and forgetfulness would not
let thee see that,

z

Against which now thou canst not close thy
eyes.
What injury could be equal to thy late
Contempt of my good counsel? When I
urged
The emperor's prodigal bounties, and en-
treated
That you would use your power to give them
limits,
Or, at the least, a due consideration
Of such as sued, and for what, ere he
sign'd it;
In opposition, you brought against me
The obedience of a wife, that ladies were not,
Being well accommodated by their lords,
To question, but much less to cross, their
pleasures;
Nor would you, though the emperor were
resolved
To give away his sceptre, hinder it,
Since 'twas done for your honour; covering,
with
False colours of humility, your ambition.
   Eud. And is this my offence?
   Pul. As wicked counsel
Is still most hurtful unto those that give it;
Such as deny to follow what is good,
In reason, are the first that must repent it.
When I please, you shall hear more; in the
mean time,
Thank your own wilful folly, that hath
changed you
From an empress to a bondwoman.
   Theo. [*within.*] Force the doors;
Kill those that dare resist.

   Enter Theodosius, Paulinus, Philanax,
     Chrysapius, *and* Gratianus.

   Eud. Dear sir, redeem me.
   Flac. O suffer not, for your own honour's
sake,
The empress, you so late loved, to be made
A prisoner in the court.
   Arcad. Leap to his lips,
You'll find them the best sanctuary.
   Flac. And try then,
What interest my reverend sister hath
To force you from them.
   Theo. What strange May-game's this?
Though done in sport, how ill this levity
Becomes your wisdom?
   Pul. I am serious, sir,
And have done nothing but what you in
honour,
And as you are yourself an emperor,
Stand bound to justify.
   Theo. Take heed; put not these
Strange trials on my patience.
   Pul. Do not you, sir,

Deny your own act: As you are a man,
And stand on your own bottom, 'twill appear
A childish weakness to make void a grant
Sign'd by your sacred hand and seal, and
strengthen'd
With a religious oath, but with my license
Never to be recall'd. For some few minutes
Let reason rule your passion, and in this
              [*Delivers the deed.*
Be pleased to read my interest: you will find
there,
What you in me call violence, is justice,
And that I may make use of what's my own,
According to my will. 'Tis your own gift,
sir;
And what an emperor gives, should stand
as firm
As the celestial poles upon the shoulders
Of Atlas, or his successor in that office,
The great Alcides.
   Theo. Miseries of more weight
Than 'tis feign'd they supported, fall upon
me.
What hath my rashness done! In this trans-
action,
Drawn in express and formal terms, I have
Given and consign'd into your hands, to use
And observe as you please, my dear Eu-
docia!
It is my deed, I do confess it is,
And, as I am myself, not to be cancell'd:
But yet you may shew mercy—and you will,
When you consider that there is no beauty
So perfect in a creature, but is soil'd
With some unbeseeming blemish. You have
labour'd
To build me up a complete prince, 'tis
granted;
Yet, as I am a man, like other monarchs
I have defects and frailties: my facility
To send petitioners with pleased looks from
me,
Is all I can be charged with; and it will
Become your wisdom, (since 'tis in your
power,)
In charity to provide I fall no further
Or in my oath, or honour.
   Pul. Royal sir,
This was the mark I aim'd at, and I glory
At the length, you so conceive it: 'twas a
weakness
To measure, by your own integrity,
The purposes of others. I have shewn you,
In a true mirror, what fruit grows upon
The tree of hoodwink'd bounty, and what
dangers
Precipitation, in the managing
Your great affairs, produceth.
   Theo. I embrace it

As a grave advertisement, and vow hereafter
Never to sign petitions at this rate.
 Pul. For mine, see, sir, 'tis cancell'd ;
  on my knees
I re-deliver what I now begg'd from you.
  [*Tears the deed.*
She is my second gift.
 Theo. Which if I part from
Till death divorce us—— [*Kisses* Eudocia.
 Eud. So, sir !
 Theo. Nay, sweet, chide not,
I am punish'd in thy looks ; defer the rest,
Till we are more private.
 Pul. I ask pardon too,
If, in my personated passion, I
Appear'd too harsh and rough.
 Eud. 'Twas gentle language,
What I was then consider'd.
 Pul. O, dear madam,
It was decorum in the scene.
 Eud. This trial,
When I was Athenais, might have pass'd,
But as I am the empress——
 Theo. Nay, no anger,
Since all good was intended.
  [*Exeunt* Theodosius, Eudocia, Arcadia,
    and Flaccilla.
 Pul. Building on
That certain base, I fear not what can follow.
  [*Exit.*
 Paul. These are strange devices, Philanax.
 Phil. True, my lord.
May all turn to the best !
 Grat. The emperor's looks
Promised a calm.
 Chry. But the vex'd empress' frowns
Presaged a second storm.
 Paul. I am sure I feel one
In my leg already.
 Phil. Your old friend, the gout ?
 Paul. My forced companion, Philanax.
 Chry. To your rest.
 Paul. Rest, and forbearing wine, with a
  temperate diet,
Though many mountebanks pretend the cure
  of t,
I have found my best physicians.
 Phil. Ease to your lordship. [*Exeunt.*

ACT IV.

SCENE I.—*A Room in the Palace.*

Enter Eudocia *and* Chrysapius.

 Eud. Make me her property !
 Chry. Your majesty
Hath just cause of distaste ; and your re-
  sentment

Of the affront, in the point of honour, cannot
But meet a fair construction.
 Eud. I have only
The title of an empress, but the power
Is by her ravish'd from me : she surveys
My actions as a governess, and calls
My not observing all that she directs,
Folly and disobedience.
 Chry. Under correction,
With grief I've long observed it ; and, if you
Stand pleased to sign my warrant, I'll deliver,
In my unfeign'd zeal and desire to serve you,
(Howe'er I run the hazard of my head for't,
Should it arrive at the knowledge of the
  princess,)
Not alone the reasons why things are thus
  carried,
But give into your hands the power to clip
The wings of her command.
 Eud. Your service this way
Cannot offend me.
 Chry. Be you pleased to know, then,
But still with pardon, if I am too bold.
Your too much sufferance imps the broken
  feathers
Which carry her to this proud height, in
  which
She with security soars, and still towers o'er
  you :
But if you would employ the strengths you
  hold
In the emperor's affections, and remember
The orb you move in should admit no star
  else,
You never would confess the managing
Of state affairs to her alone are proper,
And you sit by, a looker on.
 Eud. I would not,
If it were possible I could attempt
Her diminution, without a taint
Of foul ingratitude in myself.
 Chry. In this
The sweetness of your temper does abuse
  you ;
And you call that a benefit to yourself,
Which she, for her own ends, conferr'd
  upon you.
'Tis yielded, she gave way to your advance-
  ment ;
But for what cause ? that she might still
  continue
Her absolute sway and swing o'er the whole
  state :
And that she might to her admirers vaunt,
The empress was her creature, and the giver
To be preferr'd before the gift.
 Eud. It may be.
 Chry. Nay, 'tis most certain : whereas
  would you please

z 2

In a true glass to look upon yourself,
And view, without detraction, your own
    merits,
Which all men wonder at, you would find
    that fate,
Without a second cause, appointed you
To the supremest honour. For the princess,
She hath reign'd long enough, and her
    remove
Will make your entrance free to the posses-
    sion
Of what you were born to ; and, but once
    · resolve
To build upon her ruins, leave the engines
That must be used to undermine her great-
    ness
To my provision.
    Eud. I thank your care :
But a design of such weight must not be
Rashly determined of ; it will exact
A long and serious consultation from me.
In the meantime, Chrysapius, rest assured
I live your thankful mistress.   [*Exit.*
    Chry. Is this all?
Will the physic that I minister'd work no
    further?
I have play'd the fool ; and, leaving a calm
    port,
Embark'd myself on a rough sea of danger.
In her silence lies my safety, which how
    can I
Hope from a woman ? but the die is thrown,
And I must stand the hazard.   [*Exit.*

SCENE II.—*A Space before the Palace.*

Enter Theodosius, Philanax, Timantus,
    Gratianus, *and* Huntsmen.

    Theo. Is Paulinus
So tortured with his gout?
    Phil. Most miserably,
And it adds much to his affliction, that
The pain denies him power to wait upon
Your majesty.
    Theo. I pity him :—he is
A wondrous honest man, 'and what he
    suffers,
I know, will grieve my empress.
    Tim. He, indeed, is
Much bound to her gracious favour.
    Theo. He deserves it ;
She cannot find a subject upon whom
She better may confer it.—Is the stag
Safe lodged ?
    Grat. Yes, sir, and the hounds and hunts-
    men ready.
    Phil. He will make you royal sport. He
    is a deer
Of ten, at the least.

Enter a Countryman *with an apple.*

    Grat. Whither will this clown ?
    Tim. Stand back.
    Countr. I would zee the emperor ; why
    should you courtiers
Scorn a poor countryman ? we zweat at the
    plough
To vill your mouths, you and your curs
    might starve else :
We prune the orchards, and you cranch the
    fruit ;
Yet still you're snarling at us.
    Theo. What's the matter?
    Countr. I would look on thy zweet face.
    Tim. Unmannerly swain !
    Countr. Zwain ! though I am a zwain, I
    have a heart yet,
As ready to do service for my liege,
As any princox peacock of you all.
Zookers ! had I one of you zingle, with this
    twig
I would soo veeze you.
    Tim. Will your majesty
Hear his rude language ?
    Theo. Yes, and hold it as
An ornament, not a blemish.   O, Timantus,
Since that dread Power by whom we are,
    disdains not
With an open ear to hear petitions from us ;
Easy access in us, his deputies,
To the meanest of our subjects, is a debt
Which we stand bound to pay.
    Countr. By my granam's ghost
'Tis a holesome zaying ! our vicar could not
    mend it
In the pulpit on a Zunday.
    Theo. What's thy suit, friend ?
    Countr. Zute ! I would laugh at that. Let
    the court beg from thee,
What the poor country gives : I bring a
    present
To thy good grace, which I can call mine
    own,
And look not, like these gay volk, for a return
Of what they venture. Have I giv'n't you?
    ha ! ·
    Chry. A perilous knave.
    Countr. Zee here a dainty apple,
                    [*Presents the apple.*
Of mine own graffing ; zweet and zound, I
    assure thee.
    Theo. It is the fairest fruit I ever saw.
Those golden apples in the Hesperian or-
    chards,
So strangely guarded by the watchful dragon
As they required great Hercules to get them ;
Or those with which Hippomenes deceived
Swift-footed Atalanta, when I look

On this, deserve no wonder. You behold
The poor man and his present with con-
tempt ;
I to their value prize both : he that could
So aid weak nature by his care and labour,
As to compel a crab-tree stock to bear
A precious fruit of this large size and beauty,
Would by his industry change a petty village
Into a populous city, and from that
Erect a flourishing kingdom. Give the
fellow,
For an encouragement to his future labours,
Ten Attic talents.
Countr. I will weary heaven
With my prayers for your majesty. [*Exit.*
Theo. Philanax,
From me present this rarity to the rarest
And best of women : when I think upon
The boundless happiness that from her flows
to me,
In my imagination I am rapt
Beyond myself : but I forget our hunting.
To the forest, for the exercise of my body ;
But for my mind, 'tis wholly taken up
In the contemplation of her matchless
virtues. [*Exeunt.*

SCENE III.—*A Room in the Palace.*

Enter Eudocia, Pulcheria, Arcadia, *and*
Flaccilla.

Eud. You shall know there's a difference
between us.
Pul. There was, I am certain, not long
since, when you
Kneel'd a petitioner to me ; then you were
happy
To be near my feet ; and do you hold it now,
As a disparagement, that I side you, lady?
Eud. Since you respect me only as I was,
What I am shall be remember'd.
Pul. Does the means
I practised, to give good and saving counsels
To the emperor, and your new-stamp'd
majesty,
Still stick in your stomach?
Eud. 'Tis not yet digested,
In troth it is not. Why, good governess,
Though you are held for a grand madam,
and yourself
The first that overprize it, I ne'er took
Your words for Delphian oracles, nor your
actions
For such wonders as you make them :—there
is one,
When she shall see her time, as fit and able
To be made partner of the emperor's cares,
As your wise self, and may with justice
challenge

A nearer interest.—You have done your visit,.
So, when you please, you may leave me.
Pul. I'll not bandy
Words with your mightiness, proud one ;
only this,
You carry too much sail for your small bark,
And that, when you least think upon't, may
sink you. [*Exit.*
Flac. I am glad she's gone.
Arcad. I fear'd she would have read
A tedious lecture to us.

Enter Philanax *with the apple.*

Phil. From the emperor,
This rare fruit to the rarest.
Eud. How, my lord !
Phil. I use his language, madam ; and
that trust,
Which he imposed on me, discharged, his
pleasure
Commands my present service. [*Exit.*
Eud. Have you seen
So fair an apple !
Flac. Never.
Arcad. If the taste
Answer the beauty.
Eud. Prettily begg'd :— you should have it,
But that you eat too much cold fruit, and
that
Changes the fresh red in your cheeks to pale-
ness.

Enter a Servant.

I have other dainties for you :—You come
from
Paulinus ; how is't with that truly noble,
And honest lord, my witness at the fount,
In a word, the man to whose bless'd charity
I owe my greatness? How is't with him ?
Serv. Sprightly
In his mind ; but, by the raging of his gout,
In his body much distemper'd ; that you
pleased
To inquire his health, took off much from
his pain,
His glad looks did confirm it.
Eud. Do his doctors
Give him no hope ?
Serv. Little ; they rather fear
By his continual burning, that he stands
In danger of a fever.
Eud. To him again,
And tell him that I heartily wish it lay
In me to ease him ; and from me deliver
This choice fruit to him ; you may say to that,.
I hope it will prove physical.
Serv. The good lord
Will be o'erjoyed with the favour.
Eud. He deserves more. [*Exeunt.*

SCENE IV.—*A Room in* Paulinus' *House.*

Paulinus *discovered in a Chair, attended by
a* Surgeon.

Surg. I have done as much as art can do,
to stop
The violent course of your fit, and I hope
you feel it :
How does your honour ?
Paul. At some ease, I thank you ;
I would you could assure continuance of it,
For the moiety of my fortune.
Surg. If I could cure
The gout, my lord, without the philosopher's
stone
I should soon purchase, it being a disease
In poor men very rare, and in the rich
The cure impossible. Your many bounties
Bid me prepare you for a certain truth,
And to flatter you were dishonest.
Paul. Your plain dealing
Deserves a fee. Would there were many
more such
Of your profession ! Happy are poor
men !
If sick with the excess of heat or cold,
Caused by necessitous labour, not loose
surfeits,—
They, when spare diet, or kind nature fail
To perfect their recovery, soon arrive at
Their rest in death : but, on the contrary,
The great and noble are exposed as preys
To the rapine of physicians ; and they,
In lingering out what is remediless,
Aim at their profit, not the patient's health.
A thousand trials and experiments
Have been put upon me, and I forced to pay
dear
For my vexation ; but I am resolved
(I thank your honest freedom) to be made
A property no more for knaves to work on.—

Enter Cleon *with a parchment roll.*

What have you there?
Cle. The triumphs of an artsman
O'er all infirmities, made authentical
With the names of princes, kings, and
emperors,
That were his patients.
Paul. Some empiric.
Cle. It may be so ; but he swears, within
three days
He'll grub up your gout by the roots, and
make you able
To march ten leagues a day in complete
armour.
Paul. Impossible.
Cle. Or, if you like not him——

Surg. Hear him, my lord, for your mirth; I
will take order
They shall not wrong you.
Paul. Usher in your monster.
Cle. He is at hand.—March up : now
speak for yourself.

Enter Empiric.

Emp. I come not, right honourable, to
your presence, with any base and sordid end
of reward ; the immortality of my fame is
the white I shoot at : the charge of my most
curious and costly ingredients frayed, amount-
ing to some seventeen thousand crowns—a
trifle in respect of health—writing your noble
name in my catalogue, I shall acknowledge
myself amply satisfied.
Surg. I believe so.
Emp. For your own sake, I most heartily
wish that you had now all the diseases,
maladies, and infirmities upon you, that
were ever remembered by old Galen, Hip-
pocrates, or the later and more admired
Paracelsus.
Paul. For your good wish, I thank you !
Emp. Take me with you, I beseech your
good lordship.—I urged it, that your joy, in
being certainly and suddenly freed from
them, may be the greater, and my not-to-be-
paralleled skill the more remarkable. The
cure of the gout—a toy, without boast be it
said, my cradle-practice : The cancer, the
fistula, the dropsy, consumption of lungs
and kidneys, hurts in the brain, heart, or
liver, are things worthy my opposition ; but
in the recovery of my patients I ever overcome them. But to your gout——
Paul. Ay, marry, sir, that cured, I shall
be apter
To give credit to the rest.
Emp. Suppose it done, sir.
Surg. And the means you use, I beseech
you ?
Emp. I will do it in the plainest language,
and discover my ingredients. First, my
boteni terebinthina of Cypris, my manna,
ros cælo, coagulated with *vetulos ovorum,*
vulgarly yolks of eggs, with a little cyath or
quantity of my potable elixir, with some few
scruples of sassafras and guiacum, so taken
every morning and evening, in the space of
three days purgeth, cleanseth, and dissipateth
the inward causes of the virulent tumour.
Paul. Why do you smile ?
Surg. When he hath done I will resolve
you.
Emp. For my exterior applications, I
have these balsum-unguentulums, extracted
from herbs, plants, roots, seeds, gums, and

a million of other vegetables, the principal of which are, *Ulissipona*, or *serpentaria*, *sophia*, or *herba consolidarum*, *parthenium*, or *commanilla Romana*, *mumia transmarina*, mixed with my *plumbum philosophorum*, and *mater metallorum*, *cum ossa paraleli*, *est universale medicamentum in podagra*.

Cle. A conjuring balsamum!

Emp. This applied warm upon the pained place, with a feather of struthio-cameli, or a bird of paradise, which is everywhere to be had, shall expulse this tartarous, viscous, anatheos, and malignant dolor.

Surg. An excellent receipt! but does your lordship
Know what 'tis good for?

Paul. I would be instructed.

Surg. For the gonorrhœa, or, if you will hear it
In a plainer phrase, the pox.

Emp. If it cure his lordship
Of that by the way, I hope, sir, 'tis the better.
My medicine serves for all things, and the pox, sir,
Though falsely named the sciatica, or gout,
Is the more catholic sickness.

Paul. Hence with the rascal!
Yet hurt him not, he makes me smile, and that
Frees him from punishment.
[*They thrust him off.*

Surg. Such slaves as this
Render our art contemptible.

Enter Servant *with the apple.*

Serv. My good lord.

Paul. So soon return'd!

Serv. And with this present from
Your great and gracious mistress, with her wishes
It may prove physical to you.

Paul. In my heart
I kneel, and thank her bounty. Dear friend Cleon,
Give him the cupboard of plate in the next room,
For a reward.—[*Exeunt* Cleon *and* Servant.]
⁚ —Most glorious fruit! but made
More precious by her grace and love that sent it:
To touch it only, coming from her hand,
Makes me forget all pain. A diamond
Of this large size, (though it would buy a kingdom,)
Hewed from the rock, and laid down at my feet,
Nay, though a monarch's gift, will hold no value,

Compared with this—and yet, ere I presume
To taste it, though, sans question, it is
Some heavenly restorative, I in duty
Stand bound to weigh my own unworthiness.
Ambrosia is food only for the gods,
And not by human lips to be profaned.
I may adore it as some holy relic
Derived from thence, but impious to keep it
In my possession; the emperor only
Is worthy to enjoy it.—

Re-enter Cleon.

Go, good Cleon,
And (cease this admiration at this object,)
From me present this to my royal master,
I know it will amaze him; and excuse me
That I am not myself the bearer of it.
That I should be lame now, when with wings of duty
I should fly to the service of this empress!
Nay, no delays, good Cleon.

Cle. I am gone, sir. [*Exeunt.*

SCENE V.—*A Room in the Palace.*

Enter Theodosius, Chrysapius, Timantus, *and* Gratianus.

Chry. Are you not tired, sir?

Theo. Tired! I must not say so,
However, though I rode hard. To a huntsman,
His toil is his delight, and to complain
Of weariness, would shew as poorly in him
As if a general should grieve for a wound
Received upon his forehead, or his breast,
After a glorious victory. Lay by
These accoutrements for the chase.

Enter Pulcheria.

Pul. You are well return'd, sir,
From your princely exercise.

Theo. Sister, to you
I owe the freedom, and the use of all
The pleasures I enjoy: your care provides
For my security, and the burthen, which
I should alone sustain, you undergo,
And, by your painful watchings, yield my sleeps
Both sound and sure. How happy am I in
Your knowledge of the art of government!
And, credit me, I glory to behold you
Dispose of great designs, as if you were
A partner, and no subject of my empire.

Pul. My vigilance, since it hath well succeeded,
I am confident you allow of—yet it is not
Approved by all.

Theo. Who dares repine at that
Which hath our sufirage?

Pul. One that too well knows
The strength of her abilities can better
My weak endeavours.
　Theo. In this you reflect
Upon my empress?
　Pul. True : for, as she is
The consort of your bed, 'tis fit she share in
Your cares and absolute power.
　Theo. You touch a string
That sounds but harshly to me ; and I must
In a brother's love, advise you, that hereafter
You would forbear to move it : since she is
In her pure self a harmony of such sweetness,
Composed of duty, chaste desires, her beauty
(Though it might tempt a hermit from his
　　beads)
The least of her endowments. I am sorry
Her holding the first place, since that the
　second
Is proper to yourself, calls on your envy.
She err ! it is impossible in a thought ;
And much more speak or do what may
　offend me.
In other things I would believe you, sister ;
But, though the tongues of saints and angels
　tax'd her,
Of any imperfection, I should be
Incredulous.
　Pul. She is yet a woman, sir.
　Theo. The abstract of what's excellent in
　the sex,
But to their mulcts and frailties a mere
　stranger ;
I'll die in this belief.

Enter Cleon *with the apple.*

　Cle. Your humblest servant,
The lord Paulinus, as a witness of
His zeal and duty to your majesty,
Presents you with this jewel.
　Theo. Ha !
　Cle. It is
Preferr'd by him——
　Theo. Above his honour?
　Cle. No, sir ;
I would have said his patrimony.
　Theo. 'Tis the same.
　Cle. And he entreats, since lameness may
　excuse
His not presenting it himself, from me
(Though far unworthy to supply his place)
You would vouchsafe to accept it.
　Theo. Further off,
You've told your tale. Stay you for a reward?
Take that.　　　　　　　　*[Strikes him.*
　Pul. How's this?
　Chry. I never saw him moved thus.
　Theo. We must not part so, sir :—a guard
　upon him !

Enter Guard.

May I not vent my sorrows in the air,
Without discovery? Forbear the room !
　　[Exeunt Pul. Chry. Tim. Grat. *and*
　　　　Guard *with* Cle.
Yet be within call—What an earthquake I
　feel in me !
And on the sudden my whole fabric totters.
My blood within me turns, and through my
　veins,
Parting with natural redness, I discern it
Changed to a fatal yellow.　What an army
Of hellish furies, in the horrid shapes
Of doubts and fears, charge on me ! rise to
　my rescue,
Thou stout maintainer of a chaste wife's
　honour,
The confidence of her virtues ; be not shaken
With the wind of vain surmises, much less
　suffer
The devil Jealousy to whisper to me
My curious observation of that
I must no more remember.　Will't not be?
Thou uninvited guest, ill-manner'd monster,
I charge thee, leave me ! wilt thou force me
　to
Give fuel to that fire I would put out ?
The goodness of my memory proves my
　mischief,
And I would sell my empire, could it pur-
　chase
The dull art of forgetfulness.—Who waits
　there ?

Re-enter Timantus.

　Tim. Most sacred sir——
　Theo. Sacred, as 'tis accurs'd,
Is proper to me. Sirrah, upon your life,
Without a word concerning this, command
Eudocia to come to me. *[Exit* Tim.]
　Would I had
Ne'er known her by that name, my mother's
　name,
Or that, for her own sake, she had continued
Poor Athenais still !—No intermission !
Wilt thou so soon torment me? must I read,
Writ in the table of my memory,
To warrant my suspicion, how Paulinus
(Though ever thought a man averse **to**
　women)
First gave her entertainment, made her **way**
For audience to my sister ?—then I did
Myself observe how he was ravish'd with
The gracious delivery of her story,
Which was, I grant, the bait that first took
　me, too :—
She was his convert ; what the rhetoric was
He used, I know not ; and, since she was
　mine,

In private as in public what a mass
Of grace and favour hath she heap'd upon
   him !
And, but to-day, this fatal fruit—She's come.

Re-enter Timantus *with* Eudocia, Flaccilla,
   and Arcadia.

Can she be guilty ?
   Eud. You seem troubled, sir ;
My innocence makes me bold to ask the
   cause,
That I may ease you of it. No salute,
After four long hours' absence !
   Theo. Prithee, forgive me.— [*Kisses her.*
Methinks I find Paulinus on her lips,
And the fresh nectar that I drew from
   thence
Is on the sudden pall'd.—How have you
   spent
Your hours since I last saw you ?
   Eud. In the converse
Of your sweet sisters.
   Theo. Did not Philanax,
From me deliver you an apple ?
   Eud. Yes, sir ;
Heaven, how you frown! pray you, talk of
   something else,
Think not of such a trifle.
   Theo. How, a trifle !
Does any toy from me presented to you,
Deserve to be so slighted? do you value
What's sent, and not the sender? from a
   peasant
It had deserved your thanks.
   Eud. And meets from you, sir,
All possible respect.
   Theo. I prized it, lady,
At a higher rate than you believe ; and would
   not
Have parted with it, but to one I did
Prefer before myself.
   Eud. It was, indeed,
The fairest that I ever saw.
   Theo. It was ;
And it had virtues in it, my Eudocia,
Not visible to the eye.
   Eud. It may be so, sir.
   Theo. What did you with it?—tell me
   punctually ;
I look for a strict accompt.
   Eud. What shall I answer ? [*Aside.*
   Theo. Do you stagger? Ha !
   Eud. No, sir ; I have eaten it.
It had the pleasant'st taste !—I wonder that
You found it not in my breath.
   Theo. I'faith, I did not,
And it was wonderous strange.
   Eud. Pray you, try again.

   Theo. I find no scent of 't here : you play
   with me ;
You have it still ?
   Eud. By your sacred life and fortune,
An oath I dare not break, I have eaten it.
   Theo. Do you know how this oath binds ?
   Eud. Too well, to break it.
   Theo. That ever man, to please his brutish
   sense,
Should slave his understanding to his
   passions,
And, taken with soon-fading white and red,
Deliver up his credulous ears to hear
The magic of a Syren ; and from these
Believe there ever was, is, or can be,
More than a seeming honesty in bad woman !
   Eud. This is strange language, sir.
   Theo. Who waits ? Come all.

Re-enter Pulcheria, Philanax, Chrysapius,
   Gratianus, *and* Guard.

Nay, sister, not so near, being of the sex,
I fear you are infected too.
   Pul. What mean you ?
   Theo. To shew you a miracle, a prodigy
Which Affic never equall'd :——Can you
   think
This masterpiece of heaven, this precious
   vellum,
Of such a purity and virgin whiteness,
Could be design'd to have perjury and
   whoredom,
In capital letters, writ upon't ?
   Pul. Dear sir.
   Theo. Nay, add to this, an impudence
   beyond
All prostituted boldness. Art not dead yet ?
Will not the tempests in thy conscience rend
   thee
As small as atoms, that there may no sign
Be left thou ever wert so ? wilt thou live
Till thou art blasted with the dreadful
   lightning
Of pregnant and unanswerable proofs
Of thy adulterous twines? die yet, that I
With my honour may conceal it.
   Eud. Would long since
The Gorgon of your rage had turn'd me
   marble !
Or, if I have offended——
   Theo. If !——good angels !
But I am tame ; look on this dumb accuser.
                [*Shewing the apple.*
   Eud. Oh, I am lost !
   Theo. Did ever cormorant
Swallow his prey, and then digest it whole,
As she hath done this apple ? Philanax,
As 'tis, from me presented it ; the good lady

Swore she had eaten it; yet, I know not how,
It came entire into Paulinus' hands,
And I from him received it, sent in scorn,
Upon my life, to give me a close touch
That he was weary of thee. Was there nothing
Left thee to fee him to give satisfaction
To thy insatiate lust, but what was sent
As a dear favour from me? How have I sinn'd
In my dotage on this creature! but to her,
I have lived as I was born, a perfect virgin:
Nay, more, I thought it not enough to be
True to her bed, but that I must feed high,
To strengthen my abilities to cloy
Her ravenous appetite, little suspecting
She would desire a change.
   Eud. I never did, sir.
   Theo. Be dumb; I will not waste my breath in taxing
Thy base ingratitude. How I have raised thee
Will by the world be, to thy shame, spoke often:
But for that ribald, who held in my empire
The next place to myself, so bound unto me
By all the ties of duty and allegiance,
He shall pay dear for't, and feel what it is,
In a wrong of such high consequence, to pull down
His lord's slow anger on him!—Philanax,
He's troubled with the gout, let him be cured
With a violent death, and in the other world
Thank his physician.
   Phil. His cause unheard, sir?
   Pul. Take heed of rashness.
   Theo. Is what I command
To be disputed?
   Phil. Your will shall be done, sir:
But that I am the instrument——
   Theo. Do you murmur?
               [*Exit* Phil. *with* Guard.
What couldst thou say, if that my license should
Give liberty to thy tongue? [*Eudocia kneeling, points to* Theodosius' *sword.*] thou wouldst die? I am not
So to be reconciled. See me no more:
The sting of conscience ever gnawing on thee,
A long life be thy punishment!   [*Exit.*
   Flac. O sweet lady,
How I could weep for her!
   Arcad. Speak, dear madam, speak.
Your tongue, as you are a woman, while you live

Should be ever moving, at the least, the last part
That stirs about you.
   Pul. Though I should, sad lady,
In policy rejoice, you, as a rival
Of my greatness, are removed, compassion,
Since I believe you innocent, commands me
To mourn your fortune; credit me, I will urge
All arguments I can allege that may
Appease the emperor's fury.
   Arcad. I will grow too,
Upon my knees, unless he bid me rise,
And swear he will forgive you.
   Flac. And repent too:
All this pother for an apple!
     [*Exeunt* Pulcheria, Arcadia, *and* Flaccilla.
   Chry. Hope, dear madam,
And yield not to despair; I am still your servant,
And never will forsake you, though awhile
You leave the court and city, and give way
To the violent passions of the emperor.
Repentance, in his want of you, will soon find him:
In the mean time, I'll dispose of you, and omit
No opportunity that may invite him
To see his error.
   Eud. Oh!   [*Wringing her hands.*
   Chry. Forbear, for heaven's sake.
                   [*Exeunt.*

ACT V.

SCENE I.—*A Room in* Paulinus' *House.*

Enter Philanax, Paulinus, Guard, *and* Executioners.

   Paul. This is most barbarous! how have you lost
All feeling of humanity, as honour,
In your consent alone to have me used thus?
But to be, as you are, a looker on,
Nay, more, a principal actor in't, (the softness
Of your former life consider'd,) almost turns me
Into a senseless statue.
   Phil. Would, long since,
Death, by some other means, had made you one,
That you might be less sensible of what
You have, or are to suffer!
   Paul. Am to suffer!
Let such, whose happiness and heaven depend
Upon their present being, fear to part with
A fort they cannot long hold; mine to me is

A charge that I am weary of, all defences
By pain and sickness batter'd :—yet take
   heed,
Take heed, lord Philanax, that, for private
   spleen,
Or any false-conceived grudge against me,
(Since in one thought of wrong to you I am
Sincerely innocent,) you do not that
My royal master must in justice punish,
If you pass to your own heart thorough mine ;
The murder, as it will come out, discover'd.
   Phil. I murder you, my lord ! heaven
  . witness for me,
With the restoring of your health, I wish you
Long life and happiness : for myself, I am
Compell'd to put in execution that
Which I would fly from ; 'tis the emperor,
The high incensed emperor's will, commands
What I must see perform'd.
   Paul. The emperor !
Goodness and innocence guard me ! wheels
   nor racks
Can force into my memory the remembrance
Of the least shadow of offence, with which
I ever did provoke him. Though beloved,
(And yet the people's love is short and fatal,)
I never courted popular applause,
Feasted the men of action, or labour'd
By prodigal gifts to draw the needy soldier,
The tribunes, or centurions to a faction,
Of which I would raise up the head against
  . him.
I hold no place of strength, fortress, or
   castle,
In my command, that can give sanctuary
To malcontents, or countenance rebellion.
I have built no palaces to face the court,
Nor do my followers' braveries shame his
   train ;
And though I cannot blame my fate for want,
My competent means of life deserve no envy ;
In what, then, am I dangerous?
   Phil. His displeasure
Reflects on none of those particulars
Which you have mention'd, though some
   jealous princes
In a subject cannot brook them.
   Paul. None of these !
In what, then, am I worthy his suspicion ?
But it may, nay it must be, some informer,
To whom my innocence appear'd a crime,
Hath poison'd his late good opinion of me.
'Tis not to die, but, in the censure of
So good a master, guilty, that afflicts me.
   Phil. There is no remedy.
   Paul. No !—I have a friend yet,
To whom the state I stand in now deliver'd,
(Could the strictness of your warrant give
   way to it,)

That, by fair intercession for me, would
So far prevail, that, my defence unheard,
I should not, innocent or guilty suffer
Without a fit distinction.
   Phil. These false hopes,
My lord, abuse you. What man, when con-
   demn'd,
Did ever find a friend ? or who dares lend
An eye of pity to that star-cross'd subject
On whom his sovereign frowns ?
   Paul. She that dares plead
For innocence without a fee, the empress,
My great and gracious mistress.
   Phil. There's your error.
Her many favours, which you hoped should
   make you,
Prove your undoing. She, poor lady, is
Banish'd for ever from the emperor's pre-
   sence,
And his confirm'd suspicion, to his wrong,
That you have been over-familiar with her,
Dooms you to death. I know you under-
   stand me.
   Paul. Over-familiar !
   Phil. In sharing with him
Those sweet and secret pleasures of his bed,
Which can admit no partner.
   Paul. And is that
The crime for which I am to die ? of all .
My numerous sins, was there not one of   •
   weight
Enough to sink me, if he borrow'd not
The colour of a guilt I never saw,
To paint my innocence in a deform'd
And monstrous shape? but that it were
   profane
To argue heaven of ignorance or injustice,
I now should tax it. Had the stars that
   reign'd
At my nativity such cursed influence,
As not alone to make me miserable,
But, in the neighbourhood of her goodness
   to me,
To force contagion upon a lady,
Whose purer flames were not inferior,
To theirs when they shine brightest ! to die
  . for her,
Compared with what she suffers, is a trifle.
By her example warn'd, let all great women
Hereafter throw pride and contempt on such
As truly serve them, since a retribution
In lawful courtesies is now styled lust ;
And to be thankful to a servant's merits
Is grown a vice, no virtue.
   Phil. These complaints
Are to no purpose: think on the long flight
Your better part must make.
   Paul. She is prepared :
Nor can the freeing of an innocent

From the emperor's furious jealousy hinder
her.
—It shall out, 'tis resolved ; but to be
whisper'd
To you alone.   What a solemn preparation
Is made here to put forth an inch of taper,
In itself almost extinguish'd ! mortal poison !
The hangman's sword ! the halter !
    Phil. 'Tis left to you
To make choice of which you please.
    Paul. Any will serve
To take away my gout and life together.
I would not have the emperor imitate
Rome's monster, Nero, in that cruel mercy
He shew'd to Seneca.   When you have dis-
charged
What you are trusted with, and I have given
you
Reasons beyond all doubt or disputation,
Of the empress' and my innocence ; when I
am dead,
(Since 'tis my master's pleasure, and high
treason
In you not to obey it,) I conjure you,
By the hopes you have of happiness here-
after,
Since mine in this world are now parting
from me,
That you would win the young man to re-
pentance
Of the wrong done to his chaste wife,
Eudocia.
And if perchance he shed a tear for what
In his rashness he imposed on his true
servant,
So it cure him of future jealousy,
'Twill prove a precious balsamum, and find
me
When I am in my grave.—Now, when you
please ;
For I am ready.
    Phil. His words work strangely on me,
And I would do—but I know not what to
think on't.   [*Exeunt.*

SCENE II.—*A Room in the Palace.*

Enter Pulcheria, Flaccilla, Arcadia, Timantus, Gratianus, *and* Chrysapius.

    Pul. Still in his sullen mood ? no inter-
mission
Of his melancholy fit ?
    Tim. It rather, madam,
Increases, than grows less.
    Grat. In the next room
To his bedchamber we watch'd ; for he, by
signs,
Gave us to understand he would admit
Nor company nor conference.

    Pul. Did he take
No rest, as you could guess ?
    Chry. Not any, madam.
Like a Numidïan lion, by the cunning
Of the desperate huntsman taken in a toil,
And forced into a spacious cage, he walks
About his chamber ; we might hear him
gnash
His teeth in rage, which open'd, hollow
groans
And murmurs issued from his lips, like winds
Imprison'd in the caverns of the earth
Striving for liberty ; and sometimes throwing
His body on his bed, then on the ground,
And with such violence, that we more than
fear'd,
And still do, if the tempest of his passions
By your wisdom, be not laid, he will commit
Some outrage on himself.
    Pul. His better angel,
I hope, will stay him from so foul a mischief :
Nor shall my care be wanting.
    Tim. Twice I heard him
Say, *False Eudocia, how much art thou
Unworthy of these tears!* then sigh'd, and
straight
Roar'd out, *Paulinus! was his gouty age
To be preferr'd before my strength and youth?*
Then groan'd again, so many ways express-
ing
The afflictions of a tortured soul, that we,
Who wept in vain for what we could not help,
Were sharers in his sufferings.
    Pul. Though your sorrow
Is not to be condemn'd, it takes not from
The burthen of his miseries : we must prae-
tise,
With some fresh object, to divert his thoughts
From that they are wholly fix'd on.
    Chry. Could I gain
The freedom of access, I would present him
With this petition.—Will your highness
please
To look upon it : you will soon find there
What my intents and hopes are.

    Enter Theodosius.

    Grat. Ha ! 'tis he.
    Pul. Stand close,
And give way to his passions ; 'tis not safe
To stop them in their violent course, before
They have spent themselves.
    Theo. I play the fool, and am
Unequal to myself ; delinquents are
To suffer, not the innocent.   I have done
Nothing, which will not hold weight in the
scale
Of my impartial justice ; neither feel I
The worm of conscience upbraiding me

For one black deed of tyranny; wherefore, then,
Should I torment myself? Great Julius would not
Rest satisfied that his wife was free from fact,
But, only for suspicion of a crime,
Sued a divorce ; nor was this Roman rigour
Censured as cruel : and still the wise Italian,
That knows the honour of his family
Depends upon the purity of his bed,
For a kiss, nay, wanton look, will plough
    up mischief,
And sow the seeds of his revenge in blood.
And shall I, to whose power the law's a servant,
That stand accountable to none, for what
My will calls an offence, being compell'd,
And on such grounds, to raise an altar to
My anger ; though, I grant, it is cemented
With a loose strumpet and adulterer's gore,
Repent the justice of my fury? No.
I should not : yet still my excess of love,
Fed high in the remembrance of her choice
And sweet embraces, would persuade me that
Connivance or remission of her fault,
Made warrantable by her true submission
For her offence, might be excusable,
Did not the cruelty of my wounded honour,
With an open mouth, deny it.
    Pul. I approve of
Your good intention, and I hope 'twill
    prosper.—   [*To* Chrysapius.
He now seems calm : let us, upon our knees,
Encompass him.—Most royal sir——
                  [*They all kneel.*
    Flac. Sweet brother——
    Arcad. As you are our sovereign, by the ties of nature
You are bound to be a father in your care
To us poor orphans.
    Tim. Shew compassion, sir,
Unto yourself.
    Grat. The majesty of your fortune
Should fly above the reach of grief.
    Chry. And 'tis
Impair'd, if you yield to it.
    Theo. Wherefore pay you
This adoration to a sinful creature ?
I am flesh and blood, as you are, sensible
Of heat and cold, as much a slave unto
The tyranny of my passions, as the meanest
Of my poor subjects. The proud attributes,
By oil-tongued flattery imposed upon us,
As sacred, glorious, high, invincible,
The deputy of heaven, and in that
Omnipotent, with all false titles else,
Coin'd to abuse our frailty, though compounded,

And by the breath of sycophants applied,
Cure not the least fit of an ague in us.
We may give poor men riches, confer honours
On undeservers, raise, or ruin such
As are beneath us, and, with this puff'd up,
Ambition would persuade us to forget
That we are men : but He that sits above us,
And to whom, at our utmost rate, we are
But pageant properties, derides our weakness :
In me, to whom you kneel, 'tis most apparent.
Can I call back yesterday, with all their aids
That bow unto my sceptre? or restore
My mind to that tranquillity and peace
It then enjoy'd ?—Can I make Eudocia chaste,
Or vile Paulinus honest ?
    Pul. If I might
Without offence, deliver my opinion——
    Theo. What would you say ?
    Pul. That, on my soul, the empress
Is innocent.
    Chry. The good Paulinus guiltless.
    Grat. And this should yield you comfort.
    Theo. In being guilty
Of an offence far, far transcending that
They stand condemn'd for ! Call you this a comfort ?
Suppose it could be true,—a corsive rather,
Not to eat our dead flesh, but putrify
What yet is sound. Was murder ever held
A cure for jealousy? or the crying blood
Of innocence, a balm to take away
Her festering anguish ? As you do desire
I should not do a justice on myself,
Add to the proofs by which Paulinus fell,
And not take from them ; in your charity
Sooner believe that they were false, than I
Unrighteous in my judgment? subjects' lives
Are not their prince's tennis-balls, to be bandied
In sport away : all that I can endure
For them, if they were guilty, is an atom
To the mountain of affliction I pull'd on me,
Should they prove innocent.
    Chry. For your majesty's peace,
I more than hope they were not : the false oath
Ta'en by the empress, and for which she can
Plead no excuse, convicted her, and yields
A sure defence for your suspicion of her.
And yet, to be resolved, since strong doubts are
More grievous, for the most part, than to know
A certain loss——

Theo. 'Tis true, Chrysapius,
Were there a possible means.
Chry. 'Tis offer'd to you,
If you please to embrace it.   Some few minutes
Make truce with passion, and but read, and follow
What's there projected,—[*Delivers him a paper.*]—you shall find a key
Will make your entrance easy, to discover
Her secret thoughts; and then, as in your wisdom
You shall think fit, you may determine of her;
And rest confirm'd, whether Paulinus died
A villain or a martyr.
Theo. It may do,
Nay, sure it must; yet, howsoe'er it fall;
I am most wretched.   Which way in my wishes
I should fashion the event, I'm so distracted
I cannot yet resolve of.—Follow me;
Though in my name all names are comprehended,
I must have witnesses in what degree
I have done wrong, or suffer'd.
Pul. Hope the best, sir.   [*Exeunt.*

SCENE III.—*Another Room in the same.*
Enter Eudocia *in sackcloth, her hair loose.*

[Sings.] *Why art thou slow, thou rest of trouble, Death,*
        To stop a wretch's breath,
That calls on thee, and offers her sad heart
        A prey unto thy dart?
I am nor young nor fair; be, therefore, bold:
        Sorrow hath made me old,
Deform'd and wrinkled; all that I can crave,
        Is, quiet in my grave.
Such as live happy, hold long life a jewel;
        But to me thou art cruel,
If thou end not my tedious misery;
        And I soon cease to be.
Strike, and strike home, then; pity unto me,
In one short hour's delay, is tyranny.

Thus, like a dying swan, to a sad tune
I sing my own dirge; would a requiem follow,
Which in my penitence I despair not of,
(This brittle glass of life already broken
With misery,) the long and quiet sleep
Of death would be most welcome!—Yet, before
We end our pilgrimage, 'tis fit that we
Should leave corruption and foul sins behind us.

But with wash'd feet and hands, the heathens dare not
Enter their profane temples; and for me
To hope my passage to eternity
Can be made easy, till I have shook off
The burthen of my sins in free confession,
Aided with sorrow and repentance for them,
Is against reason.   'Tis not laying by
My royal ornaments, or putting on
This garment of humility and contrition,
The throwing dust and ashes on my head,
Long fasts to tame my proud flesh, that can make
Atonement for my soul; that must be humbled,
All outward signs of penitence else are useless.
Chrysapius did assure me he would bring me
A holy man, from whom (having discover'd
My secret crying sins) I might receive
Full absolution—and he keeps his word.

Enter Theodosius *disguised as a Friar, with* Chrysapius.

Welcome, most reverend sir, upon my knees
I entertain you.
Theo. Noble sir, forbear
The place; the sacred office that I come for
                    [*Exit* Chrysapius.
Commands all privacy.   My penitent daughter,
Be careful, as you wish remission from me,
That, in confession of your sins, you hide not
One crime, whose ponderous weight, when you would make
Your flights above the firmament, may sink you.
A foolish modesty in concealing aught,
Is now far worse than impudence to profess.
And justify your guilt, be therefore free;
So may the gates of mercy open to you!
Eud. First then, I ask a pardon, for my being
Ingrateful to heaven's bounty.
Theo. A good entrance.
Eud. Greatness comes from above, and I raised to it
From a low condition, sinfully forgot
From whence it came; and, looking on myself
In the false glass of flattery, I received it
As a debt due to my beauty, not a gift
Or favour from the emperor.
Theo. 'Twas not well.
Eud. Pride waited on unthankfulness; and no more
Remembering the compassion of the princess,
And the means she used to make me what I was,

Contested with her, and with sore eyes
  seeing
Her greater light as it dimm'd mine, I
  practised .
To have it quite put out.
  Theo. A great offence;
But, on repentance, not unpardonable.
Forward.
  Eud. O, father!—what I now must utter,
I fear, in the delivery will destroy me,
Before you have absolved me.
  Theo. Heaven is gracious;
Out with it.
  Eud. Heaven commands us to tell truth,
Yet I, most sinful wretch, forswore myself.
  Theo. On what occasion?
  Eud. Quite forgetting that
An innocent truth can never stand in need
Of a guilty lie, being on the sudden ask'd
By the emperor, my husband, for an apple
Presented by him, I swore I had eaten it;
When my grieved conscience too well knows
  I sent it
To comfort sick Paulinus, being a man
I truly loved and favour'd.
  Theo. A cold sweat,
Like the juice of hemlock, bathes me.
                                    [*Aside.*
  Eud. And from this
A furious jealousy getting possession
Of the good emperor's heart, in his rage he
  doom'd
The innocent lord to die; my perjury
The fatal cause of murder.
  Theo. Take heed, daughter,
You niggle not with your conscience, and
  religion,
In styling him an innocent, from your fear
And shame to accuse yourself. The emperor
Had many spies upon you, saw such graces,
Which virtue could not warrant, shower'd
  upon him;
Glances in public, and more liberal favours
In your private chamber-meetings, making
  way
For foul adultery; nor could he be
But sensible of the compact pass'd between
  you,
To the ruin of his honour.
  Eud. Hear me, father;
I look'd for comfort, but, in this, you come
To add to my afflictions.
  Theo. Cause not you
Your own damnation in concealing that
Which may, in your discovery, find for-
  giveness.
Open your eyes; set heaven or hell before
  you;
In the revealing of the truth, you shall

Prepare a palace for your soul to dwell in,
Stored with celestial blessings; whereas, if
You palliate your crime, and dare beyond
Playing with lightning, in concealing it.
Expect a dreadful dungeon fill'd with horror,
And never-ending torments.
  Eud. May they fall
Eternally upon me, and increase,
When that which we call Time hath lost its
  name!
May lightning cleave the centre of the earth,
And I sink quick, before you have absolv'd
  me,
Into the bottomless abyss, if ever,
In one unchaste desire, nay in a thought,
I wrong'd the honour of the emperor's bed!
I do deserve, I grant, more than I suffer,
In that my fervour and desire to please him,
In my holy meditations press'd upon me,
And would not be kept out; now to dis-
  semble,
When I shall suddenly be insensible
Of what the world speaks of me, were mere
  madness:
And, though you are incredulous, I presume,
If, as I kneel now, my eyes swoll'n with tears,
My hands heaved up thus, my stretch'd
  heart-strings ready
To break asunder, my incensed lord
(His storm of jealousy blown o'er) should
  hear me,
He would believe I lied not.
  Theo. Rise, and see him,
                        [*Discovers himself.*
On his knees with joy affirm it.
  Eud. Can this be?
  Theo. My sisters, and the rest there!—All
  bear witness,

Enter Pulcheria, Arcadia, Flaccilla, Chrysapius, Timantus, *and* Philanax.

In freeing this incomparable lady
From the suspicion of guilt, I do
Accuse myself, and willingly submit
To any penance she in justice shall
Please to impose upon me.
  Eud. Royal sir,
Your ill opinion of me's soon forgiven.
  Pul. But how you can make satisfaction to
The poor Paulinus, he being dead, in reason
You must conclude impossible.
  Theo. And in that
I am most miserable; the ocean
Of joy, which, in your innocence, flow'd
  high to me,
Ebbs in the thought of my unjust command,
By which he died. O, Philanax, (as thy
  name
Interpreted speaks thee,) thou hast ever been

A lover of the king, and thy whole life
Can witness thy obedience to my will,
In putting that in execution which
Was trusted to thee ; say but yet this once,
Thou hast not done what rashly I com-
    manded,
And that Paulinus lives, and thy reward
For not performing that which I enjoin'd
    thee,
Shall centuple whatever yet thy duty
Or merit challenged from me.
    Phil. 'Tis too late, sir :
He's dead ; and, when you know he was
    unable
To wrong you in the way that you suspected,
You'll wish it had been otherwise.
    Theo. Unable !
    Phil. I am sure he was an eunuch, and
    might safely
Lie by a virgin's side ; at four years made one,
Though, to hold grace with ladies, he con-
    ceal'd it.
The circumstances, and the manner how,
You may hear at better leisure.
    Theo. How, an eunuch !
The more the proofs are that are brought to
    clear thee,
My best Eudocia, the more my sorrows.
    Eud. That I am innocent ?
    Theo. That I am guilty
Of murder, my Eudocia. I will build
A glorious monument to his memory ;
And, for my punishment, live and die upon it,
And never more converse with men.

        Enter Paulinus.

    Paul. Live long, sir !
May I do so to serve you ! and, if that
I live does not displease you, you owe for it
To this good lord.
    Theo. Myself, and all that's mine.
    Phil. Your pardon is a payment.

    Theo. I am rapt
With joy beyond myself. Now, my Eudocia,
My jealousy puff'd away thus, in this breath
I scent the natural sweetness.   [*Kisses her.*
    Arcad. Sacred sir,
I am happy to behold this, and presume,
Now you are pleased, to move a suit, in
    which
My sister is join'd with me.
    Theo. Prithee speak it ;
For I have vow'd to hear before I grant :—
I thank your good instructions.
                    [*To* Pulcheria.
    Arcad. 'Tis but this, sir :
We have observed the falling out and in
Between the husband and the wife shews
    rarely ;
Their jars and reconcilements strangely
    take us.
    Flac. Anger and jealousy that conclude in
    kisses,
Is a sweet war, in sooth.
    Arcad. We therefore, brother,
Most humbly beg you would provide us
    husbands,
That we may taste the pleasure of 't.
    Flac. And with speed, sir ;
For so your favour's doubled.
    Theo. Take my word,
I will with all convenience ; and not blush
Hereafter to be guided by your counsels :
I will deserve your pardon.   Philanax
Shall be remember'd, and magnificent boun-
    ties
Fall on Chrysapius ; my grace on all.
Let Cleon be deliver'd, and rewarded.
My grace on all, which as I lend to you,
Return your vows to heaven, that it may
    please,
As it is gracious, to quench in me
All future sparks of burning jealousy.
                    [*Exeunt.*

EPILOGUE.

We have reason to be doubtful, whether he,
On whom (forced to it from necessity)
The maker did confer his emperor's part,
Hath given you satisfaction, in his art
Of action and delivery; 'tis sure truth,
The burthen was too heavy for his youth
To undergo:—but, in his will, we know,
He was not wanting, and shall ever owe,
With his, our service, if your favours deign
To give him strength, hereafter to sustain
A greater weight.   It is your grace that can
In your allowance of this, write him man
Before his time ; which, if you please to do,
You make the player and the poet too.

The Fatal Dowry.

DRAMATIS PERSONÆ.

Rochfort, *ex-premier president of the parliament of* Dijon.
Charalois, *a noble gentleman, son to the deceased marshal.*
Romont, *a brave officer, friend to* Charalois.
Novall senior, *premier president of the parliament of* Dijon.
Novall, *junior his son, in love with* Beaumelle.
Du Croy, *president of the parliament of* Dijon.
Charmi, *an advocate.*
Beaumont, *secretary to* Rochfort.
Pontalier, } *friends of* Novall *junior.*
Malotin, }
Liladam, *a parasite, dependent on* Novall *junior.*

Aymer, *a singer, and keeper of a music-house, also dependent on* Novall *junior.*
Advocates.
Three Creditors.
A Priest.
Tailor.
Barber.
Perfumer.
Page.
Beaumelle, *daughter to* Rochfort.
Florimel, { *servants to* Beaumelle; *the latter the secret agent of* Novall *junior.*
Bellapert, {
Presidents, Captains, Soldiers, Mourners, Gaoler, Bailiffs, Servants.

SCENE,—Dijon.

ACT I.

SCENE I.—*A Street before the Court of Justice.*

Enter Charalois *with a paper,* Romont, *and* Charmi.

Char. Sir, I may move the court to serve
  your will;
But therein shall both wrong you and myself.
  Rom. Why think you so, sir?
  Char. 'Cause I am familiar
With what will be their answer: they will say,
'Tis against law; and argue me of ignorance,
For offering them the motion.
  Rom. You know not, sir,
How in this cause, they may dispense with
  law;
And therefore frame not you their answer
  for them,
But do your parts.
  Char. I love the cause so well,
As I could run the hazard of a check for't.
  Rom. From whom?
  Char. Some of the bench, that watch to
  give it,
More than to do the office that they sit for:
But give me, sir, my fee.
  Rom. Now you are noble.
                    [*Gives him his purse.*
  Char. I shall deserve this better yet, in
  giving   .

My lord some counsel, if he please to hear it,
Than I shall do with pleading.
  Rom. What may it be, sir?
  Char. That it would please his lordship,
  as the presidents
And counsellors of court come by, to stand
Here, and but shew himself, and to some one
Or two, make his request:—there is a minute,
When a man's presence speaks in his own
  cause,
More than the tongues of twenty advocates.
  Rom. I have urged that.

Enter Rochfort *and* Du Croy.

  Char. Their lordships here are coming,
I must go get me a place. You'll find me in
  court,
And at your service.   [*Exit.*
  Rom. Now, put on your spirits.
  Du Croy. The ease that you prepare your
  self, my lord,
In giving up the place you hold in court,
Will prove, I fear, a trouble in the state,
And that no slight one.
  Roch. Pray you, sir, no more.
  Rom. Now, sir, lose not this offer'd means:
  their looks,
Fix'd on you with a pitying earnestness,
Invite you to demand their furtherance
To your good purpose:—this such a dulness,
So foolish and untimely, as——

A A

Du Croy. You know him?

Roch. I do; and much lament the sudden fall

Of his brave house. It is young Charalois,
Son to the marshal, from whom he inherits
His fame and virtues only.

Rom. Ha! they name you.

Du Croy. His father died in prison two days since.

Roch. Yes, to the shame of this ungrateful state;
That such a master in the art of war,
So noble, and so highly meriting
From this forgetful country, should, for want
Of means to satisfy his creditors
The sums he took up for the general good,
Meet with an end so infamous.

Rom. Dare you ever
Hope for like opportunity?

Du Croy. My good lord!
    [*They salute him as they pass by.*

Roch. My wish bring comfort to you!

Du Croy. The time calls us.

Roch. Good morrow, colonel!
    [*Exeunt* Rochfort *and* Du Croy.

Rom. This obstinate spleen,
You think, becomes your sorrow, and sorts well
With your black suits; but, grant me wit or judgment,
And, by the freedom of an honest man,
And a true friend to boot, I swear 'tis shameful.
And therefore flatter not yourself with hope,
Your sable habit, with the hat and cloak,
No, though the ribands help, have power to work them
To what you would: for those that had no eyes
To see the great acts of your father, will not,
From any fashion sorrow can put on,
Be taught to know their duties.

Charal. If they will not,
They are too old to learn, and I too young
To give them counsel; since, if they partake
The understanding and the hearts of men,
They will prevent my words and tears: if not,
What can persuasion, though made eloquent
With grief, work upon such as have changed natures
With the most savage beast? Blest, blest be ever
The memory of that happy age, when justice
Had no guards to keep off wrong'd innocence
From flying to her succours, and, in that,
Assurance of redress! where now, Romont,

The damn'd with more ease may ascend from hell,
Than we arrive at her. One Cerberus there
Forbids the passage, in our courts a thousand,
As loud and fertile-headed; and the client
That wants the sops to fill their ravenous throats,
Must hope for no access: why should I, then,
Attempt impossibilities; you, friend, being
Too well acquainted with my dearth of means
To make my entrance that way?

Rom. Would I were not!
But, sir, you have a cause, a cause so just,
Of such necessity, not to be deferr'd,
As would compel a maid, whose foot was never
Set o'er her father's threshold, nor within
The house where she was born, ever spake word
Which was not usher'd with pure virgin blushes,
To drown the tempest of a pleader's tongue,
And force corruption to give back the hire
It took against her. Let examples move you.
You see men great in birth, esteem, and fortune,
Rather than lose a scruple of their right,
Fawn basely upon such, whose gowns put off,
They would disdain for servants.

Charal. And to these
Can I become a suitor?

Rom. Without loss:
Would you consider, that, to gain their favours,
Our chastest dames put off their modesties,
Soldiers forget their honours, usurers
Make sacrifice of gold, poets of wit,
And men religious part with fame and goodness.
Be therefore won to use the means that may
Advance your pious ends.

Charal. You shall o'ercome.

Rom. And you receive the glory. Pray you, now practise.

Charal. 'Tis well.

Enter Novall senior, Advocates, Liladam, *and three* Creditors.

[*Tenders his petition.*] Not look on me!

Rom. You must have patience——
Offer it again.

Charal. And be again contemn'd!

Nov. sen. I know what's to be done.

    1 *Cred.* And, that your lordship
Will please to do your knowledge, we offer first

Our thankful hearts here, as a bounteous
    earnest
To what we will add.
  Nov. sen. One word more of this,
I am your enemy. Am I a man
Your bribes can work on? ha?
  Lilad. Friends, you mistake
                [Aside to Cred.
The way to win my lord ; he must not hear
    this,
But I, as one in favour, in his sight
May hearken to you for my profit.—Sir !
Pray hear them.
  Nov. sen. It is well.
  Lilad. Observe him now.
  Nov. sen. Your cause being good, and
    your proceedings so,
Without corruption I am your friend ;
Speak your desires.   •
  2 Cred. Oh, they are charitable ;
The marshal stood engaged unto us three
Two hundred thousand crowns, which, by
    his death,
We are defeated of : for which great loss
We aim at nothing but his rotten flesh ;
Nor is that cruelty.
  1 Cred. I have a son
That talks of nothing but of guns and
    armour,
And swears he'll be a soldier ; 'tis an humour
I would divert him from ; and I am told,
That if I minister to him in his drink,
Powder made of this bankrupt marshal's
    bones,
Provided that the carcass rot above ground,
'Twill cure his foolish frenzy.
  Nov. sen. You shew in it
A father's care. I have a son myself,
A fashionable gentleman, and a peaceful ;
And, but I am assured he's not so given,
He should take of it too.
  Charal. Sir !   *[Tenders his petition.*
  Nov. sen. What are you?
  Charal. A gentleman.
  Nov. sen. So are many that rake dunghills.
If you have any suit, move it in court :
I take no papers in corners.   *[Exit.*
  Rom. Yes,
As the matter may be carried—and where-
    by—
To manage the conveyance——Follow him.
  Lilad. You are rude : I say he shall not
    pass.
      [Exeunt Charalois *and* Advocates.
  Rom. You say so !
On what assurance ?
For the well cutting of his lordship's corns,
Picking his toes, or any office else
Nearer to baseness !

  Lilad. Look upon me better ;
Are these the ensigns of so coarse a fellow?
Be well advised.
  Rom. Out, rogue ! do not I know
These glorious weeds spring from the sordid
    dunghill
Of thy officious baseness? wert thou worthy
Of anything from me, but my contempt,
I would do more than this,—*[Beats him.]*—
    more, you court-spider !
  Lilad. But that this man is lawless, he
    should find
That I am valiant,
  1 Cred. If your ears are fast,
'Tis nothing. What's a blow or two? as
    much.
  2 Cred. These chastisements as useful are
    as frequent,
To such as would grow rich.
  Rom. Are they so, rascals ?
I will befriend you, then.   *[Kicks them.*
  1 Cred. Bear witness, sirs !
  Lilad. Truth, I have borne my part
    already, friends :
In the court you shall have more.   *[Exit.*
  Rom. I know you for
The worst of spirits, that strive to rob the
    tombs
Of what is their inheritance, the dead :
For usurers, bred by a riotous peace,
That hold the charter of your wealth and
    freedom
By being knaves and cuckolds ; that ne'er
    pray,
But when you fear the rich heirs will grow
    wise,
To keep their lands out of your parchment
    toils ;
And then, the devil your father's call'd upon,
To invent some ways of luxury ne'er thought
    on.
Be gone, and quickly, or I'll leave no room
Upon your foreheads for your horns to
    sprout on—
Without a murmur, or I will undo you ;
For I will beat you honest.
  1 Cred. Thrift forbid !
We will bear this, rather than hazard that.
               [Exeunt Creditors.

        Re-enter Charalois.

  Rom. I am somewhat eased in this yet.
  Char. Only friend,
To what vain purpose do I make my sorrow
Wait on the triumph of their cruelty ?
Or teach their pride, from my humility,
To think it has o'ercome? They are de-
    termined

                       A A 2

What they will do ; and it may well become
me,
To rob them of the glory they expect
From my submiss entreaties.
   Rom. Think not so, sir :
The difficulties that you encounter with
Will crown the undertaking—heaven ! you
weep :
And I could do so too, but that I know
There's more expected from the son and
friend
Of him whose fatal loss now shakes our
natures,
Than sighs or tears, in which a village nurse,
Or cunning strumpet, when her knave is
hang'd,
May overcome us. We are men, young lord,
Let us not do like women. To the court,
And there speak like your birth : wake
sleeping justice,
Or dare the axe. This is a way will sort
With what you are : I call you not to that
I will shrink from myself ; I will deserve
Your thanks, or suffer with you—O how
bravely
That sudden fire of anger shews in you !
Give fuel to it. Since you are on a shelf
Of extreme danger, suffer like yourself.
                        [*Exeunt.*

SCENE II.—*The Court of Justice.*

Enter Rochfort, Novall *senior,* Presidents,
Charmi, Du Croy, Beaumont, Advocates,
three Creditors, *and* Officers.

   Du Croy. Your lordships seated, may this
meeting prove
Prosperous to us, and to the general good
Of Burgundy !
   Nov. sen. Speak to the point.
   Du Croy. Which is
With honour to dispose the place and power
Of premier president, which this reverend
man,
Grave Rochfort, whom for honour's sake I
name,
Is purposed to resign ; a place, my lords,
In which he hath with such integrity
Perform'd the first and best parts of a judge,
That, as his life transcends all fair examples
Of such as were before him in Dijon,
So it remains to those that shall succeed him,
A precedent they may imitate, but not equal.
   Roch. I may not sit to hear this.
   Du Croy. Let the love
And thankfulness we are bound to pay to
goodness,
In this o'ercome your modesty.
   Roch. My thanks

For this great favour shall prevent your
trouble.
The honourable trust that was imposed
Upon my weakness, since you witness for
me
It was not ill discharged, I will not mention;
Nor now, if age had not deprived me of
The little strength I had to govern well
The province that I undertook, forsake it.
   Nov. sen. That we could lend you of our
years !
   Du Croy. Or strength !
   Nov. sen. Or, as you are, persuade you to
continue
The noble exercise of your knowing judg-
ment !
   Roch. That may not be ; nor can your
lordships' goodness,
Since your employments have conferr'd upon
me
Sufficient wealth, deny the use of it :
And, though old age, when one foot's in the
grave,
In many, when all humours else are spent,
Feeds no affection in them, but desire
To add height to the mountain of their riches,
In me it is not so. I rest content
With the honours and estate I now possess :
And, that I may have liberty to use
What heaven, still blessing my poor industry,
Hath made me master of, I pray the court
To ease me of my burthen, that I may
Employ the small remainder of my life
In living well, and learning how to die so.

   Enter Romont *and* Charalois.

   Rom. See, sir, our advocate.
   Du Croy. The court entreats
Your lordship will be pleased to name the
man,
Which you would have your successor, and,
in me,
All promise to confirm it.
   Roch. I embrace it
As an assurance of their favour to me,
And name my lord Novall.
   Du Croy. The court allows it.
   Roch. But there are suitors wait here, and
their causes
May be of more necessity to be heard ;
I therefore wish that mine may be deferr'd,
And theirs have hearing.
   Du Croy. If your lordship please
                     [*To* Nov. sen.
To take the place, we will proceed.
   Char. The cause
We come to offer to your lordships' censure,
Is in itself so noble, that it needs not
Or rhetoric in me that plead, or favour

From your grave lordships, to determine of
    it ;
Since to the praise of your impartial justice
(Which guilty, nay, condemn'd men, dare
    not scandal)
It will erect a trophy of your mercy,
Which married to that justice——
    Nov. sen. Speak to the cause.
    Char. I will, my lord. To say, the late
        dead marshal,
The father of this young lord here, my client,
Hath done his country great and faithful
    service,
Might task me of impertinence, to repeat
What your grave lordships cannot but re-
    member.
He, in his life, became indebted to
These thrifty men, (I will not wrong their
    credits,
By giving them the attributes they now
    merit,)
And failing, by the fortune of the wars,
Of means to free himself from his engage-
    ments,
He was arrested, and for want of bail,
Imprison'd at their suit ; and, not long after,
With loss of liberty, ended his life.
And, though it be a maxim in our laws,
All suits die with the person, these men's
    malice
In death finds matter for their hate to work
    on ;
Denying him the decent rites of burial,
Which the sworn enemies of the Christian
    faith
Grant freely to their slaves. May it there-
    fore please
Your lordships so to fashion your decree,
That, what their cruelty doth forbid, your
    pity
May give allowance to.
    Nov. sen. How long have you, sir,
Practised in court?
    Char. Some twenty years, my lord.
    Nov. sen. By your gross ignorance, it
        should appear,
Not twenty days.
    Char. I hope I have given no cause
In this, my lord.
    Nov. sen. How dare you move the court
To the dispensing with an act, confirm'd
By parliament, to the terror of all bankrupts?
Go home ; and with more care peruse the
    statutes :
Or the next motion, savouring of this bold-
    ness,
May force you, sir, to leap, against your will,
Over the place you plead at.
    Char. I foresaw this.

Rom. Why, does your lordship think the
    moving of
A cause more honest than this court had ever
The honour to determine, can deserve
A check like this?
    Nov. sen. Strange boldness !
    Rom. 'Tis fit freedom :
Or, do you conclude an advocate cannot hold
His credit with the judge, unless he study
His face more than the cause for which he
    pleads ?
    Char. Forbear.
    Rom. Or cannot you, that have the power
To qualify the rigour of the laws
When you are pleased, take a little from
The strictness of your sour decrees, enacted
In favour of the greedy creditors,
Against the o'erthrown debtor ?
    Nov. sen. Sirrah ! you that prate
Thus saucily, what are you ?
    Rom. Why, I'll tell thee,
Thou purple-colour'd man ! I am one to
    whom
Thou ow'st the means thou hast of sitting
    there,
A corrupt elder.
    Char. Forbear.
    Rom. The nose thou wear'st is my gift ;
    and those eyes,
That meet no object so base as their master,
Had been long since torn from that guilty
    head,   •
And thou thyself slave to some needy Swiss,
Had I not worn a sword, and used it better
Than, in thy prayers, thou ever didst thy
    tongue.
    Nov. sen. Shall such an insolence pass
        unpunish'd !
    Char. Hear me.
    Rom. Yet I, that, in my service done my
        country,
Disdain to be put in the scale with thee,
Confess myself unworthy to be valued
With the least part, nay, hair of the dead
    marshal ;
Of whose so many glorious undertakings,
Make choice of any one, and that the
    meanest,
Perform'd against the subtle fox of France,
The politic Louis, or the more desperate
    Swiss,
And 'twill outweigh all the good purposes,
Though put in act, that ever gownman prae-
    tised.
    Nov. sen. Away with him to prison !
    Rom. If that curses,
Urged justly, and breath'd forth so, ever fell
On those that did deserve them, let not
    mine

Be spent in vain now, that thou from this
     instant
Mayst, in thy fear that they will fall upon
     thee,
Be sensible of the plagues they shall bring
     with them.
And for denying of a little earth ,
To cover what remains of our great soldier,
May all your wives prove whores, your
     factors thieves,
And, while you live, your riotous heirs undo
     you I
And thou, the patron of their cruelty,
Of all thy lordships live not to be owner
Of so much dung as will conceal a dog,
Or, what is worse, thyself in ! And thy years,
To th' end thou mayst be wretched, I wish
     many ;
And, as thou hast denied the dead a grave,
May misery in thy life make thee desire one,
Which men and all the elements keep from
     thee !
—I have begun well ; imitate, exceed.
                         [*Aside to* Charalois.
Roch. Good counsel, were it a praise-
     worthy deed.
                 [*Exeunt officers with* Romont.
Du Croy. Remember what we are.
Charal. Thus low my duty
Answers your lordship's counsel. I will use,
In the few words with which I am to trouble
Your lordship's ears, the temper that you
     wish me ;
Not that I fear to speak my thoughts as loud,
And with a liberty beyond Romont ;
But that I know, for me, that am made up
Of all that's wretched, so to haste my end,
Would seem to most rather a willingness
To quit the burthen of a hopeless life,
Than scorn of death, or duty to the dead.
I, therefore, bring the tribute of my praise
To your severity, and commend the justice
That will not, for the many services
That any man hath done the commonwealth,
Wink at his least of ills. What though my
     father
Writ man before he was so, and confirm'd it,
By numbering that day no part of his life,
In which he did not service to his country ;
Was he to be free, therefore, from the laws
And ceremonious form in your decrees !
Or else, because he did as much as man,
In those three memorable overthrows
At Grauson, Morat, Nancy, where his
     master,
The warlike Charalois, (with whose mis-
     fortunes
I bear his name,) lost treasure, men, and life,
To be excused from payment of those sums

Which (his own patrimony spent) his zeal
To serve his country forced him to take up!
     Nov. sen. The precedent were ill.
     Charal. And yet, my lord, this much,
I know, you'll grant ; after those great
     defeatures,
Which in their dreadful ruins buried quick

                   Re-enter Officers.

Courage and hope in all men but himself,
He forced the proud foe, in his height of
     conquest,
To yield unto an honourable peace ;
And in it saved an hundred thousand lives,
To end his own, that was sure proof against
The scalding summer's heat, and winter's
     frost,
Ill airs, the cannon, and the enemy's sword,
In a most loathsome prison.
     Du Croy. 'Twas his fault
To be so prodigal.
     Nov. sen. He had from the state
Sufficient entertainment for the army.
     Charal. Sufficient, my lords ! You sit at
     home,
And, though your fees are boundless at the
     bar,
Are thrifty in the charges of the war——
But your wills be obey'd. To these I turn,
To these soft-hearted men, that wisely know
They're only good men that pay what they
     owe.
     2 Cred. And so they are.
     1 Cred. It is the city doctrine ;
We stand bound to maintain it.
     Charal. Be constant in it ;
And since you are as merciless in your
     natures,
As base and mercenary in your means
By which you get your wealth, I will not urge
The court to take away one scruple from
The right of their laws, or [wish] one good
     thought
In you, to mend your disposition with.
I know there is no music to your ears
So pleasing as the groans of men in prison ;
And that the tears of widows, and the cries
Of famish'd orphans, are the feasts that take
     you.
That to be in your danger, with more care
Should be avoided than infectious air,
The loath'd embraces of diseased women,
A flatterer's poison, or the loss of honour.—
Yet rather than my father's reverend dust
Shall want a place in that fair monument,'
In which our noble ancestors lie entomb'd,
Before the court I offer up myself
A prisoner for it. Load me with those irons

That have worn out his life; in my best strength
I'll run to the encounter of cold, hunger,
And choose my dwelling where no sun dares
  enter,
So he may be released.

  1 *Cred.* What mean you, sir?

  2 *Advo.* Only your fee again : there's so
  much said
Already in this cause, and said so well,
That, should I only offer to speak in it,,
I should be or not heard, or laugh'd at for it.

  1 *Cred.* 'Tis the first money advocate e'er
  gave back,
Though he said nothing.

  Roch. Be advised, young lord,
And well considerate ; you throw away
Your liberty and joys of life together :
Your bounty is employ'd upon a subject
That is not sensible of it, with which wise man
Never abused his goodness. The great
  virtues
Of your dead father vindicate themselves
From these men's malice, and break ope the
  prison,
Though it contain his body.

  Nov. sen. Let him alone :
If he love cords, in God's name let him
  wear them ;
Provided these consent.

  Charal. I hope they are not
So ignorant in any way of profit,
As to neglect a possibility
To get their own, by seeking it from that
Which can return them nothing but ill fame,
And curses, for their barbarous cruelties.

  3 *Cred.* What think you of the offer?

  2 *Cred.* Very well.

  1 *Cred.* Accept it by all means. Let's
  shut him up :
He is well shaped, and has a villainous
  tongue,
And, should he study that way of revenge,
As I dare almost swear he loves a wench,
We have no wives, nor never shall get
  daughters,
That will hold out against him.

  Du Croy. What's your answer?

  2 *Cred.* Speak you for all.

  1 *Cred.* Why, let our executions
That he upon the father, be return'd
Upon the son, and we release the body.

  Nov. sen. The court must grant you that.

  Charal. I thank your lordships.
They have in it confirm'd on me such glory
As no time can take from me : I am ready,
Come, lead me where you please. Captivity,
That comes with honour, is true liberty.

    [*Exeunt* Charalois, Charmi, Officers,
    · *and* Creditors.

  Nov. sen. Strange rashness !

  Roch. A brave resolution rather,
Worthy a better fortune : but, however,
It is not now to be disputed ; therefore
To my own cause. Already I have found
Your lordships bountiful in your favours
  to me,
And that should teach my modesty to end
  here,
And press your loves no further.

  Du Croy. There is nothing
The court can grant, but with assurance you
May ask it, and obtain it.

  Roch. You encourage
A bold petitioner, and 'tis not fit
Your favours should be lost : besides, 't'as
  been
A custom many years, at the surrendering
The place I now give up, to grant the
  president
One boon, that parted with it ; and, to con-
  firm
Your grace towards me, against all such as
  may   . . .
Detract my actions and life hereafter,
I now prefer it to you.

  Du Croy. Speak it freely.

  Roch. I then desire the liberty of Romont,
And that my lord Novall, whose private
  wrong
Was equal to the injury that was done
To the dignity of the court, will pardon it,
And now sign his enlargement.

  Nov. sen. Pray you demand
The moiety of my estate, or anything
Within my power, but this.

  Roch. Am I denied then
My first and last request?

  Du Croy. It must not be.

  2 *Pre.* I have a voice to give in it.

  3 *Pre.* And I.
And if persuasion will not work him to it,
We will make known our power.

  Nov. sen. You are too violent ,
You shall have my consent : but would you
  had
Made trial of my love in anything
But this, you should have found then—but
  it skills not :
You have what you desire.

  Roch. I thank your lordships.

  Du Croy. The court is up. Make way.

    [*Exeunt all but* Rochfort *and* Beaumont.

  Roch. I follow you.

  Beaumont !

  Beau. My lord.

  Roch. You are a scholar, Beaumont ;
And can search deeper into the intents of
  men,

Than those that are less knowing.—How
    appear'd
The piety and brave behaviour of
Young Charalois, to you?
    Beau. It is my wonder,
Since I want language to express it fully:
And sure the colonel——
    Roch. Fie! he was faulty.
What present money have I?
    Beau. There's no want
Of any sum a private man has use for.
    Roch. 'Tis well:
I am strangely taken with this Charalois.
Methinks, from his example the whole age
Should learn to be good, and continue so.
Virtue works strangely with us; and his
    goodness
Rising above his fortune, seems to me,
Prince-like, to will, not ask, a courtesy.
                                    [*Exeunt.*

ACT II.

SCENE I.—*A Street before the Prison.*
Enter Pontalier, Malotin, *and* Beaumont.

    Mal. 'Tis strange.
    Beau. Methinks so.
    Pont. In a man but young,
Yet old in judgment; theoric and practic
In all humanity, and, to increase the wonder,
Religious, yet a soldier; that he should
Yield his free-living youth a captive for
The freedom of his aged father's corpse,
And rather choose to want life's necessaries,
Liberty, hope of fortune, than it should
In death be kept from Christian ceremony.
    Mal. Come, 'tis a golden precedent in a
    son,
To let strong nature have the better hand,
In such a case, of all affected reason.
What years sit on this Charalois?
    Beau. Twenty-eight:
For since the clock did strike him seventeen
    old,
Under his father's wing this son hath fought,
Served and commanded, and so aptly both,
That sometimes he appear'd his father's
    father,
And never less than 's son; the old man's
    virtues
So recent in him, as the world may swear,
Nought but a fair tree could such fair fruit
    bear.
    Pont. But wherefore lets he such a bar-
    barous law,
And men more barbarous to execute it,
Prevail on his soft disposition,
That he had rather die alive for debt

Of the old man, in prison, than they should
Rob him of sepulture; considering
These monies borrow'd bought the lenders
    peace,
And all the means they enjoy, nor were
    diffused
In any impious or licentious path!
    Beau. True! for my part, were it my
    father's trunk,
The tyrannous ram-heads with their horns
    should gore it,
Or cast it to their curs, than they less
    currish,
Ere prey on me so with their lion-law,
Being in my free will, as in his, to shun it.
    Pont. Alas! he knows himself in poverty
    lost:
For, in this partial avaricious age,
What price bears honour? virtue? long ago,
It was but praised, and freezed; but now-a-
    days,
'Tis colder far, and has nor love nor praise:
The very praise now freezeth too; for
    nature
Did make the heathen far more Christian
    then,
Than knowledge us, less heathenish, Chris-
    tian.
    Mal. This morning is the funeral?
    Pont. Certainly,
And from this prison,—'twas the son's re-
    quest.
That his dear father might interment have,
See, the young son enter'd a lively grave!
    Beau. They come:—observe their order.

*Solemn music.   Enter the Funeral Pro-
    cession.   The Coffin borne by four, pre-
    ceded by a* Priest.   Captains, Lieutenants,
    Ensigns, *and* Soldiers; Mourners, Scutch-
    eons, *&c., and very good order.*   Romont
    and Charalois, *followed by the* Gaolers
    and Officers, *with* Creditors, *meet it.*

    Charal. How like a silent stream shaded
    with night,
And gliding softly, with our windy sighs,
Moves the whole frame of this solemnity!
Tears, sighs, and blacks filling the simile;
Whilst I, the only murmur in this grove
Of death, thus hollowly break forth. Vouch-
    safe
    [*To the* Bearers, *who set down the Coffin.*
To stay awhile.—Rest, rest in peace, dear
    earth!
Thou that brought'st rest to their unthank-
    ful lives,
Whose cruelty denied thee rest in death!
Here stands thy poor executor, thy son,

That makes his life prisoner to bail thy
    death ;
Who gladlier puts on this captivity,
Than virgins, long in love, their wedding
    weeds.
Of all that ever thou hast done good to,
These only have good memories ; for they
Remember best forget not gratitude.
I thank you for this last and friendly love.
                            [*To the* Soldiers.
And though this country, like a viperous
    mother,
Not only hath eat up ungratefully
All means of thee, her son, but last, thyself,
Leaving thy heir so bare and indigent,
He cannot raise thee a poor monument,
Such as a flatterer or a usurer hath ;
Thy worth, in every honest breast, builds
    one,
Making their friendly hearts thy funeral
    stone.
    Pont. Sir.
    Charal. Peace ! O, peace ! this scene is
        wholly mine.
What ! weep ye, soldiers ? blanch not.—
    Romont weeps !——
Ha ! let me see !—my miracle is eased,
The gaolers and the creditors do weep ;
Even they that make us weep, do weep
    themselves !
Be these thy body's balm ! these and thy
    virtue
Keep thy fame ever odoriferous,
Whilst the great, proud, rich, undeserving
    man,
Alive, stinks in his vices, and, being vanish'd,
The golden calf, that was an idol deck'd
With marble pillars, jet, and porphyry,
Shall quickly, both in bone and name, con-
    sume,
Though rapt in lead, spice, searcloth, and
    perfume !
    1 *Cred.* Sir.
    Charal. What ? away, for shame ! you,
        profane rogues,
Must not be mingled with these holy
    relics ;
This is a sacrifice :—our shower shall crown
His sepulchre with olive, myrrh, and bays,
The plants of peace, of sorrow, victory ;
Your tears would spring but weeds.
    1 *Cred.* Would they so !
We'll keep them to stop bottles then.
    Rom. No, keep them
For your own sins, you rogues, till you
    repent ;
You'll die else, and be damn'd.
    2 *Cred.* Damn'd—ha ! ha ! ha !
    Rom. Laugh ye ?

    3 *Cred.* Yes, faith, sir ; we would be very
        glad
To please you either way.
    1 *Cred.* Your are ne'er content,
Crying nor laughing.
    Rom. Both with a birth, ye rogues ?
    2 *Cred.* Our wives, sir, taught us.
    Rom. Look, look, you slaves ! your thank-
        less cruelty,
And savage manners of unkind Dijon,
Exhaust these floods, and not his father's
    death.
    1 *Cred.* 'Slid, sir ! what would you ? you're
        so choleric !
    2 *Cred.* Most soldiers are so, i'faith ;—let
        him alone.
They have little else to live on. We've not
    had
A penny of him, have we ?
    3 *Cred.* 'Slight ! would you have our
        hearts ?
    1 *Cred.* We have nothing but his body
        here in durance,
For all our money.
    Priest. On.
    Charal. One moment more,
But to bestow a few poor legacies,
All I have left in my dead father's rights,
And I have done. Captain, wear thou these
    spurs,
That yet ne'er made his horse run from a
    foe.
Lieutenant, thou this scarf ; and may it tie
Thy valour and thy honesty together !
For so it did in him. Ensign, this cuirass,
Your general's necklace once. You, gentle
    bearers,
Divide this purse of gold ; this other, strew
Among the poor ; 'tis all I have. Ro-
    mont——
Wear thou this medal of himself——that,
    like
A hearty oak, grew'st close to this tall pine,
Even in the wildest wilderness of war,
Whereon foes broke their swords, and tired
    themselves :
Wounded and hack'd ye were, but never
    fell'd.
For me, my portion provide in heaven !——
My root is earth'd, and I, a desolate branch,
Left scatter'd in the highway of the world,
Trod under foot, that might have been a
    column
Mainly supporting our demolish'd house.
This would I wear as my inheritance——
And what hope can arise to me from it,
When I and it are both here prisoners !
Only may this, if ever we be free,
Keep, or redeem, me from all infamy.

A DIRGE TO SOLEMN MUSIC.

Fie! cease to wonder,
Though you hear Orpheus with his ivory lute,
*   Move trees and rocks,*
Charm bulls, bears, and men more savage,
*   to be mute;*
*   Weak foolish singer, here is one*
*   Would have transformed thyself to*
*   stone.*

1 *Cred.* No further ; look to them at your
    own peril.
2 *Cred.* No, as they please : their master's
    a good man——
I would they were at the Bermudas !
Gaol. You must no further.
The prison limits you, and the creditors
Exact the strictness.
    Rom. Out, you wolvish mongrels !
Whose brains should be knock'd out, like
    dogs in July,
Lest your infection poison a whole town.
    Charal. They grudge our sorrow. Your
    ill wills, perforce,
Turn now to charity : they would not have us
Walk too far mourning ; usurers' relief
Grieves, if the debtors have too much of
    grief.   [*Exeunt.*

SCENE II.—*A Room in* Rochfort's *House.*
Enter Beaumelle, Florimel, *and* Bellapert.

    Beaumel. I prithee tell me, Florimel, why
do women marry ?
    Flor. Why truly, madam, I think, to lie
with their husbands.
    Bell. You are a fool. She lies, madam ;
women marry husbands, to lie with other
men.
    Flor. 'Faith, even such a woman wilt thou
make. By this light, madam, this wagtail
will spoil you, if you take delight in her license.
    Beaumel. 'Tis true, Florimel ; and thou
wilt make me too good for a young lady.
What an electuary found my father out for
his daughter, when he compounded you two
my women ! for thou, Florimel, art even a
grain too heavy, simply, for a waiting-
gentlewoman——
    Flor. And thou, Bellapert, a grain too
light.
    Bell. Well, go thy ways, goody wisdom,
whom nobody regards. I wonder whether
be elder, thou or thy hood ? You think,
because you served my lady's mother, are
thirty-two years old, which is a pip out, you
know——
    Flor. Well said, whirligig.

    Bell. You are deceived ; I want a peg in
the middle.—Out of these prerogatives, you
think to be mother of the maids here, and
mortify them with proverbs : go, go, govern
the sweetmeats, and weigh the sugar, that
the wenches steal none ; say your prayers
twice a day, and, as I take it, you have
performed your function.
    Flor. I may be even with you.
    Bell. Hark ! the court's broke up. Go,
help my lord out of his caroch, and
scratch his head till dinner-time.
    Flor. Well.   [*Exit.*
    Bell. Fie, madam, how you walk ! By my
maidenhead, you look seven years older than
you did this morning. Why, there can be
nothing under the sun valuable to make you
thus a minute.
    Beaumel. Ah, my sweet Bellapert, thou
        cabinet
To all my counsels, thou dost know the
        cause
That makes thy lady wither thus in youth.
    Bell. Uds-light ! enjoy your wishes : whilst
        I live,
One way or other you shall crown your will.
Would you have him your husband that you
        love,
And can it not be ? he is your servant,
        though,
And may perform the office of a husband.
    Beaumel. But there is honour, wench.
    Bell. Such a disease
There is indeed, for which ere I would
        die——
    Beaumel. Prithee, distinguish me a maid
        and wife.
    Bell. 'Faith, madam, one may bear any
man's children, t'other must bear no man's.
    Beaumel. What is a husband ?
    Bell. Physic, that, tumbling in your belly,
will make you sick in the stomach. The
only distinction betwixt a husband and a
servant, the first will lie with you when
he pleases ; the last shall lie with you when
you please. Pray tell me, lady, do you
love, to marry after, or would you marry, to
love after ?
    Beaumel. I would meet love and marriage
        both at once.
    Bell. Why then you are out of the fashion,
and will be contemn'd : for I will assure
you, there are few women in the world,
but either they have married first, and love
after ; or love first, and married after. You
must do as you may, not as you would :
your father's will is the goal you must fly
to. If a husband approach you, you would
have further off, is he you love, the less

near you? A husband in these days is but a cloak, to be oftener laid upon your bed, than in your bed.

Beaumel. Humph!

Bell. Sometimes you may wear him on your shoulder; now and then under your arm; but seldom or never let him cover you, for 'tis not the fashion.

Enter Novall *junior*, Pontalier, Malotin, Liladam, *and* Aymer.

Nov. jun. Best day to nature's curiosity, Star of Dijon, the lustre of all France! Perpetual spring dwell on thy rosy cheeks, Whose breath is perfume to our conti-nent!——
See! Flora trimm'd in her varieties.

Bell. O, divine lord!

Nov. No autumn nor no age ever ap-proach
This heavenly piece; which nature having wrought,
She lost her needle, and did then despair
Ever to work so lively and so fair!

Lilad. Uds-light! my lord, one of the purls of your band is, without all discipline, fallen out of his rank.

Nov. jun. How! I would not for a thousand crowns she had seen't. Dear Liladam, reform it.

Bell. Oh lord *per se*, lord! quintessence of honour! she walks not under a weed that could deny thee anything.

Beaumel. Prithee peace, wench; thou dost but blow the fire,
That flames too much already.

[Liladam *and* Aymer *trim* Novall, *while* Bellapert *dresses her lady.*

Aym. By gad, my lord, you have the divinest tailor in Christendom; he hath made you look like an angel in your cloth-of-tissue doublet.

Pont. This is a three-legg'd lord; there's a fresh assault. Oh! that men should spend time thus! See, see, how her blood drives to her heart, and straight vaults to her cheeks again!

Malot. What are these?

Pont. One of them there, the lower, is a good, foolish, knavish, sociable gallimaufry of a man, and has much caught my lord with singing; he is master of a music-house. The other is his dressing block, upon whom my lord lays all his clothes and fashions ere he vouchsafes them his own person: you shall see him in the morning in the Galley-foist, at noon in the Bullion, in the evening in Quirpo, and all night in——

Malot. A bawdyhouse.

Pont. If my lord deny, they deny; if he affirm, they affirm: they skip into my lord's cast skins some twice a year; and thus they flatter to eat, eat to live, and live to praise my lord.

Malot. Good sir, tell me one thing.

Pont. What's that?

Malot. Dare these men ever fight on any cause?

Pont. Oh, no! 'twould spoil their clothes, and put their bands out of order.

Nov. jun. Mistress, you hear the news? your father has resign'd his presidentship to my lord my father.

Mal. And lord Charalois
Undone for ever.

Pont. Troth, 'tis pity, sir.
A braver hope of so assured a father,
Did never comfort France.

Lilad. A good dumb mourner.

Aym. A silent black.

Nov. jun. Oh, fie upon him, how he wears his clothes!
As if he had come this Christmas from St. Omers,
To see his friends, and return'd after Twelfth-tide.

Lilad. His colonel looks finely like a drover——

Nov. jun. That had a winter lain perdue in the rain.

Aym. What, he that wears a clout about his neck,
His cuffs in's pocket, and his heart in's mouth?

Nov. jun. Now, out upon him!

Beaumel. Servant, tie my hand.
[Nov. jun. *kisses her hand.*
How your lips blush, in scorn that they should pay
Tribute to hands, when lips are in the way!

Nov. jun. I thus recant; [*Kisses her.*] yet now your hand looks white,
Because your lips robb'd it of such a right.
Monsieur Aymer, I prithee sing the song
Devoted to my mistress.

MUSIC,—AND A SONG BY AYMER.

A Dialogue between a Man and a Woman.

Man. *Set, Phœbus, set; a fairer sun doth rise*
From the bright radiance of my mis-tress' eyes
Than ever thou begat'st: I dare not look;
Each hair a golden line, each word a hook;
The more I strive, the more still I am took.

Wom. *Fair servant, come; the day these*
    eyes do lend
  To warm thy blood, thou dost so
    vainly spend,
  Come, strangle breath.
Man. *What note so sweet as this,*
  That calls the spirits to a further
    bliss ?
Wom. *Yet this out-savours wine, and this*
    perfume.
Man. *Let's die; I languish, I consume.*

    Enter Rochfort *and* Beaumont.

Beau. Romont will come, sir, straight.
Roch. 'Tis well.
Beaumel. My father !
Nov. jun. My honourable lord.
Roch. My lord Novall, this is a virtue in
you ;
So early up and ready before noon,
That are the map of dressing through all
France !
Nov. jun. I rise to say my prayers, sir ;
here's my saint.
Roch. 'Tis well and courtly :—you must
give me leave,—
I have some private conference with my
daughter ;
Pray use my garden : you shall dine with me.
Lilad. We'll wait on you.
Nov. jun. Good morn unto your lordship !
Remember, what you have vow'd—
    [*Aside to* Beaumelle.
Beaumel.—Perform I must.
    [*Exeunt all but* Rochfort *and*
    Beaumelle.
Roch. Why, how now, Beaumelle ? thou
look'st not well.
Thou art sad of late :—come, cheer thee, I
have found
A wholesome remedy for these maiden fits;
A goodly oak whereon to twist my vine,
Till her fair branches grow up to the stars.
Be near at hand.—Success crown my intent !
My business fills my little time so full,
I cannot stand to talk ; I know thy duty
Is handmaid to my will, especially
When it presents nothing but good and fit.
Beaumel. Sir, I am yours.—Oh ! if my
fears prove true,
Fate hath wrong'd love, and will destroy me
too.   [*Aside, and exit.*

    Enter Romont *and* Gaoler.

Rom. Sent you for me, sir ?
Roch. Yes.
Rom. Your lordship's pleasure ?
Roch. Keeper, this prisoner I will see
forthcoming,

Upon my word.—Sit down, good colonel.
    [*Exit* Gaoler.
Why I did wish you hither, noble sir,
Is to advise you from this iron carriage,
Which, so affected, Romont, you will wear ;
To pity, and to counsel you submit
With expedition to the great Novall :
Recant your stern contempt, and slight
neglect
Of the whole court and him, and oppor-
tunely,
Or you will undergo a heavy censure
In public, very shortly.
Rom. Reverend sir,
I have observed you, and do know you well;
And am now more afraid you know not me,
By wishing my submission to Novall,
Than I can be of all the bellowing mouths
That wait upon him to pronounce the cen-
sure,
Could it determine me torments and shame.
Submit, and crave forgiveness of a beast !——
'Tis true, this boil of state wears purple
tissue,
Is high fed, proud ; so is his lordship's
horse,
And bears as rich caparisons. I know
This elephant carries on his back not only
Towers, castles, but the ponderous republic,
And never stoops for't ; with his strong-
breath'd trunk
Snuffs others' titles, lordships, offices,
Wealth, bribes, and lives, under his ravenous
jaws :
What's this unto my freedom ? I dare die;
And therefore ask this camel, if these bless-
ings
(For so they would be understood by a man)
But mollify one rudeness in his nature,
Sweeten the eager relish of the law,
At whose great helm he sits. Helps he the
poor,
In a just business? nay, does he not cross
Every deserved soldier and scholar,
As if, when nature made him, she had made
The general antipathy of all virtue ?
How savagely and blasphemously he spake
Touching the general, the brave general
dead !
I must weep when I think on't.
Roch. Sir.
Rom. My lord,
I am not stubborn ; I can melt, you see,
And prize a virtue better than my life :
For though I be not learn'd, I ever loved
That holy mother of all issues good,
Whose white hand, for a sceptre, holds a file
To polish roughest customs ; and, in you,
She has her right : see ! I am calm as sleep.

But when I think of the gross injuries,
The godless wrong done to my general dead,
I rave indeed, and could eat this Novall;
A soulless dromedary !
Roch. Oh ! be temperate.
Sir, though I would persuade, I'll not con-
strain :
Each man's opinion freely is his own
Concerning anything, or any body ;
Be it right or wrong, 'tis at the judge's peril.

Re-enter Beaumont.

Beau. These men, sir, wait without ; my
lord is come too.
Roch. Pay them those sums upon the
table ; take
Their full releases :—stay, I want a witness.
Let me entreat you, colonel, to walk in,
And stand but by to see this money paid ;
It does concern you and your friend ; it was
The better cause you were sent for, though
said otherwise.
The deed shall make this my request more
plain.
Rom. I shall obey your pleasure, sir,
though ignorant
To what it tends.
[*Exeunt* Romont *and* Beaumont.

Enter Charalois.

Roch. Worthiest sir,
You are most welcome. Fie, no more of
this !
You have outwept a woman, noble Charalois.
No man but has or must bury a father.
Charal. Grave sir, I buried sorrow for his
death,
In the grave with him. I did never think
He was immortal—though I vow I grieve,
And see no reason why the vicious,
Virtuous, valiant, and unworthy man,
Should die alike.
Roch. They do not.
Charal. In the manner
Of dying, sir, they do not ; but all die,
And therein differ not :—but I have done.
I spied the lively picture of my father,
Passing your gallery, and that cast this water
Into mine eyes : See,—foolish that I am,
To let it do so !
Roch. Sweet and gentle nature !
How silken is this well, comparatively
To other men ! [*Aside.*] I have a suit to you,
sir.
Charal. Take it, 'tis granted.
Roch. What ?
Charal. Nothing, my lord.
Roch. Nothing is quickly granted.
Charal. Faith, my lord,

That nothing granted is even all I have,
For, all know, I have nothing left to grant.
Roch. Sir, have you any suit to me ? I'll
grant
You something, anything.
Charal. Nay, surely, I that can
Give nothing, will but sue for that again.
No man will grant me anything I sue for,
But begging nothing, every man will give it.
Roch. Sir !
The love I bore your father, and the worth
I see in you, so much resembling his,
Made me thus send for you :—and tender
here,
[*Draws a curtain and discovers a table
with money and jewels upon it.*
Whatever you will take, gold, jewels, both,.
All, to supply your wants, and free yourself.,
Where heavenly virtue in high blooded veins
Is lodged, and can agree, men should kneel
down,
Adore, and sacrifice all that they have ;
And well they may, it is so seldom seen.—
Put off your wonder, and here freely take,
Or send your servants : nor, sir, shall you use;.
In aught of this, a poor man's fee, or bribe
Unjustly taken of the rich, but what's
Directly gotten, and yet by the law.
Charal. How ill, sir, it becomes those
hairs to mock !
Roch. Mock ! thunder strike me then !
Charal. You do amaze me :
But you shall wonder too. I will not take
One single piece of this great heap. Why
should I
Borrow, that have no means to pay ? nay, am.
A very bankrupt, even in flattering hope
Of ever raising any. All my begging,
Is Romont's liberty.

Re-enter Romont *and* Beaumont, *with*
Creditors.

Roch. Here is your friend,
Enfranchised ere you spake. I give him to-
you ;
And, Charalois, I give you to your friend,
As free a man as he. Your father's debts
Are taken off.
Charal. How !
Rom. Sir, it is most true ;
I am the witness.
1 *Cred.* Yes, faith, we are paid.
2 *Cred.* Heaven bless his lordship ! I did-
think him wiser.
3 *Cred.* He a statesman ! he an ass. Pay
other men's debts !
1 *Cred.* That he was never bound for.
Rom. One more such
Would save the rest of pleaders.

Charal. Honour'd Rochfort——
Lie still, my tongue, and, blushes, scald my
  cheeks,
That offer thanks in words, for such great
  deeds.
Roch. Call in my daughter. Still I have
  a suit to you,   [*Exit* Beaumont.
Would you requite me.
Rom. With his life, I assure you.
Roch. Nay, would you make me now your
  debtor, sir——

Re-enter Beaumont *with* Beaumelle.

This is my only child: what she appears,
Your lordship well may see: her education
Follows not any; for her mind, I know it
To be far fairer than her shape, and hope
It will continue so. If now her birth
Be not too mean for Charalois, take her, take
This virgin by the hand, and call her Wife,
Endow'd with all my fortunes. Bless me so;
Requite me thus, and make me happier,
In joining my poor empty name to yours,
Than if my state were multiplied tenfold.
  Charal. Is this the payment, sir, that you
  expect!
Why, you precipitate me more in debt,
That nothing but my life can ever pay.
This beauty being your daughter, in which
  YOURS
I must conceive necessity of her virtue,
Without all dowry is a prince's aim:
Then, as she is, for poor and worthless me
How much too worthy! Waken me,
  Romont,
That I may know I dream'd, and find this
  vanish'd.
  Rom. Sure, I sleep not.
  Roch. Your sentence—life or death.
  Charal. Fair Beaumelle, can you love me?
  Beaumel. Yes, my lord.

Enter Novall *junior,* Pontalier, Malotin,
Liladam, *and* Aymer. *They all salute.*

  Charal. You need not question me if I
  can you:
You are the fairest virgin in Dijon,
And Rochfort is your father.
  Nov. jun. What's this change? [*Aside.*
  Roch. You meet my wishes, gentlemen.
  Rom. What make
These dogs in doublets here?
  Beau. A visitation, sir.
  Charal. Then thus, fair Beaumelle, I
  write my faith,
Thus seal it in the sight of heaven and men!
Your fingers tie my heart-strings with this
  touch,

In true-love knots, which nought but death
  shall loose.
And let these tears, an emblem of our loves,
Like crystal rivers individually
Flow into one another, make one source,
Which never man distinguish, less divide!
Breath marry breath, and kisses mingle souls,
Two hearts and bodies here incorporate!
And, though with little wooing I have won,
My future life shall be a wooing time,
And every day new as the bridal one.
Oh, sir! I groan under your courtesies,
More than my father's bones under his
  wrongs:
You, Curtius like, have thrown into the gulf
Of this his country's foul ingratitude,
Your life and fortunes, to redeem their
  shames.
  Roch. No more, my glory! come, let's
  in, and hasten
This celebration.
  Rom. Mal. Pont. Beau. All fair bliss
  upon it!
    [*Exeunt* Rochfort, Charalois, Ro-
    mont, Beaumont, *and* Malotin.
  Nov. jun. [*As* Beaumelle *is going out.*]
  Mistress!
  Beaumel. Oh, servant!—Virtue strengthen
  me!
Thy presence blows round my affection's
  vane:—
You will undo me, if you speak again.
                  [*Exit.*
  Lilad. Aym. Here will be sport for you!
  this works.   [*Exeunt.*
  Nov. jun. Peace! peace!
  Pont. One word, my lord Novall.
  Nov. jun. What, thou wouldst money?—
  there!
  Pont. No, I will none; I'll not be bought
  a slave,
A pander, or a parasite, for all
Your father's worth. Though you have
  saved my life,
Rescued me often from my wants, I must not
Wink at your follies: that will ruin you.
You know my blunt way, and my love to
  truth—
Forsake the pursuit of this lady's honour,
Now you do see her made another man's,
And such a man's, so good, so popular!
Or you will pluck a thousand mischiefs on
  you.
The benefits you have done me are not lost,
Nor cast away, they are purs'd here in my
  heart;
But let me pay you, sir, a fairer way,
Than to defend your vices, or to sooth
  them.

Nov. jun. Ha, ha ! what are my courses
 unto thee ?——
Good cousin Pontalier, meddle with that
That shall concern thyself.   [*Exit.*
 Pont. No more but scorn !
Move on then, stars, work your pernicious
 will :
Only the wise rule, and prevent your ill.
         [*Exit.*
[*Here a passage over the stage, while
the act is playing for the marriage
of* Charalois *with* Beaumelle, *&c.*

ACT III.

SCENE I.—*A Room in* Charalois' *House.*

Enter Novall *junior, and* Bellapert.

 Nov. jun. Fly not to these excuses ; thou
 hast been
False in thy promise—and, when I have said
Ungrateful, all is spoken.
 Bell. Good my lord,
But hear me only.
 Nov. jun. To what purpose, trifler ?
Can anything that thou canst say make void
The marriage, or those pleasures but a
 dream,
Which Charalois, oh Venus ! hath enjoy'd?
 Bell. I yet could say that you receive ad-
 vantage
In what you think a loss, would you vouch-
 safe me ;
That you were never in the way, till now,
With safety to arrive at your desires ;
That pleasure makes love to you, unattended
By danger or repentance.
 Nov. jun. That I could
But apprehend one reason how this might be!
Hope would not then forsake me.
 Bell. The enjoying
Of what you most desire, I say the enjoying,
Shall, in the full possession of your wishes,
Confirm that I am faithful.
 Nov. jun. Give some relish
How this may appear possible.
 Bell. I will,
Relish and taste, and make the banquet easy.
You say my lady's married ;
That Charalois hath enjoy'd her ;—'tis most
 true :
That, with her, he's already master of
The best part of my old lord's state—still
 better.
But, that the first or last should be your
 hinderance,
I utterly deny ; for, but observe me ;
While she went for, and was, I swear, a
 virgin, .

What courtesy could she, with her honour,
 give,
Or you receive with safety !—take me with
 you :
When I say courtesy, do not think I mean,
A kiss, the tying of her shoe or garter,
An hour of private conference ; those are
 trifles.
In this word courtesy we, that are gamesters,
 point at
The sport direct, where not alone the lover
Brings his artillery, but uses it ;
Which word expounded to you, such a
 courtesy
Do you expect, and sudden.
 Nov. jun. But he tasted
The first sweets, Bellapert.
 Bell. He wrong'd you shrewdly !
He toil'd to climb up to the phœnix' nest,
And in his prints leaves your ascent more
 easy.
I do not know, you that are perfect critics
In women's books, may talk of maiden-
 heads——
 Nov. jun. But for her marriage !
 Bell. 'Tis a fair protection
'Gainst all arrests of fear or shame for ever.
Such as are fair, and yet not foolish, study
To have one at thirteen; but they are mad
That stay till twenty. Then, sir, for the
 pleasure,
To say adultery's sweeter, that is stale ;
This only—is not the contentment more,
To say, This is my cuckold, than my rival?
More I could say— but briefly, she doats on
 you ;
If it prove otherwise, spare not ; poison me,
With the next gold you give me.

   Enter Beaumelle.

 Beaumel. How's this, servant !
Courting my woman ?
 Bell. As an entrance to
The favour of the mistress. You are to-
 gether ;
And I am perfect in my cue. [*Going.*
 Beaumel. Stay, Bellapert.
 Bell. In this I must not, with your leave,
obey you.
Your tailor and your tirewoman wait with-
 out,
And stay my counsel and direction for
Your next day's dressing. I have much to do,
Nor will your ladyship, now time is precious,
Continue idle ; this choice lord will find
So fit employment for you ! [*Exit.*
 Beaumel. I shall grow angry.
 Nov. jun. Not so ; you have a jewel in
 her, madam.

Re-enter Bellapert.

Bell. I had forgot to tell your ladyship
The closet is private, and your couch [there]
    ready ;
And, if you please that I shall lose the key,
But say so, and 'tis done.   [*Exit.*
    Beaumel. You come to chide me, servant,
        and bring with you
Sufficient warrant. You will say, and truly,
My father found too much obedience in me,
By being won too soon ; yet, if you please
But to remember all my hopes and fortunes
Had reference to his liking, you will grant,
That though I did not well towards you, I
    yet
Did wisely for myself.
    Nov. jun. With too much fervour
I have so long loved, and still love you,
    mistress,
To esteem that an injury to me,
Which was to you convenient :—that is past
My help, is past my cure. You yet may,
    lady,
In recompense of all my duteous service,
(Provided that your will answer your power,)
Become my creditress.
    Beaumel. I understand you ;
And for assurance the request you make
Shall not be long unanswered,—pray you,
    sit ;
And by what you shall hear, you'll easily
    find,
My passions are much fitter to desire,
Than to be sued to.   [*They court.*

    Enter Romont *and* Florimel *behind.*

    Flor. Sir, it is not envy
At the start my fellow has got of me in
My lady's good opinion, that's the motive
Of this discovery ; but the due payment
Of what I owe her honour.
    Rom. So I conceive it.
    Flor. I have observed too much, nor shall
        my silence
Prevent the remedy :——Yonder they are ;
I dare not be seen with you. You may do
What you think fit, which will be, I presume,
The office of a faithful and tried friend
To my young lord.   [*Exit.*
    Rom. This is no vision : ha !
    Nov. jun. With the next opportunity ?
    Beaumel. By this kiss,
And this, and this.
    Nov. jun. That you would ever swear
        thus !
    Rom. [*comes forward.*] If I seem rude,
        your pardon, lady ; yours
I do not ask : come ; do not dare to shew me

A face of anger, or the least dislike :
Put on, and suddenly, a milder look,
I shall grow rough else.
    Nov. jun. What have I done, sir,
To draw this harsh unsavoury language from
    you ?
    Rom. Done, popinjay ! why, dost thou
        think, that, if
I e'er had dreamt that thou hadst done me
    wrong,
Thou shouldst outlive it ?
    Beaumel. This is something more
Than my lord's friendship gives commission
    for.
    Nov. jun. Your presence and the place
        make him presume
Upon my patience.
    Rom. As if thou e'er wert angry
But with thy tailor ! and yet that poor shred
Can bring more to the making up of a man,
Than can be hoped from thee : thou art his
    creature ;
And did he not, each morning, new create
    thee,
Thou'dst stink, and be forgotten. I'll not
    change
One syllable more with thee, until thou bring
Some testimony, under good men s hands,
Thou art a Christian : I suspect thee strongly,
And will be satisfied ; till which time, keep
    from me.——
The entertainment of your visitation,
Has made what I intended one, a business.
    Nov. jun. So ! we shall meet.—Madam.
    Rom. Use that leg again,
And I'll cut off the other.
    Nov. jun. Very good.   [*Exit.*
    Rom. What a perfume the muskcat leaves
        behind him !
Do you admit him for a property,
To save you charges, lady ?
    Beaumel. 'Tis not useless,
Now you are to succeed him.
    Rom. So I respect you,
Not for yourself, but in remembrance of
Who is your father, and whose wife you now
    are,
That I choose rather not to understand
Your nasty scoff, than——
    Beaumel. What, you will not beat me
If I expound it to you ! Here's a tyrant
Spares neither man nor woman !
    Rom. My intents,
Madam, deserve not this ; nor do I stay
To be the whetstone of your wit : preserve it
To spend on such as know how to admire
Such colour'd stuff. In me, there now
    speaks to you,
As true a friend and servant to your honour,

And one that will with as much hazard
    guard it,
As ever man did goodness :——but then,
    lady,
You must endeavour not alone to BE,
But to APPEAR, worthy such love and ser-
    vice.
    Beaumel. To what tends this?
    Rom. Why, to this purpose, lady.
I do desire you should prove such a wife
To Charalois (and such a one he merits)
As Cæsar, did he live, could not except at ;
Not only innocent from crime, but free
From all taint and suspicion.
    Beaumel. They are base
That judge me otherwise.
    Rom. But yet be careful :
Detraction's a bold monster, and fears not
To wound the fame of princes, if it find
But any blemish in their lives to work on.
But I'll be plainer with you : had the people
Been learn'd to speak but what even now I
    saw,
Their malice out of that would raise an
    engine
To overthrow your honour. In my sight,
With yonder painted fool I frighted from
    you,
You used familiarity beyond
A modest entertainment : you embraced him
With too much ardour for a stranger, and
Met him with kisses neither chaste nor
    comely.
But learn you to forget him, as I will
Your bounties to him ; you will find it safer
Rather to be uncourtly than immodest.
    Beaumel. This pretty rag about your neck
    shews well,
And, being coarse and little worth, it speaks
    you
As terrible as thrifty.
    Rom. Madam !
    Beaumel. Yes :
And this strong belt, in which you hang
    your honour,
Will outlast twenty scarfs.
    Rom. What mean you, lady ?
    Beaumel. And [then] all else about you
    cap-à-pié,
So uniform in spite of handsomeness,
Shews such a bold contempt of comeliness,
That 'tis not strange your laundress in the
    leaguer
Grew mad with love of you.
    Rom. Is my free counsel
Answer'd with this ridiculous scorn ?
    Beaumel. These objects
Stole very much of my attention from me ;
Yet something I remember, to speak truth,

Deliver'd gravely, but to little purpose,
That almost would have made me swear
    some curate
Had stolen into the person of Romont,
And, in the praise of goodwife honesty,
Had read an homily.
    Rom. By this hand——
    Beaumel. And sword,
I will make up your oath, it will want weight
    else.——
You are angry with me, and poor I laugh
    at it.
Do you come from the camp, which affords
    only
The conversation of cast suburb whores,
To set down, to a lady of my rank,
Limits of entertainment ?
    Rom. Sure a legion
Has possest this woman !
    Beaumel. One stamp more would do well :
    yet I desire not
You should grow horn-mad till you have a
    wife.
You are come to warm meat, and perhaps
    clean linen ;
Feed, wear it, and be thankful. For me,
    know,
That though a thousand watches were set
    on me,
And you the master-spy, I yet would use
The liberty that best likes me. I will revel,
Feast, kiss, embrace, perhaps grant larger
    favours ;
Yet such as live upon my means shall know
They must not murmur at it. If my lord
Be now grown yellow, and has chose out you
To serve his jealousy this way, tell him this :
You have something to inform him. [*Exit.*
    Rom. And I will ;
Believe it, wicked one, I will. Hear, heaven,
But, hearing, pardon me !—if these fruits
    grow
Upon the tree of marriage, let me shun it,
As a forbidden sweet. An heir, and rich,
Young, beautiful, yet add to this—a wife,
And I will rather choose a spittle sinner
Carted an age before, though three parts
    rotten,
And take it for a blessing, rather than
Be fetter'd to the hellish slavery
Of such an impudence.

    Enter Beaumont *with writings.*

    Beau. Colonel, good fortune
To meet you thus ! You look sad ; but I'll
    tell you
Something that shall remove it. O, how
    happy
Is my lord Charalois in his fair bride !

Rom. A happy man, indeed!—pray you, in what?

Beau. I dare swear, you would think so good a lady
A dower sufficient.

Rom. No doubt.   But on.

Beau. So fair, so chaste, so virtuous, so— indeed,
All that is excellent!

Rom. Women have no cunning
To gull the world!   [*Aside.*

Beau. Yet, to all these, my lord,
Her father, gives the full addition of
All he does now possess in Burgundy:
These writings, to confirm it, are new seal'd,
And I most fortunate to present him with them;
I must go seek him out.   Can you direct me?

Rom. You'll find him breaking a young horse.

Beau. I thank you.   [*Exit.*

Rom. I must do something worthy Charalois' friendship.
If she were well inclined, to keep her so
Deserved not thanks; and yet, to stay a woman
Spurr'd headlong by hot lust to her own ruin,
Is harder than to prop a falling tower
With a deceiving reed.

Enter Rochfort, *speaking to a* Servant *within.*

Roch. Some one seek for me
As soon as he returns.

Rom. Her father? ha?——
How if I break this to him? sure it cannot
Meet with an ill construction: his wisdom,
Made powerful by the authority of a father,
Will warrant and give privilege to his counsels.
It shall be so.—My lord!

Roch. Your friend, Romont.
Would you aught with me?

Rom. I stand so engaged
To your so many favours, that I hold it
A breach in thankfulness, should I not discover,
Though with some imputation to myself,
All doubts that may concern you.

Roch. The performance
Will make this protestation worth my thanks.

Rom. Then, with your patience, lend me your attention:
For what I must deliver, whisper'd only,
You will with too much grief receive.

Enter Beaumelle *and* Bellapert, *behind.*

Beaumel. See, wench!
Upon my life, as I forespake, he's now

Preferring his complaint; but be thou perfect,
And we will fit him.

Bell. Fear not me; pox on him!
A captain turn informer against kissing!
Would he were hang'd up in his rusty armour!—
But, if our fresh wits cannot turn the plots
Of such a mouldy murrion on itself,
Rich clothes, choice fare, and a true friend at a call,
With all the pleasures the night yields, forsake us!

Roch. This in my daughter! do not wrong her.

Bell. Now
Begin: the game's afoot, and we in distance.

Beaumel. [*comes forward.*] 'Tis thy fault, foolish girl! pin on my veil,
I will not wear those jewels.   Am I not
Already match'd beyond my hopes? yet still
You prune and set me forth, as if I were
Again to please a suitor.

Bell. 'Tis the course
That our great ladies take.

Beaumel. A weak excuse!
Those that are better seen in what concerns
A lady's honour and fair fame, condemn it.
You wait well! in your absence, my lord's friend,
The understanding, grave, and wise Romont——

Rom. Must I be still her sport?

Beaumel. Reproved me for it;
And he has travell'd to bring home a judgment
Not to be contradicted.   You will say
My father, that owes more to years than he,
Has brought me up to music, language, courtship,
And I must use them: true; but not to offend,
Or render me suspected.

Roch. Does your fine story
Begin from this?

Beaumel. I thought a parting kiss
From young Novall would have displeased no more
Than heretofore it hath done; but I find
I must restrain such favours now; look, therefore,
As you are careful to continue mine,
That I no more be visited.   I'll endure
The strictest course of life that jealousy
Can think secure enough, ere my behaviour
Shall call my fame in question.

Rom. Ten dissemblers
Are in this subtle devil!   You believe this?

Roch. So far, that if you trouble me again
With a report like this, I shall not only

Judge you malicious in your disposition,
But study to repent what I have done
To such a nature.
   Rom. Why, 'tis exceeding well.
   Roch. And for you, daughter, off with this,
    off with it !
I have that confidence in your goodness, I,
That I will not consent to have you live
Like to a recluse in a cloister : Go,
Call in the gallants, let them make you
   merry ;
Use all fit liberty.
   Bell. Blessing upon you !
If this new preacher with the sword and
   feather
Could prove his doctrine for canonical,
We should have a fine world.   [*Exit.*
   Roch. Sir, if you please
To bear yourself as fits a gentleman,
The house is at your service ; but, if not,
Though you seek company elsewhere, your
   absence
Will not be much lamented.   [*Exit.*
   Rom. If this be
The recompense of striving to preserve
A wanton gigglet honest, very shortly
'Twill make all mankind panders.—Do you
   smile,
Good lady looseness ! your whole sex is like
   you,
And that man's mad that seeks to better any :
What new change have you next ?
   Beaumel. Oh, fear not you, sir ;
I'll shift into a thousand, but I will
Convert your heresy.
   Rom. What heresy ? speak.
   Beaumel. Of keeping a lady that is married,
From entertaining servants——

   Enter Novall *junior*, Malotin, Liladam,
    Aymer, *and* Pontalier.

——O, you are welcome !
Use any means to vex him,
And then with welcome follow me.
    [*Aside to them, and exit.*
   Nov. jun. You are tired
With your grave exhortations, colonel !
   Lilad. How is it ? faith, your lordship
   may do well
To help him to some church preferment : 'tis
The fashion now for men of all conditions,
However they have lived, to end that way.
   Aym. That face would do well in a surplice.
   Rom. Rogues,
Be silent—or——
   Pont. 'Sdeath ! will you suffer this?
   Rom. And you, the master-rogue, the
   coward rascal,
I shall be with you suddenly.

   Nov. jun. Pontalier,
If I should strike him, I know I should kill
   him ;
And therefore I would have thee beat him, for
He's good for nothing else.
   Lilad. His back
Appears to me, as it would tire a beadle ;
And then he has a knotted brow, would
   bruise
A courtlike hand to touch it.
   Aym. He looks like .
A currier when his hides grow dear.
   Pont. Take heed
He curry not some of you.
   Nov. jun. Gads me ! he's angry.
   Rom. I break no jests ; but I can break
   my sword
About your pates.

   Enter Charalois *and* Beaumont.

   Lilad. Here's more.
   Aym. Come, let's be gone :
We are beleaguer'd.
   Nov. jun. Look, they bring up their
   troops.
   Pont. Will you sit down
With this disgrace? you are abused most
   grossly.
   Lilad. I grant you, sir, we are ; and you
   would have us
Stay, and be more abused.
   Nov. jun. My lord, I'm sorry
Your house is so inhospitable, we must quit
   it.
    [*Exeunt all but* Charalois *and* Romont.
   Charal. Prithee, Romont, what caused
   this uproar?
   Rom. Nothing ;
They laugh'd, and used their scurvy wits
   upon me.
   Charal. Come, 'tis thy jealous nature :
   but I wonder
That you, which are an honest man and
   worthy,
Should foster this suspicion : no man laughs,
No one can whisper, but thou apprehend'st
His conference and his scorn reflect on thee :
For my part, they should scoff their thin wits
   out,
So I not heard them ; beat me, not being
   there.
Leave, leave these fits to conscious men, to
   such
As are obnoxious to those foolish things
As they can gibe at.
   Rom. Well, sir.
   Charal. Thou art known
Valiant without defect, rightly defined,
Which is as fearing to do injury,

B B 2

As tender to endure it ; not a brabbler,
A swearer——
   Rom. Pish, pish! what needs this, my
     lord?
If I be known none such, how vainly you
Do cast away good counsel!   I have loved
     you,
And yet must freely speak ; so young a tutor
Fits not so old a soldier as I am :
And I must tell you, 'twas in your behalf
I grew enraged thus, yet had rather die
Than open the great cause a syllable further.
   Charal. In my behalf!   Wherein hath
     Charalois
Unfitly so demean'd himself, to give
The least occasion to the loosest tongue
To throw aspersions on him? or so weakly
Protected his own honour, as it should
Need a defence from any but himself?
They are fools that judge me by my outward
     seeming.
Why should my gentleness beget abuse?
The lion is not angry that does sleep,
Nor every man a coward that can weep.
For God's sake, speak the cause.
   Rom. Not for the world.
Oh ! it will strike disease into your bones,
Beyond the cure of physic; drink your blood,
Rob you of all your rest, contract your sight,
Leave you no eyes but to see misery,
And of your own ; nor speech, but to wish
     thus,
Would I had perish'd in the prison's jaws,
From whence I was redeem'd !—'twill wear
     you old,
Before you have experience in that art
That causes your affliction.
   Charal. Thou dost strike
A deathful coldness into my heart's high heat,
And shrink'st my liver like the calenture.
Declare this foe of mine, and life's, that like
A man I may encounter and subdue it.
It shall not have one such effect in me,
As thou denouncest : with a soldier's arm,
If it be strength, I'll meet it ; if a fault
Belonging to my mind, I'll cut it off
With mine own reason, as a scholar should.
Speak, though it make me monstrous.
   Rom. I will die first.
Farewell ; continue merry, and high heaven
Keep your wife chaste !
   Charal. Hum ! Stay, and take this wolf
Out of my breast, that thou hast lodged
     there, or
For ever lose me.
   Rom. Lose not, sir, yourself,
And I will venture :—so, the door is fast.
              [*Locks the door.*
Now, noble Charalois, collect yourself,

Summon your spirits, muster all your
     strength
That can belong to man ; sift passion
From every vein, and whatsoe'er ensues,
Upbraid not me hereafter, as the cause of
Jealousy, discontent, slaughter, and ruin :
Make me not parent to sin.—You will know
This secret that I burn with?
   Charal. Devil on't,
What should it be !   Romont, I heard you
     wish
My wife's continuance of chastity.
   Rom. There was no hurt in that.
   Charal. Why, do you know
A likelihood, or possibility,
Unto the contrary ?
   Rom. I know it not, but doubt it ; these
     the grounds :
The servant of your wife now, young Novall,
The son unto your father's enemy,
(Which aggravates presumption the more,)
I have been warn'd of, touching her :—nay,
     seen them
Tied heart to heart, one in another's arms,
Multiplying kisses, as if they meant
To pose arithmetic ; or whose eyes would
Be first burnt out with gazing on the other's.
I saw their mouths engender, and their palms
Glew'd,   as if love had lock'd them ; their
     words flow
And melt each other's, like two circling
     flames,
Where chastity, like a phœnix, methought,
     buru'd,
But left the world nor ashes, nor an heir.—
Why stand you silent thus ? what cold dull
     phlegm,
As if you had no drop of choler mix'd
In your whole constitution, thus prevails,
To fix you now thus stupid, hearing this ?
   Charal. You did not see him on my couch
     within,
Like George a-horseback, on her, nor a-bed?
   Rom. No.
   Charal. Ha ! ha !
   Rom. Laugh you ! even so did your wife,
And her indulgent father.
   Charal. They were wise :
Wouldst have me be a fool?
   Rom. No, but a man.
   Charal. There is no dram of manhood to
     suspect,
On such thin airy circumstance as this ;
Mere compliment and courtship.   Was this
     tale
The hideous monster which you so con-
     ceal'd ?
Away, thou curious impertinent,
And idle searcher of such lean, nice toys !

Go, thou seditious sower of debate,
Fly to such matches, where the bridegroom
    doubts,
He holds not worth enough to countervail
The virtue and the beauty of his wife !
Thou buzzing drone, that 'bout my ears dost
    hum,
To strike thy rankling sting into my heart,
Whose venom time nor medicine could
    assuage,
Thus do I put thee off ! and, confident
In mine own innocency and desert,
Dare not conceive her so unreasonable,
To put Novall in balance against me ;
An upstart, craned up to the height he has.
Hence, busybody ! thou'rt no friend to me,
That must be kept to a wife's injury.
    Rom. Is't possible ?—farewell, fine honest
        man !
Sweet-temper'd lord, adieu ! What apoplexy
Hath knit sense up? is this Romont's re-
    ward?
Bear witness, the great spirit of thy father,
With what a healthful hope I did ad-
    minister
This potion, that hath wrought so viru-
    lently !
I not accuse thy wife of act, but would
Prevent her precipice to thy dishonour,
Which now thy tardy sluggishness will
    admit.
Would I had seen thee graved with thy
    great sire,
Ere lived to have men's marginal fingers
    point
At Charalois, as a lamented story !
An emperor put away his wife for touching
Another man ; but thou wouldst have thine
    tasted,
And keep her, I think—Phoh ! I am a fire,
To warm a dead man, that waste out myself.
Bleed—What a plague, a vengeance, is't
    to me,
If you will be a cuckold ? here, I shew
A sword's point to thee, this side you may
    shun,
Or that, the peril ; if you will run on,
I cannot help it.
    Charal. Didst thou never see me
Angry, Romont?
    Rom. Yes, and pursue a foe
Like lightning.
    Charal. Prithee, see me so no more :
I can be so again. Put up thy sword,
And take thyself away, lest I draw mine.
    Rom. Come, fright your foes with this,
        sir ! I'm your friend,
And dare stand by you thus.
    Charal. Thou art not my friend,

Or, being so, thou art mad ; I must not buy
Thy friendship at this rate. Had I just cause,.
Thou know'st I durst pursue such injury
Through fire, air, water, earth, nay, were'
    they all
Shuffled again to chaos ; but there's none.
Thy skill, Romont, consists in camps, not'
    courts.
Farewell, uncivil man ! let's meet no more :
Here our long web of friendship I untwist.
Shall I go whine, walk pale, and lock my
    wife,
For nothing, from her birth's free liberty,
That open'd mine to me ? yes ! if I do,
The name of cuckold then dog me with
    scorn !
I am a Frenchman, no Italian born.
                                        [*Exit.*
    Rom. A dull Dutch rather : fall and cool,.
        my blood !
Boil not in zeal of thy friend's hurt so high,
That is so low and cold himself in't !
    Woman,
How strong art thou ! how easily beguiled !
How thou dost rack us by the very horns !'
Now wealth, I see, change manners and the'
    man.
Something I must do mine own wrath to
    assuage,
And note my friendship to an after-age.
                                        [*Exit.*

ACT IV.

SCENE I.—*A Room in* Novall's *House.*

Novall *junior discovered seated before a'
looking-glass, with a* Barber *and* Perfumer *dressing his hair, while a* Tailor
adjusts a new suit which he wears.
Liladam, Aymer, *and a* Page *attending.*

    Nov. jun. Mend this a little : pox ! thou
hast burnt me. Oh, fie upon't ! O lard !
he has made me smell for all the world like
a flax, or a red-headed woman's chamber :
Powder, powder, powder !
    Perf. Oh, sweet lord !
    Page. That's his perfumer.
    Tail. Oh, dear lord !
    Page. That's his tailor.
    Nov. jun. Monsieur Liladam, Aymer,.
how allow you the model of these clothes?
    Aym. Admirably, admirably ; oh, sweet
lord ! assuredly it's pity the worms should
eat thee.
    Page. Here's a fine cell ! a lord, a tailor,.
a perfumer, a barber, and a pair of monsieurs : three to three ; as little wit in the'
one, as honesty in the other. 'Sfoot ! I'll

into the country again, learn to speak truth, drink ale, and converse with my father's tenants ; here I hear nothing all day, but— *Upon my soul, as I am a gentleman, and an honest man !* [*Aside.*

Aym. I vow and affirm, your tailor must needs be an expert geometrician ; he has the longitude, latitude, altitude, profundity, every dimension of your body, so exquisitely —here's a lace laid as directly as if truth were a tailor.

Page. That were a miracle. [*Aside.*

Lilad. With a hair's-breadth's error, there's a shoulder-piece cut, and the base of a pickadille in *puncto.*

Aym. You are right, monsieur ; his vestaments sit as if they grew upon him, or art had wrought them on the same loom as nature framed his lordship ; as if your tailor were deep read in astrology, and had taken measure of your honourable body with a Jacob's staff, an ephimerides.

Tail. I am bound t'ye, gentlemen.

Page. You are deceived ; they'll be bound to you : you must remember to trust them none. [*Aside.*

Nov. jun. Nay, 'faith, thou art a reasonable neat artificer, give the devil his due.

Page. Ay, if he would but cut the coat according to the cloth still. [*Aside.*

Nov. jun. I now want only my mistress' approbation, who is, indeed, the most polite, punctual queen of dressing in all Burgundy —pah ! and makes all other young ladies appear as if they came from board last week out of the country : is't not true, Liladam ?

Lilad. True, my lord ! as if anything your lordship could say could be otherwise than true.

Nov. jun. Nay, o' my soul, 'tis so ; what fouler object in the world, than to see a young, fair, handsome beauty unhandsomely dighted, and incongruently accoutred ? or a hopeful chevalier unmethodically appointed in the external ornaments of nature ? For, even as the index tells us the contents of stories, and directs to the particular chapters, even so does the outward habit and superficial order of garments (in man or woman) give us a taste of the spirit, and demonstratively point (as it were a manual note from the margin) all the internal quality and habiliment of the soul ; and there cannot be a more evident, palpable, gross manifestation of poor, degenerate, dunghilly blood and breeding, than a rude, unpolished, disordered, and slovenly outside.

Page. An admirable lecture ! oh, all you gallants, that hope to be saved by your clothes, edify, edify ! [*Aside.*

Aym. By the Lard, sweet lard, thou deservest a pension o' the state.

Page. O' the tailors : two such lords were able to spread tailors o'er the face of the whole kingdom. [*Aside.*

Nov. jun. Pox o' this glass ! it flatters.— I could find in my heart to break it.

Page. O, save the glass, my lord, and break their heads ;
They are the greater flatterers, I assure you. [*Aside.*

Aym. Flatters ! detracts, impairs—yet, put it by,
Lest thou, dear lord, Narcissus like, should'st doat
Upon thyself, and die ; and rob the world
Of nature's copy, that she works form by.

Lilad. O that I were the infanta queen of Europe !
Who, but thyself, sweet lord, should marry me ?

Nov. jun. I marry ! were there a queen o' the world, not I.
Wedlock ! no ; padlock, horselock :—I wear spurs [*He capers.*
To keep it off my heels. Yet, my Aymer,
Like a free, wanton jennet in the meadows,
I look about, and neigh, take hedge and ditch,
Feed in my neighbour's pastures, pick my choice
Of all their fair-maned mares : but married once,
A man is staked or poun'd, and cannot graze
Beyond his own hedge.

Enter Pontalier *and* Malotin.

Pont. I have waited, sir,
Three hours to speak wi' ye, and not take it well
Such magpies are admitted, whilst I dance
Attendance.

Lilad. Magpies ! what d'ye take me for ?

Pont. A long thing with a most unpromising face.

Aym. I'll never ask him what he takes me for.

Malot. Do not, sir,
For he'll go near to tell you.

Pont. Art not thou
A barber-surgeon ?

Barb. Yes, sirrah ; why ?

Pont. My lord is sorely troubled with two scabs.

Lilad. Aym. Hum——

Pont. I prithee cure him of them.

Nov. jun. Pish ! no more.
Thy gall sure's overflown ; these are my council,
And we were now in serious discourse.
Pont. Of perfume and apparel ! Can you rise,
And spend five hours in dressing-talk with these !
Nov. jun. Thou'ldst have me be a dog : up, stretch, and shake,
And ready for all day.
Pont. Sir, would you be
More curious in preserving of your honour trim,
It were more manly. I am come to wake
Your reputation from this lethargy
You let it sleep in ; to persuade, impórtune,
Nay, to provoke you, sir, to call to account
This colonel Romont, for the foul wrong
Which, like a burthen, he hath laid upon you,
And, like a drunken porter, you sleep under.
'Tis all the town talks ; and, believe it, sir,
If your tough sense persist thus, you are undone,
Utterly lost ; you will be scorn'd and baffled
By every lacquey : season now your youth
With one brave thing, and it shall keep the odour
Even to your death, beyond, and on your tomb
Scent like sweet oils and frankincense. Sir, this life,
Which once you saved, I ne'er since counted mine :
I borrow'd it of you, and now will pay it :
I tender you the service of my sword,
To bear your challenge ; if you'll write, your fate
I'll make mine own ; whate'er betide you, I,
That have lived by you, by your side will die.
Nov. jun. Ha! ha! wouldst have me challenge poor Romont?—
Fight with close breeches, thou mayst think I dare not :
Do not mistake me, coz, I am very valiant ;
But valour shall not make me such an ass.
What use is there of valour now-a-days ?
'Tis sure or to be kill'd, or to be hang'd.
Fight thou as thy mind moves thee, 'tis thy trade ;
Thou hast nothing else to do. Fight with Romont !
No ; I'll not fight, under a lord.
Pont. Farewell, sir !
I pity you,
Such living lords walk, their dead honour's graves,
For no companions fit but fools and knaves.
Come, Malotin.
[*Exeunt* Pontalier *and* Malotin.

Enter Romont.

Lilad. 'Sfoot, Colbrand, the low giant !
Aym. He has brought a battle in his face, let's go.
Page. Colbrand, d'ye call him? he'll make some of you
Smoke, I believe.
Rom. By your leave, sirs !
Aym. Are you a consort ?
Rom. Do you take me for
A fiddler? you're deceived : look ! I'll pay you.
[*Kicks them.*
Page. It seems he knows you one, he bumfiddles you so.
Lilad. Was there ever so base a fellow ?
Aym. A rascal.
Lilad. A most uncivil groom.
Aym. Offer to kick a gentleman in a nobleman's chamber ! a pox o' your man-ners !
Lilad. Let him alone, let him alone : thou shalt lose thy aim, fellow ; if we stir against thee, hang us.
Page. 'Sfoot ! I think they have the better on him, though they be kick'd, they talk so.
Lilad. Let's leave the mad ape. [*Going.*
Nov. jun. Gentlemen !
Lilad. Nay, my lord, we will not offer to dishonour you so much as to stay by you, since he's alone.
Nov. jun. Hark you !
Aym. We doubt the cause, and will not disparage you so much as to take your lordship's quarrel in hand. Plague on him, how he has crumpled our bands !
Page. I'll e'en away with them, for this soldier beats man, woman, and child.
[*Exeunt all but* Novall *jun. and* Romont.
Nov. jun. What mean you, sir? My people !
Rom. Your boy's gone, [*Locks the door.*
And your door's lock'd ; yet for no hurt to you,
But privacy. Call up your blood again :——
Be not afraid, I do beseech you, sir ;
And, therefore, come, without more cir-cumstance,
Tell me how far the passages have gone
'Twixt you and your fair mistress, Beaumelle,
Tell me the truth, and by my hope of heaven,
It never shall go further.
Nov. jun. Tell you ! why, sir, are you my confessor ?

Rom. I will be your confounder, if you do
not.   *[Draws a pocket dag.*
Stir not, nor spend your voice.
   Nov. jun. What will you do?
   Rom. Nothing but line your brain-pan,
   sir, with lead,
If you not satisfy me suddenly:
I am desperate of my life, and command
   yours.
   Nov. jun. Hold! hold! I'll speak. I vow
   to heaven and you,
She's yet untouch'd, more than her face and
   hands.
I cannot call her innocent: for, I yield,
On my solicitous wooing, she consented,
Where time and place met opportunity,
To grant me all requests.
   Rom. But may I build
On this assurance?
   Nov. jun. As upon your faith.
   Rom. Write this, sir; nay, you must.
   Nov. jun. Pox of this gun!
   Rom. Withal, sir, you must swear, and
put your oath
Under your hand, (shake not,) ne'er to
   frequent
This lady's company, nor ever send
Token, or message, or letter, to incline
This, too much prone already, yielding lady.
   Nov. jun. 'Tis done, sir.
   Rom. Let me see this first is right.
                 [Reading.
And here you wish a sudden death may light
Upon your body, and hell take your soul,
If ever more you see her, but by chance;
Much less allure her. Now, my lord, your
   hand.
   Nov. jun. My hand to this!
   Rom. Your heart else, I assure you.
   Nov. jun. Nay, there 'tis.
   Rom. So! keep this last article
Of your faith given, and, stead of threaten-
   ings, sir,
The service of my sword and life is yours.
But not a word of it :—'tis fairies' treasure,
Which but reveal'd, brings on the blabber's
   ruin.
Use your youth better, and this excellent
   form
Heaven hath bestow'd upon you. So, good
   morrow
To your lordship!   *[Exit.*
   Nov. jun. Good devil to your rogueship!
   No man's safe——
I'll have a cannon planted in my chamber,
Against such roaring rogues.

     Enter Bellapert, *hastily.*

   Bell. My lord, away!

The caroch stays: now have your wish, and
   judge
If I have been forgetful.
   Nov. jun. Hah!
   Bell. Do you stand
Humming and bahing now?   *[Exit.*
   Nov. jun. Sweet wench, I come.
Hence, fear!
I swore—that's all one; my next oath I'll
   keep
That I did mean to break, and then 'tis quit.
No pain is due to lovers' perjury:
If Jove himself laugh at it, so will I. *[Exit.*

   SCENE II.—*An outer Room in* Aymer's
             House.

   Enter Charalois *and* Beaumont.

   Beau. I grieve for the distaste, though I
   have manners
Not to inquire the cause, fallen out between
Your lordship and Romont.
   Charal. I love a friend,
So long as he continues in the bounds
Prescribed by friendship; but, when he
   usurps
Too far on what is proper to myself,
And puts the habit of a governor on,
I must and will preserve my liberty.
But speak of something else, this is a theme
I take no pleasure in. What's this Aymer,
Whose voice for song, and excellent know-
   ledge in
The chiefest parts of music, you bestow
Such praises on?
   Beau. He is a gentleman
(For so his quality speaks him) well received
Among our greatest gallants; but yet holds
His main dependence from the young lord
   Novall.
Some tricks and crotchets he has in his head,
As all musicians have, and more of him
I dare not author: but, when you have heard
   him,
I may presume your lordship so will like him,
That you'll hereafter be a friend to music.
   Charal. I never was an enemy to't, Beau-
   mont,
Nor yet do I subscribe to the opinion
Of those old captains, that thought nothing
   musical
But cries of yielding enemies, neighing of
   horses,
Clashing of armour, loud shouts, drums, and
   trumpets;
Nor, on the other side, in favour of it,
Affirm the world was made by musical dis-
   cord;
Or that the happiness of our life consists
In a well-varied note upon the lute:

I love it to the worth of't, and no
further.——
But let us see this wonder.
Beau. He prevents
My calling of him.

Enter Aymer, *speaking to one within.*

Aym. Let the coach be brought
To the back gate, and serve the banquet
up.——
My good lord Charalois! I think my house
Much honour'd in your presence.
Charal. To have means
To know you better, sir, has brought me
hither
A willing visitant ; and you'll crown my wel-
come
In making me a witness to your skill,
Which, crediting from others, I admire.
Aym. Had I been one hour sooner made
acquainted
With your intent, my lord, you should have
found me
Better provided : now, such as it is,
Pray you grace with your acceptance.
Beau. You are modest.
Aym. Begin the last new air.
    [*To the* Musicians *within.*
Charal. Shall we not see them ?
Aym. This little distance from the instru-
ments,
Will to your ears convey the harmony
With more delight.
Charal. I'll not contend.
Aym. You are tedious.
    [*To the* Musicians.
By this means shall I with one banquet
please
Two companies, those within and these gulls
here.

Citizen's SONG *of the Courtier.*

Courtier, if thou needs wilt wive,
From this lesson learn to thrive ;
If thou match a lady, that
Passes thee in birth and state,
Let her curious garments be
Twice above thine own degree ;
This will draw great eyes upon her,
Get her servants, and thee honour.

Beaumel. [*within.*] Ha! ha! ha!
Charal. How's this! it is my lady's laugh,
most certain.
When I first pleased her, in this merry
language
She gave me thanks.   [*Aside.*
Beau. How like you this?
Charal. 'Tis rare——

Yet I may be deceived, and should be sorry,
Upon uncertain suppositions, rashly
To write myself in the black list of those
I have declaim'd against, and to Romont.
    [*Aside.*
Aym. I would he were well off!——
Perhaps your lordship
Likes not these sad tunes ? I have a new
song,
Set·to a lighter note, may please you better ;·
'Tis call'd *the Happy Husband.*
Charal. Pray you, sing it.

Courtier's SONG *of the Citizen.*

Poor citizen, if thou wilt be
A happy husband, learn of me
To set thy wife first in thy shop ;
A fair wife, a kind wife, a sweet wife, sets a/
poor man up.
What though thy shelves be ne'er so bare,
A woman still is current ware ;
Each man will cheapen, foe and friend ;
But, whilst thou art at t'other end,
Whate'er thou seest, or what dost hear,
Fool, have no eye to, nor an ear ;
And after supper, for her sake,
When thou hast fed, snort, though thou wake ;·
What though the gallants call thee Mome !
Yet with thy lantern light her home ;
Then look into the town, and tell
If no such tradesmen there do well.

Beaumel. [*within.*] Ha! ha! 'tis such a
groom !
Charal. Do I hear this,
And yet stand doubtful ?
    [*Rushes into the house.*
Aym. Stay him—I am undone,
And they discover'd.
Beau. What's the matter ?
Aym. Ah !
That women, when they're well pleas'd,
cannot hold ;
But must laugh out.

Re-enter Charalois, *with his sword drawn,*
pursuing Novall *junior,* Beaumelle,
and Bellapert.

Nov. jun. Help ! save me ! murder ! mur-
der !
Beaumel. Undone, undone, for ever !
Charal. Oh, my heart !
Hold yet a little—do not hope to 'scape
By flight, it is impossible. Though I might
On all advantage take thy life, and justly ;
This sword, my father's sword, that ne'er
was drawn
But to a noble purpose, shall not now
Do the office of a hangman. I reserve it

To right mine honour, not for a revenge
So poor, that though with thee it should
    cut off
Thy family, with all that are allied
To thee in lust or baseness, 'twere still
    short of
All terms of satisfaction.   Draw !
    Nov. jun. I dare not :
I have already done you too much wrong,
To fight in such a cause.
    Charal. Why, darest thou neither
Be honest coward, nor yet valiant knave,
In such a cause ! come, do not shame thy-
    self :
Such whose bloods wrongs, or wrong done
    to themselves
Could never heat, are yet in the defence
Of their whores daring. Look on her again :
You thought her worth the hazard of your
    soul,
And yet stand doubtful, in her quarrel, to
Venture your body.
    Beau. No, he fears his clothes,
More than his flesh.
    Charal. Keep from me ! guard thy life,
Or, as thou hast lived like a goat, thou
    shalt
Die like a sheep.
    Nov. jun. Since there's no remedy,
Despair of safety now in me prove courage !
                [*They fight*, Novall *falls.*
    Charal. How soon weak wrong's o'er-
    thrown !   Lend me your hand :
Bear this to the caroch—come, you have
    taught me
To say, you must and shall?
    [*Exeunt* Beaumont *and* Bellapert, *with
        the Body of* Novall ; *followed by*
    Beaumelle.
                    I wrong you not,
You are but to keep him company you
    love.—

        Re-enter Beaumont.

Is't done ? 'tis well. Raise officers, and take
    care
All you can apprehend within the house
May be forthcoming. Do I appear much
    moved ?
    Beau. No, sir.
    Charal. My griefs are now thus to be borne;
Hereafter I'll find time and place to mourn.
                        [*Exeunt.*

        SCENE III.--*A Street.*

        Enter Romont *and* Pontalier.

    Pont. I was bound to seek you, sir.
    Rom. And, had you found me
In any place but in the street, I should

Have done,—not talked to you. Are you,
    the captain,
The hopeful Pontalier, whom I have seen
Do, in the field, such service as then made
    you
Their envy that commanded, here, at home,
To play the parasite to a gilded knave,
And, it may be, the pander?
    Pont. Without this,
I come to call you to account for what
Is past already. I, by your example
Of thankfulness to the dead general,
By whom you were raised, have practised to
    be so
To my good lord Novall, by whom I live ;
Whose least disgrace that is or may be
    offer'd,
With all the hazard of my life and fortunes
I will make good on you, or any man
That has a hand in't : and, since you allow
    me
A gentleman and a soldier, there's no doubt
You will except against me. You shall meet
With a fair enemy : you understand
The right I look for, and must have?
    Rom. I do ;
And with the next day's sun you shall hear
    from me.   [*Exeunt.*

SCENE IV.—*A Room in* Charalois' *House.*

    Enter Charalois *with a casket,* Beaumelle,
        and Beaumont.

    Charal. Pray bear this to my father, at
    his leisure
He may peruse it ; but with your best
    language
Entreat his instant presence. You have
    sworn
Not to reveal what I have done.
    Beau. Nor will I—but——
    Charal. Doubt me not ; by heaven, I will
    do nothing
But what may stand with honour. Pray
    you, leave me   [*Exit* Beaumont.
To my own thoughts.—If this be to me,
    rise ;   [Beaumelle *kneels.*
I am not worth the looking on, but only
To feed contempt and scorn ; and that from
    you,
Who, with the loss of your fair name have
    caused it,
Were too much cruelty.
    Beaumel. I dare not move you
To hear me speak.   I know my fault is far
Beyond qualification or excuse ;
That 'tis not fit for me to hope, or you
To think of mercy ; only I presume
To entreat you would be pleased to look
    upon

My sorrow for it, and believe these tears
Are the true children of my grief, and not
A woman's cunning.
   Charal. Can you, Beaumelle,
Having deceived so great a trust as mine,
Though I were all credulity, hope again
To get belief? No, no; if you look on me
With pity, or dare practise any means
To make my sufferings less, or give just
   cause
To all the world to think what I must do
Was call'd upon by you, use other ways :
Deny what I have seen, or justify
What you have done ; and, as you despe-
   rately
Made shipwreck of your faith, to be a
   whore,
Use the arms of such a one, and such de-
   fence,
And multiply the sin with impudence.
Stand boldly up, and tell me to my teeth,
That you have done but what is warranted
By great examples, in all places where
Women inhabit ; urge your own deserts,
Or want of me in merit ; tell me how
Your dower, from the low gulf of poverty,
Weighed up my fortunes to what they now
   are :
That I was purchased by your choice and
   practice,
To shelter you from shame, that you might
   sin
As boldly as securely : that poor men
Are married to those wives that bring them
   wealth,
One day their husbands, but observers
   ever.
That when, by this proud usage, you have
   blown
The fire of my just vengeance to the height,
I then may kill you, and yet say 'twas done
In heat of blood, and after die myself,
To witness my repentance.
   Beaumel. O my fate !
That never would consent that I should see
How worthy you were both of love and duty,
Before I lost you ; and my misery made
The glass in which I now behold your virtue!
While I was good, I was a part of you,
And of two, by the virtuous harmony
Of our fair minds, made one ; but, since I
   wander'd
In the forbidden labyrinth of lust,
What was inseparable is by me divided.——
With justice, therefore, you may cut me off,
And from your memory wash the remem-
   brance
That e'er I was ; like to some vicious pur-
   pose,

Which, in your better judgment, you re-
   pent of,
And study to forget.
   Charal. O Beaumelle,
That you can speak so well, and do so ill !
But you had been too great a blessing, if
You had continued chaste : see, how you
   force me
To this, because mine honour will not yield
That I again should love you.
   Beaumel. In this life
It is not fit you should : yet you shall find,
Though I was bold enough to be a strumpet,
I dare not yet live one. Let those famed
   matrons,
That are canonized worthy of our sex,
Transcend me in their sanctity of life ;
I yet will equal them in dying nobly,
Ambitious of no honour after life,
But that, when I am dead, you will forgive
   me.
   Charal. How pity steals upon me ! should
    I hear her   [*Knocking within.*
But ten words more, I were lost.—One
    knocks, go in.   [*Exit* Beaumelle.
That to be merciful should be a sin !

       Enter Rochfort.

O, sir, most welcome ! Let me take your
   cloak,
I must not be denied.—Here are your robes,
As you love justice, once more put them on.
There is a cause to be determined of,
That does require such an integrity
As you have ever used.—I'll put you to
The trial of your constancy and goodness :
And look that you, that have been eagle-eyed
In other men's affairs, prove not a mole
In what concerns yourself. Take you your
   seat ;
I will be for you presently.   [*Exit.*
   Roch. Angels guard me !
To what strange tragedy does this induction
Serve for a prologue?

Re-enter Charalois, Beaumelle, *and* Beaumont, *with Servants bearing the body of*
Novall *junior.*

   Charal. So, set it down before
The judgment seat—[*Exeunt* Servants.]—
   and stand you at the bar :
                [*To* Beaumelle.
For me, I am the accuser.
   Roch. Novall slain !
And Beaumelle, my daughter, in the place
Of one to be arraign'd !
   Charal. O, are you touch'd !
I find that I must take another course.

Fear nothing, I will only blind your eyes ;
                              [*He binds his eyes.*
For justice should do so, when 'tis to meet
An object that may sway her equal doom
From what it should be aim'd at.—Good,
      my lord,
A day of hearing.
     Roch. It is granted, speak——
You shall have justice.
     Charal. I then here accuse,
Most equal judge, the prisoner, your fair
      daughter,
For whom I owed so much to you ; your
      daughter,
So worthy in her own parts, and that worth
Set forth by yours, to whose so rare per-
      fections,
Truth witness with me, in the place of service
I almost paid idolatrous sacrifice,
To be a false adultress.
     Roch. With whom ?
     Charal. With this Novall here dead.
     Roch. Be well advised ;
And ere you say *adultress* again,
Her fame depending on it, be most sure
That she is one.
     Charal. I took them in the act :
I know no proof beyond it.
     Roch. O my heart !
     Charal. A judge should feel no passions.
     Roch. Yet remember
He is a man, and cannot put off nature.
What answer makes the prisoner ?
     Beaumel. I confess
The fact I am charged with, and yield my-
      self
Most miserably guilty.
     Roch. Heaven take mercy
Upon your soul, then ! it must leave your
      body.
Now free mine eyes ; I dare unmoved look
      on her,   [Charalois *unbinds his eyes.*
And fortify my sentence with strong reasons.
Since that the politic law provides that ser-
      vants,
To whose care we commit our goods, shall
      die
If they abuse our trust, what can you look
      for,
To whose charge this most hopeful lord
      gave up
All he received from his brave ancestors,
Or he could leave to his posterity,
His honour, wicked woman ! in whose safety
All his life's joys and comforts were lock'd
      up,
Which thy . . . lust, a thief, hath now
      stolen from him ;
And therefore——

     Charal. Stay, just judge :—may not what's
      lost
By her one fault, (for I am charitable,
And charge her not with many,) be for-
      gotten
In her fair life hereafter ?
     Roch. Never, sir.
The w   g that's done to the chaste married
      bed,
Repentant tears can never expiate ;
And be assured,—to pardon such a sin,
Is an offence as great as to commit it.
     Charal. I may not then forgive her ?
     Roch. Nor she hope it.
Nor can she wish to live : no sun shall rise,
But, ere it set, shall shew her ugly lust
In a new shape, and every one more horrid.
Nay, even those prayers which, with such
      humble fervour,
She seems to send up yonder, are beat back,
And all suits which her penitence can
      proffer,
As soon as made, are with contempt thrown
      out
Of all the courts of mercy.
     Charal. Let her die, then !
                              [*He stabs her.*
Better prepared, I'm sure, I could not take
      her,
Nor she accuse her father, as a judge
Partial against her.
     Beaumel. I approve his sentence,
And kiss the executioner. My lust
Is now run from me in that blood in which
It was begot and nourish'd.   [*Dies.*
     Roch. Is she dead, then ?
     Charal. Yes, sir ; this is her heart-blood,
      is it not ?
I think it be.
     Roch. And you have kill'd her ?
     Charal. True,
And did it by your doom.
     Roch. But I pronounced it
As a judge only, and a friend to justice ;
And, zealous in defence of your wrong'd
      honour,
Broke all the ties of nature, and cast off
The love and soft affection of a father.
I, in your cause, put on a scarlet robe
Of red-dyed cruelty ; but in return,
You have advanced for me no flag of mercy.
I look'd on you as a wrong'd husband ; but
You closed your eyes against me as a father.
O Beaumelle ! my daughter !
     Charal. This is madness.
     Roch. Keep from me !—Could not one
      good thought rise up,
To tell you that she was my age's comfort,
Begot by a weak man, and born a woman,

And could not, therefore, but partake of
　　frailty?
Or wherefore did not thankfulness step forth,
To urge my many merits, which I may
Object unto you, since you prove ungrateful,
Flint-hearted Charalois !
　　Charal. Nature does prevail
Above your virtue.
　　Roch. No ; it gives me eyes
To pierce the heart of your design against
　　me :
I find it now, it was my state was aim'd at.
A nobler match was sought for, and the
　　hours
I lived grew tedious to you : my compassion
Tow'rds you hath render'd me most mise-
　　rable,
And foolish charity undone myself.
But there's a heaven above, from whose just
　　wreak
No mists of policy can hide offenders.
　　Nov. sen. [*within.*] Force ope the doors !

　　Enter Novall *senior, with* Officers.

　　　　　　　　　　　O monster ! cannibal !
Lay hold on him.　My son, my son !—O
　　Rochfort,
'Twas you gave liberty to this bloody wolf,
To worry all our comforts :——but this is
No time to quarrel ; now give your assis-
　　tance
For the revenge——
　　Roch. Call it a fitter name,
Justice for innocent blood.
　　Charal. Though all conspire
Against that life which I am weary of,
A little longer yet I'll strive to keep it,
To shew, in spite of malice and their laws,
His plea must speed, that hath an honest
　　cause.　　　　　　　　　　　[*Exeunt.*

———

ACT V.

SCENE I.—*A Street.*

Enter Tailor, *and two* Bailiffs *with*
　　Liladam.

　　Lilad. Why, 'tis both most unconscion-
　　able and untimely,
To arrest a gallant for his clothes, before
He has worn them out : besides, you said
　　you ask'd
My name in my lord's bond but for form
　　only,
And now you'll lay me up for't !　Do not
　　think
The taking measure of a customer
By a brace of varlets, though I rather wait
Never so patiently, will prove a fashion

Which any courtier or inns-of-court-man
Would follow willingly.
　　Tail. There I believe you.
But, sir, I must have present monies, or
Assurance to secure me when I shall ;
Or I will see to your coming forth.
　　Lilad. Plague on't !
You have provided for my entrance in ;
That coming forth you talk of, concerns me.
What shall I do ? you have done me a dis-
　　grace
In the arrest, but more in giving cause
To all the street to think I cannot stand
Without these two supporters for my arms.
Pray you, let them loose me : for their satis-
　　faction,
I will not run away.
　　Tail. For theirs, you will not ;
But for your own, you would.　Look to him,
　　fellows.
　　Lilad. Why, do you call them fellows ?
　　do not wrong
Your reputation so.　As you are merely
A tailor, faithful, apt to believe in gallants,
You are a companion at a ten-crown supper,
For cloth of bodkin, and may, with one lark,
Eat up three manchets, and no man observe
　　you,
Or call your trade in question for't.　But,
　　when
You study your debt-book, and hold corre-
　　spondence
With officers of the hanger, and leave swords-
　　men,
The learn'd conclude, the tailor and the ser-
　　jeant,
In the expression of a knave and thief,
To be synonyma.　Look, therefore, to it,
And let us part in peace ; I would be loth
You should undo yourself.

　　Enter Novall *senior, and* Pontalier.

　　Tail. To let you go,
Were the next way.　But see ! here's your
　　old lord :
Let him but give his word I shall be paid,
And you are free.
　　Lilad. 'Slid !　I will put him to't.
I can be but denied ; or—what say you ?
His lordship owing me three times your debt,
If you arrest him at my suit, and let me
Go run before, to see the action enter'd :—
'Twould be a witty jest !
　　Tail. I must have earnest :
I cannot pay my debts so.
　　Pont. Can your lordship
Imagine, while I live, and wear a sword,
Your son's death shall be unrevenged ?
　　Nov. sen. I know not

One reason why you should not do like
  others :
I am sure, of all the herd that fed upon him,
I cannot see in any, now he's gone,
In pity or in thankfulness, one true sign
Of sorrow for him.
  Pont. All his bounties yet,
Fell not in such unthankful ground : 'tis true,
He had weaknesses, but such as few are free
  from ;
And, though none sooth'd them less than I,
  (for now
To say that I foresaw the dangers that
Would rise from cherishing them, were but
  untimely,)
I yet could wish the justice that you seek for,
In the revenge, had been trusted to me,
And not the uncertain issue of the laws.
It has robb'd me of a noble testimony
Of what I durst do for him :—but, however,
My forfeit life redeem'd by him, though dead,
Shall do him service.
  Nov. sen. As far as my grief
Will give me leave, I thank you.
  Lilad. O, my lord !
Oh, my good lord ! deliver me from these
  Furies.
  Pont. Arrested ! this is one of them,
  whose base
And abject flattery help'd to dig his grave :
He is not worth your pity, nor my anger.
Go to the basket, and repent.
  Nov. sen. Away !
I only know thee now to hate thee deadly :
I will do nothing for thee.
  Lilad. Nor you, captain ?
  Pont. No ; to your trade again ; put off
  this case :
It may be, the discovering what you were,
When your unfortunate master took you up,
May move compassion in your creditor.
Confess the truth.
  [*Exeunt* Novall *sen. and* Pontalier.
  Lilad. And now I think on't better,
I will.   Brother, your hand ; your hand,
  sweet brother :
I'm of your sect, and my gallantry but a
  dream,
Out of which these two fearful apparitions,
Against my will, have waked me.   This
  rich sword,
Grew suddenly out of a tailor's bodkin ;
These hangers, from my vails and fees in
  hell ;
And where as now this beaver sits, full often
A thrifty cap, composed of broad-cloth lists,
Near-kin unto the cushion where I sat,
Cross-legg'd, and yet ungarter'd, hath been
  seen :

Our breakfasts, famous for the butter'd
  loaves,
I have with joy been oft acquainted with ;
And therefore use a conscience, though it be
Forbidden in our hall towards other men,
To me, that, as I have been, will again
Be of the brotherhood.
  1 *Bail.* I know him now ;
He was a prentice to Le Robe at Orleans.
  Lilad. And from thence brought by my
  young lord, now dead,
Unto Dijon, and with him, till this hour,
Have been received here for a complete
  monsieur ;
Nor wonder at it ; for but tithe our gallants,
Even those of the first rank, and you will find
In every ten, one, peradventure two,
That smell rank of the dancing-school or
  fiddle,
The pantofle, or pressing-iron :—but here-
  after
We'll talk of this.   I will surrender up
My suits again, there cannot be much loss ;
'Tis but the turning of the lace, with one
Addition more you know of, and what wants,
I will work out.
  Tail. Then here our quarrel ends :
The gallant is turn'd tailor, and all friends.
  [*Exeunt.*

SCENE II.—*The Court of Justice.*

Enter Romont *and* Beaumont.

  Rom. You have them ready ?
  Beau. Yes, and they will speak
Their knowledge in this cause, when you
  think fit
To have them call'd upon.
  Rom. 'Tis well ; and something
I can add to their evidence, to prove
This brave revenge, which they would have
  call'd murder,
A noble justice.
  Beau. In this you express
(The breach by my lord's want of you new
  made up)
A faithful friend.
  Rom. That friendship's raised on sand,
Which every sudden gust of discontent,
Or flowing of our passions, can change,
As if it ne'er had been :—but do you know
Who are to sit on him ?
  Beau. Monsieur Du Croy,
Assisted by Charmi.
  Rom. The advocate
That pleaded for the marshal's funeral,
And was check'd for it by Novall ?
  Beau. The same.
  Rom. How fortunes that ?
  Beau. Why, sir, my lord Novall,

Being the accuser, cannot be the judge ;
Nor would grieved Rochfort, but lord Chara-
    lois,
However he might wrong him by his power,
Should have an equal hearing.
    Rom. By my hopes
Of Charalois's acquittal, I lament
That reverend old man's fortune.
    Beau. Had you seen him,
As, to my grief, I have, now promise
    patience,
And, ere it was believed, though spake by
    him
That never brake his word, enraged again
So far as to make war upon those hairs,
Which not a barbarous Scythian durst pre-
    sume
To touch, but with a superstitious fear,
As something sacred ;—and then curse his
    daughter,
But with more frequent violence, himself,
As if he had been guilty of her fault,
By being incredulous of your report,
You would not only judge him worthy pity,
But suffer with him :—but here comes the
    prisoner ;

    Enter Officers with Charalois.

I dare not stay to do my duty to him ;
Yet, rest assured, all possible means in me
To do him service, keeps you company.
                                    [*Exit.*
    Rom. It is not doubted.
    Charal. Why, yet as I came hither,
The people, apt to mock calamity,
And tread on the oppress'd, made no horns
    at me,
Though they are too familiar I deserve them.
And, knowing too what blood my sword hath
    drunk,
In wreak of that disgrace, they yet forbear
To shake their heads, or to revile me for
A murderer ; they rather all put on,
As for great losses the old Romans used,
A general face of sorrow, waited on
By a sad murmur breaking through their
    silence :
And no eye but was readier with a tear
To witness 'twas shed for me, than I could
Discern a face made up with scorn against
    me.
Why should I, then, though for unusual
    wrongs,
I chose unusual means to right those
    wrongs,
Condemn myself, as over-partial
In my own cause ?—Romont !
    Rom. Best friend, well met !
By my heart's love to you, and join to that,

My thankfulness that still lives to the dead,.
I look upon you now with more true joy,
Than when I saw you married.
    Charal. You have reason
To give you warrant for't : my falling off
From such a friendship, with the scorn that
    answered
Your too prophetic counsel, may well move
    you
To think your meeting me, going to my
    death,
A fit encounter for that hate which justly
I have deserved from you.
    Rom. Shall I still, then,
Speak truth, and be ill understood ?
    Charal. You are not.
I am conscious I have wrong'd you : and
    allow me,
Only a moral man ;—to look on you,
Whom foolishly I have abused and injured,.
Must of necessity be more terrible to me,
Than any death the judges can pronounce,
From the tribunal which I am to plead at.
    Rom. Passion transports you.
    Charal. For what I have done
To my false lady, or Novall, I can
Give some apparent cause ; but touching
    you,
In my defence, child-like, I can say nothing
But, I am sorry for't ; a poor satisfaction !
And yet, mistake me not ; for it is more
Than I will speak, to have my pardon sign'd'
For all I stand accused of.
    Rom. You much weaken
The strength of your good cause, should you
    but think,
A man for doing well could entertain
A pardon, were it offer'd : you have given
To blind and slow-paced justice wings and'
    eyes,
To see and overtake impieties,
Which, from a cold proceeding, had received'
Indulgence or protection.
    Charal. Think you so ?
    Rom. Upon my soul ! nor should the blood.
    you challenged,
And took to cure your honour, breed more:
    scruple
In your soft conscience, than if your sword
Had been sheath'd in a tiger or she-bear,
That in their bowels would have made your
    tomb.
To injure innocence is more than murder :
But when inhuman lusts transform us, then'
As beasts we are to suffer, not like men
To be lamented. Nor did Charalois ever
Perform an act so worthy the applause
Of a full theatre of perfect men,
As he hath done in this. The glory got

By overthrowing outward enemies,
Since strength and fortune are main sharers
  in it,
We cannot, but by pieces, call our own :
But, when we conquer our intestine foes,
Our passions bred within us, and of those
The most rebellious tyrant, powerful love,
Our reason suffering us to like no longer
Than the fair object, being good, deserves it,
That's a true victory ! which, were great men
Ambitious to achieve, by your example
Setting no price upon the breach of faith,
But loss of life, 'twould fright adultery
Out of their families, and make lust appear
As loathsome to us in the first consent,
As when 'tis waited on by punishment.
   Charal. You have confirm'd me. Who
  would love a woman,
That might enjoy in such a man a friend !
You have made me know the justice of my
  cause,
And mark'd me out the way how to defend it.
   Rom. Continue to that resolution constant,
And you shall, in contempt of their worst
  malice,
Come off with honour—here they come.
   Charal. I am ready.

Enter Du Croy, Charmi, Rochfort, Novall
   senior, Pontalier, *and* Beaumont.

   Nov. sen. See, equal judges, with what
  confidence
The cruel murderer stands, as if he would
Outface the court and justice !
   Roch. But look on him,
And you shall find, for still methinks I do,
Though guilt hath dyed him black, some-
  thing good in him,
That may perhaps work with a wiser man
That I have been, again to set him free,
And give him all he has.
   Char. This is not well.
I would you had lived so, my lord, that I
Might rather have continued your poor ser-
  vant,
Than sit here as your judge.
   Du Croy. I am sorry for you.
   Roch. In no act of my life I have deserved
This injury from the court, that any here,
Should thus uncivilly usurp on what
Is proper to me only.
   Du Croy. What distaste
Receives my lord ?
   Roch. You say you are sorry for him ;
A grief in which I must not have a partner.
'Tis I alone am sorry, that when I raised
The building of my life, for seventy years,
Upon so sure a ground, that all the vices

Practised to ruin man, though brought
  against me,
Could never undermine, and no way left
To send these gray hairs to the grave with
  sorrow,
Virtue, that was my patroness, betray'd me.
For, entering, nay, possessing this young
  man,
It lent him such a powerful majesty .
To grace whate'er he undertook, that freely
I gave myself up, with my liberty,
To be at his disposing. Had his person,
Lovely I must confess, or far-famed valour,
Or any other seeming good, that yet
Holds a near neighbourhood with ill, wrought
  on me,
I might have borne it better : but, when
  goodness
And piety itself in her best figure
Were bribed to my destruction, can you
  blame me,
Though I forget to suffer like a man,
Or rather act a woman ?
   Beau. Good, my lord !—
   Nov. sen. You hinder our proceeding.
   Char. And forget
The parts of an accuser.
   Beau. Pray you, remember
To use the temper which to me you promised.
   Roch. Angels themselves must break, Beau-
  mont, that promise
Beyond the strength and patience of angels.
But I have done :—My good lord, pardon
  me,
A weak old man, and pray you, add to that,
A miserable father ; yet be careful
That your compassion of my age, nor his,
Move you to anything that may disbecome
The place on which you sit.
   Char. Read the indictment.
   Charal. It shall be needless ; I myself, my
  lords,
Will be my own accuser, and confess
All they can charge me with, nor will I spare
To aggravate that guilt with circumstance,
They seek to load me with ; only I pray,
That, as for them you will vouchsafe me
  hearing,
I may
Not be denied it for myself, when I
Shall urge by what unanswerable reasons
I was compell'd to what I did, which yet,
Till you have taught me better, I repent not.
   Roch. The motion's honest.
   Char. And 'tis freely granted.
   Charal. Then I confess, my lords, that I
  stood bound,
When, with my friends, even hope itself had
  left me,

To this man's charity, for my liberty ;
Nor did his bounty end there, but began :
For, after my enlargement, cherishing
The good he did, he made me master of
His only daughter, and his whole estate.
Great ties of thankfulness, I must acknow-
ledge :
Could any one, fee'd by you, press this
further?
But yet consider, my most honour'd lords,
If to receive a favour make a servant,
And benefits are bonds to tie the taker
To the imperious will of him that gives,
There's none but slaves will receive courtesies,
Since they must fetter us to our dishonours.
Can it be call'd magnificence in a prince,
To pour down riches with a liberal hand
Upon a poor man's wants, if that must bind
him
To play the soothing parasite to his vices?
Or any man, because he saved my hand,
Presume my head and heart are at his service?
Or, did I stand engaged to buy my freedom
(When my captivity was honourable)
By making myself here, and fame hereafter,
Bondslaves to men's scorn, and calumnious
tongues?—
Had his fair daughter's mind been like her
feature,
Or, for some little blemish, I had sought
For my content elsewhere, wasting on others
My body and her dower ; my forehead then
Deserved the brand of base ingratitude :
But if obsequious usage, and fair warning
To keep her worth my love, could not pre-
serve her
From being a whore, and yet no cunning
one,
So to offend, and yet the fault kept from me,
What should I do? Let any free-born spirit
Determine truly, if that thankfulness,
Choice form, with the whole world given
for a dowry,
Could strengthen so an honest man with
patience,
As with a willing neck to undergo
The insupportable yoke of slave, or wittol.
Char. What proof have you she did play
false, besides
Your oath?
Charal. Her own confession to her father:
I ask him for a witness.
Roch. 'Tis most true.
I would not willingly blend my last words
With an untruth.
Charal. And then to clear myself,
That his great wealth was not the mark I
shot at,
But that I held it, when fair Beaumelle

Fell from her virtue, like the fatal gold
Which Brennus took from Delphos, whose
possession
Brought with it ruin to himself and army :
Here's one in court, Beaumont, by whom I
sent
All grants and writings back which made it
mine,
Before his daughter died by his own sen-
tence,
As freely as, unask'd, he gave it to me.
Beau. They are here to be seen.
Char. Open the casket.
——Peruse that deed of gift. [*To* Du Croy.
Rom. Half of the danger
Already is discharged ; the other part
As bravely ; and you are not only free
But crown'd with praise for ever !
Du Croy. 'Tis apparent.
Char. Your state, my lord, again is yours.
Roch. Not mine ;
I am not of the world. If it can prosper,
(And yet, being justly got, I'll not examine
Why it should be so fatal,) do you bestow it
On pious uses : I'll go seek a grave.
And yet, for proof I die in peace, your
pardon
I ask ; and, as you grant it me, may heaven,
Your conscience, and these judges, free you
from
What you are charged with ! So, farewell
for ever!— [*Exit.*
Nov. sen. I'll be mine own guide. Passion
nor example
Shall be my leaders. I have lost a son,
A son, grave judges ; I require his blood
From his accursed homicide.
Char. What reply you,
In your defence, for this?
Charal. I but attended
Your lordship's pleasure.—For the fact, as of
The former, I confess it ; but with what
Base wrongs I was unwillingly drawn to it,
To my few words there are some other
proofs,
To witness this for truth. When I was
married,
For there I must begin, the slain Novall
Was to my wife, in way of our French
courtship,
A most devoted servant; but yet aimed at
Nothing but means to quench his wanton
heat,
His heart being never warm'd by lawful fires,
As mine was, lords : and though, on these
presumptions,
Join'd to the hate between his house and
mine,
I might, with opportunity and ease,

c c

Have found a way for my revenge, I did
　not ;
But still he had the freedom as before,
When all was mine : and, told that he
　abused it
With some unseemly license, by my friend,
My approved friend, Romont, I gave no
　credit
To the reporter, but reproved him for it,
As one uncourtly, and malicious to him.
What could I more, my lords? Yet, after
　this,
He did continue in his first pursuit,·
Hotter than ever, and at length obtain'd it ;
But, how it came to my most certain know-
　ledge,
For the dignity of the court, and my own
　honour,
I dare not say.

Nov. sen. If all may be believed
A passionate prisoner speaks, who is so
　foolish
That durst be wicked, that will appear
　guilty?
No, my grave lords ; in his impunity,
But give example unto jealous men
To cut the throats they hate, and they will
　never
Want matter or pretence for their bad
　ends.

Char. You must find other proofs to
　strengthen these
But mere presumptions.

Du Croy. Or we shall hardly
Allow your innocence.

Charal. All your attempts
Shall fall on me like brittle shafts on armour,
That break themselves ; or waves against a
　rock,
That leave no sign of their ridiculous fury,
But foam and splinters ; my innocence, like
　these,
Shall stand triumphant, and ·your malice
　serve
But for a trumpet to proclaim my conquest.
Nor shall you, though you do the worst fate
　can,
Howe'er condemn, affright an honest man.

Rom. May it please the court, I may be
　heard ?

Nov. sen. You come not
To rail again? but do—you shall not find
Another Rochfort.

Rom. In Novall I cannot ;
But I come furnished with what will stop
The mouth of his conspiracy 'gainst the
　life
Of innocent Charalois. Do you know this
　character ?

Nov. sen. Yes, 'tis my son's.

Rom. May it please you lordships, read
　it :
And you shall find there, with what vehe-
　mency
He did solicit Beaumelle ; how he got
A promise from her to enjoy his wishes ;
How after, he abjured her company,
And yet—but that 'tis fit I spare the dead—
Like a damn'd villain, as soon as recorded,
He brake that oath :— to make this manifest,
Produce his bawds and hers.

Enter Officers with Aymer, Florimel, *and*
Bellapert.

Char. Have they ta'en their oaths?

Rom. They have, and, rather than endure
　the rack,
Confess the time, the meeting, nay, the act ;
What would you more? only this matron
　made
A free discovery to a good end ;
And therefore I sue to the court, she may not
Be placed in the black list of the delinquents.

Pont. I see by this, Novall's revenge
　needs me,
And I shall do—— 　　　　　　[*Aside.*

Char. 'Tis evident.

Nov. sen. That I
Till now was never wretched ; here's no
　place
To curse him or my stars. 　　　[*Exit.*

Char. Lord Charalois,
The injuries you have sustain'd appear
So worthy of the mercy of the court,
That, notwithstanding you have gone be-
　yond
The letter of the law, they yet acquit you.

Pont. But, in Novall, I do condemn him
—thus. 　　　　　　　[*Stabs him.*

Charal. I am slain.

Rom. Can I look on? Oh, murderous
　wretch !
Thy challenge now I answer. So! die with
　him. 　　　　　　　[*Stabs* Pontalier.

Char. A guard ! disarm him.

Rom. I yield up my sword
Unforced—-Oh, Charalois.

Charal. For shame, Romont,
Mourn not for him that dies as he hath lived,
Still constant and unmoved : what's fall'n
　upon me
Is by heaven's will, because I made myself
A judge in my own cause, without their
　warrant ;
But He that lets me know thus much in
　death,
With all good men-–forgive me ! 　[*Dies.*

A New Way to Pay Old Debts.

DRAMATIS PERSONÆ.

Lord Lovell.
Sir Giles Overreach, *a cruel extortioner.*
Frank Wellborn, *a prodigal.*
Tom Allworth, *a young gentleman, page to* Lord Lovell.
Greedy, *a hungry justice of peace.*
Marrall, *a term-driver; a creature of* Sir Giles Overreach.
Order, *steward*
Amble, *usher*
Furnace, *cook*   } *to* Lady Allworth.
Watchall, *porter*

Willdo, *a parson*
Tapwell, *an alehouse keeper.*
Creditors, Servants, &c.
Lady Allworth, *a rich widow.*
Margaret, Overreach's *daughter.*
Froth, Tapwell's *wife.*
Chambermaid.
Waiting Woman.

SCENE,—*The country near* Nottingham.

~~~~~~~

ACT I.

SCENE I.—*Before* Tapwell's *House.*

Enter Wellborn *in tattered apparel,* Tapwell, *and* Froth.

Well. No house? nor no tobacco?
Tap. Not a suck, sir;
Nor the remainder of a single can
Left by a drunken porter, all night pall'd too.
Froth. Not the dropping of the tap for your morning's draught, sir:
'Tis verity, I assure you.
Well. Verity, you brache!
The devil turn'd precisian! Rogue, what am I?
Tap. Troth, durst I trust you with a looking-glass,
To let you see your trim shape, you would quit me,
And take the name yourself.
Well. How, dog!
Tap. Even so, sir.
And I must tell you, if you but advance
Your Plymouth cloak, you shall be soon instructed
There dwells, and within call, if it please your worship,
A potent monarch, call'd the constable,
That does command a citadel call'd the stocks;
Whose guards are certain files of rusty billmen,
Such as with great dexterity will hale
Your tatter'd, lousy——
Well. Rascal! slave!
Froth. No rage, sir.

Tap. At his own peril: Do not put yourself
In too much heat, there being no water near
To quench your thirst; and sure, for other liquor,
As mighty ale, or beer, they are things, I take it,
You must no more remember; not in a dream, sir.
Well. Why, thou unthankful villain, dar'st thou talk thus!
Is not thy house, and all thou hast, my gift?
Tap. I find it not in chalk; and Timothy Tapwell
Does keep no other register.
Well. Am not I he
Whose riots fed and clothed thee? wert thou not
Born on my father's land, and proud to be
A drudge in his house?
Tap. What I was, sir, it skills not;
What you are, is apparent: now, for a farewell,
Since you talk of father, in my hope it will torment you,
I'll briefly tell your story. Your dead father,
My quondam master, was a man of worship,
Old Sir John Wellborn, justice of peace and quorum,
And stood fair to be custos rotulorum;
Bore the whole sway of the shire, kept a great house,
Relieved the poor, and so forth; but he dying,
And the twelve hundred a year coming to you,

Pont. I receive
The vengeance which my love, not built on
virtue,
Has made me worthy, worthy of.   [*Dies.*
Char. We are taught
By this sad precedent, how just soever
Our reasons are to remedy our wrongs,
We are yet to leave them to their will and
power
That, to that purpose, have authority.

For you, Romont, although in your custom,
You may plead what you did was in re-
venge
Of the dishonour done unto the court,
Yet, since from us you had not warrant for it,
We banish you the state: for these, they
shall,
As they are found guilty or innocent,
Or be set free, or suffer punishment.
[*Exeunt.*

Late master Francis, but now forlorn Well-
  born——
  Well. Slave, stop ! or I shall lose myself.
  Froth. Very hardly ;
You cannot out of your way.
  Tap. But to my story :
You were then a lord of acres, the prime
  gallant,
And I your under butler ; note the change
  now :
You had a merry time of't ; hawks and
  hounds,
With choice of running horses : mistresses
Of all sorts and all sizes, yet so hot,
As their embraces made your lordships melt ;
Which your uncle, Sir Giles Overreach, ob-
  serving,
(Resolving not to lose a drop of them,)
On foolish mortgages, statutes, and bonds,
For a while supplied your looseness, and
  then left you.
  Well. Some curate hath penn'd this in-
  vective, mongrel,
And you have studied it.
  Tap. I have not done yet :
Your land gone, and your credit not worth
  a token,
You grew the common borrower ; no man
  scaped
Your paper-pellets, from the gentleman
To the beggars on highways, that sold you
  switches
In your gallantry.
  Well. I shall switch your brains out.
  Tap. Where poor Tim Tapwell, with a
  little stock,
Some forty pounds or so, bought a small
  cottage ;
Humbled myself to marriage with my Froth
  here,
Gave entertainment——
  Well. Yes, to whores and canters,
Clubbers by night.
  Tap. True, but they brought in profit,
And had a gift to pay for what they called
  for ;
And stuck not like your mastership. The
  poor income
I glean'd from them hath made me in my
  parish
Thought worthy to be scavenger, and in time
·May rise to be overseer of the poor ;
Which if I do, on your petition, Wellborn,
I may allow you thirteen-pence a quarter,.
And you shall thank my worship.
  Well. Thus, you dog-bolt,
And thus—— [*Beats and kicks him.*
  Tap. [*to his wife.*] Cry out for help !
  Well. Stir, and thou diest :

Your potent prince, the constable, shall not
  save you.
Hear me, ungrateful hell-hound ! did not I
Make purses for you ? then you lick'd my
  boots,
And thought your holiday cloak too coarse
  to clean them.
'Twas I that, when I heard thee swear if ever
Thou couldst arrive at forty pounds, thou
  wouldst
Live like an emperor, 'twas I that gave it
In ready gold. Deny this, wretch !
  Tap. I must, sir ;
For, from the tavern to the taphouse, all,
On forfeiture of their licenses, stand bound
Ne'er to remember who their best guests were,
If they grew poor like you.
  Well. They are well rewarded
That beggar themselves to make such cuck-
  olds rich.
Thou viper, thankless viper ! impudent
  bawd !—
But since you are grown forgetful, I will help
Your memory, and tread you into mortar ;
Not leave one bone unbroken.
                          [*Beats him again.*
  Tap. Oh !
  Froth. Ask mercy.

                  Enter Allworth.

  Well. 'Twill not be granted.
  All. Hold, for my sake hold.
Deny me, Frank ! they are not worth your
  anger.
  Well. For once thou hast redeem'd them
  from this sceptre ;
But let them vanish, creeping on their knees,
And, if they grumble, I revoke my pardon.
  Froth. This comes of your prating, hus-
  band ; you presumed
On your ambling wit, and must use your
  glib tongue,
Though you are beaten lame for't.
  Tap. Patience, Froth ;
There's law to cure our bruises.
          [*They crawl off on their hands and knees.*
  Well. Sent to your mother?
  All. My lady, Frank, my patroness, my
  all !
She's such a mourner for my father's death,
And, in her love to him, so favours me,
That I cannot pay too much observance to
  her :
There are few such stepdames.
  Well. 'Tis a noble widow,
And keeps her reputation pure, and clear
From the least taint of infamy ; her life,
With the splendour of her actions, leaves no
  tongue

To envy or detraction. Prithee tell me,
Has she no suitors?
  All. Even the best of the shire, Frank,'
My lord, excepted; such as sue, and send,
And send, and sue again, but to no purpose;
Their frequent visits have not gain'd her
    presence.
Yet she's so far from sullenness and pride,
That I dare undertake you shall meet from
    her
A liberal entertainment: I can give you
A catalogue of her suitors' names.
  Well. Forbear it,
While I give you good counsel: I am bound
    to it.
Thy father was my friend; and that affection
I bore to him, in right descends to thee;
Thou art a handsome and a hopeful youth,
Nor will I have the least affront stick on thee,
If I with any danger can prevent it.
  All. I thank your noble care; but, pray
    you, in what
Do I run the hazard?
  Well. Art thou not in love?
Put it not off with wonder.
  All. In love, at my years!
  Well. You think you walk in clouds, but
    are transparent.
I have heard all, and the choice that you
    have made;
And, with my finger, can point out the north
    star
By which the loadstone of your folly's guided;
And, to confirm this true, what think you of
Fair Margaret, the only child and heir
Of Cormorant Overreach? Does it blush
    and start,
To hear her only named? blush at your want
Of wit, and reason.
  All. You are too bitter, sir.
  Well. Wounds of this nature are not to
    be cured
With balms, but corrosives. I must be plain:
Art thou scarce manumised from the porter's
    lodge,
And yet sworn servant to the pantofle,
And dars't thou dream of marriage? I fear
'Twill be concluded for impossible,
That there is now, or e'er shall be hereafter,
A handsome page, or player's boy of fourteen,
But either loves a wench, or drabs love him;
Court-waiters not exempted.
  All. This is madness.
Howe'er you have discover'd my intents,
You know my aims are lawful; and if ever
The queen of flowers, the glory of the spring,
The sweetest comfort to our smell, the
    rose,
Sprang from an envious briar, I may infer,

There's such disparity in their conditions,
Between the goodness of my soul, the
    daughter,
And the base churl her father.
  Well. Grant this true,
As I believe it, canst thou ever hope
To enjoy a quiet bed with her, whose father
Ruin'd thy state?
  All. And yours too.
  Well. I confess it.
True; I must tell you as a friend, and freely,
That, where impossibilities are apparent,
'Tis indiscretion to nourish hopes.
Canst thou imagine (let not self-love blind
    thee)
That Sir Giles Overreach, that, to make her
    great
In swelling titles, without touch of con-
    science,
Will cut his neighbour's throat, and I hope
    his own too,——
Will e'er consent to make her thine? Give
    o'er,
And think of some course suitable to thy
    rank,
And prosper in it.
  All. You have well advised me.
But, in the mean time, you, that are so
    studious
Of my affairs, wholly neglect your own:
Remember yourself, and in what plight you
    are.
  Well. No matter, no matter.
  All. Yes, 'tis much material:
You know my fortune, and my means; yet
    something
I can spare from myself, to help your wants.
  Well. How's this?
  All. Nay, be not angry; there's eight
    pieces,
To put you in better fashion.
  Well. Money from thee!
From a boy! a stipendiary! one that lives
At the devotion of a stepmother,
And the uncertain favour of a lord!
I'll eat my arms first. Howsoe'er blind
    Fortune
Hath spent the utmost of her malice on
    me;
Though I am vomited out of an alehouse,
And thus accoutred.; know not where to eat,
Or drink, or sleep, but underneath this
    canopy;
Although I thank thee, I despise thy offer:
And as I, in my madness, broke my state,
Without the assistance of another's brain,
In my right wits I'll piece it; at the worst,
Die thus, and be forgotten.
  All. A strange humour!   [*Exeunt.*

CENE II.—*A Room in* Lady Allworth's
House.

Enter Order, Amble, Furnace, *and*
Watchall.

Ord. Set all things right, or, as my name
is Order,
nd by this staff of office that commands
you,
his chain and double ruff, symbols of
power,
'hoever misses in his function,
or one whole week makes forfeiture of his
breakfast,
nd privilege in the wine-cellar.
Amb. You are merry,
ood master steward.
Furn. Let him ; I'll be angry.
Amb. Why, fellow Furnace, 'tis not twelve
o'clock yet,
or dinner taking up ; then, 'tis allow'd,
ooks, by their places, may be choleric.
Furn. You think you have spoke wisely,
goodman Amble,
Iy lady's go-before !
Ord. Nay, nay, no wrangling.
Furn. Twit me with the authority of the
kitchen !
t all hours, and all places, I'll be angry ;
nd thus provoked, when I am at my prayers
will be angry.
Amb. There was no hurt meant.
Furn. I am friends with thee ; and yet I
will be angry.
Ord. With whom ?
Furn. No matter whom : yet, now I
think on it,
am angry with my lady.
Watch. Heaven forbid, man !
Ord. What cause has she given thee ?
Furn. Cause enough, master steward.
was entertained by her to please her palate,
And, till she forswore eating, I perform'd it.
ow, since our master, noble Allworth, died,
hough I crack my brains to find out
tempting sauces,
nd raise fortifications in the pastry,
uch as might serve for models in the Low
Countries ;
Which, if they had been practised at Breda,
Spinola might have thrown his cap at it, and
ne'er took it——
Amb. But you had wanted matter there
to work on.
Furn. Matter ! with six eggs, and a strike
of rye meal,
I had kept the town till doomsday, perhaps
longer.

Ord. But what's this to your pet against
my lady ?
Furn. What's this ? marry this ; when I
am three parts roasted,
And the fourth part parboiled, to prepare her
viands,
She keeps her chamber, dines with a panada,
Or water-gruel, my sweat never thought on.
Ord. But your art is seen in the dining-
room.
Furn. By whom ?
By such as pretend love to her ; but come
To feed upon her. Yet, of all the harpies
That do devour her, I am out of charity
With none so much as the thin-gutted squire,
That's stolen into commission.
Ord. Justice Greedy ?
Furn. The same, the same : meat's cast
away upon him,
It never thrives ; he holds this paradox,
Who eats not well, can ne'er do justice well :
His stomach's as insatiate as the grave,
Or strumpets' ravenous appetites.
[*Knocking within.*
Watch. One knocks. [*Exit.*
Ord. Our late young master ! '

Re-enter Watchall *and* Allworth.

Amb. Welcome, sir.
Furn. Your hand ;
If you have a stomach, a cold bake-meat's
ready.
Ord. His father's picture in little.
Furn. We are all your servants.
Amb. In you he lives.
All. At once, my thanks to all ;
This is yet some comfort. Is my lady
stirring ?

Enter Lady Allworth, Waiting Woman,
and Chambermaid.

Ord. Her presence answers for us.
L. All. Sort those silks well.
I'll take the air alone.
[*Exeunt* Waiting Woman *and* Cham-
bermaid.
Furn. You air and air ;
But will you never taste but spoon-meat
more ?
To what use serves ?
L. All. Prithee, be not angry ;
I shall ere long ; i' the mean time, there is
gold
To buy thee aprons, and a summer suit.
Furn. I am appeased, and Furnace now
grows cool.
L. All. And, as I gave directions, if this
morning
am visited by any, entertain them

As heretofore ; but say, in my excuse,
I am indisposed.

Ord. I shall, madam.

L. All. Do, and leave me.

Nay, stay you, Allworth.

    [Exeunt Order, Amble, Furnace, *and*
    Watchall.

All. I shall gladly grow here,
To wait on your commands.

L. All. So soon turn'd courtier !

All. Style not that courtship, madam,
    which is duty
Purchased on your part.

L. All. Well, you shall o'ercome ;
I'll not contend in words. How is it with
Your noble master ?

All. Ever like himself ;
No scruple lessen'd in the full weight of
    honour :
He did command me, pardon my pre-
    sumption,
As his unworthy deputy, to kiss
Your ladyship's fair hands.

L. All. I am honour'd in
His favour to me. Does he hold his purpose
For the Low Countries ?

All. Constantly, good madam ;
But he will in person first present his service.

L. All. And how approve you of his
    course ? you are yet
Like virgin parchment, capable of any
Inscription, vicious or honourable.
I will not force your will, but leave you free
To your own election.

All. Any form you please,
I will put on ; but, might I make my choice,
With humble emulation I would follow
The path my lord marks to me.

L. All. 'Tis well answer'd,
And I commend your spirit :· you had a
    father,
Bless'd be his memory ! that some few hours
Before the will of heaven took him from me,
Who did commend you, by the dearest ties
Of perfect love between us, to my charge ;
And, therefore, what I speak, you are bound
    to hear,
With such respect as if he lived in me.
He was my husband, and howe'er you are
    not
Son of my womb, you may be of my love,
Provided you deserve it.

All. I have found you,
Most bouour'd madam, the best mother to
    me ;
And, with my utmost strengths of care and
    service,
Will labour that you never may repent
Your bounties shower'd upon me.

L. All. I much hope it.
These were your father's words : *If e'er my
    son
Follow the war, tell him it is a school,
Where all the principles tending to honour
Are taught, if truly follow'd : but for such
As repair thither, as a place in which
They do presume they may with license
    practise
Their lusts and riots, they shall never merit
The noble name of soldiers.   To dare boldly
In a fair cause, and for their country's safety,
To run upon the cannon's mouth undaunted ;
To obey their leaders, and shun mutinies ;
To bear with patience the winter's cold,
And summer's scorching heat, and not to
    faint,
When plenty of provision fails, with hunger ;
Are the essential parts make up a soldier,
Not swearing, dice, or drinking.*

All. There's no syllable
You speak, but is to me an oracle,
Which but to doubt were impious.

L. All. To conclude :
Beware ill company, for often men
Are like to those with whom they do con-
    verse ;
And, from one man I warn you, and that's
    Wellborn :
Not 'cause he's poor, that rather claims
    your pity ;
But that he's in his manners so debauch'd,
And hath to vicious courses sold himself.
'Tis true, your father loved him, while he was
Worthy the loving ; but if he had lived
To have seen him as he is, he had cast him
    off.
As you must do.

All. I shall obey in all things.

L. All. Follow me to my chamber, you
    shall have gold
To furnish you like my son, and still sup-
    plied,
As I hear from you.

All. I am still your creature.   *[Exeunt.*

    SCENE III.—*A Hall in the same.*

Enter Overreach, Greedy, Order, Amble,
    Furnace, Watchall, *and* Marrall.

Greedy. Not to be seen ! ·

Over. Still cloister'd up ! Her reason,
I hope, assures her, though she make herself
Close prisoner ever for her husband's loss,
'Twill not recover him.

Ord. Sir, it is her will,
Which we, that are her servants, ought to
    serve,
And not dispute : howe'er, you are nobly
    welcome ;

And, if you please to stay, that you may
  think so,
There came, not six days since, from Hull,
  a pipe,
Of rich Canary, which shall spend itself
For my lady's honour.
  Greedy. Is it of the right race?
  Ord. Yes, master Greedy.
  Amb. How his mouth runs o'er!
  Furn. I'll make it run, and run. Save
  your good worship!
  Greedy. Honest master cook, thy hand;
  again: how I love thee!
Are the good dishes still in being? speak,
  boy.
  Furn. If you have a mind to feed, there
  is a chine
Of beef, well season'd.
  Greedy. Good!
  Furn. A pheasant, larded.
  Greedy. That I might now give thanks
  for't!
  Furn. Other kickshaws.
Besides, there came last night, from the
  forest of Sherwood,
The fattest stag I ever cook'd.
  Greedy. A stag, man!
  Furn. A stag, sir; part of it prepared for
  dinner,
And baked in puff-paste.
  Greedy. Puff-paste too! Sir Giles,
A ponderous chine of beef! a pheasant
  larded!
And red deer too, sir Giles, and baked in
  puff-paste!
All business set aside, let us give thanks here.
  Furn. How the lean skeleton's rapt?
  Over. You know we cannot.
  Mar. Your worships are to sit on a com-
  mission,
And if you fail to come, you lose the cause.
  Greedy. Cause me no causes. I'll prove't,
  for such a dinner,
We may put off a commission: you shall
  find it
Henrici decimo quarto.
  Over. Fie, master Greedy!
Will you lose me a thousand pounds for a
  dinner,
No more, for shame! we must forget the
  belly,
When we think of profit.
  Greedy. Well, you shall o'er-rule me;
I could e'en cry now.—Do you hear, master
  cook,
Send but a corner of that immortal pasty,
And I, in thankfulness, will, by your boy,
Send you—a brace of three-pences.
  Furn. Will you be so prodigal?

Enter Wellborn.

  Over. Remember me to your lady. Who
  have we here?
  Well. You know me.
  Over. I did once, but now I will not;
Thou art no blood of mine. Avaunt, thou
  beggar!
If ever thou presume to own me more,
I'll have thee caged, and whipp'd.
  Greedy. I'll grant the warrant.
Think of pie-corner, Furnace!
  [*Exeunt* Overreach, Greedy, *and* Marrall.
  Watch. Will you out, sir?
I wonder how you durst creep in.
  Ord. This is rudeness,
And saucy impudence.
  Amb. Cannot you stay
To be serv'd, among your fellows, from the
  basket,
But you must press into the hall?
  Furn. Prithee, vanish
Into some outhouse, though it be the pigstie;
My scullion shall come to thee.

Enter Allworth.

  Well. This is rare:
Oh, here's Tom Allworth. Tom!
  All. We must be strangers;
Nor would I have you seen here for a million.
  [*Exit.*
  Well. Better and better. He contemns
  me too!

Enter Waiting Woman *and* Chambermaid.

  Woman. Foh, what a smell's here! what
  thing's this?
  Cham. A creature
Made out of the privy; let us hence, for
  love's sake,
Or I shall swoon.
  Woman. I begin to faint already.
  [*Exeunt* Waiting Woman *and* Chamber-
  maid.
  Watch. Will you know your way?
  Amb. Or shall we teach it you,
By the head and shoulders?
  Well. No; I will not stir;
Do you mark, I will not: let me see the
  wretch
That dares attempt to force me. Why, you
  slaves,
Created only to make legs, and cringe;
To carry in a dish, and shift a trencher;
That have not souls only to hope a blessing
Beyond black jacks or flagons; you, that
  were born
Only to consume meat and drink, and batten

Upon reversions !—who advances? who
Shews me the way?
 Ord. My lady !

Enter Lady Allworth, Waiting Woman,
  and Chambermaid.

 Cham. Here's the monster.
 Woman. Sweet madam, keep your glove
to your nose.
 Cham. Or let me
Fetch some perfumes may be predominant ;
You wrong yourself else.
 Well. Madam, my designs
Bear me to you.
 L. All. To me !
 Well. And though I have met with
But ragged entertainment from your grooms
 here,
I hope from you to receive that noble usage
As may become the true friend of your
 husband,
And then I shall forget these.
 L. All. I am amazed
To see, and hear this rudeness. Darest thou
 think,
Though sworn, that it can ever find belief,
That I, who to the best men of this country
Denied my presence, since my husband's
 death,
Can fall so low, as to change words with
 thee?
Thou son of infamy·! forbear my house,
And know, and keep the distance that's be-
 tween us ;
Or, though it be against my gentler temper,
I shall take order you no more shall be
An eyesore to me.
 Well. Scorn me not, good lady ;
But, as in form you are angelical,
Imitate the heavenly natures, and vouchsafe
At the least awhile to hear me. You will
 grant
The blood that runs in this arm is as noble
As that which fills your veins ; those costly
 jewels,
And those rich clothes you wear, your men's
 observance,
And women's flattery, are in you no virtues ;
Nor these rags, with my poverty, in me vices.
You have a fair fame, and, I know deserve it ;
Yet, lady, I must say. in nothing more
Than in the pious sorrow you have shewn
For your late noble husband.
 Ord. How she starts !
 Furn. And hardly can keep finger from
 the eye,
To hear him named.
 L. All. Have you aught else to say ?

 Well. That husband, madam, was once
 in his fortune
Almost as low as I ; want, debts, and quarrels
Lay heavy on him : let it not be thought
A boast in me, though I say, I relieved him.
'Twas I that gave him fashion ; mine the
 sword,
That did on all occasions second his ;
I brought him on and off with honour, lady ;
And when in all men's judgments he was
 sunk,
And, in his own hopes, not to be buoy'd up,
I stepp'd unto him, took him by the hand,
And set him upright.
 Furn. Are not we base rogues,
That could forget this ?
 Well. I confess, you made him
Master of your estate ; nor could your friends,
Though he brought no wealth with him,
 blame you for it ;
For he had a shape, and to that shape a
 mind
Made up of all parts, either great or noble ;
So winning a behaviour, not to be
Resisted, madam.
 L. All. 'Tis most true, he had.
 Well. For his sake, then, in that I was his
 friend,
Do not contemn me.
 L. All. For what's past excuse me,
I will redeem it. Order, give the gentleman
A hundred pounds.
 Well. No, madam, on no terms :
I will nor beg nor borrow sixpence of you,
But be supplied elsewhere, or want thus ever.
Only one suit I make, which you deny not
To strangers ; and 'tis this. [*Whispers to her.*
 L. All. Fie ! nothing else ?
 Well. Nothing, unless you please to charge
 your servants,
To throw away a little respect upon me.
 L. All. What you demand is yours.
 Well. I thank you, lady.
Now what can be wrought out of such a suit
Is yet in supposition : [*Aside.*]—I have said
 all ;
When you please, you may retire. [*Exit*
 Lady Allworth.]—Nay, all's forgotten ;
      [*To the* Servants.
And, for a lucky omen to my project,
Shake hands, and end all quarrels in the
 cellar.
 Ord. Agreed, agreed.
 Furn. Still merry master Wellborn.
        Exeunt.

ACT II.

SCENE I.—*A Room in* Overreach's *House.*

Enter Overreach *and* Marrall. .

Over. He's gone, I warrant thee; this commission crush'd him.

Mar. Your worships have the way on't, and ne'er miss
To squeeze these unthrifts into air: and yet,
The chapfall'n justice did his part, returning
For your advantage, the certificate,
Against his conscience, and his knowledge too,
With your good favour, to the utter ruin
Of the poor farmer.

Over. 'Twas for these good ends
I made him a justice: he that bribes his belly,
Is certain to command his soul.

Mar. I wonder,
Still with your license, why, your worship having
The power to put this thin-gut in commission,
You are not in't yourself?

Over. Thou art a fool;
In being out of office I am out of danger;
Where, if I were a justice, besides the trouble,
I might or out of wilfulness, or error,
Run myself finely into a premunire,
And so become a prey to the informer.
No, I'll have none of't; 'tis enough I keep
Greedy at my devotion: so he serve
My purposes, let him hang, or damn, I care not;
Friendship is but a word.

Mar. You are all wisdom.

Over. I would be worldly wise; for the other wisdom,
That does prescribe us a well govern'd life,
And to do right to others, as ourselves,
I value not an atom.

Mar. What course take you,
With your good patience, to hedge in the manor
Of your neighbour, master Frugal? as 'tis said
He will nor sell, nor borrow, nor exchange;
And his land, lying in the midst of your many lordships,
Is a foul blemish.

Over. I have thought on't, Marrall,
And it shall take. I must have all men sellers,
And I the only purchaser.

Mar. 'Tis most fit, sir.

Over. I'll therefore buy some cottage near his manor,
Which done, I'll make my men break ope his fences,
Ride o'er his standing corn, and in the night
Set fire on his barns, or break his cattle's legs:
These trespasses draw on suits, and suits expenses,
Which I can spare, but will soon beggar him.
When I have harried him thus two or three year,
Though he sue *in forma pauperis*, in spite
Of all his thrift and care, he'll grow behindhand.

Mar. The best I ever heard! I could adore you.

Over. Then, with the favour of my man of law,
I will pretend some title: want will force him
To put it to arbitrement; then, if he sell
For half the value, he shall have ready money,
And I possess his land.

Mar. 'Tis above wonder!
Wellborn was apt to sell, and needed not
These fine arts, sir, to hook him in.

Over. Well thought on.
This varlet, Marrall, lives too long, to upbraid me
With my close cheat put upon him. Will nor cold,
Nor hunger, kill him?

Mar. I know not what to think on't.
I have used all means; and the last night I caused
His host, the tapster, to turn him out of doors;
And have been since with all your friends and tenants,
And, on the forfeit of your favour, charged them,
Though a crust of mouldy bread would keep him from starving,
Yet they should not relieve him. This is done, sir.

Over. That was something, Marrall; but thou must go further,
And suddenly, Marrall.

Mar. Where, and when you please, sir.

Over. I would have thee seek him out, and, if thou canst,
Persuade him that 'tis better steal than beg;
Then, if I prove he has but robb'd a henroost,.

Not all the world shall save him from the gallows.
Do any thing to work him to despair ;
And 'tis thy masterpiece.
 Mar. I will do my best, sir.
 Over. I am now on my main work with the lord Lovell,
The gallant-minded, popular lord Lovell,
The minion of the people's love. I hear
He's come into the country, and my aims are
To insinuate myself into his knowledge,
And then invite him to my house.
 Mar. I have you ;
This points at my young mistress.
 Over. She must part with
That humble title, and write honourable,
Right honourable, Marrall, my right honourable daughter ;
If all I have, or e'er shall get, will do it.
I'll have her well attended ; there are ladies
Of errant knights decay'd, and brought so low,
That for cast clothes and meat will gladly serve her.
And 'tis my glory, though I come from the city,
To have their issue whom I have undone,
To kneel to mine as bondslaves.
 Mar. 'Tis fit state, sir.
 Over. And therefore, I'll not have a chambermaid
That ties her shoes, or any meaner office,
But such whose fathers were right worshipful.
'Tis a rich man's pride ! there having ever been
More than a feud, a strange antipathy,
Between us and true gentry.

Enter Wellborn.

 Mar. See, who's here, sir. -
 Over. Hence, monster ! prodigy !
 Well. Sir, your wife's nephew ,
She and my father tumbled in one belly.
 Over. Avoid my sight ! thy breath's infectious, rogue !
I shun thee as a leprosy, or the plague.—
Come hither, Marrall—this is the time to work him.   [*Aside, and exit.*
 Mar. I warrant you, sir.
 Well. By this light I think he's mad.
 Mar. Mad ! had you ta'en compassion on yourself,
You long since had been mad.
 Well. You have ta'en a course
Between you and my venerable uncle,
To make me so.
 Mar. The more pale-spirited you,

That would not be instructed. I swear deeply——
 Well. By what ?
 Mar. By my religion,
 Well. Thy religion !
The devil's creed :—but what would you have done?
 Mar. Had there been but one tree in all the shire,
Nor any hope to compass a penny halter,
Before, like you, I had outlived my fortunes,
A withe had served my turn to hang myself.
I am zealous in your cause ; pray you hang yourself,
And presently, as you love your credit.
 Well. I thank you.
 Mar. Will you stay till you die in a ditch, or lice devour you?——
Or, if you dare not do the feat yourself,
But that you'll put the state to charge and trouble,
Is there no purse to be cut, house to be broken,
Or market-woman with eggs, that you may murder,
And so dispatch the business?
 Well. Here's variety,
I must confess ; but I'll accept of none
Of all your gentle offers, I assure you.
 Mar. Why, have you hope ever to eat again,
Or drink? or be the master of three farthings?
If you like not hanging, drown yourself ; take some course
For your reputation.
 Well. 'Twill not do, dear tempter,
With all the rhetoric the fiend hath taught you.
I am as far as thou art from despair ;
Nay, I have confidence, which is more than hope,
To live, and suddenly, better than ever.
 Mar. Ha ! ha ! these castles you build in the air,
Will not persuade me or to give, or lend,
A token to you.
 Well. I'll be more kind to thee :
Come, thou shalt dine with me.
 Mar. With you !
 Well. Nay more, dine gratis.
 Mar. Under what hedge, I pray you? or at whose cost ?
Are they padders, or abram-men that are your consorts ?
 Well. Thou art incredulous ; but thou shalt dine,
Not alone at her house, but with a gallant lady ;
With me, and with a lady.

Well. I am satisfied: farewell, Tom.

All. All joy stay with you!   [*Exit.*

Re-enter Amble.

Amb. You are happily encounter'd; I yet
never
Presented one so welcome as, I know,
You will be to my lady.

Mar.   This is some vision;
Or, sure, these men are mad, to worship a
dunghill;
It cannot be a truth,

Well.   Be still a pagan,
An unbelieving infidel; be so, miscreant,
And mediate on blankets, and on dog-whips!

Re-enter Furnace.

Furn. I am glad you are come; until I
know your pleasure,
I knew not how to serve up my lady's dinner.

Mar. His pleasure! is it possible?

Well.   What's thy will?

Furn. Marry, sir, I have some browse,
and turkey chicken,
Some rails and quails, and my lady will'd
me ask you,
What kind of sauces best affect your palate,
That I may use my utmost skill to please it,

Mar. The devil's enter'd this cook: sauce
for his palate!
That, on my knowledge, for almost this
twelvemonth,
Durst wish but cheeseparings and brown
bread on Sundays.

Well. That way I like them best.   [*Aside.*

Furn. It shall be done, sir.   [*Exit.*

Well. What think you of the hedge we shall
dine under?
Shall we feed gratis?

Mar.   I know not what to think;
Pray you make me not mad.

Re-enter Order.

Ord. This place becomes you not;
Pray you walk, sir, to the dining room.

Well.   I am well here,
Till her ladyship quits her chamber.

Mar.   Well here, say you?
'Tis a rare change! but yesterday you
thought
Yourself well in a barn, wrapp'd up in
pease-straw.

*Re-enter Waiting Woman and Cham-
bermaid.*

Woman. O! sir, you are wish'd for.

Cham. My lady dream'd, sir, of you.

Woman. And the first command she gave,
after she rose.

Was, (her devotions done,) to give her notice
When you approach'd here.

Cham. Which is done, on my virtue.

Mar. I shall be converted; I begin to
grow
Into a new belief, which saints, nor angels,
Could have won me to have faith in.

Woman. Sir, my lady!

Enter Lady Allworth.

L. All. I come to meet you, and languish'd
till I saw you.
This first kiss is for form; I allow a second
To such a Wellborn.   [*Kisses Wellborn.*

Mar. To such a friend! heaven bless me!

Well. I am wholly yours; yet, madam,
if you please
To grace this gentleman with a salute—

Mar. Salute me at his bidding!

Well.   I shall receive it
As a most high favour.

L. All. Sir, you may command me.
  [*Advances to salute Marrall, who retires.*

Well. Run backward from a lady; and
such a lady!

Mar. To kiss her foot is, to poor me, a
favour
I am unworthy of.   [*Offers to kiss her foot.*

L. All. Nay, pray you rise;
And since you are so humble, I'll exalt you:
You shall dine with me to-day, at mine own
table.

Mar. Your ladyship's table! I am not
good enough
To sit at your steward's board.

L. All.   You are too modest;
I will not be denied.

Re-enter Furnace.

Furn. Will you still be babbling
Till your meat freeze on the table? the old
trick still;
My art ne'er thought on!

L. All.   Your arm, master Wellborn:—
Nay, keep us company.   [*To Marrall.*

Mar. I was ne'er so graced.
  [*Exeunt Wellborn, Lady Allworth,
Amble, Marrall, Waiting Woman,
and Chambermaid.*

Ord. So! we have play'd our parts, and
are come off well;
But if I know the mystery, why my lady
Consented to it, or why master Wellborn
Desired it, may I perish!

Furn.   Would I had
The roasting of his heart that cheated him,
And forces the poor gentleman to these
shifts!

Mar. Lady ! what lady ?
With the lady of the lake, or queen of
  fairies ?
For I know it must be an enchanted dinner.
  Well. With the lady Allworth, knave.
Mar. Nay, now there's hope
Thy brain is crack'd.
  Well. Mark there, with what respect
I am entertain'd.
  Mar. With choice, no doubt, of dog-
  whips.
Why, dost thou ever hope to pass her
  porter ?
  Well. 'Tis not far off, go with me ; trust
  thine own eyes.
Mar. Troth, in my hope, or my assurance
  rather,
To see thee curvet, and mount like a dog in
  a blanket,
If ever thou presume to pass her threshold,
I will endure thy company.
  Well. Come along then.   [*Exeunt.*

SCENE II.—*A Room in* Lady Allworth's
                House.

Enter Allworth, Waiting Woman, Chambermaid, Order, Amble, Furnace, *and*
  Watchall.

  Woman. Could you not command your
  leisure one hour longer ?
  Cham. Or half an hour ?
  All. I have told you what my haste is :
Besides, being now another's, not mine
  own,
Howe'er I much desire to enjoy you longer,
My duty suffers, if, to please myself,
I should neglect my lord.
  Woman. Pray you do me the favour
To put these few quince-cakes into your
  pocket ;
They are of mine own preserving.
· *Cham.* And this marmalade ;
'Tis comfortable for your stomach.
  Woman. And, at parting,
Excuse me if I beg a farewell from you.
  Cham. You are still before me. I move
  the same suit, sir.
          [Allworth *kisses them severally.*
  Furn. How greedy these chamberers are
  of a beardless chin !
I think the tits will ravish him.
  All. My service
To both.
  Woman. Ours waits on you.
  Cham. And shall do ever.
  Ord. You are my lady's charge, be there-
  fore careful
That you sustain your parts.

Woman. We can bear. I warrant yo
    [*Exeunt* Waiting Woman *and* Ch
        bermaid.
  Furn. Here, drink it off ; the ingredi
  are cordial,
And this the true elixir ; it hath boil'd
Since midnight for you. 'Tis the q
  essence
Of five cocks of the game, ten doze
  sparrows,
Knuckles of veal, potatoe-roots, and
  row,
Coral, and ambergris : were you two y
  older,
And I had a wife, or gamesome mistres
I durst trust you with neither : you need
  bait
After this, I warrant you, though
  journey's long ;
You may ride on the strength of this till
  morrow morning.
  All. Your courtesies overwhelm me
  much grieve
To part from such true friends ; and yet
  comfort,
My attendance on my honourable lord,
Whose resolution holds to visit my lady
Will speedily bring me back.
        [*Knocking within. Exit* Watc
  Mar. [*within.*] Dar'st thou venture
  ther ?
  Well. [*within.*] Yes, yes, and k
  again.
  Ord. 'Tis he ; disperse !
  Amb. Perform it bravely.
  Furn. I know my cue, ne'er doubt m
        [*Exeunt all but* Allwo

Re-enter Watchall, *ceremoniously intro
    ing* Wellborn *and* Marrall.

  Watch. Beast that I was, to make
  stay ! most welcome ;
You were long since expected.
  Well. Say so much
To my friend, I pray you.
  Watch. For your sake, I will, sir.
  Mar. For his sake !
  Well. Mum ; this is nothing.
  Mar. More than ever
I would have believed, though I had fo
  it in my primer.
  All. When I have given you reasons
  my late harshness,
You'll pardon and excuse me ; for, bel
  me,
Though now I part abruptly, in my serv
I will deserve it.
  Mar. Service ! with a vengeance !

By fire! for cooks are Persians, and swear
   by it,
Of all the griping and extorting tyrants
I ever heard or read of, I ne'er met
A match to sir Giles Overreach.
  Watch. What will you take
To tell him so, fellow Furnace ?
  Fur. Just as much
As my throat is worth, for that would be the
  price on't.
To have a usurer that starves himself,
And wears a cloak of one and twenty years
On a suit of fourteen groats, bought of the
  hangman,
To grow rich, and then purchase, is too
  common : ·
But this sir Giles feeds high, keeps many
  servants,
Who must at his command do any outrage ;
Rich in his habit, vast in his expenses ;
Yet he to admiration still increases
In wealth, and lordships.
  Ord. He frights men out of their estates,
And breaks through all law-nets, made to
  curb ill men,
As they were cobwebs. No man dares re-
  prove him.
Such a spirit to dare, and power to do, were
  never ·
Lodged so unluckily.

    Re-enter Amble *laughing.*

  Amb. Ha! ha! I shall burst.
  Ord. Contain thyself, man.
  Furn. Or make us partakers
Of your sudden mirth.
  Amb. Ha! ha! my lady has got
Such a guest at her table !—this term-driver,
  Marrall,
This snip of an attorney——
  Furn. What of him, man ?
  Amb. The knave thinks still he's at the
  cook's shop in Ram Alley,
Where the clerks divide, and the elder is to
  choose;
And feeds so slovenly! ·
  Furn. Is this all?
  Amb. My lady
Drank to him for fashion sake, or to please
  master Wellborn ;
As I live, he rises, and takes up a dish
In which there were some remnants of a
  boil'd capon,
And pledges her in white broth!
  Furn. Nay, 'tis like
The rest of his tribe.
  Amb. And when I brought him wine,
He leaves his stool, and, after a leg or two,
Most humbly thanks my worship.

  Ord. Risen already !
  Amb. I shall be chid.

  Re-enter Lady Allworth, Wellborn, *and*
    Marrall.

  Furn. My lady frowns.
  L.. All. You wait well!   [*To* Amble.
Let me have no more of this ; I observed
  your jeering :
Sirrah, I'll have you know, whom I think
  worthy
To sit at my table, be he ne'er so mean,
When I am present, is not your companion.
  Ord. Nay, she'll preserve what's due to
  her.
  Furn. This refreshing
Follows your flux of laughter.
  L. All. [*To* Wellborn.] You are master
Of your own will. I know so much of
  manners,
As not to inquire your purposes ; in a word,
To me you are ever welcome, as to a house
That is your own.
  Well. Mark that.   [*Aside to* Marrall.
  Mar. With reverence, sir,
An it like your worship.
  Well. Trouble yourself no further,
Dear madam ; my heart's full of zeal and
  service,
However, in my language I am sparing.
Come, master Marrall.
  Mar. I attend your worship.
    [*Exeunt* Wellborn *and* Marrall.
  L. All. I see in your looks you are sorry,
  and you know me
An easy mistress : be merry; I have forgot all.
Order and Furnace, come with me ; I must
  give you
Further directions.
  Ord. What you please.   ·
  Furn. We are ready.   [*Exeunt.*

SCENE III.—*The Country near* Lady
    Allworth's *House.*

Enter Wellborn, *and* Marrall *bare-headed.*

  Well. I think I am in a good way.
  Mar. Good ! sir ; the best way,
The certain best way.
  Well. There are casualties
That men are subject to.
  Mar. You are above them ;
And as you are already worshipful,
I hope ere long you will increase in worship,
And be, right worshipful.
  Well. Prithee do not flout me :
What I shall be, I shall be. Is't for your
  ease,
You keep your hat off?

Mar. Ease! an it like your worship!
I hope Jack Marrall shall not live so long,
To prove himself such an unmannerly beast,
Though it hail hazel-nuts, as to be cover'd
When your worship's present.

Well. Is not this a true rogue,
That, out of mere hope of a future cozenage,
Can turn thus suddenly? 'tis rank already.
                                        [Aside.

Mar. I know your worship's wise, and
    needs no counsel :
Yet if, in my desire to do you service,
I humbly offer my advice, (but still
Under correction,) I hope I shall not
Incur your high displeasure.

Well. No; speak freely.

Mar. Then, in my judgment, sir, my
    simple judgment,
(Still with your worship's favour,) I could
    wish you
A better habit, for this cannot be
But much distasteful to the noble lady,
(I say no more) that loves you : for, this
    morning,
To me, and I am but a swine to her,
Before the assurance of her wealth perfumed
    you,
You savour'd not of amber.

Well. I do now then !

Mar. This your batoon hath got a touch of
    it.——   *[Kisses the end of his cudgel.*
Yet, if you please, for change, I have twenty
    pounds here,
Which, out of my true love, I'll presently
Lay down at your worship's feet ; 'twill serve
    to buy you
A riding suit.

Well. But where's the horse?

Mar. My gelding
Is at your service : nay, you shall ride me,
Before your worship shall be put to the
    trouble
To walk afoot.   Alas ! when you are lord
Of this lady's manor, as I know you will be,
You may with the lease of glebe land, call'd
    Knave's-acre,
A place I would manure, requite your vassal.

Well. I thank thy love, but must make no
    use of it ;
What's twenty pounds?

Mar. 'Tis all that I can make, sir.

Well. Dost thou think, though I want
    clothes, I could not have them,
For one word to my lady?

Mar. As I know not that !

Well. Come, I will tell thee a secret, and
    so leave thee.
I will not give her the advantage, though
    she be

A gallant-minded lady, after we are married,
(There being no woman, but is sometimes
    froward,)
To hit me in the teeth, and say, she was
    forced
To buy my wedding-clothes, and took me on,
With a plain riding-suit, and an ambling nag,
No, I'll be furnish'd something like myself,
And so farewell : for thy suit touching
    Knave's-acre,
When it is mine, 'tis thine.   *[Exit.*

Mar. I thank your worship.
How was I cozen'd in the calculation
Of this man's fortune ! my master cozen'd too,
Whose pupil I am in the art of undoing men ;
For that is our profession ! · Well, well, master
    Wellborn,
You are of a sweet nature, and fit again to
    be cheated :
Which, if the Fates please, when you are
    possess'd
Of the land and lady, you, sans question,
    shall be.
I'll presently think of the means.
                            [Walks by musing.

Enter Overreach, *speaking to a servant*
                  within.

Over. Sirrah, take my horse.
I'll walk to get me an appetite ; 'tis but a
    mile,
And exercise will keep me from being pursey.
Ha ! Marrall ! is he conjuring? perhaps
The knave has wrought the prodigal to do
Some outrage on himself, and now he feels
Compunction in his conscience for't : no
    matter,
So it be done.   Marrall !

Mar. Sir.

Over. How succeed we
In our plot on Wellborn ?

Mar. Never better, sir.

Over. Has he hang'd or drown'd himself?

Mar. No, sir, he lives ;
Lives once more to be made a prey to you,
A greater prey than ever.

Over. Art thou in thy wits ?
If thou art, reveal this miracle, and briefly.

Mar. A lady, sir, is fall'n in love with
    him.

Over. With him? what lady?

Mar. The rich lady Allworth.

Over. Thou dolt ! how dar'st thou speak
    this ?

Mar. I speak truth.
And I do so but once a year, unless
It be to you, sir : we dined with her ladyship,
I thank his worship.

Over. His worship !

Mar. As I live, sir,
I dined with him, at the great lady's table,
Simple as I stand here ; and saw when she
    kiss'd him,
And would, at his request, have kiss'd me
    too ;
But I was not so audacious as some youths
    are,
That dare do anything, be it ne'er so absurd,
And sad after performance.
    Over. Why, thou rascal !
To tell me these impossibilities.
Dine at her table ! and kiss him ! or
    thee !——
Impudent varlet, have not I myself,
To whom great countesses' doors have oft
    flew open,   .
Ten times attempted, since her husband's
    death,
In vain, to see her, though I came—a suitor?
And yet your good solicitorship, and rogue
    Wellborn,
Were brought into her presence, feasted
    with her !——
But that I know thee a dog that cannot
    blush,
This most incredible lie would call up one,
On thy buttermilk cheeks.
    Mar. Shall I not trust my eyes, sir,
Or taste ? I feel her good cheer in my belly.
    Over. You shall feel me, if you give not
over, sirrah :
Recover your brains again, and be no more
    gull'd
With a beggar's plot, assisted by the aids
Of serving-men and chambermaids, for
    beyond these
Thou never saw'st a woman, or I'll quit you
From my employments.
    Mar. Will you credit this yet ?
On my confidence of their marriage, I offer'd
    Wellborn——
I would give a crown now I durst say his
    worship——   [*Aside.*
My nag, and twenty pounds.
    Over. Did you so, ideot !
        [*Strikes him down.*
Was this the way to work him to despair,
Or rather to cross me?
    Mar. Will your worship kill me?
    Over. No, no ; but drive the lying spirit
out of you.
    Mar. He's gone.
    Over. I have done then : now, forgetting
Your late imaginary feast and lady,
Know, my lord Lovell dines with me to-
    morrow.
Be careful nought be wanting to receive him ;
And bid my daughter's women trim her up,

Though they paint her, so she catch the
    lord, I'll thank them :
There's a piece for my late blows.
    Mar. I must yet suffer :
But there may be a time——   [*Aside.*
    Over. Do you grumble?
    Mar. No, sir.   [*Exeunt.*
        ———

ACT III.

SCENE I.—*The Country near* Overreach's
    House.
Enter Lord Lovell, Allworth, *and* Servants.

    Lov. Walk the horses down the hill :
    something in private
I must impart to Allworth.
        [*Exeunt* Servants.
    All. O, my lord,
What sacrifice of reverence, duty, watching,
Although I could put off the use of sleep,
And ever wait on your commands to serve
    them ;
What dangers, though in ne'er so horrid
    shapes,
Nay death itself, though I should run to
    meet it,
Can I, and with a thankful willingness
    suffer ;
But still the retribution will fall short
Of your bounties shower'd upon me ?
    Lov. Loving youth ;
Till what I purpose be put into act,
Do not o'erprize it ; since you have trusted me
With your soul's nearest, nay, her dearest
    secret,
Rest confident 'tis in a cabinet lock'd
Treachery shall never open. I have found
    you
(For so much to your face I must profess,
Howe'er you guard your modesty with a
    blush for't)
More zealous in your love and service to me,
Than I have been in my rewards.
    All. Still great ones,
Above my merit.
    Lov. Such your gratitude calls them :
Nor am I of that harsh and rugged temper
As some great men are taxed with, who
    imagine
They part from the respect due to their
    honours,
If they use not all such as follow them,
Without distinction of their births, like
    slaves.
I am not so condition'd : I can make
A fitting difference between my footboy,
And a gentleman by want compell'd to serve
    me.

        D D

All. 'Tis thankfully acknowledged ; you have been
More like a father to me than a master :
Pray you, pardon the comparison.

Lov. I allow it ;
And to give you assurance I am pleased in't,
My carriage and demeanour to your mistress,
Fair Margaret, shall truly witness for me,
I can command my passions.

All. 'Tis a conquest
Few lords can boast of when they are tempted
—Oh !

Lov. Why do you sigh? can you be doubtful of me?
By that fair name I in the wars have purchased,
And all my actions, hitherto untainted,
I will not be more true to mine own honour,
Than to my Allworth !

All. As you are the brave lord Lovell,
Your bare word only given is an assurance
Of more validity and weight to me,
Than all the oaths, bound up with imprecations,
Which, when they would deceive, most courtiers practise :
Yet being a man, (for, sure, to style you more
Would relish of gross flattery,) I am forced,
Against my confidence of your worth and virtues,
To doubt, nay more, to fear.

Lov. So young, and jealous !

All. Were you to encounter with a single foe,
The victory were certain ; but to stand
The charge of two such potent enemies,
At once assaulting you, as wealth and beauty,
And those too seconded with power, is odds
Too great for Hercules.

Lov. Speak your doubts and fears,
Since you will nourish them, in plainer language,
That I may understand them.

All. What's your will,
Though I lend arms against myself, (provided
They may advantage you,) must be obey'd.
My much-loved lord, were Margaret only fair,
The cannon of her more than earthly form,
Though mounted high, commanding all beneath it,
And ramm'd with bullets of her sparkling eyes,
Of all the bulwarks that defend your senses
Could batter none, but that which guards your sight.

But when the well-tuned accents of her tongue
Make music to you, and with numerous sounds
Assault your hearing, (such as Ulysses, if [he]
Now lived again, howe'er he stood the Syrens,
Could not resist,) the combat must grow doubtful
Between your reason and rebellious passions.
Add this too ; when you feel her touch, and breath
Like a soft western wind, when it glides o'er
Arabia, creating gums and spices ;
And in the van, the nectar of her lips,
Which you must taste, bring the battalia on,
Well arm'd, and strongly lined with her discourse,
And knowing manners, to give entertainment ;—
Hippolytus himself would leave Diana,
To follow such a Venus.

Lov. Love hath made you
Poetical, Allworth.

All. Grant all these beat off,
Which if it be in man to do, you'll do it,
Mammon, in Sir Giles Overreach, steps in
With heaps of ill-got gold, and so much land,
To make her more remarkable, as would tire
A falcon's wings in one day to fly over.
O my good lord ! these powerful aids, which would
Make a mis-shapen negro beautiful,
(Yet are but ornaments to give her lustre,
That in herself is all perfection,) must
Prevail for her : I here release your trust ;
'Tis happiness, enough, for me to serve you,
And sometimes, with chaste eyes, to look upon her.

Lov. Why, shall I swear?

All. O, by no means, my lord ;
And wrong not so your judgment to the world,
As from your fond indulgence to a boy,
Your page, your servant, to refuse a blessing
Divers great men are rivals for.

Lov. Suspend
Your judgment till the trial. How far is it
To Overreach' house?

All. At the most, some half hour's riding ;
You'll soon be there.

Lov. And you the sooner freed
From your jealous fears.

All. O that I durst but hope it.

[*Exeunt.*

SCENE II.—*A Room in* Overreach's
House.

Enter Overreach, Greedy, *and* Marrall.

Over. Spare for no cost; let my dressers
crack with the weight
Of curious viands.
Greedy. *Store indeed's no sore,* sir.
Over. That proverb fits your stomach,
master Greedy.
And let no plate be seen but what's pure
gold,
Or such whose workmanship exceeds the
matter
That it is made of; let my choicest linen
Perfume the room, and, when we wash, the
water,
With precious powders mix'd, so please my
lord,
That he may with envy wish to bathe so ever.
Mar. 'Twill be very chargeable.
Over. Avaunt, you drudge!
Now all my labour'd ends are at the stake,
Is't a time to think of thrift? Call in my
daughter.   [*Exit* Marrall.
And, master justice, since you love choice
dishes,
And plenty of them——
Greedy. As I do, indeed, sir,
Almost as much as to give thanks for them.
Over. I do confer that providence, with
my power
Of absolute command to have abundance,
To your best care.
Greedy. I'll punctually discharge it,
And give the best directions. Now am I,
In mine own conceit, a monarch; at the
least,
Arch-president of the boil'd, the roast, the
baked,
For which I will eat often; and give thanks
When my belly's braced up like a drum, and
that's pure justice.   [*Exit.*
Over. It must be so: should the foolish
girl prove modest,
She may spoil all; she had it not from me,
But from her mother; I was ever forward,
As she must be, and therefore I'll prepare
her.

Enter Margaret.

Alone—and let your women wait without.
Marg. Your pleasure, sir?
Over. Ha! this is a neat dressing!
These orient pearls and diamonds well placed
too!
The gown affects me not, it should have been
Embroider'd o'er and o'er with flowers of
gold;

But these rich jewels, and quaint fashion
help it.
And how below? since oft the wanton eye,
The face observed, descends unto the foot,
Which being well proportion'd, as yours is,
Invites as much as perfect white and red,
Though without art. How like you your
new woman,
The lady Downfallen?
Marg. Well, for a companion;
Not as a servant.
Over. Is she humble, Meg,
And careful too, her ladyship forgotten?
Marg. I pity her fortune.
Over. Pity her! trample on her.
I took her up in an old tamin gown,
(Even starv'd for want of twopenny chops,)
to serve thee,
And if I understand she but repines
To do thee any duty, though ne'er so servile,
I'll pack her to her knight, where I have
lodged him,
Into the counter, and there let them howl
together.
Marg. You know your own ways; but
for me, I blush
When I command her, that was once attended
With persons not inferior to myself,
In birth.
Over. In birth! why, art thou not my
daughter,
The blest child of my industry and wealth?
Why, foolish girl, was't not to make thee
great,
That I have run, and still pursue, those ways
That hale down curses on me, which I mind
not!
Part with these humble thoughts, and apt
thyself
To the noble state I labour to advance thee;
Or, by my hopes, to see thee honourable,
I will adopt a stranger to my heir,
And throw thee from my care: do not pro-
voke me.
Marg. I will not, sir; mould me which
way you please.

Re-enter Greedy.

Over. How! interrupted!
Greedy. 'Tis matter of importance.
The cook, sir, is self-will'd, and will not
learn
From my experience: there's a fawn brought
in, sir,
And, for my life, I cannot make him roast it
With a Norfolk dumpling in the belly of it;
And, sir, we wise men know, without the
dumpling
'Tis not worth three-pence.

D D 2

Over. Would it were whole in thy belly,
To stuff it out! cook it any way ; prithee,
   leave me.
Greedy. Without order for the dumpling?
Over. Let it be dumpled
Which way thou wilt ; or tell him, I will
   scald him
In his own caldron.
Greedy. I had lost my stomach
Had I lost my mistress dumpling ; I'll give
   thanks for't.   [*Exit.*
Over. But to our business, Meg; you have
   heard who dines here ?
Marg. I have, sir.
Over. 'Tis an honourable man ;
A lord, Meg, and commands a regiment
Of soldiers, and, what's rare, is one himself,
A bold and understanding one : and to be
A lord, and a good leader, in one volume,
Is granted unto few but such as rise up
The kingdom's glory.

Re-enter Greedy.

Greedy. I'll resign my office,
If I be not better obey'd.
Over. 'Slight, art thou frantic?
Greedy. Frantic! 'twould make me frantic,
   and stark mad,
Were I not a justice of peace and quorum too,
Which this rebellious cook cares not a straw
   for.
There are a dozen of woodcocks——
Over. Make thyself
Thirteen, the baker's dozen.
Greedy. I am contented,
So they may be dress'd to my mind ; he has
   found out
A new device for sauce, and will not dish
   them
With toasts and butter ; my father was a
   tailor,
And my name, though a justice, Greedy
   Woodcock ;
And, ere I'll see my lineage so abused,
I'll give up my commission.
Over. [*aloud.*] Cook!—Rogue, obey him!
I have given the word, pray you now remove
   yourself
To a collar of brawn, and trouble me no
   further.
Greedy. I will, and meditate what to eat
   at dinner.   [*Exit.*
Over. And as I said, Meg, when this gull
   disturb'd us,
This honourable lord, this colonel,
I would have thy husband.
Marg. There's too much disparity
Between his quality and mine, to hope it.

Over. I more than hope, and doubt not to
   effect it,
Be thou no enemy to thyself; my wealth
Shall weigh his titles down, and make you
   equals.
Now for the means to assure him thine, ob-
   serve me ;
Remember he's a courtier, and a soldier,
And not to be trifled with ; and, therefore,
   when
He comes to woo you, see you do not coy it :
This mincing modesty has spoil'd many a
   match
By a first refusal, in vain after hoped for.
Marg. You'll have me, sir, preserve the
   distance that
Confines a virgin?
Over. Virgin me no virgins ?
I must have you lose that name, or you lose
   me.
I will have you private—start not—I say,
   private ;
If thou art my true daughter, not a bastard,
Thou wilt venture alone with one man,
   though he came
Like Jupiter to Semele, and come off, too ;
And therefore, when he kisses you, kiss
   close.
Marg. I have heard this is the strumpet's
   fashion, sir,
Which I must never learn.
Over. Learn any thing,
And from any creature that may make thee
   great ;
From the devil himself.
Marg. This is but devilish doctrine !
          [*Aside.*
Over. Or, if his blood grow hot, suppose
   he offer
Beyond this, do not you stay till it cool,
But meet his ardour ; if a couch be near,
Sit down on't, and invite him.
Marg. In your house,
Your own house, sir ! for heaven's sake,
   what are you then ?
Or what shall I be, sir?
Over. Stand not on form ;
Words are no substances.
Marg. Though you could dispense
With your own honour, cast aside religion,
The hopes of heaven, or fear of hell ; excuse
   me,
In worldly policy, this is not the way
To make me his wife ; his whore, I grant it
   may do.
My maiden honour so soon yielded up,
Nay, prostituted, cannot but assure him
I, that am light to him, will not hold
   weight

Whene'er tempted by others; so, in judg-
ment,
When to his lust I have given up my
bonour,
He must and will forsake me.
  Over. How! forsake thee!
Do I wear a sword for fashion? or is this arm
Shrunk up, or wither'd? does there live a
man
Of that large list I have encounter'd with
Can truly say I e'er gave inch of ground
Nor purchased with his blood that did
oppose me?
Forsake thee when the thing is done! he
dares not.
Give me but proof he has enjoyed thy person,
Though all his captains, echoes to his will,
Stood arm'd by his side to justify the wrong,
And he himself in the head of his bold troop,
Spite of his lordship, and his colonelship,
Or the judge's favour, I will make him render
A bloody and a strict accompt, and force
him,
By marrying thee, to cure thy wounded
honour!
I have said it.

    Re-enter Marrall.   .

  Mar. Sir, the man of honour's come,
Newly alighted.
  Over. In, without reply;
And do as I command, or thou art lost.
                    [*Exit* Margaret.
Is the loud music I gave order for
Ready to receive him?
  Mar. 'Tis, sir.
  Over. Let them sound
A princely welcome. [*Exit* Marrall.] Rough-
ness awhile leave me;
For fawning now, a stranger to my nature,
Must make way for me.

Loud music. *Enter* Lord Lovell, Greedy,
Allworth, *and* Marrall.

  Lov. Sir, you meet your trouble.
  Over. What you are pleased to style so,
is an honour
Above my worth and fortunes.
  All. Strange, so humble.   [*Aside.*
  Over. A justice of peace, my lord.
           [*Presents* Greedy *to him.*
  Lov. Your hand, good sir.
  Greedy. This is a lord, and some think
this a favour;
But I had rather have my hand in my dump-
ling.   [*Aside.*
  Over. Room for my lord.
  Lov. I miss, sir, your fair daughter
To crown my welcome.

  Over. May it please my lord   -
To taste a glass of Greek wine first, and
suddenly
She shall attend my lord.
  Lov. You'll be obey'd, sir.
             [*Exeunt all but* Overreach.
  Over. 'Tis to my wish: as soon as come,
ask for her!
Why, Meg! Meg Overreach.—

    Re-enter Margaret.

           How! tears in your eyes!
Hah! dry them quickly, or I'll dig them out.
Is this a time to whimper? meet that great-
ness
That flies into thy bosom, think what 'tis
For me to say, My honourable daughter;
And thou, when I stand bare, to say, Put on;
Or, Father, you forget yourself. No more,
But be instructed, or expect——he comes.

  Re-enter Lord Lovell, Greedy, Allworth,
              and Marrall.

A black-brow'd girl, my lord.
       [Lord Lovell *salutes* Margaret.
  Lov. As I live, a rare one.
  All. He's ta'en already: I am lost.
                   [*Aside.*
  Over. That kiss
Came twanging off, I like it; quit the room.
      [*Exeunt all but* Over. Lov. *and* Marg.
A little bashful, my good lord, but you,
I hope, will teach her boldness.
  Lov. I am happy
In such a scholar: but——
  Over. I am past learning,
And therefore leave you to yourselves:—
remember.
        [*Aside to* Margaret, *and exit.*
  Lov. You see, fair lady, your father is
solicitous,
To have you change the barren name of
virgin
Into a hopeful wife.
  Marg. His haste, my lord,
Holds no power o'er my will.
  Lov. But o'er your duty.
  Marg. Which forced too much, may
break.
  Lov. Bend rather, sweetest:
Think of your years.
  Marg. Too few to match with yours:
And choicest fruits too soon plucked, rot
and wither.
  Lov. Do you think I am old?
  Marg. I am sure I am too young.
  Lov. I can advance you.
  Marg. To a hill of sorrow;
Where every hour I may expect to fall,

But never hope firm footing. You are noble,
I of a low descent, however rich;
And tissues match'd with scarlet suit but ill.
O, my good lord, I could say more, but that
I dare not trust these walls.
 Lov. Pray you, trust my ear then.

  Re-enter Overreach *behind, listening.*

 Over. Close at it! whispering! this is excellent!
And, by their postures, a consent on both
 parts.

   Re-enter Greedy *behind.*

 Greedy. Sir Giles, Sir Giles!
 Over. The great fiend stop that clapper!
 Greedy. It must ring out, sir, when my
belly rings noon.
The baked-meats are run out, the roast turn'd
powder.
 Over. I shall powder you.
 Greedy. Beat me to dust, I care not;
In such a cause as this, I'll die a martyr.
 Over. Marry, and shall, you barathrum of
 the shambles!   [*Strikes him.*
 Greedy. How! strike a justice of peace!
 'tis petty treason,
Edwardi quinto: but that you are my friend,
I would commit you without bail or main-
 prize.
 Over. Leave your bawling, sir, or I shall
commit you
Where you shall not dine to-day : disturb my
 lord,
When he is in discourse!
 Greedy. Is't a time to talk
When we should be munching?
 Lov. Hah! I heard some noise.
 Over. Mum, villain; vanish! shall we
 break a bargain
Almost made up?   [*Thrusts* Greedy *off.*
 Lov. Lady, I understand you,
And rest most happy in your choice, believe
 it;
I'll be a careful pilot to direct
Your yet uncertain bark to a port of safety.
 Marg. So shall your honour save two lives,
 and bind us
Your slaves for ever.
 Lov. I am in the act rewarded,
Since it is good; howe'er, you must put on
An amorous carriage towards me to delude
Your subtle father
 Marg. I am prone to that.
 Lov. Now break we off our conference.—
 Sir Giles!
Where is Sir Giles?
   [Overreach *comes forward.*

  Re-enter Allworth, Marrall, *and* Greedy.

 Over. My noble lord; and how
Does your lordship find her?
 Lov. Apt, Sir Giles, and coming;
And I like her the better.
 Over. So do I too.
 Lov. Yet should we take forts at the first
 assault,
'Twere poor in the defendant; I must con-
 firm her
With a love-letter or two, which I must have
Deliver'd by my page, and you give way to't.
 Over. With all my soul :—a towardly
 gentleman!
Your hand, good master Allworth; know
 my house
Is ever open to you.
 All. 'Twas shut till now.   [*Aside.*
 Over. Well done, well done, my honour-
 able daughter!
Thou'rt so already : know this gentle youth,
And cherish him, my honourable daughter.
 Marg. I shall, with my best care.
  [*Noise within, as of a coach.*
 Over. A coach!
 Greedy. More stops
Before we go to dinner! O my guts!

  Enter Lady Allworth *and* Wellborn.

 L. All. If I find welcome,
You share in it; if not, I'll back again,
Now I know your ends; for I come arm'd
 for all
Can be objected.
 Lov. How! the lady Allworth!
 Over. And thus attended!
  [Lovell *salutes* Lady Allworth, Lady
  Allworth *salutes* Margaret.
 Mar. No, *I am a dolt!*
The spirit of lies hath enter'd me!
 Over. Peace, Patch;
'Tis more than wonder! an astonishment
That does possess me wholly!
 Lov. Noble lady,
This is a favour, to prevent my visit,
The service of my life can never equal.
 L. All. My lord, I laid wait for you, and
 much hoped
You would have made my poor house your
 first inn :
And therefore doubting that you might
 forget me,
Or too long dwell here, having such ample
 cause,
In this unequall'd beauty, for your stay;
And fearing to trust any but myself
With the relation of my service to you,·

I borrow'd so much from my long restraint,
And took the air in person to invite you.
   Lov. Your bounties are so great, they
    rob me, madam,
Of words to give you thanks.
   L. All. Good sir Giles Overreach.
                    [*Salutes him.*
—How dost thou, Marrall? liked you my
    meat so ill,
You'll dine no more with me?
   Greedy. I will, when you please,
An it like your ladyship.
   L. All. When you please, master Greedy;
If meat can do it, you shall be satisfied.
And now, my lord, pray take into your
    knowledge
This gentleman; howe'er his outside's coarse,
               [*Presents* Wellborn.
His inward linings are as fine and fair
As any man's; wonder not I speak at large:
And howsoe'er his humour carries him
To be thus accoutred, or what taint so-
    ever,
For his wild life, hath stuck upon his fame,
He may, ere long, with boldness, rank him-
    self
With some that have contemn'd him. Sir
    Giles Overreach,
If I am welcome, bid him so.
   Over. My nephew!
He has been too long a stranger: faith you
    have,
Pray let it be mended.
       [Lovell *confers aside with* Wellborn.
   Mar. Why, sir, what do you mean?
This is *rogue* Wellborn, *monster, prodigy,*
That should hang or drown himself; no
    man of worship,
Much less your nephew.
   Over. Well, sirrah, we shall reckon
For this hereafter.
   Mar. I'll not lose my jeer,
Though I be beaten dead for't.
   Well. Let my silence plead
In my excuse, my lord, till better leisure
Offer itself to hear a full relation
Of my poor fortunes.
   Lov. I would hear, and help them.
   Over. Your dinner waits you.
   Lov. Pray you lead, we follow.
   L. All. Nay, you are my guest; come,
    dear master Wellborn.
            [*Exeunt all but* Greedy.
   Greedy. Dear Master Wellborn! So she
    said: heaven! heaven!
If my belly would give me leave, I could
    ruminate
All day on this: I have granted twenty
    warrants

To have him committed, from all prisons in
    the shire,
To Nottingham gaol; and now, *Dear*
    Master Wellborn!
And, *My good nephew!*—but I play the fool
To stand here prating, and forget my dinner.

         Re-enter Marrall.

Are they set, Marrall?
   Mar. Long since; pray you a word, sir.
   Greedy. No wording now.
   Mar. In troth, I must; my master,
Knowing you are his good friend, makes
    bold with you,
And does entreat you, more guests being
    come in
Than he expected, especially his nephew,
The table being full too, you would excuse
    him,
And sup with him on the cold meat.
   Greedy. How! no dinner,
After all my care?
   Mar. 'Tis but a penance for
A meal; besides, you broke your fast.
   Greedy. That was
But a bit to stay my stomach: a man in com-
    mission,
Give place to a tatterdemalion!
   Mar. No bug words, sir;
Should his worship hear you——
   Greedy. Lose my dumpling too,
And butter'd toasts, and woodcocks!
   Mar. Come, have patience.
If you will dispense a little with your worship,
And sit with the waiting women, you'll have
    dumpling,
Woodcock, and butter'd toasts too.
   Greedy. This revives me:
I will gorge there sufficiently.
   Mar. This is the way, sir.   [*Exeunt.*

   SCENE III.—*Another Room in* Over-
      reach's *House.*

    Enter Overreach, *as from dinner.*

   Over. She's caught! O women!—she
    neglects my lord,
And all her compliments applied to Well-
    born!
The garments of her widowhood laid by,
She now appears as glorious as the spring.
Her eyes fix'd on him, in the wine she drinks,
He being her pledge, she sends him burn-
    ing kisses,
And sits on thorns, till she be private with
    him.
She leaves my meat, to feed upon his looks:
And if in our discourse he be but named,
From her a deep sigh follows. But why
    grieve I

At this! it makes for me ; if she prove his,
All that is hers is mine, as I will work him.

Enter Marrall.

Mar. Sir, the whole board is troubled at
your rising.

Over. No matter, I'll excuse it : prithee,
Marrall,
Watch an occasion to invite my nephew
To speak with me in private.

Mar. Who! the *rogue*
The lady scorn'd to look on ?

Over. You are a wag.

Enter Lady Allworth *and* Wellborn.

Mar. See, sir, she's come, and cannot be
without him.

L. All. With your favour, sir, after a
plenteous dinner,
I shall make bold to walk a turn or two,
In your rare garden.

Over. There's an arbour too,
If your ladyship please to use it.

L. All. Come, master Wellborn.

[*Exeunt* Lady Allworth *and* Wellborn.

Over. Grosser and grósser ! now I believe
the poet
Feign'd not, but was historical, when he
wrote
Pasiphaë was enamour'd of a bull :
This lady's lust's more monstrous.—My
good lord,

Enter Lord Lovell, Margaret, *and the rest.*

Excuse my manners.

Lov. There needs none, sir Giles,
I may ere long say Father, when it pleases
My dearest mistress to give warrant to it.

Over. She shall seal to it, my lord, and
make me happy.

Re-enter Wellborn *and* Lady Allworth.

Marg. My lady is return'd.

L. All. Provide my coach,
I'll instantly away; my thanks, sir Giles,
For my entertainment.

Over. 'Tis your nobleness
To think it such.

L. All. I must do you a further wrong,
In taking away your honourable guest.

Lov. I wait on you, madam ; farewell,
good sir Giles.

L. All. Good mistress Margaret ! nay,
come, master Wellborn,
I must not leave you behind ; in sooth, I
must not.

Over. Rob me not, madam, of all joys at
once ;

Let my nephew stay behind : he shall have
my coach,
And, after some small conference between us,
Soon overtake your ladyship.

L. All. Stay not long, sir.

Lov. This parting kiss : [*Kisses* Margaret.]
you shall every day hear from me,
By my faithful page.

All. 'Tis a service I am proud of.
[*Exeunt* Lord Lovell, Lady Allworth,
Allworth, *and* Marrall.

Over. Daughter, to your chamber.—[*Exit*
Margaret.]—You may wonder, nephew,
After so long an enmity between us,
I should desire your friendship.

Well. So I do, sir ;
'Tis strange to me.

Over. But I'll make it no wonder ;
And what is more, unfold my nature to you.
We worldly men, when we see friends, and
kinsmen,
Past hope sunk in their fortunes, lend no
hand
To lift them up, but rather set our feet
Upon their heads, to press them to the
bottom ;
As, I must yield, with you I practised it :
But, now I see you in a way to rise,
I can and will assist you ; this rich lady
(And I am glad of 't) is enamour'd of you ;
'Tis too apparent, nephew.

Well. No such thing :
Compassion rather, sir.

Over. Well, in a word,
Because your stay is short, I'll have you
seen
No more in this base shape ; nor shall she
say,
She married you like a beggar, or in debt.

Well. He'll run into the noose, and save
my labour.   [*Aside.*

Over. You have a trunk of rich clothes,
not far hence,
In pawn ; I will redeem them ; and that no
clamour
May taint your credit for your petty debts,
You shall have a thousand pounds to cut
them off,
And go a free man to the wealthy lady.

Well. This done, sir, out of love, and no
ends else——

Over. As it is, nephew.

Well. Binds me still your servant.

Over. No compliments, you are staid for :
ere you have supp'd
You shall hear from me. My coach, knaves,
for my nephew.
To-morrow I will visit you.

Well. Here's an uncle

In a man's extremes! how much they do
  belie you,
That say you are hard-hearted !
  Over. My deeds, nephew,
Shall speak my love ; what men report I
  weigh not. [*Exeunt.*

ACT IV.

SCENE I.—*A Room in* Lady Allworth's
  House.

Enter Lord Lovell *and* Allworth.

  Lov. 'Tis well ; give me my cloak ; I now
  discharge you
From further service : mind your own affairs,
I hope they will prove successful.
  All. What is blest
With your good wish, my lord, cannot but
  prosper.
Let aftertimes report, and to your honour,
How much I stand engaged, for I want lan-
  guage
To speak my debt ; yet if a tear or two
Of joy, for your much goodness, can supply
My tongue's defects, I could——
  Lov. Nay, do not melt :
This ceremonial thanks to me's superfluous.
  Over. [*within.*] Is my lord stirring ?
  Lov. 'Tis he ! oh, here's your letter : let
  him in.

Enter Overreach, Greedy, *and* Marrall.

  Over. A good day to my lord !
  Lov. You are an early riser,
Sir Giles.
  Over. And reason, to attend your lordship.
  Lov. And you, too, master Greedy, up so
  soon !
  Greedy. In troth, my lord, after the sun
  is up,
I cannot sleep, for I have a foolish stomach
That croaks for breakfast. With your lord-
  ship's favour,
I have a serious question to demand
Of my worthy friend sir Giles.
  Lov. Pray you use your pleasure.
  Greedy. How far, sir Giles, and pray you
  answer me
Upon your credit, hold you it to be
From your manor-house, to this of my lady
  Allworth's ?
  Over. Why, some four mile.
  Greedy. How ! four mile, good sir
  Giles——
Upon your reputation, think better ;
For if you do abate but one half-quarter
Of five, you do yourself the greatest wrong

That can be in the world ; for four miles
  riding,
Could not have raised so huge an appetite
As I feel gnawing on me.
  Mar. Whether you ride,
Or go afoot, you are that way still provided,
An it please your worship.
  Over. How now, sirrah ? prating
Before my lord ! no difference ! Go to my
  nephew,
See all his debts discharged, and help his
  worship
To fit on his rich suit.
  Mar. I may fit you too.
Toss'd like a dog still ! [*Aside, and exit.*
  Lov. I have writ this morning
A few lines to my mistress, your fair
  daughter.
  Over. 'Twill fire her, for she's wholly
  yours already :—
Sweet master Allworth, take my ring ; 'twill
  carry you
To her presence, I dare warrant you ; and
  there plead
For my good lord, if you shall find occasion.
That done, pray ride to Nottingham, get a
  license,
Still by this token. I'll have it dispatch'd,
And suddenly, my lord, that I may say,
My honourable, nay, right honourable
  daughter.
  Greedy. Take my advice, young gentle-
  man, get your breakfast ;
'Tis unwholesome to ride fasting : I'll eat
  with you,
And eat to purpose.
  Over. Some Fury's in that gut :
Hungry again ! did you not devour, this
  morning,
A shield of brawn, and a barrel of Colches-
  ter oysters ?
  Greedy. Why, that was, sir, only to scour
  my stomach,
A kind of a preparative. Come, gentleman,
I will not have you feed like the hangman
  of Flushing,
Alone, while I am here.
  Lov. Haste your return.
  All. I will not fail, my lord.
  Greedy. Nor I, to line
My Christmas coffer.
  [*Exeunt* Greedy *and* Allworth.
  Over. To my wish : we are private.
I come not to make offer with my daughter
A certain portion, that were poor and trivial :
In one word, I pronounce all that is mine,
In lands or leases, ready coin or goods,
With her, my lord, comes to you ; nor shall
  you have

One motive, to induce you to believe
I live too long, since every year I'll add
Something unto the heap, which shall be
   yours too.
   Lov. You are a right kind father.
   Over. You shall have reason
To think me such. How do you like this
   seat?
It is well wooded, and well water'd, the acres
Fertile and rich; would it not serve for
   change,
To entertain your friends in a summer pro-
   gress?
What thinks my noble lord?
   Lov. 'Tis a wholesome air,
And well-built pile; and she that's mistress
   of it,
Worthy the large revenue.
   Over. She the mistress!
It may be so for a time: but let my lord
Say only that he likes it, and would have it,
I say, ere long 'tis his.
   Lov. Impossible.
   Over. You do conclude too fast, not
   knowing me,
Nor the engines that I work by. 'Tis not
   alone
The lady Allworth's lands, for those once
   Wellborn's,
(As by her dotage on him I know they will
   be,)
Shall soon be mine; but point out any man's
In all the shire, and say they lie convenient,
And useful for your lordship, and once more
I say aloud, they are yours.
   Lov. I dare not own
What's by unjust and cruel means extorted;
My fame and credit are more dear to me,
Than so to expose them to be censured by
The public voice.
   Over. You run, my lord, no hazard.
Your reputation shall stand as fair,
In all good men's opinions, as now;
Nor can my actions, though condemn'd for
   ill,
Cast any foul aspersion upon yours.
For, though I do contemn report myself,
As a mere sound, I still will be so tender
Of what concerns you, in all points of
   honour,
That the immaculate whiteness of your
   fame,
Nor your unquestioned integrity,
Shall e'er be sullied with one taint or spot
That may take from your innocence and
   candour.
All my ambition is to have my daughter
Right honourable, which my lord can make
   her:

And might I live to dance upon my knee
A young lord Lovell, born by her unto you,
I write *nil-ultra* to my proudest hopes.
As for possessions, and annual rents,
Equivalent to maintain you in the port
Your noble birth, and present state requires,
I do remove that burthen from your shoul-
   ders,
And take it on mine own: for, though I
   ruin
The country to supply your riotous waste,
The scourge of prodigals, want, shall never
   find you.
   Lov. Are you not frighted with the im-
   precations
And curses of whole families, made wretched
By your sinister practices?
   Over. Yes, as rocks are,
When foamy billows split themselves against
Their flinty ribs; or as the moon is moved,
When wolves, with hunger pined, howl at
   her brightness.
I am of a solid temper, and, like these,
Steer on, a constant course: with mine own
   sword,
If call'd into the field, I can make that
   right,
Which fearful enemies murmur'd at as
   wrong.
Now, for these other piddling complaints
Breath'd out in bitterness; as when they
   call me
Extortioner, tyrant, cormorant, or intruder
On my poor neighbour's right, or grand in-
   closer
Of what was common, to my private use;
Nay, when my ears are pierced with widows'
   cries,
And undone orphans wash with tears my
   threshold,
I only think what 'tis to have my daughter
Right honourable; and 'tis a powerful
   charm
Makes me insensible of remorse, or pity,
Or the least sting of conscience.
   Lov. I admire
The toughness of your nature.
   Over. 'Tis for you,
My lord, and for my daughter, I am marble;
Nay more, if you will have my character
In little, I enjoy more true delight,
In my arrival to my wealth these dark
And crooked ways, than you shall e'er take
   pleasure
In spending what my industry hath com-
   pass'd.
My haste commands me hence; in one
   word, therefore,
Is it a match?

Lov. I hope, that is past doubt now.

Over. Then rest secure ; not the hate of all mankind here,
Nor fear of what can fall on me hereafter,
Shall make me study aught but your advancement
One story higher : an earl ! if gold can do it.
Dispute not my religion, nor my faith ;
Though I am borne thus headlong by my will,
You may make choice of what belief you please,
To me they are equal ; so, my lord, good morrow.   [*Exit.*

Lov. He's gone—I wonder how the earth can bear
Such a portént ! I, that have lived a soldier,
And stood the enemy's violent charge undaunted,
To hear this blasphemous beast am bath'd all over
In a cold sweat : yet, like a mountain, he
(Confirm'd in atheistical assertions)
Is no more shaken than Olympus is
When angry Boreas loads his double head
With sudden drifts of snow.

  Enter Lady Allworth, Waiting Woman, *and* Amble.

L. All. Save you, my lord !
Disturb I not your privacy ?

Lov. No, good madam ;
For your own sake I am glad you came no sooner :
Since this bold bad man, sir Giles Overreach,
Made such a plain discovery of himself,
And read this morning such a devilish matins,
That I should think it a sin next to his
But to repeat it.

L. All. I ne'er press'd, my lord,
On others' privacies ; yet, against my will,
Walking, for health sake, in the gallery
Adjoining to your lodgings, I was made
(So vehement and loud he was) partaker
Of his tempting offers.

Lov. Please you to command
Your servants hence, and I shall gladly hear
Your wiser counsel.

L. All. 'Tis, my lord, a woman's,
But true and hearty ;—wait in the next room,
But be within call ; yet not so near to force me
To whisper my intents.

Amb. We are taught better
By you, good madam.

Woman. And well know our distance.

L. All. Do so, and talk not ; 'twill become your breeding.
    [*Exeunt* Amble *and* Woman.
Now, my good lord : if I may use my freedom,
As to an honour'd friend——

Lov. You lessen else
Your favour to me.

L. All. I dare then say thus ;
As you are noble (howe'er common men
Make sordid wealth the object and sole end
Of their industrious aims) 'twill not agree
With those of eminent blood, who are engaged
More to prefer their honours, than to increase
The state left to them by their ancestors,
To study large additions to their fortunes,
And quite neglect their births :—though I must grant,
Riches, well got, to be a useful servant,
But a bad master.

Lov. Madam, 'tis confess'd ;
But what infer you from it ?

L. All. This, my lord ;
That as all wrongs, though thrust into one scale,
Slide of themselves off, when right fills the other,
And cannot bide the trial ; so all wealth,
I mean if ill-acquired, cemented to honour
By virtuous ways achieved, and bravely purchased,
Is but as rubbish pour'd into a river,
(Howe'er intended to make good the bank,)
Rendering the water, that was pure before,
Polluted and unwholesome. I allow
The heir of sir Giles Overreach, Margaret,
A maid well qualified, and the richest match
Our north part can make boast of ; yet she cannot,
With all that she brings with her, fill their mouths,
That never will forget who was her father ;
Or that my husband Allworth's lands, and Wellborn's,
(How wrung from both needs now no repetition,)
Were real motives that more work'd your lordship
To join your families, than her form and virtues :
You may conceive the rest.

Lov. I do, sweet madam,
And long since have considered it. I know,
The sum of all that makes a just man happy
Consists in the well choosing of his wife :
And there, well to discharge it, does require
Equality of years, of birth, of fortune ;

For beauty being poor, and not cried up
By birth or wealth, can truly mix with neither.
And wealth, where there's such difference in years,
And fair descent, must make the yoke uneasy :—
But I come nearer.

L. All. Pray you do, my lord.

Lov. Were Overreach' states thrice centupled, his daughter
Millions of degrees much fairer than she is,
Howe'er I might urge precedents to excuse me,
I would not so adulterate my blood
By marrying Margaret, and so leave my issue
Made up of several pieces, one part scarlet,
And the other London blue. In my own tomb
I will inter my name first.

L. All. I am glad to hear this.——
[*Aside.*
Why then, my lord, pretend your marriage to her?
Dissimulation but ties false knots
On that straight line, by which you, hitherto,
Have measured all your actions.

Lov. I make answer,
And aptly, with a question. Wherefore have you,
That, since your husband's death, have lived a strict
And chaste nun's life, on the sudden given yourself
To visits and entertainments? think you, madam,
'Tis not grown public conference? or the favours
Which you too prodigally have thrown on Wellborn,
Being too reserved before, incur not censure?

L. All. I am innocent here ; and, on my life, I swear
My ends are good.

Lov. On my soul, so are mine
To Margaret ; but leave both to the event :
And since this friendly privacy does serve
But as an offer'd means unto ourselves,
To search each other further, you having shewn
Your care of me, I my respect to you ;
Deny me not, but still in chaste words, madam,
An afternoon's discourse.

L. All. So I shall hear you. [*Exeunt.*

SCENE II.—*Before* Tapwell's *House.*

Enter Tapwell *and* Froth.

Tap. Undone, undone ! this was your counsel, Froth.

Froth. Mine ! I defy thee : did not master Marrall
(He has marr'd all, I am sure) strictly command us,
On pain of sir Giles Overreach' displeasure,
To turn the gentleman out of doors?

Tap. 'Tis true ;
But now he's his uncle's darling, and has got
Master justice Greedy, since he fill'd his belly,
At his commandment, to do anything ;
Woe, woe to us !

Froth. He may prove merciful.

Tap. Troth, we do not deserve it at his hands.
Though he knew all the passages of our house,
As the receiving of stolen goods, and bawdry,
When he was rogue Wellborn no man would believe him,
And then his information could not hurt us ;
But now he is right worshipful again,
Who dares but doubt his testimony? methinks,
I see thee, Froth, already in a cart,
For a close bawd, thine eyes even pelted out
With dirt and rotten eggs ; and my hand hissing,
If I scape the halter, with the letter R
Printed upon it.

Froth. Would that were the worst !
That were but nine days wonder : as for credit,
We have none to lose, but we shall lose the money
He owes us, and his custom ; there's the hell on't.

Tap. He has summon'd all his creditors by the drum,
And they swarm about him like so many soldiers
On the pay day : and has found out such a NEW WAY
TO PAY HIS OLD DEBTS, as 'tis very likely
He shall be chronicled for it !

Froth. He deserves it
More than ten pageants. But are you sure his worship
Comes this way, to my lady's?
[*A cry within :* Brave master Wellborn !

Tap. Yes:—I hear him.

Froth. Be ready with your petition, and present it
To his good grace.

Enter Wellborn *in a rich habit, followed by* Marrall, Greedy, Order, Furnace, *and* Creditors ; Tapwell *kneeling, delivers his petition.*

Well. How's this ! petition'd too?——

But note what miracles the payment of
A little trash, and a rich suit of clothes
Can work upon these rascals ! I shall be,
I think, prince Wellborn.
   Mar. When your worship's married,
You may be :—I know what I hope to see you.
   Well. Then look thou for advancement.
   Mar. To be known
Your worship's bailiff, is the mark I shoot at.
   Well. And thou shalt hit it.
   Mar. Pray you, sir, dispatch
These needy followers, and for my ad-
   mittance,
Provided you'll defend me from sir Giles,
Whose service I am weary of, I'll say some-
   thing
You shall give thanks for.
   Well. Fear me not sir Giles.
   Greedy. Who, Tapwell? I remember thy
   wife brought me,
Last new-year's tide, a couple of fat turkies.
   Tap. And shall do every Christmas, let
   your worship
But stand my friend now.
   Greedy. How ! with master Wellborn?
I can do anything with him on such terms.—
See you this honest couple, they are good
   souls
As ever drew out fosset ; have they not
A pair of honest faces?
   Well. I o'erheard you,
And the bribe he promised. You are cozen'd
   in them ;
For, of all the scum that grew rich by my
   riots,
This, for a most unthankful knave, and this,
For a base bawd and whore, have worst de-
   serv'd me,
And therefore speak not for them : by your
   place
You are rather to do me justice ; lend me
   your ear :
—Forget his turkies, and call in his license
And, at the next fair, I'll give you a yoke of
   oxen
Worth all his poultry.
   Greedy. I am changed on the sudden
In my opinion ! come near ; nearer, rascal.
And, now I view him better, did you e'er see
One look so like an archknave? his very
   countenance,
Should an understanding judge but look
   upon him,
Would hang him, though he were innocent.
   Tap. Froth. Worshipful sir.
   Greedy. No, though the great Turk came,
   instead of turkies,
To beg my favour, I am inexorable.
Thou hast an ill name : besides thy musty ale,

That hath destroyed many of the king's liege
   people,
Thou never hadst in thy house, to stay men's
   stomachs,
A piece of Suffolk cheese, or gammon of
   bacon,
Or any esculent, as the learn'd call it,
For their emolument, but sheer drink only.
For which gross fault I here do damn thy
   license,
Forbidding thee ever to tap or draw ;
For, instantly, I will, in mine own person,
Command the constable to pull down thy sign,
And do it before I eat.
   Froth. No mercy?
   Greedy. Vanish !
If I shew any, may my promised oxen gore
   me !
   Tap. Unthankful knaves are ever so re-
   warded.
   [*Exeunt* Greedy, Tapwell, *and* Froth.
   Well. Speak ; what are you?
   1 *Cred.* A decay'd vintner, sir,
That might have thrived, but that your
   worship broke me
With trusting you with muskadine and eggs,
And five pound suppers, with your after
   drinkings,
When you lodged upon the Bankside.
   Well. I remember.
   1 *Cred.* I have not been hasty, nor e'er
   laid to arrest you ;
And therefore, sir——
   Well. Thou art an honest fellow,
I'll set thee up again ; see his bill paid.—
What are you?
   2 *Cred.* A tailor once, but now mere
   botcher.
I gave you credit for a suit of clothes,
Which was all my stock, but you failing in
   payment,
I was removed from the shopboard, and
   confined
Under a stall.
   Well. See him paid ; and botch no more.
   2 *Cred.* I ask no interest, sir.
   Well. Such tailors need not ;
If their bills are paid in one and twenty year,
They are seldom losers.—O, I know thy face,
                [*To* 3 Cred.
Thou wert my surgeon : you must tell no
   tales ;
Those days are done. I will pay you in
   private.
   Ord. A royal gentleman !
   Furn. Royal as an emperor !
He'll prove a brave master ; my good lady
   knew
To choose a man.

Well. See all men else discharg'd ;
And since old debts are clear'd by a new way,
A little bounty will not misbecome me ;
There's something, honest cook, for thy
good breakfasts ;
And this, for your respect ; [*To* Order.]
take't, 'tis good gold,
And I able to spare it.
Ord. You are too munificent.
Furn. He was ever so.
Well. Pray you, on before.
3 *Cred.* Heaven bless you !
Mar. At four o'clock ; the rest know
where to meet me.
[*Exeunt* Order, Furnace, *and* Creditors.
Well. Now, master Marrall, what's the
weighty secret
You promised to impart ?
Mar. Sir, time nor place
Allow me to relate each circumstance,
This only, in a word ; I know sir Giles
Will come upon you for security
For his thousand pounds, which you must
not consent to.
As he grows in heat, as I am sure he will,
Be you but rough, and say he's in your debt
Ten times the sum, upon sale of your land ;
I had a hand in't (I speak it to my shame)
When you were defeated of it.
Well. That's forgiven.
Mar. I shall deserve it : then urge him to
produce
The deed in which you pass'd it over to him,
Which I know he'll have about him, to de-
liver
To the lord Lovell, with many other writings,
And present monies : I'll instruct you further,
As I wait on your worship : if I play not my
prize
To your full content, and your uncle's much
vexation,
Hang up Jack Marrall.
Well. I rely upon thee. [*Exeunt.*

SCENE III.—*A Room in* Overreach's
House.

Enter Allworth *and* Margaret.

All. Whether to yield the first praise to
my lord's
Unequall'd temperance, or your constant
sweetness,
That I yet live, my weak hands fasten'd on
Hope's anchor, spite of all storms of despair,
I yet rest doubtful.
Marg. Give it to lord Lovell ;
For what in him was bounty, in me's duty.
I make but payment of a debt to which
My vows, in that high office register'd,
Are faithful witnesses.

All. 'Tis true, my dearest :
Yet, when I call to mind how many fair ones
Make wilful shipwreck of their faiths, and
oaths
To God and man, to fill the arms of great-
ness ;
And you rise up no less than a glorious star,
To the amazement of the world,—that hold
out
Against the stern authority of a father,
And spurn at honour, when it comes to court
you ;
I am so tender of your good, that faintly,
With your wrong, I can wish myself that
right
You yet are pleased to do me.
Marg. Yet, and ever.
To me what's title, when content is wanting?
Or wealth, raked up together with much
care,
And to be kept with more, when the heart
pines,
In being dispossess'd of what it longs for,
Beyond the Indian mines? or the smooth
brow
Of a pleased sire, that slaves me to his will ;
And so his ravenous humour may be feasted
By my obedience, and he see me great,
Leaves to my soul nor faculties nor power
To make her own election ?
All. But the dangers
That follow the repulse——
Marg. To me they are nothing ;
Let Allworth love, I cannot be unhappy.
Suppose the worst, that, in his rage, he kill
me ;
A tear or two, by you dropt on my herse,
In sorrow for my fate, will call back life
So far as but to say, that I die yours ;
I then shall rest in peace : or should he
prove
So cruel, as one death would not suffice
His thirst of vengeance, but with lingering
torments,
In mind and body, I must waste to air,
In poverty join'd with banishment ; so you
share
In my afflictions, which I dare not wish you,
So high I prize you, I could undergo them
With such a patience as should look down
With scorn on his worst malice.
All. Heaven avert
Such trials of your true affection to me !
Nor will it unto you, that are all mercy,
Shew so much rigour : but since we must
run
Such desperate hazards, let us do our best
To steer between them.
Marg. Your lord's ours, and sure ;

And though but a young actor, second me
In doing to the life what he has plotted,

Enter Overreach *behind.*

The end may yet prove happy. Now, my
Allworth.   [*Seeing her father.*
All. To your letter, and put on a seeming
anger.
Marg. I'll pay my lord all debts due to
his title ;
And when with terms, not taking from his
honour,
He does solicit me, I shall gladly hear him.
But in this peremptory, nay, commanding
way,
T' appoint a meeting, and, without my
knowledge,
A priest to tie the knot can ne'er be undone
Till death unloose it, is a confidence
In his lordship will deceive him.
All. I hope better,
Good lady.
Marg. Hope, sir, what you please: for me
I must take a safe and secure course ; I have
A father, and without his full consent,
Though all lords of the land kneel'd for my
favour,
I can grant nothing.
Over. I like this obedience :
                         [*Comes forward.*
But whatsoe'er my lord writes, must and
shall be
Accepted and embraced. Sweet master
Allworth,
You shew yourself a true and faithful servant
To your good lord ; he has a jewel of you.
How ! frowning, Meg? are these looks to
receive
A messenger from my lord? what's this?
give me it.
Marg. A piece of arrogant paper, like the
inscriptions.
Over. [*Reads.*] *Fair mistress, from your
servant learn, all joys
That we can hope for, if deferr'd, prove toys ;
Therefore this instant, and in private, meet
A husband, that will gladly at your feet
Lay down his honours, tendering them to you
With all content, the church being paid her
due.*
--Is this the arrogant piece of paper? fool !
Will you still be one ? in the name of mad-
ness what
Could his good honour write more to con-
tent you?
Is there aught else to be wish'd, after these
two,
That are already offer'd ; marriage first,

And lawful pleasure after : what would you
more?
Marg. Why, sir, I would be married like
your daughter ;
Not hurried away i' the night I know not
whither,
Without all ceremony ; no friends invited
To honour the solemnity.
All. An't please your honour,
For so before to-morrow I must style you,
My lord desires this privacy, in respect
His honourable kinsmen are afar off,
And his desires to have it done, brook not
So long delay as to expect their coming ;
And yet he stands resolv'd, with all due
pomp,
As running at the ring, plays, masks, and
tilting,
To have his marriage at court celebrated,
When he has brought your honour up to
London.
Over. He tells you true ; 'tis the fashion,
on my knowledge :
Yet the good lord, to please your peevish-
ness,
Must put it off, forsooth ! and lose a night,
In which perhaps he might get two boys on
thee.
Tempt me no further, if you do, this goad
                         [*Points to his sword.*
Shall prick you to him.
Marg. I could be contented,
Were you but by, to do a father's part,
And give me in the church.
Over. So my lord have you,
What do I care who gives you? since my
lord
Does purpose to be private, I'll not cross him.
I know not, master Allworth, how my lord
May be provided, and therefore there's a
purse
Of gold, 'twill serve this night's expense ;
to-morrow
I'll furnish him with any sums : in the mean
time,
Use my ring to my chaplain ; he is beneficed
At my manor of Got'em, and call'd parson
Willdo :
'Tis no matter for a license, I'll bear him
out in't.
Marg. With your favour, sir, what warrant
is your ring?
He may suppose I got that twenty ways,
Without your knowledge ; and then to be
refused,
Were such a stain upon me !—if you pleased,
sir,
Your presence would do better.
Over. Still perverse !

I say again, I will not cross my lord ;
Yet I'll prevent you too.—Paper and ink,
    there !
    All. I can furnish you.
    Over. I thank you, I can write then.
                                    [*Writes.*
    All. You may, if you please, put out the
    name of my lord, '
In respect he comes disguised, and only
    write,
Marry her to this gentleman.
    Over. Well advised.
'Tis done ; away ;—[Margaret *kneels.*] My
    blessing, girl ? thou hast it.
Nay, no reply, be gone :—good master
    Allworth,
This shall be the best night's work you ever
    made.
    All. I hope so, sir.   •
                [*Exeunt* Allworth *and* Margaret.
    Over. Farewell !—Now all's cocksure :
Methinks I hear already knights and ladies
Say, Sir Giles Overreach, how is it with
Your honourable daughter ! has her honour
Slept well to-night ? or, will her honour
    please
To accept this monkey, dog, or paroqueto,
(This is state in ladies,) or my eldest son
To be her page, and wait upon her trencher?
My ends, my ends are compass'd—then for
    Wellborn
And the lands ; were he once married to the
    widow——
I have him here—I can scarce contain my-
    self,
1 am so full of joy, nay, joy all over. [*Exit.*

ACT V.

SCENE I.—*A Room in* Lady Allworth's
                House.

Enter Lord Lovell, Lady Allworth, *and*
                Amble.

L. All. By this you know how strong the
    motives were
That did, my lord, induce me to dispense
A little, with my gravity, to advance
In personating some few favours to him,
The plots and projects of the down-trod
    Wellborn.
Nor shall I e'er repent, although I suffer
In some few men's opinions for't, the action ;
For he that ventured all for my dear hus-
    band,
Might justly claim an obligation from me,
To pay him such a courtesy ; which had I
Coyly, or over-curiously denied,

It might have argued me of little love
To the deceased.   •
    Lov. What you intended, Madam,
For the poor gentleman, hath found good
    success ;
For, as I understand, his debts are paid,
And he once more furnish'd for fair employ-
    ment :
But all the arts that I have used to raise
The fortunes of your joy and mine, young
    Allworth,
Stand yet in supposition, though I hope well :
For the young lovers are in wit more
    pregnant
Than their years can promise ; and for their
    desires,
On my knowledge, they are equal.
    L. All. As my wishes
Are with yours, my lord ; yet give me leave
    to fear
The building, though well grounded : to
    deceive
Sir Giles, that's both a lion and a fox
In his proceedings, were a work beyond
The strongest undertakers ; not the trial
Of two weak innocents.
    Lov. Despair not, madam :
Hard things are compass'd oft by easy
    means ;
And judgment, being a gift derived from
    heaven,
Though sometimes lodged in the hearts of
    worldly men,
That ne'er consider from whom they receive
    it,
Forsakes such as abuse the giver of it.
Which is the reason that the politic   ·
And cunning statesman, that believes he
    fathoms
The counsels of all kingdoms on the earth,
Is by simplicity oft over-reach'd.
    L. All. May he be so ! yet, in his name
    to express it,
Is a good omen.
    Lov. May it to myself
Prove so, good lady, in my suit to you !
What think you of the motion ?
    L. All. Troth, my lord,
My own unworthiness may answer for me ;
For had you, when that I was in my prime,
My virgin flower uncropp'd, presented me
With this great favour ; looking on my low-
    ness
Not in a glass of self-love, but of truth,
I could not but have thought it, as a blessing
Far, far beyond my merit.
    Lov. You are too modest,
And undervalue that which is above
My title, or whatever I call mine.

I grant, were I a Spaniard, to marry
A widow might disparage me ; but being
A true-born Englishman, I cannot find
How it can taint my honour : nay, what's
  more,
That which you think a blemish, is to me
The fairest lustre. You already, madam,
Have given sure proofs how dearly you can
  cherish
A husband that deserves you ; which con-
  firms me,
That, if I am not wanting in my care
To do you service, you'll be still the same
That you were to your Allworth : in a word,
Our years, our states, our births are not un-
  equal,
You being descended nobly, and allied so ;
If then you may be won to make me happy,
But join your lips to mine, and that shall be
A solemn contract.
  L. All. I were blind to my own good,
Should I refuse it ; [*Kisses him.*] yet, my
  lord, receive me
As such a one, the study of whose whole life
Shall know no other object but to please you.
  Lov. If I return not, with all tenderness,
Equal respect to you, may I die wretched !
  L. All. There needs no protestation, my
  lord,
To her that cannot doubt.—

Enter Wellborn, *handsomely apparelled.*

                    You are welcome, sir.
Now you look like yourself. .
  Well. And will continue
Such in my free acknowledgment, that I am
Your creature, madam, and will never hold
My life mine own, when you please to com-
  mand it.
  Lov. It is a thankfulness that well becomes
  you ;
You could not make choice of a better shape
To dress your mind in.
  L. All. For me, I am happy
That my endeavours prosper'd. Saw you of
  late
Sir Giles, your uncle ?
  Well. I heard of him, madam,
By his minister, Marrall ; he's grown into
  strange passions
About his daughter : this last night he look'd
  for
Your lordship at his house, but missing you,
And she not yet appearing, his wise head
Is much perplex'd and troubled.
  Lov. It may be,
Sweetheart, my project took. '
  L. All. I strongly hope.

Over. [*within.*] Ha ! find her, booby,
  thou huge lump of nothing,
I'll bore thine eyes out else.
  Well. May it please your lordship,
For some ends of mine own, but to with-
  draw
A little out of sight, though not of hearing,
You may, perhaps, have sport.
  Lov. You shall direct me.   [*Steps aside.*

Enter Overreach, *with distracted looks,
driving in* Marrall *before him, with a box.*

  Over. I shall sol fa you, rogue !
  Mar. Sir, for what cause
Do you use me thus ?
  Over. Cause, slave ! why, I am angry,
And thou a subject only fit for beating,
And so to cool my choler. Look to the
  writing ;
Let but the seal be broke upon the box,
That has slept in my cabinet these three
  years,
I'll rack thy soul for't.
  Mar. I may yet cry quittance,
Though now I suffer, and dare not resist.
                                [*Aside.*
  Over. Lady, by your leave, did you see
  my daughter, lady ?
And the lord her husband ? are they in your
  house ?
If they are, discover, that I may bid them
  joy ;
And, as an entrance to her place of honour,
See your ladyship on her left hand, and
  make courtsies
When she nods on you ; which you must
  receive
As a special favour.
  L. All. When I know, sir Giles,
Her state requires such ceremony, I shall
  pay it ;
But, in the meantime, as I am myself,
I give you to understand, I neither know
Nor care where her honour is.
  Over. When you once see her
Supported, and led by the lord her husband,
You'll be taught better.——Nephew. .
  Well. Sir.
  Over. No more !
  Well. 'Tis all I owe you.
  Over. Have your redeem'd rags
Made you thus insolent ?
  Well. Insolent to you !
Why, what are you, sir, unless in your years,
At the best, more than myself ?
  Over. His fortune swells him :
'Tis rank, he's married.   [*Aside.*
  L. All. This is excellent !

                                    E E

Over. Sir, in calm language, though I
  seldom use it,
I am familiar with the cause that makes you
Bear up thus bravely ; there's a certain buz
Of a stolen marriage, do you hear ? of a
  stolen marriage,
In which, 'tis said, there's somebody hath
  been cozen'd ;
I name no parties.
      Well. Well, sir, and what follows ?
      Over. Marry, this ; since you are peremp-
  tory. Remember,
Upon mere hope of your great match, I lent
  you
A thousand pounds : put me in good se-
  curity,
And suddenly, by mortgage or by statute,
Of some of your new possessions, or I'll
  have you
Dragg'd in your lavender robes to the gaol :
  you know me,
And therefore do not trifle.
      Well. Can you be
So cruel to your nephew, now he's in
The way to rise ? was this the courtesy
You did me *in pure love, and no ends else ?*
      Over. End me no ends ! engage the whole
  estate,
And force your spouse to sign it, you shall
  have
Three or four thousand more, to roar and
  swagger,
And revel in bawdy taverns.
      Well. And beg after ;
Mean you not so ?
      Over. My thoughts are mine, and free.
Shall I have security ?
      Well. No, indeed you shall not,
Nor bond, nor bill, nor bare acknowledg-
  ment ;
Your great looks fright not me.
      Over. But my deeds shall.
Outbraved !   [*Both draw.*
      L. All. Help, murder ! murder !

                Enter Servants.

      Well. Let him come on,
With all his wrongs and injuries about him,
Arm'd with his cut-throat practices to guard
  him ;
The right that I bring with me will defend
  me,
And punish his extortion.
      Over. That I had thee
But single in the field !
      L. All. You may ; but make not
My house your quarrelling scene.
      Over. Were't in a church,
By heaven and hell, I'll do't.

      Mar. Now put him to
The shewing of the deed.
                          [*Aside to* Wellborn.
      Well. This rage is vain, sir ;
For fighting, fear not, you shall have your
  hands full,
Upon the least incitement ; and whereas
You charge me with a debt of a thousand
  pounds,
If there be law, (howe'er you have no con-
  science,)
Either restore my land, or I'll recover
A debt, that's truly due to me from you,
In value ten times more than what you
  challenge.
      Over. I in thy debt !   O impudence ! did
  I not purchase   .
The land left by thy father, that rich land,
That had continued in Wellborn's name
Twenty descents ; which, like a riotous fool,
Thou didst make sale of ?   Is not here,
  inclosed,
The deed that does confirm it mine ?
      Mar. Now, now !
      Well. I do acknowledge none ; I ne'er
  pass'd over
Any such land : I grant, for a year or two
You had it in trust ; which if you do dis-
  charge,
Surrendering the possession, you shall ease
Yourself and me of chargeable suits in law,
Which, if you prove not honest, as I doubt it,
Must of necessity follow.
      L. All. In my judgment,
He does advise you well.
      Over. Good ! good ! conspire
With your new husband, lady ; second him
In his dishonest practices ; but when
This manor is extended to my use,
You'll speak in an humbler key, and sue for
  favour.
      L. All. Never : do not hope it.
      Well. Let despair first seize me.   .
      Over. Yet, to shut up thy mouth, and
  make thee give
Thyself the lie, the loud lie, I draw out
The precious evidence ; if thou canst for-
  swear
Thy hand and seal, and make a forfeit of
          [*Opens the box, and displays the bond.*
Thy ears to the pillory, see ! here's that will
  make
My interest clear—ha !
      L. All. A fair skin of parchment.
      Well. Indented, I confess, and labels too ;
But neither wax nor words.   How ! thun-
  der struck ?
Not a syllable to insult with ?   My wise
  uncle,

Is this your precious evidence, this that
   makes
Your interest clear?
   Over. I am o'erwhelmed with wonder!
What prodigy is this? what subtle devil
Hath razed out the inscription? the wax
Turn'd into dust!—the rest of my deeds
   whole,
As when they were deliver'd, and this only
Made nothing! do you deal with witches,
   rascal?
There is a statute for you, which will bring
Your neck in an hempen circle; yes, there is;
And now 'tis better thought for, cheater,
   know
This juggling shall not save you.
   Well. To save thee,
Would beggar the stock of mercy.
   Over. Marrall!
   Mar. Sir.
   Over. Though the witnesses are dead,
   your testimony
Help with an oath or two: and for thy
   master,
Thy liberal master, my good honest servant,
I know thou wilt swear anything, to dash
This cunning sleight: besides, I know thou
   art
A public notary, and such stand in law
For a dozen witnesses: the deed being
   drawn too
By thee, my careful Marrall, and deliver'd
When thou wert present, will make good
   my title.
Wilt thou not swear this?
                        [*Aside to* Marrall.
   Mar. I! no, I assure you:
I have a conscience not sear'd up like yours;
I know no deeds.
   Over. Wilt thou betray me?
   Mar. Keep him
From using of his hands, I'll use my tongue,
To his no little torment.
   Over. Mine own varlet
Rebel against me!
   Mar. Yes, and uncase you too.
The *ideot*, the *Patch*, the *slave*, the *booby*,
The *property fit only to be beaten*
For your morning exercise, your *football*, or
The *unprofitable lump of flesh*, your *drudge;*
Can now anatomise you, and lay open
All your black plots, and level with the earth
Your hill of pride: and, with these gabions
   guarded,
Unload my great artillery, and shake,
Nay pulverize, the walls you think defend
   you.
   L. All. How he foams at the mouth with
   rage!

   Well. To him again.
   Over. O that I had thee in my gripe, I
   would tear thee
Joint after joint!
   Mar. I know you are a tearer.
But I'll have first your fangs pared off, and
   then
Come nearer to you; when I have discover'd,
And made it good before the judge, what
   ways,
And devilish practices, you used to cozen
   with
An army of whole families, who yet alive,
And but enroll'd for soldiers, were able
To take in Dunkirk.
   Well. All will come out.
   L. All. The better.
   Over. But that I will live, rogue, to tor-
   ture thee,
And make thee wish, and kneel in vain, to
   die,
These swords, that keep thee from me,
   should fix here,
Although they made my body but one
   wound,
But I would reach thee.
   Lov. Heaven's hand is in this;
One bandog worry the other!   [*Aside.*
   Over. I play the fool,
And make my anger but ridiculous:
There will be a time and place, there will be,
   cowards,
When you shall feel what I dare do.
   Well. I think so:
You dare do any ill, yet want true valour
To be honest, and repent.
   Over. They are words I know not,
Nor e'er will learn. Patience, the beggar's
   virtue,

   Enter Greedy *and* Parson Willdo.

Shall find no harbour here:—after these
   storms
At length a calm appears. Welcome, most
   welcome!
There's comfort in thy looks; is the deed
   done?
Is my daughter married? say but so, my
   chaplain,
And I am tame.
   Willdo. Married! yes, I assure you.
   Over. Then vanish all sad thoughts!
   there's more gold for thee.
My doubts and fears are in the titles
   drown'd
Of my honourable, my right honourable
   daughter.
   Greedy. Here will be feasting! at least
   for a month,

E E 2

I am provided : empty guts, croak no more,
You shall be stuff'd like bagpipes, not with
   wind,
But bearing dishes.
  Over. Instantly be here ?
              [*Whispering to* Willdo.
To my wish ! to my wish ! Now you that
  plot against me,
And hoped to trip my heels up, that con-
  temn'd me,
Think on't and tremble :—[*Loud music.*]—
  they come ! I hear the music.
A lane there for my lord !
  Well. This sudden heat
May yet be cool'd, sir.
  Over. Make way there for my lord !

Enter Allworth *and* Margaret.

  Marg. Sir, first your pardon, then your
  blessing, with
Your full allowance of the choice I have
  made.
As ever you could make use of your reason,
                [*Kneeling.*
Grow not in passion ; since you may as well
Call back the day that's past, as untie the
  knot
Which is too strongly fasten'd : not to dwell
Too long on words, this is my husband.
  Over. How !
  All. So I assure you ; all the rights of
  marriage,
With every circumstance, are past. Alas !
  sir,
Although I am no lord, but a lord's page,
Your daughter and my loved wife mourns
  not for it ;
And, for right honourable son-in-law, you
  may say,
Your dutiful daughter.
  Over. Devil ! are they married ?
  Willdo. Do a father's part, and say,
  Heaven give them joy !
  Over. Confusion and ruin ! speak, and
  speak quickly,
Or thou art dead.
  Willdo. They are married.
  Over. Thou hadst better
Have made a contract with the king of fiends,
Than these :—my brain turns !
  Willdo. Why this rage to me?
Is not this your letter, sir, and these the
  words ?
Marry her to this gentleman.
  Over. It cannot—
Nor will I e'er believe it, 'sdeath ! I will not ;
That I, that, in all passages I touch'd
At worldly profit, have not left a print

Where I have trod, for the most curious
  search
To trace my footsteps, should be gull'd by
  children,
Baffled and fool'd, and all my hopes and la-
  bours
Defeated, and made void.
  Well. As it appears,
You are so, my grave uncle.
  Over. Village nurses
Revenge their wrongs with curses ; I'll not
  waste
A syllable, but thus I take the life
Which, wretched, I gave to thee.
        [*Attempts to kill* Margaret.
  Lov. [*coming forward.*] Hold, for your
  own sake !
Though charity to your daughter hath quite
  left you,
Will you do an act, though in your hopes
  lost here,
Can leave no hope for peace or rest hereafter?
Consider ; at the best you are but a man,
And cannot so create your aims, but that
  They may be cross'd.
  Over. Lord ! thus I spit at thee,
And at thy counsel ; and again desire thee,
And as thou art a soldier, if thy valour
Dares shew itself, where multitude and
  example
Lead not the way, let's quit the house, and
  change
Six words in private.
  Lov. I am ready.
  L. All. Stay, sir,
Contest with one distracted !
  Well. You'll grow like him,
Should you answer his vain challenge.
  Over. Are you pale ?
Borrow his help, though Hercules call it odds,
I'll stand against both as I am, hemm'd in
  thus.—
Since, like a Libyan lion in the toil,
My fury cannot reach the coward hunters,
And only spends itself, I'll quit the place :
Alone I can do nothing ; but I have servants,
And friends to second me ; and if I make not
This house a heap of ashes, (by my wrongs,
What I have spoke I will make good !) or
  leave
One throat uncut,—if it be possible,
Hell, add to my afflictions !   [*Exit.*
  Mar. Is't not brave sport ?
  Greedy. Brave sport ! I am sure it has ta'en
away my stomach ;
I do not like the sauce.
  All. Nay, weep not, dearest,
Though it express your pity ; what's decreed
Above, we cannot alter.

L. All. His threats move me
No scruple, madam.

Mar. Was it not a rare trick,
An it please your worship, to make the deed
    nothing?
I can do twenty neater, if you please
To purchase and grow rich; for I will be
Such a solicitor and steward for you,
As never worshipful had.

Well. I do believe thee;
But first discover the quaint means you used
To raze out the conveyance?

Mar. They are mysteries
Not to be spoke in public: certain minerals
Incorporated in the ink and wax.—
Besides, he gave me nothing; for I still fed me
With hopes and blows; and that was the in-
    ducement
To this conundrum. If it please your worship
To call to memory, this mad beast once
    caused me
To urge you, or to drown or hang yourself;
I'll do the like to him, if you command me.

Well. You are a rascal! he that dares be
    false
To a master, though unjust, will ne'er be true
To any other. Look not for reward
Or favour from me; I will shun thy sight
As I would do a basilisk's: thank my pity,
If thou keep thy ears; howe'er, I will take
    order
Your practice shall be silenced.

Greedy. I'll commit him,
If you will have me, sir.

Well. That were to little purpose;
His conscience be his prison. Not a word,
But instantly be gone.

Ord. Take this kick with you.

Amb. And this.

Furn. If that I had my cleaver here,
I would divide your knave's head.

Mar. This is the haven
False servants still arrive at.   *[Exit.*

Re-enter Overreach.

L. All. Come again!

Lov. Fear not, I am your guard.

Well. His looks are ghastly.

Willdo. Some little time. I have spent,
    under your favours,
In physical studies, and if my judgment err
    not,
He's mad beyond recovery: but observe him,
And look to yourselves.

Over. Why, is not the whole world
Included in myself? to what use then
Are friends and servants? Say there were a
    squadron
Of pikes, lined through with shot, when I am
    mounted
Upon my injuries, shall I fear to charge
    them?
No: I'll through the battalia, and that
    routed,
    [Flourishing his sword sheathed.
I'll fall to execution.—Ha! I am feeble:
Some undone widow sits upon mine arm,
And takes away the use of 't; and my sword,
Glued to my scabbard, with wrong'd or-
    phans' tears,
Will not be drawn. Ha! what are these?
    sure, hangmen,
That come to bind my hands, and then to
    drag me
Before the judgment-seat: now they are new
    shapes,
And do appear like Furies, with steel whips
To scourge my ulcerous soul. Shall I then
    fall
Ingloriously, and yield? no; spite of Fate,
I will be forced to hell like to myself.
Though you were legions of accursed
    spirits,
Thus would I fly among you.
    [Rushes forward, and flings himself
        on the ground.

Well. There's no help;
Disarm him first, then bind him.

Greedy. Take a mittimus,
And carry him to Bedlam.

Lov. How he foams!

Well. And bites the earth!

Willdo. Carry him to some dark room,
There try what art can do for his recovery.

Marg. O my dear father!
    [They force Overreach off.

All. You must be patient, mistress.

Lov. Here is a precedent to teach wicked
    men,
That when they leave religion, and turn
    atheists,
Their own abilities leave them. Pray you take
    comfort,
I will endeavour you shall be his guardians
In his distractions: and for your land, master
    Wellborn,
Be it good or ill in law, I'll be an umpire
Between you, and this, the undoubted heir
Of sir Giles Overreach: for me, here's the
    anchor
That I must fix on.

All. What you shall determine,
My lord, I will allow of.

Well. 'Tis the language
That I speak too; but there is something
    else
Beside the repossession of my land,

And payment of my debts, that I must practise.
I had a reputation, but 'twas lost
In my loose course; and until I redeem it
Some noble way, I am but half made up.
It is a time of action; if your lordship
Will please to confer a company upon me,
In your command, I doubt not, in my service
To my king and country, but I shall do something
That may make me right again.
    Lov. Your suit is granted,
And you loved for the motion.

    Well. [coming forward.] *Nothing wants then*
But your allowance—and in that our all
Is comprehended; it being known, nor we,
Nor he that wrote the comedy, can be free,
Without your manumission; which if you
Grant willingly, as a fair favour due
To the poet's, and our labours, (as you may,)
For we despair not, gentlemen, of the play:
We jointly shall profess your grace hath might
To teach us action, and him how to write.
                    [Exeunt.

The City Madam.

DRAMATIS PERSONÆ.

Lord Lacy.
Sir John Frugal, *a merchant.*
Sir Maurice Lacy, *son to lord* Lacy.
Mr. Plenty, *a country gentleman.*
Luke Frugal, *brother to sir* John.
Goldwire *senior,* } *two gentlemen.*
Tradewell *senior,* }
Goldwire *junior,* } *their sons, apprentices*
Tradewell *junior,* } *to sir* John Frugal.
Stargaze, *an astrologer.*
Hoyst, *a decayed gentleman.*
Fortune, } *decayed merchants.*
Penury, }
Holdfast, *steward to sir* John Frugal.

Ramble, } *two hectors.*
Scuffle, }
Ding'em, *a pimp.*
Gettall, *a box-keeper.*
Page, Sheriff, Marshal, Serjeants.
Lady Frugal.
Anne, } *her daughters.*
Mary, }
Milliscent, *her woman.*
Shave'em, *a courtezan.*
Secret, *a bawd.*
Orpheus, Charon, Cerberus, Chorus,
Musicians, Porters, Servants.

SCENE,—London.

ACT I.

SCENE I.—*A Room in Sir* John Frugal's *House.*

Enter Goldwire *junior and* Tradewell *junior.*

Gold. The ship is safe in the Pool then?
Trade. And makes good
In her rich fraught, the name she bears,
The *Speedwell:*
My master will find it; for, on my certain knowledge,
For every hundred that he ventured in her,
She hath return'd him five.
Gold. And it comes timely;
For, besides a payment on the nail for a manor
Late purchased by my master, his young daughters
Are ripe for marriage.
Trade. Who? Nan and Mall?
Gold. Mistress Anne and Mary, and with some addition,
Or 'tis more punishable in our house
Than *scandalum magnatum.*
Trade. 'Tis great pity
Such a gentleman as my master (for that title
His being a citizen cannot take from him)
Hath no male heir to inherit his estate,
And keep his name alive.
Gold. The want of one,
Swells my young mistresses, and their madam-mother,

With hopes above their birth, and scale their dreams are
Of being made countesses; and they take state,
As they were such already. When you went
To the Indies, there was some shape and proportion
Of a merchant's house in our family; but since
My master, to gain precedency for my mistress,
Above some elder merchants' wives, was knighted,
'Tis grown a little court in bravery,
Variety of fashions, and those rich ones:
There are few great ladies going to a mask
That do outshine ours in their every-day habits.
Trade. 'Tis strange, my master, in his wisdom, can
Give the reins to such exorbitance.
Gold. He must,
Or there's no peace nor rest for him at home:
I grant his state will bear it; yet he's censured
For his indulgence, and, for sir John Frugal,
By some styled sir John Prodigal.
Trade. Is his brother,
Master Luke Frugal, living?
Gold. Yes; the more
His misery, poor man!
Trade. Still in the counter?

Gold. In a worse place. He was redeem'd
    from the hole,
To live, in our house, in hell; since, his base
    usage
Consider'd, 'tis no better. My proud lady
Admits him to her table ; marry, ever
Beneath the salt, and there he sits the sub-
    ject
Of her contempt and scorn ; and dinner
    ended,
His courteous nieces find employment for him
Fitting an under-prentice, or a footman,
And not an uncle.
    Trade. I wonder, being a scholar
Well read, and travell'd, the world yielding
    means
For men of such desert, he should endure it.
    Gold. He does, with a strange patience ;
    and to us,
The servants, so familiar, nay humble !

Enter Stargaze, Lady Frugal, Anne, Mary,
    and Milliscent, *in several affected postures,*
    with looking-glasses at their girdles.

I'll tell you—but I am cut off. Look these
Like a citizen's wife and daughters ?
    Trade. In their habits
They appear other things : but what are the
    motives
Of this strange preparation ?
    Gold. The young wagtails
Expect their suitors : the first, the son and
    heir
Of the lord Lacy, who needs my master's
    money,
As his daughter does his honour; the second,
    Mr. Plenty,
A rough-hewn gentleman, and newly come
To a great estate ; and so all aids of art
In them's excusable.
    L. Frug. You have done your parts here :
To your study ; and be curious in the search
Of the nativities.   [*Exit* Stargaze.
    Trade. Methinks the mother,
As if she could renew her youth, in care,
Nay curiosity, to appear lovely,
Comes not behind her daughters.
    Gold. Keeps the first place ;
And though the church-book speak her fifty,
    they
That say she can write thirty, more offend
    er,
Than if they tax'd her honesty : t'other day,
A tenant of hers, instructed in her humour,
But one she never saw, being brought before
    her,
For saying only, *Good young mistress, help*
    me

To the speech of your lady-mother, so far
    pleased her,
That he got his lease renew'd for't.
    Trade. How she bristles !
Prithee, observe her.
    Mill. As I hope to see
A country knight's son and heir walk bare
    before you
When you are a countess, as you may be
    one
When my master dies, or leaves trading ;
    and I, continuing
Your principal woman, take the upper hand
Of a squire's wife, though a justice, as I
    must
By the place you give me ; you look now as
    young
As when you were married.
    L. Frug. I think I bear my years well.
    Mill. Why should you talk of years?
    Time hath not plough'd
One furrow in your face ; and were you not
    known
The mother of my young ladies, you might
    pass
For a virgin of fifteen.
    Trade. Here's no gross flattery !
Will she swallow this?
    Gold. You see she does, and glibly.
    Mill. You never can be old ; wear but a
    mask
Forty years hence, and you will still seem
    young
In your other parts. What a waist is here !
    O Venus !
That I had been born a king ! and here a
    hand
To be kiss'd ever ;—pardon my boldness,
    madam.
Then, for a leg and foot, you will be courted
When a great grandmother.
    L. Frug. These, indeed, wench, are not
So subject to decayings as the face ;
Their comeliness lasts longer.
    Mill. Ever, ever !
Such a rare featured and proportion'd
    madam,
London could never boast of.
    L. Frug. Those that your ladyship gave order,
    Mill. Those that your ladyship gave order,
    should
Be made of the Spanish perfum'd skins ?
    L. Frug. The same.
    Mill. I sent the prison-bird this morning
    for them ;
But he neglects his duty.
    Anne. He is grown
Exceeding careless.
    Mary. And begins to murmur

At our commands, and sometimes grumbles
　　to us,
He is, forsooth, our uncle !
　L. Frug.　He is your slave,
And as such use him.
　Anne.　Willingly ; but he's grown
Rebellious, madam.
　Gold.　Nay, like hen, like chicken.
　L. Frug.　I'll humble him.

Enter Luke, *with shoes, garters, fans, and*
roses.

　Gold.　Here he comes, sweating all over :
He shews like a walking frippery.
　L. Frug.　Very good, sir :
Were you drunk last night, that you could
　　rise no sooner,
With humble diligence, to do what my
　　daughters
And woman did command you ?
　Luke.　Drunk, an't please you !
　L. Frug.　Drunk, I said, sirrah ! dar'st
thou, in a look,
Repine or grumble ?　Thou unthankful
　　wretch,
Did our charity redeem thee out of prison,
(Thy patrimony spent,) ragged and lousy,
When the sheriff's basket, and his broken
　　meat,
Were your festival-exceedings ! and is this
So soon forgotten ?
　Luke.　I confess I am
Your creature, madam.
　L. Frug.　And good reason why
You should continue so.
　Anne.　Who did new clothe you ?
　Marg.　Admitted you to the dining-room ?
　Mill.　Allow'd you
A fresh bed in the garret ?
　L. Frug.　Or from whom
Received you spending money ?
　Luke.　I owe all this
To your goodness, madam ; for it you have
　　my prayers,
The beggar's satisfaction : all my studies
(Forgetting what I was, but with all duty
Remembering what I am) are how to please
　　you.
And if in my long stay I have offended,
I ask your pardon ; though you may con-
　　sider,
Being forced to fetch these from the Old
　　Exchange,
These from the Tower, and these from
　　Westminster,
I could not come much sooner.
　Gold.　Here was a walk
To breathe a footman !
　Anne.　'Tis a curious fan.

　Mary.　These roses will shew rare : would
'twere in fashion
That the garters might be seen too !
　Mill.　Many ladies
That know they have good legs, wish the
　　same with you ;
Men that way have the advantage.
　Luke.　I was with
The lady, and delivered her the satin
For her gown, and velvet for her petti-
　　coat ;
This night she vows she'll pay you.
　　　　　　　　　　[Aside to Goldwire.
　Gold.　How I am bound
To your favour, master Luke !
　Mill.　As I live, you will
Perfume all rooms you walk in.
　L. Frug.　Get your fur,
You shall pull them on within. *[Exit* Luke.
　Gold.　That servile office
Her pride imposes on him.
　Sir John. [*within.*] Goldwire ! Trade-
well !
　Trade.　My master calls.—We come, sir.
　　　　　　[Exeunt Goldwire *and* Tradewell.

Enter Holdfast, *and* Porters *with*
baskets, &c.

　L. Frug.　What have you brought there ?
　Hold.　The cream o' the market ;
Provision enough to serve a garrison.
I weep to think on't : when my master got
His wealth, his family fed on roots and
　　livers,
And necks of beef on Sundays.——
But now I fear it will be spent in poultry ;
Butcher's-meat will not go down.
　L. Frug.　Why, you rascal, is it
At your expense ? what cooks have you pro-
　　vided ?
　Hold.　The best of the city : they've
wrought at my lord mayor's.
　Anne.　Fie on them ! they smell of Fleet-
lane, and Pie-corner.
　Mary.　And think the happiness of man's
life consists
In a mighty shoulder of mutton.
　L. Frug.　I'll have none
Shall touch what I shall eat, you grumbling
　　cur,
But Frenchmen and Italians ; they wear
　　satin,
And dish no meat but in silver.
　Hold.　You may want, though,
A dish or two when the service ends.
　L. Frug.　Leave prating ;
I'll have my will : do you as I command you.
　　　　　　　　　　　　　　[Exeunt.

SCENE II.—*The Street before* Frugal's
House.

Enter Sir Maurice Lacy *and* Page.

Sir Maur. You were with Plenty?
Page. Yes, sir.
Sir Maur. And what answer
Return'd the clown?
Page. Clown, sir! he is transform'd,
And grown a gallant of the last edition;
More rich than gaudy in his habit; yet
The freedom and the bluntness of his
    language
Continues with him. When I told him that
You gave him caution, as he loved the peace
And safety of his life, he should forbear
To pass the merchant's threshold, until you,
Of his two daughters, had made choice of
    her
Whom you design'd to honour as your wife,
He smiled in scorn.
Sir Maur. In scorn!
Page. His words confirm'd it;
They were few, but to this purpose: *Tell
    your master,*
*Though his lordship in reversion were now
    his,*
It cannot awe me. I was born a freeman,
And will not yield, in the way of affection,
Precedence to him: I will visit them,
Though he sate porter to deny me entrance:
*When I meet him next, I'll say more to his
    face.*
Deliver thou this: then gave me a piece,
To help my memory, and so we parted.
Sir Maur. Where got he this spirit?
Page. At the academy of valour,
Newly erected for the institution
Of elder brothers; where they are taught
    the ways,
Though they refuse to seal for a duellist,
How to decline a challenge. He himself
Can best resolve you.

Enter Plenty *and three* Servants.

Sir Maur. You, sir!
Plenty. What with me, sir?
How big you look! I will not loose a hat
To a hair's breadth: move your beaver, I'll
    move mine;
Or if you desire to prove your sword, mine
    hangs
As near my right hand, and will as soon out;
    though I keep not
A fencer to breathe me. Walk into Moor-
    fields—
I dare look on your Toledo. Do not shew
A foolish valour in the streets, to make

Work for shopkeepers and their clubs, 'tis
    scurvy,
And the women will laugh at us.
Sir Maur. You presume
On the protection of your hinds.
Plenty. I scorn it:
Though I keep men, I fight not with their
    fingers,
Nor make it my religion to follow
The gallant's fashion, to have my family
Consisting in a footman and a page,
And those two sometimes hungry. I can
    feed these,
And clothe them too, my gay sir.
Sir Maur. What a fine man
Hath your tailor made you!
Plenty. 'Tis quite contrary,
I have made my tailor, for my clothes are.
    paid for
As soon as put on; a sin your man of title
Is seldom guilty of; but Heaven forgive it!
I have other faults, too, very incident
To a plain gentleman: I eat my venison
With my neighbours in the country, and
    present not
My pheasants, partridges, and growse to
    the usurer;
Nor ever yet paid brokage to his scrivener.
I flatter not my mercer's wife, nor feast her
With the first cherries, or peascods, to pre-
    pare me
Credit with her husband, when I come to
    London.
The wool of my sheep, or a score or two of
    fat oxen
In Smithfield, give me money for my expenses.
I can make my wife a jointure of such lands
    too
As are not encumber'd; no annuity
Or statute lying on them. This I can do,
An it please your future honour, and why,
    therefore,
You should forbid my being suitor with you,
My dullness apprehends not.
Page. This is bitter.   [*Aside.*
Sir Maur. I have heard you, sir, and in
    my patience shewn
Too much of the stoic. But to parley further,
Or answer your gross jeers, would write me
    coward.
This only,—thy great-grandfather was a
    butcher,
And his son a grazier; thy sire, constable
Of the hundred, and thou the first of your
    dunghill
Created gentleman. Now you may come
    on, sir,
You and your thrashers.
Plenty. Stir not, on your lives.

This for the grazier,—this for the butcher.
                        [They fight.
Sir Maur. So, sir !
Page. I'll not stand idle ; draw ! [*to the*
    Servants.] my little rapier,
Against your bumb blades ! I'll one by one
    dispatch you,
Then house this instrument of death and
    horror.

Enter Sir John Frugal, Luke, Goldwire
    junior, and Tradewell *junior.*

Sir John. Beat down their weapons. My
    gate ruffian's hall ! .
What insolence is this?
Luke. Noble sir Maurice,
Worshipful master Plenty——
Sir John. I blush for you.
Men of your quality expose your fame
To every vulgar censure ! this at midnight,
After a drunken supper in a tavern,
(No civil man abroad to censure it,)
Had shewn poor in you ; but in the day, and
    view
Of all that pass by, monstrous !
Plenty. Very well, sir ;
You look'd for this defence.
Sir Maur. 'Tis thy protection ;
But it will deceive thee.
Sir John. Hold, if you proceed thus,
I must make use of the next justice's power,
And leave persuasion ; and in plain terms
    tell you,

Enter Lady Frugal, Anne, Mary, *and*
    Milliscent.

Neither your birth, sir Maurice, nor your
    wealth,
Shall privilege this riot. See whom you have
    drawn
To be spectators of it ! can you imagine
It can stand with the credit of my daughters,
To be the argument of your swords ? i'the
    street too?
Nay, ere you do salute, or I give way
To any private conference, shake hands
In sign of peace : he that draws back, parts
    with
My good opinion. [*They shake hands.*]
    This is as it should be.
Make your approaches, and if their affection
Can sympathise with yours, they shall not
    come,
On my credit, beggars to you. I will hear
What you reply within.
Sir Maur. May I have the honour
To support you, lady ?   [*To* Anne.
Plenty. I know not what's supporting,

But by this fair hand, glove and all, I love
    you.   [*To* Mary.
                  [*Exeunt all but* Luke.

Enter Hoyst, Penury, *and* Fortune.

Luke. You are come with all advantage.
    I will help you
To the speech of my brother.
For. Have you moved him for us ?
Luke. With the best of my endeavours,
    and I hope
You'll find him tractable.
Pen. Heaven grant he prove so !
Hoyst. Howe'er, I'll speak my mind.

Enter Lord Lacy.

Luke. Do so, master Hoyst.
Go in : I'll pay my duty to this lord,
And then I am wholly yours.
    [*Exeunt* Hoyst, Penury, *and* Fortune.
              Heaven bless your honour !
L. Lacy. Your hand, master Luke : the
    world's much changed with you
Within these few months ; then you were
    the gallant :
No meeting at the horse-race, cocking,
    hunting,
Shooting, or bowling, at which master Luke
Was not a principal gamester, and com-
    panion
For the nobility.
Luke. I have paid dear
For those follies, my good lord ; and 'tis but
    justice
That such as soar above their pitch, and
    will not
Be warn'd by my example, should, like me,
Share in the miseries that wait upon it.
Your honour, in your charity, may do well
Not to upbraid me with those weaknesses,
Too late repented.
L. Lacy. I nor do, nor will ;
And you shall find I'll lend a helping hand
To raise your fortunes : how deals your
    brother with you ?
Luke. Beyond my merit, I thank his
    goodness for't.
I am a free man, all my debts discharged ;
Nor does one creditor, undone by me,
Curse my loose riots. I have meat and
    clothes,
Time to ask heaven remission for what's
    past ;
Cares of the world by me are laid aside,
My present poverty's a blessing to me ;
And though I have been long, I dare not say
I ever lived till now.
L. Lacy. You bear it well ;
Yet as you wish I should receive for truth

What you deliver, with that truth acquaint
  me
With your brother's inclination. I have
  heard,
In the acquisition of his wealth, he weighs
  not
Whose ruins he.builds upon.
  Luke. In that, report
Wrongs him, my lord. He is a citizen,
And would increase his heap, and will not lose
What the law gives him : such as are worldly
  wise
Pursue that track, or they will ne'er wear
  scarlet.
But if your honour please to know his temper,
You are come opportunely. I can bring you
Where you, unseen, shall see and hear his
  carriage
Towards some poor men, whose making, or
  undoing,
Depends upon his pleasure.
  L. Lacy. To my wish :
I know no object that could more content me.
                              [*Exeunt.*

SCENE III.—*A Counting-room in* Frugal's
              House.

Enter Sir John Frugal, Hoyst, Fortune,
    Penury, *and* Goldwire *junior.*

  Sir John. What would you have me do?
reach me a chair.
When I lent my monies I appear'd an angel;
But now I would call in mine own, a devil.
  Hoyst. Were you the devil's dam, you
must stay till I have it,
For as I am a gentleman——

Re-enter Luke, *behind, with* Lord Lacy,
    whom he places near the door.

  Luke. There you may hear all.
  Hoyst. I pawn'd you my land for the tenth
part of the value :
Now, 'cause I am a gamester, and keep or-
  dinaries,
And a livery punk or so, and trade not with
The money-mongers' wives, not one will be
  bound for me :
'Tis a hard case ; you must give me longer
  day,
Or I shall grow very angry.
  Sir John. Fret, and spare not.
I know no obligation lies upon me
With my honey to feed drones. But to the
  purpose,
How much owes Penury?
  Gold. Two hundred pounds :
His bond three times since forfeited.
  Sir John. Is it sued ?

  Gold. Yes, sir, and execution out against
him.
  Sir John. For body and goods ?
  Gold. For both, sir.
  Sir John. See it served.
  Pen. I am undone ; my wife and family
Must starve for want of bread.
  Sir John. More infidel thou,
In not providing better to support them.
What's Fortune's debt ?
  Gold. A thousand, sir.
  Sir John. An estate
For a good man ! You were the glorious
  trader,
Embraced all bargains ; the main venturer
In every ship that launch'd forth ; kept your
  wife
As a lady ; she had her caroch, her choice
Of summer houses, built with other men's
  monies
Ta'en up at interest, the certain road
To Ludgate in a citizen. Pray you acquaint
  me,
How were my thousand pounds employ'd ?
  For. Insult not
On my calamity ; though, being a debtor,
And a slave to him that lends, I must endure
  it.
Yet hear me speak thus much in my defence ;
Losses at sea, and those, sir, great and
  many,
By storms and tempests, not domestical riots
In soothing my wife's humour, or mine own,
Have brought me to this low ebb.
  Sir John. Suppose this true,
What is't to me ? I must and will have my
  money,
Or I'll protest you first, and, that done,
  have
The statute made for bankrupts served upon
  you.
  For. 'Tis in your power, but not in mine
  to shun it.
  Luke [*comes forward.*] Not as a brother,
    sir, but with such duty,
As I should use unto my father, since
Your charity is my parent, give me leave
To speak my thoughts.
  Sir John. What would you say?
  Luke. No word, sir,
I hope, shall give offence ; nor let it relish
Of flattery, though I proclaim aloud,
I glory in the bravery of your mind,
To which your wealth's a servant. Not that
  riches
Is, or should be, contemn'd, it being a
  blessing
Derived from heaven, and by your industry
Pull'd down upon you ; but in this, dear sir,

You have many equals : such a man's possessions
Extend as far as yours ; a second hath
His bags as full ; a third in credit flies
As high in the popular voice : but the distinction
And noble difference by which you are
Divided from them, is, that you are styled,
Gentle in your abundance, good in plenty ;
And that you feel compassion in your bowels
Of others' miseries, (I have found it, sir,
Heaven keep me thankful for't !) while they are curs'd
As rigid and inexorable.
    Sir John. I delight not
To hear this spoke to my face.
    Luke. That shall not grieve you.
Your affability, and mildness, clothed
In the garments of your [thankful] debtors' breath,
Shall everywhere, though you strive to conceal it,
Be seen and wonder'd at, and in the act
With a prodigal hand rewarded. Whereas, such
As are born only for themselves, and live so,
Though prosperous in worldly understandings,
Are but like beasts of rapine, that, by odds
Of strength, usurp, and tyrannize o'er others
Brought under their subjection.
    L. Lacy. A rare fellow !
I am strangely taken with him.
    Luke. Can you think, sir,
In your unquestion'd wisdom, I beseech you,
The goods of this poor man sold at an outcry,
His wife turn'd out of doors, his children forced
To beg their bread ; this gentleman's estate,
By wrong extorted, can advantage you ?
    Hoyst. If it thrive with him, hang me, as it will damn him,
If he be not converted.
    Luke. You are too violent.——
Or that the ruin of this once brave merchant,
For such he was esteem'd, though now decay'd,
Will raise your reputation with good men ?
But you may urge, (pray you pardon me, my zeal
Makes me thus bold and vehement,) in this
You satisfy your anger, and revenge
For being defeated. Suppose this, it will not
Repair your loss, and there was never yet
But shame and scandal in a victory,
When the rebels unto reason, passions, fought it.

Then for revenge, by great souls it was ever
Contemn'd, though offered ; entertain'd by none
But cowards, base and abject spirits, strangers
To moral honesty, and never yet
Acquainted with religion.
    L. Lacy. Our divines
Cannot speak more effectually.
    Sir John. Shall I be
Talk'd out of my money ?
    Luke. No, sir, but entreated
To do yourself a benefit, and preserve
What you possess entire.
    Sir John. How, my good brother ?
    Luke. By making these your beadsmen.
When they eat,
Their thanks, next heaven, will be paid to your mercy ;
When your ships are at sea, their prayers will swell
The sails with prosperous winds, and guard them from
Tempests, and pirates ; keep your warehouses
From fire, or quench them with their tears.
    Sir John. No more.
    Luke. Write you a good man in the people's hearts,
Follow you everywhere.
    Sir John. If this could be——
    Luke. It must, or our devotions are but words.
I see a gentle promise in your eye,
Make it a blessed act, and poor me rich,
In being the instrument.
    Sir John. You shall prevail ;
Give them longer day : but, do you hear, no talk of't.
Should this arrive at twelve on the Exchange,
I shall be laugh'd at for my foolish pity,
Which money-men hate deadly. Take your own time,
But see you break not. Carry them to the cellar ;
Drink a health, and thank your orator.
    Pen. On our knees, sir.
    For. Honest master Luke !
    Hoyst. I bless the counter, where
You learn'd this rhetoric.
    Luke. No more of that, friends.
    [*Exeunt* Luke, Hoyst, Fortune, *and* Penury. Lord Lacy *comes forward.*
    Sir John. My honourable lord.
    L. Lacy. I have seen and heard all.
Excuse my manners, and wish heartily
You were all of a piece. Your charity to your debtors,

I do commend ; but where you should express
Your piety to the height, I must boldly tell
    you,
You shew yourself an atheist.
    Sir John. Make me know
My error, and for what I am thus censured,
And I will purge myself, or else confess
A guilty cause.
    L. Lacy. It is your harsh demeanour
To your poor brother.
    Sir John. Is that all?
    L. Lacy. 'Tis more
Than can admit defence. You keep him as
A parasite to your table, subject to
The scorn of your proud wife ; an underling
To his own nieces : and can I with mine
    honour
Mix my blood with his, that is not sensible
Of his brother's miseries?
    Sir John. Pray you, take me with you ;
And let me yield my reasons why I am
No opener-handed to him. I was born
His elder brother, yet my father's fondness
To him, the younger, robb'd me of my birth-
    right:
He had a fair estate, which his loose riots
Soon brought to nothing; wants grew heavy
    on him,
And when laid up for debt, of all forsaken,
And in his own hopes lost, I did redeem him.
    L. Lacy. You could not do less.
    Sir John. Was I bound to it, my lord?
What I possess I may, with justice, call
The harvest of my industry. Would you
    have me,
Neglecting mine own family, to give up
My estate to his disposure?
    L. Lacy. I would have you,
What's pass'd forgot, to use him as a brother;
A brother of fair parts, of a clear soul,
Religious, good, and honest.
    Sir John. Outward gloss
Often deceives, may it not prove so in him !
And yet my long acquaintance with his
    nature
Renders me doubtful ; but that shall not
    make
A breach between us : let us in to dinner,
And what trust, or employment you think fit,
Shall be conferr'd upon him : if he prove
True gold in the touch, I'll be no mourner
    for it.
    L. Lacy. If counterfeit, I'll never trust my
    judgment.   [*Exeunt.*

ACT II.

SCENE I.—*A Room in* Sir John Frugal's
                House.

Enter Luke, Holdfast, Goldwire *junior, and*
                Tradewell *junior.*

    Hold. The like was never seen.
    Luke. Why in this rage, man ?
    Hold. Men may talk of country-christ-
masses, and court-gluttony,
Their thirty-pound butter'd eggs, their pies
    of carps' tongues,
Their pheasants drench'd with ambergris,
    the carcases
Of three fat wethers bruised for gravy, to
Make sauce for a single peacock ; yet their
    feasts
Were fasts, compared with the city's.
    Trade. What dear dainty
Was it, thou murmur'st at ?
    Hold. Did you not observe it?
There were three sucking pigs serv'd up in
    a dish,
Ta'en from the sow as soon as farrowed,
A fortnight fed with dates, and muskadine,
That stood my master in twenty marks apiece,
Besides the puddings in their bellies, made
Of I know not what.—I dare swear the
    cook that dress'd it
Was the devil, disguised like a Dutchman.
    Gold. Yet all this
Will not make you fat, fellow Holdfast.
    Hold. I am rather
Starv'd to look on't. But here's the mis-
    chief—though
The dishes were raised one upon another,
As woodmongers do.billets, for the first,
The second, and third course, and most
    of the shops
Of the best confectioners in London ran-
    sack'd,
To furnish out a banquet ; yet my lady
Call'd me penurious rascal, and cried out,
There was nothing worth the eating.
    Gold. You must have patience,
This is not done often.
    Hold. 'Tis not fit it should ;
Three such dinners more would break an
    alderman,
And make him give up his cloak : I am
    resolv'd
To have no hand in't. I'll make up my
    accompts,
And since my master longs to be undone,
The great fiend be his steward : I will pray,
And bless myself from him !   [*Exit.*
    Gold. The wretch shews in this
An honest care.

Luke. Out on him ! with the fortune
Of a slave he has the mind of one. How-
    ever
She bears me hard, I like my lady's humour,
And my brother's suffrage to it. They are
    now
Busy on all hands ; one side eager for
Large portions, the other arguing strictly
For jointures and security ; but this
Being above our scale, no way concerns us.
How dull you look ! in the mean time, how
    intend you
To spend the hours?
    Gold. We well know how we would,
But dare not serve our wills.
    Trade. Being prentices,
We are bound to attendance.
    Luke. Have you almost served out
The term of your indentures, yet make con-
    science
By starts to use your liberty ! Hast thou
    traded   [*To* Tradewell.
In the other world, exposed unto all dangers,
To make thy master rich, yet dar'st not take
Some portion of the profit for thy pleasure ?
Or wilt thou, [*to* Gold.] being keeper of
    the cash,
Like an ass that carries dainties, feed on
    thistles ?
Are you gentlemen born, yet have no gallant
    tincture
Of gentry in you ? you are no mechanics,
Nor serve some needy shopkeeper, who
    surveys
His every-day takings : you have in your
    keeping
A mass of wealth, from which you may take
    boldly,
And no way be discover'd. He's no rich man
That knows all he possesses, and leaves
    nothing
For his servants to make prey of. I blush
    for you,
Blush at your poverty of spirit ; you,
The brave sparks of the city !
    Gold. Master Luke,
I wonder you should urge this, having felt
What misery follows riot.
    Trade. And the penance.
You endur'd for't in the counter.
    Luke. You are fools,
The case is not the same ; I spent mine own
    money,
And my stock being small, no marvel 'twas
    soon wasted ;
But you, without the least doubt or suspicion,
If cautelous, may make bold with your
    master's.
As, for example, when his ships come home,

And you take your receipts, as 'tis the
    fashion,
For fifty bales of silk you may write forty ;
Or for so many pieces of cloth of bodkin,
Tissue, gold, silver, velvets, satins, taffetas,
A piece of each deducted from the gross
Will ne'er be miss'd, a dash of a pen will
    do it.
    Trade. Ay, but our fathers' bonds, that
    lie in pawn
For our honesties, must pay for't.
    Luke. A mere bugbear,
Invented to fright children ! As I live,
Were I the master of my brother's fortunes,
I should glory in such servants. Didst thou
    know
What ravishing lechery it is to enter
An ordinary, cap-à-pie, trimm'd like a gal-
    lant,
For which, in trunks conceal'd, be ever
    furnish'd ;
The reverence, respect, the crouches,
    cringes,
The musical chime of gold in your cramm'd
    pockets,
Commands from the attendants, and poor
    porters——
    Trade. O rare !
    Luke. Then sitting at the table with
The braveries of the kingdom, you shall hear
Occurrents from all corners of the world,
The plots, the counsels, the designs of
    princes,
And freely censure them ; the city wits
Cried up, or decried, as their passions lead
    them ;
Judgment having nought to do there.
    Trade. Admirable !
    Luke. My lord no sooner shall rise out of
    his chair,
The gaming lord I mean, but you may
    boldly,
By the privilege of a gamester, fill his room,
For in play you are all fellows ; have your
    knife
As soon in the pheasant ; drink your health
    as freely,
And, striking in a lucky hand or two,
Buy out your time.
    Trade. This may be ; but suppose
We should be known?
    Luke. Have money and good clothes,
And you may pass invisible. Or, if
You love a madam-punk, and your wide
    nostril
Be taken with the scent of cambric smocks,
Wrought and perfumed——
    Gold. There, there, master Luke,
There lies my road of happiness !

Luke. Enjoy it.
And pleasure stolen, being sweetest, apprehend
The raptures of being hurried in a coach
To Brentford, Staines, or Barnet.
Gold. 'Tis enchanting.
I have proved it.
Luke. Hast thou?
Gold. Yes, in all these places
I have had my several pagans billeted
For my own tooth, and after ten-pound suppers
The curtains drawn, my fiddlers playing all night
The shaking of the sheets, which I have danced
Again and again with my cockatrice :—
master Luke,
You shall be of my counsel, and we two sworn brothers ;
And therefore I'll be open. I am out now
Six hundred in the cash, yet if on a sudden
I should be call'd to account, I have a trick
How to evade it, and make up the sum.
Trade. Is't possible?
Luke. You can instruct your tutor.
How, how, good Tom?
Gold. Why, look you. We cash-keepers
Hold correspondence, supply one another
On all occasions : I can borrow for a week
Two hundred pounds of one, as much of a second,
A third lays down the rest ; and, when they want,
As my master's monies come in I do repay it :
Ka me, ka thee!
Luke. An excellent knot! 'tis pity
It e'er should be unloosed ; for me it shall not.
You are shewn the way, friend Tradewell, you may make use on't,
Or freeze in the warehouse, and keep company
With the cater, Holdfast.
Trade. No, I am converted.
A Barbican broker will furnish me with outside,
And then, a crash at the ordinary !
Gold. I am for
The lady you saw this morning, who indeed is
My proper recreation.
Luke. Go to, Tom ;
What did you make me?
Gold. I'll do as much for you,
Employ me when you please.
Luke. If you are enquired for,
I will excuse you both.
Trade. Kind master Luke !
Gold. We'll break my master to make you. You know——

Luke. I cannot love money. Go, boys !
[*Exeunt* Goldwire *and* Tradewell.
When time serves,
It shall appear I have another end in't.
[*Exit.*

SCENE II.—*Another Room in the same.*

Enter Sir John Frugal, Lord Lacy, Sir
Maurice Lacy, Plenty, Lady Frugal,
Anne, Mary, *and* Milliscent.

Sir John. Ten thousand pounds a piece
I'll make their portions,
And after my decease it shall be double,
Provided you assure them, for their jointures,
Eight hundred pounds per annum, and entail
A thousand more upon the heirs male
Begotten on their bodies.
L. Lacy. Sir, you bind us
To very strict conditions.
Plenty. You, my lord,
May do as you please : but to me it seems strange,
We should conclude of portions, and of jointures,
Before our hearts are settled.
L. Frug. You say right :
There are counsels of more moment and importance,
On the making up of marriages, to be
Consider'd duly, than the portion or the jointures,
In which a mother's care must be exacted ;
And I, by special privilege, may challenge
A casting voice.
L. Lacy. How's this?
L. Frug. Even so, my lord ;
In these affairs I govern.
L. Lacy. Give you way to't?
Sir John. I must, my lord.
L. Frug. 'Tis fit he should, and shall.
You may consult of something else, this province
Is wholly mine.
Sir Maur. By the city custom, madam?
L. Frug. Yes, my young sir ; and both must look my daughters
Will hold it by my copy.
Plenty. Brave, i' faith !
Sir John. Give her leave to talk, we have the power to do ;
And now touching the business we last talk'd of,
In private, if you please.
L. Lacy. 'Tis well remember'd :
You shall take your own way, madam.
[*Exeunt* Lord Lacy *and* Sir John Frugal.
Sir Maur. What strange lecture
Will she read unto us ?
L. Frug. Such as wisdom warrants

From the superior bodies. Is Stargaze ready
With his several schemes ?
Mill. Yes, madam, and attends
Your pleasure.
· *Sir Maur.* Stargaze ! lady : what is he ?
L. Frug. Call him in.—[*Exit* Milliscent.]
—You shall first know him, then admire
him
For a man of many parts, and those parts
rare ones.
He's every thing, indeed ; parcel physician,
And as such prescribes my diet, and foretels
My dreams when I eat potatoes ; parcel poet,
And sings encomiums to my virtues sweetly ;
My antecedent, or my gentleman-usher,
And as the stars move, with that due pro-
portion
He walks before me : but an absolute master
In the calculation of nativities ;
Guided by that ne'er-erring science call'd,
Judicial astrology.
Plenty. Stargaze ! sure
I have a penny almanack about me
Inscribed to you, as to his patronness,
In his name publish'd.
L. Frug. Keep it as a jewel.
Some statesmen that I will not name are
wholly
Govern'd by his predictions ; for they serve
For any latitude in Christendom,
As well as our own climate.

Re-enter Milliscent, *followed by* Stargaze,
with two schemes.

Sir Maur. I believe so.
Plenty. Must we couple by the almanack?
L. Frug. Be silent ;
And ere we do articulate, much more
Grow to a full conclusion, instruct us
Whether this day and hour, by the planets,
promise
Happy success in marriage.
Star. *In omni*
Parte, et toto.
Plenty. Good learn'd sir, in English ;
And since it is resolved we must be cox-
combs,
Make us so in our own language.
Star. You are pleasant :
Thus in our vulgar tongue then.
L. Frug. Pray you observe him.
Star. Venus, in the west angle, the house
of marriage the seventh house, in trine of
Mars, in conjunction of Luna ; and Mars
almuthen, or lord of the horoscope.
Plenty. Hey-day !
L. Frug. The angels' language ! I am
ravish'd : forward.
Star. Mars, as I said, lord of the horo-

scope, or geniture, in mutual reception of
each other ; she in her exaltation, and he in
his triplicite trine, and face, assure a for-
tunate combination to Hymen, excellent,
prosperous, and happy.
L. Frug. Kneel, and give thanks.
[*The* Women *kneel.*
Sir Maur. For what we understand not ?
Plenty. And have as little faith in ?
L. Frug. Be incredulous ;
To me, 'tis oracle.
Star. Now for the sovereignty of my future
ladies, your daughters, after they are married.
Plenty. Wearing the breeches, you mean?
L. Frug. Touch that point home :
It is a principal one, and, with London
ladies,
Of main consideration.
Star. This is infallible : Saturn out of all dignities in his detriment and fall, combust : and
Venus in the south angle elevated above him,
lady of both their nativities, in her essential
and accidental dignities ; occidental from
the sun, oriental from the angle of the east,
in cazini of the sun, in her joy, and free
from the malevolent beams of infortunes ; in
a sign commanding, and Mars in a constel-
lation obeying ; she fortunate, and he dejected : the disposers of marriage in the
radix of the native in feminine figures, argue,
foretel, and declare rule, pre-eminence, and
absolute sovereignty in women.
L. Frug. Is't possible !
Star. 'Tis drawn, I assure you, from the
aphorisms of the old Chaldeans, Zoroastes
the first and greatest magician, Mercurius
Trismegistus, the later Ptolemy, and the
everlasting prognosticator, old Erra Pater.
L. Frug. Are you yet satisfied ?
Plenty. In what ?
L. Frug. That you
Are bound to obey your wives ; it being so
Determined by the stars, against whose
influence
There is no opposition.
Plenty. Since I must
Be married by the almanack, as I may be,
'Twere requisite the services and duties
Which, as you say, I must pay to my wife,
Were set down in the calendar.
Sir Maur. With the date
Of my apprenticeship.
L. Frug. Make your demands ;
I'll sit as moderatrix, if they press you
With over-hard conditions.
Sir Maur. Mine hath the van ;
I stand your charge, sweet.
Star. Silene.

F F

Anne. I require first,
And that, since 'tis in fashion with kind
  husbands,
In civil manners you must grant, my will
In all things whatsoever, and that will
To be obey'd, not argued.
  L. Frug. And good reason.
  Plenty. A gentle *imprimis!*
  Sir Maur. This in gross contains all :
But your special items, lady.
  Anne. When I am one,
And you are honour'd to be styled my hus-
  band,
To urge my having my page, my gentleman-
  usher,
My woman sworn to my secrets, my caroch
Drawn by six Flanders mares, my coachman,
  grooms,
Postillion, and footmen.
  Sir Maur. Is there aught else
To be demanded?
  Anne. Yes, sir, mine own doctor.
French and Italian cooks, musicians,
  songsters,
And a chaplain that must preach to please
  my fancy :
A friend at court to place me at a masque ;
The private box ta'en up at a new play,
For me and my retinue ; a fresh habit,
Of a fashion never seen before, to draw
The gallants' eyes, that sit on the stage, upon
  me ;
Some decayed lady for my parasite,
To flatter me, and rail at other madams ;
And there ends my ambition.
  Sir Maur. Your desires
Are modest, I confess !
  Anne. These toys subscribed to,
And you continuing an obedient husband,
Upon all fit occasions you shall find me
A most indulgent wife.
  L. Frug. You have said ; give place,
And hear your younger sister.
  Plenty. If she speak
Her language, may the great fiend, booted
  and spurr'd,
With a sithe at his girdle, as the Scotchman
  says,
Ride headlong down her throat !
  Sir Maur. Curse not the judge,
Before you hear the sentence.
  Mary. In some part
My sister hath spoke well for the city
  pleasures,
But I am for the country's ; and must say,
Under correction, in her demands
She was too modest.
  Sir Maur. How like you this exordium ?
  Plenty. Too modest, with a mischief !

Mary. Yes, too modest :
I know my value, and prize it to the worth,
My youth, my beauty——
  Plenty. How your glass deceives you !
  Mary. The greatness of the portion I
  bring with me,
And the sea of happiness that from me
  flows to you.
  Sir Maur. She bears up close.
  Mary. And can you, in your wisdom,
Or rustical simplicity, imagine
You have met some innocent country girl,
  that never
Look'd further than her father's farm, nor
  knew more
Than the price of corn in the market ; or at
  what rate
Beef went a stone ? that would survey your
  dairy,
And bring in mutton out of cheese and
  butter?
That could give directions at what time of
  the moon
To cut her cocks for capons against Christmas,
Or when to raise up goslings ?
  Plenty. These are arts
Would not misbecome you, though you
  should put in
Obedience and duty.
  Mary. Yes, and patience,
To sit like a fool at home, and eye your
  thrashers ;
Then make provision for your slavering
  hounds,
When you come drunk from an alehouse,
  after hunting
With your clowns and comrades, as if all
  were yours,
You the lord paramount, and I the drudge ;
The case, sir, must be otherwise.
  Plenty. How, I beseech you?
  Mary. Marry, thus : I will not, like my
  sister, challenge
What's useful or superfluous from my hus-
  band,
That's base all o'er ; mine shall receive
  from me
What I think fit ; I'll have the state convey'd
Into my hands, and he put to his pension,
Which the wise viragos of our climate prac-
  tise ;—
I will receive your rents.
  Plenty. You shall be hang'd first.
  Mary. Make sale or purchase : nay, I'll
  have my neighbours
Instructed, when a passenger shall ask,
Whose house is this? (though you stand
  by) to answer,
The lady Plenty's. Or who owns this manor?

The lady Plenty. Whose sheep are these, whose oxen?
The lady Plenty's.
Plenty. A plentiful pox upon you!
Mary. And when I have children, if it be inquired
By a stranger, whose they are?—they shall still echo,
My lady Plenty's, the husband never thought on.
Plenty. In their begetting: I think so.
Mary. Since you'll marry
In the city for our wealth, in justice, we
Must have the country's sovereignty.
Plenty. And we nothing.
Mary. A nag of forty shillings, a couple of spaniels,
With a sparhawk, is sufficient, and these too,
As you shall behave yourself, during my pleasure,
I will not greatly stand on. I have said, sir,
Now if you like me, so.
L. Frug. At my entreaty,
The articles shall be easier.
Plenty. Shall they, i' faith?
Like bitch, like whelps.
Sir Maur. Use fair words.
Plenty. I cannot;
I have read of a house of pride, and now I have found one:
A whirlwind overturn it!
Sir Maur. On these terms,
Will your minxship be a lady?
Plenty. A lady in a morris:
I'll wed a pedlar's punk first——
Sir Maur. Tinker's trull,
A beggar without a smock.
Plenty. Let monsieur almanack,
Since he is so cunning with his Jacob's staff,
Find you out a husband in a bowling-alley.
Sir Maur. The general pimp to a brothel.
Plenty. Though that now
All the loose desires of man were raked up in me,
And no means but thy maidenhead left to quench them,
I would turn cinders, or the next sow-gelder,
On my life, should lib me, rather than embrace thee.
Anne. Wooing do you call this!
Mary. A bear-baiting rather.
Plenty. Were you worried, you deserve it, and I hope
I shall live to see it.
Sir Maur. I'll not rail, nor curse you:
Only this, you are pretty peats, and your great portions

Add much unto your handsomeness; but as
You would command your husbands, you are beggars,
Deform'd and ugly.
L. Frug. Hear me.
Plenty. Not a word more.
    [*Exeunt* Sir Maurice Lacy *and* Plenty.
Anne. I ever thought it would come to this.
Mary. We may
Lead apes in hell for husbands, if you bind us
To articulate thus with our suitors.
    [*Both speak weeping.*
Star. Now the cloud breaks,
And the storm will fall on me.   [*Aside.*
L. Frug. You rascal! juggler!
    [*She breaks* Stargaze's *head, and beats him.*
Star. Dear madam.
L. Frug. Hold you intelligence with the stars,
And thus deceive me!
Star. My art cannot err;
If it does, I'll burn my astrolabe. In mine own star
I did foresee this broken head, and beating;
And now your ladyship sees, as I do feel it,
It could not be avoided.
L. Frug. Did you?
Star. Madam,
Have patience but a week, and if you find not
All my predictions true, touching your daughters,
And a change of fortune to yourself, a rare one,
Turn me out of doors. These are not the men the planets
Appointed for their husbands; there will come
Gallants of another metal.
Mill. Once more trust him.
Anne. Mary. Do, lady-mother.
L. Frug. I am vex'd, look to it;
Turn o'er your books; if once again you fool me,
You shall graze elsewhere: come, girls.
Star. I am glad I scaped thus.
    [*Aside. Exeunt.*

SCENE III.—*Another Room in the same.*

Enter Lord Lacy *and* Sir John Frugal.

L. Lacy. The plot shews very likely.
Sir John. I repose
My principal trust in your lordship; 'twill prepare
The physic I intend to minister
To my wife and daughters.
L. Lacy. I will do my parts,
To set it off to the life.

F F 2

Enter Sir Maurice Lacy, *and* Plenty.

Sir John. It may produce
A scene of no vulgar mirth. Here come the
    suitors ;
When we understand how they relish my
    wife's humours,
The rest is feasible.
L. Lacy. Their looks are cloudy.
Sir John. How sits the wind? are you
    ready to launch forth
Into this sea of marriage?
Plenty. Call it rather,
A whirlpool of afflictions.
Sir Maur. If you please
To enjoin me to it, I will undertake
To find the north passage to the Indies
    sooner,
Than plough with your proud heifer.
Plenty. I will make
A voyage to hell first.—
Sir John. How, sir !
Plenty. And court Proserpine,
In the sight of Pluto, his three-headed porter,
Cerberus, standing by, and all the Furies
With their whips to scourge me for't, than
    say, I Jeffrey
Take you, Mary, for my wife.
L. Lacy. Why, what's the matter?
Sir Maur. The matter is, the mother (with
    your pardon,
I cannot but speak so much) is a most un-
    sufferable,
Proud, insolent lady.
Plenty. And the daughters worse.
The dam in years had the advantage to be
    wicked,
But they were so in her belly.
Sir Maur. I must tell you,
With reverence to your wealth, I do begin
To think you of the same leaven.
Plenty. Take my counsel ;
'Tis safer for your credit to profess
Yourself a cuckold, and upon record,
Than say they are your daughters.
Sir John. You go too far, sir.
Sir Maur. They have so articled with us !
Plenty. And will not take us
For their husbands, but their slaves ; and so
    aforehand
They do profess they'll use us.
Sir John. Leave this heat :
Though they are mine, I must tell you, the
    perverseness
Of their manners (which they did not take
    from me, ·
But from their mother) qualified, they de-
    serve
Your equals.

Sir Maur. True ; but what's bred in the
    bone,
Admits no hope of cure.
Plenty. Though saints and angels
Were their physicians.
Sir John. You conclude too fast,
Plenty. God be wi' you ! I'll travel three
    years, but I'll bury
This shame that lives upon me.
Sir Maur. With your license,
I'll keep him company.
L. Lacy. Who shall furnish you
For your expenses.
Plenty. He shall not need your help,
My purse is his ; we were rivals, but now
    friends,
And will live and die so.
Sir Maur. Ere we go, I'll pay
My duty as a son.
Plenty. And till then leave you.
    [*Exeunt* Sir Maurice, Lacy, *and* Plenty.
L. Lacy. They are strangely moved.
Sir John. What's wealth, accompanied
With disobedience in a wife and children ?
My heart will break.
L. Lacy. Be comforted, and hope better :
We'll ride abroad ; the fresh air and dis-
    course
May yield us new inventions.
Sir John. You are noble,
And shall in all things, as you please, com-
    mand me.   [*Exeunt.*

ACT III.

SCENE I.—*A Room in* Secret's *House.*

Enter Shave'em *and* Secret.

Secret. Dead doings, daughter.
Shave. Doings ! sufferings, mother :
[For poor] men have forgot what doing is ;
And such as have to pay for what they do,
Are impotent, or eunuchs.
Secret. You have a friend yet,
And a striker too, I take it.
Shave. Goldwire is so, and comes
To me by stealth, and, as he can steal,
    maintains me
In clothes, I grant ; but alas ! dame, what's
    one friend ?
I would have a hundred ;—for every hour,
    and use,
And change of humour I am in, a fresh one :
'Tis a flock of sheep that makes a lean wolf
    fat,
And not a single lambkin. I am starv'd,
Starv'd in my pleasures ; I know not what
    a coach is,
To hurry me to the Burse, or Old Exchange :

The neathouse for musk-melons, and the
gardens,
Where we traffic for asparagus, are, to me,
In the other world.
Secret. There are other places, lady,
Where you might find customers..
Shave. You would have me foot it
To the dancing of the ropes, sit a whole
afternoon there
In expectation of nuts and pippins ;
Gape round about me, and yet not find a
chapman
That in courtesy will bid a chop of mutton,
Or a pint of drum-wine for me.
Secret. You are so impatient !
But I can tell you news will comfort you,
And the whole sisterhood.
Shave. What's that?
Secret. I am told
Two ambassadors are come over : a French
monsieur,
And a Venetian, one of the clarissimi,
A hot-rein'd marmoset. Their followers,
For their countries' honour, after a long
vacation,
Will make a full term with us.
Shave. They indeed are
Our certain and best customers :—[*knocking
within.*]—Who knocks there ?
Ramb. [*within.*] Open the door.
Secret. What are you?
Ramb. [*within.*] Ramble.
Scuff. [*within.*] Scuffle.
Ramb. [*within.*] Your constant visitants.
Shave. Let them not in ;
I know them, swaggering, suburbian roarers,
Sixpenny truckers.
Ramb. [*within.*] Down go all your win-
dows,
And your neighbours' too shall suffer.
Scuff. [*within.*] Force the doors!
Secret. They are outlaws, mistress
Shave'em, and there is
No remedy against them. What should you
fear?
They are but men ; lying at your close ward,
You have foil'd their betters.
Shave. Out, you bawd ! you care not
Upon what desperate service you employ me,
Nor with whom, so you have your fee.
Secret. Sweet lady-bird,
Sing in a milder key.

Exit, and re-enters with Ramble *and*
Scuffle.

Scuff. Are you grown proud ?
Ramb. I knew you a waistcoateer in the
garden alleys,
And would come to a sailor's whistle.

Secret. Good sir Ramble,
Use her not roughly ; she is very tender.
Ramb. Rank and rotten, is she not?
[*Shave'em draws her knife.*
Shave. Your spittle rogueships
[*Ramble draws his sword.*
Shall not make me so.
Secret. As you are a man, squire Scuffle,
Step in between them : a weapon of that
length,
Was never drawn in my house.
Shave. Let him come on.
I'll scour it in your guts, you dog !
Ramb. You brache !
Are you turn'd mankind ? you forgot I gave
you,
When we last join'd issue, twenty pound——
Shave. O'er night,
And kick'd it out of me in the morning. I
was then
A novice, but I know to make my game
now.
Fetch the constable.

Enter Goldwire *junior, disguised like a
Justice of Peace,* Ding'em *like a Constable, and* Musicians *like Watchmen.*

Secret. Ah me ! here's one unsent for,
And a justice of peace, too.
Shave. I'll hang you both, you rascals !
I can but ride :—you for the purse you cut
In Paul's at a sermon ; I have smoak'd
you, ha !
And you for the bacon you took on the
highway,
From the poor market woman, as she rode
From Rumford.
Ramb. Mistress Shave'em.
Scuff. Mistress Secret,
On our knees we beg your pardon.
Ramb. Set a ransome on us.
Secret. We cannot stand trifling : if you
mean to save them,
Shut them out at the back-door.
Shave. First, for punishment,
They shall leave their cloaks behind them ;
and in sign
I am their sovereign, and they my vassals,
For homage kiss my shoe-sole, rogues, and
vanish ! [*Exeunt* Ramble *and* Scuffle.
Gold. My brave virago! The coast's clear;
strike up.
[Goldwire, *and the rest discover them-
selves.*
Shave. My Goldwire made a justice !
Secret. And your scout
Turn'd constable, and the musicians watch-
men !

Gold. We come not to fright you, but to
make you merry :
A light lavolta. [*They dance.*
Shave. I am tired ; no more.
This was your device ?
Ding. Wholly his own ; he is
No pig-sconce, mistress.
Secret. He has an excellent headpiece.
Gold. Fie ! no, not I ; your jeering gallants
say,
We citizens have no wit.
Ding. He dies that says so :
This was a masterpiece.
Gold. A trifling stratagem,
Not worth the talking of.
Shave. I must kiss thee for it,
Again, and again. [*They kiss.*
Ding. Make much of her. Did you
know
What suitors she had since she saw you——
Gold. I' the way of marriage?
Ding. Yes, sir ; for marriage, and the other
thing too ;
The commodity is the same. An Irish lord
offer'd her
Five pound a week.
Secret. And a cashier'd captain, half
Of his entertainment.
Ding. And a new-made courtier,
The next suit he could beg.
Gold. And did my sweet one
Refuse all this, for me ?
Shave. Weep not for joy ;
'Tis true. Let others talk of lords and com-
manders,
And country heirs for their servants ; but
give me
My gallant prentice ! he parts with his money
So civilly and demurely, keeps no account
Of his expenses, and comes ever furnish'd. –
I know thou hast brought money to make
up
My gown and petticoat, with the appurte-
nances.
Gold. I have it here, duck ; thou shalt
want for nothing.
Shave. Let the chamber be perfumed ;
and get you, sirrah, [*To* Ding'em.
His cap and pantofles ready.
Gold. There's for thee,
And thee : that for a banquet.
Secret. And a caudle
Again you rise.
Gold. There. [*Gives them money.*
Shave. Usher us up in state.
Gold. You will be constant ?
Shave. Thou art the whole world to me.
[*Exeunt ;* Gold. *and* Shave. *embracing,
music playing before them.*

SCENE II.—*A Room in* Sir John Frugal's
House.

Enter Luke.

Anne. [*within.*] Where is this uncle ?
L. Frug. [*within.*] Call this beadsman-
brother ;
He hath forgot attendance.
Mary. [*within.*] Seek him out ;
Idleness spoils him.
Luke. I deserve much more
Than their scorn can load me with, and 'tis
but justice
That I should live the family's drudge,
design'd
To all the sordid offices their pride
Imposes on me ; since, if now I sat
A judge in mine own cause, I should conclude
I am not worth their pity. Such as want
Discourse, and judgment, and through weak-
ness fall,
May merit man's compassion ; but I,
That knew profuseness of expense the parent
Of wretched poverty, her fatal daughter,
To riot out mine own, to live upon
The alms of others, steering on a rock
I might have shunn'd ! O Heaven ! it is not
fit
I should look upward, much less hope for
mercy.

Enter Lady Frugal, Anne, Mary, Stargaze,
and Milliscent.

L. Frug. What are you devising, sir ?
Anne. My uncle is much given
To his devotion.
Mary. And takes time to mumble
A paternoster to himself.
L. Frug. Know you where
Your brother is ? it better would become you
(Your means of life depending wholly on him)
To give your attendance.
Luke. In my will I do :
But since he rode forth yesterday with lord
Lacy,
I have not seen him.
L. Frug. And why went not you
By his stirrup ? How do you look ! were his
eyes closed,
You'd be glad of such employment.
Luke. 'Twas his pleasure
I should wait your commands, and those I
am ever
Most ready to receive.
L. Frug. I know you can speak well ;
But say, and do.

Enter Lord Lacy.

Luke. Here comes my lord.

L. Frug. Further off :
You are no companion for him, and his
  business
Aims not at you, as I take it,
Luke. Can I live
In this base condition !
                 [He stands aside.
L. Frug. I hope, my lord,
You had brought master Frugal with you ;
  for I must ask
An account of him from you.
  L. Lacy. I can give it, lady ;
But with the best discretion of a woman,
And a strong fortified patience, I desire you
To give it hearing.
Luke. My heart beats.
L. Frug. My lord, you much amaze me.
L. Lacy. I shall astonish you. The noble
  merchant,
Who, living, was, for his integrity
And upright dealing, (a rare miracle
In a rich citizen,) London's best honour ;
Is——I am loth to speak it.
  Luke. Wonderous strange !
  L. Frug. I do suppose the worst ; not
  dead, I hope?
L. Lacy. Your supposition's true, your
  hopes are false ;
He's dead.
  L. Frug. Ah me !
Anne. My father !
Mary. My kind father !
Luke. Now they insult not.
L. Lacy. Pray hear me out.
He's dead ; dead to the world and you, and,
  now,
Lives only to himself.
  Luke. What riddle's this?
  L. Frug. Act not the torturer in my
  afflictions ;
But make me understand the sum of all
That I must undergo.
  L. Lacy. In few words take it :
He is retired into a monastery,
Where he resolves to end his days.
  Luke. More strange.
  L. Lacy. I saw him take post for Dover,
  and the wind
Sitting so fair, by this he's safe at Calais,
And ere long will be at Lovain.
  L. Frug. Could I guess
What were the motives that induced him
  to it,
'Twere some allay to my sorrows.
  L. Lacy. I'll instruct you,
And chide you into that knowledge ; 'twas
  your pride
Above your rank, and stubborn disobe-
  dience

Of these your daughters, in their milk suck'd
  from you :
At home the harshness of his entertainment,
You wilfully forgetting that your all
Was borrow'd from him ; and to hear
  abroad
The imputations dispers'd upon you,
And justly too, I fear, that drew him to
This strict retirement : and, thus much said
  for him,
I am myself to accuse you.
  L. Frug. I confess
A guilty cause to him ; but, in a thought,
My lord, I ne'er wrong'd you.
  L. Lacy. In fact, you have.
The insolent disgrace you put upon
My only son, and Plenty, men that loved
Your daughters in a noble way, to wash off
The scandal, put a resolution in them
For three years travel.
  L. Frug. I am much grieved for it.
  L. Lacy. One thing I had forgot ; your
  rigour to
His decay'd brother, in which your flatteries,
Or sorceries, made him a co-agent with you,
Wrought not the least impression.
  Luke. Hum ! this sounds well.
  L. Frug. 'Tis now past help : after these
  storms, my lord,
A little calm, if you please.
  L. Lacy. If what I have told you,
Shew'd like a storm, what now I must de-
  liver,
Will prove a raging tempest. His whole
  estate,
In lands and leases, debts and present
  monies,
With all the movables he stood possess'd of,
With the best advice which he could get for
  gold
From his learned counsel, by this formal
  will
Is pass'd o'er to his brother.—*[Giving the*
  will to Luke, *who comes forward.*]—With
  it take
The key of his counting-house. Not a groat
  left you,
Which you can call your own.
  L. Frug. Undone for ever !
  Anne. Mary. What will become of us?
  Luke. Hum !   *[Aside.*
  L. Lacy. The scene is changed,
And he that was your slave, by Fate ap-
  pointed
    [Lady Frugal, Mary, and Anne *kneel.*
Your governor : you kneel to me in vain,
I cannot help you : I discharge the trust
Imposed upon me. This humility,
From him may gain remission, and, perhaps,

Forgetfulness of your barbarous usage to
  him.
L. Frug. Am I come to this?
L. Lacy. Enjoy your own, good sir,
But use it with due reverence.   I once heard
  you
Speak most divinely in the opposition
Of a revengeful humour ; to these shew it,
And such who then depended on the mercy
Of your brother, wholly now at your devo-
  tion,
And make good the opinion I held of you,
Of which I am most confident.
  Luke. Pray you rise,   [*Raises them.*
And rise with this assurance, I am still,
As I was of late, your creature ; and if raised
In anything, 'tis in my power to serve you,
My will is still the same.   O my good lord !
This heap of wealth which you possess me of,
Which to a worldly man had been a blessing,
And to the messenger might with justice
  challenge
A kind of adoration, is to me
A curse I cannot thank you for ; and, much
  less,
Rejoice in that tranquillity of mind
My brother's vows must purchase. I have
  made
A dear exchange with him : he now enjoys
My peace and poverty, the trouble of
His wealth conferr'd on me, and that a
  burthen
Too heavy for my weak shoulders.
  L. Lacy. Honest soul,
With what feeling he receives it !
  L. Frug. You shall have
My best assistance, if you please to use it,
To help you to support it.
  Luke. By no means ;
The weight shall rather sink me, than you
  part
With one short minute from those lawful
  pleasures
Which you were born to, in your care to aid
  me :
You shall have all abundance. In my nature,
I was ever liberal ; my lord, you know it ;
Kind, affable.—And now methinks I see
Before my face the jubilee of joy,
When 'tis assured my brother lives in me,
His debtors, in full cups, crown'd to my
  health,
With pæans to my praise will celebrate !
For they well know 'tis far from me to take
The forfeiture of a bond : nay, I shall blush,
The interest never paid after three years,
When I demand my principal : and his
  servants,
Who from a slavish fear paid their obedience,

By him exacted, now, when they are mine,
Will grow familiar friends, and as such use
  me ;
Being certain of the mildness of my temper,
Which my change of fortune, frequent in
  most men,
Hath not the power to alter.
  L. Lacy. Yet take heed, sir,
You ruin not, with too much lenity,
What his fit severity raised.
  L. Frug. And we fall from
That height we have maintain'd.
  Luke. I'll build it higher,
To admiration higher.   With disdain
I look upon these habits, no way suiting
The wife and daughters of a knighted citizen
Bless'd with abundance.
  L. Lacy. There, sir, I join with you ;
A fit decorum must be kept, the court
Distinguish'd from the city.
  Luke. With your favour,
I know what you would say ; but give me
  leave
In this to be your advocate. You are wide,
Wide the whole region, in what I purpose.
Since all the titles, honours, long descents,
Borrow their gloss from wealth, the rich with
  reason
May challenge their prerogatives : and it
  shall be
My glory, nay a triumph, to revive,
In the pomp that these shall shine, the memory
Of the Roman matrons, who kept captive
  queens
To be their handmaids.   And when you
  appear,
Like Juno, in full majesty, and my nieces,
Like Iris, Hebe, or what deities else
Old poets fancy, (your cramm'd wardrobes
  richer
Than various nature's,) and draw down the
  envy
Of our western world upon you ; only hold
  me
Your vigilant Hermes with aërial wings,
(My caduceus, my strong zeal to serve you,)
Prest to fetch in all rarities may delight you,
And I am made immortal.
  L. Lacy. A strange frenzy !   [*Aside.*
  Luke. Off with these rags, and then to
  bed ; there dream
Of future greatnesss, which, when you awake,
I'll make a certain truth : but I must be
A doer, not a promiser.   The performance
Requiring haste, I kiss your hands, and
  leave you.   [*Exit.*
  L. Lacy. Are we all turn'd statues? have
  his strange words charm'd us ?
What muse you on, lady ?

L. Frug. Do not trouble me.
L. Lacy. Sleep you too, young ones?
Anne. Swift-wing'd time till now
Was never tedious to me. Would 'twere
night!
Mary. Nay, morning rather.
L. Lacy. Can you ground your faith
On such impossibilities? have you so soon
Forgot your good husband?
L. Frug. He was a vanity
I must no more remember.
L. Lacy. Excellent!
You, your kind father?
Anne. Such an uncle never
Was read of in story!
L. Lacy. Not one word in answer
Of my demands?
Mary. You are but a lord; and know,
My thoughts soar higher.
L. Lacy. Admirable! I'll leave you
To your castles in the air.—When I relate
this,
It will exceed belief; but he must know it.
                              [*Aside, and exit.*
Star. Now I may boldly speak. May it
please you, madam,
To look upon your vassal; I foresaw this,
The stars assured it.
L. Frug. I begin to feel
Myself another woman.
Star. Now you shall find
All my predictions true, and nobler matches
Prepared for my young ladies.
Mill. Princely husbands.
Anne. I'll go no less.
Mary. Not a word more;
Provide my night-rail.
Mill. What shall we be to morrow!
                              [*Exeunt.*

SCENE III.—*Another Room in the same.*

Enter Luke.

Luke. 'Twas no fantastic object, but a
truth,
A real truth; nor dream: I did not slumber,
And could wake ever with a brooding eye
To gaze upon't! it did endure the touch;
I saw and felt it! Yet what I beheld
And handled oft, did so transcend belief,
(My wonder and astonishment pass'd o'er,)
I faintly could give credit to my senses.
Thou dumb magician,—[*Taking out a key.*]
—that without a charm
Didst make my entrance easy, to possess
What wise men wish, and toil for! Hermes'
moly,
Sibylla's golden bough, the great elixir,
Imagined only by the alchemist,

Compared with thee are shadows,—thou
the substance,
And guardian of felicity! No marvel,
My brother made thy place of rest his bosom,
Thou being the keeper of his heart, a
mistress ·
To be hugg'd ever! In by-corners of
This sacred room, silver in bags, heap'd up
Like billets saw'd and ready for the fire,
Unworthy to hold fellowship with bright
gold
That flow'd about the room, conceal'd itself.
There needs no artificial light; the splen-
dour
Makes a perpetual day there, night and
darkness
By that still-burning lamp for ever banish'd!
But when, guided by that, my eyes had made
Discovery of the caskets, and they open'd,
Each sparkling diamond, from itself, shot
forth
A pyramid of flames, and, in the roof,
Fix'd it a glorious star, and made the place
Heaven's abstract, or epitome!—rubies,
sapphires,
And ropes of orient pearl, these seen, I
could not
But look on with contempt. And yet I
found,
What weak credulity could have no faith in,
A treasure far exceeding these: here lay
A manor bound fast in a skin of parchment,
The wax continuing hard, the acres melting;
Here a sure deed of gift for a market-town,
If not redeem'd this day, which is not in
The unthrift's power: there being scarce one
shire
In Wales or England, where my monies are
not
Lent out at usury, the certain hook
To draw in more. I am sublimed! gross
earth
Supports me not; I walk on air!—Who's
there?

Enter Lord Lacy, *with* Sir John Frugal,
Sir Maurice Lacy, *and* Plenty, *painted
and disguised as Indians.*

Thieves! raise the street! thieves!
L. Lacy. What strange passion's this!
Have you your eyes? do you know me?
Luke. You, my lord,
I do: but this retinue, in these shapes too,
May well excuse my fears. When 'tis your
pleasure
That I should wait upon you, give me leave
To do it at your own house, for I must tell
you,

Things as they now are with me well con-
sider'd,
I do not like such visitants.
   L. Lacy. Yesterday,
When you had nothing, praise your poverty
for't,
You could have sung secure before a thief;
But now you are grown rich, doubts and
suspicions,
And needless fears, possess you. Thank a
good brother;
But let not this exalt you.
   Luke. A good brother!
Good in his conscience, I confess, and wise,
In giving o'er the world. But his estate,
Which your lordship may conceive great, no
way answers
The general opinion : alas!
With a great charge, I am left a poor man
by him.
   L. Lacy. A poor man, say you?
   Luke. Poor, compared with what
'Tis thought I do possess. Some little land,
Fair household furniture, a few good debts,
But empty bags, I find : yet I will be
A faithful steward to his wife and daughters;
And, to the utmost of my power, obey
His will in all things.
   L. Lacy. I'll not argue with you
Of his estate, but bind you to performance
Of his last request, which is, for testimony
Of his religious charity, that you would
Receive these Indians, lately sent him from
Virginia, into your house ; and labour,
At any rate, with the best of your en-
deavours,
Assisted by the aids of our divines,
To make them Christians.
   Luke. Call you this, my lord,
Religious charity ; to send infidels,
Like hungry locusts, to devour the bread
Should feed his family? I neither can,
Nor will consent to't.
   L. Lacy. Do not slight it ; 'tis
With him a business of such consequence,
That should he only hear 'tis not embraced,
And cheerfully, in this his conscience aiming
At the saving of three souls, 'twill draw him
o'er
To see it himself accomplish'd.
   Luke. Heaven forbid
I should divert him from his holy purpose,
To worldly cares again ! I rather will
Sustain the burthen, and, with the converted,
Feast the converters, who, I know, will prove
The greater feeders.
   Sir John. Oh, *ha, enewah Chrish bully
leika.*
   Plenty. Enaula.

   Sir Maur. Harrico botikia bonnery.
   Luke. Ha ! in this heathen language,
How is it possible our doctors should
Hold conference with them, or I use the
means
For their conversion ?
   L. Lacy. That shall be no hindrance
To your good purposes : they have lived
long
In the English colony, and speak our
language
As their own dialect ; the business does
concern you :
Mine own designs command me hence. Con-
tinue,
As in your poverty you were, a pious
And honest man.   *[Exit.*
   Luke. That is, interpreted,
A slave and beggar.
   Sir John. You conceive it right ;
There being no religion, nor virtue,
But in abundance, and no vice but want.
All deities serve Plutus.
   Luke. Oracle !
   Sir John. Temples raised to ourselves in
the increase
Of wealth and reputation, speak a wise
man;
But sacrifice to an imagined Power,
Of which we have no sense but in belief,
A superstitious fool.
   Luke. True worldly wisdom !
   Sir John. All knowledge else is folly.
   Sir Maur. Now we are yours,⎤
Be confident your better angel is ⎬
Enter'd your house.   ⎦
   Plenty. There being nothing in
The compass of your wishes, but shall end
In their fruition to the full.
   Sir John. As yet,
You do not know us ; but when you under-
stand
The wonders we can do, and what the ends
were
That brought us hither, you will entertain us
With more respect.
   Luke. There's something whispers to me
These are no common men. [*Aside.*]—My
house is yours,
Enjoy it freely : only grant me this,
Not to be seen abroad till I have heard
More of your sacred principles. Pray enter:
You are learned Europeans, and we worse
Than ignorant Americans.
   Sir John. You shall find it.   *[Exeunt.*

————

ACT IV.

SCENE I.—*A Room in* Frugal's *House.*

Enter Ding'em, Gettall, *and* Holdfast.

Ding. Not speak with him! with fear
survey me better,
Thou figure of famine!

Gett. Coming, as we do,
From his quondam patrons, his dear ingles
now,
The brave spark Tradewell—

Ding. And the man of men
In the service of a woman, gallant Goldwire!

Enter Luke.

Hold. I know them for his prentices,
without
These flourishes.—Here are rude fellows, sir.

Ding. Not yours, you rascal!

Hold. No, don pimp; you may seek them
In Bridewell, or the hole; here are none of
your comrogues.

Luke. One of them looks as he would cut
my throat:
Your business, friends?

Hold. I'll fetch a constable;
Let him answer him in the stocks.

Ding. Stir, an thou dar'st:
Fright me with Bridewell and the stocks!
they are fleabitings
I am familiar with.   [*Draws.*

Luke. Pray you put up:
And, sirrah, hold your peace.

                             [*To* Holdfast.

Ding. Thy word's a law,
And I obey. Live, scrape-shoe, and be
thankful.
Thou man of muck and money, for as such
I now salute thee, the suburbian gamesters
Have heard thy fortunes, and I am, in person,
Sent to congratulate.

Gett. The news hath reach'd
The ordinaries, and all the gamesters are
Ambitious to shake the golden golls
Of worshipful master Luke. I come from
Tradewell,
Your fine facetious factor.

Ding. I from Goldwire:
He and his Helen have prepared a banquet,
With the appurtenances, to entertain thee;
For, I must whisper in thine ear, thou art
To be her Paris: but bring money with
thee,
To quit old scores.

Gett. Blind chance hath frown'd upon
Brave Tradewell: he's blown up, but not
without
Hope of recovery, so you supply him

With a good round sum. In my house, I can
assure you,
There's half a million stirring.

Luke. What hath he lost?

Gett. Three hundred.

Luke. A trifle.

Gett. Make it up a thousand,
And I will fit him with such tools as shall
Bring in a myriad.

Luke. They know me well,
Nor need you use such circumstances for
them:
What's mine, is theirs. They are my friends,
not servants,
But in their care to enrich me; and these
courses,
The speeding means. Your name, I pray
you?

Gett. Gettall.
I have been many years an ordinary-keeper,
My box my poor revenue.

Luke. Your name suits well
With your profession. Bid him bear up; he
shall not
Sit long on Penniless-Bench.

Gett. There spake an angel!

Luke. You know mistress Shave'em?

Gett. The pontifical punk?

Luke. The same. Let him meet me there
some two hours hence:
And tell Tom Goldwire I will then be with
him,
Furnish'd beyond his hopes; and let your
mistress
Appear in her best trim.

Ding. She will make thee young,
Old Æson: she is ever furnish'd with
Medea's drugs, restoratives. I fly
To keep them sober till thy worship come;
They will be drunk with joy else.

Gett. I'll run with you.

               [*Exeunt* Ding'em *and* Gettall.

Hold. You will not do as you say, I hope?

Luke. Enquire not;
I shall do what becomes me.—[*Knocking
within.*]—To the door.

                             [*Exit* Holdfast.

New visitants!

Re-enter Holdfast.

                   What are they?

Hold. A whole batch, sir,
Almost of the same leaven: your needy
debtors,
Penury, Fortune, Hoyst.

Luke. They come to gratulate
The fortune fallen upon me.

Hold. Rather, sir,
Like the others, to prey on you.

Luke. I am simple ; they
Know my good nature : but let them in,
   however.
Hold. All will come to ruin ! I see beg-
gary
Already knocking at the door.—You may
   enter—   [*Speaking to those without.*
But use a conscience, and do not work upon
A tender-hearted gentleman too much ;
'Twill shew like charity in you.

   Enter Fortune, Penury, *and* Hoyst.

Luke. Welcome, friends :
I know your hearts and wishes ; you are
   glad
You have changed your creditor.
   Pen. I weep for joy,
To look upon his worship's face.
   For. His worship's !
I see lord mayor written on his forehead ;
The cap of maintenance, and city sword,
Borne up in state before him.
   Hoyst. Hospitals,
And a third Burse, erected by his honour.
   Pen. The city poet on the pageant day
Preferring him before Gresham.
   Hoyst. All the conduits
Spouting canary sack.
   For. Not a prisoner left,
Under ten pounds.
   Pen. We, his poor beadsmen, feasting
Our neighbours on his bounty.
   Luke. May I make good
Your prophecies, gentle friends, as I'll en-
   deavour,
To the utmost of my power !
   Hold. Yes, for one year,
And break the next.
   Luke. You are ever prating, sirrah.
Your present business, friends ?
   For. Were your brother present,
Mine had been of some consequence ; but
   now
The power lies in your worship's hand, 'tis
   little,
And will, I know, as soon as ask'd, be
   granted.
   Luke. 'Tis very probable.
   For. The kind forbearance
Of my great debt, by your means, Heaven
   be prais'd for't !
Hath raised my sunk estate.   I have two
   ships,
Which I long since gave for lost, above my
   hopes
Return'd from Barbary, and richly freighted.
   Luke. Where are they ?
   For. Near Gravesend.
   Luke. I am truly glad of it.

For. I find your worship's charity, and
   dare swear so.
Now may I have your license, as I know
With willingness I shall, to make the best
Of the commodities, though you have exe-
   cution,
And after judgment, against all that's
   mine,
As my poor body, I shall be enabled
To make payment of my debts to all the
   world,
And leave myself a competence.
   Luke. You much wrong me,
If you only doubt it.   Yours, master Hoyst ?
   Hoyst. 'Tis the surrendering back the
   mortgage of
My lands, and on good terms, but three
   days' patience ;
By an uncle's death I have means left to
   redeem it,
And cancel all the forfeited bonds I seal'd
   to,
In my riots, to the merchant ; for I am
Resolv'd to leave off play, and turn good
   husband.
   Luke. A good intent, and to be cherish'd
   in you.
Yours, Penury ?
   Pen. My state stands as it did, sir ;
What I owed I owe, but can pay nothing to
   you.
Yet, if you please to trust me with ten pounds
   more,
I can buy a commodity of a sailor,
Will make me a freeman.   There, sir, is his
   name ;
And the parcels I am to deal for.
                    [*Gives him a paper.*
   Luke. You are all so reasonable
In your demands, that I must freely grant
   them.
Some three hours hence meet me on the
   exchange,
You shall be amply satisfied.
   Pen. Heaven preserve you !
   For. Happy were London, if, within her
   walls,
She had many such rich men !
   Luke. No more ; now leave me :
I am full of various thoughts.—[*Exeunt*
   Fortune, Hoyst, *and* Penury.]—Be
   careful, Holdfast ;
I have much to do.
   Hold. And I something to say,
Would you give me hearing.
   Luke. At my better leisure.
Till my return look well unto the Indians ;
In the mean time, do you as this directs you.
                 [*Gives him a paper. Exeunt.*

SCENE II.—*A Room in* Shave'em's
House.

Enter Goldwire *junior,* Tradewell *junior,*
Shave'em, Secret, Gettall, *and* Ding'em.

Gold. All that is mine is theirs. Those
were his words?

Ding. I am authentical.

Trade. And that *I should not
Sit long on Penniless-Bench ?*

Gett. But suddenly start up
A gamester at the height, and cry *At all!*

Shave. And did he seem to have an inclination
To toy with me?

Ding. He wish'd you would put on
Your best habiliments, for he resolv'd
To make a jovial day on't.

Gold. Hug him close, wench,
And thou mayst eat gold and amber. I well
know him
For a most insatiate drabber : he hath given,
Before he spent his own estate, which was
Nothing to the huge mass he's now possess'd
of,
A hundred pound a leap.

Shave. Hell take my doctor !
He should have brought me some fresh oil
of talc ;
These ceruses are common.

Secret. Troth, sweet lady,
The colours are well laid on.

Gold. And thick enough :
I find that on my lips.

Shave. Do you so, Jack Sauce !
I'll keep them further off.

Gold. But be assured first
Of a new maintainer, ere you cashier the
old one.
But bind him fast by thy sorceries, and thou
shalt
Be my revenue ; the whole college study
The reparation of thy ruin'd face ;
Thou shalt have thy proper and bald-headed
coachman ;
Thy tailor and embroiderer shall kneel
To thee, their idol : Cheapside and the Ex-
change
Shall court thy custom, and thou shalt forget
There e'er was a St. Martin's : thy procurer
Shall be sheath'd in velvet, and a reverend
veil
Pass her for a grave matron. Have an eye to
the door,
And let loud music, when this monarch enters,
Proclaim his entertainment.

Ding. That's my office.
                    [*Flourish of cornets within.*
The consort's ready.

Enter Luke.

Trade. And the god of pleasure,
Master Luke, our Comus, enters.

Gold. Set your face in order,
I will prepare him.—Live I to see this day,
And to acknowledge you my royal master ?

Trade. Let the iron chests fly open, and
the gold,
Rusty for want of use, appear again !

Gett. Make my ordinary flourish !

Shave. Welcome, sir,
To your own palace !   [*The music plays.*

Gold. Kiss your Cleopatra,
And shew yourself, in your magnificent
bounties,
A second Antony !

Ding. All the nine worthies !

Secret. Variety of pleasures wait upon you,
And a strong back !

Luke. Give me leave to breathe, I pray
you.
I am astonish'd ! all this preparation
For me? and this choice modest beauty
wrought
To feed my appetite ?

All. We are all your creatures.

Luke. A house well furnish'd !

Gold. At your own cost, sir,
Glad I the instrument. I prophesied
You should possess what now you do, and
therefore
Prepared it for your pleasure. There's no
rag
This Venus wears, but, on my knowledge, was
Derived from your brother's cash : the lease
of the house,
And furniture, cost near a thousand, sir.

Shave. But now you are master both of it
and me,
I hope you'll build elsewhere.

Luke. And see you placed,
Fair one, to your desert. As I live, friend
Tradewell,
I hardly knew you, your clothes so well
become you.
What is your loss? speak truth.

Trade. Three hundred, sir.

Gett. But, on a new supply, he shall recover
The sum told twenty times o'er.

Shave. There's a banquet,
And after that a soft couch, that attends you.

Luke. I couple not in the daylight. Expectation
Heightens the pleasure of the night, my
sweet one !
Your music's harsh, discharge it ; I have
provided

A better consort, and you shall frolic it
In another place.   [*The music ceases.*
  Gold. *But have you brought gold, and*
    store, sir?
  Trade. I long to *Ware the caster!*
  Gold. I to appear
In a fresh habit.
  Shave. My mercer and my silkman
Waited me, two hours since.
  Luke. I am no porter,
To carry so much gold as will supply
Your vast desires, but I have ta'en order for
  you ;

  Enter Sheriff, Marshal, *and* Officers.

You shall have what is fitting, and they
  come here
Will see it perform'd.—Do your offices: you
  have
My lord chief-justice's warrant for't.
  Sher. Seize them all,
  Shave. The city marshal !
  Gold. And the sheriff ! I know him.
  Secret. We are betray'd.
  Ding. Undone.
  Gett. Dear master Luke.
  Gold. You cannot be so cruel ; your per-
    suasion
Chid us into these courses, oft repeating,
Shew yourselves city-sparks, and hang up
  money !
  Luke. True ; when it was my brother's, I
    contemn'd it ;
But now it is mine own, the case is alter'd.
  Trade. Will you prove yourself a devil?
    tempt us to mischief,
And then discover it ?
  Luke. Argue that hereafter :
In the mean time, master Goldwire, you
  that made
Your ten-pound suppers ; kept your punks
  at livery
In Brentford, Staines, and Barnet, and this,
  in London ;
Held correspondence with your fellow-
  cashiers,
Ka me, ka thee ! and knew, in your ac-
  compts,
To cheat my brother ; if you can, evade me.
If there be law in London, your father's
  bonds
Shall answer for what you are out.
  Gold. You often told us
It was a bugbear.
  Luke. Such a one as shall fright them
Out of their estates, to make me satisfaction
To the utmost scruple. And for you, madam,
My Cleopatra, by your own confession,

Your house, and all your moveables, are
  mine ;
Nor shall you nor your matron need to
  trouble
Your mercer, or your silkman ; a blue gown,
And a whip to boot, as I will handle it,
Will serve the turn in Bridewell ; and these
  soft hands,
When they are inured to beating hemp, be
  scour'd
In your penitent tears, and quite forget their
  powders
And bitter almonds.
  Shave. Secret. Ding. Will you show no
    mercy ?
  Luke. I am inexorable.
  Gett. I'll make bold
To take my leave ; the gamesters stay my
  coming.
  Luke. We must not part so, gentle master
    Gettall.
Your box, your certain income, must pay
  back
Three hundred, as I take it, or you lie by it.
There's *half a million stirring in your*
  house,
This a poor trifle.—Master shrieve and
  master marshal,
On your perils, do your offices.
  Gold. Dost thou cry now
                        [*To* Tradewell.
Like a maudlin gamester after loss? I'll suffer
Like a Roman, and now, in my misery,
In scorn of all thy wealth, to thy teeth tell
  thee
Thou wert my pander.
  Luke. Shall I hear this from
My prentice ?
  Mar. Stop his mouth.
  Sher. Away with them.
      [*Exeunt* Sheriff, Marshal, *and* Officers,
        with Gold. Trade. Shave. Secret. Gett.
        and Ding.
  Luke. A prosperous omen in my entrance
    to
My alter'd nature ! these house thieves re-
  moved,
And what was lost, beyond my hopes, re-
  cover'd,
Will add unto my heap ; increase of wealth
Is the rich man's ambition, and mine
Shall know no bounds. The valiant Macedon
Having in his conceit subdued one world,
Lamented that there were no more to con-
  quer :
In my way, he shall be my great example.
And when my private house, in cramm'd
  abundance,
Shall prove the chamber of the city poor,

And Genoa's bankers shall look pale with
    envy
When I am mentioned, I shall grieve there is
No more to be exhausted in one kingdom.
Religion, conscience, charity, farewell!
To me you are words only, and no more ;
All human happiness consists in store.
                           [Exit.

SCENE III.—*A Street.*

Enter Serjeants *with* Fortune, Hoyst, *and*
        Penury.

For. At master Luke's suit ! the action
    twenty thousand !
1 *Serj.* With two or three executions,
    which shall grind you
To powder, when we have you in the counter.
For. Thou dost belie him, varlet ! he,
    good gentleman,
Will weep when he hears how we are used.
1 *Serj.* Yes, millstones.
Pen. He promised to lend me ten pound
    for a bargain,
He will not do it this way.
2 *Serj.* I have warrant
For what I have done. You are a poor fellow,
And there being little to be got by you,
In charity, as I am an officer,
I would not have seen you, but upon com-
    pulsion,
And for mine own security.
3 *Serj.* You are a gallant,
And I'll do you a courtesy, provided
That you have money : for a piece an hour,
I'll keep you in the house till you send for
    bail.
2 *Serj.* In the mean time, yeoman, run
    to the other counter,
And search if there be aught else out against
    him.
3 *Serj.* That done, haste to his creditors :
    he's a prize,
And as we are city pirates by our oaths,
We must make the best on't.
Hoyst. Do your worst, I care not.
I'll be removed to the Fleet, and drink and
    drab there
In spite of your teeth.   I now repent I ever
Intended to be honest.

Enter Luke.

3 *Serj.* Here he comes
You had best tell so.
For. Worshipful sir,
You come in time to free us from these ban-
    dogs.
I know you gave no way to't.
Pen. Or if you did,
'Twas but to try our patience.

Hoyst. I must tell you
I do not like such trials.
Luke. Are you serjeants,
Acquainted with the danger of a rescue,
Yet stand here prating in the street? the
    counter
Is a safer place to parley in.
For. Are you in earnest?
Luke. Yes, faith ; I will be satisfied to a
    token,
Or, build upon't, you rot there.
For. Can a gentleman
Of your soft and silken temper, speak such
    language?
Pen. So honest, so religious ?
Hoyst. That preach'd
So much of charity for us to your brother ?
Luke. Yes, when I was in poverty it
    shew'd well ;
But I inherit with his state, his mind,
And rougher nature. I grant then, I talk'd,
For some ends to myself conceal'd, of pity,
The poor man's orisons, and such like no-
    things :
But what I thought you all shall feel, and
    with rigour ;
Kind master Luke says it.   Who pays for
    your attendance?
Do you wait gratis ?
For. Hear us speak.
Luke. While I,
Like the adder, stop mine ears : or did I
    listen,
Though you spake with the tongues of
    angels to me,
I am not to be alter'd.
For. Let me make the best
Of my ships, and their freight.
Pen. Lend me the ten pounds you pro-
    mised.
Hoyst. A day or two's patience to redeem
    my mortgage,
And you shall be satisfied.
For. To the utmost farthing.
Luke. I'll shew some mercy ; which is,
    that I will not
Torture you with false hopes, but make you
    know
What you shall trust to.—Your ships to my
    use
Are seized on.—I have got into my hands
Your bargain from the sailor, 'twas a good one
For such a petty sum.—I will likewise take
The extremity of your mortgage, and the
    forfeit
Of your several bonds ; the use and principal
Shall not serve.—Think of the basket,
    wretches,
And a coal-sack for a winding-sheet.

For. Broker!
Hoyst. Jew!
For. Imposter!
Hoyst. Cut-throat!
For. Hypocrite!
Luke. Do, rail on;
Move mountains with your breath, it shakes
　　not me.
Pen. On my knees I beg compassion. My
　　wife and children
Shall hourly pray for your worship.
For. Mine betake thee
To the devil, thy tutor.
Pen. Look upon my tears.
Hoyst. My rage.
For. My wrongs.
Luke. They are all alike to me;
Entreaties, curses, prayers, or imprecations.
Do your duties, serjeants; I am elsewhere
　　look'd for.　　　　　　　[*Exit.*
3 *Serj.* This your kind creditor!
2 *Serj.* A vast villain, rather.
Pen. See, see, the serjeants pity us! yet
　　he's marble.
Hoyst. Buried alive!
For. There's no means to avoid it.
　　　　　　　　　　　　[*Exeunt.*

SCENE IV.—*A Room in* Sir John Frugal's
　　　　　　　House.

Enter Holdfast, Stargaze, *and* Milliscent.

Star. Not wait upon my lady?
Hold. Nor come at her;
You find it not in your almanack.
Mill. Nor I have license
To bring her breakfast?
Hold. My new master hath
Decreed this for a fasting-day. She hath
　　feasted long,
And, after a carnival, Lent ever follows.
Mill. Give me the key of her wardrobe.
　　You'll repent this;
I must know what gown she'll wear.
Hold. You are mistaken,
Dame president of the sweetmeats; she and
　　her daughters
Are turn'd philosophers, and must carry all
Their wealth about them; they have clothes
　　laid in their chamber,
If they please to put them on, and without
　　help too,
Or they may walk naked. You look, master
　　Stargaze,
As you had seen a strange comet, and had
　　now foretold,
The end of the world, and on what day:
　　and you,
As the wasps had broke into the gallipots,
And eaten up your apricots.

L. Frug. [*within.*] Stargaze! Milliscent!
Mill. My lady's voice.
Hold. Stir not, you are confined here.
Your ladyship may approach them, if you
　　please;
But they are bound in this circle.　[*Aloud.*
L. Frug. [*within.*] Mine own bees
Rebel against me! When my kind brother
　　knows this,
I will be so revenged!
Hold. The world's well alter'd.
He's your kind brother now; but yesterday
Your slave and jesting-stock.

Enter Lady Frugal, Anne, *and* Mary, *in
　　coarse habits, weeping.*

Mill. What witch hath transform'd you?
Star. Is this the glorious shape your
　　cheating brother
Promised you should appear in?
Mill. My young ladies
In buffin gowns, and green aprons! tear
　　them off;
Rather shew all than be seen thus.
Hold. 'Tis more comely,
I wis, than their other whim-whams.
Mill. A French hood too,
Now, tis out of fashion! a fool's cap would
　　show better.
L. Frug. We are fool'd indeed! by whose
　　command are we used thus?

Enter Luke.

Hold. Here he comes can best resolve you.
L. Frug. O, good brother!
Do you thus preserve your protestation to
　　me?
Can queens envy this habit? or did Juno
E'er feast in such a shape?
Anne. You talk'd of Hebe,
Of Iris, and I know not what; but were
　　they
Dress'd as we are? they were sure some
　　chandler's daughters
Bleaching linen in Moorfields.
Mary. Or Exchange wenches,
Coming from eating pudding-pies on a
　　Sunday,
At Pimlico, or Islington.
Luke. Save you, sister!
I now dare style you so: you were before
Too glorious to be look'd on, now you appear
Like a city matron; and my pretty nieces
Such things as were born and bred there.
　　Why should you ape
The fashions of court-ladies, whose high
　　titles,
And pedigrees of long descent, give warrant

For their superfluous bravery? 'twas mon-
strous :
Till now you ne'er look'd lovely.
  L. Frug. Is this spoken
In scorn !
  Luke. Fie ? no ; with judgment. I make
good
My promise, and now shew you like your-
selves,
In your own natural shapes; and stand
resolved
You shall continue so.
  L. Frug. It is confess'd, sir.
  Luke. Sir ! sirrah : use your old phrase, I
can bear it.
  L. Frug. That, if you please, forgotten,
we acknowledge
We have deserv'd ill from you ; yet despair
not,
Though we are at your disposure, you'll
maintain us
Like your brother's wife and daughters.
  Luke. 'Tis my purpose.
  L. Frug. And not make us ridiculous.
  Luke. Admired rather,
As fair examples for our proud city dames,
And their proud brood to imitate. Do not
frown ;
If you do, I laugh, and glory that I have
The power, in you, to scourge a general vice,
And raise up a new satirist : but hear gently,
And in a gentle phrase I'll reprehend
Your late disguised deformity, and cry up
This decency and neatness, with the advan-
tage
You shall receive by't.
  L. Frug. We are bound to hear you.
  Luke. With a soul inclined to learn. Your
father was
An honest country farmer, goodman
Humble,
By his neighbours ne'er call'd Master. Did
your pride
Descend from him ? but let that pass : your
fortune,
Or rather your husband's industry, advanced
you
To the rank of a merchant's wife. He made
a knight,
And your sweet mistress-ship ladyfied, you
wore
Satin on solemn days, a chain of gold,
A velvet hood, rich borders, and sometimes
A dainty miniver cap, a silver pin,
Headed with a pearl worth three-pence, and
thus far
You were privileged, and no man envied it ;
It being for the city's honour that
There should be a distinction between

The wife of a patrician, and plebeian.
  Mill. Pray you, leave preaching, or choose
some other text ;
Your rhetoric is too moving, for it makes
Your auditory weep.
  Luke. Peace, chattering magpie !
I'll treat of you anon :—but when the height
And dignity of London's blessings grew
Contemptible, and the name lady-mayoress
Became a by-word, and you scorn'd the
means
By which you were raised, my brother's fond
indulgence,
Giving the reins to it ; and no object pleased
you
But the glittering pomp and bravery of the
court ;
What a strange, nay monstrous, metamor-
phosis follow'd !
No English workman then could please your
fancy,
The French and Tuscan dress your whole
discourse ;
This bawd to prodigality, entertain'd
To buzz into your ears what shape this
countess
Appear'd in the last masque, and how it drew
The young lord's eyes upon her ; and this
usher
Succeeded in the eldest prentice' place,
To walk before you——
  L. Frug. Pray you, end.
  Hold. Proceed, sir ;
I could fast almost a prenticeship to hear
you,
You touch them so to the quick.
  Luke. Then, as I said,
The reverend hood cast off, your borrow'd
hair,
Powder'd and curl'd, was by your dresser's
art
Form'd like a coronet, hang'd with dia-
monds,
And the richest orient pearl ; your carcanets
That did adorn your neck, of equal value :
Your Hungerland bands, and Spanish quellio
ruffs ;
Great lords and ladies feasted to survey
Embroider'd petticoats ; and sickness feign'd,
That your night rails of forty pounds a piece
Might be seen, with envy, of the visitants ;
Rich pantofles in ostentation shewn,
And roses worth a family : you were served
in plate,
Stirr'd not a foot without your coach, and
going
To church, not for devotion, but to shew
Your pomp, you were tickled when the
beggars cried,

G G

Heaven save your honour ! this idolatry
Paid to a painted room.
Hold. Nay, you have reason
To blubber, all of you.
Luke. And when you lay
In childbed, at the christening of this minx,
I well remember it, as you had been
An absolute princess, since they have no
more,
Three several chambers hung, the first with
arras,
And that for waiters ; the second crimson
satin,
For the meaner sort of guests ; the third of
scarlet
Of the rich Tyrian die ; a canopy
To cover the brat's cradle ; you in state,
Like Pompey's Julia.
L. Frug. No more, I pray you.
Luke. Of this, be sure, you shall not. I'll
cut off
Whatever is exorbitant in you,
Or in [your] daughters, and reduce you to
Your natural forms and habits ; not in re-
venge
Of your base usage of me, but to fright
Others by your example : 'tis decreed
You shall serve one another, for I will
Allow no waiter to you. Out of doors
With these useless drones !
Hold. Will you pack ?
Mill. Not till I have
My trunks along with me.
Luke. Not a rag ; you came
Hither without a box.
Star. You'll shew to me,
I hope, sir, more compassion.
Hold. Troth I'll be
Thus far a suitor for him : he hath printed
An almanack, for this year, at his own
'charge ;
Let him have the impression with him, to
set up with.
Luke. For once I'll be entreated ; let it be
Thrown to him out of the window.
Star. O cursed stars
That reign'd at my nativity ! how have you
cheated
Your poor observer !
Anne. Must we part in tears ?
Mary. Farewell, good Milliscent !
L. Frug. I am sick, and meet with
A rough physician. O my pride and scorn !
How justly am I punish'd !
Mary. Now we suffer
For our stubbornness and disobedience
To our good father.
Anne. And the base conditions
We imposed upon our suitors.

Luke. Get you in,
And caterwaul in a corner.
L. Frug. There's no contending.
[Lady Frugal, Anne, *and* Mary, *go
off at one door,* Stargaze *and*
Milliscent *at the other.*
Luke. How
Lik'st thou my carriage, Holdfast ?
Hold. Well in some parts ;
But it relishes, I know not how, a little
Of too much tyranny.
Luke. Thou art a fool :
He's cruel to himself, that dares not be
Severe to those that used him cruelly.
[*Exeunt.*

ACT V.

SCENE I.—*A Room in* Sir John Frugal's
House.

Enter Luke, Sir John Frugal, Sir Maurice
Lacy, *and* Plenty.

Luke. You care not then, as it seems, to
be converted
To our religion ?
Sir John. We know no such word,
Nor power but the devil, and him we serve
for fear,
Not love.
Luke. I am glad that charge is saved.
Sir John. We put
That trick upon your brother, to have means
To come to the city. Now, to you, we'll
discover
The close design that brought us, with
assurance,
If you lend your aids to furnish us with that
Which in the colony was not to be pur-
chased,
No merchant ever made such a return
For his most precious venture, as you shall
Receive from us ; far, far above your hopes,
Or fancy, to imagine.
Luke. It must be
Some strange commodity, and of a dear
value,
(Such an opinion is planted in me
You will deal fairly,) that I would not
hazard :
Give me the name of it.
Sir Maur. I fear you will make
Some scruple in your conscience, to grant it.
Luke. Conscience ! no, no ; so it may be
done with safety,
And without danger of the law.
Plenty. For that,
You shall sleep securely : nor shall it di-
minish,

But add unto your heap such an increase.
As what you now possess shall appear an atom,
To the mountain it brings with it.
Luke. Do not rack me
With expectation.
Sir John. Thus then in a word:
The devil—why start you at his name ? if you
Desire to wallow in wealth and worldly honours,
You must make haste to be familiar with him.—
This devil, whose priest I am, and by him made
A deep magician, (for I can do wonders,)
Appear'd to me in Virginia, and commanded,
With many stripes, for that's his cruel custom,
I should provide, on pain of his fierce wrath,
Against the next great sacrifice, at which,
We, grovelling on our faces, fall before him,
Two Christian virgins, that, with their pure blood,
Might dye his horrid altars ; and a third,
In his hate to such embraces as are lawful,
Married, and with your ceremonious rites,
As an oblation unto Hecate,
And wanton Lust, her favourite.
Luke. A devilish custom !
And yet why should it startle me?—There are
Enough of the sex fit for this use ; but virgins,
And such a matron as you speak of, hardly
To be wrought to it.
Plenty. A mine of gold, for a fee,
Waits him that undertakes it and performs it.
Sir Maur. Know you no distressed widow, or poor maids,
Whose want of dower, though well born, makes them weary
Of their own country ?
Sir John. Such as had rather be
Miserable in another world, than where
They have surfeited in felicity?
Luke. Give me leave—— [*Walks aside.*
I would not lose this purchase. A grave matron !
And two pure virgins ! Umph ! I think my sister,
Though proud, was ever honest ; and my nieces,
Untainted yet. Why should not they be shipp'd
For this employment? they are burthensome to me,
And eat too much ; and if they stay in London,
They will find friends that, to my loss, will force me

To composition : 'twere a masterpiece,
If this could be effected. They were ever
Ambitious of title : should I urge,
Matching with these they shall live Indian queens,
It may do much : but what shall I feel here,
Knowing to what they are design'd ? they absent,
The thought of them will leave me. It shall be so.—— . [*Returns.*
I'll furnish you, and, to endear the service,
In mine own family, and my blood too.
Sir John. Make this good, and your house shall not contain
The gold we'll send you.
Luke. You have seen my sister,
And my two nieces?
Sir John. Yes, sir.
Luke. These persuaded
How happily they shall live, and in what pomp,
When they are in your kingdoms, for you must
Work them a belief that you are kings——
Plenty. We are so.
Luke. I'll put it in practice instantly. Study you
For moving language. Sister ! nieces !

Enter Lady Frugal, Anne, *and* Mary.

How !
Still mourning ? dry your eyes, and clear these clouds
That do obscure your beauties. Did you believe
My personated reprehension, though
It shew'd like a rough anger, could be serious?
Forget the fright I put you in : my end,
In humbling you, was to set off the height
Of honour, principal honour, which . my studies,
When you least expect it, shall confer upon you !
Still you seem doubtful : be not wanting to
Yourselves, nor let the strangeness of the means,
With the shadow of some danger, render you Incredulous.
L. Frug. Our usage hath been such,
As we can faintly hope that your intents
And language are the same.
Luke. I'll change those hopes
To certainties.
Sir John. With what art he winds about them ! [*Aside.*
Luke. What will you say, or what thanks shall I look for,
If now I raise you to such eminence, as

G G 2

The wife and daughters of a citizen
Never arrived at! many, for their wealth, I
grant,
Have written ladies of honour, and some few
Have higher titles, and that's the furthest rise
You can in England hope for. What think
you,
If I should mark you out a way to live
Queens in another climate?
   Anne. We desire
A competence.
   Mary. And prefer our country's smoke
Before outlandish fire.
   L. Frug. But should we listen
To such impossibilities, 'tis not in
The power of man to make it good.
   Luke. I'll do it:
Nor is this seat of majesty far removed;
It is but to Virginia.
   L. Frug. How! Virginia!
High heaven forbid! Remember, sir, I be-
seech you,
What creatures are shipp'd thither.
   Anne. Condemn'd wretches,
Forfeited to the law.
   Mary. Strumpets and bawds,
For the abomination of their life,
Spew'd out of their own country.
   Luke. Your false fears
Abuse my noble purposes. Such indeed
Are sent as slaves to labour there; but you,
To absolute sovereignty. Observe these men,
With reverence observe them: they are
kings of
Such spacious territories and dominions,
As our Great Britain measured will appear
A garden to it.
   Sir Maur. You shall be adored there
As goddesses.
   Sir John. Your litters made of gold,
Supported by your vassals, proud to bear
The burthen on their shoulders. ·
   Plenty. Pomp, and ease,
With delicates that Europe never knew,
Like pages shall wait on you.
   Luke. If you have minds
To entertain the greatness offer'd to you,
With outstretch'd arms, and willing hands,
embrace it.
But this refused, imagine what can make you
Most miserable here; and rest assured,
In storms it falls upon you: take them in,
And use your best persuasion. If that fail,
I'll send them aboard in a dry fat.
   [*Exeunt all but* Sir John Frugal *and*
Luke.
   Sir John. Be not moved, sir;
We'll work them to your will. Yet, ere we
part,

Your worldly cares deferr'd, a little mirth
Would not misbecome us.
   Luke. You say well: and now
It comes into my memory, 'tis my birthday,
Which with solemnity I would observe,
But that it would ask cost.
   Sir John. That shall not grieve you.
By my art I will prepare you such a feast,
As Persia, in her height of pomp and riot,
Did never equal; and such ravishing music
As the Italian princes seldom heard
At their greatest entertainments. Name
your guests.
   Luke. I must have none.
   Sir John. Not the city senate?
   Luke. No;
Nor yet poor neighbours: the first would
argue me
Of foolish ostentation, and the latter
Of too much hospitality; a virtue
Grown obsolete, and useless. I will sit
Alone, and surfeit in my store, while others
With envy pine at it; my genius pamper'd
With the thought of what I am, and what
they suffer
I have mark'd out to misery.
   Sir John. You shall:
And something I will add you yet conceive
not,
Nor will I be slow-paced.
   Luke. I have one business,
And, that dispatch'd, I am free.
   Sir John. About it, sir,
Leave the rest to me.
   Luke. Till now I ne'er loved magic.
   [*Exeunt.*

SCENE II.—*Another Room in the same.*

Enter Lord Lacy, Goldwire *senior, and*
Tradewell *senior.*

   L. Lacy. Believe me, gentlemen, I never
was
So cozen'd in a fellow. He disguised
Hypocrisy in such a cunning shape
Of real goodness, that I would have sworn
This devil a saint. M. Goldwire, and M.
Tradewell,
What do you mean to do? Put on.
   Gold. With your lordship's favour.
   L. Lacy. I'll have it so.
   Trade. Your will, my lord, excuses
The rudeness of our manners.
   L. Lacy. You have received
Penitent letters from your sons, I doubt not
   Trade. They are our only sons.
   Gold. And as we are fathers,
Remembering the errors of our youth,
We would pardon slips in them.

Trade. And pay for them
In a moderate way.
Gold. In which we hope your lordship
Will be our mediator.
L. Lacy. All my power

Enter Luke, *richly dressed.*

You freely shall command ; 'tis he ! You
are well met,
And to my wish,—and wonderous brave !
your habit
Speaks you a merchant royal.
Luke. What I wear
I take not upon trust.
L. Lacy. Your betters may,
And blush not for't.
Luke. If you have nought else with me
But to argue that, I will make bold to leave
you.
L. Lacy. You are very peremptory ; pray
you stay :—
I once held you
An upright honest man.
Luke. I am honester now
By a hundred thousand pound, I thank my
stars for't,
Upon the Exchange ; and if your late
opinion
Be alter'd, who can help it? Good my lord,
To the point ; I have other business than to
talk
Of honesty, and opinions.
L. Lacy. Yet you may
Do well, if you please, to shew the one, and
merit
The other from good men, in a case that now
Is offer'd to you.
Luke. What is it? I am troubled.
L. Lacy. Here are two gentlemen, the
fathers of
Your brother's prentices.
Luke. Mine, my lord, I take it.
L. Lacy. Goldwire, and Tradewell.
Luke. They are welcome, if
They come prepared to satisfy the damage
I have sustain'd by their sons.
Gold. We are, so you please
To use a conscience.
Trade. Which we hope you will do,
For your own worship's sake.
Luke. Conscience, my friends,
And wealth, are not always neighbours.
Should I part
With what the law gives me, I should suffer
mainly
In my reputation ; for it would convince me
Of indiscretion : nor will you, I hope, move
me
To do myself such prejudice.

L. Lacy. No moderation?
Luke. They cannot look for't, and pre-
serve in me
A thriving citizen's credit. Your bonds lie
For your sons' truth, and they shall answer all
They have run out : the masters never pros-
per'd
Since gentlemen's sons grew prentices :
when we look
To have our business done at home, they are
Abroad in the tennis-court, or in Partridge-
alley,
In Lambeth Marsh, or a cheating ordinary,
Where I found your sons. I have your
bonds, look to't.
A thousand pounds apiece, and that will
hardly
Repair my losses.
L. Lacy. Thou dar'st not shew thyself
Such a devil !
Luke. Good words.
L. Lacy. Such a cut-throat ! I have
heard of
The usage of your brother's wife and
daughters ;
You shall find you are not lawless, and that
your monies
Cannot justify your villainies.
Luke. I endure this.
And, good my lord, now you talk in time of
monies,
Pay in what you owe me. And give me
leave to wonder
Your wisdom should have leisure to consider
The business of these gentlemen, or my
carriage
To my sister, or my nieces, being yourself,
So much in my danger.
L. Lacy. In thy danger?
Luke. Mine.
I find in my counting-house a manor pawn'd,
Pawn'd, my good lord ; Lacy manor, and
that manor
From which you have the title of a lord,
An it please your good lordship ! You are
a nobleman ;
Pray you pay in my monies : the interest
Will eat faster in't, than aquafortis in iron.
Now though you bear me hard, I love your
lordship.
I grant your person to be privileged
From all arrests ; yet there lives a foolish
creature
Call'd an under-sheriff, who, being well
paid, will serve
An extent on lords or lowns' land. Pay
it in :
I would be loth your name should sink, or
that

Your hopeful son, when he returns from
   travel,
Should find you my lord-without-land. You
   are angry
For my good counsel : look you to your
   bonds ; had I known
Of your coming, believ't, I would have had
   serjeants ready.
Lord, how you fret ! but that a tavern's
   near,
You should taste a cup of muscadine in my
   house,
To wash down sorrow ; but there it will do
   better :
I know you'll drink a health to me. [*Exit.*
L. Lacy. To thy damnation.
Was there ever such a villain ! heaven for-
   give me
For speaking so unchristianly, though he
   deserves it.
   Gold. We are undone.
   Trade. Our families quite ruin'd.
   L. Lacy. Take courage, gentlemen ; com-
   fort may appear,
And punishment overtake him, when he
   least expects it.   [*Exeunt.*

SCENE III.—*Another Room in the same.*

   Enter Sir John Frugal *and* Holdfast.

Sir John. Be silent, on your life.
Hold. I am o'erjoy'd.
Sir John. Are the pictures placed as I
   directed ?
Hold. Yes, sir.
Sir John. And the musicians ready?
Hold. All is done
As you commanded.
   Sir John. [*goes to the door.*] Make haste ;
   and be careful ;
You know your cue, and postures?
   Plenty. [*within.*] We are perfect.
Sir John. 'Tis well. The rest are come,
   too?
   Hold. And disposed of
To your own wish.

   Enter Servants *with a rich banquet.*

Sir John. Set forth the table : so !
A perfect banquet. At the upper end,
His chair in state : he shall feast like a
   prince.
   Hold. And rise like a Dutch hangman.

        Enter Luke.

Sir John. Not a word more——
How like you the preparation ? Fill your
   room,
And taste the cates ; then in your thought
   consider

A rich man, that lives wisely to himself,
In his full height of glory.
   Luke. I can brook
No rival in this happiness. How sweetly
These dainties, when unpaid for, please my
   palate ?
Some wine. Jove's nectar ! Brightness to
   the star
That govern'd at my birth ! shoot down
   thy influence,
And with a perpetuity of being
Continue this felicity, not gain'd
By vows to saints above, and much less
   purchased
By thriving industry ; nor fallen upon me
As a reward to piety, and religion,
Or service to my country : I owe all
This to dissimulation, and the shape
I wore of goodness. Let my brother number
His beads devoutly, and believe his alms
To beggars, his compassion to his debtors,
Will wing his better part, disrobed of flesh,
To soar above the firmament. I am well ;
And so I surfeit here in all abundance,
Though styled a cormorant, a cut-throat, Jew,
And prosecuted with the fatal curses
Of widows, undone orphans, and what else
Such as malign my state can load me with,
I will not envy it. You promised music.
   Sir John. And you shall hear the strength
   and power of it,
The spirit of Orpheus raised to make it good,
And, in those ravishing strains, with which
   he moved
Charon and Cerberus to give him way,
To fetch from hell his lost Eurydice.
—Appear ! swifter than thought ! [*Aloud.*

Music.   Enter at one door, Cerberus, *at the
   other,* Charon, Orpheus, *and Chorus.*

   Luke. 'Tis wonderous strange !
   [*They represent the story of* Orpheus,
   with dance and gesture.
Sir John. Does not the object and the
   accent take you?
   Luke. A pretty fable. [*Exe.* Orph. *and*
   the rest.] But that music should
Alter, in fiends, their nature, is to me
Impossible ; since, in myself, I find,
What I have once decreed shall know no
   change.
   Sir John. You are constant to your pur-
   poses ; yet I think
That I could stagger you.
   Luke. How ?
   Sir John. Should I present
Your servants, debtors, and the rest that
   suffer

By your fit severity, I presume the sight
Would move you to compassion.
Luke. Not a mote.
The music that your Orpheus made was
harsh,
To the delight I should receive in hearing
Their cries and groans : if it be in your
power,
I would now see them.
Sir John. Spirits, in their shapes,
Shall shew them as they are : but if it
should move you ?—
Luke. If it do, may I ne'er find pity !
Sir John. Be your own judge.——
Appear ! as I commanded.

Sad Music. Enter Goldwire *junior, and*
Tradewell *junior, as from prison ;* For-
tune, Hoyst, *and* Penury ; *Serjeants with*
Tradewell *senior, and* Goldwire *senior ;—
these followed by* Shave'em, *in a blue gown,*
Secret, *and* Ding'em ; *they all kneel to*
Luke, *lifting up their hands.* Stargaze
is seen, with a pack of almanacks, and
Milliscent.

Luke. Ha, ha, ha !
This move me to compassion, or raise
One sign of seeming pity in my face !
You are deceived : it rather renders me
More flinty, and obdurate. A south wind
Shall sooner soften marble, and the rain
That slides down gently from his flaggy
wings,
O'erflow the Alps, than knees, or tears, or
groans,
Shall wrest compunction from me. 'Tis my
glory
That they are wretched, and by me made so ;
It sets my happiness off : I could not triumph
If these were not my captives.—Ha ! my
tarriers,
As it appears, have seized on these old foxes,
As I gave order ; new addition to
My scene of mirth : ha, ha !—They now
grow tedious,
Let them be removed.
        [*Exeunt* Gold. *and the rest.*
          Some other object, if
Your art can shew it.
Sir John. You shall perceive 'tis bound-
less.
Yet one thing real, if you please ?
Luke. What is it ?
Sir John. Your nieces, ere they put to
sea, crave humbly,
Though absent in their bodies, they may
take leave
Of their late suitors' statues.

Enter Lady Frugal, Anne, *and* Mary.
Luke. There they hang :
In things indifferent, I am tractable.
Sir John. There pay your vows, you have
liberty.
Anne. O sweet figure   [*kneels.*
Of my abused Lacy ! when removed
Into another world, I'll daily pay
A sacrifice of sighs to thy remembrance ;
And with a shower of tears strive to wash off
The stain of that contempt my foolish pride
And insolence threw upon thee.
Mary. I had been
Too happy, if I had enjoyed the substance ;
But far unworthy of it, now I fall
Thus prostrate to thy statue.   [*kneels.*
L. Frug. My kind husband,   [*kneels.*
(Bless'd in my misery,) from the monastery
To which my disobedience confined thee,
With thy soul's eye, which distance cannot
hinder,
Look on my penitence. O, that I could
Call back time past ! thy holy vow dis-
pensed,
With what humility would I observe
My long-neglected duty !
Sir John. Does not this move you?
Luke. Yes, as they do the statues, and
her sorrow
My absent brother. If, by your magic art,
You can give life to these, or bring him hither
To witness her repentance, I may have,
Perchance, some feeling of it.
Sir John. For your sport,
You shall see a masterpiece. Here's nothing
but
A superficies ; colours, and no substance.
Sit still, and to your wonder and amazement,
I'll give these organs. This the sacrifice,
To make the great work perfect.
        [*Burns incense, and makes mystical*
          gesticulations. Sir Maurice Lacy
          and Plenty *give signs of anima-
          tion.*
Luke. Prodigious !
Sir John. Nay, they have life, and mo-
tion. Descend !
        [Sir Maurice Lacy, *and* Plenty *de-
          scend and come forward.*
And for your absent brother,—this wash'd
off,
Against your will you shall know him.
        [*Discovers himself.*
Enter Lord Lacy, *with* Goldwire *senior
and junior,* Tradewell *senior and junior,
the* Debtors, *&c. &c. as before.*
Luke. I am lost.
Guilt strikes me dumb.

Sir John. You have seen, my lord, the pageant?

L. Lacy. I have, and am ravish'd with it.

Sir John. What think you now Of this clear soul? this honest, pious man? Have I stripp'd him bare, or will your lordship have A further trial of him? 'Tis not in A wolf to change his nature.

L. Lacy. I long since Confess'd my error.

Sir John. Look up; I forgive you, And seal your pardons thus. [*Raises and embraces* Lady Frugal, Anne, *and* Mary.

L. Frug. I am too full Of joy, to speak it.

Anne. I am another creature; Not what I was.

Mary. I vow to shew myself, When I am married, an humble wife, Not a commanding mistress.

Plenty. On those terms, I gladly thus embrace you. [*To* Mary.

Sir Maur. Welcome to My bosom: as the one half of myself, I'll love and cherish you. [*To* Anne.

Gold. jun. Mercy!

Trade. jun. and the rest. Good sir, mercy!

Sir John. This day is sacred to it. All shall find me, As far as lawful pity can give way to't, Indulgent to your wishes, though with loss Unto myself.—My kind and honest brother, Looking into yourself, have you seen the Gorgon? What a golden dream you have had, in the possession Of my estate!—but here's a revocation That wakes you out of it. Monster in nature! Revengeful, avaricious atheist, Transcending all example!—but I shall be A sharer in thy crimes, should I repeat them— What wilt thou do? turn hypocrite again, With hope dissimulation can aid thee? Or that one eye will shed a tear in sign Of sorrow for thee? I have warrant to Make bold with mine own, pray you uncase: this key, too, I must make bold with. Hide thyself in some desart, Where good men ne'er may find thee; or in justice Pack to Virginia, and repent; not for Those horrid ends to which thou didst design these.

Luke. I care not where I go: what's done, with words Cannot be undone. [*Exit.*

L. Frug. Yet, sir, shew some mercy; Because his cruelty to me and mine, Did good upon us.

Sir John. Of that at better leisure, As his penitency shall work me. Make you good Your promised reformation, and instruct Our city dames, whom wealth makes proud, to move In their own spheres; and willingly to confess, In their habits, manners, and their highest port, A distance 'twixt the city and the court.

[*Exeunt.*

The Guardian.

PROLOGUE.

After twice putting forth to sea, his fame
Shipwreck'd in either, and his once-known name
In two years silence buried, perhaps lost
In the general opinion ; at our cost
(A zealous sacrifice to Neptune made
For good success in his uncertain trade)
Our author weighs up anchors, and once more
Forsaking the security of the shore,
Resolves to prove his fortune : what 'twill be,
Is not in him, or us, to prophesie ;
You only, can assure us : yet he pray'd
This little, in his absence, might be said,
Designing me his orator.   He submits
To the grave censure of those abler wits
His weakness ; nor dares he profess that when
The critics laugh, he'll laugh at them agen.
(Strange self-love in a writer!)   He would know
His errors as you find them, and bestow
His future studies to reform from this,
What in another might be judged amiss.
And yet despair not, gentlemen ; though he fear
His strengths to please, we hope that you shall hear
Some things so writ, as you may truly say
He hath not quite forgot to make a play,
As 'tis with malice rumour'd : his intents
Are fair ; and though he want the compliments
Of wide-mouth'd promisers, who still engage,
Before their works are brought upon the stage,
Their parasites to proclaim them : this last birth,
Deliver'd without noise, may yield such mirth,
As, balanced equally, will cry down the boast
Of arrogance, and regain his credit lost.

DRAMATIS PERSONÆ.

Alphonso, *king of* Naples.
Duke Montpensier, *general of* Milan.
Severino, *a banished nobleman.*
Monteclaro, *his brother-in-law (supposed dead,) disguised under the name of* Laval.
Durazzo, *the* GUARDIAN.
Caldoro, *his nephew and ward, in love with* Calista.
Adorio, *a young libertine.*
Camillo,
Lentulo, } Neapolitan *gentlemen.*
Donato,

Cario, *cook to* Adorio.
Claudio, *a confidential servant to* Severino.
Captain.
Banditti.
Servants.
Iölante, *wife to* Severino.
Calista, *her daughter, in love with* Adorio.
Mirtilla, Calista's *maid.*
Calipso, *the confident of* Iölante.
Singers, Countrymen.

SCENE,—*Partly at* Naples, *and partly in the adjacent country.*

ACT I.

SCENE I.—Naples. *A Grove.*

Enter Durazzo, Camillo, Lentulo, Donato, *and two* Servants.

Dur. Tell me of his expenses ! Which of you
Stands bound for a gazet? he spend his own ;
And you impertinent fools or knaves, (make choice
Of either title, which your signiorships please,)
To meddle in't.
   Camil. Your age gives privilege
To this harsh language.
   Dur. My age ! do not use
That word again ; if you do, I shall grow young,
And swinge you soundly : I would have you know
Though I write fifty odd, I do not carry
An almanack in my bones to pre-declare
What weather we shall have ; nor do I kneel
In adoration, at the spring and fall,
Before my doctor, for a dose or two
Of his restoratives, which are things, I take it,
You are familiar with.
   Camil. This is from the purpose.
   Dur. I cannot cut a caper, or groan like you
When I have done, nor run away so nimbly
Out of the field : but bring me to a fence-school,
And crack a blade or two for exercise,
Ride a barb'd horse, or take a leap after me,
Following my hounds, or hawks, (and, by your leave,
At a gamesome mistress,) and you shall confess
I am in the May of my abilities,
And you in your December.
   Lent. We are glad you bear
Your years so well.
   Dur. My years ! no more of years ;
If you do, at your peril.
   Camil. We desire not
To prove your valour.
   Dur. 'Tis your safest course.
   Camil. But as friends to ycur fame and reputation,
Come to instruct you, your too much in-dulgence
To the exorbitant waste of young Caldoro,
Your nephew and your ward, hath rendered you
But a bad report among wise men in Naples.
   Dur. Wise men !—in your opinion ; but to me,

That understand myself and them, they are
Hide-bounded money-mongers : they would have me
Train up my ward a hopeful youth, to keep
A merchant's book ; or at the plough, and clothe him
In canvas or coarse cotton ; while I fell
His woods, grant leases, which he must make good
When he comes to age, or be compelled to marry
With a cast whore and three bastards ; let him know
No more than how to cipher well, or do
His tricks by the square root ; grant him no pleasure
But quoits and nine-pins ; suffer him to con-verse
With none but clowns and cobblers : as the Turk says,
Poverty, old age, and aches of all seasons,
Light on such heathenish guardians !
   Don. You do worse
To the ruin of his state, under your favour,
In feeding his loose riots.
   Dur. Riots ! what riots ?
He wears rich clothes, I do so ; keeps
   horses, games, and wenches ;
'Tis not amiss, so it be done with decorum :
In an heir 'tis ten times more excusable
Than to be over-thrifty.   Is there aught else
That you can charge him with ?
   Camil. With what we grieve for,
And you will not approve.
   Dur. Out with it, man.
   Camil. His rash endeavour, without your consent,
To match himself into a family
Not gracious with the times.
   Dur. 'Tis still the better ;
By this means he shall scape court visitants,
And not be eaten out of house and home
In a summer progress : but does he mean to marry ?
   Camil. Yes, sir, to marry.
   Dur. In a beardless chin
'Tis ten times worse than wenching.   Family !
   whose family ?
   Camil. Signor Severino's.
   Dur. How ! not he that killed
The brother of his wife, as it is rumour'd,
Then fled upon it ; since proscribed, and chosen
Captain of the Banditti ; the king's pardon
On no suit to be granted ?
   Lent. The same, sir.
   Dur. This touches near : how is his love return d
By the saint he worships ?

Don. She affects him not,
But dotes upon another.
Dur. Worse and worse.
Camil. You know him, young Adorio.
Dur. A brave gentleman !
What proof of this ?
Lent. I dogg'd him to the church ;
Where he, not for devotion, as I guess.
But to make his approaches to his mistress,
Is often seen.
Camil. And would you stand conceal'd
Among these trees, for he must pass this
    green,
The matins ended, as she returns home,
You may observe the passages.
Dur. I thank you ;
This torrent must be stopt.
Don. They come.
Camil. Stand close.   [*They stand aside.*

Enter Adorio, Calista, Mirtilla, *and*
    Caldoro *muffled.*

Calis. I know I wrong my modesty.
Ador. And wrong me,
In being so importunate for that
I neither can nor must grant.
Calis. A hard sentence !
And to increase my misery, by you,
Whom fond affection hath made my judge,
Pronounced without compassion. Alas, sir,
Did I approach you with unchaste desires,
A sullied reputation ; were deform'd,
As it may be I am, though many affirm
I am something more than handsome——
Dur. I dare swear it.
Calis. Or if I were no gentlewoman, but
    bred coarsely,
You might, with some pretence of reason,
    slight
What you should sue for.
Dur. Were he not an eunuch,
He would, and sue again ; I am sure I
    should.
Pray look in my collar, a flea troubles me :
Hey-day ! there are a legion of young Cupids
At barley-break in my breeches.
Calis. Hear me, sir ;
Though you continue, nay increase your
    scorn,
Only vouchsafe to let me understand
What my defects are ; of which once con-
    vinced,
I will hereafter silence my harsh plea,
And spare your further trouble.
Ador. I will tell you,
And bluntly, as my usual manner is.
Though I were a woman-hater, which I am
    not,

But love the sex,—for my ends, take me with
    you ;
If in my thought I found one taint or blemish
In the whole fabric of your outward features,
I would give myself the lie. You are a
    virgin
Possess'd of all your mother could wish in
    you ;
Your father Severino's dire disaster
In killing of your uncle, which I grieve for,
In no part taking from you. I repeat it,
A noble virgin, for whose grace and favours
The Italian princes might contend as rivals ;
Yet unto me, a thing far, far beneath you,
(A noted libertine I profess myself,)
In your mind there does appear one fault so
    gross,
Nay, I might say unpardonable at your
    years,
If justly you consider it, that I cannot
As you desire, affect you.
Calis. Make me know it,
I'll soon reform it.
Ador. Would you'd keep your word !
Calis. Put me to the test.
Ador. I will. You are too honest,
And, like your mother, too strict and re-
    ligious,
And talk too soon of marriage; I shall break,
If at that rate I purchase you. Can I part
    with
My uncurb'd liberty, and on my neck
Wear such a heavy yoke ? hazard my for-
    tunes,
With all the expected joys my life can yield
    me,
For one commodity, before I prove it ?
Venus forbid on both sides ! let crook'd
    hams,
Bald heads, declining shoulders, furrow'd
    cheeks,
Be awed by ceremonies : if you love me
In the way young people should, I'll fly to
    meet it,
And we'll meet merrily.
Calis. 'Tis strange such a man
Can use such language.
Ador. In my tongue my heart
Speaks freely, fair one. Think on't, a close
    friend,
Or private mistress, is court rhetoric ;
A wife, mere rustic solecism : so good mor-
    row !
    [Adorio *offers to go,* Caldoro *comes
        forward and stops him.*
Camil. How like you this ?
Dur. A well-bred gentleman !
I am thinking now if ever in the dark,
Or drunk, I met his mother : he must have

Some drops of my blood in him, for at his years
I was much of his religion.

　Camil. Out upon you !
　Don. The colt's tooth still in your mouth !
　Dur. What means this whispering?
　Ador. You may perceive I seek not to displant you,
Where you desire to grow ; for further thanks,
'Tis needless compliment.
　Cald. There are some natures
Which blush to owe a benefit, if not
Received in corners; holding it an impairing
To their own worth, should they acknow-
　ledge it.
I am made of other clay, and therefore must
Trench so far on your leisure, as to win you
To lend a patient ear, while I profess
Before my glory, though your scorn, Calista,
How much I am your servant.
　Ador. My designs
Are not so urgent, but they can dispense
With so much time.
　Camil. Pray you now observe your nephew.
　Dur. How he looks ! like a school-boy that had play'd the truant,
And went to be breech'd.
　Cald. Madam !
　Calis. A new affliction :
Your suit offends as much as his repulse,
It being not to be granted.
　Mirt. Hear him, madam ;
His sorrow is not personated ; he deserves
Your pity, not contempt.
　Dur. He has made the maid his ;
And, as the master of *the Art of Love*
Wisely affirms, it is a kind of passage
To the mistress' favour.
　Cald. I come not to urge
My merit to deserve you, since you are,
Weigh'd truly to your worth, above all value:
Much less to argue you of want of judgment
For following one that with wing'd feet flies
　from you,
While I, at all parts, without boast, his equal,
In vain pursue you ; bringing those flames with me,
Those lawful flames, (for, madam, know, with other
I never shall approach you,) which Adorio,
In scorn of Hymen and religious rites,
With atheistical impudence contemns ;
And in his loose attempt to undermine
The fortress of your honour, seeks to ruin
All holy altars by clear minds erected
To virgin honour.
　Dur. My nephew is an ass ;

What a devil hath he to do with virgin honour,
Altars, or lawful flames, when he should tell her
They are superstitious nothings ; and speak to the purpose,
Of the delight to meet in the old dance,
Between a pair of sheets ; my grandam call'd it,
The Peopling of the World.
　Calis. How, gentle sir !
To vindicate my honour? that is needless ;
I dare not fear the worst aspersion malice
Can throw upon it.
　Cald. Your sweet patience, lady,
And more than dove-like innocence, render you
Insensible of an injury, for which
I deeply suffer. Can you undergo
The scorn of being refused ? I must confess
It makes for my ends ; for had he embraced
Your gracious offers tender'd him, I had been
In my own hopes forsaken ; and if yet
There can breathe any air of comfort in me,
To his contempt I owe it : but his ill
No more shall make way for my good intents,
Than virtue, powerful in herself, can need
The aids of vice.
　Ador. You take that license, sir,
Which yet I never granted.
　Cald. I'll force more ;
Nor will I for my own ends undertake it,
As I will make apparent, but to do
A justice to your sex, with mine own wrong
And irrecoverable loss. To thee I turn,
Thou goatish ribald, in whom lust is grown
Defensible, the last descent to hell,
Which gapes wide for thee : look upon this lady,
And on her fame, (if it were possible,
Fairer than she is,) and if base desires,
And beastly appetite, will give thee leave,
Consider how she sought thee, how this lady,
In a noble way, desired thee. Was she fashion'd
In an inimitable mould, (which Nature broke,
The great work perfected,) to be made a slave
To thy libidinous twines, and, when com-
　manded,
To be used as physic after drunken surfeits !
Mankind should rise against thee : what even now
I heard with horror, shewed like blasphemy,
And as such I will punish it.
　　[*Strikes* Adorio, *the rest rush for-*
　　　　ward ; they all draw.
　Calis. Murder !

Mirt. Help!

Dur. After a whining prologue, who
would have look'd for
Such a rough catastrophe? Nay, come on,
fear nothing:
Never till now my nephew! and do you
hear, sir?
(And yet I love thee too) if you take the
wench now,
I'll have it posted first, then chronicled,
Thou wert beaten to it.

Ador. You think you have shewn
A memorable masterpiece of valour
In doing this in public, and it may
Perhaps deserve her shoe-string for a favour:
Wear it without my envy; but expect,
For this affront, when time serves, I shall
call you
To a strict accompt.   [*Exit.*

Dur. Hook on, follow him, harpies!
You may feed upon this business for a month,
If you manage it handsomely: .
    [*Exeunt* Camillo, Lentulo, *and* Donato.
                When two heirs quarrel,
The swordmen of the city shortly after
Appear in plush, for their grave consultations
In taking up the difference; some, I know,
Make a set living on't. Nay, let him go,
Thou art master of the field; enjoy thy
fortune
With moderation: for a flying foe,
Discreet and provident conquerors build up
A bridge of gold. To thy mistress, boy! if
I were
In thy shirt, how I could nick it!

Cald. You stand, madam,
As you were rooted, and I more than fear
My passion hath offended: I perceive
The roses frighted from your cheeks, and
paleness
To usurp their room; yet you may please to
ascribe it
To my excess of love, and boundless ardour
To do you right; for myself I have done
nothing.
I will not curse my stars, howe'er assured
To me you are lost for ever: for suppose
Adorio slain, and by my hand, my life
Is forfeited to the law, which I contemn,
So with a tear or two you would remember
I was your martyr, and died in your service.

Cal. Alas, you weep! and in my just
compassion
Of what you suffer, I were more than marble,
Should I not keep you company: you have
sought
My favours nobly, and I am justly punish'd,
In wild Adorio's contempt and scorn,
For my ingratitude, it is no better,

To your deservings: yet such is my fate,
Though I would, I cannot help it. O
Caldoro!
In our misplaced affection I prove
Too soon, and with dear-bought experience,
Cupid
Is blind indeed, and hath mistook his
arrows.
If it be possible, learn to forget,
(And yet that punishment is too light,) to
hate,
A thankless virgin: practise it; and may
Your due consideration that I am so,
In your imagination, disperse
Loathsome deformity upon this face
That hath bewitch'd you! more I cannot say,
But that I truly pity you, and wish you
A better choice, which, in my prayers,
Caldoro,
I ever will remember.
            [*Exeunt* Calista *and* Mirtilla.

Dur. 'Tis a sweet rogue.
Why, how now! thunderstruck?

Cald. I am not so happy:
Oh that I were but master of myself!
You soon should see me nothing.

Dur. What would you do?

Cald. With one stab give a fatal period
To my woes and life together.

Dur. For a woman!
Better the kind were lost, and generation
Maintain'd a new way.

Cald. Pray you, sir, forbear
This profane language.

Dur. Pray you, be you a man,
And whimper not like a girl: all shall be well,
As I live it shall; this is no hectic fever,
But a love-sick ague, easy to be cured,
And I'll be your physician, so you subscribe
To my directions. First, you must change
This city whorish air, for 'tis infected,
And my potions will not work here; I must
have you
To my country villa: rise before the sun,
Then make a breakfast of the morning
dew,
Served up by nature on some grassy hill;
You'll find it nectar, and far more cordial
Than cullises, cock-broth, or your distilla-
tions
Of a hundred crowns a quart.

Cald. You talk of nothing.

Dur. This ta'en as a preparative, to
strengthen
Your queasy stomach, vault into your saddle;
With all this flesh I can do it without a
stirrup:—
My hounds uncoupled, and my huntsmen
ready,

You shall hear such music from their tunable
  mouths,
That you shall say the viol, harp, theorbo,
Ne'er made such ravishing harmony ; from
  the groves
And neighbouring woods, with frequent
  iterations,
Enamour'd of the cry, a thousand echoes
Repeating it.
  Cald. What's this to me ?
  Dur. It shall be,
And you give thanks for't. In the afternoon,
For we will have variety of delights,
We'll to the field again, no game shall rise
But we'll be ready for't : if a hare, my grey-
  hounds
Shall make a course ; for the pie or jay, a
  sparhawk
Flies from the fist ; the crow so near pursued,
Shall be compell'd to seek protection under
Our horses' bellies ; a hearn put from her
  siege,
And a pistol shot off in her breech, shall
  mount
So high, that, to your view, she'll seem to soar
Above the middle region of the air :
A cast of haggard falcons, by me mann'd,
Eyeing the prey at first, appear as if
They did turn tail ; but with their labouring
  wings
Getting above her, with a thought their
  pinions
Cleaving the purer element, make in,
And by turns bind with her ; the frighted
  fowl,
Lying at her defence upon her back,
With her dreadful beak a while defers her
  death,
But by degrees forced down, we part the
  fray,
And feast upon her.
  Cald. This cannot be, I grant,
But pretty pastime.
  Dur. Pretty pastime, nephew !
'Tis royal sport. Then, for an evening flight,
A tiercel gentle, which I call, my masters,
As he were sent a messenger to the moon,
In such a place flies, as he seems to say,
See me, or see me not ! the partridge sprung,
He makes his stoop ; but wanting breath, is
  forced
To cancelier ; then, with such speed as if
He carried lightning in his wings, he strikes
The trembling bird, who even in death
  appears
Proud to be made his quarry.
  Cald. Yet all this
Is nothing to Calista.
  Dur. Thou shalt find

Twenty Calistas there ; for every night,
A fresh and lusty one ; I'll give thee a ticket,
In which my name, Durazzo's name, sub-
  scribed,
My tenants' nut-brown daughters, whole-
  some girls,
At midnight shall contend to do thee service.
I have bred them up to't ; should their
  fathers murmur,
Their leases are void, for that is a main point
In my indentures ; and when we make our
  progress,
There is no entertainment perfect, if
This last dish be not offer'd.
  Cald. You make me smile.
  Dur. I'll make thee laugh outright.—My
  horses, knaves !
'Tis but six short hours riding : yet ere night
Thou shalt be an alter'd man.
  Cald. I wish I may, sir.   [*Exeunt.*

SCENE II.—*A Room in* Severino's *House.*
    Enter Iölante, Calista, Calipso, *and*
            Mirtilla.

  Iöl. I had spies upon you, minion ; the
  relation
Of your behaviour was at home before you :
My daughter to hold parley, from the
  church too,
With noted libertines ! her fame and favours
The quarrel of their swords !
  Calis. 'Twas not in me
To help it, madam.
  Iöl. No ! how have I lived ?
My neighbour knows my manners have
  been such,
That I presume I may affirm, and boldly,
In no particular action of my life
I can be justly censured.
  Calip. Censured, madam !
What lord or lady lives, worthy to sit
A competent judge on you ?
  Calis. Yet black detraction
Will find faults where they are not.
  Calip. Her foul mouth
Is stopp'd, you being the object : give me
  leave
To speak my thoughts, yet still under cor-
  rection ;
And if my young lady and her woman hear
With reverence, they may be edified.
You are my gracious patroness and sup-
  portress,
And I your poor observer, nay, your creature,
Fed by your bounties ; and but that I know
Your honour detests flattery, I might say,
And with an emphasis, you are the lady
Admired and envied at, far, far above
All imitation of the best of women

That are or ever shall be.   This is truth :
I dare not be obsequious ; and 'twould ill
Become my gravity, and wisdom glean'd
From your oraculous ladyship, to act
The part of a she-parasite.
   Iöl. If you do,
I never shall acknowledge you.
   Calis. Admirable !
This is no flattery !   [*Aside to* Mirt.
   Mirt. Do not interrupt her :
'Tis such a pleasing itch to your lady-
   mother,
That she may peradventure forget us,
To feed on her own praises.
   Iöl. I am not
So far in debt to age, but if I would
Listen to men's bewitching sorceries,
I could be courted.
   Calip. Rest secure of that.
All the braveries of the city run mad for you,
And yet your virtue's such, not one attempts
   you.
   Iöl. I keep no mankind servant in my
   house,
In fear my chastity may be suspected :
How is that voiced in Naples?
   Calip. With loud applause,
I assure your honour.
   Iöl. It confirms I can
Command my sensual appetites.
   Calip. As vassals to
Your more than masculine reason, that com-
   mands them :
Your palace styled a nunnery of pureness,
In which not one lascivious thought dares
   enter,
Your clear soul standing centinel.
   Mirt. Well said, Echo !   [*Aside.*
   Iöl. Yet I have tasted those delights
   which women
So greedily long for, know their titillations ;
And when, with danger of his head, thy
   father
Comes to give comfort to my widow'd sheets,
As soon as his desires are satisfied,
I can with ease forget them.
   Calip. Observe that,
It being indeed remarkable : 'tis nothing
For a simple maid, that never had her hand
In the honey-pot of pleasure, to forbear it ;
But such as have lick'd there, and lick'd
   there often,
And felt the sweetness of t——
   Mirt. How her mouth runs o'er
With rank imagination !   [*Aside.*
   Calip. If such can,
As urged before, the kickshaw being offer'd,
Refuse to take it, like my matchless madam,
They may be sainted.

   Iöl. I'll lose no more breath
In fruitless reprehension ; look to it :
I'll have thee wear this habit of my mind,
As of my body.
   Calip. Seek no other precedent :
In all the books of *Amadis de Gaul,*
The *Palmerins,* and that true Spanish story,
The *Mirror of Knighthood,* which I have
   read often,
Read feelingly, nay more, I do believe in't,
My lady has no parallel.
   Iöl. Do not provoke me :
If, from this minute, thou e'er stir abroad,
Write letter, or receive one ; or presume
To look upon a man, though from a window,
I'll chain thee like a slave in some dark
   corner ;
Prescribe thy daily labour, which omitted,
Expect the usage of a fury from me,
Not an indulgent mother.—Come, Calipso.
   Calip. Your ladyship's injunctions are so
   easy,
That I dare pawn my credit my young lady
And her woman shall obey them.
            [*Exeunt* Iölante *and* Calipso.
   Mirt. You shall fry first
For a rotten piece of touchwood, and give
   fire
To the great fiend's nostrils, when he smokes
   tobacco !
Note the injustice, madam ; they would
   have us,
Being young and hungry, keep perpetual
   Lent,
And the whole year to them a carnival.
Easy injunctions, with a mischief to you !
Suffer this and suffer all.
   Calis. Not stir abroad !
The use and pleasure of our eyes denied us!
   Mirt. Insufferable.
   Calis. Nor write, nor yet receive
An amorous letter !
   Mirt. Not to be endured.
   Calis. Nor look upon a man out of a
   window !
   Mirt. Flat tyranny, insupportable tyranny,
To a lady of your blood.
   Calis. She is my mother,
And how should I decline it ?
   Mirt. Run away from't ;
Take any course.
   Calis. But without means, Mirtilla,
How shall we live ?
   Mirt. What a question's that ! as if
A buxom lady could want maintenance
In any place in the world, where there are
   men,
Wine, meat, or money stirring.
   Calis. Be you more modest,

Or seek some other mistress : rather than
In a thought or dream I will consent to
　aught
That may take from my honour, I'll endure
More than my mother can impose upon me.
　Mirt. I grant your honour is a specious
　　dressing,
But without conversation of men,
A kind of nothing. I will not persuade you
To disobedience : yet my confessor told me
(And he, you know, is held a learned clerk)
When parents do enjoin unnatural things,
Wise children may evade them. She may as
　well
Command when you are hungry, not to eat,
Or drink, or sleep : and yet all these are
　easy,
Compared with the not seeing of a man,
As I persuade no further ; but to you
There is no such necessity ; you have the
　means
To shun your mother's rigour.
　Calis. Lawful means ?
　Mirt. Lawful, and pleasing too ; I will
　　not urge
Caldoro's loyal love, you being averse to't ;
Make trial of Adorio.
　Calis. And give up
My honour to his lust !
　Mirt. There's no such thing
Intended, madam ; in few words, write to
　him
What slavish hours you spend under your
　mother ;
That you desire not present marriage from
　him,
But as a noble gentleman to redeem you
From the tyranny you suffer. With your
　letter
Present him some rich jewel; you have one,
In which the rape of Proserpine, in little,
Is to the life express'd : I'll be the messenger
With any hazard, and at my return,
Yield you a good account of't.
　Calis. 'Tis a business
To be consider'd of.
　Mirt. Consideration,
When the converse of your lover is in
　question,
Is of no moment : if she would allow you
A dancer in the morning to well breathe you,
A songster in the afternoon, a servant
To air you in the evening ; give you leave
To see the theatre twice a week, to mark
How the old actors decay, the young sprout
　up,
(A fitting observation,) you might bear it ;
But not to see, or talk, or touch a man,
Abominable !

　Calis. Do not my blushes speak
How willingly I would assent ?
　Mirt. Sweet lady,
Do something to deserve them, and blush
　after.　　　　　　　　　　　　*[Exeunt.*

　　　　　　　　────────

ACT II.

SCENE I.—*The same. A Street near*
　　　　Severino's House.

Enter Iölante *and* Calipso.

　Iöl. And are these Frenchmen, as you say,
　　such gallants ?
　Calip. Gallant and active ; their free
　　breeding knows not
The Spanish and Italian preciseness
Practised among us ; what we call immodest,
With them is styled bold courtship : they
　dare fight
Under a velvet ensign, at fourteen.
　Iöl. A petticoat, you mean ?
　Calip. You are in the right ;
Let a mistress wear it under an armour of
　proof,
They are not to be beaten off.
　Iöl. You are merry, neighbour.
　Calip. I fool to make you so : pray you
　　observe them,
They are the forward'st monsieurs ; born
　physicians
For the malady of young wenches, and
　ne'er miss :
I owe my life to one of them. When I was
A raw young thing, not worth the ground I
　trod on,
And long'd to dip my bread in tar, my lips
As blue as salt-water, he came up roundly
　to me,
And cured me in an instant ; Venus be
　praised for't !

Enter Alphonso, Montpensier, Laval, Cap-
　tain, *and* Attendants.

　Iöl. They come, leave prating.
　Calip. I am dumb, an't like your honour.
　Alph. We will not break the league con-
　　firm'd between us
And your great master : the passage of his
　army
Through all our territories lies open to him ;
Only we grieve that your design for Rome
Commands such haste, as it denies us means
To entertain you as your worth deserves,
And we would gladly tender.
　Mont. Royal Alphonso,
The king my master, your confederate,
Will pay the debt he owes, in fact, which I

Want words t'express. I must remove to-
night ;
And yet, that your intended favours may not
Be lost, I leave this gentleman behind me,
To whom you may vouchsafe them, I dare
say,
Without repentance. I forbear to give
Your majesty his character ; in France
He was a precedent for arts and arms,
Without a rival, and may prove in Naples
Worthy the imitation.
    [*Introduces* Laval *to the king.*
Calip. Is he not, madam,
A monsieur in print ? what a garb was there!
 O rare !
Then, how he wears his clothes ! and the
 fashion of them !
A main assurance that he is within
All excellent : by this, wise ladies ever
Make their conjectures.
 Iöl. Peace, I have observed him
From head to foot.
 Calip. Eye him again, all over.
 Lav. It cannot, royal sir, but argue me
Of much presumption, if not impudence,
To be a suitor to your majesty,
Before I have deserved a gracious grant,
By some employment prosperously achieved.
But pardon, gracious sir : when I left France
I made a vow to a bosom friend of mine,
(Which my lord general, if he please, can
 witness,)
With such humility as well becomes
A poor petitioner, to desire a boon
From your magnificence.
    [*He delivers a petition.*
 Calip. With what punctual form
He does deliver it !
 Iöl. I have eyes : no more.
 Alph. For Severino's pardon !—you must
 excuse me,
I dare not pardon murder.
 Lav. His fact, sir,
Ever submitting to your abler judgment,
Merits a fairer name : he was provoked,
As by unanswerable proofs it is confirm'd,
By Monteclaro's rashness ; who repining
That Severino, without his consent,
Had married Iölante, his sole sister,
(It being conceal'd almost for thirteen years,)
Though the gentleman, at all parts, was his
 equal,
First challeng'd him, and, that declined, he
 gave him
A blow in public.
 Mont. Not to be endured,
But by a slave.
 Lav. This, great sir, justly weigh'd,
You may a little, if you please, take from

The rigour of your justice, and express
An act of mercy.
 Iöl. I can hear no more.
This opens an old wound, and makes a new
 one.
Would it were cicatrized ! wait me.
 Calip. As your shadow.
    [*Exeunt* Iölante *and* Calipso.
 Alph. We grant you these are glorious
 pretences,
Revenge appearing in the shape of valour,
Which wise kings must distinguish : the
 defence
Of reputation, now made a bawd
To murder ; every trifle falsely styled
An injury, and not to be determined
But by a bloody duel : though this vice
Hath taken root and growth beyond the
 mountains,
(As France, and, in strange fashions, her ape,
England, can dearly witness with the loss
Of more brave spirits, than would have stood
 the shock
Of the Turk's army,) while Alphonso lives
It shall not here be planted. Move me no
 further
In this ; in what else suiting you to ask,
And me to give, expect a gracious answer :
However, welcome to our court. Lord
 General,
I'll bring you out of the ports, and then
 betake you
To your good fortune.
 Mont. Your grace overwhelms me.
         [*Exeunt.*

SCENE II.—*A Room in* Severino's *House.*

  Enter Calipso *and* Iölante.

 Calip. You are bound to favour him :
 mark you how he pleaded
For my lord's pardon.
 Iöl. That's indeed a tie ;
But I have a stronger on me.
 Calip. Say you love
His person, be not asham'd of't ; he's a man,
For whose embraces, though Endymion
Lay sleeping by, Cynthia would leave her
 orb,
And exchange kisses with him.
 Iöl. Do not fan
A fire that burns already too hot in me ;
I am in my honour sick, sick to the death,
Never to be recovered.
 Calip. What a coil's here
For loving a man ! It is no Africk wonder :
If, like Pasiphaë, you doted on a bull,
Indeed 'twere monstrous ; but in this you
 · have

          H H

A thousand thousand precedents to excuse
   you.
A seaman's wife may ask relief of her neigh-
   bour,
When her husband's bound to the Indies,
   and not blamed for't ;
And many more besides of higher calling,
Though I forbear to name them. You
   have a husband ;
But, as the case stands with my lord, he is
A kind of no husband ; and your ladyship
As free as a widow can be. I confess,
If ladies should seek change, that have their
   husbands
At board and bed, to pay their marriage
   duties,
(The surest bond of concord,) 'twere a fault,
Indeed it were : but for your honour, that
Do lie alone so often—body of me !
I am zealous in your cause—let me take
   breath.

   Iöl. I apprehend what thou wouldst say,
   I want all
As means to quench the spurious fire that
   burns here.

   Calip. Want means, while I, your creature, live ! I dare not
Be so unthankful.

   Iöl. Wilt thou undertake it ?
And, as an earnest of much more to come,
Receive this jewel, and purse cramm'd full
   of crowns.——
How dearly I am forced to buy dishonour !
                          [*Aside.*

   Calip. I would do it gratis, but 'twould
   ill become
My breeding to refuse your honour's bounty ;
Nay, say no more, all rhetoric in this
Is comprehended ; let me alone to work him.
He shall be yours ; that's poor, he is already
At your devotion. I will not boast
My faculties this way, but suppose he were
Coy as Adonis, or Hippolytus,
And your desires more hot than Cytherea's,
Or wanton Phædra's, I will bring him chain'd
To your embraces, glorying in his fetters :
I have said it.

   Iöl. Go, and prosper ; and imagine
A salary beyond thy hopes.

   Calip. Sleep you
Secure on either ear ; the burthen's yours
To entertain him, mine to bring him hither.
                          [*Exeunt.*

SCENE III.—*A Room in* Adorio's *House.*

   Enter Adorio, Camillo, Lentulo, *and*
         Donato.

   Don. Your wrong's beyond a challenge,
   and you deal

Too fairly with him, if you take that way
To right yourself.

   Lent. The least that you can do,
In the terms of honour, is, when next you
   meet him,
To give him the bastinado.

   Cam. And that done,
Draw out his sword to cut your own throat !
   No,
Be ruled by me, shew yourself an Italian,
And having received one injury, do not put
   off
Your hat for a second ; there are fellows that,
For a few crowns, will make him sure, and so,
With your revenge, you prevent future mis-
   chief.

   Ador. I thank you, gentlemen, for your
   studied care
In what concerns my honour ; but in that
I'll steer my own course. Yet, that you may
   know
You are still my cabinet counsellors, my
   bosom
Lies open to you ; I begin to feel
A weariness, nay, satiety of looseness,
And something tells me here, I should repent
My harshness to Calista.

        Enter Cario, *hastily.*

   Camil. When you please,
You may remove that scruple.

   Ador. I shall think on't.

   Car. Sir, sir, are you ready ?

   Ador. To do what ?
I am sure 'tis not yet dinner-time.

   Car. True ; but I usher
Such an unexpected dainty bit for breakfast,
As yet I never cook'd : 'tis not botargo,
Fried frogs, potatoes marrow'd, cavear,
Carps' tongues, the pith of an English chine
   of beef,
Nor our Italian delicate, oil'd mushrooms,
And yet a drawer-on too ; and if you shew
   not
An appetite, and a strong one, I'll not say
To eat it, but devour it, without grace too,
(For it will not stay a preface,) I am shamed,
And all my past provocatives will be jeer'd
   at.

   Ador. Art thou in thy wits ? what new-
   found rarity
Hast thou discover'd ?

   Car. No such matter, sir ;
It grows in our own country.

   Don. Serve it up,
I feel a kind of stomach.

   Camil. I could feed too.

   Car. Not a bit upon a march ; there's
   other lettuce

For your coarse lips ; this is peculiar only
For my master's palate : I would give my
    whole year's wages,
With all my vails, and fees due to the kitchen,
But to be his carver.
   Ador. Leave your fooling, sirrah,
And bring in your dainty.
   Car. 'Twill bring in itself,
It has life and spirit in it ; and for proof,
Behold ! Now fall to boldly ; my life on't,
It comes to be tasted.

        Enter Mirtilla.

   Camil. Ha ! Calista's woman ?
   Lent. A handsome one, by Venus.
   Ador. Pray you forbear :—
You are welcome, fair one.
   Don. How that blush becomes her !
   Ador. Aim your designs at me ?
   Mirt. I am trusted, sir,
With a business of near consequence, which
   I would
To your private ear deliver.
   Car. I told you so.
Give her audience on your couch ; it is fit
   state
To a she-ambassador.
   Ador. Pray you, gentlemen,
For awhile dispose of yourselves, I'll straight
   attend you.
        [*Exeunt* Camil. Lent. *and* Don.
   Car. Dispatch her first for your honour:
   the quickly doing——
You know what follows.
   Ador. Will you please to vanish ?
            [*Exit* Carlo.
Now, pretty one, your pleasure? you shall
   find me
Ready to serve you ; if you'll put me to
My oath, I'll take it on this book.
         [*Offers to kiss her.*
   Mirt. O sir,
The favour is too great, and far above
My poor ambition ; I must kiss your hand
In sign of humble thankfulness.
   Ador. So modest !
   Mirt. It well becomes a maid, sir. Spare
   those blessings
For my noble mistress, upon whom with
   justice,
And, with your good allowance, I might add
With a due gratitude, you may confer them ;
But this will better speak her chaste desires,
        [*Delivers a letter.*
Than I can fancy what they are, much less
With moving language, to their fair deserts,
Aptly express them. Pray you read, but
   with
Compassion, I beseech you : if you find

The paper blurr'd with tears fallen from her
   eyes,
While she endeavour'd to set down that
   truth
Her soul did dictate to her, it must chal-
   lenge
A gracious answer.
   Ador. O the powerful charms
By that fair hand writ down here ! not like
   those
Which dreadfully pronounced by Circe,
   changed
Ulysses' followers into beasts ; these have
An opposite working, I already feel,
But reading them, their saving operations ;
And all those sensual, loose, and base
   desires,
Which have too long usurp'd, and tyran-
   nized
Over my reason, of themselves fall off.
Most happy metamorphosis ! in which
The film of error that did blind my judgment,
And seduced understanding, is removed.
What sacrifice of thanks can I return
Her pious charity, that not alone
Redeems me from the worst of slavery;
The tyranny of my beastly appetites,
To which I long obsequiously have bow'd ;
But adds a matchless favour, to receive
A benefit from me, nay, puts her goodness
In my protection?
   Mirt. Transform'd !—it is
A bless'd metamorphosis, and works
I know not how on me.   [*Aside.*
   Ador. My joys are boundless,
Curb'd with no limits : for her sake, Mirtilla,
Instruct me how I presently may seal
To those strong bonds of loyal love, and
   service,
Which never shall be cancell'd.
   Mirt. She'll become
Your debtor, sir, if you vouchsafe to answer
Her pure affection.
   Ador. Answer it, Mirtilla !
With more than adoration I kneel to it.
Tell her, I'll rather die a thousand deaths.
Than fail, with punctuality, to perform,
All her commands.
   Mirt. I am lost on this assurance,
Which, if 'twere made to me, I should have
   faith in't,
As in an oracle : ah me ! [*Aside.*] She pre-
   sents you
This jewel, her dead grandsire's gift, in
   which,
As by a true Egyptian hieroglyphic,
(For so I think she call'd it,) you may be
Instructed what her suit is you should do,
And she with joy will suffer.

Ador. [*looking at the trinket.*] Heaven be
  pleased
To qualify this excess of happiness
With some disaster, or I shall expire
With a surfeit of felicity.   With what art
The cunning lapidary hath here express'd
The rape of Proserpine !   I apprehend
Her purpose, and obey it ; yet not as
A helping friend, but a husband I will meet
Her chaste desires with lawful heat, and warm
Our Hymenæal sheets with such delights
As leave no sting behind them.
    Mirt. I despair then.   [*Aside.*
    Ador. At the time appointed say, wench,
      I'll attend her,
And guard her from the fury of her mother,
And all that dare disturb her.
    Mirt. You speak well ;
And I believe you.
    Ador. Would you aught else?
    Mirt. I would carry
Some love-sign to her ; and now I think on
  it,
The kind salute you offer'd at my entrance,
Hold it not impudence that I desire it,
I'll faithfully deliver it.
    Ador. O, a kiss !
You must excuse me, I was then mine own,
Now wholly hers : the touch of other lips
I do abjure for ever : but there's gold
To bind thee still my advocate.   [*Exit.*
Mirt. Not a kiss !
I was coy when it was offer'd, and now justly,
When I beg one am denied.   What scorch-
  ing fires
My loose hopes kindle in me ! shall I be
False to my lady's trust, and, from a servant,
Rise up her rival ?   His words have be-
  witch'd me,
And something I must do, but what ?—'tis
  yet
An embryon, and how to give it form,
Alas, I know not.   Pardon me, Calista,
I am nearest to myself, and time will teach
  me
To perfect that which yet is undetermined.
                                  [*Exit.*

SCENE IV.—*The Country.   A Forest.*

    Enter Claudio *and* Severino.

    Claud. You are master of yourself ; yet,
      if I may,
As a tried friend in my love and affection,
And a servant in my duty, speak my thoughts
Without offence, i'the way of counsel to you ;
I could allege, and truly, that your purpose
For Naples, cover'd with a thin disguise,
Is full of danger.
    Sev. Danger, Claudio !

'Tis here, and everywhere, our forced com-
  panion :
The rising and the setting sun beholds us
Environ'd with it ; our whole life a journey
Ending in certain ruin.
    Claud. Yet we should not,
Howe'er besieg'd, deliver up our fort
Of life, till it be forced.
    Sev. 'Tis so indeed
By wisest men concluded, which we should
Obey as Christians ; but when I consider
How different the progress of our actions
Is from religion, nay, morality,
I cannot find in reason, why we should
Be scrupulous that way only ; or like meteors
Blaze forth prodigious terrors, till our stuff
Be utterly consumed, which once put out,
Would bring security unto ourselves,
And safety unto those we prey upon.
O Claudio ! since by this fatal hand
The brother of my wife, bold Monteclaro,
Was left dead in the field, and I proscribed
After my flight, by the justice of the king,
My being hath been but a living death,
With a continued torture.
    Claud. Yet in that,
You do delude their bloody violence
That do pursue your life.
    Sev. While I, by rapines,
Live terrible to others as myself——
What one hour can we challenge as our own,
Unhappy as we are, yielding a beam
Of comfort to us? Quiet night, that brings
Rest to the labourer, is the outlaw's day,
In which he rises early to do wrong,
And when his work is ended, dares not sleep:
Our time is spent in watches to entrap
Such as would shun us, and to hide ourselves
From the ministers of justice, that would
  bring us
To the correction of the law.   O, Claudio,
Is this a life to be preserv'd, and at
So dear a rate ? But why hold I discourse
On this sad subject, since it is a burthen
We are mark'd to bear, and not to be shook
  off
But with our human frailty ? in the change
Of dangers there is some delight, and there-
  fore
I am resolved for Naples.
    Claud. May you meet there
All comforts that so fair and chaste a wife
As Fame proclaims her, without parallel,
Can yield to ease your sorrows !
    Sev. I much thank you ;
Yet you may spare those wishes, which with
  joy
I have proved certainties, and from their want
Her excellencies take lustre.

Claud. Ere you go yet,
Some charge unto your squires not to fly out
Beyond their bounds, were not impertinent :
For though that with a look you can com-
mand them,
In your absence they'll be headstrong.
Sev. 'Tis well thought on,
I'll touch my horn,—[*Blows his horn.*]—they
know my call.
Claud. And will,
As soon as heard, make in to't from all
quarters,
As the flock to the shepherd's whistle.

Enter Banditti.

1 *Ban.* What's your will?
2 *Ban.* Hail sovereign of these woods !
3 *Ban.* We lay our lives
At your highness' feet.
4 *Ban.* And will confess no king,
Nor laws but what come from your mouth ;
and those
We gladly will subscribe to.
Sev. Make this good,
In my absence, to my substitute, to whom
Pay all obedience as to myself ;
The breach of this in one particular
I will severely punish : on your lives,
Remember upon whom with our allowance
You may securely prey, with such as are
Exempted from your fury.
Claud. 'Twere not amiss,
If you please, to help their memory ; besides,
Here are some newly initiated.
Sev. To these
Read you the articles ; I must be gone :
Claudio, farewell ! [*Exit.*
Claud. May your return be speedy !
1 *Ban.* Silence ; out with your table-books.
2 *Ban.* And observe.
Claud. [reads.] *The cormorant that lives
in expectation*
*Of a long-wish'd for dearth, and, smiling,
grinds*
*The faces of the poor, you may make spoil of;
Even theft to such is justice.*
3 *Ban.* He's in my tables.
*Claud. The grand encloser of the commons,
for*
*His private profit or delight, with all
His herds that graze upon't, are lawful prize.*
4 *Ban.* And we will bring them in, al-
though the devil
Stood roaring by, to guard them.
*Claud. If a usurer,
Greedy, at his own price, to make a pur-
chase,
Taking advantage upon bond or mortgage
From a prodigal, pass through our territories,*

*In the way of custom, or of tribute to us,
You may ease him of his burthen.*
2 *Ban.* Wholesome doctrine.
*Claud. Builders of iron mills, that grub
up forests
With timber trees for shipping.*
1 *Ban.* May we not
Have a touch at lawyers ?
Claud. By no means ; they may
Too soon have a gripe at us ; they are angry
hornets,
Not to be jested with.
3 *Ban.* This is not so well.
*Claud. The owners of dark shops, that
vent their wares,
With perjuries; cheating vintners, not con-
tented
With half in half in their reckonings, yet
cry out,
When they find their guests want coin, 'Tis
late, and bed-time.
These ransack at your pleasures.*
3 *Ban.* How shall we know them ?
Claud. If they walk on foot, by their rat-
colour'd stockings,
And shining-shoes ; if horsemen, by short
boots,
And riding-furniture of several counties.
2 *Ban.* Not one of the list escapes us.
*Claud. But for scholars,
Whose wealth lies in their heads, and not
their pockets,
Soldiers that have bled in their country's
service;
The rent-rack'd farmer, needy market folks;
The sweaty labourer, carriers that transport
The goods of other men, are privileged;
But, above all, let none presume to offer
Violence to women, for our king hath sworn,
Who that way's a delinquent, without mercy
Hangs for't, by martial law.*
All. Long live Severino,
And perish all such cullions as repine
At his new monarchy !
Claud. About your business,
That he may find, at his return, good cause
To praise your care and discipline.
All. We'll not fail, sir. [*Exeunt.*

SCENE IV.—Naples. *A Street.*

Enter Laval *and* Calipso.

Lav. Thou art sure mistaken ; 'tis not
possible
That I can be the man thou art employ'd to.
Calip. Not you the man ! you are the man
of men,
And such another, in my lady's eye,
Never to be discover'd.

Lav. A mere stranger,
Newly arrived !
Calip. Still the more probable,
Since ladies, as you know, affect strange dainties,
And brought far to them. This is not an age
In which saints live ; but women, knowing women,
That understand their *summum bonum* is
Variety of pleasures in the touch,
Derived from several nations ; and if men would
Be wise by their example——
Lav. As most are :
'Tis a coupling age !
Calip. Why, sir, do gallants travel?
Answer that question ; but, at their return,
With wonder to the hearers, to discourse of
The garb and difference in foreign females,
As the lusty girl of France, the sober German,
The plump Dutch frow, the stately dame of Spain ;
The Roman libertine, and sprightful Tuscan,
The merry Greek, Venetian courtezan,
The English fair companion, that learns something
From every nation, and will fly at all :—
I say again, the difference betwixt these
And their own country gamesters.
Lav. Aptly urged.
Some make that their main end : but may I ask,
Without offence to your gravity, by what title ·
Your lady, that invites me to her favours,
Is known in the city?
Calip. If you were a true-born monsieur,
You would do the business first, and ask that after.
If you only truck with her title, I shall hardly
Deserve thanks for my travail ; she is, sir,
No single-ducat trader, nor a beldam
So frozen up, that a fever cannot thaw her ;
No lioness by her breath.
Lav. Leave these impertinencies,
And come to the matter.
Calip. Would you be as forward,
When you draw for the upshot ! she is, sir,
a lady,
A rich, fair, well-complexion'd, and what is
Not frequent among Venus' votaries,
Upon my credit, which good men have trusted,
A sound and wholesome lady, and her name is
Madonna Iölante.
Lav. Iölante !
I have heard of her ; for chastity, and beauty,
The wonder of the age.
Calip. Pray you, not too much

Of chastity ; fair and free I do subscribe to,
And so you'll find her.
Lav. Come, you are a base creature ;
And, covering your foul ends with her fair name,
Give me just reason to suspect you have
A plot upon my life.
Calip. A plot ! very fine !
Nay, 'tis a dangerous one, pray you beware of't ;
'Tis cunningly contriv'd : I plot to bring you
Afoot, with the travel of some forty paces,
To those delights which a man not made of snow
Would ride a thousand miles for. You shall be
Received at a postern door, if you be not cautious,
By one whose touch would make old Nestor young,
And cure his hernia ; a terrible plot !
A kiss then ravish'd from you by such lips
As flow with nectar, a juicy palm more precious
Than the famed Sibylla's bough, to guide you safe
Through mists of perfumes to a glorious room,
Where Jove might feast his Juno ; a dire plot !
A banquet I'll not mention, that is common :
But I must not forget, to make the plot
More horrid to you, the retiring bower,
So furnish'd as might force the Persian's envy,
The silver bathing-tub, the cambric rubbers,
The embroider'd quilt, the bed of gossamer
And damask roses ; a mere powder plot
To blow you up ! and last, a bed-fellow,
To whose rare entertainment all these are
But foils and settings off.
Lav. No more ; her breath
Would warm an eunuch.
Calip. I knew I should heat you :
Now he begins to glow !
Lav. I am flesh and blood,
And I were not man if I should not run the hazard,
Had I no other ends in't. I have consider'd
Your motion, matron.
Calip. My *plot*, sir, *on your life*,
For which I am deservedly suspected
For a base and dangerous woman ! Fare you well, sir,
I'll be bold to take my leave.
Lav. I will along too.
Come, pardon my suspicion : I confess
My error ; and eyeing you better, I perceive

There's nothing that is ill that can flow from
   you ;
I am serious, and, for proof of it, I'll purchase
Your good opinion.   [*Gives her his purse.*
   Calip. I am gentle natured,
And can forget a greater wrong upon   .
Such terms of satisfaction.
   Lav. What's the hour?
   Calip. Twelve.
   Lav. I'll not miss a minute.
   Calip. I shall find you
At your lodging?
   Lav. Certainly; return my service,
And for me kiss your lady's hands.
   Calip. At twelve
I'll be your convoy.
   Lav. I desire no better.   [*Exeunt.*

ACT III.

SCENE I.—*The Country.*

Enter Durazzo, Caldoro, *and* Servant.

   Dur. Walk the horses down the hill; I
   have a little
To speak in private.   [*Exit* Servant.
   Cald. Good sir, no more anger.
   Dur. Love do you call it ! madness, wil-
ful madness ;
And since I cannot cure it, I would have you
Exactly mad.   You are a lover already,
Be a drunkard too, and after turn small poet,
And then you are mad, katexokên the mad-
   man.
   Cald. Such as are safe on shore may
   smile at tempests ;
But I, that am embark'd, and every minute
Expect a shipwreck, relish not your mirth :
To me it is unseasonable.
   Dur. Pleasing viands
Are made sharp by sick palates. I affect
A handsome mistress in my gray beard as
   well
As any boy of you all ; and on good terms
Will venture as far i' the fire, so she be
   willing
To entertain me ; but ere I would dote,
As you do, where there is no flattering hope
Ever t' enjoy her, I would forswear wine,
And kill this lecherous itch with drinking
   water,
Or live, like a Carthusian, on poor John,
Then bathe myself night by night in marble
   dew,
And use no soap but camphire-balls.
   Cald. You may,
(And I must suffer it,) like a rough surgeon,
Apply these burning caustics to my wounds

Already gangrened, when soft unguents
   would
Better express an uncle with some feeling
Of his nephew's torments.
   Dur. I shall melt, and cannot
Hold out if he whimper. O that this young
   fellow,
Who, on my knowledge, is able to beat a
   man,
Should be baffled by this blind imagined
   boy,
Or fear his bird-bolts !   [*Aside.*
   Cald. You have put yourself already
To too much trouble, in bringing me thus
   far :
Now, if you please, with your good wishes,
   leave me
To my hard fortunes.
   Dur. I'll forsake myself first.
Leave thee ! I cannot, will not ; thou shalt
   have
No cause to be weary of my company,
For I'll be useful ; and, ere I see thee perish,
Dispensing with my dignity and candour,
I will do something for thee, though it
   savour
Of the old squire of Troy. As we ride, we
   will
Consult of the means : bear up.
   Cald. I cannot sink,
Having your noble aids to buoy me up ;
There was never such a guardian.
   Dur. How is this?
Stale compliments to me ! when my work's
   done,
Commend the artificer, and then be thankful.
      [*Exeunt.*

SCENE II.—Naples. *A Room in* Severino's *House.*

Enter Calista *richly habited, and* Mirtilla
in the gown which Calista *first wore.*

   Calis. How dost thou like my gown?
   Mirt. 'Tis rich and courtlike.
   Calis. The dressings too are suitable?
   Mirt. I must say so,
Or you might blame my want of care.
   Calis. My mother
Little dreams of my intended flight, or that
These are my nuptial ornaments.
   Mirt. I hope so.
   Calis. How dully thou reply'st ! thou dost
   not envy
Adorio's noble change, or the good fortune
That it brings to me ?
   Mirt. My endeavours that way
Can answer for me.
   Calis. True ; you have discharged
A faithful servant's duty, and it is

By me rewarded like a liberal mistress :
I speak it not to upbraid you with my
  bounties,
Though they deserve more thanks and cere-
  mony
Than you have yet express'd.
  Mirt. The miseries
Which, from your happiness, I am sure to
  suffer,
Restrain my forward tongue ; and, gentle
  madam,
Excuse my weakness, though I do appear
A little daunted with the heavy burthen
I am to undergo : when you are safe,
My dangers, like to roaring torrents, will
Gush in upon me ; yet I would endure
Your mother's cruelty ; but how to bear
Your absence, in the very thought confounds
  me.
Since we were children I have loved and
  serv'd you ;
I willingly learned to obey, as you
Grew up to knowledge, that you might
  command me ;
And now to be divorced from all my com-
  forts !—
Can this be borne with patience ?
  Calis. The necessity
Of my strange fate commands it ; but I vow
By my Adorio's love, I pity thee.
  Mirt. Pity me, madam ! a cold charity ;
You must do more, and help me.
  Calis. Ha ! what said you ?
I *must ?* is this fit language for a servant ?
  Mirt. For one that would continue your
  poor servant,
And cannot live that day in which she is
Denied to be so. Can Mirtilla sit
Mourning alone, imagining those pleasures
Which you, this blessed Hymeneal night,
Enjoy in the embraces of your lord,
And my lord too, in being yours? (already
As such I love and honour him.) Shall a
  stranger
Sew you in a sheet, to guard that maidenhead
You must pretend to keep ; and 'twill be-
  come you ?
Shall another do those bridal offices,
Which time will not permit me to remember,
And I pine here with envy ? pardon me,—
I must and will be pardon'd,—for my pas-
  sions
Are in extremes ; and use some speedy means
That I may go along with you, and share
In those delights, but with becoming dis-
  tance ;
Or by his life, which as a saint you swear by,
I will discover all !
  Calis. Thou canst not be

So treacherous and cruel, in destroying
The building thou hast raised.
  Mirt. Pray you do not tempt me,
For 'tis resolv'd.
  Calis. I know not what to think of t.
In the discovery of my secrets to her,
I have made my slave my mistress ; I must
  sooth her,
There's no evasion else. [*Aside.*] Prithee,
  Mirtilla,
Be not so violent, I am strangely taken
With thy affection for me ; 'twas my purpose
To have thee sent for.
  Mirt. When ?
  Calis. This very night ;
And I vow deeply I shall be no sooner
In the desired possession of my lord,
But by some of his servants I will have thee
Convey'd unto us.
  Mirt. Should you break !
  Calis. I dare not.
Come, clear thy looks, for instantly we'll
  prepare
For our departure.
  Mirt. Pray you, forgive my boldness,
Growing from my excess of zeal to serve you.
  Calis. I thank thee for't.
  Mirt. You'll keep your word ?
  Calis. Still doubtful !   [*Exit.*
  Mirt. 'Twas this I aim'd at, and leave the
    rest to fortune.   [*Exit, following.*

SCENE III.—*A Room in* Adorio's *House.*

Enter Adorio, Camillo, Lentulo, Donato,
    Cario, *and* Servants.

  Ador. Haste you unto my villa, and take
    all
Provision along with you, and for use
And ornament, the shortness of the time
Can furnish you ; let my best plate be set
    out,
And costliest hangings ; and, if't be possible,
With a merry dance to entertain the bride,
Provide an epithalamium.
  Car. Trust me
For belly timber : and for a song, I have
A paper-blurrer, who on all occasions,
For all times, and all seasons, hath such
    trinkets
Ready in the deck : it is but altering
The names, and they will serve for any bride,
Or bridegroom, in the kingdom.
  Ador. But for the dance ?
  Car. I will make one myself, and foot it
    finely ;
And summoning your tenants at my dresser,
Which is, indeed, my drum, make a rare
    choice

Of the able youth, such as shall sweat suffi-
  ciently;
And smell too, but not of amber, which, you
  know, is
The grace of the country-hall.
  Ador. About it, Cario,
And look you be careful.
  Car. For mine own credit, sir.
    [*Exeunt* Cario *and* Servants.
  Ador. Now, noble friends, confirm your
  loves, and think not
Of the penalty of the law, that does forbid
The stealing away an heir : I will secure
  you,
And pay the breach of't.
  Camil. Tell us what we shall do,
We'll talk of that hereafter.
  Ador. Pray you be careful
To keep the west gate of the city open,
That our passage may be free, and bribe the
  watch
With any sum ; this is all.
  Don. A dangerous business !
  Camil. I'll make the constable, watch,
  and porter drunk,
Under a crown.
  Lent. And then you may pass while they
  snore,
Though you had done a murder.
  Camil. Get but your mistress,
And leave the rest to us.
  Ador. You much engage me :
But I forget myself.
  Camil. Pray you, in what, sir?
  Ador. Yielding too much to my affection,
Though lawful now, my wounded reputation
And honour suffer: the disgrace, in taking
A blow in public from Caldoro, branded
With the infamous mark of coward, in de-
  laying
To right myself, upon my cheek grows
  fresher ;
That's first to be consider'd.
  Camil. If you dare
Trust my opinion, (yet I have had
Some practice and experience in duels,)
You are too tender that way : can you answer
The debt you owe your honour till you meet
Your enemy from whom you may exact it?
Hath he not left the city, and in fear
Conceal'd himself, for aught I can imagine?
What would you more?
  Ador. I should do.
  Camil. Never think on't,
'Till fitter time and place invite you to it :
I have read Caranza, and find not in his
  Grammar
Of quarrels, that the injured man is bound
To seek for reparation at an hour ;

But may, and without loss, till he hath settled
More serious occasions that import him,
For a day or two defer it.
  Ador. You'll subscribe
Your hand to this ?
  Camil. And justify't with my life ;
Presume upon't.
  Ador. On, then ; you shall o'er-rule me.
    [*Exeunt.*

SCENE IV.—*A Room in* Severino's *House.*

  Enter Iölante *and* Calipso.

  Iöl. I'll give thee a golden tongue, and
  have it hung up,
Over thy tomb, for a monument.
  Calip. I am not prepared yet
To leave the world ; there are many good
  pranks
I must dispatch in this kind before I die :
And I had rather, if your honour please,
Have the crowns in my purse.
  Iöl. Take that.
  Calip. Magnificent lady !
May you live long, and, every moon, love
  change,
That I may have fresh employment ! you
  know what
Remains to be done ?
  Iöl. Yes, yes ; I will command
My daughter and Mirtilla to their chamber.
  Calip. And lock them up ; such liquorish
  kitlings are not
To be trusted with our cream. Ere I go,
  I'll help you
To set forth the banquet, and place the can-
  died eringoes
Where he may be sure to taste them ; then
  undress you,
For these things are cumbersome, when you
  should be active :
A thin night mantle to hide part of your
  smock,
With your pearl embroider'd pantofles on
  your feet,
And then you are arm'd for service ! nay,
  no trifling,
We are alone, and you know 'tis a point of
  folly
To be coy to eat when meat is set before
  you.   [*Exeunt.*

SCENE V.—*A Street before* Severino's
  House.

  Enter Adorio *and* Servant.

  Ador. 'Tis eleven by my watch, the hour
  appointed.
Listen at the door—hear'st thou any stirring?
  Serv. No, sir ;
All's silent here.

Ador. Some cursed business keeps
Her mother up. I'll walk a little circle,
And shew where you shall wait us with the
　　horses,
And then return. This short delay afflicts
　　me,
And I presume to her it is not pleasing.
　　　　　　　　　　　　　[*Exeunt.*

Enter Durazzo *and* Caldoro.

Dur. What's now to be done? prithee
　let's to bed, I am sleepy;
And here's my hand on't, without more ado,
By fair or foul play we'll have her to-morrow
In thy possession.
　　Cald. Good sir, give me leave
To taste a little comfort in beholding
The place by her sweet presence sanctified.
She may perhaps, to take air, ope the case-
　　ment,
And looking out, a new star to be gazed on
By me with adoration, bless these eyes,
Ne'er happy but when she is made the object.
　　Dur. Is not here fine fooling!
　　Cald. Thou great queen of love,
Or real or imagined, be propitious
To me, thy faithful votary! and I vow
To erect a statue to thee, equal to
Thy picture, by Apelles' skilful hand
Left as the great example of his art;
And on thy thigh I'll hang a golden Cupid,
His torches flaming, and his quiver full,
For further honour!
　　Dur. End this waking dream,
And let's away.

Enter from the house Calista *and* Mirtilla.

　　Calis. Mirtilla!
　　Cald. 'Tis her voice!
　　Calis. You heard the horses' footing?
　　Mirt. Certainly.
　　Calis. Speak low. My lord Adorio!
　　Cald. I am dumb.
　　Dur. The darkness friend us too! Most
　　honour'd madam,
Adorio, your servant.
　　Calis. As you are so,
I do command your silence till we are
Further remov'd; and let this kiss assure you
(I thank the sable night that hides my
　　blushes)
I am wholly yours.
　　Dur. Forward, you micher!
　　Mirt. Madam,
Think on Mirtilla! 　　[*Goes into the house.*
　　Dur. I'll not now enquire
The mystery of this, but bless kind fortune
Favouring us beyond our hopes: yet, now
　　I think on't,

I had ever a lucky hand in such smock
　night-work. 　　　　　　　[*Exeunt.*

Enter Adorio *and* Servant.

Ador. This slowness does amaze me:
　she's not alter'd
In her late resolution?
　　Iöl. [*within.*] Get you to bed,
And stir not on your life, till I command you.
　　Ador. Her mother's voice! listen.
　　Serv. Here comes the daughter.

Re-enter Mirtilla, *hastily.*

　　Mirt. Whither shall I fly for succour?
　　Ador. To these arms,
Your castle of defence, impregnable,
And not to be blown up: how your heart
　　beats!
Take comfort, dear Calista, you are now
In his protection that will ne'er forsake you:
Adorio, your changed Adorio, swears
By your best self, an oath he dares not break,
He loves you, loves you in a noble way,
His constancy firm as the poles of heaven.
I will urge no reply, silence becomes you;
And I'll defer the music of your voice,
Till we are in a place of safety.
　　Mirt. O blest error! 　　[*Aside. Exeunt.*

Enter Severino.

　　Sev. 'Tis midnight: how my fears of cer-
　　tain death,
Being surprised, combat with my strong
　　hopes
Raised on my chaste wife's goodness! I am
　　grown
A stranger in the city, and no wonder,
I have too long been so unto myself:
Grant me a little truce, my troubled soul——
I hear some footing, ha!

Enter Laval *and* Calipso.

　　Calip. That is the house,
And there's the key: you'll find my lady
　　ready
To entertain you; 'tis not fit I should
Stand gaping by while you bill: I have
　　brought you on,
Charge home, and come off with honour.
　　　　　　　　　　　　　[*Exit.*
　　Sev. It makes this way.
　　Lav. I am much troubled, and know not
　　what to think
Of this design.
　　Sev. It still comes on.
　　Lav. The watch!
I am betray'd.
　　Sev. Should I now appear fearful,
It would discover me; there's no retiring.

My confidence must protect me ; I'll appear
As if I walk'd the round.—Stand !

Lav. I am lost.

Sev. The word ?

Lav. Pray you forbear ; I am a stranger,
And missing, this dark stormy night, my way
To my lodging, you shall do a courteous office
To guide me to it.

Sev. Do you think I stand here
For a page or a porter ?

Lav. Good sir, grow not so high :
I can justify my being abroad ; I am
No pilfering vagabond, and what you are
Stands yet in supposition ; and I charge you,
If you are an officer, bring me before your captain ;
For if you do assault me, though not in fear
Of what you can do alone, I will cry murder,
And raise the streets.

Sev. Before my captain, ha !
And bring my head to the block. Would we were parted,
I have greater cause to fear the watch than he.

Lav. Will you do your duty?

Sev. I must close with him :—
Troth, sir, whate'er you are, (yet by your language,
I guess you a gentleman,) I'll not use the rigour
Of my place upon you : only quit this street,
For your stay here will be dangerous ; and good night !

Lav. The like to you, sir ; l'll grope out my way
As well as I can. O damn'd bawd !—Fare you well, sir. [*Exit.*

Sev. I am glad he's gone ; there is a secret passage,
Unknown to my wife, through which this key will guide me
To her desired embraces, which must be,
My presence being beyond her hopes, most welcome. [*Exit.*

SCENE VI.—*A Room in* Severino's *House.*

Iölante *is heard speaking behind a curtain.*

Iöl. I am full of perplex'd thoughts. Imperious blood,
Thou only art a tyrant ; judgment, reason,
To whatsoever thy edicts proclaim,
With vassal fear subscribe against themselves.
I am yet safe in the port, and see before me,
If I put off, a rough tempestuous sea,
The raging winds of infamy from all quarters
Assuring my destruction ; yet my lust

Swelling the wanton sails, (my understanding
Stow'd under hatches,) like a desperate pilot,
Commands me to urge on. My pride, my pride,
Self-love, and over-value of myself,
Are justly punish'd : I, that did deny
My daughter's youth allow'd and lawful pleasures,
And would not suffer in her those desires
She suck'd in with my milk, now in my waning
Am scorch'd and burnt up with libidinous fire,
That must consume my fame ; yet still I throw
More fuel on it.

Enter Severino *before the curtain.*

Sev. 'Tis her voice, poor turtle :
She's now at her devotions, praying for
Her banish'd mate ; alas, that for my guilt
Her innocence should suffer ! But I do
Commit a second sin in my deferring
The ecstacy of joy that will transport her
Beyond herself, when she flies to my lips,
And seals my welcome.—[*Draws the curtain, and discovers* Iölante *seated, with a rich banquet, and tapers, set forth.*]—
Iölante !

Iöl. Ha !
Good angels guard me !

Sev. What do I behold !
Some sudden flash of lightning strike me blind,
Or cleave the centre of the earth, that I
May living find a sepulchre to swallow
Me and my shame together !

Iöl. Guilt and horror
Confound me in one instant ; thus surprised,
The subtilty of all wantons, though abstracted,
Can shew no seeming colour of excuse,
To plead in my defence. [*Aside.*

Sev. Is this her mourning?
O killing object ! The imprison'd vapours
Of rage and sorrow make an earthquake in me ;
This little world, like to a tottering tower,
Not to be underpropp'd ;—yet in my fall,
I'll crush thee with my ruins.
[*Draws a poniard.*

Iöl. [*kneeling.*] Good sir, hold :
For, my defence unheard, you wrong your justice,
If you proceed to execution ;
And will, too late, repent it.

Sev. Thy defence !
To move it, adds (could it receive addition)

Ugliness to the loathsome leprosy
That, in thy being a strumpet, hath already
Infected every vein, and spreads itself
Over this carrion, which would poison vul-
    tures
And dogs, should they devour it.   Yet, to
    stamp
The seal of reprobation on thy soul,
I'll hear thy impudent lies, borrow'd from
    hell,
And prompted by the devil, thy tutor, whore!
Then send thee to him.   Speak.
    Iöl. Your Gorgon looks
Turn me to stone, and a dead palsy seizes
My silenced tongue.
    Sev. O Fate, that the disease
Were general in women, what a calm
Should wretched men enjoy !   Speak, and
    be brief,
Or thou shalt suddenly feel me.
    Iöl. Be appeased, sir,
Until I have deliver'd reasons for
This solemn preparation.
    Sev. On, I hear thee.
    Iöl. With patience ask your memory;
    'twill instruct you,
This very day of the month, seventeen years
    since,
You married me.
    Sev. Grant it, what canst thou urge
From this ?
    Iöl. That day, since your proscription, sir,
In the remembrance of it annually,
The garments of my sorrow laid aside,
I have with pomp observed.
    Sev. Alone !
    Iöl. The thoughts
Of my felicity then, my misery now,
Were the invited guests; imagination
Teaching me to believe that you were pre-
    sent,
And a partner in it.
    Sev. Rare ! this real banquet
To feast your fancy : fiend ! could fancy
    drink off
These flaggons to my health, or the idle
    thought,
Like Baal, devour these delicates ? the room
Perfumed to take his nostrils ! this loose
    habit,
Which Messalina would not wear, put on
To fire his lustful eyes ! Wretch, am I
    grown
So weak in thy opinion, that it can
Flatter credulity that these gross tricks
May be foisted on me? Where's my daughter?
    where
The bawd your woman? answer me.—
    Calista !

Mirtilla ! they are disposed of, if not
    murder'd,
To make all sure ; and yet methinks your
    neighbour,
Your whistle, agent, parasite, Calipso,
Should be within call, when you hem, to
    usher in
The close adulterer.   [*Lays hands on her.*
    Iöl. What will you do ?
    Sev. Not kill thee, do not hope it ; I am
    not
So near to reconcilement.   Ha ! this scarf,
The intended favour to your stallion, now
Is useful : do not strive ;—[*He binds her.*]—
    thus bound, expect
All studied tortures my assurance, not
My jealousy, thou art false, can pour upon
    thee.
In darkness howl thy mischiefs ; and if rank-
    ness
Of thy imagination can conjure
The ribald [hither,] glut thyself with him ;
I will cry *Aim !* and in another room
Determine of my vengeance.   Oh, my heart-
    strings !   [*Exit with the tapers.*
    Iöl. Most miserable woman ! and yet
    sitting
A judge in mine own cause upon myself,
I could not mitigate the heavy doom
My incens'd husband, must pronounce upon
    me.
In my intents I am guilty, and for them
Must suffer the same punishment, as if
I had, in fact, offended.
    Calip. [*within.*] Bore my eyes out,
If you prove me faulty ; I'll but tell my lady
What caused your stay, and instantly pre-
    sent you.

                Enter Calipso.

How's this? no lights !   What new device?
    will she play
At blindman's-buff ?—Madam !
    Iöl. Upon thy life,
Speak in a lower key.
    Calip. The mystery
Of this, sweet lady ? where are you ?
    Iöl. Here, fast bound.
    Calip. By whom ?
    Iöl. I'll whisper that into thine ear,
And then farewell for ever.——
    Calip. How ! my lord ?
I am in a fever: horns upon horns grow on
    him ! ,
Could he pick no hour but this to break a
    bargain
Almost made up?
    Iöl. What shall we do ?

Calip. Betray him ;
I'll instantly raise the wateh.
Iöl. And so make me
For ever infamous.
Calip. The gentleman,
The rarest gentleman is at the door,
Shall he lose his labour? Since that you
must perish,
'Twill shew a woman's spleen in you to fall
Deservedly ; give him his answer, madam.
I have on the sudden in my head a strange
whim ;
But I will first unbind you. [*Frees Iöl.*
Iöl. Now what follows?
Calip. I will supply your place ; [*Iöl.
binds Calip.*] and, bound, give me
Your mantle, take my night-gown ; send
away
The gentleman satisfied. I know my lord
Wants power to hurt you, I perhaps may get
A kiss by the bargain, and all this may prove
But some neat love-trick : if he should grow
furious,
And question me, I am resolved to put on
An obstinate silence. Pray you dispatch the
gentleman,
His courage may cool.
Iöl. I'll speak with him, but if
To any base or lustful end, may mercy
At my last gasp forsake me ! [*Exit.*
Calip. I was too rash,
And have done what I wish undone : say he
should kill me?
I have run my head in a fine noose, and I
smell
The pickle I am in ! 'las, how I shudder
Still more and more ! would I were a she
Priapus,
Stuck up in a garden to fright away the
crows,
So I were out of the house ! she's at her
pleasure,
Whate'er she said ; and I must endure the
torture—
He comes ; I cannot pray, my fears will kill
me.

Re-enter Severino *with a knife in his hand,
throwing open the doors violently.*

Sev. It is a deed of darkness, and I need
No light to guide me ; there is something
tells me
I am too slow-paced in my wreak, and trifle
In my revenge. All hush'd ! no sigh nor
groan,
To witness her compunction ! can guilt sleep,
And innocence be open-eyed ? even now,
Perhaps, she dreams of the adulterer,

And in her fancy hugs him. Wake, thou
strumpet,
And instantly give up unto my vengeance
The villain that defiles my bed ; discover
Both what and where he is, and suddenly,
That I may bind you face to face, then sew
you
Into one sack, and from some steep rock
hurl you
Into the sea together; do not play with
The lightning of my rage ; break stubborn
silence,
And answer my demands ; will it not be ?
I'll talk no longer ; thus I mark thee for
A common strumpet.
[*Strikes at her with the knife.*
Calip. Oh !
Sev. Thus stab these arms
That have stretch'd out themselves to grasp
a stranger.
Calip. Oh !
Sev. This is but an induction ; I will draw
The curtains of the tragedy hereafter :
Howl on, 'tis music to me. [*Exit.*
Calip. He is gone.
A *kiss* and *love-tricks!* he hath villainous
teeth,
May sublimed mercury draw them ! if all
dealers
In my profession were paid thus, there
would be
A dearth of cuckolds. Oh my nose ! I *had*
one :
My arms, my arms ! I dare not cry for fear;
Cursed desire of gold, how art thou punish'd !

Enter Iölante.

Iöl. Till now I never truly knew myself,
Nor by all principles and lectures read
In chastity's cold school, was so instructed
As by her contrary, how base and deform'd
Loose appetite is ; as in a few short minutes
This stranger hath, and feelingly, deliver'd.
Oh ! that I could recall my bad intentions,
And be as I was yesterday, untainted
In my desires, as I am still in fact,
I thank his temperance ! I could look un-
daunted
Upon my husband's rage, and smile at it,
So strong the guards and sure defences are
Of armed innocence ; but I will endure
The penance of my sin, the only means
Is left to purge it. The day breaks.—
Calipso !
Calip. Here, madam, here.
Iöl. Hath my lord visited thee ?
Calip. Hell take such visits ! these stabb'd
arms, and loss

Of my nose you left fast on, may give you a
relish
What a night I have had of't, and what you
had suffered,
Had I not supplied your place.

Iöl. I truly grieve for't;
Did not my husband speak to thee?

Calip. Yes, I heard him,
And felt him, *ecce signum*, with a mischief!
But he knew not me; like a true-bred Spartan
boy,
With silence I endured it; he could not get
One syllable from me.

Iöl. Something may be fashion'd
From this; invention help me! I must be
sudden. 　　　　　　　　[*Unbinds her.*
Thou art free, exchange, quick, quick! now
bind me sure,
And leave me to my fortune.

Calip. Pray you consider
The loss of my nose; had I been but carted
for you,
Though wash'd with mire and chamber-lie,
I had
Examples to excuse me: but my nose,
My nose, dear lady!

Iöl. Get off, I'll send to thee.
　　　　　　　　　　　　[*Exit* Calipso.
If so, it may take; if it fail, I must
Suffer whatever follows.

Re-enter Severino *with the knife and taper.*

Sev. I have search'd
In every corner of the house, yet find not
My daughter, nor her maid; nor any print
Of a man's footing, which, this wet night,
would
Be easily discern'd, the ground being soft,
At his coming in or going out.

Iol. 'Tis he,
And within hearing; heav'n forgive this
feigning,
I being forced to't to preserve my life,
To be better spent hereafter!

Sev. I begin
To stagger, and my love, if it knew how,
(Her piety heretofore and fame remember'd,)
Would plead in her excuse.

Iöl. [*aloud.*] You blessed guardians
Of matrimonial faith, and just revengers
Of such as do in fact offend against
Your sacred rites and ceremonies; by all titles
And holy attributes you do vouchsafe
To be invoked, look down with saving pity
Upon my matchless sufferings!

Sev. At her devotions:
Affliction makes her repent.

Iöl. Look down
Upon a wretched woman, and as I

Have kept the knot of wedlock, in the temple
By the priest fasten'd, firm; (though in loose
wishes
I yield I have offended;) to strike blind
The eyes of jealousy, that see a crime
I never yet committed, and to free me
From the unjust suspicion of my lord,
Restore my martyr'd face and wounded arms
To their late strength and beauty.

Sev. Does she hope
To be cured by miracle?

Iöl. This minute I
Perceive with joy my orisons heard and
granted.
You ministers of mercy, who unseen,
And by a supernatural means, have done
This work of heavenly charity, be ever
Canonized for't!

Sev. I did not dream, I heard her,
And I have eyes too, they cannot deceive
me:
If I have no belief, in their assurance,
I must turn sceptic. Ha! this is the hand,
And this the fatal instrument: these drops
Of blood, that gush'd forth from her face
and arms,
Still fresh upon the floor. This is some-
thing more
Than wonder or amazement; I profess
I am astonish'd.

Iöl. Be incredulous still,
And go on in your barbarous rage, led to it
By your false guide, suspicion; have no faith
In my so long tried loyalty, nor believe
That which you see; and for your satisfac-
tion,
My doubted innocence cleared by miracle,
Proceed; these veins have now new blood,
if you
Resolve to let it out.

Sev. I would not be fool'd
With easiness of belief, and faintly give
Credit to this strange wonder; 'tis now
thought on:
In a fitter place and time I'll sound this
further. 　　　　　　　　　　[*Aside.*
How can I expiate my sin? or hope,
　　　　　　　　　　　　[*Unties her.*
Though now I write myself thy slave, the
service
Of my whole life can win thee to pronounce
Despair'd-of pardon? Shall I kneel? that's
poor,
Thy mercy must urge more in my defence,
Than I can fancy; wilt thou have revenge?
My heart lies open to thee.

Iöl. This is needless
To me, who in the duty of a wife,
Know I must suffer.

Sev. Thou art made up of goodness,
And from my confidence that I am alone
The object of thy pleasures, until death
Divorce us, we will know no separation.
Without inquiring why, as sure thou wilt
    not,
Such is thy meek obedience, thy jewels
And choicest ornaments pack'd up, thou
    shalt
Along with me, and as a queen be honour'd
By such as style me sovereign. Already
My banishment is repeal'd, thou being
    present ;
The Neapolitan court a place of exile
When thou art absent : my stay here is
    mortal,
Of which thou art too sensible, I perceive it;
Come, dearest Iölante, with this breath
All jealousy is blown away. [*Embraces her.*
Iöl. Be constant. [*Exeunt.*

ACT IV.

SCENE I.—*The Country.*

*A Noise within, as of a horse fallen ;—then
enter* Durazzo, Caldoro, *and* Servant,
with Calista *in their arms.*

Dur. Hell take the stumbling jade !
Cald. Heaven help the lady !
Serv. The horse hath broke his neck.
Dur. Would thine were crack'd too,
So the lady had no harm ! Give her fresh
    air,
'Tis but a swoon.
Cald. 'Tis more, she's dead.
Dur. Examine
Her limbs if they be whole : not too high,
    not too high,
You ferret ; this is no coney-burrow for you.
How do you find her?
Cald. No breath of comfort, sir : too
    cruel fate !
Had I still pined away, and linger'd under
The modesty of just and honest hopes
After a long consumption, sleep and death
To me had been the same ; but now, as
    'twere,
Possess'd of all my wishes, in a moment
To have them ravish'd from me! suffer
    shipwreck
In view of the port ! and, like a half-starv'd
    beggar,
No sooner in compassion clothed, but
    coffin'd !
Malevolent destinies, too cunning in
Wretched Caldoro's tortures ! O Calista,
If thy immortal part hath not already
Left this fair palace, let a beam of light

Drawn from thine eye, in this Cimmerian
    darkness,
To guide my shaking hand to touch the
    anchor
Of hope in thy recovery.
Calis. Oh !
Dur. She lives ;
Disturb her not : she is no right-bred woman,.
If she die with one fall ; some of my ac-
    quaintance
Have ta'en a thousand merrily, and are still
Excellent wrestlers at the close hug.
Cald. Good sir——
Dur. Prithee be not angry, I should speak
    thus if
My mother were in her place.
Cald. But had you heard
The music of the language which she used
To me, believed Adorio, as she rode
Behind me ; little thinking that she did
Embrace Caldoro——
Calis. Ah, Adorio !
Dur. Leave talking, I conceive it.
Calis. Are you safe ?
Cald. And raised, like you, from death to
    life, to hear you.
Calis. Hear my defence then, ere I take
    my veil off,
A simple maid's defence, which, looking on
    you,
I faintly could deliver ; willingly
I am become your prize, and therefore use
Your victory nobly ; heaven's bright eye, the
    sun,
Draws up the grossest vapours, and I hope
I ne'er shall prove an envious cloud to
    darken
The splendour of your merits. I could urge
With what disdain, nay scorn, I have de-
    clined
The shadows of insinuating pleasures
Tender'd by all men else, you only being
The object of my hopes : that cruel prince
To whom the olive-branch of peace is offer'd,.
Is not a conqueror, but a bloody tyrant,
If he refuse it ; nor should you wish a
    triumph,
Because Calista's humble : I have said,
And now expect your sentence.
Dur. What a throng
Of clients would be in the court of Love,
Were there many such she-advocates !. Art
    thou dumb?
Canst thou say nothing for thyself?
Cald. [*Kneels.*] Dear lady,
Open your eyes, and look upon the man,
The man you have elected for your judge,
Kneeling to you for mercy.
Calis. I should know

This voice, and something more than fear I
  am
Deceived ; but now I look upon his face,
I am assured I am wretched.
  Dur. Why, good lady?
Hold her up, she'll fall again before her time
  else.
The youth's a well-timber'd youth, look on
  his making ;
His hair curl'd naturally ; he's whole-chested
  too,
And will do his work as well, and go through
  stitch with't,
As any Adorio in the world, my state on't !
A chicken of the right kind ; and if he prove
  not
A cock of the game, cuckold him first, and
  after
Make a capon of him.
  Calis. I'll cry out a rape,
If thou unhand me not ; would I had died
In my late trance, and never lived to know
I am betray'd !
  Dur. To a young and active husband !
Call you that treachery? there are a shoal of
Young wenches i'the city, would vow a pil-
  grimage
Beyond Jerusalem, to be so cheated.—
To her again, you milksop ! violent storms
Are soon blown over.
  Calis. How could'st thou, Caldoro,
With such a frontless impudence arm thy
  hopes
So far, as to believe I might consent
To this lewd practice? have I not often told
  thee,
Howe'er I pitied thy misplaced affection,
I could not answer it ; and that there was
A strong antipathy between our passions,
Not to be reconciled?
  Cald. Vouchsafe to hear me
With an impartial ear, and it will take from
The rigour of your censure. Man was mark'd
A friend, in his creation, to himself,
And may with fit ambition conceive
The greatest blessings and the highest
  honours
Appointed for him, if he can achieve them
The right and noble way : I grant you were
The end of my design, but still pursued
With a becoming modesty, heaven at length
Being pleased, and not my arts, to further it.
  Dur. Now he comes to her : on, boy !
  Cald. I have served you
With a religious zeal, and borne the burthen
Of your neglect, if I may call it so,
Beyond the patience of a man : to prove this,
I have seen those eyes with pleasant glances
  play

Upon Adorio's, like Phœbe's shine
Gilding a crystal river ; and your lip
Rise up in civil courtship to meet his,
While I bit mine with envy : yet these
  favours,
Howe'er my passions raged, could not pro-
  voke me
To one act of rebellion against
My loyalty to you, the sovereign
To whom I owe obedience.
  Calis. My blushes
Confess this for a truth.
  Dur. A flag of truce is
Hung out in this acknowledgement.
  Cald. I could add,
But that you may interpret what I speak
The malice of a rival, rather than
My due respect to your deserts, how faintly
Adorio hath return'd thanks to the bounty
Of your affection, ascribing it
As a tribute to his worth, and not in you
An act of mercy : could he else, invited
(As by your words I understood) to take you
To his protection, grossly neglect
So gracious an offer, or give power
To Fate itself to cross him? O, dear madam,
We are all the balls of time, toss'd to and
  fro,
From the plough unto the throne, and back
  again :
Under the swing of destiny mankind suffers,
And it appears, by an unchanged decree,
You were appointed mine ; wise nature al-
  ways
Aiming at due proportion : and if so,
I may believe with confidence, heaven, in
  pity
Of my sincere affection, and long patience,
Directed you, by a most blessed error,
To your vow'd servant's bosom.
  Dur. By my holidam,
Tickling philosophy !
  Calis. I am, sir, too weak
To argue with you ; but my stars have better,
I hope, provided for me.
  Cald. If there be
Disparity between us, 'tis in your
Compassion to level it.
  Dur. Give fire
To the mine, and blow her up.
  Calis. I am sensible
Of what you have endured ; but on the
  sudden,
With my unusual travel, and late bruise,
I am exceeding weary. In yon grove,
While I repose myself, be you my guard ;
My spirits with some little rest revived,
We will consider further : for my part,
You shall receive modest and gentle answers

To your demands, though short, perhaps, to make you
Full satisfaction.
    Cald. I am exalted
In the employment,; sleep secure, I'll be
Your vigilant centinel.
    Calis. But I command you,
And as you hope for future grace, obey me,
Presume not with one stolen kiss to disturb
The quiet of my slumbers ; let your temperance,
And not your lust, watch o'er me.
    Cald. My desires
Are frozen, till your pity shall dissolve them.
    Dur. Frozen ! think not of frost, fool, in the dog-days.
Remember the old adage, and make use of t,
Occasion's bald behind.
    Calis. Is this your uncle ?
    Cald. And guardian, madam : at your better leisure,
When I have deserved it, you may give him thanks
For his many favours to me.
    Calis. He appears
A pleasant gentleman.
         [*Exeunt* Caldoro *and* Calista.
    Dur. You should find me so,
But that I do hate incest : I grow heavy ;
Sirrah, provide fresh horses ; I'll seek out
Some hollow tree, and dream till you return,
Which I charge you to hasten.
    Serv. With all care, sir.   [*Exeunt.*

SCENE II.—*The Country. A Room in* Adorio's *House.*

Enter Cario, *with several* Villagers, Musicians, &c.

    Car. Let your eyes be rivetted to my heels, and miss not
A hair's breadth of my footing ; our dance has
A most melodious note, and I command you
To have ears like hares this night, for my lord's honour,
And something for my worship ; your reward is
To be drunk-blind like moles, in the wine-cellar ;
And though you ne'er see after, 'tis the better ;
You were born for this night's service. And, do you hear,
Wire-string and cat-gut men, and strong-breath'd hoboys,
For the credit of your calling, have not your instruments
To tune when you should strike up ; but twang it perfectly,

As you would read your neck-verse ; and you, warbler,
Keep your wind pipe moist, that you may not spit and hem,
When you should make division. How I sweat !
Authority is troublesome ;—[*A horn within.*]
    —they are come,
I know it by the cornet that I placed
On the hill to give me notice : marshal yourselves
I'the rear ; the van is yours.

    Enter Adorio, Mirtilla, Camillo, Dentulo, *and* Donato

             Now chant it sprightly.

    SONG, *between* Juno *and* Hymen.

        Juno *to the* Bride.

Enter a maid ; but made a bride,
    Be bold, and freely taste
The marriage banquet, ne'er denied
    To such as sit down chaste.
Though he unloose thy virgin zone,
    Presumed against thy will,
Those joys reserved to him alone,
    Thou art a virgin still.

    Hymen *to the* Bridegroom.

Hail, bridegroom, hail! thy choice thus made,
    As thou wouldst have her true,
Thou must give o'er thy wanton trade,
    And bid loose fires adieu.
That husband who would have his wife
    To him continue chaste,
In her embraces spends his life,
    And makes abroad no waste.

    Hymen *and* Juno.

Sport then like turtles, and bring forth
    Such pledges as may be
Assurance of the father's worth,
    And mother's purity.
Juno doth bless the nuptial bed ;
    Thus Hymen's torches burn.
Live long, and may, when both are dead,
    Your ashes fill one urn !

    Ador. A well-penn'd ditty.
    Camil. Not ill sung.
    Ador. What follows ?   [*to the dancers.*
    Car. Use your eyes.   If ever—now your master-piece !

        A DANCE.

    Ador. 'Tis well perform'd ; take that, but not from me,
'Tis your new lady's bounty, thank her for it ;
All that I have is hers.

                    I I

Car. I must have three shares
For my pains and properties, the rest shall
    be
Divided equally.   [*Exeunt* Cario, Villagers, &c.
    Mirt. My real fears
Begin, and soon my painted comforts vanish,
In my discovery.
    Ador. Welcome to your own!
You have (a wonder in a woman) kept
Three long hours silence; and the greater,
    holding
Your own choice in your arms; a blessing
    for which
I will be thankful to you: nay, unmask,
And let mine eye and ears together feast,
Too long by you kept empty. Oh, you want
Your woman's help, I'll do her office for you.
                      [*Takes off her mask.*
Mirtilla!
    Camil. It is she, and wears the habit
In which Calista three days since appeared,
As she came from the temple.
    Lent. All this trouble
For a poor waiting-maid!
    Don. We are grossly gull'd.
    Ador. Thou child of impudence, answer
    me, and truly,
Or, though the tongues of angels pleaded
    mercy,
Tortures shall force it from thee.
    Mirt. Innocence
'Is free, and open-breasted; of what crime
Stand I accused, my lord?
    Ador. What crime! no language
Can speak it to the height; I shall become
Discourse for fools and drunkards. How
    was this
Contrived? who help'd thee in the plot?
    discover.
Were not Calista's aids in't?
    Mirt. No, on my life;
Nor am I faulty.
    Ador. No! What May-game's this?
Didst thou treat with me for thy mistress'
    favours,
To make sale of thine own?
    Mirt. With her and you
I have dealt faithfully: you had her letter
With the jewel I presented: she received
Your courteous answer, and prepared herself
To be removed by you: and howsoever
You take delight to hear what you have done,
From my simplicity, and make my weakness
The subject of your mirth, as it suits well
With my condition, I know you have her
In your possession.
    Ador. How! has she left
Her mother's house?

Mirt. You drive this nail too far.
Indeed she deeply vow'd, at her departure,
To send some of your lordship's servants for
    me,
(Though you were pleased to take the pains
    yourself,)
That I might still be near her, as a shadow
To follow her, the substance.
    Ador. She is gone then?
    Mirt. This is too much; but, good my
    lord, forgive me,
I come a virgin hither to attend
My noble mistress, though I must confess,
I look with sore eyes upon her good fortune,
And wish it were mine own.
    Ador. Then, as it seems,
You do yourself affect me?
    Mirt. Should she hear me,
And in her sudden fury kill me for't,
I durst not, sir, deny it; since you are
A man so form'd, that not poor I alone,
But all our sex like me, I think, stand bound
To be enamour'd of you.
    Ador. O my fate!
How justly am I punish'd, in thee punish'd,
For my defended wantonness! I, that scorn'd
The mistress when she sought me, now I
    would
Upon my knees receive her, am become
A prey unto her bondwoman, my honour too
Neglected for this purchase. Art thou one of
    those
Ambitious servingwomen, who, contemning
The embraces of their equals, aim to be
The wrong way ladyfied, by a lord? was there
No forward page or footman in the city,
To do the feat, that in thy lust I am chosen
To be the executioner? dar'st thou hope
I can descend so low?
    Mirt. Great lords sometimes
For change leave calver'd salmon, and eat
    sprats:
In modesty I dare speak no more.
    Camil. If 'twere
A fish-day, though you like it not, I could
    say
I have a stomach, and would content myself
With this pretty whiting-mop.
    Ador. Discover yet
How thou cam'st to my hands.
    Mirt. My lady gone,
Fear of her mother's rage, she being found
    absent,
Moved me to fly; and quitting of the house,
You were pleased, unask'd, to comfort me;
    (I used
No sorceries to bewitch you;) then vouch-
    safed
(Thanks ever to the darkness of the night!)

To hug me in your arms ; and I had wrong'd
My breeding near the court, had I refused it.
  Ador. This is still more bitter. Canst thou
    guess to whom
Thy lady did commit herself?
  Mirt. They were
Horsemen, as you are.
  Ador. In the name of wonder,
How could they pass the port, where you
    expected
My coming?
  Camil. Now I think upon't, there came
Three mounted by, and, behind one, a
    woman
Embracing fast the man that rode before her.
  Lent. I knew the men ; but she was veil'd.
  Ador. What were they?
  Lent. The first the lord Durazzo, and the
    second,
Your rival, young Caldoro ; it was he
That carried the wench behind him.
  Don. The last a servant,
That spurr'd fast after them.
  Ador. Worse and worse ! 'twas she !
Too much assurance of her love undid me.
Why did you not stay them ?
  Don. We had no such commission.
  Camil. Or say we had, who durst lay
    fingers on
The angry old ruffian?
  Lent. For my part, I had rather
Take a baited bull by the horns.
  Ador. You are sure friends
For a man to build on !
  Camil. They are not far off,
Their horses appear'd spent too ; let's take
    fresh ones,
And coast the country ; ten to one we find
    them.
  Ador. I will not eat nor sleep, until I have
    them :
Moppet, you shall along too.
  Mirt. So you please
I may keep my place behind you, I'll sit fast,
And ride with you all the world o'er.
  Camil. A good girl !   [*Exeunt.*

SCENE III.—Naples. *A Street.*

Enter Laval *and* Calipso.

  Lav. Her husband? Severino?
  Calip. You may see
His handywork by my flat face ; no bridge
Left to support my organ, if I had one :
The comfort is, I am now secure from the
    crincomes,
I can lose nothing that way.
  Lav. Dost thou not know
What became of the lady?
  Calip. A nose was enough to part with,

I think, in the service ; I durst stay no
    longer :
But I am full assured the house is empty,
Neither poor lady, daughter, servant left
    there.
I only guess he hath forced them to go with
    him
To the dangerous forest, where he lives like
    a king,
Among the banditti ; and how there he hath
    used them,
Is more than to be fear'd.
  Lav. I have play'd the fool,
And kept myself too long conceal'd, sans
    question,
With the danger of her life. Leave me——
    the king !

Enter Alphonso *and* Captain.

  Calip. The surgeon must be paid.
  Lav. Take that.   [*Gives her money.*
  Calip. I thank you ;
I have got enough by my trade, and I will
    build
An hospital only for noseless bawds,
('Twill speak my charity,) and be myself
The governess of the sisterhood.   [*Exit.*
  Alph. I may
Forget this in your vigilance hereafter !
But as I am a king, if you provoke me
The second time with negligence of this kind,
You shall deeply smart for't.
  Lav. The king's moved.
  Alph. To suffer
A murderer, by us proscribed, at his pleasure
To pass and repass through our guards !
  Capt. Your pardon
For this, my gracious lord, binds me to be
More circumspect hereafter.
  Alph. Look you be so :
Monsieur Laval, you were a suitor to me
For Severino's pardon.
  Lav. I was so, my good lord.
  Alph. You might have met him here, to
    have thank'd you for't,
As now I understand.
  Lav. So it is rumour'd ;
And hearing in the city of his boldness,
I would not say contempt of your decrees,
As then I pleaded mercy, under pardon,
I now as much admire the slowness of
Your justice (though it force you to some
    trouble)
In fetching him in.
  Alph. I have consider'd it.
  Lav. He hath of late, as 'tis suspected,
    done
An outrage on his wife, forgetting nature
To his own daughter ; in whom, sir, I have

Some nearer interest than I stand bound to
In my humanity, which I gladly would
Make known unto your highness.

Alph. Go along,
You shall have opportunity as we walk :
See you what I committed to your charge,
In readiness, and without noise.

Capt. I shall, sir. [*Exeunt.*

ACT V.

SCENE I.—*The Forest.*

Enter Claudio *and all the* Banditti, *making
a guard;* Severino *and* Iölante *with
oaken-leaved garlands;* Singers.

SONG, Entertainment of the Forest's Queen.

*Welcome, thrice welcome to this shady green,
Our long-wish'd Cynthia, the forest's queen,
The trees begin to bud, the glad birds sing
In winter, changed by her into the spring.
          We know no night,
          Perpetual light
                Dawns from your eye.
          You being near,
          We cannot fear,
                Though Death stood by.
From you our swords take edge, our hearts
     grow bold;
From you in fee their lives your liegemen
     hold.
These groves your kingdom, and our law
     your will;
Smile, and we spare; but if you frown, we
     kill.
          Bless then the hour
          That gives the power
          In which you may,
          At bed and board,
          Embrace your lord
          Both night and day.
Welcome, thrice welcome to this shady green,
Our long-wished Cynthia, the forest's queen!*

Sev. Here, as a queen, share in my sove-
reignty :
The iron toils pitch'd by the law to take
The forfeiture of my life, I have broke
     through,
And secure in the guards of these few
     subjects,
Smile at Alphonso's fury ; though I grieve
     for
The fatal cause, in your good brother's loss,
That does compel me to this course.

Iöl. Revive not
A sorrow long since dead, and so diminish

The full fruition of those joys, which now
I stand possess'd of : womanish fear of
     danger
That may pursue us, I shake off, and with
A masculine spirit.

Sev. 'Tis well said.

Iöl. In you, sir,
I live ; and when, or by the course of nature,
Or violence, you must fall, the end of my
Devotions is, that one and the same hour
May make us fit for heaven.

Sev. I join with you .
In my votes that way : but how, Iölante,
You that have spent your past days, slum-
     bering in
The down of quiet, can endure the hardness
And rough condition of our present being,
Does much disturb me.

Iöl. These woods, Severino,
Shall more than seem to me a populous city.
You being present ; here are no allurements
To tempt my frailty, nor the conversation
Of such whose choice behaviour, or dis-
     course,
May nourish jealous thoughts.

Sev. True, Iölante ;
Nor shall suspected chastity stand in need
     here,
To be clear'd by miracle. -

Iöl. Still on that string !
It yields harsh discord.

Sev. I had forgot myself,
And wish I might no more remember it.
The day wears, sirs, without one prize
     brought in
As tribute to your queen : Claudio, divide
Our squadron in small parties, let them watch
All passages, that none escape without
The payment of our customs.

Claud. Shall we bring in
The persons, with the pillage?

Sev. By all means ;
Without reply, about it : we'll retire
          [*Exeunt* Claudio *and the rest.*
Into our cave, and there at large discourse
Our fortunes past, and study some apt means
To find our daughter ; since, she well dis-
     posed of,
Our happiness were perfect.

Iöl. We must wait
With patience heaven's pleasure.

Sev. 'Tis my purpose. [*Exeunt.*

SCENE II.—*Another part of the forest.*

Enter Lentulo *and* Camillo.

Lent. Let the horses graze, they are spent.

Camil. I am sure I'm sleepy,
And nodded as I rode : here was a jaunt

I' the dark through thick and thin, and all
  to no purpose !
What a dulness grows upon me !
  Lent. I can hardly
Hold ope mine eyes to say so. How did we
  lose
Adorio?   *[They sit down.*
  Camil. He, Donato, and the wench,
That cleaves to him like birdlime, took the
  right hand :
But this place is our rendezvous.
  Lent. No matter,
We'll talk of that anon——heigh ho !
                [Falls asleep.
  Camil. He's fast already.
Lentulo !—I'll take a nap too.
                [Falls asleep.

  Enter Adorio, Mirtilla, *and* Donato.

  Ador. Was ever man so crost ?
  Mirt. So blest ; this is
The finest wild-goose chase !   *[Aside.*
  Ador. What's that you mutter ?
  Mirt. A short prayer, that you may find
  your wish'd-for love,
Though I am lost for ever.
  Don. Pretty fool !
Who have we here ?
  Ador. This is Camillo.
  Mirt. This signior Lentulo.
  Ador. Wake them.
  Don. They'll not stir,
Their eyelids are glued, and mine too : by
  your favour,
I'll follow their example.   *[Lies down.*
  Ador. Are you not weary ?
  Mirt. I know not what the word means,
  while I travel
To do you service.
  Ador. You expect to reap
The harvest of your flattery ; but your hopes
Will be blasted, I assure you.
  Mirt. So you give leave
To sow it, as in me a sign of duty,
Though you deny your beams of gracious
  favour
To ripen it, with patience I shall suffer.
  Ador. No more ; my resolution to find
Calista, by what accident lost I know not,
Binds me not to deny myself what nature
Exacteth from me : to walk alone afoot
(For my horse is tired) were madness, I must
  sleep.
You could lie down too ?
  Mirt. Willingly ; so you please
To use me——
  Ador. Use thee !
  Mirt. As your pillow, sir ;
I dare presume no further. Noble sir,

Do not too much contemn me ; generous feet
Spurn not a fawning spaniel.
  Ador. Well ; sit down.
  Mirt. I am ready, sir.
  Ador. So nimble !
  Mirt. Love is active,
Nor would I be a slow thing : rest secure, sir ;
On my maidenhead, I'll not ravish you.
  Ador. For once,
So far I'll trust you.
        [Lays his head on her lap.
  Mirt. All the joys of rest
Dwell on your eyelids ; let no dream disturb
Your soft and gentle slumbers ! I cannot sing,
But I'll talk you asleep ; and I beseech you
Be not offended, though I glory in
My being thus employ'd ; a happiness
That stands for more than ample satisfaction
For all I have or can endure.— He snores,
And does not hear me ; would his sense of
  feeling
Were bound up too ! I should——I am all
  fire.
Such heaps of treasure offer'd as a prey,
Would tempt a modest thief ; I can no longer
Forbear—I'll gently touch his lips, and leave
No print of mine :—*[Kisses him.]* ah !—I
  have heard of nectar,
But till now never tasted it ; these rubies
Are not clouded by my breath : if once again
I steal from such a full exchequer, trifles
Will not be miss'd ;—*[Kisses him again.]*—
  I am entranced : our fancy,
Some say, in sleep works stronger ; I will
  prove
How far my——   *[Falls asleep.*

      Enter Durazzo.

  Dur. My bones ache,.
I am exceeding cold too ; I must seek out
A more convenient truckle-bed. Ha ! do I
  dream ?
No, no, I wake. Camillo, Lentulo,
Donato this, and, as I live, Adorio
In a handsome wench's lap ! a whoreson !
  you are
The best accommodated. I will call
My nephew and his mistress to this pageant ;
The object may perhaps do more upon her,
Than all Caldoro's rhetoric. With what
Security they sleep ! sure Mercury
Hath travell'd this way with his charming-
  rod.
Nephew ! Calista ! Madam !

    Enter Caldoro *and* Calista.

  Cald. Here, sir. Is
Your man return'd with horses ?

Dur. No, boy, no ;
But here are some you thought not of.
Calis. Adorio !
Dur. The idol that you worshipped.
Calis. This Mirtilla !
I am made a stale.
Dur. I knew 'twould take.   [*Aside.*
Calis. False man !
But much more treacherous woman ! 'Tis
      apparent,
They jointly did conspire against my weak-
      ness,
And credulous simplicity, and have
Prevail'd against it.
Cald. I'll not kill them sleeping ;
But, if you please, I'll wake them first, and
      after
Offer them as a fatal sacrifice,
To your just anger.
Dur. You are a fool ; reserve
Your blood for better uses.
Calis. My fond love
Is changed to an extremity of hate ;
His very sight is odious.
Dur. I have thought of
A pretty punishment for him and his com-
      rades,
Then leave him to his harlotry ; if she
      prove not
Torture enough, hold me an ass. Their
      horses
Are not far off, I'll cut the girths and
      bridles,
Then turn them into the wood ; if they can
      run,
Let them follow us as footmen.   Wilt thou
      fight
For what's thine own already !
Calis. In his hat
He wears a jewel, which this faithless
      strumpet,
As a salary of her lust, deceived me of ;
He shall not keep't to my disgrace, nor
      will I
Stir till I have it.
Dur. I am not good at nimming ;
And yet that shall not hinder us : by your
      leave, sir ;
'Tis restitution : pray you all bear witness
I do not steal it ; here 'tis.
            Takes off Adorio's *hat, and removes*
                  the jewel, which he gives to Calista.
Calis. Take it,—not
As a mistress' favour, but a strong assurance
I am your wife.   [*Gives it to* Caldoro.
Cald. O heaven !
Dur. Pray in the church.
Let us away.   Nephew, a word ; have you
      not

Been billing in the brakes, ha ! and so de-
      serv'd
This unexpected favour?
Cald. You are pleasant.
      Exeunt Durazzo, Caldoro, *and* Calista.
Ador. As thou art a gentleman, kill me
      not basely ;   [*Starts up; the rest awake.*
Give me leave to draw my sword.
Camil. Ha ! what's the matter?
Lent. He talk'd of's sword.
Don. I see no enemy near us,
That threatens danger.
Mirt. Sure 'twas but a dream.
Ador. A fearful one.   Methought Cal-
      doro's sword
Was at my throat, Calista frowning by,
Commanding him, as he desired her fa-
      vour,
To strike my head off.
Camil. Mere imagination
Of a disturbed fancy.
Mirt. Here's your hat, sir.
Ador. But where's my jewel?
Camil. By all likelihood lost,
This troublesome night.
Don. I saw it when we came
Unto this place.
Mirt. I look'd upon't myself,
When you reposed.
Ador. What is become of it?
Restore it, for thou hast it ;   do not put
      me
To the trouble to search you.
Mirt. Search me !
Ador. You have been,
Before your lady gave you entertainment,
A night-walker in the streets.
Mirt. How, my good lord !
Ador. Traded in picking pockets, when
      tame gulls,
Charm'd with your prostituted flatteries,
Deign'd to embrace you.
Mirt. Love, give place to anger.
Charge me with theft, and prostituted
      baseness !
Were you a judge, nay more, the king, thus
      urged,
To your teeth I would say, 'tis false.
Ador. This will not do.
Camil. Deliver it in private.
Mirt. You shall be
In public hang'd first, and the whole gang
      of you.
I steal what I presented !
Lent. Do not strive.
Ador. Though thou hast swallow'd it,
      I'll rip thy entrails,
But I'll recover it.   . [*Seizes her.*
Mirt. Help, help !

Claudio *and two* Banditti *rush upon them with pistols.*

Ador. A new plot!

Claud. Forbear, libidinous monsters! if you offer
The least resistance, you are dead. If one
But lay his hand upon his sword, shoot all.

Ador. Let us fight for what we have, and if you can
Win it, enjoy it.

Claud. We come not to try
Your valour, but for your money; throw down your sword,
Or I'll begin with you: so! if you will
Walk quietly without bonds, you may, if not
We'll force you.—[Fear not,] thou shalt have no wrong,
But justice against these. [*To* Mirtilla.

1 *Ban.* We'll teach you, sir,
To meddle with wenches in our walks.

2 *Ban.* It being
Against our canons.

Camil. Whither will you lead us?

Claud. You shall know that hereafter.—
Guard them sure. [*Exeunt.*

SCENE III.—*Another part of the Forest.*

Enter Alphonso *disguised as an old Man,* Laval *and* Captain.

Alph. Are all the passages stopp'd?

Capt. And strongly mann'd;
They must use wings, and fly, if they escape us.

Lav. But why, great sir, you should expose your person
To such apparent danger, when you may
Have them brought bound before you, is beyond
My apprehension.

Alph. I am better arm'd
Than you suppose: besides, it is confirm'd
By all that have been robb'd, since Severino
Commanded these banditti, (though it be
Unusual in Italy,) imitating
The courteous English thieves, for so they call them,
They have not done one murder: I must add too,
That, from a strange relation I have heard
Of Severino's justice, in disposing
The preys brought in, I would be an eye-witness
Of what I take up now but on report:
And therefore 'tis my pleasure that we should,
As soon as they encounter us, without
A shew of opposition, yield.

Lav. Your will
Is not to be disputed.

Alph. You have placed
Your ambush so, that, if there be occasion,
They suddenly may break in?

Capt. My life upon't.

Alph. We cannot travel far, but we shall meet
With some of these good fellows; and be. sure
You do as I command you,

Lav. Without fear, sir. [*Exeunt.*

SCENE IV.—*Another part of the Forest.*

Enter Severino *and* Iölante.

Sev. 'Tis true; I did command Calista should not,
Without my knowledge and consent, assisted
By your advice, be married; but your
Restraint, as you deliver it, denying
A grown-up maid the modest conversation
Of men, and warrantable pleasures, relish'd.
Of too much rigour, which, no doubt, hath. driven her
To take some desperate course.

Iöl. What then I did
Was, in my care, thought best.

Sev. So I conceive it;
But where was your discretion to forbid
Access, and fit approaches, when you knew
Her suitors noble, either of which I would
Have wish'd my son-in-law? Adorio,
However wild, a young man of good parts,.
But better fortunes: his competitor,
Caldoro, for his sweetness of behaviour,
Staidness, and temperance, holding the first place
Among the gallants most observed in Naples;.
His own revenues of a large extent,
But in the expectation of his uncle
And guardian's entradas, by the course
Of nature to descend on him, a match
For the best subject's blood, I except none
Of eminence in Italy.

Iöl. Your wishes,
Howe'er a while delay'd, are not, I hope,
Impossibilities.

Sev. Though it prove so,
Yet 'tis not good to give a check to fortune,.
When she comes smiling to us.—Hark! this cornet [*Cornet within.*
Assures us of a prize; there sit in state,
'Tis thy first tribute.

Iöl. Would we might enjoy
Our own as subjects!

Sev. What's got by the sword,
Is better than inheritance: all those kingdoms
Of Alexander were, by force, extorted,
Though gilded o'er with glorious styles of conquest:

His victories but royal robberies,
And his true definition a thief,
When circled with huge navies, to the terror
Of such as plough'd the ocean, as the pirate,
Who, from a narrow creek, puts off for
    prey
In a small pinnace :—[*Cornet within.*]—
    From a second place
New spoil brought in !—[*Cornet within.*]—
  . from a third party ! brave !
This shall be register'd a day of triumph,
Design'd by fate to honour thee.——

        Enter Claudio.

               Welcome, Claudio !

Good booty, ha?

*Enter at different sides, various parties of
  the* Banditti ; *one with* Adorio, Lentulo,
  Donato, Camillo, Mirtilla ; *another with*
  Durazzo, Caldoro, Calista; *and the rest
  with* Alphonso, Laval, *and* Captain.

  Claud. Their outsides promise so ;
But yet they have not made discovery
Of what they stand possest of.
  Sev. Welcome all ;
Good· boys ! you have done bravely, if no
    blood
Be shed in the service.
  I *Ban.* On our lives, no drop, sir.
  Sev. 'Tis to my wish.
  Iöl. My lord !
  Sev. No more ; I know them.
  Iöl. My daughter, and her woman too !
  Sev. Conceal
Your joys.
  Dur. Fallen in the devil's mouth !
  Calis. My father,
And mother ! to what fate am I reserved?
  Cald. Continue mask'd ; or grant that
    you be known,
From whom can you expect a gentle sen-
    tence,
If you despair a father's ?
  Ador. I perceive now
Which way I lost my jewel.
  Mirt. I rejoice
I'm clear'd from theft ; you have done me
    wrong, but I,
Unask'd, forgive you.
  Dur. 'Tis some comfort yet,
The rivals, men and women, friends and
    foes, are
Together in one toil.
  Sev. You all look pale,
And by your private whisperings and soft
    murmurs,
Express a general fear : pray you shake it off;
For understand you are not fallen into

The hands of a Busiris or a Cacus,
Delighted more in blood than spoil, but
  . given up
To the power of an unfortunate gentle-
    man,
Not born to these low courses, howsoever
My fate, and just displeasure of the king,
Design'd me to it : you need not to doubt
A sad captivity here, and much less fear,
For profit, to be sold for slaves, then shipp'd
Into another country ; in a word,
You know the proscribed Severino, he,
Not unacquainted, but familiar with
The most of you.—Want in myself I know
    not ;
But for the pay of these my squires, who eat
Their bread with danger purchased, and
    must be
With others' fleeces clothed, or live exposed
To the summer's scorching heat and winter's
    cold ;
To these, before you be compell'd, (a word
I speak with much unwillingness,) deliver
Such coin as you are furnish'd with.
  Dur. A fine method !
This is neither begging, borrowing, nor
    robbery ;
Yet it hath a twang of all of them : but one
    word, sir.
  Sev. Your pleasure.
  Dur. When we have thrown down our
    muck,
What follows?
  Sev. Liberty, with a safe convoy,
To any place you choose.
  Dur. By this hand, you are
A fair fraternity ! for once I'll be
The first example to relieve your convent.
There's a thousand crowns, my vintage,
    harvest, profits,
Arising from my herds, bound in one bag,
Share it among you.
  Sev. You are still the jovial,
And good Durazzo.
  Dur. To the offering ; nay,
No hanging an a—, this is their wedding-
    day :
What you must do spite of your hearts, do
    freely
For your own sakes.
  Camil. There's mine.
  Lent. Mine.
  Don. All that I have.
  Cald. This, to preserve my jewel.
  Ador. Which I challenge :
Let me have justice, for my coin I care not.
  Lav. I will not weep for mine.
  Capt. Would it were more.
    [*They all throw down their purses.*

Sev. Nay, you are privileged; but why,
old father,   [*To the* King.
Art thou so slow? thou hast one foot in the
grave,
And, if desire of gold do not increase
With thy expiring lease of life, thou shouldst
Be forwardest.   · ·
   Alph. In what concerns myself,
I do acknowledge it; and I should lie,
A vice I have detested from my youth, ·
If I denied my present store, since what·
I have about me now weighs down in value,
Almost a hundred fold, whatever these
Have laid before you: see! I do groan
under   [*Throws down three bags.*
The burthen of my treasure: nay, 'tis gold;
And if your hunger of it be not sated · ·
With what already I have shewn unto you,
Here's that shall glut it. In this casket are
Inestimable jewels, diamonds
Of such a piercing lustre, as struck blind
The amazed lapidary, while he labour'd
        [*Opens the casket.*
To honour his own art in setting them:
Some orient pearls too, which the queen of
Spain
Might wear as ear-rings, in remembrance of
The day that she was crown'd.
   Sev. The spoils, I think,
Of both the Indies!
   Dur. The great sultan's poor,
If parallel'd with this Crœsus.
   Sev. Why dost thou weep?
   Alph. From a most fit consideration of
My poverty; this, though restored, will not
Serve my occasions.
   Sev. Impossible!
   Dur. May be he would buy his passport
up to heaven;
And then this is too little; though, in the
journey,
It were a good viaticum.
   Alph. I would make it
A means to help me thither: not to wrong
you
With tedious expectation, I'll discover
What my wants are, and yield my reasons
   for them.
I have two sons, twins, the true images
Of what I was at their years; never father
Had fairer or more promising hopes in his
Posterity: but, alas! these sons, ambitious
Of glittering honour, and an after-name,
Achieved by glorious, and yet pious actions,
(For such were their intentions,) put to sea:
They had a well-rigg'd bottom, fully mann'd,
An old experienced master, lusty sailors,
Stout landmen, and what's something more
   than rare,

They did agree, had one design, and that was
In charity to redeem the Christian slaves . ·
Chain'd in the Turkish servitude.
   Sev. A brave aim!
   Dur. A most heroic enterprise; I languish ·
To hear how they succeeded. ·
   Alph. Prosperously,
At first, and to their wishes: divers gallies
They boarded, and some strong forts near
   the shore ·
They suddenly surprised; a thousand cap-·
   tives,
Redeem'd from the oar, paid their glad
   vows and prayers
For their deliverance: their ends acquired,
And making homeward in triumphant man-
   ner,
For sure the cause deserved it——
   Dur. Pray you end here;
The best, I fear, is told, and that which
   follows
Must conclude ill.
   Alph. Your fears are true, and yet
I must with grief relate it. Prodigal fame,
In every place, with her loud trump, pro-
   claiming
The greatness of the action, the pirates
Of Tunis and Argiers laid wait for them · ·
At their return: to tell you what resistance
They made, and how my poor sons fought,
   would but
Increase my sorrow, and, perhaps, grieve
   you
To hear it passionately described unto you.
In brief, they were taken, and for the great
   loss
The enemy did sustain, their victory
Being with much blood bought, they do
   endure ·
The heaviest captivity wretched men
Did ever suffer. O my sons! my sons!
To me for ever lost! lost, lost for ever! ·
   Sev. Will not these heaps of gold, added
   to thine,
Suffice for ransome?
   Alph. For my sons it would;
But they refuse their liberty, if all
That were engaged with them, have not
   their irons,
With theirs, struck off, and set at liberty
   with them;
Which these heaps cannot purchase.
   Sev. Ha! the toughness · ·
Of my heart melts. Be comforted, old father;
I have some hidden treasure, and if all
I and my squires these three years have laid
   up,
Can make the sum up, freely take't.

Dur. I'll sell
Myself to my shirt, lands, moveables ; and
  thou
Shalt part with thine too, nephew, rather
  than
Such brave men shall live slaves.
  2 Ban. We will not yield to't.
  3 Ban. Nor lose our parts.
  Sev. How's this !
  2 Ban. You are fitter far
To be a churchman, than to have command
Over good fellows.
  Sev. Thus I ever use [*Strikes them down.*
Such saucy rascals ; second me, Claudio.—
Rebellious ! do you grumble? I'll not leave
One rogue of them alive.
  Alph. Hold ;—give the sign.
                      [*Discovers himself.*
  All. The king !
  Sev. Then I am lost.
  Claud. The woods are full
Of armed men.
  Alph. No hope of your escape
Can flatter you.
  Sev. Mercy, dread sir !   [*Kneels.*
  Alph. Thy carriage
In this unlawful course appears so noble,
Especially in this last trial, which
I put upon you, that I wish the mercy
You kneel in vain for might fall gently on
  you :
But when the holy oil was pour'd upon
My head, and I anointed king, I swore
Never to pardon murder.   I could wink at
Your robberies, though our laws call them
  death,
But to dispense with Monteclaro's blood
Would ill become a king ; in him I lost
A worthy subject, and must take from you
A strict account of't.   'Tis in vain to move;
My doom's irrevocable.
  Lav. Not, dread sir,
If Monteclaro live.
  Alph. If ! good Laval.
  Lav. He lives in him, sir, that you thought
Laval.   [*Discovers himself.*
Three years have not so alter'd me, but you
  may
Remember Monteclaro.
  Dur. How !
  Iöl. My brother !
  Calis. Uncle !
  Mont. Give me leave : I was
Left dead in the field, but by the duke
  Montpensier,
Now general at Milan, taken up,
And with much care recover'd.
  Alph. Why lived you
So long conceal'd ?

Mont. Confounded with the wrong
I did my brother, in provoking him
To fight, I spent the time in France that I
Was absent from the court, making my exile
The punishment imposed upon myself,
For my offence.
  Iöl. Now, sir, I dare confess all :
This was the guest invited to the banquet,
That drew on your suspicion.
  Sev. Your intent,
Though it was ill in you, I do forgive ;
The rest I'll hear at leisure.   Sir, your sen-
  tence.
  Alph. It is a general pardon unto all,
Upcn my hopes, in your fair lives hereafter,
You will deserve it.
  Sev. Claud. and the rest. Long live great
    Alphonso !
  Dur. Your mercy shewn in this ; now, if
  you please,
Decide these lovers' difference.
  Alph. That is easy ;
I'll put it to the women's choice, the men
Consenting to it.
  Calis. Here I fix then, never.
To be removed.   [*Embraces* Caldoro.
  Cald. 'Tis my *nil ultra,* sir.
  Mirt. O, that I had the happiness to say
So much to you ! I dare maintain my love
Is equal to my lady's.
  Ador. But my mind
A pitch above yours : marry with a servant
Of no descent or fortune !
  Sev. You are deceived :
Howe'er she has been train'd up as a servant,
She is the daughter of a noble captain,
Who, in his voyage to the Persian gulf,
Perish'd by shipwreck ; one I dearly loved.
He to my care intrusted her, having taken
My word, if he return'd not himself,
I never should discover what she was ;
But it being for her good, I will dispense
  with't.
So much, sir, for her blood ; now for her
  portion :
So dear I hold the memory of my friend,
It shall rank with my daughter's.
  Ador. This made good,
I will not be perverse.
  Dur. With a kiss confirm it.
  Ador. I sign all concord here ; but must
  to you, sir,
For reparation of my wounded honour,
The justice of the king consenting to it,
Denounce a lawful war.
  Alph. This in our presence !
  Ador. The cause, dread sir, commands
  it : though your edicts
Call private combats, murders : rather than

Sit down with a disgrace, arising from
A blow, the bonds of my obedience shook
   off,
I'll right myself.
   Cald. I do confess the wrong,
Forgetting the occasion, and desire
Remission from you, and upon such terms
As by his sacred majesty shall be judged
Equal on both parts.

Ador. I desire no more.
   Alph. All then are pleased ; it is the
   glory of
A king to make and keep his subjects
   happy :
For us, we do approve the Roman maxim,
To save one citizen is a greater prize
Than to have kill'd in war ten enemies.
                        [Exeunt..

EPILOGUE.

I am left to enquire, then to relate
To the still-doubtful author, at what rate
His merchandise are valued. If they prove
Staple commodities, in your grace and love
To this last birth of his Minerva, he
Vows (and we do believe him) seriously,
Sloth cast off, and all pleasures else declined,
He'll search with his best care, until he find
New ways, and make good in some labour'd song,
Though he grow old, Apollo still is young.
Cherish his good intentions, and declare
By any signs of favour, that you are
Well pleased, and with a general consent ;
And he desires no more encouragement.

A Very Woman ;

or,

The Prince of Tarent.

PROLOGUE.

To such, and some there are, no question, here,
Who, happy in their memories, do bear
This subject, long since acted, and can say,
Truly, we have seen something like this play.
Our author, with becoming modesty, -   :
(For in this kind he ne'er was bold,) by me,
In his defence thus answers, By command,
He undertook this task, nor could it stand
With his low fortune to refuse to do
What, by his patron, he was call'd unto :
For whose delight and yours, we hope, with care
He hath review'd it ; and with him we dare
Maintain to any man, that did allow   .
'Twas good before, it is much better'd now :
Nor is it, sure, against the proclamation
To raise new piles upon an old foundation.
So much to them deliver'd ; to the rest,
To whom each scene is fresh, he doth protest,
Should his Muse fail now a fair flight to make,
He cannot fancy what will please or take.

DRAMATIS PERSONÆ.

Viceroy of Sicily.
Don Pedro, *his son.*
Duke of Messina.
Don Martino Cardenes, *his son.*
Don John Antonio, *prince of* Tarent.
Captain of the castle of Palermo.
Paulo, *a physician.*
Cuculo, *the Viceroy's steward.*
Two Surgeons.
Apothecary.
Citizens.
Slave-merchant.
Servant.

Page.
An English S*lave.*
Slaves.
Moors.
Pirates.
Sailors.
Almira, *the Viceroy's daughter.*
Leonora, *duke of* Messina's *niece.*
Borachia, *wife to* Cuculo, *governess of* Leo-
    nora *and* Almira.
Two Waiting Women.
A good and evil Genius, Servants, Guard,
        Attendants, &c.

SCENE,—Palermo.

ACT I.

SCENE I.—*A Room in the* Viceroy's
Palace.

Enter Pedro *meeting* Leonora.

Pedro. My worthiest mistress ! this day
cannot end

But prosperous to Pedro, that begins
With this so wish'd encounter.
    Leon. Only servant,
To give you thanks in your own courtly
    language,
Would argue me more ceremonious
Than heartily affected ; and you are

Too well assured, or I am miserable,
Our equal loves have kept one rank too long,
To stand at distance now. ·   ·
   Pedro. You make me happy   ·
In this so wise reproof, which I receive ·
As a chaste favour from you, and will ever
Hold such a strong command o'er my desires,
That though my blood turn rebel to my
   reason,
I never shall presume to seek aught from
   you,
But what (your honour safe) you well may
   grant me,
And virtue sign the warrant.
   Leon. Your love to me
So limited, will still preserve your mistress
Worthy her servant,' and in your restraint
Of loose affections, bind me faster to you ·
But there will be a time when we may wel-
   come
Those wish'd for· pleasures, as heaven's
   greatest blessings,   .
When·that the viceroy, your most noble
   father, ·
And the duke my uncle, and to that, my
   guardian,   .   ·
Shall by their free consent confirm them
   lawful. ··
   Pedro. You ever shall direct, and I obey
   you, :
Is my sister stirring yet ?
   Leon. Long since.
·*Pedro.* Some business
With her, join'd to my service to yourself,
Hath brought me hither ; pray you vouch-
   safe the favour· ·   .
To acquaint her with so much.
   Leon. I am prevented.

Enter Almira, *and two Waiting· Women
dressing her.* ·

   Alm. Do the rest here, my cabinet is too
   hot ;
This room is cooler. · Brother ! · ·
   Pedro. Morrow, sister ! ·
Do-I not come unseasonably ?
   Alm. Why, good brother ?
   Pedro. Because you are not yet fully made,
   up, ·
Nor fit for visitation.' There are ladies,
And great ones, that will hardly grant access,
On any terms, to their own fathers, as
They are themselves, nor· willingly be seen
Before they have ask'd counsel of their
   doctor
How the ceruse will appear, newly laid on,
When they ask blessing. ·.
   Alm. Such, indeed, there are
That would be still young, in despite of time ;

That in the wrinkled winter of their age
Would force a seeming April of fresh beauty,
As if it were within the power of art
To frame a second nature : but for me,
And for your mistress I dare say as much,
The faces, and the teeth you see, we slept
   with.
   · *Pedro.* Which is not frequent, sister, with
   some ladies.   ·
   Alm. You spy no sign of any night-mask
   · here,
(Tie on my carcanet,) nor does your nostril
Take in the scent of strong perfumes, to stifle
The sourness of our breaths as we are fasting:
You're in a lady's chamber, gentle brother,
And not in your apothecary's shop.
We use the women, you perceive, that serve
   us,
Like servants, not like such as do create
   us :—
Faith, search our pockets, and, if you find
   there
Comfits of ambergris to help our kisses,
Conclude us faulty.
   Pedro. You are pleasant, sister,
And I am glad to find you so disposed ;
You will the better hear me.
   Alm. What you please, sir.
   Pedro. I am entreated by the prince of
   Tarent, :
Don John Antonio——
   Alm. Would you would choose
Some other subject. ·
   · *Pedro.* Pray you, give me leave,
For his desires are fit for you to hear, ··
As for me to prefer. This prince of Tarent
(Let it not wrong him that I call him friend)
Finding your choice of don Cardenes liked of
By both your fathers, and his hopes cut off,
Resolves to leave Palermo.
   Alm. He does well ;
That I hear gladly.
   Pedro. How this prince came hither,
How bravely furnish'd, how attended on,
How he hath borne himself here, with what
   charge
He hath continued ; his magnificence   .
In costly banquets, curious masques, rare
   presents,   . · ·
And of all sorts, you cannot but remember.
   Alm. Give me my gloves.
   Pedro. Now, for reward of all
His cost, his travel, and his duteous service,
He does entreat that you will please he may
Take his leave of you, and receive the favour
Of kissing of your hands.·
   Alm. You are his friend, .
And shall discharge the part of one to tell
   him

That he may spare the trouble ; I desire not
To see or hear more of him.
 Pedro. Yet grant this,
Which a mere stranger, in the way of court-
ship,
Might challenge from you.
 Alm. And obtain it sooner.
 Pedro. One reason for this would do well.
 Alm. My will
Shall now stand for a thousand. Shall I lose
The privilege of my sex, which is my will,
To yield a reason like a man? or you,
Deny your sister that which all true women
Claim as their first prerogative, which nature
Gave to them for a law, and should I break it,
I were no more a woman?
 Pedro. Sure, a good one
You cannot be, if you put off that virtue
Which best adorns a good one, courtesy
And affable behaviour. Do not flatter
Yourself with the opinion that your birth,
Your beauty, or whatever false ground else
You raise your pride upon, will stand against
The censure of just men.
 Alm. Why, let it fall then ;
I still shall be unmoved.
 Leon. And, pray you, be you so.
       [*Aside to* Pedro.
 Alm. What jewel's that?
 1 *Wom.* That which the prince of
Tarent——
 Alm. Left here, and you received with-
out my knowledge !
I have use of't now. Does the page wait
without,
My lord Cardenes sent to inquire my health?
 1 *Wom.* Yes, madam.
 Alm. Give it him, and, with it, pray him
To return my service to his lord, and mine.
 Pedro. Will you so undervalue one that has
So truly loved you, to bestow the pledge
Of his affection, being a prince, upon
The servant of his rival?
 Leon. 'Tis not well.
Faith, wear it, lady : send gold to the boy,
'Twill please him better.
 Alm. Do as I command you.
      [*Exit* Waiting Woman.
I will keep nothing that may put me in mind
Don John Antonio ever loved, or was ;
Being wholly now Cardenes'.
 Pedro. In another
This were mere barbarism, sister; and in
you,
(For I'll not sooth you,) at the best, 'tis
rudeness.
 Alm. Rudeness !
 Pedro. Yes, rudeness ; and, what's worse,
the want

Of civil manners ; nay, ingratitude
Unto the many and so fair deservings
Of don Antonio. Does this express
Your breeding in the court, or that you call
The viceroy father? a poor peasant's
daughter,
That ne'er had conversation but with beasts,
Or men bred like them, would not so far
shame
Her education.
 Alm. Pray you, leave my chamber ;
I know you for a brother, not a tutor.
 Leon. You are too violent, madam.
 Alm. Were my father
Here to command me, (as you take upon
you
Almost to play his part,) I would refuse it.
Where I love, I profess it ; where I hate,
In every circumstance I dare proclaim it.
Of all that wear the shapes of men, I loath
That prince you plead for ; no antipathy
Between things most averse in nature, holds
A stronger enmity than his with mine ;
With which rest satisfied :—If not, your
anger
May wrong yourself, not me.
 Leon. My lord Cardenes !
 Pedro. Go : in soft terms, if you persist
thus, you
Will be one——

    Enter Cardenes.

 Alm. What one? pray you, out with it.
 Pedro. Why, one that I shall wish a
stranger to me,
That I might curse you ; but——
 Car. Whence grows this heat?
 Pedro. Be yet advised, and entertain him
fairly,
For I will send him to you ; or no more
Know me a brother.
 Alm. As you please.
 Pedro. Good morrow.   [*Exit.*
 Car. Good morrow, and part thus ! you
seem moved too :
What desperate fool durst raise a tempest
here,
To sink himself?
 Alm. Good sir, have patience ;
The cause, though I confess I am not
pleased,
No way deserves your anger.
 Car. Not mine, madam,
As if the least offence could point at you,
And I not feel it : as you have vouchsafed
me
The promise of your heart, conceal it not,
Whomsoever it concerns.
 Alm. It is not worth

So serious an inquiry: my kind brother
Had a desire to learn me some new court-
    ship,
Which I distasted ; that was all.
    Car. Your brother !
In being yours, with more security
He might provoke you ; yet, if he hath past
A brother's bounds——
    Leon. What then, my lord?
    Car. Believe it,
I'll call him to accompt for't.
    Leon. Tell him so.
    Alm. No more.
    Leon. Yes, thus much ; though my modesty
Be call'd in question for it, in his absence
I will defend him : he hath said nor done,
But what don Pedro well might say or do ;
Mark me, don Pedro ! in which understand
As worthy, and as well as can be hoped for
Of those that love him best—from don
    Cardenes.
    Car. This to me, cousin !
    Alm. You forget yourself.
    Leon. No, nor the cause in which you
    did so, lady,
Which is so just that it needs no concealing
On Pedro's part.
    Alm. What mean you?
    Leon. I dare speak it,
If you dare hear it, sir : he did persuade
Almira, your Almira, to vouchsafe
Some little conference with the prince of
    Tarent,
Before he left the court ; and, that the world
Might take some notice, though he prosper'd
    not
In this so loved design, he was not scorn'd,
He did desire the kissing of her hand,
And then to leave her :—this was much !
    Car. 'Twas more
Than should have been urged by him ; well
    denied,
On your part, madam, and I thank you for't.
Antonio had his answer, I your grant ;
And why your brother should prepare for
    him
An after-interview, or private favour,
I can find little reason.
    Leon. None at all,
Why you should be displeased with't.
    Car. His respect
To me, as, things now are, should have
    weigh'd down
His former friendship : 'twas done indis-
    creetly,
I would be loath to say, maliciously,
To build up the demolish'd hopes of him
That was my rival.   What had he to do,
If he view not my happiness in your favour

With wounded eyes, to take upon himself
An office so distasteful?
    Leon. You may ask
As well, what any gentleman has to do
With civil courtesy.
    Alm. Or you, with that
Which at no part concerns you.   Good my
    lord,
Rest satisfied, that I saw him not, nor will ;
And that nor father, brother, nor the world,
Can work me unto anything but what
You give allowance to—in which assurance,
With this, I leave you.
    Leon. Nay, take me along ;
You are not angry too ?
    Alm. Presume on that.
        [*Exit, followed by* Leonora.
    Car. Am I assured of her, and shall again
Be tortured with suspicion to lose her,
Before I have enjoy'd her ! the next sun
Shall see her mine ; why should I doubt,
    then ? yet,
To doubt is safer than to be secure.
But one short day !   Great empires in less
    time
Have suffer'd change : she's constant—but a
    woman ;
And what a lover's vows, persuasions, tears,
May, in a minute, work upon such frailty,
There are too many and too sad examples.
The prince of Tarent gone, all were in safety ;
Or not admitted to solicit her,
My fears would quit me : 'tis my fault, if I
Give way to that ; and let him ne'er desire
To own what's hard [to win,] that dares not
    guard it.——
Who waits there?

        Enter Servants *and* Page.

    Serv. Would your lordship aught ?
    Car. 'Tis well
You are so near.

        Enter Antonio *and a* Servant.

    Ant. Take care all things be ready
For my remove.
    Serv. They are.   [*Exit.*
    Car. We meet like friends,
No more like rivals now : my emulation
Puts on the shape of love and service to you.
    Ant. It is return'd.
    Car. 'Twas rumoured in the court
You were to leave the city, and that won me
To find you out.   Your excellence may
    wonder
That I, that never saw you, till this hour,
But that I wish'd you dead, so willingly
Should come to wait upon you to the ports ;

And there, with hope you never will look
  back,
Take my last farewell of you.
  Ant. Never look back!
  Car. I said so; neither is it fit you should;
And may I prevail with you as a friend,
You never shall; nor, while you live, here-
after
Think of the viceroy's court, or of Palermo,
But as a grave, in which the prince of Tarent
Buried his honour.
  Ant. You speak in a language
I do not understand.
  Car. No! I'll be plainer.
What madman, that came hither with that
  pomp
Don John Antonio did, that exact courtier
Don John Antonio, with whose brave fame
  only
Great princesses have fall'u in love, and died;
That came with such assurance, as young
  Paris
Did to fetch Helen, being sent back, con-
temn'd,
Disgraced, and scorn'd, his large expense
  laugh'd at,
His bravery scoff'd, the lady that he courted
Left quietly in possession of another,
(Not to be named that day a courtier
Where he was mention'd,) the scarce-known
  Cardenes,
And he to bear her from him!—that would
  ever
Be seen again (having got fairly off)
By such as will live ready witnesses
Of his repulse and scandal?
  Ant. The grief of it,
Believe me, will not kill me: all man's
  honour
Depends not on the most uncertain favour
Of a fair mistress.
  Car. Troth, you bear it well.
You should have seen some that were
  sensible
Of a disgrace, that would have raged, and
  sought
To cure their honour with some strange
  revenge:
But you are better temper'd; and they
  wrong
The Neapolitans in their report,
That say they are fiery spirits, uncapable
Of the least injury, dangerous to be talk'd
  with
After a loss; where nothing can move you,
But, like a stoic, with a constancy
Words nor affronts can shake, you still go on,
And smile when men abuse you.
  Ant. If they wrong

Themselves, I can; yet, I would have you
  know,
I dare be angry.
  Car. 'Tis not possible.
A taste of t would do well; and I'd make
  trial
What may be done. Come hither, boy.—You
  have seen
This jewel, as I take it?
  Ant. Yes; 'tis that
I gave Almira.
  Car. And in what esteem
She held it, coming from your worthy self,
You may perceive, that freely hath bestow'd it
Upon my page.
  Ant. When I presented it,
I did not indent with her, to what use
She should employ it.
  Car. See the kindness of
A loving soul! who, after this neglect,
Nay, gross contempt, will look again upon
  her,
And not be frighted from it.
  Ant. No, indeed, sir;
Nor give way longer—give way, do you
  mark,
To your loose wit, to run the wild-goose
  chase,
Six syllables further. I will see the lady,
That lady that dotes on you, from whose
  hate
My love increases, though you stand elected
Her porter, to deny me.
  Car. Sure you will not.
  Ant. Yes, instantly: your prosperous
  success
Hath made you insolent; and for her sake
I have thus long forborne you, and can yet
Forget it and forgive it, ever provided,
That you end here; and, for what's past re-
  calling,
That she make intercession for your pardon,
Which, at her suit, I'll grant.
  Car. I am much unwilling
To move her for a trifle—bear that too,
                [*Strikes him.*
And then she shall speak to you.
  Ant. Men and angels,
Take witness for me, that I have endured
More than a man!—
         [*They fight;* Cardenes *falls.*
          O do not fall so soon,
Stand up—take my hand—so! when I have
  printed,
For every contumelious word, a wound here,
Then sink for ever.
  Car. Oh, I suffer justly!
  1 *Serv.* Murder! murder! murder!
                      [*Exit.*

2 Serv. Apprehend him.
3 Serv. We'll all join with you.
Ant. I do wish you more ;
My fury will be lost else, if it meet not
Matter to work on : one life is too little
For so much injury.   --

Re-enter Almira, Leonora, *and* Servant.

Alm. O my Cardenes !
Though dead, still my Cardenes ! Villains,
    cowards,
What do ye check at ? can one arm, and that
A murderer's, so long guard the curs'd
    master,
Against so many swords made sharp with
    justice ?
    1 Serv. Sure he will kill us all ; he is a
    devil.
    2 Serv. He is invulnerable.
Alm. Your base fears
Beget such fancies in you. Give me a sword,
    [*Snatches a sword from the* Servant.
This my weak arm, made strong in my re-
    venge,
Shall force a way to't.   [*Wounds* Antonio.
Ant. Would it were deeper, madam !
The thrust, which I would not put by, being
    yours,
Of greater force, to have pierced through
    that heart
Which still retains your figure !—weep still,
    lady ;
For every tear that flows from those grieved
    eyes,
Some part of that which maintains life, goes
    from me ;
And so to die were in a gentle slumber·
To pass to paradise : but you envy me   .
So quiet a departure from my world,
My world of miseries ; therefore, take my
    sword,
And, having kill'd me with it, cure the
    wounds
It gave Cardenes.
    [*Gives* Almira *his sword.*

Re-enter Pedro.

Pedro. 'Tis too true : ˙was ever
Valour so ill employed !
Ant. Why stay you, lady?
Let not soft pity work on your hard nature ;
You cannot do a better office to
The dead Cardenes, and I willingly
Shall fall a ready sacrifice to appease him,
Your fair hand offering it.
Alm. Thou couldst ask nothing
But this, which I would grant.
    [*Attempts to wound him.*
    Leon. Flint-hearted lady !

Pedro. Are you a woman, sister !
    [*Takes the sword from her.*
Alm. Thou art not
A brother, I renounce that title to thee ;
Thy hand is in this bloody act ; 'twas this,
For which that savage homicide was sent
    hither.
Thou equal Judge of all things ! if that blood,
And innocent blood——
Pedro. [Best sister.]
Alm. Oh, Cardenes !
How is my soul rent between rage and sor-
    row,
That it can be that such an upright cedar
Should violently be torn up by the roots,
Without an earthquake in that very moment
To swallow them that did it !
Ant. The hurt's nothing ;
But the deep wound is in my conscience,
    friend,
Which sorrow in death only can recover.
Pedro. Have better hopes.

Enter Viceroy, Duke of Messina, Captain,
    Guard, *and* Servants.

Duke. My son, is this the marriage
I came to celebrate ? false hopes of man !
I come to find a grave here.
Alm. I have wasted
My stock of tears, and now just anger help
    me
To pay, in my revenge, the other part
Of duty, which I owe thee. O, great sir,
Not as a daughter now, but a poor widow,
Made so before she was a bride, I fly
To your impartial justice : the offence
Is death, and death in his most horrid form;
Let not, then, title, or a prince's name,
(Since a great crime is, in a great man,
    greater,)
Secure the offender.
Duke. Give me life for life,
As thou wilt answer it to the great king,
Whose deputy thou art here.
Alm. And speedy justice. ·
Duke. Put the damn'd wretch to torture.
Alm. Force him to
Reveal his curs'd confederates, which spare
    not,
Although you find a son among them.   .
Vice. How !
Duke. Why bring you not the rack forth?
Alm. Wherefore stands
The murderer unbound ?
Vice. Shall I have hearing ?
Duke. Excellent lady, in this you express
Your true love to the dead.
Alm. All love to mankind
From me, ends with him.

                                K K

Vice. Will you hear me yet?
And first to you; you do confess the fact
With which you stand charged?
  Ant. I will not make worse
What is already ill, with vain denial.
  Vice. Then understand, though you are
      prince of Tarent,
Yet, being a subject to the king of Spain,
No privilege of Sicily can free you
(Being convict by a just form of law)
From the municipal statutes of that kingdom,
But as a common man, being found guilty,
Must suffer for it.
  Ant. I prize not my life
So much, as to appeal from anything
You shall determine of me.
  Vice. Yet despair not
To have an equal hearing; the exclaims
Of this grieved father, nor my daughter's
      tears,
Shall sway me from myself; and, where
      they urge
To have you tortured, or led bound to
      prison,
I must not grant it.
  Duke. No!
  Vice. I cannot, sir;
For men of his rank are to be distinguish'd
From other men, before they are condemn'd,
From which (his cause not heard) he yet
      stands free:
So take him to your charge, and, as your life,
See he be safe.
  Capt. Let me die for him else.
    [*Exeunt* Pedro, *and* Capt. *and* Guard
        with Ant.
  Duke. The guard of him should have
      been given to me.
  Alm. Or unto me.
  Duke. Bribes may corrupt the captain.
  Alm. And our just wreak, by force, or
      cunning practice,
With scorn prevented.
  Car. Oh!
  Alm. What groan is that?
  Vice. There are apparent signs of life yet
      in him.
  Alm. Oh that there were! that I could
      pour my blood
Into his veins!
  Car. Oh, oh!
  Vice. Take him up gently.
  Duke. Run for physicians.
  Alm. Surgeons.
  Duke. All helps else.
  Vice. This care of his recovery, timely
      practised,
Would have express'd more of a father in
      you,

Than your impetuous clamours for revenge.
But I shall find fit time to urge that further,
Hereafter, to you; 'tis not fit for me
To add weight to oppress'd calamity.
    [*Exeunt.*

———

ACT II.

SCENE I.—*A Room in the Castle.*

Enter Pedro, Antonio, *and* Captain.

  Ant. Why should your love to me, having
      already
So oft endured the test, be put unto
A needless trial? have you not, long since,
In every circumstance and rite of friendship,
Outgone all precedents the ancients boast of,
And will you yet move further?
  Pedro. Hitherto
I have done nothing (howsoe'er you value
My weak endeavours) that may justly claim
A title to your friendship, and much less
Laid down the debt, which, as a tribute due
To your deservings, not I, but mankind
Stands bound to tender.
  Ant. Do not make an idol
Of him that should, and without supersti-
      tion,
To you build up an altar. O my Pedro!
When I am to expire, to call you mine,
Assures a future happiness: give me leave
To argue with you, and, the fondness of
Affection struck blind, with justice hear me:
Why should you, being innocent, fling your
      life
Into the furnace of your father's anger,
For my offence? or, take it granted (yet
'Tis more than supposition) you prefer
My safety 'fore your own, so prodigally
You waste your favours, wherefore should
      this captain,
His blood and sweat rewarded in the favour
Of his great master, falsify the trust
Which, from true judgment, he reposes in
      him,
For me a stranger?
  Pedro. Let him answer that,
He needs no prompter: speak your thoughts,
      and freely.
  Capt. I ever loved to do so, and it shames
      not
The bluntness of my breeding: from my
      youth
I was train'd up a soldier, one of those
That in their natures love the dangers more,
Than the rewards of danger. I could add,
My life, when forfeited, the viceroy pardon'd
But by his intercession; and therefore,
It being lent by him, I were ungrateful,

Which I will never be, if I refused
To pay that debt at any time demanded.
Pedro. I hope, friend, this will satisfy you.
Ant. No, it raises
More doubts within me.   Shall I, from the
    school
Of gratitude, in which this captain reads
The text so plainly, learn to be unthankful?
Or, viewing in your actions the idea   .
Of perfect friendship, when it does point to
    me
How brave a thing it is to be a friend,
Turn from the object?   Had I never loved
The fair Almira for her outward features,
Nay, were the beauties of her mind sus-
    pected,   .
And her contempt and scorn painted before
    me,
The being your sister would anew inflame
    me,   .
With much more impotence to dote upon
    her:
No, dear friend, let me in my death confirm,
(Though you in all things else have the pre-
    cedence,)
I'll die ten times, ere one of Pedro's hairs
Shall suffer in my cause.
Pedro. If you so love me,
In love to that part of my soul dwells in you,
(For though two bodies, friends have but one
    soul,)
Lose not both life and me.

Enter a Servant.

Serv. The prince is dead.   [*Exit.*
Ant. If so, shall I leave Pedro here to
    answer
For my escape? as thus I clasp thee, let
The viceroy's sentence find me.
Pedro. Fly, for heaven's sake !
Consider the necessity ; though now
We part, Antonio, we may meet again,
But death's division is for ever, friend.

Enter another Servant.

Serv. The rumour spread, sir, of Martino's
    death,
Is check'd ; there's hope of his recovery.
                                [*Exit.*
Ant. Why should I fly, then, when I may
    enjoy,
With mine own life, my friend?
Pedro. That's still uncertain,
He may have a relapse ; for once be ruled,
    friend :
He's a good debtor that pays when 'tis due ;
A prodigal, that, before it is required,
Makes tender of it.

Enter Sailors.

1 Sail. The bark, sir, is ready.
2 Sail. The wind sits fair.
3 Sail. Heaven favours your escape.
                        [*Whistles within.*
Capt. Hark, how the boatswain whistles
    you aboard !
Will nothing move you?
Ant. Can I leave my friend?
Pedro. I must delay no longer ; force him
    hence.
Capt. I'll run the hazard of my fortunes
    with you.
Ant. What violence is this?—hear but my
    reasons.
Pedro. Poor friendship that is cool'd with
    arguments !
Away, away !
Capt. For Malta.
Pedro. You shall hear
All our events.
Ant. I may sail round the world,
But never meet thy like.   Pedro !
Pedro. Antonio !
Ant. I breathe my soul back to thee.
Pedro. In exchange,
Bear mine along with thee.
Capt. Cheerly, my hearts !
        [*Exeunt* Captain *and* Sailors *with*
                Antonio.
Pedro. He's gone : may pitying heaven his
    pilot be,
And then I weigh not what becomes of me.
                                [*Exit.*

SCENE II.—*A Room in the* Viceroy's *Palace.*

Enter Viceroy, Duke of Messina, *and* Attendants.

Vice. I tell you right, sir.
Duke. Yes, like a rough surgeon,
Without a feeling in yourself you search
My wounds unto the quick, then pre-declare
The tediousness and danger of the cure,
Never remembering what the patient suffers,
But you preach this philosophy to a man
That does partake of passion, and not
To a dull stoic.
Vice. I confess you have
Just cause to mourn your son ; and yet, if
    reason
Cannot yield comfort, let example cure.
I am a father too, my only daughter
As dear in my esteem, perhaps as worthy,.
As your Martino, in her love to him
As desperately ill, either's loss equal ;
And yet I bear it with a better temper :
                                      K K 2

Enter Pedro.

Which, if you please to imitate, 'twill not
   wrong
Your piety, nor your judgment.
  Duke. We were fashion'd
In different moulds. I weep with mine own
   eyes, sir,
Pursue my ends too ; pity to you's a cordial,
Revenge to me ; and that I must and will
   have,
If my Martino die.
  Pedro. Your *must* and *will,*
Shall in your full-sailed confidence deceive
   you.   [*Aside.*
Here's doctor Paulo, sir.

Enter Paulo *and two* Surgeons.

  Duke. My hand ! you rather
Deserve my knee, and it shall bend as to
A second father, if your saving aids
Restore my son.
  Vice. Rise, thou bright star of knowledge,
Thou honour of thy art, thou help of nature,
Thou glory of our academies !
  Paul. If I blush, sir,
To hear these attributes ill-placed on me,
It is excusable. I am no god, sir,
Nor holy saint that can do miracles,
But a weak, sinful man : yet, that I may,
In some proportion, deserve these favours
Your excellencies please to grace me with,
I promise all the skill I have acquired
In simples, or the careful observation
Of the superior bodies, with my judgment
Derived from long experience, stand ready
To do you service.
  Duke. Modestly replied.
  Vice. How is it with your princely patient ?
  Duke. Speak,
But speak some comfort, sir.
  Paul. I must speak truth :
His wounds though many, heaven so guided
   yet
Antonio's sword, it pierced no part was
   mortal.
These gentlemen, who worthily deserve
The names of surgeons, have done their
   duties :
The means they practised, not ridiculous
   charms
To stop the blood ; no oils, nor balsams
   bought
Of cheating quack-salvers, or mountebanks,
By them applied : the rules by Chiron taught,
And Æsculapius, which drew upon him
The Thunderer's envy, they with care pur-
   :sued,
Heaven prospering their endeavours.

  Duke. There is hope, then,
Of his recovery ?
  Paul. But no assurance ;
I must not flatter you.   That little air
Of comfort that breathes towards us {for I
   dare not
Rob these t'enrich myself) you owe their
   care ;
For, yet, I have done nothing.
  Duke. Still more modest ;
I will begin with them : to either give
Three thousand crowns.
  Vice. I'll double your reward :
See them paid presently.
  1 *Surg.* This magnificence
With equity cannot be conferr'd on us ;
'Tis due unto the doctor.
  2 *Surg.* True ; we were
But his subordinate ministers, and did only
Follow his grave directions.
  Paul. 'Tis your own :
I challenge no part in it.
  Vice. Brave on both sides !
  Paul. Deserve this, with the honour that
   will follow,
In your attendance.
  2 *Surg.* If both sleep at once,
'Tis justice both should die.
             [*Exeunt* Surgeons.
  Duke. For you, grave doctor,
We will not in such petty sums consider
Your high deserts ; our treasury lies open,
Command it as your own.
  Vice. Choose any castle,
Nay, city, in our government, and be lord
   of't.
  Paul. Of neither, sir ; I am not so am-
   bitious :
Nor would I have your highnesses secure.
We have but faintly yet begun our journey ;
A thousand difficulties and dangers must be
Encounter'd, ere we end it : though his
   hurts,
I mean his outward ones, do promise fair,
There is a deeper one, and in his mind,
Must be with care provided for ; melan-
   choly,
And at the height, too, near akin to mad-
   ness,
Possesses him ; his senses are distracted,
Not one, but all ; and, if I can collect them,
With all the various ways invention
Or industry e'er practised, I shall write it
My masterpiece.
  Duke. You more and more engage me.
  Vice. May we not visit him ?
  Paul. By no means, sir ;
As he is now, such courtesies come un-
   timely :

I'll yield you reason for't. Should he look
on you,
It will renew the memory of that
Which I would have forgotten ; your good
prayers
And those I do presume shall not be wanting
To my endeavours, are the utmost aids
I yet desire your excellencies should grant
me.
So, with my humblest service——
Duke. Go, and prosper.   [*Exit* Paulo.
Vice. Observe his piety ;—I have heard,
how true
I know not, most physicians, as they grow
Greater in skill, grow less in their religion ;
Attributing so much to natural causes,
That they have little faith in that they
cannot
Deliver reason for : this doctor steers
Another course—but let this pass. If you
please,
Your company to my daughter.
Duke. I wait on you.   [*Exeunt.*

SCENE III.—*Another Room in the same.*

Enter Leonora *and* Waiting Women.

Leon. Took she no rest to-night?
1 *Wom.* Not any, madam ;
I am sure she slept not. If she slumber'd,
straight,
As if some dreadful vision had appear'd,
She started up, her hair unbound, and with
Distracted looks staring about the chamber,
She asks aloud, *Where is Martino? where
Have you conceal'd him?* sometimes names
Antonio,
Trembling in every joint, her brows con-
tracted,
Her fair face as 'twere changed into a curse,
Her hands held up thus ; and, as if her
words
Were too big to find passage through her
mouth,
She groans, then throws herself upon her
bed,
Beating her breast.
Leon. 'Tis wonderous strange.
2 *Wom.* Nay, more ;
She that of late vouchsafed not to be seen,
But so adorn'd as if she were to rival
Nero's Poppæa, or the Egyptian queen,
Now, careless of her beauties, when we offer
Our service, she contemns it.
Leon. Does she not
Sometimes forsake her chamber?
2 *Wom.* Much about
This hour ; then, with a strange unsettled
gait,
She measures twice or thrice the gallery,

Silent, and frowning, (we dare not speak to
her,)
And then returns.—She's come, pray you,
now observe her.

Enter Almira *in black, carelessly habited.*

Alm. Why are my eyes fix'd on the
ground, and not
Bent upwards? ha ! that which was mortal of
My dear Martino, as a debt to nature,
I know this mother earth hath sepulchred ;
But his diviner part, his soul, o'er which
The tyrant Death, nor yet the fatal sword
Of curs'd Antonio, his instrument,
Had the least power, borne upon angels' wings
Appointed to that office, mounted far
Above the firmament.
Leon. Strange imagination !
Dear cousin, your Martino lives.
Alm. I know you,
And that in this you flatter me ; he's dead,
As much as could die of him :—but look
yonder !
Amongst a million of glorious lights
That deck the heavenly canopy, I have
Discern'd his soul, transform'd into a star.
Do you not see it?
Leon. Lady !
Alm. Look with my eyes.
What splendour circles it ! the heavenly
archer,
Not far off distant, appears dim with envy,
Viewing himself outshined.   Bright con-
stellation !
Dart down thy beams of pity on Almira,
And, since thou find'st such grace where
now thou art,
As I did truly love thee on the earth,
Like a kind harbinger, prepare my lodging,
And place me near thee !
Leon. I much more than fear
She'll grow into a frenzy.
Alm. How? what's this !
A dismal sound ! come nearer, cousin ; lay
Your ear close to the ground,—closer, I pray
you.
Do you howl? are you there, Antonio? —
Leon. Where, sweet lady?
Alm. In the vault, in hell, on the infernal
rack,
Where murderers are tormented ;—yerk
him soundly,
'Twas 'Rhadamanth's sentence ;—do your
office, Furies.—
How he roars ! What ! _ plead_to_me to
mediate for you !
I'm deaf, I cannot hear you.
Leon. 'Tis but fancy,
Collect yourself.

Alm. Leave babbling ; 'tis rare music !
Rhamnusia plays on a pair of tongs
Red hot, and Proserpine dances to the
    consort ;
Pluto sits laughing by too.   So ! enough :
I do begin to pity him.
    Leon. I wish, madam,
You would shew it to yourself.
    2 Wom. Her fit begins
To leave her.
    Alm. Oh my brains ! are you there,
    cousin ?
    Leon. Now she speaks temperately.   I
    am ever ready
To do you service : how do you?
    Alm. Very much troubled.
I have had the strangest waking dream of hell
And heaven—I know not what.
    Leon. My lord your father
Is come to visit you ; as you would not
    grieve him
That is so tender of you, entertain him
With a becoming duty.

    Enter Viceroy, Duke of Messina, Pedro,
        and Attendants.

    Vice. Still forlorn !
No comfort, my Almira ?
    Duke. In your sorrow,
For my Martino, madam, you have express'd
All possible love and tenderness ; too much
    of it
Will wrong yourself, and him.   He may
    live, lady,
(For we are not past hope,) with his future
    service,
In some part to deserve it.
    Alm. If heaven please
To be so gracious to me, I will serve him
With such obedience, love, and humbleness,
That I will rise up an example for
Good wives to follow : but until I have
Assurance what fate will determine of me,
Thus, like a desolate widow, give me leave
To weep for him ; for, should he die, I have
    vow'd
Not to outlive him ; and my humble suit is,
One monument may cover us, and Antonio
(In justice you must grant me that) be
    offer'd
A sacrifice to our ashes.
    Vice. Prithee put off
These sad thoughts ; both shall live, I doubt
    it not,
A happy pair.

    Enter Cuculo, *and* Borachia.

    Cuc. O sir, the foulest treason
That ever was discover'd !

    Vice. Speak it, that
We may prevent it.
    Cuc. Nay, 'tis past prevention :
Though you allow me wise, (in modesty,
I will not say oraculous,) I cannot help it.
I am a statesman, and some say a wise one ;
But I could never conjure, nor divine
Of things to come.
    Vice. Leave fooling : to the point ;
What treason ?
    Cuc. The false prince, don John Antonio,
Is fled.
    Vice. It is not possible.
    Pedro. Peace, screech-owl.
    Cuc. I must speak, and it shall out, sir ;
    the captain
You trusted with the fort is run away too.
    Alm. O miserable woman ! I defy
All comfort : cheated too of my revenge !
As you are my father, sir, and you my
    brother,
I will not curse you ; but I dare, and will
    say,
You are unjust and treacherous.—If there be
A way to death, I'll find it.   [*Exit.*
    Vice. Follow her,
She'll do some violent act upon herself ;
Till she be better temper'd, bind her hands,
And fetch the doctor to her.—
    [*Exeunt* Leonora, *and* Waiting Women.
                        Had not you
A hand in this?
    Pedro: I, sir ! I never knew
Such disobedience.
    Vice. My honour's touch'd in't :
Let gallies be mann'd forth in his pursuit,
Search every port and harbour ; if I live,
He shall not 'scape thus.
    Duke. Fine hypocrisy !
Away, dissemblers ! 'tis confederacy
Betwixt thy son, and self, and the false cap-
    tain.
He could not thus have vanish'd else.   You
    have murder'd
My son amongst you, and now murder jus-
    tice :
You know it most impossible he should live,
Howe'er the doctor, for your ends, dissem-
    bled,
And you have shifted hence Antonio.
    Vice. Messina, thou'rt a crazed and
    grieved old man,
And being in my court, protected by
The law of hospitality, or I should
Give you a sharper answer : may I perish,
If I knew of his flight !
    Duke. Fire, then, the castle.
Hang up the captain's wife and children.
    Vice. Fie, sir !

Pedro. My lord, you are uncharitable;
capital treasons
Exact not so much.
  Duke. Thanks, most noble signior !
We ever had your good word and your love.
  Cuc. Sir, I dare pass my word, my lords
are clear
Of any imputation in this case
You seem to load them with.
  Duke. Impertinent fool !——
No, no; the loving faces you put on,
Have been but grinning visors : you have
juggled me
Out of my son, and out of justice too ;
But Spain shall do me right, believe me,
Viceroy :
There I will force it from thee by the king.
He shall not eat nor sleep in peace for me,
Till I am righted for this treachery.
  Vice. Thy worst, Messina ! since no rea-
son can
Qualify thy intemperance ; the corruption
Of my subordinate ministers cannot wrong
My true integrity. Let privy searchers
Examine all the land.
  Pedro. Fair fall Antonio !   [*Aside.*
  [*Exeunt* Viceroy, Pedro, *and* Attendants.
  Cuc. This is my wife, my lord ; troth speak
your conscience,
Is't not a goodly dame?
  Duke. She is no less, sir ;
I will make use of these : may I entreat you
To call my niece.
  Bora. With speed, sir.   [*Exit* Borachia.
  Cuc. You may, my lord, suspect me
As an agent in these state-conveyances :
Let signior Cuculo, then, be never more,
For all his place, wit, and authority,
Held a most worthy, honest gentleman.

      Re-enter Borachia *with* Leonora.

  Duke. I do acquit you, signior. Niece,
you see
To what extremes I am driven ; the cunning
viceroy,
And his son Pedro, having express'd too
plainly
Their cold affections to my son Martino :
And therefore I conjure thee, Leonora,
By all thy hopes from me, which is my
dukedom
If my son fail,—however, all thy fortunes ;
Though heretofore some love hath past
betwixt
Don Pedro, and thyself, abjure him now :
And as thou keep'st Almira company,
In this her desolation, so in hate
To this young Pedro, for thy cousin's love,
Be her associate ; or assure thyself,

I cast thee like a stranger from my blood.
If I do ever hear thou see'st, or send'st
Token, or receiv'st message—by yon heaven,
I never more will own thee !
  Leon. O, dear uncle !
You have put a tyrannous yoke upon my
heart,
And it will break it.   [*Exit.*
  Duke. Gravest lady, you
May be a great assister in my ends.
I buy your diligence thus :—divide this
couple,
Hinder their interviews ; feign 'tis her will
To give him no admittance, if he crave it ;
And thy rewards shall be thine own desires :
Whereto, good sir, but add your friendly aids,
And use me to my uttermost.
  Cuc. My lord,
If my wife please, I dare not contradict.
Borachia, what do you say?
  Bora. I say, my lord,
I know my place ; and be assured, I will
Keep fire and tow asunder.
  Duke. You in this
Shall much deserve me.   [*Exit.*
  Cuc. We have ta'en upon us
A heavy charge : I hope you'll now forbear
The excess of wine.
  Bora. I will do what I please.
This day the market's kept for slaves ; go you,
And buy me a fine-timber'd one to assist me ;
I must be better waited on.
  Cuc. Anything,
So you'll leave wine.
  Bora. Still prating !
  Cuc. I am gone, duck.   [*Exit.*
  Bora. Pedro ! so hot upon the scent ! I'll
fit him.

            Re-enter Pedro.

  Pedro. Donna Borachia, you most happily
Are met to pleasure me.
  Bora. It may be so ;
I use to pleasure many. Here lies my way,
I do beseech you, sir, keep on your voyage.
  Pedro. Be not so short, sweet lady, I must
with you.
  Bora. With me, sir ! I beseech you, sir—
why, what, sir,
See you in me?
  Pedro. Do not mistake me, lady ;
Nothing but honesty.
  Bora. Hang honesty !
Trump me not up with honesty : do you
mark, sir,
I have a charge, sir, and a special charge, sir,
And 'tis not honesty can win on me, sir.
  Pedro. Prithee conceive me rightly.
  Bora. I conceive you !

Pedro. But understand.

Bora. I will not understand, sir,
I cannot, nor I do not understand, sir.

Pedro. Prithee, Borachia, let me see my mistress,
But look upon her ; stand you by.

Bora. How's this !
Shall I stand by ? what do you think of me?
Now, by the virtue of the place I hold,
You are a paltry lord to tempt my trust thus :
I am no Helen, nor no Hecuba,
To be deflower'd of my loyalty
With your fair language.

Pedro. Thou mistak'st me still.

Bora. It may be so, my place will bear
me out in't,
And will mistake you still, make you your
best on't.

Pedro. A pox upon thee ! let me but behold
her.

Bora. A plague upon you ! you shall never
see her.

Pedro. This is a crone in grain ! thou art
so testy—
Prithee, take breath, and know thy friends.

Bora. I will not,
I have no friends, nor I will have none this
way :
And, now I think on't better, why will you
see her ?

Pedro. Because she loves me dearly, I her
equally.

Bora. She hates you damnably, most
wickedly,
Build that upon my word, most wickedly ;
And swears her eyes are sick when they
behold you.
How fearfully have I heard her rail upon you,
And cast and rail again ; and cast again ;
Call for hot waters, and then rail again !

Pedro. How ! 'tis not possible.

Bora. I have heard her swear
(How justly, you best know, and where the
cause lies)
That you are—I shame to tell it—but it must
out—
Fie, fie ! why, how have you deserv'd it ?

Pedro. I am what?

Bora. The beastliest man—why, what a
grief must this be ?
(Sir-reverence of the company)—a rank
whoremaster :
Ten livery whores, she assured me on her
credit,
With weeping eyes she spake it, and seven
citizens,
Besides all voluntaries that serve under you,
And of all countries.

Pedro. This must needs be a lie.

Bora. Besides, you are so careless of your
body,
Which is a foul fault in you.

Pedro. Leave your fooling,
For this shall be a fable : happily,
My sister's anger may grow strong against
me,
Which thou mistak'st.

Bora. She hates you very well too,
But your mistress hates you heartily :—look
upon you !
Upon my conscience, she should see the
devil first,
With eyes as big as saucers ; when I but
named you,
She has leap'd back thirty feet : if once she
smell you,
For certainly you are rank, she says, extreme rank,
And the wind stand with you too, she's
gone for ever !

Pedro. For all this, I would see her.

Bora. That's all one.
Have you new eyes when those are scratch'd
out, or a nose
To clap on warm ? have you proof against
a piss-pot,
Which, if they bid me, I must fling upon
you ?

Pedro. I shall not see her, then, you say ?

Bora. It seems so.

Pedro. Prithee, be thus far friend then,
good Borachia,
To give her but this letter, and this ring,
And leave thy pleasant lying, which I pardon :
But leave it in her pocket ; there's no harm
in't.
I'll take thee up a petticoat, will that please
thee ?

Bora. Take up my petticoat ! I scorn the
motion,
I scorn it with my heels ; take up my petticoat !

Pedro. And why thus hot ?

Bora. Sir, you shall find me hotter,
If you take up my petticoat.

Pedro. I'll give thee a new petticoat.

Bora. I scorn the gift—take up my petti-
coat !
Alas ! my lord, you are too young, my lord,
Too young, my lord, to circumcise me that
way.
Take up my petticoat ! I am a woman,
A woman of another way, my lord,
A gentlewoman : he that takes up my petti-
coat,
Shall have enough to do, I warrant him,
I would fain see the proudest of you all so
lusty.

Pedro. Thou art disposed still to mistake
  me.
Bora. Petticoat !
You shew now what you are ; but do. your
  worst, sir.
Pedro. A wild-fire take thee !
Bora. I ask no favour of you,
And so I leave you ; and withal, I charge you
In my own name, for, sir, I'd have you know
  it,
In this place I present your father's person,
Upon your life, not dare to follow me,
For if you do——   [*Exit.*
Pedro. Go ! and the pox go with thee,
If thou hast so much moisture to receive
  them !
For thou wilt have them, though a horse
  bestow them.
I must devise a way—for I must see her,
And very suddenly ; and, madam petticoat,
If all the wit I have, and this can do,
I'll make you break your charge, and your
  hope too.   ——   [*Exit.*

ACT III.
SCENE I.—*The Slave Market.*

Enter Slave-merchant *and* Servant, *with*
Antonio *and* Captain *disguised, and
dressed as* Slaves, English Slave, *and
divers other* Slaves.

Merch. Come, rank yourselves, and stand
  out handsomely.
—Now ring the bell, that they may know
  my market.
Stand you two here ; [*To* Antonio *and the*
  Captain.] you are personable men,
And apt to yield good sums, . if. women
  cheapen.
Put me that pig-complexion'd fellow behind,
He will spoil my sale else ; the slave looks
  .like famine.
Sure he was got in a cheese-press, the whey
  runs out on's nose yet.
.He will not yield above a peck of oysters—
If I can get a quart of wine in too, you are
  gone, sir :
Why sure, thou hadst no father.
  1 *Slave.* Sure I know not.
  Merch. No, certainly ; a March frog
  [leap'd] thy mother ;
Thou'rt but a monster-paddock.—Look who
  comes, sirrah.—   [*Exit* Servant.
And next prepare the song, and do it lively.—
Your tricks too, sirrah, they are ways to
  catch the buyer, [*To the* English Slave.
And if you do them well, they'll prove good
  dowries.—
How now ?

Re-enter Servant.

Serv. They come, sir, with their bags full
  loaden.
Merch. Reach me my stool. O ! here
  they come.

Enter Paulo, Apothecary, Cuculo, *and*
      Citizens.

Cuc. That's he.
He never fails monthly to sell his slaves here ;
He buys them presently upon their taking,
And so disperses them to every market.
  Merch. Begin the song, and chant it
  merrily.

A SONG, *by one of the* Slaves.

Well done.
  Paul. Good morrow !
  Merch. Morrow to you, signiors !
  Paul. We come to look upon your slaves,
  and buy too,
If we can like the persons, and the prices.
  Cuc. They shew fine active fellows.
  Merch. They are no less, sir,
And people of strong labours.
  Paul. That's in the proof, sir.
  Apoth. Pray what's the price of this red-
  bearded fellow?
If his gall be good, I have certain uses for
  him.
  Merch. My sorrel slaves are of a lower price,
Because the. colour's faint :—fifty chequins,
  sir.
  Apoth. What be his virtues ?
  Merch. He will poison rats ;
Make him but angry, and his eyes kill spiders ;
Let him but, fasting, spit upon a toad,
And presently it bursts, and dies ; his dreams
  kill :
He'll run you in a wheel, and draw up water,
But if his nose drop in't, 'twill kill an army.
When you have worn him to the bones with
  uses,
Thrust him into an oven luted well,
Dry him, and beat him, flesh and bone, to
  powder,
And that kills scabs, and aches of all climates.
  Apoth. Pray at what distance may I talk
  to him ?
  Merch. Give him but sage and butter in
  a morning,
And there's no fear : but keep him from all
  women,
For there his poison swells most.
  Apoth. I will have him.
Cannot he breed a plague too ?
  Merch. Yes, yes, yes,
Feed him with fogs ; *probatum.*—Now to
  you, sir.

Do you like this slave?
[*Pointing to* Antonio.
Cuc. Yes, if I like his price well.
Merch. The price is full an hundred,
  nothing bated.
Sirrah, sell the Moors there :—feel, he's high
  and lusty,
And of a gamesome nature ; bold, and secret,
Apt to win favour of the man that owns him,
By diligence and duty : look upon him.
Paul. Do you hear, sir?
Merch. I'll be with you presently.—
Mark but his limbs, that slave will cost you
  fourscore ;   [*Pointing to the* Captain.
An easy price—turn him about, and view
  him.—
For these two, sir? why, they are the finest
  children——
Twins, on my credit, sir.—Do you see this
  boy, sir?
He will run as far from you in an hour——
1 *Cit.* Will he so, sir?
Merch. Conceive me rightly,—if upon an
  errand,
As any horse you have.
2 *Cit.* What will this girl do?
Merch. Sure no harm at all, sir,
For she sleeps most an end.
Cit. An excellent housewife.
Of what religion are they?
Merch. What you will, sir,
So there be meat and drink in't : they'll do
  little
That shall offend you, for their chief desire
Is to do nothing at all, sir.
Cuc. A hundred is too much.
Merch. Not a doit bated :
He's a brave slave, his eye shews activeness ;
Fire and the mettle of a man dwell in him.
Here is one you shall have——
Cuc. For what?
Merch. For nothing,
And thank you too.
Paul. What can he do?
Merch. Why, anything that's ill,
And never blush at it : he's so true a thief,
That he'll steal from himself, and think he
  has got by it.
He stole out of his mother's belly, being an
  infant
And from a lousy nurse he stole his nature,
From a dog his look, and from an ape his
  nimbleness ;
He will look in your face and pick your
  pockets,
Rob ye the most wise rat of a cheese-paring;
There, where a cat will go in, he will follow,
His body has no backbone. Into my com-
  pany

He stole, for I never bought him, and will
  steal into yours,
An you stay a little longer. Now, if any of
  you
Be given to the excellent art of lying,
Behold, before you here, the masterpiece !
He'll outlie him that taught him, monsieur
  devil,
Offer to swear he has eaten nothing in a
  twelvemonth,
When his mouth's full of meat.
Cuc. Pray keep him, he's a jewel ;
And here's your money for this fellow.
Merch. He's yours, sir.
Cuc. Come, follow me.
                        [*Exit with* Antonio.
Cit. Twenty chequins for these two.
Merch. For five and twenty take them.
Cit. There's your money ;
I'll have them, if it be to sing in cages.
Merch. Give them hard eggs, you never
  had such blackbirds.
Cit. Is she a maid, dost think?
Merch. I dare not swear, sir :
She is nine year old, at ten you shall find
  few here.
Cit. A merry fellow ! thou say'st true.
Come, children.
                    [*Exit with the two* Moors.
Paul. Here, tell your money ; if his life
  but answer
His outward promises, I have bought him
  cheap, sir.
Merch. Too cheap, o' conscience : he's a
  pregnant knave ;
Full of fine thought, I warrant him.
Paul. He's but weak-timber'd.
Merch. 'Tis the better, sir ;
He will turn gentleman a great deal
  sooner.
Paul. Very weak legs.
Merch. Strong, as the time allows, sir.
Paul. What's that fellow?
Merch. Who, this? the finest thing in all
  the world, sir,
The punctuallest, and the perfectest ; an
  English metal,
But coin'd in France : *Your servant's ser-*
  vant, sir!
Do you understand that? or *your shadow's*
  servant!
Will you buy him to carry in a box? Kiss
  your hand, sirrah ;—
Let fall your cloak on one shoulder ;—face
  to your left hand ;—
Feather your hat ;—slope your hat ;—now
  charge.—Your honour,
What think you of this fellow?
Paul. Indeed, I know not ;

I never saw such an ape before : but, hark you,
Are these things serious in his nature ?
Merch. Yes, yes ;
Part of his creed : come, do some more devices.
Quarrel a little, and take him for your enemy,
Do it in dumb show. Now observe him nearly.
    [*The* English Slave *practises his postures.*
Paul. This fellow's mad, stark mad.
Merch. Believe they are all so :
I have sold a hundred of them.
Paul. A strange nation !
What may the women be ?
Merch. As mad as they,
And, as I have heard for truth, a great deal madder :
Yet, you may find some civil things amongst them,
But they are not respected. Nay, never wonder ;
They have a city, sir,—I have been in it,
And therefore dare affirm it, where, if you saw
With what a load of vanity 'tis fraughted,
How like an everlasting morris-dance it looks,
Nothing but hobby-horse, and maid Marian,
You would start indeed.
Paul. They are handsome men ?
Merch. Yes, if they would thank their maker,
And seek no further ; but they have new creators,
God-tailor, and god-mercer : a kind of Jews, sir,
But fall'n into idolatry ; for they worship
Nothing with so much service, as the cow-calves.
Paul. What do you mean by cow-calves ?
Merch. Why, their women.
Will you see him do any more tricks ?
Paul. 'Tis enough, I thank you ;
But yet I'll buy him, for the rareness of him :
He may make my princely patient mirth, and that done,
I'll chain him in my study, that at void hours
I may run o'er the story of his country.
Merch. His price is forty.
Paul. Hold—I'll once be foolish,
And buy a lump of levity to laugh at.
Apoth. Will your worship walk ?
Paul. How now, apothecary,
Have you been buying too ?
Apoth. A little, sir,
A dose or two of mischief.
Paul. Fare ye well, sir,
As these prove, we shall look the next wind for you.

Merch. I shall be with you, sir.
Paul. Who bought this fellow ?
2 Cit. Not I.
Apoth. Nor I.
Paul. Why does he follow us, then ?
Merch. Did not I tell you he would steal to you ?
2 Cit. Sirrah,
You mouldy-chaps ! know your crib, I would wish you,
And get from whence you came.
1 Slave. I came from no place.
Paul. Wilt thou be my fool ? for fools, they say, will tell truth.
1 Slave. Yes, if you will give me leave, sir, to abuse you,
For I can do that naturally.
Paul. And I can beat you.
1 Slave. I should be sorry else, sir.
Merch. He looks for that, as duly as his victuals,
And will be extreme sick when he is not beaten.
He will be as wanton, when he has a bone broken,
As a cat in a bowl on the water.
Paul. You will part with him ?
Merch. To such a friend as you, sir.
Paul. And without money ?
Merch. Not a penny, signior ;
And would he were better for you !
Paul. Follow me, then ;
The knave may teach me something.
1 Slave. Something that
You dearly may repent ; howe'er you scorn me,
The slave may prove your master.
Paul. Farewell once more !
Merch. Farewell ! and when the wind serves next, expect me.   [*Exeunt.*

SCENE II.—*A Room in the* Viceroy's *Palace.*

Enter Cuculo *and* Antonio.

Cuc. Come, sir, you are mine, sir, now ;
you serve a man, sir,
That, when you know more, you will find——
Ant. I hope so.
Cuc. What dost thou hope ?
Ant. To find you a kind master.
Cuc. Find you yourself a diligent true servant,
And take the precept of the wise before you,
And then you may hope, sirrah. Understand,
You serve me—what is ME ? a man of credit.
Ant. Yes, sir.
Cuc. Of special credit, special office ; hear first
And understand again, of special office :

A man that nods upon the thing he meets,
And that thing bows.

Ant. 'Tis fit it should be so, sir.

Cuc. It shall be so: a man near all importance.
Dost thou digest this truly?

Ant. I hope I shall, sir.

Cuc. Besides, thou art to serve a noble mistress,
Of equal place and trust. Serve usefully,
Serve all with diligence, but her delights;
There make your stop. She is a woman, sirrah,
And though a cull'd out virtue, yet a woman.
Thou art not troubled with the strength of blood,
And stirring faculties, for she'll shew a fair one?

Ant. As I am a man, I may; but as I am your man,
Your trusty, useful man, those thoughts shall perish.

Cuc. 'Tis apt, and well distinguish'd. The next precept,
And then, observe me, you have all your duty;
Keep, as thou'dst keep thine eye-sight, all wine from her,
All talk of wine.

Ant. Wine is a comfort, sir.

Cuc. A devil, sir! let her not dream of wine;
Make her believe there neither is, nor was wine;
Swear it.

Ant. Will you have me lie?

Cuc. To my end, sir:
For if one drop of wine but creep into her,
She is the wisest woman in the world straight,
And all the women in the world together
Are but a whisper to her; a thousand iron mills
Can be heard no further than a pair of nut-crackers.
Keep her from wine; wine makes her dangerous.
Fall back—my lord Don Pedro!

Enter Pedro.

Pedro. Now, master Office,
What is the reason that your vigilant Greatness,
And your wife's wonderful Wiseness, have lock'd up from me
The way to see my mistress? Whose dog's dead now,
That you observe these vigils?

Cuc. Very well, my lord.
Belike, we observe no law then, nor no order,

Nor feel no power, nor will, of him that made them,
When state-commands thus slightly are disputed.

Pedro. What state command? dost thou think any state
Would give thee anything but eggs to keep,
Or trust thee with a secret above lousing?

Cuc. No, no, my lord, I am not passionate;
You cannot work me that way, to betray me.
A point there is in't, that you must not see, sir,
A secret and a serious point of state too;
And do not urge it further, do not, lord,
It will not take; you deal with them that wink not.
You tried my wife. Alas! you thought she was foolish,
Won with an empty word; you have not found it.

Pedro. I have found a pair of coxcombs, that I am sure on.

Cuc. Your lordship may say three :—I am not passionate.

Pedro. How's that?

Cuc. Your lordship found a faithful gentlewoman,
Strong, and inscrutable as the viceroy's heart;
A woman of another making, lord:
And, lest she might partake with woman's weakness,
I've purchased her a rib to make her perfect,
A rib that will not shrink, nor break in the bending.
This trouble we are put to, to prevent things,
Which your good lordship holds but necessary.

Pedro. A fellow of a handsome and free promise,
And much, methinks, I'm taken with his countenance.—
Do you serve this yeoman, porter?
　　　　　　　　　　　　　[*To* Antonio.

Cuc. Not a word.
Basta! Your lordship may discourse your freedom;
He is a slave of state, sir, so of silence.

Pedro. You are very punctual, state-cut, fare ye well;
I shall find time to fit you too, I fear not.
　　　　　　　　　　　　　[*Exit.*

Cuc. And I shall fit you, lord : you would be billing;
You are too hot, sweet lord, too hot.—Go you home,
And there observe these lessons I first taught you.
Look to your charge abundantly; be wary,
Trusty and wary; much weight hangs upon me,

Watchful and wary too! this lord is dan-
gerous,
Take courage and resist : for other uses,
Your mistress will inform you. Go, be
faithful,
And, do you hear? no wine.
Ant. I shall observe, sir. [*Exeunt.*

SCENE III.—*Another Room in the same.*

Enter Paulo *and* Surgeons.

Paul. He must take air.
1 S*urg.* Sir, under your correction,
The violence of motion may make
His wounds bleed fresh.
2 S*urg.* And he hath lost already
Too much blood, in my judgment.
Paul. I allow that ;
But to choke up his spirits in a dark room,
Is far more dangerous. He comes ; no
questions.

Enter Cardenes.

Car. Certain we have no reason, nor that
soul
Created of that pureness books persuade us :
We understand not; sure, nor feel that
sweetness
That men call virtue's chain to link our
actions.
Our imperfections form, and flatter us ;
A will to rash and rude things is our reason,
And that we glory in, that makes us guilty.
Why did I wrong this man ? unmanly wrong
him ?
Unmannerly ? He gave me no occasion.
In all my heat how noble was his temper !
And, when I had forgot both man and man-
hood,
With what a gentle bravery did he chide me !
And, say he had kill'd me, whither had I
travell'd ?
Kill'd me in all my rage—oh, how it shakes
me !
Why didst thou do this, fool? a woman
taught me,
The devil and his angel, woman, bade me.—
I am a beast, the wildest of all beasts,
And like a beast I make my blood my
master.
Farewell, farewell, forever, name of mistress !
Out of my heart I cross thee ; love and
women
Out of my thoughts.
Paul. Ay, now you shew your manhood.
Car. Doctor, believe me, I have bought
my knowledge,
And dearly, doctor :——they are dangerous
creatures,

They sting at both ends, doctor ; worthless
creatures,
And all their loves and favours end in ruins.
Paul. To man, indeed.
Car. Why, now thou tak'st me rightly.
What can they shew, or by what act deserve
us,
While we have Virtue, and pursue her
beauties !
Paul. And yet I've heard of many virtuous
women.
Car. Not many, doctor ; there your read-
ing fails you :
Would there were more, and in their loves
less dangers !
Paul. Love is a noble thing without all
doubt, sir.
Car. Yes, and an excellent—to cure the
itch.   [*Exit.*
1 S*urg.* Strange melancholy !
Paul. By degrees 'twill lessen :
Provide your things.
2 S*urg.* Our care shall not be wanting.
                              [*Exeunt.*

SCENE IV.—*A Room in* Cuculo's *House.*

Enter Leonora *and* Almira.

Leon. Good madam, for your health's
sake clear those clouds up,
That feed upon your beauties like diseases.
Time's hand will turn again, and what he
ruins
Gently restore, and wipe off all your sorrows.
Believe you are to blame, much to blame,
lady ;
You tempt his loving care whose eye has
number'd
All our afflictions, and the time to cure
them :
You rather with this torrent choak his mercies,
Than gently slide into his providence.
Sorrows are well allow'd, and sweet nature,
Where they express no more than drops on
lilies ;
But, when they fall in storms, they bruise
our hopes ;
Make us unable, though our comforts meet
us,
To hold our heads up : Come, you shall
take comfort ;
This is a sullen grief becomes condemn'd
men,
That feel a weight of sorrow through their
souls :
Do but look up. Why, so !—is not this
better,
Than hanging down your head still like a
violet,

And .dropping out those sweet eyes for a
wager?
Pray you, speak a little.
   Alm. Pray you, desire no more ;
And, if you love me, say no more.
   Leon. How fain,
If I would be as wilful, and partake in't,
Would you destroy yourself! how often, lady,
Even of the same disease have you cured
   me,
And shook me out on't ; chid me, tumbled
   me,
And forced my hands, thus?
   Alm. By these tears, no more.
   Leon. You are too prodigal of them. Well,
   I will not ;
For though my love bids me transgress your
   will,
I have a service to your sorrows still.
                   [*Exeunt.*

SCENE V.—*A Hall in the same.*

Enter Pedro *and* Antonio.

   Ant. Indeed, my lord, my place is not so
   near :
I wait below stairs, and there sit, and wait
Who comes to seek accesses ; nor is it fit, sir,
My rudeness should intrude so near their
   lodgings.
   Pedro. Thou mayst invent a way, 'tis but
   a trial,
But carrying up this letter, and this token,
And giving them discreetly to my mistress,
The lady Leonora : there's my purse,
Or anything thou'lt ask me ; if thou knew'st
   me,
And what I may be to thee for this
   courtesy——
   Ant. Your lordship speaks so honestly,
   and freely,
That by my troth I'll venture.
   Pedro. I dearly thank thee.
   Aut. And it shall cost me hard ; nay, keep
   your purse, sir,
For, though my body's bought, my mind
   was never.
Though I am bound, my courtesies are no
   slaves.
   Pedro. Thou shouldst be truly gentle.
   Ant. If I were so,
The state I am in bids you not believe it.
But to the purpose, sir ; give me your letter,
And next your counsel, for I serve a crafty
   mistress.
   Pedro. And she must be removed, thou
   wilt else ne'er do it.
   Ant. Ay, there's the plague : think, and
   I'll think awhile too.

   Pedro. Her husband's suddenly fallen sick?·
   Ant. She cares not ;
If he were dead, indeed, it would do better..
   Pedro. Would he were hang'd !
   Ant. Then she would run for joy, sir.
   Pedro. Some lady crying out?
   Ant. She has two already.
   Pedro. Her house afire?
   Ant. *Let the fool, my husband, quench it.*
This will be her answer.—This may take ; it
   will, sure.
Your lordship must go presently, and send me
Two or three bottles of your best Greek wine,
The strongest and the sweetest.
   Pedro. Instantly :
But will that do?
   Ant. Let me alone to work it.
                   [*Exit* Pedro.
Wine I was charged to keep by all means
   from her ;   .
All secret locks it opens, and all counsels,
That I am sure, and gives men all accesses.
Pray heaven she be not loving when she's
   drunk now !
For drunk she shall be, though my pate pay
   for it.
She'll turn my stomach then abominably.
She has a most wicked face, and that lewd
   face
Being a drunken face, what face will there
   be !——
She cannot ravish me. Now, if my master
Should take her so, and know I minister'd,
What will his wisdom do ? I hope be drunk
   too,
And then all's right. Well, lord, to do thee
   service
Above these puppet-plays, I keep a life
   yet——
Here come the executioners.

   Enter Servant *with bottles.*

                  You are welcome;
Give me your load, and tell my lord I am
   at it.
   Serv. I will, sir ; speed you, sir. [*Exit.*
   Ant. Good speed on all sides !
'Tis strong, strong wine : O, the yaws that
   she will make !
Look to your stern, dear mistress, and steer
   right,
Here's that will work as high as the Bay of
   Portugal.
Stay, let me see—I'll try her by the nose first ;
For, if she be a right sow, sure she ll find it.
She is yonder by herself, the ladies from her.
Now to begin my sacrifice :—[*pours out some
   of the wine.*]—she stirs, and vents it.
O, how she holds her nose up like a jennet

In the wind of a grass mare ! she has it full
   now,
And now she comes.— I'll stand aside awhile.

Enter Borachia.

Bora. [*snuffing.*] 'Tis wine ! ay, sure 'tis
   wine ! excellent strong wine !
In the must, I take it : very wine ! this way
   too.
Ant. How true she hunts ! I'll make the
   train a little longer.
                          [*Pours out more wine.*
Bora. Stronger and stronger still ! still !
   blessed wine !
Ant. Now she hunts hot.
Bora. All that I can for this wine !
This way it went, sure.
Ant. Now she's at a cold scent.
Make out your doubles, mistress. O, well
   hunted !
That's she ! that's she !
Bora. O, if I could but see it !
Oh what a precious scent it has !—but handle
   it !
Ant. Now I'll untappice.
                  [*Comes forward with the bottle.*
Bora. What's that ? still 'tis stronger.
Why, how now, sirrah ! what's that ? answer
   quickly,
And to the point.
Ant. 'Tis wine, forsooth, good wine,
Excellent Candy wine.
Bora. 'Tis well, forsooth !
Is this a drink for slaves ? why, saucy sirrah,
(Excellent Candy wine !) draw nearer to me,
Reach me the bottle : why, thou most de-
   bauch'd slave——
Ant. Pray be not angry, for with all my
   service
And pains, I purchased this for you, (I dare
   not drink it,)
For you a present ; only for your pleasure ;
To shew in little what a thanks I owe
The hourly courtesies your goodness gives me.
Bora. And I will give thee more ; there,
   kiss my hand on't.
Ant. I thank you dearly—for your dirty
   favour :
How rank it smells ?   [*Aside.*
Bora. By thy leave, sweet bottle,
And sugar-candy wine, I now come to thee ;
Hold your hand under.
Ant. How does your worship like it ?
Bora. Under again—again—and now
   come kiss me ;
I'll be a mother to thee : come, drink to me.
Ant. I do beseech your pardon.
Bora. Here's to thee, then ;
I am easily entreated for thy good.

'Tis naught for thee, indeed ; 'twill make thee
   break all ;
Thou hast a pure complexion : now, for me
'Tis excellent, 'tis excellent for me.
Son slave, I've a cold stomach, and the
   wind——
Ant. Blows out a cry at both ends.
Bora. Kiss again.
Cherish thy lips, for thou shalt kiss fair ladies ;
Son slave, I have them for thee ; I'll shew
   thee all.
Ant. Heaven bless mine eyes !
Bora. Even all the secrets, son slave,
In my dominion.
Ant. Oh ! here come the ladies ;
Now to my business.

Enter Leonora *and* Almira *behind.*

Leon. This air will much refresh you.
Alm. I must sit down.
Leon. Do, and take freer thoughts,
The place invites you ; I'll walk by like your
   sentinel.
Bora. And thou shalt be my heir, I'll leave
   thee all,
Heaven knows to what 'twill mount to ; but
   abundance :
I'll leave thee two young ladies—what think
   you of that, boy !—
                        [*Antonio goes to* Leonora.
Where is the bottle ?—two delicate young
   ladies :
But first you shall commit with me ; do you
   mark, son ?
And shew yourself a gentleman, that's the
   truth, son.
Ant. Excellent lady, kissing your fair
   hand,
And humbly craving pardon for intruding,
This letter, and this ring——
Leon. From whom, I pray you, sir ? .
Ant. From the most noble, loving lord,
   don Pedro,
The servant of your virtues.
Bora. And prithee, good son slave, be wise
   and circumspect,
And take heed of being o'ertaken with too
   much drink ;
For it is a lamentable sin, and spoils all :
Why, 'tis the damnablest thing to be drunk,
   son !
Heaven can't endure it. And hark you, one
   thing I'd have done :
Knock my husband on the head, as soon as
   may be,
For he is an arrant puppy, and cannot per-
   form——
Why, where the devil is this foolish bottle ?
Leon. I much thank you ;

And this, sir, for your pains.
　　　　　　　　　[*Offers him her purse.*
　Ant. No, gentle lady;
That I can do him service is my merit,
My faith, my full reward.
　Leon. Once more, I thank you.
Since I have met so true a friend to goodness,
I dare deliver to your charge my answer:
Pray you, tell him, sir, this night I do invite
　him
To meet me in the garden; means he may find,
For love, they say, wants no abilities.
　Ant. Nor shall he, madam, if my help may
　prosper;
So everlasting love and sweetness bless
　you!—
She's at it still, I dare not now appear to her.
　Alm. What fellow's that?
　Leon. Indeed I know not, madam;
It seems of some strange country by his habit;
Nor can I shew you by what mystery
He wrought himself into this place, pro-
　hibited.
　Alm. A handsome man.
　Leon. But of a mind more handsome.
　Alm. Was his business to you?
　Leon. Yes, from a friend you wot of.
　Alm. A very handsome fellow,
And well demean'd.
　Leon. Exceeding well; and speaks well.
　Alm. And speaks well, too?
　Leon. Ay, passing well, and freely,
And, as he promises, of a most clear nature;
Brought up, sure, far above his shew.
　Alm. It seems so:
I would I'd heard him, friend. Comes he
　again?
　Leon. Indeed I know not if he do.
　Alm. 'Tis no matter.
Come, let's walk in.
　Leon. I am glad you have found your
　tongue yet.
　　　　　　　[*Exeunt* Leonora *and* Almira.
　　　　　Borachia *sings.*
　Cuc. [*within.*] My wife is very merry; sure
　'twas her voice:
Pray heaven there be no drink in't, then I
　allow it.
　Ant. 'Tis sure my master.
　　　　　Enter Cuculo.
　　　　　　Now the game begins;
Here will be spitting of fire o' both sides
　presently;
'Send me but safe deliver'd!
　Cuc. O, my heart aches!
My head aches too: mercy o' me, she's
　perish'd!
She has gotten wine! she is gone for ever!

　Bora. Come hither, ladies, carry your
　bodies swimming;
Do your three duties, then—then fall behind
　me.
　Cuc. O, thou pernicious rascal! what
　hast thou done?
　Ant. I done! alas, sir, I have done nothing.
　Cuc. Sirrah,
How came she by this wine?
　Ant. Alas, I know not.
　Bora. Who's that, that talks of wine there?
　Ant. Forsooth, my master.
　Bora. Bring him before me, son slave.
　Cuc. I will know it.
This bottle, how this bottle?
　Bora. Do not stir it;
For, if you do, by this good wine, I'll knock
　you,
I'll beat you damnably, yea and nay, I'll
　beat you;
And, when I have broke it 'bout your head,
　do you mark me?
Then will I tie it to your worship's tail,
And all the dogs in the town shall follow you.
No question, I would advise you, how I came
　by it;
I will have none of these points handled now.
　Cuc. She'll ne'er be well again while the
　world stands.
　Ant. I hope so.　　　　　　　[*Aside.*
　Cuc. How dost thou, lamb?
　Bora. Well, God-a-mercy.
Belwether, how dost thou? Stand out, son
　slave,
Sit you here, and before this worshipful
　audience
Propound a doubtful question; see who's
　drunk now.
　Cuc. Now, now it works; the devil now
　dwells in her.
　Bora. Whether the heaven or the earth
　be nearer the moon?
Or what's the natural reason, why a woman
　longs
To make her husband cuckold? Bring me
　your cousin
The curate now, that great philosopher,
He that found out a pudding had two ends,
That learned clerk, that notable gymnoso-
　phist;
And let him with his Jacob's-staff discover
What is the third part of three farthings,
Three halfpence being the half, and I am
　satisfied.
　Cuc. You see she hath learning enough,
　if she could dispose it.
　Bora. Too much for thee, thou logger-
　head, thou bull-head!
　Cuc. Nay, good Borachia.

Bora. Thou a sufficient statesman !
A gentleman of learning ! hang thee, dog-whelp ;
Thou shadow of a man of action,
Thou scab o' the court ! go sleep, you drunken rascal,
You debauch'd puppy ; get you home, and sleep, sirrah ;
And so will I : son slave, thou shalt sleep with me.,
  Cuc. Prithee, look to her tenderly.
  Bora. No words, sirrah,
Of any wine, or anything like wine, .
Or anything concerning wine, or by wine,
Or from, or with wine. Come, lead me like a countess.
  Cuc. Thus must we bear, poor men ! there is a trick in't ;
But, when she is well again, I'll trick her for it.   [*Exeunt.*

ACT IV.
SCENE I.—*A Room in the* Viceroy's *Palace.*

Enter Pedro.

Pedro. Now, if this honest fellow do but prosper,
I hope I shall make fair return. I wonder
I hear not from the prince of Tarent yet,
I hope he's landed well, and to his safety ;
The winds have stood most gently to his purpose.

Enter Antonio.

My honest friend !
  Ant. Your lordship's poorest servant.
  Pedro. How hast thou sped ?
  Ant. My lord, as well as wishes.
My way hath reach'd your mistress, and deliver'd
Your loveletter, and token ; who, with all joy,
And virtuous constancy, desires to see you :
Commands you this night, by her loving power,
To meet her in the garden.
  Pedro. Thou hast made me ;
Redeem'd me, man, again from all my sorrows ;
Done above wonder for me. Is it so ?
  Ant. I should be now too old to learn to lie, sir,
And, as I live, I never was good flatterer.
  Pedro. I do see something in this fellow's face still,
That ties my heart fast to him. Let me love thee,
Nay, let me honour thee for this fair service :
And if I e'er forget it——

Ant. Good my lord,
The only knowledge of me is too much bounty :
My service, and my life, sir.
  Pedro. I shall think on't ;
But how for me to get access ?
  Ant. 'Tis easy ;
I'll be your guide, sir, all my care shall lead you ;
My credit's better than you think.
  Pedro. I thank you,
And soon I'll wait your promise.
  Ant. With all my duty.   [*Exeunt.*

SCENE II.—*A Bed-room in the same.*

Enter Viceroy, Duke, Paulo, *and* Cuculoi

Paulo. All's as I tell you, princes ; you shall here
Be witness to his fancies, melancholy,
And strong imagination of his wrongs.
His inhumanity to don Antonio
Hath rent his mind into so many pieces
Of various imaginations, that,
Like the celestial bow, this colour now's
The object, then another, till all vanish.
He says a man might watch to death, or fast,
Or think his spirit out ; to all which humours
I do apply myself, checking the bad,
And cherishing the good. For these, I have
Prepared my instruments, fitting his chamber
With trapdoors, and descents ; sometimes presenting
Good spirits of the air, bad of the earth,
To pull down or advance his fair intentions.
He's of a noble nature, yet sometimes
Thinks that which, by confederacy, I do,
Is by some skill in magic.

Enter Cardenes, *a book in his hand.*
          Here he comes
Unsent. I do beseech you, what do you read, sir?
  Car. A strange position, which doth much perplex me :
That every soul's alike a musical instrument,
The faculties in all men equal strings,
Well or ill handled ; and those sweet or harsh.   [*Exit* Paulo.
How like a fiddler I have play'd on mine then !
Declined the high pitch of my birth and breeding,
Like the most barbarous peasant ; read my pride
Upon Antonio's meek humility,
Wherein he was far valianter than I.
Meekness, thou wait'st upon courageous spirits,
Enabling sufferance past inflictions.

                       L L

In patience Tarent overcame me more
Than in my wounds : live then, no more to
    men,
Shut daylight from thine eyes, here cast
    thee down,   [*Falls on the bed.*
And with a sullen sigh breathe forth thy soul—

Re-enter Paulo *disguised as a Friar.*

What art ? an apparition, or a man ?
    Paul. A man, and sent to counsel thee.
    Car. Despair
Has stopt mine ears ; thou seem'st a holy
    friar.
    Paul. I am ; by doctor Paulo sent, to
    tell thee
Thou art too cruel to thyself, in seeking
To lend compassion and aid to others.
My order bids me comfort thee. I have
    heard all
Thy various, troubled passions : hear but
    my story.
In way of youth I did enjoy one friend,
As good and perfect as heaven e'er made
    man ;
This friend was plighted to a beauteous
    woman,
(Nature proud of her workmanship,) mutual
    love
Possess'd them both, her heart in his breast
    lodged,
And his in hers.
    Car. No more of love, good father,
It was my surfeit, and I loath it now,
As men in fevers meat they fell sick on.
    Paul. Howe'er, 'tis worth your hearing.
This betroth'd lady,
(The ties and duties of a friend forgotten,)
Spurr'd on by lust, I treacherously pursued;
Contemn'd by her, and by my friend re-
    proved,
Despised by honest men, my conscience
    sear'd up,
Love I converted into frantic rage ;
And by that false guide led, I summon'd him
In this bad cause, his sword 'gainst mine, to
    prove
If he or I might claim most right in love.
But fortune, that does seld or never give
Success to right and virtue, made him fall
Under my sword.   Blood, blood, a friend's
    dear blood,
A virtuous friend's, shed by a villain, me,
In such a monstrous and unequal cause,
Lies on my conscience.
    Car. And durst thou live,
After this, to be so old ? 'tis an illusion
Raised up by charms : a man would not
    have lived.
Art quiet in thy bosom ?

    Paul. As the sleep
Of infants.
    Car. My fault did not equal this ;
Yet I have emptied my heart of joy,
Only to store sighs up.   What were the arts
That made thee live so long in rest ?
    Paul. Repentance
Hearty, that cleansed me ; reason then con-
    firm'd me,
I was forgiven, and took me to my beads.
                                        [*Exit.*
    Car. I am in the wrong path ; tender
    conscience
Makes me forget mine honour : I have done
No evil like this, yet I pine ; whilst he,
A few tears of his true contrition tender'd,
Securely sleeps.   Ha ! where keeps peace of
    conscience,
That I may buy her?—nowhere ; not in
    life.
'Tis feign'd that Jupiter two vessels placed,
The one with honey fill'd, the other gall,
At the entry of Olympus ; Destiny,
There brewing these together, suffers not
One man to pass, before he drinks this mix-
    ture.
Hence it is we have not an hour of life
In which our pleasures relish not some pain,
Our sours some sweetness.   Love doth taste
    of both ;
Revenge, that thirsty dropsy of our souls,
Which makes us covet that which hurts us
    most,
Is not alone sweet, but partakes of tartness.
    Duke. Is't not a strange effect ?
    Vice. Past precedent.
    Cuc. His brain-pan's perish'd with his
    wounds : go to,
I knew 'twould come to this.
    Vice. Peace, man of wisdom.
    Car. Pleasure's the hook of evil ; ease of
    care,
And so the general object of the court ;
Yet some delights are lawful.   Honour is
Virtue's allow'd ascent ; honour, that clasps
All-perfect justice in her arms, that craves
No more respect than what she gives, that
    does
Nothing but what she'll suffer.—This dis-
    tracts me ;
But I have found the right : had don An-
    tonio
Done that to me, I did to him, I should
    have kill'd him ;
The injury so foul, and done in public,
My footman would not bear it ; then in
    honour
Wronging him so, I'll right him on myself :
There's honour, justice, and full satisfaction

Equally tender'd ; 'tis resolved, I'll do it.
[*They rush forward and disarm him.*
They take all weapons from me.
Duke. Bless my son !

Re-enter Paulo, *dressed like a Soldier, and
the* English Slave *like a Courtier.*

Vice. The careful doctor's come again.
Duke. Rare man !
How shall I pay this debt ?
Cuc. He that is with him,
Is one o' the slaves he lately bought, he said,
To accommodate his cure : he's English born,
But French in his behaviour ; a delicate slave.
Vice. The slave is very fine.
Cuc. Your English slaves
Are ever so ; I have seen an English slave
Far finer than his master : there's a state-
point,
Worthy your observation.
Paul. On thy life,
Be perfect in thy lesson : fewer legs, slave.
Car. My thoughts are search'd and
answer'd ; for I did
Desire a soldier and a courtier,
To yield me satisfaction in some doubts
Not yet concluded of.
Paul. Your doctor did
Admit us, sir.
Slave. And we are at your service ;
Whate'er it be, command it.
Car. You appear
A courtier in the race of LOVE ; how far
In honour are you bound to run ?
Slave. I'll tell you,
You must not spare expense, but wear gay
clothes,
And you may be, too, prodigal of oaths,
To win a mistress' favour ; not afraid
To pass unto her through her chambermaid.
You may present her gifts, and of all sorts,
Feast, dance, and revel; they are lawful
sports :
The choice of suitors you must not deny her,
Nor quarrel, though you find a rival by her:
Build on your own deserts, and ever be
A stranger to love's enemy, jealousy,
For that draws on——
Car. No more ; this points at me ;
[*Exit* English Slave.
I ne'er observed these rules. Now speak, old
soldier,
The height of HONOUR?
Paul. No man to offend,
Ne'er to reveal the secrets of a friend ;
Rather to suffer than to do a wrong ;
To make the heart no stranger to the
tongue ;
Provoked, not to betray an enemy,

Nor eat his meat I choak with flattery ;
Blushless to tell wherefore I wear my scars,
Or for my conscience, or my country's wars ;
To aim at just things; if we have wildly run
Into offences, wish them all undone :
'Tis poor, in grief for a wrong done, to die,
Honour, to dare to live, and satisfy.
Vice. Mark, how he winds him.
Duke. Excellent man !
Paul. Who fights
With passions, and o'ercomes them, is en-
dued
With the best virtue, passive fortitude.
[*Exit.*
Car. Thou hast touch'd me, soldier ; oh !
this honour bears
The right stamp ; would all soldiers did
profess
Thy good religion ! The discords of my soul
Are tuned, and make a heavenly harmony :
What sweet peace feel I now ! I am ravish'd
with it.
Vice. How still he sits ! [*Music.*
Cuc. Hark ! music.
Duke. How divinely
This artist gathers scatter'd sense ; with
cunning
Composing the fair jewel of his mind,
Broken in pieces, and nigh lost before.

Re-enter Paulo, *dressed like a Philosopher,
accompanied by a good and evil Genius,
who sing a song in alternate stanzas :
during the performance of which* Paulo
goes off, and returns in his own shape.

Vice. See Protean Paulo in another shape.
Paul. Away, I'll bring him shortly per-
fect, doubt not.
Duke. Master of thy great art !
Vice. As such we'll hold thee.
Duke. And study honours for him.
Cuc. I'll be sick
On purpose to take physic of this doctor.
[*Exeunt all but* Cardenes *and* Paulo.
Car. Doctor, thou hast perfected a body's
cure
To amaze the world, and almost cured a mind
Near frenzy. With delight I now perceive,
You, for my recreation, have invented
The several objects, which my melancholy
Sometimes did think you conjured, other-
whiles
Imagined them chimæras. You have been
My friar, soldier, philosopher,
My poet, architect, physician ;
Labour'd for me, more than your slaves for
you,
In their assistance : in your moral song
L L 2

Of my good Genius and my bad, you have
  won me
A cheerful heart, and banish'd discontent ;
There being nothing wanting to my wishes,
But once more, were it possible, to behold
Don John Antonio.
  Paul. There shall be letters sent
Into all parts of Christendom, to inform him
Of your recovery, which now, sir, I doubt
  not.
  Car. What honours, what rewards can I
  heap on you !
  Paul. That my endeavours have so well
  succeeded,
Is a sufficient recompense. Pray you retire, sir;
Not too much air so soon.
  Car. I am obedient.   [*Excunt.*

SCENE III.—*A Room in* Cuculo's *House.*

    Enter Almira *and* Leonora.

  Leon. How strangely
This fellow runs in her mind !   [*Aside.*
  Alm. Do you hear, cousin ?
  Leon. Her sadness clean forsaken !
  Alm. A poor slave
Bought for my governess, say you ?
  Leon. I hear so.
  Alm. And, do you think, a Turk ?
  Leon. His habit shows it ;
At least bought for a Turk.
  Alm. Ay, that may be so.
  Leon. What if he were one naturally ?
  Alm. Nay, 'tis nothing,
Nothing to the purpose ; and yet, methinks,
  'tis strange
Such handsomeness of mind, and civil out-
  side,
Should spring from those rude countries. ·
  Leon. If it be no more,
I'll call our governess, and she can shew you.
  Alm. Why, do you think it is ?
  Leon. I do not think so.
  Alm. Fie ! no, no, by no means ; and to
  tell thee truth, wench,
I am truly glad he is here, be what he will :
Let him be still the same he makes a shew of ;
For now we shall see something to delight us.
  Leon. And heaven knows, we have need
  on't.
  Alm. Heigh ho ! my heart aches.
Prithee, call in our governess.—[*Exit*
  Leonora.] Plague o' this fellow !
Why do I think so much of him ? how the
  devil
Creep'd he into my head ? and yet, beshrew
  me,
Methinks I have not seen—I lie, I have seen
A thousand handsomer, a thousand
  sweeter.——

But say this fellow were adorn'd as they are,
Set off to shew and glory !—What's that to
  me ?
Fie, what a fool am I ! what idle fancies
Buz in my brains !

    Re-enter Leonora *with* Borachia.

  Bora. And how doth my sweet lady ?
  Leon. She wants your company to make
  her merry.
  Bora. And how does master Pug, I pray
  you, madam ?
  Leon. Do you mean her little dog ?
  Bora. I mean his worship.
  Leon. Troubled with fleas a little.
  Bora. Alas, poor chicken !
  Leon. She's here, and drunk, very fine
  drunk, I take it ;
I found her with a bottle for her bolster,
Lying along, and making love.
  Alm. Borachia,
Why, where hast thou been, wench ? she
  looks not well, friend.
Art not with child ?
  Bora. I promise ye, I know not ;
I am sure my belly's full, and that's a shrewd
  sign :
Besides I am shrewdly troubled with a tiego
Here in my head, madam ; often with this
  tiego,
It takes me very often.
  Leon. I believe thee.
  Alm. You must drink wine.
  Bora. A little would do no harm, sure.
  Leon. 'Tis a raw humour blows into your
  head ;
Which good strong wine will temper.
  Bora. I thank your highness.
I will be ruled, though much against my
  nature ;
For wine I ever hated from my cradle :
Yet, for my good——
  Leon. Ay, for your good, by all means.
  Alm. Borachia, what new fellow's that
  thou hast gotten ?
(Now she will sure be free) that handsome
  stranger ?
  Bora. How much wine must I drink, an't
  please your ladyship ?
  Alm. She's finely greased !—Why, two or
  three round draughts, wench.
  Bora. Fasting ?
  Alm. At any time.
  Bora. I shall hardly do it :
But yet I'll try, good madam.
  Leon. Do ; 'twill work well.
  Alm. But, prithee answer me, what is this
  fellow ?

Bora. I'll tell you two : but let it go no
further.

Leon. No, no, by no means.

Bora. May I not drink before bed too?

Leon. At any hour.

Bora. And say in the night it take me?

Alm. Drink then : but what's this man?

Bora. I'll tell ye, madam,
But pray you be secret ; he's the great Turk's
   .son, for certain,
And a fine Christian ; my husband bought
him for me :
He's circumsinged.

Leon. He's circumcised, thou wouldst say.

Alm. How dost thou know?

Bora. I had an eye upon him :
But even as sweet a Turk, an't like your
  ladyship,
And speaks ye as pure pagan :—I'll assure ye,
My husband had a notable pennyworth of
him ;
And found me but the Turk's own son, his
own son
By father and mother, madam !

Leon. She's mad-drunk.

Alm. Prithee, Borachia, call him ; I would
  see him,
And tell thee how I like him.

Bora. As fine a Turk, madam,
For that which appertains to a true Turk——

Alm. Prithee, call him.

Bora. He waits here at the stairs :—Son
slave ! come hither.

Enter Antonio.

Pray you give me leave a little to instruct him,
He's raw yet in the way of entertainment.
Son slave, where's the other bottle?

 Ant. In the bedstraw ;
I hid it there.

Bora. Go up, and make your honours.
Madam, the tiego takes me now, now,
  madam ;
I must needs be unmannerly.

Alm. Pray you be so.

Leon. You know your cure.

Bora. In the bedstraw?

Ant. There you'll find it.
                [*Exit* Borachia.

Alm. Come hither, sir : how long have you
  served here?

Ant. A poor time, madam, yet, to shew
  my service.

Alm. I see thou art diligent.

Ant. I would be, madam ;
*'Tis all the portion left me, that and truth.

 Alm. Thou art but young.

Ant. Had fortune meant me so,

Excellent lady, time had not much wrong'd
me.

Alm. Wilt thou serve me?

Ant. In all my prayers, madam,
Else such a misery as mine but blasts you.

Alm. Beshrew my heart, he speaks well ;
  wondrous honestly.   [*Aside.*

Ant. Madam, your loving lord stays for
you.

Leon. I thank you.
Your pardon for an hour, dear friend.

Alm. Your pleasure.

Leon. I dearly thank you, sir.   [*Exit.*

Ant. My humblest service.
She views me narrowly, yet sure she knows
me not :
I dare not trust the time yet, nor I must not.
                [*Aside.*

Alm. You are not as your habit shews?

Ant. No, madam,
His hand, that, for my sins, lies heavy on me,
I hope will keep me from being a slave to
the devil.

Alm. A brave clear mind he has, and nobly
  season'd.
What country are you of?

Ant. A Biseau, lady.

Alm. No doubt, a gentleman,

Ant. My father thought so.

Alm. Ay, and I warrant thee, a right fair
woman
Thy mother was :—he blushes, that confirms it.
Upon my soul, I have not seen such sweetness !
I prithee, blush again.

Ant. 'Tis a weakness, madam,
I am easily this way woo'd to.

Alm. I thank you.
Of all that e'er I saw, thou art the perfectest.   [*Aside.*
Now you must tell me, sir, for now I long
for't.——

Ant. What would she have?

Alm. The story of your fortune,
The hard and cruel fortune brought you
hither.

Ant. That makes me stagger ; yet I hope
  I'm hid still.——   [*Aside.*
That I came hither, madam, was the fairest.

Alm. But how this misery you bear, fell on
  you?

Ant. *Infandum, regina, jubes renovare
dolorem.*

Alm. Come, I will have it ; I command you,
  tell it,
For such a speaker I would hear for ever.

Ant. Sure, madam, 'twill but make you
  sad and heavy,

Because I know your goodness full of pity;
And 'tis so poor a subject too, and to your
    ears,
That are acquainted with things sweet and
    easy,
So harsh a harmony.
    Alm. I prithee speak it.
    Ant. I ever knew obedience the best
    sacrifice.
Honour of ladies, then, first passing over
Some few years of my youth, that are im-
    pertinent,
Let me begin the sadness of my story,
Where I began to lose myself, to love first.
    Alm. 'Tis well, go forward; some rare
    piece I look for.
    Ant. Not far from where my father lives,
    a lady,
A neighbour by, bless'd with as great a
    beauty
As nature durst bestow without undoing,
Dwelt, and most happily, as I thought then,
And bless'd the house a thousand times she
    dwelt in.
This beauty, in the blossom of my youth,
When my first fire knew no adulterate in-
    cense,
Nor I no way to flatter, but my fondness;
In all the bravery my friends could shew me,
In all the faith my innocence could give me,
In the best language my true tongue could
    tell me,
And all the broken sighs my sick heart lend
    me,
I sued, and serv'd : long did I love this lady,
Long was my travail, long my trade to win
    her ;
With all the duty of my soul I served her.—
    Alm. How feelingly he speaks! [*Aside.*]—
    And she loved you too?
It must be so.
    Ant. I would it had, dear lady ;
This story had been needless, and this place,
I think, unknown to me.
    Alm. Were your bloods equal?
    Ant. Yes, and I thought our hearts too.
    Alm. Then she must love.
    Ant. She did—but never me ; she could
    not love me,
She would not love, she hated : more, she
    scorn'd me,
And in so poor and base a way abused me,
For all my services, for all my bounties,
So bold neglects flung on me.
    Alm. An ill woman!
Belike you found some rival in your love,
    then?
    Ant. How perfectly she points me to my
    story !   [*Aside.*

Madam, I did ; and one whose pride and
    anger,
Ill manners, and worse mien, she doted on,
Doted to my undoing, and my ruin.
And, but for honour to your sacred beauty,
And reverence to the noble sex, though she
    fall,
As she must fall that durst be so unnoble,
I should say something unbeseeming me.
What out of love, and worthy love, I gave her,
Shame to her most unworthy mind! to fools,
To girls, and fiddlers, to her *boys* she flung,
And in disdain of me.
    Alm. Pray you take me with you.
Of what complexion was she?
    Ant. But that I dare not
Commit so great a sacrilege gainst virtue,
She look'd not much unlike——though far,
    far short.
Something, I see, appears—your pardon,
    madam—
Her eyes would smile so, but her eyes would
    cozen ;
And so she would look sad : but yours is pity,
A noble chorus to my wretched story ;
Hers was disdain and cruelty.
    Alm. Pray heaven,
Mine be no worse! he has told me a strange
    story,   [*Aside.*
And said 'twould make me sad! he is no
    liar.—
But where begins this poor state? I will have
    all,
For it concerns me truly.
    Ant. Last, to blot me
From all remembrance what I had been to
    her,
And how, how honestly, how nobly served
    her,
'Twas thought she set her gallant to dispatch
    me.
'Tis true, he quarrell'd without place or
    reason :
We fought, I kill'd him ; heaven's strong
    hand was with me.—
For which I lost my country, friends, ac-
    quaintance,
And put myself to sea, where a pirate took me,
Forcing this habit of a Turk upon me,
And sold me here.
    Alm. Stop there awhile ; but stay still.
                    [*Walks aside.*
In this man's story, how I look, how
    monstrous !
How poor and naked now I shew ! what don
    John,
In all the virtue of his life, but aim'd at,
This thing hath conquer'd with a tale, and
    carried.

Forgive me, thou that guid'st me ! never
   conscience
Touch'd me till now, nor true love : let me
   keep it.

Re-enter Leonora *with* Pedro.

Leon. She is there. Speak to her, you will
   find her alter'd.
Pedro. Sister, I am glad to see you, but
   far gladder,
To see you entertain your health so well.
Alm. I am glad to see you too, sir, and
   shall be gladder
Shortly to see you all.
Pedro. Now she speaks heartily.
What do you want?
Alm. Only an hour of privateness ;
I have a few thoughts--
Pedro. Take your full contentment,
We'll walk aside again ; but first to you,
   .friend,
Or I shall much forget myself: my best
   friend,
Command me ever, ever—you have won it.
Ant. Your lordship overflows me.
Leon. 'Tis but due, sir,
      [*Exeunt* Leonora *and* Pedro.
Alm. He's there still. Come, sir, to your
   last part now,
Which only is your name, and I dismiss you.
Why, whither go you?
Ant. Give me leave, good madam,
Or I must be so seeming rude to take it.
Alm. You shall not go, I swear you shall
   not go :
I ask you nothing but your name ; you have
   one,
And why should that thus fright you?
Ant. Gentle madam,
I cannot speak ; pray pardon me, a sickness,
That takes me often, ties my tongue : go
   from me,
My fit's infectious, lady.
Alm. Were it death
In all his horrors, I must ask and know it ;
Your sickness is unwillingness. Hard heart,
To let a lady of my youth, and place,
·Beg thus long for a trifle !
Ant. Worthiest lady,
Be wise, and let me go ; you'll bless me for it,
Beg not that poison from me that will kill you.
Alm. I only beg your name, sir.
Ant. That will choak you ;
I do beseech you, pardon me.
Alm. I will not.
Ant. You'll curse me when you hear it.
Alm. Rather kiss thee ;
Why shouldst thou think so?
Ant. Why ! I bear that name,

And most unluckily as now it happens,
(Though I be innocent of all occasion,)
That, since my coming hither, people tell me
You hate beyond ·forgiveness : now, heaven
   knows
So much respect, although I am a stranger,
Duty, and humble zeal, I bear your sweet-
   ness,
That for the world I would not grieve your
   goodness :
I'll change my name, dear madam.
Alm. People lie,
And wrong thy name ; thy name may save
   all others,
And make that holy to me, that I hated :
Prithee, what is't ?
Ant. Don John Antonio.——
What will this woman do, what thousand
   changes
Run through her heart and hands? no fix'd
   thought in her !
She loves for certain now, but now I dare not.
Heaven guide me right !   [*Aside.*
Alm. I am not angry, sir,
With you, nor with your name ; I love it
   rather,
And shall respect you—you deserve—for
   this time
I license you to go : be not far from me,
I shall call for you often.
Ant. I shall wait, madam.   [*Exit.*

Enter Cuculo.

Alm. Now, what's the news with you?
Cuc. My lord your father
Sent me to tell your honour, prince Martino
Is well recovered, and in strength.
Alm. Why, let him.——
The stories and the names so well agreeing,
And both so noble gentlemen.   [*Aside.·*
Cuc. And more, an't please you—
Alm. It doth not please me, neither more
   nor less on't.
Cuc. They'll come to visit you.
Alm. They shall break through the doors
   then.   [*Exit.*
Cuc. Here's a new trick of state ; this
   shews foul weather ;
But let her make it when she please, I'll
   gain by it.   [*Exit.*

ACT V.

SCENE I.—*A Street.*

Enter Pirates, *and the* Slave *that followed*
Paulo.

1 *Pir.* Sold for a slave, say'st thou?
Slave. 'Twas not so well :

Though I am bad enough, I personated
Such base behaviour, barbarism of manners,
With other pranks that might deter the
    buyer,
That the market yielded not one man that
    would
Vouchsafe to own me.
    1 *Pir.* What was thy end in it ?
    Slave. To be given away for nothing, as
    I was
To the viceroy's doctor ; with him I have
    continued
In such contempt, a slave unto his slaves ;
His horse and dog of more esteem : and from
That villainous carriage of myself, as if
I'd been a lump of flesh without a soul,
I drew such scorn upon me, that I pass'd,
And pried in every place, without observance.
For which, if you desire to be made men,
And by one undertaking, and that easy,
You are bound to sacrifice unto my sufferings,
The seed I sow'd, and from which you shall
    reap
A plentiful harvest.
    1 *Pir.* To the point ; I like not
These castles built in the air.
    Slave. I'll make them real,
And you the Neptunes of the sea ; you shall
No more be sea-rats.
    1 *Pir.* Art not mad?
    Slave. You have seen
The star of Sicily, the fair Almira,
The viceroy's daughter, and the beauteous
    ward
Of the duke of Messina ?
    1 *Pir.* Madam Leonora.
    Slave. What will you say, if both these
    princesses,
This very night, for I will not delay you,
Be put in your possession?
    1 *Pir.* Now I dare swear
Thou hast maggots in thy brains, thou
    wouldst not else,
Talk of impossibilities.
    Slave. Be still
Incredulous.
    1 *Pir.* Why, canst thou think we are able
To force the court ?
    Slave. Are we able to force two women,
And a poor Turkish slave ? Where lies
    your pinnace ?
    1 *Pir.* In a creek not half a league hence.
    Slave. Can you fetch ladders,
To mount a garden wall?
    2 *Pir.* They shall be ready.
    Slave. No more words then, but follow
    me ; and if
I do not make this good, let my throat pay
    for't.

    1 *Pir.* What heaps of gold these beauties
        would bring to us
From the great Turk, if it were possible
That this could be effected !
    Slave. If it be not,
I know the price on't.
    1 *Pir.* And be sure to pay it.   [*Exeunt.*

SCENE II.—*A Room in* Cuculo's *House.*

    Enter Antonio *with a letter in his hand.*

    Ant. Her fair hand threw this from the
        window to me,
And as I took it up, she said, *Peruse it,
And entertain a fortune offer'd to thee.*—
What may the inside speak?—
                [*Breaks it open, and reads.*
                        *For satisfaction
Of the contempt I shew'd don John Antonio,
Whose name thou bear'st, and in that dearer
    to me,
I do profess I love thee*—How !—tis so—
*I love thee ; this night wait me in the garden,
There thou shalt know more*—subscribed,
                            Thy Almira.
Can it be possible such levity
Should wait on her perfections ! when I was
Myself, set off with all the grace of greatness,
Pomp, bravery, circumstance, she hated me,
And did profess it openly ; yet now,
Being a slave, a thing she should in reason
Disdain to look upon ; in this base shape,
And, since I wore it, never did her service,
To dote thus fondly !—and yet I should glory
In her revolt from constancy, not accuse it,
Since it makes for me.   But, ere I go further,
Or make discovery of myself, I'll put her
To the utmost trial.   *In the garden!* well,
There I shall learn more.   Women, giddy
    women !
In her the blemish of your sex you prove,
There is no reason for your hate or love.
                                    [*Exit.*

SCENE III.—*A Garden belonging to the
                same.*

        Enter Almira, Leonora, *and two
                Waiting Women.*

    Leon. At this
Unseasonable time to be thus brave,
No visitants expected ! you amaze me.
    Alm. Are these jewels set forth to the best
        advantage,
To take the eye?
    1 *Wom.* With our best care.
    2 *Wom.* We never
Better discharged our duties.
    Alm. In my sorrows,
A princess' name (I could perceive it) struck

A kind of reverence in him, and my beauty,
As then neglected, forced him to look on me
With some sparks of affection ; but now,
When I would fan them to a glorious flame,
I cannot be too curious. I wonder
He stays so long.'   [*Aside.*
Leon. These are strange fancies.
  Alm. Go,
Entreat—I do forget myself—command
My governess' gentleman — her slave, I
  should say, .
To wait me instantly ;—[*Exit* 1 Woman.]—
  and yet already
He's here ; his figure graven on my heart,
Never to be razed out.

        Enter Pirates, *and the* Slave.

Slave. There is the prize.
Is it so rich that you dare not seize upon it ?
Here I begin.   [*Seizes* Almira.
  Alm. Help ! villain !
1 *Pir.* You are mine.   [*Seizes* Leonora.
2 *Pir.* Though somewhat coarse, you'll
  serve, after a storm,
To bid fair weather welcome.
                          [*Seizes* 2 Woman.
Leon. Ravisher !
Defend me, heaven !
  Alm. No aid near !
2 *Wom.* Help !
Slave. Dispatch.
No glove nor handkerchief to stop their
  mouths ?
Their cries will reach the guard, and then
  we are lost.

    Re-enter 1 *Woman, with* Antonio.

Ant. What shrieks are these ? from
  whence ? O blessed saints,
What sacrilege to beauty ! do I talk,
When 'tis almost too late to do !—[*Forces a
  sword from the* Slave.]—Take that.
Slave. All set upon him.
1 *Pir.* Kill him.
Ant. You shall buy
My life at a dear rate, you rogues.

    Enter Pedro, Cuculo, Borachia, *and*
                  Guard.

Cuc. Down with them !
Pedro. Unheard-of treason !
Bora. Make in, loggerhead ;
My son slave fights like a dragn p : take my
  bottle,
Drink courage out on't.
Ant. Madam, you are free.
Pedro. Take comfort, dearest mistress.
  Cuc. O you micher,
Have you a hand in this?

Slave. My aims were high ;
Fortune's my enemy . to die's the worst,
And that I look for.
  1 *Pir.* Vengeance on your plots !
Pedro. The rack at better leisure shall
  force from them
A full discovery : away with them.
  Cuc. Load them with irons.
Bora. Let them have no wine
          [*Exit* Guard *with* Pirates *and* Slave.
To comfort their cold hearts.
Pedro. Thou man of men !
Leon. A second Hercules.
Alm. An angel thus disguised.
Pedro. What thanks?
Leon. What service ?
Bora. He shall serve me, by your leave,
  no service else.
Ant. I have done nothing but my duty,
  madam ;
And if the little you have seen exceed it,
The thanks due for it pay my watchful master,
And this my sober mistress.
  Bora. He speaks truth, madam,
I am very sober.
  Pedro. Far beyond thy hopes
Expect reward.
  Alm. We'll straight to court, and there
It is resolved what I will say and do.
I am faint, support me.
  Pedro. This strange accident
Will be heard with astonishment. Come,
  friend,
You have made yourself a fortune, and
  deserve it.   [*Exeunt.*

SCENE IV.—*A Room in the* Viceroy's
                Palace.

      Enter Viceroy, Duke *of* Messina, *and*
                  Paulo.

Duke. Perfectly cured !
Paul. As such I will present him :
The thanks be given to heaven.
  Duke. Thrice-reverend man,
What thanks but will come short of thy
  desert ?
Or bounty, though all we possess were given
  thee,
Can pay thy merit? I will have thy statue
Set up in brass.
  Vice. Thy name made the sweet subject
Of our best poems ; thy unequall'd cures
Recorded to posterity.
  Paul. Such false glories
(Though the desire of fame be the last
  weakness
Wise men put off) are not the marks I shoot
  at :

But, if I have done anything that may chal-
lenge
Your favours, mighty princes, my request is,
That for the good of such as shall succeed
me,
A college for physieiaus may be
With care and cost erected, in which no man
May be admitted to a fellowship,
But such as by their vigilant studies shall
Deserve a place there ; this magnificence,
Posterity shall thank you for.
   Vice. Rest assured,
In this, or any boon you please to ask,
You shall have no repulse.
   Paul. My humblest service
Shall ne'er be wanting. Now, if you so
please,
I'll fetch my princely patient, and present
him.
   Duke. Do ; and imagine in what I may
serve you,
And, by my honour, with a willing hand
I will subscribe to't.   [*Exit* Paulo.

  Enter Pedro, Almira, Leonora, Antonio,
   Cuculo, Borachia, *and* Guard.

   Cuc. Make way there.
   Vice. My daughter !
How's this ! a slave crown'd with a civic
garland !
The mystery of this ?
   Pedro. It will deserve
Your hearing and attention : such a truth
Needs not rhetorical flourishes, and therefore
With all the brevity and plainness that
I can, I will deliver it. If the old Romans,
When of most power and wisdom, did decree
A wreath like this to any common soldier
That saved a citizen's life, the bravery
And valour of this man may justly challenge
Triumphant laurel. This last night a crew
Of pirates brake in signior Cuculo's house,
With violent rudeness seizing on my sister,
And my fair mistress ; both were in their
power,
And ready to be forced hence, when this man,
Unarm'd, came to their rescue, but his
courage
Soon furnish'd him with weapons ; in a word,
The lives and liberties of these sweet ladies,
You owe him for: the rovers are in bold,
And ready, when you please, for punishment.
   Vice. As an induction of more to come,
Receive this favour.
   Duke. With myself, my son
Shall pay his real thanks. He comes ; ob-
serve now
Their amorous meeting.

   Re-enter Paulo *with* Cardenes.

   Car. I am glad you are well, lady.
   Alm. I grieve not your recovery.
   Vice. So coldly !
   Duke. Why fall you off?
   Car. To shun captivity, sir.
I was too long a slave, I'll now be free.
   Alm. 'Tis my desire you should. Sir, my
affection
To him was but a trifle, which I play'd with
In the childhood of my love ; which now,
grown older,
I cannot like of.
   Vice. Strange inconstancy !
   Car. 'Tis judgment, sir, in me, or a true
debt
Tender'd to justice, rather. My first life,
Loaden with all the follies of a man,
Or what could take addition from a woman,
Was by my headstrong passions, which o'er-
ruled
My understanding, forfeited to death :
But this new being, this my second life,
Begun in serious contemplation of
What best becomes a perfect man, shall
never
Sink under such weak frailties.
   Duke. Most unlook'd for !
   Paul. It does transcend all wonders.
   Car. 'Tis a blessing
I owe your wisdom, which I'll not abuse :
But if you envy your own gift, and will
Make me that wretched creature which I was,
You then again shall see me passionate,
A lover of poor trifles, confident
In man's deceiving strength, or falser fortune ;
Jealous, revengeful, in unjust things daring,
Injurious, quarrelsome, stored with all
diseases
The beastly part of man infects his soul with,
And to remember what's the worst, once
more
To love a woman ; but till that time never.
                    [*Exit.*
   Vice. Stand you affected so to men,
Almira ?
   Alm. No, sir ; if so, I could not well dis-
charge
What I stand bound to pay you, and to
nature.
Though prince Martino does profess a hate
To womankind, 'twere a poor world for
women,
Were there no other choice, or all should
follow
The example of this new Hippolytus :
There are men, sir, that can love, and have
loved truly ;

Nor am I desperate but I may deserve
One that both can and will so.
 Vice. My allowance
Shall rank with your good liking, still pro-
 vided
Your choice be worthy.
 Alm. In it I have used
The judgment of my mind, and that made
 clearer
With calling oft to heaven it might be so.
I have not sought a living comfort from
The reverend ashes of old ancestors ;
Nor given myself to the mere name and titles
Of such a man, that, being himself nothing,
Derives his substance from his grandsire's
 tomb :
For wealth, it is beneath my birth to think
 on't,
Since that must wait upon me, being your
 daughter ;
No, sir, the man I love, though he wants all
The setting forth of fortune, gloss and
 greatness,
Has in himself such true and real goodness,
His parts so far above his low condition,
That he will prove an ornament, not a
 blemish,
Both to your name and family.
 Pedro. What strange creature
Hath she found out ?
 Leon. I dare not guess.
 Alm. To hold you
No longer in suspense, this matchless man,
That saved my life and honour, is my hus-
 band,
Whom I will serve with duty.
 Bora. My son slave !
 Vice. Have you your wits?
 Bora. I'll not part with him so.
 Cuc. This I foresaw too.
 Vice. Do not jest thyself
Into the danger of a father's anger.
 Alm. Jest, sir ! by all my hope of comfort
 in him,
I am most serious. Good sir, look upon
 him
But let it be with my eyes, and the care
You should owe to your daughter's life and
 safety,
Of which, without him, she's uncapable,
And you'll approve him worthy.
 Vice. O thou shame
Of women ! thy sad father's curse and
 scandal !
With what an impious violence thou tak'st
 from him,
His few short hours of breathing !
 Paul. Do not add, sir,
Weight to your sorrow in the ill-bearing of it.

 Vice. From whom, degenerate monster,
 flow these low
And base affections in thee? what strange
 philtres
Hast thou received? what witch with damned
 spells
Deprived thee of thy reason? Look on me,
Since thou art lost unto thyself, and learn,
From what I suffer for thee, what strange
 tortures
Thou dost prepare thyself.
 Duke. Good sir, take comfort ;
The counsel you bestow'd on me, make use of.
 Paul. This villain, (for such practices in
 that nation
Are very frequent,) it may be, hath forced,
By cunning potions, and by sorcerous
 charms,
This frenzy in her.
 Vice. Sever them.
 Alm. I grow to him.
 Vice. Carry the slave to torture, and wrest
 from him,
By the most cruel means, a free confession
Of his impostures.
 Alm. I will follow him,
And with him take the rack.
 Bora. No ; hear me speak,
I can speak wisely : hurt not my son slave,
But rack or hang my husband, and I care not ;
For I'll be bound body to body with him,
He's very honest, that's his fault.
 Vice. Take hence
This drunken beast.
 Bora. Drunk ! am I drunk? bear witness.
 Cuc. She is indeed distemper'd.
 Vice. Hang them both,
If e'er more they come near the court.
 Cuc. Good sir,
You can recover dead men ; can you cure
A living drunkenness ?
 Paul. 'Tis the harder task :
Go home with her, I'll send you something
 that
Shall once again bring her to better temper,
Or make her sleep for ever.
 Cuc. Which you please, sir.
    [*Exeunt* Cuculo *and* Borachia.
 Vice. Why linger you? rack him first, and
 after break him
Upon the wheel.
 Pedro. Sir, this is more than justice.
 Ant. Is't death in Sicily to be beloved
Of a fair lady ?
 Leon. Though he be a slave,
Remember yet he is a man.
 Vice. I am deaf
To all persuasions :—drag him hence.
    [*The* Guard *carry off* Antonio.

Alm. Do, tyrant,
No more a father, feast thy cruelty
Upon thy daughter; but hell's plagues fall
    on me,
If I inflict not on myself whatever
He can endure for me!
    Vice. Will none restrain her?
    Alm. Death hath a thousand doors to let
        out life,
I shall find one. If Portia's burning coals,
The knife of Lucrece, Cleopatra's aspics,
Famine, deep waters, have the power to
    free me
From a loath'd life, I'll not an hour outlive
    him.
    Pedro. Sister!
    Leon. Dear cousin!
        [*Exit* Almira, *followed by* Pedro *and*
            Leon.
    Vice. Let her perish.
    Paul. Hear me:
The effects of violent love are desperate,
And therefore in the execution of
The slave be not too sudden. I was present
When he was bought, and at that time myself
Made purchase of another; he that sold them
Said that they were companions of one
    country;
Something may rise from this to ease your
    sorrows.
By circumstance I'll learn what's his con-
    dition;
In the mean time use all fair and gentle
    means,
To pacify the lady.
    Vice. I'll endeavour,
As far as grief and anger will give leave,
To do as you direct me.
    Duke. I'll assist you.   [*Exeunt.*

SCENE V.—*A Room in the Prison.*

Enter Pedro *and* Keeper.

    Pedro. Hath he been visited already?
    Keep. Yes, sir,
Like one of better fortune; and to increase
My wonder of it, such as repair to him,
In their behaviour rather appear
Servants, than friends to comfort him.
    Pedro. Go fetch him.   [*Exit* Keeper.
I am bound in gratitude to do more than wish
The life and safety of a man that hath
So well deserved me.

Re-enter Keeper *with* Antonio *in his former
    dress, and* Servant.

    Keep. Here he is, my lord.
    Pedro. Who's here? thou art no conjurer
        to raise

A spirit in the best shape man e'er appeared in,
My friend, the prince of Tarent! doubts,
    forsake me!
I must and will embrace him.
    Ant. Pedro holds
One that loves life for nothing, but to live
To do him service.
    Pedro. You are he, most certain.
Heaven ever make me thankful for this
    bounty.
Run to the Viceroy, let him know this rarity.
                    [*Exit* Keeper.
But how you came here thus—yet, since I
    have you,
Is't not enough I bless the prosperous means
That brought you hither?
    Ant. Dear friend, you shall know all;
And though, in thankfulness, I should begin
Where you deliver'd me——
    Pedro. Pray you pass that over,
That's not worth the relation.
    Ant. You confirm
True friends love to do courtesies, not to hear
    them.
But I'll obey you. In our tedious passage
Towards Malta—I may call it so, for hardly
We had lost the ken of Sicily, but we were
Becalm'd, and hull'd so up and down twelve
    hours;
When, to our more misfortunes, we descried
Eight well-mann'd galleys making amain for
    us,
Of which the arch Turkish pirate, cruel
    Dragut,
Was admiral: I'll not speak what I did
In our defence, but never man did more
Than the brave captain that you sent forth
    with me:
All would not do; courage oppress'd with
    number,
We were boarded, pillaged to the skin, and
    after
Twice sold for slaves; by the pirate first, and
    after
By a Maltese to signior Cuculo,
Which I repent not, since there 'twas my
    fortune
To be to you, my best friend, some ways
    useful—
I thought to cheer you up with this short
    story,
But you grow sad on't.
    Pedro. Have I not just cause,
When I consider I could be so stupid,
As not to see a friend through all disguises;
Or he so far to question my true love,
To keep himself conceal'd?
    Ant. 'Twas fit to do so,
And not to grieve you with the knowledge of

What then I was ; where now I appear to you,
Your sister loving me, and Martino safe,
Like to myself and birth.

Pedro. May you live long so !
How dost thou, honest friend? (your trustiest
servant)
Give me thy hand :—I now can guess by
whom
You are thus furnish'd.

Ant. Troth he met with me
As I was sent to prison, and there brought me
Such things as I had use of.

Pedro. Let's to court,
My father never saw a man so welcome,
As you'll be to him.

Ant. May it prove so, friend ! [*Exeunt.*

SCENE VI.—*A Room in the* Viceroy's
Palace.

Enter Viceroy, Duke of Messina, Cardenes,
Paulo, Captain, Almira, Leonora, Waiting
Women, *and* Attendants.

Vice. The slave changed to the prince of
Tarent, says he?

Capt. Yes, sir, and I the captain of the fort,
Worthy of your displeasure, and the effect of't,
For my deceiving of the trust your excellency
Reposed in me.

Paul. Yet since all hath fallen out
Beyond your hopes, let me become a suitor,
And a prevailing one, to get his pardon.

Alm. O, dearest Leonora, with what fore-
head
Dare I look on him now? too powerful Love,
The best strength of thy unconfined empire
Lies in weak women's hearts : thou art feign'd
blind,
And yet we borrow our best sight from thee.
Could it be else, the person still the same,
Affection over me such power should have,
To make me scorn a prince, and love a slave?

Car. But art thou sure 'tis he?

Capt. Most certain, sir.

Car. Is he in health, strong, vigorous, and
as able
As when he left me dead?

Capt. Your own eyes, sir,
Shall make good my report.

Car. I am glad of it,
And take you comfort in it, sir, there's hope,
Fair hope left for me, to repair mine honour.

Duke. What's that?

Car. I will do something, that shall speak me
Messina's son.

Duke. I like not this :—one word, sir.
[*Whispers the* Viceroy.

Vice. We'll prevent it.—
Nay, look up my Almira ; now I approve

Thy happy choice ; I have forgot my anger ;
I freely do forgive thee.

Alm. May I find
Such easiness in the wrong'd prince of Tarent I
then were happy.

Leon. Rest assured you shall.

Enter Antonio, Pedro, *and* Servant.

Vice. We all with open arms haste to
embrace you.

Duke. Welcome, most welcome !

Car. Stay.

Duke. 'Twas this I fear'd.

Car. Sir, 'tis best known to you, on what
strict terms
The reputation of men's fame and honours
Depends in this so punctual age, in which
A word that may receive a harsh construction,
Is answer'd and defended by the sword :
And you, that know so much, will, I presume,
Be sensibly tender of another's credit,
As you would guard your own.

Ant. I were unjust else.

Car. I have received from your hands
wounds, and deep ones,
My honour in the general report
Tainted and soil'd, for which I will demand
This satisfaction—that you would forgive
My contumelious words and blow, my rash
And unadvised wildness first threw on you.
Thus I would teach the world a better way,
For the recovery of a wounded honour,
Than with a savage fury, not true courage,
Still to run headlong on.

Ant. Can this be serious?

Car. I'll add this, he that does wrong, not
alone
Draws, but makes sharp, his enemy's sword
against
His own life and his honour. I have paid
for't ;
And wish that they who dare most, would
learn from me,
Not to maintain a wrong, but to repent it.

Paul. Why, this is like yourself.

Car. For further proof,
Here, sir, with all my interest, I give up
This lady to you.

Vice. Which I'll make more strong
With my free grant.

Alm. I bring mine own consent,
Which will not weaken it.

All. All joy confirm it !

Ant. Your unexpected courtesies amaze
me,
Which I will study with all love and service
To appear worthy of.

Paul. Pray you, understand, sir,
There are a pair of suitors more, that gladly

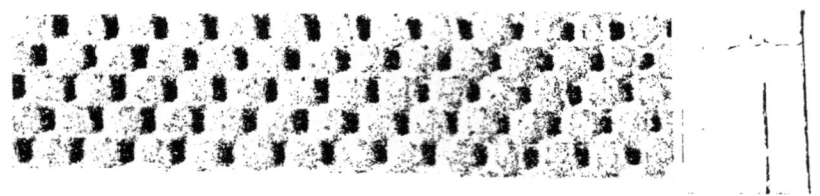

Would hear from you as much as the pleased
    viceroy
Hath said unto the prince of Tarent.
   Duke. Take her;
Her dowry shall be answerable to
Her birth, and your desert.
   Pedro. You make both happy.
   Ant. One only suit remains; that you
    would please
To take again into your highness' favour,

This honest captain: let him have your
   grace;
What's due to his much merit, shall from
   me
Meet liberal rewards.
   Vice. Have your desire.
   Ant. Now may all here that love, as they
   are friends
To our good fortunes, find like prosperous
   ends.   *[Exeunt.*

EPILOGUE.

Custom, and that a law we must obey,
In the way of epilogue bids me something say,
Howe'er to little purpose, since we know,
If you are pleased, unbegg'd you will bestow
A gentle censure: on the other side,
If that this play deserve to be decried
In your opinions, all that I can say
Will never turn the stream the other way.
Your gracious smiles will render us secure;
Your frowns without despair we must endure.

The Bashful Lover.

PROLOGUE.

This from our author, far from all offence
To abler writers, or the audience
Met here to judge his poem. He, by me,
Presents his service, with such modesty
As well becomes his weakness. 'Tis no crime,
He hopes, as we do, in this curious time,
To be a little diffident, when we are
To please so many with one bill of fare.
Let others, building on their merit, say
You're in the wrong, if you move not that way
Which they prescribe you; as you were bound to learn
Their maxims, but uncapable to discern
'Twixt truth and falsehood. Ours had rather be
Censured by some for too much obsequy,
Than tax'd of self opinion. If he hear
That his endeavours thrived, and did appear
Worthy your view, (though made so by your grace,
With some desert,) he, in another place,
Will thankfully report, one leaf of bays
Truly conferr'd upon this work, will raise
More pleasure in him, you the givers free,
Than garlands ravish'd from the virgin tree.

DRAMATIS PERSONÆ.

Gonzaga, *duke of* Mantua.
Lorenzo, *duke of* Tuscany.
Uberti, *prince of* Parma.
Farneze, *cousin to* Gonzaga.
Alonzo, *the ambassador, nephew to* Lorenzo.
Manfroy, *a lord of* Mantua.
Octavio, *formerly general to* Gonzaga, *but now in exile.*
Gothrio, *his servant.*
Galeazzo, *a* Milanese *prince, disguised under the name of* Hortensio.
Julio, *his attendant.*

Pisano, } Florentine *officers.*
Martino, }
Captains.
Milanese *Ambassador.*
Doctor.
Matilda, *daughter to* Gonzaga.
Beatrice, *her waiting woman.*
Maria, *daughter to* Octavio, *disguised as a page, and called* Ascanio.
Waiting Women.
Captains, Soldiers, Guard, Attendants, Page, &c.

SCENE,—*Partly in the City of* Mantua, *and partly in the dutchy.*

ACT I.

SCENE I.—Mantua. *A Space before the Palace.*

Enter Hortensio *and* Julio.

Jul. I dare not cross you, sir, but I would gladly
(Provided you allow it) render you
My personal attendance.

Hort. You shall better
Discharge the duty of an honest servant,
In following my instructions, which you have
Received already, than in questioning
What my intents are, or upon what motives
My stay's resolved in Mantua : believe me,
That servant overdoes, that's too officious ;
And, in presuming to direct your master,

You argue him of weakness, and yourself
Of arrogance and impertinence.

Jul. I have done, sir ;
But what my ends are——

Hort. Honest ones, I know it.
I have my bills of exchange, and all pro-
visions,
Entrusted to you ; you have shown yourself
Just and discreet, what would you more ? and
yet,
To satisfy in some part your curious care,
Hear this, and leave me. I desire to be
Obscured ; and, as I have demean'd myself
These six months past in Mantua, I'll con-
tinue
Unnoted and unknown, and, at the best,
Appear no more than a gentleman, and a
stranger,
That travels for his pleasure.

Jul. With your pardon,
This hardly will hold weight, though I should
swear it,
With your noble friends and brother.

Hort. You may tell them,
Since you will be my tutor, there's a rumour,
Almost cried up into a certainty,
Of wars with Florence, and that I am de-
termined
To see the service : whatever I went forth,
Heaven prospering my intents, I would come
home
A soldier, and a good one.

Jul. Should you get
A captain's place, nay, colonel's, 'twould add
little
To what you are ; few of your rank will follow
That dangerous profession.

Hort. 'Tis the noblest,
And monarchs honour'd in it : but no more,
On my displeasure.

Jul. Saints and angels guard you !
                                    [*Exit.*
Hort. A war, indeed, is threaten'd, nay,
expected,
From Florence ; but it is 'gainst me already
Proclaim'd in Mantua ; I find it here,
No foreign, but intestine war : I have
Defied myself, in giving up my reason
A slave to passion, and am led captive
Before the battle's fought : I fainted, when
I only saw mine enemy, and yielded,
Before that I was charged ; and, though
defeated,
I dare not sue for mercy. Like Ixion,
I look on Juno, feel my heart turn cinders
With an invisible fire ; and yet, should she
Deign to appear clothed in a various cloud,
The majesty of the substance is so sacred,
I durst not clasp the shadow. I behold her

With adoration, feast my eye, while all
My other senses starve ; and, oft frequenting
The place which she makes happy with her
presence,
I never yet had power with tongue or pen
To move her to compassion, or make known
What 'tis I languish for ; yet I must gaze still,
Though it increase my flame :—however, I
Much more than fear I am observed, and
censured
For bold intrusion.   [*Walks by.*

Enter Beatrice *and* Ascanio.

Beat. Know you, boy, that gentleman ?
Asc. Who ? monsieur Melancholy ? hath
not your honour
Mark'd him before ?
Beat. I have seen him often wait
About the princess' lodgings, but ne'er guess'd
What his designs were.
Asc. No ! what a sigh he breath'd now !
Many such will blow up the roof : cn my
small credit
There's gunpowder in them.
Beat. How, crack ! gunpowder ?
He's flesh and blood, and devils only carry
Such roaring stuff about them : you cannot
prove
He is or spirit or conjurer.
Asc. That I grant,
But he's a lover, and that's as bad ; their sighs
Are like petards, and blow all up.
Beat. A lover !
I have been in love myself, but never found
yet
That it could work such strange effects.
Asc. True, madam,
In women it cannot ; for when they miss the
enjoying
Of their full wishes, all their sighs and
heigh-hoes,
At the worst, breed tympanies, and these are
cured too
With a kiss or two of their saint, when he
appears
Between a pair of sheets : but, with us men,
The case is otherwise.
Beat. You will be breech'd, boy,
For your physical maxims.—But how are
you assured,
He is a lover ?
Asc. Who, I ? I know with whom too :
But that is to be whisper'd.   [*Whispers.*
Beat. How ! the princess !
The unparallel'd Matilda ! some proof of it ;
I'll pay for my intelligence.
                            [*Gives* Asc. *money.*
Asc. Let me kiss

Your honour's hand ; 'twas ever fair, but now
Beyond comparison.
   Beat. I guess the reason ;
A giving hand is still fair to the receiver.
   Asc. Your ladyship's in the right ; but to
    the purpose.
He is my client, and pays his fees as duly
As ever usurer did, in a bad cause,
To his man of law ; and yet I get, and
    take them
Both easily and honestly : all the service
I do him, is, to give him notice when
And where the princess will appear; and that
I hope's no treason. If you miss him, when
She goes to the vesper or the matins, hang
    me ;
Or when she takes the air, be sure to find him
Near her coach, at her going forth, or
    coming back :
But if she walk, he's ravish'd. I have seen
    him
Smell out her footing like a lime-hound, and
    nose it
From all the rest of her train.
   Beat. Yet I ne'er saw him
Present her a petition.
   Asc. Nor e'er shall :
He only sees her, sighs, and sacrifices
A tear or two—then vanishes.
   Beat. 'Tis most strange :
What a sad aspéct he wears ! but I'll make
    use of't.
The princess is much troubled with the
    threats
That come from Florence ; I will bring her
    to him,
The novelty may afford her sport, and help
To purge deep melancholy. Boy, can you
    stay
Your client here for the third part of an hour?
I have some ends in't.
   Asc. Stay him, madam ! fear not:
The present receipt of a round sum of crowns,
And that will draw most gallants from their
    prayers,
Cannot drag him from me.
   Beat. See you do.   [*Exit.*
   Asc. Ne'er doubt me.
I'll put him out of his dream.—Good mor-
    row, signior.
   Hort. My little friend, good morrow.
    Hath the princess
Slept well to-night ?
   Asc. I hear not from her women
One murmur to the contrary.
   Hort. Heaven be praised for't !
Does she go to church this morning?
   Asc. Troth, I know not ;
I keep no key of her devotion, signior.

   Hort. Goes she abroad? pray tell me.
   Asc. 'Tis thought rather,
She is resolv'd to keep her chamber.
   Hort. Ah me !
   Asc. Why do you sigh? if that you have
    a business
To be dispatch'd in court, shew ready money,
You shall find those that will prefer it for
    you.
   Hort. Business! can any man have busi-
    ness, but
To see her; then admire her, and pray for her,
She being composed of goodness? for myself,
I find it a degree of happiness
But to be near her, and I think I pay
A strict religious vow, when I behold her ;
And that's all my ambition.
   Asc. I believe you:
Yet, she being absent, you may spend some
    hours
With profit and delight too. After dinner,
The duke gives audience to a rough am-
    bassador,
Whom yet I never saw, nor heard his title,
Employ'd from Florence ; I'll help you to
    a place,
Where you shall see and hear all.
   Hort. 'Tis not worth
My observation.
   Asc. What think you of
An excellent comedy, to be presented
For his entertainment ? he that penn'd it is
The poet of the time, and all the ladies,
(I mean the amorous and learned ones,)
Except the princess, will be there to grace it.
   Hort. What's that to me ? without her all
    is nothing ;
The light that shines in court Cimmerian
    darkness ;
I will to bed again, and there contemplate
On her perfections.

   Re-enter Beatrice *with* Matilda, *and two*
    Waiting Women.

   Asc. Stay, sir, see ! the princess,
Beyond our hopes.
   Hort. Take that. [*Gives him money.*]—As
    Moors salute
The rising sun with joyful superstition,
I could fall down and worship.——O my
    heart !
Like Phœbe breaking through an envious
    cloud,
Or something which no simile can express,
She shews to me: a reverent fear, but
    blended
With wonder and amazement, does possess
    me.
Now glut thyself, my famish'd eye !
                   M M

Beat. That's he,
An't please your excellence.
  1 *Wom.* Observe his posture,
But with a quarter-look.
  2 *Wom.* Your eye fix'd on him,
Will breed astonishment.
  Matil. A comely gentleman!
I would not question your relation, lady,
Yet faintly can believe it. How he eyes me!
Will he not speak?
  Beat. Your excellence hath deprived him
Of speech and motion.
  Matil. 'Tis most strange.
  Asc. These fits
Are usual with him.
  Matil. Is it not, Ascanio,
A personated folly! or he a statue?
If it be, it is a masterpiece; for man
I cannot think him.
  Beat. For your sport, vouchsafe him
A little conference.
  Matil. In compassion rather:
For should he love me, as you say, (though
    hopeless,)
It should not be return'd with scorn; that
    were
An inhumanity, which my birth nor honour
Could privilege, were they greater.   Now I
    perceive
He has life and motion in him.   To whom,
    lady,
Pays he that duty?
      [*Hortensio, bowing, offers to go off.*
  Beat. Sans doubt, to yourself.
  Matil. And whither goes he now?
  Asc. To his private lodging,
But to what end I know not; this is all
I ever noted in him.
  Matil. Call him back:
In pity I stand bound to counsel him,
Howe'er I am denied, though I were willing,
To ease his sufferings.
  Asc. Signior! the princess
Commands you to attend her.
  Hort. [*Returns.*] How! the princess!
Am I betray'd?
  Asc. What a lump of flesh is this!
You are betray'd, sir, to a better fortune
Than you durst ever hope for.   What a
    Tantalus
Do you make yourself! the flying fruit stays
    for you,
And the water that you long'd for, rising up
Above your lip, do you refuse to taste it?
Move faster, sluggish camel, or I'll thrust
This goad in your breech: had I such a
    promising beard,
I should need the reins, not spurs.
  Matil. You may come nearer.

Why do you shake, sir?   If I flatter not
Myself, there's no deformity about me,
Nor any part so monstrous, to beget
An ague in you.
  Hort. It proceeds not, madam,
From guilt, but reverence.
  Matil. I believe you, sir;
Have you a suit to me?
  Hort. Your excellence
Is wondrous fair.
  Matil. I thank your good opinion.
  Hort. And I beseech you that I may have
    license
To kneel to you.
  Matil. A suit I cannot cross.
  Hort. I humbly thank your excellence.
                              [*Kneels.*
  Matil. But what,
As you are prostrate on your knee before me,
Is your petition?
  Hort. I have none, great princess.
  Matil. Do you kneel for nothing?
  Hort. Yes, I have a suit,
But such a one, as, if denied, will kill me.
  Matil. Take comfort: it must be of some
    strange nature,
Unfitting you to ask, or me to grant,
If I refuse it.
  Hort. It is, madam——
  Matil. Out with't.
  Hort. That I may not offend you, this is all,
When I presume to look on you.
  Asc. A flat eunuch!
To look on her? I should desire myself
To move a little further.
  Matil. Only that?
  Hort. And I beseech you, madam, to
    believe
I never did yet with a wanton eye;
Or cherish one lascivious wish beyond it.
  Beat. You'll never make good courtier, or
    be
In grace with ladies.
  1 *Wom.* Or us waiting women,
If that be your *nil ultra*.
  2 *Wom.* He's no gentleman,
On my virginity, it is apparent:
My tailor has more boldness; nay, my shoe-
    maker
Will fumble a little further, he could not have
The length of my foot else.
  Matil. Only to look on me!
Ends your ambition there?
  Hort. It does, great lady,—
And that confined too, and at fitting distance:
The fly that plays too near the flame burns in it.
As I behold the sun, the stars, the temples,
I look on you, and wish it were no sin
Should I adore you.

Matil. Come, there's something more in't;
And since that you will make a goddess of me,
As such a one I'll tell you, I desire not
The meanest altar raised up to mine honour
To be pull'd down ; I can accept from you,
Be your condition ne'er so far beneath me,
One grain of incense with devotion offer'd,
Beyond all perfumes, or Sabæan spices,
By one that proudly thinks he merits in it :
I know you love me. ·
Hort. Next to heaven, madam, ·
And with as pure a zeal. That, we behold
With the eyes of contemplation, but can
Arrive no nearer to it in this life ;
But when that is divorced, my soul shall
      serve yours,
And witness my affection.
Matil. Pray you, rise ;
But wait my further pleasure,
            [Hort. *rises and walks aside.*

Enter Farneze *and* Uberti. ·

Farn. I'll present you,
And give you proof I am your friend, a true
      one ;
And in my pleading for you, teach the age,
That calls, erroneously, friendship but a
      name,
It is a substance.—Madam, I am bold
To trench so far upon your privacy,
As to desire my friend (let not that wrong him,
For he's a worthy one) may have the honour
To kiss your hand.
Matil. His own worth challenges
A greater favour.
Farn. Your acknowledgment
Confirms it, madam. If you look on him
As he's built up a man, without addition
Of fortune's liberal favours, wealth or titles,
He doth deserve no usual entertainment :
But, as he is a prince, and for your service
Hath left fair Parma, that acknowledges
No other lord, and, uncompell'd, exposes
His person to the dangers of the war,
Ready to break in storms upon our heads ;
In noble thankfulness you may vouchsafe him
Nearer respect, and such grace as may
      nourish,
Not kill, his amorous hopes.
Matil. Cousin, you know
I am not the disposer of myself,
The duke my father challenges that power :
Yet thus much I dare promise ; prince Uberti
Shall find the seed of service that he sows,
Falls not on barren ground.
Uber. For this high favour
I am your creature, and profess I owe you
Whatever I call mine. [*They walk aside.*

Hort. This great lord is
A suitor to the princess.
Asc. True, he is so.
Hort. Fame gives him out too for a brave
      commander.
Asc. And in it does him but deserved right ;
The duke hath made him general of his horse,
On that assurance.
Hort. And the lord Farneze,
Pleads for him, as it seems.
Asc. 'Tis too apparent :
And, this consider'd, give me leave to ask
What hope have you, sir ?
Hort. I may still look on her,
Howe'er he wear the garland.
Asc. A thin diet,
And will not feed you fat, sir.
Uber. I rejoice,
Rare princess, that you are not to be won
By carpet-courtship, but the sword ; with this
Steel pen I'll write on Florence' helm how
      much
I can, and dare do for you.
Matil. 'Tis not question'd.
Some private business of mine own disposed of,
I'll meet you in the presence.
· *Uber.* Ever your servant.
            [*Exeunt* Uberti *and* Farneze.
Matil. Now, sir, to you. You have ob-
      served, I doubt not,
For lovers are sharp-sighted, to what purpose
This prince solicits me ; and yet I am not
So taken with his worth, but that I can
Vouchsafe you further parle. The first com-
      mand
That I'll impose upon you, is to hear ·
And follow my good counsel : I am not ·
Offended that you love me, persist in it,
But love me virtuously ; such love may spur
      you
To noble undertakings, which achieved,
Will raise you into name, preferment,
      honour :
For all which, though you ne'er enjoy my
      person,
(For that's impossible,) you are indebted
To your high aims : visit me when you
      please,
I do allow it, nor will blush to own you,
So you confine yourself to what you promise,
As my virtuous servant.
Beat. Farewell, sir ! you have
An unexpected cordial.
Asc. May it work well !
            [*Exeunt all but* Hort.
Hort. *Your love*—yes, so she said, *may
      spur you to*
Brave undertakings: adding this, *You may
Visit me when you please.* Is this allow'd me,

And any act, within the power of man,
Impossible to be effected? no:
I will break through all oppositions that
May stop me in my full career to honour :
And, borrowing strength to do, from her
    high favour,
Add something to Alcides' greatest labour.
                                    [*Exit.*

SCENE II.—*The same.   A State-room in
    the Palace.*

Enter Gonzaga, Uberti, Farneze, Manfroy,
    and Attendants.

Gon. This is your place ; and, were it in
    our power,   [*Leads* Uberti *to the state.*
You should have greater honour, prince of
    Parma ;
The rest know theirs.—Let some attend
    with care
On the ambassador, and let my daughter
Be present at his audience.
                        [*Exeunt* Attendants.
—Reach a chair,
We'll do all fit respects ; and, pray you,
    put on
Your milder looks, you are in a place where
    frowns
Are no prevailing agents.   [*To* Uberti.

Enter at one door Alonzo *and* Attendants :
    Matilda, Beatrice, Ascanio, Hortensio,
    and Waiting Women, *at the other.*

Asc. I have seen
More than a wolf, a Gorgon !   [*Swoons.*
Gon. What's the matter?
Matild. A page of mine is fallen into a
    swoon ;
Look to him carefully.
                    [Ascanio *is carried out.*
Gon. Now, when you please,
The cause that brought you hither?
Alon. The protraction
Of my dispatch forgotten, from Lorenzo,
The Tuscan duke, thus much to you,
    Gonzaga,
The duke of Mantua. By me, his nephew,
He does salute you fairly, and entreats
(A word not suitable to his power and
    greatness)
You would consent to tender that which he,
Unwillingly, must force, if contradicted.
Ambition, in a private man a vice,
Is, in a prince, the virtue.
Gon. To the purpose ;
These ambages are impertinent.
Alon. He demands
The fair Matilda, for I dare not take
From her perfections, in a noble way ;
And in creating her the comfort of

His royal bed, to raise her to a height
Her flattering hopes could not aspire, where
    she
With wonder shall be gazed upon, and live
The envy of her sex.
Gon. Suppose this granted.
Uber. Or, if denied, what follows?
Alon. Present war,
With all extremities the conqueror can
Inflict upon the vanquish'd.
Uber. Grant me license
To answer this defiance. What intelligence
Holds your proud master with the will of
    heaven,
That, ere the uncertain die of war be thrown,
He dares assure himself the victory?
Are his unjust invading arms of fire?
Or those we put on in defence of right,
Like chaff, to be consumed in the encounter?
I look on your dimensions, and find not
Mine own of lesser size ; the blood that fills
My veins, as hot as yours ; my sword as sharp,
My nerves of equal strength, my heart as
    good ;
And, confident we have the better cause,
Why should we fear the trial?
Far. You presume
You are superior in numbers ; we
Lay hold upon the surest anchor, virtue ;
Which, when the tempest of the war roars
    loudest,
Must prove a strong protection.
Gon. Two main reasons
(Seconding those you have already heard)
Give us encouragement ; the duty that
I owe my mother-country, and the love
Descending to my daughter. For the first,
Should I betray her liberty, I deserv'd
To have my name with infamy razed from
The catalogue of good princes ; and I should
Unnaturally forget I am a father,
If, like a Tartar, or for fear or profit,
I should consign her, as a bondwoman,
To be disposed of at another's pleasure ;
Her own consent or favour never sued for,
And mine by force exacted. No, Alonzo,
She is my only child, my heir ; and, if
A father's eyes deceive me not, the hand
Of prodigal nature hath given so much to
    her,
As, in the former ages, kings would rise up
In her defence, and make her cause their
    quarrel :
Nor can she, if that any spark remain
To kindle a desire to be possess'd
Of such a beauty, in our time, want swords
To guard it safe from violence.
Hort. I must speak,
Or I shall burst ; now to be silent were

A kind of blasphemy : if such purity,
Such innocence, an abstract of perfection,
The soul of beauty, virtue, in a word,
A temple of things sacred, should groan
  under
The burthen of oppression, we might
Accuse the saints, and tax the Powers above
  us
Of negligence or injustice.——Pardon, sir,
A stranger's boldness, and in your mercy
  call it
True zeal, not rudeness. In a cause like this,
The husbandman would change his plough-
  ing-irons
To weapons of defence, and leave the earth
Untill'd, although a general dearth should
  follow :
The student would forswear his book, the
  lawyer
Put off his thriving gown, and, without pay,
Conclude this cause is to be fought, not
  pleaded.
The women will turn Amazons, as their sex
In her were wrong'd ; and boys write down
  their names
In the muster-book for soldiers.
  Gon. Take my hand :
Whate'er you are, I thank you. How are
  you call'd ?
  Hort. Hortensio, a Milanese.
  Gon. I wish
Mantua had many such.—My lord am-
  bassador,
Some privacy, if you please ; Manfroy, you
  may
Partake it, and advise us.
                    [*They walk aside.*
  Uber. Do you know, friend,
What this man is, or of what country ?
  Farn. Neither.
  Uber. I'll question him myself. What are
  you, sir?
  Hort. A gentleman.
  Uber. But if there be gradation
In gentry, as the heralds say, you have
Been over-bold in the presence of your
  betters.
  Hort. My betters, sir !
  Uber. Your betters. As I take it,
You are no prince.
  Hort. 'Tis fortune's gift you were born one;
I have not heard that glorious title crowns
  you,
As a reward of virtue : it may be,
The first of your house deserv'd it ; yet his
  merits
You can but faintly call your own.
  Matil. Well answer'd.
  Uber. You come up to me.

  Hort. I would not turn my back,
If you were the duke of Florence, though
  you charged me
I' the head of your troops.
  Uber. Tell me in gentler language,
Your passionate speech induces me to think
  so,
Do you love the princess ?
  Hort. Were you mine enemy,
Your foot upon my breast, sword at my
  throat,
Even then I would profess it. The ascent
To the height of honour is by arts or arms ;
And if such an unequall'd prize might fall
On him that did deserve best in defence
Of this rare princess in the day of battle,
I should lead you a way would make your
  greatness
Sweat drops of blood to follow.
  Uber. Can your excellence
Hear this without rebuke from one unknown?
Is he a rival for a prince ?
  Matil. My lord,
You take that liberty I never gave you.
In justice you should give encouragement
To him, or any man, that freely offers
His life to do me service, not deter him ;
I give no suffrage to it. Grant he loves me,
As he professes, how are you wrong'd in it ?
Would you have all men hate me but your-
  self ?
No more of this, I pray you : if this gentle-
  man
Fight for my freedom, in a fit proportion
To his desert and quality, I can
And will reward him ; yet give you no cause
Of jealousy or envy.
  Hort. Heavenly lady !
  Gon. No peace but on such poor and base
  conditions !
We will not buy it at that rate : return
This answer to your master : Though we
  wish'd
To hold fair quarter with him, on such terms
As honour would give way to, we are not
So thunderstruck with the loud voice of war,
As to acknowledge him our lord before
His sword hath made us vassals : we long
  since
Have had intelligence of the unjust gripe
He purposed to lay on us ; neither are we
So unprovided as you think, my lord ;
He shall not need so seek us ; we will meet
  him,
And prove the fortune of a day, perhaps
Sooner than he expects.
  Alon. And find repentance,
When 'tis too late. Farewell.
              [*Exit with* Farnezo.

Gon. No, my Matilda,
We must not part so. Beasts and birds of
     prey,
To their last gasp, defend their brood; and
     Florence,
Over thy father's breast shall march up to
     thee,
Before he force affection.   The arms
That thou must put on for us and thyself,
Are prayers and pure devotion, which will
Be heard, Matilda. Manfroy, to your trust
We do give up the city, and my daughter;
On both keep a strong guard—No tears,
     they are ominous.
O my Octavio, my tried Octavio,
In all my dangers! now I want thy service,
In passion recompensed with banishment.
Error of princes, who hate virtue when
She's present with us, and in vain admire her
When she is absent!—'tis too late to think
     on't.
The wish'd-for time is come, princely Uberti,
To shew your valour; friends, being to do,
     not talk,
All rhetoric is fruitless, only this,
Fate cannot rob you of deserv'd applause,
Whether you win or lose in such a cause.
                              [*Exeunt.*

————

ACT II.

SCENE I.—Mantua. *A Room in the
          Palace.*

Enter Matilda, Beatrice, *and* Waiting
          Women.

Matil. No matter for the ring I ask'd you
     for.
The boy not to be found?
Beat. Nor heard of, madam.
1 *Wom.* He hath been sought and search'd
     for, house by house,
Nay, every nook of the city, but to no pur-
     pose.
2 *Wom.* And how he should escape hence,
     the lord Manfroy
Being so vigilant o'er the guards, appears
A thing impossible.
Matil. I never saw him,
Since he swoon'd in the presence, when my
     father
Gave audience to the ambassador: but I feel
A sad miss of him; on any slight occasion,
He would find out such pretty arguments
To make me sport, and with such witty
     sweetness
Deliver his opinion, that I must
Ingenuously confess his harmless mirth,

When I was most oppress'd with care,
     wrought more
In the removing of't, than music on me.
Beat. An't please your excellence, I have
     observed him
Waggishly witty; yet, sometimes, on the
     sudden,
He would be very pensive; and then talk
So feelingly of love, as if he had
Tasted the bitter sweets of't.
1 *Wom.* He would tell, too,
A pretty tale of a sister, that had been
Deceived by her sweetheart; and then,
     weeping, swear
He wonder'd how men could be false.
2 *Wom.* And that
When he was a knight, he'd be the ladies'
     champion,
And travel o'er the world to kill such lovers,
As durst play false with their mistresses.
Matil. I am sure
I want his company.

Enter Manfroy.

Man. There are letters, madam,
In post come from the duke; but I am
     charged,
By the careful bringer, not to open them
But in your presence.
Matil. Heaven preserve my father!
Good news, an't be thy will!
Man. Patience must arm you
Against what's ill.
Matil. I'll hear them in my cabinet.
                              [*Exeunt.*

SCENE II.—*The Dutchy of* Mantua.
          Gonzaga's *Camp.*

Enter Hortensio *and* Ascanio.

Hort. Why have you left the safety of the
     city,
And service of the princess, to partake
The dangers of the camp? and at a time too
When the armies are in view, and every
     minute
The dreadful charge expected?
Asc. You appear
So far beyond yourself, as you are now,
Arm'd like a soldier, (though I grant your
     presence
Was ever gracious,) that I grow enamour'd
Of the profession: in the horror of it,
There is a kind of majesty.
Hort. But too heavy
To sit on thy soft shoulders, youth; retire
To the duke's tent, that's guarded.
Asc. Sir, I come
To serve you; knight-adventurers are allow'd

Their pages, and I bring a will that shall
Supply my want of power.

Hort. To serve me, boy !
I wish, believe it, that 'twere in my nerves
To do thee any service ; and thou shalt,
If I survive the fortune of this day,
Be satisfied I am serious.

Asc. I am not
To be put off so, sir. Since you do neglect
My offer'd duty, I must use the power
I bring along with me, that may command
you :
You have seen this ring—

Hort. Made rich by being worn
Upon the princess' finger.

Asc. 'Tis a favour
To you, by me sent from her : view it better ;
But why coy to receive it ?

Hort. I am unworthy
Of such a blessing, I have done nothing
yet
That may deserve it ; no commander's blood
Of the adverse party hath yet died my sword
Drawn out in her defence. I must not
take it.
This were a triumph for me when I had
Made Florence' duke my prisoner, and
compell'd him
To kneel for mercy at her feet.

Asc. 'Twas sent, sir,
To put you in mind whose cause it is you
fight for ;
And, as I am her creature, to revenge
A wrong to me done.

Hort. By what man ?

Asc. Alonzo.

Hort. The ambassador ?

Asc. The same.

Hort. Let it suffice.
I know him by his armour and his horse ;
And if we meet——[*Trumpets sound.*]—I
am cut off, the alarum
Commands me hence : sweet youth, fall off.

Asc. I must not ;
You are too noble to receive a wound
Upon your back, and, following close be-
hind you,
I am secure ; though I could wish my bosom
Were your defence.

Hort. Thy kindness will undo thee.
[*Exeunt.*

SCENE III.—*The same.* Lorenzo's *Camp.*

Enter Lorenzo, Alonzo, Pisano, *and*
Martino.

Lor. We'll charge the main battalia, fall
you
Upon the van · preserve your troops entire,

To force the rear : he dies that breaks his
ranks,
Till all be ours, and sure.

Pis. 'Tis so proclaim'd. [*Exeunt.*

Fighting and alarum. Enter Hortensio,
Ascanio, *and* Alonzo.

Hort. 'Tis he, Ascanio :—Stand !

Alon. I never shunn'd
A single opposition ; but tell me
Why, in the battle, of all men, thou hast
Made choice of me ?

Hort. Look on this youth ; his cause
Sits on my sword.

Alon. I know him not.

Hort. I'll help
Your memory. [*They fight.*

Asc. What have I done ? I am doubtful
To whom to wish the victory ; for, still
My resolution wavering, I so love
The enemy that wrong'd me, that I cannot,
Without repentance, wish success to him
That seeks to do me right.—[*Alonzo falls.*]
—Alas, he's fall'n !
As you are gentle, hold, sir ! or, if I want ·
Power to persuade so far, I conjure you
By her loved name I am sent from.

Hort. 'Tis a charm
Too strong to be resisted : he is yours.
Yet, why you should make suit to save that
life
Which you so late desired should be cut
off,
For injuries received, begets my wonder.

Asc. Alas ! we foolish, spleenful boys
would have
We know not what ; I have some private
reasons,
But now not to be told.

Hort. Shall I take him prisoner ?

Asc.. By no means, sir ; I will not save
his life,
To rob him of his honour : when you give,
Give not by halves. One short word, and I
follow. [*Exit* Hortensio.
My lord Alonzo, if you have received
A benefit, and would know to whom you
owe it,
Remember what your entertainment was
At old Octavio's house, one you call'd
friend,
And how you did return it. [*Exit.*

Alon. I remember
I did not well ; but it is now no time
To think upon't : my wounded honour calls
For reparation, I must quench my fury
For this disgrace, in blood, and some shall
smart for't. [*Exit.*

SCENE IV.—*The same. A Forest.*

Alarum continued. Enter Uberti, *and*
Farneze *wounded.*

Farn. O prince Uberti, valour cannot
save us ;
The body of our army's pierced and broken,
The wings are routed, and our scatter'd troops
Not to be rallied up.

Uber. 'Tis yet some comfort,
The enemy must say we were not wanting
In courage or direction ; and we may
Accuse the Powers above as partial, when
A good cause, well defended too, must suffer
For want of fortune.

Farn. All is lost ; the duke
Too far engaged, I fear, to be brought off:
Three times I did attempt his rescue, but
With odds was beaten back ; only the
stranger,
I speak it to my shame, still follow'd him,
Cutting his way ; but 'tis beyond my hopes,
That either should return.

Uber. That noble stranger,
Whom I, in my proud vanity of greatness,
As one unknown contemn'd, when I was
thrown
Out of my saddle by the great duke's lance,
Horsed me again, in spite of all that made
Resistance ; and then whisper'd in mine ear,
*Fight bravely, prince Uberti, there's no way
else,*
To the fair Matilda's favour.

Farn. 'Twas done nobly.

Uber. In you, my bosom-friend, I had
call'd it noble :
But such a courtesy from a rival merits
The highest attribute.

Enter Hortensio *and* Gonzaga.

Farn. Stand on your guard ;
We are pursued.

Uber. Preserv'd ! wonder on wonder.

Farn. The duke in safety !

Gon. Pay your thanks, Farneze,
To this brave man, if I may call him so,
Whose acts were more than human. If
thou art
My better angel, from my infancy
Design'd to guard me, like thyself appear,
For sure thou'rt more than mortal.

Hort. No, great sir,
A weak and sinful man ; though I have done
you
Some prosperous service that hath found your
favour,
I am lost to myself : but lose not you
The offer'd opportunity to delude
The hot-pursuing enemy ; these woods,

Nor the dark veil of night, cannot conceal you,
If you dwell long here. You may rise again;
But I am fallen for ever.

Farn. Rather borne up
To the supreme sphere of honour.

Uber. I confess
My life your gift.

Gon. My liberty.

Uber. You have snatch'd
The wreath of conquest from the victor's head,
And do alone, in scorn of Lorenzo's fortune,
Though we are slaved, by true heroic valour
Deserve a triumph.

Gon. From whence then proceeds
This poor dejection ?

Hort. In one suit I'll tell you,
Which I beseech you grant :—I loved your
daughter ;
But how? as beggars in their wounded fancy,
Hope to be monarchs : I long languish'd for
her,
But did receive no cordial, but what
Despair, my rough physician, prescribed me.
A length her goodness and compassion
found it ;
And, whereas I expected, and with reason,
The distance and disparity consider'd
Between her birth and mine, she would con-
temn me,
The princess gave me comfort.

Gon. In what measure?

Hort. She did admit me for her knight
and servant,
And spurr'd me to do something in this battle,
Fought for her liberty, that might not blemish
So fair a favour.

Gon. This you have perform'd,
To the height of admiration.

Uber. I subscribe to't,
That am your rival.

Hort. You are charitable :
But how short of my hopes, nay, the assurance
Of those achievements which my love and
youth
Already held accomplish'd, this day's fortune
Must sadly answer. What I did, she gave me
The strength to do ; her piety preserved
Her father, and her gratitude for the dangers
You threw yourself into for her defence,
Protected you by me her instrument :
But when I came to strike in mine own cause,
And to do something so remarkable,
That should at my return command her
thanks
And gracious entertainment, then, alas !
I fainted like a coward. I made a vow, too,
(And it is register'd,) ne'er to presume
To come into her presence, if I brought not
Her fears and dangers bound in fetters to her,

Which now's impossible. —— Hark! the enemy
Makes his approaches: save yourselves: this only
Deliver to her sweetness; I have done
My poor endeavours, and pray her not repent
Her goodness to me. May you live to serve her,
This loss recover'd, with a happier fate!
And make use of this sword: arms I abjure,
And conversation of men; I'll seek out
Some unfrequented cave, and die love's martyr. [*Exit hastily.*

Gon. Follow him.

Uber. 'Tis in vain; his nimble feet
Have borne him from my sight.

Gon. I suffer for him.

Farn. We share in it; but must not, sir, forget
Your means of safety.

Uber. In the war I have served you,
And to the death will follow you.

Gon. 'Tis not fit,
We must divide ourselves. My daughter——
If I retain yet
A sovereign's power o'er thee, or friend's with you,
Do, and dispute not; by my example change
Your habits: as I thus put off my purple,
Ambition dies; this garment of a shepherd,
Left here by chance, will serve; in lieu of it,
I leave this to the owner. Raise new forces,
And meet me at St. Leo's fort; my daughter,
As I commanded Manfroy, there will meet us.
The city cannot hold out, we must part:
Farewell, thy hand.

Farn. You still shall have my heart.
[*Exeunt.*

SCENE V.—*The same. Another part of the Forest.*

Enter Lorenzo, Alonzo, Pisano, Martino, Captains, *and* Soldiers.

Lor. The day is ours, though it cost dear; yet 'tis not
Enough to get a victory, if we lose
The true use of it. We have hitherto
Held back your forward swords, and in our fear
Of ambushes, deferr'd the wish'd reward
Due to your bloody toil: but now give freedom,
Nay, license to your fury and revenge;
Now glut yourselves with prey; let not the night,
Nor these thick woods, give sanctuary to
The fear-struck hares, our enemies: fire these trees,

And force the wretches to forsake their holes,
And offer their scorch'd bodies to your swords,
Or burn them as a sacrifice to your angers.
Who brings Gonzaga's head, or takes him prisoner,
(Which I incline to rather, that he may
Be sensible of those tortures, which I vow
To inflict upon him for denial of
His daughter to our bed,) shall have a blank,
With our hand and signet made authentical,
In which he may write down himself, what wealth
Or honours he desires.

Alon. The great duke's will
Shall be obey'd.

Pisan. Put it in execution.

Mart. Begirt the wood, and fire it.

Sold. Follow, follow! [*Exeunt.*

SCENE VI.—*The same. Another part of the same.*

Enter Farneze, *disguised as a* Florentine Soldier.

Farn. Uberti, prince Uberti! O my friend,
Dearer than life! I have lost thee. Cruel fortune,
Unsatisfied with our sufferings! we no sooner
Were parted from the duke, and e'en then ready
To take a mutual farewell, when a troop
Of the enemy's horse fell on us; we were forced
To take the woods again, but, in our flight,
Their hot pursuit divided us: we had been happy
If we had died together. To survive him,
To me is worse than death; and therefore should not
Embrace the means of my escape, though offer'd.
When nature gave us life she gave a burthen,
But at our pleasure not to be cast off,
Though weary of it; and my reason prompts me,
This habit of a Florentine, which I took
From a dying soldier, may keep me unknown,
Till opportunity mark me out a way
For flight, and with security.

Enter Uberti.

Uber. Was there ever
Such a night of horror?

Farn. My friend's voice! I now
In part forgive thee, fortune.

Uber. The wood flames,
The bloody sword devours all that it meets,
And death in several shapes rides here in triumph.

I am like a stag closed in a toil, my life,
As soon as found, the cruel huntsman's
      prey :
Why fliest thou, then, what is inevitable?
Better to fall with manly wounds before
Thy cruel enemy, than survive thine honour:
And yet to charge him, and die unrevenged,
Mere desperation.
      Farn. Heroic spirit !
      Uber. Mine own life I contemn, and would
      not save it
But for the future service of the duke,
And safety of his daughter ; having means,
If I escape, to raise a second army ;
And, what is nearest to me, to enjoy
My friend Farneze.
      Farn. I am still his care.
      Uber. What shall I do? if I call loud, the
      foe
That hath begirt the wood, will hear the
      sound.
Shall I return by the same path ? I cannot,
The darkness of the night conceals it from
      me ;
Something I must resolve.
      Farn. Let friendship rouse
Thy sleeping soul, Farneze : wilt thou suffer
Thy friend, a prince, nay, one that may set
      free
Thy captived country, perish, when 'tis in
Thy power, with this disguise, to save his life?
Thou hast lived too long, therefore resolve
      to die ;
Thou hast seen thy country ruin'd, and thy
      master
Compell'd to shameful flight ; the fields and
      woods
Strew'd o'er with carcases of thy fellow-
      soldiers :
The miseries thou art fallen in, and before
Thy eyes the horror of this place, and
      thousand
Calamities to come ; and after all these,
Can any hope remain ? shake off delays :
Dost thou doubt yet?   To save a citizen,
The conquering Roman in a general
Esteem'd the highest honour : can it be then
Inglorious to preserve a prince? thy friend?—
Uberti, prince Uberti ! [*Aloud.*] use this
      means
Of thy escape ;—
      [*Pulls off his Florentine uniform,
      and casts it before* Uberti.
      conceal'd in this, thou mayst
Pass through the enemy's guards : the time
      denies
Longer discourse ; thou hast a noble end,
Live, therefore, mindful of thy dying friend.
                                    [*Exit.*

      Uber. Farneze, stay thy hasty steps !
      Farneze !
Thy friend Uberti calls thee : 'tis in vain;
He's gone to death an innocent, and makes
      life,
The benefit he confers on me, my guilt.
Thou art too covetous of another's safety,
Too prodigal and careless of thine own.
'Tis a deceit in friendship to enjoin me
To put this garment on, and live, that he
May have alone the honour to die nobly.
O cruel piety, in our equal danger
To rob thyself of that thou giv'st thy friend !
It must not be ; I will restore his gift,
And die before him.   How? where shall I
      find him?——
Thou art o'ercome in friendship ; yield,
      Uberti,
To the extremity of the time, and live :
A heavy ransome ! but it must be paid.
I will put on this habit : pitying heaven,
As it loves goodness, may protect my friend,
And give me means to satisfy the debt
I stand engaged for ; if not, pale despair,
I dare thy worst ; thou canst but bid me die,
And so much I'll force from an enemy.
                                    [*Exit.*

      SCENE VII.—*The same.* Lorenzo's
                              Camp.

Enter Alonzo *and* Pisano, *with* Farneze
bound; Soldiers *with torches,* Farneze's
sword in one of the Soldier's *hands.*

      Alon. I know him, he's a man of ransome.
      Pisan. True ;
But if he live, 'tis to be paid to me.
      Alon. I forced him to the woods.
      Pisan. But my art found him ;
Nor will I brook a partner in the prey
My fortune gave me.
      Alon. Render him, or expect
The point of this.
      Pisan. Were it lightning, I would meet it,
Rather than be outbraved.
      Alon. I thus decide
The difference.
      Pisan. My sword shall plead my title.
                                    [*They fight.*

Enter Lorenzo, Martino, Captains, *and*
                        Attendants.

      Lor. Ha ! where learn'd you this disci-
      pline? my commanders
Opposed 'gainst one another! what blind fury
Brings forth this brawl? Alonzo and Pisano
At bloody difference ! hold, or I tilt
At both as enemies.—Now speak ; how grew
This strange division ?
      Pisan. Against all right,

By force Alonzo strives to reap the harvest
Sown by my labour.
   Alon. Sir, this is my prisoner,
The purchase of my sword, which proud Pisano,
That hath no interest in him, would take
   from me.
   Pisan. Did not the presence of the duke
   forbid me,
I would say——
   Alon. What?
   Pisan. 'Tis false.
   Lor. Before my face!
Keep them asunder. And was this the cause
Of such a mortal quarrel, this the base
To raise your fury on? the ties of blood,
Of fellowship in arms, respect, obedience
To me, your prince and general, no more
Prevailing on you? this a price for which
You would betray our victory, or wound
Your reputation with mutinies,
Forgetful of yourselves, allegiance, honour?—
This is a course to throw us headlong down
From that proud height of empire, upon
   which
We were securely seated. Shall division
O'erturn what concord built? if you desire
To bathe your swords in blood, the enemy
Still flies before you: would you have spoil?
   the country
Lies open to you. O unheard-of madness!
What greater mischief could Gonzaga wish
   us,
Than you pluck on our heads? no, my
   brave leaders,
Let unity dwell in our tents, and discord
Be banish'd to our enemies.
   Alon. Take the prisoner,
I do give up my title.
   Pisan. I desire
Your friendship, and will buy it; he is yours.
             [*They embrace.*
   Alon. No man's a faithful judge in his
   own cause;
Let the duke determine of him: we are
   friends, sir.
   Lor. Shew it in emulation to o'ertake
The flying foe; this cursed wretch disposed of,
With our whole strength we'll follow.
      [*Exeunt* Alonzo *and* Pisano *embracing.*
   Farn. Death at length
Will set a period to calamity:
I see it in this tyrant's frowns haste to me.

   Enter Uberti, *habited like a* Florentine
   Soldier, *and mixes with the rest.*

   Lor. Thou machine of this mischief, look
   to feel
Whate'er the wrath of an incensed prince

Can pour upon thee: with thy blood I'll
   quench
(But drawn forth slowly) the invisible flames
Of discord—by thy charms first fetch'd from
   hell,
Then forced into the breasts of my com-
   manders.
Bring forth the tortures.
   Uber. Hear, victorious duke,
The story of my miserable fortune,
Of which this villain (by your sacred tongue
Condemned to die) was the immediate cause:
And, if my humble suit have justice in it,
Vouchsafe to grant it.
   Lor. Soldier, be brief, our anger
Can brook no long delay.
   Uber. I am the last
Of three sons, by one father got, and train'd
   up
With his best care, for service in your wars:
My father died under his fatal hand,
And two of my poor brothers. Now I hear,
Or fancy, wounded by my grief, deludes me,
Their pale and mangled ghosts crying for
   vengeance
On perjury and murder. Thus the case
   stood:
My father, (on whose face he durst not look
In equal mart,) by his fraud circumvented,
Became his captive; we, his sons, lamenting
Our old sire's hard condition, freely offer'd
Our utmost for his ransome: that refused,
The subtile tyrant, for his cruel ends,
Conceiving that our piety might ensnare us,
Proposed my father's head to be redeem'd,
If two of us would yield ourselves his slaves.
We, upon any terms, resolved to save him,
Though with the loss of life which he gave
   to us,
With an undaunted constancy drew lots
(For each of us contended to be one)
Who should preserve our father; I was
   exempted,
But to my more affliction. My brothers
Deliver'd up, the perjured homicide,
Laughing in scorn, and by his hoary locks
Pulling my wretched father on his knees,
Said, *Thus receive the father you have ran-*
   somed!
And instantly struck off his head.
   Lor. Most barbarous!
   Farn. I never saw this man.
   Lor. One murmur more,
I'll have thy tongue puli'd out.—Proceed.
   Uber. Conceive, sir,
How thunderstruck we stood, being made
   spectators
Of such an unexpected tragedy:
Yet this was a beginning, not an end

To his intended cruelty ; for, pursuing
Such a revenge as no Hyrcanian tigress,
Robb'd of her whelps, durst aim at, in a
    moment,
Treading upon my father's trunk, he cut off
My pious brothers' heads, and threw them
    at me.
Oh, what a spectacle was this ! what moun-
    tain
Of sorrow overwhelm'd me ! my poor heart-
    strings,
As tenter'd by his tyranny, crack'd ; my knees
Beating 'gainst one another, groans and
    tears
Blended together follow'd ; not one passion
Calamity ever yet express'd, forgotten.——
Now, mighty sir, (bathing your feet with
    tears,)
Your suppliant's suit is, that he may have
    leave,
With any cruelty revenge can fancy,
To sacrifice this monster, to appease
My father's ghost, and brothers'.
    Lor. Thou hast obtain'd it :
Choose any torture, let the memory
Of what thy father and thy brothers suffer'd,
Make thee ingenious in it ; such a one,
As Phalaris would wish to be call'd his.
Martino, guarded with your soldiers, see
The execution done ; but bring his head,
On forfeiture of your own, to us : our presence
Long since was elsewhere look'd for.
        [*Exit, with* Captains *and* Attendants.
    Mart. Soldier, to work ;
Take any way thou wilt for thy revenge,
Provided that he die : his body's thine,
But I must have his head.
    Uber. I have already
Concluded of the manner. O just heaven,
The instrument I wish'd for offer'd me !
    Mart. Why art thou rapt thus ?
    Uber. In this soldier's hand
I see the murderer's own sword, I know it ;
Yes, this is it by which my father and
My brothers were beheaded : noble captain,
Command it to my hand.—[*Takes* Farneze's
    sword from the Soldier.]—Stand forth
    and tremble !
This weapon, of late drunk with innocent
    blood,
Shall now carouse thine own : pray, if thou
    canst,
For, though the world shall not redeem thy
    body,
I would not kill thy soul.
    Farn. Canst thou believe
There is a heaven, or hell, or soul ? thou hast
    none,
In death to rob me of my fame, my honour,

With such a forged lie. Tell me, thou hang-
    man,
Where did I ever see thy face ? or when
Murder'd thy sire or brothers ? look on me,
And make it good : thou dar'st not.
    Uber. Yes, I will   [*He unbinds his arms.*
In one short whisper ; and that told, thou
    art dead.
I am Uberti : take thy sword, fight bravely ;
We'll live or die together.
    Mart. We are betray'd.
        [Martino *is struck down, the* Soldiers
            run off.
    Farn. And have I leave once more, brave
    prince, to ease
My head on thy true bosom?
    Uber. I glory more
To be thy friend, than in the name of prince,
Or any higher title.
    Farn. My preserver !
    Uber. The life you gave to me I but return ;
And pardon, dearest friend, the bitter lan-
    guage
Necessity made me use.
    Farn. O, sir, I am
Outdone in all ; but comforted, that none
But you can wear the laurel.
    Uber. Here's no place
Or time to argue this ; let us fly hence.
    Farn. I follow.   [*Exeunt.*
    Mart. [*rises.*] A thousand Furies keep you
    company !
I was at the gate of [hell,] but now I feel
My wound's not mortal ; I was but astonish'd ;
And, coming to myself, I find I am
Reserv'd for the gallows : there's no looking
    on
The enraged duke, excuses will not serve ;
I must do something that may get my pardon ;
If not, I know the worst, a halter ends all !
                            [*Exit.*

_____

ACT III.

SCENE I.—The Dutchy of Mantua.—*A*
part of the Country near Octavio's *Cottage.*
    Enter Octavio, *a book in his hand.*
    Oct. 'Tis true, by proof I find it, human
    reason
Views with such dim eyes what is good or ill,
That if the great Disposer of our being
Should offer to our choice all worldly bless-
    ings,
We know not what to take. When I was
    young,
Ambition of court-preferment fired me :
And, as there were no happiness beyond it,
I labour'd for't, and got it ; no man stood

In greater favour with his prince ; I had
Honours and offices, wealth flow'd in to me,
And, for my service both in peace and war,
The general voice gave out I did deserve them.
But, O vain confidence in subordinate great-
ness !
When I was most secure it was not in
The power of fortune to remove me from
The flat I firmly stood on, in a moment
My virtues were made crimes, and popular
favour,
(To new-raised men still fatal) bred suspicion
That I was dangerous : which no sooner
enter'd
Gonzaga's breast, but straight my ruin
follow'd.
My offices were ta'en from me, my state
seized on :
And, had I not prevented it by flight,
The jealousy of the duke had been removed
With the forfeiture of my head.
  Hort. [*within.*] Or shew compassion,
Or I will force it.
  Oct. Ha ! is not poverty safe ?
I thought proud war, that aim'd at kingdoms'
ruins,
The sack of palaces and cities, scorn'd
To look on a poor cottage.

Enter Hortensio *with* Ascanio *in his arms,*
Gothrio *following.*

  Goth. What would you have ?
The devil sleeps in my pocket ; I have no
cross
To drive him from it. Be you or thief or
soldier,
Or such a beggar as will not be denied,
My scrip, my tar-box, hook, and coat, will
prove
But a thin purchase ; if you turn my inside
outwards,
You'll find it true.
  Hort. Not any food ? [*Searches his scrip.*
  Goth. Alas ! sir,
I am no glutton, but an under-shepherd ;
The very picture of famine ; judge by my
cheeks else :
I have my pittance by ounces, and starve
myself,
When I pay a pensioner, an ancient mouse,
I have, a crumb a meal.
  Hort. No drop left ? [*Takes his bottle.*
Drunkard ! hast thou swill'd up all ?
  Goth. How ! drunkard, sir ?
I am a poor man, you mistake me, sir,
Drunkard's a title for the rich, my betters ;
A calling in repute : some sell their lands for't,
And roar, *Wine's better than money.* Our
poor beverages

Of buttermilk or whey allayed with water,
Ne'er raise our thoughts so high. Drunk, I
had never
The credit to be so yet.
  Hort. Ascanio,
Look up, dear youth ; Ascanio, did thy
sweetness
Command the greedy enemy to forbear
To prey upon it, and I thank my fortune
For suffering me to live, that in some part
I might return thy courtesies, and now,
To heighten my afflictions, must I be
Enforced, no pitying angel near to help us,
Heaven deaf to my complaints too, to behold
thee
Die in my arms for hunger? no means left
To lengthen life 'a little ! I will open
A vein, and pour my blood, not yet corrupted
With any sinful act, but pure as he is,
Into his famish'd mouth.
  Oct. [*comes forward.*] Young man, forbear
Thy savage pity ; I have better means
To call back flying life.
      [*Pours a cordial into the mouth of*
Ascanio.
  Goth. You may believe him ;
It is his sucking-bottle, and confirms,
An old man's twice a child; his nurse's milk
Was ne'er so chargeable, should you put in
too
For soap and candles : though he sell his
flock for't,
The baby must have this dug : he swears
'tis ill
For my complexion; but wondrous comfort-
able
For an old man, that would never die.
  Oct. Hope well, sir ;
A temperate heat begins to thaw his numb-
ness ;
The blood too by degrees takes fresh posses-
sion
On his pale cheek ; his pulse beats high :
stand off,
Give him more air, he stirs.
      [Gothrio *steals the bottle.*
  Goth. And have I got thee,
Thou bottle of immortality ! [*Aside.*
  Asc. Where am I ?
What cruel hand hath forced back wretched
life ?
Is rest in death denied me?
  Goth. O sweet liquor ! [*Drinks.*
Were here enough to make me drunk, I might
Write myself gentleman, and never buy
A coat of the heralds. [*Aside.*
  Oct. How now, slave !
  Goth. I was fainting,
A clownlike qualm seized on me ; but I am

Recover'd, thanks to your bottle, and begin
To feel new stirrings, gallant thoughts : one
  draught more
Will make me a perfect signior.
  Oct. A tough cudgel
Will take this gentle itch off ; home to my
  cottage,
See all things handsome.
  Goth. Good sir, let me have
The bottle along to smell to : O rare per-
  fume !   [*Exit.*
  Hort. Speak once more, dear Ascanio.—
How he eyes you,
Then turns away his face ! look up, sweet
  youth ;
The object cannot hurt you ; this good man,
Next heaven, is your preserver.
  Asc. Would I had perish'd
Without relief, rather than live to break
His good old heart with sorrow. O my
  shame !
My shame, my never-dying shame !
  Oct. I have been
Acquainted with this voice, and know the
  face too :——
'Tis she, 'tis too apparent ; O my daughter !
I mourn'd long for thy loss, but thus to find
  thee,
Is more to be lamented.
  Hort. How ! your daughter ?
  Oct. My only child ; I murmur'd against
  heaven
Because I had no more, but now I find
This one too many.—Is Alonzo glutted
              [*Maria weeps.*
With thy embraces ?
  Hort. At his name, a shower
Of tears falls from her eyes ; she faints again.
Grave sir, o'er-rule your passion, and defer
The story of her fortune. On my life
She is a worthy one ; her innocence
Might be abused, but mischief's self wants
  power
To make her guilty. Shew yourself a father
In her recovery ; then as a judge,
When she hath strength to speak in her own
  cause,
You may determine of her.
  Oct. I much thank you
For your wise counsel : you direct me, sir,
As one indebted more to years, and I,
As a pupil, will obey you : not far hence
I have a homely dwelling ; if you please there
To make some short repose, your enter-
  tainment,
Though coarse, shall relish of a gratitude,
And that's all I can pay you. Look up, girl,
Thou art in thy father's arms.
  Hort. She's weak and faint still—

O spare your age ! I am young and strong,
  and this way
To serve her is a pleasure, not a burthen :
              [*Takes her in his arms.*
Pray you, lead the way.
  Oct. The saints reward your goodness !
              [*Exeunt.*

SCENE II.—*The same. Another part of
              the Country.*

Enter Maufroy, *and* Matilda *disguised.*

  Matil. No hope of safety left ?
  Man. We are descried.
  Matil. I thought that, cover'd in this poor
  disguise,
I might have pass'd unknown.
  Man. A diamond,
Though set in horn, is still a diamond,
And sparkles as in purest gold. We are fol-
  low'd :
Out of the troops that scour'd the plains, I
  saw
Two gallant horsemen break forth, (who, by
  their
Brave furniture and habiliments for the war,
Seem'd to command the rest,) spurring hard
  towards us.
See with what winged speed they climb the
  hill,
Like falcons on the stretch to seize the prey !
Now they dismount, and on their hands and
  knees
O'ercome the deep ascent that guards us from
  them.
Your beauty hath betray'd you ; for it can
No more be night when bright Apollo shines
In our meridian, than that be conceal'd.
  Matil. It is my curse, not blessing ; fatal to
My country, father, and myself. Why did you
Forsake the city ?
  Man. 'Twas the duke's command :
No time to argue that ; we must descend.
If undiscover'd your soft feet, unused
To such rough travel, can but carry you
Half a league hence, I know a cave which will
Yield us protection.
  Matil. I wish I could lend you
Part of my speed ; for me, I can outstrip
Daphne or Atalanta.
  Man. Some good angel
Defend us, and strike blind our hot pursuers !
              [*Exeunt.*

Enter Alonzo *and* Pisano.

  Alon. She cannot be far off : how
  gloriously
She shew'd to us in the valley !
  Pisan. In my thought,
Like to a blazing comet.

Alon. Brighter far:
Her beams of beauty made the hill all fire;
From whence removed, 'tis cover'd with
thick clouds.
But we lose time ; I'll take that way.
Pisan. I, this. [*Exeunt severally.*

SCENE III.—*The same. A Wood.*

Enter Hortensio.

Hort. 'Tis a degree of comfort in my
sorrow,
I have done one good work in reconciling
Maria, long hid in Ascanio's habit,
To griev'd Octavio. What a sympathy
I found in their affections! she with tears
Making a free confession of her weakness,
In yielding up her honour to Alonzo,
Upon his vows to marry her ; Octavio,
Prepared to credit her excuses, nay,·
To extenuate her guilt ; she the delinquent,
And judge, as 'twere, agreeing.—But to me,
The most forlorn of men, no beam of comfort
Deigns to appear ; nor can I, in my fancy,
Fashion a means to get it : to my country
I am lost for ever, and 'twere impudence
To think of a return ; yet this I could
Endure with patience, but to be divorced
From all my joy on earth, the happiness
To look upon the excellence of nature,
That is perfection in herself, and needs not
Addition or epithet, rare Matilda,
Would make a saint blaspheme. Here,
Galeazzo,
In this obscure abode, 'tis fit thou shouldst
Consume thy youth, and grow old in la-
menting
Thy star-cross'd fortune, in this shepherd's
habit ;
This hook thy best defence, since thou
couldst use,
When thou didst fight in such a princess'
cause,
Thy sword no better.. [*Lies down.*

Enter Alonzo *and* Pisano *with* Matilda.

Matil. Are you men, or monsters?
Whither will you drag me? can the open ear
Of heaven be deaf, when an unspotted maid
Cries out for succour !
Pisan. 'Tis in vain ; cast lots
Who shall enjoy her first.
Alon. Flames rage within me,
And, such a spring of nectar near to quench
. them !
My appetite shall be cloy'd first : here I stand,
Thy friend, or enemy ; let me have prece-
dence,
I write a friend's name in my heart; deny it,
As an enemy I defy thee.

Pisan. Friend or foe
In this alike I value, I disdain
To yield priority ; draw thy sword.
Alon. To sheath it
In thy ambitious heart.
Matil. O curb this fury,
And hear a wretched maid first speak.
Hort. I am marble.
Matil. Where shall I seek out words, or·
how restrain
My enemies rage, or lovers'? oh, the latter
Is far more odious : did not your lust
Provoke you, for that is its proper name,
My chastity were safe ; and yet I tremble·
more
To think what dire effects lust may bring
forth,
Than what, as enemies, you can inflict, .
And less I fear it. Be friends to yourselves,
And enemies to me ; better I fall
A sacrifice to your atonement, than
Or one or both should perish. I am the cause
Of your division ; remove it, lords,
And concord will spring up : poison this face
That hath bewitch'd you, this grove cannot
want
Aspics or toads; creatures, though justly·
call'd,
For their deformity, the scorn of nature,·
More happy than myself with this false beauty
(The seed and fruit of mischief) you admire
so.
I thus embrace your knees, and yours, a
suppliant,
If tigers did not nurse you, or you suck
The milk of a fierce lioness, shew compassion
Unto yourselves in being reconciled,
And pity to poor me, my honour safe,
In taking loath'd life from me.
Pisan. What shall we do?
Or end our difference in killing her,
Or fight it out?
Alon. To the last gasp. I feel
The moist tears on my cheeks, and blush to·
find
A virgin's plaints can move so.
Pisan. To prevent
Her flight while we contend, let's bind her
fast
To this cypress-tree.
Alon. Agreed.
Matil. It does presage
My funeral rites. [*They bind* Matilda.
Hort. I shall turn atheist
If heaven see and suffer this : why did I
Abandon my good sword? with unarm'd
hands
I cannot rescue her. Some angel pluck me
From the apostacy I am falling to,

And by a miracle lend me a weapon
To underprop falling honour.
Pisan. She is fast :
Resume your arms.
    Alon. Honour, revenge, the maid too,
Lie at the stake.
    Pisan. Which thus I draw.
            [*They fight,* Pisano *falls.*
    Alon. All's mine,
But bought with some blood of mine own.
Pisano,
Thou wert a noble enemy, wear that laurel
In death to comfort thee : for the reward,
'Tis mine now without rival.
    [Hortensio *snatches up* Pisano's *sword.*
    Hort. Thou art deceived ;
Men will grow up like to the dragon's teeth
From Cadmus' helm, sown in the field of
    Mars,
To guard pure chastity from lust and rape.
Libidinous monster, satyr, faun, or what
Does better speak thee, slave to appetite,
And sensual baseness ; if thy profane hand
But touch this virgin temple, thou art dead.
    Matil. I see the aid of heaven, though
    slow, is sure.
    Alon. A rustic swain dare to retard my
    pleasure !
    Hort. No swain, Alonzo, but her knight
    and servant
To whom the world should owe and pay
    obedience ;
One that thou hast encounter'd, and shrunk
    under
His arm ; that spared thy life in the late battle,
At the intercession of the princess' page.
Look on me better.
    Matil. 'Tis my virtuous lover !
Under his guard 'twere sin to doubt my safety.
    Alon. I know thee, and with courage will
    redeem
What fortune then took from me.
    Hort. Rather keep
            [*They fight,* Alonzo *falls.*
Thy compeer company in death.—Lie by him,
A prey for crows and vultures : these fair
    arms,   [*He unbinds* Matilda.
Unfit for bonds, should have been chains to
    make
A bridegroom happy, though a prince, and
    proud
Of such captivity : whatsoe'er you are,
I glory in the service I have done you ;
But I entreat you pay your vows and prayers,
For preservation of your life and honour,
To the most virtuous princess, chaste Matilda.
I am her creature, and what good I do
You truly may call hers ; what's ill, mine
    own.

    Matil. You never did do ill, my virtuous
    servant ;
Nor is it in the power of poor Matilda,
To cancel such an obligation as,
With humble willingness, she must sub-
    scribe to.
    Hort. The princess? ha !
    Matil. Give me a fitter name,
Your manumised bondwoman, but even now
In the possession of lust, from which
Your more than brave,—heroic valour
    bought me :
And can I then, for freedom unexpected,
But kneel to you, my patron ?
    Hort. Kneel to me !
For heaven's sake rise ; I kiss the ground
    you tread on,
My eyes fix'd on the earth ; for I confess
I am a thing not worthy to look on you,
Till you have sign'd my pardon.
    Matil. Do you interpret
The much good you have done me, an
    offence?
    Hort. The not performing your injunc-
    tions to me,
Is more than capital : your allowance of
My love and service to you, with admission
To each place you made paradise with your
    presence,
Should have enabled me to bring home
    conquest ;
Then, as a sacrifice, to offer it
At the altar of your favour : had my love
Answer'd your bounty, or my hopes, an army
Had been as dust before me ; whereas I,
Like a coward, turn'd my back, and durst
    not stand
The fury of the enemy.
    Matil. Had you done
Nothing in the battle, this last act deserves
    more
Than I, the duke my father joining with me,
Can ever recompense. But take your plea-
    sure ;
Suppose you have offended in not grasping
Your boundless hopes, I thus seal on your lips
A full remission.
    Hort. Let mine touch your foot,
Your hand's too high a favour.
    Matil. Will you force me
To ravish a kiss from you ?   [*Kisses him.*
    Hort. I am entranced.
    Matil. So much desert and bashfulness
    should not march
In the same file. Take comfort ; when you
    have brought me
To some place of security, you shall find
You have a seat here, in a heart that hath
Already studied and vow'd to be thankful.

Hort. Heaven make me so! oh, I am
overwhelm'd
With an excess of joy! Be not too prodigal,
Divinest lady, of your grace and bounties,
At once; if you are pleased, I shall enjoy
them,
Not taste them, and expire.
Matil. I'll be more sparing. [*Exeunt.*

Enter Octavio, Gothrio, *and* Maria.

Oct. What noise of clashing swords, like
armour fashion'd
Upon an anvil, pierced mine ears; the echo
Redoubling the loud sound through all the
vallies?
This way the wind assures me that it came.
Goth. Then with your pardon, I'll take this.
Oct. Why, sirrah?
Goth. Because, sir, I will trust my heels
before
All winds that blow in the sky: we are
wiser far
Than our grandsires were, and in this I'll
prove it;
They said, *Haste to the beginning of a feast,*
There I am with them; *but to the end of a
fray—*
That is apocryphal; 'tis more canonical,
Not to come there at all; after a storm
There are still some drops behind.
Mar. Pure fear hath made
The fool a philosopher.
Oct. See, Maria, see!
I did not err; here lie two brave men wel-
tering
In their own gore.
Mar. A pitiful object.
Goth. I am in a swoon to look on't.
Oct. They are stiff already.
Goth. But are you sure they are dead?
Oct. Too sure, I fear.
Goth. But are they stark dead?
Oct. Leave prating.
Goth. Then I am valiant, and dare come
nearer to them.
This fellow without a sword shall be my
patient. [*Goes to* Pisano.
Oct. Whate'er they are, humanity com-
mands us
To do our best endeavour. Run, Maria,
To the neighbour spring for water; you
will find there
A wooden dish, the beggar's plate, to bring
it. [*Exit* Maria.
Why dost not, dull drone, bend his body,
and feel
If any life remain?
Goth. By your leave, he shall die first,
And then I'll be his surgeon.

Oct. Tear ope his doublet,
And prove if his wounds be mortal.
Goth. Fear not me, sir:
Here's a large wound.—[*Feels his pocket.*]—
How it is swoln and imposthumed!
This must be cunningly drawn out; should
it break, [*Pulls out his purse.*
'Twould strangle him. What a deal of foul
matter's here!
This hath been long a gathering. Here's a
gash too
On the rim of his belly,—[*Feels his side
pocket.*]—it may have matter in it.
He was a choleric man, sure; what comes
from him [*Takes out his money.*
Is yellow as gold:—how! troubled with the
stone too?
[*Seeing a diamond ring on his finger.*
I'll cut you for this.
Pisan. Oh, oh! [*Starts up.*
Goth. He roars before I touch him.
Pisan. Robb'd of my life?
Goth. No, sir, nor of your money,
Nor jewel; I keep them for you:—if I had been
A perfect mountebank, he had not lived
To call for his fees again.
Oct. Give me leave—there's hope
Of his recovery.
[*Quits* Pisano *and goes to* Alonzo.
Goth. I had rather bury him quick,
Than part with my purchase; let his ghost
walk, I care not.

Re-enter Maria *with a dish of water.*

Oct. Well done, Maria; lend thy helping
hand.
He hath a deep wound in his head, wash off
The clotted blood: he comes to himself.
Alon. My lust!
The fruit that grows upon the tree of lust!
With horror now I taste it.
Oct. Do you not know him?
Mar. Too soon. Alonzo! oh me! though
disloyal,
Still dear to thy Maria.
Goth. So they know not
My patient, all's cocksure; I do not like
The Romanish restitution. [*Aside.*
Oct. Rise, and leave him.
Applaud heaven's justice.
Mar. 'Twill become me better,
To implore its saving mercy.
Oct. Hast thou no gall?
No feeling of thy wrongs?
Mar. Turtles have none;
Nor can there be such poison in her breast
That truly loves, and lawfully.
Oct. True, if that love
Be placed on a worthy subject. What he is,

N N

In thy disgrace is published ; heaven hath
    mark'd him
For punishment, and 'twere rebellious mad-
    ness
In thee to attempt to alter it : revenge,
A sovereign balm for injuries, is more proper
To thy robb'd honour. Join with me, and
    thou
Shalt be thyself the goddess of revenge,
This wretch, the vassal of thy wrath : I'll
    make him,
While yet he lives, partake those torments
    which,
For perjured lovers, are prepared in hell,
Before his curs'd ghost enter it. This oil,
Extracted and sublimed from all the simples
The earth, when swoln with venom, e'er
    brought forth,
Pour'd in his wounds, shall force such
    anguish as
The Furies whips but imitate ; and when
Extremity of pain shall hasten death,
Here is another that shall keep in life,
And make him feel a perpetuity
Of lingering tortures.
    Goth. Knock them both o' th' head, I say,
An it be but for their skins ; they are em-
    broider'd,
And will sell well in the market.
    Mar. Ill-look'd devil,
Tie up thy bloody tongue.—O sir ! I was
    slow
In beating down those propositions which
You urge for my revenge ; my reasons being
So many, and so forcible, that make
Against yours, that until I had collected
My scatter'd powers, I waver'd in my choice
Which I should first deliver. Fate hath
    brought
My enemy (I can faintly call him so)
Prostrate before my feet ; shall I abuse
The bounty of my fate, by trampling on him?
He alone ruin'd me, nor can any hand
But his rebuild my late demolish'd honour.
If you deny me means of reparation,
To satisfy your spleen, you are more cruel
Than ever yet Alonzo was ; you stamp
The name of strumpet on my forehead, which
Heaven's mercy would take off ; you fan the
    fire,
E'en ready to go out ; forgetting that
'Tis truly noble, having power to punish,
Nay, kinglike, to forbear it. I would pur-
    chase
My husband by such benefits as should make
    him
Confess himself my equal, and disclaim
Superiority.
    Oct. My blessing on thee !

What I urged was a trial ; and my grant
To thy desires shall now appear, if art
Or long experience can do him service.
Nor shall my charity to this be wanting,
Howe'er unknown: help me, Maria: you, sir,
Do your best to raise him.—So !
    Goth. He's wondrous heavy ;
But the porter's paid, there's the comfort.
    Oct. 'Tis but a trance,
And 'twill forsake both.
    Mar. If he live, I fear not
He will redeem all, and in thankfulness
Confirm he owes you for a second life,
And pay the debt, in making me his wife.
    [*Exeunt* Octavio *and* Maria *with* Alonzo,
        and Gothrio *with* Pisano.

———

ACT IV.

SCENE I.—Lorenzo's *Camp under the*
        Walls of Mantua.

Enter Lorenzo *and* Captains.

    Lor. Mantua is ours ; place a strong
    garrison in it,
To keep it so ; and as a due reward
To your brave service, be our governour in it.
    1 *Capt.* I humbly thank your excellence.
                            [*Exit.*
    Lor. Gonzaga
Is yet out of our gripe ; but his strong fort,
St. Leo, which he holds impregnable
By the aids of art, as nature, shall not long
Retard our absolute conquest. The escape
Of fair Matilda, my supposed mistress,
(For whose desired possession 'twas given out
I made this war,) I value not ; alas !
Cupid's too feeble-eyed to hit my heart,
Or could he see, his arrows are too blunt
To pierce it ; his imagined torch is quench'd
With a more glorious fire of my ambition
To enlarge my empire : soft and silken
    amours,
With carpet courtship, which weak princes
    style
The happy issue of a flourishing peace,
My toughness scorns. Were there an abstract
    made
Of all the eminent and canonized beauties
By truth recorded, or by poets feign'd,
I could unmoved behold it ; as a picture,
Commend the workmanship, and think no
    more on't ;
I have more noble ends. Have you not
    heard yet
Of Alonzo, or Pisano?
    2 *Capt.* My lord, of neither.
    Lor. Two turbulent spirits unfit for dis-
    cipline,

Much less command in war; if they were lost,
I should not pine with mourning.

Enter Martino *and* Soldiers *with* Matilda
and Hortensio.

Mart. Bring them forward :
This will make my peace, though I had kill'd
  his father ;
Besides the reward that follows.
  Lor. Ha, Martino !
Where is Farneze's head? dost thou stare!
  and where
The soldier that desired the torture of him?
  Mart. An't please your excellence——
  Lor. It doth not please us ;
Are our commands obey'd ?
  Mart. Farneze's head, sir,
Is a thing not worth your thought, the sol-
  dier's less, sir :
I have brought your highness such a head !
  a head
So well set on too ! a fine head——
  Lor. Take that,   [*Strikes him.*
For thy impertinence : what head, you rascal?
  Mart. My lord, if they that bring such
  presents to you
Are thus rewarded, there are few will strive
To be near your grace's pleasures : but I know
You will repent your choler. Here's the head :
And now I draw the curtain, it hath a face
  too,
And such a face——
  Lor. Ha !
  Mart. View her all o'er, my lord,
My company on't, she's sound of wind and
  limb,
And will do her labour tightly, a *bona roba:*
And for her face, as I said, there are five
  hundred
City-dubb'd madams in the dukedom, that
  would part with
Their jointures to have such another :—hold
  up your head, maid.
  Lor. Of what age is the day?
  Mart. Sir, since sunrising
About two hours.
  Lor. Thou liest ; the sun of beauty,
In modest blushes on her cheeks, but now
Appear'd to me, and in her tears breaks forth,
As through a shower in April ; every drop
An orient pearl, which, as it falls, congeal'd,
Were ear-rings for the Catholic king, [to be]
Worn on his birthday.
  Mart. Here's a sudden change !
  Lor. Incensed Cupid, whom even now I
  scorn'd,
Hath ta'en his stand, and by reflection shines
(As if he had two bodies, or indeed

A brother-twin whom sight cannot dis-
  tinguish)
In her fair eyes :—see, how they head their
  arrows
With her bright beams ! now frown, as if my
  heart,
Rebellious to their edicts, were unworthy,
Should I rip up my bosom, to receive
A wound from such divine artillery !
  Mart. I am made for ever.   [*Aside.*
  Matil. We are lost, dear servant.
  Hort. Virtue's but a word ;
Fortune rules all.
  Matil. We are her tennis-balls.
  Lor. Allow her fair, her symmetry and
  features
So well proportion'd, as the heavenly object
With admiration would strike Ovid dumb,
Nay, force him to forget his faculty
In verse, and celebrate her praise in prose.
What's this to me? I that have pass'd my
  youth
Unscorch'd with wanton fires, my sole delight
In glittering arms, my conquering sword my
  mistress,
Neighing of barbed horse, the cries and
  groans
Of vanquish'd foes suing for life, my music :
And shall I, in the autumn of my age,
Now, when I wear the livery of time
Upon my head and beard, suffer myself
To be transform'd, and like a puling lover,
With arms thus folded up, echo *Ah me's!*
And write myself a bondman to my vassal ?
It must not, nay, it shall not be : remove
The object, and the effect dies. Nearer,
  Martino.
  Mart. I shall have a regiment : colonel
  Martino,
I cannot go less.
  Lor. What thing is this thou hast brought
  me ?
  Mart. What thing? heaven bless me ! are
  you a Florentine,
Nay, the great duke of Florentines, and
  having had her
So long in your power, do you now ask what
  she is ?   ·
Take her aside and learn : I have brought
  you that
I look to be dearly paid for.
  Lor. I am a soldier,
And use of women will, Martino, rob
My nerves of strength.
  Mart. All armour and no smock ?
Abominable ! a little of the one with the
  other
Is excellent : I ne'er knew general yet,
Nor prince that did deserve to be a worthy,

N N 2

But he desired to have his sweat wash'd off
By a juicy bedfellow.
   Lor. But say she be unwilling
To do that office?
   Mart. Wrestle with her, I will wager
Ten to one on your grace's side.
   Lor. Slave, hast thou brought me
Temptation in a beauty not to be
With prayers resisted; and, in place of
   counsel
To master my affections, and to guard
My honour, now besieged by lust, with the
   arms
Of sober temperance, mark me out a way
To be a ravisher? Would thou hadst shewn
   me
Some monster, though in a more ugly form
Than Nile or Afric ever bred! The basilisk,
Whose envious eye yet never brook'd a neigh-
   bour,
Kills but the body; her more potent eye
Buries alive mine honour: Shall I yield thus?
And all brave thoughts of victory and
   triumphs,
The spoils of nations, the loud applauses
Of happy subjects, made so by my conquests;
And, what's the crown of all, a glorious name
Insculp'd on pyramids to posterity,
Be drench'd in Lethe, and no object take me
But a weak woman, rich in colours only,
Too delicate a touch, and some rare features
Which age or sudden sickness will take from
. her!
And where's then the reward of all my ser-
   vice,
Love-soothing passions, nay, idolatry
I must pay to her? Hence, and with thee
  take
This second but more dangerous Pandora,
Whose fatal box, if open'd, will pour on me
All mischiefs that mankind is subject to.
To the desarts with this Circe, this Calypso,
This fair enchantress! let her spells and
   charms
Work upon beasts and thee, than whom wise
   nature
Ne'er made a viler creature.
   Matil. Happy exile!
   Hort. Some spark of hope remains yet.
   Mart. Come, you are mine now.
I will remove her where your highness shall
   not
Or see or hear more of her: what a sum
Will she yield for the Turk's seraglio!
   Lor. Stay, I feel
A sudden alteration.
   Mart. Here are fine whimsies.
   Lor. Why should I part with her? can any
   foulness

Inhabit such a clean and gorgeous palace?
The fish, the fowl, the beasts, may safer
   leave
The elements they were nourish'd in, and live,
Than I endure her absence; yet her presence
Is a torment to me: why do I call it so?
My sire enjoy'd a woman, I had not been
   else;
He was a complete prince, and shall I blush
To follow his example? Oh! but my choice,
Though she gave suffrage to it, is beneath
   me:
But even now, in my proud thoughts, I
   scorn'd
A princess, fair Matilda; and is't decreed
For punishment, I straight must dote on one,
What, or from whence, I know not? Grant
   she be
Obscure, without a coat or family,
Those I can give: and yet, if she were noble,
My fondness were more pardonable.—Mar-
   tino,
Dost thou know thy prisoner?
   Mart. Do I know myself?
I kept that for the l'envoy; 'tis the daughter
Of your enemy, duke Gonzaga.
   Lor. Fair Matilda!
I now call to my memory her picture,
And find this is the substance; but her painter
Did her much wrong, I see it.
   Mart. I am sure
I tugg'd hard for her, here are wounds can
   witness,
Before I could call her mine.
   Lor. No matter how:
Make thine own ransome, I will pay it for her.
   Mart. I knew 'twould come at last.
   Matil. We are lost again.
   Hort. Variety of afflictions!
   Lor. That his knee,
That never yet bow'd to mortality, [*Kneels.*
Kisses the earth happy to bear your weight,
I know, begets your wonder; hear the reason,
And cast it off:—your beauty does com-
   mand it.
Till now, I never saw you; fame hath been
Too sparing in report of your perfections,
Which now with admiration I gaze on.
Be not afraid, fair virgin; had you been
Employ'd to mediate your father's cause,
My drum had been unbraced, my trumpet
   hung up;
Nor had the terror of the war e'er frighted
His peaceful confines; your demands had
   been,
As soon as spoke, agreed to: but you'll
   answer, .
And may with reason, words make no satis-
   faction

For what's in fact committed. Yet, take
comfort,
Something my pious love commands me do,
Which may call down your pardon.
 Matil. This expression
Of reverence to your person better suits
 [*Raises* Lorenzo, *and kneels.*
With my low fortune. That you deign to
love me,
My weakness would persuade me to believe,
Though conscious of mine own unworthiness :
You being as the liberal eye of heaven,
Which may shine where it pleases, let your
beams
Of favour warm and comfort, not consume
me !
For, should your love grow to excess, I dare
not
Deliver what I fear.
 Lor. Dry your fair eyes ;
I apprehend your doubts, and could be angry,
If humble love could warrant it, you should
Nourish such base thoughts of me. Heaven
bear witness,
And, if I break my vow, dart thunder at me,
You are, and shall be, in my tent as free
From fear of violence, as a cloister'd nun
Kneeling before the altar. What I purpose
Is yet an embryon ; but, grown into form,
I'll give you power to be the sweet disposer
Of blessings unexpected ; that your father,
Your country, people, children yet unborn
too,
In holy hymns, on festivals, shall sing
The triumph of your beauty. On your hand
Once more I swear it :—O imperious Love,
Look down, and, as I truly do repent,
Prosper the good ends of thy penitent !
 [*Exeunt.*

SCENE II.—*The Dutchy. A Room in*
Octavio's *Cottage.*

Enter Octavio, *disguised as a* Priest, *and*
Maria.

 Oct. You must not be too sudden, my
Maria,
In being known : I am, in this friar's habit,
As yet conceal'd. Though his recovery
Be almost certain, I must work him to
Repentance by degrees ; when I would have
you
Appear in your true shape of sorrow, to
Move his compassion, I will stamp thus,——
then,
You know to act your part.
 Mar. I shall be careful. [*Exit.*
 Oct. If I can cure the ulcers of his mind,
As I despair not of his body's wounds,
Felicity crowns my labour.—Gothrio !

Enter Gothrio.

 Goth. Here, sir.
 Oct. Desire my patients to leave their
chamber,
And take fresh air here : how have they slept ?
 Goth. Very well, sir.
I would we were so rid of them.
 Oct. Why ?
 Goth. I fear one hath
The art of memory, and will remember
His gold and jewels : could you not minister
A potion of forgetfulness ? What would
gallants
That are in debt give me for such a receipt,
To pour in their creditors' drink ?
 Oct. You shall restore all,
Believe 't, you shall :—will you please to
walk ?
 Goth. Will you please to put off
Your holy habit, and spiced conscience ? one,
I think, infects the other. [*Exit.*
 Oct. I have observed
Compunction in Alonzo ; he speaks little,
But full of retired thoughts : the other is
Jocund and merry ; no doubt, because he
hath
The less accompt to make here.

Enter Alonzo.

 Alon. Reverend sir,
I come to wait your pleasure ; but, my
friend,
Your creature I should say, being so myself,
Willing to take further repose, entreats
Your patience a few minutes.
 Oct. At his pleasure ;
Pray you sit down ; you are faint still.
 Alon. Growing to strength,
I thank your goodness : but my mind is
troubled,
Very much troubled, sir, and I desire,
Your pious habit giving me assurance
Of your skill and power that way, that you
would please
To be my mind's physician.
 Oct. Sir, to that
My order binds me ; if you please to unload
The burthen of your conscience, I will
minister
Such heavenly cordials as I can, and set you
In a path that leads to comfort.
 Alon. I will open
My bosom's secrets to you. That I am
A man of blood, being brought up in the wars,
And cruel executions, my profession
Admits not to be question'd ; but in that,
Being a subject, and bound to obey
Whate'er my prince commanded, I have left

Some shadow of excuse : with other crimes,
As pride, lust, gluttony, it must be told,
I am besmear'd all over.
    Oct. On repentance,
Mercy will wash it off.
    Alon. O sir, I grant
These sins are deadly ones ; yet their fre-
    queney
With wicked men makes them less dreadful
    to us.
But I am conscious of one crime, with which
All ills I have committed from my youth
Put in the scale, weigh nothing ; such a crime,
So odious to heaven and man, and to
My sear'd-up conscience so full of horror,
As penance cannot expiate.
    Oct. Despair not.
'Tis impious in man to prescribe limits
To the divine compassion : out with it.
    Alon. Hear then, good man, and when
    that I have given you
The character of it, and confess'd myself
The wretch that acted it, you must repent
The charity you have extended towards me.
Not long before these wars began, I had
Acquaintance ('tis not fit I style it friendship,
That being a virtue, and not to be blended
With vicious breach of faith) with the lord
    Octavio,
The minion of his prince and court, set off
With all the pomp and circumstance of
    greatness :
To this then happy man I offer'd service,
And with insinuation wrought myself
Into his knowledge, grew familiar with him,
Ever a welcome guest. This noble gentleman
Was bless'd with one fair daughter, so he
    thought,
And boldly might believe so, for she was
In all things excellent without a rival,
Till I, her father's mass of wealth before
My greedy eyes, but hoodwink'd to mine
    honour,
With far more subtile arts than perjured Paris
E'er practised on poor credulous Oenone,
Besieged her virgin fort, in a word, took it,
No vows or imprecation forgotten
With speed to marry her.
    Oct. Perhaps, she gave you
Just cause to break those vows.
    Alon. She cause ! alas,
Her innocence knew no guilt, but too much
    favour
To me, unworthy of it : 'twas my baseness,
My foul ingratitude—what shall I say more?
The good Octavio no sooner fell
In the displeasure of his prince, his state
Confiscated, and he forced to leave the court,
And she exposed to want ; but all my oaths

And protestation of service to her,
Like seeming flames raised by enchantment,
    vanish'd ;
This, this sits heavy here.
    Oct. He speaks as if
He were acquainted with my plot.—You
    have reason
To feel compunction, for 'twas most inhuman
So to betray a maid.
    Alon. Most barbarous.
    Oct. But does your sorrow for the fact beget
An aptness in you to make satisfaction
For the wrong you did her ?
    Alon. Gracious heaven ! an aptness ?
It is my only study : since I tasted
Of your compassion, these eyes ne'er were
    closed,
But fearful dreams cut off my little sleep ;
And, being awake, in my imagination
Her apparition haunted me.
    Oct. 'Twas mere fancy.   [*He stamps.*
    Alon. 'Twas more, grave sir—nay, 'tis——
    now it appears !
        Enter Maria, *in white.*
    Oct. Where ?
    Alon. Do you not see there the gliding
    shadow
Of a fair virgin ? that is she, and wears
The very garments that adorn'd her, when
She yielded to my crocodile tears : a cloud
Of fears and diffidence then so chased away
Her purer white and red, as it foretold
That I should be disloyal. Blessed shadow !
For 'twere a sin, far, far exceeding all
I have committed, to hope only that
Thou art a substance ; look on my true sorrow,
Nay, soul's contrition : hear again those vows
My perjury cancell'd, stamp'd in brass, and
    never
To be worn out.
    Mar. I can endure no more ;
Action, not oaths, must make me reparation :
I am Maria.
    Alon. Can this be ?
    Oct. It is,
And I Octavio.
    Alon. Wonder on wonder !
How shall I look on you, or with what fore-
    head
Desire your pardon ?
    Mar. You truly shall deserve it
In being constant.
    Re-enter Gothrio, *with the purses of* Alonzo
        and Pisano.
    Oct. If you fall not off,
But look on her in poverty with those eyes
As, when she was my heir in expectation,
You thought her beautiful.

Alon. She is in herself
Both Indies to me.
Goth. Stay, she shall not come
A beggar to you, my sweet young mistress !
no,
She shall not want a dower : here's white and
red
Will ask a jointure ; but how you should
make her one,
Being a captain, would beget some doubt,
If you should deal with a lawyer.
Alon. I have seen this purse.
Goth. How the world's given—I dare not
say, to lying,
Because you are a soldier ; you may say as
well,
This gold is mark'd too : you, being to re-
ceive it,   .
Should ne'er ask how I got it. I'll run for a
priest
To dispatch the matter ; you shall not want
a ring,
I have one for the purpose.—[*Gives* Pisano's
ring to Alonzo.]—Now, sir, I think I'm
honest.   [*Exit.*
Alon. This ring was Pisano's.
Oct. I'll dissolve this riddle
At better leisure : the wound given to my
daughter,
Which, in your honour, you are bound to
cure,
Exacts our present care.
Alon. I am all yours, sir.   [*Exeunt.*

SCENE III.—*The same. The Castle of*
St. Leo.

Enter Gonzaga, Uberti, *and* Manfroy.

Gon. Thou hast told too much to give
assurance that
Her honour was too far engaged, to be
By human help redeem'd : if thou hadst
given
Thy sad narration this full period,
She's dead, I had been happy.
Uber. Sir, these tears
Do well become a father, and my eyes
Would keep you company as a forlorn lover,
But that the burning fire of my revenge
Dries up those drops of sorrow. We once
more,
Our broken forces rallied up, and with
Full numbers strengthen'd, stand prepared
t'endure
A second trial ; nor let it dismay us
That we are once again to affront the fury
Of a victorious army ; their abuse
Of conquest hath disarm'd them, and call'd
down

The Powers above to aid us. I have read
Some piece of story, yet ne'er found but that.
The general, that gave way to cruelty,
The profanation of things sacred, rapes
Of virgins, butchery of infants, and
The massacre in cold blood of reverend age,
Against the discipline and law of arms,
Did feel the hand of heaven lie heavy on him,
When most secure. We have had a late
example,
And let us not despair but that, in Lorenzo,
It will be seconded.
Gon. You argue well,
And 'twere a sin in me to contradict you :
Yet we must not neglect the means that's
lent us,
To be the ministers of justice.   '
Uber. No, sir :
One day given to refresh our wearied troops,
Tired with a tedious march, we'll be no .
longer
Coop'd up, but charge the enemy in his
trenches,
And force him to a battle. [*Shouts within.*
Gon. Ha ! how's this ?
In such a general time of mourning, shouts,
And acclamations of joy ?
     [*Cry within,* Long live the princess !
          long live Matilda !
Uber. Matilda !
The princess' name, Matilda, oft re-echoed !

Enter Farneze.

Gon. What speaks thy haste ?
Farn. More joy and happiness
Than weak words can deliver, or strong faith
Almost give credit to : the princess lives ;
I saw her, kiss'd her hand.
Gon. By whom deliver'd ?
Farn. This is not to be staled by my
report,
This only must be told :—As I rode forth
With some choice troops, to make discovery
Where the enemy lay, and how intrench'd,
a leader
Of the adverse party, but unarm'd, and in
His hand an olive branch, encounter'd me :
He shew'd the great duke's seal, that gave
him power
To parley with me ; his desires were, that
Assurance for his safety might be granted
To his royal master, who came as a friend,.
And not as an enemy, to offer to you
Conditions of peace. I yielded to it.
This being return'd, the duke's prætorium
open'd,
When suddenly, in a triumphant chariot
Drawn by such soldiers of his own as were,
For insolence after victory, condemn'd

Unto this slavish office, the fair princess
Appear'd, a wreath of laurel on her head,
Her robes majestical, their richness far
Above all value, as the present age
Contended that a woman's pomp should dim
The glittering triumphs of the Roman
    Cæsars.   [*Music without.*
—I am cut off; no cannon's throat now
    thunders,
Nor fife nor drum beat up a charge; choice
    music
Ushers the parent of security,
Long-absent peace.
    Man. I know not what to think on't.
    Uber. May it poise the expectation!

Loud music. Enter Soldiers *unarmed, bearing olive branches,* Captains, Lorenzo,
Matilda *crowned with a wreath of laurel,
and seated in a chariot drawn by* Soldiers;
followed by Hortensio *and* Martino.

    Gon. Thus to meet you,
Great duke of Tuscany, throws amazement
    on me;
But to behold my daughter, long since
    mourn'd for,
And lost even to my hopes, thus honour'd
    by you,
With an excess of comfort overwhelms me:
And yet I cannot truly call myself
Happy in this solemnity, till your highness
Vouchsafe to make me understand the motive
That, in this peaceful way, hath brought
    you to us.
    Lor. I must crave license first; for know,
    Gonzaga,
I am subject to another's will, and can
Nor speak nor do without permission from
    her,
My curled forehead, of late terrible
To those that did acknowledge me their lord,
Is now as smooth as rivers when no wind stirs;
My frowns or smiles, that kill'd or saved,
    have lost
Their potent awe, and sweetness: I am
    transform'd
(But do not scorn the metamorphosis)
From that fierce thing men held me; I am
    captived,
And, by the unresistible force of beauty,
Led hither as a prisoner. Is't your pleasure
    that
I shall deliver those injunctions which
Your absolute command imposed upon me,
Or deign yourself to speak them?
    Matil. Sir, I am
Your property, you may use me as you
    please;

But what is in your power and breast to do,
No orator can dilate so well.
    Lor. I obey you.
That I came hither as an enemy,
With hostile arms, to the utter ruin of
Your country, what I have done makes ap-
    parent;
That fortune seconded my will, the late
Defeature will make good: that I resolved
To force the sceptre from your hand, and
    make
Your dukedom tributary, my surprisal
Of Mantua, your metropolis, can well wit-
    ness;
And that I cannot fear the change of fate,
My army flesh'd in blood, spoil, glory, con-
    quest,
Stand ready to maintain: yet, I must tell you
By whom I am subdued, and what's the
    ransome
I am commanded to lay down.
    Gon. My lord,
You humble yourself too much; it is fitter
You should propose, and we consent.
    Lor. Forbear,
The articles are here subscribed and sign'd
By my obedient hand: all prisoners,
Without a ransome, set at liberty;
Mantua to be deliver'd up, the rampires
Ruin'd in the assault, to be repair'd;
The loss the husbandman received, his crop
Burnt up by wanton license of the soldier,
To be made good;—with whatsoever else
You could impose on me, if you had been
The conqueror, I your captive.
    Gon. Such a change
Wants an example: I must owe this favour
To the clemency of the old heroic valour,
That spared when it had power to kill; a
    virtue
Buried long since, but raised out of the grave
By you, to grace this latter age.
    Lor. Mistake not
The cause that did produce this good effect,
If as such you receive it: 'twas her beauty,
Wrought first on my rough nature; but the
    virtues
Of her fair soul, dilated in her converse,
That did confirm it.
    Matil. Mighty sir, no more:
You honour her too much, that is not worthy
To be your servant.
    Lor. I have done, and now
Would gladly understand that you allow of
The articles propounded.
    Gon. Do not wrong
Your benefits with such a doubt; they are
So great and high, and with such reverence
To be received, that, if I should profess

I hold my dukedom from you, as your vassal,
Or offer'd up my daughter as you please
To be disposed of, in the point of honour,
And a becoming gratitude, 'twould not cancel
The bond I stand engaged for :—but accept
Of that which I can pay, my all is yours, sir;
Nor is there any here, (though I must grant
Some have deserved much from me,) for so far
I dare presume, but will surrender up
Their interest to that your highness shall
Deign to pretend a title.

Uber. I subscribe not
To this condition.

Farn. The services
This prince hath done your grace in your
    most danger,
Are not to be so slighted.

Hort. 'Tis far from me
To urge my merits, yet, I must maintain,
Howe'er my power is less, my love is more ;
Nor will the gracious princess scorn to ac-
    knowledge
I have been her humble servant.

Lor. Smooth your brows,
I'll not encroach upon your right, for that
    were
Once more to force affection, (a crime
With which should I the second time be
    tainted,
I did deserve no favour,) neither will I
Make use of what is offer'd by the duke,
Howe'er I thank his goodness. I'll lay by
My power, and though I should not brook
    a rival,
(What we are, well consider'd,) I'll descend
To be a third competitor ; he that can
With love and service best deserve the gar-
    land,
With your consent let him wear it ; I de-
    spair not
The trial of my fortune.

Gon. Bravely offer'd,
And like yourself, great prince.

Uber. I must profess
I am so taken with it, that I know not
Which way to express my service.

Hort. Did I not build
Upon the princess' grace, I could sit down,
And hold it no dishonour.

Matil. How I feel
My soul divided ! all have deserved so well,
I know not where to fix my choice.

Gon. You have
Time to consider : will you please to take
Possession of the fort? then, having tasted
The fruits of peace, you may at leisure prove,
Whose plea will prosper in the court of Love.
                                    [*Exeunt.*

ACT V.

SCENE I.—Mantua. *A Room in the
                Palace.*

Enter Alonzo, Octavio, Pisano, Maria, *and*
            Gothrio.

Alon. You need not doubt, sir, were not
    peace proclaim'd
And celebrated with a general joy,
The high displeasure of the Mantuan duke,
Raised on just grounds, not jealous suppo-
    sitions,
The saving of our lives (which, next to heaven,
To you alone is proper) would force mercy
For an offence, though capital.

Pisan. When the conqueror
Uses entreaties, they are arm'd commands
The vanquish'd must not check at.

Mar. My piety pay the forfeit,
If danger come but near you ! I have heard
My gracious mistress often mention you,
When I served her as a page, and feelingly
Relate how much the duke her sire repented
His hasty doom of banishment, in his rage
Pronounced against you.

Oct. In a private difference,
I grant that innocence is a wall of brass,
And scorns the hottest battery ; but, when
The cause depends between the prince and
    subject,
'Tis an unequal competition ; Justice
Must lay her balance by, and use her sword
For his ends that protects it. I was banish'd,
And, till revoked from exile, to tread on
My sovereign's territories with forbidden feet,
The severe letter of the law calls death ;
Which I am subject to, in coming so near
His court and person. But my only child
Being provided for, her honour salved too,
I thank your noble change, I shall endure
Whate'er can fall, with patience.

Alon. You have used
That medicine too long ; prepare yourself
For honour in your age, and rest secure of't.

Mar. Of what is your wisdom musing?

Goth. I am gazing on
This gorgeous house ; our cote's a dishclout
    to it ;
It has no sign,—what do you call't?

Mar. The court ;
I have lived in't a page.

Goth. Page ! very pretty :
May I not be a page ? I am old enough,
Well-timber'd too, and I've a beard to
    carry it :
Pray you, let me be your page ; I can swear
    already,
Upon your pantofle.

Mar. What?

Goth. That I'll be true
Unto your smock.

Mar. How, rascal!

Oct. Hence, and pimp
To your rams and ewes; such foul pollution is
To be whipt from court; I have now no more
   use of you;
Return to your trough.

Goth. Must I feed on husks,
Before I have play'd the prodigal?

Oct. No, I'll reward
Your service; live in your own element,
Like an honest man; all that is mine in the
   cottage,
I freely give you.

Goth. Your bottles too, that I carry
For your own tooth!

Oct. Full as they are.

Mar. And gold,   [*Gives him her purse.*
That will replenish them.

Goth. I am made for ever.
This was done i'the nick.

Oct. Why in the nick?

Goth. O sir!
'Twas well for me that you did reward my
   service
Before you enter'd the court; for 'tis reported
There is a drink of forgetfulness, which once
   tasted,
Few masters think of their servants, who,
   grown old,
Are turu'd off, like lame hounds and hunting
   horses,
To starve on the commons.   [*Exit.*

Alon. Bitter knave!

   Enter Martino.

              There's craft
In the clouted shoe.—Captain!

Mart. I am glad to kiss
Your valiant hand, and yours; but pray you,
   take notice,
My title's changed, I am a colonel.

Pisan. A colonel! where's your regiment?

Mart. Not raised yet;
All the old ones are cashier'd, and we are now
To have a new militia: all is peace here,
Yet I hold my title still, as many do
That never saw an enemy.

Alon. You are pleasant,
And it becomes you. Is the duke stirring?

Mart. Long since,
Four hours at least, but yet not ready.

Pisan. How!

Mart. Even so; you make a wonder of't,
   but leave it:
Alas, he is not now, sir, in the camp,
To be up and arm'd upon the least alarum;

There's something else to be thought on:
   here he comes,
With his officers, new-rigg'd.

Enter Lorenzo, *as from his chamber, with a
looking-glass;* Doctor, Gentleman, *and*
Page *employed about his person.*

Alon. A looking-glass!
Upon my head, he saw not his own face
These seven years past, but by reflection
From a bright armour.

Mart. Be silent, and observe.

Lor. So, have you done yet?
Is your building perfect?

Doct. If your highness please,
Here is a water.

Lor. To what use? my barber
Hath wash'd my face already.

Doct. But this water
Hath a strange virtue in't, beyond his art;
It is a sacred relic, part of that
Most powerful juice, with which Medea made
Old Æson young.

Lor. A fable! but suppose
I should give credit to it, will it work
The same effect on me?

Doct. I'll undertake
This will restore the honour'd hair that grows
Upon your highness' head and chin, a little
Inclining unto gray.

Lor. Inclining! doctor.

Doct. Pardon me, mighty sir, I went too
   far,
Not gray at all;—I dare not flatter you—
'Tis something changed; but this applied will
   help it
To the first amber-colour, every hair
As fresh as when, your manhood in the prime,
Your grace arrived at thirty.

Lor. Very well.

Doct. Then here's a precious oil, to which
   the maker
Hath not yet given a name, will soon fill up
These dimples in your face and front. I
   grant
They are terrible to your enemies, and set off
Your frowns with majesty; but you may
   please
To know, as sure you do, a smooth aspect,
Softness and sweetness, in the court of Love,
Though dumb, are the prevailing orators.

Lor. Will he new-create me?

Doct. If you deign to taste too,
Of this confection.

Lor. I am in health, and need
No physic.

Doct. Physic, sir! An empress,
If that an empress' lungs, sir, may be tainted
With putrefaction, would taste of it,

hat night on which she were to print a kiss
pon the lips of her long-absent lord,
eturning home with conquest.

Lor. 'Tis predominant
ver a stinking breath, is it not, doctor?

Doct. Clothe the infirmity with sweeter
language:
I'is a preservative that way.

Lor. You are, then,
dmitted to the cabinets of great ladies,
nd have the government of the borrow'd
beauties
f such as write near forty.

Doct. True, my good lord,
And my attempts have prosper'd.

Lor. Did you never
Minister to the princess?

Doct. Sir, not yet;
he's in the April of her youth, and needs
not
The aids of art, my gracious lord; but in
The autumn of her age I may be useful,
And sworn her highness' doctor, and your
grace
Partake of the delight.—

Lor. Slave! witch! impostor!
[*Strikes him down.*
Mountebank! cheater! traitor to great
nature,
In thy presumption to repair what she,
In her immutable decrees, design'd
For some few years to grow up, and then
wither!
Or is't not crime enough thus to betray
The secrets of the weaker sex, thy patients,
But thou must make the honour of this age,
And envy of the time to come, Matilda,
Whose sacred name I bow to, guilty of
A future sin in thy ill-boding thoughts,
Which for a perpetuity of youth
And pleasure she disdains to act, such is
Her purity and innocence!
[*Sets his foot on the* Doctor's *breast.*

Alon. Long since
I look'd for this l'envoy.

Mart. Would I were well off!
He's dangerous in these humours.

Oct. Stand conceal'd.

Doct. O sir, have mercy! in my thought
I never
Offended you.

Lor. Me! most of all, thou monster!
What a mock-man property in thy intent
Wouldst thou have made me? a mere pathic
. to
Thy devilish art, had I given suffrage to it.
Are my gray hairs, the ornament of age,
And held a blessing by the wisest men,
And for such warranted by holy writ,

To be conceal'd, as if they were my shame?
Or plaister up these furrows in my face,
As if I were a painted bawd or whore?
By such base means if that I could ascend
To the height of all my hopes, their full frui-
tion
Would not wipe off the scandal: no, thou
wretch!
Thy cozening water and adulterate oil
I thus pour in thine eyes, and tread to dust
Thy loath'd confection with thy trumperies:—
Vanish for ever!

Mart. You have your fee, as I take it,
Dear domine doctor! I'll be no sharer with
you. [*Exit* Doctor.

Lor. I'll court her like myself; these rich
adornments
And jewels, worn by me, an absolute prince,
My order too, of which I am the sovereign,
Can meet no ill construction; yet 'tis far
From my imagination to believe
She can be taken with sublimed clay,
The silk-worm's spoils, or rich embroideries:
Nor must I borrow helps from power or
greatness,
But as a loyal lover plead my cause;
If I can feelingly express my ardour,
And make her sensible of the much I suffer
In hopes and fears, and she vouchsafe to·
take
Compassion on me,—ha! compassion?
The word sticks in my throat: what's here,.
that tells me
I do descend too low? rebellious spirit,
I conjure thee to leave me! there is now
No contradiction or declining left,
I must and will go on.

Mart. The tempest's laid;
You may present yourselves.
[*Alonzo and* Pisano *come forward..*

Alon. My gracious lord.

Pisan. Your humble vassal.

Lor. Ha! both living?

Alon. Sir,
We owe our lives to this good lord, and·
make it
Our humble suit——

Lor. Plead for yourselves: we stand
Yet unresolved whether your knees or prayers·
Can save the forfeiture of your own heads:
Though we have put our armour off, your
pardon
For leaving of the camp without our license,
Is not yet sign'd. At some more fit time
wait us.
[*Exeunt* Lorenzo, Gentleman, *and* Page.

Alon. How's this?

Mart. 'Tis well it is no worse; I met with·
A rougher entertainment, yet I had

Good cards to shew. He's parcel mad ;
    you'll find him
Every hour in a several mood ; this foolish
    love
·Is such a shuttlecock ! but all will be well,
When a better fit comes on him, never doubt
    it.   [*Exeunt.*

SCENE II.—*Another Room in the same.*

Enter Gonzaga, Uberti, Farneze, *and*
            Manfroy.

Gon. How do you find her ?
Uber. Thankful for my service,
·And yet she gives me little hope ; my rival
Is too great for me.
Gon. The great duke, you mean ?
Uber. Who else ? the Milanese, although
    he be
A complete gentleman, I am sure despairs
More than myself.
Farn. A high estate, with women,
Takes place of all desert.
Uber. I must stand my fortune.

Enter Lorenzo *and* Attendants.

Man. The duke of Florence, sir.
Gon. Your highness' presence
Answers my wish. Your private ear :—I
    have used
My best persuasion, with a father's power,
To work my daughter to your ends ; yet she,
Like a small bark on a tempestuous sea,
Toss'd here and there by opposite winds,
    resolves not
At which port to put in. This prince's merits,
Your grace and favour ; nor is she unmindful
Of the brave acts (under your pardon, sir,
I needs must call them so) Hortensio
Hath done to gain her good opinion of him ;
All these together tumbling in her fancy,
Do much distract her. I have spies upon
    her,
And am assured this instant hour she gives
Hortensio private audience ; I will bring you
Where we will see and hear all.
Lor. You oblige me.
Uber. I do not like this whispering.
Gon. Fear no foul play.   [*Exeunt.*

SCENE III.—*Another Room in the same.*

Enter Hortensio, Beatrice, *and two*
            Waiting Women.

1 *Wom.* The princess, sir, long since ex-
    pected you ;
And, would I beg a thanks, I could tell you
    that
'I have often moved her for you.
Hort. I am your servant.

Enter Matilda.

Beat. She's come ;. there are others I must
    place to hear
The conference.   [*Aside, and exit.*
1 *Wom.* Is't your excellency's pleasure
That we attend you ?
Matil. No ; wait me in the gallery.
1 *Wom.* Would each of us, wench, had a
    sweetheart too
To pass away the time !
2 *Wom.* There I join with you.
                    [*Exeunt* Waiting Women.
Matil. I fear this is the last time we shall
    meet.
Hort. Heaven forbid !

Re-enter above Beatrice *with* Lorenzo,
        Gonzaga, Uberti, *and* Farneze.

Matil. O my Hortensio !
In me behold the misery of greatness,
And that which you call beauty. Had I
    been
Of a more low condition, I might
Have call'd my will and faculties mine own,
Not seeing that which was to be beloved
With others' eyes : but now, ah me, most
    wretched
And miserable princess, in my fortune,
To be too much engaged for service done me !
It being impossible to make satisfaction
To my so many creditors ; all deserving,
I can keep touch with none.
Lor. A sad exordium.
Matil. You loved me long, and without
    hope (alas,
I die to think on't !) Parma's prince, invited
With a too partial report of what
I was, and might be to him, left his country,
To fight in my defence. Your brave achieve-
    ments
I' the war, and what you did for me, un-
    spoken,
Because I would not force the sweetness of
Your modesty to a blush, are written here :
And, that there might be nothing wanting to
Sum up my numerous engagements, (never
In my hopes to be cancell'd,) the great duke,
Our mortal enemy, when my father's country
Lay open to his fury, and the spoil
Of the victorious army, and I brought
Into his power, hath shewn himself so noble,
So full of honour, temperance, and all virtues
That can set off a prince, that, though I
    cannot
Render him that respect I would, I am bound
In thankfulness to admire him.
Hort. 'Tis acknowledged,
And on your part to be return'd.

Matil. How can I,
/ithout the brand of foul ingratitude
o you, and prince Uberti?
Hort. Hear me, madam,
nd what your servant shall with zeal deliver,
s a Dædalean clew may guide you out of
'his labyrinth of distraction. He that loves
is mistress truly, should prefer her honour
nd peace of mind, above the glutting of
is ravenous appetite: he should affect her,
ut with a fit restraint, and not take from
her
o give himself: he should make it the height
f his ambition, if it lie in
is stretch'd-out nerves to effect it, though
she fly in
n eminent place, to add strength to her
wings,
nd mount her higher, though he fall himself
ito the bottomless abyss; or else
he services he offers are not real,
But counterfeit.
Matil. What can Hortensio
Infer from this?
Hort. That I stand bound in duty,
(Though in the act I take my last farewell
Of comfort in this life,) to sit down willingly,
And move my suit no further. I confess,
While you were in danger, and heaven's
mercy made me
Its instrument to preserve you, (which your
goodness
Prized far above the merit,) I was bold
To feed my starv'd affection with false hopes
I might be worthy of you: for know, madam,
How mean soever I appear'd in Mantua,
I had in expectation a fortune,
Though not possess'd of't, that encouraged
me
With confidence to prefer my suit, and not
To fear the prince Uberti as my rival.
Gon. I ever thought him more than what
he seem'd.
Lor. Pray you, forbear.
Hort. But when the duke of Florence
Put in his plea, in my consideration
Weighing well what he is, as you must grant
him
A Mars of men in arms, and, those put off,
The great example for a kingly courtier
To imitate; annex to these his wealth,
Of such a large extent, as other monarchs
Call him the king of coin; and, what's
above all,
His lawful love, with all the happiness
This life can fancy, from him flowing to you;
The true affection which I have ever borne
you,
Does not alone command me to desist,

But, as a faithful counsellor, to advise you
To meet and welcome that felicity,
Which hastes to crown your virtues.
Lor. We must break off this parley:
Something I have to say.   [*Exeunt above.*
Matil. In tears I thank
Your care of my advancement; but I dare
not
Follow your counsel. Shall such piety
Pass unrewarded? such a pure affection,
For any ends of mine, be undervalued?
Avert it, heaven! I will be thy Matilda,
Or cease to be; no other heat but what
Glows from thy purest flames, shall warm this
bosom,
Nor Florence, nor all monarchs of the earth,
Shall keep thee from me.

Re-enter below Lorenzo, Gonzaga, Uberti,
Farneze, *and* Manfroy.

Hort. I fear, gracious lady,
Our conference hath been overheard.
Matil. The better:
Your part is acted; give me leave at distance
To zany it.—Sir, on my knees thus prostrate
Before your feet——
Lor. This must not be, I shall
Both wrong myself and you in suffering it.
Matil. I will grow here, and weeping thus
turn marble,
Unless you hear and grant the first petition
A virgin, and a princess, ever tendered:
Nor does the suit concern poor me alone,
It hath a stronger reference to you,
And to your honour; and, if you deny it,
Both ways you suffer. Remember, sir, you
were not
Born only for yourself, heaven's liberal hand
Design'd you to command a potent nation,
Gave you heroic valour, which you have
Abused, in making unjust war upon
A neighbour-prince, a Christian; while the
Turk,
Whose scourge and terror you should be,
securely
Wastes the Italian confines: 'tis in you
To force him to pull in his horned crescents,
And 'tis expected from you.
Lor. I have been
In a dream, and now begin to wake.
Matil. And will you
Forbear to reap the harvest of such glories,
Now ripe, and at full growth, for the em-
braces
Of a slight woman? or exchange your
triumphs
For chamber-pleasures, melt your able
nerves

(That should with your victorious sword
   make way
Through the armies of your enemies) in
   loose
And wanton dalliance? be yourself, great sir,
The thunderbolt of war, and scorn to sever
Two hearts long since united ; your example
May teach the prince Uberti to subscribe
To that which you allow of.
   Lor. The same tongue
That charm'd my sword out of my hand,
   and threw
A frozen numbness on my active spirit,
Hath disenchanted me. Rise, fairest prin-
   cess !
And, that it may appear I do receive
Your counsel as inspired from heaven, I will
Obey and follow it : I am your debtor,
And must confess you have lent my weaken'd
   reason
New strengths once more to hold a full
   command
Over my passions. Here, to the world,
I freely do profess that I disclaim
All interest in you, and give up my title,
Such as it is, to you, sir ; and, as far
As I have power, thus join your hands.
   Gon. To yours
I add my full consent.
   Uber. I am lost, Farneze.
   Farn. Much nearer to the port than you
   suppose :—
In me our laws speak, and forbid this con-
   tract.
   Matil. Ah me, new stops !
   Hort. Shall we be ever cross'd thus?
   Farn. There is an act upon record, con-
   firm'd
By your wise predecessors, that no heir
Of Mantua (as questionless the princess
Is the undoubted one) must be join'd in
   marriage,
But where the match may strengthen the
   estate
And safety of the dukedom. Now, this
   gentleman,
However I must style him honourable,
And of a high desert, having no power
To make this good in his alliance, stands
Excluded by our laws ; whereas this prince,
Of equal merit, brings to Mantua
The power and principality of Parma :
And   , since the great duke hath let
   therefore
His plea, there lives no prince that justlier
   can
Challenge the princess' favour.
   Lor. Is this true, sir?
   Gon. I cannot contradict it.

Enter Manfroy.

   Man. There's an ambassador
From Milan, that desires a present audience ;
His business is of highest consequence,
As he affirms : I know him for a man
Of the best rank and quality.
   Hort. From Milan !
   Gon. Admit him.

Enter Ambassador, *and* Julio *with a letter,
which he presents on his knee to* Hortensio.

               How ! so low ?
   Amb. I am sorry, sir,
To be the bringer of this heavy news ;
But since it must be known——
   Hort. Peace rest with him !
I shall find fitter time to mourn his loss.
My faithful servant too !
   Jul. I am o'erjoy'd,
To see your highness safe.
   Hort. Pray you, peruse this,
And there you'll find that the objection,
The lord Farneze made, is fully answer'd.
   Gon. The great John Galeas dead !
   Lor. And this his brother,
The absolute lord of Milan !
   Matil. I am revived.
   Uber. There's no contending against des-
   tiny :
I wish both happiness.

Enter Alonzo, Maria, Octavio, Pisano, *and*
Martino.

   Lor. Married, Alonzo !
I will salute your lady, she's a fair one,
And seal your pardon on her lips.
                    [*Kisses* Maria.
   Gon. Octavio !
Welcome e'en to my heart. Rise, I should
   kneel
To thee for mercy.
   Oct. The poor remainder of
My age shall truly serve you.
   Matil. You resemble
A page I had, Ascanio.
   Mar. Your highness' servant still.
   Lor. All stand amazed
At this unlook'd-for meeting ; but defer
Your several stories. Fortune here hath
   shown
Her various power ; but virtue, in the end,
Is crown'd with laurel : Love hath done his
   parts too ;
And mutual friendship, after bloody jars,
Will cure the wounds received in our wars.
                         [*Exeunt.*

EPILOGUE.

Pray you, gentlemen, keep your seats; something I would
Deliver to gain favour, if I could,
To us, and the still doubtful author. He,
When I desired an epilogue, answer'd me,
"'Twas to no purpose: he must stand his fate,
Since all entreaties now would come too late;
You being long since resolved what you would say
Of him, or us, as you rise, or of the play."
A strange old fellow! yet this sullen mood
Would quickly leave him, might it be understood
You part not hence displeased. I am design'd
To give him certain notice: if you find
Things worth your liking, shew it. Hope and fear,
Though different passions, have the self-same ear.

The Old Law.

DRAMATIS PERSONÆ.

Evander, *duke of* Epire.
Cratilus, *the executioner.*
Creon, *father to* Simonides.
imonides, } *young courtiers.*
Cleanthes, }
Lysander, *husband to* Eugenia, *and uncle to* Cleanthes.
Leonides, *father to* Cleanthes.
Gnotho, *the clown.*
Lawyers.
Courtiers.
Dancing-master.

Butler, }
Bailiff, }
Tailor, } *Servants to* Creon.
Coachman, }
Footman, }
Cook, }
Clerk. }
Drawer.
Antigona, *wife to* Creon.
Hippolita, *wife to* Cleanthes.
Eugenia, *wife to* Lysander, *and mother to* Parthenia.
Parthenia.
Agatha, *wife to* Gnotho.
Old women, wives to Creon's *servants.*
Courtezan.
Fiddlers, Servants, Guard, &c.

SCENE,—Epire.

ACT I.

SCENE I.—*A Room in* Creon's *House.*

Enter Simonides *and two* Lawyers.

Sim. Is the law firm, sir?
1 *Law.* The law! what more firm, sir,
More powerful, forcible, or more permanent?
Sim. By my troth, sir,
I partly do believe it; conceive, sir,
You have indirectly answered my question.
I did not doubt the fundamental grounds
Of law in general, for the most solid;
But this particular law that me concerns,
Now, at the present, if that be firm and strong,
And powerful, and forcible, and permanent?
I am a young man that has an old father.
2 *Law.* Nothing more strong, sir.
It is—*Secundum statutum principis, confirmatum cum voce senatus, et voce reipublicæ;* nay, *consummatum et exemplificatum.*
Is it not in force,
When divers have already tasted it,
And paid their lives for penalty?
Sim. 'Tis true.
My father must be next; this day completes
Full fourscore years upon him.
2 *Law.* He is here, then,
Sub pœna statuti : hence I can tell him,
Truer than all the physicians in the world,
He cannot live out to-morrow; this
Is the most certain climacterical year—

'Tis past all danger, for there's no escaping it.
What age is your mother, sir!
Sim. Faith, near her days too;
Wants some two of threescore.
1 *Law.* So! she'll drop away
One of these days too: here's a good age now,
For those that have old parents, and rich inheritance!
Sim. And, sir, 'tis profitable for others too:
Are there not fellows that lie bedrid in their offices,
That younger men would walk lustily in?
Churchmen, that even the second infancy
Hath silenced, yet have spun out their lives so long,
That many pregnant and ingenious spirits
Have languish'd in their hoped reversions,
And died upon the thought? and, by your leave, sir,
Have you not places fill'd up in the law,
By some grave senators, that you imagine
Have held them long enough, and such spirits as you,
Were they removed, would leap into their dignities?
1 *Law. Dic quibus in terris, et eris mihi magnus Apollo.*
Sim. But tell me, faith, your fair opinion:
Is't not a sound and necessary law,
This, by the duke enacted?
1 *Law.* Never did Greece,

Our ancient seat of brave philosophers,
'Mongst all her *nomothetæ* and lawgivers,
Not when she flourish'd in her sevenfold
   sages,
Whose living memory can never die,
Produce a law more grave and necessary.
  Sim. I am of that mind too.
  2 *Law.* I will maintain, sir,
Draco's oligarchy, that the government
Of community reduced into few,   ·
Framed a fair state ; Solon's *chreokopia*,
That cut off poor men's debts to their rich
   creditors,
Was good and charitable, but not full,
   allow'd ;
His *scisactheia* did reform that error,
His honourable senate of Areopagitæ.
Lycurgus was more loose, and gave too free
And licentious reins unto his discipline ;
As that a young woman, in her husband's
   weakness,
Might choose her able friend to propagate ;
That so the commonwealth might be supplied
With hope of lusty spirits. Plato did err,
And so did Aristotle, in allowing
Lewd and luxurious limits to their laws :
But now our Epire, our Epire's Evander,
Our noble and wise prince, has hit the law
That all our predecessive students
Have miss'd, unto their shame.

Enter Cleanthes.

  Sim. Forbear the praise, sir,
'Tis in itself most pleasing :—Cleanthes !
O, lad, here's a spring for young plants to
   flourish !
The old trees must down kept the sun from
   us ;
We shall rise now, boy.
  Clean. Whither, sir, I pray ?
To the bleak air of storms, among those trees
Which we had shelter from ?
  Sim. Yes, from our growth
Our sap and livelihood, and from our fruit.
What ! 'tis not jubilee with thee yet, I think,
Thou look'st so sad on't. How old is thy
   father ?
  Clean. Jubilee ! no, indeed ; 'tis a bad
   year with me.
  Sim. Prithee, how old's thy father ? then
   I can tell thee.
  Clean. I know not how to answer you,
   Simonides ;
He is too old, being now exposed
Unto the rigour of a cruel edict ;
And yet not old enough by many years,
'Cause I'd not see him go an hour before me.
  Sim. These very passions I speak to my
   father.

Come, come, here's none but friends here,
  we may speak
Our insides freely ; these are lawyers, man,
And shall be counsellors shortly.
  Clean. They shall be now, sir,
And shall have large fees if they'll under-
   take
To help a good cause, for it wants assistance;
Bad ones, I know, they can insist upon.
  1 *Law.* Oh, sir, we must undertake of both
   parts ;
But the good we have most good in.
  Clean. Pray you, say,
How do you allow of this strange edict ?
  1 Law. *Secundum justitiam ;* by my faith,
   sir,
The happiest edict that ever was in Epire.
  Clean. What, to kill innocents, sir ? it
   cannot be,
It is no rule in justice there to punish.
  1 *Law.* Oh, sir,
You understand a conscience, but not law.
  Clean. Why, sir, is there so main a difference ?
  1 *Law.* You'll never be good lawyer if you
   understand not that.
  Clean. I think, then, 'tis the best to be a
   bad one.
  1 *Law.* Why, sir, the very letter and the
sense both do overthrow you in this statute,
which speaks, that every man living to fourscore years, and women to threescore, shall
then be cut off as fruitless to the republic,
and law shall finish what nature linger'd at.
  Clean. And this suit shall soon be dispatch'd in law ?
  1 *Law.* It is so plain it can have no demur,
The church-book overthrows it.
  Clean. And so it does ;
The church-book overthrows it, if you read
  it well.
  1 *Law.* Still you run from the law into
error :
You say it takes the lives of innocents,
I say no, and so says common reason ;
What man lives to fourscore, and woman to
  three,
That can die innocent ?
  Clean. A fine law evasion !
Good sir, rehearse the whole statute to me.
  Sim. Fie ! that's too tedious ; you have
  already
The full sum in the brief relation.
  Clean. Sir,
'Mongst many words may be found contra-
  dictions ;
And these men dare sue and wrangle with a
  statute,
If they can pick a quarrel with some error.

o o

2 *Law.* Listen, sir, I'll gather it as brief as I can for you:

Anno primo Evandri, Be it for the care and good of the commonwealth, (for divers necessary reasons that we shall urge,) thus peremptorily enacted,——

Clean. A fair pretence, if the reasons foul it not!

2 Law. *That all men living in our dominions of Epire, in their decayed nature, to the age of fourscore, or women to the age of threescore, shall on the same day be instantly put to death, by those means and instruments that a former proclamation, had to this purpose, through our said territories dispersed.*

· *Clean.* There was no woman in this senate, certain.

1 *Law.* *That these men, being past their bearing arms, to aid and defend their country; past their manhood and likelihood, to propagate any further issue to their posterity; and as well past their councils (whose overgrown gravity is now run into dotage) to assist their country; to whom, in common reason, nothing should be so wearisome as their own lives, as they may be supposed tedious to their successive heirs, whose times are spent in the good of their country: yet wanting the means to maintain it; and are like to grow old before their inheritance (born to them) come to their necessary use, be condemned to die: for the women, for that they never were a defence to their country; never by counsel admitted to assist in the government of their country; only necessary to the propagation of posterity, and now, at the age of threescore, past that good, and all their goodness: it is thought fit (a quarter abated from the more worthy member) that they be put to death, as is before recited: provided that for the just and impartial execution of this our statute, the example shall first begin in and about our court, which ourself will see carefully performed; and not, for a full month following, extend any further into our dominions. Dated the sixth of the second month, at our Palace Royal in Epire.*

Clean. A fine edict, and very fairly gilded! And is there no scruple in all these words, To demur the law upon occasion?

Sim. Pox! 'tis an unnecessary inquisition; Prithee set him not about it.

2 *Law.* Troth, none, sir: It is so evident and plain a case, There is no succour for the defendant.

Clean. Possible! can nothing help in a good case?

1 *Law.* Faith, sir, I do think there may be a hole, Which would protract; delay, if not remedy.

Clean. Why, there's some comfort in that; good sir, speak it.

1 *Law.* Nay, you must pardon me for that, sir.

Sim. Prithee, do not; It may ope a wound to many sons and heirs, That may die after it.

Clean. Come, sir, I know How to make you speak :—will this do it? [*Gives him his purse.*

1 *Law.* I will afford you my opinion, sir.

Clean. Pray you, repeat the literal words expressly, The time of death.

Sim. 'Tis an unnecessary question; prithee let it alone.

2 *Law.* Hear his opinion, 'twill be fruitless, sir.

That man, at the age of fourscore, and woman at threescore, shall the same day be put to death.

1 *Law.* Thus I help the man to twenty-one years more.

Clean. That were a fair addition.

1 *Law.* Mark it, sir; we say, man is not at age Till he be one and twenty; before, 'tis infancy, And adolescency; now, by that addition, Fourscore he cannot be, till a hundred and one.

Sim. Oh, poor evasion! He is fourscore years old, sir.

1 *Law.* That helps more, sir; He begins to be old at fifty, so, at fourscore, He's but thirty years old; so, believe it, sir, He may be twenty years in declination; And so long may a man linger and live by it.

Sim. The worst hope of safety that e'er I heard! Give him his fee again, 'tis not worth two deniers.

1 *Law.* There is no law for restitution of fees, sir.

Clean. No, no, sir; I meant it lost when it was given.

Enter Creon *and* Antigona.

Sim. No more, good sir, Here are ears unnecessary for your doctrine.

1 *Law.* I have spoke out my fee, and I have done, sir.

Sim. O my dear father!

Creon. Tush! meet me not in exclaims; I understand the worst, and hope no better.

A fine law ! if this hold, white heads will be
    cheap,
And many watchmen's places will be vacant ;
Forty of them I know my seniors,
That did due deeds of darkness too :——their
    country
Has watch'd them a good turn for't,
And ta'en them napping now :
The fewer hospitals will serve too, many
May be used for stews and brothels ; and
    those people
Will never trouble them to fourscore.
    Ant. Can you play and sport with sorrow,
    sir ?
    Creon. Sorrow ! for what, Antigona ? for
    my life ?
My sorrow is I have kept it so long well,
With bringing it up unto so ill an end.
I might have gently lost it in my cradle,
Before my nerves and ligaments grew strong,
To bind it faster to me.
    Sim. For mine own sake,
I should have been sorry for that:
    Creon. In my youth
I was a soldier, no coward in my age ;
I never turn'd my back upon my foe ;
I have felt nature's winters, sicknesses,
Yet ever kept a lively sap in me
To greet the cheerful spring of health again.
Dangers, on horse, on foot, [by land,] by
    water,
I have scaped to this day ; and yet this day,
Without all help of casual accidents,
Is only deadly to me, 'cause it numbers
Fourscore years to me. Where is the fault
    now ?
I cannot blame time, nature, nor my stars,
Nor aught but tyranny. Even kings them-
    selves
Have sometimes tasted an even fate with me.
He that has been a soldier all his days,
And stood in personal opposition
'Gainst darts and arrows, the extremes of heat
And pinching cold, has treacherously at
    home,
In's secure quiet, by a villain's hand
Been basely lost, in his star's ignorance :——
And so must I die by a tyrant's sword.
    1 *Law.* Oh, say not so, sir, it is by the law.
    Creon. And what's that, but the sword of
    tyranny,
When it is brandish'd against innocent lives?
I am now upon my deathbed, and 'tis fit
I should unbosom my free conscience,
And shew the faith I die in :—I do believe
'Tis tyranny that takes my life.
    Sim. Would it were gone
By one means or other ! what a long day
Will this be ere night ?   [*Aside.*

    Creon. Simonides.
    Sim. Here, sir,—weeping.
    Creon. Wherefore dost thou weep ?
    Clean. 'Cause you make no more haste to
    your end.   [*Aside.*
    Sim. How can you question nature so un-
    justly?
I had a grandfather, and then had not you
True filial tears for him?
    Clean. Hypocrite ?
A disease of drought dry up all pity from him,
That can dissemble pity with wet eyes !
    Creon. Be good unto your mother, Si-
    monides.
She must be now your care.
    Ant. To what end, sir ?
The bell of this sharp edicts tolls for me,.
As it rings out for you.—I'll be as ready,
With one hour's stay, to go along with you.,
    Creon. Thou must not, woman, there are·
    years behind,
Before thou canst set forward in this voyage ;.
And nature, sure, will now be kind to all :
She has a quarrel in't, a cruel law
Seeks to prevent her, she ·will therefore fight
    in't,
And draw out life even to her longest thread :.
Thou art scarce fifty-five.
    Ant. So many morrows !
Those five remaining years I'll turn to days,.
To hours, or minutes, for your company.
'Tis fit that you and I, being man and wife,'
Should walk together arm in arm.
    Sim. I hope
They'll go together ; I would they would,.
    i'faith,
Then would her thirds be saved too. [*Aside.*]
    —The day goes away, sir.
    Creon. Why wouldst thou have me gone,
    Simonides?
    Sim. O my heart ! Would you have me·
    gone before you, 'sir,
You give me such a deadly wound ?.
    Clean. Fine rascal !
    Sim. Blemish my duty so with such a·
    question ?
Sir, I would haste me to the duke for mercy ;.
He that's above the law may mitigate
The rigour of the law. · How a good meaning·
May be corrupted by a misconstruction !
    Creon. Thou corrupt'st mine ; I. did not·
    think thou mean'st so. ·
    Clean. You were in the more error.
    ·   [*Aside:.*
    Sim. The words wounded me.
    Clean. 'Twas pity thou died'st not on't:
    Sim. I have been ransacking the helps of·
    law,
Conferring with these learned advocates :.

If any scruple, cause, or wrested sense
Could have been found out to preserve your
    life,
It had been bought, though with your full
    estate,
Your life's so precious to me!--but there's
    none.
    1 *Law.* Sir, we have canvass'd her from
        top to toe,
Turn'd her upside down, thrown her upon
    her side,
Nay, open'd and dissected all her entrails,
Yet can find none : there's nothing to be
    hoped,
But the duke's mercy.
    Sim. I know the hope of that ;
He did not make the law for that purpose.
    Creon. Then to this hopeless mercy last
        I go ;
I have so many precedents before me,
I must call it hopeless : Antigona,
See me delivered up unto my deathsman,
And then we'll part ;—five years hence I'll
    look for thee.
    Sim. I hope she will not stay so long
        behind you.   [*Aside.*
    Creon. Do not bate him an hour by grief
        and sorrow,
Since there's a day prefix'd, hasten it not.
Suppose me sick, Antigona, dying now,
Any disease thou wilt may be my end,
Or when death's slow to come, say tyrants
    send. [*Exeunt* Creon *and* Antigona.
    Sim. Cleanthes, if you want money, to-
        morrow use me ;
I'll trust you while your father's dead.
                    [*Exit, with the* Lawyers.
    Clean. Why, here's a villain,
Able to corrupt a thousand by example !
Does the kind root bleed out his liveli-
    hood
In parent distribution to his branches,
Adorning them with all his glorious fruits,
Proud that his pride is seen when he's un-
    seen ;
And must not gratitude descend again,
To comfort his old limbs in fruitless winter?
Improvident, or at least partial nature !
(Weak woman in this kind,) who, in thy last
    teeming,
Forgettest still the former, ever making
The burthen of thy last throes the dearest
    darling !
O yet in noble man reform [reform] it,
And make us better than those vegetives,
Whose souls die with them. Nature, as thou
    art old,
If love and justice be not dead in thee,
Make some the pattern of thy piety ;

Lest all do turn unnaturally against thee,
And thou be blamed for our oblivious

    Enter Leonides *and* Hippolita.

And brutish reluctations ! Ay, here's the
    ground
Whereon my filial faculties must build
An edifice of honour, or of shame,
To all mankind.
    Hip. You must avoid it, sir,
If there be any love within yourself :
This is far more than fate of a lost game
That another venture may restore again ;
It is your life, which you should not subject
To any cruelty, if you can preserve it.
    Clean. O dearest woman, thou hast
        doubled now
A thousand times thy nuptial dowry to me !—
Why, she whose love is but derived from me,
Is got before me in my debted duty.
    Hip. Are you thinking such a resolution,
        sir ?
    Clean. Sweetest Hippolita, what love
        taught thee
To be so forward in so good a cause ?
    Hip. Mine own pity, sir, did first instruct
        me,
And then your love and power did both
    command me.
    Clean. They were all blessed angels to
        direct thee ;
And take their counsel. How do you fare,
    sir ?
    Leon. Cleanthes, never better ; I have
        conceived
Such a new joy within this old bosom,
As I did never think would there have en-
    ter'd.
    Clean. Joy call you it ? alas ! 'tis sorrow,
        sir,
The worst of sorrows, sorrow unto death.
    Leon. Death ! what is that, Cleanthes ? I
        thought not on't,
I was in contemplation of this woman :
'Tis all thy comfort, son ; thou hast in her
A treasure invaluable, keep her safe.
When I die, sure 'twill be a gentle death,
For I will die with wonder of her virtues ;
Nothing else shall dissolve me.
    Clean. 'Twere much better, sir,
Could you prevent their malice.
    Leon. I'll prevent them,
And die the way I told thee, in the wonder
Of this good woman. I tell thee there's
    few men
Have such a child : I must thank thee for
    her.
That the strong tie of wedlock should do
    more,

Than nature in her nearest ligaments
Of blood and propagation ! I should never
Have begot such a daughter of my own :
A daughter-in-law ! law were above nature,
Were there more such children.

Clean. This admiration
Helps nothing to your safety ; think of that,
    sir.

Leon. Had you heard her, Cleanthes, but
    labour
In the search of means to save my forfeit
    life,
And knew the wise and the sound preserva-
    tions
That she found out, you would redouble all
My wonder, in your love to her.

Clean. The thought,
The very thought, sir, claims all that from me,
And she is now possest of 't : but, good sir,
If you have aught received from her advice,
Let's follow it ; or else let's better think,
And take the surest course.

Leon. I'll tell thee one ;
She counsels me to fly my severe country ;
To turn all into treasure, and there build up
My decaying fortunes in a safer soil,
Where Epire's law cannot claim me.

Clean. And, sir,
I apprehend it as a safest course,
And may be easily accomplished ;
Let us be all most expeditious.
Every country where we breathe will be our
    own,
Or better soil ; heaven is the roof of all,
And now, as Epire's situate by this law,
There is 'twixt us and heaven a dark eclipse.

Hip. Oh, then avoid it, sir ; these sad
    events
Follow those black predictions.

Leon. I prithee peace ;
I do allow thy love, Hippolita,
But must not follow it as counsel, child ;
I must not shame my country for the law.
This country here hath bred me, brought
    me up,
And shall I now refuse a grave in her ?
I am in my second infancy, and children
Ne'er sleep so sweetly in their nurse's cradle,
As in their natural mother's.

Hip. Ay, but, sir,
She is unnatural ; then the stepmother's
To be preferr'd before her.

Leon. Tush ! she shall
Allow it me in despite of her entrails.
Why, do you think how far from judgment
    'tis,
That I should travel forth to seek a grave
That is already digg'd for me at home,
Nay, perhaps find it in my way to seek it ?—

How have I then sought a repentant sorrow ?
For your dear loves, how have I banish'd you
From your country ever ? With my base
    attempt,
How have I beggar'd you in wasting that
Which only for your sakes I bred together ;
Buried my name in Epire which I built
Upon this frame, to live for ever in ?
What a base coward shall I be, to fly from
That enemy which every minute meets me,
And thousand odds he had not long van-
    quish'd me
Before this hour of battle ! Fly my death !
I will not be so false unto your states,
Nor fainting to the man that's yet in me :
I'll meet him bravely ; I cannot (this know-
    ing) fear
That, when I am gone hence, I shall be there.
Come, I have days of preparation left.

Clean. Good sir, hear me :
I have a genius that has prompted me,
And I have almost form'd it into words——
'Tis done, pray you observe them ; I can
    conceal you ;
And yet not leave your country.

Leon. Tush ! it cannot be,
Without a certain peril on us all.

Clean. Danger must be hazarded, rather
    than accept
A sure destruction. You have a lodge, sir,
So far remote from way of passengers,
That seldom any mortal eye does greet with't;
And yet so sweetly situate with thickets,
Built with such cunning labyrinths within,
As if the provident heavens, foreseeing
    cruelty,
Had bid you frame it to this purpose only.

Leon. Fie, fie ! 'tis dangerous,—and trea-
    son too,
To abuse the law.

Hip. 'Tis holy care, sir,
Of your dear life, which is your own to keep,
But not your own to lose, either in will
Or negligence.

Clean. Call you it treason, sir ?
I had been then a traitor unto you,
Had I forgot this ; beseech you, accept of it ;
It is secure, and a duty to yourself.

Leon. What a coward will you make me !

Clean. You mistake ;
'Tis noble courage, now you fight with
    death ;
And yield not to him till you stoop under
    him.

Leon. This must needs open to discovery,
And then what torture follows ?

Clean. By what means, sir ?
Why, there is but one body in all this
    counsel.

Which cannot betray itself : we two are one,
One soul, one body, one heart, that think
　　one thought ;
And yet we two are not completely one,
But as I have derived myself from you.——
Who shall betray us where there is no
　　second?
　　Hip. You must not mistrust my faith,
　　though my sex plead
Weakness and frailty for me.
　　Leon. Oh, I dare not.
But where's the means that must make
　　answer for me?
I cannot be lost without a full account,
And what must pay that reckoning?
　　Clean. Oh, sir, we will
Keep solemn obits for your funeral ;
We'll seem to weep, and seem to joy withal,
That death so gently has prevented you
The law's sharp rigour ; and this no mortal
　　ear shall
Participate the knowledge of.
　　Leon. Ha, ha, ha !
This will be a sportive fine demur,
If the error be not found.
　　Clean. Pray doubt of none.
Your company and best provision,
Must be no further furnish'd than by us ;
And, in the interim, your solitude may
Converse with heaven, and fairly [so] prepare
[For that] which was too violent and raging
Thrown headlong on you.
　　Leon. Still, there are some doubts
Of the discovery ; yet I do allow it.
　　Hip. Will you not mention now the cost
　　and charge,
Which will be in your keeping !
　　Leon. That will be somewhat,
Which you might save too.
　　Clean. With his will against him,
What foe is more to man than man himself?
Are you resolved, sir?
　　Leon. I am, Cleanthes :
If by this means I do get a reprieve,
And cozen death awhile, when he shall come
Armed in his own power to give the blow,
I'll smile upon him then, and laughing go.
　　　　　　　　　　　　　　　　[Exeunt.

　　　　　　　　ACT II.

　　SCENE I.—*Before the Palace.*

Enter Evander, Courtiers, *and* Cratilus.

　　Evan. Executioner !
　　Crat. My lord.
　　Evan. How did old Diocles' take his
　　death?

　　Crat. As weeping brides receive their
　　joys at night ;
With trembling, yet with patience.
　　Evan. Why, 'twas well.
　　1 *Court.* Nay, I knew my father would
　　do well, my lord,
Whene'er he came to die ; I'd that opinion
　　of him,
Which made me the more willing to part
　　from him ;
He was not fit to live in the world, indeed
Any time these ten years, my lord,
But I would not say so much.
　　Evan. No! you did not well in't,
For he that's all spent, is ripe for death at
　　all hours,
And does but trifle time out.
　　1 *Court.* Troth, my lord,
I would I'd known your mind nine years ago.
　　Evan. Our law is fourscore years, because
　　we judge
Dotage complete then, as unfruitfulness
In women, at threescore ; marry, if the son
Can, within compass, bring good solid proofs
Of his own father's weakness, and unfitness
To live, or sway the living, though he want
　　five
Or ten years of his number, that's not it ;
His defect makes him fourscore, and 'tis fit
He dies when he deserves ; for every act
Is in effect then, when the cause is ripe.
　　2 *Court.* An admirable prince ! how rarely
　　he talks !
Oh that we'd known this, lads ! What a
　　time did we endure
In two-penny commons, and in boots twice
　　vamp'd !
　　1 *Court.* Now we have two pair a week,
　　and yet not thankful ;
'Twill be a fine world for them, sirs, that
　　come after us.
　　2 *Court.* Ay, an they knew it.
　　1 *Court.* Peace, let them never know it.
　　3 *Court.* A pox, there be young heirs will
　　soon smell't out.
　　2 *Court.* 'Twill come to them by instinct,
　　man : may your grace
Never be old, you stand so well for youth !
　　Evan. Why now, methinks, our court
　　looks like a spring,
Sweet, fresh, and fashionable, now the old
　　weeds are gone.
　　1 *Court.* It is as a court should be :
Gloss and good clothes, my lord, no matter
　　for merit;
And herein your law proves a provident act,
When men pass not the palsy of their
　　tongues,
Nor colour in their cheeks.

Evan. But women,
By that law, should live long, for they're
ne'er past it.
  1 *Court.* It will have heats though, when
they see the painting
Go an inch deep i'the wrinkle, and take up
A box more than their gossips : but for
men, my lord,
That should be the sole bravery of a palace,
To walk with hollow eyes and long white
beards,
As if a prince dwelt in a land of goats ;
With clothes as if they sat on their backs on
purpose
To arraign a fashion, and condemn't to exile;
Their pockets in their sleeves, as if they laid
Their ear to avarice, and heard the devil
whisper !
Now ours lie downward, here, close to the
  · flank ;
Right spending pockets, as a son's should be,
That lives i'the fashion ; where our diseased
fathers,
Worried with the sciatica and aches,
Brought up your paned hose first, which
ladies laugh'd at,
Giving no reverence to the place lies ruin'd :
They love a doublet that's three hours a
buttoning,
And sits so close makes a man groan again,
And his soul mutter half a day ; yet these
are those,
That carry sway and worth : prick'd up in
  · clothes,
Why should we fear our rising ?
  Evan. You but wrong
Our kindness, and your own deserts, to doubt
on't.
Has not our law made you rich before your
time?
Our countenance then can make you honour-
able.
  1 *Court.* We'll spare for no cost, sir, to
appear worthy.
  Evan. Why you're i'the noble way then,
  · for the most
Are but appearers ; worth itself is lost,
And bravery stands for't.

Enter Creon, Antigona, *and* Simonides.

  1 *Court.* Look, look, who comes here !
I smell death, and another courtier,
Simonides.
  2 *Court.* Sim !
  Sim. Pish ! I'm not for you yet,
Your company's too costly; after the old man's
Dispatch'd, I shall have time to talk with you;
I shall come into the fashion you shall see too,

After a day or two ; in the mean time,
I am not for your company.
  Evan. Old Creon, you have been expected
long ;
Sure you're above fourscore.
  Sim. Upon my life,
Not four and twenty hours,· my lord ; I
search'd
The church-book yesterday. Does your grace
think
I'd let my father wrong the law, my lord ?
'Twere pity o' my life then ! no, your act
Shall not receive a minute's wrong by him,
While I live, sir; and he's so just himself too,
I know he would not offer't :—here he
stands.
  Creon. 'Tis just I die, indeed; for I confess
I am troublesome to life now, and the state
Can hope for nothing worthy from me now,
Either in force or counsel; I've o' late
Employ'd myself quite from the world,
and he
That once begins to serve his Maker faith-
  · fully,
Can never serve a worldly prince well after ;
'Tis clean another way.
  Ant. Oh, give not confidence
To all he speaks, my lord, in his own injury.
His preparation only for the next world,
Makes him talk wildly, to his wrong, of this;
He is not lost in judgment.
  Sim. She spoils all again.   [*Aside.*
  Ant. Deserving any way for state employ-
ment.
  Sim. Mother——
  Ant. His very household laws prescribed
at home by him,
Are able to conform seven Christian king-
doms,
They are so wise and virtuous.
  Sim. Mother, I say——
  Ant. I know your laws extend not to
desert, sir,
But to unnecessary years ; and, my lord,
His are not such ; though they show white,
they are worthy,
Judicious, able, and religious.
  Sim. Mother,
I'll help you to a courtier of nineteen.
  Ant. Away, unnatural !
  Sim. Then I am no fool, sure,
For to be natural at such a time
Were a fool's part, indeed.
  Ant. Your grace's pity,
And 'tis but fit and just.
  Creon. The law, my lord,
And that's the justest way.
  Sim. Well said, father, i'faith !
Thou wert ever juster than my mother still.

Evan. Come hither, sir.

Sim. My lord.

Evan. What are those orders?

Ant. Worth observation, sir,
So please you hear them read.

Sim. The woman speaks she knows not
what, my lord :
He make a law, poor man! he bought a
TABLE, indeed,
Only to learn to die by't, there's the busi-
ness, now ;
Wherein there are some precepts for a son
too,
How he should learn to live, but I ne'er
look'd on't :
For, when he's dead, I shall live well enough,
And keep a better TABLE than that, I trow.

Evan. And is that all, sir?

Sim. All, I vow, my lord ;
Save a few running admonitions
Upon cheese-trenchers, as——
Take heed of whoring, shun it ;
'Tis like a cheese too strong of the runnet.
And such calves' maws of wit and admonition,
Good to catch mice with, but not sons and
heirs ;
They are not so easily caught.

Evan. Agent for death !

Crat. Your will, my lord?

Evan. Take hence that pile of years,
Forfeit before with unprofitable age,
And, with the rest, from the high promon-
tory,
Cast him into the sea.

Creon. 'Tis noble justice !
         [*Exit* Grat. *with* Creon.

Ant. 'Tis cursed tyranny !

Sim. Peace ! take heed, mother ;
You've but short time to be cast down your-
self ;
And let a young courtier do't, an you be wise,
In the mean time.

Ant. Hence, slave !

Sim. Well, seven-and-fifty,
You have but three years to scold, then
comes your payment.
         [*Exit* Antigona.

1 *Court.* Simonides.

Sim. Pish, I'm not brave enough to hold
you talk yet,
Give a man time, I have a suit a making.

2 *Court.* We love thy form first ; brave
clothes will come, man.

Sim. I'll make them come else, with a
mischief to them,
As other gallants do, that have less left them.
         [*Recorders within.*

Evan. Hark ! whence those sounds ?
what's that ?

1 *Court.* Some funeral,
It seems, my lord ; and young Cleanthes
follows.

Enter a Funeral Procession ; the hearse fol-
lowed by Cleanthes *and* Hippolita, *gaily*
dressed.

Evan. Cleanthes !

2 *Court.* 'Tis, my lord, and in the place
Of a chief mourner too, but strangely habited.

Evan. Yet suitable to his behaviour ;
mark it :
He comes all the way smiling, do you ob-
serve it ;
I never saw a corse so joyfully followed :
Light colours and light cheeks !—who should
this be ?
'Tis a thing worth resolving.

Sim. One, belike,
That doth participate this our present joy.

Evan. Cleanthes.

Clean. Oh, my lord !

Evan. He laugh'd outright now ;
Was ever such a contrariety seen
In natural courses yet, nay profess'd openly ?

1 *Court.* I have known a widow laugh
closely, my lord,
Under her handkerchief, when t'other part
Of her old face has wept like rain in sun-
shine ;
But all the face to laugh apparently,
Was never seen yet.

Sim. Yes, mine did once.

Clean. 'Tis, of a heavy time, the joy-
full'st day
That ever son was born to.

Evan. How can that be ?

Clean. I joy to make it plain,—my father's
dead.

Evan. Dead !

2 *Court.* Old Leonides !

Clean. In his last month dead :
He beguiled cruel law the sweetliest,
That ever age was blest to.——
It grieves me that a tear should fall upon't,
Being a thing so joyful, but his memory
Will work it out, I see ; when his poor
heart broke,
I did not do so much : but leap'd for joy
So mountingly, I touch'd the stars, me-
thought ;
I would not hear of blacks, I was so light,
But chose a colour, orient like my mind :
For blacks are often such dissembling
mourners,
There is no credit given to't ; it has lost
All reputation by false sons and widows.
Now I would have men know what I re-
semble,

A truth, indeed ; 'tis joy clad like a joy,
Which is more honest than a cunning grief,
That's only faced with sables for a show,
But gawdy-hearted : When I saw death come
So ready to deceive you, sir,—forgive me,
I could not choose but be entirely merry,
And yet to see now !—of a sudden,
Naming but death, I shew myself a mortal,
That's never constant to one passion long.
I wonder whence that tear came, when I
  smiled
In the production on't ; sorrow's a thief,
That can, when joy looks on, steal forth a
  grief.
But, gracious leave, my lord ; when I've
  perform'd
My last poor duty to my father's bones,
I shall return your servant.
  Evan. Well, perform it,
The law is satisfied ; they can but die :
And by his death, Cleanthes, you gain well,
A rich and fair revenue.
  [*Flourish. Exeunt* Duke, Courtiers, *&c.*
  Sim. I would I had e'en
Another father, condition he did the like.
  Clean. I have past it bravely now ; how
  blest was I,
To have the duke in sight ! now 'tis con-
  firm'd,
Past fear or doubts confirm'd : on, on I say,
Him that brought me to man, I bring to clay.
  [*Exit Funeral Procession, followed by*
  Cleanthes *and* Hippolita.
  Sim. I am rapt now in a contemplation,
Even at the very sight of yonder hearse ;
I do but think what a fine thing 'tis now
To live, and follow some seven uncles
  thus,
As many cousin-germans, and such people,
That will leave legacies ; pox ! I'd see them
  hang'd else,
Ere I'd follow one of them, an they could
  find the way.
Now I've enough to begin to be horrible
  covetous.

  Enter Butler, Tailor, Bailiff, Cook, Coachman, *and* Footman.

  But. We come to know your worship's
  pleasure, sir,
Having long serv'd your father, how your
  good will
Stands towards our entertainment.
  Sim. Not a jot, i'faith :
My father wore cheap garments, he might
  do't ;
I shall have all my clothes come home to-
  morrow,

They will eat up all you, an there were more
  of you, sirs.
To keep you six at livery, and still munching !
  Tail. Why, I'm a tailor ; you have most
  need of me, sir.
  Sim. Thou mad'st my father's clothes,
  that I confess ;
But what son and heir will have his father's
  tailor,
Unless he have a mind to be well laugh'd at?
Thou'st been so used to wide long-side
  things, that when
I come to truss, I shall have the waist of my
  doublet
Lie on my buttocks, a sweet sight !
  But. I a butler.
  Sim. There's least need of thee, fellow ; I
shall ne'er drink at home, I shall be so drunk
  abroad.
  But. But a cup of small beer will do well
next morning, sir.
  Sim. I grant you ; but what need I keep
so big a knave for a cup of small beer ?
  Cook. Butler, you have your answer :
marry, sir, a cook
I know your mastership cannot be without.
  Sim. The more ass art thou to think so ;
for what should I do with a mountebank,
no drink in my house ?—the banishing the
butler might have been a warning for thee,
unless thou mean'st to choak me.
  Cook. In the meantime you have choak'd
me, methinks.
  Bail. These are superfluous vanities,
indeed,
And so accounted of in these days, sir ;
But then, your bailiff to receive your rents——
  Sim. I prithee hold thy tongue, fellow, I
shall take a course to spend them faster than
thou canst reckon them ; 'tis not the rents
must serve my turn, unless I mean to be
laugh'd at ; if a man should be seen out of
slash-me, let him ne'er look to be a right
gallant. But, sirrah, with whom is your
business ?
  Coach. Your good mastership.
  Sim. You have stood silent all this while,
like men
That know your strengths : in these days,
none of you
Can want employment ; you can win me
wagers,
Footman, in running races.
  Foot. I dare boast it, sir.
  Sim. And when my bets are all come in,
and store,
Then, coachman, you can hurry me to my
whore.
  Coach. I'll firk them into foam else.

Sim. Speaks brave matter :
And I'll firk some too, or't shall cost hot
  water.
    [*Exeunt* Simonides, Coachman, *and*
      Footman.
Cook. Why, here's an age to make a cook
  a ruffian, .
And scald the devil indeed ! do strange mad
  things,
Make mutton-pasties of dog's flesh,
Bake snakes for lamprey pies, and cats for
  conies.
  But. Come, will you be ruled by a butler's
advice once? for we must make up our fortunes somewhere now, as the case stands :
let's e'en, therefore, go seek out widows of
nine and fifty, an we can, that's within a
year of their deaths, and so we shall be
sure to be quickly rid of them ; for a year's
enough of conscience to be troubled with a
wife, for any man living.
  Cook. Oracle butler ! oracle butler ! he puts
down all the doctors o' the name. [*Exeunt.*

SCENE II.—*A room in* Creon's *House.*

    Enter Eugenia *and* Parthenia.

Eug. Parthenia.
Parth. Mother.
Eug. I shall be troubled
This six months with an old clog ; would
  the law
Had been cut one year shorter !
  Parth. Did you call, forsooth ?
  Eug. Yes, you must make some spoonmeat
for your father,   [*Exit* Parthenia.
And warm three nightcaps for him. Out
  upon't !
The mere conceit turns a young woman's
  stomach.
His slippers must be warm'd, in August too,
And his gown girt to him in the very dog-days,
When every mastiff lolls out's tongue for heat.
Would not this vex a beauty of nineteen now?
Alas ! I should be tumbling in cold baths now,
Under each armpit a fine bean-flower bag,
To screw out whiteness when I list——
And some sev'n of the properest men in the
  dukedom
Making a banquet ready i' the next room for
  me ;
Where he that gets the first kiss is envied,
And stands upon his guard a fortnight after.
This is a life for nineteen ! 'tis but justice :
For old men, whose great acts stand in their
  minds,
And nothing in their bodies, do ne'er think
A woman young enough for their desire ;
And we young wenches, that have mother-
  wits,

And love to marry muck first, and man after,
Do never think old men are old enough,
That we may soon be rid o' them ; there's
  our quittance.
I've waited for the happy hour this two years,
And, if death be so unkind to let him live
  still,
All that time I have lost.

    Enter Courtiers.

1 Court. Young lady !
2 Court. O sweet precious bud of beauty !
Troth, she smells over all the house, methinks.
  1 Court. The sweetbriar's but a counterfeit to her——
It does exceed you only in the prickle,
But that it shall not long, if you'll be ruled,
  lady.
  Eug. What means this sudden visitation,
  gentlemen ?
So passing well perfumed too ! who's your
  milliner ?
  1 Court. Love, and thy beauty, widow.
  Eug. Widow, sir ?
  1 Court. 'Tis sure, and that's as good : in
  troth we're suitors ;
We come a wooing, wench ; plain dealing's
  best.
  Eug. A wooing ! what, before my husband's dead?
  2 Court. Let's lose no time ; six months
  will have an end ;
I know't by all the bonds that e'er I made
  yet.
  Eug. That's a sure knowledge ; but it
  holds not here, sir.
  1 Court. Do not we know the craft of you
  young tumblers ?
That when you wed an old man, you think
  upon
Another husband as you are marrying of
  him ;—
We, knowing your thoughts, made bold to
  see you.

    Enter Simonides *richly drest, and*
      Coachman.

  Eug. How wondrous right he speaks !
  'twas my thought, indeed.
  Sim. By your leave, sweet widow, do you
  lack any gallants ?
  Eug. Widow, again ! 'tis a comfort to be
  call'd so.
  1 Court. Who's this? Simonides ?
  2 Court. Brave Sim, i' faith !
  Sim. Coachman !
  Coach. Sir.

Sim. Have an especial care of my new
  mares ;
They say, sweet widow, he that loves a horse
  well,
Must needs love a widow well.—When dies
  thy husband ?
Is't not July next ?
Eug. Oh, you are too hot, sir !
Pray cool yourself, and take September with
  you.
Sim. September ! oh, I was but two bows
  wide.
1 *Court.* Simonides.
Sim. I can entreat you, gallants, I'm in
  fashion too.

          Enter Lysander.

Lys. Ha ! whence this herd of folly ? what
  are you ?
Sim. Well-willers to your wife : pray 'tend
  your book, sir ;
We've nothing to say to you, you may go die,
For here be those in place that can supply.
Lys. What's thy wild business here ?
Sim. Old man, I'll tell thee ;
I come to beg the reversion of thy wife :
I think these gallants be of my mind too.—
But thou art but a dead man, therefore what
should a man do talking with thee ? Come,
widow, stand to your tackling.
Lys. Impious blood-hounds !
Sim. Let the ghost talk, ne'er mind him.
Lys. Shames of nature !
Sim. Alas, poor ghost ! consider what the
  man is.
Lys. Monsters unnatural ! you that have
  been covetous
Of your own father's death, gape you for
  mine now ?
Cannot a poor old man, that now can reckon
Even all the hours he has to live, live quiet,
For such wild beasts as these, that neither
  hold
A certainty of good within themselves,
But scatter others' comforts that are ripen'd
For holy uses ? is hot youth so hasty,
It will not give an old man leave to die,
And leave a widow first, but will make one,
The husband looking on ? May your de-
  structions
Come all in hasty figures to your souls !
Your wealth depart in haste, to overtake
Your honesties, that died when you were
  infants !
May your male seed be hasty spendthrifts too,
Your daughters hasty sinners, and diseased
Ere they be thought at years to welcome
  misery !
And may you never know what leisure is,

But at repentance !—I am too uncharitable,
Too foul ; I must go cleanse myself with
  prayers.
These are the plagues of fondness to old men,
We're punish'd home with what we dote upon.
                                        [*Exit.*
Sim. So, so ! the ghost is vanish'd : now,
  your answer, lady.
Eug. Excuse me, gentlemen ; 'twere as
  much impudence
In me, to give you a kind answer yet,
As madness to produce a churlish one.
I could say now, come a month hence, sweet
  gentlemen,
Or two, or three, or when you will, indeed ;
But I say no such thing : I set no time,
Nor is it mannerly to deny any.
I'll carry an even hand to all the world :
Let other women make what haste they will,
What's that to me? but I profess unfeignedly,
I'll have my husband dead before I marry ;
Ne'er look for other answer at my hands.
Sim. Would he were hang'd, for my part,
  looks for other !
Eug. I'm at a word.
Sim. And I am at a blow, then ;
I'll lay you o' the lips, and leave you.
                                    [*Kisses her.*
1 *Court.* Well struck, Sim.
Sim. He that dares say he'll mend it, I'll
  strike him.
1 *Court.* He would betray himself to be a
  botcher,
That goes about to mend it.
Eug. Gentlemen,
You know my mind ; I bar you not my
  house :
But if you choose out hours more seasonably,
You may have entertainment.

          Re-enter Parthenia.

Sim. What will she do hereafter, when
  she is a widow,
Keeps open house already?
              [*Exeunt* Simonides *and* Courtiers.
Eug. How now, girl !
Parth. Those feather'd fools that hither
  took their flight,
Have grieved my father much.
Eug. Speak well of youth, wench,
While thou'st a day to live ; 'tis youth must
  make thee,
And when youth fails, wise women will
  make it ;
But always take age first, to make thee
  rich :
That was my counsel ever, and then youth
Will make thee sport enough all thy life
  after.

'Tis the time's policy, wench ; what is't to
　bide
A little hardness for a pair of years, or so ?
A man whose only strength lies in his
　breath,
Weakness in all parts else, thy bedfellow,
A cough o' the lungs, or say a wheezing
　matter ;
Then shake off chains, and dance all thy life
　after ?
Parth. Every one to their liking ; but I
　say
An honest man's worth all, be he young or
　gray.
Yonder's my cousin.   [*Exit.*

　　　　　Enter Hippolita.

Eug. Art, I must use thee now ;
Dissembling is the best help for a virtue,
That ever women had ; it saves their credit
　oft.
Hip. How now, cousin !
What, weeping ?
Eug. Can you blame me, when the time
Of my dear love and husband now draws on ?
I study funeral tears against the day
I must be a sad widow.
Hip. In troth, Eugenia, I have cause to
　weep too ;
But, when I visit, I come comfortably,
And look to be so quited :—yet more sob-
　bing ?
Eug. Oh !
The greatest part of your affliction's past,
The worst of mine's to come ; I have one to
　die ;
Your husband's father is dead, and fixed in
　his
Eternal peace, past the sharp tyrannous
　blow.
Hip. You must use patience, coz.
Eug. Tell me of patience !
Hip. You have example for't, in me and
　many.
Eug. Yours was a father-in-law, but mine
　a husband :
O, for a woman that could love, and live
With an old man, mine is a jewel, cousin ;
So quietly he lies by one, so still !
Hip. Alas ! I have a secret lodged within
　me,
Which now will out in pity :—I cannot hold.
　　　　　　　　　　　　　　　　[*Aside.*
Eug. One that will not disturb me in my
　sleep
For a whole month together, less it be
With those diseases age is subject to,
As aches, coughs, and pains, and these,
　heaven knows,

Against his will too :—he's the quietest man,
Especially in bed.
Hip. Be comforted.
Eug. How can I, lady?
None know the terror of an husband's loss,
But they that fear to lose him.
Hip. Fain would I keep it in, but 'twill
　not be ;
She is my kinswoman, and I am pitiful.
I must impart a good, if I know it once,
To them that stand in need on't ; I'm like
　one
Loves not to banquet with a joy alone,
My friends must partake too. [*Aside.*]—
　Prithee, cease, cousin ;
If your love be so boundless, which is rare,
In a young woman, in these days, I tell you,
To one so much past service as your hus-
　band,
There is a way to beguile law, and help you ;
My husband found it out first.
Eug. Oh, sweet cousin !
Hip. You may conceal him, and give out
　his death
Within the time ; order his funeral too ;
We had it so for ours, I praise heav'n for't,
And he's alive and safe.
Eug. O blessed coz,
How thou revivest me !
Hip. We daily see
The good old man, and feed him twice a
　day.
Methinks, it is the sweetest joy to cherish
　him,
That ever life yet shew'd me.
Eug. So should I think,
A dainty thing to nurse an old man well !
Hip. And then we have his prayers and
　daily blessing ;
And we two live so lovingly upon it,
His son and I, and so contentedly,
You cannot think unless you tasted on't.
Eug. No, I warrant you. Oh, loving
　cousin,
What a great sorrow hast thou eased me of ?
A thousand thanks go with thee !
Hip. I have a suit to you,
I must not have you weep when I am gone.
　　　　　　　　　　　　　　　　[*Exit.*
Eug. No, if I do ne'er trust me. Easy fool,
Thou hast put thyself into my power for
　ever ;
Take heed of angering of me : I conceal !
I feign a funeral ! I keep my husband !
'Las ! I've been thinking any time these two
　years,
I have kept him too long already.—
I'll go count o'er my suitors, that's my
　business,

And prick the man down ; I've six months
to do't,
But could dispatch it in one, were I put to't.
[Exit.

ACT III.

SCENE I.—*Before the Church.*

Enter Gnotho *and* Clerk.

Gnoth. You have search'd over the parish-
chronicle, sir?

Clerk. Yes, sir ; I have found out the true
age and date of the party you wot on.

Gnoth. Pray you, be cover'd, sir.

Clerk. When you have shewed me the
way, sir.

Gnoth. Oh, sir, remember yourself, you
are a clerk.

Clerk. A small clerk, sir.

Gnoth. Likely to be the wiser man, sir ;
for your greatest clerks are not always so, as
'tis reported.

Clerk. You are a great man in the parish,
sir.

Gnoth. I understand myself so much the
better, sir ; for all the best in the parish pay
duties to the clerk, and I would owe you
none, sir.

Clerk. Since you'll have it so, I'll be the
first to hide my head.

Gnoth. Mine is a capcase : now to our business in hand. Good luck, I hope ; I long to
be resolved.

Clerk. Look you, sir, this is that cannot
deceive you :
This is the dial that goes ever true ;
You may say *ipse dixit* upon this witness,
And it is good in law too.

Gnoth. Pray you, let's hear what it speaks.

Clerk. Mark, sir.—*Agatha, the daughter
of Pollux,* (this is your wife's name, and the
name of her father,) *born*——

Gnoth. Whose daughter, say you?

Clerk. The daughter of Pollux.

Gnoth. I take it his name was Bollux.

Clerk. Pollux the orthography, I assure
you, sir ; the word is corrupted else.

Gnoth. Well, on sir,—of Pollux ; now come
on, Castor.

Clerk. *Born in an.* 1540, and now 'tis 99.
By this infallible record, sir, (let me see,)
she's now just fifty-nine, and wants but one.

Gnoth. I am sorry she wants so much.

Clerk. Why, sir? alas, 'tis nothing ; 'tis
but so many months, so many weeks, so
many——

Gnoth. Do not deduct it to days, 'twill be
the more tedious ; and to measure it by
hourglasses were intolerable.

Clerk. Do not think on it, sir ; half the
time goes away in sleep, 'tis half the year in
nights.

Gnoth. O, you mistake me, neighbour, I
am loth to leave the good old woman ; if
she were gone now it would not grieve me,
for what is a year, alas, but a lingering torment? and were it not better she were out of
her pain ? It must needs be a grief to us
both.

Clerk. I would I knew how to ease you,
neighbour !

Gnoth. You speak kindly, truly, and if you
say but Amen to it, (which is a word that I
know you are perfect in,) it might be done.
Clerks are the most indifferent honest men,
—for to the marriage of your enemy, or the
burial of your friend, the curses or the blessings to you are all one ; you say Amen to
all.

Clerk. With a better will to the one than
the other, neighbour : but I shall be glad to
say Amen to anything might do you a
pleasure.

Gnoth. There is, first, something above your
duty : [*Gives him money.*] now I would have
you set forward the clock a little, to help the
old woman out of her pain.

Clerk. I will speak to the sexton ; but the
day will go ne'er the faster for that.

Gnoth. Oh, neighbour, you do not conceit
me, not the jack of the clock-house ; the
hand of the dial, I' mean.—Come, I know
you, being a great clerk, cannot choose but
have the art to cast a figure.

Clerk. Never, indeed, neighbour ; I never
had the judgment to cast a figure.

Gnoth. I'll shew you on the back side of
your book, look you,—what figure's this?

Clerk. Four with a cipher, that's forty.

Gnoth. So ! forty ; what's this, now ?

Clerk. The cipher is turn'd into 9 by adding the tail, which makes forty-nine.

Gnoth. Very well understood : what is't
now?

Clerk. The four is turn'd into three ; 'tis
now thirty-nine.

Gnoth. Very well understood ; and can you
do this again ?

Clerk. Oh ! easily, sir.

Gnoth. A wager of that ! let me see the
place of my wife's age again.

Clerk. Look you, sir, 'tis here, 1540.

Gnoth. Forty drachmas, you do not turn
that forty into thirty-nine.

Clerk. A match with you.

Gnoth. Done ! and you shall keep stakes
yourself : there they are.

Clerk. A firm match—but stay, sir, now I

consider it, I shall add a year to your wife's age ; let me see—*Scirophorion* the 17,—and now 'tis *Hecatombaion* the 11. If I alter this, your wife will have but a month to live by law.

Gnoth. That's all one, sir ; either do it, or pay me my wager.

Clerk. Will you lose your wife before you lose your wager ?

Gnoth. A man may get two wives before half so much money by them ; will you do it ?

Clerk. I hope you will conceal me, for 'tis flat corruption.

Gnoth. Nay, sir, I would have you keep counsel ; for I lose my money by't, and should be laugh'd at for my labour, if it should be known.

Clerk. Well, sir, there !—'tis done ; as perfeet a 39 as can be found in black and white : but mum, sir,—there's danger in this figure-casting.

Gnoth. Ay, sir, I know that : better men than you have been thrown over the bar for as little ; the best is, you can be but thrown out of the belfry.

Enter the Cook, Tailor, Bailiff, *and* Butler.

Clerk. Lock close, here comes company ; asses have ears as well as pitchers.

Cook. Oh, Gnotho, how is't ? here's a trick of discarded cards of us ! we were rank'd with coats, as long as old master lived.

Gnoth. And is this then the end of serving-men ?

Cook. Yes, 'faith, this is *the end of serving men :* a wise man were better serve one God than all the men in the world.

Gnoth. 'Twas well spoke of a cook. And are all fallen into fasting-days and Ember-weeks, that cooks are out of use ?

Tail. And all tailors will be cut into lists and shreds ; if this world hold, we shall grow both out of request.

But. And why not butlers as well as tailors ? if they can go naked, let them neither eat nor drink.

Clerk. That's strange, methinks, a lord should turn away his tailor, of all men :— and how dost thou, tailor ?

Tail. I do so, so ; but, indeed, all our wants are long of this publican, my lord's bailiff ; for had he been rent-gatherer still, our places had held together still, that are now seam-rent, nay crack'd in the whole piece.

Bail. Sir, if my lord had not sold his lands that claim his rents, I should still have been the rent-gatherer.

Cook. The truth is, except the coachman and the footman, all serving-men are out of request.

Gnoth. Nay, say not so, for you were never in more request than now, for requesting is but a kind of a begging ; for when you say, I beseech your worship's charity, 'tis all one as if you say I request it ; and in that kind of requesting, I am sure serving-men were never in more request.

Cook. Troth, he says true : well, let that pass, we are upon a better adventure. I see, Gnotho, you have been before us ; we came to deal with this merchant for some commodities.

Clerk. With me, sir ? anything that I can.

But. Nay, we have looked out our wives already : marry, to you we come to know the prices, that is, to know their ages ; for so much reverence we bear to age, that the more aged, they shall be the more dear to us.

Tail. The truth is, every man has laid by his widow ; so they be lame enough, blind enough, and old enough, 'tis good enough.

Clerk. I keep the town-stock ; if you can but name them, I can tell their ages to a day.

All. We can tell their fortunes to an hour, then.

Clerk. Only you must pay for turning of the leaves.

Cook. Oh, bountifully.—Come, mine first.

But. The butler before the cook, while you live ; there's few that eat before they drink in a morning.

Tail. Nay, then the tailor puts in his needle of priority, for men do clothe themselves before they either drink or eat.

Bail. I will strive for no place ; the longer ere I marry my wife, the older she will be, and nearer her end and my ends.

Clerk. I will serve you all, gentlemen, if you will have patience.

Gnoth. I commend your modesty, sir ; you are a bailiff, whose place is to come behind other men, as it were in the bum of all the rest.

Bail. So, sir ! and you were about this business too, seeking out for a widow ?

Gnoth. Alack ! no, sir ; I am a married man, and have those cares upon me that you would fain run into.

Bail. What, an old rich wife ! any man in this age desires such a care.

Gnoth. 'Troth, sir, I'll put a venture with you, if you will ; I have a lusty old quean to my wife, sound of wind and limb, yet I'll give out to take three for one at the marriage of my second wife.

Bail. Ay, sir, but how near is she to the law?

Gnoth. Take that at hazard, sir; there must be time, you know, to get a new. Unsight, unseen, I take three to one.

Bail. Two to one I'll give, if she have but two teeth in her head.

Gnoth. A match; there's five drachmas for ten at my next wife.

Bail. A match.

Cook. I shall be fitted bravely: fifty-eight, and upwards; 'tis but a year and a half, and I may chance make friends, and beg a year of the duke.

But. Hey, boys! I am made sir butler; my wife that shall be wants but two months of her time; it shall be one ere I marry her, and then the next will be a honey moon.

Tail. I outstrip you all; I shall have but six weeks of Lent, if I get my widow, and then comes eating-tide, plump and gorgeous.

Gnoth. This tailor will be a man, if ever there were any.

Bail. Now comes my turn, I hope, good-man Finis, you that are still at the end of all, with a *so be it*. Well now, sirs, do you venture there as I have done; and I'll venture here after you: Good luck, I beseech thee!

Clerk. Amen, sir.

Bail. That deserves a fee already—there 'tis; please me, and have a better.

Clerk. Amen, sir.

Cook. How, two for one at your next wife! is the old one living?

Gnoth. You have a fair match, I offer you no foul one; if death make not haste to call her, she'll make none to go to him.

But. I know her, she's a lusty woman; I'll take the venture.

Gnoth. There's five drachmas for ten at my next wife.

But. A bargain.

Cook. Nay, then we'll be all merchants: give me.

Tail. And me.

But. What, has the bailiff sped?

Bail. I am content; but none of you shall know my happiness.

Clerk. As well as any of you all, believe it, sir.

Bail. Oh, clerk, you are to speak last always.

Clerk. I'll remember't hereafter, sir. You have done with me, gentlemen?

Enter Agatha.

All. For this time, honest register.

Clerk. Fare you well then; if you do, I'll cry Amen to it.   [*Exit.*

Cook. Look you, sir, is not this your wife?

Gnoth. My first wife, sir.

But. Nay, then we have made a good match on't; if she have no froward disease, the woman may live this dozen years by her age.

Tail. I'm afraid she's broken-winded, she holds silence so long.

Cook. We'll now leave our venture to the event; I must a wooing.

But. I'll but buy me a new dagger, and overtake you.

Bail. So we must all; for he that goes a wooing to a widow without a weapon, will never get her.

·   [*Exeunt all but* Gnotho *and* Agatha.

Gnoth. Oh, wife, wife!

Aga. What ail you, man, you speak so passionately?

Gnoth. 'Tis for thy sake, sweet wife: who would think so lusty an old woman, with reasonable good teeth, and her tongue in as perfect use as ever it was, should be so near her time?—but the Fates will have it so.

Aga. What's the matter, man? you do amaze me.

Gnoth. Thou art not sick neither, I warrant thee.

Aga. Not that I know of, sure.

Gnoth. What pity 'tis a woman should be so near her end, and yet not sick!

Aga. Near her end, man! tush, I can guess at that;
I have years good yet of life in the remainder;
I want two yet at least of the full number;
Then the law, I know, craves impotent and useless,
And not the able women.

Gnoth. Ay, alas! I see thou hast been repairing time as well as thou couldst; the old wrinkles are well filled up, but the vermilion is seen too thick, too thick—and I read what's written in thy forehead; it agrees with the church-book.

Aga. Have you sought my age, man? and, I prithee, how is it?

Gnoth. I shall but discomfort thee.

Aga. Not at all, man, when there's no remedy, I will go, though unwillingly.

Gnoth. 1539. Just; it agrees with the book: you have about a year to prepare yourself.

Aga. Out, alas! I hope there's more than so.   But do you not think a reprieve might be gotten for half a score—an 'twere but five years, I would not care? an able woman, methinks, were to be pitied.

Gnoth. Ay, to be pitied, but not help'd ; no hope of that : for, indeed, women have so blemish'd their own reputations now-a-days, that it is thought the law will meet them at fifty very shortly.

Aga. Marry, the heavens forbid !

Gnoth. There's so many of you, that, when you are old, become witches ; some profess physic, and kill good subjects faster than a burning fever; and then school-mistresses of the sweet sin, which commonly we call bawds, innumerable of that sort : for these and such causes 'tis thought they shall not live above fifty.

Aga. Ay, man, but this hurts not the good old women.

Gnoth. Faith, you are so like one another, that a man cannot distinguish them : now, were I an old woman, I would desire to go before my time, and offer myself willingly, two or three years before. Oh, those are brave women, and worthy to be commended of all men in the world, that, when their husbands die, they run to be burnt to death with them : there's honour and credit ! give me half a dozen such wives.

Aga. Ay, if her husband were dead before, 'twere a reasonable request ; if you were dead, I could be content to be so.

Gnoth. Fie ! that's not likely, for thou hadst two husbands before me.

Aga. Thou wouldst not have me die, wouldst thou, husband ?

Gnoth. No, I do not speak to that purpose ; but I say what credit it were for me and thee, if thou wouldst ; then thou shouldst never be suspected for a witch, a physician, a bawd, or any of those things : and then how daintily should I mourn for thee, how bravely should I see thee buried ! when, alas, if he goes before, it cannot choose but be a great grief to him to think he has not seen his wife well buried. There such virtuous women in the world, but too few, too few, who desire to die seven years before their time, with all their hearts.

Aga. I have not the heart to be of that mind ; but, indeed, husband, I think you would have me gone.

Gnoth. No, alas ! I speak but for your good and your credit ; for when a woman may die quickly, why should she go to law for her death ? Alack, I need not wish thee gone, for thou hast but a short time to stay with me : you do not know how near 'tis,— it must out ; you have but a month to live by the law.

Aga. Out, alas !

Gnoth. Nay, scarce so much.

Aga. Oh, oh, oh, my heart ! [*Swoons.*

Gnoth. Ay, so ! if thou wouldst go away quietly, 'twere sweetly done, and like a kind wife ; lie but a little longer, and the bell shall toll for thee.

Aga. Oh my heart, but a month to live !

Gnoth. Alas, why wouldst thou come back again for a month ? I'll throw her down again—oh ! woman, 'tis not three weeks ; I think a fortnight is the most.

Aga. Nay, then I am gone already.
[*Swoons.*

Gnoth. I would make haste to the sexton now, but I am afraid the tolling of the bell will wake her again. If she be so wise as to go now—she stirs again ; there's two lives of the nine gone.

Aga. Oh ! wouldst thou not help to recover me, husband ?

Gnoth. Alas, I could not find in my heart to hold thee by thy nose, or box thy cheeks ; it goes against my conscience.

Aga. I will not be thus frighted to my death, I'll search the church records : a fortnight !
'Tis too little of conscience, I cannot be so near ;
O time, if thou be'st kind, lend me but a year.
[*Exit.*

Gnoth. What a spite's this, that a man cannot persuade his wife to die in any time with her good will ? I have another bespoke already ; though a piece of old beef will serve to breakfast, yet a man would be glad of a chicken to supper. The clerk, I hope, understands no Hebrew, and cannot write backward what he hath writ forward already, and then I am well enough.
'Tis but a month at most, if that were gone,
My venture comes in with her two for one :
'Tis use enough o' conscience for a broker—
if he had a conscience. [*Exit.*

SCENE II.—*A Room in* Creon's *House.*

Enter Eugenia *at one door,* Simonides *and* Courtiers *at the other.*

Eug. Gentlemen courtiers.

1 *Court.* All your vow'd servants, lady.

Eug. Oh, I shall kill myself with infinite laughter !
Will nobody take my part ?

Sim. An't be a laughing business,
Put it to me, I'm one of the best in Europe ;
My father died last too, I have the most cause.

Eug. You have pick'd out such a time, sweet gentlemen,
To make your spleen a banquet.

Sim. Oh, the jest !
Lady, I have a jaw stands ready for't,
I'll gape half way, and meet it.
Eug. My old husband,
That cannot say his prayers out for jealousy,
And madness at your coming first to woo
me——
Sim. Well said.
1 *Court.* Go on.
2 *Court.* On, on.
Eug. Takes counsel with
The secrets of all art, to make himself
Youthful again.
Sim. How ! youthful? ha, ha, ha !
Eug. A man of forty-five he would fain
seem to be,
Or scarce so much, if he might have his will,
indeed.
Sim. Ay, but his white hairs, they'll be-
tray his hoariness.
Eug. Why, there you are wide : he's not
the man you take him for,
Nor will you know him when you see him
again ;
There will be five to one laid upon that.
1 *Court.* How !
Eug. Nay, you did well to laugh faintly
there ;
I promise you, I think he'll outlive me now,
And deceive law and all.
Sim. Marry, gout forbid !
Eug. You little think he was at fencing-
school
At four o'clock this morning.
Sim. How, at fencing-school !
Eug. Else give no trust to woman.
Sim. By this light,
I do not like him, then ; he's like to live
Longer than I, for he may kill me first, now.
Eug. His dancer now came in as I met
you.
1 *Court.* His dancer, too !
Eug. They observe turns and hours with
him ;
The great French rider will be here at ten,
With his curveting horse.
2 *Court.* These notwithstanding,
His hair and wrinkles will betray his age.
Eug. I'm sure his head and beard, as he
has order'd it,
Look not past fifty now : he'll bring't to
forty
Within these four days, for nine times an
hour
He takes a black lead comb, and kembs it
over :
Three quarters of his beard is under fifty ;
There's but a little tuft of fourscore left,
All o' one side, which will be black by Monday.

Enter Lysander.

And, to approve my truth, see where he
comes !
Laugh softly, gentlemen, and look upon him.
[*They go aside.*
Sim. Now, by this hand, he's almost
black i' the mouth, indeed.
1 *Court.* He should die shortly, then.
Sim. Marry, methinks he dyes too fast
already,
For he was all white but a week ago.
1 *Court.* Oh ! this same coney-white takes
an excellent black.
Too soon, a mischief on't !
2 *Court.* He will beguile
Us all, if that little tuft northward turn
black too.
Eug. Nay, sir, I wonder 'tis so long a
turning.
Sim. May be some fairy's child held
forth at midnight,
Has piss'd upon that side.
1 *Court.* Is this the beard ?
Lys. Ah, sirrah? my young boys, I shall
be for you :
This little mangy tuft takes up more time
Than all the beard beside. Come you a
wooing,
And I alive and lusty? you shall find
An alteration, jack-boys ; I have a spirit yet,
(An I could match my hair to't, there's the
fault,)
And can do offices of youth yet lightly ;
At least, I will do, though it pain me a
little.
Shall not a man, for a little foolish age,
Enjoy his wife to himself? must young court
tits
Play tomboys' tricks with her, and he live?
ha !
I have blood that will not bear't ; yet, I
confess,
I should be at my prayers—but where's the
dancer, there !

Enter Dancing-master.

Mast. Here, sir.
Lys. Come, come, come, one trick a day,
And I shall soon recover all again.
Eug. 'Slight, an you laugh too loud, we
are all discover'd.
Sim. And I have a scurvy grinning laugh
o' mine own,
Will spoil all, I am afraid.
Eug. Marry, take heed, sir.
Sim. Nay, an I should be hang'd I cannot
leave it ;
Pup !—there 'tis. [*Bursts into a laugh.*
P P

Eug. Peace ! oh peace !

Lys. Come, I am ready, sir.
I hear the church-book's lost where I was
born too,
And that shall set me back one twenty years ;
There is no little comfort left in that :
And—then my three court-codlings, that
look parboil'd,
As if they came from Cupid's scalding-
house——

Sim. He means me specially, I hold my
life.

Mast. What trick will your old worship
learn this morning, sir?

Lys. Marry, a trick, if thou couldst teach
a man,
To keep his wife to himself ; I'd fain learn
that.

Mast. That's a hard trick, for an old man
specially ;
The horse-trick comes the nearest.

Lys. Thou say'st true, i' faith,
They must be horsed indeed, else there's no
keeping them,
And horse-play at fourscore is not so ready.

Mast. Look you, here's your worship's
horse-trick, sir.   [*Gives a spring.*

Lys. Nay, say not so,
'Tis none of mine ; I fall down horse and
man,
If I but offer at it.

Mast. My life for yours, sir.

Lys. Say'st thou me so?   [*Springs aloft.*

Mast. Well offer'd, by my viol, sir.

Lys. A pox of this horse-trick ! 't has
play'd the jade with me,
And given me a wrench i' the back.

Mast. Now here's your inturn, and your
trick above ground.

Lys. Prithee, no more, unless thou hast a
mind
To lay me under-ground ; one of these tricks
Is enough in a morning.   .

Mast. For your galliard, sir,
You are complete enough, ay, and may
challenge
The proudest coxcomb of them all, I'll stand
to't.

Lys. Faith, and I've other weapons for the
rest too :
I have prepared for them, if e'er I take
My Gregories here again.

Sim. Oh ! I shall burst,
I can hold out no longer.

Eug. He spoils all.   [*They come forward.*

Lys. The devil and his grinners ! are you
come ?
Bring forth the weapons, we shall find you
play ;

All feats of youth too, jack-boys, feats of
youth,
And these the weapons, drinking, fencing,
dancing :
Your own road-ways, you clyster-pipes ! I
am old, you say, .
Yes, parlous old, kids, an you mark me well !
This beard cannot get children, you lank
suck-eggs,
Unless such weasels come from court to
help us.
We will get our own brats, you letcherous
dog-bolts !

Enter a Servant *with foils, and glasses.*

Well said, down with them ; now we shall
see your spirits.
What ! dwindle you already ?

2 Court. I have no quality.

Sim. Nor I, unless drinking may be
reckon'd for one.

1 Court. Why, Sim, it shall.

Lys. Come, dare you choose your weapon
now ?

1 Court. I? dancing, sir, an you will be
so hasty.

Lys. We're for you, sir.

2 Court. Fencing, I.

Lys. We'll answer you too.

Sim. I am for drinking ; your wet weapon
there.

Lys. That wet one has cost many a princox life ;
And I will send it through you with a powder !

Sim. Let it come, with a pox ! I care not,
so't be drink.
I hope my guts will hold, and that's e'en all
A gentleman can look for of such trillibubs.

Lys. Play the first weapon ; come strike,
strike, I say.
Yes, yes, you shall be first ; I'll observe
court rules :
Always the worst goes foremost, so 'twill
prove, I hope.
              [*1* Courtier *dances a galliard.*
So, sir ! you've spit your poison ; now come I.
Now, forty years go backward and assist me,
Fall from me half my age, but for three
minutes,
That I may feel no crick ! I will put fair for't,
Although I hazard twenty sciaticas.
                                      [*Dances.*
So, I have hit you.

1 Court. You've done well, i'faith, sir.

Lys. If you confess it well, 'tis excellent,
And I have hit you soundly ; I am warm now:
The second weapon instantly.

2 Court. What, so quick, sir ?
Will you not allow yourself a breathing-time?

Lys. I've breath enough at all times, Lu-
eifer's musk-cod,
To give your perfumed worship three venues:
A sound old man puts his thrust better home,
Than a spiced young man : there I.
[They fence.
2 Court. Then have at you, fourscore.
Lys. You lie, twenty, I hope, and you
shall find it.
Sim. I'm glad I miss'd this weapon, I'd
had an eye
Popt out ere this time, or my two butter-
teeth
Thrust down my throat instead of a flap-
dragon.
Lys. There's two, pentweezle.
[Hits him.
Mast. Excellently touch'd, sir.
2 Court. Had ever man such luck ! speak
your opinion, gentlemen.
Sim. Methinks your luck's good that your
eyes are in still ;
Mine would have dropt out like a pig's half
roasted.
Lys. There wants a third—and there it is
again ! *[Hits him again.*
2 Court. The devil has steel'd him.
Eug. What a strong fiend is jealousy !
Lys. You are dispatch'd, bear-whelp.
Sim. Now comes my weapon in.
Lys. Here, toadstool, here.
'Tis you and I must play these three wet
venues.
Sim. Venues in Venice glasses ! let them
come,
They'll bruise no flesh, I'm sure, nor break
no bones.
2 Court. Yet you may drink your eyes out,
sir.
Sim. Ay, but that's nothing ;
Then they go voluntarily : I do not
Love to have them thrust out, whether they
will or no.
Lys. Here's your first weapon, duck's-
meat.
Sim. How ! a Dutch what-do-you-call-'em,
Stead of a German faulchion ! a shrewd
weapon,
And, of all things, hard to be taken down :
Yet down it must, I have a nose goes into't ;
I shall drink double, I think.
1 Court. The sooner off, Sim.
Lys. I'll pay you speedily,——with a
trick
I learnt once amongst drunkards, here's a
half-pike. *[Drinks.*
Sim. Half-pike comes well after Dutch
what-do-you-call-'em,
They'd never be asunder by their good will.

1 Court. Well pull'd of an old fellow !
Lys. Oh, but your fellows
Pull better at a rope.
1 Court. There's a hair, Sim,
In that glass.
Sim. An't be as long as a halter, down
it goes ;
No hair shall cross me. *[Drinks.*
Lys. I'll make you stink worse than your
polecats do :
Here's long-sword, your last weapon.
[Offers him the glass.
Sim. No more weapons.
1 Court. Why, how now, Sim ? bear up,
thou shamest us all, else.
Sim. 'Slight I shall shame you worse, an
I stay longer.
I have got the scotomy in my head already,
The whimsey : you all turn round—do not
you dance, gallants?
2 Court. Pish ! what's all this? why, Sim,
look, the last venue.
Sim. No more venues go down here, for
these two
Are coming up again.
2 Court. Out ! the disgrace of drinkers !
Sim. Yes, 'twill out,
Do you smell nothing yet ?
1 Court. Smell !
Sim. Farewell quickly, then ;
You will do, if I stay. *[Exit.*
1 Court. A foil go with thee !
Lys. What, shall we put down youth at
her own virtues ?
Beat folly in her own ground ? wondrous
much !
Why may not we be held as full sufficient
To love our own wives then, get our own
children,
And live in free peace till we be dissolv'd,
For such spring butterflies that are gaudy-
wing'd,
But no more substance than those shamble
flies
Which butchers' boys snap between sleep
and waking ?
Come but to crush you once, you are but
maggots,
For all your beamy outsides !

Enter Cleanthes.

Eug. Here's Cleanthes,
He comes to chide ;—let him alone a little,
Our cause will be revenged ; look, look, his
face
Is set for stormy weather ; do but mark
How the clouds gather in it, 'twill pour down
straight.

P P 2

Clean. Methinks, I partly know you,
  that's my grief.
Could you not all be lost? that had been
  handsome ;
But to be known at all, 'tis more than
  shameful.
Why, was not your name wont to be
  Lysander?
Lys. 'Tis so still, coz.
Clean. Judgment, defer thy coming ! else
  this man's miserable.
Eug. I told you there would be a shower
  anon.
  2 *Court.* We'll in, and hide our noddles.
    [*Exeunt* Eugenia *and* Courtiers.
Clean. What devil brought this colour to
  your mind,
Which, since your childhood, I ne'er saw
  you wear?
[Sure] you were ever of an innocent gloss
Since I was ripe for knowledge, and would
  you lose it,
And change the livery of saints and angels
For this mixt monstrousness : to force a
  ground
That has been so long hallowed like a temple,
To bring forth fruits of earth now ; and turn
  back
To the wild cries of lust, and the complexion
Of sin in act, lost and long since repented !
Would you begin a work ne'er yet attempted,
To pull time backward?
See what your wife will do ! are your wits
  perfect ?
Lys. My wits !
Clean. I like it ten times worse, for't had
  been safer
Now to be mad, and more excusable :
I hear you dance again, and do strange follies.
Lys. I must confess I have been put to
  some, coz.
Clean. And yet you are not mad ! pray,
  say not so ;
Give me that comfort of you, that you are
  mad,
That I may think you are at worst ; for if
You are not mad, I then must guess you have
The first of some disease was never heard of,
Which may be worse than madness, and
  more fearful :
You'd weep to see yourself else, and your care
To pray, would quickly turn you white again.
I had a father, had he lived his month out,
But to have seen this most prodigious folly,
There needed not the law to have him cut off ;
The sight of this had proved his executioner,
And broke his heart : he would have held it
  equal
Done to a sanctuary,—for what is age ‾

But the holy place of life, chapel of ease
For all men's wearied miseries ? and to rob·
That of her ornament, it is accurst
As from a priest to steal a holy vestment,
Ay, and convert it to a sinful covering.
                              [*Exit* Lysander.
I see 't has done him good ; blessing go·
  with it,
Such as may make him pure again.

                Re-enter Eugenia.

Eug. 'Twas bravely touch'd, i' faith, sir.
Clean. Oh, you are welcome.
Eug. Exceedingly well handled.
Clean. 'Tis to you I come ; he fell but in·
  my way.
Eug. You mark'd his beard, cousin ?
Clean. Mark me.
Eug. Did you ever see a hair so changed ?·
Clean. I must be forced to wake her
  loudly too,
The devil has rock'd her so fast asleep :—
  Strumpet !
Eug. Do you call, sir ?
Clean. Whore i
Eug. How do you, sir ?
Clean. Be I ne'er so well,
I must be sick of thee ; thou art a disease
That stick'st to the heart,—as all such
  women are.
Eug. What ails our kindred ?
Clean. Bless me, she sleeps still !
What a dead modesty is in this woman,
Will never blush again ! Look on thy work
But with a Christian eye, 'twould turn thy
  heart
Into a shower of blood, to be the cause
Of that old man's destruction, think upon't,
Ruin eternally ; for, through thy loose follies,
Heaven has found him a faint servant lately :
His goodness has gone backward, and en-
  gender'd
With his old sins again ; he has lost his
  prayers,
And all the tears that were companions with
  them :
And like a blindfold man, (giddy and
  blinded,)
Thinking he goes right on still, swerves but
  one foot,
And turns to the same place where he set
  out ;
So he, that took his farewell of the world,
And cast the joys behind him, out of sight,
Summ'd up his hours, made even with time
  and men,
Is now in heart arrived at youth again,
All by thy wildness : thy too hasty lust
Has driven him to this strong apostasy.

Immodesty like thine was never equall'd :
I've heard of women, (shall I call them so ?)
Have welcomed suitors ere the corpse were
  cold ;
But thou, thy husband living :—thou'rt too
  bold.
Eug. Well, have you done now, sir ?
Clean. Look, look ! she smiles yet.
Eug. All this is nothing to a mind re-
  solved ;
Ask any woman that, she'll tell you so much :
You have only shewn a pretty saucy wit,
Which I shall not forget, nor to requite it.
You shall hear from me shortly.
Clean. Shameless woman !
I take my counsel from thee, 'tis too honest,
And leave thee wholly to thy stronger
  master :
Bless the sex o' thee from thee ! that's my
  prayer.
Were all like thee, so impudently common,
No man would e'er be found to wed a
  woman.   [*Exit.*
Eug. I'll fit you gloriously.
He that attempts to take away my pleasure,
I'll take away his joy ; and I can sure.
His conceal'd father pays for't : I'll e'en tell
Him that I mean to make my husband next,
And he shall tell the duke—mass, here he
  comes.

Re-enter Simonides.

Sim. He has had a bout with me too.
Eug. What ! no ? since, sir ?
Sim. A flirt, a little flirt ; he call'd me
  strange names,
But I ne'er minded him.
Eug. You shall quit him, sir,
When he as little minds you.
Sim. I like that well.
I love to be revenged when no one thinks of
  me ;
There's little danger that way.
Eug. This is it then ;
He you shall strike your stroke shall be pro-
  found,
And yet your foe not guess who gave the
  wound.
Sim. O' my troth I love to give such
  wounds.   [*Exeunt.*

ACT IV.

SCENE I.—*Before a Tavern.*

Enter Gnotho, Butler, Bailiff, Tailor, Cook,
  Drawer, *and* Courtezan.

Draw. Welcome, gentlemen, will you not
draw near ? will you drink at door, gentlemen ?
But. Oh ! the summer air is best.
Draw. What wine will't please you drink,
gentlemen ?
But. De Clare, sirrah.   [*Exit* Drawer.
Gnoth. What, you're all sped already,
bullies ?
Cook. My widow's o' the spit, and half
ready, lad ; a turn or two more, and I have
done with her.
Gnoth. Then, cook, I hope you have
basted her before this time.
Cook. And stuck her with rosemary too, to
sweeten her ; she was tainted ere she came
to my hands. What an old piece of flesh
of fifty-nine, eleven months, and upwards !
she must needs be fly-blown.
Gnoth. Put her off, put her off, though
you lose by her ; the weather's hot.
Cook. Why, drawer !

Re-enter Drawer.

Draw. By and by :—here, gentlemen,
here's the quintessence of Greece ; the sages
never drunk better grape.
Cook. Sir, the mad Greeks of this age can
taste their Palermo as well as the sage
Greeks did before them.—Fill, lick-spiggot.
Draw. *Ad imum,* sir.
Gnoth. My friends, I must doubly invite
you all, the fifth of the next month, to the
funeral of my first wife, and to the marriage
of my second, my two to one ; this is she.
Cook. I hope some of us will be ready
for the funeral of our wives by that time, to
go with thee : but shall they be both of a
day ?
Gnoth. Oh ! best of all, sir ; where sorrow
and joy meet together, one will help away
with another the better. Besides, there will
be charges saved too ; the same rosemary
that serves for the funeral, will serve for the
wedding.
But. How long do you make account to
be a widower, sir ?
Gnoth. Some half an hour ; long enough
o' conscience. Come, come, let's have some
agility ; is there no music in the house ?
Draw. Yes, sir, here are sweet wire-
drawers in the house.
Cook. Oh ! that makes them and you
seldom part ; you are wine-drawers, and
they wire-drawers.
Tail. And both govern by the pegs too.
Gnoth. And you have pipes in your consort too.
Draw. And sack-buts too, sir.
But. But the heads of your instruments

differ ; yours are hogs-heads, theirs cittern and gittern-heads.

Bail. All wooden heads ; there they meet again.

Cook. Bid them strike up, we'll have a dance, Gnotho ; come, thou shalt foot it too.
　　　　　　　　　　　　　　[Exit Drawer.

Gnoth. No dancing with me, we have Siren here.

Cook. Siren ! 'twas Hiren, the fair Greek, man.

Gnoth. Five drachmas of that. I say Siren, the fair Greek, and so are all fair Greeks.

Cook. A match ; five drachmas her name was Hiren.

Gnoth. Siren's name was Siren, for five drachmas.

Cook. 'Tis done.

Tail. Take heed what you do, Gnotho.

Gnoth. Do not I know our own country-women, Siren and Nell of Greece, two of the fairest Greeks that ever were?

Cook. That Nell was Helen of Greece too.

Gnoth. As long as she tarried with her husband, she was Ellen ; but after she came to Troy, she was Nell of Troy, or Bonny Nell, whether you will or no.

Tail. Why, did she grow shorter when she came to Troy?

Gnoth. She grew longer, if you mark the story. When she grew to be an ell, she was deeper than any yard of Troy could reach by a quarter ; there was Cressid was Troy weight, and Nell was avoirdupois ; she held more, by four ounces, than Cressida.

Bail. They say she caused many wounds to be given in Troy.

Gnoth. True, she was wounded there herself, and cured again by plaister of Paris ; and ever since that has been used to stop holes with.

　　　　　Re-enter Drawer.

Draw. Gentlemen, if you be disposed to be merry, the music is ready to strike up ; and here's a consort of mad Greeks, I know not whether they be men or women, or between both ; they have, what do you call them, wizards on their faces.

Cook. Vizards, good man lick-spiggot.

But. If they be wise women, they may be wizards too.

Draw. They desire to enter amongst any merry company of gentlemen-good-fellows, for a strain or two.

　　Enter old Women *and* Agatha *in masks.*

Cook. We'll strain ourselves with them,

say ; let them come, Gnotho ; now for the honour of Epire !

Gnoth. No dancing with me, we have Siren here.

　　[A dance by the old Women *and* Aga-tha ; *they offer to take the men, all agree except* Gnotho, *who sits with the* Courtezan..

Cook. Ay ! so kind ! then every one his wench to his several room ; Gnotho, we are all provided now as you are.

　　[Exeunt all but Gnotho, Courtezan, *and* Agatha.

Gnoth. I shall have two, it seems : away! I have Siren here already.

Aga. What, a mermaid?

　　　　　　　　　[Takes off her mask.

Gnoth. No, but a maid, horse-face : oh, old woman ! is it you ?

Aga. Yes, 'tis I ; all the rest have gulled themselves, and taken their own wives, and shall know that they have done more than they can well answer ; but I pray you, hus-band, what are you doing ?

Gnoth. Faith, thus should I do, if thou wert dead, old Ag, and thou hast not long to live, I'm sure : we have Siren here.

Aga. Art thou so shameless, whilst I am living, to keep one under my nose ?

Gnoth. No, Ag, I do prize her far above thy nose ; if thou wouldst lay me both thine eyes in my hand to boot, I'll not leave her : art not ashamed to be seen in a tavern, and hast scarce a fortnight to live ? oh, old woman, what art thou? must thou find no time to think of thy end?

Aga. O, unkind villain !

Gnoth. And then, sweetheart, thou shalt have two new gowns ; and the best of this old woman's shall make thee raiment for the working days.

Aga. O, rascal ! dost thou quarter my clothes already too?

Gnoth. Her ruffs will serve thee for no-thing but to wash dishes ; for thou shalt have thine of the new fashion.

Aga. Impudent villain ! shameless harlot!

Gnoth. You may hear, she never wore any but rails all her lifetime.

Aga. Let me come, I'll tear the strumpet from him.

Gnoth. Dar'st thou call my wife strumpet, thou preterpluperfect tense of a woman ! I'll make thee do penance in the sheet thou shalt be buried in ; abuse my choice, my two-to-one !

Aga. No, unkind villain, I'll deceive thee yet,

I have a reprieve for five years of life ;
I am with child.

Court. Cud so, Gnotho, I'll not tarry so
long ; five years! I may bury two husbands
by that time.

Gnoth. Alas ! give the poor woman leave
to talk, she with child ! ay, with a puppy :
as long as I have thee by me, she shall not
be with child, I warrant thee.

Aga. The law, and thou, and all, shall
find I am with child.

Gnoth. I'll take my corporal oath I begat
it not, and then thou diest for adultery.

Aga. No matter, that will ask some time
in the proof.

Gnoth. Oh ! you'd be stoned to death,
would you ? all old women would die o' that
fashion with all their hearts ; but the law
shall overthrow you the other way, first.

Court. Indeed, if it be so, I will not linger
so long, Gnotho.

Gnoth. Away, away ! some botcher has
got it ; 'tis but a cushion, I warrant thee :
the old woman is *loth to depart;* she never
sung other tune in her life.

Court. We will not have our noses bored
with a cushion, if it be so.

Gnoth. Go, go thy ways, thou old almanack at the twenty-eighth day of December,
e'en almost out of date ! Down on thy
knees, and make thee ready ; sell some of
thy clothes to buy thee a death's head, and
put upon thy middle finger ; your least considering bawd does so much ; be not thou
worse, though thou art an old woman, as
she is : I am cloy'd with old stock-fish,
here's a young perch is sweeter meat by
half ; prithee, die before thy day, if thou
canst, that thou mayst not be counted a
witch.

Aga. No, thou art a witch, and I'll prove
it ; I said I was with child, thou knew'st no
other but by sorcery : thou said'st it was a
cushion, and so it is ; thou art a witch for't,
I'll be sworn to't.

Gnoth. Ha, ha, ha! I told thee 'twas a
cushion. Go, get thy sheet ready ; we'll see
thee buried as we go to church to be married. [*Exeunt* Gnotho *and* Courtezan.

Aga. Nay, I'll follow thee, and shew myself a wife. I'll plague thee as long as I live
with thee ; and I'll bury some money before
I die, that my ghost may haunt thee after-
ward. [*Exit.*

SCENE II.—*The Country. A Forest.*

Enter Cleanthes.

Clean. What's that ? oh, nothing but the
whispering wind

Breathes through yon churlish hawthorn, that
grew rude,
As if it chid the gentle breath that kiss'd it.
I cannot be too circumspect, too careful ;
For in these woods lies hid all my life's
treasure,
Which is too much never to fear to lose,
Though it be never lost : and if our watch-
fulness
Ought to be wise and serious 'gainst a thief
That comes to steal our goods, things all
without us,
That prove vexation often more than com-
fort ;
How mighty ought our providence to be,
To prevent those, if any such there were,
That come to rob our bosom of our joys,
That only make poor man delight to live!
Pshaw ! I'm too fearful—fie, fie ! who can
hurt me?
But 'tis a general cowardice, that shakes
The nerves of confidence ; he that hides
treasure,
Imagines every one thinks of that place,
When 'tis a thing least minded ; nay, let
him change
The place continually ; where'er it keeps,
There will the fear keep still : yonder's the
storehouse
Of all my comfort now—and see ! it sends
forth

Enter Hippolita, *from the wood.*

A dear one to me :—Precious chief of
women,
How does the good old soul? has he fed
well?

Hip. Beshrew me, sir, he made the
heartiest meal to day—
Much good may't do his health.

Clean. A blessing on thee,
Both for thy news and wish !

Hip. His stomach, sir,
Is better'd wondrously, since his concealment.

Clean. Heaven has a blessed work in't.
Come, we are safe here ;
I prithee call him forth, the air's much whole-
somer.

Hip. Father !

Enter Leonides.

Leon. How sweetly sounds the voice of a
good woman !
It is so seldom heard, that, when it speaks,
It ravishes all senses. Lists of honour !
I've a joy weeps to see you, 'tis so full,
So fairly fruitful.

Clean. I hope to see you often and return

Loaded with blesssings, still to pour on
　　some ;
I find them all in my contented peace,
And lose not one in thousands, they are dis-
　　perst
So gloriously, I know not which are
　　brightest.
I find them, as angels are found, by legions :
First, in the love and honesty of a wife,
Which is the chiefest of all temporal bless-
　　ings ;
Next in yourself, which is the hope and joy
Of all my actions, my affairs, my wishes ;
And lastly, which crowns all, I find my soul
Crown'd with the peace of them, the eternal
　　riches,
Man's only portion for his heavenly mar-
　　riage !
　Leon. Rise, thou art all obedience, love,
　　and goodness.
I dare say that which thousand fathers can-
　　not,
And that's my precious comfort, never son
Was in the way more of celestial rising :
Thou art so made of such ascending virtue,
That all the powers of hell can't sink thee.
　　　　　　　　[*A horn sounded within.*
　Clean. Ha !
　Leon. What was't disturb'd my joy?
　Clean. Did you not hear,
As afar off ?
　Leon. What, my excellent comfort ?
　Clean. Nor you?
　Hip. I heard a——　　　　[*A horn.*
　Clean. Hark, again !
　Leon. Bless my joy,
What ails it on a sudden ?
　Clean. Now ? since lately ?
　Leon. 'Tis nothing but a symptom of thy
　　care, man.
　Clean. Alas ! you do not hear well.
　Leon. What was't, daughter ?
　Hip. I heard a sound, twice.　　[*A horn.*
　Clean. Hark ! louder and nearer :
In, for the precious good of virtue, quick,
　　sir !
Louder and nearer yet ! at hand, at hand !
　　　　　　　　　　[*Exit* Leonides.
A hunting here ? 'tis strange ! I never knew
Game followed in these woods before.

　　Enter Evander, Simonides, Courtiers,
　　　　　and Cratilus.

　Hip. Now let them come, and spare not.
　Clean. Ha ! 'tis—is't not the duke ?—look
　　sparingly.
　Hip. 'Tis he, but what of that ? alas, take
　　heed, sir,
Your care will overthrow us.

　Clean. Come, it shall not:
Let's set a pleasant face upon our fears,
Though our hearts shake with horror.—Ha,
　　ha, ha !
　Evan. Hark !
　Clean. Prithee, proceed ;
I am taken with these light things infinitely,
Since the old man's decease ; ha !—so they
　　parted ? ha, ha, ha !
　Evan. Why, how should I believe this ?
　　look, he's merry
As if he had no such charge : one with that
　　care
Could never be so ; still he holds his temper,
And 'tis the same still (with no difference)
He brought his father's corpse to the grave
　　with ;
He laugh'd thus then, you know.
　1 *Court.* Ay, he may laugh,
That shews but how he glories in his cunning ;
And is, perhaps, done more to advance his
　　wit,
That only he has over-reach'd the law,
Than to express affection to his father.
　Sim. He tells you right, my lord, his own
　　cousin-german
Reveal'd it first to me ; a free-tongued woman,
And very excellent at telling secrets.
　Evan. If a contempt can be so neatly
　　carried,
It gives me cause of wonder.
　Sim. Troth, my lord,
'Twill prove a delicate cozening, I believe :
I'd have no scrivener offer to come near it.
　Evan. Cleanthes.
　Clean. My loved lord.
　Evan. Not moved a whit,
Constant to lightness still ! 'Tis strange to
　　meet you
Upon a ground so unfrequented, sir :
This does not fit your passion ; you're for
　　mirth,
Or I mistake you much.
　Clean. But finding it
Grow to a noted imperfection in me,
For anything too much is vicious,
I come to these disconsolate walks, of pur-
　　pose,
Only to dull and take away the edge on't.
I ever had a greater zeal to sadness,
A natural propension, I confess,
Before that cheerful accident fell out—
If I may call a father's funeral cheerful,
Without wrong done to duty or my love.
　Evan. It seems, then, you take pleasure
　　in these walks, sir.
　Clean. Contemplative content I do, my
　　lord :
They bring into my mind oft meditations

So sweetly precious, that, in the parting,
I find a shower of grace upon my cheeks,
They take their leave so feelingly.

Evan. So, sir!

Clean. Which is a kind of grave delight,
my lord.

Evan. And I've small cause, Cleanthes,
to afford you
The least delight that has a name.

Clean. My lord!

Sim. Now it begins to fadge.

1 *Court.* Peace! thou art so greedy, Sim.

Evan. In your excess of joy you have ex-
press'd
Your rancour and contempt against my law :
Your smiles deserve a fining; you have pro-
fess'd
Derision openly, e'en to my face,
Which might be death, a little more in-
censed.
You do not come for any freedom here,
But for a project of your own :—
But all that's known to be contentful to thee,
Shall in the use prove deadly. Your life's
mine,
If ever your presumption do but lead you
Into these walks again,—ay, or that woman;
I'll have them watched o' purpose.
[Cleanthes *retires from the wood, fol-
lowed by* Hippolita.

1 *Court.* Now, now, his colour ebbs and
flows.

Sim. Mark hers too.

Hip. Oh, who shall bring food to the poor
old man, now!

Speak somewhat, good sir, or we're lost for
ever.

Clean. Oh, you did wonderous ill to call
me again.
There are not words to help us ; if I entreat,
'Tis found ; that will betray us worse than
silence :

Prithee let heaven alone, and let's say nothing.

1 *Court.* You have struck them dumb, my
lord.

Sim. Look how guilt looks !
I would not have that fear upon my flesh,
To save ten fathers.

Clean. He is safe still, is he not?

Hip. Oh, you do ill to doubt it.

Clean. Thou art all goodness.

Sim. Now does your grace believe?

Evan. 'Tis too apparent.

Search, make a speedy search ; for the imposture
Cannot be far off, by the fear it sends.

Clean. Ha !

Sim. He has the lapwing's cunning, I am
afraid,

That cries most when she's furthest from the
nest.

Clean. Oh, we are betray'd.

Hip. Betray'd, sir !

Sim. See, my lord,
It comes out more and more still.
[Simonides *and* Courtiers *enter the
wood.*

Clean. Bloody thief!
Come from that place; 'tis sacred, homicide!
'Tis not for thy adulterate hands to touch it.

Hip. Oh miserable virtue, what distress
Art thou in at this minute !

Clean. Help me, thunder,
For my power's lost ! angels, shoot plagues,
and help me !
Why are these men in health, and I so heart-
sick?
Or why should nature have that power in me
To levy up a thousand bleeding sorrows,
And not one comfort? only make me lie
Like the poor mockery of an earthquake
here,
Panting with horror,
And have not so much force in all my ven-
geance,
To shake a villain off me.

Re-enter Simonides *and* Courtiers *with*
Leonides.

Hip. Use him gently,
And heaven will love you for it.

Clean. Father ! oh father ! now I see thee
full
In thy affliction ; thou'rt a man of sorrow,
But reverendly becom'st it, that's my com-
fort :
Extremity was never better graced,
Than with that look of thine ; oh ! let me
look still,
For I shall lose it ; all my joy and strength
[*Kneels.*
Is e'en eclipsed together : I transgress'd
Your law, my lord, let me receive the sting
on't :
Be once just, sir, and let the offender die :
He's innocent in all, and I am guilty.

Leon. Your grace knows, when affection
only speaks,
Truth is not always there; his love would draw
An undeserved misery on his youth,
And wrong a peace resolv'd, on both parts
sinful.
'Tis I am guilty of my own concealment,
And, like a worldly coward, injured heaven
With fear to go to't :—now I see my fault,
I am prepared with joy to suffer for it.

Evan. Go, give him quick dispatch, let
him see death :

And your presumption, sir, shall come to
  judgment.
        [*Exeunt* Evander, Courtiers, Simo-
            nides; *and* Cratilus *with* Leonides.
Hip. He's going ! oh, he's gone, sir !
Clean. Let me rise.
Hip. Why do you not then, and follow ?
Clean. I strive for it,
Is there no hand of pity that will ease me,
And take this villain from my heart awhile ?
                                    [*Rises.*
Hip. Alas ! he's gone.
Clean. A worse supplies his place then,
A weight more ponderous ; I cannot follow.
Hip. Oh misery of affliction !
Clean. They will stay
Till I can come ; they must be so good ever,
Though they be ne'er so cruel :
My last leave must be taken, think of that,
And his last blessing given ; I will not lose
That for a thousand consorts.
Hip. That hope's wretched.
Clean. The unutterable stings of fortune !
All griefs are to be borne save this alone,
This, like a headlong torrent, overturns
The frame of nature :
For he that gave us life first, as a father,
Locks all his natural sufferings in our blood,
The sorrows that he feels are our heart's too,
They are incorporate to us.
Hip. Noble sir !
Clean. Let me behold thee well.
Hip. Sir !
Clean. Thou should'st be good,
Or thou'rt a dangerous substance to be
  lodged
So near the heart of man.
Hip. What means this, dear sir ?
Clean. To thy trust only was this blessed
  secret
Kindly committed, 'tis destroy'd, thou seest ;
What follows to be thought on't ?
Hip. Miserable !
Why, here's the unhappiness of woman still ;
That, having forfeited in old times her trust,
Now makes their faiths suspected that are
  just.
Clean. What shall I say to all my sorrows
  then,
That look for satisfaction ?

                Enter Eugenia.

Eug. Ha, ha, ha ! cousin.
Clean. How ill dost thou become this
  time !
Eug. Ha, ha, ha !
Why, that's but your opinion ; a young
  wench
Becomes the time at all times.

Now, coz, we are even : an you be remem-
  ber'd,
You left a *strumpet* and a *whore* with me,
And such fine field-bed words, which could.
  not cost you
Less than a father.
Clean. Is it come that way ?
Eug. Had you an uncle,
He should go the same way too.
Clean. Oh eternity,
What monster is this fiend in labour with ?
Eug. An ass-colt with two heads, that's
  she and you :
I will not lose so glorious a revenge,
Not to be understood in't ; I betray'd him ;
And now we are even, you'd best keep you so.
Clean. Is there not poison yet enough to
  kill me ?
Hip. Oh, sir, forgive me ; it was I betray'd.
  him.
Clean. How !
Hip. I.
Clean. The fellow of my heart ! 'twill speed
  me, then.
Hip. Her tears that never wept, and mine
  own pity
Even cozen'd me together, and stole from me
This secret, which fierce death should not
  have purchased.
Clean. Nay, then we are at an end ; all
  we are false ones,
And ought to suffer. I was false to wisdom,
In trusting woman ; thou wert false to faith,
In uttering of the secret ; and thou false
To goodness, in deceiving such a pity :
We are all tainted some way, but thou worst,
And for thy infectious spots ought'st to die
  first.   [*Offers to kill* Eugenia.
Eug. Pray turn your weapon, sir, upon
  your mistress,
I come not so ill friended :—rescue, servants !

        Re-enter Simonides *and* Courtiers.

Clean. Are you so whorishly provided ?
Sim. Yes, sir,
She has more weapons at command than
  one.
Eug. Put forward, man, thou art most
  sure to have me.
Sim. I shall be surer, if I keep behind,
  though.
Eug. Now, servants, shew your loves.
Sim. I'll shew my love, too, afar off.
Eug. I love to be so courted, woo me
  there.
Sim. I love to keep good weapons,
  though ne'er fought with.
I'm sharper set within than I am without.
Hip. Oh gentlemen ! Cleanthes !

Eug. Fight! upon him!

Clean. Thy thirst of blood proclaims thee now a strumpet.

Eug. 'Tis dainty, next to procreation fitting;
I'd either be destroying men or getting.

Enter Guard.

1 *Officer.* Forbear, on your allegiance, gentlemen.
He's the duke's prisoner, and we seize upon him
To answer this contempt against the law.

Clean. I obey fate in all things.

Hip. Happy rescue!

Sim. I would you'd seized upon him a minute sooner, it had saved me a cut finger: I wonder how I came by't, for I never put my hand forth, I'm sure; I think my own sword did cut it, if truth were known; may be the wire in the handle: I have lived these five and twenty years and never knew what colour my blood was before. I never durst eat oysters, nor cut peck-loaves.

Eug. You've shewn your spirits, gentlemen; but you
Have cut your finger.

Sim. Ay, the wedding-finger too, a pox on't!

Court. You'll prove a bawdy bachelor, Sim, to have a cut upon your finger, before you are married.

Sim. I'll never draw sword again, to have such a jest put upon me.   . [*Exeunt.*

ACT V.

SCENE I.—*A Court of Justice.*

Enter Simonides *and* Courtiers, *sword and mace carried before them.*

Sim. Be ready with your prisoner; we'll sit instantly,
And rise before eleven, or when we please;
Shall we not, fellow-judges?

1 *Court.* 'Tis committed
All to our power, censure, and pleasure, now;
The duke hath made us chief lords of this sessions,
And we may speak by fits, or sleep by turns.

Sim. Leave that to us, but, whatsoe'er we do,
The prisoner shall be sure to be condemn'd;
Sleeping or waking, we are resolved on that,
Before we sit upon him!

2 *Court.* Make you question
If not?—Cleanthes! and an enemy!

Nay a concealer of his father too!
A vile example in these days of youth.

Sim. If they were given to follow such examples;
But sure I think they are not: howsoever,
'Twas wickedly attempted; that's my judgment,
And it shall pass whilst I am in power to sit.
Never by prince were such young judges made,
But now the cause requires it: if you mark it;
He must make young or none; for all the old ones ·
He hath sent a fishing—and my father's one,.
I humbly thank his highness.

Enter Eugenia.

1 *Court.* Widow!

Eug. You almost hit my name now, gentlemen;
You come so wonderous near it, I admire you
For your judgment.

Sim. My wife that must be! She.

Eug. My husband goes upon his last hour now.

1 *Court.* On his last legs, I am sure.

Sim. September the seventeenth—
I will not bate an hour on't, and to-morrow
His latest hour's expired.

2 *Court.* Bring him to judgment;
The jury's panell'd, and the verdict given
Ere he appears; we have ta'en a course for · that.

Sim. And officers to attach the gray young man,
The youth of fourscore: Be of comfort, lady,
You shall no longer bosom January;
For that I will take order, and provide
For you a lusty April.

Eug. The month that ought, indeed,
To go before May.

1 *Court.* Do as we have said,
Take a strong guard, and bring him into · court.
Lady Eugenia, see this charge performed,
That, having his life forfeited by the law,
He may relieve his soul.

Eug. Willingly.
From shaven chins never came better justice ·
Than these ne'er touch'd by razor.   [*Exit.*

Sim. What you do,
Do suddenly, we charge you, for we purpose
To make but a short sessions:—a new business!

Enter Hippolita.

1 *Court.* The fair Hippolita! now what's · your suit?

Hip. Alas! I know not how to style you
yet;
To call you judges doth not suit your years,
Nor heads and beards shew more an-
tiquity;—
Yet sway yourselves with equity and truth,
And I'll proclaim you reverend, and repeat
Once in my lifetime I have seen grave heads
Placed upon young men's shoulders.

2 Court. Hark! she flouts us,
And thinks to make us monstrous.

Hip. Prove not so;
For yet, methinks, you bear the shapes of
men;
(Though nothing more than merely beauty
serves
To make you appear angels,) but if you
crimson
Your name and power with blood and
cruelty,
Suppress fair virtue, and enlarge bold vice,
Both against heaven and nature, draw your
sword,
Make either will or humour turn the soul
Of your created greatness, and in that
Oppose all goodness, I must tell you there
You are more than monstrous; in the very
act,
You change yourselves to devils.

1 Court. She's a witch;
Hark! she begins to conjure.

Sim. Time, you see,
Is short, much business now on foot:—shall I
Give her her answer?

2 Court. None upon the bench,
More learnedly can do it.

Sim. He, he, hem! then list:
I wonder at thine impudence, young hus-
wife,
That thou darest plead for such a base
offender.
Conceal a father past his time to die!
What son and heir would have done this
but he?

1 Court. I vow, not I.

Hip. Because ye are parricides;
And how can comfort be derived from such
That pity not their fathers?

2 Court. You are fresh and fair; practise
young women's ends;
When husbands are distress'd, provide them
friends.

Sim. I'll set him forward for thee without
fee:
Some wives would pay for such a courtesy.

Hip. Times of amazement! what duty,
goodness dwell——
I sought for charity, but knock at hell.
[*Exit.*

Re-enter Eugenia, *and* Guard, *with* Lysander.

Sim. Eugenia come! command a second
guard
To bring Cleanthes in; we'll not sit long;
My stomach strives to dinner.

Eug. Now, servants, may a lady be so bold
To call your power so low?

Sim. A mistress may,
She can make all things low; then in that
language
There can be no offence.

Eug. The time's now come
Of manumissions, take him into bonds,
And I am then at freedom.

2 Court. This the man!
He hath left off o' late to feed on snakes;
His beard's turn'd white again.

1 Court. Is't possible these gouty legs
danced lately,
And shatter'd in a galliard?

Eug. Jealousy
And fear of death can work strange prodigies.

2 Court. The nimble fencer this, that
made me tear
And traverse 'bout the chamber?

Sim. Ay, and gave me
Those elbow healths, the hangman take him
for't!
They'd almost fetch'd my heart out: the
Dutch what-you-call,
I swallow'd pretty well; but the half-pike
Had almost pepper'd me; but had I ta'en
long-sword,
Being swollen, I had cast my lungs out.

A Flourish. Enter Evander *and* Cratilus.

1 Court. Peace, the duke!

Evan. Nay, back t' your seats: who's
that?

2 Court. May't please your highness, it is
old Lysander.

Evan. And brought in by his wife! a
worthy precedent.
Of one that no way would offend the law,
And should not pass away without remark.
You have been look'd for long.

Lys. But never fit
To die till now, my lord. My sins and I
Have been but newly parted; much ado
I had to get them leave me, or be taught
That difficult lesson how to learn to die.
I never thought there had been such an act,
And 'tis the only discipline we are born for:
All studies else are but as circular lines,
And death the centre where they must all
meet.
I now can look upon thee, erring woman,

And not be vex'd with jealousy ; on young
    men,
And no way envy their delicious health,
Pleasure, and strength ; all which were once
    mine own,
And mine must be theirs one day.
    Evan. You have tamed him.
    Sim. And know how to dispose him ;
    that, my liege,
Hath been before determined. You confess
Yourself of full age ?
    Lys. Yes, and prepared to inherit——
    Eug. Your place above.
    Sim. Of which the hangman's strength
Shall put him in possession.
    Lys. 'Tis still cared
To take me willing and in mind to die ;
And such are, when the earth grows weary
    of them,
Most fit for heaven.
    Sim. The court shall make his mittimus,
And send him thither presently : i' the mean
    time——
    Evan. Away to death with him.
       [*Exit* Cratilus *with* Lysander.

Enter Guard *with* Cleanthes, Hippolita
    following, weeping.

    Sim. So ! see another person brought to
    the bar.
    1 *Court.* The arch-malefactor.
    2 *Court.* The grand offender, the most
    refractory
To all good order ; 'tis Cleanthes, he——
    Sim. That would have sons grave fathers,
    ere their fathers
Be sent unto their graves.
    Evan. There will be expectation
In your severe proceedings against him ;
His act being so capital.
    Sim. Fearful and bloody ;
Therefore we charge these women leave the
    court,
Lest they should swoon to hear it.
    Eug. I, in expectation
Of a most happy freedom.   [*Exit.*
    Hip. I, with the apprehension
Of a most sad and desolate widowhood.
                    [*Exit.*
    1 *Court.* We bring him to the bar——
    2 *Court.* Hold up your hand, sir.
    Clean. More reverence to the place than
    to the persons :
To the one I offer up a [spreading] palm
Of duty and obedience, as to heaven,
Imploring justice, which was never wanting
Upon that bench whilst their own fathers sat ;
But unto you, my hands contracted thus,
As threatening vengeance against murderers,

For they that kill in thought, shed innocent
    blood.——
With pardon of your highness, too much
    passion
Made me forget your presence, and the place
I now am call'd to.
    Evan. All our majesty
And power we have to pardon or condemn,
Is now conferr'd on them.
    Sim. And these we'll use,
Little to thine advantage.
    Clean. I expect it :
And, as to these, I look no mercy from them,
And much less mean to entreat it, I thus now
Submit me to the emblems of your power,
The sword and bench : but, my most
    reverend judges,
Ere you proceed to sentence, (for I know
You have given me lost,) will you resolve me
    one thing ?
    1 *Court.* So it be briefly question'd.
    2 *Court.* Shew your honour ;
Day spends itself apace.
    Clean. My lords, it shall.
Resolve me, then, where are your filial tears,
Your mourning habits, and sad hearts be-
    come,
That should attend your fathers' funerals ?
Though the strict law (which I will not accuse,
Because a subject) snatch'd away their lives,
It doth not bar you to lament their deaths :
Or if you cannot spare one sad suspire,
It doth not bid you laugh them to their
    graves,
Lay subtle trains to antedate their years,
To be the sooner seized of their estates.
Oh, time of age ! where's that Æneas now,
Who letting all his jewels to the flames ;
Forgetting country, kindred, treasure, friends,
Fortunes and all things, save the name of son,
Which you so much forget, godlike Æneas,
Who took his bedrid father on his back,
And with that sacred load (to him no burthen)
Hew'd out his way through blood, through
    fire, through [arms,]
Even all the arm'd streets of bright-burning
    Troy,
Only to save a father ?
    Sim. We've no leisure now,
To hear lessons read from Virgil ; we are past
    school,
And all this time thy judges.
    2 *Court.* It is fit
That we proceed to sentence.
    1 *Court.* You are the mouth,
And now 'tis fit to open.
    Sim. Justice, indeed,
Should ever be close-ear'd, and open-
    mouth'd ;

That is to hear a little and speak much.
Know then, Cleanthes, there is none can be
A good son and bad subject ; for, if princes
Be called the people's fathers, then the
  subjects
Are all his sons, and he that flouts the prince,
Doth disobey his father : there you are gone.
  1 *Court.* And not to be recover'd.
  Sim. And again——
  2 *Court.* If he be gone once, cail him not
  again.
  Sim. I say again, this act of thine expresses
A double disobedience : as our princes
Are fathers, so they are our sovereigns too ;
And he that doth rebel 'gainst sovereignty,
Doth commit treason in the height of degree :
And now thou art quite gone.
  1 *Court.* Our brother in commission,
Hath spoke his mind both learnedly and
  neatly,
And I can add but little ; howsoever,
It shall send him packing.
He that begins a fault that wants example,
Ought to be made example for the fault.
  Clean. A fault ! no longer can I hold
  myself
To hear vice upheld and virtue thrown down.
A fault ! judge, I desire, then, where it lies,
In those that are my judges, or in me :
Heaven stands on my side, pity, love, and
  duty.
  Sim. Where are they, sir? who sees them
  but yourself ?
  Clean. Not you ; and I am sure,
You never had the gracious eyes to see them.
You think that you arraign me, but I hope
To sentence you at the bar.
  2 *Court.* That would shew brave.
  Clean. This were the judgment-seat we
  [stand at] now !
Of the heaviest crimes that ever made up
  [sin],
Unnaturalness, and inhumanity,
You are found foul and guilty, by a jury
Made of your father's curses, which have
  brought
Vengeance impending on you ; and I, now,
Am forced to pronounce judgment on my
  judges.
The common laws of reason and of nature
Condemn you, *ipso facto;* you are parricides,
And if you marry, will beget the like,
Who, when they are grown to full maturity,
Will hurry you, their fathers, to their graves.
Like traitors, you take council from the
  living,
Of upright judgment you would rob the bench,
(Experience and discretion snatch'd away
From the earth's face,) turn all into disorder,

Imprison virtue, and infranchise vice,
And put the sword of justice in the hands
Of boys and madmen.
  Sim. Well, well, have you done, sir?
  Clean. I have spoke my thoughts.
  Sim. Then I'll begin and end.
  Evan. 'Tis time I now begin—
Here your commission ends.
Cleanthes, come you from the bar.   Because
I know you are severally disposed, I here
Invite you to an object will, no doubt,
Work in you contrary effects.—Music !

  Loud music. Enter Leonides, Creon,
  Lysander, *and other old men.*

  Clean. Pray, heaven, I dream not ! sure
  he moves, talks comfortably,
As joy can wish a man.   If he be changed,
(Far above from me,) he's not ill entreated ;
His face doth promise fullness of content,
And glory hath a part in't.
  Leo. Oh my son !
  Evan. You that can claim acquaintance
  with these lads,
Talk freely.
  Sim. I can see none there that's worth
One hand to you from me.
  Evan. These are thy judges, and by their
  grave law
I find thee clear, but these delinquents guilty.
You must change places, for 'tis so decreed :
Such just pre-eminence hath thy goodness
  gain'd,
Thou art the judge now, they the men
  arraign'd.   [*To* Cleanthes.
  1 *Court.* Here's fine dancing, gentlemen.
  2 *Court.* Is thy father amongst them ?
  Sim. Oh, pox ! I saw him the first thing
  I look'd on.
Alive again ! 'slight, I believe now a father
Hath as many lives as a mother.
  Clean. 'Tis full as blessed as 'tis wonderful.
Oh ! bring me back to the same law again,
I am fouler than all these ; seize on me,
  officers,
And bring me to new sentence.
  Sim. What's all this ?
  Clean. A fault not to be pardon'd,
Unnaturalness is but sin's shadow to it.
  Sim. I am glad of that ; I hope the case
  may alter,
And I turn judge again.
  Evan. Name your offence.
  Clean. That I should be so vile
As once to think you cruel.
  Evan. Is that all ?
'Twas pardon'd ere confess'd : you that have
  sons,
If they be worthy, here may challenge them.

Creon. I should have one amongst them,
  had he had grace
To have retained that name.
Sim. I pray you, father.   [*Kneels.*
Creon. That name, I know,
Hath been long since forgot.
Sim. I find but small comfort in remem-
bering it now.
Evan. Cleanthes, take your place with
  these grave fathers,
And read what in that table is inscribed.
                              [*Gives him a paper.*
Now set these at the bar,
And read, Cleanthes, to the dread and terror
Of disobedience and unnatural blood.
  Clean. [*reads.*] *It is decreed by the grave
and learned council of Epire, that no son
and heir shall be held capable of his inheritance at the age of one and twenty, unless he
be at that time as mature in obedience, manners, and goodness.*
  Sim. Sure I shall never be at full age,
then, though I live to an hundred years ; and
that's nearer by twenty than the last statute
allow'd.
  1 *Court.* A terrible act !
  *Clean. Moreover, it is enacted that all
sons aforesaid, whom either this law, or
their own grace, shall reduce into the true
method of duty, virtue, and affection, [shall
appear before us] and relate their trial and
approbation from Cleanthes, the son of
Leonides*—from me, my lord !
  Evan. From none but you, as fullest.
  Proceed, sir.
  *Clean. Whom, for his manifest virtues,
we make such judge and censor of youth, and
the absolute reference of life and manners.*
  Sim. This is a brave world ! when a man
should be selling land he must be learning
manners. Is't not, my masters?

Enter Eugenia.

  Eug. What's here to do? my suitors at
  the bar !
The old band shines again : oh miserable !
                              [*She swoons.*
  Evan. Read the law over to her, 'twill
  awake her :
'Tis one deserves small pity.
  *Clean. Lastly, it is ordained, that all such
wives now whatsoever, that shall design their
husband's death, to be soon rid of them, and
entertain suitors in their husbands' lifetime*——
  Sim. You had best read that a little
louder ; for, if anything, that will bring her
to herself again, and find her tongue.
  Clean. Shall not presume, on the penalty

*of our heavy displeasure, to marry within
ten years after.*
  Eug. That law's too long by nine years
  and a half,
I'll take my death upou't, so shall most
  women.
  *Clean. And those incontinent women so
offending, to be judged and censured by Hippolita, wife to Cleanthes.*
  Eug. Of all the rest, I'll not be judged by
  her.

Re-enter Hippolita.

  Clean. Ah ! here she comes.   Let me
  prevent thy joys,
Prevent them but in part, and hide the rest ;
Thou hast not strength enough to bear them,
  else.
  Hip. Leonides !   [*She faints.*
  Clean. I fear'd it all this while ;
I knew 'twas past thy power.   Hippolita !
What contrariety is in women's blood !
One faints for spleen and anger, she for grace.
  Evan. Of sons and wives we see the
  worst and best.
May future ages yield Hippolitas
Many ; but few like thee, Eugenia !
Let no Simonides henceforth have a fame,
But all blest sons live in Cleanthe's name—
                              [*Harsh music within.*
Ha ! what strange kind of melody was that?
Yet give it entrance, whatsoe'er it be,
This day is all devote to liberty.

Enter Fiddlers, Gnotho, Courtezan, Cook,
Butler, &c., *with the* Old Women, Agatha,
*and one bearing a bridecake for the wed-
ding.*

  Gnoth. Fiddlers, crowd on, crowd on ; let
no man lay a block in your way.—Crowd on,
I say.
  Evan. Stay the crowd awhile; let's know
the reason of this jollity.
  Clean. Sirrah, do you know where you are?
  Gnoth. Yes, sir ; I am here, now here,
  and now here again, sir.
  Lys. Your hat is too high crown'd, the
  duke in presence.
  Gnoth. The duke ! as he is my sovereign,
I do give him two crowns for it, and that's
equal change all the world over : as I am
lord of the day (being my marriage-day the
second) I do advance my bonnet.   Crowd on
afore.
  Leon. Good sir, a few words, if you will
  vouchsafe them ;
Or will you be forced ?
  Gnoth. Forced ! I would the duke himself
  would say so.

Evan. I think he dares, sir, and does ; if
    you stay not,
You shall be forced.

Gnoth. I think so, my lord, and good
reason too ; shall not I stay when your grace
says I shall? I were unworthy to be a bridegroom in any part of your highness's dominions, then : will it please you to taste of
the wedlock-courtesy ?

Evan. Oh, by no means, sir ; you shall not
deface so fair an ornament for me.

Gnoth. If your grace please to be cakated,
say so.

Evan. And which might be your fair
bride, sir ?

Gnoth. This is my two-for-one that must
be the *uxor uxoris*, the remedy *doloris*, and
the very *syceum amoris.*

Evan. And hast thou any else ?

Gnoth. I have an older, my lord, for
other uses.

Clean. My lord,
I do observe a strange decorum here :
These that do lead this day of jollity,
Do march with music and most mirthful
    cheeks ;
Those that do follow, sad, and woefully,
Nearer the haviour of a funeral,
Than of a wedding.

Evan. 'Tis true ; pray expound that, sir.

Gnoth. As the destiny of the day falls out,
my lord, one goes to wedding, another goes
to hanging ; and your grace, in the due consideration, shall find them much alike ; the one
hath the ring upon her finger, the other the
halter about her neck. *I take thee, Beatrice,*
says the bridegroom ; *I take thee, Agatha,*
says the hangman ; and both say together, *to
have and to hold, till death do part us.*

Evan. This is not yet plain enough to my
    understanding.

Gnoth. If further your grace examine it,
you shall find I shew myself a dutiful subject, and obedient to the law, myself, with
these my good friends, and your good subjects, our old wives, whose days are ripe,
and their lives forfeit to the law : only
myself, more forward than the rest, am
already provided of my second choice.

Evan. Oh ! take heed, sir, you'll run
    yourself into danger ;
If the law finds you with two wives at once,
There's a shrewd premunire.

Gnoth. I have taken leave of the old, my
lord. I have nothing to say to her ; she's
going to sea, your grace knows whither,
better than I do : she has a strong wind
with her, it stands full in her poop ; when
you please, let her disembogue.

Cook. And the rest of her neighbours with
her, whom we present to the satisfaction of
your highness' law.

Gnoth. And so we take our leaves, and
leave them to your highness.—Crowd on.

Evan. Stay, stay, you are too forward. Will
    you marry,
And your wife yet living?

Gnoth. Alas ! she'll be dead before we can
get to church. If your grace would set her
in the way, I would dispatch her : I have a
venture on't, which would return me, if
your highness would make a little more
haste, two for one.

Evan. Come, my lords, we must sit again ;
    here's a case
Craves a most serious censure.

Cook. Now they shall be dispatch'd out of
    the way.

Gnoth. I would they were gone once ; the
time goes away.

Evan. Which is the wife unto the forward
    bridegroom ?

Aga. I am, an it please your grace.

Evan. Trust me, a lusty woman, able-
    bodied,
And well-blooded cheeks.

Gnoth. Oh, she paints, my lord ; she was
a chambermaid once, and learn'd it of her
lady.

Evan. Sure I think she cannot be so old.

Aga. Truly I think so too, an't please
your grace.

Gnoth. Two to one with your grace of
that ! she's threescore by the book.

Leon. Peace, sirrah, you are too loud.

Cook. Take heed, Gnotho : if you move
the duke's patience, 'tis an edge-tool ; but a
word and a blow, he cuts off your head.

Gnoth. Cut off my head ! away, ignorant !
he knows it cost more in the hair ; he does
not use to cut off many such heads as mine :
I will talk to him too ; if he cut off my head,
I'll give him my ears. I say my wife is at
full age for the law, the clerk shall take his
oath, and the church-book shall be sworn
too.

Evan. My lords, I leave this censure to you.

Leon. Then first, this fellow does deserve
    punishment,
For offering up a lusty able woman,
Which may do service to the common-
    wealth,
Where the law craves one impotent and use-
    less.

Creon. Therefore to be severely punished,
For thus attempting a second marriage,
His wife yet living.

Lys. Nay, to have it trebled ;

That even the day and instant when he
  should mourn,
As a kind husband, at her funeral,
He leads a triumph to the scorn of it ;
Which unseasonable joy ought to be punish'd
  With all severity.
  But. The fiddles will be in a foul case too,
  by and by.
  Leon. Nay, further ; it seems he has a
  venture
Of two for one at his second marriage,
Which cannot be but a conspiracy
Against the former.
  Gnoth. A mess of wise old men !
  Lys. Sirrah, what can you answer to all
  these ?
  Gnoth. Ye are good old men, and talk as
age will give you leave. I would speak
with the youthful duke himself ; he and I
may speak of things that shall be thirty or
forty years after you are dead and rotten.
Alas ! you are here to-day, and gone to sea
to-morrow.
  Evan. In troth, sir, then I must be plain
  with you.
The law that should take away your old
  wife from you,
The which I do perceive was your desire,
Is void and frustrate ; so for the rest :
There has been since another parliament,
Has cut it off.
  Gnoth. I see your grace is disposed to be
pleasant.
  Evan. Yes, you might perceive that ; I
  had not else
Thus dallied with your follies.
  Gnoth. I'll talk further with your grace
when I come back from church ; in the mean
time, you know what to do with the old
women.
  Evan. Stay, sir, unless in the mean time
  you mean
I cause a gibbet to be set up in your way,
And hang you at your return.
  Aga. O gracious prince !
  Evan. Your old wives cannot die to-day
by any law of mine ; for aught I can say to
  them,
They may, by a new edict, bury you,
And then, perhaps, you'll pay a new fine too.
  Gnoth. This is fine, indeed !
  Aga. O gracious prince ! may he live a
  hundred years more.
  Cook. Your venture is not like to come in
to-day, Gnotho.
  Gnoth. Gave me the principal back.
  Cook. Nay, by my troth, we'll venture still
—and I'm sure we have as ill a venture of
it as you ; for we have taken old wives of

purpose, that we had thought to have put
away at this market, and now we cannot
utter a pennyworth.
  Evan. Well, sirrah, you were best to discharge your new charge, and take your old
one to you.
  Gnoth. Oh music ! no music, but prove
  most deleful trumpet ;
Oh bride ! no bride, but thou mayst prove
  a strumpet ;
Oh venture ! no venture, I have, for one,
  now none ;
Oh wife ! thy life is saved when I hoped it
  had been gone.
Case up your fruitless strings ; no penny, no
  wedding ;
Case up thy maidenhead ; no priest, no
  bedding :
Avaunt, my venture ! ne'er to be restored,
Till Ag, my old wife, be thrown overboard :
Then come again, old Ag, since it must
  be so ;
Let bride and venture with woful music go.
  Cook. What for the bridecake, Gnotho?
  Gnoth. Let it be mouldy, now 'tis out of
  season,
Let it grow out of date, currant, and reason ;
Let it be chipt and chopt, and given to
  chickens.
No more is got by that, than William
  Dickins
Got by his wooden dishes.
Put up your plums, as fiddlers put up pipes,
The wedding dash'd, the bridegroom weeps
  and wipes.
Fiddlers, farewell ! and now, without perhaps,
Put up your fiddles as you put up scraps.
  Lys. This passion has given some satis-
faction yet. My lord, I think you'll pardon
him now, with all the rest, so they live
honestly with the wives they have.
  Evan. Oh ! most freely ; free pardon to all.
  Cook. Ay, we have deserved our pardons,
if we can live honestly with such reverend
wives, that have no motion in them but their
tongues.
  Aga. Heaven bless your grace ! you are a
just prince.
  Gnoth. All hopes dash'd ; the clerk's
  duties lost,
My venture gone ; my second wife divorced ;
And which is worst, the old one come back
  again !
Such voyages are made now-a-days !
Besides these two fountains of fresh water,
I will weep two salt out of my nose. Your
grace had been more kind to your young
subjects—heaven bless and mend your laws,
that they do not gull your poor countrymen:

Q Q

but I am not the first, by forty, that has been undone by the law. 'Tis but a folly to stand upon terms; I take my leave of your grace, as well as mine eyes will give me leave: I would they had been asleep in their beds when they opened them to see this day! Come Ag, come Ag.

[Exeunt Gnotho *and* Agatha.

Creon. Were not you all my servants?

Cook. During your life, as we thought, sir; but our young master turn'd us away.

Creon. How headlong, villain, wert thou in thy ruin!

Sim. I followed the fashion, sir, as other young men did. If you were as we thought you had been, we should ne'er have come for this, I warrant you. We did not feed, after the old fashion, on beef and mutton, and such like.

Creon. Well, what damage or charge you have run yourselves into by marriage, I cannot help, nor deliver you from your wives; them you must keep; yourselves shall again return to me.

All. We thank your lordship for your love, and must thank ourselves for our bad bargains.   [*Exeunt.*

Evan. Cleanthes, you delay the power of law,
To be inflicted on these misgovern'd men,
That filial duty have so far transgress'd.

Clean. My lord, I see a satisfaction
Meeting the sentence, even preventing it,
Beating my words back in their utterance.
See, sir, there's salt sorrow bringing forth fresh
And new duties, as the sea propagates.
The elephants have found their joints too——
                              [*They kneel.*
Why, here's humility able to bind up
The punishing hands of the severest masters,
Much more the gentle fathers'.

Sim. I had ne'er thought to have been brought so low as my knees again; but since there's no remedy, fathers, reverend fathers, as you ever hope to have good sons and heirs, a handful of pity! we confess we have deserved more than we are willing to receive at your hands, though sons can never deserve too much of their fathers, as shall appear afterwards.

Creon. And what way can you decline your feeding now?
You cannot retire to beeves and muttons sure.

Sim. Alas! sir, you see a good pattern for that, now we have laid by our high and lusty meats, and are down to our marrow-bones already.

Creon. Well, sir, rise to virtues: we'll bind you now;   [*They rise.*
You that were too weak yourselves to govern,
By others shall be govern'd.

Lys. Cleanthes,
I meet your justice with reconcilement:
If there be tears of faith in woman's breast,
I have received a myriad, which confirms me
To find a happy renovation.

Clean. Here's virtue's throne,
Which I'll embellish with my dearest jewels
Of love and faith, peace and affection!
This is the altar of my sacrifice,
Where daily my devoted knees shall bend.
Age-honoured shrine! time still so love you,
That I so long may have you in mine eye
Until my memory lose your beginning!
For you, great prince, long may your fame survive,
Your justice and your wisdom never die,
Crown of your crown, the blessing of your land,
Which you reach to her from your regent hand!

Leon. O Cleanthes, had you with us tasted
The entertainment of our retirement,
Fear'd and exclaim'd on in your ignorance,
You might have sooner died upon the wonder,
Than any rage or passion for our loss.
A place at hand we were all strangers in,
So sphered about with music, such delights,
Such viands and attendance, and once a day
So cheered with a royal visitant,
That oft times, waking, our unsteady fancies
Would question whether we yet lived or no,
Or had possession of that paradise
Where angels be the guard!

Evan. Enough, Leonides,
You go beyond the praise; we have our end,
And all is ended well: we have now seen
The flowers and weeds that grow about our court.

Sim. If these be weeds, I'm afraid I shall wear none so good again as long as my father lives.

Evan. Only this gentleman we did abuse
With our own bosom: we seem'd a tyrant,
And he our instrument. Look, 'tis Cratilus,
                    [*Discovers* Cratilus.
The man that you supposed had now been travell'd;
Which we gave leave to learn to speak,
And bring us foreign languages to Greece.
All's joy, I see; let music be the crown:
And set it high, "The good needs fear no law,
It is his safety, and the bad man's awe."
                    [*Flourish. Exeunt.*

[*Now for the first time printed in Massinger's Works.*]

Believe as you List.

PROLOGUE.

So far our author is from arrogance
That he craves pardon for his ignorance
In story. If you find what's Roman here,
Grecian or Asiatic, draw too near
A late and sad example, 'tis confest
He's but an English scholar; at his best
A stranger to cosmography, and may err
In the country's names, the shape and character
Of the person he presents. Yet he is bold
In me to promise, be it new or old,
The tale is worth the hearing; and may move
Compassion, perhaps deserve your love
And approbation. He dares not boast
His pains and care, or what books he hath tost
And turned to make it up. The rarity
Of the events in this strange history,
Now offered to you, by his own confession
Must make it good, and not his weak expression.
You sit his judges, and like judges be
From favour to his cause, or malice, free;
Then, whether he hath hit the white or miss'd,
As the title speaks, Believe you as you list!

DRAMATIS PERSONÆ.

Antiochus, *king of the* Lower Asia, *a fugitive.*
A Stoic Philosopher, *friend to* Antiochus.
Chrysalus, Syrus, Geta, *ungrateful servants of* Antiochus.
Berecinthius, *a flamen of* Cybele.
First, Second, *and* Third Merchants, *born subjects of* Antiochus.
Flaminius, *the Roman Ambassador at* Carthage.
Calistus, Demetrius, } *Freedmen of* Flaminius.
Amilcar, *Prince of the* Carthaginian *Senate.*
Hanno, Asdrubal, Carthalo, Carthaginian *Senators.*
Lentulus, *successor of* Flaminius *at* Carthage.

Titus, *head of* Flaminius' *intelligence department.*
Prusias, *King of* Bithynia.
Philoxenus, *tutor and minister of* Prusias.
Metellus, *Proconsul of* Lusitania.
Sempronius, *a Captain.*
Marcellus, *a noble Roman, Proconsul of* Sicily.
Jailor, Officer, Captain, &c.
Queen *of* Prusias.
Courtezan.
Cornelia, *a noble Roman lady, wife to* Marcellus.
Moorish Waiting Woman.
Guards, *&c., &c.*

SCENE,—Carthage, Bithynia, Callipolis, Syracuse.

ACT I.

SCENE I.—*The neighbourhood of* Carthage.

Enter Antiochus *and a* Stoic.

Stoic. You're now in sight of Carthage, that great city,
Which, in her empire's vastness, rivals Rome
At her proud height; two hours will bring you thither.
Make use of what you've learn'd in your long travails,
And from the golden principles, read to you

In the Athenian Academie, stand resolved
For either fortune. You must now forget
The contemplations of a private man,
And put in action that which may comply
     with
The majesty of a monarch.
     Ant.   How that title,
That glorious attribute of majesty,
That troublesome, though most triumphant
     robe
Designed me in my birth, which I have worn
With terror and astonishment to others,
Affrights *me* now ! O memory ! memory
Of what I was once when the Eastern world
With wonder, in my May of youth, look'd
     on me.
Ambassadors of the most potent kings,
With noble emulation, contending
To court my friendship, their fair daughters
     offered
As pledges to assure it, with all pomp
And circumstance of glory. Rome herself,
And Carthage, emulous whose side I should
Confirm in my protection. O remembrance,
With what ingenious cruelty and tortures,
Out of a due consideration of
My present low and desperate condition,
Dost thou afflict me now.
     Stoic.   You must oppose
(For so the stoic discipline commands you)
That wisdom with your patience fortified,
Which holds dominion over fate, against
The torrent of your passion.
     Ant.   I should,
I do confess I should, if I could drink up
That river of forgetfulness poets dream of.
But still in dreadful forms, (philosophy
     wanting
Power to remove them,) all those innocent
     spirits,
Borrowing again their bodies, gashed with
     wounds,
(Which strewed Achaia's bloody plains, and
     made
Rivulets of gore) appear to me, exacting
A strict account of my ambitious folly,
For the exposing of twelve thousand souls,
Who fell that fatal day, to certain ruin ;
Neither the counsel of the Persian king
Prevailing with me; nor the grave advice
Of my wise enemy, Marcus Seaurus, hinder-
     ing
My desperate enterprise—too late repented.
Methinks I now look on my butchered army!
     Stoic. This is mere melancholy.
     Ant.   O, 'tis more, sir ;
Here, there, and everywhere they do pur-
     sue me!
The genius of my country made a slave,

Like a weeping mother, seems to kneel be-
     fore me,
Wringing her manacled hands ! The hope-
     ful youth
And bravery of my kingdom, in their pale
And ghastly looks, lamenting that they were
Too soon by my means forced from their
     sweet being :
Old [He]sper with his fierce beams [scorc]h-
     ing in vain
Their [wives, their sisters, and their tender
     daughters]
Trained up in all delights, or sacred to
The chaste Diana's rites, compelled to
     bow to
The soldiers' lusts, or at an outcry sold
Under the spear like beasts—to be spurned
     and trod on
By their proud mistresses, the Roman
     matrons !
O, sir, consider then if it can be
In the constancy of a stoic to endure
What now I suffer ?
     Stoic.   Two and twenty years
Travailing o'er the world, you've paid the
     forfeit
Of this engagement : shed a sea of tears
In your sorrow for it : and now, being called
     from
The rigour of a strict philosopher's life
By the cries of your poor country, you are
     bound
With an obedient cheerfulness to follow
The path that you are entered in, which will
Guide you out of a wilderness of horror,
To the flourishing plains of safety, the just
     gods
Smoothing the way before you.
     Ant.   Though I grant
That all impossibilities are easy
To their omnipotence, give me leave to fear
The more than doubtful issue. Can it fall.
In the compass of my hopes—the lordly
     Romans,
So long possessed of Asia, their plea
Made good by conquest, and that ratified
With their religious authority,
The propagation of the commonwealth
To whose increase they're sworn to, will e'er
     part with
A prey so precious, and so dearly purchased ?
A tigress circled with her famished whelps
Will sooner yield a lamb, snatched from the
     flock,
To the dumb oratory of the ewe
Than Rome restore one foot of earth that may
Diminish her vast empire !
     Stoic.   In her will
This may be granted, but you have a title

So strong and clear that there's no colour left
To varnish Rome's pretences. Add this, sir,
The Asian princes, warned by your example,
And yet unconquered, never will consent
That such a foul example of injustice
Shall, to the scandal of the present age,
Hereafter be recorded. They in this
Are equally engaged with you, and must,
Though not in love to justice, for their safety
In policy assist, guard, and protect you.
And, you may rest assured, neither the king
Of Parthia, the Gauls, nor big-boned Germans,
Nor this great Carthage, grown already
  jealous
Of Rome's encroaching empire, will cry *Aim*
To such an usurpation, which must
Take from their own security. Besides
Your mother was a Roman ; for her sake,
And the families from which she is derived,
You must find favour.
   Ant.   For her sake ! Alas, sir,
Ambition knows no kindred. Right and
  lawful
Was never yet found as a marginal note
In the black book of profit. I am sunk
Too low to be buoyed up, it being held
A foolish weakness and disease in statists,
In favour of a weak man, to provoke
Such as are mighty. The imperious waves
Of my calamities have already fallen
   .   .   .   .   .   .

[Here is a sad hiatus in the manuscript.]

To them enter Chrysalus, Syrus, Geta, *servants of* Antiochus, *who revile him, and rob and strip him.*
      [The hiatus continues.]
          [*Exeunt all but* Antiochus.
   Anti.   .   .   .   .
[Farewell my h]opes ; despair with sable
  wings
[Sail-stretch'd ab]ove my head : the gold
  with which
[   ] us furnished me to supply my wants,
[And] make my first appearance like myself
[Have these] disloyal villains ravished from
  me.
Wretch that I was to tempt their abject minds
With such a purchase. Can I, in this weed,
Without the gold to fee an advocate
To plead my royal title, nourish hope
Of a recovery ? Forlorn majesty,
Wanting the outer gloss and ceremony
To give it lustre, meets no more respect
Than knowledge with the ignorant. Ha !
  what is
Contained in this waste paper ? 'Tis endorsed
To the no-king Antiochus ; and subscribed
No more thy servant, but superior, Chrysalus.

What am I fallen to ? There is something
  writ more.
Why this small piece of silver ? What I read
  may
Reveal the mystery :—*Forget thou wert ever
Called king Antiochus. With this charity
I enter thee a beggar.* Too tough heart
Will nothing break thee? O that now I stood
On some high pyramid, from whence I might
Be seen by the whole world, and with a voice
Louder than thunder pierce the ears of proud
And secure greatness with the true relation
Of my remarkable story, that my fall
Might not be fruitless, but still live the great
Example of man's frailty. I that was
Born and bred up a king, whose frown or
  smile
Spake death or life ; my will a law ; my
  person
Environed with an army : now exposed
To the contempt and scorn of my own slave,
Who in his pride, as a god compared with
  me,
Bids me become a beggar ! But complaints
  are weak
And womanish. I will like a palm tree grow
Under my [own] huge weight. Nor shall the
  fear
Of death or torture that dejection bring,
Make me [or] live or die less than a king !
                      [*Exit.*

SCENE II.—*A Street in* Carthage.

Enter Berecinthius (*with three petitions,*)
    and three Merchants *of* Asia.

   1 *Merch.* We are grown so contemptible
  he disdains
To give us hearing.
   2 *Merch.* Keeps us at such a distance,
And with his Roman gravity declines
Our suit for conference, as with much more
  ease
We might make our approaches to the
  Parthian,
Without a present, than work him to have
A feeling of our grievances.
   3 *Merch.*   A statesman !
The devil, I think, who only knows him truly,
Can give his character. When he is to deter-
  mine
A point of justice, his words fall in measure
Like plummets of a clock, observing time
And just proportion.
   1 *Merch.*   But when he is
To speak in any cause concerns himself,
Or Rome's republic, like a gushing torrent,
Not to be stopp'd in its full course, his
  reasons,
Delivered like a second Mercurie,

Break in, and [bear down] whatsoever is
Opposed against them.
 2 *Merch.*   When he smiles, let such
Beware as have to do with him, for then,
Sans doubt, he's bent on mischief.
 Berec.   As I am
Cybele's flamen (whose most sacred image,
Drawn thus in pomp, I wear upon my
breast),
I am privileged, nor is it in his power
To do me wrong ; and he shall find I can
Think, and aloud too, when I am not at
Her altar kneeling. Mother of the gods !
 what is he ?
At his best but a patrician of Rome,
His name Titus Flaminius ; and speak mine,
Berecinthius, arch-flamen to Cybele,
It makes as great a sound.
 3 *Merch.*   True ; but his place, sir,
And the power it carries in it, as Rome's
legate,
Gives him pre-eminence o'er you.
 Berec.   Not an atom.
When moral honesty and *jus gentium* fail
To lend relief to such as are oppressed,
Religion must use her strength. I'm perfect
In these notes you gave me. Do they con-
tain at full,
Your grievances and losses.
 1 *Merch.*   Would they were
As well redressed, as they are punctually
Delivered to you.
 Berec.   Say no more, they shall
And to the purpose.
 2 *Merch.*   Here he comes.
 Berec.   Have at him.

 Enter Flaminius *with two freedmen,*
  Calistus *and* Demetrius.

 Flam. Blow away these troublesome
 and importunate drones,
I've embryons of greater consequence
In my imaginations to which
I must give life and form, not now vouchsafing
To hear their idle buzzes.
 2 *Merch.*   Note you that ?
 Berec. Yes, I do note it ; but the Flamen
is not
So light to be removed by a groom's breath.
I must, and will, speak, and I thus confront
him.
 Flam. But that the image of the god-
dess, which
Thou wear'st upon thy breast, protects thy
rudeness,
'T had forfeited thy life. Dost thou not tremble
When an incensed Roman frowns ?
 Berec.   I see
No Gorgon in your face.

 Flam. Must I speak in thunder
Before thou wilt be awed ?
 Berec.   I rather look
For reverence from thee if thou respectest
The goddess' power, and in her name I
 charge thee
To give me hearing. If these lions roar,
For thy contempt of her expect a vengeance
Suitable to thy pride.
 Flam.   Thou shalt o'ercome,
There's no contending with thee.
 3 *Merch.*   Hitherto
The Flamen hath the better.
 1 *Merch.*   But I fear
He will not keep it.
 Berec.   Know you these men's
faces ?
 Flam. Yes, yes, poor Asiatics.
 Berec.   Poor ! They are made so
By your Roman tyranny and oppression.
 Flam. . . . [to task]
If arrogantly you presume to take
The Roman government, your goddess can-
 not
Give privilege to it, and you'll find and feel
'Tis little less than treason, Flamen.
 Berec.   Truth
In your pride is so interpreted : these poor
 men,
These Asiatic merchants, whom you look
 on
With such contempt and scorn, are they to
 whom
Rome owes her bravery : their industrious
 search
To the farthest Inde, with danger to them-
 selves
Brings home security to you—to you—un-
 thankful :
Your magazines are from their sweat sup-
 plied :
The legions with which you fright the world
Are from their labour paid : the Tyrian
 fish,
Whose blood dyes your proud purple, in the
 colour
Distinguishing the senator's garded robe
From a plebeian habit, their nets catch :
The diamond hewed from the rock, the
 pearl
Dived for into the bottom of the sea,
The sapphire, ruby, jacinth, amber, coral,
And all rich ornaments of your Latian
 dames
Are Asian spoils. They are indeed the
 nurses
And sinews of your war, and without them
What could you do ? Your handkercher——
 Flam.   Wipe your face,

You're in a sweat. The weather's hot, take heed
Of melting your fat kidneys.
   Berec.   There's no heat
Can thaw thy frozen conscience.
   Flam.   To it again ;
I am not mov'd.
   Berec.   I see it. If you had
The feeling of a man you would not suffer
These men, who have deserved so well, to
  sink
Under the burthen of their wrongs. If they
Are subjects, why enjoy they not the right
And privilege of subjects ? What defence
Can you allege for your connivance to
The Carthaginian gallies, who forced from
  them
The prize they took, belonging not to them
Nor their confederates ?
   Flam.   With reverence
To your so sacred goddess, I must tell you
You're grown presumptuous ; and, in your demands,
A rash and saucy Flamen. Meddle with
Your juggling mysteries, and keep in awe
Your gelded ministers. Shall I yield account
Of what I do to you ?
   1 *Merch.*   He smiles in frown.
   2 *Merch.* Nay then I know what follows.
   3 *Merch.*   In his looks
A tempest rises.
   Flam.   How dare you complain,
Or in a look repine? Our government
Hath been too easy, and the yoke, which Rome
In her accustomed lenity imposed
Upon your stubborn necks, begets con-
  tempt.
Hath our familiar commérce and trading,
Almost as with our equals, taught you to
Dispute our actions? Have you quite forgot
What we are, and you ought to be? Shall vassals
Capitulate with their lords?
   2 *Merch.*   I vow he speaks
In his own dialect.
   Flam.   'Tis too frequent, wretches,
To have the vanquished hate the conqueror,
And from us needs no answer. Do I not know
How odious the lordly Roman is
To the despiséd Asian ; and that
To gain your liberty you would pull down
The altars of your gods, and like the giants
Raise a new war gainst heaven.
   1 *Merch.*   Terrible !
   Flam. Did you not give assurance of this,
  when
Giddy Antiochus died, and rather than

Accept us guardians of your orphan king-
  dom,
When the victorious Scaurus with his sword
Pleaded the Roman title, with our vote,
You did exclaim against us as the men
That sought to lay an unjust gripe upon
Your territories ; never remembering that
In the brass-leaved book of fate it was set
  down
The earth should know no sovereign but
  Rome.
Yet you repine, and rather choose to pay
Homage and fealty to the Parthian,
The Egyptian Ptolemy, or indeed any,
Than bow unto the Roman.
   Berec.   And perhaps
Our government in them had been more
  gentle,
Since yours is insupportable.
   Flam.   If thou wert not
In a free state, the tongue that belloweth forth
These blasphemies should be seared. For
you—presume not [*To the* Merchants.
To trouble me, hereafter. If you do,
You shall with horror to your proudest hopes
Feel really that we have iron hammers
To pulverize rebellion, and that
We dare use you as slaves. Be you, too,
  warned, sir,   [*To* Beree.
And this is my last caution. I have seen
A murmurer, like yourself, for his attempting
To raise sedition in Rome's provinces,
Hang'd up in such a habit !
      [*Exeunt* Flaminius *and freedmen.*
   Berec.   I have took
Poison in at my ears, and I shall burst
If it come not up in my reply.
   1 *Merch.*   He's gone, sir.
   Berec. He durst not stay me. If he had,
he'd found
I would not swallow my spittle.
   2 *Merch.*   As we must
Our wrongs and our disgraces.
   3 *Merch.*   O, the wretched
Condition that we live in ! Made the anvil
On which Rome's tyrannies are shaped and
  fashioned.
   1 *Merch.* But our calamities there's nothing
left us,
Which we can call our own.
   2 *Merch.*   Our wives and daughters
Lie open to their lusts, and such as should be
Our judges dare not right us.
   3 *Merch.*   O, Antiochus !
Thrice happy were the men whom fate ap-
  pointed
To fall with thee in Achaia.

2 Merch. They have set
A period to their miseries.
1 Merch. We survive
To linger out a tedious life ; and death——
We call in vain what flies us.
Berec. If religion
Be not a mere word only, and the gods
Are just, we shall find a delivery
When least expected.

       Enter Antiochus.

  1 Merch. 'Tis beyond all hope, sir.
Berec. Ha ! who is this ?
Ant. Your charity to a poor man
As you are Asians.
  2 Merch. Pray you observe him.
  3 Merch. I am amazed !
  1 Merch. I thunderstrook !
Berec. What are you ?
Ant. The King Antiochus.
  2 Merch. Or some deity
That hath assumed his shape ?
Berec. He only differs
In the colour of his hair, and age.
Ant. Consider
What two and twenty years of misery
Can work upon a wretch : that long time
  spent too
Under distant zeniths, and the change you
  look on
Will not deserve your wonder.
  1 Merch. His own voice !
  2 Merch. His very countenance, his fore-
  head, eyes !
  3 Merch. His nose, his very lip !
Berec. His stature, speech !
  1 Merch. His very hand, leg, foot !
  2 Merch. The moles upon
His face and hands.
  3 Merch. The scars caused by his hurts
On his right brow and head.
Berec. The hollowness
Of his under jaw, occasioned by the loss
Of a tooth pulled out by his chirurgion.
  1 Merch. To confirm us, tell your chirurgion's name
When he served you.
Ant. You all knew him as I
Do you : Demetrius Castor.
  2 Merch. Strange.
  3 Merch. But
Most infallibly true.
Berec. So many marks
Confirming us, we'll pay for our distrust
A sacrifice for his safety.
  1 Merch. May Rome smile !
  2 Merch. And Asia once more flourish !
  3 Merch. You the means, sir !

Ant. Silence your shouts : I will give
  stronger proofs
Than these exterior marks when I appear
Before the Carthaginian senators, .
With whom I have held more intelligence
And private counsels than with all the kings
Of Asia or Afric : I'll amaze them
With the wonder of my story.
Berec. Yet, until
Your majesty be furnished like yourself,
To a neighbour village——
Ant. Where you please. The omen
Of this encounter promises a good issue : .
And, our gods pleased, oppressed Asia,
When aid is least expected, may shake off
The insulting Roman bondage, and in me
Gain and enjoy her pristine liberty.
                        [*Exeunt.*

—————

· ACT II.

SCENE I.—Carthage. *A Room in the*
          House of Flaminius.

Enter Flaminius *and his freedman* Calistus.

  Flam. A man that styles himself Antiochus
  say you ?
  Calis. Not alone styled so, but as such
  received
And honoured by the Asians.
Flam. Two impostors,
For their pretension to that fatal name,
Already have paid dear ; nor shall this third
Escape unpunished.
Calis. I will exact your wisdom
With an Herculean arm (the cause requires it)
To strangle this new monster in the birth.
For, on my life, he hath delivered to
The credulous multitude such reasons why
They should believe he is the true Antiochus
That, with their gratulations for his safety,
And wishes for his restitution, freely
Offer the hazard of their lives and fortunes
To do him service.
Flam. Poor seducéd fools !
However 'tis a business of such weight
I must not sleep in 't. Is he now in Carthage?
  Calis. No, sir ; removed to a grange some
  two miles off ;
And there the malcontents, and such, whose
  wants
With forfeited credits make them wish a
  change
Of the Roman government, in troops flock
To him.
  Flam. With one puff—thus—will I dis-
  perse and scatter
This heap of dust. Here take my ring. By
  this

Entreat my friend Amilcar to procure
A mandate from the Carthaginian senate
For the apprehension of this impostor, ·
And with all possible speed. [*Exit* Calistus.
      Howe'er I know
The rumour of Antiochus' death uncertain,
It much imports the safety of great Rome
To have it so believed.

     Enter Demetrius.

  Dem.   There wait without
Three fellows I ne'er saw before, who much
Importune their access. They swear they
  bring
Business along with 'em that deserves your
  care,
It being for the safety of the republic,
And quiet of the provinces. They are full
Of gold—I've felt their bounty.
  Flam.   Such are welcome.
Give them admittance. In this various play
Of state and policy, there is no property
But may be useful.

   Enter Chrysalus, Geta, *and* Syrus.

     Now, friends, what design
Carries you to me?
  Geta.   My most honoured lord——
  Syrus. May't please your mightiness——
  Flam. · Let one speak for all.
I cannot brook this discord.
  Chrys.   As our duties
Command us, noble Roman, having dis-
  covered
A dreadful danger, with the nimble wings
Of speed approaching to the state of Rome,
We hold it fit you should have the first notice,
That you may have the honour to prevent it.
  Flam. I thank you; but instruct me what
  form wears
The danger that you speak of.
  Chrys.   It appears
In the shape of King Antiochus.
  Flam.   How! Is he
Rose from the dead?
  Chrys.   Alas! he never died, sir;
He at this instant lives—the more the pity
He should survive, to the disturbance of
Rome's close and politic counsels in the
  getting
Possession of his kingdom, which he would
Recover (simple as he is) the plain
And downright way of justice.
  Flam.   Very likely.
But how are you assured this is Antiochus,
And not a counterfeit? Answer that.
  Chrys.   I serv'd him
In the Achaian war, where, his army routed,

And the warlike Romans hot in their exe-
  cution,
To shun their fury he and his minions were
(Having cast off their glorious armour) forced
To hide themselves as dead, with fear and
  horror,
Among the slaughtered carcases. I lay by
  them,
And rose with them at midnight. Then
  retiring
Unto their ships, we sailed to Corinth: thence
To India, where he spent many years
With their gymnosophists. There I waited
  on him,
And came thence with him. But, at length,
  tired out
With an unrewarded service, and affrighted
In my imagination with the dangers,
Or rather certain ruins, in pursuing
His more than desperate fortunes, we forsook
  him.
  Flam. A wise and politic fellow! Give me
  thy hand.
Thou'rt sure of this?
  Chrys.   As of my life.
  Flam.   And this is
Known only to you three?
  Chrys.   There's no man lives else
To witness it.
  Flam.   The better: but inform me,
And, as you would oblige me to you, truly,
Where did you leave him?
  Syrus.   For the payment of
Our long and tedious travail, we made bold
To rifle him.
  Flam.   Good!
  Geta.   And so disabling him
Of means to claim his right, we hope
  despair
Hath made him hang himself.
  Flam.   It had been safer
If you had done it for him. But as it is,
You are honest men. You have revealed this
  secret
To no man but myself?
  Chrys.   Nor ever will.
  Flam. I will take order that you never
  shall.   [*Aside.*
And, since you have been true unto the
  state,
I'll keep you so. I'm even now considering
How to advance you.
  Chrys.   What a pleasant smile
His honour throws upon us.
  Geta.   We are made.
  Flam. And now 'tis found out, that no
  danger may
Come near you, should the robbery be dis-
  covered,

Which the Carthaginian laws, you know, call death,
My house shall be your sanctuary.

Syrus.   There's a favour!

Flam. And that our entertainment come not short
Of your deservings, I commit you to
My secretary's care. See that they want not,
Among their other delicates——

Chrys.   Mark that!

Flam. —A sublimated pill of mercuric,
For sugar to their wine.

Dem.   I understand you.

Flam. Attend these honest men, as if they were
Made Roman citizens. And be sure, at night,
I may see 'em well-lodged.—Dead in the vault, I mean,
Their gold is thy reward.

                              [*Aside to* Demetrius.

Dem.   Believe it done, sir.

Flam. And when 'tis known how I have recompensed
(Though you were treacherous to your own king,)
The service done to Rome, I hope that others
Will follow your example. Enter, friends ;
I'll so provide that when you next come forth,
You shall not fear who sees you.

Chrys.   Was there ever
So sweet a tempered Roman ?

Flam.   You shall find it.

                                        [*Exeunt.*

Ha ! what's the matter? Do I feel a sting here,
For what is done to these poor snakes ? My reason
Will easily remove it. That assures me,
That, as I am a Roman, to preserve
And propagate her empire, though they were
My father's sons, they must not live to witness
Antiochus is in being. The relation
The villain made, in every circumstance
Appeared so like to truth, that I began
To feel an inclination to believe
What I must have no faith in. By my birth
I am bound to serve thee, Rome, and what I do,
Necessity of state compels me to.   [*Exit.*

SCENE II.—*The Senate Hall in* Carthage.

Enter Amilcar, Hanno, Asdrubal, *and* Carthalo.

Amil. To steer a middle course 'twixt these extremes,
Exacts our serious care.

Hanno.   I know not which way
I should incline.

Amil.   The reasons this man urges,
To prove himself Antiochus, are so pregnant,
And the attestation of his countrymen
In every circumstance so punctual,
As not to show him our compassion were
An act of barb'rous cruelty.

Carth.   Under correction,
Give me leave to speak my thoughts. We're bound to weigh
Not what we should do in the point of honour,
Swayed by our pity, but what may be done
With the safety of the state.

Asd.   Which is, indeed,
The main consideration : for, grant
This is the true Antiochus, without danger,
Nay, almost certain ruin to ourselves,
We cannot yield him favour or protection.

Hanno. We've fear'd and felt the Roman power, and must
Expect, if we provoke him, a return
Not limited to the quality of the offence,
But left at large to his interpretation,
Which seldom is confined. Who knows not that
The tribute Rome receives from Asia, is
Her chief supportance ; other provinces
Hardly defray the charge by which they are
Kept in subjection. They, in name, perhaps,
Render the Roman terrible ; but his strength
And power to do hurt, without question, is
Derived from Asia. And can we hope then,
That such as lend their aids to force it from them,
Will be held for less than capital enemies,
And, as such, pursued and punished ?

Carth.   I could wish
We were well rid of him.

Asd.   The surest course
Is to deliver him into the hands
Of bold Flaminius.

Hanno.   And so oblige
Rome, for a matchless benefit.

Amil.   If my power
Were absolute, as 'tis but titular,
And that confined too, being by you elected
Prince of the Senate only for a year,
I would oppose your counsels, and not labour
With arguments to confute them. Yet, however,
Though a fellow-patriot with you, let it not savour
Of usurpation, though in my opinion
I cross your abler judgments. Call to mind
Our grandsires' glories (though not seconded
With due imitation), and remember

With what expense of coin, as blood, they
  did
Maintain their liberty, and kept the scale
Of empire even 'twixt Carthage and proud
  Rome ;
And though the Punic faith is branded by
Our enemies, our confederates and friends,
And seventeen kings, our feodaries, found it
As firm as fate. Our strengths upon the sea
Exceeding theirs—and our land soldiers
In number far above theirs, though inferior
In arms and discipline (to our shame we
  speak it)
And then for our cavallery, in the champaign
How often have they brake their piles, and
  routed
Their coward legions.
  Hanno.   This, I grant, is not
To be contradicted.
  Amil.   If so we find it
In our records, and that this state hath been
The sanctuary to which mighty kings
Have fled to for protection, and found it,
Let it not to posterity be told
That we so far degenerate from the race
We are derived, as in a servile fear
Of the Roman power, in a kind to play the
  bawds
To their ravenous lusts, by yielding up a
  man,
That wears the shape of our confederate,
To their devouring gripe, whose strong
  assurance
Of our integrity and impartial doom
Hath made this seat his altar.
  Carth.   I join with you
In this opinion, but no farther than
It may be done with safety.
  Asd.   In his ruins
To bury ourselves, you needs must grant
  to be
An inconsiderate pity, no way suiting
With a wise man's reason.
  Carth.   Let us face to face
Hear the accuser and accused, and then,
As either's arguments work on us, determine
As the respect of our security
Or honour shall invite us.
  Amil.   From the Senate,
Entreat the Roman, Titus Flaminius
To assist us with his counsel.
  Hanno.   And let the prisoner
Be brought into the court.
  Amil.   The gods of Carthage
Direct us the right way !

Enter Flaminius.

  Asd.   With what gravity
He does approach us.

  Carth.   As he would command,
Not argue his desires.
  Amil.   May it please your lordship
To take your place.
  Flam.   In civil courtesy
As I am Titus Flaminius, I may thank you;
But, sitting here as Rome's ambassador,
(In which you are honoured,) to instruct
  you in
Her will, (which you are bound to serve,
  not argue)
I must not borrow—that were poor—but
  take
As a tribute due to her, that's justly styled
The mistress of this earthly globe, the bold-
  ness
To reprehend your slow progression in
Doing her greatness right. That she believes,
In me, that this impostor was suborned
By the conquered Asiatics, in their hopes
Of future liberty, to usurp the name
Of dead Antiochus, should satisfy
Your scrupulous doubts ; all proofs beyond
  this being
Merely superfluous.
  Carth.   My lord, my lord,.
You trench too much upon us.
  Asd.   We are not
Led by an implicit faith.
  Hanno.   Nor, though we would
Preserve Rome's amity, must not yield up
The freedom of our wills and judgments to
Quit or condemn, as we shall be appointed
By her imperious pleasure.
  Carth.   We confess not,
Nor ever will, she hath a power above us.
Carthage is still her equal.
  Amil.   If you can
Prove this man an impostor, he shall suffer
As he deserves. If not, you shall perceive
You have no empire here.
  Hanno.   Call in the pris'ner :
Then, as you please, confront him.
  Flam.   This neglect
Hereafter will be thought on.
  Amil.   We shall stand
The danger howsoever. When we did,
His cause unheard, at your request commit
This king or this impostor, you received
More favour than we owed you.
  Officer [*within*]. Room for the prisoner !

Enter Antiochus, *habited as a king,* Berecinthius, *the three* Merchants, *and a* Guard.

  Ant. This shape, that you have put me
  in, suits ill
With the late austereness of my life.
  Berec.   Fair gloss
Wrongs not the richest stuff, but sets it off,

And let your language, high and stately,
   speak you
As you were born—a king.
   Ant.   Health to the Senate.
We do suppose your duties done.   Sit still.
Titus Flaminius, we remember you.
As you are a public minister from Rome
You may sit covered.
   Flam.   How !
   Ant.   But as we are
A potent king in whose court you have waited
And sought our favour, you betray your pride,
And the more than saucy rudeness of your
   manners.
A bended knee, remembering what we are,
Much better had become you.
   Flam.   Ha !
   Ant.   We said it :
But fall from our own height to hold dis-
   course
With a thing so far beneath us.
   Berec.   Admirable !
   Amil. The Roman looks as he had seen
   the wolf.
How his confidence awes him.
   Asd.   Be he what he will,
He bears him like a king ; and I must tell
   you
I am amazed too.
   Ant.   Are we so transformed
From what we were, since our disaster in
The Grecian enterprise, that you gaze upon us
As some strange prodigy ne'er seen in Afric.
Antiochus speaks to you, the King Antiochus,
And challenges a retribution in
His entertainment of the love and favours
Extended to you.   Call to memory
Your true friend and confederate, who re-
   fused
In his respect to you the proffered amity
Of the Roman people.   Hath this vile en-
   chanter
Environed me with such thick clouds in your
Erroneous belief, from his report
That I was long since dead, that, being
   present,
The beams of majesty cannot break through
The foggy mists, raised by his wicked charms,
To lend you light to know me ? I cite you,
My lord Amilcar : now I look on you
As prince of the senate, but, when you were
   less,
I've seen you in my court assisted by
Grave Hanno, Asdrubal, and Carthalo,
The pillars of the Carthaginian greatness.
I know you all.   Antiochus ne'er deserved
To be thus slighted.
   Amil.   Not so. We in you
Look on the figure of the King Antiochus,

But, without stronger proofs than yet you
   have
Produced to make us think so, cannot near
   you
But as a man suspected.
   Ant.   Of what guilt?
   Flam. Of subornation and imposture.
   Ant.   Silence
This fellow's saucy tongue. O Majesty !
How soon a short eclipse hath made thy
   splendour,
As it had never shined on these, forgotten !
But you refuse to hear me as a king,
Deny not yet, in justice, what you grant
To common men, free liberty without
His interruption (having heard what he
Objects against me) to acquit myself
Of that, which, in his malice, I am charged
   with.
   Amil. You have it.
   Ant.   As my present fortune wills me
I thank your goodness. Rise thou cursed
   agent
Of mischief, and accumulate in one heap
All engines, by the devil thy tutor fashioned
To ruin innocence. In poison steep
Thy bloodied tongue, and let thy words, as
   full
Of bitterness as malice, labour to
Seduce these noble hearers. Make me, in
Thy coinéd accusation, guilty of
Such crimes, whose names my innocence
   ne'er knew,
I'll stand the charge. And when that thou
   hast shot
All arrows in thy quiver, feathered with
Slanders, and aimed with cruelty, in vain,
My truth, though yet concealed, the moun-
   tains of
Thy glosséd fictions in her strength re-
   moved,
Shall in a glorious shape appear, and show
Thy painted mistress, falsehood, when
   stripped bare
Of borrowed and adulterate colours, in
Her own shape and deformity.
   Berec.   I am ravished !
   1 *Merch.* O, more than royal sir !
   Amil.   Forbear.
   2 *Merch.*   The monster
Prepares to speak.
   Berec.   And still that villainous smile
Ushers his following mischiefs.
   Flam.   Since the assurance,
From one of my place, quality, and rank,
Is not sufficient with you to suppress
This bold seductor, and to acquit our state
From the least tyrannous imputation,
I will forget awhile I am a Roman,

Whose arguments are warranted by his
  sword
And not filled from his tongue.   This crea-
  ture here,
That styles himself Antiochus, I know
For an apostata Jew, though others say
He is a cheating Greek called Pseudolus,
And keeps a whore in Corinth.   But I'll
  come
To real proofs ; reports and rumours being
Subjects unsuitable with my gravity .
To speak, or yours to hear.   'Tis most ap-
  parent
The king Antiochus was slain in Greece ;
His body, at his subjects' suit, delivered ;
His ashes, from the funeral pile, raked up,
And in a golden urn preserved, and kept
In the royal monument of the Asian
  kings.
Such was the clemency of Marcus Seaurus,
The Roman conqueror, whose triumph was
Graced only with his statue.   But suppose
He had survived (which is impossible)
Can it fall in the compass of your reason
That this impostor (if he were the man
Which he with impudence affirms he is)
Would have wandered two and twenty
  tedious years
Like a vagabond o'er the world, and not
  have tried
Rome's mercy as a suppliant.
  Hanno.   Shrewd suspicions.
  Flam. A mason of Callipolis, heretofore,
Presumed as far, and was, like this im-
  postor,
By slavish Asians followed.   And a second,
A Cretan of a base condition, did
Maintain the like.   All ages have been fur-
  nished
With such as have usurped upon the names
And persons of dead princes.   Is it not
As evident as the day this wretch, instructed
By these poor Asians (sworn enemies
To the majesty of Rome) but personates
The dead Antiochus : hired to it by these
To stir up a rebellion, which they call
Delivery or restoring..   And will you,
Who, for your wisdom, are esteemed the
  sages
And oracles of Afric, meddle in
The affairs of this affronter, which no
  monarch,
Less rash and giddy than Antiochus was,
Would undertake.
  Ant.   Would I were dead, indeed,
Rather than hear this, living !
  Flam.   I confess
He hath some marks of king Antiochus, but
The most of 'em artificial.   Then observe

What kind of men they are that do abet
  him :
Proscribed and banished persons : the ring-
  leader
Of this seditious troop a turbulent Flamen,
Grown fat with idleness——
  Berec.   That's I.
  Flam.   And puffed up
With the wind of his ambition.
  Berec.   With reverence to
[This place,] thou liest.   I am grown to this
  bulk
By being   .   .   .   .   .
       .   .   .   .   .
  Amil.   I [bow to] your goddess.   She
Defends you from a whipping.
  Hanno.   Take him off,
He does disturb the court.
  Berec.   I'll find a place yet
Where I will roar my wrongs out.
        [*Exeunt* Officers *with* Berecinthius.
  Flam.   As you have,
In the removing of that violent fool,
Given me a taste of your severity,
Make it a feast, and perfect your great jus-
  tice
In the surrendering up this false pretender
To the correction of the law, and let him
Undergo the same punishment, which others
Have justly suffered that preceded him
In the same machination.
  Ant.   As you wish
A noble memory to after times
Reserve one ear for my defence, and let not—
For your own wisdoms let not—that belief,
This subtle fiend would plant, be rooted in
  you
Till you have heard me.   Would you know
  the truth,
And real cause, why poor Antiochus hath
So long concealed himself?   Though in the
  opening
A wound, in some degree by time closed up,
I shall pour scalding oil and sulphur in it,
I will, in the relation of my
To be lamented story, punctually
Confute my false accuser.   Pray you conceive,
As far as your compassion will permit,
How great the grief and agony of my soul
  was,
When I considered that the violence
Of my ill-reined ambition had made Greece
The fatal sepulchre of so many thousands
Of brave and able men, that might have
  stood
In opposition for the defence
Of mine own kingdom, and a ready aid
For my confed'rates.   After which rout,
And my retreat in a disguise to Athens,

The shame of this disgrace, though I then had
The forehead of this man, would have deterred me
From being ever seen where I was known ;
And such was then my resolution.
   Amil. This granted, whither went you?
   Ant.   As a punishment
Imposed upon myself, and equal to
My wilful folly, giving o'er the world,
I went into a desert.
   Flam.   This agrees
With the dead slaves' report ; but I must
contemn it.   [*Aside.*
   Amil. What drew you from that austere life ?
   Asd.   Clear that.
   Ant. The counsel of a grave philosopher
Wrought on me to make known myself the man
That I was born. And, of all potentates
In Afric, to determine of the truth
Of my life and condition I preferred
The commonwealth of Carthage.
   Flam.   As the fittest
To be abused.
   Ant.   This is not fair.
   Amil.   My lord,
If not entreat, I must command your silence,
Or absence—which you please.
   Flam.   So peremptory ?
   Ant. To vindicate myself from all suspicion
Of forgery and imposture, in this scroll,
Writ with my royal hand, you may peruse
A true memorial of all circumstances,
Answers, despatches, doubts, and difficulties
Between myself and your ambassadors,
Sent to negociate with me.
   Amil.   Fetch the records.
   Ant. 'Tis my desire you should.   Truth
seeks the light.
And, when you have compared them, if you find them
In any point of moment differing,

Enter one with the books.

Conclude me such a one, as this false man
Presents me to you. But, if you perceive
Those private passages, in my cabinet argued,   .
And, but to your ambassadors and myself,
Concealed from all men, in each point agreeing,
Judge if a cheating Greek, a Pseudolus,
Or an apostata Jew, could e'er arrive at
Such deep and weighty secrets.
   Hanno.   To a syllable
They are the same.

   Amil.   It cannot be but this is
The true Antiochus !
   Flam.   A magician rather, ·
And hath the spirit of Python.
   Carth.   These are toys.
   Ant. You see he will omit no trifle, that
His malice can lay hold of, to divert
Your love and favour to me. Now for my
   death :   .
The firmest base on which he builds the strength
Of his assertions : if you please to weigh it,
With your accustom'd wisdom, you'll perceive
'Tis merely fabulous.   Had they meant fairly
And, as a truth, would have it so confirmed
To the doubtful Asians, why did they not
Suffer the carcase they affirmed was mine
To be viewed by such men as were interested
In the great cause, that were bred up with me,
And were familiar with the marks I carried
Upon my body, and not rely upon
Poor prisoners taken in the war, from whom,
In hope of liberty and reward, they drew
Such depositions as they knew would make
For their dark ends. Was anything more easy
Than to suppose a body, and that placed on
A solemn hearse,—with funeral pomp to inter it
In a rich monument ; and, then, proclaim
This is the body of Antiochus,
King of the lower Asia !
   Flam.   · Rome's honour
Is taxed in this of practise and corruption !
I'll hear no more. In your determinations,
Consider what it is to hold and keep her
Your friend or enemy.   [*Exit* Flaminius.
   Amil.   We wish we could
Receive you as a king, since your relation
Hath wrought so much upon us that we do
Incline to that belief. But since we cannot
As such protect you, but with certain danger,
Until you are by other potent nations
Proclaimed for such, our fitting caution
Cannot be censured, though we do entreat
You would elsewhere seek justice.
   Ant.   Where ? when 'tis
Frighted from you by power?
   Amil.   And yet take comfort.
Not all the threats of Rome shall force us to
Deliver you. The short time that you stay
In Carthage you are safe. No more a prisoner—
You are enlarged. With full security
Consult of your affairs. In what we may

We are your friends. Break up the court.
  [*Exeunt all but* Antiochus *and the three*
    Merchants.
  1 *Merch.*   Dear sir,
Take courage in your liberty. The world
Lies open to you.
  2 *Merch.*   We shall meet with comfort
When most despaired of by us.
  Ant.   Never, never !
Poor men, though fallen, may rise, but
    kings like me,
If once by fortune slaved, are ne'er set free.
                      [*Exeunt.*

ACT III.

SCENE I.—*House of* Flaminins *at Carthage.*
Enter Flaminius (*with two letters*), Calistus,
    and Demetrius.

  Flam. You gave him store of gold with
    the instructions
That I prescribed him ?
  Cal.   Yes, my lord, and on
The forfeiture of my credit with your honour,
Titus will do his parts, and dive into
Their deepest secrets.
  Flam.   Men of place pay dear
For their intelligence. It eats out of the
    profit
Of their employment. But, in a design
Of such weight, prodigality is a virtue.
The fellow was of trust that you despatched
To Rome with the packets?
  Dem.   Yes, sir, he flies—not rides.
By this, if his access answer his care,
He is upon return.
  Flam.   I am on the stage,
And if now, in the scene imposed upon me,
So full of change—nay, a mere labyrinth
Of politic windings—I show not myself
A Prótean actor, varying every shape
With the occasion, it will hardly poise
The expectation. I'll so place my nets
That, if this bird want wings to carry him,
At one flight, out of Afric, I shall catch him.
Calistus !
  Cal.   Sir.
  Flam.   Give these at Syracusa
To the proconsul Marcellus. Let another post
To Sardinia with these. You have the picture
Of the impostor ?
  Dem.   Drawn to the life, my lord.
  Flam.   Take it along with you. I have
    commanded,
In the senate's name, that they man out
    their gallies,
And not to let one vessel pass without
A strict examination. The sea

Shall not protect him from me. I've charged
    too
The garrisons, that keep the passages
By land, to let none 'scape, that come from
    Carthage,
Without a curious search.

        Enter Lentulus.

  Lent.   I will excuse
My visit without preparation. Fear not——
  Flam. Who have we here?
  Lent. When you have viewed me better
You will resolve yourself.
  Flam.   My good lord Lentulus !
  Lent. You name me right. The speed
    that brought me hither
As you see accoutred—and without a train
Suitable to my rank—may tell your lordship
That the design admits no vacant time
For compliment. Your advertisements have
    been read
In open court. The consuls and the senate
Are full of wonder and astonishment
At the relation. Your care is much
Commended, and will find a due reward,
When what you have so well begun is ended.
In the meantime with their particular thanks
They thus salute you. You'll find there that
    they
(Their good opinion of me far above
My hopes or merits) have appointed me
Your successor in Carthage, and commit
Unto your abler trust the prosecution
Of this impostor.
  Flam.   As their creature ever
I shall obey, and serve them. I will leave
My freedman to instruct you in the course
Of my proceedings. You shall find him able
And faithful, on my honour.
  Lent.   I receive him
At his due value. Can you guess yet
    whither
This creature tends. By some passengers I
    met
I was told howe'er the state denies to yield him
To our dispose, they will not yet incense us
By giving him protection.
  Flam.   Ere long,
I hope I shall resolve you. To my [aid]

        Enter Titus.

Here comes my true discoverer. Be brief,
And labour not with circumstance to endear
The service thou hast done me.
  Titus.   As your lordship
Commanded me, in this Carthaginian habit
I made my first approaches, and delivered
The gold was given me, as a private present,
Sent from the lord Amilcar for his viaticum

To another country. For I did pretend
I was his menial servant.
  Flam.   Very well.
  Titus. 'Twas entertained almost with
     sacrifice,
And I, as one most welcome, was admitted
Into their turbulent counsel. Many means
Were there propounded, whither, and to
     whom,
Their king Antiochus (for so they style him)
Should fly for safety. One urged to the
     Parthian,
A second into Egypt, and a third
To the Batavian. But, in conclusion,
The corpulent Flamen, that would govern
     all,
And in his nature would not give allowance
To any proposition that was not
The child of his own brain, resolved to
     carry
Their May-game prince, covered with a
     disguise,
To Prusias king of Bithynia. His opinion
Carried it ; and thither, without pause or
     stay,
To thank my lord for his bounty, they are
     gone—
Upon my certain knowledge, for I rid
Two days and nights along, that I might
     not build
Upon suppositions. By this they are
At their journey's end.
  Flam. With my thanks, there's thy reward.
I will take little rest until I have
Soured his sweet entertainment. You have
     been
In the court of this Prusias. Of what temper
     is he?
  Lent. A well disposed and noble gentle-
     man,
And very careful to preserve the peace
And quiet of his subjects.
  Flam.   I shall find him
The apter to be wrought on. Do you know
     who is
His special favourite ?
  Lent.   One that was his tutor,
A seeming politician, and talks often
The end of his ambition is to be
A gentleman of Rome.
  Flam.   I shall fit him, fear not.
Your travail's ended—mine begins : I take
     my leave.
Formality of manners now is useless :
I long to be a horseback.
  Lent.   You have my wishes
For a fair success.
  Flam.   My care shall not be wanting.
                        [*Exeunt.*

SCENE II.—*Capital of* Prusias, *king of
            Bithynia.*

Enter Antiochus *and the three* Merchants.

  1 *Merch.* This tedious journey, from your
     majesty's
Long discontinuance of riding hard,
With weariness hath dull'd your spirits.
  2 *Merch.*   The Flamen,
His corpulency considered, hath held out
Beyond imagination.
  3 *Merch.*   As often
As he rode down a hill I did expect
The chining of his horse.
  Ant.   I wonder more
How mine sustained his burden, since the
     weight
That sits on my more heavy heart would
     crack
The sinews of an elephant.
  2 *Merch.*   'Tis said
That beast hath strength to carry six armed
     men
In a turret on his back.
  Ant.   True. But the sorrow
Of a wretched and forsaken king like me
Is far more ponderous.
  1 *Merch.*   O part not, sir,
From your own strength by yielding to
     despair.
I am most confident Berecinthius will,
From the great king Prusias—in his good-
     ness great—
Bring comfort to you.   [*Flourish.*
  Ant.   I am prepared, however.
Lower I cannot fall.

         Enter Berecinthius.

  3 *Merch.*   Ha ! these are signs
Of a glorious entertainment—not contempt !
  Berec. Bear up, sir. I have done you
     simple service :
I thank my eloquence and boldness for it.
When would a modest silent fool effect
What I have done? But such men are not
     born
For great employments. The fox, that
     would confer
With a lion without fear, must see him often.
O for a dozen of rubbers and a bath,
And yet I need no tub since I drench
     myself
In mine own balsam.
  1 *Merch.*   Balsamum? It smells
Like a tallow chandler's shop.
  Berec.   Does it so ? thou thin-gut !
Thou thing without moisture ! But I have
     no time

To answer thee. The great king—by my
   means, sir—
Ever remember that—·in his own person,
With his fair consort and a gallant train,
                     [*Flourish.*
Are come to entertain you.
   Ant.   Jove! if thou art
Pleased that it shall be so—
   Berec.   Change not Jove's purpose
In your slowness to receive it. In your car-
   riage
Express yourself. They come.

Enter Prusias, *his* Queen, *and* Philoxenus.

   Prusias.   The strong assurance
You gave at Carthage to confirm you are
The king Antiochus (for so much, from
My agent there I've heard) commands me to
Believe you are so. And however they,
Awed by the Roman greatness, durst not
   lend you
Aid or protection; in me you shall find
A surer guard. I stand on mine own bases,
Nor shall or threats or prayers deter me
   from
Doing a good deed in itself rewarded;
You are welcome to my bosom.
   Ant.   All that yet
I can return you, sir, is thanks, expressed
In tears of joy, to find here that compassion
Hath not forsook the earth.
   Queen.   Alas, good king,
I pity him!
   Prus.   This lady, sir, your servant,
Presents her duty to you.
   Ant.   Pray you forgive me.
Calamity, my too long rude companion,
Hath taught me, gracious madam, to forget
Civility and manners.   [*Kisses her.*
   Queen.   I ne'er touched
But the king, my husband's lips, and, as I
   live,
He kisses very like him.
   Prus.   Here is one
I dare present to you, for a knowing man
In politic designs. But he is present,
I should say more else.
   Ant.   Your assistance, sir,
To raise a trod-down king, will well become
   you.
   Philox. What man can do that is fami-
   liar with
The deep directions of Xenophon,
Or Aristotle's politics, besides
Mine own collections, which some prefer,
And with good reason, as they say, before
   'em,
Your highness may expect.
   Prus.   We will at leisure,

Consider of the manner and the means
How to restore you to your own.
   Queen.   And till then
Suppose yourself in your own court.
   Ant.   The gods
Be sureties for the payment of this debt
I stand engaged. Your bounties overwhelm
   me.
    [*Flourish. Exeunt all but* Berecin-
    thius, *and the* Merchants.
   Berec. Ay! marry this is as it should be!
   Ha!
After these storms raised by this Roman
   devil,
Titus Flaminins—you know whom I mean—
Are we got into the port once. I must
   purge.
   1 *Merch.* Not without cause.
   Berec.   Or my increasing belly
Will metamorphose me into the shape
Of a great tortoise, and I shall appear
A cipher, a round man, or what you will.
Now jeer at my bulk, and spare not.
   1 *Merch.*   You are pleasant.
   Berec. Farce thy lean ribs with hope, and
   thou wilt grow to
Another kind of creature. When our king is
Restored, let me consider, as he must be,
And I the principal means, I'll first grow
   rich,
Infinite rich, and build a strange new temple
To the goddess that I·worship, and so bind
   her
To prosper all my purposes.
   2 *Merch.*   Be not rapt so.
   Berec. Prithee, do not trouble me. First
   I will expel
The Romans out of Asia. And, so breaking
Their reputation in the world, we will
Renew our league with Carthage. Then
   draw to
Our party the Egyptian Ptolemy,
And great Arsaces' issue. I will be
The general, and march to Rome, which
   taken,
I'll fill proud Tiber with the carcases
Of men, women, and children. Do not per-
   suade me,—
I'll show no mercy!
   3 *Merch.* Have the pow'r to hurt first.
   Berec. Then by the senators, whom I'll
   use as horses,
I will be drawn in a chariot, made for my
   bulk,
In triumph to the capitol, more admired
Than Bacchus was in India. Titus Fla-
   minius
Our enemy, led like a dog in a chain,
As I descend or reascend in state,

Shall serve for my foot-stool. I will conjure him
If revenge hath any spells.

Enter Flaminius *with* Demetrius.

Flam.   Command the captain
To wait me with his galley at the next port.
I'm confident I shall fraught him.
            [*Exit* Demetrius.
   1 *Merch.*   You are conjuring,
And see what you have raised.
   Berec.   Cybele save me!
I do not fear me, Pluto, though thou hast
Assumed a shape not to be matched in
   Cocytus!
Why dost thou follow me?
   Fiam.   Art thou mad?
   Berec.   Thou com'st
To make me so. How my jelly quakes.
   Avaunt!
What have I to do with thee?
   Flam.   You'll know at leisure.
The time is now too precious.
            [*Exit* Flaminius.
   Berec.   'Tis vanished.
Sure, 'twas an apparition.
   1 *Merch.*   I fear
A fatal one to us.
   2 *Merch.*   We may easily guess at
The cause that brings him hither.
   3 *Merch.*   Now, if ever,
Confirm the king——
   1 *Merch.*   Against this battery
New works are to be raised, or we are
   ruined.
   Berec. What think you of this rampire?
   'twill hold out!
And he shall shoot through an' through it but
   I'll cross him.   [*Exeunt.*

     SCENE III.—*Court of* Prusias.

     Enter Flaminius *and* Philoxenus.

   Flam. What we have said, the consuls
   will make good,
And the glad senate ratify.
   Philox.   They have so
Obliged me for this favour, that there is not
A service of that difficulty, from which
I would decline. In this rest confident,
I am your own—and sure.
   Flam.   You shall do, sir,
A noble office in it. And, however
We thank you for the courtesy, the profit
And certain honours, the world's terror,
   Rome,
In thankfulness cannot but shower upon you,
Are wholly yours. How happy I esteem
Myself, in this employment, to meet with
A wise and provident statesman.

   Philox.   My good lord!
   Flam. I flatter not in speaking truth. You
   are so,
And, in this prompt alacrity, confirm it.
Since a wise forecast in the managing
Worldly affairs is the true wisdom—rashness,
The schoolmistress of idiots. You well know
Charity begins at home, and that we are
Nearest unto ourselves. Fools build upon
Imaginary hopes, but wise men ever
On real certainties. A tender conscience,
Like a glowworm, shows a seeming fire in
   darkness,
But, set near to the glorious light of honour,
It is invisible. As you are a statesman—
And a master in that art—you must remove
All rubs—tho' with a little wrong some-
   times—
That may put by the bias of your counsels
From the fair mark they aim at.
   Philox.   You are read well
In worldly passages.
   Flam.   I barter with you
Such trifles as I have. But, if you pleased,
You could instruct me that philosophy
And policy, in states, are not such strangers
As men o'er curious and precise would have
   them.
But to the point. With speed get me access
To the king your pupil. And 'tis well for him
That he hath such a tutor.—Rich Bithynia
Was never so indebted to a patriot,
And vigilant watchman, for her peace and
   safety,
As to yourself.
   Philox.   Without boast I may whisper
I have done something in that way.
   Flam.   All, in all!
Fame, filling her loud trump with truth,
   proclaims it!
But, when it shall be understood you are
The principal means, by which a dangerous
   serpent,
Warm'd in your sovereign's bosom, is de-
   livered
To have his sting and venomous teeth pulled
   out;
And the ruin, in a willing grant, avoided,
Which in detaining him falls on the king-
   dom,
Not Prusias alone, but his saved people,
Will raise your providence altars!
   Philox.   Let me entreat
Your patience some few minutes. I'll bring
   the king
In person to you.
   Flam.   Do, and, this effected,
Think of the ring you are privileged to wear
When a Roman gentleman; and, after that,

·Of provinces and purple !

[*Exit* Philoxenus.

I must smile now
In my consideration with what glibness
My flatteries, oiled with hopes of future
      greatness,
Are swallowed by this dull pate. But it is
      not
Worth the observation. Most of our seem-
      ing statesmen
Are caught in the same noose.

Prusias and Philoxenus *approaching.*

                      Returned so soon—
And the king with him ! But his angry
      forehead
Furrowed with frowns. No matter, I am
      for him.
Prus. From the people of Rome—so
quick ? Hath he brought with him
Letters of credence, and authority
To treat with us ?
Philox.   I read them.
Prus.   What can he
Propound which I must fear to hear ? I
      would
·Continue in fair terms with that warlike
      nation,
Ever provided I wrong not myself
In the least point of honour.
Philox.   To the full
He will instruct your majesty.
Flam.   So may
Felicity, as a page, attend your person,
As you embrace the friendly counsel sent
      you
From the Roman senate.
Prus.   With my thanks to you
Their instrument, if the advice be such,
As by this preparation you would have me
·Conceive it is, I shall—and 'twill become
      me—
Receive it as a favour.
Flam.   Know then, Rome,
In her pious care that you may still increase
The happiness you live on ; and your sub-
      jects,
Under the shadow of their own vines, eat
The fruit they yield them—their soft musical
      feasts
·Continuing, as they do yet, unaffrighted
With the harsh noise of war—entreats as low
As her known power and majesty can
      descend,
You would return, with due equality,
A willingness to preserve what she hath con-
      quered
From change and innovation.

Prus.   I attempt not
To trouble her, nor ever will.
Flam.   Fix there !
Or if, for your own good, you will move
      further,
Make Rome your thankful debtor by sur-
      rendering
Into her hands the false impostor, that
Seeks to disturb her quiet.
Prus.   This I looked for :
And that I should find mortal poison
      wrapp'd up
In your candied pills. Must I, because you
      say so,
Believe that this most miserable king is
A false affronter ? who, with arguments
Unanswerable, and near miraculous proofs,
Confirms himself the true Antiochus.
Or is it not sufficient that you Romans,
In your unsatisfied ambition, have
Seized with an unjust gripe on half the
      world,
Which you call conquest ? If that I consent
      not
To have my innocence soiled with that pol-
      lution
You are willingly smeared o'er with——
Flam.   Pray you, hear me——
Prus. I will be first heard. Shall I, for
      your ends,
Infringe my princely word ? or break the
      laws
Of hospitality ? defeat myself
Of the certain honour to restore a king
Unto his own ? and what you Romans have
Extorted and keep from him ? Far be't from
      · me !
I will not buy your amity at such loss.
So it be to all after times remembered
I held it not sufficient to live
As one born only for myself, and I
Desire no other monument !
Flam.   I grant
It is a specious thing to leave behind us
A fair report, though in the other world
We have no feeling of it : and to lend
A desperate, though fruitless, aid to such
As Fate, not to be altered, hath marked out
Examples of calamity, may appear
A glorious ornament : but here's a man,
The oracle of your kingdom, that can tell
      you,
When there's no probability it may be
Effected, 'tis mere madness to attempt it.
Philox. A true position.
Flam.   Your inclination
Is honourable, but your power deficient,
To put your purpose into act.
Prus.   My power ?

R R 2

Flam. Is not to be disputed, if weighed
truly
With the petty kings your neighbours; but,
when balanced
With the globes and sceptres of my mistress
Rome,
Will but——I spare comparisons, but you
build on
Your strength to justify the fact. Alas,
It is a feeble reed, and leaning on it
Will wound your hand much sooner than
support you.
You keep in pay, 'tis true, some peace-
trained troops,
Which awe your neighbours; but consider,
when
Our eagles shall display their sail-stretched
wings,
Hovering o'er our legions, what defence
Can you expect from yours?
    Philox.   Urge that point home.
    Flam. Our old victorious bands are ever
ready;
And such, as are not our confed'rates,
tremble,
To think where next the storm shall fall,
with horror.
Philoxenus knows it. Will you to help one
You should contemn, and is not worth your
pity,
Pull it on your own head? Your neighbour
Carthage
Would smile to see your error. Let me paint
The danger to you ere it come. Imagine
Our legions, and the auxiliary forces
Of such as are our friends and tributaries,
Drawn up—Bithynia covered with our
armies—
All places promising defence blocked up
With our armed troops—the siege con-
tinuing—
Famine within and force without disabling
All opposition—then the army entered!
As victory is insolent, the rapes
Of virgins and grave matrons—reverend old
men
With their last groans accusing you—your
city
And palace sacked——
    Philox.   Dear sir!
    Flam.   And you yourself
Captived; and, after that, chained by the
neck;
Your matchless queen, your children, officers,
friends,
Waiting, as scorns of fortune, to give lustre
To the victor's triumph.
    Philox.   I am in a fever
To think upon it.

    Flam.   As a friend I have delivered,
And more than my commission warrants me,
This caution to you. But now—Peace—or
War?
If the first I entertain it. If the latter,
I'll instantly defy you!
    Philox.   Pray you say *Peace*, sir.
    Prus. On what conditions?
    Flam.   The delivery
Of this seducer and his complices.
On no terms else—and suddenly.
    Prus.   How can I
Dispense with my faith given?
    Philox.   I'll yield you reasons.
    Prus. Let it be *Peace* then, oh. Pray you
call in   [*Exit* Philoxenus.
The wretched man. In the meantime I'll
consider
How to excuse myself.
    Flam.   While I, in silence,
Triumph in my success, and meditate
On the reward that crowns it. A strong
army
Could have done no more than I alone, and
with
A little breath, have effected.

Enter Queen, Antiochus, Berecinthius, *the
three* Merchants, Philoxenus, *and* Deme-
triu°.

    Ant.   Goodness guard me!
Whom do I look on? Sir, come further from
him.
He is infectious; so swollen with mischief,
And strange impieties; his language too
So full of siren sorceries, if you hear him
There is no touch of moral honesty,
Though rampired in your soul, but will fly
from you.
The mandrake's shrieks, the aspick's deadly
tooth,
The tears of crocodiles, or the basilisk's eye
Kill not so soon, nor with that violence
As he who, in his cruel nature, holds
Antipathy with mercy.
    Prus.   I am sorry——
    Ant. Sorry—for what? That you had an
intent
To be a good and just prince? Are com-
passion
And charity grown crimes?
    Prus.   The gods can witness
How much I would do for you. And but that
Necessity of state——
    Ant.   Make not the gods
Guilty of your breach of faith! From *them*
you find not
Treachery commanded; and the state, that
seeks

Strength from disloyalty, in the quicksands
    which
She trusteth in, is swallowed.   'Tis in vain
To argue with you.   If I am condemned,
Defences come too late.   What do you
    purpose
Shall fall on poor Antiochus?
   Prus.   For my
Security—there being no means left else—
Against my will I must deliver you.
   Ant.   To whom?

Enter Guard.

   Prus. To Rome's ambassador.
   Ant.   O, the Furies
Exceed not him in cruelty !   Remember
I am a king !   your royal guest !   Your right
    hand,
The pawn and pledge that should defend me
    from
My bloody enemy !   Did you accuse
The Carthaginian senate for denying
Aid and protection to me—giving hope
To my despairing fortunes ?   Or but now
Raise me to make my fall more terrible ?
Did you tax them of weakness, and will
    you
So far transcend them in a coward fear,
Declaimed against by your own mouth ?   O,
    sir,
If you dare not give me harbour, set me safe
    yet
In any desert, where this serpent's hisses
May not be heard ; and to the gods I'll speak
    you
A prince both wise and honourable.
   Prus.   Alas !
It is not in my power.
   Ant.   As an impostor
Take off my head then.   At the least—so far—
Prove merciful.   Or with any torture ease me
Of the burthen of a life : rather than yield me
To this politic state hangman.
   Flam.   This to me is
A kind of ravishing music !
   Queen.   I have lived
For many years, sir, your obedient handmaid,
Nor ever in a syllable presumed
To cross your purpose.   But now, with a
    sorrow
As great almost as this poor king's, beholding
Your poverty of spirit—for it does
Deserve no better name—I must put off
Obsequiousness and silence, and take to me
The warrant and authority of your queen,
And, as such, give you counsel.
   Prus.   You displease me.
   Queen. The physic promising health is
    ever bitter.

Hear me.   Will you that are a man—nay
    more,
A king of men—do that, forced to it by fear,
Which common men would scorn ?   I am a
    woman—
A weak and feeble woman—yet before
I would deliver up my bondwoman,
And have it told I did it by constraint,
I would endure to have these hands cut off,
These eyes pull'd out——
   Prus.   I'll hear no more.
   Queen.   Do then,
As a king should.
   Prus.   Away with her !
              [They bear off the Queen.
   Flam.   My affairs
Exact a quick despatch.
   Prus.   He's yours.   Conceive
What I would say.   Farewell.
        [Exeunt Prusias *and* Philoxenus.
   Ant.   That I had been
Born deaf !   I will not grace thy triumph,
    tyrant,
With one request of favour.
          [Exit Antiochus *guarded.*
   Berec.   My good lord !
   Flam. Your will, dear Flamen ?
   Berec.   I perceive you are like
To draw a great charge upon you.   My fat
    bulk,
And these my lions, will not be kept for a
    little.
Nor would we be chargeable.   And, there-
    fore, kissing
Your honoured hands, I take my leave.
   Flam.   By no means,
I have been busy, but I shall find leisure
To treat with you in another place.
   Berec.   I would not
Put your lordship to the trouble.
   Flam.   It will be
A pleasure rather.   Bring them all away.
   Berec. The comfort is, whether I drown or
    hang
I shall not be long about it.   I'll preserve
The dignity of my family.
   Flam.   'Twill become you.
                 [Exeunt omnes.

———

ACT IV.

SCENE I.—*A Street in* Callipolis.

Enter Metellus, *Proconsul of* Lusitania, *and*
    Sempronius, *a Captain.*

   Met. A revolt in Asia ?
   Semp.   Yes.   On the report
The long-thought dead Antiochus lives.
   Met.   I heard

Such a one appeared in Carthage, but sup-
     pressed
By Titus Flaminius, my noble friend,
Who, by his letters, promised me a visit
If his designs, as I desire they may,
Succeeded to his wishes.
     Semp.   Till you behold him
I can bring your honour, if you please, where
     you
May find fair entertainment.
     Met.   From whom, captain?
     Semp. A new rigg'd pinnace, that put off
     from Corinth,
And is arrived among us—tight and yare—
Nor comes she to pay custom for her fraught,
But to impose a tax, on such as dare
Presume to look on her, which smock
     gamesters offer
Sooner than she demands it.
     Met.   Some fresh courtezan
Upon mine honour !
     Semp.   You are i' the right, my lord.
     Met. And there lies your intelligence?
     Semp.   True, my good lord.
'Tis a discovery will not shame a captain
When he lies in garrison. Since I was a
     trader
In such commodities I never saw
Her equal. I was ravished with the object,
And, would you visit her, I believe you'd
     write
Yourself of my opinion.
     Met.   Fie upon thee !
I am old.
     Semp. And therefore have the greater use
Of such a cordial. All Medea's drugs,
And her charms to boot, that made old
     Æson young,
Were nothing to her touch. Your viper wine,
So much in practice with grey-bearded
     gallants,
But vappa to the nectar of her lips.
She hath done miracles since she came. A
     usurer,
Full of the gout, and more diseases than
His crutches could support, used her rare
     physic
But one short night, and rising in the morn-
     ing, he
Danced a lavolta !
     Met.   Prithee, leave thy fooling,
And talk of something else.
     Semp.   The whole world yields not
Apter discourse. She hath all the qualities
Conducing to the sport ; sings like a siren ;
Dances, as the gross element of earth
Had no part in her ; her discourse, so full
Of eloquence and prevailing, there is nothing
She asks to be denied her. Had she desired

My captain's place, I had cashier'd myself :
And, should she beg your proconsulship, if
     you heard her,
'Twere hers upon my life.
     Met.   She should be damned first,.
And her whole tribe !

     Enter Flaminius.

               My lord Flaminius, welcome !
I have long been full of expectation
Of your great design, and hope a fair success
Hath crowned your travail in your bringing
     in
This dangerous impostor.
     Flam.   At the length
I have him and his complices.
     Met.   I'll not now
Enquire how you achieved him, but would
     know,
Since 'tis referr'd to you, what punishment
Should fall upon him ?
     Flam.   If you please, in private,
I will acquaint you.
     Met.   Captain, let me entreat you
To meditate on your woman in the next
     room.
We may have employment for you.
     Semp.   I'd rather
She would command my service.
                    [*Exit* Sempronius.
     Met.   Pray you sit.
     Flam. Now, my good lord, I ask your
     grave advice
What course to take.
     Met.   That, in my judgment, needs not
Long consultation. He is a traitor,
And, his process framed, must, as a traitor,
     suffer
A death due to his treason.
     Flam.   There's much more
To be considered, there being a belief,
Dispersed almost through Asia, that he is
The true Antiochus ; and we must decline
The certain scandal it will draw upon
The Roman government, if he die the man
He is by the most received to be ; and there-
     fore,
Till that opinion be removed, we must
Use some quaint practice, that may work
     upon
His hopes or fears, to draw a free confession
That he was suborned to take on him the
     name
He still maintains.
     Met. That, torture will wrest from him.
I know no readier way.
     Flam.   If you had seen
His carriage in Carthage and Bithynia
You would not think so. Since I had him in

My power I have used all possible means that might
Force him into despair, and so to do
A violence on himself. He hath not tasted
These three days any sustenance, and still
Continues fasting.

Met.   Keep him to that diet
Some few hours more.

Flam.   I am of opinion rather,
Some competence offered him, and a place of rest,
Where he might spend the remnant of his days
In pleasure and security, might do more
Than fear of death or torture.

Met.   It may be
There are such natures : and now I think upon't,
I can help you to a happy instrument
To motion it. Your ear.   [*Whispers.*

Flam.   'Tis wondrous well,
And may prove fortunate.

Met.   'Tis but a trial.
However, I will send for her.

Flam.   Pray you do.
She shall have my directions.

Met.   What botches
Are made in the shop of policy !

Flam.   So they cover
The nakedness we must conceal, it skills not.
          [*Exeunt.*

SCENE II.—*The Prison in* Callipolis.

Enter Jailor, *with a poniard and a halter.*

Jailor. Why should I feel compuncion for that
Which yields me profit ? Ha ! a prisoner's tears
Should sooner pierce flint, or Egyptian marble
Than move us to compassion. Yet I know not
Why, the sufferings of this miserable man
Work strangely on me. Some say he is a king.
It may be so; but, if they hold out thus,
I'm sure he's like to die a beggar's death,
And starve for hunger. I am, by a servant
Of the lord Flaminius, strictly commanded,
Before I have raised him out of the dungeon, to
Lay these instruments in his view. To what end
I'm not to enquire, but I am certain,
After his long fast, they are viands that
Will hardly be digested. Do you hear, sir ?

Ant. [*below.*] If thou'rt my death'sman, welcome !

Jailor.   I so pity you
That I wish I had commission, as you rise,
To free you from all future misery,
To knock your brains out.

Ant.   Would thou hadst !
Jailor.   You have
The liberty to air yourself, and that
Is all I can afford you. Fast, and be merry';
I am elsewhere called on.   [*Exit* Jailor.

Ant.   Death ! as far as faintness
Will give me leave to chide thee, I am angry
Thou comest not at me. No attendance ?
Famine,
Thy meagre harbinger, flatters me with hope
Of thy so wished arrival, yet thy coming
Is still deferred. Why? Is it in thy scorn
To take a lodging here ? I am a king,
And know that not the potent sceptre, nor the guards
Of faithful subjects ; neither threats nor prayers
Of friends or kindred ; nor yet walls of brass
Or iron, should their proud height knock at the moon,
Can stop thy passage, when thou art resolved
To force thy entrance : yet a king, in reason,
By the will of fate severed from common men,
Should have the privilege and prerogative,
When he is willing, to disrobe himself
Of this cobweb garment, life, to have thee ready
To do thy fatal office. What have we here ?

Enter Flaminius, Metellus, *and* Sempronius
          above.

A poniard, and a halter ! From the objects
I am easily instructed to what end
They were prepared. Either will serve the turn
To ease the burthen of a wretched life.
Or thus [*lifts the dagger*] or thus [*lifts the halter*] in death ! I must commend
The Roman courtesy. How am I grown
So cheap and vile in their opinion that
I am denied an executioner ?
Will not the loss of my life quit the cost ?
O rare frugality ! Will they force me to
Be mine own hangman ? Every slave, that's guilty
Of crimes not to be named, receives such favour
By the judge's doom, and is my innocence—
The oppressed innocence of a star-crossed king—
Held more contemptible ? My better angel,
Though wanting power to alter fate, discovers
Their hellish purposes. Yes—yes—'tis so.
My body's death will not suffice, they aim at
My soul's perdition. And shall I, to shun
A few more hours of misery, betray her ?
No, she is free still, and shall so return
From whence she came, and in her pureness triumph.

Their tyranny chained and fettered——
     [*Sinks back from weakness.*
 Flam.   O, the devil!
Thou art weak. This will not do.
    [*Orders the* Jailor *to take in food.*
 Met.   Mark how he'll stand
The second charge.
 Semp. The honour is reserved
For the pretty tempting friend I brought—
my life on't.

Enter Jailor, *with brown bread, and a
  wooden dish of water.*

 Jailor. Here, sir, take this. Tho' coarse
it will kill hunger.
It is your daily pittance. Yet, when you
 please,
Your commons may be mended.
 Ant.   Show me the way.
 Jailor. Confess yourself to be a cozening
 knave—
The matter's feasible. But, if you will be
Still king of the crickets, feed on this and live.
You shall not say we starved you.
     [*Exit* Jailor.
 Ant. Stay, I beseech thee,
And take thy cruel pity back again
To him that sent it. This is a tyranny
That doth transcend all precedents. My soul,
But even now, this lump of clay, her prison,
Of itself, in the want of nourishment, opening,
Had shook off her sick feathers, and prepared
Herself to make a noble flight, as set
At liberty, and now this reparation
Again immures. You! for whose curious
 palates
The elements are ransacked, look upon
This bill of fare, by my penurious steward,
Necessity, served to a famished king;
And, warned by my example, when your tables
Crack not with the weight of deer, and far-
 fetched dainties,
Dispute not with heaven's bounties. What
 shall I do?
If I refuse to touch and taste these coarse
And homely cakes, I hasten my own fate,
And so, with willingness, embrace a sin
I hitherto have fled from. No—I'll eat;
And if, at this poor rate, life can continue,
I will not throw it off.
 Flam. I pine with envy
To see his constancy. [*A lute is heard.*
 Met. Bid your property enter
And use her subtlest magic.
 Semp. I have already
Acquainted her with her cue. The music
 ushers
Her personal appearance. [*A song.*
 Ant. From what hand

And voice do I receive this charity?
It is unusual at such a feast:
But I miscall it. 'Tis some new-found engine
Mounted to batter me! Ha!

   Enter Courtezan.

 Court.   If I were not
More harsh and rugged in my disposition
Than thy tormentors, these eyes had out-
 stripped
My tongue, and, with a shower of tears, had
 told you
Compassion brings me hither.
 Ant.   That I could
Believe so much, as, by my miseries!
(An oath I dare not break) I gladly would;
Pity methinks, I know not how, appears
So lovely in you.
 Court. It being spent upon
A subject, in each circumstance deserving
An universal sorrow, tho' 'tis simple
It cannot be deformed. May I presume
To kiss your royal hand, for sure you are not
Less than a king!
 Ant. Have I one witness living
Dares only think so much?
 Court. I do believe it,
And will die in that belief; and nothing
 more
Confirms it than your patience, not to be
Found in a meaner man. Not all the trim
Of the majesty you were born to, tho' set off
With pomp and glorious lustre, showed you
 in
Such full perfection as, at this instant,
Shines round about you, in your constant
 bearing
Your adverse fortune—a degree beyond
All magnanimity that ever was
Canonized by mankind!
 Ant.   Astonishment
And wonder seizes on me. Pray what are
 you?
 Court. Without your pity—nearer to the
 grave
Than the malice of prevailing enemies
Can hurry you.
 Ant. My pity! I will part with
So much from what I have engrossed to
 mourn
Mine own afflictions, as—I freely grant it.
Will you have me weep before I know the
 cause
In which I may serve you?
 Court. You already have
Spent too much of that stock. Pray you,
 first hear me,
And wrong not my simplicity with doubts
Of that I shall deliver. I am a virgin——

Semp. If I had not toyed with her myself,
I should now believe her !
   Court. And, tho' not of the eagle's brood, descended
From a noble family.
   Semp.   Her mother sold her
To a Corinthian lecher at thirteen,
As 'tis reported.
   Met.   Be silent, I command you.
   Ant. To be a virgin, and so well derived,
In my opinion, fair one, are not things
To be lamented.
   Court.   If I had not fallen
From my clear height of chastity—I confess it—
In my too forward wishes. That, sir, is
A sin I am guilty of ! I am in love, sir,—
Impotently mad in love—and my desires
Not to be stopped in their career.
   Ant.   With whom
Are you so taken ?
   Court.   With your own dear self, sir,
Behold me not with such a face of wonder :
It is too sad a truth. The story of
Your most deplorable fortune at the first warmed me
With more than modest heats ; but, since I saw you,
I am all fire, and shall turn cinders, if
You show not mercy to me.
   Ant.   Foolish creature,
If I could suppose this true, and met your wishes
With   equal   ardour,——as I am, what shadow
Of seeming hope is left you to arrive at
The port you long for ?
   Court.   If you will be good
Unto yourself the voyage is accomplished.
It is but putting off a poisoned shirt,   .
Which in the wearing eats into your flesh,
And must, against your will, be soon forced from you :—
The malice of your enemies tendering to you
More true security, and safety, than
The violence of your friends' and servants' wishes
Could heap upon you.
   Ant.   'Tis impossible.
Clear this dark mystery, for yet, to me,
You speak in riddles.
   Court.   I will make it easy
To your understanding, and thus—sweeten
it   [*Offers to kiss him.*
In the delivery. 'Tis but to disclaim,
With the continual cares that wait upon it,
The title of a king.
   Ant.   Devil Flaminius !
I find you here !

   Court.   Why do you turn away ?
The counsel that I offer, if you please
To entertain it, as long-wished companions,
In her right hand, brings liberty and a calm,
After so many storms. And you no sooner
Shall, to the world, profess you were suborned
To this imposture—tho' *I* still believe
It is a truth—but, with a free remission
For the offence, I, as your better genius,
Will lead you, from this place of horror, to
A paradise of delight, to which compared,
Thessalian Tempe, or that garden, where
Venus with her revived Adonis spend
Their pleasant hours, and make from their embraces
A perpetuity of happiness,
Deserve not to be named. There, in an arbour,
Of itself supported o'er a bubbling spring,
With purple hyacinths and roses covered,
We will enjoy the sweets of life ; nor shall
Arithmetic sum up the varieties of
Our amorous dalliance. Our viands such,
As not alone shall nourish appetite,
But strengthen our performance. And, when call'd for,
The quiristers of the air shall give us music :
And, when we slumber, in a pleasant dream
You shall behold the mountains of vexations
Which you have heaped upon the Roman tyrants
In your free resignation of your kingdom,
And smile at their afflictions.
   Ant.   Hence, you siren !
   Court. Are you displeased ?
   Ant.   Were all your flatteries
Aimed at this mark ? Will not my virtuous anger,
Assisted by contempt and scorn, yield strength
To spurn thee from me ? But thou art some whore—
Some common whore—and, if thou hast a soul,
(As in such creatures it is more than doubted)
It hath its being in thy wanton veins,
And will, with thy expense of blood, become
Like that of sensual beasts !
   Met.   This will not do.
   Ant. How did my enemies lose themselves to think,
A painted prostitute with her charms could conquer
What malice, at the height, could not subdue.
Is all their stock of malice so consumed,
As, out of penury, they are forced to use
A whore for their last agent ?
   Court.   If thou wert

Ten times a king thou liest. I am a lady—
A gamesome lady—of the last edition ;
And, tho' I physic noblemen, no whore.
   Met. He hath touched her freehold !
   Semp.   Now let her alone,
And she will worry him.
   Court.   Have I lived to have
My courtesies refused ? That I had leave
To pluck thy eyes out !
Are you so coy? Thou art a man of snow,
And thy father got thee in the wane of the
   moon !
But scorn me not. 'Tis true I was set on
By the higher powers ; but now, for all the
   wealth
In Asia, thou shalt not have the favour,
Though, prostrate on the earth, thou wouldst
   implore it
To kiss my shoestring.

       Enter Jailor *and others.*

   Flam.   We lose time, my lord.
   Court. Foh ! how he stinks ! I will not
   wear a rag more
That he hath breathed on.
   Met.   Without more ado
Let him have his sentence.
   Flam.   Drag him hence.
   Ant.   Are *you* there ?
Nay then——
   Flam. I will not hear him speak. My
   anger
Is lost. Why linger you?
   Ant.   Death ends all,
   . however !   [*Exeunt.*

SCENE III.---*Place of Execution*, Callipolis.

    Enter Officers, *leading in* Berecinthius
    and 1st Merchant, *with halters.*

   Berec. What a skeleton they've made of
me ! Starve me first,
And hang me after ! Is there no conscience
   extant
To a man of my order? They have de-
   graded me,
Ta'en away my lions, and to make me roar
   like them
They've pared the flesh off from my fingers'
   ends,
And then laughed at me ! I've been kept
   in darkness
These five long days—no visitants but devils,
Or men in shapes more horrid, coming at
   me.
A chafing dish of coals and a butcher's knife
I found set by me—and, inquiring why,
I was told that I had flesh enough of mine
   own,
And, if that I were hungry, I might freely

Eat mine own carbonadoes, and be chro-
   nicled
For a cannibal never read of !
   Off.   Will you walk, sir ?
   Berec. I shall come too soon, tho' I creep,
   to such a breakfast !
I ever use to take my portion sitting :
Hanging in the air, it is not physical.
   Off.   Time flies away, sir.
   Berec. Why let him fly, sir. Or, if you
   please to stay him,
And bind up the bold knave's wings, make
   use of my collar.
There's substance in it, I can assure your
   worship,
And I thank your wisdom that you make
   distinction
Between me and this starveling. He goes
   to it
Like a greyhound for killing of sheep in a
   twopenny slip,
But here's a cable will weigh up an anchor,
And yet, if I may have fair play, ere I die
Ten to one I shall make it crack.
   Off.   What would you have, sir ?
   Berec. My ballast about me. I shall ne'er
   sail well else
To the other world. My bark you see wants
   stowage.
But give me half a dozen hens, and a loin of
   veal
To keep it steady, and you may spare the
   trouble
Of pulling me by the legs, or setting the knot
Under mine ear. This drum, well braced,
   defies
Such foolish courtesies.
   1 *Merch.*   This mirth, good Flamen,
Is out of season. Let us think of Elysium
If we die honest men ; or what we—there—
Shall suffer from the furies.
   Berec.   Thou'rt a fool
To think there are or gods or goddesses,
For the latter, if that they had any power,
Mine, being the mother of them, would have
   helped me.
They are things we make ourselves. Or,
   grant there should be
A hell, or an Elysium, sing I cannot
To Orpheus' harp in the one, nor dance in
   the other.
But—if there be a Cerberus, if I serve not
To make three sops for his three heads, that
   may serve
For something more than an ordinary break-
   fast,
The cur is devilish hungry. Would I had
Run away with your fellow merchants, I had
   then

Provided for my frame. Yet, as I am,
I have one request to make, and that, my
   friends,
Concerns my body, which I pray you grant,
And then I shall die in peace.
  Off.   What is it?
  Berec.   Marry,
That you would be suitors to the proconsul
   for me
That no covetous Roman, after I am dead,
May beg to have my skin flayed off, and stuff it
With straw like an alligator, and then show it
In fairs and markets for a monster. Tho'
I know the sight will draw more fools to
   gape on't
Than a camel or an elephant, aforehand
I tell you, if you do, my ghost shall haunt you.
  Off. You shall have burial, fear not.
  Berec.   And room enough
To tumble in, I pray you, tho' I take up
More grave than Alexander. I have ill luck
If I stink not as much as he, and yield the
   worms
As large a supper.
  1 *Merch.*   Are you not mad to talk thus?
  Berec. I came crying into the world, and
   am resolved
To go out merrily—therefore despatch me.
                        [*Exeunt.*

    SCENE IV.—Proconsul's *House at*
           Callipolis.

    Enter Metellus *and* Flaminius.

  Met. There was never such constancy.
  Flam.   You give it
Too fair a name. 'Tis foolish obstinacy,
For which he shall, without my pity, suffer.
What we do for the service of the republic,
And propagation of Rome's glorious empire,
Needs no defence, and we shall wrong our
   judgments
To feel compunction for it. Have you given
   order,
According to the sentence, that the impostor,
Riding upon an ass, his face turned to
The hinder part, may in derision be
Brought through Callipolis?
  Met.   Yes. And a paper
Upon his head, in which, with capital letters,
His faults are inscribed, and by three trum-
   peters
Proclaimed before him; and—that done—to
   have him
Committed to the gallies. Here comes
   Sempronius,

    Enter Sempronius.

To whom I gave the charge.

  Semp.   I have performed it
In every circumstance.
  Flam.   How do the people
Receive it?
  Semp.   As an act of cruelty,
And not of justice. It drew tears from all
The sad spectators. His demeanour was
In the whole progress worth the observation,
But, in one thing, most remarkable.
  Flam.   What was that?
  Semp. When the city-clerk with a loud
   voice read the cause
For which he was condemned, in taking on
   him
The name of a king, with a settled coun-
   tenance
The miserable man replied, *I am so;*
But when he touched his being a cheating
   Jew,
His patience moved, with a face full of anger
He boldly said, '*Tis false.* I never saw
Such magnanimity.
  Flam.   Frontless impudence rather!
  Met. Or anything else you please.
  Flam.   Have you forced on him
The habit of a slave?
  Semp.   Yes, and in that,
Pardon my weakness, still there does appear
A kind of majesty in him.
  Flam.   You look on it
With the eyes of foolish pity that deceives
   you.
  Semp. This way he comes; and, I believe,
   when you see him,
You'll be of my opinion.
  Off. (*within*).   Make way there.

  Enter Officers *leading in* Antiochus, *his*
   head shaved, in the habit of a slave.

  Ant. Fate! 'tis thy will it should be thus,
   and I
With patience obey it. Was there ever,
In all precedent maps of misery,
Calamity so drawn out to the life
As she appears in me? In all the changes
Of fortune, such a metamorphosis
Antiquity cannot show us! Men may read
   there
Of kings deposed, and some in triumph led
By the proud insulting Roman. Yet they
   were
Acknowledged such, and died so. My sad
   fate
Is of worse condition, and Rome
To me more barbarous than ere yet to any
Brought in subjection. Is it not sufficient
That the locks of this our royal head are
   shaved off—

My glorious robes changed to this slavish
habit—
This hand, that grasped a sceptre, manacled—
Or that I have been, as a spectacle,
Exposed to public frown, if to make perfect
This cruel reckoning I am not compelled
To live beyond this, and, with stripes, be
forced
To stretch my shrunk-up sinews at an oar,
In the company of thieves and murderers—
My innocence, and their guilt, no way dis-
tinguished,
But equal in our sufferings?
    Met.   You may yet
Redeem all, and be happy.
    Flam.   But, persisting
In this imposture, think but what it is
To live in hell on earth, and rest assur'd
It is your fatal portion.
    Ant.   Do what you please!
I am in your power, but still Antiochus,
King of the lower Asia—no impostor—
That, four and twenty years since, lost a
battle,
And ·challenge now mine own, which
tyrannous Rome
With violence keeps from me.
    Flam.   Stop his mouth!
    Ant. This is the very truth; and if I live
Thrice Nestor's years in torture, I will speak
No other language.
    Met.   I begin to melt.
    Flam. To the galley with him!
    Ant.   Every place shall be
A temple to my penitence in me!
                     [Exeunt.

ACT V.

SCENE I.—Syracuse.

Enter Marcellus, *proconsul of* Sicily (*with a
letter*), *and the* 2nd *and* 3rd Merchants.

    Mar. Upon your recantation this Gal-
lerien
Was not Antiochus, you had your pardons
Signed by the senate?
    2 *Merch.*   Yes, my lord.
    Mar.   Troth, tell me,
And freely—I am no informer—did you
Believe and know him such, or raised that
rumour
For private ends of your own?
    3 *Merch.*   May it please your excellence
To understand, the fear of death wrought
on us,
In a kind, to turn apostatas: besides,
Having proved our testimonies could not
help him,
We studied our safeties.

    2 *Merch.*   A desire too
Of the recovery of our own, kept from us
With strong hand, by his violent persecutor,
Titus Flaminius, when he was at Carthage,
Urged us to seek redress; nor was it fit
We should oppose great Rome.
    Mar.   In worldly wisdom
You are excusable. But——
    3 *Merch.*   We beseech your honour
Press us no further.
    Mar.   I do not purpose it.
Do you know what this contains?
              [Holding up the letter.
    2 *Merch.*   No, my good lord.
    3 *Merch.* Perhaps we b[ring the warra]nt
for our [deat]hs,
As 'tis said of Bellerophon, yet we durst not
Presume to open it.
    Mar.   'Twas manners in you.
But I'll discharge you of that fear. There is
Nor hurt intended to you.
    3 *Merch.*   We thank your lordship.
    Mar. How is the service of Flaminius
spoke of
In Rome?
    2 *Merch.*   With admiration, and many
Divine great honours to him.
    Mar.   The people's voice
Is not oraculous ever. Are you sure
The galley in which your supposed king is
chained
Was bound for Syracusa?
    3 *Merch.*   She is now
In the port, my lord.
    Mar.   Titus Flaminius in her?
    3 *Merch.* Upon my certain knowledge.
    Mar.   Keep yourselves
Concealed till you are called for. When
least hoped for
You shall have justice.
    2 *Merch.*   Your honour's vassals ever.
              [Exeunt Merchants.
    Mar. Here, here, it is apparent that the
poet
Wrote truth, tho' no proof else could be
alleged
To make it good, that though the heavens
lay open
To human wishes, and the fates were bound
To sign what we desire, such clouds of
error
Involve our reason, we'd still beg a curse,
And not a blessing. How many, born unto
Ample possessions, and, like petty kings,
Disposing of their vassals, sated with
The peace and quiet of a country life,
Carried headlong with ambition, contend
To wear the golden fetters of employment,
Presuming there's no happiness but in

The service of the state.   But when they
  have tried,
By a sad experience, the burthen of them,
When 'tis not in their power, at any rate,
They would redeem their calm security,
Mortgaged in wantonness.   Alas ! what are
  we,
That govern provinces, but preys exposed
To every subtle spy ; and when we have,
Like sponges, sucked in wealth, we are
  squeezed out
By the rough hand of the law ; and, failing in
One syllable of our commission, with
The loss of what we got with toil, we draw
What was our own in question.   You come
  timely,

    Enter Cornelia, *with a* Moor-woman.

To turn my tired thoughts from a sad dis-
  course
That I had with myself.
    Corn.   I rather fear, sir,
I bring an argument along with me
That will increase, not lessen, such con-
  ceptions
As I found with you.
    Mar.   Why, sweet ! what's the matter?
    Corn. When I but name Antiochus, tho' I
  spare,
To make a brief relation, how he died,
Or what he is, if he now live, a sigh,
And seconded with a tear, I know, must fall
As a due tribute to him.
    Mar.   Which I pay
Without compulsion.   But why do you
Lance this old sore?
    Corn. .   The occasion commands it,
And now I would forget it, I am forced,
In thankfulness, to call to memory
The favours for which we must ever owe him.
You had the honour, in his court at Sardis,
To be styled his friend, an honour Rome
  and Carthage
Were rivals for, and did deserve the envy
Of his prime miuions and favourites :
His natural subjects planted in his favour
Or rooted up, as your dislike or praise
Reported them——the good king holding
  what   \
You spake to be oraculous, and not
To be disputed.   His magnificent gifts
Confirmed his true affection, which you were
More weary to receive than he to give :
Yet still he studied new ones.
    Mar.   Pray you no more.
    Corn. O 'tis a theme, sir, I could ever dwell
  on.
But since it does offend you, I will speak
Of what concerns myself. He did not blush,

In the height of his felicity, to confess
Fabricius, my lord and father, for
His much-loved kinsman, and as such ob-
  served him.
You may please to remember too, when, at
A public sacrifice, made to the gods
After a long infection, in which
The Asian kings and queens were his
  assistants,
With what respect and grace he did receive
  me.
And, at a solemn tilting, when he had
Put on the richest armour in the world,
Smiling he said——his words are still, and
  shall be,
Writ in the tablet of my heart——*Fair
  cousin,*
So he began (and then *you* thought me fair
  too),
Since I am term'd a soldier, 'twere a solecism,
*In the language of the war, to have no mis-
  tress,*
And therefore, as a prosperous omen to
My undertakings, I desire to fight—
So you with willingness give suffrage to it—
Under your gracious colours : and, then,
  loosening
A scarf tied to mine arm, he did entreat me
To fasten it on his.   O, with what joy
I did obey him, rapt, beyond myself,
In my imagination, to have
So great a king my servant !
    Mar.   You had too·
Some private conference.
    Corn.   And you gave way to it
Without a sign of jealousy, and dispensed
  with
The Roman gravity.
    Mar.   Would I could again
Grant you like opportunity ; but why
Is this remembered now ?
    Corn.   It does prepare
A suit I have, which you must not deny me,
To see the man, who, as it is reported,
In the exterior parts nature hath drawn
As his perfect copy.   There must be some-
  thing in him
Remarkable in his resemblance only
Of King Antiochus' features.
    Mar.   'Twas my purpose,

    Enter Flaminius *and* Demetrius.

And so much, my Cornelia, Flaminius
Shall not deny us.
    Flam.   As my duty binds me,
My stay here being but short, I come, un-
  sent for
To kiss your lordship's hands.
    Mar.   I answer you

In your own language, sir. And yet your
stay here
May be longer than you think.   [*Aside.*
Flam.   Most honoured madam,
I cannot stoop too low in tendering of
My humblest service.
Corn.   You disgrace your courtship
By overacting it, my lord.   I look not
For such observance.
Flam.   I am most unhappy,
If that your excellence make any scruple
Of doubt you may command me.
Corn.   This assurance
·Gives me encouragement to entreat a favour,
In which, my lord being a suitor with me,
I hope shall find a grant.
Flam.   Tho' all that's mine
Be comprehended in it.
Mar.   Your promise, sir,
Shall not so far engage you.   In respect
Of some familiar passages between
King Antiochus, when he lived, and us,
And, tho' it needs not, for farther proof
That this is an impostor, we desire
Some conference with him.
Flam.   For your satisfaction
I will dispense a little with the strictness
Of my commission. Sirrah! Will the captain
To bring him to the proconsul.
Corn.   His chains took off :
That I entreat too.   Since I would not look
on
The image of a king I so much honoured
Bound like a slave.
Flam.   See this great lady's will
Be punctually obeyed.   [*Exit* Demetrius.
Mar.   Your wisdom, sir,
Hath done the state a memorable service,
In strangling, in the birth, this dreadful
monster ;
And, tho' with some, your cruel usage of
him—
(For so they call your fit severity)
They find a harsh interpretation, wise men
In judgment must applaud it.
Flam.   Such as are
Selected instruments for deep designs,
As things unworthy of them must not feel
Or favours or affections.   Tho' I know
The ocean of your apprehensions needs not
The rivulet of my poor cautions, yet,
Bold from my long experience, I presume
(As a symbol of my zeal, and service to
you)
To leave this counsel.   When you are, my
lord,
Graced, or distasted by the state, remember
Your faculties are the state's, and not your
own.

And, therefore, have a care the empty
sounds
Of *friend* or *enemy* sway you not beyond
The limits are assigned you. We, with ease,
Swim down the stream, but to oppose the
torrent
Is dangerous, and to go more, or less,
Than we are warranted, fatal.
Mar.   With my thanks
For your so grave advice, I'll put in practice
On all occasions what you deliver,
And study 'em as aphorisms.   In the mean
time,
Pray you attempt such entertainment as
Syracusa can present you.   When the im-
postor
Arrives let us have notice.   Pray you walk,
sir.   [*Exeunt.*

SCENE II.—*Hall in* Syracuse.

Enter Antiochus, Captain, *and* Soldiers.

Capt. Wait at the palace gate.   There is
no fear now
Of his escape. I'll be myself his guardian
Till you hear further from me.
Ant.   What new engine
Hath cruelty found out to raise against
This poor demolished rampire?   It is
levelled
With the earth already. Will they triumph in
The ruins they have made ; or is there yet
One masterpiece of tyranny in store
Beyond that I have suffered?   If thou be
A vial of affliction, not poured out yet
Upon this sinful head, I am prepared,
And will look on the cloud before it break
Without astonishment.   Scorn me not,
captain,
As a vain braggart, I will make this good,
And I have strength to do it. I am armed
With such varieties of defensive weapons,
Lent to me from my passive fortitude,
That there's no torment, of a shape so horrid
Can shake my constancy !   Where lies the
scene now ?
Tho' the hangings of the stage were con-
gealed gore,
The chorus flinty executioners,
And the spectators, if it could be, more
Inhuman than Flaminius, the cue given,
The principal actor's ready.
Capt.   If I durst
I could show my compassion.
Ant.   Take heed, captain,
Pity in Roman officers is a crime
To be punished more than murther in cold
blood.
Bear up. To tell me where I am, I take it,
Is no offence.

Capt.   You are in Syracusa—
In the court of the Proconsul.
Ant.   Who? Marcellus.
Capt. That noble Roman. By him you are
    sent for,
But to what end I'm ignorant.
Ant.   Ha ! He was
My creature, and, in my prosperity, proud
To hold dependence of me, tho' I grand him
With the title of a friend ; and his fair lady
In courtship styled my mistress. Can *they* be
Infected with such barbarism as to make me
A spectacle for their sport?

Enter Marcellus, Flaminius, Cornelia,
    Moor-woman, *and* Servants.

Capt.   They are here, and soon
They will resolve you.
Mar.   Be reserved, and let not
The near resemblance of his shape transport
    you
Beyond yourself. Though I confess the
    object
Does much amaze me.
Corn.   You impose, my lord,
What I want power to bear.
Mar.   Let my example,
Though your fierce passions make war
    against it,
Strengthen your reason.
Ant.   Have you taken yet
A full view of me ? In what part do I
Appear a monster ?
Corn.   His own voice !
Ant.   Forbear.
Tho' I were an impostor, as this fellow
Labours you to believe, you break the laws
Of fair humanity in adding to
Affliction at the height ; and I must tell you
The reverence, you should pay unto the shape
Of King Antiochus, may challenge pity
As a due debt—not scorn. Wise men
    preserve
Dumb pictures of their friends, and look
    upon them
With feeling and affection, yet not hold it
A foolish superstition. But there is
In thankfulness a greater tye on you
To show compassion.
Mar.   Were it possible
Thou couldst be King Antiochus——
Ant.   What then ?
Mar. I should both say and do——
Ant.   Nothing for me
(As far as my persuasion could prevent it)
Not suiting with the quality and condition
Of one, that owes his loyalty to Rome.
And, since it is, by the inscrutable will

Of fate, determined that the royalties
Of Asia must be conferred upon her—
For what offence I know not—'tis in vain
For men to oppose it. You express, my
    lord,
A kind of sorrow for me, in which, madam,
You seem to be a sharer. That you may
Have some proof to defend it, for your
    mirth's sake
I'll play the juggler, or more subtle gipsy,
And to your admiration reveal
Strange mysteries to you, which, as you are
    Romans,
You must receive for cunning tricks, but give
No farther credit to them.
Flam.   At your peril
You may give him hearing. But to have
    faith in him
Neighbours to treason. Such an impudent
    slave
Was never read of.
Mar.   I dare stand his charms
With open ears—speak on.
Ant.   If so, have at you !
Can you call to your memory when you were
At Sardis with Antiochus, before
His Grecian expedition, what he,
With his own hands, presented you as a
    favour,
No third man by to witness it?
Mar.   Give me leave
To recollect myself. Yes—sure 'twas so—
He gave me a fair sword.
Ant.   'Tis true, and you
Vowed never to part from it. Is it still
In your possession ?
Mar.   The same sword I have,
And, while I live, will keep.
Ant.   Will you not say,
It being four and twenty years since you
Were master of that gift, if now I know it,
Among a thousand others, that I have
The art of memory?
Mar.   I shall receive it
As no common sleight. Sirrah ! Fetch all
    the swords
For mine own use in my armoury, and, do
    you hear,   [*Whispers.*
Do as I give directions.
Servant.   With all care, sir,
                              [*Exit* Servant.
Ant. To entertain the time until your
    servant
Returns. There is no syllable that passed
Between you and Antiochus, which I could
    not
Articulately deliver. You must still
Be confident that I am an impostor,
Or else the trick is nothing.

Enter Servant *with many swords.*

Corn.   Can this be?
Ant. O welcome, friend. Most choice and
curious swords,
But mine is not among them.
Marc.   Bring the rest!

Enter another Servant *with more swords.*

Ant. Aye! this is it.   This is the sword I
gave you
Before I went to Greece.   Be not amazed
Nor let this trifle purchase a belief
I am Antiochus. Here is one will assure you
These are but juggling tricks of an affronter.
Flam. They are no more.   A contract's
sealed between
The devil and this seducer, at the price
Of his damned soul. And his familiar
Dæmon
Acquaints him with these passages.
Marc.   I know not
But I am thunderstrook.
Corn.   I can contain
Myself no longer.
Ant.   Stay, dear madam.   Though
Credulity be excusable in your sex
To take away all colour of guilt in you,
You shall have stronger proofs.   The scarf
you gave me,
As a testimony you adopted me
Into your service, I wore on mine armour,
When I fought with Marcus Scaurus ; and
mine eye
Hath on the sudden found a precious jewel
You deigned to receive from me. [The
armlet]
Which you wear on your sleeve.
Corn.   I acknowledge
It was the king Antiochus' gift.
Ant.   I will
Make a discovery of a secret in it
Of which you yet are ignorant.   Pray you
trust it,
For king Antiochus' sake, into my hands.
I thank your readiness. Nay dry your eyes.
You hinder else the faculty of seeing
The cunning of the lapidary.   I can
Pull out the stone, and under it you shall
find
My name, and cipher I then used, engraven.
Corn. 'Tis most apparent. Tho' I lose
my life for it,
These knees shall pay their duty.
Ant.   By no means ;
For your own sake be still incredulous,
Since your faith cannot save me.   I should
know

This Moorish woman. Yes. 'Tis she. Thou
wert
One of my laundry, and thou wast called
Zanthia
While thou wert mine.   I'm glad thou'st
lighted on
So gracious a mistress.
Moor-woman.   Mine own king!
O let me kiss your feet. What cursed villains
Have thus transformed you?
Flam.   'Tis not safe, my lord,
To suffer this.
Marc.   I am turu'd statue, or
All this is but a vision.
Ant.   Your ear, madam,
                        [*Speaks aside.*
Since what I now shall say is such a secret
As is known only to yourself and me,
And must exclude a third—tho' your own
lord,
From being of the counsel.   Having gained
Access, and privacy with you, my hot blood
(No friend to modest purposes) prompted me
With pills of poisoned language, candied o'er
With hopes of future greatness, to attempt
The ruin of your honour.   I enforced then
My power to justify the ill, and pressed
You with mountainous promises of love and
service.
But when the building of your faith and
virtue
Began to totter, and a kind of grant
Was offered, my then sleeping temperance
Began to rouse itself ; and, breaking through
The obstacles of lust, when most assured
To enjoy a pleasant hour, I let my suit fall,
And, with a gentle reprehension, taxed
Your forward proneness—but with many
vows
Ne'er to discover it, which heaven can witness
I have and will keep faithfully.
Corn.   This is
The king Antiochus, as sure as I am
The daughter of my mother.
Marc.   Be advised.
Flam. This is little less than treason !
Corn.   They are traitors—
Traitors to innocence and oppressed justice—
That dare affirm the contrary.
Marc.   Pray you temper
The violence of your passion.

.   .   .   .   .   ˘.
Corn.   [Do] but express
Your thankfulness for his so many [favours]:
And labour that the senate may restore him
Unto his own.   I'll die else.
Ant.   Live long, madam,
To nobler and more profitable uses.
I am a falling structure : and desire not

Your honours should be buried in my ruins.
Let it suffice. My lord, you must not see
The sun, if, in the policy of state,
It is forbidden. With compassion '
Of what a miserable king hath suffered
Preserve me in your mem'ry.

Flam. You stand as
This sorc'rer had bewitched you. Drag him to
His oar, and let his weighty chains be
    doubled.

Marc. For my sake let the poor man
    have what favour
You can afford him.

Flam. Sir, you must excuse me.
You have abused the liberty I gave you,
                    [*To* Antiochus.
But, villain, you pay dear for't. I will trust
The execution of his punishment
To no man but myself. His cries and groans
Shall be my hourly music. So, my lord,
I take my leave abruptly.

Corn. May all plagues,
That ever followed tyranny, pursue thee !

Marc. Pray you stay a little.

Flam. On no terms.

Marc. Yield so much
To my entreaties.

Flam. Not a minute, for
Your government !

Marc. I will not purchase, sir,
Your company at such a rate. And yet
Must take the boldness upon me to tell you
You must, and shall, stay.

Flam. How !

Marc. Nay, what is more,
As a prisoner—not a guest. Look not so
    high,
I'll humble your proud thoughts.

Flam. You dare not do this
Without authority.

Marc. You shall find I have
Sufficient warrant, with detaining you,
To take this man into my custody.
Tho' 'tis not in my power, whate'er you are,
To do you further favour, I thus free you
Out of this devil's paws.

Ant. I take it as
A lessening of my torments.

Flam. You shall answer
This in another place.

Marc. But you shall, here,

Yield an account without appeal for what
You have already done. You may peruse.
    [Does it] [*Hands him the letter.*
Shake you already? Do you find I have
[The warran]t? Call in the Asian merchants.

Enter the two Merchants *and a* Guard.

2 Merch. [.   .] now to be hanged
3 Merch. [.   .] him that pities thee
Flam. [.   .] accusers
Marc. .   .   .
.   die and will prove that you took bribes
Of the Carthaginian merchants, to detain
Their lawful prize ; and, for your sordid
    ends,
Abused the trust, committed by the state,
To right their vassals. The wise senate, as
They will reward your good and faithful
    service,
Cannot, in justice, without punishment
Pass o'er your ill. Guiltiness makes you
    dumb.
But, 'till that I have leisure, and you find
Your tongue——to prison with him !

Flam. I prove too late,
As heaven is merciful, man's cruelty
Never escapes unpunished.
            [*Exeunt with* Flaminius.

Ant. How a smile
Labours to break forth from me. But
    what is
Rome's pleasure shall be done with me?

Marc. Pray you think, sir,
"Tis a Roman—not your constant friend—
    that tells you
You are confined unto the Gyaræ
With a strong guard upon you.

Re-enter Guard.

Ant. Then 'tis easy
To prophecy I have not long to live,
Though the manner how I shall die is un-
    certain.
Nay, weep not. Since 'tis not in you to
    help me,
These showers of tears are fruitless. May
    my story
Teach potentates humility, and instruct
Proud monarchs, tho' they govern human
    things,
A greater power does raise, or pull down,
    kings.

EPILOGUE.

The end of epilogues is to enquire
The censure of the play, or to desire
Pardon for what's amiss. In his intent
The maker vows that he is innocent.

S S

And, for me and my fellows, I protest,
And you may believe me, we have done our best ;
And reason too we should, but whether you
Conceive we have with care discharg'd what's due
Rests yet in supposition, you may
If you please resolve us. If our fate this day
Prove prosperous ; and you too vouchsafe to give
Some sign your pleasure is this work shall live,
We will find out new ways for your delight,
And, to our power, ne'er fail to do you right.

POEMS

ON SEVERAL OCCASIONS.

To my Honorable ffreinde Sr. ffrancis ffoliambe
Knight and Baronet.

Sr. with my service I præsent this booke,
  A trifle, I confesse, but pray you looke
Upon the sender, not his guift, with your
  Accustomde favor, and then 't will indure
Your serch the better. Somethinge there
  may bee
You 'l finde in the perusall fit for mee
To give to one I honor, and may pleade,
  In your defence, though you descende to
  reade

A Pamplet of this nature. May it prove
  In your free iudgement, though not worth,
  your llove,
Yet fit to finde a pardon, and I'll say
  Upon your warrant that it is a play.

      Ever at your commaundment,

        PHILIP MASSINGER.

To my judicious and learned Friend the Author, [James Shirley] *upon his inge-*
nious Poem, the Grateful Servant, *a Comedy, published in* 1630.

THOUGH I well know, that my obscurer
  name
Listed with theirs who here advance thy
  fame,
Cannot add to it, give me leave to be,
Among the rest a modest votary
At the altar of thy Muse. I dare not
  raise
Giant hyperboles unto thy praise ;
Or hope it can find credit in this age,
Though I should swear, in each triumphant
  page
Of this thy work there's no line but of
  weight,
And poesy itself shewn at the height :
Such common places, friend, will not agree
With thy own vote, and my integrity.

I'll steer a mid way, have clear truth my
  guide,
And urge a praise which cannot be denied.
Here are no forced expressions, no rack'd
  phrase ;
No Babel compositions to amaze
The tortured reader ; no believed defence
To strengthen the bold Atheist's insolence ;
No obscene syllable, that may compel
A blush from a chaste maid ; but all so well
Express'd and order'd, as wise men must
  say
It is a grateful poem, a good play :
And such as read ingeniously, shall find
Few have outstripp'd thee, many halt
  behind.

        PHILIP MASSINGER.
           S S 2

To his Son, J[ames] S[mith] upon his Minerva.

Thou art my son; in that my choice is
  spoke:
Thine with thy father's Muse strikes equal
  stroke.
It shew'd more art in Virgil to relate,
And make it worth the hearing, his gnat's
  fate,
Than to conceive what those great minds
  must be
That sought, and found out, fruitful Italy.
And such as read and do not apprehend,
And with applause, the purpose and the
  end
Of this neat poem, in themselves confess
A dull stupidity and barrenness.

Methinks I do behold, in this rare birth,
A temple built up to facetious Mirth,
Pleased Phœbus smiling on it: doubt not,
  then,
But that the suffrage of judicious men
Will honour this Thalia; and, for those
That praise sir Bevis, or what's worse in
  prose,
Let them dwell still in ignorance. To write
In a new strain, and from it raise delight,
As thou in this hast done, doth not by
  chance,
But merit, crown thee with the laurel
  branch.
                          PHILIP MASSINGER.

SERO· SED SERIO.

To the Right Honourable my most singular good, Lord and Patron, Philip *Earl of*
Pembroke and Montgomery, Lord-Chamberlain of His Majesty's Household,
&c. upon the deplorable and untimely Death of his late truly noble Son, Charles
Lord Herbert, &c.

'Twas fate, not want of duty, did me wrong;
Or, with the rest, my hymenæal song
Had been presented, when the knot was tied
That made the bridegroom and the virgin
  bride
A happy pair. I curs'd my absence then
That hinder'd it, and bit my star-cross'd
  pen,
Too busy in stage-blanks, and trifling rhyme,
When such a cause call'd, and so apt a time
To pay a general debt; mine being more
Than they could owe, who since, or hereto-
  fore,
Have labour'd with exalted lines to raise
Brave piles, or rather pyramids of praise
To Pembroke and his family: and dare I,
Being silent then, aim at an elegy?
Or hope my weak Muse can bring forth one
  verse
Deserving to wait on the sable hearse
Of your late hopeful Charles? his obsequies
Exact the mourning of all hearts and eyes
That knew him, or loved virtue. He that
  would
Write what he was, to all posterity, should

Have ample credit in himself, to borrow,
Nay, make his own, the saddest accents
  sorrow
Ever express'd, and a more moving quill,
Than Spenser used when he gave Astrophil
A living epicedium. For poor me,
By truth I vow it is no flattery,
I from my soul wish, (if it might remove
Grief's burthen, which too feelingly you
  prove,)
Though I have been ambitious of fame,
As poets are, and would preserve a name,
That, my toys burnt, I had lived unknown
  to men,
And ne'er had writ, nor ne'er to write
  again.
Vain wish, and to be scorn'd! can my foul
  dross,
With such pure gold be valued? or the loss
Of thousand lives like mine, merit to be
The same age thought on, when his destiny
Is only mentioned? no, my lord, his fate,
Is to be prized at a higher rate;
Nor are the groans of common men to be
Blended with those, which the nobility

Vent hourly for him. That great ladies mourn
His sudden death, and lords vie at his urn
Drops of compassion ; that true sorrow, fed
With showers of tears, still bathes the widow'd bed
Of his dear spouse ; that our great king and queen
(To grace your grief) disdain'd not to be seen
Your royal comforters ; these well become
The loss of such a hope, and on his tomb
Deserve to live : but, since no more could be
Presented, to set off his tragedy,
And with a general sadness, why should you
(Pardon my boldness!) pay more than his due,
Be the debt ne'er so great ? No stoic can,
As you were a loving father, and a man,
Forbid a moderate sorrow ; but to take
Too much of it, for his or your own sake

If we may trust divines, will rather be
Censured repining, than true piety.
I still presume too far, and more than fear
My duty may offend, pressing too near
Your private passions. I thus conclude,
If now you shew your passive fortitude,
In bearing this affliction, and prove
You take it as a trial of heaven's love
And favour to you, you ere long shall see
Your second care return'd from Italy,
To bless his native England, each rare part,
That in his brother lived, and joy'd your heart,
Transferr'd to him ; and to the world make known
He takes possession of what's now his own.

> Your honour's
> most humble
> and faithful servant,
> PHILIP MASSINGER.

DEDICATIONS TO THE PLAYS.

The Unnatural Combat.

To my much Honoured Friend, Anthony Sentleger, *of Oakham in Kent, Esq.*

SIR,

THAT the patronage of trifles, in this kind, hath long since rendered dedications, and inscriptions obsolete, and out of fashion, I perfectly understand, and cannot but ingenuously confess, that I walking in the same path, may be truly argued by you of weakness, or wilful error: but the reasons and defences, for the tender of my service this way to you, are so just, that I cannot (in my thankfulness for so many favours received) but be ambitious to publish them. Your noble father, Sir Warham Sentleger (whose remarkable virtues must be ever remembered) being, while he lived, a master, for his pleasure, in poetry, feared not to hold converse with divers, whose necessitous fortunes made it their profession, among which, by the clemency of his judgment, I was not in the last place admitted. You (the heir of his honour and estate) inherited his good inclinations to men of my poor quality, of which I cannot give any ampler testimony, than by my free and glad profession of it to the world. Besides (and it was not the least encouragement to me) many of eminence, and the best of such, who disdained not to take notice of me, have not thought themselves disparaged, I dare not say honoured, to be celebrated the patrons of my humble studies. In the first file of which, I am confident, you shall have no cause to blush, to find your name written. I present you with this old tragedy, without prologue or epilogue, it being composed in a time (and that too, peradventure, as knowing as this) when such by-ornaments were not advanced above the fabric of the whole work. Accept it, I beseech you, as it is, and continue your favour to the author,

Your Servant,
PHILIP MASSINGER.

The Duke of Milan.

To the Right Honourable, and much esteemed for her high birth, but more admired for her virtue, the Lady Catherine Stanhope, *wife to Philip Lord Stanhope, Baron of Shelford.*

MADAM,

IF I were not most assured that works of this nature have found both patronage and protection amongst the greatest princesses of Italy, and are at this day cherished by persons most eminent in our kingdom, I should not presume to offer these my weak and imperfect labours at the altar of your favour. Let the example of others, more knowing, and more experienced in this kindness (if my boldness offend) plead my pardon, and the rather, since there is no other means left me (my misfortunes having cast me on this course) to publish to the world (if it hold the least good opinion of me) that I am ever your ladyship's creature. Vouchsafe, therefore, with the never-failing clemency of your noble disposition, not to contemn the tender of his duty, who, while he is, will ever be

An humble Servant to your
Ladyship, and yours,
PHILIP MASSINGER.

The Bondman.

To the Right Honourable, my singular good Lord, Philip Earl of Montgomery, *Knight of the most Noble Order of the Garter, &c.*

RIGHT HONOURABLE,

HOWEVER I could never arrive at the happiness to be made known to your lordship, yet a desire, born with me, to make a tender of all duties and service to the noble family of the Herberts, descended to me as an inheritance from my dead father, Arthur Massinger. Many years he happily spent in the service of your honourable house, and died a servant to it ; leaving his to be ever most glad and ready, to be at the command of all such as derive themselves from his most honoured master, your lordship's most noble father. The consideration of this encouraged me (having no other means to present my humblest service to your honour) to shroud this trifle under the wings of your noble protection ; and I hope, out of the clemency of your heroic disposition, it will find, though perhaps not a welcome entertainment, yet, at the worst, a gracious pardon. When it was first acted, your lordship's liberal suffrage taught others to allow it for current, having received the undoubted stamp of your lordship's allowance : and if in the perusal of any vacant hour, when your honour's more serious occasions shall give you leave to read it, it answer, in your lordship's judgment, the report and opinion it had upon the stage, I shall esteem my labours not ill employed, and, while I live, continue

The humblest of those that

truly honour your lordship,

PHILIP MASSINGER.

The Renegado.

To the Right Honourable George Harding, *Baron Berkeley, of Berkeley Castle, and Knight of the Honourable Order of the Bath.*

MY GOOD LORD,

To be honoured for old nobility, or hereditary titles, is not alone proper to yourself, but to some few of your rank, who may challenge the like privilege with you : but in our age to vouchsafe (as you have often done) a ready hand to raise the dejected spirits of the contemned sons of the Muses ; such as would not suffer the glorious fire of poesy to be wholly extinguished, is so remarkable and peculiar to your lordship, that with a full vote and suffrage, it is acknowledged that the patronage and protection of the dramatic poem, is yours, and almost without a rival. I despair not therefore, but that my ambition to present my service in this kind, may in your clemency meet with a gentle interpretation. Confirm it, my good lord, in your gracious acceptance of this trifle ; in which, if I were not confident there are some pieces worthy the perusal, it should have been taught an humbler flight ; and the writer, your countryman, never yet made happy in your notice and favour, had not made this an advocate to plead for his admission among such as are wholly and sincerely devoted to your service. I may live to tender my humble thankfulness in some higher strain ; and till then, comfort myself with hope, that you descend from your height to receive

Your honour's commanded servant,

PHILIP MASSINGER.

The Roman Actor.

To my much honoured and most true Friends, Sir Philip Knyvet, Knt. and Bart. and to Sir Thomas Jeay, *Knt., and* Thomas Bellingham, *of Newtimber, in Sussex, Esq.*

How much I acknowledge myself bound for your so many and extraordinary favours conferred upon me, as far as it is in my power, posterity shall take notice : I were most unworthy of such noble friends, if I should not, with all thankfulness, profess and own them. In the composition of this Tragedy you were my only supporters, and it being now by your principal encouragement to be turned into the world, it cannot walk safer than under your protection. It hath been happy in the suffrage of some learned and judicious gentlemen when it was presented, nor shall they find cause, I hope, in the perusal, to repent them of their good opinion of it. If the gravity and height of the subject distaste such as are only affected with jigs and ribaldry, (as I presume it will,) their condemnation of me and my poem, can no way offend me : my reason teaching me, such malicious and ignorant detractors deserve rather contempt than satisfaction. I ever held it the most perfect birth of my Minerva ; and therefore in justice offer it to those that have best deserved of me ; who, I hope, in their courteous acceptance will render it worth their receiving, and ever, in their gentle construction of my imperfections, believe they may at their pleasure dispose of him, that is wholly and sincerely

Devoted to their service,

PHILIP MASSINGER.

The Great Duke of Florence.

To the truly honoured, and my noble Favourer, Sir Robert Wiseman, *Knt., of Thorrell's-Hall, in Essex.*

SIR,

As I dare not be ungrateful for the many benefits you have heretofore conferred upon me, so I have just reason to fear that my attempting this way to make satisfaction (in some measure) for so due a debt, will further engage me.' However, examples encourage me. The most able in my poor quality have made use of Dedications in this nature, to make the world take notice (as far as in them lay) who and what they were that gave supportment and protection to their studies, being more willing to publish the doer than receive a benefit in a corner. For myself, I will freely, and with a zealous thankfulness, acknowledge, that for many years I had but faintly subsisted, if I had not often tasted of your bounty. But it is above my strength and faculties to celebrate to the desert your noble inclination, and that made actual, to raise up, or, to speak more properly, to re-build the ruins of demolished poesie. But that is a work reserved, and will be, no doubt, undertaken, and finished, by one that can to the life express it. Accept, I beseech you, the tender of my service, and in the list of those you have obliged to you, contemn not the name of

Your true and faithful honourer,

PHILIP MASSINGER.

The Maid of Honour.

To my most honoured Friends, Sir Francis Foljambe, *Knt. and Bart. and* Sir Thomas Bland, *Knt.*

THAT you have been, and continued so for many years, since you vouchsafed to own me, patrons to me and my despised studies, I cannot but with all humble thankfulness acknowledge : and living, as you have done, inseparable in your friendship, (notwithstanding all differences, and suits in law arising between you,) I held it as impertinent as absurd, in the presentment of my service in this kind, to divide you. A free confession of a debt in a meaner man, is the amplest satisfaction to his superiors ; and I heartily wish, that the world may take notice, and from myself, that I had not to this time subsisted, but that I was supported by your frequent courtesies and favours. When your more serious occasions will give you leave, you may please to peruse this trifle, and peradventure find something in it that may appear worthy of your protection. Receive it, I beseech you, as a testimony of his duty who, while he lives, resolves to be
Truly and sincerely devoted to your service,
PHILIP MASSINGER.

The Picture.

To my honoured and selected Friends, of the Noble Society of the Inner Temple.

IT may be objected, my not inscribing their names, or titles, to whom I dedicate this poem, proceedeth either from my diffidence of their affection to me, or their unwillingness to be published the patrons of a trifle. To such as shall make so strict an inquisition of me, I truly answer, The play, in the presentment, found such a general approbation, that it gave me assurance of their favour to whose protection it is now sacred ; and they have professed they so sincerely allow of it, and the maker, that they would have freely granted that in the publication, which, for some reasons, I denied myself. One, and that is a main one ; I had rather enjoy (as I have done) the real proofs of their friendship, than, mountebank-like, boast their numbers in a catalogue. Accept it, noble Gentlemen, as a confirmation of his service, who hath nothing else to assure you, and witness to the world, how much he stands engaged for your so frequent bounties ; and in your charitable opinion of me believe, that you now may, and shall ever command,
Your Servant,
PHILIP MASSINGER.

The Emperor of the East.

To the Right Honourable, and my especial good Lord, John Lord Mohun, *Baron of Okehampton, &c.*

MY GOOD LORD,
LET my presumption in styling you so, (having never deserved it in my service,) from the clemency of your noble disposition, find pardon. The reverence due to the name of Mohun, long since honoured in three earls of Somerset, and eight barons of Munster, may challenge from all pens a deserved celebration. And the rather in respect those titles were not purchased, but conferred, and continued in your ancestors, for many virtuous, noble, and still living actions ; nor ever forfeited or tainted, but when the iniquity of those times laboured the depression of approved goodness, and in wicked policy held it fit that loyalty and faith, in taking part with the true prince, should be degraded and mulcted. But this admitting no further dilation in this place, may your lordship please, and with all possible brevity, to understand the reasons why I am, in humble thankfulness, ambitious.

to shelter this poem under the wings of your honourable protection. My worthy friend, Mr. Aston Cockayne, your nephew, to my extraordinary content, delivered to me that your lordship, at your vacant hours, sometimes vouchsafed to peruse such trifles of mine as have passed the press, and not alone warranted them in your gentle suffrage, but disdained not to bestow a remembrance of your love, and intended favour to me. I profess to the world, I was exalted with the bounty, and with good assurance, it being so rare in this age to meet with one noble name, that, in fear to be censured of levity and weakness, dares express itself a friend or patron to contemned poetry. Having, therefore, no means else left me to witness the obligation in which I stand most willingly bound to your lordship, I offer this Tragi-comedy to your gracious acceptance, no way despairing, but that with a clear aspect you will deign to receive it, (it being an induction to my future endeavours,) and that in the list of those, that to your merit truly admire you, you may descend to number   Your lordship's faithful honourer,

PHILIP MASSINGER.

A New Way to Pay Old Debts.

To the Right Honourable, Robert Earl of Carnarvon, *Master Falconer of England.*

My Good Lord,

PARDON, I beseech you, my boldness, in presuming to shelter this Comedy under the wings of your lordship's favour and protection. I am not ignorant (having never yet deserved you in my service) that it cannot but meet with a severe construction, if, in the clemency of your noble disposition, you fashion not a better defence for me, than I can fancy for myself. All I can allege is, that divers Italian princes, and lords of eminent rank in England, have not disdained to receive and read poems of this nature ; nor am I wholly lost in my hopes, but that your honour (who have ever expressed yourself a favourer, and friend to the Muses) may vouchsafe, in your gracious acceptance of this trifle, to give me encouragement to present you with some laboured work, and of a higher strain, hereafter. I was born a devoted servant to the thrice noble family of your incomparable lady, and am most ambitious, but with a becoming distance, to be known to your lordship, which, if you please to admit, I shall embrace it as a bounty, that while I live shall oblige me to acknowledge you for my noble patron, and profess myself to be,

Your honour's true servant,

PHILIP MASSINGER.

The City Madam.

To the truly Noble and Virtuous Lady Ann Countess of Oxford.

Honoured Lady,

In that age when wit and learning were not conquered by injury and violence, this poem was the object of love and commendations, it being composed by an infallible pen, and censured by an unerring auditory. In this epistle I shall not need to make an apology for plays in general, by exhibiting their antiquity and utility : in a word, they are mirrors or glasses which none but deformed faces, and fouler consciences fear to look into. The encouragement I had to prefer this dedication to your powerful protection proceeds from the universal fame of the deceased author, who, (although he composed many,) wrote none amiss, and this may justly be ranked among his best. I have redeemed it from the teeth of Time, by committing of it to the press, but more in imploring your patronage. I will not slander it with my praises, it is commendation enough to call it MASSINGER'S ; if it may gain your allowance and pardon, I am highly gratified, and desire only to wear the happy title of,   Madam,

Your most humble servant,

ANDREW PENNYCUICKE.

GLOSSARIAL INDEX.

a means left column ; *b* right column.

ABRAM-MEN. 396 *b*.
An Abram-man was an impudent impostor who, under the garb and appearance of a lunatic, rambled about the country, and compelled, as Decker says, the servants of small families " to give him, through fear, whatever he demanded."

ABSURD. 331 *a*.
In logical phraseology, is a term used when false conclusions are drawn from the opponent's premises.

ABUSE. 270 *a*.
"You abuse me :" *i.e.*, you practise on my credulity with a forged tale. The word often occurs in this sense.

ALBA REGALIS. 286 *a*, 305 *a*.
The town where the kings of Hungary were anciently crowned. Whitehall is often called so by writers of the seventeenth century.

ALTAR. 176 *b*.
" That binds no further than to the altar," is not an allusion to the married state, but to the saying of Pericles. that he would support the interests of his friend *as far as the altar ; i.e.*, as far as his respect for the gods would permit.

AMSTERDAM. 133 *b*.
The toleration allowed to religious sects of all denominations had, in Massinger's time, filled Amsterdam with fanatics from every country in Europe. To this aggregation of zealots there are perpetual allusions in our old writers.

ANAXARETE. 209 *a*.
The story of Iphis and Anaxarete is beautifully told by Ovid (" Met." xiv.—698 *et seq.*) Massinger has followed his leader *pari passu.*

ANGEL. 10 *b*.
This word is frequently used for *Bird*, by our old writers. " Roman angel," therefore, means the eagle, the military ensign.

APES. 115 *a*.
Our ancestors certainly excelled us in the education which they bestowed on their animals. Banks s horse far surpassed all that have been brought up in the academy of Mr. Astley, and the apes of these days are mere clowns to their progenitors. The apes of Massinger's time were gifted with a pretty smattering of politics and philosophy. In the " Parson's Wedding" we have an allusion to one that would frown when the Pope's name was mentioned ; and in " Ram Alley" to another (or the same), that would hold up his hand at the word Geneva.

APOSTATA. 27 *b*, 32 *a*, 38 *b*, 40 *b*, 605 *a*, 606 *a*, 620 *a*.
Our old writers usually said *apostata, statua, &c.*, where we now say *apostate, statue.* The metre is often absolutely destroyed by the editors in attempting to alter the spelling.

APPLE. 344 *b*.
The ancients attached a certain degree of mystical consequence to the presentation of an apple ; which they universally agreed to consider as a tacit confession of passion, accepted and returned.

AT ALL ! 445 *a*.
This expression occurs in Skelton's bold and animated description of Ryotte, the prototype of a gamester :—
" With that came Ryotte, rushing all at ones
A rustic galande, to ragged and to rente,
And on the borde he whirled a pair of bones,
Quater, trey, dews l he chattered as he went,
Now *have at all*, by St. Thomas of Kent."—
Bouge of Court.

ATHEISM. 270 *b*.
Our old writers seem to have used such words as profaneness, blasphemy, *atheism*, &c., with a laxity which modern practice does not acknowledge. They applied them to any extraordinary violation of moral or natural decorum.

ATONEMENT. 88 *b*, 543 *b*.
Reconciliation. To atone is often used in this sense by Shakspeare and others.

AVENTINE. 195 *a*.
My security, my defence. The Aventine was a post of great strength. It is used in this metaphorical sense by Fletcher, and others of our old dramatists.

BAKEHOUSE. 186 *a*.
The *conduit* and the *bakehouse* in the age of Massinger were the general rendezvous of gossips of both sexes : they are so still in most country towns.

BANDOG. 12 *b*.
A dog so fierce as to require to be chained up, as the name implies.

BANQUET. 46 *b*, 101 *b*, 430 *b*.
A banquet was what we now call a dessert, and was composed of fruit, sweetmeats, &c. It was usually placed in a separate room, to which the guests removed as soon as they had dined. The common place of banqueting was the garden-house, or arbour, with which almost every dwelling was once furnished.

BARATHRUM. 406 *a*.
" Barathrum of the shambles " is taken literally from Horace.
" Pernicies et tempestas, barathrumque macelli."
The word is used by Shirley and others in the classical sense of an abyss or devouring gulf.
[I have no doubt that when Meg Merrilies called Dominie Sampson " You black *barrowtram* of the kirk," preparatory to the order " Gape, sinner, and swallow," Sir Walter Scott was thinking of this word, and not of " the side of a wheelbarrow," as interpreted in the Glossary to the Waverley novels.]

BARLEY-BREAK. 30 *b*, 185 *a*.
A game played by six people (three of each sex), who were coupled by lot. A piece of ground was then chosen, and divided into three compartments, of which the middle one was called Hell. It was the object of the couple condemned to this division to catch the others who advanced from the two extremities.
[" At *barley-break* her sweet swift foot to try," is a line in the " Arcadia."]

BASES. 292 *b*.
Seem to have been some kind of quilted and ornamented covering for the thighs. Highlanders wear a kind of *bases* at this day. [Qy., the French word, *bas*. stockings.]

BASKET. 382 *a*, 393 *b*, 425 *a*.
The allusions are to the basket in which the broken bread and meat was distributed to the poor at the porter's lodge of great houses. The "sheriff's basket" was that in which the victuals were sent to the prisons from the sheriff's table.

BEADSMEN. 429 *b*, 438 *b*.
Is pure Saxon, and means prayers men, *i.e.*, such as are engaged, in consequence of past or present favours, to pray for their benefactors. The name was formerly given with great propriety to the inhabitants of almshouses, and, in general, to the objects of our public charities.

BEARING-DISHES. 420 *a*.
Means solid, substantial dishes, like the "portly viands" spoken of at 46 *a*.

BECCO. 318 *b*.
Is rendered by the commentators on our old plays a *cuckold*. The Italians generally use it for one accessary to his own disgrace, and in this sense Massinger employs it.

BEGGING ESTATES. 324 *a*.
A severe sarcasm on the avidity of the courtiers. The estates of many condemned persons were *begged* with scandalous precipitancy by the favourites of the day; and, what is worse, were justly suspected in more than one instance to have constituted the principal part of the crime for which the possessors suffered.

BEGLERBEG. 150 *a*.
Chief governor of a city.

BEND HER BODY. 77 *b*, 545 *a*.
To try if there be any life in it. In "The Maid's Tragedy,"

"I've heard if there be any life, but *bow*
The body thus, and it will show itself."

BIND. 462 *a*.
"And by turns *bind* with her." This exquisite description of rural amusements is from the hand of a great master. I lament that it is so technical; but in Massinger's time this language was perfectly familiar to the audience who heard it, in a greater or less degree, in every play that came before them. A hawk is said to *bind* when she seizes her prey.

BISOGNION. 272 *a*.
A necessitous person, a beggar. In our old writers it frequently occurs as a term of contempt.—[The *Bezonian* of Ancient Pistol.]

BLACKS. 360 *b*, 568 *b*.
Constantly used by our old writers for mourning weeds.

BLASPHE'MOUS. 237 *a*.
The word was constantly thus accented by Sidney, Spenser, and others, and with strict regard to its Greek derivation.

BLUE GOWN. 446 *b*, 455 *a*.
The livery of Bridewell.

BOMAN. 446 *b*.
In the language of Alsatia a gallant fellow; but most probably, in this instance, a misprint for Roman, which reading is here adopted.

BOX-KEEPER. 422 *Dram. Pers.*
The groom-porter of a gambling-house. This important character never plays, but is seated on a box or elevated chair, where he declares the state of the game, the odds, and the success of the parties.

BRACHES. 58 *a*, 388 *a*, 437 *b*.
The *Gentleman's Recreation* says "Braches is a *mannerly name* for hound bitches," and, adds Gifford, "*for all others.*"

BREDA. 391 *a*.
This was one of the most celebrated sieges of the time. Spinola sat down before the town on the 26th August, 1624, and it did not surrender till the 1st July, 1625. Tobacco was sold for 100 florins the lb.

BROADSIDE (to shew). 165 *b*.
Gifford adduces this as an illustration of the familiarity of our ancestors with nautical language. It is here offered with great propriety to prove that the fugitives thought themselves out of danger of pursuit—*they bore up in the wind*, which checked their course.

BUCK. 26 *a*.
To *buck* is to wash clothes by laying them on a smooth plank or stone, and beating them with a pole flattened at the sides.

BUG-WORDS. 407 *b*.
Frightful, terrific words,—in the same way as *bug* bear.

BURSE. 436 *b*.
The New Exchange, which was then full of shops, where all kinds of finery for the ladies, trinkets, ornaments, &c., were sold.

BUTLER. 570 *a*.
"Oracle Butler!" He alludes to Dr. W. Butler, a very celebrated physician of Queen Elizabeth's time.

CALVERED SALMON. 266 *b*, 482 *b*.
Appears to have differed very little from pickled salmon, as the directions are to "boil it in vinegar, with oil and spices."

CANCELIER. 462 *a*.
"Is when a high-flown hawk in her stooping, turneth two or three times upon the wing, to recover herself before she seizeth upon her prey."

CANDOUR. 183 *a*, 471 *b*.
Massinger uses "candour" in both these places as synonymous with "honour," or fairness of reputation.

CAPITULATE. 599 *a*.
To draw up articles. So Shakspeare:
"The Archbishop's Grace of York, Douglas, and Mortimer,
Capitulate against us, and are up."

CARANZA. 44 *a*, 473 *a*.
This man wrote a treatise on duelling, which seems to have been the *Vade Mecum* of the punctilious gallants about the Court of James I. He is frequently mentioned by Beaumont and Fletcher, and Jonson.

CASTER. 446 *a*.
"I long to *ware* the *caster*." When at a gaming-table a *setter* supposes himself to possess more money than the *caster*, it is usual for him, on putting his stake into the ring, to cry *Ware Caster!* The caster then declares at all under such a sum, ten, twenty, or fifty pounds, for instance ; or else to place against the stakes of certain setters the corresponding sums, and cry *Ware, covered only!*

CASTING. 315 *a*.
"When the hawk will come to the lure, then give her every night *stones*, till you find her stomach good: after that, proffer her *casting*, to make her cleanse and purge her gorge."

CAT-STICK. 260 *b*.
This is what is now called a buck-stick, used by children in the game of tip-cat or kit-cat.

CAUTELOUS. 110 *b*.
This word occurs continually in the sense of *wary*, suspicious, over-circumspect.

CENSURE. 129 a, 249 a, 494 a, 526 epi.,
587 a, 592 b, 625 epi., 634.
Our ancestors used this word precisely as we do
judgment: sometimes for a quality of the mind, sometimes for a judicial determination. [It was so used even
in Congreve's time ("Old Batch.," iv. 5). At page 625
Mr. Crofton Croker reads "conjure," which is meaning-
less.]

CERUSES. 493 a.
Ceruse is white paint for the complexion. No one
has yet been successful in procuring oil from *talc*, although many have pretended to do so, and have sold
the preparations to those who desire to be "beautiful
for ever."

CHAMBERS. 165 a.
Small pieces of ordnance, such as are still fired in the
Park on rejoicing days.

CHAPINES. 136 a.
A kind of clogs with thick cork soles, which the ladies
wear on their shoes when they go abroad. They are
mentioned by Shakspeare, and most of our old dramatists.

CHARMS. 233 a.
"Can charms be writ on such pure rubies." This
alludes to a very old opinion that some sorts of gems
(from an inherent sanctity) could not be profaned, or
applied to the purposes of magic.

CHEESE-TRENCHERS. 568 a.
Before the general introduction of books, our ancestors were careful to dole out instruction in many ways.
Hangings, pictures, *trenchers*, knives, wearing apparel,
everything—in a word—that was capable of containing
a short sentence, was turned to account.

CHIAUS. 150 a.
An officer in the Turkish court, who performs the
duty of an usher.

CHINING. 608 b.
To *chine* is to cut through the backbone. Mr.
Crofton Croker reads "chining of the *fork*," but it is
evident from what follows that the beast, not the rider,
is referred to.

CHREOKOPIA. 561 a.
Signifies the cutting off that part of a debt which
arises from the interest of the sum lent.

CHUFFS. 78 b.
Coarse unmannered clowns; at once sordid and
wealthy.

CIRCULAR. 333 b.
Full and perfect—a latinism.

CIVIL. 161 a, 427 a.
Civil, in Massinger, as well as in his contemporaries,
alludes to the political regulations, customs, and habits
of the City, as distinguished from the Court; sometimes,
indeed, it takes a wider range, and comprises a degree
of civilization, or moral improvement, as opposed to a
state of barbarism or pure nature.

CLEMM'D. 205 a.
To have the entrails shrunk up with hunger, so as to
cling together—metaphorically, to be starved.

COATS. 574 a.
What we now call *court-cards*.

COLON. 36 b, 293 a.
The largest of the human intestines. "To satisfy
colon" means to satisfy hunger. It frequently occurs
in the same sense in our old poets.

COMMODITIES. 112 a.
Wares, of which needy borrowers made what they
could.—["the old masters and curious old sherry" of
the usurers of the present day.]

COME OFF. 58 a.
"Will you come off, sir?" *i.e.*, Will you pay, sir?
The word is used by all our old dramatic writers.

CONCEITED. 110 b.
Facetious, witty. Abounding with *conceits*, not conceit.

CONDUIT. 186 a.
See BAKEHOUSE.

CONSTANTLY. 248 b.
"So constantly;" with such unshaken patience, such
immovable resolution.

CORSIVE. 227 a, 349 b.
Our old authors used *corsive* or *corrosive* indifferently, as suited the verse.

COUNSEL. 79 a, 214 a.
Is used for *secrecy*.

COUNTERFEIT GOLD THREAD. 112 a.
See MOMPESSON.

COURTSHIP. 83 a, 85 b, 228 a, 245 b, 494 a.
The court paid to rank, court-policy, court-breeding,
the grace and elegance learned in courts.

CRACK. 36 a, 528 b.
An arch, sprightly boy. The word is of constant oc-
currence in our old plays.

CRINCOMES. 483 a.
Calipso's meaning is that, having already lost her
nose, she is secured from one of the evils, still known
among the vulgar by the name which she assigns to it.

CRONE. 36 a.
This word, which, as Johnson says, means an old
toothless ewe, is constantly used for an old woman.

CROWD. 591 b.
Another word for *fiddle*.

CROWNS O' THE SUN. 36 b, 176 b.
The best kind of crown then struck. They had a
star (sun) on one side.

CRY AIM! 105 a, 135 a, 597 a.
A phrase taken from archery. "When any one had
challenged another to shoot at the butts, the standers
by used to cry "Aim" to encourage the shooting.

CUPID AND DEATH. 26 b.
This is a beautiful allusion to a little poem among
the Elegies of Secundus. The fable is very ancient.

CULLIONS. 469 b.
Abject wretches: a term taken from the Italians,
and strongly expressive of contempt.

CURIOSITY. 424 a.
Here, as in many other passages of these plays, signifies scrupulous attention, anxiety.

CURIOUS IMPERTINENT. 372 b.
An allusion to the title of one of Cervantes's novels,
which were much read in Massinger's time.

CURIOUSNESS. 53 a, 166 b.
Refined and over-scrupulous consideration of the
subject.

DAG. 376 a.
A pocket-pistol. Their introduction is mentioned by
Knolles in his "History of the Turks."

DALLIANCE. 23 b.
Hesitation, delay.

DANGER. 358 *b*, 453 *b*.
To be in your *danger* meant to be in your *debt*. So Portia:
"You stand within his danger, do you not?"

DEAD-PAYS. 57 *b*.
The collusory practices here alluded to appear not to have been unfrequent—Sir W. Davenant mentions many similar corruptions in the "war department" of his time.

DEAF. 613 *b*.
[Mr. Crofton Croker reads *dumb*, but the change seems required by the sense. It *may*, however, be the correct word, and have been used as meaning not merely muteness, but the mental state generally of what we call the "*dumb* creation." Antiochus in short may have wished that he had been born "a beast wanting *discourse of reason*."]

DECIMO-SEXTO. 49 *a*, 260 *b*.
This expression in both places applied to a page. Gifford says that no author, with whom he is acquainted, repeats himself so frequently, and with so little ceremony as Massinger.

DECK. 472 *b*.
"Ready in the *deck*" means in *the heap*, the *gross*. In our old poets a pack of cards is called a *deck*.

DECLINE. 255 *a*.
Here means to divert from their course.

DEDUCT. 573 *a*.
"Do not *deduct* it to days." A latinism from *deducere*, to bring it down, or reduce it to days.

DEER OF TEN. 340 *a*.
A deer that has ten branches to his horns, which they have at three years old.

DEFENDED. 482 *b*.
Forbidden, interdicted, as in the French. The word occurs in this sense in many of our old writers.

DEFENSIBLE. 460 *b*.
Become an object of justification rather than of shame.

DEGREES. 207 *b*.
Scalæ Gemoniæ. Abrupt and rugged precipices on the Aventine, where the bodies of state criminals were flung.—*See* GEMONIES.

DEMEANS. 284 *b*.
Here used for means, as demerits for merits. [*Qy.* Demesnes.]

DEPART. 136 *a*.
Depart and part were anciently synonymous. Thus Ben Jonson—
"He that *departs* with his own honesty
For vulgar praise, does it too dearly buy."

DEPENDENCIES. 254 *b*.
"Masters of dependencies" were a set of needy bravoes, who undertook to ascertain the authentic grounds of a quarrel, and in some cases to settle it for the timorous or unskilful.

DERIVE. 603 *a*.
Verb neuter, *to come from.*—JOHNSON.

DISCLOSE. 258 *b*.
Constantly used by our old writers for *hatch*.

DISSOLVE. 90 *b*, 209 *b*.
"Dissolve this doubtful riddle." Our old writers used *dissolve* and *solve* indiscriminately; or if they made any difference it was in favour of the former.

DISTASTE. 52 *b*, 135 *b*, 622 *a*.
Displease. The word perpetually recurs in this sense; as also in that of *dislike*. It is so used by Congreve.

DISTEMPERED. 65 *b*.
Intoxicated. It is used thus in "Hamlet," and by Shirley in "The Grateful Servant."

DIVERT. 227 *a*.
The motives that *divert* us, *i.e.*, turn us aside from following your advice.

DRESSER. 46 *b*, 472 *b*.
In both these places the dresser is called the cook's drum. It was formerly customary for the cook, when dinner was ready, to knock on the dresser with his knife by way of summoning the servants to carry it into the hall. Thus Suckling—
"Just in the nick the cook knocked thrice,
And all the waiters in a trice
His summons did obey."

ELENCHS. 331 *a*.
A sophistical refutation of a position maintained by an opponent.

EMPIRIC. 342 *b*.
Massinger's empiric may be considered as the fruitful parent of the quack, which for the two last centuries has poisoned us in the closet and entertained us on the stage. It may be doubted whether Massinger ever fell into Molière's hands, but there is so striking a resemblance between a passage in the "Malade Imaginaire" and this before us, that it is difficult to believe the coincidence accidental.
Toinette. Je voudrais que vous eussiez toutes les maladies que je viens de dire ; que vous fussiez abandonné de tous les medecins, désespéré, à l'agonie, pour vous montrer l'excellence de mes remèdes, et l'envie que j'aurais de vous rendre service.
Argan. Je vous suis obligé, monsieur, des bontés que vous avez pour moi, etc.

ENTRADAS. 487 *b*.
Rents, revenues.

EQUAL MART. 539 *b*.
A vile translation of *in æquo marte*, in equal fight.

ESTRIDGE TRAIN. 57 *b*, 263 *b*.
Ostrich tail. There is some humour in this lively apostrophe to the bird.

EXTENDED. 418 *b*, 453 *b*.
"This manor is extended to my use," *i.e.*, *seized*. It is a legal phrase, and occurs continually.

EYASSES. 315 *a*.
A young hawk newly taken out of the nest, and not able to prey for himself.

FADGE. 585 *a*.
To suit—to fit.

FARCE. 609 *b*.
To stuff—a culinary term.

FAULT. 126 *b*, 577 *b*.
Misfortune. That the word anciently had this meaning could be proved by many examples.

FESTIVAL-EXCEEDINGS. 314 *a*, 425 *a*.
At the Middle Temple an additional dish to the regular dinner is still called "Exceedings."

FEWTERER. 260 *b*, 314 *b*.
A name which frequently occurs in our old treatises on Hunting. He was the person who took charge of the dogs immediately under the huntsman.

FINE-NESS. 152 *b*.
Subtle and ingenious device. Johnson and Gifford concur in reprobating the introduction of the word *finesse* into our language as quite unnecessary.

FLIES. 10 *a.*
This word is used by Ben Jonson, a close and devoted imitator of the ancients, for a domestic parasite, a familiar, &c.

FOR. 29 *b.*
" But far enough *for* reaching." The word *for* occurs perpetually in these plays in the sense of *prevention.* It is so used by every writer of Massinger's age.

FREQUENT. 195 *a.*
"'Tis *frequent* in the city," a latinism, for 'tis currently reported in the city.

FREQUENT. 197 *b.*
" Frequent senate," a latinism for a " full house."

FRIPPERY. 425 *a.*
An old clothes shop. The word is pure French, but occurs in most of our ancient dramatists.

FUR. 425 *b.*
" Get your fur " to put under her feet while she tried on the shoes, says M. Mason. Gifford characteristically adds, " *Grande certamen !* was not the fur a piece of undressed skin, such as is sometimes used by ladies of the present day in lieu of a shoeing horn?"

FEERING. 81 *b.*
[Gifford printed *feeling.* I have made the change with some hesitation.]

GABEL. 326 *a.*
This spirit of imposition is well touched on by Donne :
——————— shortly, boys shall not play
At span-counter, or blow point, but shall pay
Toll to some courtier.—Sat. iv.

GALLERIEN.
A galley slave.—*French.*

GALLIARD. 578 *a.*
Is described by Sir John Davies as a " swift and wandering dance with lofty turns and capriols in the air."

GARDED ROBE. 194 *b,* 598 *b.*
A laced or bordered robe.

GAZET. 266.
A Venetian coin (gazetta) worth about three farthings of our money. The petty Italian courant, or written summary of intelligence was originally sold for this sum; hence it derived the name which is now common to all the newspapers of Europe.

GEMONIES. 207 *b.*
The Gemonies (*Scalæ Gemoniæ*) were abrupt and rugged precipices on the Aventine, where the bodies of state criminals were flung, and whence, after they had been exposed to the insults of the rabble, they were dragged to the Tiber, which flowed at the foot of the hill.

GENEVA PRINT. 65 *a.*
Alluding to the spirituous liquor so called.

GLORIOUS. 39 *a,* 55*a,* 227 *b.*
Vain, boastful, ostentatious, Vaunting.

GO BY ! 278 *b.*
This is an allusion to the " Spanish Tragedy;" the constant butt of all the writers of those times, who seem to be a little uneasy, notwithstanding their scoffs at its popularity.

GOLD AND STORE. 296 *a,* 446 *a.*
This expression, which is taken from an old ballad, frequently occurs in these plays.

GO NO LESS. 441 *a,* 547 *b.*
This is a gaming phrase, and means I will not play for a smaller stake.

GOLLS. 443 *a.*
A cant word for hands, or rather fists. It occurs continually in our old writers.

GOOD. 358 *b,* 442 *a.*
Luke here alludes to the mercantile sense of the word *good,* i.e. *rich.*

GOOD FELLOWS. 487 *b,* 490 *a.*
A cant name by which highwaymen and thieves have been long pleased to denominate themselves; and which has been given them, in courtesy, by others.

GOVERNOR'S PLACE. 7 *a.*
From the Latin, *ne sis mihi tutor.*

GRANSON. 358 *a.*
The " memorable overthrow" of Granson took place March 3rd, 1476; that of Morat, June 22nd, in the same year; and that of Nancy, January 5th, 1477. In this Charles (or, as he is here called, Charalois), Duke of Burgundy, fell, and the subtle fox of France, the politic Louis XI., shortly after seized upon the defenceless duchy.

GREAT—wholesale. 318 *b.*

GREEN APRON. 134 *a.*
It should be observed that this colour is appropriated to the descendants of Mahomet. To "land at Tunis," or any other town professing the Mahometan religion, in a green dress at this day would place the wearer's safety in danger.

GREGORIES. 578 *a.*
Gifford leaves this word unexplained. Gregorie was a famous barber and wigmaker of Massinger's day. Bishop Hall, for some similar reason, I suppose, uses *Rogerians* for false scalps.

GUARD. 288 *b.*
Posture of defence.

GYARÆ. 625 *b.*
Gyaros or Gyara was a small island in the Ægæan sea. Under the Romans it was used as a place of banishment, and was one of the most dreaded spots employed for that purpose.

HAND. 153 *b.*
"Hand with my will " means go hand-in-hand, co-operate, with my will.

HAWKING. 315 *a.*
Humanity has seldom obtained a greater triumph in the animal world than in the abolition of this most execrable pursuit, compared to which cock-fighting and bull-baiting are innocent amusements; and this not so much on account of the game killed in the open field, as of the immense number of domestic animals sacrificed to the instruction of the hawk. The blood runs cold while we peruse the calm directions of the brutal falconer to impale, tie down, fasten by the beak, break the legs and wings of living pigeons, hens, and sometimes herons, for the hourly exercise of the hawk, who was thus enabled to pull them to pieces without resistance.

HELL. 424 *a.*
The *hole* was one of the wretched departments of a gaol, in which prisoners, who could not afford to pay for better accommodations, were obliged to take up their residence. The darkest part of this *hole* was called *hell*—a dungeon within a dungeon in some prisons.— *See* " Howard's Reports."

HORNED MOONS. 143 *b*.
This elegant allusion to the impress of the Turkish standards is beautifully varied in the "Knight of Malta" by Fletcher.
" And all their silver crescents then I saw,
Like falling meteors spent, and set for ever
Under the cross of Malta."

HOSE. 240 *a*, 567 *a*.
Hose are breeches; *paned hose* are breeches composed of small squares or panels. [Perhaps, rather, breeches with openings in the cloth where pieces of stuff of other colours were inserted.]

HUMANITY. 360 *a*.
Polite literature. The term is still preserved in the Scotch universities.

HUNT'S UP. 76 *a*.
Was a lesson on the horn, played under the windows of sportsmen, to call them up in the morning. It was probably sufficiently obstreperous, for it is frequently applied by our old writers, as in this place, to any noise or clamour of an awakening or alarming nature.

IMP. 165 *a*, 221 *b*, 226 *a*.
To *imp* " is to insert into the wing of a hawk, or other bird, in place of one that is broken." To this practice our old writers, who seem to have been, in the language of the present day, keen sportsmen, perpetually allude. There is a passage in Tomkis's " Albumazar" which would be admired even in the noblest scenes of Shakspeare :
How slow the day slides on ! when we desire
Time's haste, he seems to lose a match with lobsters;
And when we wish him stay, *he imps his wings
With feathers plumed with thought!*

IMPOTENT. 48 *a*, 227 *b*, 499 *a*, 617 *a*.
Wild, fierce, uncontrollable in his passions : this is a latinism, *impotens amoris*, and is a very strong expression. Horace applies the word to Cleopatra.

INGLES. 443 *a*.
Bosom friends, associates.

IPHIS. 209 *a*.
Vide Anaxarete.

KA ME, KA THEE ! 432 *a*.
Is a Scotch proverb, and means, indulge or serve me, and I'll serve thee in my turn. It is not uncommon in our old dramas.

KATEXOKÉN. 471 *a*.
Supereminently—the Greek κατέξοχην.

KEEPER OF THE DOOR. 184 *a*.
This was one of the thousand synonyms of a bawd or pander.

LACHRYMÆ. 254 *b*, 318 *b*.
Was the title of a musical work, composed by John Douland, a celebrated lutanist in the time of James I. It is alluded to in the *Knight of the burning Pestle*.

LADY OF THE LAKE. 397 *a*.
This is a very prominent character in *Morte Arthur*, and in many of our old romances. She seems to be the Circe of the dark ages ; and is frequently mentioned by our old dramatists.

LAMIA. 24 *b*.
The sorceress, the hag. The word is pure Latin.

LANCE PREZADO. 260 *a*.
" The lowest range, and meanest officer in an army is called the lance presado or prezado, who is the leader or governor of half a file ; and therefore is called a middleman, or captain over four."—*The Soldier's Accidence*. [The lowest rank at the present time among non-commissioned officers is *lance* corporal.]

LAVENDER ROBES. 418 *a*.
Clothes just redeemed out of pawn. To lay a thing in lavender was a common phrase for pawning it.

LAVOLTA. 168 *a*, 243 *a*, 438 *a*, 614 *a*.
Lavolta (literally the *turn*) was a dance, originally imported with many others from Italy. It is frequently mentioned by our old writers, with whom it was a favourite ; and is so graphically described by Sir John Davies, in his *Orchestra*, that all further attempts to explain it must be superfluous.
"Yet is there one, the most delightful kind,
A lofty jumping or a leaping round,
Where, arm-in-arm, two dancers are entwined,
And whirl themselves in strict embracements bound."
Our countrymen, who seem to be lineally descended from Sisyphus, and who, at the end of every century, usually have their work to do over again, after proudly importing from Germany the long-exploded trash of their own nurseries, have just brought back from the same country, and with an equal degree of exultation, the well-known *lavolta* of their grandfathers under the mellifluous name of *waltz*.

LEAGUER LAUNDRESS. 285 *b*, 369 *a*.
Camp washerwoman. *Leaguer* is the Dutch, or rather Flemish, word for a camp; and was one of the new-fangled terms introduced from the Low Countries.

LENT. 159 *b*.
Massinger alludes to the custom which all good Catholics had of confessing themselves at Easter. Good Friday and Easter Sunday are almost the only two days on which the French and Italian sailors ever think of repairing to a confessional.

L'ENVOY. 548 *b*, 555 *b*.
Conclusion, termination, main import.

LEPER. 171 *a*.
" A leper with a clap-dish (to give notice
He is infectious)."
This explains the origin of the custom to which our old writers have such frequent allusions. The leprosy was once very common here, and the old poets seldom mention a leper without noticing at the same time his constant accompaniments, the cup and clapper. Thus Henryson—
" Thus shalt thou go begging from hous to hous
With cuppe and clapper like a Lazarous."
The clapper was not, as some imagine, an instrument solely calculated for making a noise ; it was simply the cover of the cup or dish, which the poor wretch opened and shut with a loud clap at the doors of the well-disposed.

LETS. 7 *a*, 61 *a*.
Impediments, obstacles.

LIGHTLY. 117 *a*.
Commonly, usually.

LIME-HOUND. 529 *a*.
The common hound.

LIONS. 598 *b*, 613 *b*, 618 *a*.
Cybele was often represented in a chariot drawn by lions. The old Flamen wore her " sacred image drawn thus in pomp" upon his breast. Hence his frequent references to his lions.

LITTLE LEGS. 506 *b*.
Slender legs seem at this time to have been considered as one of the characteristics of a fine gentleman. Jonson expressly says so in the " Poetaster," —" a man borne upon little legs is always a gentleman born."

LOOKING-GLASSES. 424 *a*.
It appears from innumerable passages in our old writers that it was customary, not only for ladies, but for gentlemen, to carry mirrors about them.

LOTH TO DEPART. 583 *a.*
There was anciently both a tune and a dance of this name.

LUDGATE. 428 *b.*
This prison was anciently appropriated to the freemen of the city and to clergymen. It was taken down in Nov. 1760.

MAGNIFICENT. 329 *b.*
Constantly used by Massinger for *munificent.*

MANDRAKES. 35 *a.*
Mandrakes have a soporific quality, and were used by the ancients when they wanted a narcotic of the most powerful kind. To this there are perpetual allusions in our old writers.

MANKIND. 437 *b.*
Masculine, mannish. It sometimes carried with it the stronger sense of violent, ferocious, wicked.

MARMOSET. 437 *a.*
A small monkey.

MERMAID. 582 *b.*
The mermaids of the writer's time had succeeded to the syrens of the ancients, and possessed all their musical as well as seductive qualities. Mermaid also was one of the thousand cant terms which served to denote a strumpet; and to this perhaps Agatha alludes.

MICHER. 474 *a.*
To mich is to lurk.

MINERVA. 220 *a.*
This attachment of Domitian to Minerva is an historical fact. He chose her at an early period of his life for his protectress, multiplied her statues to a great extent, and had always a strong reliance on her favour.

MISTRESSES. 129 *a,* 168 *a,* 621 *b,* 623 *a.*
Servant and Mistress signified in the language of Massinger's time, a lover and the object of his affections. Let me now call the reader's attention to the exquisite melody of this speech (*Charles* in Scene v. Act 1 of "Parliament of Love, p. 168 *a* "). Nothing is forced, nothing is inverted; plainness and simplicity are all the aids of which the poet has availed himself; yet a more perfect specimen of flowing, elegant, and rhythmical modulation is not to be found in the English language. The sprightliness, energy, and spirit, which pervade the remainder of this scene, are worthy of all praise.

MOMPESSON, SIR GILES. 395 *b.*
Was undoubtedly the prototype of Sir Giles Overreach. He and one Michel had obtained of the facile James a patent for the sole manufacturing of gold and silver thread, which they abused to the most detestable purposes. This is specially alluded to in the "Bondman," Act ii. scene 3. His character will be found in Wilson's "Life and Reign of James I." *sub anno* 1621. When the cup of his iniquities was full, and the House of Commons ordered his apprehension (3rd March, 1620), he made his escape beyond sea On the 30th of the same month a proclamation was issued, banishing him from the king's dominions, and degrading him from knighthood. His associate, Sir Francis Michel (Justice Greedy), was also degraded, fined a thousand pounds, carried on horseback through the principal streets (his face to the tail), and imprisoned for life.

MORAT. 358 *a.*
Vide Cranson.

MUSICIANS. 376 *b.*
In these lines there is an allusion to another profession (of a less honourable nature), which in those days was commonly added to that of music-master.

NANCY. 358 *a.*
Vide Cranson.

NEAT-HOUSE. 437 *a.*
The Neat-house was a celebrated garden and nursery near Chelsea.

NIMMING. 486 *a.*
The word is pure Saxon, and means to *take,* to *seize.* It is found in all our old writers, and, indeed, is still in use as a cant term for stealing.

NO CUNNING QUEAN. 100 *b.*
In our author's time, as is justly observed by Warburton, "the negative, in common speech, was used ironically to express the excess of a thing."

OIL OF ANGELS. 82 *a.*
It may be just necessary to observe that this is a pleasant allusion to the gold coin of that name.

OLYMPUS. 411 *a.*
Either Massinger or his transcriber has mistaken Olympus for Parnassus. It may be the former; for in trusting to their memory, such slips are not unusual in our old writers, who were, indeed, little solicitous of accuracy in these trivial matters.

ORC. 220 *b.*
A fabulous sea monster, depicted on most of the charts of Massinger's time. The whale of our old romances.

OUT. 170 *b.*
"I'll not out for a second."
[*I.e.* it is evident from the sequel that Novall *did* take up the bet, the Edinburgh Reviewers maintained that the word "not" in this line should have been omitted. Gifford successfully defended his reading, and proved beyond all question that the meaning of "I'll not out" was "I'll not be found wanting."]

OUTCRY. 429 *a,* 596 *b.*
A public auction. [The word is still used by our countrymen in India.]

OWE. 5 *a,* 108 *a,* 141 *b.*
To *own.*
"No sound that the earth owes."—*Tempest.*

PACKING. 239 *b.*
Insidious contrivance; iniquitous collusion. The word is thus used by Shakspeare, and others, [and the term is preserved in "packing a jury."]

PADDER. 396 *b.*
A lurker about the highways, a foot-pad.

PANTOFLE. 49 *a.*
"Ere I was sworn to the pantofle" means before I was taken from my first menial service, and made attendant on a lady.

PARALLEL. 88 *b.*
"And, but herself, admits no parallel."
This idea, in the much ridiculed form of
"None but himself can be his parallel,"
is familiar to every one as a verse of Theobald's; but not only is it found in Massinger, but twenty instances of it could be adduced from his contemporaries.

PARALLELS. 258 *b.*
The word seems to be used here for *radii.* Other writers of the time fell into the same error.

PARTED. 11 *b,* 244 *b.*
Favoured, or endowed, with a part, or parts.

PARTHIAN. 597 *b.*
Mr. Crofton Croker prints *Parthenon.*

T T

PASH. 10 *b*.
To strike a thing with such force as to crush it to pieces.

PASSIONATE. 226 *a*, 575 *b*.
Plaintive, full of sorrow, deeply affected.

PASSION. 561 *a*, 593 *b*.
Pathetic speech, or exclamation.

PASTRY FORTIFICATIONS. 391 *a*.
The cooks of Elizabeth and James took great pride in the construction of these fortifications; [and in later days Gibraltar and Seringapatam were similarly commemorated. The earth-works of Todleben were not picturesque enough for the purpose.]

PATCH. 9 *b*, 406 *b*, 419 *a*.
Patch was the cant name of a fool kept by Cardinal Wolsey; and who has had the honour of transmitting his appellation to a very numerous body of descendants; he being "*a notable fool* in his time."

PEEVISH. 20 *b*.
Foolish. Mrs. Quickly says of her fellow servant, "His worst fault is that he is given to prayer: he is something *peevish* that way." "Your peevishness," 415 *b*, means *you*—his daughter.

PESCARA. 70 *b*.
The Marquis was indeed a "great soldier," a fortunate commander, an able negociator. in a word one of the chief ornaments of a period which abounded in extraordinary characters.

PIG-SCONCE. 438 *a*.
A heavy, dull-pated fellow.

PLACE. 462 *a*, 557 *a*.
In falconry means the greatest elevation which a bird of prey attains in its flight. This lends additional force to Shakspeare's line—
"A falcon towering in his pride of *place*."

PLEURISY OF GOODNESS. 55 *a*.
Superabundance of goodness.

PLYMOUTH CLOAK. 388 *a*.
An old expression for a *cudgel*. Davenant says—
"Whose cloak, at Plymouth spun, was crab-tree wood."

POET. 620 *b*.
"The poet wrote truth"—Mr. Crofton Croker prints *post*.

POOR JOHN. 133 *b*, 298 *b*.
Hake dried and salted.

PORTER'S LODGE. 82 *b*, 390 *a*.
The porter's lodge in great houses was the usual place of punishment for the domestics.

PORTS. 2 *b*, 163 *a*.
The *gates* of a city, as in Edinburgh.

POSSESS. 235 *b*.
Acquaint, inform. In this sense the word perpetually occurs in our old writers.

POWER OF THINGS. 195 *b*.
A Latinism—that. now sways the world, *rerum potestas*.

PRACTICE. 187 *a*, 252 *a*.
Insidious trick, stratagem, artifice.

PREST. 440 *b*.
Ready, prepared.

PREVENT. 139 *b*, 406 *a*, 416 *a*, 563 *b*.
Anticipate, from the Latin. It is so used in the Psalms, "Mine eyes *prevent* the night-watches."

PROVANT SWORD. 254 *b*.
A plain, unornamented sword, such as the army is supplied with.

PUT ON. 185 *b*, 405 *b*, 452 *b*.
De covered; a frequent expression in these plays.

PUT ON YOUR SPIRITS. 353 *b*.
Rouse, animate them.

QUALITY. 197 *b*, 292 *b*, 376 *b*, 630.
Used in a general sense for any occupation, calling, or condition of life, but more peculiarly appropriated by our old writers to that of a player.

QUELLIO RUFFS. 449 *b*.
Ruffs for the neck, a corruption of *cuello*.

QUIRPO. 363 *a*.
Quirpo (cuerpo) is an undress. The Spaniards, from whom we borrowed the word, apply it to a person in a light jacket, without his cabot or cloak; but our old dramatists, who use the expression upon all occasions, mean by it any state from nakedness to imperfect clothing. Gifford could not satisfy himself as to the meaning of *Gallyfoist* and *Bullion* in this passage.

RAGGED CLIFFS. 188 *a*.
This expressive epithet is from Scripture. "To go into the clefts of the rocks, and into the tops of the ragged rocks."—*Isaiah* ii. 21. Massinger is frequently indebted to this source.

RAM ALLEY. 399 *a*.
Ram Alley is one of the avenues into the Temple from Fleet Street. The stink from its cook-shops is spoken of by Barrey in his comedy (1611).

REMARKABLE. 43 *b*.
Had in Massinger's time a more dignified sound, and a more appropriate meaning than it bears at present. With him it constantly stands for surprising, highly striking, or observable in an uncommon degree.

REMEMBER. 122 *b*, 172 *b*, 472 *a*.
Is used for *cause to remember*, put in mind of.

RESOLVED. 77 *a*, 318 *a*.
Convinced. Thus Shakspeare—
"By heavens! I am *resolved*
That Clifford's manhood lies upon his tongue."

REST ON IT. 103 *a*.
Fixed, determined on it. Taken from the gaming-table.

RIDE. 437 *b*.
"I can but ride"—*i.e.*, I know the worst of my punishment; I can but be carted for a strumpet.

RIVO. 145 *b*.
This interjection is frequently introduced by our old poets, and generally as an incitement to boisterous mirth and revelry.

ROARER. 139 *a*.
A cant term for what we now call a blusterer, or bully.

ROSES. 425 *a*, 449 *b*.
These were not the flowers of that name, but knots of ribands to be fixed on the shoes. They were of preposterous size, and extremely dear.

ROUSE. 65 *b*, 111 *a*.
A *rouse* was a large glass in which a health was given, the drinking of which by the rest of the company formed a *carouse*.

SACRED. 344 *b*.
Theodosius alludes to the Latin word *sacer*.

ST. MARTIN'S. 445 a.

The parish of St. Martin appears, from the old histories of London, to have been distinguished successively for a sanctuary, a bridewell, a spittle, and an almshouse. Which of them was to be driven from the mind of Mistress Shave'em by the full tide of prosperity which is here anticipated, must be left to the sagacity of the reader.

SANZACKE. 150 a.

Governor of a city.

SCARABS. 78 b.

Beetles.

SCARLET. 428 a.

"Or they will ne'er wear scarlet," i.e., never rise to city honours. Our old writers have innumerable allusions to the *scarlet* gowns of the mayors and aldermen of London.

SCOTOMY. 579 b.

From the Greek; a dizziness or swimming in the head.

SEEK TO. 62 a, 290 a.

To supplicate, entreat, have earnest recourse to. Thus in 2 Chron. xvi. 12, we read, "And Asa was diseased in his feet, yet in his disease he *sought* not *to* the Lord, but *to* his physicians."

SEISACTHEIA. 561 a.

Σεισαχθεια. *i.e.*, a shaking off a burthen; metaphorically an abolition of debt.

SERVANT. 52 a, 168 a, 621 b, 623 a.

Vide Mistress.

SHADOWS. 46 a.

It was considered, Plutarch says, as a mark of politeness, to let an invited guest know that he was at liberty to bring a friend or two with him ; a permission that was, however, sometimes abused. These friends the Romans called *shadows* (*umbræ*), a term which Massinger has very happily explained.

SHAPE. 131 a, 178 a, 207 a, 209 a, 337 b, 603 b, 607 a.

Dress, habit—derived from the phraseology of the theatre.

SHEW WATER. 253 a.

Shew water, to clear his sight. This was a proverbial periphrasis for a bribe, which, in Massinger's days, was found to be the only collyrium for the eyes of a courtier.

SIEGE. 462 a.

"*Hern at siege* is when you find a hern standing by the water side watching for prey or the like."

SKILLS NOT. 65 b, 192 a, 194 a, 615 a.

Matters not, signifies not.

SLEEPS MOST AN END. 506 a.

Almost perpetually—without intermission.

SLEEP ON EITHER EAR. 466 a.

This idea is derived from Terence, "*in aurem utramvis dormire*," and means to sleep soundly, free from care.

SORT 20 b.

"*Sort* of rogues," a set, or pack of rogues. Of constant recurrence in our old writers.

SPITTLE. 309 b, 369 b, 437 b.

The earlier editors in each instance changed this word to *Spital ;* but our old writers carefully distinguished between the two. With them, a hospital, or spital, signified a charitable institution for the advantage of poor, infirm, and aged persons, an almshouse in short ; while *Spittles* were mere lazarhouses, receptacles for wretches in the leprosy, and other loathsome diseases, the consequence of debauchery and Vice. [Thus Ancient Pistol, "News have I that my Doll is dead i' the *Spittle* of malady of France."]

SQUIRE O' DAMES. 183 b, 323 a.

This honourable term was degraded by our old dramatists to mean a pander.

START-UP. 315 a.

A coarse kind of half boot or spatterdash with thick soles ; the *paro* of the ancients,

STATE. 102 a, 251 a.

The *state* was a raised platform, on which was placed a chair with a canopy over it. The word occurs perpetually in our old writers. It is used by Dryden, but seems to have been growing obsolete while he was writing : in the first edition of Mac Fleckno, the monarch is placed on a *state :* in the subsequent ones he is seated, like his fellow kings, on a *throne :* it occurs also, and I believe for the last time, in Swift : " As she affected not the grandeur of a *state* with a canopy, she thought there was no offence in an elbow chair."— *Hist. of John Bull,* c. i.

STATES. 247 a.

Statesmen, men of power, &c., a common acceptation of the word.

STONES. 315 a.

Vide Casting.

STOOLS, TO BRING WITH ONE, 50 b, 266 b.

The singular custom of uninvited or unexpected guests bringing seats with them, is frequently noticed by the writers of Massinger's time. [In the army at this day "camp fashion" means that the guest should bring not chair only, but plate, knife, fork, spoon, and glass likewise.]

STRANGELY GUARDED. 340 b.

Perhaps this ought to be *strongly* guarded.

STRENGTHS. 155 b, 164 b, 339 b.

Castles, strong places, and, metaphorically, defences.

STRIKER. 58 a.

A striker is a wencher. The word occurs again in the " Parliament of Love."

SUPPLANT. 154 b.

To trip up, to overthrow ; a Latinism.

SWEATING SICKNESS. 58 a.

This alludes to a species of plague (*sudor anglicus*) peculiar, the physicians say, to this country, where it made dreadful ravages in the 16th century. It is frequently mentioned by our old writers.

SWORN SERVANTS. 204 b.

In Massinger's time the attendants of the great, who maintained them in considerable numbers, took an oath of fidelity on their entering into service.

TAILORS. 381 b.

Our old writers abound in allusion to the quantity of bread devoured by tailors.

TAINT. 184 a.

To break, in a derogatory sense. It is used in the same way in " Every Man out of his Humour."

TAKE UP. 228 a, 317 b.

Stop, check yourself. [*Shut up,* in the slang of 1868.]

TALL. 32 b, 46 b.

Tall, in the language of our old writers, meant stout, or, rather, bold and fearless : but they abused the word (of which they seem fond) in a great variety of senses A *tall man of his hands,* was a great fighter ; a *tall man of his tongue,* a licentious speaker ; and a *tall trencherman,* a hearty feeder.

TAMIN. 403 *b*.
A coarse linsey-woolsey stuff, still worn by the poor of this country, under the name of *taminy*, or, rather, *tammy*: a corruption, I suppose, of *etamine*, Fr., which has the same meaning.

THING OF THINGS. 111 *b*.
A literal translation of *Ens Entium*.

TIMARIOTS. 284 *a*.
The Turkish Cavalry, a sort of feudal yeomanry, who hold their lands on condition of service.

TOKEN. 389 *a*, 447 *b*.
During the reign of Elizabeth, and down to Charles II., very little copper money was coined. For the convenience of the public, tradesmen were permitted to strike *tokens*, as they were called. The value generally was about one farthing.

TRILLIBUBS. 578 *b*.
A cant word for anything of a trifling nature.

TRIPE. 266 *b*.
A tripe shop. To "carry my own stool" is explained elsewhere.

UNCIVIL. 373 *b*.
Unacquainted with the usages and customs of *civil*, or municipal ife.

UNEQUAL. 348 *b*.
Unjust.

UNTAPPICE. 511 *a*.
To discover one's self. A hunting frame for turning the game out of a bag, or driving it out of a cover.

USES. 254 *b*, 335 *a*.
An expression adopted by our old dramatists from the Puritans, who usually divided their discourses into *doctrines* and *uses*. By the former they meant the explanation of their subject; and by the latter the practical inferences drawn from it.

VARLETS. 381 *a*.
So our old writers call the sheriff's officers.

VIRBIUS. 209 *a*.
The name given to Hippolytus, after he was restored to life by Æsculapius. He was so called, say the critics, "quod inter *viros bis* fuerit."

VOLEY. 304 *b*.
"What we spake on the voley," a literal translation of the French phrase *à la volée*, which signifies at random, or inconsiderately. [The word is preserved in the technical language of the racquet-court.]

VOTES. 484 *b*.
Prayers. I do not know who led the way to this pedantic adoption of the Latin word (*votum*), but I find it in Jonson, and in others before his time.

VAPPA. 614 *a*.
Palled wine that has lost its strength (Latin).

WAISTCOATEER. 437 *a*.
It appears from innumerable passages in our old plays that *waistcoater* was a cant term for a strumpet of the lowest kind; probably given to them from their usually appearing, either through choice or necessity, in a succinct habit.

WHERE. 168 *b*, 354 *a*, 389 *a*, 496 *a*, 525 *a*, 567 *a*.
Constantly used for *whereas*.

WHILE. 219 *b*.
Until : a very common acceptation of the word in our old writers.

WHITING MOP. 482 *b*.
A young whiting. Puttenham says "We call little fishes that be not come to their full growth moppes, as whiting moppes, gurnard moppes, &c."

WITNESS. 333 *a*.
The puritan word for sponsor.

WORK OF GRACE. 152 *b*.
This is a reverential description of the elevation of the host; and could only be written by a man on whom that awful act of pious daring had made a deep and lasting impression.

WREAK. 135 *a*.
To revenge. So Spenser:
" Another's wrongs to *wreak* upon thyself."

YAW. 510 *b*.
Yaw is that unsteady motion which a ship makes in a great swell, when in steering she inclines to the right or left of her course.

YELLOW. 87 *a*.
" I should wear yellow breeches." Be jealous; yellow, with our old poets, being the livery of jealousy; probably because it was that of Hymen.

ZANY. 557 *b*.
To imitate. So Lovelace:
" As I have seen an arrogant baboon
With a small piece of glass *zany* the sun."

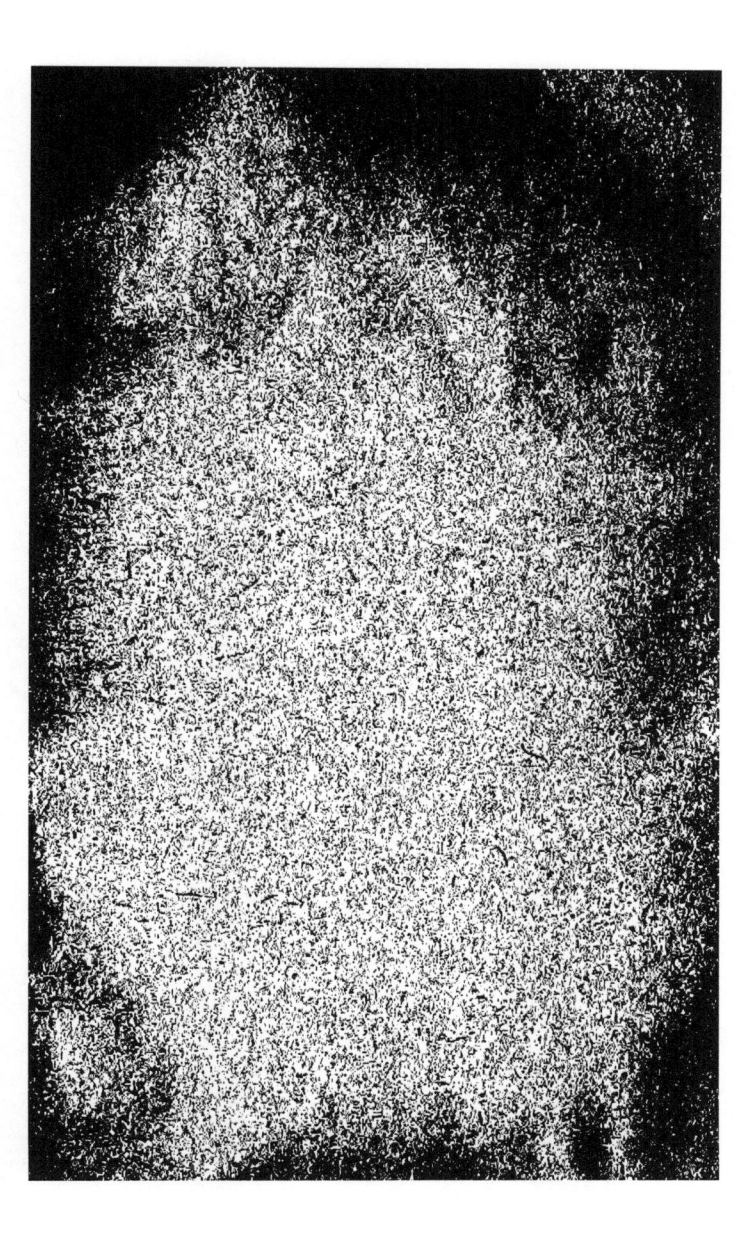

Lightning Source UK Ltd.
Milton Keynes UK
UKHW021828190219
337363UK00005BB/869/P